A History of

COLONIAL AMERICA

HARPER'S HISTORICAL SERIES

Under the Editorship of

GUY STANTON FORD

A History
of COLONIAL
AMERICA

by

OLIVER PERRY CHITWOOD, Ph.D., LL.D

PROFESSOR EMERITUS OF HISTORY

WEST VIRGINIA UNIVERSITY

SECOND EDITION

Harper & Brothers Publishers

NEW YORK

A History of
COLONIAL AMERICA
SECOND EDITION

————➤➤❯❮❮————

Copyright 1931, 1948, by
HARPER & BROTHERS
Printed in the U. S. A.

————➤➤❯❮❮————

E-B

To the Memory of My Parents

HENRY CLAY CHITWOOD
GILLIE ANNE DIVERS CHITWOOD

CONTENTS

CONTENTS

ILLUSTRATIONS

(*will be found following page 426*)

ix

MAPS

EDITOR'S FOREWORD

THE appearance of another edition of a widely used textbook on the history of the nation's formative years has a significance greater than usually attaches to the success of a publishing enterprise. It means, when put together with other signs, that to find out what the American way of life really means we are turning to a study of the first half of our history measured in years. It was in the years from 1607 to 1789 that the pioneers of the Atlantic seaboard under the influence of a new environment reshaped their European heritage to create a new kind of man, the American, under a new kind of government that epitomized their experience as colonists and guided their course as a nation. It is well to know the later years when millions of new settlers poured in and the stream of old and new colonials filled an inland empire and crossed desert and mountain range to reach an ocean whose further shores were the goal of the first discoverers. It is well to know all this and to know the building of a material power that carries, whether we will or no, world-wide responsibilities. It is better to understand what we know of all these later decades that bulk so large in our teaching and thinking. That understanding of America as we know it and as we would have the world know it is to be found in the ideals shaped by the last colonials and the first nation makers like Franklin, Jefferson, Hamilton, Adams, Madison, and Washington. The world order we seek amid today's confusions and conflicts may yet be found in an adaptation of the charter they framed out of their colonial and post-Revolutionary experience seasoned by a knowledge rare among statesmen in any day of the world's great political thinkers. The principles governing men in their relations with each other and of state with state were theirs. The testing and interpretation of the solution wrought out in the half of our nation's life covered by this book have been and will be the core of American history. The products of our technology and mass production may sustain peoples in distress and give us unexampled well-being. But neither we nor they can live by bread alone. We shall be lifted and lift others with us by our loyalty to the spirit and the letter of the chartered liberties and representative government bequeathed to us by the generations from the Mayflower Compact to the preamble of the Constitution and the Bill of Rights.

No history that frees the student to look at the present in the perspective of the past can be a manual for ancestor worship. But it can fortify him by telling the story of men and women, human like himself, who struggled against the adversity of nature and their own limitations to achieve something that time has tested and found good. That is the story this book tells. Its reëditing and other signs I cannot detail here are cheering indications that the history of the formative years of the nation is again finding its rightful place in the curriculums of our colleges and universities.

GUY STANTON FORD

PREFACE TO THE FIRST EDITION

THIS volume is intended primarily for the college student, though it is hoped that it will also be of interest to the general reader. In the narrative part of the work I have given an account of the principal events that occurred in the discovery and exploration of the continent, the settlement of the Atlantic Slope, the international contest for possession of the interior, the occupation of the transmontane region, and the secession of the colonies from the empire. As one of the main purposes of the work is to show how an old civilization was adapted to a new environment, considerable space is devoted to economic and social life, political institutions, and the problems growing out of the relations between the dominions and the homeland. A special effort has also been made to acquaint the reader with the most outstanding figures in the early history of our country. To this end numerous character sketches have been drawn, which portray the personality of the leading actors in the colonial and Revolutionary drama.

A number of maps are inserted, each at the place where it can be referred to with the least inconvenience. These maps are simplified by the omission of all names except those that are referred to in the context or are necessary for an easy understanding of the narrative.

A good deal of space has been allotted to bibliographical aids. The purpose of the "Selected Readings" is to list references on short topics for the guidance of college students and others who do not have time to make a study of the more comprehensive works. Nearly all of the selections that are starred are interesting, and most of them are of the proper length for assignment as parallel reading. In the "Bibliographical Notes" are given lists and appraisals of such secondary authorities and primary sources as will enable serious students, without waste of time, to enter upon an intensive study of such topics as they may be interested in.

Unusual emphasis has been placed on the notes and references given at the bottom of the pages. The longer notes are intended to serve two purposes. One is to amplify or explain certain statements made in the text which either treat the topics under discussion very briefly or else presuppose a knowledge of related facts that all readers may not possess. The other is to present opposing views on certain points on which the authorities are not in entire agreement. The references cited in the shorter footnotes are mostly to primary sources, though quite a number of them are to secondary authorities. Those of the former class are put in as an aid to the student who may wish to find his way easily to accessible primary sources. Most of these references are to documentary collections or source books that can be found in any good college library. As a rule, references to secondary authorities indicate that I have leaned heavily on the passages cited, having borrowed either the language or the thought of the author.

In the preparation of this volume I have been favored with the counsel of a number of scholars, all of whom have offered important suggestions for the improvement of the work. In acknowledging my indebtedness to these, I wish especially to express my appreciation of the assistance rendered by Dean Guy Stanton Ford, of the Graduate School of the University of Minnesota, the editor of the series to which this history belongs. A very careful reading of the entire manuscript enabled him to make a number of discriminating criticisms that were indispensable. All of the manuscript, or nearly all of it, was also read by Professor David Dale Johnson, head of the English Department of West Virginia University, and Dean Elbert Jay Benton, of the Graduate School of Western Reserve University, both of whom offered valuable suggestions; the former as to style, and the latter as to factual content. One or more chapters were read by each of the following scholars: Professors Charles M. Andrews, of Yale University; Robert D. W. Connor, of the University of North Carolina; Harold U. Faulkner, of Smith College; Percy S. Flippin, of Coker College; Louis K. Koontz, of the University of California at Los Angeles; Charles C. Tansill, of the American University; T. J. Wertenbaker, of Princeton University; Dr. Charles O. Paullin and Dr. Edmund C. Burnett, of the Carnegie Institution of Washington, D. C.; and Professors Charles H. Ambler, John D. Barnhart, James M. Callahan, Carl M. Frasure, John F. Sly, and Dean Wilson P. Shortridge, of West Virginia University. In most cases the topics examined by each of these historians belong to the field in which he holds high rank as a specialist, and, therefore, the emendations suggested by them have proved most useful. It is to be understood, however, that none of these specialists is in any way responsible for any errors that may have crept into the book.

I wish also to express my appreciation of the courteous assistance given me by the officials of the Library of Congress, where most of the material for this work was collected.

OLIVER PERRY CHITWOOD

West Virginia University
   May 15, 1931

PREFACE TO THE SECOND EDITION

In this revision of the original work the following changes have been made:

The elimination of minor errors which have been revealed by the use of the book as a college text. These corrections, although of considerable number, have involved only slight changes.

The modification of a few original statements to bring them in line with recent research embodied in monographs and books published since 1930. These revisions, although not numerous, are important in that they correct wrong impressions. They have, however, been kept within the original framework.

The addition of two chapters (XXXIV and XXXV) to continue the narrative to 1789. In preparing this extra material I have leaned heavily on Chapters XV and XVI of *A Short History of the American People*, by O. P. Chitwood and Frank L. Owsley. There have been liberal borrowings as to factual content and in some passages the method of expression has been followed with little or no change. For this privilege we are indebted to the courtesy of D. Van Nostrand Company, the publishers of *A Short History*. I wish also to acknowledge my indebtedness to Dr. D. D. Johnson, Professor Emeritus of English, West Virginia University, for valuable assistance in the preparation of one of these chapters.

A slight change in three of the original maps and the addition of three maps and one chart. The map showing the English continental colonies in 1760 is taken from Faulkner's *American Economic History*, and the two maps showing the vote distribution in the ratification of the Constitution come from Harper's *Atlas of American History*; both published by Harper & Brothers.

The insertion of pictures illustrating the life of the people.

The revision of the Bibliographical Notes so as to bring them up to date. A few of the older titles have been omitted and others, published since 1930, have been added.

The enlargement of the Index, mainly by including items covering the new material.

March, 1948   O.P.C.

Part I:

THE ORIGIN AND DEVELOPMENT
OF THE COLONIES

A HISTORY OF
COLONIAL AMERICA

CHAPTER I

THE BACKGROUND OF COLONIAL AMERICAN
HISTORY

THE colonial history of North America is really a chapter in the The Eu-history of Europe. It is an account of the attempt to transplant a ropean mature civilization from an old to a new world. (The culture of back-the new continent naturally developed along somewhat different ground lines from that of the old, but the likenesses between parent and lonial child were greater than their differences.) The political and social history ideals and institutions, as well as the manners and customs, of Europe were brought over by the colonists, and the changes made in adapting them to the new environment were slow and gradual. To understand the early history of our country it is, therefore, necessary to know something about conditions in Europe at the time America was born into the family of civilized communities.

(As the colonies that later became the United States were all the daughters—either by birth or adoption—of England and, therefore, derived their institutions mainly from that country, a knowledge of England is more important for our purposes than that of any other European nation) But important contributions to our colonial history were also made by some of the peoples of continental Europe. Many of the early explorers were from Spain, France, the Netherlands, and Italy, and emigrants from the Netherlands, Sweden, Germany, Switzerland, and France played an important part in the planting and development of the original thirteen colonies. (Moreover, certain great movements on the Continent, like the Protestant Reformation and the religious wars, either stimulated emigration to America or exerted a marked influence on the religious and social views of the early settlers.) It will, therefore, be necessary at times to preface the

narrative of events and the discussion of institutions in the colo
nies with an account of such European events and movements as
are vitally related to our early history.

CONTINENTAL EUROPE AT THE BEGINNING OF THE SIXTEENTH CENTURY

Italy and
Germany

At the time America was discovered Italy and Germany were
only geographical terms. Each country was divided into a number
of small states, and in neither of them had an effective general
government been established. In Italy local jealousies caused
frequent disputes between the little principalities, which kept
them constantly in a state of military weakness and invited the
aggression of their powerful neighbors. The rulers both of
France and Spain laid claim to portions of Italy, and for decades
the peninsula was the battleground on which these two powers
fought out their rivalries. This divided condition of Italy had
not prevented her people from playing the leading part in the
Renaissance movement, but it rendered impossible that governmental assistance on a large scale which was necessary to promote exploration and colonization. Therefore, while many explorers were Italians, hardly any of them sailed under the flag
of their own country, and so the governments of Italy took no
part officially in the exploration and colonization of the New
World. The spirit of disunion in Germany was aggravated by
the Protestant Reformation, which divided the people into two
antagonistic religious parties. Moreover, by the Reformation
movement the attention of the people was directed into ecclesiastical and religious rather than geographical channels. Hence
while other nations were sailing strange seas and blazing trails
in a new world, Germany was exploring in the realm of the spirit
and trying to find a better way to the New Jerusalem. But
though official Germany had no share in the occupation of the
New World, the German people did take an important part in the
colonization of America. The hardships to which the people were
subjected, largely because their governments were too weak to
protect them against foreign aggression, caused numbers of them
to leave the fatherland and settle in the colonies that other nations
had established.

France

Germany and Italy were not the only regions which feudal
disintegration had split up into numerous petty states. France,
too, in the Middle Ages had been divided into a number of small

feudal districts. The counts and dukes who controlled these little principalities were virtually independent, though they gave a nominal allegiance to the French king, who, according to the feudal theory, was their overlord or suzerain. But the king had only nominal authority outside of the domain that he controlled as feudal lord. (By the end of the fifteenth century the kings of France had consolidated their power and extended their authority over the whole of France. The power of the monarchy had gradually increased until now it was the strongest in Europe.)

Portugal

(The countries of continental Europe that are of especial interest to the student of early American history are Spain and Portugal, as they are the ones that took the lead in showing Europe the way to America.\ To understand how and why they played such an important part in discovery and exploration we have to note briefly some of the events in their previous history. In the eighth century the Spanish peninsula was overrun by the Mohammedan Moors. The native Christian population was brought under the rule of the Mohammedans or driven back into the mountains. The mountain strongholds became centers of opposition to the conquerors, and soon the Christians began to throw off the foreign yoke and gradually to regain the land of their fathers. In the long and bitter fight between the Christians and the Mohammedans the latter gradually lost ground until by the middle of the thirteenth century (1266) they had been deprived of all of their territory except the mountainous kingdom of Granada in the south. Out of the territory thus wrested from the Moors there grew up a number of little Christian states. One of the most important of these was Portugal, which had reached its present territorial limits by 1263. By the opening of the sixteenth century this little principality had attained an importance out of all proportion to its size. It had had a succession of able rulers, and in the fifteenth century was able to play a leading part in the explorations along the African coast.

The other small Christian states were gradually consolidated into larger ones, and by the end of the thirteenth century two of these principalities, Castile and Aragon, contained within their limits the greater part of the territory of the peninsula. These two kingdoms were united by a marriage (1469) between Isabella of Castile and Ferdinand, prospective ruler of Aragon. Ferdinand and Isabella now had the territorial basis for a great nation. Other portions of the Spanish peninsula were afterward

Spain

acquired by these able sovereigns, and Granada, the last Moorish state, was conquered and annexed to Castile (1492). All of the Spanish peninsula except Portugal had now been brought under the authority of the joint sovereigns.[1] The Spanish sovereigns were thus in a position at the end of the fifteenth century to encourage and support the explorations and discoveries in America which were destined to add to Spain a great empire in the New World.

The Netherlands

Next to the English the Dutch have probably had the greatest influence of any of the European peoples on the early history of the United States. At the middle of the sixteenth century the term Netherlands, or Low Countries, was applied to the region now comprised approximately within the countries of Belgium and the Netherlands and consisted of seventeen provinces loosely held together by a common ruler. In 1555 Philip II of Spain became the ruler of the Low Countries. The Protestant movement had already come to the Netherlands and had made many converts. In his effort to stamp out this heresy, Philip carried out a most cruel policy of persecution through the Inquisition and imposed unreasonable taxes and other burdens on the people. As a result there broke out a revolt (1568) that proved to be one of the bravest fights for political and religious freedom known to history. For a while all sections of the Low Countries were united in their opposition to the Spanish king, but later the southern Catholic provinces came to an understanding with Philip and thus remained under Spanish control. The seven northern provinces, now thoroughly Protestant in religion, continued the fight under the heroic leadership of William the Silent until their independence was recognized by Spain.

The Renaissance

In Europe the transition from the mediæval to the modern era was marked by a great intellectual upheaval, which in turn was followed by an ecclesiastical revolution. The first of these movements is known as the Renaissance; the second, as the Protestant Reformation. The Renaissance started in Italy and it grew out of an increased interest in the study of Latin and Greek. A knowledge of these languages was cultivated by a few people, mainly the clergy, throughout the Middle Ages. But in Italy in the fourteenth century scholars began to study Latin and afterward Greek with an enthusiasm that amounted almost

[1] For map illustrating the unification of Spain, see Bolton, H. E., *History of the Americas*, p. 13.

to a religion. This enthusiasm they were able to impart to others, and as a result the Italian states, and later the other countries of western Europe, were swept by a great revival of learning. The classics were so thoroughly mastered that the treasures stored away in them were liberated by the scholars and appropriated by the people because at this juncture printing was invented (about the middle of the fifteenth century), and this greatly aided in disseminating and popularizing the new learning. The interest in the classics was not confined to language and literature, but extended also to the philosophy, science, and art of the ancients. There was, therefore, a great awakening in architecture, painting, and sculpture.

The Renaissance was not merely the revival of an old civilization, but also the beginning of a new. The new ideas acquired from the study of the Greek and Latin writings acted as a tonic on the mind and stimulated originality in thought and initiative in action, and this activity showed itself in all the various fields of mental endeavor. It led to a renewed interest in geography. The invention of the compass and astrolabe made possible longer voyages on the ocean, and these in turn extended the knowledge of geography and whetted the desire for information as to the unexplored portions of the globe.

(The chief significance of the Renaissance for our purposes lies in the fact that it gave a new spirit to Europe.) It inspired the people with optimism, self-reliance, a feeling of freedom from conventional restraints, and an adventurous faith. It rejuvenated the mind of Europe and arrested the tendency toward intellectual senility, toward which mediæval theology and scholastic philosophy were pushing it. The stream of classical learning was a veritable fountain of youth to those who drank from it. Whenever the new learning got a firm hold on a people it gave a severe shock to conservatism and enabled the progressives to wrest from the standpatters the leadership in thought and action. (It was this progressive and daring attitude of mind that furnished Europe with the spiritual equipment needed in venturing upon expeditions that led to the discovery of new lands and new routes to the old ones.)

(In the beginning of the sixteenth century the people in all of Europe west of Russia and the Balkan peninsula, except the Moors in Spain and the Jews, belonged to the Roman Catholic) The Reformation

Church. In the Balkan peninsula there were some Turks and Albanians who were Mohammedans. The rest of the population of the Balkans and all the Russians belonged to the Greek Catholic Church. The Christian church had been divided into these two branches since the eleventh century. The western church was well organized with the pope at its head. Thanks to its efficient organization, it was able to preserve its unity throughout the Middle Ages, though there had been occasional outbursts of heresy, all of which, however, the authorities had been able to suppress.

Early in the sixteenth century there broke out in Germany an ecclesiastical revolt under the leadership of Martin Luther that resulted in a permanent division of the church. The movement started as a protest (1517) against what Luther considered improper practices of the church, and apparently he had at first no intention of forming a new denomination and making a "rent in the seamless robe of Christ." But the breach between Luther and his opponents soon became so wide that there was no possibility of bridging it over with a compromise. The pope excommunicated Luther (1520) and so put an end to all hope that the two parties might become reconciled to each other. From that time until the present, western Christendom has been divided into the two rival camps of Protestants and Catholics, the former being the followers of Luther and other reformers and the latter the adherents of the old faith. Next year (1521) Luther was also condemned by the emperor, Charles V, in the Edict of Worms.[2] By this edict Luther was declared an outlaw and his life forfeited. But Charles was so busy with his wars and other interests that the edict was not enforced in Germany. Lutheranism, being thus left free to expand, spread rapidly in the North German states and soon had overrun the Scandinavian countries.

Calvin at
Geneva

(Soon after Luther started his revolt in the church, Ulrich Zwingli began to attack the authority of Rome at Zurich, in Switzerland) His views were readily accepted by his compatriots, and in a short time several Swiss cantons had thrown off their allegiance to the old church. From Switzerland the new doctrines found their way to Geneva. In 1536 John Calvin, an able French-

---

[2] Charles, besides being king of Spain and other lands, was at the head of the Holy Roman Empire, a name used to designate the loose and weak union of the German states.

man, took charge of the reform movement there and this city soon became Protestant. Geneva was under his control for a number of years, and during this time his religious views were enforced by the state.

Calvin had an exceptionally logical mind, and he was the ablest writer among the early Protestant theologians. His great theological treatise, *The Institutes of the Christian Religion*, was regarded by his Catholic opponents as the "Koran of the heretics." Owing largely to the fine literary quality of his writings, his works, more than those of any of the other reformers, were accepted in the sixteenth and seventeenth centuries as a correct formulation of the Protestant doctrines. Geneva also became an asylum for religious exiles from other lands, most of whom were imbued with Calvin's ideas as to religion. *Calvin formulates the Protestant doctrines*

John Calvin was the great moral and religious teacher of our ancestors. It is doubtful whether any man who has lived since the days of the Apostle Paul has influenced American thinking along ecclesiastical and ethical lines more than has the great Genevan theologian. In colonial times his theological views were the basis of the doctrines held by the Congregationalists, the Presbyterians, most of the Baptists, the adherents of the Dutch Reformed and German Reformed Churches, and a good many of the Anglicans. To these denominations belonged the great majority of the people in colonial days. Besides, some of the sects, like the Quakers, Mennonites, and Dunkards, that did not accept his theological views, lived up to his rigid standard of morality. *The influence of John Calvin*

Calvin taught that Adam by his sin had brought condemnation and spiritual death upon all his progeny, and that, therefore, no one is able to raise himself from his fallen condition by his own efforts. But Christ came and died and made it possible for some who are spiritually dead to be revived by the Holy Spirit, who moves upon the heart and quickens it into life. This redemptive experience, however, is not open to all mankind. No one has it unless he is called of God, and God calls only certain ones who have been elected from the foundation of the world. The elect are predestined to be saved, and all others are predestined to be lost, and there is nothing the non-elect sinner can do to put himself in the favored class. *Calvin's doctrine*

Calvin believed in the infallibility of the Bible—that the authors of the Scriptures were the "sure and authentic amanuenses of the Holy Spirit."[3] In his interpretation of the Old and New Testament he emphasized the sovereignty of God and denied the freedom of the human will. Despite the fact that man is not a free agent morally, the Christian is under a binding obligation to live up to a high ethical code; for correct moral behavior is an evidence of God's call, and it is by right living that we make sure of our calling and election. Moreover, if one is really chosen of God the consciousness of this great favor creates within him an overpowering desire to achieve a character worthy of this high calling and thus not grieve the Holy Spirit that has brought about his redemption. Calvin insisted, therefore, upon the practice of a stern morality and reined up his followers to the most rigid discipline. Amusements were frowned upon and undue prominence was given to the serious side of life. The chief end of man was, he taught, "to know and do the will of God."

Calvinism has been favorable to the progress of civil liberty. The belief that God is all-powerful and man comparatively insignificant made the adherents of this doctrine bold toward human rulers and defiant toward their commands when these conflicted with their rights and principles. The followers of the Genevan reformer, who considered themselves as belonging to the elect, had a lofty disdain of "mortal peril and earthly grandeur." "Taught that they were kings by the election of God and priests by the imposition of his hands, they despised the puny and vicious monarchs of this earth."[4] Besides, in Calvin's plan for the government of the church there was an element of democracy inasmuch as there was a provision that laymen were to have a voice in the choice of their pastors. Circumstances in Geneva were such that Calvin was unable to realize fully his theory as to the power of the people in church affairs, but his teachings on this point had a democratic tendency.

Protestantism with doctrines and church government as formulated by Calvin, Luther, and others spread throughout western Europe and became especially strong in Switzerland, the Low Countries, the Scandinavian Peninsula, England, and Scotland.

The French Protestants, or Huguenots, as they were called,

[3] For an excellent statement of Calvin's theological opinions, with numerous quotations from his writings, see WALKER, W., *John Calvin*, ch. 15.

[4] SMITH, P., *The Age of the Reformation*, pp. 167-168. See also FISHER, G. P., *The Reformation*, p. 208.

unfortunately allowed their cause to become entangled with the ambitions of some politicians who were scheming for power. As a result, there was a long series of civil wars characterized by conspiracies and assassinations on both sides. Finally, Henry of Navarre, the leader of the Protestants, came to the throne of France, and it looked as if the long contest would end in victory for the Huguenots. (But Henry was satisfied that a heretic king would never be recognized by the Catholic leaders and the great mass of the people, who were Catholics. So to put an end to bloodshed and secure for himself a comfortable seat on the throne, he changed his religious allegiance and became a Catholic. This ended the strife and saved France, though it struck a severe blow to Protestantism. However, Henry did not entirely forget his old supporters, but in the Edict of Nantes (1598) gave them a considerable measure of toleration.)

Protestantism in France

England in the Sixteenth Century

The end of the fifteenth century found England with a strong kingship. The feudal system there had never gone as far toward anarchy as it had in France and Germany. (But under the weak rule of Henry VI there began (1455) a terrible civil struggle, known as the Wars of the Roses, which gave England an experience of the evils of feudal disorder. When these wars ended (1485), Henry VII came to the throne as the first Tudor king.) Circumstances were now favorable for the establishment of a strong monarchy, and under him the authority of the crown was almost absolute. The people were tired of civil strife and anarchy and were willing to purchase peace and order by a partial sacrifice of their liberties.)

England under the Tudors

The strong monarchy founded by the first Tudor sovereign was passed on to his son, Henry VIII, under whom the powers of the crown were still further enlarged. By separating the English church from that of Rome and putting himself at its head, Henry VIII brought the ecclesiastical organization under his control. Besides, the suppression of the monasteries and the confiscation of their property gave him the means with which to attach to himself the new nobility, which was largely his own creation. (So under Henry VIII the monarchy was more nearly absolute than it has been in any other period of English history.) Absolutism acquired so much force under the first two Tudors that it ran cn its own momentum during the reigns of their

immediate successors, Edward VI and Mary, and being reinforced by the vigorous policy of Elizabeth, continued until the
end of her long reign.

Henry VIII, although he was an orthodox Catholic in his
theological views, got into a quarrel with the pope, which resulted in the separation of the English church from that of
Rome.[5] Henry had his subservient Parliament pass an Act of
Supremacy (1534), which placed the king at the head of the
independent English church. This change did not make the
church Protestant, but it prepared the way for reforms in the
direction of Protestantism that came later. Under Henry's successor, Edward VI, Protestantism became the established religion
of the kingdom. A Confession of Faith and a Book of Common
Prayer embodying Protestant doctrines were adopted and all the
people were compelled to accept them. Edward's successor, Mary
(1553-58), who was a devout adherent of the old faith, brought
England back into the Catholic fold. There was not only a return
to the teachings of Catholicism, but the authority of the pope
was also recognized. Under Elizabeth (1558-1603) Protestantism was restored and the Acts of Supremacy and Uniformity
were passed (1559), which made the Anglican the established
church of the realm. By the former of these laws the queen was
declared the head of the church and by the latter conformity to
the doctrines of the Articles of Faith (now reduced to thirty-
nine) and the Prayer Book was required of all ministers. The
state church was supported by taxation, and all other religious
denominations had no legal standing.

In the meantime Scotland had, under the leadership of John
Knox, been converted to Protestantism. Knox was a follower of
John Calvin. A majority of the Scotch became Presbyterians,
who were more radically Protestant than the adherents of the
Church of England. The Irish remained loyal to the old church.

[5] This quarrel arose over the effort of Henry to get rid of his first
wife, Catherine of Aragon, in order that he might marry Anne
Boleyn, one of her ladies in waiting. In fairness to Henry it ought to
be said, however, that his infatuation for Anne Boleyn was not the
only reason that he wanted a divorce from Catherine. All of Catherine's children had died in childhood except one daughter and she
was of rather frail health. Henry was anxious to have a son to succeed him, and there was no hope of this as long as Catherine remained
as the royal consort.

a more efficient form of organization.] It enabled men of small, as well as those of large, means to take part in the great projects of the day. Moreover, wealth at that time was venturesome and patriotic, and the capitalists were willing to hazard their newly-acquired gains in promoting commercial and colonial expansion.

The economic progress that characterized the reign of Elizabeth was purchased at a high cost to the laboring class. The sudden increase in the world's supply of precious metals, due to the stream of gold and silver that had been flowing into Europe from the Spanish possessions in America, had caused a considerable increase in prices. Wages had not been raised in the same proportion, and so the laboring classes were finding it difficult to procure the means of living. Moreover, during the sixteenth century landlords were diverting a considerable amount of their lands from the cultivation of grain to the pasturage of sheep.[6] This change deprived many agricultural laborers of employment. The dissolution of the monasteries by Henry VIII in this same century had also helped to aggravate the troubles of the poor, as some of the monasteries were better landlords than the nobles who took over their lands. These monasteries had also served as charitable agencies and had done much to relieve the suffering caused by pauperism. The laboring classes could not better their condition, for they were unorganized and were completely at the mercy of the nobility and gentry who controlled the local and national government. There were thus at the beginning of the seventeenth century a large number of laborers who could not find employment. As they were accustomed to hard work, they were well suited to pioneering in a new world. There was also available an abundance of capital ready to organize itself into

[6] The explanation for the inclosures of the fifteenth and sixteenth centuries usually given by historians is that the high price of wool of that period made sheep-raising more profitable than farming. Miss Harriett Bradley, in her monograph on *The Enclosures in England*, takes exception to this view. She points out that "the price of wool fell during the fifteenth century, and failed to rise as rapidly as that of wheat in the sixteenth century." The real reason for the inclosures, she thinks, was that the lands which were converted into sheep pastures had been worn out and were no longer adapted to successful agriculture. See BRADLEY, HARRIETT, *The Enclosures in England* (Columbia University *Studies in History Economics and Public Law*, lxxx, no. 2, ch. 1)

The Anglican Church as organized under Elizabeth w
acceptable to all the people. There were quite a number wh
to the beliefs and practices of the Roman Catholic commu
and still acknowledged the pope as the head of the church. At
opposite extreme from the conservative Catholics were a gro
of radical Protestants, known as Puritans.) They considered th
Anglicans too conservative in ritual and doctrine and not rigid
enough in their moral standards. The established church, they
thought, had not gone far enough away from Rome—was too
much like that of the Catholics, as to both church government
and religious practices. The Puritans wanted to simplify the administration of the church and do away with what they called
popish customs in worship. They also wished to purify the establishment of what they deemed errors in doctrine.

Among the refugees at Geneva there were quite a number of
Protestants from England who had been driven from home by the
persecutions under Queen Mary. When these exiles returned to
the homeland they brought with them religious notions more
radically Protestant than those held by a majority of the adherents
of the state church. It was from these radicals and others of like
belief that the Puritan dissenters were recruited. (The English
Puritans of the early seventeenth century were indoctrinated
with the political, as well as the theological, philosophy of Calvinism and did not overlook its democratic leanings; for they
were quick to resent any infringement of their rights by their
rulers.)

The earl
Puritan
indoctri-
nated by
Calvin

(The sixteenth century was for England a period not only
important intellectual and religious changes, but also one
marked economic development.) The discovery and exploitatic
America had opened up new opportunities for trade an
greatly increased the amount of gold and silver availa
circulation as money. While agriculture was still the mai
tion of the people at the end of the century, the manu
woolens was a growing industry, especially in the s
counties, which furnished many of the emigrants
These economic changes had greatly enhanced the
nation. This new wealth was not equally distri
merchants received more, and the laborers an
lower classes less, than would have been the
apportionment. (During this century the Engli
the Dutch the idea of the joint-stock company

joint-stock companies for the financing of colonization ventures. Besides, the stirring events of the reign of Elizabeth brought forward men of courage, vision, patriotism, and daring initiative. These stood ready either to search out new lands or to lead settlers to occupy them when found.

At the end of the sixteenth century the people of England were divided into clearly distinguished classes. At the top of the social ladder were the nobility, who with the higher clergy had a monopoly of the seats in the House of Lords. The next class included the professional men, scholars, military leaders, and the landed gentry. The most influential group in this class was the gentry. It consisted of the large landholders, many of whom were quite wealthy. Although they were comparatively few in number, they held a very prominent place in both the local and general government. It was from this group that the justices of the peace were selected and the membership of the House of Commons was largely recruited. The men belonging to the two higher classes enjoyed the distinction of being called "gentlemen," which means that they did not have to work with their hands for a living. Another group which might be considered as a separate class was that of the merchants, or the bourgeois.[7] It had grown rapidly in numbers and importance during the reign of Elizabeth as a result of the rapid commercial expansion of that exciting period. It played a large part in the occupation of America by furnishing most of the capital by which British colonial ventures were financed. Next in social rank came the yeomanry, comprising those persons who owned and cultivated small farms. This class was quite numerous and constituted the backbone of English society. These independent landowners enjoyed the right of suffrage, and they composed the bulk of the rural voters. Just below the yeomanry in social position was the class that was made up of the tenant farmers in the country and the mechanics and smaller tradespeople in the towns. These were denied the privilege of voting and so exerted little influence on the government, though some of them filled minor offices in the towns and rural parishes. Still lower in the scale both economically and socially were the farm laborers. The members of this very numerous class were dependent upon their daily earnings

Social classes

[7] This group is sometimes classed with that of the professional men. See TRAIL, H. D., *Social England*, iii, pp. 377-383.

for a living, and the families of many of them were often in dire poverty.[8]

The lines that separated the people into distinct classes, while clearly drawn, were not insuperable barriers. The last half of the sixteenth century was a period of rapid economic changes, and consequently there was a frequent shifting of the social boundaries. Individuals, by a betterment of their economic status, were constantly rising to higher social levels. Unfortunately, however, this rearrangement of society did not change to any considerable extent the aristocratic ideals of the people. The humbler classes were still despised and were not accorded as generous a treatment as they deserved.

Extent
of the
English
dominions
at the end
of the
sixteenth
century

At the end of the sixteenth century the English dominions were restricted to what are now England and Wales and a district in the eastern part of Ireland, which had been held since the time of Henry II. Scotland was entirely separate from England until James I came to the English throne (1603). He was already king of Scotland, and when he succeeded to the English crown the two kingdoms were joined in a personal union. But the two countries still remained separate as to government, and for another century the king was the only common bond that held them together. In 1707 under Queen Anne an act of union was passed providing for a common Parliament for both England and Scotland. From that time until the present, the whole island of Great Britain has been united under one government.

The intellectual awakening experienced by the English people in the latter part of the sixteenth century gave to their culture a fresh vigor that served it in good stead in its struggle to gain a foothold in the New World. A decadent civilization would not have been equal to the hostile influences of the wilderness and so would not have taken root in the new soil. To the first settlers in America the unharnessed natural resources appeared in a very different light from that in which they are viewed by their descendants after having been exploited and appropriated to the uses of man. Nature in her untamed state was in pioneer days more often a tyrannical mistress than an obedient servant, and the natural environment was too harsh to permit the survival of a transplanted civilization unless it showed signs of exceptional vitality. As the history of the American colonies is largely an

[8] For a contemporary account of the social classes in England, see WEST, W. M., *A Source Book in American History*, pp. 1-3.

account of the attempt to effect a mutual adjustment between a full-grown civilization and its wilderness environment, it is necessary to take a glance at the physical geography of the region first occupied by our ancestors.

PHYSICAL GEOGRAPHY OF NORTH AMERICA

That portion of the present United States which was occupied and held by the English colonists is divided into two sections, the Atlantic Slope and the Appalachian Highland.[9] The Atlantic Slope lies between the Appalachian Mountains and the coast and extends all the way from the northern limits of New England to Florida. It is divided into two parts, the Tidewater Belt and the Piedmont Plateau. *The Atlantic Slope*

The former is an alluvial plain extending from the ocean westward to the waterfalls that usually separate the navigable from the unnavigable portions of the streams. As the boundary between the Tidewater and Piedmont sections is determined by these falls, it is known as the fall line. Throughout the Tidewater Belt the elevation above sea-level is so slight that the tide goes up the rivers all the way to the falls. But at these points there is usually an abrupt break, and the deep quiet streams suddenly become shallow and swift-flowing rivers. The rapids that mark the transition afford valuable water power. In New England the fall line is so close to the sea that there is a very small extent of coastal plain. From New York southward it broadens out until it attains a width of about two hundred miles in Georgia. There are rich bottom lands along the rivers, but with this exception the soil is generally of only moderate fertility and in some places is quite poor. A good deal of the region is swampy and unhealthful, especially in the south. *The Tidewater Belt*

The Piedmont Plateau extends all the way from New England to Alabama and attains a width in the middle section of about one hundred and fifty miles. Being well drained, the whole region is comparatively free from marshes and the climate is healthful and delightful. The soil is generally fertile, and especially so in the river valleys. *The Piedmont Plateau*

The Appalachian Highland is an elevated region consisting of mountains, plateaus, and valleys extending from northern New England to central Alabama and central Georgia. There are only *The Appalachian Highland*

[9] For a physical map of North America, see SHEPHERD, W. R., *Historical Atlas*, pp. 186-187.

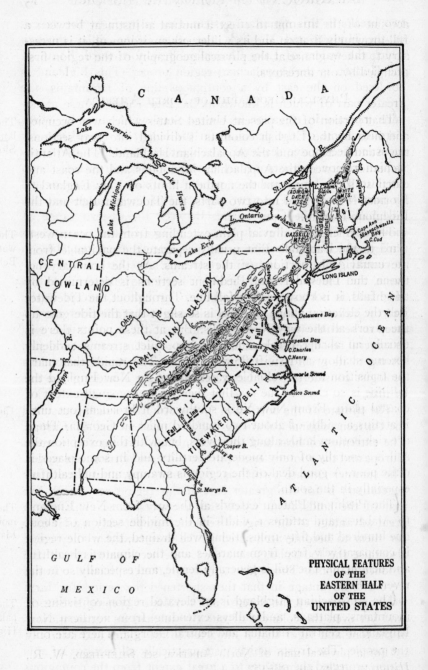

PHYSICAL FEATURES
OF THE
EASTERN HALF
OF THE
UNITED STATES

two breaks in this mountain system. One is made by the valleys of the Hudson and Mohawk, the other is the valley through which the waters of Lake Champlain flow northward. South of the Hudson is the Appalachian region proper. This highland is bordered on the east by a continuous line of mountains, the greater part of which is known as the Blue Ridge. These mountains increase in elevation as we go southward, until in North Carolina some of the peaks attain the height of more than six thousand feet above sea-level. The western portion of the Appalachian region consists of an elevated plateau traversed from north to south by a number of parallel mountain ranges separated by narrow valleys. The most important of these ranges are the Alleghany and the Cumberland. Between the eastern range of mountains and the western plateau is located the Appalachian Valley, which "under different names extends from the Hudson to central Alabama." It is underlaid to a large extent with limestone, and the soil is very fertile. The rest of the Appalachian Highland is not especially adapted to agriculture, except in the narrow valleys, as many of the hills and mountain sides are too steep to be cultivated profitably. This region was and still is rich in mineral resources such as coal, iron, petroleum, and natural gas. Owing to its great natural resources and good climate, a modern geologist considers it the finest section in the world for the use of man.

The climate of the portion of North America which comprised the thirteen original colonies is quite similar to that of Europe. The extremes of heat and cold are greater here than in western Europe and the winters, except in the southern portion, are colder. The summer climate (which is most important, as it determines vegetation) is for the greater part of this region very much like that of the lands from which our ancestors came. This was a great advantage to the original settlers. For not only was it easy for them to become acclimated in the new land, but they could also raise the food plants that they were accustomed to use and produce at home. The colder winters in the continental colonies were a disadvantage in that they shortened the period for farm work and increased the expense and trouble of keeping live-stock. And yet even the coldness of our climate had its compensations in the tone and vigor that it imparted to the bodies and minds of the people. The frosts which visit practically all sections of this region protected the settlers to a great extent from the contagious

Climate

fevers which otherwise would have come to them from the tropics. The diseases here were also those to which the Europeans were accustomed and to which they had acquired a partial immunity.

Forests Nearly all of the territory within the present limits of the United States east of the prairies was originally covered over with valuable forests.[10] There were in this region great numbers of hardwood, or deciduous, trees and also several varieties of conifers, or softwood trees. Among the most important varieties of the former class may be mentioned the oak, hickory, elm, maple, chestnut, walnut, and ash. Of the latter class the most important were the long-leaved, or yellow, pine in the south and the short-leaved, or white, pine in the north. The last-named has been the most valuable commercially of all our trees. It was found not only in the northern colonies, but also on the Appalachian Mountains nearly to their southern limit. The first settlers probably considered the trees an obstacle rather than an aid to settlement, owing to the amount of labor required to clear them off the land. And yet the forest was a great blessing both to the Indian and the early settler. It was not only a source of supply of wood for fuel and of lumber for building purposes (and in some places for export), but it also furnished acorns and other feed for hogs and was an invaluable hunting-ground for wild animals.

Animal life The wild game found in forest and stream was the main dependence of the Indian for food and was an important supplement to the domestic supply of the European immigrant. The wild animals also furnished both with furs and skins, which were used as clothing and constituted one of the most important of all the exports from the colonies. Among the important fur-bearing animals may be mentioned the beaver, otter, mink, muskrat, sable, and skunk. Of these, the most important was the beaver. It was widely distributed and more of its skins have been taken than of any other North American animal. There were also in the greatest plenty wild fowl of the most edible varieties, such as pigeons, ducks, geese, quail, and turkeys. Fish and oysters were also of great value to both the Indians and the colonists. Oysters

---

[10] It is said that the Valley of Virginia and portions of the Carolina Piedmont were without trees when the Europeans first came. These sections and the small patches used by the Indians for farming were practically the only breaks in the forest.

were found everywhere on the coasts and in the salt-water bays and streams. Fish were plentiful not only in these same waters, but were also caught in large quantities in the fresh-water streams and lakes.

The Original Inhabitants of North America

When North America was first seen by Europeans, the number of Indians within the present United States, including Alaska, was, according to the best estimates, a little more than one million. The Indians had made almost no impression on the great natural resources of the continent. The coal, iron, and most of the other minerals had not been touched by them. They had little more than begun to clear the forest even, for much of the land tilled by them was along the streams and was naturally free from trees. In short, middle North America under their control was making almost no contribution toward the progress of civilization. Nor have the Indians made any substantial contribution to the civilization that we now have in the United States, though they did render valuable aid to the colonists in the early stages of settlement. They taught the newcomers how to clear the land and plant and cultivate corn and tobacco. They acted as guides for the first settlers through the trackless forest, and procured for them most of the furs that were exported to Europe. They showed the colonials how to make maple sugar, to hunt and trap wild animals, and to dress their skins. From the Indians the whites learned how to make the birch-bark canoe, which was an invaluable aid in penetrating the wilderness. To them we are also indebted for many euphonious names for our rivers, lakes, and mountains, which have given a tinge of poetry to American geography.[11] Aside from these contributions, American life has not been modified by Indian influence. The red men, however, have taken a keen interest in the effort of the Europeans to tame the wilderness and exploit its natural resources. During the time that this long contest has been going on they have sometimes played the part of allies and sometimes of enemies of civilization, while at others they have looked on with the disinterestedness of unofficial observers.

[11] For an excellent brief discussion of the influence of the Indians upon the life and the customs of the colonists, see WERTENBAKER, T. J., *The First Americans*, pp. 308-310.

The question naturally arises, why did they live in this good land for centuries without making any substantial advance in civilization? It was not due to a lack of native ability, for the great personalities that have come to the front in Indian history show that the race was not lacking in mental vigor. One explanation for their backwardness is that they had no beasts of burden or milch cattle, their only domestic animal being the dog. Agriculture is the basis of civilization everywhere, and extensive agriculture is well-nigh impossible when all the work is to be done with crude tools by the unaided strength of man. Then, too, the Indians were cut off from the Old World centers of culture and had no opportunity to learn from those who had advanced beyond them in civilization.[12] Whatever the explanation, the fact remains that the aboriginal inhabitants of our part of this continent failed to appreciate and exploit the richest gifts that nature has ever bestowed upon any land.

SELECTED READINGS

1. Social Conditions in Europe at the Opening of the Sixteenth Century.—Higby, C. P., *History of Europe*, *ch. 1.
2. The Protestant and Catholic Reformations.—Sellery, G. C., and Krey, A. C., *Medieval Foundations of Western Civilization*, *ch. 21.
3. The Renaissance.—An article by Symonds, J. A., in the *Encyclopedia Britannica* (very good).
4. The Physical Divisions of the United States.—Johnson, E. R., and others, eds., *History of Domestic and Foreign Commerce of the United States*, i, pp. *9-13; Powell, J. W., *Physiographic Regions of the United States* (*National Geographic Monographs*).
5. The Atlantic Slope.—Brigham, A. P., *Geographic Influences*, pp. *70-76 (for an excellent relief map of the northern Appalachian region and the accompanying coastal plain see opposite p. 76).
6. The Appalachian Highland.—Brigham, *op. cit.*, pp. 76-104.
7. The Physical Geography of the South.—Phillips, U. B., *Life and Labor in the Old South*, *ch. 1.

[12] It is hardly probable that the natives of the eastern half of the present United States had enough contacts with the Indians of Mexico and Central and South America to be influenced by the superior civilization of the latter groups of people.

8. Original Forest.—Whitney, J. D., in *Encyclopedia Britannica,* 9th ed., xxiii, pp. *859-863; or 14th ed., xxii, pp. *714-723.
9. Animal Life.—Russell, I. C., *North America,* pp. 269-298; Shaler, N. S., *The United States of America,* i, pp. *485-509.
10. Part Played by the Rivers in Exploration and Settlement.— Semple, Ellen C., *American History and Its Geographic Conditions* (1933 ed.), ch. 2.
11. The Influence of the Appalachian Barrier upon Colonial History. —*Ibid.,* *ch. 3.
12. Indians.—Shaler, *op. cit.,* i., pp. *33-34; Payne, E. J., *History of the New World Called America,* i, pp. *287-292.

CHAPTER II

THE DISCOVERY OF AMERICA

The
Norse
discov-
eries

PROBABLY the first explorers of the western Atlantic were the Northmen, or Norsemen, bold seamen, whose courage and daring compensated for what they lacked in the knowledge of navigation. The Norsemen were a race of fearless warriors, as well as bold sailors, who during the Middle Ages occupied the Danish and Scandinavian peninsulas. Life in the cold northland was too tame and unattractive to satisfy such an adventurous people, and so we find that in the ninth and tenth centuries numerous bands of them left the homeland to seek their fortunes in far-off regions. Not satisfied with the opportunities for conquest offered by the settled portions of Europe, these restless adventurers soon began to turn their attention to the unclaimed islands in the northern Atlantic. A settlement was made by them in Iceland in 874, and a century later (about 985) a colony was planted in Greenland under the leadership of Eric the Red, who had been exiled from Iceland on account of manslaughter.[1]

Vinland

As the Norse occupation of Iceland was permanent and that of Greenland lasted for about four centuries, these islands were doubtless used as a base for still further exploration into the uncharted seas to the west of them. Indeed these bold sea-rovers would have been untrue to their character had they not continued their advance to the west and reached the continent of North America. That this was actually done is attested by some very reliable Norse traditions. According to these traditions, the son of Eric the Red, Leif Ericsson, left the court of Norway in the year 1000 to take Christianity to his father's settlement in Greenland. On the voyage to Greenland he was driven out of his course and came to a land hitherto unknown. He found wheat and grapes growing wild, and the latter were so abundant that he called the new country Vinland. An effort was made to plant a settlement and voyages were kept up between Vinland and Greenland for

[1] OLSON, J. E., and BOURNE, E. G., eds., *The Northmen, Columbus, and Cabot*, pp. 15-17, 45-46.

about twelve years. However, the difficulties of founding and sustaining a colony in this far-off region were so great that the attempt proved unsuccessful and was finally given up.

The story of Vinland would probably have been forgotten had it not been kept alive by the Icelandic sagas, which are our main source of information for the history of the Norse discoveries. The sagas that tell of the discoveries on the mainland of North America were not written until the fourteenth and early fifteenth centuries. As they are so far removed in time from the events related by them, there has been a doubt in the minds of some scholars as to whether they should be accepted as trustworthy historical documents. But the sagas as we now have them are based on documents that are much older than themselves. Besides, the Vinland voyage is spoken of by Adam of Bremen, who wrote before 1076 and whose work is still extant.[2] There is, therefore, enough evidence to satisfy most modern scholars as to the fact of the Norse discoveries, though there is still great uncertainty as to the location of Vinland. About all we can say with reasonable certainty is that it was located somewhere between the southern coast of New England and the coast of Labrador.

The Norse discoveries have for us only an antiquarian interest, for they are in no way related to the subsequent history of America. It is not unlikely that Columbus had heard of Leif's

Signifi- cance of the Norse discov- eries

[2] For an account of Leif's discovery of Vinland, as given in the Saga of Eric the Red, which is the most trustworthy of the traditions that have come down to us, see OLSON and BOURNE, *op. cit.*, pp. 23-26. An excellent summary of this saga is given by FISCHER, JOSEPH, in his *The Discoveries of the Norsemen in America*, pp. 17-19. According to the story contained in the *Flatey Book*, the new land was first sighted by Biarni Herjulfson. For this account, see OLSON and BOURNE, *op. cit.*, pp. 47-49. Modern scholarship is inclined to discredit this latter story and accord to Leif the honor of discovering Vinland. Some historians, however, are still of the opinion that the account related in the *Flatey Book* is the most trustworthy. Prominent among those who hold this view is Geoffrey Gathorne-Hardy. The story of the Norse discoveries, as believed by him, is summarized excellently in his *Norse Discoveries*, pp. 16-17. For the later voyages and attempts at colonization, see OLSON and BOURNE, *op. cit.*, pp. 31-42, 54-56, 59-64. Adam of Bremen's statement regarding Vinland is given in *ibid.*, pp. 67-68. For an account of Adam of Bremen and his work, see FISCHER, *op. cit.*, pp. 1-4.

famous voyage, as he was probably in Iceland before 1492. But if he were acquainted with the story of Vinland, in all probability it had no effect in inciting him to his great endeavor. The Norse traditions spoke of an undeveloped land whose chief attractions were wild wheat and wild grapes; such a country would have had no charms for Columbus, who dreamed of the Indies, where gold and spices in abundance could be easily procured.

Europe not ready to occupy America until the modern era

It was well that the first attempt at colonization in America was abandoned, for Europe was not yet ready for so great an undertaking. The sailors of that day did not have the compass to direct their voyages nor the astrolabe to assist them in computing latitude. The science of navigation was in its infancy, and though fearless seamen did occasionally make long voyages with nothing but the stars to guide them, regular communication between a distant colony and the homeland was out of the question. Moreover, the Europeans did not have gunpowder at that early date and their weapons were not much better than those of the American Indians. It would, therefore, have been a marvel if a band of Europeans could have held their own anywhere on the American continent against the hostility of the natives. The civilization of western Europe was not yet ready to clear out for itself a place in the sun in an unfriendly wilderness. It had to wait until science had equipped it with the tools and armed it with the weapons that would enable it to demonstrate its economic and military superiority over American savagery.

Incorrect notions of the East held by Europeans in the Middle Ages

That part of the known or partially known world that excited the liveliest interest was the Far East—central, eastern, and southeastern Asia. During the Middle Ages this far-off region was a twilight zone about which Europeans had only vague and incorrect notions. The Crusades widened out the known area and stimulated curiosity as to the unexplored regions of the farther East. In the later Middle Ages a few missionaries and travelers made journeys into this distant land and, returning, gave marvelous accounts of their experiences.[3] From these accounts and

[3] The most noted of these accounts is the one written by Marco Polo, who returned to Venice in 1295 after having traveled in the Far East for about twenty years. In his narrative the wealth of Cipangu (Japan) and the Spice Islands appears fabulous. See BROOKS, NOAH, *The Story of Marco Polo* (1898). For accounts of other mediæval travelers, see *The Travels of Sir John Mandeville*.

other stories transmitted orally the Europeans received an exaggerated idea of the wealth of Cipangu (Japan), Cathay (China), and the Spice Islands. The lanes of light let in by these journeys were not wide enough to give the West a correct view of the East; but the meager and incorrect knowledge afforded by them gave the imagination material with which to paint a picture of conditions in that far-away land. This picture, it is needless to say, was made in brighter colors than the facts would warrant. By it the Far East was portrayed as a land of romance and fabulous wealth, of gold, spices, precious stones, valuable woods, beautiful birds, strange animals, and still stranger men. Historical criticism was not yet born and there were no meddlesome scholars to disturb the comfortable credulity of the people by checking up on these beautiful stories.

Moreover, romance was reinforced by economic motives in arousing a lively interest in the Orient. Along with the increase of knowledge that came to Europe with the Renaissance there came also an increase in wealth, and the Europeans of the fifteenth century were able to indulge in luxuries that were not produced at home. The foreign products for which there was the greatest demand were silks, spices, drugs, precious stones, rugs, and ornamental woods. These articles came from China, Japan, and the East Indies. They were collected in the East by native merchants and carried to such centers as Calicut, Malacca, and other ports on the coasts of India and China. From there they were transported partly by sea and partly overland to the Mediterranean ports.[4] *The mediæval trade-routes to the East*

After these products reached the cities on the eastern end of the Mediterranean they were bought up by Spanish, French, and Italian merchants and by them distributed throughout the principal ports of Europe. It is needless to say that this method of conveying goods from the East to Europe was very expensive and dangerous. To the ordinary costs of transportation there had

---

For a most readable account of the voyages of Marco Polo and the elder Polos, see FISKE, J., *Discovery of America*, i, pp. 280-287.

Fiske regards Marco Polo's book as one of the most important ever written. He was the first traveler to go all the way across Asia, and his book is the first description we have of China based on information gained from personal experience.

[4] For a map showing these trade-routes, see *Harper's Atlas of American History*, p. 1.

to be added those arising from the natural hazards incident to travel over mountains and deserts in seasons of excessive heat and cold and the danger of attack from robber bands in the ungoverned districts through which the caravans passed. The need for a better means of reaching the East was therefore strongly felt by the people of Europe, and this need led to the attempt to discover a sea-route to the Indies. To reach India by sea it was necessary to sail around Africa or else plunge boldly into the unexplored waters of the West and thus reach the other side of the world. Both of these remarkable feats were accomplished by navigators at the end of the fifteenth century, and the nations to which we are indebted for these two great achievements are Portugal and Spain.

Prince Henry encourages exploration

By the middle of the fourteenth century the Canary, Madeira, and Azores Islands had been discovered, and the west coast of Africa was known as far south as Cape Bojador.[5] Italian navigators had taken the lead in these early explorations, but Portuguese seamen were the first to push into the unknown region south of Cape Bojador and make the explorations that led to the discovery of a sea-route to India. The early Portuguese explorers were greatly aided and encouraged by Prince Henry the Navigator, who was a younger son of King John I and was closely related to the three rulers who came after his father. Prince Henry built an astronomical laboratory on the promontory of Sagres, the extreme southern point of Portugal, and surrounded himself with men who were interested in map-making and the study of geography and navigation (1419-60). He encouraged exploration in the southern seas, and seamen trained in his school pushed farther and farther toward the south along the western coast of Africa.

Portuguese seamen find a sea-route to India

It was not, however, until a quarter of a century after the death of Prince Henry that Bartholomew Diaz passed the most southerly point of Africa. In 1486 Diaz was sailing along the western coast of Africa when a violent storm arose which blew him steadily southward and for thirteen days he was out of sight of land. When land again appeared he found that he had passed

[5] BEAZLEY, C. R., *The Dawn of Modern Geography* (1260-1420), pp. 411, 414, 420. An Italian map (the *Laurentian Portolano*) of 1351 shows how much of the western coast of Africa was known at that time. For a description of this map see pp. 523-524. For a reproduction of that part of it that deals with the western coast of Africa see opposite p. 422.

by the southern cape and was then more than two hundred miles   Diaz
to the east of it. On returning he passed in sight of the southern
headland, which he called the Cape of Storms. This name, however, was soon afterward changed by King John II to that of the
Cape of Good Hope because it gave promise of a sea-route to
India.

This expectation was realized twelve years later (1498), when   Vasco da
Vasco da Gama reached Calicut in India and thus solved the   Gama
problem of a sea-route to the East. The new water-route quickly
superseded the old Asiatic trade-routes and they soon fell into
disuse. The king of Portugal was greatly elated over the fact
that one of his own subjects was the first to find a waterway to
the real land of spices. The prestige gained for his country by
this voyage came as a consolation prize at a time when it was
experiencing regret and chagrin at having failed to avail itself
of a greater opportunity, which had been seized by its rival in the
field of discovery. For in the meantime Columbus had made his
historic voyage with the aid of the Spanish sovereigns, after
having been refused support by the king of Portugal.

By the beginning of the last decade of the fifteenth century the   Europe
Europeans had advanced far enough in the science of navigation   was ready
to be able to find the New World, and in the arts of peace and   for the
war to appropriate it in the face of a strenuous opposition on   discovery
the part of the natives. All that was now needed was a leader of   and colo-
vision and daring to push ahead and show the way. Columbus   nization
proved to be such a leader.   of Amer-
                                                                    ica by
Columbus had a vivid imagination, which was the source of an   the end of
unfailing stream of enthusiasm, and an ample flow of eloquence   the fif-
by which he was able to impart this enthusiasm to others. Among   teenth
his other outstanding characteristics which were favorable to his   century
rôle as pathfinder of the seas, were self-confidence, courage, perseverance, strong will-power, and a firm, unwavering conviction   Colum-
as to the ultimate success of his undertaking. He was also de-   bus: His
voutly religious and was earnestly desirous of taking Christianity character
to heathen lands. It is true that his religion did not always inspire
him to live up to the highest standards of moral conduct. It did
not, for example, restrain him from indulging in an over-fond-
ness for wealth and fame; but it did fire his ambition with a holy
zeal that raised his venture to the plane of a crusade. To a man
of his imaginative temperament the pictures of the East that
were current in his day made a great appeal. If he could find a

waterway to this magic land of gold and spices and perhaps discover new islands on the way, he would be able to gratify his craving for glory, his desire for gain, and his curiosity as to the unknown world, and at the same time be instrumental in spreading Christianity in heathen countries. His undertaking would thus afford him, as he hoped, an opportunity to serve both God and mammon.

His views regarding the shape and size of the earth

Columbus was a native of Genoa, one of the leading city-republics of Italy. The great Renaissance movement was at its height in Italy in the time of his childhood and youth, and it is natural that he should have caught something of the awakening spirit of the age. In him the new spirit took the form of an ardent interest in geography and navigation. He went on a number of voyages and thus acquired considerable experience as a seaman before addressing himself to his great task. He was also up-to-date in his geographical notions and believed that the earth is round and, therefore, that China and India could be reached by sailing westward. This theory as to the shape of the earth was not original with Columbus. It was held by scholars among the ancient Greeks and Romans and was not entirely lost sight of even in the Middle Ages. We do not know just when or how it came to be accepted by Columbus. He was probably familiar with the views of the ancient geographers and he read carefully the *Imago Mundi*, a work compiled by Pierre d'Ailly (published in 1480), in which the doctrine of the sphericity of the earth is taught.

His ideas were not, however, more advanced than those of other leading geographers of his day, and the glory of his great achievement comes not from the originality of his views, but from the courage and faith that enabled him to stake his career on a belief that others held only as an academic opinion. Columbus was in error as to the size of the earth, as he believed it to be smaller than it is. This was fortunate for the success of his enterprise; for if he had realized how far the Indies are to the west from Europe he could not have been so enthusiastic as to the success of his undertaking, and he would have been unable to persuade a crew to accompany him on so long a voyage unless he had deceived them as to its probable length.

To fit out ships for a long sea voyage required more money than Columbus could raise, and he realized that he could not make the great experiment without first enlisting the support of a ruler of one of the European powers. He first asked financial aid from King John of Portugal, who kept him waiting for a number of years and finally decided that the scheme was too visionary to risk money on. Cast down but not wholly discouraged, Columbus now laid his plans before the Spanish sovereigns, Ferdinand and Isabella, rulers of Aragon and Castile, and after a long period of patient waiting received a decision in his favor. His persuasive eloquence and undaunted persistence doubtless made a favorable impression on these sovereigns, and Queen Isabella was so completely won over that she became an enthusiastic champion of the undertaking.

> The Spanish court agrees to finance the undertaking

By the commission granted by Isabella, Columbus received the title of admiral and was made viceroy of all new lands that he might discover.[6] For financing the expedition an appropriation was granted out of the royal treasury and a requisition was made on the city of Palos. The friends of the admiral furnished one-eighth of the amount needed and were to receive a like proportion of the profits. With the royal backing it was easy to procure and equip the vessels needed for the voyage, but it was difficult to get seamen to volunteer for so hazardous an undertaking. In order to make up the crews, amounting to ninety in all, it was necessary to offer criminals pardon for their offenses and debtors release from their obligations on condition that they would agree to enlist.

Columbus expected to find new lands as well as a western water-route to India, as is evidenced by the fact that his commission authorized him to govern such unclaimed regions as he might add to the Spanish empire. At that time the imagination of the people had placed in the western seas such fabled islands as Antillia, St. Brandon, and Brazil. The traditions regarding the existence of these islands were probably based on voyages made by unknown seamen. Columbus, of course, knew of these traditions and doubtless talked with sailors who had made voyages into the uncharted waters of the West.[7]

> Columbus expected to find new lands as well as a sea-route to the Indies

[6] For the articles of agreement between the Spanish sovereigns and Columbus, see OLSON and BOURNE, *op. cit.*, pp. 77-84.

[7] For a map of Columbus's time showing the location of imaginary islands in the Atlantic, see RICHMAN, I. B., *The Spanish Conquerors*, p. 12.

Recent scholarship has raised doubts as to whether the main motive behind Columbus's first voyage was the hope of finding undis-

The
historic
voyage

When all was ready the expedition, consisting of three small vessels, the *Pinta*, *Niña*, and *Santa Maria*, set sail from Palos (August 3, 1492) and made for the Canaries, the plan being to sail directly west from these islands and thus reach Japan. The incidents of the voyage are too well known to need repetition. Suffice it to say that the admiral showed the same persistence and courage in carrying out his great plan that he had exhibited in his effort to win the support of the Portuguese and Spanish rulers. His unwavering determination to sail on despite the fears and murmurings of his crew, and his refusal to become discouraged even after he had passed without any signs of land the point at which he expected to find Japan, have won for him a deservedly high place in the hero-worship of every modern schoolboy. Nothing short of genius can account for the calm assurance with which he pursued his course under circumstances that would have discouraged any ordinary man. It is true they encountered no real dangers, for the weather was fine, and if the demon of fear had not haunted the crew this late summer voyage would have been a delightful excursion. But to ignorant sailors, who with the eye of the imagination saw in the unknown Sea of Darkness one horror after another, the fears within were worse than would have been the encounter with real dangers from without.

The
land-
fall

Finally they came within plain view of land and their fears and deferred hopes gave way to wild excitement and ecstatic joy. The new land proved to be one of the Bahama Islands, which Columbus called San Salvador and which was probably the one now known as Watling Island. On Friday, October 12, 1492, they made a very dramatic landing. The officers and men crowded around the admiral, the former embracing him and the latter throwing themselves at his feet to beg his pardon. This emotional display was witnessed by brown, naked savages, who looked on in silence and wonder at these strange beings, who, they thought, had come down from the skies.

Other
islands
discovered

After visiting other islands of the Bahama group Columbus steered southward and sailed along the coasts of Cuba and Haiti. In these islands he noticed a luxuriant vegetation and enjoyed the beautiful landscapes, but saw no signs of the spices and "rose-colored pearls" of the East. The East had been pictured as a land in which the people, clad in silk and wearing pearls and other

covered lands or a western sea-route to India. For a discussion of this question see Bibliographical Notes, p. 715.

jewels, lived in populous cities adorned with magnificent palaces. On the islands just discovered there were villages of rude huts in which dwelt naked savages living in primitive squalor, with no signs of luxury.[8] To identify this new-found region with the fabulous East required a stretch of the imagination that would be well-nigh impossible in this practical age. But in the mind of a romantic dreamer like the great admiral the wish can father almost any kind of thought, and he sincerely believed that he had found the way to the land of spices. Haiti was supposed to be Cipangu, and Cuba a part of the mainland of Asia. It was this belief that prompted him to send two envoys into the interior of Cuba to find the ruler of Cathay or some prince who was the rival of the Great Khan, and bear to him the greetings of the sovereigns of Castile and Aragon.[9] Although these messengers could gather no information regarding the Great Khan, Columbus still believed that the Indies had been reached and so he called the natives Indians, a name which has ever since been applied to the aborigines of the Western World. When it was later found that these islands were not the East Indies they were appropriately named the West Indies.

The discoveries of this famous voyage might easily lead to a controversy between Spain and Portugal. For Portugal was at this time claiming all the "islands in the region from the Canaries towards Guinea." This claim had been confirmed by a series of papal bulls and had been recognized by Spain in a treaty signed in 1479.[10] According to Portuguese interpretation of this agreement, Portugal was to have all lands discovered in the southern, or equatorial, waters. But it was this very region that Columbus

The papal line of demarcation

---

[8] Several abridgments of the Journal of Columbus's first voyage were made by his contemporaries. The longest of these, probably made by Las Casas, is given in OLSON and BOURNE, *op. cit.*, pp. 89-258. The first published account that we have of this famous expedition is the letter that Columbus wrote to Louis de Santangel on his return (published first in April, 1493). For this letter, see *ibid.*, pp. 263-272.

[9] OLSON and BOURNE, *op. cit.*, pp. 134-137.

[10] The Latin texts of these bulls and English translations of them are given in DAVENPORT, FRANCES G., *European Treaties Bearing on the History of the United States and its Dependencies to 1648*, pp. 13-32 (note especially pp. 23-24, 31). For the original text of the treaty between Portugal and Spain and the English translation of it, see pp. 36-48, especially p. 44.

hoped to explore in future voyages. If the islands to be found by him were to be incorporated into the Spanish empire it would be necessary to transfer to Spain in advance the rights to that region now claimed by Portugal. And this was what was done.

The pope, Alexander VI, was a native of Aragon and was bound to Spain by both sentiment and self-interest. As he had already received a number of favors from Ferdinand and expected more, he was willing to do him a good turn, apparently at the risk of infringing upon grants made by his predecessors to Portugal. Accordingly, he issued four bulls in 1493, by which he divided the unknown world between Portugal and Spain. A line of demarcation was drawn one hundred leagues west of the Azores and Cape Verde Islands; Spain was to have all lands not held by a Christian people found west of this line, and Portugal was thereby restricted to the territory east of it. King John of Portugal naturally was not satisfied with this arrangement, for it did not, as he considered, give his country its rightful share of the new lands. Some diplomatic negotiations between the rulers of these two Catholic countries were, therefore, necessary before a final agreement was reached. These negotiations led to a treaty between Spain and Portugal (signed June, 1494), by which the line of demarcation was pushed westward to three hundred and seventy leagues from the Azores and the Cape Verde Islands and was accepted by both countries.[11]

The other colonizing nations paid no attention to the division; for neither France nor England at this time recognized the temporal power of the pope outside of the Papal States. A remark made by Francis I of France to Charles I of Spain showed his contemptuous estimate of these bulls as a basis for the blanket claim to the non-Christian world set up by his neighboring sovereigns. Francis is reported to have said to Charles: "Your

[11] In the first bull there was this reservation in Portugal's favor: "That by this our gift, grant, assignment, and investiture no right acquired by any Christian prince is hereby to be understood to be withdrawn or taken away." This reservation does not appear in the other two bulls. See DAVENPORT, *op. cit.*, pp. 62-63, 68, 77. For the Latin texts of these bulls and English translations of them, see *ibid.*, pp. 58-83. For the text and an English translation of the treaty of 1494 between Spain and Portugal, see pp. 86-100, especially p. 95. The text of one of the papal bulls is given in HART, A. B., *American History Told by Contemporaries*, i, pp. 40-43.

Majesty and the king of Portugal have divided the world between you, offering no part of it to me. Show me, I pray you, the will of our father Adam, so that I may see if he has really made you his only universal heirs."[12]

Columbus made three other voyages. On the second of these later expeditions (1498) he discovered the mainland of South America at the mouth of the Orinoco River. Thinking that so large a stream of fresh water could not come from an island, he concluded that he had found a new continent. As he believed

Later voyages of Columbus

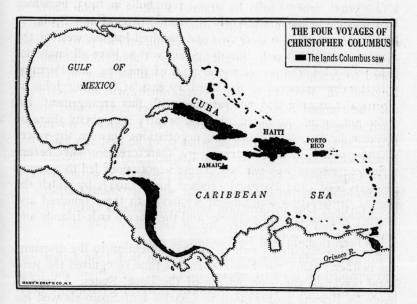

THE FOUR VOYAGES OF CHRISTOPHER COLUMBUS
■ The lands Columbus saw

GULF OF MEXICO

CUBA

HAITI

PORTO RICO

JAMAICA

CARIBBEAN SEA

Orinoco R.

MANN'N DRAF'G CO.,N.Y.

that the islands to the north belonged to that group which is off the east or southern coast of Asia, he still entertained the hope of reaching Asia by sailing farther west around the northern end of this newly-discovered continent. In order to find such a water-route he made his fourth and last voyage (1502). On this expedition he sailed along the southeastern coast of North America from Honduras to Panama, vainly looking for a strait that would lead into Asiatic waters.[13]

[12] Quoted in the *Journal of Negro History*, ix, p. 5.
[13] Dr. Chanca, of Seville, the surgeon of the expedition, wrote an account of Columbus's second voyage. This is given in OLSON and BOURNE, *op. cit.*, pp. 282-313. For another contemporary account

While Columbus was impatiently awaiting the decision of the Spanish court his brother Bartholomew was urging Henry VII of England to pledge his support to the plan of the great navigator. If we are to believe the statement attributed to Ferdinand, the son of Columbus, he was successful in getting a promise of assistance from the king. This promise, if made, came too late, however, for when Bartholomew reached Paris on his way to Spain he learned that his brother had returned from a successful voyage to the Indies. Henry was still interested in discovery and a few years later (1496) he granted a patent to John Cabot, a Venetian navigator, authorizing him to search for unknown lands in the east, north, and west, and conferring on him power to rule over any islands that he might discover. Cabot, like Columbus, hoped to reach Cathay and the Spice Islands. Leaving Bristol, England, in May, 1497, he steered northward and westward until he reached the coast of North America. He sailed southward along the coast for three hundred leagues and then returned to England. It is not known at what point he first saw land, but it was somewhere north of New England and probably not far from Cape Breton Island. Next year he made a second voyage and probably skirted the coast as far south as South Carolina or even farther. Our information regarding Cabot's second voyage is meager and there is no record of his return. For this reason it has been thought that he was lost at sea.[14]

Formerly, scholars were of the opinion that John Cabot was accompanied on his first voyage by his son Sebastian, and there is some evidence to support this belief. Recent scholarship, however, is not satisfied with this evidence and is skeptical as to whether Sebastian Cabot had any connection with his father's discoveries.[15]

---

of this voyage, see THACHER, J. B., *Christopher Columbus*, ii, pp. 244-262. For Las Casas's account of the third voyage, based on Columbus's Journal, see OLSON and BOURNE, *op. cit.*, pp. 319-366. Columbus's own account of his fourth voyage is given in pp. 389-418.

[14] For easily accessible primary sources for the Cabot voyages, see OLSON and BOURNE, *op. cit.*, pp. 423-430, and *Old South Leaflets*, nos. 37 and 115.

[15] For a discussion of the evidence bearing on the Cabot controversy, with extracts from the sources, see WINSOR, J., *Narrative*

The Cabot voyages were the basis of the claim of England to North America. They also marked out a route to the Newfoundland fisheries and a regular trade was soon established between England and these newly-found regions. Ships from Spain,

and Critical History, iii, pp. 7-58, and WEARE, G. E., *Cabot's Discovery of North America.*

There are three easily accessible documents that bear on the question as to whether Sebastian Cabot accompanied his father on either or both of his voyages. These are (1) the letters patent granted to John Cabot by Henry VII, (2) the Cabot Map, and (3) the Cabot Portrait. In the king's patent, authority to enter upon the voyage is granted to "John Cabot, citizen of Venice, to Lewis, Sebastian, and Santius, sons of the said John." But there are no contemporary documents that enable us to determine whether the sons accompanied their father. For these instructions see *Old South Leaflets*, no. 37.

There is in the National Library in Paris a large map of the world engraved on metal. One of the inscriptions of the map states that it was made by Sebastian Cabot in 1544. There are a number of legends on it, in both Latin and Spanish. One of these, Legend No. 8, which refers to Newfoundland, says in part: "This country was discovered by John Cabot, a Venetian, and Sebastian Cabot, his son, in the year of our Lord Jesus Christ, MCCCCXCIV." (The number is probably a misprint for 1497.) Winsor thinks that Sebastian Cabot was undoubtedly responsible for this inscription. If this view is correct we are bound to believe that Sebastian Cabot was with his father on one of his voyages, or else charge him with downright falsehood. For a description of this map, see WINSOR, *op. cit.*, iii. pp. 20-24. For the text of the inscription see *ibid.*, p. 21, and CHANNING, *op. cit.*, i, p. 36.

There was originally in the royal gallery in Whitehall a portrait bearing the name of Sebastian Cabot. This portrait was obtained by Richard Biddle, of Pittsburgh, and was destroyed when his library was burned in 1845. But two copies of it had been made and they are still preserved in this country. On this picture there is this Latin inscription: "The picture of Sebastian Cabot, an Englishman, son of John Cabot, a Venetian, Knight (Militis Avrati), the first discoverer of the New World under Henry VII, King of England." In all probability this picture is authentic and Sebastian Cabot is responsible for the legend. But it will be noticed that it is impossible to tell whether the author of the inscription meant to say that John Cabot or his son was the discoverer of America, though the arrangement of the words would indicate that the former was intended.

Portugal, and France were also actively engaged in the New-foundland fisheries during the sixteenth century. For his magnificent service to the British empire, John Cabot was rewarded by the parsimonious king with a bounty of ten pounds and an annual pension of twenty pounds.

The naming of America   The new continent discovered by Columbus barred the way to the Indies, and numerous attempts were soon made to find a waterway around or across it. In one of these expeditions, conducted by a Portuguese sailor in 1501, the coast of South America was followed from latitude 5° to 32° south. One of the men who accompanied the Portuguese captain on this voyage was the Florentine, Amerigo Vespucci, who is generally known by his Latinized name, Americus Vespucius. Vespucius wrote two private letters to friends in which he gave interesting accounts of the regions visited by him on this voyage and three others made by him. These accounts were translated into Latin, the literary language of that day, before any description of Columbus's discovery of the mainland of South America had been given in the Latin language. He thus got ahead of Columbus in reaching the reading public with his account of the continent south of the West Indies. Besides, he claimed—falsely, according to some modern authorities[16]—to have made his first voyage in 1497, a

---

For a copy of this portrait, see WINSOR, *op. cit.*, iii, p. 5; for a description of it, *ibid.*, pp. 31-32; for the inscription on it, *ibid.*, p. 31, and CHANNING, *op. cit.*, i, p. 85. For a discussion of the other evidence bearing on this controversy, with extracts from the sources, see WINSOR, *op. cit.*, iii, pp. 7-58, and WEARE, G. E., *Cabot's Discovery of North America*, especially pp. 94-100, 155-156, 165-168, 171-209.

If a student who has plenty of leisure should decide to spend it in making a thorough study of the documents and the discussions bearing on this disputed point he would probably come to this conclusion: We are positively certain that John Cabot discovered North America in 1497, but whether he was or was not accompanied by his son Sebastian we cannot with certainty tell.

[16] Some modern scholars, however, think that Americus Vespucius made a very important voyage in the year 1497-98 (see Bibliographical Notes, p. 716).

For a good map of the voyages of discovery of Columbus, Cabot, Vespucius, and others, see SELLERY, G. C., and KREY, A. C., *Medieval Foundations of Western Civilization*, facing p. 550.

year before Columbus discovered South America. In this way he was given the credit, which rightfully belonged to Columbus, of having discovered South America, or "Mundus Novus," the "New World," as he called it.

In 1507 Martin Waldseemüller published a short treatise on geography together with one of Vespucius's letters, in which he spoke of this new world as having been discovered by Americus Vespucius. He suggested that the new continent, known as "Mundus Novus," be named "Amerige" or "America," in honor of its discoverer. His suggestion was readily accepted, and soon the name of America became attached to the southern continent. At first it applied only to the region south of the Isthmus of Panama. The lands north of the Isthmus were still known for a time as the Indies, but later the northern mainland received the name of North America. Then the term "America" was made to apply to the whole region, and what was originally known as "Mundus Novus" became South America.

Selected Readings

1. Trade Routes to the East.—Cheyney, E. P., *European Background of American History,* *ch. 2 (see also A. H. Lybyer in *English Historical Review,* iii, pp. 577-578).
2. The Norse Discoveries.—Channing, E., *History of the United States,* i, pp. *1-16.
3. Personal Traits of Columbus.—Morison, S. E., *Admiral of the Ocean Sea,* pp. *43-48.
4. Contemporary Authorities on Columbus.—*Ibid.,* pp. *48-53.
5. Columbus.—Bourne, E. G., *Spain in America,* *chs. 2-4; Richman, I. B., *The Spanish Conquerors,* *ch. 2; Channing, E., *op. cit.,* i, pp. 12-27; Biggar, H. P., "The New Columbus," in the *Annual Report* of the American Historical Association for 1912, pp. *97-104.
6. The Landfall.—Morison, *op. cit.,* *ch. 16; Olson, J. E., and Bourne, E. G., *The Northmen, Columbus, and Cabot,* pp. *263-272 (Columbus's account).
7. The Cabots.—Bourne, E. G., *Spain in America,* pp. *55-61; Winship, G. P., *Cabot Bibliography,* pp. *xi-xvi; Olson, J. E., and Bourne, E. G., *op. cit.* (primary source), pp. 423-450.
8. The Naming of America.—Channing, E., *op. cit.,* i, pp. *42-47; Bourne, E. G., article in *American Historical Review,* x, pp. *41-51.

CHAPTER III

EARLY EXPLORATIONS AND INTERNATIONAL RIVALRIES IN AMERICA

SPANISH EXPLORATION AND OCCUPATION OF AMERICA

Spanish colonies in the West Indies

SPAIN was prompt to reinforce by colonization the claim to the New World conferred upon her by the Columbian discovery and the papal grant. Indeed, Spanish colonization had begun in America before Ferdinand and Isabella learned that a new world had been found. For on leaving for Spain on the return from his first voyage (January 4, 1493) Columbus had left forty-four members of his crew at a place called La Navida (the Nativity) on the northern coast of Haiti. This little colony was destroyed by the Indians, but in a few years a number of permanent settlements had been established in the West Indies. By the middle of the second decade of the sixteenth century a good start had been made toward the occupation of Puerto Rico, Jamaica, and Cuba, as well as Haiti.

The exploration and occupation of the mainland of North and South America

But the energy and enthusiasm so characteristic of the Spanish leaders of that day were demanding wider opportunities for self-expression than were afforded by colonization in the West Indian islands. Numerous exploring expeditions were made along the coasts of both Americas, and by 1525 the "entire Atlantic shore from the Straits of Magellan to Nova Scotia had been explored by expeditions made in the name of Spain."[1] One bold adventurer, Balboa, had crossed the Isthmus of Panama and discovered the Pacific Ocean (1513), and the Spanish flag had been carried around the world (1519-22) in the famous voyage made by Magellan and his men.[2] The incentives that promoted these ven-

[1] BOLTON, H. E., and MARSHALL, T. M., *The Colonization of North America*, p. 26.

[2] For maps showing the voyage of Magellan, as well as those of other great navigators of his day, see SHEPHERD, W. R., *Atlas*, pp. 107-110. A contemporary account of the famous voyage was written by Antonio Pigafetta, one of the men who was with Magellan on his world voyage. This account has been translated into English by

38

tures were the desire to curb the rivalry of other nations, especially that of Portugal, promote trade and colonization, and find a sea-route to India.

These explorations soon led to the establishment of colonies on the mainland in both North and South America. Spain took possession of all of South America except Brazil, which was settled by Portugal. During the first three decades of the sixteenth century the Spaniards also made considerable headway toward the occupation and exploration of Central America and Mexico.[3] The success of the Spaniards in Mexico was greatly aided by the dissensions among the natives, many of whom took sides with their conquerors against their fellow-countrymen. The invaders in this region were led by Hernando Cortez, a man of genius and exceptional courage, who disregarded all considerations of justice and humanity and allowed his ambition to ride to its goal rough-shod over the most sacred rights of the natives. Nor were the other leaders much, if any, better. Lured on by the appetite for gain, which was always kept on keen edge by rumors of gold mines, these unscrupulous conquerors marched through the land exploiting the natives with ruthless abandon. To this nefarious work some of these Spanish conquistadors prostituted a romantic courage and a spirit of adventure that deserved much better employment.

In shining contrast to the brutalities of the cut-throat military leaders were the labors of the humble monks who went among the Indians to teach them Catholic Christianity. Both by precept and by example they presented Christianity as a religion of love and sacrificial service, many of them sealing their testimony with their life's blood. To the untutored native this new religion must have offered bewildering contrasts far beyond his power of comprehension. For on the one hand he saw a small band of its adherents who preached and practiced the gospel of love and helpfulness; while the majority of the Christians with whom he

Labors of the Spanish missionaries

F. A. Robertson (2 vols.). In this edition are given on opposite pages both the Spanish original and the English translation. For an account of the experiences of Magellan and his crew while going through the Strait of Magellan, see pp. 63-65; for their sufferings, see pp. 83-85.

[3] For maps showing the location of Spanish settlements in Central America and Mexico, see BOLTON, H. E., and MARSHALL, T. M., *The Colonization of North America*, pp. 30, 35.

came in contact proclaimed by their acts the evangel of hate and exploitation. That the spirit of vengeance generated in his heart by the acts of the latter group should have found an outlet in the killing of his real friends of the former group is deplorable, but in no sense unnatural. Ignorant Indians should not be too severely condemned if they regarded the servants of the God of a Cortez as priests of the devil. Moreover, the strenuous demands made on the savages by the missionaries aroused the opposition of the former to the well-intentioned policy of the latter. When the Spanish conquerors pushed northward and occupied territory within the present limits of the United States, the friars went

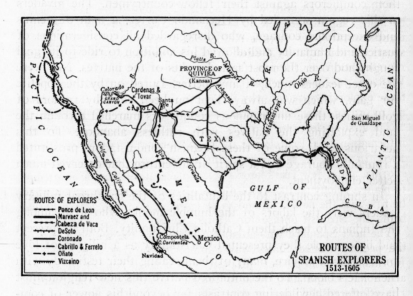

ROUTES OF EXPLORERS'
Ponce de Leon
Narvaez and
Cabeza de Vaca
DeSoto
Coronado
Cabrillo & Ferrelo
Oñate
Vizcaino

ROUTES OF
SPANISH EXPLORERS
1513-1605

along with them, as they had done in Mexico and Central America, and met with the same experiences as they had had in the former regions.

Spanish explorations within the present United States
The occupation of the West Indies and Mexico gave Spain convenient bases from which she could begin the exploration of the eastern and western portions of the present United States. The Spanish king asserted his right to all of North America now included within the limits of the United States, basing his claim originally on the discoveries of Columbus and the action of the pope in dividing the Western Hemisphere between his country and Portugal by the line of demarcation (1493). The original

title was reinforced by the explorations made in this region in the sixteenth century and by a few settlements planted in this century and the early part of the next one.[4]

Of the early Spanish adventurers who were active in exploring the territory now belonging to the United States, probably none were more important than Hernando de Soto and Francisco de Coronado. Driven on by the hope of finding precious metals, these bold adventurers blazed trails into the interior of the northern continent. The former made extensive explorations in the southeastern and south central portions of the present United States, which region was known by the Spaniards as Florida.[5] The latter,

[4] The eastern coast of what is now the United States had probably been seen and marked out by navigators by the beginning of the sixteenth century; for there is still extant a map made in 1502 which shows the southeastern portion of North America, including a crude representation of Florida (for a reproduction of this map, see WINSOR, J., *Narrative and Critical History*, ii, p. 118). Just who these explorers were and why they were so modest as to leave behind no record of their achievement, we have no means of determining.

The first explorer to visit this region about whom we have definite information was Juan Ponce de Leon, former governor of Puerto Rico. In 1513 he sailed along the eastern and western coasts of Florida, and a few years later (1521) made an unsuccessful attempt to plant a colony on the western coast. It was the Easter season when he first saw the new land, and so he called it Florida (*pascua florida* being the Spanish phrase for Easter Sunday).

The next Spaniard who attempted to explore the southern part of the present United States was Panfilo de Narvaez. He landed in Florida, near Tampa Bay, in 1528, with a large number of settlers and soldiers, and undertook to conquer and colonize the country. His efforts resulted in complete failure and Narvaez was drowned. The survivors of the expedition, now reduced to fifteen, threw themselves on the mercy of the Indians. Finally, after five years of wandering, four of these survivors, under the leadership of Cabeza de Vaca, reached the Spanish settlements in Mexico.

For Vaca's account of the expedition, see HODGE, F. W., and LEWIS, T. H., *Spanish Explorers in the Southern United States* (*Original Narratives of Early American History*), pp. 14-126. See also *The Journey of Alvar Nuñez Cabeza de Vaca* (*The Trail Makers* series), written by Vaca and translated by Fanny Bandelier.

[5] De Soto secured from the Spanish king an appointment as governor of Cuba with permission to explore and settle Florida at his own expense. Landing at Tampa in 1539 with 625 men, he began

operating from Mexico as a base, traversed a wide area in the southwestern part of our country.[6] These expeditions greatly ex-

a three years' march through the tangled forests and swamps of the southern part of North America. In his relations with the natives he displayed a foolish cruelty which aroused their bitter enmity and caused them to put up a brave fight against the invaders. The Spaniards also suffered from disease and endured the great hardships that are incident to travel in a wilderness beset with savage enemies. In all of these difficulties their great leader showed an unwavering perseverance and a heroic devotion to his purpose. Being led on by Indian stories of gold, the expedition went northward through the present states of Georgia and South Carolina and into what is now North Carolina. De Soto then turned to the southwest and continued his course until finally he reached the Mississippi River (1541).

This was the first time that the Mississippi had ever been crossed by a white man. The Spaniards were stopped by this stream for a month, but finally, after having built barges, they were able to cross it. The journey westward was then resumed and was continued until the Arkansas region was reached. De Soto's men were unwilling to go farther toward the west and he returned to the Mississippi. Here he died in the spring of 1542 and was buried in the great river discovered by him.

His followers, now sick of the dangers and sufferings incident to exploration, were anxious to exchange the hardships of aimless wandering in the wilderness for the comforts of settled life. Therefore, after making hasty preparations, they left for the Spanish settlements in the southwest. They sailed down the river and along the Gulf of Mexico, and about one-half of the original number reached the Spanish settlement of Panuco in Mexico.

As an exhibition of courage and daring this expedition was considered by Professor Bourne as the most remarkable one in the history of North America. But its importance in the development of our country is not to be measured by the degree of courage and energy displayed by De Soto and his followers. Men like De Soto, with their feverish ambition and useless activity, do not often affect very appreciably the stream of history, though they do sometimes contribute to it a tinge of color that adds very much to its picturesqueness. This expedition, however, appeals to our interest not only because of the thrilling adventures experienced by the leader and the men, but also because it affords us a fine example of the methods pursued by the typical Spanish explorer.

For an account of De Soto's expedition, written by one of the men who took part in it, see HODGE and LEWIS, *op. cit.,* pp.

tended the geographical knowledge of Europeans regarding North America and strengthened Spain's claim to the southern half of it.

135-272. For the reproduction of a contemporary map, probably made by one of De Soto's men, which shows the territory covered by his expedition, see *ibid.*, opposite p. 132.

[6] In Mexico there circulated among the Spanish settlers Indian stories regarding cities in the north that were rich in gold and silver. These Indian legends, interwoven with European folk tales, created the belief among the Spaniards in Mexico that to the north were the Seven Cities of Cibola, from which gold and silver could be procured in abundance. As these rumors were so persistent, Mendoza, the able viceroy of New Spain, as Mexico was then called, decided to have some of his men undertake the discovery and conquest of these rich cities. Francisco Vasquez de Coronado was chosen for this important task, and an expedition worthy of so promising an undertaking was easily fitted out, as everyone wanted to share in the venture.

From the great number of volunteers that offered, about two hundred and seventy men were selected and were well equipped with the implements of war. With the Spanish soldiers there also went hundreds of Indian allies. The expedition was "attended by a thousand horses, an immense herd of cattle and mules, and a great flock of sheep." Such a large number of men and animals could not travel in one body in the wilderness, and Coronado had to divide his forces. With a small number of picked men he went ahead of the main force, hoping soon to reach the Seven Cities. After enduring great hardships from a lack of food and drink, they came to one of the Zuñi villages. This was captured, but not until after the inhabitants had put up a brave fight. Soon thereafter the other Zuñi pueblos were discovered. The Spaniards were, however, sorely disappointed at what they had found; for not only had they failed to find gold and silver in these settlements, but the communal dwellings of the Indians fell far below the expectations that had been aroused by the stories about the fabulous cities of Cibola. Despite his disillusionment, however, Coronado kept going farther and farther into the interior, being led on by false reports of gold circulated by the Indians. In this way he explored a large part of the continent, going as far east as central Kansas. In these long journeys he traversed an endless plain, tenanted by hunchback cows, and acquired a fund of valuable information regarding the heart of the American continent. But inasmuch as he had found neither gold nor fabled cities, he returned to Mexico (1541) with a sense of utter failure and quickly fell into obscurity. He had also solved the riddle of the Seven Cities and put an end to that fiction. But this contribution to knowledge did not raise him to favor, for he had substituted a prosaic fact

Explora-
tions
along
the
Pacific
coast

The Pacific coast as far as Oregon was also explored by the Spaniards before the middle of the century (by 1543).[7]

for a poetic dream, and truth is rarely welcome when it has to be purchased at the cost of disillusionment.

While Coronado was engaged in the major venture of exploring the interior of the continent, three smaller exploring expeditions were led into the southwest into the Colorado River region. In one of these, led by Don Garcia Lopez de Cardenas, the Grand Canyon was discovered. This wonder of nature made a profound impression on the exploring party. As they looked down the gorge the water at the bottom seemed to be more than a mile below and the stream appeared to be only about six feet wide, although they were told by the Indians that it had a width of half a league. Three of the men went down at the least difficult place about one-third of the distance, and returned to make an enthusiastic report on the grandeur of the scenery. They were of the opinion that the Indian estimate as to the width of the river was correct and declared that some rocks, which appeared from the top to be about as high as a man, were larger than the great tower of Seville.

The best contemporary account of the explorations of Coronado is the one that was written by Pedro de Castañeda, who took part in the expedition. This account is given, with explanatory notes, in HODGE, F. W., and LEWIS, T. H., *Spanish Explorers in the Southern United States*, pp. 285-387. Some documentary material relating to the expedition is also given in *Old South Leaflets*, no. 20; *American History Leaflets*, no. 13; and WINSHIP, G. P., *The Journey of Coronado, 1540-1542* (*Trail Makers* series). For an excellent modern map showing the route of Coronado's expedition, as well as the routes of the subsidiary expeditions, see HODGE and LEWIS, *op. cit.*, opposite page 280.

For a contemporary description of the Grand Canyon as it appeared to this exploring party, see HODGE and LEWIS, *op. cit.*, p. 309. Contemporary accounts of the explorations in the Colorado region can be found in *ibid.*, pp. 302-310.

[7] In 1542 Mendoza sent out an expedition to explore the Pacific coast. The command of the ships was at first intrusted to Juan Rodriquez Cabrillo, but at his death (January, 1543) it passed to Bartolomé Ferrelo, who had been chief pilot. The expedition sailed along the coast until it reached a point near the mouth of the Rogue River in the southwestern part of Oregon. For a contemporary account of this voyage, see BOLTON, H. E., ed., *Spanish Explorations in the Southwest* (*Original Narratives*), pp. 13-39. For a summary of Cabrillo's diary made by Professor Bolton, see pp. 5-10. In 1602 an expedition under the command of Sebastián Vizcaino

Spanish activity in the north was not confined to exploration and gold-hunting. During the first six decades of the sixteenth century a number of attempts at settlement were made within the present limits of the United States. One of these colonizing ventures was at San Miguel, thought by some writers to have been on the site later occupied by Jamestown. It is more probable, however, that this colony was planted on the Pedee River in South Carolina. None of these early efforts at settlement were successful, and at the beginning of the year 1562 there was not a white man of any nationality on the soil of the present United States. Philip II was discouraged over these failures and had ordered that no more attempts at colonization be made in Florida for the time being.

Spanish settlements in the present United States

But France was now contesting Spain's claim to America. Not only had Frenchmen been active in exploring the Atlantic coast, but they were now engaged in planting a settlement in territory that Spain had staked off for herself (see pp. 48-49 below). To meet this new danger the Spanish government felt that it would have to reinforce its rights in Florida by colonization. Accordingly, Pedro Menendez de Avilés, a well-known naval officer, was sent over as governor of Florida with instructions to expel the French from Spanish territory and plant a colony. Menendez was successful in both endeavors. Not only did he defeat the French and destroy their colony, but he also founded the town of St. Augustine (September, 1565), which proved to be the first permanent settlement made by Europeans within the present limits of the United States.[8] In a few years Spanish posts were located along the coast all the way from Port Royal, South Carolina, to the southern end of Florida. A monastery was established at St. Augustine, and from it monks went out to found island missions all along the Georgia and Florida coast. Before the end of the century a permanent settlement had also been established in New Mexico.[9]

St. Augustine

sailed along the California and Oregon coasts to Cape Blanco, a short distance beyond the mouth of the Rogue River. For contemporary accounts of Vizcaino's voyage, see *ibid.*, pp. 52-103, 105-122, noting especially pp. 105-109. For a fine map showing the voyages on the Pacific coast, see *ibid.*, at the beginning of the volume.

[8] LOWERY, W., *The Spanish Settlements within the Present Limits of the United States*, ii, pp. 158-159.

[9] In 1598 a settlement was made by Juan de Oñate at the pueblo

The extent of territory in continental North America north of Mexico actually occupied by Spain in the sixteenth century is small as compared with the amount of energy expended by Spanish leaders in exploring this region. The reason why Spain's explorations in the north were followed up by comparatively few settlements was that she was already engaged in too many great undertakings and had only a small surplus population to support colonization. Besides attempting a big rôle in Europe, she had settled considerable portions of South America, southern North America, and the West Indies. In 1574 there were about two hundred Spanish towns in North and South America, having a total white population of 160,000 or more. In addition to these there were about 5,000,000 Indians under Spanish control. The conquest of Peru, Mexico, and the other southern regions had enriched the Spanish adventurers and had caused a stream of gold and silver to flow into the homeland. It was natural, therefore, that enterprising Spaniards would devote their energies to the exploitation of the southern regions, where the returns were quick and large, rather than incur the hazards of colonization in the north, which, at the most, could only promise remote and uncertain returns.[10]

FRANCE CONTESTS SPAIN'S CLAIM TO NORTH AMERICA

The first quarter of the sixteenth century had hardly ended before France began to contest the exclusive right of Spain and Portugal to the New World. At that time France was in good and regular standing in the Catholic Church, but its worldly-minded and free-thinking ruler, Francis I, did not recognize that the pope had any authority to apportion the newly-discovered lands, and so laughed at the claims of Spain and Portugal based on the papal line of demarcation) (see pp. 32-33). He felt free, therefore, to encourage French exploration in the New World. Already French fishermen had been plying their trade off the coast of Newfoundland, probably since the beginning of the six-

---

of Caypa, which was known as San Juan. This settlement was at first used as a base by Oñate for his explorations, but in a few years he moved his headquarters to Santa Fé.

[10] For an excellent brief account of Spanish achievements in the sixteenth century, see BOLTON, H. E., and MARSHALL, T. M., *The Colonization of North America*, pp. 75-76. For a fuller account, see BOURNE, E. G., *Spain in America*, ch. 13.

teenth century, but no explorations had been made with the sanction and support of the government.

The first French explorer to visit the American shores under the auspices of the French king was Giovanni da Verrazano, a

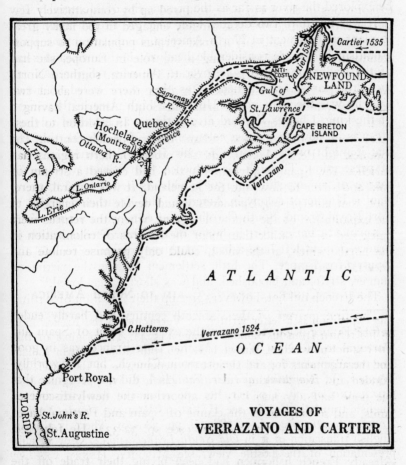

VOYAGES OF
VERRAZANO AND CARTIER

native of Florence. In 1524 he crossed the Atlantic with the hope of finding a waterway across North America to India and China. He sailed along the coast, probably from Cape Fear to Newfoundland, stopping at New York Harbor and Narragansett Bay. Returning to France, he dropped back into that obscurity from which he had emerged to make this one voyage.[11]

[11] The statement made above regarding the voyage of Verrazano is questioned by some scholars. Our chief source of information for

Cartier

Ten years later Francis I sent out Jacques Cartier to search for a waterway to China. In his first voyage (1534) he discovered and named the Gulf of St. Lawrence. He led two other expeditions into the St. Lawrence region, in the course of which he explored the river as far as the present site of Montreal.[12]

Ribaut and Laudonnière

It was not until two decades later that the French again tried to plant a settlement in North America. In the meantime Protestantism had made considerable headway in France, and some of the leading men had gone over to the new religion. Among the Protestants, or Huguenots, as they were called, Admiral Coligny was the most noted. He held a high place in the esteem of the king, Charles IX, and at one time was his chief adviser. He was anxious to plant a colony in the New World, thinking that it might prove a refuge for his fellow-Huguenots in times of persecution. Through his influence Jean Ribaut was put in charge of an expedition (1562) which sailed from France to plant a Huguenot colony in America. The Frenchmen landed at Port Royal Sound, South Carolina, and established a post which was named Charles Fort in honor of the king. On his return to France, Ribaut left here a band of thirty volunteers to hold the country for France. The little settlement became the victim of hunger, strife, and bloodshed, and was shortly abandoned.[13]

The French did not, however, give up their intention of settling

---

this expedition is a letter written by Verrazano to the French king on his return from his famous voyage (1524). The original of this letter is not now extant, but we have two translations of it in Italian. For the arguments for and against the genuineness of this letter, see WINSOR, J., *Narrative and Critical History*, iv, pp. 17-28, and CHANNING, *op. cit.*, i, p. 111. For one version of this letter and an English translation of it, see HAKLUYT, RICHARD, *Early English Voyages to America*, ed. of 1889, ii, pp. 389-401. There is also an English translation of it in *Old South Leaflets*, no. 17. For an able presentation of the hostile view, see MURPHY, HENRY C., *The Voyage of Verrazano*. DE COSTA, B. F., *The Voyage of Verrazano, the Explorer*, is friendly to Verrazano. A copy of the Verrazano Map is reproduced in WINSOR, *op. cit.*, iv, p. 26.

[12] For contemporary accounts of Cartier's voyages, see BURRAGE, H. S., *Early English and French Voyages* (*Original Narratives*), pp. 4-31, 37-88, 93-102.

[13] For an account of these events, written by Laudonnière, who accompanied the expedition, see HAKLUYT, RICHARD, ed., *The Principal Navigations, Voyages, etc.*, 1889 edition, xiii, pp. 417-441.

in Florida, and in 1564 Laudonnière, another Huguenot, led a large expedition to the St. John's River. A settlement was begun on this river about five miles from the mouth, which was called Fort Caroline. The settlers made no effort to cultivate the soil, but spent their energies in hunting for gold and in participating in the quarrels between Indian tribes. This improvidence and the violent quarrels that broke out among them soon brought the colonists to the verge of starvation. They were preparing to return home when Ribaut arrived with seven ships and six hundred men. All plans for abandoning the settlement were now canceled.

In the meantime Philip II of Spain had learned of the French settlement in Florida and had determined to destroy it.[14] For this ruthless task Philip selected Pedro Menendez de Avilés, "the bloodiest Spaniard that ever cursed American soil—and one of the ablest."[15] Menendez effected a landing about fifty miles south of Fort Caroline and began to lay the foundations of St. Augustine. He next made an attack on the French post after a strenuous march across country through swamps and tangled forests. As the French were taken by surprise, the fort was captured without resistance and only a few of the garrison escaped. Most of the captives were killed, and this wholesale butchery was approved by the Spanish king, Philip II.[16]

[14] There were strong reasons, from Philip's point of view, why a Huguenot colony should not be allowed to take root in that part of America. The settlement might easily become—as it actually did—a base for piratical attacks on the Spanish West Indies. Besides, these colonists were adherents of a heretical sect and subjects of a rival power. As heretics they had no right to live anywhere, and as Frenchmen they should not be allowed to take possession of land that belonged to Spain by right of discovery and exploration. To strangle the infant colony in its cradle would, therefore, be to perform a good service for both the Catholic Church and the Spanish empire (see HAKLUYT, RICHARD, *Voyages*, xiii, pp. 454, 504-511).

[15] CHANNING, E., *History of the United States*, i, p. 98.

[16] PARKMAN, FRANCIS, *Pioneers of France in the New World*, chs. 3-8. Numerous quotations from the sources are given in this lengthy account. For contemporary accounts, see also BURRAGE, H. S., ed., *Early English and French Voyages (Original Narratives)*, pp. 122-124.

Nothing was done by the French government to avenge this wrong, although all parties in France were aroused by the massacre. Catherine de' Medici, the queen mother, who was dominating the

In this way ended for the time the attempt of the French to contest the claim of Spain to the continent of North America. The sixteenth century was nearing its end before another effort at American colonization was made by France.

ENGLAND AND SPAIN CLASH IN EUROPE AND AMERICA

Spain's easy victory over France in this first clash between European powers in North America left the former in undisturbed possession of that continent for only a short time. For soon another rival entered the lists against her that was destined to curb her ambition and limit her expansion toward the north. This new rival was England. At the beginning of the sixteenth century England was backward in commerce, industry, and wealth, and therefore did not rank as one of the great European nations. But from this time on her people increased rapidly in numbers and wealth, and by the time Queen Elizabeth came to the throne (1558) this little country had become a great power. The British navy and merchant marine had increased in size and importance and a generation of seamen had grown up to whom "no land was uninhabitable and no sea unnavigable."[17] During the last half of the sixteenth century—which was covered approximately by the reign of Elizabeth—the Renaissance, which had come to England at the end of the fifteenth century, was at its height in the British Isles and was stimulating thought and action in every field of endeavor. It was a time when Spenser, Marlowe, Bacon, Shakespeare, and other literary lights were creating the Golden Age of English literature. By this time Protestantism was firmly intrenched among the British people, and the Reformation movement was still young enough to retain much of its nascent zeal and was thus able to impart a religious tinge to every great movement. The set time had thus come for

young king at the time, was restrained by her fears of Philip, and felt that in the divided state of France she could do nothing except to make use of high words in protest against the act. But one Frenchman, Dominique de Gourgues, was unwilling for this atrocity to go unavenged, and with an expedition of three small ships, fitted out at his own expense, he attacked the Spanish fort on the St. John's and put the garrison to the sword (1567) (HAKLUYT, RICHARD, *The Principal Navigations, Voyages, etc.*, xiii, pp. 524-525).

[17] FORMAN, S. E., *Advanced American History*, p. 19.

the English people to go forward and possess the land that had been pointed out to them by the Cabot voyages.

The English people had, however, been slow to press the claim that had been bequeathed to them by John Cabot. Indeed, but for the activity of the British merchants and seamen who conducted trading and fishing expeditions to the coast of Newfoundland, no connection between North America and the British Isles would have been maintained during the first half of the sixteenth century. It was not until after the accession of Queen Elizabeth that there grew up an active interest in expansion to the west. Protestantism had created a feeling of hostility toward Spain, the leading Catholic power of the world, and the people were ready to dispute the claims of Spain and Portugal to the lands of the New World. The two men who were chiefly instrumental in arousing this interest in America and this hostility to Spain were John Hawkins and Francis Drake. *Hawkins and Drake arouse the English to an interest in colonization*

These bold seamen were related to each other, and in courage, initiative, patriotism, and in their hatred of the Spaniards they were kindred spirits. Both were very religious, according to the standard of the time—a standard, however, allowing many practices that did not square with New Testament ethics. Of these daring sea-dogs Sir John Hawkins was the first to defy the trade regulations of Spain and thereby arouse the hostility of that power toward his country. As a patriotic Englishman with strong Protestant prejudices he had, to begin with, no love for a nation that was both the rival of his own country and the chief protagonist of Catholicism. This dislike was converted into bitter hatred when his business as a slave-trader brought him into unpleasant relations with Spanish officials. Like so many other great men of that age, he combined the outward piety of a saint with the inner and real brutality of a murderer. Although he would not scruple at kidnapping Negroes and perpetrating other cruelties toward his fellow-beings, this religious robber laid down for his men pious rules of conduct, among which were "Serve God daily" and "Love one another."[18] *John Hawkins*

In 1562 he entered upon a remarkable career as a slave-merchant, and during the next half-decade (1562-68) he transported three cargoes of Negroes from the African coast to the Spanish

[18] Quoted in INGRAM, J. R., *History of Slavery and Serfdom*, pp. 146-147.

colonies in America.[19] To sell slaves in America was a violation of the laws of Spain, as the commercial regulations of that country were so framed as to give to its own subjects a monopoly of the trade with the American colonies. But to weaken a great Catholic power in the New World was considered good policy for an Englishman and a Protestant. So he was encouraged in his course by both patriotism and business considerations.

Francis Drake

Of the semi-piratical sea-dogs that went from England to sail the Spanish Main the greatest was Francis Drake. Like Hawkins, Drake was a strong Protestant and was strict in his observance of the outward forms of religion. He used a pious phraseology in his dealings with his men, and was doubtless sincere in his religious professions; but his religion seems never to have functioned properly when he was in sight of a Spanish merchant vessel. At any rate, he plundered Spanish ships and laid Spanish American towns under contribution, apparently without any qualms of conscience, at a time when England and Spain were nominally at peace. The queen, however, did not punish him for these acts, but on the contrary encouraged him by receiving a share of the plunder and by knighting him.

The most famous of Drake's voyages was the one that took him around the world. Leaving England in 1577 with five ships, he sailed for the Strait of Magellan, hoping to find Spanish treasure ships on the western coast of South America. This long journey was attended by hardships that aroused dissatisfaction and mutiny among his crews, and his ships and men dwindled in number until only one vessel, the *Pelican*, was with him when he emerged upon the Pacific Ocean (1578). Sailing northward along the western coast of South America, he seized great treasures from the Spaniards. One ship taken was so heavily loaded with silver, gold, and precious stones that it required a week to transfer the cargo from the captured vessel to the *Pelican*. These plunderings had aroused the Spaniards, and Drake knew that he could not escape them if he should try to return by the Strait of Magellan. So he pursued his journey still further northward and explored the coast of California, looking for a strait across the

[19] For contemporary accounts of the last two of these voyages, see BURRAGE, H. S., *Early English and French Voyages*, pp. 114-132, 137-148. The best contemporary account we have of the third voyage, written by one of Hawkins's men, is given in WILLIAMSON, J. A., *Sir John Hawkins*, appendix, pp. 493-534.

the continent. He called the country New Albion, thinking that the poetic name of his own country was appropriate for this new land because of the white cliffs and banks observed by him.[20] Finding no waterway to the eastward, he boldly struck across the Pacific and went to the Spice Islands. Here he loaded his ship with pepper and returned to England by way of the Cape of Good Hope. He had thus completed the second voyage around the world.[21]

The historic voyage of Drake brought prestige and wealth to his country, but did not in any way strengthen her claim to lands in the New World. This could be done only by permanent occupation. The first attempt to plant an English colony in America was made by Sir Humphrey Gilbert, who received a patent from Queen Elizabeth (1578) authorizing him to explore and settle "remote heathen and barbarous lands, countreys and territories not actually possessed by any Christian prince or people."[22] It was his purpose to find the northwest passage to the Pacific and plant settlements on it. In 1583 he sailed to the New World and made an unsuccessful effort to plant a settlement on Newfoundland. While the expedition was returning home the little vessel in which he sailed suddenly sank with all on board.[23] **Gilbert**

Gilbert's patent rights descended to his half-brother, Walter Raleigh, a romantic favorite of the queen, who shared his brother's ambition to plant a colony in the New World. He sent out an expedition under Philip Amadas and Arthur Barlowe to explore the coast of North America before deciding on a place for settlement. They landed on the coast of North Carolina in July (1584) and were charmed with the beauty afforded by a region clothed in rich midsummer vegetation. After a sojourn of two months they returned home, giving a glowing account of the country, which they represented as "the most plentiful, sweet, **Raleigh**

[20] BURRAGE, H. S., *Early English and French Voyages,* p. 171.

[21] For an accessible collection of documents on Drake's famous voyage, with a discussion of the sources, see WAGNER, H. R., *Sir Francis Drake's Voyage around the World,* pp. 229-452.

[22] HAKLUYT, RICHARD, *The Principal Navigations, Voyages, etc.,* 1904 ed., viii, p. 17.

[23] For a contemporary account of Sir Humphrey Gilbert's attempt at colonization, see BURRAGE, H. S., *Early English and French Voyages,* pp. 179-222.

fruitful, and wholesome of all the world."[24] This report excited a lively interest in the new land, to which was given the name of Virginia in honor of Elizabeth, the Virgin Queen.

Encouraged by the success of his first exploring venture, Raleigh sent out a year later a second expedition to explore and colonize Virginia. This expedition consisted of a fleet of seven ships under the command of Sir Richard Grenville, who had instructions to plant a settlement and put Ralph Lane in charge of it. Accordingly, Lane was left on Roanoke Island with about one hundred emigrants (1585). Owing to the mismanagement of their leader and the hostility of the natives, by the beginning of the next summer (1586) the existence of the colony was threatened by famine. At this juncture Sir Francis Drake, who was returning from one of his raids in the Spanish Main, stopped at Roanoke Island with his fleet well loaded with Spanish plunder. He was in a generous mood toward his unfortunate fellow-countrymen and offered to give to Lane any assistance that he might ask. The emigrants were unanimous in the desire to return home, and all of them were put on board Drake's ships and taken back to England.[25]

The "Lost Colony" of Roanoke Island

Nothing daunted by his first failure, Raleigh made preparations for another attempt at colonization. The interest of capitalists and prospective settlers was secured by offering them stock in a company that had been formed on the basis of Raleigh's patent. One hundred and fifty emigrants, including seventeen women, were sent over in three ships, and the expedition gave every promise of success. A plan of government for a permanent colony was devised and John White was appointed governor. When they reached the coast of Carolina (1587) they selected the ill-fated Roanoke Island as the place for their settlement. Among the

[24] For an account of this voyage, written by Barlowe, see BURRAGE, op. cit., pp. 227-241.

[25] Ibid., pp. 246-271, 276-277.

A few weeks after the colony was deserted Grenville arrived with three ships and fresh supplies. After hunting for some time for the first settlers and not being able to find any of them, he returned to England, but left fifteen men on the island to hold it until they could be reinforced. When the next contingent of settlers came over (a year later) no trace of these men could be found. We know that two of them had been killed by the Indians, but the fate of the others is unknown (ibid., pp. 276-278, 288).

women who came over was the daughter of Governor White, Eleanor, who was married to Ananias Dare, one of the governor's assistants. Shortly after their arrival at Roanoke, a daughter was born to this couple, who was appropriately named Virginia. Virginia Dare was thus the first white child born in English America.

Governor White did not remain long in the colony, for he felt it his duty to go back to England with the returning ships to urge that more supplies be sent over at once. When he arrived at Southampton after a long voyage he found England all agog with excitement over the threatened attack of the Spanish Armada, and he was not able to secure a prompt compliance with his request. However, in a few months, thanks to the influence of Raleigh, White was able to start to Virginia with two small vessels (April, 1588). But these ships were attacked by Spanish warships at Madeira and were so badly crippled that they had to return to England. Raleigh's second attempt to send relief to the colony also failed, and White was not able to return to America until 1591.[26] When he reached Roanoke Island the settlers were nowhere to be seen, though their homes were still standing. The only hint as to their fate was the word "Croatoan," which he found cut in the bark of a tree. This was the name of a friendly tribe of Indians that lived at the other end of Pamlico Sound.[27] It is not known whether the lost colonists were killed by the Indians or absorbed by them. The fate of the "Lost Colony" is one of the unsolvable problems with which some modern historians amuse themselves in their moments of leisure. But so far, all the efforts in this direction have been no more fruitful than the study of a cross-word puzzle, for all the theories advanced as to the fate of White's colonists are nothing more than idle conjectures.

It will be remembered that Protestantism in the early decades

[26] Raleigh had spent an immense amount of money on his colonial venture and had gotten nothing in return. He was, therefore, willing to share the expense and responsibility of colonizing Virginia with other capitalists. In 1589 there was a reorganization of his company, according to which he surrendered still more of his rights under his patent. But the new organization was also very slow to get the funds necessary to send out the supply ships. See CHANNING, *op. cit.*, ii, pp. 129-130; DOYLE, J. A., *English Colonies in America*, i, p. 72.

[27] White's account of these events is given in BURRAGE, H. S., *Early English and French Voyages*, pp. 282-300, 305-320.

of its youthful enthusiasm gained rapidly on Catholicism. For a while the Catholics did not show their accustomed ability to meet an emergency. But soon they awoke from their lethargy and began to take vigorous measures to meet the new danger. Some of the abuses in the practices of the church were reformed, but no important concessions in doctrine were made to the new heresy. A general council of the church was held at Trent (1545-63), and the old doctrines were reaffirmed and defined. The Catholics now had a body of clearly-stated beliefs which served as a platform on which they could make an active campaign, and so they became aggressive and began to regain the lost territory. One of the chief agencies in bringing about this successful result was the Jesuit Order, a new organization (recognized by the pope in 1540), which was aflame with energy and enthusiasm.

The Protestants were divided among themselves on many points, but were a unit in regarding the Catholic denomination as their common enemy. Under such conditions it was natural that the friction between the two great Christian bodies would generate a dangerous amount of heat, which might at any time flame up into war. At that time, too, both Protestants and Catholics believed in the union of church and state, and both were willing to use the material weapon of government in fighting their spiritual battles. The state was glad to ally itself with the church and to have patriotism bolstered up with denominational prejudice and fired with religious zeal. Every international contest of this period, therefore, had a religious aspect, and every religious struggle had a political side. At no other time in the modern period has the unholy alliance between religion and politics been carried to a more dangerous extreme.

In such a state of affairs the Catholics naturally regarded the king of the leading Catholic power as their champion, and the Protestants looked for leadership to the ruler of the strongest Protestant nation. Philip II of Spain and Elizabeth of England were thus chosen by circumstances to lead, respectively, the Catholic and Protestant causes. The former assumed his rôle with a serious mind and acted from conviction as well as from considerations of policy. The latter played her part light-heartedly, not having any deep religious convictions to interfere seriously with policy.

But despite the tenseness of the religious situation it was to the highest interest of both nations to maintain friendly relations with each other. English merchants were carrying on a lucrative trade with the Netherlands, which were now under the control of Philip, and a war with Spain would dry up this source of gain. On the other hand, Philip's ships had to pass through the English Channel to reach the Spanish Netherlands, and a war with England would thus jeopardize his communications with his possessions in the Low Countries. Both rulers appreciated the mutual advantages of a policy of peace, and the religious antagonism of the two countries would probably never have led to war had it not allied itself with political and commercial rivalry.

Unfortunately, Philip allowed his zeal for the Catholic cause to override the prudential restraints imposed upon him by the interests of his own country. He encouraged the Jesuits and disloyal English Catholics to intrigue against Elizabeth, with a view to bringing England back into the Catholic fold with Mary Stuart, the dethroned Scottish queen, on the throne. These intrigues and the plots growing out of them aroused a strong anti-Spanish feeling in England and drove the government into a policy of persecuting Catholics at home and of supporting the Protestant cause abroad. The growing ill-feeling between Protestant England and Catholic Spain afforded an opportunity to loyal British seamen, like Drake and Hawkins, to defy the Spanish trade regulations and plunder Spanish vessels in the name of patriotism and religion. Moreover, these raids, which were encouraged by Elizabeth, exasperated Philip and spurred him on to further acts of hostility. Elizabeth, too, was ready to do what she could to weaken her rival, and in 1585 sent troops to the Netherlands to aid the Protestant rebels in their heroic struggle against Spain. Philip now decided to throw off the mask of friendship and make preparations for war.

Causes of the war between England and Spain

A great fleet was prepared, which was thought to be invincible, and hence was known as the Invincible Armada. In the summer of 1588 this proud fleet sailed into the British Channel, hoping to pass through to Flanders to convoy to England or Scotland the Duke of Parma and his army, which had been making a fine showing against the Dutch rebels. With these troops and his Invincible Armada Philip would be in a position to make a joint land and naval attack on Britain, and soon the heretic kingdom would be at his disposal. As Mary Stuart had been recently executed (February, 1587), the crown of England would be given to his favorite daughter, Isabella.

The defeat of the Armada

But in his calculation he failed to take into proper account the most important factor in the situation—the British navy. It was now composed of light and quick-moving ships, manned by experienced seamen and led by able and courageous commanders, such as Drake, Hawkins, and other famous sea-dogs. The Spanish ships outnumbered their English competitors, but were heavy and unwieldy, poorly equipped, and under the command of an incompetent leader. After a running fight for some days the two fleets met in a hard-fought battle off Gravelines (July, 1588), in which the Armada was badly defeated and forced to flee northward through the North Sea. "North, and still north, round by the surf-lashed Orkneys, then down the wild coasts of the Hebrides and Ireland, went the forlorn Armada, losing ships and men at every stage, until at last the remnant straggled into Spanish ports."[28]

Results of the battle   This English victory had an important bearing on the history of America. It lowered the morale of the Spanish seamen and enhanced the prestige of the British fleet. With her new rank as a naval power England was in a position to appropriate by colonization a large portion of North America in the face of Spain's claim to the whole continent. Spain was now in a chastened mood and not inclined to press her claims to the point of risking a dangerous clash with the British navy. The defeat of the great Armada thus made the New World safe for English colonization.

SELECTED READINGS

1. Magellan.—Bourne, E. G., *Spain in America*, *ch. 9; Fiske, J., *The Discovery of America*, ii, pp. *184-211.
2. Balboa.—Bourne, *Spain in America*, pp. *108-112.
3. Narvaez and De Vaca.—Channing, *op. cit.*, i, pp. *62-67; Bourne, E. G., *Spain in America*, pp. *159-162; *Old South Leaflets*, no. 39.
4. De Soto.—Channing, *op. cit.*, i, pp. *67-72; Bourne, *op. cit.*, pp. *162-168; *Old South Leaflets*, no. 36.
5. Coronado.—Channing, *op. cit.*, i, pp. 72-84; Bourne, *op. cit.*, pp. *169-173.
6. The Founding of St. Augustine.—Lowery, W., *The Spanish Settlements within the Present Limits of the United States* (1531-61), pp. *147, 158-159; *Old South Leaflets*, no. 89, especially pp. *10-14.
7. Spanish Achievements in the Seventeenth Century.—Bolton, H.

[28] Wood, W., *Elizabethan Sea-Dogs*, p. 191.

E., and Marshall, T. M., *The Colonization of North America*, pp. *75-76; Bourne, *op. cit.*, *ch. 20.

8. Spanish Policy toward the Indians.—Priestley, H. I., *The Coming of the White Man*, *ch. 5.

9. Verrazano.—Fiske, J., *The Dutch and Quaker Colonies*, i, pp. 60-68; *Old South Leaflets*, no. 17.

10. Cartier.—Munro, W. B., *Crusaders of New France*, *ch. 2; Channing, *op. cit.*, i, pp. *92-94.

11. Fort Carolina and Its Destruction by the Spaniards.—Channing, *op. cit.*, i, pp. *94-100; Bourne, *op. cit.*, *ch. 12. Bourne's position with reference to Gourgues's expedition (as given in pp. 187-189) is not accepted by the most recent scholarship. See Lowery, *op. cit.*, pp. 324-336, 454-457.

12. Sir John Hawkins.—Channing, *op. cit.*, i, pp. *115-119; Hart, A. B., *American History Told by Contemporaries*, i, pp. *75-81; Wood, W., *Elizabethan Sea-Dogs*, ch. 5 (interesting; quotes at length from sources, but rather long for class assignment).

13. Sir Francis Drake.—Channing, *op. cit.*, i, pp. *119-122; Hart, A. B., *American History Told by Contemporaries,* i, pp. *81-88; Wood, W., *Elizabethan Sea-Dogs*, chs. 6-10 and 12 (interesting, but too long).

14. Gilbert and Raleigh.—Wood, *op. cit.*, *ch. 11; Hart, *op. cit.*, pp. *89-95; *Old South Leaflets*, nos. 92 and 119; Channing, *op. cit.*, i, pp. *122-130.

CHAPTER IV

VIRGINIA FROM PLANTATION TO ROYAL PROVINCE

THE sixteenth century had come to an end before England had gained a foothold in America. The failure of the attempts at settlement just described showed that the planting of a colony was too big a venture for any individual. The risks were so great that they should be shared by a number of persons. A company, with stockholders of limited liability, was, therefore, the only proper private agency to undertake so great an enterprise as colonization. But this corporation should be associated with the government in order that the colony founded by it might be linked up properly with the homeland and protected against foreign aggression.

Motives for English colonization:

At this time there were a number of reasons for colonization that would strongly appeal both to the king and to patriotic capitalists. Prominent among these may be mentioned the following:

(1) Expectation of finding gold in Virginia

(1) The expectation of finding gold and silver in Virginia.— The Spaniards had been reaping a great harvest of gold in tropical America, and their success inflamed the English with the desire to get their share of the treasures of the New World. This was one of the main motives that led to the settlement at Jamestown. It was unfortunate for the infant colony that there was so much interest in gold-hunting, for it used up the energies of the early settlers in a bootless quest at a time when they were badly needed in raising food supplies. This misplaced effort was one of the causes of the terrible sufferings that the early settlers experienced from a shortage of food.[1]

---

[1] For an excellent discussion of the motives of English colonization, see BRUCE, P. A., *Economic History of Virginia*, i, ch. 1. For the best contemporary discussion, see HAKLUYT, RICHARD, *Discourse on Western Planting*. This work is reprinted in the Maine Historical Society *Collections*, second series (*Documentary History*), ii, pp. 3-161. An excellent summary of the whole treatise is given on pp. 3-5. Extracts from HAKLUYT's *Discourse* and other contemporary tracts

(2) The hope of finding a waterway across the continent to the Indies.—In the early decades of the seventeenth century it was still believed that Asia was not far west of the eastern coast of North America. The James and York rivers in their lower reaches look more like ocean straits than rivers, and the probability that they might lead across what was thought to be a comparatively narrow strip of land to the Pacific Ocean seemed not unreasonable. The first settlers were encouraged in this hope by the persistent statements of the Indians about the western sea and rivers having their sources near it. These stories were too numerous and came from too many different sources to be explained by the desire of the natives to lead their white enemies away on a fool's errand. There must have been some basis of fact on which these reports rested. The Indians probably had in mind the Great Lakes and possibly the Gulf of Mexico when they spoke of the great western sea; but the settlers interpreted these statements as referring to the South Sea, or the Pacific Ocean. The planting of a colony in America would promote the discovery of this waterway. Besides, settlements situated on this strait would become wealthy by commerce, and the nation controlling such a strait would have a great advantage over its competitors in the trade with the East. It would mean as much for a nation to control such a strait as it now does for England to own the Suez Canal or the United States to possess the Panama Canal.

(2) The hope of finding a waterway to the Pacific

(3) The determination to challenge Spain's claim to North America.—England and Spain both claimed the territory of the present United States on the basis of discoveries made under their respective flags, but up to the middle of the sixteenth century neither had supported its claim by successful colonization. The nation that would first occupy the territory would have the advantage of the nine points of the law that always go with possession. Spain, having got the start on her rival by planting a colony in Florida (1565), might soon extend her occupation northward on the Atlantic, as she afterward did on the Pacific coast. An English colony in Virginia would check this expansion and serve to stake off a good portion of America for England before Spain had preëmpted the ground.

(3) The determination to challenge Spain's claim to all of North America

are given in WEST, W. M., *Source Book*, pp. 4-19, and in PEASE, T. C., and ROBERTS, A. S., *Selected Readings in American History*, pp. 1-4.

(4) The hope of producing raw materials in America for English manufactures

(4) The hope of producing in the New World certain raw materials and other articles that England was buying from other countries.—Among these commodities were lumber, silks, spices, copper, iron, timber for ship-building, pitch, tar, rosin, and other naval stores. It was not always easy to procure these products, as the countries from which they came sometimes imposed restrictions on the trade in them. Besides, to procure them money had to be sent out of the country, and so the balance of trade was disturbed. If these necessary articles could be produced in an English colony the supply would be more dependable and the money spent for them would all be kept within the empire. The illimitable forests in the New World and the other natural resources made this hope quite reasonable so far as some of these commodities were concerned.

(5) Belief that America would afford a market for British manufactures

(5) The belief that America would afford a market for British manufactures.—In England at this time the chief manufacture was that of coarse woolens. It was at first thought that the Indians would buy coarse cloth and thereby stimulate the woolen industry. This expectation was not realized, but it was still hoped that the colonists would demand enough cloth and clothing to encourage the industry in the homeland.

(6) The hope that colonization would increase the British merchant marine and strengthen the navy

(6) The hope that colonization would increase the English merchant marine and strengthen the navy.—The trade between the colonies and the homeland would require more ships, and this increase in the merchant marine would, in turn, strengthen the navy, for the skill acquired by the sailors on merchant vessels could be employed by the navy in time of war.

(7) Colonization would provide a vent for surplus population

(7) The need of finding a vent for the surplus population.— Not only could criminals and other undesirables be gotten rid of by being sent off to the New World, but many worthy poor people who could not get employment in England could also find a home there. This latter class was large in England at that time, owing to the economic changes which had taken place in the reign of Elizabeth (see pp. 11-12).

(8) The religious motive.—The desire to convert the heathen natives to Christianity also figured to some slight extent in colonization. The men who risked their capital in the colonizing venture at Jamestown were probably actuated only in a secondary way, if at all, by religious considerations, but the religious leaders who supported the undertaking had a real interest in the spiritual welfare of the natives and emphasized the importance of evan-

gelizing them. The religious motive was, however, a more important factor in the planting of later colonies, such as Plymouth,
Massachusetts, Rhode Island, Maryland, and Pennsylvania.[2]

Although Raleigh had failed in his attempt at colonization, he
still claimed the exclusive right under his patent to exploit
America. Despite this claim, however, several trading and exploring expeditions went from England to the New World in the
opening years of the seventeenth century. One of the most important of these was the one conducted by George Weymouth in
1604. He visited the shores of New England near the mouth of
the Kennebec River, and on his return gave an enthusiastic account of the country. This account aroused a new interest in
colonization and led to the formation of a joint-stock company.

This company, whose stockholders were merchants, knights,
and gentlemen, received a charter from the king in 1606, which
authorized it to make settlements in America. The patentees were
grouped into two divisions, and in a sense there were really two
companies. One of these was composed mainly of capitalists from
London and is generally known as the London Company. The
other drew its membership mostly from Plymouth and is known
as the Plymouth Company. The former was given the right to
plant a colony anywhere between the 34th and 41st parallels of
north latitude; the latter, anywhere between the 38th and 45th
parallels. There was, therefore, a zone three degrees wide open
to both groups. The possibility of a conflict between the two
companies in this overlapping zone was guarded against by a
provision that neither one should occupy the land within one
hundred miles of a settlement already made by the other. Each
Company was given the land extending fifty miles north and fifty
miles south of its first settlement and one hundred miles into
the interior.[3]

[2] While these motives are listed by an able contemporary as the
reasons for colonization, it is hardly probable that the British government was in the beginning consciously influenced by all of these
considerations. The establishment of the English plantations in
America was not the outgrowth of a well-thought-out plan, but was
largely the result of accident. Some of these reasons were doubtless
an afterthought and only served to influence British policy after
colonization was well under way.

[3] For the full text of this charter, see THORPE, F. N., *The Federal
and State Constitutions, Colonial Charters,* etc., pp. 3783-3789. The

Provisions for the government of the colonies

In making this grant of land the king did not surrender his right to govern the American settlements. A council resident in England and appointed by the king was to have general supervision over both colonies. In each colony there was to be a local council, appointed in the first instance by the general council. The local council was a self-perpetuating body; it had power to fill vacancies and remove members for just cause and also to elect its president, who was to be chosen annually. The local council was to govern the colony according to the laws of England, and was not to pass ordinances affecting life or limb. But with the exception of these two restrictions its powers were almost absolute. In it were vested all the functions of government, legislative, judicial, and executive. The settlers and their descendants were to have all the "liberties, franchises, and immunities" enjoyed by Englishmen of the homeland. This clause and others of a similar character mentioned in other charters are the basis of the claim that the colonists had all the rights and privileges conferred by the English common law. But these high-sounding phrases meant little or nothing to the first immigrants, for most of them were under the power of irresponsible officials and were not able to assert effectively their rights as free-born Englishmen.

Rivalry of Spain

The territory granted by the king was all claimed by Spain, and the Spanish ambassador at the English court protested against the proposed expedition. James was usually overanxious to please the Spanish government, but on this occasion he displayed unexpected independence of spirit. He paid no heed to the Spanish protest, declaring in effect that he did not recognize Spain's blanket claim to the unsettled lands of North America.

Zuñiga, the Spanish ambassador, realized that the English colony would be a bar to Spanish expansion in America and urged his sovereign, Philip III, to strangle it in its infancy.[4] While Philip did not dare to carry out this advice fully, still two Spanish expeditions were sent against Jamestown in the earliest years of its history. One turned back after reaching Chesapeake Bay (1609), but a second had the boldness to go all the way to the English settlement (1611). Nothing of importance, however,

---

greater part of the text is also given in BROWN, A., *The Genesis of the United States*, pp. 52-63, and MACDONALD, WILLIAM, *Select Charters*, pp. 1-11.

[4] BROWN, A., *Genesis of the United States*, i, pp. 117, 120, 123-124, 140, 196, 259.

happened except that the colonists seized three Spaniards and the Spanish ships went away with one English captive.[5] Nevertheless, it increased the feeling of uneasiness among the Virginia settlers, for they had from the beginning feared a Spanish attack and these episodes added to their alarm.

It is difficult for us to understand at this distance the hesitant and timid policy pursued by Spain toward the defenseless settlement. To explain this weakness and vacillation we have to remember that when the Spanish Armada was so badly defeated in 1588 the morale of the Spanish navy was also seriously crippled. After this great disaster the Spanish people entertained a fear of the British navy that exercised a very wholesome restraint on their actions whenever British interests were concerned. Besides, for some time it looked as if the Jamestown settlement would perish, and King Philip III would thus be saved the trouble of putting an end to it. The king, therefore, pursued a policy of watchful waiting until he finally awoke to the fact that the young colony had grown strong enough to offer a dangerous resistance to attack and that Spain had lost the opportunity of enforcing her claim to Virginia.

An expedition sent out by the Plymouth Company landed at the mouth of the Kennebec River in August, 1607. Here they built a fort which they named St. George and left forty-four men to hold it. After a winter of terrible suffering the settlement was abandoned and no further effort to plant a colony was made by the Plymouth Company for some years.[6]

An attempt at settlement made by the Plymouth Company

The London Company was more persistent in its efforts, and as a result succeeded in planting the first permanent English colony in America. In December, 1606, this corporation sent out from London three small vessels,[7] carrying one hundred and twenty emigrants, under the command of Christopher Newport, an experienced seaman. The journey to the Virginia coast was a long and trying one, as the expedition went the old route by way

Jamestown founded

---

[5] *Ibid.*, i, p. 507. For an account of these events by John Clark, the English captive, in Spanish and in English translation, see article by WRIGHT, IRENE A., in the *American Historical Review*, xxv, pp. 460-479.

[6] For a contemporary account of this attempt at settlement, see THAYER, H. O., *The Sagadahoc Colony*, pp. 35-86.

[7] The names of these vessels were the *Goodspeed*, the *Discovery*, and the *Sarah Constant.*

of the Canaries and the West Indies. A sea voyage in that day was not only an uncomfortable experience, but was also a hazardous undertaking. The passengers and crew were crowded in the small vessels with no adequate provision for fresh air and with little or no regard for other sanitary requirements. It was also very difficult to keep the ships supplied with proper food and drinking-water on these long journeys. It is not surprising, therefore, that sixteen of the emigrants died on this first voyage.

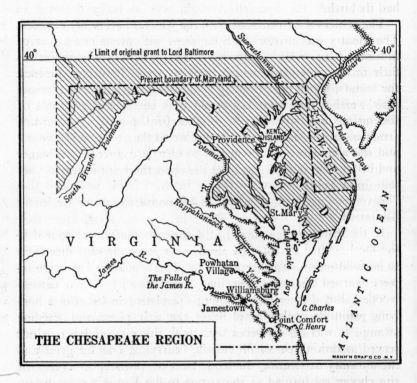

THE CHESAPEAKE REGION

Finally, on April 26, more than four months after leaving London, they came in sight of the two capes at the mouth of Chesapeake Bay, which they called Henry and Charles in honor of the two sons of the English king. Passing into the bay, they soon approached another cape between the bay and a great river. They were now satisfied that they were near the end of their voyage, and were so rejoiced over it that they named the headland Point Comfort. To the river, which was known by the Indians as Powhatan, they gave the name of James in honor of their king. Going up the James for about thirty-two miles, they landed on a peninsula May 14, 1607 (May 24 new style) and began a settlement which they called Jamestown. The number of emigrants who landed was a little over one hundred and consisted entirely of men and boys, as it was more than a year before the first women came to Virginia. They began at once to build a palisaded fort for protection, a storehouse, a church, and a row of log huts for dwellings. In this way the United States had its birth.[8]

The settlers were charmed with the natural beauty of Virginia. The country was covered with big trees with grape vines as large as a man's leg swinging between them. In some places there was little or no underbrush and a carriage could be driven through the forests. When the newcomers walked out to enjoy the glorious May weather they were entranced with the crystal clearness of the springs and streams, the singing of the birds, the verdant freshness of the spring vegetation, the beauty of the wild flowers, and the abundance of the wild strawberries "four times bigger and better than ours in England." One of these enthusiasts (Captain John Smith) went so far as to say of this new land that "heaven and earth never agreed better to frame a place for man's habitation."[9] *The beauty of the country*

In the instructions issued by the general council in England to the local council in Virginia there were some sensible directions to be followed in choosing a site for a settlement.[10] The colonists were warned against places that were swampy or too densely wooded. But despite this warning the place selected was a low-lying peninsula in the James River near a large malaria-breeding swamp. It was also covered over with magnificent trees, which served as lurking-places for hostile Indians and added greatly to the difficulty of clearing the land. In other respects, however, the site chosen conformed to the requirements laid down in the in- *Nature of the site chosen for the settlement*

---

[8] For an account of this voyage written by George Percy, who took a prominent part in planting the settlement, see TYLER, L. G., *Narratives of Early Virginia (Original Narratives)*, pp. 5-23. For two other contemporary accounts, see *ibid.*, pp. 32-36, 121-126.

[9] *Ibid.*, pp. 16, 81.

[10] These instructions are given in the main in FISKE, JOHN, *Old Virginia and Her Neighbors*, i, pp. 75-79. For the full text of the instructions see BROWN, A., *Genesis of the United States*, pp. 65-75; also ARBER, E., *Works of Captain John Smith*, i, xxxiii-xxxvii.

structions. The peninsula (now an island) was almost entirely surrounded by water. It was, therefore, easy to defend, and there was abundant space for the safe anchorage of their boats.

The Indian menace

The Indians in this region belonged to the Algonquin race, and were united into a confederacy ruled over by Powhatan. There were thirty-four tribes under his authority, which extended from the Roanoke River to the head of Chesapeake Bay. These Indians had already come in contact with English and Spanish traders and were hostile to the whites. They regarded the settlement at Jamestown as an infringement upon their territory and would have destroyed it if they had been able. This hostility was responsible for much of the suffering of the first settlers. It is true that in the early years only a few whites were actually killed by the natives, but they were considerably restrained by fear of the Indians from the activities that were necessary to procure an adequate food supply. The forest was alive with game and the river and the bay abounded in fish and oysters, but fear of the Indians prevented their taking full advantage of these sources of food.

Friction in the council

To these difficulties were added those arising from strife and faction in the governing council. Seven men had been appointed to the local council, prominent among whom were Edward Maria Wingfield, John Smith, and Captain Newport. This list was kept by Newport in a sealed package, with instructions not to break the seals until after they had reached the shores of Virginia.[11] Wingfield and Smith got into a quarrel on the voyage over and the latter was put in irons. He was released after they reached Virginia, but the quarrel continued and there were bitter partisans on both sides. As a result of these and other bickerings two presidents of the council were deposed, two councilors removed, and one shot for mutiny, all in a comparatively short time.[12] These dissensions prevented that coöperation on the part of the rulers which was needed for the effective management of the colony, and this misgovernment was responsible for much of the hardship that the settlers had to undergo.

Disease and death

There were other causes of suffering, however, over which the

[11] BROWN, A., *op. cit.*, p. 77; TYLER, L. G., ed., *Narratives of Early Virginia*, p. 123.

[12] TYLER, L. G., *op. cit.*, pp. 36-37, 41, 147; BROWN. A., *op. cit.*, pp. 167, 168; ARBER, E., *Works of Captain John Smith*, pp. 432, 435.

council had no control. When the warm days of August set in, disease and famine began their deadly work and wrought such havoc that at one time "the living were scarce able to bury the dead."[13] Twice during the year 1608 Newport made return trips to Jamestown, bringing new emigrants and supplies; but despite these efforts the number of settlers continued to decline rapidly.

These troublous times brought to the front a man who proved himself a leader of real ability. This was Captain John Smith. He had had quite a romantic and thrilling career in the Old World. If we can believe his own account, portions of which are corroborated by other sources, he had fought against the Turks and on one occasion had killed three of them in single combat. Later he was enslaved by the Turks and in fighting his way to freedom he showed a cool-headed daring that would have done credit to one of King Arthur's knights. Accounts of other experiences and hair-breadth escapes are related by him, some of which sound like the stories about Sindbad the Sailor.

His career in America was also one of thrilling adventure, according to the accounts that he has left us. Of his writings, the most valuable for the student of Virginia history are two pamphlets which describe Virginia and detail the early events in the history of the colony. These works entitle him to the honor of being the father of American history. They give us valuable information as to the natural resources and physical geography of primeval Virginia, including a map of the lower Chesapeake Bay that is remarkably accurate,[14] and also relate interesting stories regarding his adventures with the Indians and his schemes for outwitting them. A fuller work, entitled *The General History of Virginia,* includes writings by Smith and compilations made by him of the writings of others. According to the accounts given in the *General History,* Pocahontas, the beautiful young daughter of Powhatan, was infatuated with him and more than once saved his life.[15]

Smith played a prominent part in the early bickerings at Jamestown and was at one time sentenced to be hanged. He was saved from this fate only by the timely arrival of Captain Newport (January, 1608). Later he triumphed over his enemies and became the real ruler of the colony. When the other councilors died

John Smith

[13] TYLER, L. G., *op. cit.,* p. 36.
[14] For a reproduction of this map, see ARBER, *op. cit.,* p. 385.
[15] *Ibid.,* pp. 400, 530-531; see also TYLER, L. G., *op. cit.,* p. 326.

he refused to have their places filled and at one time he was the sole councilor. During this time he ruled the colony as a benevolent despot. Under his directions a blockhouse was built, a well was dug, twenty cabins were erected, and from thirty to forty acres planted in corn.[16] He also procured corn from the natives and thus saved the settlers from starvation. His firm policy toward the Indians inspired in them a wholesome respect for the English. When the gold fever struck the colony and all the other leaders lost their heads, Smith opposed the expenditure of effort in the search for gold at a time when the chief concern of the colonists should have been the raising of corn.[17] He advised the Company to forego its immediate profits and pursue a policy that would put the colony on a firm footing. If his advice had been taken, much of the suffering endured by the first settlers might have been spared them.

Smith was boastful and self-confident and aroused bitter enmities, as has already been shown. Even before he reached Virginia he had created enough antagonism among his associates to get himself in irons, and from that day until this he has been the center of controversy. The violent personal quarrels of his lifetime have been followed in later years by a warm academic dispute among scholars as to his proper place in history. Today historians are lined up for and against him, and in their attack and defense show a feeling akin to that exhibited by his friends and enemies in those trying days that witnessed the birth pangs of the Virginia colony. Some consider him a charlatan and trouble-breeder; they are inclined to put a low estimate on his achievements at Jamestown and to regard his writings as the self-advertising vaporings of an unreliable braggart. Others look upon him as the savior of the colony and accept his writings as quite trustworthy and authoritative history. The disagreement has been characterized by so much heat that it is not easy for the unbiased but untrained student to distinguish between prejudice and argument and thus arrive at a correct appraisal of Smith's real place in history.

Impartial and unemotional scholarship, however, inclines to the friendly rather than to the hostile view. It admits that Smith was fond of a good story whenever he was the hero of it; that in his writings he was not restrained by any considerations of modesty

[16] Tyler, L. G., *op. cit.*, p. 185.
[17] *Ibid.*, pp. 136-137.

or over-conscientiousness as to fact from reserving for himself the center of the stage; and that he was contentious and got into more quarrels with his associates than even an energetic policy of pure devotion to the colony would warrant. The unbiased scholar of today accepts, but with some deductions and reservations, his account of the early history of Virginia, though he is not free from an honest skepticism as to the details of some of the stories. An impartial estimate of his achievements as a leader at Jamestown would also accord to him a place of prime importance in the early history of the colony.[18]

The experiences through which the little colony had passed during the first two years of its existence were enough to discourage the most optimistic of its supporters. The Company had been playing a losing game in Virginia and naturally was not satisfied with the result. Although a good deal of money had been spent, the appalling death-rate among the immigrants had not been arrested and the infant settlement was still hovering between life and death.

Reasons for the sufferings of the early colonists

The reason frequently given for this failure is the fact that many of the first settlers were gentlemen and, therefore, were not willing to engage in the manual labor that is necessary to start

[18] The following estimate made by an eminent historian of Virginia seems to be sustained by the facts in Smith's career: "That this great man was egotistic and self-assertive it is impossible to deny, but that he was brave, steadfast, sagacious, and far-seeing no one will question who approaches the study of his career with the critical faculty free from all prejudice. His example and his teachings were in every instance marked by the highest practical wisdom. His services in the first settlement of Virginia were of incalculable value in their influence, and the general voice of the Colony and the State has not been incorrect in proclaiming him the real founder of the community." See BRUCE, P. A., *Economic History of Virginia in the Seventeenth Century*, i, p. 31, note.

The following eulogy on his character was given by one of the Jamestown settlers: "What shall I say, but thus we lost him, that in all his proceedings, made justice his first guide and experience his second, even hating baseness, sloth, pride and indignity more than any dangers; that never allowed more for himself than his soldiers with him; that upon no danger would send them where he would not lead them himself; . . . that loved action more than words, and nated falsehood and covetousness worse than death" (ARBER, *op. cit.*, pp. 485-486).

a new colony. This, however, does not explain the failure, for these gentlemen were of an adventurous spirit and of a character suited to pioneering.[19] The main reasons were disease and famine. The immigrants underwent a costly experience in becoming acclimated, or in passing through the "seasoning" process, as the early writers termed it. The swamps and lowlands near Jamestown were favorable breeding-places for malaria, and this disease was especially prevalent. Besides, the plague was brought over from London by later arrivals. Much of the illness that proved fatal would not have been so had not the power of the colonists to combat disease been weakened by the malnutrition of their bodies through a lack of proper food.

It is easy to understand why there was always a scarcity of food. The ships of that day were so small that there was little cargo space for supplies above what was necessary for the passengers and crew. For this reason it was very difficult and well-nigh impossible to keep the settlers supplied properly with food from the homeland. They were, therefore, mainly dependent upon the grain that they could raise themselves or procure from the natives. Some provisions were obtained from the Indians, but their stock of food was generally small and they were very reluctant to share it with the English intruders who had come to rob them of their hunting-lands.

If the colonists had gone to work energetically in the very beginning and devoted all their time to raising food crops, they could have supplied themselves after the first year. There are several reasons to account for their failure to do so. In the first place, the regulations of the Company required that the men should all work together and put what they made in a common storehouse. This arrangement took away the main incentive to labor, the hope of individual gain. The quarrels among the rulers

[19] One of the early writers, in speaking of the gentlemen as colonists, says: "Let no man think that the President or these gentlemen spent their time as common wood-hackers at felling of trees, or such like other labours, or that they were pressed to anything as hirelings or common slaves; for what they did (being but once a little inured), it seemed, and they conceited it, only as a pleasure and a recreation. Yet 30 or 40 of such voluntary Gentlemen would doe more in a day than 100 of the rest that must be pressed to it by compulsion" (TYLER, L. G., op. cit., p. 157).

were also unfavorable to coöperative effort on the part of the workers.

The impatient desire of the Company for returns on their investment was also largely responsible for the scarcity of food. Twice during the year 1608 Captain Newport, in obedience to instructions from the Company, brought return cargoes from Virginia. In the spring he loaded up with lumber and in December with tar, pitch, iron ore, and other articles. At both times the colonists had to stop their work to get these products ready for shipment. Newport also employed the settlers in his hunt for gold and in search of Raleigh's lost colony. In the spring of 1608 the gold fever struck the plantation and the council put the settlers to digging an ore which was supposed to contain gold but which proved to be worthless. Besides, a good deal of valuable time was consumed in exploring the bay and rivers in the effort to find a waterway across the continent. As a result of all of these outside activities only four acres of corn were planted in the spring of 1608.

To the drawbacks that came from bad management there were added the misfortunes that arose from ill luck and accident. In January, 1608, a fire broke out which destroyed most of the buildings in the fort. These had to be rebuilt in midwinter and many people died of exposure. In the spring of the following year the store of corn was largely destroyed by rats and what was left was found to be rotten. Added to all these calamities was the constant fear of the Indians, which kept the settlers from ranging the forest for game.[20]

Such a state of affairs called loudly for a change in the management of the colony. All classes interested in the colonizing venture had reason to be dissatisfied with the results so far attained. Friends of the settlers who had perished in the far-away wilderness had a right to question a policy that had proved so inefficient, and the stockholders of the Company were also dissatisfied because they had no voice in the management of an enterprise in which their capital was invested. So in 1609 a new charter was granted, by which the responsibility for governing the colonists was gradually transferred from the crown to the Company.[21]

The second charter

[20] *Ibid.*, pp. 135-136, 185.
[21] For the text of this charter, see THORPE, F. N., *op. cit.*, pp. 3790-3802. It is given in abbreviated form in MACDONALD, W., *Select Charters*, pp. 11-16.

By this second charter, however, the government of the colony was, in the beginning, still to be in the hands of the appointees of the crown; for the treasurer and council, whose names were mentioned in the king's patent, now had the same powers in the general management of affairs as did the general council under the first charter. But under the new patent vacancies in this governing body were to be filled by the Company, and so ultimately the governing council would be made up entirely of appointees of the Company. The grant of land was also enlarged by this second charter. The Company was now to have all the land two hundred miles north and two hundred miles south of Old Point Comfort and extending west and northwest to the Pacific Ocean.

The third charter

By the third charter granted by the king (1612) the Company was given still more powers of government and the Bermuda Islands were added to the territorial grant.[22] The treasurer and stockholders were to hold meetings every week or oftener, at which the less important business was to be transacted. For the appointment of officials and the transaction of the more important business, the council and Company were to meet four times a year in great and general courts.

Change in the local government

After receiving the second charter, the Company appointed a governor to take the place of the council at Jamestown, and gave him absolute authority in the local government of the colony. The change was a wise one, as it did away with the dissensions that had characterized the local administration. The governor had the assistance of a council of six men, but these new councilors were to be advisers only and were not to limit his authority.[23]

The wreck of the Sea Venture

Lord Delaware was selected as the first governor, but as he was not able to leave England just at this time, Sir Thomas Gates was sent over to act in his stead until he should arrive later. Along with Gates there went (June, 1609) a large expedition of nine ships carrying about six hundred new emigrants, including women and children. The fleet was shipwrecked and one of the vessels was lost at sea. Another, the *Sea Venture*, which had on board about one hundred and fifty people, including Governor Gates and Sir George Somers, was separated from the others and

[22] For abbreviated text of the third charter, see MacDonald, W., *op. cit.*, pp. 17-23. For the full text, see Thorpe, *op. cit.*, p. 3802 *et seq.*

[23] For the commission to Lord Delaware, see Brown, *op. cit.*, pp. 376-384.

was finally driven to the Bermuda Islands. Thanks to the heroic efforts of Sir George Somers and the crew, all on board were safely landed. After a sojourn of nine months on one of these beautiful islands, they sailed for Jamestown in two rough boats which they had constructed by prolonged and patient effort.[24]

In the meantime the other seven ships had weathered the storm and proceeded to Jamestown with about four hundred passengers. They landed in the sickly season (August) and some of them were already afflicted with the London plague. The provisions brought in by these ships had gotten wet and most of them had spoiled on the voyage. Many of these new immigrants were worthless characters, described by a contemporary writer as "unruly gallants, packed thither by their friends to escape ill destinies."[25] Among the new arrivals were several men who had figured prominently in the old quarrels and had taken sides against Smith. The latter was by no means cordial to these old enemies and refused to surrender his authority to them. The result was that old quarrels were revived and Smith was hampered in his efforts in behalf of the colony by the opposition of his enemies. These new recruits, therefore, only aggravated a situation that was already bad enough.

In September Smith was badly burned by an explosion of gunpowder, and his enemies, taking advantage of his helplessness, trumped up charges against him and had him deposed from the presidency. Moreover, he could not get the proper medical attention in Virginia for his burns, and so he decided to take passage in a returning ship for England.[26] When he sailed for England in October there was no one left in Virginia who was strong enough to cope with the situation. The settlers were hemmed in at Jamestown by the Indians, who were so bold as to come up to the settlement and drive off hogs and deer belonging to the colonists. The result of these conditions was a period of famine during the winter of 1609-10 known as the "Starving Time." Food became so scarce that the people ate with great relish their horses and dogs and all the mice and snakes they could find about the fort. To such straits were they brought by hunger that human bodies were eaten. During this terrible winter the number of the

The "Starving Time"

[24] For Somers's account of the shipwreck and the sojourn in the Bermudas, see *ibid.*, pp. 400-402.

[25] ARBER, *op. cit.*, p. 162.

[26] *Ibid.*, pp. 484-485.

colonists was reduced from five hundred to about sixty.[27] This was the most tragic experience endured by any group of pioneers who had a part in laying the foundations of the present United States.

Arrival
of Gates
at James-
town

It was in this awful plight that Gates and Somers with their fellow-refugees from Bermuda found the languishing colony when they sailed up the James River in May, 1610. They had to witness a terrible scene as they neared Jamestown. When they pulled up to the landing they were met by the few half-starved and half-demented survivors who were able to straggle down to the wharf. On going ashore they found that the houses had fallen into disrepair, the doors were off their hinges, and the palisades of the fort fallen down.[28] Some of them had even torn down their own houses and burned the lumber, being "not able, as they pretended, to step into the woods to gather other fire-wood."

The set-
tlement
aban-
doned, but
shortly
afterward
restored
by Lord
Delaware

As Gates by his commission was authorized to act as governor until the arrival of Lord Delaware, he at once took charge of affairs in the colony. But only a small quantity of supplies had been brought from the Bermudas and it was necessary to abandon Jamestown. The settlers were placed on board the pinnaces brought by Gates from the Bermudas, and all started down the river with the intention of going to the fishing-stations in New-foundland. Some of the "intemperate and malicious people" wished to wipe out every trace of their terrible sufferings by burning the town. This Gates determined to prevent and remained on shore until all were on board, "when, about noon, giving a farewell with a peale of small shott, he sett sayle." Before they reached the mouth of the river they were met by Lord Delaware, who was coming to the relief of the famine-stricken colony with supplies and fresh immigrants. Gates's vessels were now turned back and the work of colonization was started anew at Jamestown.[29]

Lord Delaware was just the man for such a situation as was now confronting him. The irresponsible idlers and "unruly gallants" among the immigrants needed a master and they found it in the serious-minded governor. He was kind but strict, and he realized that the colonists needed a leader who would hold them

[27] *Ibid.*, pp. 498-499. See also TYLER, L. G., *op. cit.*, pp. 294-296.
[28] BROWN, *op. cit.*, p. 405.
[29] *Ibid.*, pp. 400-413.

to a rigid discipline. On landing at Jamestown he first repaired
to the ruined church to hear a sermon by the chaplain, and then
he announced his policy to the settlers, speaking in no uncertain
terms as to what he would expect of them. He reminded them
that all their sufferings had been caused by their indolence and
improvidence, and he expressed the hope that such faults would
not again crop out, lest he should be compelled "to draw the
sword of justice to cut off such delinquents, which [he] would
much rather draw in their defence."[30] Under his wise management the colony was reëstablished on a firmer basis, though
disease and famine continued to make great inroads on the lives
of the people. Lord Delaware himself became ill and had to return
to England in the spring of 1611. From that time until 1618 he
governed Virginia through deputies.

The most noted of these early deputy governors was Thomas
Dale, who administered the colony for several years with the
title of High Marshal. He enforced the strictest military discipline and subjected the people to untold cruelties. Cruel and
inhuman punishments were inflicted without trial by jury and
sometimes for trivial offenses. Among the penalties to which they
were subjected were hanging, burning, and breaking on the
wheel. Some of them were hanged for "stealing to satisfy their
hunger." One case is given in which a lawbreaker "had a bodkin
thrust through his tongue and was chained to a tree until he
perished." Many of the settlers found the government intolerable;
some of them committed suicide, while others hid themselves
away in holes dug in the ground in order to escape its horrors.[31]

When we view the administration of the high marshal at this
distance we are at first inclined to regard it as an inexcusable
despotism. But while passing judgment on his severe rule we
must remember that the ills of the colony were such as could not
be remedied except by heroic treatment. Many of the settlers that
Dale and his successors had to deal with would not work except
when driven to it by the taskmaster. But even after making due
allowance for the character of the settlers under his control, we

Thomas Dale

---

[30] *Ibid.*, p. 407; TYLER, L. G., *op. cit.*, pp. 296-301.

[31] For a brief account of Dale's administration, see CHITWOOD,
O. P., *Justice in Colonial Virginia* (Johns Hopkins University
Studies, 23rd series), pp. 13-16. For the text of Dale's Laws, see
FORCE, P., *Tracts*, iii, pp. 9-27. See also TYLER, L. G., *op. cit.*, pp.
302-321.

are bound to admit that he erred greatly on the side of severity in subjecting the people to such a merciless system of government. The most that can be said in excuse for this reign of terror is that it acted as a schoolmaster to give the idle and irresponsible laborers the discipline they needed to prepare them for the freedom that came to them a few years later.

Dale's policy, however, was not altogether one of repression, but it included a number of constructive measures of great value to the colony. In his dealings with the Indians he acted with a firmness that overawed them and a craftiness that outwitted them. His methods did not always square with the highest ethical standards, but they were successful in allaying the strife between the natives and the whites. Powhatan's daughter, Pocahontas, was kidnapped and kept at Jamestown as a hostage. It was here that she met John Rolfe, a prominent planter, whom she afterward married (1614).[32] In this way the old chief was bound to a peace policy by family ties. Dale also modified the system of working in common and made everyone depend upon his own labor for his support. He allowed the settlers small allotments of land to be cultivated independently. They had to pay a heavy rent for the use of this acreage and in addition had to give the Company a month's work out of each year. As this plan made an appeal to the self-interest of the laborers and thereby gave them a motive for work, it was more successful than the old one of unrestricted communism.[33]

It was in Dale's administration that the cultivation of tobacco was begun. In 1612 John Rolfe was successful in raising and curing a crop of tobacco and thereby demonstrated that Virginia could compete with Spain in the production of the nicotine plant. The colony now had a valuable money crop for export, and was thus placed on a firm economic basis. There was, even at that early date, a great demand for the fragrant herb, both in England and on the Continent, and the growing of it was a very profitable industry. At once the colony took on new life and tobacco became the leading product.

The charter of 1609 provided for two kinds of stockholders,

[32] TYLER, L. G., *op. cit.*, pp. 239-244, 307-310; STEDMAN, E. C., and HUTCHINSON, E. M., *A Library of American Literature*, i, pp. 17-21.

[33] TYLER, L. G., *op. cit.*, p. 312.

"planters" and "adventurers." The former were those who went to Virginia as settlers; the latter those who invested capital in the enterprise but remained in England. Everyone who put in twelve pounds and ten shillings was credited with one share of stock. As the meetings of the stockholders were all held in London, the government of the Company was entirely in the hands of the adventurers. Every person over ten years of age who came to Virginia also received one share of stock. The planters were to work for the Company for seven years, receiving food, clothing, and shelter during the period, and a promise that each one would be given one hundred acres of land for himself and each member of his family at the expiration of the term. At the end of the seven-year period all the possessions of the Company were to be divided among all the stockholders, including planters as well as adventurers, in proportion to the amount of stock held by each. Theoretically, therefore, the planters were freemen holding stock in the Company. Practically, however, they were servants of the Company, as controlled by the English stockholders. Under the harsh rule of such governors as Dale and Argall their condition was little better than that of slaves.

"Planters" and "adventurers"

Under the charter of 1612 the sessions of the Company were important political meetings. The stockholders soon divided into two parties, the court party and "the country," or "patriot," party. The former wished to continue martial rule, while the latter wanted the colonists set free. The country party were more numerous than their opponents and soon were able to dominate the policy of the Company. When they got control they ordered that the planters should all be freed at the expiration of the joint-stock agreement, November, 1616. The deputy governor, however, failed to obey this instruction, and it was not until the arrival of Yeardley as governor in April, 1619, that the new policy was carried out. Martial law was now declared at an end and the settlers set free. Land was also given to them in accordance with the promise made to them in 1609.

End of martial law

When Yeardley arrived (1619) he brought with him instructions, issued the preceding November, directing him to give the people a voice in making the laws. These instructions have been called, somewhat extravagantly, perhaps, the "Magna Carta of America." In obedience to this order of the Company, the first legislative assembly in America was convened at Jamestown, July

Beginning of representative government

30, 1619 (old style).[34] This body was composed of the governor and his council and two representatives from each of the eleven plantations, or boroughs. The first meeting was held in the church. The governor, sitting in the midst of his council, who were ranged on his right and left, welcomed the burgesses, as the representatives were called, in the choir of the church. After the opening prayer, the burgesses went to the body of the church and the meeting entered upon its work. In this way representative government had its birth in America. The assembly thus organized developed into a bicameral legislature like the English Parliament, the governor and council being the upper house, and the burgesses, corresponding to the Commons in England, constituting the lower house.[35]

Intro-
duction
of slavery

In this same memorable year of 1619 a Dutch vessel appeared at Jamestown with twenty Negroes on board.[36] They were huddled together in close quarters and the settlers bought them largely out of kindness. It is contended by a high authority on the history of slavery (Professor J. C. Ballagh) that these Negroes were sold into servitude rather than into slavery.[37] But even if this view is correct, it was not long before Negro servitude had developed into slavery. This event may, therefore, properly be regarded as the beginning of African slavery in English America. American slavery and American democracy were thus twin born at Jamestown, and in their infancy both were rocked in the Cradle of the Republic.

Wives
sent over
for the
colonists
by the
Company

There were no women in Virginia for more than a year after the beginning of the settlement at Jamestown, the first to arrive being Mrs. Forrest and her maid, Anne Burras, who landed in September, 1608. Two months later Anne Burras was married to John Laydon and this was the first marriage solemnized in Eng-

[34] Brief quotations from Yeardley's commission directing him to establish an assembly are given in BROWN, ALEXANDER, *The First Republic*, pp. 293-309. A part of his instructions, dealing with land distribution, the establishment of a college, and other important affairs, is given in the *Virginia Magazine of History and Biography*, ii, pp. 154-165.

[35] For an account of the first meeting of the assembly written by John Pory, the speaker, see TYLER, L. G., *op. cit.*, pp. 249-278.

[36] ARBER, *op. cit.*, p. 541; TYLER, L. G., *op. cit.*, p. 337.

[37] For a discussion of this point, see BALLAGH, J. C., *History of Slavery in Virginia*, pp. 28-34.

lish America.[38] A year later a daughter, named Virginia, was born to them, who was the first white child born in the colony. Later expeditions brought over quite a number of women and children, but there was still a scarcity of women as late as 1619. To meet the demand for wives the Company sent over this year and at different times thereafter a number of unmarried young women of good character. These girls were carefully chosen, properly chaperoned, and apparently were well suited to the men who were blazing a trail for civilization in the New World. On arriving at Jamestown they were free to accept or reject any offer of marriage that might be made to them, but when a marriage was arranged for, each prospective husband had to pay one hundred and twenty pounds of tobacco (more than five hundred dollars in our present money) for his bride, to compensate the Company for the cost of transportation. But despite this high tax on matrimony, these young maidens had no difficulty in finding husbands.[39]

There was no great amount of fighting between the colonists and the Indians during the first fifteen years, as Powhatan at an early date was brought into friendly relations with the whites, and this friendship was cemented by the marriage of his daughter to John Rolfe (1614). At his death in 1618 he was succeeded by Opechancanough, who hated the English and resented their occupation of Indian lands. At first, however, he dissembled his wrath, and the settlers, lulled into a false security by the outward appearances of friendship, did not take the proper precautions to prevent a possible outbreak. Encouraged by the carelessness and unpreparedness of the colonists, Opechancanough formed a deep-laid and carefully concealed plot for their destruction. In 1622 his followers made a simultaneous attack on a number of outlying settlements and killed about three hundred and fifty of the whites. This massacre thoroughly aroused the Virginians and they wreaked so terrible a vengeance on the Indians that they remained quiet thereafter for more than twenty years.[40]

In 1644 another outbreak occurred, which was also instigated

Indian massacres

---

[38] TYLER, L. G., *op. cit.*, pp. 155, 160.

[39] TYLER, L. G., *op. cit.*, p. 339.

[40] For a contemporary account of this Indian massacre and the vengeance taken by the whites on their savage foes, see NEILL, E. D., *The Virginia Company*, pp. 317-321, 363-367; also TYLER, L. G., *op. cit.*, pp. 357-364.

by Opechancanough. He was now old and blind but had not lost his desire for revenge. The Civil War in England gave him, he thought, the opportunity to destroy the English colony. Accordingly, he fell upon the settlers and in two days over three hundred were killed. Again the whites were aroused and determined to inflict dire punishment on the savages. Opechancanough was captured and shot and the Indians were so severely chastised that they agreed to leave the region between the York and the James rivers, and Tidewater Virginia was thus freed of further menace from the savages.

The charter of the Company annulled

The authority conferred on the Virginia Company by the second and third charters had greatly increased its power, and soon its quarterly meetings in London had become important enough to attract the notice of the king. The most important position in the Virginia Company was that of treasurer, or president. For the first twelve years this place was held by Sir Thomas Smith; but as he was president of four other companies, some of the stockholders felt that he was not devoting enough attention to affairs in Virginia. The opposition became so strong that it prevented his reëlection in 1619 and Sir Edwin Sandys was chosen in his stead, though the latter remained at the head of the Company for only one year. Sandys was very energetic in his efforts to promote the prosperity of the colony and deserved a longer lease of power than was accorded him. But the king was opposed to him because of the liberal political views that he had expressed in Parliament, and looked upon him as his greatest enemy. He therefore refused to allow the election of Sandys, and in an outburst of temper said, "Choose the devil if you will, but not Sir Edwin Sandys."[41] When the election of 1620 was held there were nearly five hundred members of the Company in attendance. The majority of these were in favor of reëlecting Sir Edwin Sandys, despite the known opposition of the crown, as they were greatly pleased with the management of the colony under his leadership. But just as the vote was to be taken a representative of James who was present announced that the king positively forbade the choice of Sandys. The latter thereupon had his name withdrawn, as he was unwilling for his candidacy to embroil the Company in a quarrel with the crown. The Earl of Southampton, who was in favor of the policy of Sandys and

[41] WOODNOTH, ARTHUR, *A Short Collection of Remarkable Passages* (1651), pp. 7-8; NEILL, E. D., *The Virginia Company*, p. 185.

therefore in disfavor with the king, was then elected by acclamation amid shouts of enthusiastic approval. This action of the Company was a bold rebuke to James for his illegal interference, an affront which he would be slow to forget. The Earl of Southampton continued as treasurer from this time until the charter was annulled in 1624, and so the liberal policy inaugurated in 1618 was carried out during the last half-decade of the Company's existence.

Sir Thomas Smith, Sir Edwin Sandys, and the Earl of Southampton all belonged to the "country," or "patriot," party. But Smith was disgruntled over his defeat, and he now joined the party in opposition to the policy of Sandys and his supporters, and later his opposition went to the extreme of advocating the forfeiture of the charter of the Company. There were thus serious dissensions in the corporation, and grave charges against the management of the colony were brought before the king. Because of circumstances largely beyond its control, the Company had become virtually bankrupt by the summer of 1621. It did not, however, adjust its colonial policy to its financial straits. Instead of devoting its meager resources to furnishing food supplies, live-stock, and agricultural equipment for the settlers, it kept sending more and more emigrants to Virginia. Proper care was not used in the selection of these emigrants and many of them were not suited to colonization. In this way the colony was overrun with settlers for whom adequate food supplies and housing facilities had not been provided.

The anxiety of the Company for immediate returns caused the diversion of the energies of the colonists from the raising of food to the making of experiments in the manufacture of iron, the culture of silk, and other like projects. James probably welcomed these complaints; for Sir Edwin Sandys by his opposition in Parliament had incurred the ill-will of the king and brought the Company into disfavor with him. He may also have still been feeling the smart to his pride caused by the rebuke administered to him on the occasion of the first election of the Earl of Southampton, and the independence of spirit that the members of the Company had been exhibiting in recent years was a constant challenge to Stuart tyranny. Moreover, James was now having trouble with Parliament, and about one hundred stockholders of the Company belonged to that obstreperous body.

The king appointed a committee to look into the affairs of the Company.[42] After having made investigations in London and Virginia, the committee presented a report to the Court of King's Bench which was an indictment of the management of the Company. There had been an appalling death-rate among the settlers, because of famine, disease, and an Indian massacre. These calamities were not all the result of the normal hazards of pioneering in a new world, but were to a considerable extent brought on by bad management. A decision was promptly rendered by the court annulling the charter (June 16, 1624).[43] Virginia now became a royal province and the king took the place of the Company in the government of the colony.

The Virginia settlers gave the Company strong support in this fight for its life, and they regarded the decision against it as a plain perversion of justice. Still the change was a necessary one if the colony was to develop as it should. A corporation is never the proper body to exercise governmental powers over a group of people. For the chief aim of a corporation is gain, whereas the purpose of government is, or should be, the welfare of the people. Although the king at this time was arbitrary and incompetent, still he represented the state, and the management of the colony under him and his successors was in the long run more nearly in accordance with the principles of good government than it could have been had it continued under the control of a company

[42] According to the older authorities on colonial history, James was encouraged in his opposition by the Spanish minister at London, who played upon his fears by pointing out that the meetings of the corporation would prove a "seminary for a seditious Parliament." This wily diplomat, it was said, had a great deal of influence with James, who at this time was obsessed with the foolish idea of arranging a marriage between Prince Charles and the daughter of the King of Spain. The credibility of this tradition is contested by Dr. W. F. Craven, who has made a careful appraisal of the evidence. He has also given us a definitive account of the last six years of the Virginia Company. See his *Dissolution of the Virginia Company: The Failure of a Colonial Experiment* (1932).

[43] Massachusetts Historical Society *Collections,* 4th series, ix, pp. 60-73; TYLER, L. G., *op. cit.,* pp. 431-460. For a good account of the events that led to the annulment of the charter, with numerous quotations from the documents, see WERTENBAKER. T. J., *Virginia under the Stuarts,* pp. 54-59.

whose policy was necessarily narrowed by considerations of profit and loss. Moreover, by establishing a representative assembly, Sandys, Southampton, and their associates had provided a defense against imperial tyranny and had thus made it safe for Virginia to be placed under the rule of the Stuarts.[44]

Selected Readings

1. The Founding of Virginia.—Eggleston, E., *The Beginners of a Nation,* book i, *ch. 2.
2. John Smith as a Writer.—Tyler, M. C., *American Literature During Colonial Times,* i, *ch. 2.
3. The Career of John Smith.—Bruce, P. A., *The Virginia Plutarch,* i, *ch. 2.
4. John Smith's Adventures in Virginia as Related by Himself.— Stedman, E. C., and Hutchinson, E. M., *Library of American Literature,* i, pp. *3-6, 10-14.
5. The Princess Pocahontas.—Bruce, P. A., *The Virginia Plutarch,* i, *ch. 3 (reproduction of a portrait painted from life, opposite p. 30).
6. The Harsh Rule of Dale.—Chitwood, O. P., *Justice in Colonial Virginia* (Johns Hopkins University *Studies,* 23rd series), pp. *13-16; Bruce, P. A., *The Virginia Plutarch,* i, *ch. 4 (favorable to Dale).
7. John Rolfe and His Method of Curing Tobacco.—Andrews, M. P., *Virginia, the Old Dominion,* pp. *69-73.
8. The First Meeting of the Assembly.—Tyler, L. G., ed., *Narratives of Early Virginia,* pp. *249-278 (this is an account written by John Pory, the first speaker). See also Andrews, C. M., *The Colonial Period of American History,* ii, *ch. 9.
9. The Indian Massacre of 1622.—Tyler, L. G., ed., *Narratives of Early Virginia,* pp. *357-369 (contemporary account).
10. Hospitality in Virginia.—Stanard, Mary N., *Colonial Virginia, Its People and Customs,* pp. *118-135.
11. Amusements in Virginia.—*Ibid.,* pp. *136-165.

[44] Yeardley's commission was granted in 1618 while Sir Thomas Smith was still treasurer, but it owed its liberal provisions mainly to Sir Edwin Sandys. This is explained by the fact that during the last two years of his administration Smith's health was poor, and Sandys, who served as his assistant, "did in a manner wholie supplie Smythe's place." Quoted in Brown, *op. cit.,* ii, p. 993.

CHAPTER V

THE OLD DOMINION AND MARYLAND

THE annulment of the charter of the Virginia Company made no important change in the government of the colony except that now the governor and council were appointed by the king instead of by the Company. There was also for the first four years no provision for the continuance of the representative assembly. But by 1629 the House of Burgesses had been renewed, and it continued from this time until the end of the colonial period.[1]

Governor Harvey deposed

The governor's council, which apparently was an advisory body at first, soon won for itself an important place in the government. Instead of servilely acquiescing in the policy of the king's representative, the councilors frequently opposed him with courage and boldness. In 1635 they went so far as to depose a governor and arrest him and send him back to England. The official so humiliated was Sir John Harvey, who had supported Lord Baltimore in his controversy with William Claiborne and had disregarded the privileges of the council and assembly (see pp. 101-102).[2] King Charles was astonished at this bold procedure on the part of the council and made known to that body his strong disapproval of its usurpation of authority by sending Harvey back as governor and summoning the leaders among the insurgents to England to answer for this offense.

Governor Berkeley

The position of governor in Virginia was no sinecure at this time, for it took a man of courage and tact to uphold the interests of the crown and at the same time to get along with the proud-spirited councilors and representatives who constituted the assembly. It was sometimes difficult to find a person who could serve these two masters acceptably, and often unsuitable appointments were made. But in the choice of William Berkeley as governor (1642) the king was able to select a man after his own

[1] HENING, W. W., *Virginia Statutes at Large*, i, pp. 129-130.

[2] NEILL, E. D., *The Founders of Maryland*, pp. 52-53. For a defense of Harvey's policy by a contemporary, see HALL, C. C., ed., *Narratives of Early Maryland*, p. 60.

heart and one who could hold his own with the aristocracy that dominated the Virginia colony. Berkeley was a staunch royalist and a narrow churchman, whose views as to the government of church and state were in complete harmony with those of the king and the primate of England. Moreover, he had courage, decision of character, an outspoken candor, and other qualities that won the respect, if not the affection, of the Virginians. Under such leadership it was natural that the government in the colony should carry out the same policy of intolerance toward Protestant dissenters as was practiced in England at that time by Archbishop Laud, the primate of the Anglican Church. In Virginia, as in the homeland, Puritans felt the heavy hand of the law, and about one thousand of them left the province for Maryland.

In thus persecuting Nonconformists, Berkeley was proving himself an apt pupil of his royal master, Charles I, who had come to the throne in 1625. Charles, like his father, James I, ruled arbitrarily, and soon there arose a violent disagreement between him and Parliament as to the respective powers of each. By 1640 the contest had become a struggle between the crown and Parliament to decide whether the former or the latter was the supreme authority in the government of England. The Parliament that assembled in this year was in no mood to yield its rights. It refused to be dissolved and remained in session for more than twelve years, and so is known as the Long Parliament. The breach between Parliament and the king widened into a civil war (1642), which is known as the Puritan Revolution. Charles's adherents were called Cavaliers; the supporters of Parliament were known as Roundheads because the Puritans, who were all on the side of Parliament, wore their own hair cut short instead of wigs. At first the Cavaliers won more battles than the Puritans, but later the Roundheads were successful and the king was forced to surrender (May, 1646). After remaining a captive for nearly three years, Charles was executed by order of Parliament (January 30, 1649), and a republic was then established under the name of the Commonwealth.

Parliament was now in complete control, but it was not long before Oliver Cromwell, the leading general of the army, took charge of the government and for five years (1653-58) ruled England with the title of Lord Protector. Cromwell's policy was characterized by efficiency at home and firmness abroad, but good order was purchased at the cost of military rule, and the people were reined up to Puritan standards of conduct, which were too strict for the average Englishman. After Cromwell's death the government was very unsettled for more than a year, and there soon developed a strong sentiment in favor of a restoration of the old régime. Accordingly, Charles II was invited to return to the throne of his fathers (1660).

Virginia loyal to the king in the Civil War

(The planter aristocracy of Virginia, led by Governor Berkeley, were outspoken in their support of the Stuart cause and in their opposition to the Puritan party.) So strong was this feeling that when Charles was executed (1649), Berkeley was able to carry the assembly with him in denouncing the murder of the king and in recognizing Charles II as the rightful ruler of the British empire.[3] This loyalty to the exiled prince won for Virginia the title of the Old Dominion. This sentiment in favor of the lost cause made the colony a desirable retreat for Cavaliers, and a considerable number of them emigrated thither after the king was beheaded.[4]

Parliament could not allow such a defiance of its authority to go unnoticed, and so it passed a law prohibiting trade with Virginia and the other rebellious colonies (1650). Two years later commissioners were appointed who, with the support of a squadron of war vessels, were to demand the submission of the Chesapeake colonies. When these ships appeared in Virginia waters

[3] HENING, W. W., op. cit., i, pp. 360, 361; WERTENBAKER, T. J., Virginia under the Stuarts, p. 95.

[4] According to the older authorities, the coming of the Cavaliers to Virginia had a marked influence on the social life of the province. These new emigrants, it was held, came mostly from the gentry, many of them being younger sons of noblemen. They brought their patrician ideals and modes of living with them and thus raised Virginia society to a higher plane of aristocracy than that enjoyed by the other provinces. But the importance of the immigration of the Cavaliers has been overestimated, if we are to accept the conclusions of Professor T. J. Wertenbaker, who has made a special study of the subject. He thinks that the number of Cavaliers who came to Virginia is not so great as the older authorities would have us believe, and that a majority of those who did come were recruited, not from the gentry, as was formerly believed, but from the middle class. The new theory is discussed at length by WERTENBAKER, T. J., in his Patrician and Plebeian in Virginia. For a defense of the old theory, see STANARD, MARY N., Colonial Virginia, pp. 49-52, and The Story of Virginia's First Century, pp. 218-221.

Berkeley called together the militia and determined to put up a fight for the lost Stuart cause. But the councilors and burgesses, seeing the folly of resistance, overruled the belligerent governor and so the colony submitted without opposition (1652).

The terms of the surrender were very reasonable and even generous, so much so that the privileges granted to the recalcitrant colonists seem like the rewards of victory rather than the penalties of defeat. Berkeley, of course, had to give up the governorship and go into retirement, and the authority of the Long Parliament was recognized. The Puritan party was now in control, but the Anglicans were not deprived of their right to worship as they pleased, being allowed even to pray for the king if they should do it privately. The people were to have a stronger voice in the government than they had had before. The governor and councilors were to be chosen by the House of Burgesses, composed of the people's representatives, and no taxes were to be levied without the consent of that body.[5] Virginia had now virtually become an independent republic with little more than a pledge of allegiance to bind it to the mother country, for no further effort was made by either Parliament or Cromwell to regulate affairs in the colony. This period of self-government lasted for eight years, and during it the colony prospered and increased rapidly in population.

Virginia under the Commonwealth

The generous treatment accorded the Virginians by Parliament and Cromwell apparently did not produce in them a change of heart toward the Commonwealth, for they remained loyal to the Stuarts and were ready at the first opportunity to go back under their authority. After Cromwell's death the assembly showed its royalist sentiments by choosing Berkeley as governor (March, 1660), about two months before Charles II was proclaimed in England, and this election was confirmed by a commission from the king a few months later.

Berkeley recalled to the governorship

Berkeley was popular during the ten-year period of his first administration, but he was now hopelessly reactionary in his ideas of government. Apparently it had never dawned upon him that eight years of self-government had wrought any change in the attitude of the people toward their rulers. He was narrow-minded, ill-tempered, and overbearing, and these faults had been

His tyrannical rule

[5] For the terms of these agreements, see HENING, W. W., *op. cit.*, i, pp. 363-368; also HART, A. B., *American History Told by Contemporaries*, i, pp. 235-236.

aggravated by defeat and the other disappointments that come with increasing years. Intolerant to begin with, he was made more so by the humiliation to which he had been subjected by Puritan supremacy in England and America. In other respects also his character and outlook on life had not improved with age. As he approached the end of his career his increasing years had brought on a senility which was hardening his faults and softening his virtues. His principles had degenerated into prejudices and his covetousness had grown into rapacity. Probably no other man in the British empire was at this time better fitted by temperament and belief to carry out in America a policy of Stuart tyranny in church and state. He was arbitrary in government and zealous in the enforcement of the regulations against religious heretics. The Quakers now felt the weight of his intolerance just as had the Puritans in his early career, and they were driven out of the colony into North Carolina.

The governors of Virginia were usually restrained from tyranny by the council and the assembly. But in the case of Berkeley these bodies offered no effective resistance to his arbitrary rule. The assembly was elected at a time when enthusiasm for the restored monarch was at its height and was therefore in sympathy with royal authority. Berkeley was so well pleased with its attitude that he did not call for a new election for ten years or more.[6] Any change in the feeling of the people was not reflected in the assembly, as the representatives had gone for a decade or longer without receiving a new mandate from their constituents. Besides, both the House of Burgesses and the council were bound to the governor by ties of self-interest. The governor had a number of offices at his disposal and he distributed them among councilors and burgesses in such a way as to win their support. He thus built up a powerful political machine and conducted the government in the interest of the upper classes.

Nor did the people have any voice in the local government, as the justices of the peace who administered affairs in the counties were appointed by the governor with little or no regard for the wishes of the people. Moreover, the people had lost their old right of choosing the governing body of the parish, for the vestries

[6] It is certain that the assembly lasted ten years, 1666-76, and very probably from 1661 to 1676. There is some evidence, however, to indicate that a new election was held in 1666 (see WERTENBAKER, T. J., *Virginia under the Stuarts*, pp. 135-136).

had become self-perpetuating bodies, as vacancies were now filled by the vestries themselves.[7] Both justices of the peace and vestrymen usually belonged to the upper class and so were socially and politically allied with the men who controlled the provincial government under the dictation of Berkeley.

Under such conditions it was only natural that the unprivileged class should grow dissatisfied and cool off in its enthusiasm for the king and his representative, the governor. Besides, the policy of Charles II toward the Virginians had from the very beginning been such as to subject the loyalty of all classes to a severe strain. Instead of considering their faithfulness to him as a reason for gratitude, he seemed to regard it as affording him the opportunity to impose on their good nature. While he was in exile he granted to Lord Hopton and several other noblemen the tract of land lying between the Rappahannock and Potomac Rivers, known as the Northern Neck. The proprietors were to receive reversions, remainders, escheats, and fees, and were given authority to dispose of all unappropriated lands. The people of Virginia, especially those living in this region, were strongly opposed to this grant, as it would retard the growth of northern Virginia and give rise to a conflict between the authority of the proprietors and the government at Jamestown. Accordingly, agents were sent to England to protest against the patent and buy the rights of the grantees. To provide a fund for this purchase the assembly levied a tax of fifty pounds of tobacco per poll. The terms of the grant were later modified, but the extra tax burden occasioned by it added greatly to the discontent of the people.[8]

In 1673 Charles II again showed his utter indifference to the rights of the people of the colony by making two of his favorites, Lords Culpeper and Arlington, proprietors of Virginia and granting to them for the period of thirty-one years the ownership of the escheated lands, with the right to appoint sheriffs, surveyors, and other officials, and placed under their control the church patronage, for the whole province.[9] Fortunately this unfair arrangement was not fully and permanently carried out. Later

Unfair treatment of Virginia by Charles II

---

[7] West, W. M., *Source Book in American History*, pp. 329-330; *Virginia Magazine of History and Biography*, ii, pp. 166-173, 289-292.

[8] WERTENBAKER, T. J., *Virginia under the Stuarts*, p. 126.

[9] For the text of the patent granted to Lords Culpeper and Arlington, see HENING, W. W., *op. cit.*, ii, pp. 569-578.

(1681 and 1683) Thomas Lord Culpeper purchased the claims of the other proprietors of both groups and shortly thereafter (1684) he sold all his rights to the crown except his ownership of ungranted lands in the Northern Neck. These landed rights were held by his heirs until the end of the colonial era.[10]

Other grievances of the people

The Virginians thus had just ground for dissatisfaction with their government. To make matters worse, there were poor crops for a few years beginning in 1670, and the winter of 1672-73 was an unusually severe one. The Dutch wars of 1664 and 1672 also added greatly to the distress of the people. Tobacco ships were seized by the Dutch and trade between Virginia and England became hazardous. The result was stagnation in commerce, which had the result of lowering the price of tobacco and raising the prices of articles bought by the planters from abroad. The dissatisfaction of the poor was also increased by the heavy taxes and the unfair method of distributing them. All taxes for both local and provincial expenditures were levied on the basis of the number of tithables in a family, every male person and every female slave over sixteen years of age and every female servant that worked in the fields being rated as a tithable.[11] At a later time when the slaves had increased in number and when the wealth of a planter was usually in proportion to the number of slaves owned, this method of taxation was approximately just. But at this time it put too heavy a burden on the poor planter and favored the large landholder. Moreover, the money so raised was wasted by unwise expenditures.

The Navigation Act of 1660

Another grievance was the Navigation Act of 1660. It was especially unjust to Virginia, for in her case there were no compensating advantages to offset the burdens as there were in the case of New England.[12]

Discontent was thus becoming dangerous. As the masses of the people had no voice in either the provincial or the local gov-

[10] *Ibid.*, ii, pp. 518-522; ANDREWS, C. M., *Colonial Period of American History,* ii, pp. 234 ff.

[11] At certain times the age limit for slaves that were tithable was lower than sixteen years, and by some of the laws all male servants imported into the colony were tithable. HENING, W. W., *Statutes at Large,* i, pp. 361, 454; ii, pp. 170, 296; iii, 258-259; iv, p. 133; vi, pp. 40-41.

[12] For an explanation as to how this law affected the tobacco planters of Virginia and Maryland, see pp. 506-507.

ernment, they had no legal means of expressing the resentment that was gradually rising over their grievances. The right to vote, which under the Commonwealth was enjoyed by all freemen, was now (1670) restricted to freeholders, and thus many of the people were disfranchised. Besides, as the assembly was acting as a permanent body, there was no chance for those who could vote to make effective their protests against the way affairs were being conducted. It was thus a government by and for the governor and the privileged patrician class. Their control was so complete that there was no opening through which the steam of discontent could escape. Under such conditions an explosion was inevitable.

(This discontent came to a head when Berkeley refused to pursue as aggressive a policy against the Indians as the settlers on the frontier demanded.) In 1675 the Indians began to show signs of dangerous unrest, and all the outlying plantations were threatened by attack. The frontiersmen sent a petition to the governor asking that a military commander be appointed by him to lead them against their savage foes. "But instead of granting this petition the governor by proclamation under great penalty forbade the petitioning for the future."[13]

The people dissatisfied with Berkeley's Indian policy

The people in Charles City County thereupon took up arms and asked Nathaniel Bacon, Jr., to lead them against the enemy. Bacon was easily persuaded to accept the offer, as he was strongly in favor of an aggressive policy toward the Indians and had been

Beginning of the rebellion

[13] WEST, W. M., *A Source Book in American History*, pp. 92, 324-325; ANDREWS, C. M., *Narratives of the Insurrections*, pp. 16-19, 105-107, 109.

It is difficult for us to understand why the governor failed so completely to appreciate the seriousness of the situation. The most charitable explanation is that his conservatism, now supported by the inertia of old age, caused him to dread the horrors of an Indian war and urged him to pursue a waiting policy with the hope that such a calamity could be averted. But the simple-minded frontiersmen, whose wives and children were left to the tender mercies of bloodthirsty savages, attributed his dilatoriness to more unworthy motives. To them it appeared that Berkeley's consideration for the Indians arose from the fear that a war with them would interfere with the fur trade, in which he was financially interested. The accusation was made by some of the war-party that the governor was anxious only "that no bullits would pierce beaver skins" (*ibid.*, p. 20).

aroused to fresh anger by the recent murder of his overseer by the savages. Berkeley regarded Bacon's attack on the Indians without his permission as a defiance of his authority and so denounced him as a rebel and traitor. The rebellion had now begun and the people had found a leader of exceptional ability, who had the boldness not only to attack the Indians, but also to put up a strong fight against an oppressive oligarchy.

Nathaniel Bacon

Nathaniel Bacon was a brilliant young man with influential family connections both in Virginia and in England. Although he had been in the colony only about fourteen months, he had been honored with membership in the governor's council, which position he now held. He was thus allied both socially and politically with the ruling class, though destiny had assigned him the rôle of tribune of the people and chief opponent of the provincial aristocracy. Impetuous and high-spirited, self-confident and courageous, ambitious and energetic, he was not the man to submit tamely to the infringement of his rights by either the savages or the patrician rulers. Moreover, he had the gift of eloquence and by stirring speeches could arouse his followers to a high pitch of enthusiasm for and devotion to his cause. There is no evidence to show that his opposition to the governor in the beginning was prompted by any motive other than the desire to protect the colonists from the savages, but his enemies charged him with a selfish ambition which impelled him to attack the established order in the hope that he might angle for fame more successfully in troubled waters. He had wasted his patrimony before coming to Virginia, they asserted, and the unsettled condition of his finances gave a tinge of recklessness to his courage. If this estimate is correct he was remarkably successful in deceiving his followers, for there is no doubt that he was the idol of the plain people.[14]

Bacon forces Berkeley to give him a commission to attack the Indians

After his return from his first campaign against the Indians, Bacon marched on Jamestown with an armed force of five hundred men. With these troops he was able to overawe the assembly and compel the governor to appoint him general of the forces against the Indians.[15] As Bacon's permit to fight the Indians had

[14] *Ibid.*, pp. 41, 109-110.

[15] Berkeley faced the situation with the fine spirit of bravery that he showed in every emergency, and refused to be frightened by the young hotspur, who, flushed with a sense of victory, was strutting around in the little capital. With a courage worthy of a better cause the aged governor advanced toward Bacon with bared bosom and

been granted under duress, the governor did not regard it as binding, and so shortly afterward once more denounced him as a rebel and traitor. He also tried to rally the people to his support against Bacon, but they regarded the young leader as their rightful defender against the savages and most of them refused to take up arms against him. Feeling that his personal safety, as well as the success of his cause, demanded that his adherents be bound to him by an oath of allegiance, Bacon met a number of his followers (August, 1676) at Middle Plantation (now Williamsburg) and induced them to take an oath to support him against the governor and also against the forces of the crown until the king could be correctly informed as to the state of affairs in Virginia.[16]

The oath taken by Bacon's followers at Middle Plantation

Bacon now attacked Berkeley (September, 1676), who had collected a nondescript army made up of a motley crowd of men drawn to his standard by generous offers of pay. This undisciplined rabble was no match for Bacon's patriotic troops, and Berkeley was defeated and driven from the town. Thereupon, Bacon, fearing lest Berkeley would return and again make the capital a rendezvous, set fire to the village and destroyed every house, including the church. Lawrence, one of Bacon's chief lieutenants, started the conflagration by burning his own house, and Bacon himself set fire to the church.[17]

Bacon defeats Berkeley at Jamestown and then burns the town

Unfortunately for his cause, Bacon lived to enjoy his triumph for only a short time, for he was soon stricken with fever and dysentery and died in little over a month after his victory at

Death of Bacon and the failure of the rebellion

cried out: "Here! Shoot me. 'Fore God, fair mark. Shoot!" Bacon, however, had not come to wreak vengeance on an old man, but to extort from him a permit to fight the Indians. Berkeley realized that both he and the assembly were completely in the power of the young rebel, and, swallowing his pride, yielded to the demands of Bacon and his followers (*ibid.*, p. 29).

[16] For the provisions of this oath, see *ibid.*, p. 122. See also pp. 35, 58-63.
We are not sure just how far Bacon intended to carry his opposition to the king's representative. If we can accept the unsupported statement of one John Coode, with whom Bacon discussed his plans, we would think that he planned a complete separation of Virginia from the British empire and hoped to be joined in this movement for independence by North Carolina and Maryland. See *ibid.*, p. 139, note.

[17] *Ibid.*, pp. 68-71, 130, 135-136, 140.

Berkeley's
cruelty
toward
the rebels

Jamestown (October, 1676).[18] There was no leader able to take his place, and Berkeley was now easily successful. The aged governor, allowing his desire for revenge to run away with his judgment, gave free rein to his spite and so signalized his victory by a cruel severity toward the rebels. He had about twenty-three of the leaders hanged and the estates of a number of others confiscated. His vengeance would even have gone to still greater lengths had not the assembly put a curb on him by petitioning that an end be made to bloodshed.[19]

In the meantime the king had sent over three commissioners with an army of about eleven hundred men to investigate conditions in Virginia and put down the revolt. When the commissioners arrived the rebellion had been quelled and their main duty was to check the vengeance of the governor. They were, therefore, soon at odds with Berkeley, and the latter was summoned to England by the king to explain his conduct. He lived only a short time after his return to England, his end probably being hastened by chagrin and humiliation over the disapproval of his conduct by his royal master. Charles is reported to have said: "That old fool has hanged more men in that naked country than I have for the death of my father."[20]

Results of
the rebel-
lion

(The significance of Bacon's Rebellion arises from the fact that it was the first instance in Virginia history in which the common people rose against not only the royal governor, but also the rule of the privileged class) Most of the aristocracy were aligned with Berkeley, while Bacon's followers were drawn mainly from the common people, many of whom were from the outlying settlements. It was, therefore, largely a struggle between patrician and plebeian and of the frontier against the older part of the colony. Despite the brave fight that the people put up against the privileged class, the immediate results of the uprising were disappointing, though the ultimate outcome was favorable to their rights. On the verge of the outbreak, Berkeley yielded to the pressure of the situation and called a new assembly, which did away with the restrictions on voting, thus giving back the suffrage to all freemen, and passed other reforms. These laws were all repealed by order of the king,[21] but some of the more important ones were reënacted by subsequent assemblies.

The government of Virginia from this time to the Revolution

[18] *Ibid.*, p. 139.   [19] *Ibid.*, pp. 38-39.   [20] *Ibid.*, p. 40.
[21] HENING, W. W., *Virginia Statutes at Large*, ii, pp. 380-381.

of 1688 was about what one could expect under the restored Stuarts. Lord Culpeper became governor shortly after Berkeley left Virginia, and he in turn was followed by Lord Howard of Effingham. Each of these placemen was of a type similar to that of his royal master. They were both rapacious and arbitrary, and the latter was exceptionally incompetent. Their instructions required them to limit the suffrage to freeholders and householders and deprive the assembly of the right of initiative in legislation. An attempt was thus made to fasten Stuart autocracy firmly on Virginia. But the effort was not successful. The House of Burgesses, under the leadership of some able and patriotic patricians, made a courageous fight for the rights of the colony and succeeded in putting some salutary restraints on Stuart tyranny. The House of Burgesses, it is true, had lost some of its privileges, but it held on to the right to initiate legislation and vote taxes. Besides, in the struggle it had acquired an experience and self-confidence that proved a valuable asset in future contests with the representatives of the crown.

The rights of the colony championed by the House of Burgesses

But the opposition to British misrule was not confined to the constitutional fight waged by the assembly. The price of tobacco was so low that there was a strong feeling in favor of limiting the output, with the hope that this would raise the price. When the assembly met with the expectation of adopting some measures for restricting the planting of tobacco, it was dissolved by the governor acting under instructions from the king. Thereupon the people in some of the counties took the law into their own hands and tried to prevent the overproduction of tobacco by destroying the growing crop on the plantations. This outbreak is known as the Tobacco Rebellion. It soon attained such serious proportions that Lord Culpeper was ordered by the king to return to Virginia and take over in person the duties of governor, which had been exercised by his deputy. Culpeper took vigorous measures against the rioters, having two of the leaders hanged, and then the trouble quieted down.

The Tobacco Rebellion

MARYLAND

Sir George Calvert enjoyed the high esteem of James I, thanks to his advocacy of the Spanish marriage, and for several years was principal secretary of state under him. In 1625 he announced his adherence to the Catholic faith and resigned his post; for as a sincere Catholic he could not subscribe to the oath that office-

Maryland granted to Lord Baltimore as proprietor

holders had to take acknowledging the supremacy of the king in the government of the church. By changing his faith he did not, however, forfeit his standing with James, who, as an evidence of his favor, created him Baron of Baltimore, in the Irish peerage. Calvert had for some years been interested in colonization, and after giving up his secretaryship he made an unsuccessful attempt (1627) to plant a colony in Newfoundland on land that had been granted to him by the king. After he and his family had spent one winter in this northern region, he decided that he would seek a warmer climate for his colonizing venture. Accordingly, in 1632 he received from Charles I a patent for a large boundary of land inclosing the northern half of Chesapeake Bay. George Calvert died before the grant was consummated, and the charter was issued to his son, Cecilius Calvert, the second Lord Baltimore (June, 1632).

Provisions of the charter

By this charter Lord Baltimore was made the proprietor of a province that extended from the Potomac on the south to the fortieth parallel on the north, and from the Atlantic Ocean westward to the meridian that passes through the source of the Potomac River. To this new province the king gave the name of Maryland, in honor of the queen, Henrietta Maria. The patent made Lord Baltimore and his heirs landlords of a vast extent of territory, with authority to dispose of the land on such terms as they should see fit to lay down. They were also given large governmental powers over the people who should settle in the colony, and Maryland was thus to be a constitutional monarchy, with the lord proprietor playing the rôle of king. The only restrictions on his power were that all laws must be in harmony with the laws of England, and the proprietor in making them must have "the advice, assent, and approbation of the freemen or the greater part of them or their delegates or deputies." The colony did not have to pay any taxes to the English government, and about the only bond that was to hold this little principality to the homeland was the proprietor's pledge of allegiance to the British government.[22]

Lord Baltimore sends out an expedition to plant a colony

Lord Baltimore was not slow to take advantage of the privileges granted him in this patent, and in little more than a year his plans were all arranged for entering upon his colonizing venture. Two small vessels, the *Ark* and the *Dove*, were ready to

[22] For the text of the charter, see HALL, C. C., *Narratives of Early Maryland*, pp. 101-112, especially pp. 103-104, 105, 110, 111.

transport the two or three hundred[23] prospective settlers, of whom about twenty were gentlemen and the remainder laborers. The proprietor had originally intended to lead the expedition in person; but owing to the opposition that members of the old Virginia Company were making to his enterprise, he felt that he had better remain in England to defend his charter rights. Two of his brothers, however, were sent over with the emigrants, and one of them, Leonard Calvert, was made governor of the province. There also went along two Jesuit priests, one of whom, Father Andrew White, wrote an interesting account of the voyage.[24] The governor and his advisers, as well as most of the influential men, were Catholics, while the majority of the laborers were Protestants. The expedition left England in December, 1633, but it was not until the following March that they reached the mouth of the Potomac River. After going up this broad and beautiful stream for a few leagues they passed into one of its northern tributaries, the St. George's River, and selected a site for their first settlement near its eastern bank, about six miles above its mouth (March 27, 1634). To the village which they established here they gave the name of St. Mary's.

They were very fortunate in the choice of a site on which to lay the foundations of the colony. The place chosen was a high bluff overlooking the river, with no malaria-breeding swamp near by, as was the case at Jamestown.[25] A contemporary gives the following account of the advantages of the location: "This place he [Governor Calvert] found to be a very commodious situation for a town, in regard the land is good, the air wholesome and pleasant, the river affords a safe harbor for ships of any burden, and a very bold shore; fresh water and wood there is in great plenty, and the place so naturally fortified, as with little difficulty, it will be defended from any enemy."[26] The first settlers were also

St. Mary's

---

[23] The number of emigrants on these two ships, according to the estimate of Dr. L. G. Tyler, was three hundred laborers and twenty gentlemen. A very trustworthy contemporary, however, gives the total number of laborers as two hundred. See TYLER, L. G., *The English in America*, p. 126; also *Narratives of Early Maryland*, p. 70.

[24] For Father White's account of the voyage, see HALL, C. C., *Narratives of Early Maryland*, pp. 29-32.

[25] For contemporary accounts of the founding of St. Mary's, see *ibid.*, pp. 39-42, 71-77.

[26] *Ibid.*, p. 73.

very favorably impressed with the surrounding country, and their descriptions of its beauty and productivity, its crystal springs and tall trees, and its birds and animals, sound very much like the effusions of John Smith and his compatriots when they first landed in Virginia. Of the Potomac River, Father White says: "This is the sweetest and greatest river I have seen, so that the Thames is but a little finger to it." He speaks of the soil as being so favorable to the growth of vegetation "that we cannot set down a foot without but tread on strawberries, raspberries, fallen mulberry vines, acorns, walnuts, sassafras, etc., and those in the wildest woods."[27]

No starving time at St. Mary's

The colony prospered from the start, and in six months it was as firmly established as Virginia had been in as many years. There are several reasons to account for this. Owing to the healthfulness of the location the settlers never suffered from disease as they did in the first years of the Virginia colony. The Indians living around St. Mary's had been harassed by the Susquehannas on the north and were on the point of moving to the south bank of the Potomac. They were, therefore, glad to sell their cleared lands to the newcomers. By cultivating these fields and others cleared by themselves, the settlers were able to raise a good crop of corn, despite the lateness of their arrival. The Indians also had a good supply of corn, which they freely sold to the whites for trinkets. Moreover, the settlers were able to get certain needed supplies from Virginia and New England.[28] The colonists at St. Mary's also profited by the experience of the Jamestown pioneers and were thus able to avoid many of the mistakes made by the latter. In Maryland the proportion of laborers to gentlemen was much larger than it had at first been in Virginia, and the incentive for work was greater, as the system of working in common was never attempted, but each laborer was allowed to enjoy his own earnings. For these various reasons St. Mary's never had a starving time and never experienced the suffering that characterized the early years at Jamestown and Plymouth.

The Virginians protest against the Maryland grant

Maryland was carved out of territory that originally belonged to Virginia, and she thus became the oldest daughter of the mother of colonies and states. Unfortunately, the mother colony

[27] *Ibid.*, pp. 40, 45. For another contemporary account of the country, see *ibid.*, pp. 77-83.

[28] *Ibid.*, pp. 75-77.

did not rejoice at the advent of her promising offspring, and for a time the feeling between parent and child was not such as should characterize family relations. The trouble arose from the fact that all the land covered by Lord Baltimore's patent was within the limits of the grant made to the Virginia Company in 1609. It is true that when the charter of the Virginia Company was revoked all ungranted lands came into possession of the king, but both James and Charles had promised not to disturb the interest of either planter or adventurer in any part of the territory formerly conveyed by the charter of 1609.[29] The Virginians, therefore, had a right to expect that the jurisdiction of their province would be extended over all the territory formerly owned by the Company. But these promises did not confer any legal title, however binding they may have been in equity, and Charles did not usually allow a mere promise to stand between him and a desired policy. So the Virginians had to acquiesce in this infringement of their rights.

They did not, however, yield with as good a grace as would be expected of subjects who a little later became noted for their loyalty to this same king. Not only were they unwilling to lose so large a boundary of land, but it was especially galling that their loss should be the gain of the hated Papists. Lord Baltimore had encountered this feeling before his expedition sailed and was determined to do all he could to allay it. In his instructions to the first colonists he directed them to avoid every occasion of friction with the Virginia authorities.[30]

The controversy between William Claiborne and Lord Baltimore

The proprietor had reason to use the utmost tact in dealing with the Virginians, who had strengthened their claim to the Chesapeake region by planting a settlement in the upper reaches of the bay. For before Lord Baltimore had received his patent, William Claiborne, a prominent Virginian, had established a trading post on Kent Island, in the Chesapeake Bay, which had speedily developed into a thriving village. By the time St. Mary's was founded, the settlement on Kent Island numbered about one hundred inhabitants, was represented in the assembly at Jamestown, and had been brought under the jurisdiction of the Virginia courts. But it was undoubtedly within the limits of the Maryland grant, and Governor Calvert called on Claiborne to acknowledge the authority of Lord Baltimore. The latter referred

---

[29] *Maryland Archives*, iii, p. 19; also HALL, C. C., *op. cit.*, p. 189.
[30] For these instructions, see *ibid.*, pp. 16-23.

the claim of the proprietor to the Virginia council, and that body decided that Kent Island belonged to Virginia as properly "as did any other part of the country given by his majesty's patent in 1609."[31] Claiborne thereupon refused to recognize the authority of Lord Baltimore, and a violent controversy arose, which led to fighting between the two parties, with bloodshed on both sides.[32] After the dispute had been going on for some time the authorities in England took a hand in it and decided that Kent Island rightfully belonged under the jurisdiction of Lord Baltimore. In this way the quarrel was put to rest for the time being, though Claiborne felt aggrieved and was resolved upon revenge whenever circumstances should take a turn in his favor.

Maryland intended as a refuge for Catholics

Lord Baltimore was actuated by two motives in planting his colony. One was to build up a landed estate in America and the other to afford an asylum for his fellow-Catholics, who were persecuted in England. The laws in England against Catholics at this time were very severe, and it was thought that many of them would be anxious to leave for Maryland. Lord Baltimore was, however, disappointed in this expectation, as only a comparatively small number ever came to his province and the Protestants were always largely in the majority. The English laws against Catholics were not strictly enforced by James I, and even more lenient treatment was expected at the hands of Charles I, whose wife was a Catholic. The lord proprietor was therefore not able to induce a large number of his coreligionists to exchange the comforts of the Old World for the hardships of the New.

Religious toleration

The provisions relating to religion in the charter are vague, and it is difficult to determine exactly what authority in church affairs the king wished to confer on the proprietor. By the terms of the patent, the proprietor had the right to appoint ministers for the churches and chapels dedicated and consecrated according to the ecclesiastical laws of England.[33] This provision apparently applied only to Anglican churches, but there was nothing in it to prevent the establishment of Catholic and dissenting Prot-

[31] HENING, W. W., *Virginia Statutes at Large*, i, p. 154; BROWNE, W. H., *Archives of Maryland*, iii, p. 53.

[32] NEILL, E. D., *Founders of Maryland*, pp. 51-52; BROWNE, W. H., *George and Cecilius Calvert*, pp. 69-70, 74; HALL, C. C., *op. cit.*, pp. 150-155.

[33] For the clause in the charter regarding religion, see HALL, C. C., *op. cit.*, p. 103.

estant churches, though the proprietor would have no voice in choosing the ministers for such churches. The proprietor, therefore, had large powers in the control of the religious policy of the colony. It is to the credit of Cecilius Calvert and his successors that they used their authority in the interest of religious toleration, and from the beginning required their representatives in Maryland to allow religious freedom to all Christians.

This liberal policy was necessary to attract settlers, and it was the only one by which Catholics could be shielded against persecution in Maryland. Whether Cecilius Calvert, in granting religious freedom to his colonists, was actuated solely or mainly by these considerations or was prompted by a broad-minded tolerance, we are unable to say. At any rate, he inaugurated a plan for dealing with the religious problem that was far in advance of the thought of his day. The wise religious policy of the proprietors was embodied in law in the famous Toleration Act of 1649. This statute prescribed the death penalty for the crime of blasphemy against any Person of the Holy Trinity, and provided that no one professing belief in Christ should be in "any waies troubled, Molested or discountenanced for or in respect of his or her religion, nor in the free exercise thereof."[34]

Lord Baltimore's liberal religious policy attracted a good many Protestants to Maryland. The most numerous of these were the Puritans who had come in from Virginia as a result of persecution by Governor Berkeley. There had always been considerable Puritan sentiment in Virginia of the Nonconformist type, and in the sixteen-forties there grew up in southeastern Virginia a strong feeling in favor of separation from the Anglican Church. By the aid of three ministers who had come down from New England in response to an invitation from these Separatists, independent congregations were organized in the region bordering on the Nansemond and Elizabeth rivers. Such a religious irregularity was too much for the conservatism of Governor Berkeley, and he determined to force these bold heretics back into conformity with the Church of England. The persecutions to which they were subjected caused a great many of them to leave Virginia for Maryland during the years 1644-49. They were welcomed in the latter province by Lord Baltimore, and were granted

The Puritan emigration from Virginia to Maryland

[34] The text of this law is given in part in MacDonald, W., *Select Charters*, pp. 105-106. For the full text, see Browne, W. H., *Archives of Maryland*, i, pp. 244-247.

lands on the Severn and Patuxent rivers in a productive district, afterward known as Anne Arundel County (the county was so named in honor of Lady Baltimore). The Puritans, however, gave to their settlement the name of Providence (now Annapolis) "with feelings like those which had led Roger Williams to give that comforting name to his settlement on Narragansett Bay."[35]

These new recruits abused the hospitality which Lord Baltimore had accorded them and increased the difficulties that he was already experiencing in the management of the colony. For they frequently opposed the policy advocated by him or his representative, the governor, and caused him a good deal of trouble. As the Protestants were in the majority they could easily dominate the assembly and thereby thwart the measures proposed by the governor or proprietor. Besides, their presence was a constant menace to the authority of the proprietor. For if they should ever receive encouragement from England, they might revolt and deprive him of his governmental powers in the province. This possible danger became an actual one when the Civil War in England resulted in a victory for the Puritans and afforded that party an opportunity to assert its power in both England and America.

Lord Baltimore deprived of his governmental authority

Maryland had never been in opposition to Parliament, as had Virginia, and the proprietor's representative in the colony, Lieutenant-Governor Stone, was in favor of the Parliamentary party. But despite the willingness of the proprietor to accept the results of the Puritan Revolution, his province was put on the list of those colonies that were disloyal to the Commonwealth, and the commissioners sent over by the Council of State were directed to reduce Maryland as well as Virginia to submission. One of the commissioners was Claiborne, who now had an opportunity to avenge the grievances that he had long been harboring against Lord Baltimore. When the commissioners appeared at St. Mary's and demanded that Maryland declare its allegiance to the English Commonwealth, Governor Stone promptly complied and agreed to recognize the authority of Parliament (1652). He would not

[35] FISKE, J., *Old Virginia and Her Neighbors*, i, p. 291. For a good brief contemporary account of the Puritan settlement at Providence, see HALL, C. C., *op. cit.*, pp. 235, 254-255. See also LATANÉ, J. H., *Early Relations between Virginia and Maryland* (Johns Hopkins University *Studies*, xiii), pp. 40-49.

agree, however, to stop issuing writs and warrants in the name of the lord proprietary, as he felt that to discontinue this practice would be to violate his oath of office. Thereupon he was removed from office and the duties of his position were intrusted to six councilors. Lord Baltimore was also deprived of his governmental powers, though he was allowed to retain all his property rights.[36] The commissioners soon realized that in deposing Stone they had gone too far, and in response to a request from the people, restored him to the governorship three months later.[37]

The Puritans were still not satisfied, and two years later (1654) they rebelled against Governor Stone and deposed him, being encouraged in their rebellion by Claiborne and the other commissioners. A new assembly was convened, which was entirely dominated by the radical Protestants. The Toleration Act was now amended so as to deprive practically all classes but the Puritans of religious freedom and the right to vote. In the meantime Cromwell had dissolved the Long Parliament and had put himself at the head of the English government with the title of Lord Protector. Lord Baltimore contended that this change in the home government had annulled the acts of the commissioners by which he had been deprived of his power in Maryland and had restored to him his full proprietary rights. Accordingly, he instructed Stone to assert his authority by force if necessary. There was a clash between the two factions which culminated in a stiff battle and Stone was defeated and imprisoned.[38]

But the Puritans had failed in an effort to win the support of Cromwell, who took sides with Lord Baltimore, and in 1657 the

Civil war in Maryland

[36] Lord Baltimore put up an able defense of his rights, but there was little or no hope that a Puritan government in England would allow an American province to remain under the control of a Catholic proprietor. For the presentation of his case, see HALL, C. C., *op. cit.*, pp. 167-180. For an answer to these arguments, see *ibid.*, pp. 187-230.

[37] See HALL, C. C., *op. cit.*, p. 185. According to Fiske, Stone agreed to yield on the question of writs and that was why he was restored (see p. 294). For a very clear and readable account of all the trouble regarding the Puritans, see FISKE, *op. cit.*, i, pp. 287-296.

[38] For a contemporary account of this battle, with the events that led up to it, from the Puritan point of view, see HALL, C. C., *op. cit.*, pp. 235-246. For a contemporary account favorable to Stone and his party, see *ibid.*, pp. 254-267. It is needless to say that the two accounts are contradictory on important details.

latter regained control of his province. The Toleration Act of 1649 was now restored (1657), and the policy of religious freedom was continued until the Calvert family was again deprived of its governmental powers by another revolution (1689).

The government

Cecilius Calvert never visited Maryland, as he had hoped to do. His first representative in the province was his brother Leonard, who held the office of governor until 1647. The powers of the governor were about the same as they were in Virginia and other royal provinces. He could convene and dissolve the assembly, prepare measures for its consideration, and veto bills passed by it. He appointed most of the officers in the government and was chief justice. A council assisted him in the performance of his administrative duties and sat with him as judge in the most important court of justice. Both governor and the councilors were appointed by the proprietor.

The charter provided that the people were to have a voice in the government, and an assembly was held in 1635. At first all the freeholders sat in this assembly. But soon new settlements were established, and it became inconvenient for all the citizens to attend the meetings held at St. Mary's. This led to the practice of allowing absentees to vote through proxies, as is the custom today with corporations. But this system of voting easily lent itself to abuse. A few officeholders or ring politicians could always get together enough proxies to give them an undue influence in the assembly. As an example of the abuse of the system, Giles Brent in 1641 brought to the assembly enough votes to insure his control of the body during the entire session. Therefore, proxies soon gave way to representatives, and by 1650 Maryland had a regular representative assembly of two houses, like its prototype in Virginia. The upper house consisted of the governor and council and persons specially summoned by the governor; the lower, of the representatives of the people. At first the proprietor claimed the sole right to propose laws. The representatives of the people would not, however, agree to this curtailment of their authority, and the opposition was so strong that the proprietor had to yield the point and acknowledge the right of the assembly to initiate legislation.

The Jesuits

The first priests of the Catholic faith in Maryland were the Jesuits, and they labored in their new vineyard with the zeal that is characteristic of their order. They were active in their efforts to convert not only the Indians, but also the Protestant settlers, and in both endeavors they met with considerable success. At one time (1638) they were able to report to their superior in Rome that nearly all the Protestant emigrants who had come over that year had been converted to Catholicism.[39] They also began to buy lands from the Indians for their society without the permission of the Maryland authorities. This was a plain violation of Lord Baltimore's rights under the charter, which gave him full power to dispose of all lands. The proprietor was so aroused by this encroachment upon his rights that he appealed to the authorities at Rome, asking them to recall the Jesuit missionaries and send over secular priests in their stead. The quarrel was settled, however, by the Jesuits acceding to his demands and agreeing to give up their lands and hold them as tenants of the proprietor.

SELECTED READINGS

1. William Berkeley.—Bruce, P. A., *The Virginia Plutarch,* i, *ch. 6 (for copy of an original portrait, see opposite p. 78).
2. Nathaniel Bacon.—Wertenbaker, T. J., *Torchbearer of the Revolution,* *ch. 2.
3. Economic Conditions in Virginia on the Eve of Bacon's Rebellion. —*Ibid.,* *ch. 1.
4. The Causes of Bacon's Rebellion.—Wertenbaker, *Virginia under the Stuarts,* *ch. 6.
5. Prologue to the Rebellion.—Wertenbaker, *Torchbearer of the Revolution,* *ch. 5.
6. The Catholic Migration.—Eggleston, E., *The Beginners of a Nation,* book iii, *ch. 1.
7. Father White's Account of the Voyage to Maryland.—Hall, C. C., ed., *Narratives of Early Maryland,* pp. 29-45 (contemporary account).
8. The Founding of St. Mary's.—*Ibid.,* pp. 39-42, *71-77 (contemporary accounts).
9. The Toleration Act of 1649.—West, W. M., *Source Book in American History,* pp. *102-105.
10. Conditions in the Province of Maryland in 1666.—Hall, C. C., ed., *Narratives of Early Maryland,* pp. 340-365 (contemporary account).
11. Conflict between the Puritans and the Catholics.—Fiske, J., *Old Virginia and Her Neighbors,* pp. *287-296.
12. Proprietary Maryland.—Andrews, C. M., *The Colonial Period of American History,* ii, *ch. 8.

[39] HALL, C. C., *op. cit.,* p. 120.

CHAPTER VI

THE MIGRATION OF PURITANISM FROM OLD TO NEW ENGLAND

The Council for New England and the land granted to it

THE Plymouth Company, as we have seen, made an unsuccessful effort to plant a colony at the mouth of the Kennebec River in 1607. From that time until the coming of the Pilgrims no permanent settlement was made by the English people in what is now New England. But in the early years of the seventeenth century this region was frequently visited by English traders and fishermen. Prominent among these early seamen was Captain John Smith, of Virginia fame, who explored the northeastern coast of the present United States. He wrote a description and drew a map of the land visited by him, to which he gave the name of New England.[1] By these voyages a knowledge of the coast of New England was gained, and English capitalists were aroused to an interest in its resources and to a realization of the opportunities afforded by its fisheries and fur trade.

Among those who appreciated most fully the possibilities of this region was Sir Ferdinando Gorges, who was a stockholder in the Plymouth Company. Gorges and some of the other stockholders decided to reorganize the old Plymouth Company, and they succeeded in getting a charter from the king for a new corporation (1620), which was known as the Council for New England. By this patent there was granted to this company all the land lying between the 40th and 48th parallels of north latitude and extending from the Atlantic to the Pacific Ocean.[2] The charter also conferred on the Company the right to govern all the colonies that they might plant in this extensive region. But the Council for New England was not especially interested in colonization. Its policy was to grant its lands in large tracts to

[1] For a reproduction of Smith's map of New England, see WINSOR, J., *Narrative and Critical History of America*, iii, between pp. 198-199.

[2] The text of this patent is given in part in MACDONALD, W., *Select Charters*, pp. 24-33.

its own stockholders and other individuals and companies. By
1635 it had disposed of most of its holdings and was ready to
surrender its charter. Of these grants the most important were
those that were made to the Puritans who founded the colonies
of Plymouth and Massachusetts.

As has already been shown (see p. 10), Protestantism had **The**
become the accepted religion of the majority of the English peo- **English**
ple by the time Elizabeth came to the throne (1558). The group **Puritans**
of Protestants that had the largest membership was the one that
adhered to the Anglican communion. This denomination was
accepted as the state church and all other forms of worship were
forbidden. But the Anglicans were too conservative in ritual and
doctrine and not rigid enough in their moral standards to suit
some of the radical Protestants. There were at that time many
ardent religionists who considered that the Anglicans had not
gone far enough away from Rome—that they were too much like
the Roman Catholics, as to both church government and religious
practices. They wanted to simplify the administration of the
church and do away with what they called popish customs in
worship. They also wished to purify the establishment of what
they deemed errors in doctrine. These ultra-Protestants were
called Puritans.

There were, however, wide divergencies in opinion among the
Puritans themselves, and it is difficult to frame a definition that
exactly fits them. They all accepted the theological tenets and
ethical views of John Calvin[3] and imposed upon themselves a
more severe standard of conduct than was thought necessary by
the average professing Christian. They were especially strict in
their observance of the Sabbath, and they regarded as wicked
some forms of amusement that we now consider innocent. Like
all people with deep convictions, they saw the serious side of life
and their seriousness sometimes degenerated into gloom. Often-
times they emphasized the obligations of religion rather than the
joy that comes from communion with God. In consequence, their
outward demeanor was such that frequently they appeared to
outsiders as being clothed in "the spirit of heaviness" rather than
with "the garment of praise."

They were, however, a wholesome and much-needed element
in the English society of that day; for like the prophet Amos of
old, they thundered their protests against the evil practices of a

[3] See pp. 7-8.

frivolous and immoral age. "Luckily the more extreme of the Puritans were thoroughgoing fanatics; for nothing less than a good dose of fanaticism seemed likely to purge England of its social evils."[4] Their standards were too rigid for the man of average spirituality, who generally wants a cheap religion, one that does not cost him too much in the way of self-denial. Moreover, in their devotion to religion the Puritans left too little room in their interests for the æsthetic and other influences that are promotive of real culture. "Their religion was a narrow Hebraism, which kept open its windows toward Jerusalem, but closed every other avenue to the soul."[5]

Separatists

Among the various types of Puritans there were two classes that took the leading part in the settlement of New England. These were the Nonconformists and the Separatists. The former were dissatisfied with some of the doctrines and ritual of the state church, but hoped to bring it into harmony with their beliefs by introducing certain reforms. Their policy was to fight from within and not to sever their connection with the establishment. The latter were more radical. Their views were so different from those of the Anglicans that they were unwilling to be associated with them in a church relation. Therefore, they separated from the Church of England and formed independent churches. It was for this reason that they were called Separatists, or Independents. They believed that each congregation, or group of worshipers, should choose its minister and manage its own religious affairs without the interference of a bishop or other ecclesiastical authority. This method of ecclesiastical administration is known as the congregational. The first settlers of New England, the Pilgrims, were of the latter class; the founders of Massachusetts at first belonged to the Nonconformist party, but soon after coming to America they too withdrew from the Anglican denomination. The congregational form of church government was thus adopted in both of these colonies.

The Pilgrims

In the beginning of the seventeenth century (1602), a group of Separatists in northern England withdrew from the Anglican communion and at the village of Gainsborough began to worship together as an independent church. A few years later (1606) this congregation divided into two groups, one of which met for

[4] ADAMS, J. T., *The Founding of New England*, p. 74.

[5] JAMESON, J. F., Introduction to Johnson's *Wonder-Working Providence*, p. 16.

worship at Scrooby, in Nottinghamshire. Most of the members of this congregation were people from the obscure walks of life, such as "had only been used to a plaine countrie life, and the innocent trade of husbandrey."[6] But this little band of earnest Christians, after having received recruits from near-by villages, included in its membership four men of exceptional character and ability. These were the ministers, Richard Clifton and John Robinson, and two influential laymen, William Brewster and William Bradford. The last-named was only about sixteen years old when the church was organized at Scrooby, but his deep piety and sound common sense, coupled with good habits of study, soon won for him a prominent place in the leadership of the congregation. The other three were older than Bradford and had enjoyed better opportunities for education than he, as all of them had attended the University of Cambridge. Robinson was a graduate of this university and was unusually broad-minded for that age. The unconventional views held by these earnest Puritans were not shared by their neighbors, and "they were both scoffed and scorned by the prophane multitude."[7] Besides, their meetings were illegal, for a recent act of Parliament (1593) had made it unlawful for any person to absent himself from the worship of the established church or to attend any other religious services.[8] The law was enforced against the Scrooby Separatists, though rather perfunctorily, and they had to endure a persecution which they considered humiliating and which made them greatly fear for their future safety.[9]

In order to escape these persecutions and the religious contamination incident to association with their heretical neighbors

[6] BRADFORD, WILLIAM, *History of Plymouth Plantation (Original Narratives)*, p. 33.

[7] *Ibid.*, p. 30.

[8] For the provisions of this law, see PROTHERO, G. W., *Select Statutes*, pp. 89-90. For an abstract of the provisions of the act, see CHANNING, E., *op. cit.*, i, p. 283.

[9] While the penalties inflicted by the authorities were neither numerous nor very severe for that day, they were regarded by young Bradford as a cruel persecution. In speaking of the punishments to which they were subjected he said: "For some were taken and clapt up in prison, others had their houses beset and watched night and day, and hardly escaped their hands; and the most were fain to leave their houses and habitations, and the means of their livelihood" (BRADFORD, *op. cit.*, p. 32).

of the Anglican faith, they left their native land and went to the Netherlands (1607-08), where all Christians were allowed religious freedom. They first stopped at Amsterdam. In this city they found a number of their fellow-countrymen who had left the homeland on account of religious dissent. A variety of theological views were upheld by these groups of refugees, and the Pilgrim Separatists soon found the religious atmosphere uncongenial to their beliefs. Accordingly, after a year's residence in Amsterdam they moved on to Leyden. In this famous university town they spent the remainder of their sojourn in the Netherlands. The group of believers was formally organized into a church, and Robinson, who had joined the Scrooby congregation just before the emigration from England, became their pastor, and Brewster was chosen elder.[10] They were quite happy in their church relations in Leyden, and they made a favorable impression on their Dutch neighbors by their diligence, honesty, and reliability. This is shown by a public statement made by the magistrates to the effect that "these English have lived amongst us now this twelve years, and yet we never had any suit or accusation come against any of them."[11]

Why the Pilgrims left the Netherlands

But living conditions were hard for them in this foreign country. Most of them had been peasant farmers in England and were not trained for the occupations by which their Dutch neighbors thrived. This lack of skill and their alien citizenship excluded them from membership in the craft guilds, which monopolized the remunerative trades. Therefore, they had to eke out a scant living by hard, unskilled labor, and their children had to assume tasks that were too heavy for their tender years. Worst of all, they noticed that the allurements and temptations of the city were enticing their children away from parental authority and into extravagance and immorality. Moreover, these Separatists, despite their nonconformity in religion, were English at heart and believed in English customs and institutions. Here they were surrounded by a people whose language was strange and uncouth, and whose fashions and ways were quite different from those to which they had been accustomed. They realized that if their children were to be brought up with English manners and ideals it would be necessary for them to leave this foreign country. Besides, they believed that by going to a new and unoccupied land

[10] USHER, R. G., *The Pilgrims and their History*, p. 40.
[11] BRADFORD, *op. cit.*, p. 42.

they could best promote the cause of true religion; for they hoped to lay the foundation "for the propagating and advancing of the gospel of the Kingdom of Christ in those remote parts of the world." For these and other reasons they decided to leave the Netherlands and go to the New World.[12]

It was their plan to settle within the limits of the territory owned by the Virginia Company, and to carry out this purpose it was necessary to get a patent from this corporation. The Virginia Company was glad to encourage settlement on its domains, and Sir Edwin Sandys, who was at that time at its head, was kindly disposed toward the Puritans. They had, therefore, no difficulty in getting a patent authorizing them to plant a colony on the Company's grant. They then tried to obtain a promise from King James, confirmed by the broad seal, that they would be allowed to practice their religion without interference. James would not enter into any written agreement, but gave them to understand "that he would connive at them and not molest them, provided they carried themselves peaceably."[13]

King James gives them permission to settle in America

The next step was to devise a plan for financing the venture. As the Pilgrims were too poor to purchase and equip a ship for the expedition, an arrangement was made with some London merchants to supply the money for the voyage. A joint-stock company was organized which was composed of two kinds of stockholders, adventurers and planters. The former were the capitalists who furnished the money, and the latter were the settlers. The stock was divided into shares, each of which was rated at ten pounds. The adventurers were given shares in proportion to the amount of capital subscribed by each, and every emigrant over sixteen years of age was to have one share for going to America and an additional share if he contributed money or provisions to the amount of ten pounds. The partnership was to continue for seven years, and during this period all the profits accruing from trade, fishing, and the work of the colonists were to be put into the common stock. The settlers were to be supported from this common fund, and at the end of the seven-year period the profits, capital, land, and all other property of the

The agreement with the London partners

[12] For the motives that prompted the Pilgrims to leave the Netherlands, see BRADFORD, *op. cit., pp.* 44-46, and YOUNG, A., *Chronicles of the Pilgrim Fathers*, p. 381. Bradford's account is also to be found in *American History Leaflets*, no. 29, pp. 7-11.

[13] BRADFORD, *op. cit.*, p. 51; YOUNG, A., *op. cit.*, pp. 382-383.

company were to be distributed among the adventurers and planters in proportion to the number of shares held by each.[14]

The voyage of the Mayflower

Finally after a good many difficulties had been met and overcome, all the preparations were made for the first Puritan emigration to the New World. In every crisis they had been encouraged and heartened by their minister, John Robinson, though he did not go with them to New England. More than half of the congregation had been left in Leyden, and it was decided that the pastor should remain with the larger group. According to the plan, some of the Separatists at Leyden were to be brought over to Southampton, where they would be joined by others of their faith from London, and both groups would set sail for America. On July 31 (1620) thirty-five of the Pilgrims left Leyden to embark on the *Speedwell* for Southampton. The day of their departure was a solemn occasion not only for those who were going but also for those whom they were leaving behind. Most of the day was spent in prayer and in listening to an encouraging sermon by Pastor Robinson. When the time came to leave, they were accompanied by many of their brethren to Delft Haven. Here, after affecting scenes of farewell, with the benediction of their beloved pastor resting upon them, they took passage in the *Speedwell* for Southampton,[15] where they found fellow-Pilgrims from London awaiting them.

About one hundred and twenty emigrants embarked (August 15) on the *Speedwell*, and a larger vessel, the *Mayflower*, for the transatlantic voyage. But the *Speedwell* was leaky and twice the expedition had to return for repairs. Finally, the ill-fated *Speedwell* was abandoned and all of the passengers—now reduced to one hundred and two—were put on board the *Mayflower*, and a final start was made, this time from Plymouth (September 16, 1620).[16] Of the passengers on the *Mayflower*, the most noted were William Brewster, the elder for the Leyden group; Miles Standish, afterward noted as the military leader of the Pilgrims;

[14] For the terms of this agreement, see BRADFORD, *op. cit.*, pp. 66-67; WEST, W. M., *Source Book*, pp. 114-115.

[15] For a good account of the departure from Leyden, see BRADFORD, *op. cit.*, pp. 78-80; also YOUNG, *op. cit.*, p. 384.

[16] For a list of those who sailed in the *Mayflower*, see BRADFORD, *op. cit.*, pp. 407-409. For two names not included in this list see BANKS, C. H., *The English Ancestry and Homes of the Pilgrim Fathers*, pp. 7-9.

John Carver, who was to be the governor; and William Bradford, who was destined to play the leading part in the early history of the colony.

After a long and stormy voyage they came in sight of Cape Cod, having gone farther north than they had planned. Turning southward with the purpose of going down to the Hudson River region, they encountered "dangerous shoals and roaring breakers," and so they returned to Cape Cod and made a temporary landing at Provincetown (November 21). The *Mayflower* remained in the harbor here while exploring expeditions were sent out to find a suitable place for a settlement. On December 21 the

The founding of Plymouth

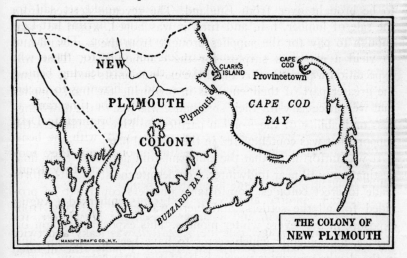

THE COLONY OF
NEW PLYMOUTH

exploring party landed at Plymouth and decided that it would be a proper place for the location of their colony. The harbor was good for shipping and near by were a number of corn-fields that had been cleared by the Indians. Five days later the *Mayflower* came up and anchored in the harbor. After spending several days in locating the most desirable site for a settlement, the emigrants began hurriedly to put up buildings to shelter themselves from the winter storms.[17] The Pilgrims called their settlement Plymouth, as the place at which it was made had been so named by John Smith on his map of New England.

[17] BRADFORD, *op. cit.*, pp. 104-105. For a detailed contemporary account of the exploring expeditions that preceded the landing at Plymouth, see *Mourt's Relation*, in YOUNG, A., *Chronicles of the Pilgrim Fathers*, pp. 125-162.

Unfavorable location of Plymouth

The region about Plymouth was not well suited to agriculture as to either soil or climatic conditions. At first sight it appears strange that the Pilgrim Fathers should have selected such a place for their settlement, when fertile lands under sunny skies were open to them. A partial explanation lies in the fact that they did not plan a colony of the usual type, but rather a fishing and trading station. It was expected that the men of the settlement would devote the greater part of their time to cutting lumber, fishing, and trading with the Indians, and as small amount as possible to the building of houses and the growing of crops. Most of the food and other commodities needed by the settlers were to be brought over from England. The revenue derived from the sale of lumber, fish, and furs, it was hoped, would be great enough to pay for the supplies brought from the homeland and to yield a generous surplus for the common chest. That this expectation was not realized and the early colonists had to expend the greater part of their energies in procuring the food supplies that were necessary for their sustenance was due to the unwillingness or inability of the London partners to give the planters the support that was contemplated in the original plan.

Hardships experienced by the settlers

It was unfortunate that the emigrants did not reach their final destination until near midwinter. For despite the strenuous efforts made to erect cottages, comfortable quarters could not be provided for all the settlers, and there was great suffering from exposure in the severe winter months. This exposure brought on disease, an epidemic which seems to have been contagious, and in the depths of winter nearly half of the little company died.[18] In the time of greatest distress there were but six or seven well persons to care for the sick and bury the dead. But this little band of helpers braced themselves for their task and nursed and provided for the needs of the sick with a kindly sympathy and a self-forgetful devotion that won for them an exalted place in the esteem of their brethren. They, "to their great commendations be it spoken, spared no pains, night nor day, but with abundance of toil and hazard of their own health, fetched them wood, made them fires, drest their meat, made their beds, washed their loathsome clothes, cloathed and unclothed them . . . and all this willingly and cheerfully, without any grudging in the least."[19] Promi-

[18] *Ibid.*, pp. 197-198.
[19] BRADFORD, *op. cit.*, p. 108.

nent in this heroic group were the elder, William Brewster, and the military leader, Captain Miles Standish.

During this time of distress they were not disturbed by the Indians. A plague had killed most of the natives who had lived around Plymouth, and the few survivors were so broken in spirit that they dared not venture an attack on the whites. The latter, however, were not aware of this and remained in constant dread of the savages, who lurked around timidly, showing themselves only at a distance. Finally, in March one of the Indians, Samoset, walked boldly into the settlement and spoke to them in broken English, telling them of the disease that had destroyed his people. He promised to bring to them another Indian, Squanto by name, who had been in England and could speak better English than himself. True to his promise, Samoset some days later reappeared at Plymouth, bringing with him not only Squanto, but also his chief, Massasoit, who had made a journey of forty miles to visit the Englishmen. The Indian sachem was cordially received and was induced to sign a treaty of friendship with the Pilgrims that lasted over fifty years.[20] Squanto remained at Plymouth and was of great service to the colonists. He acted as guide and interpreter and showed them how to raise corn and procure fish and other commodities.[21] In the spring the *Mayflower* returned to England and the settlers were now left to their own resources.

No trouble from the Indians

In April, 1621, Governor Carver died, and William Bradford was chosen as his successor. This was a very wise choice. In him the zeal for the cause of religion was combined with a practical common sense and a poise of character that eminently fitted him for leadership in a Puritan commonwealth striving to establish itself in the face of the obstacles incident to pioneer life. The people showed their appreciation of his services by keeping him in the governor's chair for more than thirty years.[22]

The plan of working in common, which was at first tried at Plymouth, proved unsatisfactory here as it had at Jamestown. Single men objected to having the fruits of their labor consumed by other men's wives and children, and married men were unwilling for their wives to be burdened with the task of cooking, washing, and sewing for the community. The industrious and capable

The plan of working in common tried and abandoned

[20] *Mourt's Relation,* in YOUNG, A., *op. cit.,* pp. 182-194.

[21] BRADFORD, *op. cit.,* pp. 110-111, 115-116, 118.

[22] From 1621 to 1657 he was annually chosen governor for every term except those of the years 1633, 1634, 1636, 1638, and 1644.

felt that they were being imposed upon by the idle and inefficient. So there was general dissatisfaction, and the plan of working in common was abandoned in 1623. In that year every settler was granted for temporary use as much land as it was thought he could cultivate, and the next year each family was given one acre for a period of seven years. By this arrangement the colonists were made responsible individually for the support of their families, but were allowed to reap the fruits of their own labor. The new policy proved to be a wise one, as there was now less cause for friction and a greater incentive to labor. "The women now wente willingly into the field, and tooke their litle-ons with them to set corne, which before would aledg weakness, and inabilities."[23] In making this change Governor Bradford was violating the letter of the agreement with the London partners, but was really serving their best interests as well as those of the planters, for the reform was necessary to prevent the failure of the enterprise. Moreover, the adventurers had not carried out their obligation to supply the planters with food from England, and it was now evident that the original plan of establishing a trading post would have to give way to that of founding a self-sustaining colony.

The partnership with the London capitalists dissolved

The partnership between the Pilgrims and the London adventurers proved to be an unsatisfactory arrangement for both parties. The London capitalists, like all promoters of colonization in that day, were anxious for profits and were sorely disappointed over the poor prospects of getting any substantial return on their investment. The planters, on the other hand, felt that their English partners had not given them the financial support that they had a right to expect. The adventurers were, therefore, willing to sell their interests to the settlers on favorable terms, and the latter were anxious to be released from the restraints and obligations imposed by the partnership. So an arrangement was made (1627) whereby the adventurers gave up all their rights in the colony for the sum of 1,800 pounds, to be paid in nine annual installments.[24] As the seven-year period was now up, the settlers apportioned among themselves the live-stock and the tillable land near Plymouth, leaving only the meadow and infertile lands to be held in common. A few years later (1633) the meadow was also

[23] BRADFORD, *op. cit.*, p. 146.
[24] *Ibid.*, pp. 122-123, 213-216.

divided up. In this way individual ownership of land, which
had been partially accepted before, was now completely adopted.

The colony was now resting on a firm basis, although its   Agree-
growth had been slow, and was enjoying a profitable trade with   ment with
the Indians. Bradford, Standish, and other leaders entered into   the "Un-
an agreement with the settlers whereby the former, known as   dertakers"
"Undertakers," assumed the obligation to the London capitalists
and the other indebtedness of the colony and promised to supply
the settlers with certain necessities from England at a specified
price. In return for these services the Undertakers were given a
monopoly of the trading privileges of the colony, and the vessels
and other facilities needed for carrying on this trade were turned
over to them.[25] Bradford and his colleagues assumed control over
the posts that had been established at Cape Cod, Cape Ann, and
on the Kennebec River, and continued the traffic in fish and furs
which had already been begun with the natives. So successful
were they in the management of this business that the profits
from it enabled them after some years to discharge all of the
indebtedness to the London merchants.

During the first decade of its history Plymouth was the only
settlement in the colony; but in 1630 the people began to occupy
the outlying districts, and ten years later the colony included ten
towns, each of which was organized into a church as well as a
civic community.

As Plymouth was outside the limits of the Virginia Company,   Govern-
the patent that had been granted to the Pilgrims by this corpora-   ment
tion was of no value. The settlers, therefore, had no legal title
to the land and no authority for organizing a government. It
was not long, however, before a valid title to the land was obtained (1621) in the form of a patent issued to the London
partners by the Council for New England. Later (1630) New
Plymouth (by which name the colony was known to differentiate
it from the town) received from the Council for New England
a patent which enlarged the former land grant and gave definite
limits to the colony.[26] But the Council for New England probably

[25] For the terms of the agreement between the Undertakers and
the colonists, see BRADFORD, *op. cit.*, pp. 227-228; also USHER, R. G.,
The Pilgrims and their History, p. 153.

[26] For the text of the patent of 1630, see THORPE, F. N., *The
Federal and State Constitutions, Colonial Charters*, etc., pp. 1841-
1846.

had no right to confer any governmental authority on its grantees, and, as New Plymouth never received a royal charter, it is more than doubtful as to whether its government ever rested on a strictly legal basis at any time during the entire period of its separate existence.[27]

The Mayflower Compact

The Pilgrim Fathers, however, were not inclined to forego the necessary benefits of government because of a technical defect as to their political status, but proceeded to establish a government on the basis of that important natural right, the consent of the governed. When it became known that the settlement would be in New England some of the company announced that they would not obey the leaders, whose authority under the patent did not extend beyond the limits of Virginia. To quiet this dissatisfaction forty-one of the men entered into a solemn covenant that they would make just and equal laws and would yield obedience to the same. This agreement was signed in the cabin of the vessel while it was anchored in Provincetown Harbor, and is known as the Mayflower Compact. The signers of the Compact declared their allegiance to King James, and had no idea of setting up an independent republic.[28] Their intention was to organize themselves into a body politic and provide such governmental machinery as would be necessary to keep order and prevent revolt. The Mayflower Compact was the first of a number of plantation covenants signed by groups of New Englanders on establishing civil governments for themselves. In entering into this agreement

---

This patent was issued to William Bradford and the other leaders associated with him. They acted as trustees for the settlers until 1641, when they gave over the patent to the freemen of the colony assembled in general court.

[27] The authority to make laws and exercise jurisdiction over the people was enumerated in the list of privileges granted in the patent of 1630 (see THORPE, *op. cit.,* p. 1842) ; the best legal opinion of that day, however, inclined to the belief that the right to establish a government in the colonies could only be conferred by a *direct* grant of the king.

For the text of the patent of 1621, see Massachusetts Historical Society *Collections,* 4th series, ii, pp. 158-163.

[28] For the text of the Mayflower Compact see WEST, W. M., *Source Book in American History,* pp. 116-117. The Compact was signed by all the adult males except eight servants and one other man, and all who did not sign were probably ill.

the Pilgrim Fathers were extending to civil affairs the principle of the church covenant which was behind the mutual pledge by which the members of every Congregational church bound themselves together in fraternal association.

There were other meetings of the freemen from time to time in the early years, and so the Mayflower Compact served as a sort of constitutional basis for a regular primary assembly, which was known as the General Court. This assembly met once a year for the election of the governor, assistants, and other officials, and at other times for the transaction of important business. It levied the taxes, acted as a court of justice, made laws, and carried out certain administrative measures. Origin of the General Court

In the early years the General Court was composed of the governor and his assistants and all the "freemen," or voters, who took the trouble to meet with them. Not all of the people, however, were classed as freemen, but only those who had had this privilege conferred upon them by the General Court. After the settlements had begun to spread out and new towns had grown up, applicants for the rights of active citizenship had to receive the endorsement of the freemen of their own towns before they were admitted as freemen by the General Court.

By 1639 the colony had expanded to the point at which it was no longer practicable for all the freemen to attend all the meetings of the General Court, and so the representative system was adopted. From that time on deputies from the towns sat with the governor and assistants to form the General Court. Once a year, however, the citizens met in a primary assembly, called the Court of Election, to choose the officers of the colony. At this meeting freemen could be represented by proxies. The General Court in the Plymouth colony was never divided into two houses, as was the case in nearly all of the other colonies.

During the first winter after the landing at Plymouth the government was administered by John Carver as governor. When Bradford succeeded him in the spring of 1621 he had not entirely recovered from the disease that had destroyed so many of the colonists, and on account of his physical condition the new executive was given an assistant.[29] The duties of the governor increased so rapidly that in a few years it was deemed necessary to raise the number of assistants to five and later (1663) to seven. The The governor and assistants

[29] OSGOOD, H. L., op. cit., i, p. 292; MORTON, NATHANIEL, New England Memorial (ed. by LORD, A. E., 1903), p. 31.

governor and assistants acted as a court of justice for the entire colony, having jurisdiction in the more important causes, and carried out the ordinary measures of administration. The General Court was the supreme authority in the government, but it dealt only with matters of special importance and left details of administration to the governor and assistants. The assistants were usually the leading men in the colony and enjoyed the high esteem of their fellow-citizens. While their term of office, as well as that of the governor, was one year, they were usually reëlected, and so in most cases they held their places during good behavior.

Place in history of the Pilgrims

The colony of New Plymouth did not play a leading rôle in the history of colonial New England. The people remained comparatively poor and were never noted for any marked achievement in art, literature, or scholarship. They were even lacking in that business initiative which is so characteristic of New Englanders generally. Plymouth was entirely overshadowed by the neighboring Puritan colonies of Connecticut and Massachusetts Bay, and was finally (1691) absorbed by the latter. At the end of the seventy-year period of its separate existence the total population of the colony was only seven thousand.

There are a number of reasons to account for the backwardness of New Plymouth as compared with the other Puritan commonwealths. In the first place, the colony was restricted in area and a good portion of the land was not well suited to agriculture, being marshy or sandy. In the second place, New Plymouth was not well located for the fur trade. In the first decade the fur-bearing animals were thinned out in the near-by regions, and there were no waterways connecting the colony with the fresh hunting-grounds of the distant interior. Nor was the town of Plymouth able to compete on equal terms with the more northerly posts in trade and fishing, for the harbor of Plymouth was too shallow for the larger vessels used in commerce and fishing. Another cause of the slow development of the colony was the fact that it did not have a constituency in England from which to draw immigrants. The type of Separatism professed by the Pilgrims soon went out of vogue in the mother country. The theological views of the Pilgrims remained about the same as they were in the beginning, while their dissenting brethren in the homeland had grown either more radical or more conservative. There was, therefore, no considerable body of believers in England who were in accord with the views of the Pilgrims.

But the Pilgrim Fathers have enjoyed a place in the esteem of later Americans out of all proportion to the importance of the colony established by them. This has been due partly to the fact that they were the pioneers among the Puritan colonists and were the first to establish in the New World the congregational form of worship and church government. As the Congregational later became the established church of Connecticut and Massachusetts, the Pilgrim pioneers thus became the fathers of the Puritan ecclesiastical system of New England. But the main reason that they have gotten such a hold on American sentiment is that their early career affords us one of the finest examples known to history of heroic devotion to a high ideal. The persecutions they suffered in England, the economic hardships they endured in Holland, and the privations and dangers they encountered in the American wilderness have a halo of sanctity thrown around them because they were all incurred in the name of religion.

SELECTED READINGS

1. Puritanism.—Adams, J. T., *The Founding of New England*, ch. 4 (an unfriendly account). For an impartial and readable discussion, see Macy, John, in *Harpers Magazine* for May, 1927. See also Morison, S. E., *Builders of the Bay Colony*, pp. *54-58. For the traditional view, see Eggleston, E., *The Beginners of a Nation*, part ii, *ch. 1.

2. Motives that Prompted the Pilgrims to Leave the Netherlands.— *American History Leaflets*, no. 29, pp. *7-11 (a contemporary account).

3. The Signing of the Treaty with Massasoit.—Young, Alexander, *Chronicles of the Pilgrim Fathers*, pp. *182-194 (a contemporary account).

4. The Pilgrim Migration.—Eggleston, Edward, *The Beginners of a Nation*, part ii, *ch. 3.

5. William Bradford as a Writer.—Tyler, M. C., *History of American Literature during the Colonial Time*, pp. *116-126.

6. Life of William Bradford by Cotton Mather.—*Old South Leaflets*, no. 77.

7. Character Estimate of Elder Brewster by William Bradford.— Bradford's *History*, pp. *376-380. See also Banks, C. E., *The English Ancestry and Homes of the Pilgrim Fathers*, pp. 35-39.

8. A Contemporary Account of Plymouth.—Jameson, J. F., *Narratives of New Netherland*, pp. *110-113.

9. Social Life in the Pilgrim Colony.—Crawford, Mary C., *In the*

Days of the Pilgrim Fathers, *ch. 12, or Usher, R. G., *The Pilgrims and their History,* ch. 17. Contemporary accounts: Hart, A. B., *American History Told by Contemporaries,* i, pp. 349-359, or West, W. M., *A Source Book in American History,* pp. 120-124.

CHAPTER VII

THE ESTABLISHMENT OF PURITANISM IN NEW ENGLAND

THE colony of Massachusetts Bay grew out of a fishing-post which was established in 1623 at Cape Ann, on the present site of Gloucester. The settlement was financed by a group of business men in Dorchester, England, who felt that farming might be combined with fishing and fur trading carried on from this post. But the site chosen was not well suited to either farming or fishing and the venture soon proved unsuccessful. With bankruptcy facing them, the Dorchester promoters withdrew all financial support from the undertaking, and most of the settlers returned to England (1626). The few remaining (about thirty, including women and children) moved southward to Naumkeag, or Salem, as it was afterward called.[1]

The beginning of the Massachusetts Bay Colony

Prominent among those who had been active in promoting the Cape Ann experiment was the Reverend John White, of Dorchester, an Anglican minister with Puritan leanings. He saw an opportunity to use the settlement at Salem as a base for religious instruction to the European fishermen who frequented that region, and as a center for missionary work among the Indians. He and some of the other Dorchester associates therefore made an earnest effort to get a patent and procure funds for putting the colony on a firm financial basis. The support of influential men was enlisted, and a new company was organized, known as the New England Company. Through the influence of the Earl of Warwick, a patent was granted in 1628 to this group of adventurers by the Council for New England. By this patent the company was to receive all the land extending from three miles south of the Charles River to three miles north of the Merrimac River and westward to the Pacific Ocean.[2]

The New England Company

---

[1] YOUNG, A., *Chronicles of Massachusetts Bay,* pp. 5-6, 11-12; HUBBARD, W., *General History of New England* (Massachusetts Historical Society *Collections,* 2nd series, v, pp. 105-108, 110-111).

[2] This patent has been lost, but some of its provisions are recited in

Endicott goes to Salem as governor of the colony

The new company sent over about forty emigrants to reinforce the settlement at Salem, and with them John Endicott, who was to be the governor of the colony.[3] The government thus established did not, however, rest on a strictly legal basis, for the Council for New England probably had no authority to confer governmental powers on its grantees. Moreover, the New England Company was soon involved in a controversy over the right to its land. The Council for New England had been lavish and even reckless in disposing of its territory, and in consequence the limits of one grant frequently overlapped those of another. As a result of this recklessness on the part of the Council for New England, the territory held by the Company was claimed by other grantees who could trace their title to a patent which antedated that of 1628.

The Massachusetts Bay Company: Provisions of the Charter of 1629

In order to put an end to all doubt as to their governmental powers and their landed rights, the Company decided to apply to the king for a charter of incorporation which would end all disputes as to land ownership and governmental authority. Again the Earl of Warwick used his influence to favor the New England enterprise, and a royal charter was obtained on March 4, 1629. In this way the New England Company was merged into a new organization known as the Massachusetts Bay Company. By this charter the new Company was confirmed in the possession of the territory which had been granted the original patentees by the Council for New England, and the stockholders, who were called "freemen," were given authority to govern the settlers. The whole body of freemen was to meet four times a year in what were known as "Great and General Courts." These meetings corresponded to the Quarter Courts of the Virginia Company. To these General Courts were granted authority to admit new members to the Company, select officers, and make such laws and ordinances as were necessary for the management of the corporation and the government of the colony. There was also to be a governor, deputy governor, and eighteen assistants. These were

---

the royal charter of 1629. See THORPE, F. N., *Colonial Charters*, pp. 1847-1848.

[3] Professor Andrews was doubtful as to the terms of the patent of 1628 and even questioned whether such a patent was ever issued by the Council for New England. See ANDREWS, C. M., *The Colonial Period of American History*, i, pp. 356 ff.

to be chosen by the General Court at the Easter term, and this session was known as the Court of Election. The governor, deputy governor, and assistants were to be a sort of committee of the General Court and were to perform such duties as should be imposed upon them by the latter. They were to meet once a month or oftener "for dispatching such business as concerned the Company or plantations." Their meetings corresponded to the ordinary courts of the Virginia Company. There was a provision that the authority of the king must be recognized and all laws passed for the colony must be in harmony with the laws of England. Except for these restrictions the Company was given almost unlimited power in the government of the colony.[4]

The Company began at once to make provision for the government of the settlers in Massachusetts. Endicott was continued as governor, and a deputy governor and a council of eleven were chosen to assist him. To these representatives of the Company was intrusted full power to govern the colonists. The plantation remained under this management for about a year.[5]

The Company assumes control of the colony in Massachusetts

Up to this point the Massachusetts colony was not essentially different in character from the one that had been planted in Virginia. Religion had not figured prominently as a motive in its foundation. It is true that a majority of the stockholders of the Company were Puritans, but the colony had been established not as a refuge for persecuted religious sectaries, but rather as a commercial venture to promote fishing, fur trading, and agriculture, the hope of gain being the main motive.

But events in England were now taking such a turn as to give the New England enterprise a religious aspect. Charles I was ruling highhandedly in both church and state. In the same year in which the Massachusetts charter was granted he dissolved Parliament and started upon a ten-year period of personal rule without the aid of Parliament. The king was controlled in church affairs by the advice of William Laud, now Bishop of London and soon to be placed at the head of the Anglican Church as Archbishop of Canterbury. As Laud was an ardent supporter of the state church and was determined to maintain its authority at all costs, he made life very uncomfortable for Nonconformists.

Puritan dissatisfaction with political, religious, and economic conditions in England

[4] For the text of this charter, see THORPE, *Colonial Charters*, pp. 1846-1860.

[5] See *Massachusetts Bay Colonial Records*, i, p. 42; YOUNG, A., *Chronicles of Massachusetts Bay*, pp. 192-196.

Charles's government, therefore, was very displeasing to those who believed in the rights of Parliament and the doctrines and practices of Puritanism. Such conditions were favorable to a great Puritan emigration. Moreover, unfavorable economic conditions were at this time a cause of dissatisfaction in the eastern and southeastern counties of England, where Puritanism was especially strong. In these sections cloth-making was an important industry, and the prosperity of the people was largely bound up with it. During the period from 1625 to 1630 this business was suffering a great decline, and there was considerable economic unrest among all classes. There was thus in these counties a strong desire on the part of both Nonconformists and persons of other faiths to go to a new country where land could easily be obtained and the necessaries and comforts of life might be secured. Among the rank and file of the emigrants, this economic motive was probably the chief incentive that prompted the Great Migration, although dissatisfaction with political and religious conditions in England may have been the strongest inducement among the leaders.

The Cambridge Agreement

This emigration was also facilitated by an important change in the management of the Company. The charter of 1629 differed in one very important particular from the form of patent usually granted to the colonizing corporations of that day—there was no provision requiring that the headquarters of the Company should be in England, and so the stockholders could hold their meetings in New England if they chose to do so. Now there were some prominent Puritans in England who were willing to settle in New England provided they were given control of the Company, and a pledge to this effect was made by John Winthrop and eleven other Nonconformist leaders. In a written agreement signed at Cambridge the latter promised to go to America with their families if the government of the colony could be transferred to them (August 26, 1629). This would mean that the meetings of the Company in the future would be held in New England instead of Old England. The Company promptly accepted this arrangement and proceeded to effect the transfer. All the officers who were unwilling to go to the New World resigned, and their places were filled by prospective emigrants. Winthrop was chosen governor of the Company and colony, and after he and his followers were settled in Massachusetts, the meetings of the Company were all held in Boston or some other town in

Massachusetts instead of in London. The control of the Company and the management of the colony had now passed into the hands of the Puritans.[6]

The economic, political, and religious situation was creating so much dissatisfaction in England that the Puritan leaders found no difficulty in enlisting a large number of emigrants for the New World. So many left in 1630 that the exodus is known as the Great Migration. In the spring of this year eleven ships were sent to Massachusetts, and by the end of summer about one thousand settlers had been brought over. This was not only the largest number of colonists that had ever left the homeland in any single year for the New World, but it also contained a larger proportion of men of means and influence than had any other contingent of emigrants.[7] Other ships came later in the year, bringing over more emigrants.

The Great Migration

The leader of the Great Migration was the new governor, John Winthrop, and no other man in all England was better fitted to act "as the Moses of the great Puritan exodus."[8] He was now in the prime of life, being only forty-two years old. He was a man of means and influence and considerable education, as he had attended the University of Cambridge, though he was not a graduate. His character was that of the typical Puritan of the best class, having practically all the virtues and some of the defects that are characteristic of that religion. He was grave, dignified, and self-controlled, and had a cool, calculating temperament, which generally ruled out impulsiveness in action. Religion was the ruling influence of his life, and he constantly saw the hand of God in the ordinary routine of daily affairs. Unfortunately, however, his religion was not free from the taint of intolerance, and his inability to rise above the spirit of his age in this respect was responsible for his connection with a policy of persecution in Massachusetts that has cast a shadow on his fame.

John Winthrop

Part played by Winthrop in the history of Massachusetts

The history of the Bay Colony for the first two decades after the Great Migration centers around Winthrop. During this entire period, except for a few years, he was governor and easily the

[6] *Massachusetts Bay Colonial Records*, i, pp. 49-51, 52, 58-61; HART, A. B., *American History Told by Contemporaries*, i, pp. 371-372; YOUNG, A., *Chronicles of Massachusetts Bay*, pp. 281-282.

[7] YOUNG, *Chronicles*, pp. 310-330; HART, A. B., *Commonwealth History of Massachusetts*, i, p. 100.

[8] FISKE, JOHN, *New France and New England*, p. 102.

leading figure in the colony. To him more than any other one man the plantation was indebted for its establishment and for the character of its early development. Moreover, he found time to write a *History of New England,* covering the period from 1630 to 1649, which is the best contemporary account we have of early Massachusetts. It will be observed that Winthrop's place in the history of colonial Massachusetts was similar to that of Bradford in the history of New Plymouth.

It would seem that a man so well established in the homeland as was Winthrop would not be willing to pull up in the middle of his career and run the hazards of beginning life all over again in the New World. But the situation in England at this time was not to his liking. Not only did he disapprove of the policy of the established church and the arbitrary rule of the king, but he had also lost his office as an attorney in the Court of Wards.[9] Besides, there were economic reasons for making a change. Although possessed of a comfortable estate, his family was expensive and he found it difficult to maintain the standard of living set for his class. Then, too, he felt that he had a capacity for government and an ambition to use it, and there was no opportunity, he thought, for exercising this talent in England. But probably the main motive was the religious one—the desire to establish a Puritan commonwealth in the New World—to erect "a bulwark against the kingdom of antichrist which the Jesuits labor to rear up in those parts."[10]

Winthrop supersedes Endicott as governor

Winthrop found the colony at Salem in "a sad and unexpected condition." One-fourth of the settlers had died during the previous winter and many of the survivors were weak and sick.[11] Winthrop's arrival did not solve the food problem, for he had by a mistake failed to bring as many supplies as were needed. There was, therefore, a danger that the great increase in numbers would add to the risks of famine. Fortunately, Winthrop had the wisdom to meet the emergency successfully. One of the vessels, the *Lyon,* was sent back with instructions to return with provisions as speedily as possible, and about two hundred of the new-comers returned home.

New settlements

The outlook at Salem was so uninviting that Winthrop and most of his followers moved to Charlestown, which had recently

[9] WINTHROP, R. C., *Life and Letters of John Winthrop,* i, p. 303.
[10] *Ibid.,* i, p. 309.
[11] *Ibid.,* ii, p. 28.

been settled. The colonists began to scatter and soon there were settlements at Boston, Charlestown, Watertown, Lynn, Medford, Dorchester, and Roxbury. Despite Winthrop's precautions, there was a great deal of suffering after the winter started, and by the beginning of the new year, two hundred had died. The *Lyon* returned in February with supplies, and soon other vessels came to their relief, including one from the Virginia colony.[12]

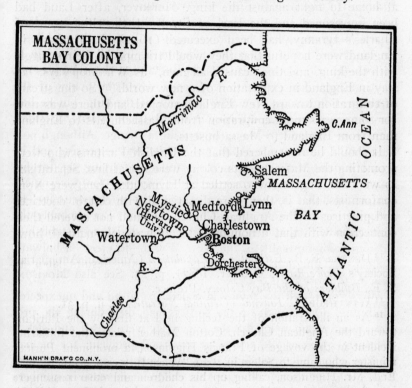

After the first year, the colony was firmly established, and although at times there was a scarcity of food, the Massachusetts settlers never suffered from famine as did the Virginia pioneers. Few emigrants, however, came over during the next two years. They were frightened away by the reports of famine that the colony had already endured and by the rigid discipline maintained by the Massachusetts authorities. In 1633 emigration again set

Emigration to Massachusetts discouraged by the Civil War in England

[12] YOUNG, A., *Chronicles of the First Planters of the Colony of Massachusetts Bay*, pp. 311-330; HUBBARD, W., *op. cit.* (Massachusetts Historical Society *Collections*, 2nd series, v, p. 139).

in and continued until the Long Parliament opened in 1640. The colony developed rapidly during this period. In 1643 the population of Massachusetts Bay was from fourteen to sixteen thousand, probably as much as all the rest of British America put together.[13] This wholesale emigration had been encouraged by Archbishop Laud's policy of persecution of the Puritans. When the king and Parliament came to blows the Puritans were needed at home to fight against the king. Moreover, after Laud had been imprisoned and the Earl of Strafford, the chief agent of Charles's tyranny, had been executed (1641) the Puritans in England were hopeful that they would triumph in their struggle with the king, and this "caused all men," as Winthrop says, "to stay in England in expectation of a new world."[14] So the stream of emigration toward New England stopped, and there was now for some years more emigration from Massachusetts to England than from England to Massachusetts.

Congregationalism established in the Massachusetts Bay Colony

It should be remembered that the English Puritans who were promoting the Massachusetts colony were not at first Separatists, as were the Pilgrims who settled at Plymouth. They were Nonconformists, that is, they were dissatisfied with certain doctrines and practices of the Anglican Church, but had not severed their connection with that denomination.[15] It was only natural, how-

[13] DEXTER, F. B., *Estimates of Population* (American Antiquarian Society's *Proceedings*, October, 1887), p. 25. See also MORISON, S. E., *Builders of the Bay Colony*, Preface.

[14] WINTHROP, J., *Journal* (*Original Narratives*), ii, p. 31.

[15] As an illustration of the feeling held at first by the Puritans toward the Anglican Church, Cotton Mather relates the following incident in the voyage of Francis Higginson, a prominent Puritan minister who came to Salem in 1629. "When they came to the Land's End, Mr. Higginson, calling up his children and other passengers into the stern of the ship, to take their last sight of England, said, 'We will not say, as the Separatists were wont to say at their leaving of England, Farewell, Babylon! Farewell, Rome! But we will say Farewell, dear England! Farewell, the Church of God in England, and all the Christian friends there. We do not go to New England as Separatists from the Church of England, though we cannot but separate from the corruptions in it. But we go to practice the positive part of church reformation, and propagate the Gospel in America.' And so he concluded with a fervent prayer for the king, and Church and State, in England" (MATHER, COTTON, *Magnalia*, i, p. 328). See also MORISON, S. E., *Builders of the Bay Colony*, p. 37.

ever, that the slender tie that bound the Puritans to the home church, which had already been strained almost to the breaking-point by the persecuting policy of Archbishop Laud, would be snapped when they had crossed the Atlantic and set up a self-governing republic. Independence in religion would be the logical corollary of the virtual independence in government which they were to enjoy under their charter. John Endicott, the first governor of Massachusetts, favored a declaration of ecclesiastical independence, as he was a zealous Puritan and strongly opposed to the Anglican doctrines. In the summer of 1629, with the assistance of a Separatist minister from Plymouth, he established at Salem the congregational form of church government modeled after that of Plymouth.[16] The example set by Endicott was followed by Winthrop, for he organized a Congregational church at Charlestown soon after his arrival there.[17] Other churches were soon organized, and in every town there was an independent Congregational church.[18]

The removal of the seat of the Company from Old to New England closed the proprietary period and made Massachusetts Bay a corporate colony. Prior to this time there had been both a governor of the Company and a governor of the colony, but now both of these places were filled by the same man. In choosing John Winthrop for this responsible position the stockholders had made a wise selection. The transfer of the government from Old to New England had changed a meeting of stockholders into a colonial legislature, and had caused a corporation to develop into a commonwealth.

Massachusetts becomes a corporate colony

When the clause conferring on the "freemen" the authority to

For other contemporary statements showing the attitude of the early Massachusetts settlers toward the Anglican Church, see WERTENBAKER, *op. cit.*, p. 89.

[16] BRADFORD, WILLIAM, *History of Plymouth Plantation*, pp. 51-52; MORTON, NATHANIEL, *New England's Memorial* (DAVIS, J., ed., 1826), pp. 143-148.

[17] BRADFORD, *op. cit.*, pp. 271-272; WINTHROP, J., *op. cit.*, i, pp. 51-52.

[18] While the New England church was Congregational in belief and practice from the beginning, this term was not applied to it until later. The word "Congregational," as applied to the church, was used as early as 1642, but the term "Congregationalism" seems not to have come into use until the next century. See *New English Dictionary*.

govern the colony was inserted, it was meant to apply to the stock-holders of the corporation holding meetings in London. But the turn that events had recently taken had resulted in placing this power in the hands of the few freemen who had emigrated to New England. The number of freemen in the colony at first was slightly over a dozen,[19] including the governor, deputy governor, and eight assistants. To these few men was thus intrusted the power to "correct, govern, punish, pardon, and rule all the king's subjects within the limits of their patent."

An increase in the number of freemen is requested

There were in Massachusetts by the end of the year of the Great Migration about two thousand settlers, and to assume that they would contentedly submit to being ruled by a dozen men would be to expect too much even in that aristocratic age. When the freemen met in October, 1630, to hold the first session of the General Court a petition was presented to that body asking that over a hundred other settlers be admitted as freemen.[20] Winthrop and his associates were now placed in an embarrassing dilemma. For not only did the petitioners have reason behind their request, but they were also in a position to weaken the colony by leaving it if their rights were denied them. To the north in the regions now known as Maine and New Hampshire, and to the south in the colony of New Plymouth, were inviting lands to which they could easily emigrate. Policy, therefore, demanded that some concessions be made to these complainants in order to keep them in the colony.

This request granted, but the government is put in the hands of the governor and assistants

On the other hand, to admit them to an equal share in the government with the old stockholders would be to swamp the General Court with new members and thus deprive the old leaders of their control of the colony. In considering such a move a dangerous innovation Winthrop and his friends were not actuated by purely selfish considerations. For they had come to America primarily to establish a Puritan commonwealth, and the experiment might easily fail unless those who were most interested in its success could control the government. The situation was, therefore, one that called for tact and compromise. The settlers must be given a voice in the government without jeopardizing the con-

[19] In October, 1630, after several freemen had died, there were left only ten, including the governor (YOUNG, A., *Chronicles of Massachusetts*, p. 319).

[20] *Massachusetts Bay Colony Records*, i, pp. 79-80.

trol of the old leaders. It was, accordingly, decided at this first meeting that thereafter the freemen should only have power to elect the assistants and the latter would choose the governor and deputy governor. By this arrangement all the powers of government, executive, legislative, and judicial, were turned over to the governor, deputy governor, and assistants, and the ordinary freemen were deprived of the power to interfere seriously with the rule of the Puritan oligarchy. Having thus safeguarded the aristocracy against the dangers of democracy, the court admitted (May, 1631) one hundred and eighteen new members to the rights of freemen. But as a further safeguard in favor of the aristocracy it voted that in the future only church members should be admitted to the freedom of the colony. This qualification on the suffrage remained in force until after the Restoration.[21] Additions to the list of voters were made from time to time on this basis, and the freemen continued to increase in number. At no time, however, did all the male citizens have the right of suffrage, but this privilege was enjoyed by only a minority belonging principally to the upper and middle classes.[22]

But these arrangements did not satisfy the people. Next year (1632) the citizens of Watertown, acting under the leadership of their minister, protested against the payment of taxes levied by the board of assistants, stating that the power to make laws and levy taxes belongs to the people. This protest was severely frowned upon by the authorities, but in this same year the right

The people demand a stronger voice in the government, and the General Court becomes a representative assembly

[21] *Ibid.*, 79, 87; WEST, W. M., *Source Book in American History*, p. 180.

In 1664, acting under pressure from the British government, the General Court made a technical, though not a substantial, change in the religious test for voters. With this slight modification, the practice of imposing the test of church membership for voting continued until the charter was annulled (1684) (OSGOOD, H. L., *American Colonies in the Seventeenth Century*, i, p. 212).

[22] There is some difference of opinion among the authorities as to the proportion of the people that enjoyed the right of suffrage. Mr. J. T. Adams thinks that only about one-fifth of the male adults were granted this privilege, while Professor S. E. Morison contends (and supports his contention with strong arguments) that the proportion of voters was generally larger. See ADAMS, J. T., *The Founding of New England*, p. 395, and MORISON, S. E., *Builders of the Bay Colony*, pp. 339-341.

to elect the governor and deputy governor was restored to the whole body of freemen.[23] The governor and assistants were now a sort of parliament for the colony, and Winthrop thought that the freemen should have no further power than that of choosing this board.

But Winthrop's aristocratic ideas of government were not accepted by the great majority of the settlers. Moreover, the governor and assistants were exercising power that under the charter was vested in the whole body of freemen meeting as a General Court. While it is more than likely that most of the settlers did not know the provisions of the charter, as the governor kept it locked up in his chest, it is very probable that the leaders of the discontented element did know that Winthrop and his associates had usurped power in violation of the charter. At any rate, by 1634 the opposition was well organized. In that year two deputies were chosen from each town to meet and consider the measures that were to be taken up by the General Court, soon to meet for the annual election of officers. On coming together, the deputies asked to see the charter. When this was produced they pointed out that the lawmaking power belonged to the General Court. Winthrop tried to persuade them that it was not feasible to carry out this provision. This clause was put in when the number of freemen was small, and it would not, he maintained, be practicable for all the freemen to meet in a primary assembly to make laws, and the colony was as yet not ready for the establishment of a representative assembly. But the trend toward popular control was again too strong to be curbed by the aristocratic governor, and the General Court, which convened a few weeks later (May, 1634) for the annual election, enacted that thereafter the voters in each town should choose deputies to represent them in all meetings of the Court except the one in which the officers were

[23] WINTHROP, J., op. cit., i, pp. 74, 79.

In this same year (1632) two men were appointed by each town to be present at the next meeting of the Court of Assistants to advise with the governor and magistrates "about the raising of a public stock" (WINTHROP, op. cit., i, p. 79). But as no further mention of these representatives is made either in WINTHROP'S Journal or the Colony Records, there is no proof that they ever met (OSGOOD, H. L., American Colonies in the Seventeenth Century, i, pp. 156-157).

chosen.[24] "From and after this time the General Court of Massachusetts consisted of the assistants and the deputies."[25]

At first the deputies and assistants sat together as one house, and for two years no serious friction arose between them, although the deputies, being more numerous, could outvote the assistants. Then a dispute arose as to the method of voting, when in 1634 the inhabitants of Newtown asked permission to leave and settle on the Connecticut River. A majority of the deputies were in favor of granting them permission to do so; but this action of theirs was negatived by a vote against it by a majority of the assistants. The deputies claimed that the assistants had no right to veto a measure supported by a majority of the whole General Court, contending that deputies and assistants should vote not as bodies but as individuals. A good deal of feeling was aroused, as the magistrate saw in this claim of the people's representatives a menace to the supremacy of the governing aristocracy. A day of fasting was appointed and Cotton preached a sermon in which he supported the contention of the assistants. This silenced for the time the opposition to the magistrates, and two years later it was definitely settled that all acts of the General Court should require the assent of the majority of both the deputies and assistants. That is, either group could negative the action of the other. The assistants and deputies still, however, sat together for some years thereafter.[26]

The two parts of the General Court decide to vote as bodies and not as individuals

Only one more step, that of dividing the General Court into two bodies, had now to be taken, and a full-grown bicameral assembly would be formed. A rather trivial incident led to the separation, and so, as Winthrop phrases it, "there fell out a great business upon a very small occasion." A civil suit between two Boston litigants was carried by appeal to the General Court (1642), which was at that time the highest judicial tribunal in the colony.[27] The deputies and assistants were deadlocked over

The General Court divides into two houses

[24] WINTHROP, J., *op. cit.*, i, pp. 122-123, 125.

[25] OSGOOD, H. L., *American Colonies in the Seventeenth Century,* i, p. 157.

[26] WINTHROP, J., *op. cit.*, i, pp. 132-134.

[27] This suit grew out of a dispute that had arisen between one Mrs. Sherman and a Mr. Keayne, a wealthy and unpopular shopkeeper of Boston. Mrs. Sherman brought suit against Keayne for the recovery of a stray sow, alleging that it had been stolen by the defendant. A majority of the deputies and a small majority of the whole assembly

the question, as a majority of the former were for the plaintiff and a majority of the latter for the defendant. Finally, after two years of high excitement, it was decided (1644) that the General Court should thereafter sit and vote as two chambers, each having the right to initiate bills, which could be passed only by a majority vote in both houses.[28]

Composition of the General Court

From this time on the legislature of Massachusetts was a body of two houses. The governor and assistants constituted the upper house, and the deputies the lower. The first charter provided that there should be eighteen assistants, but usually the actual number was less than the full quota, generally about one-half. The number was kept small in order that the dignity of the office might be maintained. The assistants, or magistrates, were the leading men in the colony and were usually chosen from the wealthy families of Boston and near-by towns.[29] They exerted a great influence in the government. Their term of office was only one year, but when a magistrate was once chosen he was generally reëlected from year to year, so that the members of the upper house of the General Court virtually held their position by life-tenure. The Rev. Mr. Cotton, a prominent minister of Boston, contended that a magistrate should not be turned into a private man without just cause any more than a private man should be put out of his freehold.[30]

decided in favor of the plaintiff and a majority of the assistants for the defendant. As the plaintiff was a poor woman and the defendant a close-fisted, wealthy man, the sympathies of the people were with the former, and a great deal of opposition to the negative voice of the assistants was aroused. This was clearly another instance of the people arraying themselves through their representatives, the deputies, against the control of the aristocracy. The ruling clique was alarmed at these symptoms of democracy, and so great was the excitement that a meeting was held and attended by nearly all the ministers and magistrates of the colony and many of the deputies. The deadlock seemed hopeless when, happily, the case was settled out of court (WINTHROP, J., op. cit., ii, pp. 64-66, 116-119).

[28] Massachusetts Colonial Records, ii, pp. 58-59; WINTHROP, J., op cit., ii, pp. 120-121.

[29] On one occasion a deputy made a motion in the assembly that two of the oldest assistants be dropped from the list on the ground that they were poor (WINTHROP, J., op. cit., ii, p. 49).

[30] Ibid., i, pp. 124-125. In 1636 two magistrates were chosen for life, but the practice was abandoned nine years later (ibid., p. 178).

In the early years when the General Court sat as one body it was presided over by the governor. After it was divided into two houses the governor became the presiding officer of the board of assistants, and the deputies elected a speaker to preside over them. The number of regular meetings of the General Court was specified by law, but the governor could call extra sessions. However, he could not dissolve the body without its consent, and had no power of veto, though he had a deciding vote in case of a tie. Deputies were heavily fined for absence and tardiness at assemblies. No one could serve as a deputy unless he was orthodox in religion, and any freeman knowingly voting for a candidate not having this qualification was to be fined. *Presiding officers*

After the General Court became a representative body (1634), it still met once a year as a primary assembly to elect the governor, deputy governor, and assistants. This meeting was known as the Court of Election. All freemen were at first expected to attend this session in person. The method of voting was at first by a show of hands; but the written ballot soon came into use.[31] *Method of electing deputies*

The primary assembly soon proved impracticable even for election purposes. Not only did voters living in frontier towns find it inconvenient to go to Boston for these meetings, but their families were exposed to Indian attack while they were away. So in 1636 the Court voted that freemen living in distant settlements could send in their votes by proxy, and the proxy system was soon extended so as to include all towns. Even this plan had its drawbacks, and later it was provided that freemen could cast their votes in their respective towns and have their deputies take them to the General Court and have them counted there.[32]

[31] HAYNES, C. H., *Representation and Suffrage in Massachusetts* (Johns Hopkins University *Studies*, 12th series), p. 30; McKINLEY, A. E., *The Suffrage Franchise in the Thirteen English Colonies in America*, pp. 307-311.

[32] This last change made it necessary to devise a system of nominating candidates to be voted on by the people in their precincts. As well-organized political parties had not come into existence, the voters in the town needed some guidance in casting their ballots, otherwise votes would be scattered too widely and thrown away on impossible candidates. More than one plan was tried, but the one most generally employed was a kind of legislative caucus. The members of the General Court would select a list of candidates to be voted upon by the freemen in the towns. For a while the freemen in the towns also

The
Body of
Liberties

Before leaving the flagship the freemen had voted that the assistants should exercise the powers of the English justices of the peace. Most of them had been magistrates in the homeland, and they proceeded to perform their old functions in the New World. In administering justice the magistrates were governed sometimes by the English common law and at others by the precepts of the Bible. This practice gave wide discretion to the judges and imparted an element of uncertainty to their decisions. There arose, therefore, a demand for the codification of the laws, in order that the people might know what were their rights and duties, and that the judges might be bound down to definite principles in rendering their decisions. In response to this demand there was prepared and adopted (1641) a code of laws known as the Body of Liberties.[33] Additions to this collection were afterward made, and in 1648 the enlarged code was published under the title of *The Laws and Liberties of Massachusetts*. These laws are based largely on the statute and common law of England, though in the penalties prescribed for criminal offenses they show a marked influence of the Mosaic code.[34]

Character
of the
government

The government established under the first charter was that of an autonomous republic. Under it Massachusetts was nominally a part of the British empire, but was virtually an independent state. It was not, however, a democracy, but rather a theocratic aristocracy. The small minority who exercised the right of suffrage usually submitted deferentially to the leadership of a few prominent men. These latter constituted an aristocracy of wealth and culture, dominated by Puritan ideals in religion. It was the

---

assisted in making out this preliminary slate (HAYNES, *op. cit.*, pp. 31-32; CHANNING, *op. cit.*, i, p. 350).

[33] These laws had been compiled by Rev. Nathaniel Ward, of Ipswich. After having been amended by the General Court they had been sent out to be discussed in the various town meetings. Again they were brought before the General Court for final revision and adoption (1641). They were to continue in force for three years, and at the end of this time they were to be revised in the light of the knowledge gained by the experience in this period (WINTHROP, J., *op. cit.*, ii, pp. 48-49). For the text of this code of laws, see *Old South Leaflets*, no. 164.

[34] *The Laws and Liberties of Massachusetts* have recently (1929) been reprinted by the Henry E. Huntingdon Library, with an explanatory introduction by Max Farrand.

government of the best, as the New Englander would interpret the word. The clergy exerted a powerful influence in the administration. The ministers were usually men of intellectual power and would have made their voices heard in any society in any age. But they were especially influential in the Bay Colony because as expounders of religion they were esteemed to be well versed in the principles of government, inasmuch as the political ideals of the Puritans were derived to a considerable extent from the teachings of the Bible. Besides, the clergy decided upon the merits of applicants for church membership and thus indirectly passed upon the qualifications for voting.

At first sight it would seem that such a government—an aristocracy limited by a potential democracy—would be almost ideal. The ruling clique was free from the vice that is usually the curse of oligarchies, namely, the disposition to exploit the masses for the material advantage of the privileged class. The administration was both honest and efficient, but its policy was narrow, shortsighted, and too conservative for a pioneer community. It insisted too much on conformity and bristled with tyranny whenever there was a departure from the orthodox beliefs or practices. The leaders, who had been the champions of nonconformity in Old England, had now become ardent advocates of a rigid standpattism. Under such a régime there was little chance for initiative and individuality. Many of the emigrants that had already come to the New World and more who were expecting to come were people of strong individuality. This narrow policy, therefore, was unacceptable to many actual and possible settlers and so tended to discourage a normal growth in population. Some of the finest men in the colony found the atmosphere too close for them and left, either to return to the mother country or else to find homes in other colonies. Others who were minded to go to America refused to settle in Massachusetts because of its narrow and intolerant policy.

In Massachusetts church and state were so closely associated that religious heresy might easily become political disloyalty. The rulers were, therefore, very intolerant of nonconformity in religion, not only because it was dangerous in itself, but also because they feared that it might undermine the foundations of the state. In its effort to silence religious and political dissent the government soon encountered the opposition of a few leaders whose principles were a challenge to the established order in both church

The expulsion of Roger Williams

and state. Prominent in this list of dissenters was Roger Williams, a brilliant and eloquent young minister, well educated and possessed of a very attractive personality, but lacking in judgment and mental poise. William Bradford very properly described him as "a man godly and zealous, having many precious parts, but very unsettled in judgment."[35] He was courageous and frank and spoke his mind freely, though always in a spirit of kindness. His unquestioned sincerity and his other fine qualities won the esteem of a small circle of devoted friends and adherents, though his pronounced individuality, the fickleness of his opinions, and his lack of ability as a politician kept him from winning a large popular following.

Because of his likable disposition, his deep piety, and his zeal for the Puritan cause, he at first found favor in the eyes of the orthodox church leaders. But he was a radical Separatist, and independence in religion was an obsession with him. Moreover, he had a conscience that was sensitive almost to the point of morbidity, and so he found it difficult to adjust his angular views to the accepted opinion of any community. It was not long, therefore, before he began to give out opinions which were regarded by the Puritan leaders as a dangerous menace to their cherished ideals in both religion and government and some of which are considered unsafe even by modern thinkers.

He believed that church and state should be entirely separate and that the government should not interfere in any way with the religious views or practices of the individual. He even went so far as to say that the magistrates should not punish such offenses as idolatry, blasphemy, perjury, and Sabbath-breaking, and that a Christian magistrate ought not to administer an oath in court to an unregenerate person. It is needless to say that such radical views gave a severe shock to the orthodoxy of that day. But he went still farther and declared that the Company's title to its land was not valid, as it rested on a charter from the king and the king had no right to dispose of Indian lands.[36] If this latter doctrine had been accepted by the authorities all land titles would have been declared invalid.

These startling opinions Williams boldly and eloquently proclaimed, and the magistrates, fearing that much mischief would result from them if he were allowed to remain longer in the

[35] BRADFORD, WILLIAM, *History of Plymouth Plantation,* p. 299.
[36] WINTHROP, J., *op. cit.,* i, pp. 57, 61-62, 116, 117, 119, 149.

colony, took steps to get rid of the trouble-maker. He was accordingly banished from Massachusetts by the General Court, and the authorities later planned to send him back to England.[37] Learning of this, he fled and took refuge with his friends, the Indians of the Narragansett region. While with the Indians he suffered terrible hardships from cold and hunger, being, as he expressed it, "sorely tossed for fourteen weeks in a bitter winter season, not knowing what bread or bed did mean."[38] Finally he and five of his friends reached the present site of Providence and there founded a settlement (June, 1636), which was the beginning of the colony of Rhode Island.

When the controversy between Williams and his opponents is viewed in the light of twentieth-century opinion, Williams seems to have had the better of the argument. For while we regard some of his positions as untenable and consider that he exalted minor theological differences into undue importance, yet his views as to religious liberty and the relation of church and state are in the main accepted as political axioms by modern Americans. Not only was Williams more liberal in his opinions than his persecutors, but he had behind his fight a saintliness of character and a mildness of temper that gave great weight to his arguments. Despite his inability to make a comfortable adjustment to his religious environment and despite the strife that so often resulted from this maladjustment, Williams was not fond of fighting for its own sake. In his disagreements with his compatriots he was actuated by loyalty to principle rather than by contrariness of disposition. His disputations with his opponents were usually carried on without personal bitterness and he harbored no enmity against his persecutors.[39]

Despite his popularity as a speaker, Williams had not succeeded in winning to his cause the permanent support of a large and influential following. His expulsion, therefore, did not shake

Mrs. Anne Hutchinson

[37] *Ibid.*, i, pp. 154, 155, 157, 162-163, 168; *Rhode Island Colonial Records*, i, p. 13, note.

[38] Quoted by PALFREY, J. G., *History of New England*, i, p. 421.

[39] COBB, S. H., *The Rise of Religious Liberty in America*, pp. 428-429.

Winthrop once wrote to him: "Sir, we have often tried your patience but could never conquer it." Quoted by PALFREY, *op. cit.*, p. 417, note. This note also gives other contemporary statements regarding his forgiving spirit.

the colony to its foundations. The cutting out of the political and religious heresy advocated by him was a disagreeable and even painful operation, but the constitution of Puritan orthodoxy in the youthful commonwealth was so vigorous that it soon recovered from the shock. The established order was, however, soon subjected to a greater strain, when there arose a noted controversy over the teachings of Mrs. Anne Hutchinson. In this case heresy was able to muster such strength as to menace seriously the supremacy if not the very existence of orthodoxy.[40]

Mrs. Hutchinson was the wife of a well-to-do man of good standing in Boston. She was a woman of exceptional ability and had endeared herself to the other women of the community by acts of helpfulness in cases of illness and other occasions of distress. She was a good conversationalist and was not averse to making use of this gift.[41] Being of a religious turn of mind, she was naturally interested in theological discussion, and soon she became the center of a group of women to whom she explained her religious views.[42] Her notions regarding theology differed from those held by Winthrop and others among the orthodox party. The differences between her beliefs and those of her opponents would be considered today too unimportant to cause a denominational breach; but at that time religion was the most serious concern of life, and theological differences had a significance out of proportion to their present-day importance.[43]

[40] For an account of this controversy, see ADAMS, C. F., *Three Episodes of Massachusetts History*, i. The sources are given at length in the *Publications of the Prince Society*. BELL, E. H., *John Wheelright*, gives some documents bearing on the part played by the Rev. John Wheelright, Mrs. Hutchinson's brother-in-law. See also ADAMS, C. F., ed., *Antinomianism in the Colony of Massachusetts Bay,* for documents on this controversy. The subject is also discussed, but more briefly, in WINTHROP, J., *op. cit.,* i, pp. 195-196, 240, 243-251, 260-261, 263-265.

[41] "She knew much; but she talked out of all proportion to her knowledge" (ADAMS, C. F., *Three Episodes of Massachusetts History*, i, p. 395).

[42] For a good brief contemporary unfriendly account of Mrs. Hutchinson up to her trial, with a brief statement of her beliefs, see *Antinomian Controversy*, pp. 157-164.

[43] For a statement of the views of Mrs. Hutchinson, as her enemies understood them, see WINTHROP, *op. cit.,* i, pp. 244-246. It is difficult for the average reader to find out from these pages just what her

Mrs. Hutchinson was a woman whose opinions had jagged edges, and consequently they did not fit into the groove that orthodoxy had hollowed out. If she were living today she would be quite happy and useful, for in our complex society a woman of her type easily finds a niche into which she can fit her personality with perfect comfort. But in Puritan New England the number of pigeonholes into which opinions could be put were few in number and all labeled by the properly-constituted authorities. Any opinion, therefore, that did not fit one of these pigeonholes was of necessity excluded from the cabinet of tolerance. The doctrine preached by Mrs. Hutchinson was thought to be something like a heresy that had appeared in the Christian church in former times, known as Antinomianism.[44] Partly because of this alleged similarity and partly because their opponents wanted to give them a bad name, the Hutchinsonians were called Antinomians by the orthodox party.

Yet these differences in doctrine were not so great but that a peaceful settlement of the dispute might have been effected if the religious quarrel had not gotten into politics. Owing to the close union that then existed between church and state in Massachusetts, practically every religious question of importance had also a political side. The colony was divided into two rival camps, and the Hutchinsonians were at first in the ascendency, as nearly the entire membership of the Boston church had embraced their

---

beliefs were, as they are vague and hard to understand. She considered that one of the preachers, Mr. Wilson, talked too much about works and not enough about the grace of God as the cause of salvation. She also taught that the Holy Spirit illumines the heart of every true believer and enables him to understand what is truth. To Winthrop and the orthodox party this was equivalent to saying that the modern Christian receives a revelation from God. This was, they maintained, to deny that the Bible is the only source of inspiration. Her views regarding illumination were also similar to those held by the heretical Quakers and Baptists.

[44] There have appeared at various times in the history of the Christian Church, going back probably as early as the first century, sects that have believed that the presence of the Holy Spirit in the heart frees one from the obligations of the moral law. This doctrine is generally known as Antinomianism. The term Antinomian probably originated with Luther, being used by him to stigmatize a theological opponent who taught that a regenerate person is free from the Mosaic Law and is under the Gospel alone.

views.[45] Their cause was strengthened by the adhesion of the young governor, Henry Vane, who had great influence in Massachusetts because of his prominent family connections in England.[46] But in the spring of 1637 Winthrop was elected governor after a very stormy meeting of the Court of Election, and the orthodox party was put in control of the government. This victory was strengthened by the departure of Vane for England in August, and the fate of the heretics was now sealed. Mrs. Hutchinson was tried before the General Court and sentenced to banishment from the colony.[47] She was afterward excommunicated from the church.[48] She with her husband and some of her followers went to Rhode Island and settled on the island of Aquidneck, while others of her party went north under the leadership of her brother-in-law, Rev. John Wheelwright, and founded a colony in New Hampshire.

The conviction of Mrs. Hutchinson cannot be charged entirely to honest bigotry. We would like to be able to say that her judges had reluctantly condemned her from a mistaken but honest sense of duty, believing that her presence in the colony would endanger the purity of religious doctrine. But, unfortunately, it has to be said that while this was one of the motives for the action of the General Court, personal and partisan feeling was also another important influence. Winthrop was the governor and president of the General Court at the time of her trial, and has merited a good deal of the condemnation that attaches to this perversion of justice. He was a bitter enemy of Mrs. Hutchinson and would by modern standards have been debarred from sitting on her case. But he not only presided at her trial, but acted as both judge and prosecutor. This event has, therefore, served to put Winthrop on trial as well as Mrs. Hutchinson. For while it led to the arraignment of the latter before the General Court, it has also arraigned the former before the tribunal of history, and

[45] *Antinomian Controversy in Massachusetts*, p. 80.

[46] Governor Vane was the son of Sir Henry Vane, who was at that time a member of the Privy Council (WINTHROP, J., *op. cit.*, i, pp. 161-162).

[47] A fine contemporary account of this trial is given in the *Antinomian Controversy in Massachusetts*, pp. 164-180. For another report of the same trial, see *ibid.*, pp. 235-284.

[48] For two contemporary reports of the church trial, see *ibid.*, pp. 217-228 and 285-336.

while Mrs. Hutchinson was unjustly sentenced to banishment by the former court, Winthrop has been justly condemned by the latter tribunal of having acted from personal spite and narrow intolerance.

It was not long before the Massachusetts authorities were again called on to deal with heresy. Soon after the expulsion of Mrs. Hutchinson, the Baptists began to come to New England. Rhode Island, owing to its liberal religious policy, became the stronghold of this radical sect. It would be easy for this dangerous heresy to spread to Massachusetts, and the General Court took precautions to prevent such a calamity. A law was passed in 1644 decreeing the penalty of banishment for all who should hold to Baptist doctrines.[49] Six years later three prominent Baptists came to Massachusetts to visit at the home of one of their brethren. While they were there one of them, Dr. John Clarke, gave a religious talk for the benefit of his host and a few friends who had come in to hear him. Before he had finished his sermon he was rudely interrupted by constables, who arrested him and his two companions. They were then brought before the Court of Assistants, and fined after an unfair trial, in the course of which Governor Endicott, who presided over the court, stormed at them like a ruffian.

Persecution of the Baptists

Clarke and one of his companions had their fines paid by friends and were able to return to their homes in Rhode Island. But one of them, Obadiah Holmes, felt called upon to suffer for his faith and refused to accept the offer of a friend to discharge his fine. Consequently, he was given thirty lashes with a three-corded whip. He received this cruel treatment in the beautiful spirit and quiet demeanor of a New Testament martyr.[50]

But it was toward the Friends, or Quakers, as they were called, that Puritan intolerance went to the greatest lengths. The orthodox Puritan regarded the unconventional religious opinions and social practices of these radical mystics not as interesting eccentricities, but as symptoms of a dangerous political and religious heresy. It was only natural, therefore, that the authorities in New

Persecution of the Quakers

---

[49] *Massachusetts Colonial Records*, ii, p. 85; WINTHROP, J., *op. cit.*, ii, pp. 177, 259-260. For the beliefs of the Baptists, see p. 526.

[50] For an account of the arrest, trial, and punishment of these three men, written by Dr. John Clarke, see Massachusetts Historical Society *Collections*, 4th series, ii, pp. 27-32, 37-38, 42-52. For Obadiah Holmes's account of his punishment, see *ibid.*, pp. 45-52.

England should take steps to protect their people from the dangerous contamination of these wild heretics, who were frowned upon by all denominations.

In 1658 the commissioners of the New England Confederation recommended that all of the members of the Confederation expel the Quakers and inflict the death penalty on those that returned.[51] This suggestion was accepted in part by all of the Puritan colonies, and in all of them there were laws providing the penalties of fine, whipping, and banishment for Quakers.[52] In New Haven those that returned after having been expelled three times were to have their tongues bored through with a hot iron.[53] In Massachusetts, the full recommendation of the commissioners was accepted, and in this colony the laws provided the death penalty for Quakers who should return after banishment. Nor was this provision intended merely as a gesture to frighten away these undesirable radicals; for under it four Quakers were executed, one of them being a woman.[54] The Quakers made complaint to the king against the Massachusetts government for its cruel policy toward them, and Charles II wrote to the Massachusetts authorities ordering them to cease inflicting the death penalty and corporal punishment on Quakers. In obedience to this order the General Court omitted these penalties from their laws against Quakers (November, 1661), though corporal punishment was revived against them later.[55] Rhode Island, true to the principles of Roger Williams as to religious freedom, never enacted any laws against Quakers, believing that persecution would only cause them to multiply more rapidly.[56]

[51] New Plymouth Colony Records, x, p. 212.

[52] Ibid., xi, pp. 100-101, 121, 127, 129-130, 177, 205, 206; Connecticut Colony Public Records, i, pp. 283-284, 303, 324; Massachusetts Bay Colonial Records, iv, pp. 277-278, 383, 384, 419.

[53] New Haven Colonial Records, iii, pp. 238-241.

[54] Massachusetts Colonial Records, iv, pp. 383-384, 419. For persecution of Quakers in other colonies, see pp. 529-530.

[55] Ibid., iv, 34, 165-166.

[56] Rhode Island Colonial Records, i, pp. 377, 378, 396-397.

For a contemporary account of the persecution of the Quakers see BISHOP, GEORGE, New England Judged (1703), pp. 47-73, 85-86, 88-95, 112-126 (note especially pp. 121-126), 137-138, 160-166, 172-205. For an excellent modern account, with quotations from and specific references to the sources, see JONES, R. M., The Quakers in the American Colonies, chs. 3-6.

Selected Readings

1. The Great Puritan Exodus.—Andrews, C. M., *The Colonial Period of American History*, ii, *ch. 8.

2. John Winthrop.—Tyler, M. C., *History of American Literature During the Colonial Time*, pp. *128-136; *Old South Leaflets*, no. 77, pp. 9-24; Hart, A. B., *Commonwealth History of Massachusetts*, i, pp. *159-167; Morison, S. E., *Builders of the Bay Colony*, *ch. 3.

3. Mrs. Anne Hutchinson.—Eggleston, E., *op. cit.*, pp. *327-341; Channing, *op. cit.*, i, pp. *368-377; Adams, C. F., *Three Episodes of Massachusetts History*, i, pp. 381-406.

4. The Quakers in New England.—Osgood, H. L., *The American Colonies in the Seventeenth Century*, i, pp. *269-289; Jones, R. M., *The Quakers in the American Colonies*, chs. 3-6; Richman, I. B., *Rhode Island, Its Making and Its Meaning*, ii, pp. *77-102.

5. Persecution of the Baptists in Massachusetts.—Massachusetts Historical Society *Collections*, 4th series, ii, pp. 27-32, 37-38, *42-52 (contemporary accounts); also Richman, *Rhode Island, Its Making and Its Meaning*, pp. *60-77.

6. Social Life in New England.—Ford, J., in the *Commonwealth History of Massachusetts*, i, *ch. 10.

7. Women of Massachusetts.—Tapley, Harriet S., in *Commonwealth History*, i, *ch. 11.

8. The Beginnings of Harvard College.—*Commonwealth History*, i, pp. *342-357.

CHAPTER VIII

THE EXPANSION OF PURITANISM IN NEW ENGLAND

CONNECTICUT

Puritan-
ism
spreads
over New
England

THE establishment of the colonies of New Plymouth and Massachusetts Bay gave Puritanism a firm foothold in America. From
these two starting-points Puritanism spread toward the north,
south, and west into the unoccupied areas of New England. The
reasons for this expansion in the New World were very much
the same as the motives that prompted the original emigration
from the Old. Religious dissent and the desire for economic betterment figured in both movements. The former was an important
factor in the emigration southward and to some extent in that
northward which led to the establishment of settlements in Rhode
Island and New Hampshire, while the latter was the dominant
one in the westward movement that resulted in the formation of
the colonies of Connecticut and New Haven.

The new Puritan commonwealths all bore a family likeness to
the parent republic, Massachusetts, though the similarity was less
marked in some of them than in the others. New Hampshire at
first showed signs of juvenile waywardness, for in the early
years some of her towns did not live up to the family traditions
in either church or state. Later, however, conditions became more
stable, and the northern colony was regarded as a member of the
New England family of commonwealths in good and regular
standing. Rhode Island, however, was considered the black sheep
of the Puritan fold, and at no time did she enjoy the parental
blessing. Connecticut and New Haven, on the other hand, were
dutiful daughters from the beginning, and their political and
religious institutions always bore the stamp of unimpeachable
orthodoxy.

It was not long before the Puritans of Massachusetts Bay and
New Plymouth heard of the Connecticut Valley with its fine
opportunities for trade and farming. It was reported that there
were broad bottoms along the Connecticut River which were

both more fertile and more easily cultivated than were the lands The Con-
of the older settlements. Soon, therefore, the lure of the west necticut
began to make its appeal to the pioneering spirit of the New Valley
Englanders, and they felt impelled to reinforce their claim to this by both
goodly land by occupation. The Dutch, too, appreciated the value the Eng-
of this region and claimed it as a part of New Netherland. These lish and
two rival claimants, therefore, entered into a race for the advan- the Dutch
tage that is conferred by possession.

In the beginning the Dutch ran slightly ahead of their The
opponents, as they were the first to strengthen their title by Dutch
occupation. They bought a tract of land from the Pequot Indians build a
and in 1633 built on it at the present site of Hartford a fortified fort at
post, which they called Fort Good Hope. When this move of the Hartford
Dutch was reported to Governor Winthrop of Massachusetts, he
sent a message to Van Twiller, the Dutch governor of New
Netherland, protesting against his action and asserting the right
of the English to all the Connecticut region. Van Twiller replied
courteously that the question of the ownership of the disputed
territory was a matter to be settled by the British and Dutch
home authorities, and he thought that pending such a settlement
the colonists of both nations should live peaceably as "good
neighbors in these heathenish countries."[1]

The Massachusetts governor took no further action at this
time, but New Plymouth decided to contest the Dutch claim. In
this same year of 1633, shortly after the Dutch had established
themselves at Fort Good Hope, a small party of emigrants from
New Plymouth ascended the river to make a settlement. When
they reached the Dutch post the commander threatened to fire on
them if they did not stop. But they paid no heed to this threat
and went on, landing ten miles farther up at a place later known
as Windsor. Here they hastily erected a building and surrounded
it with a palisade. They were thus in a position to defend themselves against Indian and, if need be, Dutch attack. Soon afterward the authorities at New Amsterdam sent an armed force to
drive the newcomers away, but when they arrived they found that
the English were well fortified and so they went back without
molesting them.[2]

In the meantime a number of farmers in Massachusetts had

[1] BRODHEAD, J. R., *History of the State of New York*, first part,
pp. 234, 238-240; WINTHROP, J., *op. cit.*, i, p. 109.

[2] BRADFORD, WILLIAM, *History of Plymouth Plantation (Original
Narratives)*, pp. 299-302; WINTHROP, J., *op. cit.*, pp. 109-110.

Emigrants from Massachusetts settle on the Connecticut River

become interested in the westward movement started by their Pilgrim brethren and were now anxious to acquire homesteads in the fertile meadows on the Connecticut. So in 1635 a number of people from the Bay Colony moved westward and settled at Wethersfield, Windsor, and Hartford.[3] The following summer (1636) the little river settlements were reinforced by the coming of the entire church congregations from Dorchester,[4] Watertown,

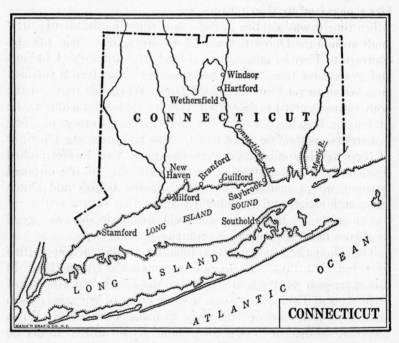

CONNECTICUT

and Newtown, which settled respectively at Windsor, Wethersfield, and Hartford. The Newtown (or Cambridge) congregation was under the leadership of its ministers, Thomas Hooker and Samuel Stone. They marched through the wilderness, driving their hogs and cattle along in true pioneer fashion. Arriving at the Connecticut, after having spent a fortnight in going the one hundred miles, they settled around the Dutch fort. The members of the Roxbury church had also come out and settled at Springfield, higher up on the river. There were now four towns on the

[3] WINTHROP, J., *op. cit.*, i, pp. 132-135; *Massachusetts Bay Colony Records*, i, pp. 146, 148.

[4] BRADFORD, WILLIAM, *History of Plymouth Plantation*, pp. 323-337.

Connecticut: Wethersfield, Hartford, Windsor, and Springfield, the last-named being within the present limits of Massachusetts. In the other three settlements there was by the spring of 1637 a population of about eight hundred.

The Dutch had apparently lost out in the contest for the disputed territory, but they still claimed all the Connecticut region and regarded the English colonists as trespassers. Fort Good Hope remained in Dutch hands for nearly two decades, during which time it was a thorn in the side of the English settlers. The lands around the Dutch fort were not being cultivated, and it was contrary to Puritan ideas of economy to see so much good corn and grass land lying idle. Therefore, the New Englanders encroached upon the Dutch territory from time to time, using it for both farming and grazing purposes.[5] As there was a good deal of friction between the Puritans and their Dutch neighbors, the Connecticut authorities tried to buy these lands, but the governor of New Netherland would not consider their offer. In 1654, when England and Holland were in a state of war, the Connecticut government appropriated all Dutch property within the colony, and so the Dutch lost control of their fort.[6]

The Dutch give up their claim to the Connecticut region

The territory occupied by the Connecticut settlers was owned by a group of Puritan proprietors, among whom were Lord Say and Sele and Lord Brooke. These patentees had been granted the land (1631) by the Earl of Warwick, who is said to have received it from the Council for New England. In the autumn of 1635 the proprietors sent over John Winthrop, Jr., with a commission as governor of "the river Connecticut, with the places adjoining thereunto."[7] Winthrop built a fort at the mouth of the river and garrisoned it with twenty men. The Dutch, too, were planning to seize the mouth of the river, and a vessel from New Amsterdam appeared before the new fort, but seeing that the English had anticipated them, they returned to New Amsterdam without challenging the newcomers. A few years later this military post was made into a plantation and named Saybrook, in honor of the two leading proprietors.[8]

The Saybrook settlement

[5] JAMESON, J. F., ed., *Narratives of New Netherland*, p. 203.

[6] MORGAN, F., and others, *Connecticut as a Colony and as a State*, i, pp. 87, 89, 90, 92, 96.

[7] For text of Winthrop's commission, see TRUMBULL, BENJAMIN, *Complete History of Connecticut to 1764*, i, pp. 497-499.

[8] WINTHROP, J., *op. cit.*, i, p. 308.

The Puritan emigrants to Connecticut were governed for the first year by their leaders acting under a commission granted to them by the Massachusetts General Court.[9] This commission had, of course, no legal force outside of the limits of Massachusetts, and only one of the towns, Springfield, was within the jurisdiction of that colony. But the exact boundaries of Massachusetts were not then known, and the settlers accepted the authority thus constituted without question.

In May, 1637, the inhabitants of the three towns, Windsor, Hartford, and Wethersfield, organized themselves into a self-governing colony known as Connecticut. A General Court was created consisting of six assistants and nine representatives, three from each town.[10] In the following year the General Court, as thus constituted, adopted a number of laws, known as the "Fundamental Orders." They are a sort of constitution, as they provided for the organization of the government, but they did not limit the power of the General Court as the Constitution of the United States restricts the power of Congress. It was formerly held that this constitution was adopted by a vote of the people meeting as a primary assembly, but recent scholarship is not satisfied with the evidence on which this contention is based. The "Fundamental Orders," which recognized no authority of king or Parliament, were "the constitution under which Connecticut was governed for [nearly] two hundred years."[11]

The governmental machinery provided for by this constitution was copied from that of Massachusetts. There was a General Court consisting of the governor, assistants, and deputies. The General Court held two sessions a year. One of these was a primary assembly consisting of all the freemen, at which meeting the governor and assistants were chosen. The other session was for ordinary legislative, judicial, and administrative business, and was attended only by the governor, the assistants, and the depu-

[9] *Massachusetts Colonial Records*, i, pp. 170-171.

[10] *Connecticut Colonial Records*, i, p. 9.

[11] TRUMBULL, B., *Complete History of Connecticut to 1764*, i, p. 100; *Connecticut Colonial Records*, i, pp. 20-21; preamble of the "Fundamental Orders," MORGAN, *op. cit.*, p. 149.

Professor Andrews, who is a very high authority on New England colonial history, doubts whether this constitution was ever adopted by the people. See ANDREWS, C. M., *The Fathers of New England*, pp. 62-63.

ties. Four deputies were chosen from each of the three towns, and other towns were later given representatives by the General Court. It will be seen that the assembly was a representative body from the beginning and was not evolved from the primary assembly as was the case in Plymouth.

In the choice of deputies all the inhabitants of the towns were to have a voice, but in electing the governor and the magistrates no one could vote except those who had been admitted as "freemen" by the General Court. The assembly sat as one body until 1698, when it was divided into two houses, the governor and assistants forming the upper house, and the deputies the lower.[12]

The local government of Connecticut was also quite similar to that of Massachusetts, the township being the chief unit of local administration.

The settlements in Rhode Island and Connecticut had brought the New Englanders into contact with two powerful Indian tribes, the Narragansetts and the Pequots. The former, living in Rhode Island, were friendly because of the kindly treatment accorded them by Roger Williams. But the Pequots were inclined to be unfriendly to the whites from the beginning. The smoldering opposition was stirred into active hostility by a cruel act of injustice on the part of the Massachusetts authorities. In the spring of 1637 war began by an attack by the Indians on Wethersfield. Connecticut was assisted in the war by the Massachusetts authorities and the Indians were completely crushed. At the Mystic River, Captain Mason surprised and captured their stronghold. The wigwams were burned and men, women, and children perished in the flames. Of the four hundred Indians in the fort all but five were killed, and this great victory was won with the loss of only two white men.[13]

The Pequot War

[12] The text of the "Fundamental Orders" is given in MORGAN, F., *First Settlements in Connecticut*, pp. 149-155.

[13] For three accounts of the Pequot War written by men who participated in it, see Massachusetts Historical Society *Collections*. Captain Mason's account is given in the 2nd series, viii, pp. 130-153; Lion Gardiner's, in the 3rd series, iii, pp. 36-160; Captain John Underhill's, in the 3rd series, vi, pp. 3-28.

The Pequots tried to win over as allies their old enemies, the Narragansetts. If they had succeeded, not only the Connecticut towns, but all the other settlements in New England, would have been in danger from Indian attack. They were defeated in this endeavor by

The Pequots were so thoroughly defeated that the nation was completely destroyed, and the two hundred survivors were absorbed by the Mohegans and the Narragansetts. The captives, men, women, and children, were enslaved. Some of them were kept in New England and some were sold into the West Indies. This terrible victory relieved the Connecticut settlers from danger from the Indians for forty years, and removed the barrier to further expansion. Other settlements were now made and by the middle of the century (1653) the colony of Connecticut contained twelve towns, one of them being on Long Island.

New Haven

The founding of New Haven

Soon after the Pequot War was over, the second colony within the present limits of Connecticut was established. This plantation was founded by a number of English Puritans under the leadership of John Davenport, a minister, and Theophilus Eaton, a wealthy merchant. They came to America to establish a new Puritan commonwealth, which, they hoped, would develop into a profitable trading community. They landed in Boston in the summer of 1637 while the Antinomian controversy was raging, and

---

Roger Williams, who had great influence with the Narragansetts because of the justice and fairness that had always characterized his dealings with them. When Governor Vane of Massachusetts called on him to use his influence with the Narragansetts against the Pequot alliance, he set out, "all alone in a poore canow, and to cut through a stormie wind with great seas, every minute in hazard of life, to the Sachem's house." When he appeared before Miantonomoh and Canonicus, the Narragansett chiefs, he found messengers from the Pequots already on the ground. But he succeeded in persuading his friends against joining the Pequots and they became allies of the whites. In performing this great service to New England Roger Williams was actuated partly by the desire to do a good turn for his friend (Governor Vane) and partly by the wish to protect the Rhode Island settlement from disaster. We are bound to believe, however, that he was moved to a considerable extent by the spirit of magnanimity that takes pleasure in returning good for evil. This noble deed must have had the effect of heaping coals of fire on the heads of his old enemies. Apparently they were deeply humiliated by the necessity of calling on him, for only one of the Massachusetts writers of that day mentions the part played by Williams on this occasion. See Williams's letter to Mason, Massachusetts Historical Society *Collections*, 1st series, i, p. 277.

Davenport was drawn into it as an able defender of the orthodox position. As their company of about fifty families included a number of large landholders and wealthy merchants, all of the Puritan belief, the Massachusetts authorities gave them a warm welcome and offered them every inducement to settle within their jurisdiction. This they declined to do as they wanted to carry out their original plan of founding a separate community. Doubtless, too, the Antinomian heresy, with which Massachusetts at this time was so deeply tainted, jarred uncomfortably on their orthodoxy and created an atmosphere that was uncongenial to them.[14]

They remained at Boston, however, until the next spring, and in the meantime they had sought out and found a suitable location for settlement. The place selected was known by the Indians as Quinnipiack, which was on a good harbor on Long Island Sound, thirty miles west of the mouth of the Connecticut River. In the spring of 1638 they laid out their town on lands that had been purchased from the Indians, and to it they gave the name of New Haven. Large and stately houses were erected on streets that crossed one another at right angles and divided the town into nine equal squares, with an ample market space in the center.

The little republic naturally looked to Davenport and Eaton for leadership, and the latter played a rôle in New Haven similar to that of John Winthrop in Massachusetts. He was chosen the first governor and was annually reëlected until the year of his death, a period of seventeen years. Other settlements were soon made, and these had by 1644 all federated with the town of New Haven to form the colony of New Haven. The government organized for the enlarged state was modeled after that of the Bay Colony. Church membership was a requisite for voting, and there was no provision for trial by jury, probably because such a practice was unknown to the Mosaic law.[15]

Establishment of the government

There were thus two autonomous republics within the present limits of Connecticut, each having a government based on a written constitution. These governments, however, rested on no

[14] WINTHROP, J., *op. cit.*, i, pp. 223, 230-231, 247, 265.

[15] For the organization of the government, see *New Haven Colonial Records*, i, pp. 11-16, 20-21, 110 n., 112. For the text of the constitution of the colony, see ATWATER, E. E., *History of New Haven*, pp. 185-188; also *New Haven Colonial Records*, i, pp. 112-116. See also CALDER, ISABEL M., "John Cotton and the New Haven Colony," an article in the *New England Quarterly*, iii, pp. 82-94.

legal basis, as they had never been authorized by any properly constituted authority.[16] Moreover, New Haven had no patent conferring title to her lands, and there was reason for questioning the grant that had been made to Connecticut. It is true that in both jurisdictions the lands had been bought from the Indians, but these purchases conferred no title in English law.

During the Civil War, the home authorities were inclined to let the little commonwealths in New England go their own way, but when Charles II came to the throne (1660), the situation changed decidedly. The Connecticut settlers tried to win the king's favor and secure a charter that would legalize their government and confirm them in the possession of their lands. Their governor, John Winthrop, Jr., was sent to England to present the case of the colony and, if possible, obtain a royal patent.[17] Through his efforts a charter was secured (1662),[18] which granted to Connecticut all the land from the boundary of Massachusetts south to the Atlantic and from the Narragansett River west to the Pacific Ocean. This grant was made in utter disregard of the claims of New Netherland and New Haven. The charter also conferred upon the colonists the right to govern this territory. It

[16] In 1632, the Earl of Warwick, then president of the Council for New England, deeded the land between the Narragansett Bay and the Connecticut River to Lord Say and Sele, Lord Brooke, and some other prominent Puritans. These grantees are known as the Warwick Patentees. The early settlers in Connecticut based their rights to the land on an understanding with the Warwick Patentees. Professor Andrews questioned the validity of the grant to the Warwick Patentees because there is no evidence that the Earl of Warwick had received a patent from the Council for New England for this land. But even if the deed to the Connecticut pioneers was valid as to landed rights it did not furnish a legal basis for the establishment of a government. Later (1644) one of the Warwick Patentees sold to the Connecticut colony the town of Saybrook to which he had a rather doubtful claim. ANDREWS, C. M., *The Colonial Period of American History,* ii, pp. 77, 120 ff., 128, note; COLEMAN, R. V., *The Old Patent of Connecticut;* LOVE, W. D., *The Colonial History of Hartford,* pp. 17-23; *Connecticut Colonial Records,* i, pp. 266-270; *Massachusetts Bay Colony Records,* i, pp. 170-171.

[17] *Connecticut Colonial Records,* i, p. 367. For Winthrop's instructions, see *ibid.,* i, pp. 580-581.

[18] This charter is given in part in WEST, W. M., *Source Book in American History,* pp. 290-293; in full in THORPE, F. N., *Colonial Charters,* i, pp. 529-536.

made no change in the form of government already established, but only gave it a legal basis. The New Haven towns on the mainland were included within the boundaries established by this charter. New Haven was therefore absorbed by Connecticut and ceased to exist as a separate colony.

We are at a loss to explain how Charles was induced to confer such a favor on a group of Puritans, especially when we remember that the grant carried with it the recognition of the virtual autonomy of an American commonwealth. A partial explanation lies in the character of the agent sent over by Connecticut, John Winthrop, Jr., who was a worthy son of the Massachusetts statesman.[19] He was well educated, widely traveled, and had a very attractive personality. From his experience and knowledge of the world he had gained a polish which rendered his contacts with others easy and agreeable. He therefore "knew how to speak to a Stuart in his own language."[20]

John Winthrop, Jr.

RHODE ISLAND

The colony of Rhode Island and Providence Plantations was founded by religious radicals who could not conform to Puritan doctrine and practice in Massachusetts. Their attitude toward Puritanism in New England was like that of the Puritans toward Anglicanism in Old England. In the colony of Massachusetts, where Puritanism was quickly standardized into a stereotyped orthodoxy, these new nonconformists came in conflict with the established order and were excluded from the commonwealth. Roger Williams was one of the early leaders of these new dissenters and the pioneer of the expansive movement southward. On being expelled from the Bay Colony, he took refuge with the Narragansett Indians, from whose chiefs, Canonicus and Miantónomoh, he procured a small boundary of land at the head of Narragansett Bay.[21] Here in the spring of 1636 he and a few friends planted a settlement, to which he gave the name of Provi-

The founding of Providence

[19] The place of the younger Winthrop in the public life of Connecticut was very much the same as that held by his father in the Bay Colony, and the people of Connecticut showed their high regard for him by electing him governor for seventeen successive terms (MORISON, S. E., *Builders of the Bay Colony*, p. 283).

[20] *Ibid.*, p. 284.

[21] For Williams's account of his movements after leaving Salem, see *Publications of the Narragansett Club*, vi, p. 335. See also CHAPIN, H. M., ed., *Documentary History of Rhode Island*, 1916, pp. 19, 28.

dence because he regarded the opportunity to settle down and enjoy his religious convictions without molestation as a special favor of Providence.[22] This was the first permanent settlement made within the present limits of Rhode Island.[23]

Organization of the government in Providence

These first settlers had no authority to establish a government. They were, therefore, in the same situation as were the Pilgrim Fathers when they landed at Plymouth. Like the Pilgrims, these Providence men entered into a compact pledging obedience to all laws and regulations that should be made by a majority of the householders, but "only in civil affairs."[24] The government thus established was a pure democracy and was carried on by all the heads of families meeting once in a fortnight for the settling of any administrative, legislative, and judicial questions that might arise. Under this arrangement there was perfect freedom in religion and a minimum of restraint in civil affairs.[25]

The infant colony was not equal to the responsibility of so much freedom, and sometimes the settlers allowed their liberty to degenerate into license. In the early years Providence was a sort of Adullam's Cave, to which the dissatisfied and undesirable element from the orthodox communities had resorted, and Williams's influence was not always strong enough to restrain this motley crowd and keep it within the bounds of law and order. At one time conditions were so unsettled that he compared the disorderly society to a "tertian ague."

Portsmouth

The next two settlements in the Narragansett region were made by the followers of Mrs. Anne Hutchinson on the island of Aquidneck, later known as Rhode Island. The first of these was made by a group of eighteen persons under the leadership of William Coddington at Portsmouth on the northern part of the island. They, too, entered into a plantation covenant, agreeing to be governed by the principles of the Bible. The governmental machinery to be employed in applying these principles to daily life was closely modeled after that of Massachusetts. The chief official, however, was given the title, not of governor, as in

---

[22] *Ibid.*, 1916, pp. 17-23.

[23] One white man, William Blackstone, was already living in the Narragansett region when Williams settled at Providence (ADAMS, J. T., *The Founding of New England*, p. 184).

[24] The text of this agreement is given in CARPENTER, E. J., *Roger Williams*, p. 134. see also CHAPIN, *op. cit.*, 1916, pp. 37-38, 45.

[25] *Ibid.*, 1916, pp. 32-33.

Massachusetts, but of judge, according to Old Testament usage.[26] Mrs. Hutchinson, who had settled at Portsmouth, soon discovered that she was still within the reach of the Massachusetts authorities, for a meddling committee from Boston came to the island to probe into her religious belief and bring her to repentance.[27] Moreover, her restless spirit did not settle down into quiet contentment in her new home, and after the death of her

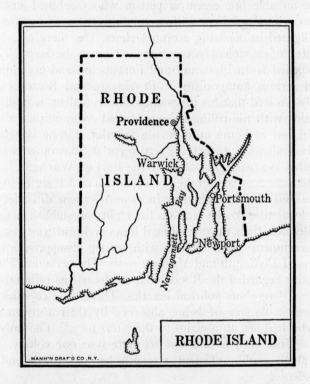

RHODE
Providence
Warwick
ISLAND
Narragansett Bay
Portsmouth
Newport

RHODE ISLAND

MANH'N DRAF'G CO .N.Y.

husband she left Rhode Island and moved to the western end of Long Island, within the jurisdiction of the Dutch. She had now escaped the annoying inquisitions of the Boston clergy but had run into a greater danger. The Indians, who were at war with the Dutch, made an attack on her home and killed her and nearly all of her family (1643).[28]

The extreme individualism that had brought the Hutchin-

[26] *Ibid.*, 1916, pp. 49-52, 59; *ibid.*, 1919, pp. 16-19, 21, 69.
[27] *Ibid.*, 1919, pp. 87-90.
[28] WINTHROP, J., *op. cit.*, ii, pp. 138, 276-277.

Newport

sonians into trouble in Massachusetts bred dissensions in this their own little Bible commonwealth, and soon there was a secession from Portsmouth. The malcontents moved to the southern part of the island and established a plantation, which they called Newport.[29]

Warwick

A fourth plantation was established on the western shore of Narragansett Bay, twelve miles from Providence, by Samuel Gorton, an able but eccentric person who combined unconventional religious opinions with a combativeness of temperament that delighted in opposing accepted views. He, therefore, became the center of a violent controversy wherever he went. He had been expelled from Plymouth and Portsmouth and his views had aroused serious antagonism in Providence and Boston. Gorton probably realized that his pronounced individualism would always be at odds with the ruling class in settled communities, and that he could feel at home only on the frontier, for he bought land from the Indians and started a settlement at Shawomet, which he later called Warwick, in honor of the Earl of Warwick.[30]

The federation of the four colonies

There were now within the present limits of Rhode Island four separate and distinct colonies. In none of them did the people have a legal title to the land or the right to establish a government. Besides, their unconventional ideas and practices in religion and government were viewed with strong disapproval by the Puritans of Plymouth and Massachusetts. The orthodox Puritans of that day regarded the Rhode Island colonists as religious anarchists and dangerous political heretics. These little colonies were, therefore, in danger of being absorbed by their Puritan neighbors, who had set up a claim to their territory.[31] The only safeguard against such a fate was to unite into one colony, for in union alone could sufficient strength be had to defend their independence.

The first step toward federation was taken in 1640, when the two island settlements united under one government.[32] Later Roger Williams was sent to England by Providence and the island plantations to secure a charter that would unite them and

[29] CHAPIN, op. cit., 1919, pp. 55-60, 69.

[30] Ibid., 1916, pp. 168-169, 187-188, 192-197; HART, A. B., American History Told by Contemporaries, i, pp. 398-401; GORTON, S., Simplicities Defence, pp. 73-75, 83-84.

[31] CHAPIN, op. cit., 1916, pp. 227, 229-230.

[32] Ibid., 1919, pp. 94-96.

place them on a firm legal basis.[33] The Civil War had begun before the arrival of Williams in England, and he conducted his negotiations with the commissioners to whom Parliament had delegated the management of colonial affairs. He succeeded in getting from the commissioners (1644) a charter which gave the Rhode Island colonies a legal title to their lands and the right to federate and form a joint government.[34] Three years later (1647) the voters from Providence, Newport, and Portsmouth acted upon the charter and formed a union, to which Warwick was admitted.

The government thus established was modeled after that of Massachusetts. There was to be a governor or president; a board of four assistants, one from each colony; and an assembly composed of representatives from each of the four colonies. All of these were to be elected annually by the freeholders. The charter conferred upon the inhabitants the right to make laws, which must conform as far as possible to those of England. The Rhode Island government had two novel features. There was a provision for the initiative and referendum. The voters in any town could propose measures, which would become laws on being confirmed by the legislature; and those proposed by the assembly might be accepted or rejected by the freeholders of the towns.

Government of the confederation

The troubles of the colony did not end, however, when the charter was secured. As the population consisted largely of the "otherwise minded"—people who held tenaciously to their opinions and valued liberty more highly than order and security— dissensions were still rife, and the settlements were split with feuds and arrayed against each other by jealousies. The little commonwealth had a checkered career until 1663, when the government was put on a firm basis by another charter, granted this time by Charles II. This second charter was necessary because Charles could hardly be expected to recognize as legal a patent granted by a rebellious Parliament that was responsible for the execution of his father. So Rhode Island through her agent, Dr. John Clarke, petitioned the crown for a new charter. Charles was favorably inclined to this request because the granting of it would aid him in curbing the ambitions of Massachusetts and enable him to reward the loyalty of the little colony, which had been so

The second charter

[33] *Ibid.*, 1916, pp. 163-164, 212.

[34] For text of this charter see *ibid.*, 1916, pp. 214-217; also *Rhode Island Colonial Records*, i, pp. 143-146.

prompt in welcoming him to the throne. The government established by the royal charter was virtually the same as that under which they had all along been living. The new patent had a provision that no one should be in "any wise molested, punished, disquieted, or called in question for any differences of opinion in matters of religion." This charter was so well suited to the people of Rhode Island that it served as their colonial and state constitution until 1842.[35]

For the provision in the patent regarding religious freedom the credit is due not to the king or his advisers, but to the Rhode Island settlers, who had already practiced the principle before it had been embodied in the charter. To Roger Williams more than to anyone else do we owe this important step toward religious freedom. He was the first man in America who taught and practiced the modern doctrine of complete religious tolerance and that of the entire separation of church and state. To this idea of religious liberty he adhered not only when he was the victim of intolerance, but also with equal firmness when he was in a position to make others suffer for their beliefs. His attitude toward the Quakers illustrates this. He abhorred the doctrines of this sect, but was strongly opposed to the state's taking any measures against them. The Rhode Islanders were indoctrinated by him with these broad views, and it is to them that we are indebted for this important chapter in the history of religious liberty in America.[36]

[35] For the text of the charter, slightly abbreviated, see MacDonald, W., *Select Charters*, pp. 126-133.

[36] The following statement, in Williams's own words, shows that his idea as to the relation of church and state was identical with ours today:

"That ever I should speak or write a Tittle that tends to such infinite Liberty of Conscience, is a Mistake; and which I have ever disclaimed and abhorred. To prevent such Mistakes, I at present shall only propose this Case. . . . There goes many a Ship to Sea, with many a Hundred Souls in one Ship, whose Weal and Woe is common: and is a true Picture of a Common-Wealth, or an human Combination, or Society. It hath fallen out sometimes, that both *Papists* and *Protestants*, *Jews* and *Turks*, may be embarqued into one Ship. Upon which Supposal, I do affirm, that all the Liberty of Conscience that ever I pleaded for, turns upon these two Hinges, that none of the *Papists, Protestants, Jews* or *Turks,* be forced to come to the Ship's Prayers or Worship: nor secondly, compelled from their own

New Hampshire

The first settlement in New Hampshire was made by David Thomson in 1623 at Little Harbor, on the site of the present town of Rye. Three years later Thomson left New Hampshire for Boston, and it is uncertain whether the plantation was deserted or was merged into the colony founded a few years later on or near the same site and known at first as Strawberry Bank and later as Portsmouth. Another settlement was planted in New Hampshire on the Piscataqua in the sixteen-twenties.[37] This was at Dover, some miles above Portsmouth. In the latter part of the next decade Puritanism began its expansive movement northward, and Puritan emigrants, both heterodox and orthodox, began to come into this region from Massachusetts. In 1638 John Wheelwright, a follower of Anne Hutchinson, who had been exiled from Massachusetts at the time of the Antinomian controversy, led a party of thirty-five fellow-heretics and settled at Exeter, where they established an orderly government and for three years maintained an independent jurisdiction. Soon

---

particular Prayers or Worship, if they practice any. I further add, that I never denied, that notwithstanding this Liberty, the Commander of this Ship ought to command the Ship's Course; Yea, and also command that Justice, Peace, and Sobriety, be kept and practiced, both among the Seamen and all the Passengers. If any Seaman refuse to perform their Service, or Passengers to pay their Freight; . . . if any refuse to help in Person or Purse, towards the Common Charges, or Defence; . . . if any refuse to obey the common Laws and Orders of the Ship, concerning their common Peace and Preservation; . . . if any shall mutiny and rise up against their Commanders, and Officers; . . . if any shall preach or write, that there ought to be no Commanders, nor Officers, because all are equal in Christ, therefore no Masters, nor Officers, no Laws, nor Orders, no Corrections, nor Punishments . . . I say, I never denied, but in such Cases, whatever is pretended, the Commander or Commanders may judge, resist, compel, and punish such Transgressors according to their Deserts and Merits" (CHAPIN, op. cit., 1916, p. 35).

For a good contemporary account of the views of Roger Williams and of his career in New England, see MORTON, NATHANIEL, New England's Memoriall, 1669 (ed. by Arthur Lord, 1903), pp. 78-81.

[37] Some authorities think that Dover was settled in 1623. Others think it was established a few years later.

afterward some orthodox Puritans from Massachusetts founded the town of Hampton as an outpost of the Bay Colony.[38]

Maine and New Hampshire granted to Mason and Gorges

In the meantime virtually all of the present states of Maine and New Hampshire had been granted by the Council for New England to Sir Ferdinando Gorges and Captain John Mason and their associates. In 1629 Mason and Gorges divided their terri-

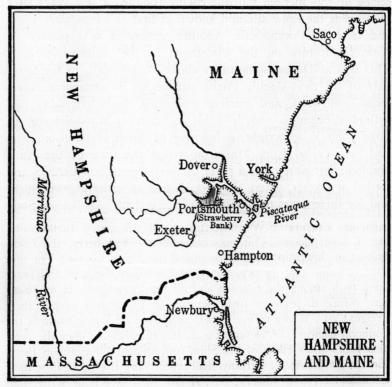

tory, the former taking the portion south and west of the Piscataqua and the latter that between this river and the Kennebec. Mason's possessions received the name of New Hampshire in honor of his native shire in England.[39]

[38] For contemporary accounts of the planting of these early settlements, see *New Hampshire Provincial Papers*, i, pp. 108-109, 118-126, 128-137, 146-153.

[39] *Massachusetts Colonial Records*, i, pp. 236, 259; *New Hampshire Provincial Papers*, i, pp. 10-15; JENNESS, J. S., *Documents Relating to the History of New Hampshire*, pp. 3-7.

The religious differences between the early New Hampshire towns were too great to permit of a voluntary federation into one commonwealth such as was later made in Rhode Island. Portsmouth was Anglican in religion and Dover was both Anglican and Puritan. Exeter and Hampton were both Puritan, though the early settlers in the former were heterodox in belief. Hampton had from the beginning recognized the jurisdiction of Massachusetts and was sending a representative to Boston to the General Court. The other three had each adopted a plantation covenant and had thus set up an independent jurisdiction. But these little states were not strong enough to stand alone, and Massachusetts seized the opportunity of extending her protection and authority over these weak communities.

Massachu setts asserts authority over the northern towns

By the terms of the royal charter (1629) the northern boundary of Massachusetts was defined as three miles north of the Merrimac River "or to the northward of any and every part thereof." Massachusetts interpreted this clause as giving her a just claim to all the territory south of a line drawn from a point three miles north of the most northerly reach of the Merrimac River eastward to the Atlantic Ocean and westward to the Pacific. Such an interpretation would put all of the New Hampshire-Maine settlements within her jurisdiction. The heirs of Mason protested against this claim, but were unable to prevent the Bay Colony from gaining control of these northern towns. The case of Puritan Massachusetts was strengthened and that of the Mason proprietors weakened by the struggle that was then going on in England between the king and the Puritan party. The New Hampshire settlements (1641-43) accepted the authority of Massachusetts, and so were placed under her jurisdiction.[40] Robert Mason, the grandson and legatee of Captain John Mason, protested against this assumption of authority on the part of the Bay Colony as an infringement upon his proprietary rights. Massachusetts, however, paid no heed to this complaint and continued to assert her authority over the New Hampshire settlements for about thirty-six years. These northern towns were allowed to send representatives to the General Court at Boston, but the requirement of church membership for voting was not imposed upon them.

The question as to the authority of the Bay Colony over New

[40] *New Hampshire Provincial Papers*, i, pp. 131, 155-156, 158-160.

Hampshire was finally brought up before the Lords Chief Justices of the King's Bench and Common Pleas, who decided (1677) that Massachusetts had no jurisdiction over New Hampshire. Two years later (1679) the king made New Hampshire a separate royal province. The colony became a part of the Dominion of New England in 1686 and remained under this jurisdiction until the downfall of Andros (1689). There was then a period of uncertainty in the government for a while, but in 1692 the royal authority was reëstablished and was continued from that time until the Revolution. Like the other crown colonies, New Hampshire had a governor and council appointed by the king and an assembly elected by the people. After 1692 New Hampshire had no connection with Massachusetts except that from 1699 to 1741 both provinces had the same governor.

MAINE

In the region east of the Piscataqua River there were only a few English settlements prior to 1640. In 1639 Gorges received a charter from the king which confirmed his claim to this territory, enlarged his grant, and conferred upon him powers of government similar to those enjoyed by the proprietor of Maryland.[41] He outlined a scheme of government for his colony which was ludicrously elaborate, considering the small number of people to whom it applied. His attempt to establish a strong proprietary province in New England was not successful. Massachusetts was able to make good her claim to the Maine settlements, and between 1652 and 1658 she annexed all of them. By 1672 she had extended her authority to the Penobscot River. Ferdinando Gorges, a grandson of the first patentee, contested the claim of the Bay Colony and put up a stiff fight with the British authorities for his rights. Finally in 1677 the Privy Council decided against Massachusetts, and she thereupon bought out the heirs of Gorges. From this time until 1691 she ruled Maine under the authority of a proprietor. When the new charter was granted to Massachusetts in 1691, Maine was joined with her and the northern limits were pushed up to the St. Croix River. From this time until long after the Revolution (1820) Maine remained under the jurisdiction of Massachusetts.

[41] For the text of this charter, see LIBBY, C. T., ed., *Province and Court Records of Maine*, i, pp. 9-29.

THE NEW ENGLAND CONFEDERATION

Events in England just prior to the Puritan Revolution kept the English king so busy that New England was neglected and the colonies were virtually independent. During the Commonwealth period the Puritan authorities in the homeland were not inclined to restrict the liberties of their coreligionists in America, and so they did not molest the New England colonies in the enjoyment of their independence. These plantations continued to increase in number, and New England was thus gradually developing into a group of little self-governing republics. By the end of the fourth decade of the seventeenth century there were four independent colonies within the present limits of Rhode Island and two each within the present states of Connecticut and Massachusetts. *New England tends to split up into small states*

This was an undesirable tendency, and if it had not been checked it would have rendered the New England settlements too weak to cope with the dangers that environed them. There were three ways by which this tendency might be arrested. One was for the British government to assert its power and unite all of these settlements under its authority; another was for one strong colony to absorb the others; and the third was to form a bigger political unit by federation. *How this tendency was arrested*

The first of these methods was not attempted until after the Restoration. In the meantime both of the others were tried. Massachusetts claimed the territory occupied by the Maine and New Hampshire colonists, and was able to make good this claim, temporarily as to the latter and permanently as to the former. She also showed an aggressive attitude toward her other neighbors. It was by the third method that the four plantations of Rhode Island were federated into a commonwealth, and the Puritan colonies were united to form the New England Confederation.

Controversies had arisen between the Puritan colonies over boundaries and trade, and there was always the possible danger from attack by the Dutch, the French, and the Indians. It was, therefore, desirable that they devise some plan whereby they might coöperate more effectively for the amicable settlement of disputes among themselves and for mutual protection against the common enemy. Such coöperation was made possible by the fact that all the Puritan colonies had the same political and religious *Circumstances favorable to the formation of the Confederation* ideals and maintained almost identical political and ecclesiastical organizations. The only barrier, therefore, that separated them was distance. This obstacle was great enough to render impracticable a union into one commonwealth, but it did permit of a federation of states. Moreover, the dispute that had begun between the king and Parliament was in the early 'forties paralyzing the home government and rendering it unable to afford protection to the New England colonies or to prevent their taking such action as they desired. The times were, therefore, favorable for the formation of a league of friendship.

Members of the Confederation

Such a league was formed in 1643. It was composed of the colonies of Connecticut, New Haven, New Plymouth, and Massachusetts. The settlements in Maine were not admitted because, as Winthrop says, of the disorderly character of their government.[42] But probably the main reason was the desire on the part of Massachusetts to annex this district, which purpose would be frustrated if Maine were recognized as a separate colony. This desire of future annexation was also probably the reason for refusing to admit Rhode Island to the Confederation, though the orthodox Puritan colonies had a strong feeling of dislike for the southern province because of the political and religious heresy of its inhabitants.[43]

Purpose of the union and powers of the Confederation

The name of the union was that of "The United Colonies of New England." The Confederation was to be "a firm and perpetual league of friendship and amity, for offence and defence, mutual advice and succor upon all just occasions, both for preserving and propagating the truths and liberties of the Gospel, and for their own mutual safety and welfare." The governmental machinery of the league consisted of eight commissioners, two from each colony. The commissioners were appointed by the General Courts and all must be church members. They were to hold one regular meeting each year and extra sessions at such times as occasion might require. These meetings were to be held alternately in the principal towns of the member colonies. The commissioners had power to declare war, make peace, divide the spoils of war, and apportion quotas of men and financial burdens among the members. They were also "authorized to take measures for the prevention of quarrels between the colonies; to see that escaped servants, prisoners, and fugitives from justice, flee-

[42] WINTHROP, J., *op. cit.*, ii, pp. 98-99.
[43] ADAMS, J. T., *The Founding of New England*, p. 227.

ing from one colony to another should be returned, that the administration of justice should be speedy and sure; and that Indian affairs should be justly regulated." Six affirmative votes were necessary for all decisions. When this number of commissioners could not agree upon a measure it was to be submitted to the General Courts of the member states.[44]

This union was a loose confederation. Its decisions were really only advisory, as it had no power to carry them out or to raise the revenue that was necessary to enforce them. It helped, however, toward bringing about a certain measure of unity of action between the New England colonies and was an interesting experiment in American federation. It lasted for forty years and was of some use in promoting coöperation against the Indians in King Philip's War.[45] — Nature of the union

One bar to the success of the experiment was the great inequality of the members as to importance and population, coupled with their equality in the league. Massachusetts had a population greater than the other three members combined, and was not always willing to accept the decisions of the other three. In 1653 the commissioners voted a war against the Dutch of New Netherland on the ground that they were conspiring with the Indians against the Connecticut colonists. In the war Massachusetts would have had to contribute more men and money than all three of the other confederates, although she was remote from the danger. Besides, she did not consider the evidence sufficient to convict the Dutch of the charge. Consequently, she refused to abide by the decision of the commissioners, reserving for herself the right to determine whether the league had exceeded its authority. From this time on the General Court of Massachusetts claimed and exercised the right to judge for itself whether or not the decisions of the commissioners were "just according to God" and therefore whether they should be obeyed or disregarded. The prestige and influence of the confederacy were greatly weakened by having its acts thus nullified by its most important member. — The Confederation weakened by action of Massachusetts

Despite this loss of prestige the commissioners continued to meet regularly once a year until 1664. In that year New Haven was absorbed by Connecticut, and the membership of the Con- — Later history of the Confederation

[44] For the text of the Articles of Confederation, see MacDonald, W., *Select Charters*, pp. 94-101.

[45] For acts of the Commissioners of the Confederation from 1643 to 1679, see *Plymouth Colony Records*, ix and x.

federation was reduced to three. Moreover, Charles II was firmly seated on his throne by this time and was able to protect his colonies in New England from external attack and to settle disputes arising between them. There was thus less need for an agency like the Confederation to perform these functions. Besides, the king looked with disfavor upon a political organization that ignored him and acted as if New England was independent. For these reasons the regular meetings were now made triennial. These continued until 1684, when Massachusetts lost her charter and the Confederation came to an end.

KING PHILIP'S WAR

At the beginning of the last quarter of the seventeenth century strife arose between the whites and the savages in a number of the colonies. In New England this friction culminated in the outbreak known as King Philip's War, and in Virginia it led to the Indian troubles which brought on Bacon's Rebellion. These Indian wars were the conflicts of two economic systems. The chief occupation of the Indians was hunting, which called for wide forests and scanty population; the main occupation of the English was agriculture, which demanded cleared areas and the sacrifice of the forest. These two antagonistic economic systems cannot exist side by side, and so war between their champions was inevitable. As the English population kept increasing and the area of cleared lands encroached more and more on the original forest, the native saw his hunting-grounds gradually shrinking. The economic basis of his very existence was thus being undermined, and self-preservation demanded that the foreigner be driven out.

Part played by Philip

In New England the struggle at this time was the most bloody and prolonged that occurred in any of the colonies. It was called King Philip's War after Philip, a prominent leader of one of the belligerent tribes.[46] The New Englanders incurred the enmity of

---

[46] There are a number of contemporary accounts of King Philip's War. The best of these are given in LINCOLN, C. H., ed., *Narratives of the Indian Wars*, pp. 7-167. Longer accounts, but not so impartial, are HUBBARD, WILLIAM, *The History of the Indian Wars in New England*, 2 vols. (most of the work is devoted to Philip's War; first published in 1677; edited by DRAKE, S. G., 1865); and CHURCH, THOMAS, *The Entertaining History of Philip's War* (first published in 1716; edited by DRAKE and published in 1827). *The Old Indian*

Philip by their unfairness and lack of tact in dealing with him, and had aroused general dissatisfaction among the red men by the high-handed way in which they had treated them. The land-hunger of the Puritans was leading them into a policy of encroachment upon the Indian lands. The savages were brought under their strict laws and were punished when they violated them, the penalties often taking the form of land confiscations. The Indians also viewed with alarm the rapid growth of the white population in New England, which was now four times as great as their own. The English settlements were also so situated that the Indians were virtually surrounded by them.[47]

The time was thus ripe for a united effort on the part of the natives against their white rivals. All that was needed to start the conflict was a leader, and so the hour for Philip's revenge had struck. He negotiated with the chiefs of other tribes and planned a simultaneous uprising of all of them in New England. The war started by an attack of the Wampanoags on Swanzea (June, 1675). It spread rapidly and soon the savages throughout New England were in arms against their English neighbors.

The war was poorly managed by the latter; they had no able leaders and it was difficult to get enough soldiers. But the odds, both as to resources and numbers, were overwhelmingly against the Indians, and in little more than a year the backbone of the war was broken (1676). It lasted two years longer in the frontier districts of Maine and New Hampshire, being terminated there by a treaty (1678) by which the whites agreed to pay tribute to the Indians. Defeat of the Indians

The victorious Puritans took a heavy revenge on the conquered foe. Philip's body was quartered and hung up on trees, and those of the captives who were considered most guilty were executed, while some were parceled out among the New Englanders as servants, and others were sent to the West Indies and sold into slavery. Among this latter class were the wife and nine-year-old son of Philip.

The war subjected the resources of New England to a heavy

Chronicle, edited by DRAKE (1867), is a collection of tracts written at the time of Philip's War. Some of these are reprinted in ANDREWS, C. M., ed., Narratives of the Insurrections.

[47] For a contemporary account of the causes and results of King Philip's War, see HART, A. B., American History Told by Contemporaries, i, pp. 458-460.

strain. It was especially severe on the frontier districts, and it took Maine fifty years to recover from it. In New England generally, one-sixteenth of the men of military age had been killed. "In Massachusetts sixteen towns were wholly destroyed, or abandoned, and four in Rhode Island."[48] However, the damage, except for Maine, was temporary, and a permanent gain had been

Results won by greatly weakening the Indian menace and removing the barrier to expansion. It was fortunate for the New Englanders that the Indian danger came at this time rather than fifteen years later. For at the latter date the French were fighting the English, and the savages would have been reinforced by allies that would have rendered them doubly formidable.

Selected Readings

1. First Settlements in Connecticut.—Morgan, F., and others, editors, *Connecticut as a Colony and as a State,* i, *chs. 4 and 5; Palfrey, J. G., *History of New England,* i, pp. *445-454.

2. Adoption of the "Fundamental Orders."—Osgood, H. L., *American Colonies in the Seventeenth Century,* i, pp. 305-307; Andrews, C. M., *Fathers of New England,* pp. *61-64.

3. Thomas Hooker.—Parrington, V. L., *The Colonial Mind,* pp. *53-62.

4. John Winthrop, Jr.—Morison, S. E., *Builders of the Bay Colony,* *ch. 9.

5. How the People Lived in Early Days.—Clark, G. L., *A History of Connecticut,* *ch. 8.

6. The Rise and Fall of the New Haven Colony.—Andrews, C. M., *The Colonial Period of American History,* ii, ch. 5.

7. The "Blue Laws" of New Haven.—Morgan, *op. cit.,* i, *ch. 23. (For these laws as given by Dr. Peters, see Peters, S., *General History of Connecticut* (1877 ed.), pp. 57-61.)

8. Religion and Morals in the New Haven Colony.—Atwater, E. E., *History of the Colony of New Haven,* *ch. 12.

9. Domestic and Social Life in New Haven.—Atwater, *op. cit.,* *ch. 16.

10. The Stuarts and the Regicides.—Atwater, *op. cit.,* ch. 18.

[48] ADAMS, J. T., *The Founding of New England,* p. 363.
For a list of the towns attacked in Philip's War, with a statement as to the number of lives lost and the amount of property destroyed in each, see HUBBARD, WILLIAM, *Indian Wars,* ii, pp. 39-54. A fine brief summary (by a contemporary) of the damage done in the war is given in LINCOLN, ed., *op. cit.,* pp. 97-99, and CHURCH, THOMAS, *King Philip's War,* p. 127.

11. The New England Confederation.—Channing, *History of the United States,* i, pp. *415-420. For fuller accounts, see Adams, J. T., *The Founding of New England,* *ch. 9, or Osgood, *op. cit.,* i, ch. 10, especially pp. *392-406.

12. Character Estimate of Roger Williams.—Ernst, James E., *Roger Williams, New England Firebrand,* *ch. 7; Richman, I. B., *Rhode Island, Its Making and Its Meaning,* ii, pp. *276-286; Carpenter, E. J., *Roger Williams,* pp. *243-246.

13. King Philip's War.—Adams, J. T., *The Founding of New England,* *ch. 14.

14. The Experiences of a Puritan Matron while a Prisoner of the Indians.—Lincoln, C. H., ed., *Narratives of the Indian Wars,* pp. *118-167. (This story not only shows how the Indians treated their captives, but it also reveals the fine way in which the Puritan spirit at its best reacted to mental anguish and physical suffering.)

CHAPTER IX

GOVERNMENT AND LAW

BY THE middle of the seventeenth century the English people had cleared out small areas of settlement in the Chesapeake region, in New England, and in the West Indies and had planted here many of the political institutions to which they had been accustomed in the homeland. Even at this early period the foundations of American government were firmly laid, and provincial and local administration had in continental North America assumed the form that it retained with slight modification as long as the colonies were a part of the British empire. At this point, therefore, we should take a cross-sectional view of the English constitution as it was at the beginning of the seventeenth century and note the changes that were made in those portions of it that were transplanted to the new soil.

Political Institutions in England about 1600

The general government: The King

At the time English colonization began in America the general government in England was in the hands of the king, the Privy Council, and Parliament. The king at that time was not a figurehead, as he is today, but a ruler with real authority. In fact, just prior to this period the Tudor sovereigns had been exercising almost absolute authority, and the first two Stuarts arrogated to themselves all the powers enjoyed by their predecessors. It is true that the extravagant pretensions of James I and Charles I were not allowed, and the crown was shorn of much of its former power by the Puritan Revolution; but the king still held at the time of the Restoration (1660) an important place in the home government and was the highest authority in the management of the colonies.

The Privy Council

In the performance of his duties the king generally acted on the advice of the Privy Council. This body held a place in the government which corresponded roughly to that now filled by the Cabinet. The Privy Council was composed of from eighteen to twenty members, including many of the men who held the leading positions in imperial administration. It met nearly every day and performed a great variety of duties. Its activities extended to all parts of the empire, and it was especially concerned with those outlying districts that were under the authority of the crown but were not covered by the ordinary machinery of government. When the colonies were founded they naturally came under the oversight of this important body.

Parliament then as now consisted of the House of Lords and the House of Commons. The former had a membership of about fifty, all of whom belonged to the nobility or higher clergy. The House of Commons was composed of five hundred or more representatives chosen two from each shire and one or two representatives from each of about three hundred towns. The distribution of seats was arbitrary, and no effort had been made to apportion representation according to population. The qualifications for voting, the method of election, and the unequal distribution of seats all tended to give the upper and middle classes control of this assembly.

Parliament

The county was the largest and most important unit of local administration and jurisdiction. Each county had a court of its own and also constituted a district for a national circuit court. The county also served as a convenient area on which to base national taxation and representation in the House of Commons.

The county an important unit of local government

The officials of the county were the lord lieutenant, the sheriff and his deputies, the coroner, the justices of the peace, and the keeper of the rolls and his deputy, generally known as the clerk of the peace. At the head of the list in rank stood the lord lieutenant, whose chief function was to look after military affairs, though often duties of a civil nature were also assigned him.

County officials

Next to the lord lieutenant in dignity and above him in real importance came the sheriff. There was usually one sheriff for each county, who was appointed by the king from a list of three eligibles selected by the Privy Council. He was frequently a knight and always belonged to the class from which knights were selected. The duties of the sheriff were similar to those that now engage that official. He had to arrange for juries and see that they were ready for the circuit court that met twice a year in each county. He had to attend the sessions of this court and execute its orders either in person or through his deputies. These same services were also performed by him or his deputies for the quarter courts held by the justices. Another important responsi-

The sheriff

bility imposed upon this man of all work was that of holding court himself once a month for the trial of petty civil cases. This county court, as it was called, was, however, declining in importance at the time colonization began in America. It was the sheriff's duty to appoint the jailer and supervise the management of the jail; to preside over the elections for Parliament and send in the returns; and to perform such other tasks as might be assigned to him from time to time by the king.

Justices of the peace

In every county there were from twenty to sixty justices of the peace appointed by the Lord Chancellor. They were usually selected from the rural gentry and were always men of property and influence. Although the pay was purely nominal and the duties onerous, the office seems never to have been shunned, as was the case with that of the sheriff. This was probably due to the fact that the position of justice carried a certain social prestige with it and gave the impression that its incumbent was performing a patriotic service.

The duties of the justices were numerous and were all the time increasing; for upon them was placed the obligation of enforcing new statutes. Contemporary writers take five or six hundred pages to list the various functions with which they were charged. Their powers were both administrative and judicial. Among the former were the construction and supervision of roads and bridges, the binding out of apprentices, the licensing of alehouses, the regulation of wages, etc. In their judicial capacity they sat regularly four times a year and sometimes oftener as a court of quarter sessions. This court had no civil jurisdiction, but heard all sorts of criminal cases except murder, treason, and certain other high crimes. They made use of both petit and grand juries in arriving at decisions.

Subdivisions of the county

The smallest subdivision of the county was known as a vill, town or township, tithing, parish, or manor, and these terms were frequently used interchangeably to designate the smallest unit of local government.[1] Of these terms only three—the township or

[1] This variety in the use of terms to designate the smallest unit of local government was due in part to a diversity in the practice of administering the affairs of the rural communities. Local institutions had grown up at a time when there was no strong central government to reduce them to uniformity; hence they had the diversities which were characteristic of the different customs and laws out of

town, the parish, and the manor—have any real significance for us, as they are the only ones that figure to any considerable extent in the local government of the English continental colonies. The manor had become almost obsolete by the end of the sixteenth century, and we might disregard it entirely had not several efforts been made to transplant it to America. These attempts were for the most part unsuccessful, and in only a very few of the colonies were manors established.[2]

The term most generally employed in the Elizabethan era for the smallest subdivision of the county was the parish, which was a unit of both ecclesiastical and civil administration. The chief officials of the parish were the churchwardens, the overseer of the poor, the surveyor of the roads, and the constable, or petty constable, as he was called to distinguish him from the high constable. The most important of these officials was the constable, whose functions were about the same as those of his successor of today. He had to perform certain duties for the parish, make arrests, and carry out the orders of the justices of the peace, the sheriff, and other officials of the county.[3] His term of office was one year, and he was chosen in some parishes by the lord of the manor or court leet, in others by the vestry, and in some cases

The parish (marginal note)

which they had grown (CHEYNEY, E. P., *A History of England from the Defeat of the Armada to the Death of Elizabeth*, ii, pp. 396-397).

The parish or township was the subdivision of a larger unit of administration known as the hundred, or wapentake. The hundred was one of the oldest of the administrative divisions but had become unimportant by the beginning of the seventeenth century. It was still used, however, for certain military and financial purposes. The hundred had so little vitality in the homeland that it did not take deep root when it was transplanted to America.

[2] A manor was an area of land occupied by a group of people over whom the lord of the manor exercised a certain measure of judicial and economic authority. Among the privileges of the lord was the right to hold courts baron and courts leet, which were meetings of all the tenants or people living on the manor. The court baron met every three weeks or oftener, while the court leet met only twice a year and then at the call of the lord of the manor. The court leet had more power than the court baron; it could elect petty officials as well as perform certain other duties (CHEYNEY, *History of England*, etc., ii, pp. 397-398).

[3] For a list of the duties of the constable from a primary source, see CHEYNEY, E. P., *loc. cit.*, ii, p. 404.

by the justices of the peace. The churchwardens were also important parish officials. There were generally from two to four in each parish, chosen annually, usually by the parishioners in their vestry meeting at Easter. To them were intrusted the control of religious affairs and the management of church buildings and other property belonging to the parish. They also collected the taxes of the parish, and in conjunction with the overseer of the poor looked after and cared for the poor. The vestry was a meeting of all the householders of the parish and was theoretically the most democratic body known to English practice. It had power to appoint the parish officials and assign duties to them, make by-laws, and vote the parish levy. In the time of Elizabeth the meetings of the vestry seem not to have been held regularly, and when held were probably attended by few except the leading men of the parish. It was, therefore, not as democratic a body in actual practice as it appeared in political theory.

Most of the local political institutions thus briefly sketched followed the English flag to the New World, and out of them have evolved the local governments of both colonial and modern America. Some of these institutions had already lost much of their vitality and so never took deep root when they were transplanted to a new soil. This was especially the case with reference to those that rested on the feudal notions of the Middle Ages. Others, however, grew into newness of life in the bracing atmosphere of the new environment, while still others have developed along different lines from those marked out by conditions in the homeland. Consequently, not only did the colonial constitutions differ in their later forms from their British prototype, but even the foundation stones of British political theory were rearranged before they were built in to form the base of American institutions.

GOVERNMENT IN THE COLONIES

Similarity between the political institutions of England and Virginia

It was in Virginia, where British institutions were first planted, that the general and local government of the colony exhibited its greatest similarity to the English prototype. Indeed, in civic and social life the likeness between the mother country and her oldest American daughter was so marked that a contemporary writer observed that the latter had been created "from a rib taken from Britain's side."[4] By 1619, when the assembly was created, gov-

[4] *Journal of the Burgesses, Va., 1712-1726,* p. 250.

ernment in Virginia had begun to crystallize into permanent form. There was now a governor, corresponding to the king in England, a council of state, whose duties were similar to those of the Privy Council and House of Lords, and the House of Burgesses, which claimed a place in the constitution of Virginia similar to that held by the House of Commons in the government of England.

The governor was the chief executive, and many of his powers were about the same as those that are exercised by that official in the American states of today. He was the representative of the home authorities and had to carry out their instructions as well as execute the laws of the colonial assembly. He was commander-in-chief of the military and naval forces, and could make all military and quite a number of civil appointments. As representative of the king, who was at the head of the British church, he had general supervision over religious affairs and was supposed to induct all ministers into their livings, though this latter power was not recognized by the vestries. He presided over the council when it sat as a court of justice[5] or upper house of assembly, and with the consent of the council appointed court officials and justices of the peace. He could call, prorogue, and dissolve the assembly and could veto finally any measure passed by it. At the opening session of the assembly he would make a speech proposing certain measures that either he or the home authorities wished to have passed. He could remit fines and forfeitures, pardon all crimes except treason and willful murder, and grant reprieves in these cases.[6]

The governor

In the autonomous republics of New England the duties and powers of the chief executive were similar to those just enumerated, though his authority was not so great as it was in Virginia and the other royal provinces. He could not dissolve or prorogue the assembly nor veto acts passed by it. His power over the militia was also not quite so great as it was in the royal colonies.

In Virginia, the governor was appointed by the Company be-

[5] SPOTSWOOD, ALEXANDER, *Official Letters*, ii, p. 14; HARTWELL, BLAIR, and CHILTON, *The Present State of Virginia* (1727), pp. 20, 21.

[6] DINWIDDIE, ROBERT, *Papers*, i, pp. 384, 385.

Pardons for treason and willful murder could be granted only by the king in council, which meant in actual practice the Privy Council.

fore 1624 and by the crown after that time.[7] The term of his office was indefinite, being determined by the pleasure of the sovereign. In the self-governing colonies of New England the governors were chosen by the people for a term of one year. They were eligible to reëlection, however, and often an able administrator would serve a number of terms. In the proprietary colonies the governor was appointed by the proprietors, and his position in the government was quite similar to that of the chief executive in the royal provinces.

The council in Virginia

Next to the governor in the administration came the council, varying in size but usually numbering about twelve or thirteen. The council in Virginia had authority to advise the governor, and curb him if necessary in the performance of his administrative duties. Some of the powers delegated to the governor by the crown could be exercised by him only with the consent of the council. The councilors were judges of the superior court and constituted the upper house of the assembly. Appointments to the council were made on the recommendation of the governor by the Company in the earliest years and by the king after the charter had been annulled.[8] They were usually men of means and influence, for only those who were possessed of considerable estates were eligible to this high office.[9] They were not chosen for any definite period, but were recommissioned whenever a new governor was appointed or a new king came to the throne. The old councilors, however, were usually continued in office by the new commissions, and so they virtually held their positions during good behavior. They not only received pay for their services, but also had a monopoly of most of the places of honor and profit in the colony. Each one was usually the commander of the militia in his own county with the rank of colonel.

The council, owing to the prominence of its members and their family connections, had great influence in the colony and was able to make its power felt in the government. Nor were the councilors slow in asserting their rights, for they often took an

---

[7] During the Commonwealth period (1652-1660) the governor was chosen by the House of Burgesses for a term of one year (KAYE, P. L., *The Colonial Executive prior to the Restoration*, p. 28).

[8] During the Commonwealth period councilors were chosen by the House of Burgesses (CHITWOOD, O. P., *Justice in Colonial Virginia*, p. 41).

[9] SPOTSWOOD, *op. cit.*, ii, pp. 39, 41, 55.

attitude of strenuous opposition to the measures proposed by the governor. Indeed, in the contests between the Virginia council and the representative of the crown, the history of the struggles of the ancient English kings with their barons was, in a small way, repeating itself. Sometimes these barons of Virginia and their allies carried their opposition to the governor to the point of procuring his dismissal.

In the New England commonwealths, the board of assistants had a place in the government similar to that of the Virginia council. It advised the governor in the performance of his administrative duties, constituted the upper house of the assembly, and acted as the provincial court. Councilors in the proprietary colonies were chosen by the proprietors and were intrusted with very much the same duties and powers as they were in the royal provinces.[10]

The board of assistants in New England

The General Assembly of Virginia, which was called into being in 1619 by Governor Yeardley, had soon (probably by 1638) become a bicameral legislature. The governor and his council were the upper house, and the burgesses, chosen by the qualified voters (in the early years by the freemen), constituted the lower house. After 1661 the laws provided that each county should send two representatives to the House of Burgesses. The towns of Jamestown, Williamsburg, and Norfolk and the College of William and Mary also had one representative each. Measures passed by both houses of the assembly and accepted by the governor were sent to England to be confirmed or rejected by the Company before 1624 and by the king after that time.[11] Besides being a lawmaking body, the assembly was also for some time a court of justice, and it continued to be the highest court of appeal in the colony until 1682.[12]

The Virginia assembly

[10] There are, however, a few exceptions to this rule. In Pennsylvania prior to 1701 the council was chosen by the voters, and in the Carolinas until near the end of the seventeenth century one-half of the councilors were chosen by the assembly. In Massachusetts, too, after 1691 the councilors were elected by the assembly. See OSGOOD, H. L., *The American Colonies in the Seventeenth Century*, ii, p. 217; *The Shaftesbury Papers*, pp. 323, 327.

[11] During the Commonwealth period no power of veto was exercised by the authorities in England, as Virginia was during that time an autonomous republic like the New England commonwealths.

[12] HENING, W. W., *Statutes at Large* (Va.), i, pp. 398, 476;

The General Court in Massachusetts

The General Court of Massachusetts (under the first charter) was the model copied by all the self-governing colonies of New England in establishing their legislatures. As considerable space has already been devoted to the evolution of this assembly (see pp. 134-139), no further discussion of the topic is deemed necessary at this point.

Before the end of the seventeenth century there was an assembly in every one of the continental colonies. All of these legislatures were bicameral, though later the council in Pennsylvania lost its legislative power, and from the beginning of the eighteenth century (1701) the Pennsylvania assembly was a body of one house.

The county in Virginia

The one important unit of local administration in colonial Virginia was the county, and the chief place in the local governmental machinery was held by the monthly, or county, court. Monthly courts were established as early as 1624, and ten years later the province was divided into eight shires, or counties, in each of which a court was to be held every month. New counties were formed as the area of settlement expanded, and each one was provided with a court as soon as it was organized. The members of the county court were at first known as commissioners of the monthly court, but afterwards were honored with the title of justice of the peace. The office was one of dignity and was usually filled by men of influence and ability. Except for a short time during the Commonwealth period, the justices were appointed by the governor, generally with the consent of the council.[13] They were not chosen for any definite period, and it seems that their commissions could be terminated at the discretion of the governor. But it was the usual practice for the governor, in issuing new commissions, to name the old members, and so the justices practically held their positions during good behavior.[14]

HARTWELL, BLAIR, and CHILTON, *Present State of Virginia*, pp. 25, 26; *Sainsbury MSS., 1640-1691*, p. 387; CHITWOOD, O. P., *Justice in Colonial Virginia*, ch. 1.

[13] For one year during the Commonwealth period the House of Burgesses had authority to appoint justices of the peace and later for about two years could confirm appointments made by the governor and council (HENING, *op. cit.*, i, pp. 372, 376, 402, 480).

[14] SPOTSWOOD, *op. cit.*, i, p. 193; DINWIDDIE, *op. cit.*, i, p. 383; CHITWOOD. O. P., *Justice in Colonial Virginia*, ch. 3.

The number of justices to a county varied at different times and in different counties, but generally ranged from eight to eighteen.

The duties of the county court were both administrative and judicial. The justices could decide certain minor criminal and civil cases individually, and when they met collectively as a county court they had a wider jurisdiction in both civil and criminal causes. This local tribunal consisted of all the justices of the county, and four were the necessary quorum for the transaction of business. All decisions were reached by a majority vote of the judges present.[15] Petit juries were called on to decide matters of fact, and offenses were brought before the court by means of presentments and indictments made by the churchwardens and the grand jury.

The judicial duties of the justices of the peace

In addition to deciding cases, the justices had to look after the business affairs of the county. They ordered the opening of new roads and saw that surveyors appointed by them kept the highways cleared. The levy of the county was apportioned by them, and the lists of tithables[16] were sometimes taken either by themselves or by officers chosen by them for that purpose. The justices also licensed taverns, regulated the prices at which drinks could be sold, and issued certificates for land grants.[17]

Administrative duties of the county court

The chief administrative official of the county was the sheriff, many of whose duties were about the same as those that are now performed by that official in the modern American commonwealth. He collected the taxes, executed the orders and sentences of the courts and the assembly, made arrests, summoned jurors and others to court, and served as keeper of the county jails. Every county was divided into precincts, in each of which there was a constable, appointed by the county court. It was the duty of the constable to collect fines, make arrests, whip criminals, and secure the return of runaway slaves and servants.[18] Another important officer of the county was the clerk of the county court, who performed about the same functions and exercised about the same influence in the county as does his successor of today.

County officials

The county held about the same place in the local government

[15] HENING, *op. cit.*, i, p. 125.

[16] For an explanation of the term "tithable," see p. 92.

[17] CHITWOOD, *Justice in Colonial Virginia*, pp. 91-92. See also pp. 446-447.

[18] JERNEGAN, M. W., *The American Colonies*, p. 77; HENING, *op. cit.*, i, pp. 333, 452, 465; ii, pp. 83, 412; iii, p. 264; vi, pp. 247, 523-524, 566; viii, p. 181.

The
county
in other
colonies

in North Carolina and Maryland as it did in Virginia. In South Carolina county government was not effectively organized until near the end of the colonial period.[19] In time counties were formed in all of the other colonies, though they never played so important a part in local administration in the northern and middle sections as they did in the Chesapeake region. The county did not appear in New England until the township had become well established, and it never superseded the latter as the chief unit of local government. Here it was, however, the basis for the organization of the county court and served as a larger militia unit, the township being the smaller. The county court performed certain minor administrative duties and exercised jurisdiction in a certain class of civil and criminal cases.[20] In the Middle colonies the county was more important as a unit of local government than it was in New England, but less so than it was in the South.

The
parish in
Virginia

The parish was a unit of church organization and also the smallest rural district having a political organization. It was usually a subdivision of the county, though sometimes the limits of the parish overlapped those of the county. In Virginia, as in England, the affairs of the parish, both civic and religious, were managed by the vestry; but the vestry was quite a different body in Virginia from what it had been in the homeland. As we have seen, in England it was, in theory at least, composed of all the parishioners meeting in a primary assembly; in Virginia it was a group of the leading men in the parish, usually twelve in number, who held their places virtually for life or during good behavior.

In Virginia when a parish was first formed and after a vestry had been dissolved the new vestrymen were chosen by the qualified voters of the parish; but it became the practice in Virginia and for a time in North Carolina for vacancies in the vestry to be filled by the vestrymen themselves.[21] The vestry looked after

[19] In South Carolina, soon after the first permanent settlement was made, the province was divided into three counties. But these large areas were not organized as counties in the usual sense of the term.

[20] After 1691, the county court in Massachusetts was divided into two tribunals.

[21] HENING, W. W., *Statutes at Large* (Va.), i, pp. 240, 290-291; ii, pp. 25, 44-45; iv, p. 304; v, p. 76; vi, pp. 386, 518; vii, p. 132; ix, p. 98.

religious affairs, supervised the morals of the community, apportioned the parish levy, cared for the poor, and performed certain
other administrative duties. Two churchwardens were chosen
annually by the vestrymen (in conjunction with the minister)
from among their number, and to them were delegated many of
the duties that were incumbent upon the vestry as a whole. The
churchwardens also had to present to the county court all persons
guilty of breaches of the moral and religious code, such as drunkenness, blasphemy, immorality, and Sabbath-breaking, and to collect and dispose of the fines imposed for such offenses.[22]

In New England the township, or town, was the chief unit The
of local administration. Each town was a miniature colony, and township
enjoyed considerable local autonomy under its own ecclesiasti- in New
cal and civic organization.[23] In all the New England colonies, England
the towns were under the authority of the colonial government,
and their powers were strictly defined by the legislative assembly.
These powers included the right to choose their officials, to organize churches, to distribute their lands, to make by-laws,
punish minor criminal offenses, and in general to look after the
local interests of the community. The town was also the unit for
representation in the General Court, for levying and collecting
taxes, and for organizing the militia.

In Massachusetts there was also a court in each of several of
the more important towns. This court was composed of a resident
assistant and other associate justices selected by the General
Court. Its jurisdiction extended to all civil causes involving
amounts not in excess of ten pounds and to all criminal cases "not
concerning life, member, or banishment." Civil causes involving
amounts of forty shillings and under could be decided by a single
magistrate without a jury. In all cases appeals lay from these town
courts to the Court of Assistants, the highest tribunal in the
colony. For the towns in which no assistant resided three commissioners were appointed by the General Court for hearing
minor civil and criminal causes.[24] Moreover, the selectmen in
small towns exercised minor judicial functions.

[22] For the religious duties performed by the vestrymen, see p. 521.
[23] For an account of the organization of the township and the land
system in New England, see pp. 442-443.
[24] *Massachusetts Colony Records*, i, pp. 174-175; *Laws and Liberties of Massachusetts* (Huntingdon Library ed.), pp. 8-9.
At first the General Court and the Court of Assistants were the

The town meeting   The chief organ of local government in the New England town was the town meeting. This was a primary assembly composed of all the citizens, and attendance at the meetings was compulsory. Once a year the citizens met to choose their local officials and their representatives in the General Court. They were also called together from time to time to transact other important business, such as levying taxes, making distributions of land, enacting by-laws, and adopting regulations for the schools and churches.

The selectmen   But the town meeting was an unwieldy body and could only direct the affairs of the community in a general way. To the selectmen it delegated the power of carrying out in detail the policies adopted by it. These officials ranged in number from three to twenty-one or more and were chosen annually by the town meeting. They were responsible to the town meeting and had only such powers as had been delegated to them by that body. Any business, however, might be referred to them, and often their delegated powers covered the entire range of activities engaged in by the town meeting except the election of the more important officials and the levying of local taxes.

In the Middle colonies also the township was employed as a unit of administration, but it never played there so important a part in local government as it did in New England.

City government   Outside of New England the government of the larger towns was modeled after that of the English cities, or boroughs, of that day, though in most of the colonial towns the people exerted an influence in the government which they were unable to do in the English boroughs. In a few of the American towns the governing body was a close corporation, as it was in the English city.[25] The form of administration provided for by the charter

only courts in Massachusetts. After the General Court became a representative assembly (1634) it gradually became more and more a legislative body and the Court of Assistants became the highest tribunal in the colony. This place it retained throughout the seventeenth century.

[25] The towns and cities in England at the beginning of the colonial era had no uniform system of government. The character of the administration in each was determined by a charter, which in some cases went back to the early Middle Ages. In some of the towns the mayor and aldermen were elected by the taxpayers; in others they were chosen by a small number of privileged voters; while in others the people had no voice at all in selecting their officials, the governing

of Williamsburg affords a good example of the kind of government that was characteristic of this type of town. By this charter the local administration was intrusted to a mayor, recorder, six aldermen, and the members of the common council, and the people had no voice whatever in the selection of any of these officials. The king appointed the first mayor, recorder, and aldermen, who elected twelve councilmen to hold office during good behavior. It was by a vote of these officials that all vacancies in these various offices were filled. In the other type of colonial cities and towns the councilmen were elected by the qualified voters, and in all but two of them the aldermen were chosen in like manner. The aldermen and councilmen in this second class of towns were chosen for a definite term, in most cases the term being one year.[26]

In two particulars the local institutions of Maryland reproduced the practice of the mother country more exactly than did the Old Dominion; for here both the hundred and the manor took root and were real units of local administration. The Maryland hundred was a subdivision of the parish, and in that respect was unlike its prototype in the homeland, which was a larger district than the parish. The hundred in Maryland was employed during the entire colonial period as a unit for levying taxes and organizing the militia, and before the Commonwealth period as a basis of representation in the assembly.[27]

The hundred

The manor owed its importance in Maryland to the feudal notions of the lord proprietary, who reserved for himself at least two manorial estates in each county. He also created other manors by granting large estates to certain individuals and conferring on

The manor

---

boards filling vacancies in their membership by coöptation. As a rule the government of the towns was in the hands of a very small minority of the people.

[26] Among the cities belonging to this class were Williamsburg, Norfolk, Annapolis, and Philadelphia. See FAIRLIE, J. A., *Municipal Administration*, pp. 72-77.

For the charter of Williamsburg, see *William and Mary College Quarterly*, 1st series, x, pp. 84-91. The charter of Norfolk can be found in the appendix of INGLE, E., *Local Institutions of Virginia* (Johns Hopkins University *Studies*, 3rd series). For the charter of Philadelphia, granted by Penn in 1689, see *The Charters and Acts of Assembly of the Province of Pennsylvania*, i, pp. 10-14.

[27] WILHELM, L. W., *Local Institutions of Maryland* (Johns Hopkins University *Studies*, 3rd series), pp. 39-63.

them the rights and privileges enjoyed by lords of manors in England. The manor was an area of land containing from one to fifteen thousand acres, on which lived the lord of the manor or his representative, and his tenants. The lord of the manor had certain privileges not enjoyed by the ordinary grantee of land. Chief among these was the right to hold court leet and court baron. The court leet was a meeting of the tenants held twice a year for the hearing of petty criminal cases and the transaction of other business. The court baron was likewise a people's court, meeting at the call of the landlord's steward for the trial of minor civil cases and the settlement of agrarian disputes.[28]

LAW AND JUSTICE

The common law in the colonies

During the seventeenth century there was a general prejudice against lawyers throughout the colonies, and the practice of the legal profession was discouraged by a number of legislative enactments. Most of the judges were also without legal training, and so neither bench nor bar was versed in the English common law. In the first half of the colonial era judicial decisions could not, therefore, have followed closely the precedents of English practice even if there had been a disposition to do so. Moreover, the English common law "was a technical system adapted to a settled community; it took the colonies some time to reach the stage of social organization which the common law expressed." Even when the common law was called into requisition in this early period it was those provisions that deal with public rather than private rights that were most often appealed to. Later, in the eighteenth century, "with a more jealous supervision of colonial development by the mother country, the introduction of law books, and the growth of a trained bench and bar, a more general reception of the private law principles of England was brought about."[29]

It is true, however, that in all the colonies, even in the seventeenth century, the courts in rendering decisions were influenced by the principles of the English common law, though not to the

[28] *Ibid.*, pp. 29-33. The charter to the Carolina proprietors also provided for the creation of manors, and there were some manorial estates in the province of New York. These latter included the patroonships established under Dutch rule and some great landed estates that had been created by grants from the English governors.

[29] REINSCH, P. S., *English Common Law in the Early American Colonies*, p. 58.

extent as was formerly thought. In actual practice the early judges had to rely for guidance mainly on the provincial statutes and their own sense of right. In all the colonies but Maryland the statutes were codified at an early date, and their provisions could easily be learned even by untrained judges. Some of the statutes were in harmony with English legal principles, while some of them were antagonistic to them. In cases not covered by these codes the common law was resorted to in some of the colonies, and the Bible in others. Where the Puritan influence was strong, especially in New England and East Jersey, the Mosaic code was in criminal cases frequently appealed to as subsidiary law.

The punishment for crime in colonial days seems unreasonably severe when judged by modern ideas of justice, but the criminal laws were generally milder in America than they were in England at the same time. The number of capital offenses was much smaller in the colonial codes than in the English statutes, but larger than in our laws today. In the early days, blasphemy was punishable by death in Connecticut, in New Haven, and in Maryland under the rule of the Catholic proprietors.[30] Hog-stealing in Virginia for the third offense was also a capital crime. Even in Pennsylvania, despite the humanitarian sentiment of the Quakers, there were fourteen capital offenses.

Punishment for crime

The usual method of inflicting the death penalty was by hanging, but occasionally a criminal was burned. The penalties for minor offenses were fines, whippings, duckings, and confinement in the stocks and pillory. In Virginia every county was required to build stocks, a ducking-stool, and a pillory. The offender was sometimes required to stand with his ears nailed to the pillory and have them cut off at the end of the appointed time. Whippings in Virginia did not usually exceed thirty-nine lashes, but they were given on the "bare back well laid on." A few cases are recorded, however, in which a culprit was punished with a hundred or more stripes.

Other inhuman methods of punishment employed, especially in the earliest years, were branding the cheek or forehead with a hot iron and boring the tongue through with a hot iron. Persons who had slandered their neighbors or been guilty of the sin of unchastity were sometimes compelled to acknowledge their fault

[30] It is more than likely, however, that there were no executions for blasphemy in any of the colonies.

while standing in church with a sheet wrapped around them. Sometimes a unique punishment was devised to fit the offense. The court of a Virginia county once sentenced a man who had gotten drunk to stand at the door of the church "with a great pot tied about his neck."[31] Torture was sometimes employed in New Amsterdam to induce supposed criminals to confess their guilt.

In the colonies the contemporary English practice obtained of confining debtors in prison when they failed to meet their financial obligations. But in Virginia they, as well as criminals except those charged with felony, were allowed the freedom of the prison grounds if they gave bond not to go beyond them. The amount of freedom thus allowed enabled the prisoner to keep up his health by fresh air and exercise. At one time in Virginia debtors were accustomed to build their houses inside the prison limits and thus live at home while serving out their prison sentences.[32]

Suffrage in the colonies

The right to vote was not extended to all freemen at any time during the colonial period except in a very few colonies, and in these only for certain periods in the seventeenth century. The suffrage was restricted by property, religious, and other qualifications. In the self-governing colonies of New England no one had a voice in the election of the governor, deputy governor, or other provincial officials except those who had been admitted to membership in the corporation that constituted the colony, though residents who were not full citizens usually voted in local elections. As a rule, the privilege of taking part in general elections was conferred by a vote of the General Court, and in some cases the application for this right had to be indorsed by the town meeting of the community in which the applicant lived before it could come before the General Court. The practice of requiring voters to become members of the corporation ceased in Massachusetts when it became a royal province (1691), but was continued in Connecticut and Rhode Island throughout the entire colonial period.

In New Haven and in Massachusetts up to 1664, only members

---

[31] STANARD, MARY N., *Colonial Virginia*, p. 330. For other unusual methods of punishment, see CHITWOOD, O. P., *Justice in Colonial Virginia* (Johns Hopkins University *Studies*, 23rd series), pp. 88-91.

[32] *Ibid.*, p. 112. See also HENING, *op. cit.*, i. p. 341; ii, pp. 19, 77; iii, pp. 15, 268; viii, p. 120.

of the established church were granted the right of suffrage.[33]
Connecticut and Plymouth had no technical requirement of this
kind, but in the seventeenth century probably few persons would
ever be admitted to the corporation except those who were members of a Congregational church or in sympathy with it. Rhode
Island had a law in the eighteenth century requiring all voters
to be professed Christians, and a like provision is found in a
South Carolina enactment made at a later date (1716). Quakers
were denied the right of suffrage in Plymouth and Massachusetts
during a good part of the seventeenth century. They were also
kept from the polls in other colonies at certain periods by their
refusal to take the oaths required by voters. In some colonies,
however, this impediment was removed by the enactment of
statutes which provided that the affirmation of a Quaker should
meet the requirement of the oath. About the middle of the seventeenth century the Baptists were almost as unpopular as the
Quakers and were not much better off as to suffrage rights than
this despised sect. But the religious denominations that fared
the worst in suffrage restrictions were the Catholics and the Jews.
After the Revolution of 1688, laws were passed in five of the
colonies (Maryland, New York, Virginia, Rhode Island, and
South Carolina) disfranchising Catholics, and they were probably not allowed to vote in most of the other jurisdictions. The
Jews were disfranchised almost as widely, and from 1687 to 1759
there were laws in four colonies (Pennsylvania, New York,
Rhode Island, and South Carolina) withholding the ballot from
them.

In the eighteenth century property rather than religion was
the basis of the suffrage, but the property qualification was generally higher than it had been in the previous century. This
narrowing of the suffrage was due partly to the desire of the
colonies to conform their practice to English usage in obedience
to instructions from the home authorities and partly to favor the
landholding aristocracy that generally controlled the provincial
governments. In six of the colonies the possession of real estate
was required for voting, while in the others the qualification could
be met by the ownership of either personal or real property.[34]

[33] See p. 135, note 21.
[34] For a table showing the qualifications for voting in the various
colonies just prior to the Revolution, see PORTER, K. H., *A History of
Suffrage in the United States*, p. 13.

Despite these restrictions, the voters in America constituted a greater proportion of the entire population than they did in the mother country. The main reason for this was that in the colonies, owing to the cheapness of land and the fine economic opportunity offered by the new country, the people could acquire the property necessary to qualify them for the suffrage more easily than they could in the homeland.

Woman suffrage was not allowed in any of the colonies, though one instance of a woman's voting in a town election is recorded. The one thus favored was Lady Deborah Moody, of Long Island (1655).[35] So far as the records show, only one other colonial woman, Mrs. Margaret Brent, of Maryland (1648),[36] ever wanted to vote. Laws excluding Negroes from the suffrage appear in the eighteenth century, but they were confined to the provinces south of the Potomac River.[37]

The common people probably had a stronger voice in their government in the English colonies than they did in any other part of the world at that time. But the colonial governments were not run either by the people or for the people. In every colony the legislature was controlled by the large landholders and prosperous merchants who lived in the older settlements, and the laws passed were in the interest of this privileged class without due regard to the rights of the laborers and small farmers. Consequently, the members of this latter class bore more of the burdens and enjoyed fewer of the benefits of government than they would have done under a fair and equal system of administration. Especially unjust was the treatment accorded the settlers on the frontier. They were not allowed an equitable representation in the assembly, and were not properly provided for as to road improvement, bridge construction, local administration of justice, and

[35]McKinley, A. E., *The Suffrage Franchise in The Thirteen English Colonies in America*, pp. 192-193; *New York Colonial Documents*, xiv, pp. 299-300, 329.

One instance is also recorded which shows that some women in Providence, R. I. (1640), participated in some of the political rights of landholders, though there is no mention of their voting (*Rhode Island Colonial Records*, i, pp. 27-31).

[36] *Maryland Archives, Assembly, 1638-1664*, p. 215.

[37] At one time (1701) Negroes were allowed to vote in South Carolina, but this was an irregular and illegal procedure (McKinley, *op. cit.*, p. 137).

military defense against the Indians. The patrician leader in the Tidewater Belt "was fierce for liberty for himself and his class, but lukewarm and even hostile to liberty for other citizens and classes."[38]

SELECTED READINGS

1. The English County and Its Officers (1600-50).—Cheyney, E. P., *European Background of American History*, *ch. 14.
2. The Justice of the Peace in England.—Cheyney, E. P., *A History of England from the Defeat of the Armada*, ii, ch. 37.
3. English Parish or Township Government (1500-1650).—Cheyney, E. P., *European Background*, *ch. 16; also Cheyney, E. P., *History of England*, ii, ch. 41.
4. Suffrage in the Colonies.—Bishop, C. F., *History of Elections in the American Colonies*, ch. 2 (for advanced students) ; McKinley, A. E., *The Suffrage Franchise in the Thirteen English Colonies in America*, *ch. 15.
5. The County System in New Jersey.—Howard, G. E., *Local Government in the Colonies*, pp. *365-367.
6. The Towns of New Netherland.—McKinley, A. E., in *American Historical Review*, vi, pp. *1-18.
7. The New England Town.—Wertenbaker, T. J., *The First Americans*, pp. *83-86.
8. The Ducking-Stool.—Earle, Alice M., *Curious Punishments of Bygone Days*, *ch. 1.
9. The Whipping-Post.—*Ibid.*, *ch. 6.
10. Public Penance.—*Ibid.*, *ch. 9.

[38] JERNEGAN, M. W., *The American Colonies*, pp. 288-293.

CHAPTER X

NEW NETHERLAND, NEW YORK, AND NEW SWEDEN

The rise of the Dutch Republic

WHEN the Dutch asserted their independence of Spain in 1581 (see p. 4) they formed a loose union of provinces somewhat like the American union under the Articles of Confederation. There was a federal legislative body known as the States General, but it did not have a great deal of power. Despite the weakness of the general government, the Dutch Republic soon became one of the leading powers of Europe in commerce and industry. The heroic struggle for independence released an unusual amount of energy and intellectual force, which led to an advance in art, literature, and science that put the little republic in the van of European progress. Such an enterprising people were not content to confine their activities to the homeland, but demanded a share in the trade with the East and the New World. In 1602 the Dutch East India Company received a charter from the States General and at once entered upon an active trade with the East.

Henry Hudson

In their trading ventures in the East, the Dutch East India Company met considerable opposition from the Portuguese, who still tried to monopolize the sea route around Africa. The Dutch Company, therefore, wished to find a northwest route to the Indies. In 1609 the Company sent over Henry Hudson, an Englishman, to hunt for a waterway leading across the American continent to China. In his ship, the *Half-Moon*, Hudson sailed along the American coast from Newfoundland to Virginia. He then turned northward and entered New York harbor with the hope that it was the entrance to the strait connecting with the Pacific. Turning into the Great River of the Mountains, for eleven days the *Half-Moon* glided leisurely upstream, while the Dutch seamen enjoyed the beauty of the wonderful scenery afforded by steep cliffs, fertile valleys, and distant mountains. After reaching a point some miles above the present site of Albany, Hudson was convinced by the shallows that this waterway was not the northwest passage, and he made no further effort to explore the river.[1]

While he had failed to find the strait to China, Hudson had succeeded in exploring from its mouth to the head of navigation the noble river that rightfully bears his name. On this expedition was also based the claim of the Dutch Republic to one of the finest portions of North America. The Dutch were quick to appreciate the opportunities for fur trading offered by the Hudson region, and a brisk trade with the Indians began in 1610, which continued throughout the decade. Traders were sent over by Dutch merchants to traffic with the Indians. They explored Long Island Sound, entered the Connecticut River, and pushed eastward along the New England coast as far as the present site of Salem, and southward as far as Cape May and up the Delaware River to the mouth of the Schuylkill.

The merchants who had promoted these explorations now organized themselves into a company and obtained from the States General a charter granting to them a monopoly of the fur trade in New Netherland for three years. The territory designated as New Netherland included all the land lying between the fortieth and forty-fifth parallels of latitude. In the latter part of 1614 a stockaded post, known as Fort Nassau, was erected near the present site of Albany.[2] About the same time or a little earlier, a few rude huts were also built on Manhattan Island for the convenience of the traders.[3] To these two centers the Indians brought their peltries to exchange them for gaudy trinkets.

The monopoly privileges of the Company were not renewed at the end of the three-year period (1618), and the American trade was thrown open to all Netherlanders. It was not long, however, before there was organized another and more important company, known as the Dutch West India Company, which received a very liberal charter from the States General in 1621. It was given authority to trade and plant settlements anywhere on the coast of

[1] For two contemporary accounts of Hudson's voyages, see JAMESON, J. F., ed., *Narratives of New Netherland*, pp. 6-9, 16-28.

[2] *Ibid.*, p. 47.

[3] O'CALLAGHAN, E. B., *History of New Netherland*, i, pp. 76-77.
Brodhead thinks that it is doubtful as to whether a settlement was made at Manhattan at this time. For the evidence in favor of his view, see BRODHEAD, J. R., *History of the State of New York*, appendix, p. 755.

Africa or in America, with the power to govern such colonies as it might establish.[4]

Up to this time Dutch interests in America had been purely commercial, and no effort at permanent colonization had been made. Now, however, plans were formed for colonizing New Netherland with a view to its permanent occupation. In the spring of 1624 the ship *New Netherland* brought over about thirty families, a majority of whom were Walloons—that is, descendants of Protestant refugees from the Spanish Netherlands (now Belgium). These emigrants came from sturdy stock and possessed the moral qualities that were needed to face the perils of pioneer life. The expedition was under the command of Cornelis May, who had been appointed as the first governor, or director, of New Netherland. The settlers first landed on Manhattan Island, but were soon distributed by their leaders in order that as much territory as possible might be occupied. The greater part of them ascended the Hudson to the present site of Albany and established the post of Fort Orange, near Fort Nassau, which had fallen into disrepair. A few families located on the Delaware River, opposite the mouth of the Schuylkill, where they planted a temporary settlement, known as Fort Nassau.[5]

[4] For an English translation of the text of the charter to the Dutch West India Company, see O'CALLAGHAN, E. B., *History of New Netherland*, i, pp. 399-407. The Dutch text and an English translation of it are given in VAN LAER, A. J. F., *Van Rensselaer Bowier Manuscripts*, pp. 86-115.

[5] For contemporary accounts of the settlement made in 1624, see JAMESON, *op. cit.*, pp. 75-76, 304, and O'CALLAGHAN, E. B., *Documentary History of New York*, iii, pp. 49-51.

According to one account by a contemporary, given late in life from memory, a half-dozen men were sent to the mouth of the Connecticut River and eight men were left on Manhattan Island to hold it. In this year or a little later a small fort was also built on Nut (now known as Governor's) Island.

Accounts of these first settlements given by the older historians (such as Channing, Greene, Jernegan, and Bolton and Marshall) should be checked with and corrected by referring to later discussions, such as those given in the works of Flick and Andrews. See FLICK, ALEXANDER C., ed., *History of the State of New York*, i, pp. 234-243; and ANDREWS, C. M., *The Colonial Period of American History*, iii, pp. 71-75.

From the beginning, a constant intercourse was kept up between New Netherland and the mother country. Food supplies, horses, cattle, hogs, and sheep were brought from the homeland, and to it were sent from the New World furs, tobacco, and maize.[6] A number of additional immigrants came over in 1625, and by the end of that year the population of the American settlements had increased to about two hundred. In 1626 a settlement was made on the lower end of Manhattan Island, where the construction of a blockhouse (Fort Amsterdam) had already begun. In this same year the island of Manhattan was bought from the Indians for about twenty-four dollars by Peter Minuit, the third governor of the colony.[7] Forty log houses were quickly erected, and this village, now known as New Amsterdam, became the capital of New Netherland. The colony was now established on a permanent basis and was beginning to enjoy a measure of prosperity. To meet the growing demand for labor, Negro slavery was introduced at an early date (1625 or 1626).

The governmental power of the Company over any settlements that might be made in New Netherland was almost absolute, being limited only by a reservation on the part of the States General of the right to hold a slight supervisory control over them. The authority of the Company was exercised through a board of directors resident in Holland and a director and council in New Amsterdam. The West India Company thus held about the same relation to New Netherland as did the Virginia Company to the Virginia colony, and the position of the director at New Amsterdam was very much like that of the governor of a British province. The director in New Netherland, however, had more authority than the governor in the English colonies, as there was no representative assembly to limit his power.[8] Besides, his au-

Government

----

[6] JAMESON, *op. cit.,* pp. 82-87.

[7] *Liberty Bell Leaflets,* no. 1.

[8] While a regular system of representation was never organized in New Netherland, still there were at times bodies of men chosen by the people which assisted the director in an advisory capacity. These groups, however, were not legislative assemblies. In 1653 a representative assembly was convened with the consent of Director Stuyvesant. This body was composed of two delegates each from eight towns and villages and was called together to devise means to prevent the depredations that British privateers were committing

thority was not checked to any considerable degree by the local council, and the Company's board of directors in Holland was too far away to exercise a close supervision over his acts. Consequently, the director was usually an autocratic ruler. His position, however, was a very difficult one, and in no case was it filled with entire satisfaction either to the colonists or to the Company. It is difficult to appraise accurately the character of the rule of the Dutch governors, owing to the violent controversies that have raged around them and the divergence of opinion among historians as to their merits and abilities. We are safe in saying, however, that as a rule they were incompetent and in one or two cases dishonest.

Indian troubles   The Dutch had a great deal of trouble with the Indians who lived about Manhattan Island. For the bad feeling that existed between the whites and the natives the whites were largely to blame. The strife was started in 1640 when Director Kieft carried out some unwise and cruel measures against the Indians.[9] From that time until the end of Dutch rule there was intermittent war between the natives and the whites. These unnecessary wars weakened the resources of the colony and were largely responsible for the slowness of its development.

Friendship with the Iroquois   The Dutch were, however, more fortunate in their dealings with the Iroquois, or Five Nations, who lived in the region extending north and south of the Mohawk River. Cordial relations existed between these Indians and the Dutch from the beginning. This friendship proved a valuable asset to the latter, as it protected them from attack by the French in Canada and greatly aided in the promotion of the fur trade. For the Iroquois would sell to the Dutch traders not only the furs procured by their own

along the coast. This convention was soon dissolved by Stuyvesant because it was more interested in stating the rights of the people and protesting against their grievances than in carrying out the director's program (O'CALLAGHAN, E. B., *History of New Netherland*, ii, p. 242 et seq.). In the last year of Dutch rule another convention was held, which was composed of two delegates from each town. It, too, got into a controversy with the governor, and was unable to accomplish anything (OSGOOD, H. L., *American Colonies in the Seventeenth Century*, ii, p. 158).

[9] For a contemporary account—unfriendly to Director Kieft— showing how the Indian wars started, see JAMESON, *op. cit.*, pp. 213-214, 226-229. For an account of the same in which Kieft's side of the case is presented, see *ibid.*, pp. 273-284.

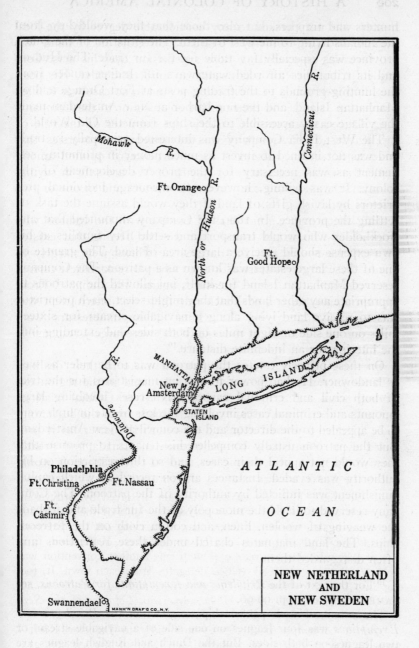

NEW NETHERLAND
AND
NEW SWEDEN

hunters and trappers, but also those that they would buy from the Indians living to the west of them. The situation of the Dutch province was especially favorable for the fur trade. The Hudson and its tributaries afforded waterways for Indian canoes from the hunting-grounds to the trading posts at Fort Orange and on Manhattan Island, and the fine harbor at New Amsterdam made the village easily accessible to the ships from the Old World.

Patroons   The West India Company was interested principally in trade and was not inclined to invest as much money in promoting settlement as was necessary for the proper development of the colony. It was willing, however, to encourage individual proprietors by lavish gifts of land if they would assume the task of settling the province. In 1629 the Company announced that any stockholder who would transport and settle fifty families at his own expense should receive a large area of land. The grantee of one of these large estates was known as a patroon. The Company reserved Manhattan Island for itself, but allowed the patroons to appropriate any other lands that they might select. Each proprietor was to receive land lying along a navigable stream for sixteen miles on one side or eight miles on both sides and extending into the interior for an indefinite distance.[10]

On these princely estates the patroon was to be ruler as well as landowner. He had power to appoint magistrates for the trial of both civil and criminal causes. Civil cases involving large amounts and criminal cases involving the loss of life or limb were to be appealed to the director and the council at New Amsterdam. But the patroon usually compelled his tenants to promise that they would not appeal their cases, and so this restriction on his authority was evaded. Instances are on record in which capital punishment was inflicted by authority of the patroon. The Company reserved to itself the monopoly of the fur trade and forbade the weaving of woolen, linen, and cotton cloth on the patroonships. The land magnates chafed under these restrictions and often disregarded them.

[10] For the text of the *Privileges and Exemptions for Patroons*, see JAMESON, *op. cit.*, pp. 90-96.

The extent of each patroonship as given in the *Privileges and Exemptions* was four leagues on one side of a navigable stream or two leagues on both sides. But the Dutch and English leagues are not the same in length; hence the apparent discrepancy between this statement and the one above (p. 91).

As soon as the Company announced its proposal, lands were promptly taken up and large patroonships were created. Some of the prominent stockholders who got the first information regarding the scheme hurried instructions to their agents in New Netherland and thereby secured for themselves the best lands. One stockholder received the whole of Staten Island and planted a colony there.[11] But the most noted, and the only really successful, patroonship was Rensselaerswyck, founded by and named for Kiliaen van Rensselaer, a pearl merchant of Amsterdam, who received a grant from the Company and enlarged it by buying other lands adjacent to it. In this way he and his associates got possession of a large boundary of land surrounding Fort Orange (but not including it, as it was reserved for the Company) and covering more than two modern counties.

The patroon system was not a success. Despite favorable conditions of soil and climate, agents, patroons, and tenants all seemed dissatisfied with their lot. The reason for this was that the system itself was wrong. It was an effort to transplant to America a mediæval feudal land policy that was not suited to New World conditions. Land was too plentiful and easy to get for tenants to bind their freedom by accepting the terms of the patroons. Not only were neighboring provinces offering lands to settlers on easy terms, but the Dutch Company itself in the charter of *Privileges and Exemptions* promised to give to emigrants in complete ownership all the land that they could improve.[12] Consequently, most of the settlers in New Netherland were not tenants but freeholders, as they were in other colonies, and the greater part of the land held by the patroons was unoccupied.

The Delaware region was considered by the Dutch as a part of New Netherland, and, as we have seen, Fort Nassau was erected by them on the east side of the Delaware River in 1624. The first attempt to establish a settlement within the present limits of Delaware was made by a group of stockholders of the Dutch West India Company, who had received from the Company a boundary of land southwest of Delaware Bay. Under the leadership of De Vries, one of the proprietors, thirty emigrants came over in 1631 and established themselves near Cape Henlopen at a place which they called Swannendael (now Lewes). The settlement was protected by a palisade, crops were planted

The occupation of the Delaware region

[11] JAMESON, *op. cit.*, pp. 199, 205, 211.
[12] *Ibid.*, p. 94.

in the spring, and the little colony started out under promising auspices. Unfortunately, however, the leader whom De Vries left in charge on his return to Holland aroused the enmity of the Indians, and the colony was completely destroyed by them before the end of the second year.[13] This tragedy ended the first attempt to colonize Delaware, as the proprietors made no effort to renew the settlement.

New
Sweden:
Organiza-
tion of a
trading
company
in Sweden

The first successful attempt to plant a colony in what is now the State of Delaware was made by the Swedes. The failure of the Dutch to support their claim by further settlement left this territory open to other nations, and Sweden was the first power to seize the opportunity which Holland had neglected. Sweden's great king, Gustavus Adolphus, had become interested in colonization by the reported opportunities for wealth in the American fur trade. But he was the leading figure in the Thirty Years' War, and his participation in this great conflict during the last years of his reign prevented him from carrying out his plans for colonial expansion.

After his death (1632), Oxenstiern, who administered the government in the name of the young Queen Christina, decided to stake off a claim for his country in America. With his encouragement and support, a Swedish trading company was organized, which was to act as an agency of the government in establishing a colony in the New World. At this time Peter Minuit, who had been forced out of his position as director at New Amsterdam, was at Stockholm and offered to lead the expedition. His offer was accepted, and under his leadership two vessels, carrying about fifty emigrants, were sent to the Delaware region in 1638. On arriving at their destination the colonists bought lands from the Indians and laid claim to the western shore of Delaware Bay and River from Cape Henlopen to the present site of Philadelphia and the eastern, or Jersey, shore from Cape May to a point opposite Chester, Pennsylvania. By later purchases the northern boundary was advanced slightly on the eastern side of the river, and on the western shore it was pushed up to Trenton Falls. To this region was given the name of New Sweden.[14]

---

[13] *Ibid.*, pp. 313-314; MYERS, A. C., ed., *Narratives of Early Pennsylvania, West New Jersey, and Delaware,* pp. 15-17.

[14] For an excellent account of the founding of the Swedish colony, written by Rev. Israel Acrelius in 1759, see MYERS, *op. cit.*, pp. 57·

The first settlement was made at the present site of Wilmington (1638) and was called Fort Christina in honor of the queen.
Other forts were built and about a dozen small settlements were
established, though they were little more than trading centers.
These posts were scattered along a length of about thirty-five
miles north and south of Fort Christina and were mostly on the
western side of the river.[15] In 1643 the seat of government was
moved to one of the islands at the mouth of the Schuylkill River,
near the site of Philadelphia. The brisk fur trade carried on with
the Indians aroused the jealousy of the Dutch at New Amsterdam. The Swedes, however, were not at this time a colonizing
people, and few emigrants from the homeland came to New
Sweden. In order to encourage the growth of the colony the
government sent over a number of convicts, who were bound to
the service of the Company for a few years and then became
free. The colony grew very slowly. At no time in its history did
the number of settlers equal four hundred, and a portion of these
were Dutch and Finns.[16]

*The estab-
lishment
of the
colony*

As soon as the Dutch in New Amsterdam heard that the
Swedes had occupied the Delaware region a protest was sent to
them by the governor, William Kieft, declaring that the land
held by the Swedes belonged to New Netherland. The Swedes
ignored the protest and the Dutch did not back it up with force.
It was more than a decade before the New Amsterdam authorities
began again to contest the right of the Swedes to the Delaware
region. This acquiescence on the part of the Dutch governor was
due to the desire of the home authorities to keep on good terms
with the Swedish government. The Thirty Years' War was going
on in Europe at this time, and England, Sweden, and the United
Netherlands, being Protestant powers, looked upon Spain and

*New
Sweden
conquered
by the
Dutch*

---

64. For a short contemporary account, see *ibid.*, pp. 86-89. For a
map of New Sweden showing the boundaries, see JOHNSON, AMAN-
DUS, *The Swedish Settlements on the Delaware*, i, opposite p. 164.

[15] For a contemporary list of the settlements and the number of
inhabitants of each, see MYERS, *op. cit.*, pp. 110-114. For a map showing the location of these settlements, see JOHNSON, *op. cit.*, ii, opposite
p. 496. For a contemporary map of New Sweden (made in 1655),
see *ibid.*, opposite p. 514. This map is also found in LINDESTROM,
Geographia Americæ, opposite p. 156.

[16] Governor Rising gives the population of the entire province in
1654, as 370 (MYERS, *op. cit.*, p. 149).

the papacy as common enemies. As long as this great struggle continued, it was necessary for these countries to maintain cordial relations with one another. They were, therefore, unwilling to allow their conflicting interests in America to jeopardize the good understanding which was so necessary to their mutual safety in Europe. This explains not only the tolerance of the Dutch toward the alleged trespassing of the Swedes, but also the forbearance of the English toward the Dutch and the Swedes, both of whom were holding lands claimed by England.

But the Thirty Years' War ended in 1648, and by this time the danger to Europe from Spain in alliance with the Catholic Church was no longer strongly felt by the Protestant allies. So the bond that had hitherto held them together began to loosen and colonial rivalries now became active. The Dutch governor, Peter Stuyvesant, was ready to reassert the authority of the Dutch over the territory held by their southern neighbors, and the Swedes were in no condition to put up a real defense against their assailants. Not only did they have a very small fighting force, but there was at Fort Christina but one round of gunpowder. The weakness of the colony was not due to the bad management of the governors, but to the failure of the Company and the Swedish authorities to give it proper support. When the Dutch vessels came up the Delaware River, carrying six or seven hundred men, the Swedish forts surrendered without firing a shot (1655) and New Sweden became a part of New Netherland. By the terms of the surrender the settlers were not to be disturbed in the possession of their lands, and such as wished to do so could return to Sweden.[17]

Peter Stuyvesant the last of the Dutch governors   The last and most picturesque of the Dutch governors, or directors, was Peter Stuyvesant, who was at the head of the government in New Netherland from 1647 to the end of Dutch rule (1664). He came to this important position with some administrative experience, as he had been governor of the island of Curaçoa. The task that he had assumed on becoming director in New Netherland was a difficult one and called for exceptional wisdom, tact, and ability, qualities not possessed to any considerable extent by the new governor.

[17] For good contemporary accounts of conditions in New Sweden prior to the Dutch conquest, see MYERS, *op. cit.*, pp. 65-81, 95-116, 120-129, 136-151, 156-165. For an excellent account of the surrender of New Sweden, written by Johan Rising, who was governor of the colony at the time, see *ibid.*, pp. 170-176.

He was not, however, entirely lacking in those traits of character that make for success in administration. He was courageous, intensely loyal to his country and the interests of the Company, and probably law-honest, though he was too covetous to be honest in the absolute sense. With his good qualities were combined a number of faults, and this combination of good and evil in his personality reminds one of Sir William Berkeley of Virginia. His rigid conservatism, autocratic notions of government, narrow intolerance, and the inability to throw off his Old World prejudices or to adapt them to New World conditions rendered him incompetent for any administrative position in a frontier community. His quick temper and overbearing disposition led him at times into asserting his authority in a manner that made him seem ridiculous. Indeed, it is more than likely that to the liberty-loving colonists—especially those that were blessed with a sense of humor—this testy martinet, blustering around on his wooden leg, appeared more like the caricature of a tyrant than a real despot.

Unfortunately, his subjects, as he regarded the citizens, were not all impressed with the humorous side of his tyranny. There were a number of them who felt the weight of his severity. He was especially harsh with the adherents of dissenting religious denominations; for he and the leading ministers of the Dutch Reformed Church were determined that no public worship should be allowed except such as conformed to the practices of the established church (the Dutch Reformed). In carrying out this policy he forbade the Lutherans to engage in public worship, fined and banished Baptists, and inflicted severe penalties on the Quakers.[18] Such an intolerant policy was contrary to the traditions of the Dutch Republic, which prided itself on offering an asylum for the persecuted. The Company, therefore, did not approve of Stuyvesant's severity against dissenters and advised him to allow freedom of conscience to the people.[19]

Despite his shortcomings, Stuyvesant's administration was marked by several important achievements. He grappled in vigorous fashion with a number of problems, and in some instances

[18] See O'CALLAGHAN, op. cit., i, pp. 320-321, 348-355; JAMESON, op. cit., pp. 393-394, 400-401; and American Historical Record, i, pp. 4-8.

[19] For a quotation from this instruction, see JAMESON, op. cit., p. 400, note.

Settlement
of the
boundary
dispute
between
Connec-
ticut and
New
Nether-
land

was able to solve them. The aggressive New Englanders were pushing westward and encroaching more and more on the Company's territory, while the Swedes were gradually appropriating Dutch lands in the south. If these aggressions were not checked, New Netherland would soon shrink into such limits that the remaining area would be too small to form the basis of a great Dutch commonwealth.

The director was not afraid to attack these knotty problems. He had no difficulty in solving the Swedish problem, as has been shown above. But even before this was done, he had undertaken to adjust the differences that had arisen between New Netherland and New England. The big-stick method employed against New Sweden would not work in this case, as the New Englanders outnumbered the New Netherlanders by more than sixteen to one.[20] He had, therefore, to resort to diplomacy. A meeting was arranged between the director and the commissioners of the New England Confederation (1650), at which an agreement was entered into settling for the time being the points at issue.

One cause of dispute had been the location of the boundary between Connecticut and New Netherland. This was settled by dividing Long Island between the claimants and fixing the boundary on the mainland at a line ten miles east of the Hudson.[21] This treaty was never ratified by the British home authorities and was, therefore, not legally binding, but it did serve for a while as a *modus vivendi* between the Dutch and English colonists.

Unpopular
measures
carried
out by the
director

Director Stuyvesant tried also to carry out certain internal reforms (or rather measures, as all of them were not reforms), such as the putting down of smuggling, the prohibition of the sale of arms and intoxicants to the Indians, the regulation of the fur trade, and the collection of a high customs duty.[22] Some of

[20] Stuyvesant estimated that the New Englanders were fifty times as numerous as the New Netherlanders. Dr. Jameson, however, thinks that this is an exaggeration and that the populations of the two sections in 1647 were, respectively, about 25,000 and 1,500. See JAMESON, *op. cit.*, p. 459, also note.

[21] For the text of this agreement see O'CALLAGHAN, *op. cit.*, ii, pp. 151-155.

[22] One of the paternal measures of the director was the effort to regulate the liquor traffic by restricting the sale of drinks on Sunday to certain hours. Some attempt at curbing the intemperance

these measures were unwise in themselves, and all of them were carried out with a lack of tact that aroused antagonism. The program of the director had, to a considerable extent, been laid out for him in the instructions issued by the Company, and so he was not altogether to blame for the unwise policies of his administration. But he got the blame for everything and so became very unpopular with an influential element in New Amsterdam.[23]

While Stuyvesant was wrestling unsuccessfully with his internal difficulties, a new danger arose from without—the threat of invasion by an English force. The territory held by the Dutch had all along been claimed by the British on the basis of the Cabot discoveries, and for many years they had protested against the Dutch occupation. New Netherland split the English continental colonies into two divisions and rendered it more difficult for the English government to enforce its commercial regulations in America. Dutch trading-vessels were carrying tobacco from the Chesapeake colonies to European markets and were distributing throughout the British colonies goods brought to New Amsterdam from foreign ports. This was in plain violation of the Navigation Law, by the terms of which this carrying trade was

England asserts a claim to New Netherland

---

of the people should have been made, for nearly one-fourth of the houses in New Amsterdam were "Brandy shops, Tobacco or Beer houses." The wet sentiment in the town was, however, so strong that the citizens paid scant heed to Stuyvesant's well-intentioned effort in favor of temperance. See O'CALLAGHAN, *Laws of New Netherland*, p. 93.

For a picture of New Amsterdam, engraved in 1651, see ANDREWS W. L., *New Amsterdam, New Orange, New York*, opposite p. 31. For other contemporary pictures of the town of New York, see *Views of Early New York* (Colonial Order of the Acorn), opposite p. 27 for 1671; opposite p. 89 for 1735; opposite p. 111 for the end of the colonial period.

[23] For a severe indictment of the policy not only of Stuyvesant, but of the Company as well, see JAMESON, *op. cit.*, pp. 320-352, especially pp. 337-352. For the *Memorial* which accompanied this *Remonstrance*, suggesting remedies, see *New York Colonial Documents*, i, pp. 259-261. For an answer to these complaints made by a partisan of Stuyvesant, see JAMESON, *op. cit.*, pp. 359-377. For the grievances complained of by the convention composed of delegates from eight towns and villages (1653), see O'CALLAGHAN, E. B., *History of New Netherland*, ii, pp. 243-246.

all to be reserved to English and colonial ships. Besides, England and Holland were rivals on the sea. As long as the Thirty Years' War lasted, this rivalry was held in abeyance, for those two Protestant powers had to maintain friendly relations with each other at a time when Protestantism was engaged in a mighty contest with Catholicism. But soon after this great struggle was ended by the Treaties of Westphalia (1648), the *entente cordiale* between the Dutch and the English governments came to an end and a free rein was given to commercial jealousies. In such a state of feeling it could hardly be expected that Britain would long abstain from asserting her claim to the Hudson River region.

New Netherland threatened by English attack

England and the Netherlands were led by their conflicting commercial and colonial interests into three wars with each other during the quarter century following the Peace of Westphalia (1648). The first of these began in 1652 under the Protectorate of Cromwell. After the war had been going on in Europe for about two years, an effort was made to wrest New Netherland from the Dutch. An expedition was sent to New England (1654), where recruits were to be enlisted and the joint English and American force was to proceed against New Amsterdam. The New Englanders welcomed the opportunity of taking away from the Dutch the territory coveted by them and they volunteered freely for the service. When everything was about ready and the expedition was on the point of leaving Boston for New Amsterdam, word was received that England and Holland had made peace. New Netherland was thus given a longer lease of life, and Stuyvesant was left in control for about another decade.

New Netherland taken over by the English

In the meantime Charles II had ascended the throne (1660). A more rigid policy of enforcing the commercial regulations was now entered upon, with the hope of giving English and colonial ships a monopoly of the trade between the colonies and the mother country. As New Amsterdam was the center of the illegal trade carried on by Dutch ships, the British government was now more anxious than ever to annex New Netherland to the British empire. This plan of the home authorities was supported by the desire of Connecticut and New Haven settlers to expand westward into the territory held by the Dutch. Connecticut had received a charter from the king (1662) which gave the Pacific Ocean as her western limit. On the basis of this patent Connecticut was claiming all the lands in New Netherland except those already occupied by the Dutch settlers.[24] Her people were thus anxious to brush aside the agreement of 1650 and so remove the barriers to their westward expansion. As both colonial and imperial interests would be advanced by the assertion of British control over New Netherland, the fate of the latter colony was sealed.

Charles, having decided to annex the Dutch territory to his possessions, granted New Netherland to his brother James, the Duke of York, and made preparations to conquer it. Four ships, carrying a considerable body of troops, recruited largely from volunteers in New England, appeared before New Amsterdam (August, 1664), and demanded the surrender of the colony to the English king. The expedition was led by Colonel Richard Nicolls, who had been appointed by the Duke of York as his deputy governor. When Nicolls called on Stuyvesant to surrender, the latter showed signs of fight and at first refused. But he was not in a position to put up an effective defense against the threatened attack, as the odds were overwhelmingly against him. The fort had fallen into disrepair and there was a scarcity of gunpowder and provisions in the town. The Company had failed to lend proper support to its colony, and this neglect was largely responsible for the weak condition of its defenses.[25] Moreover, as we have seen, Governor Stuyvesant had alienated the good will of many of the people by his arbitrary measures, and there was no strong, united public sentiment in favor of him. His position was still further weakened by the fact that a large part of the population of the province was English and preferred British to Dutch rule. Nicolls offered generous terms to the people, who were in favor of accepting them instead of jeopardizing their lives and property by a foolish resistance. The director was thus forced to surrender the province without striking a blow.[26]

New Netherland now became a proprietary province, as James, Duke of York and Albany, had been made proprietor of New Netherland and other territory granted to him by a patent issued by the king in March, 1664. His domain included all the land

Territory granted to the Duke of York

[24] JAMESON, *op. cit.*, p. 441.

[25] For an excellent account of the weakness of the town and province and the responsibility for this condition, see Stuyvesant's report to the States General, JAMESON, *op. cit.*, pp. 458-466.

[26] For the terms of the surrender, see *New York Colonial Documents*, ii, pp. 250-253.

between the Connecticut and Delaware rivers, together with northeastern Maine, Long Island, and other islands along the New England coast. He also claimed authority over the few Dutch and Swedes who were located on the western side of the Delaware, on the ground that the territory occupied by them had been a part of New Netherland. Later, however, he yielded all his rights to Delaware and Pennsylvania to William Penn and granted New Jersey to Sir George Carteret and Lord Berkeley. Moreover, the Maine district and the islands along the New England coast, except Long Island, were soon taken from under his authority and placed under the jurisdiction of Massachusetts.

The duke was also unable to establish the eastern boundary of his province at the Connecticut River. For if this were done Massachusetts and Connecticut would be deprived of territory that had been granted to them by their charters, and naturally they contested the claim. This dispute was afterward settled by an agreement fixing the boundary between New York and these two provinces at its present location. James's grant had been so trimmed down by these changes that it now included only Long Island and a narrow strip of territory along the Hudson River. Later, however, thanks to the efforts of Governor Dongan, the ablest of James's deputies, the Iroquois Indians were brought within the British sphere of influence, and the limits of the province were extended westward to Lake Ontario. Governor Dongan also encroached upon Penn's rights in Pennsylvania and raised a boundary dispute with him, which was finally settled by making the southern boundary of the province the forty-second parallel, the present boundary between New York and Pennsylvania.

Powers of the proprietor

By the charter the Duke of York was given power to make laws and govern the people of his province. The only limitations on his authority were that all laws and ordinances were to be in harmony with the laws of England, and appeals were to be allowed from the provincial courts to the Privy Council. There was no provision for a representative assembly. The proprietor was thus almost an absolute monarch in his province.[27] James never came to America himself, but delegated his large authority to a gov-

[27] For the text of the charter to the Duke of York, granted by the king in 1664, see THORPE, F. N., *Charters*, pp. 1637-1640. For the text of the charter as renewed in 1674, see *ibid.*, pp. 1641-1644. The first of these patents is given in abbreviated form in MacDonald, W., *Select Charters*, pp. 137-139.

ernor and council whom he had chosen to represent him in the province.

The first man to hold the responsible position of governor was Colonel Richard Nicolls, who showed exceptional wisdom and tact in the exercise of the autocratic power intrusted to him. It was fortunate that James made such a wise choice, for the situation called for a man of real ability. The social and religious differences of the people created problems that required careful handling. The population of the province, even at this early date, was made up of representatives of a number of different nationalities.[28] Of these the Dutch were probably more numerous than any other group. They lived mostly on Manhattan Island, at Fort Albany, and on the western end of Long Island. By the terms of the surrender they had been promised freedom of worship, protection of their property rights, and a continuance of some of their customs. The eastern end of Long Island and Westchester on the mainland had been settled by New Englanders, who were demanding all the rights of Englishmen. There was also a variety of religions. The Dutch belonged to the Dutch Reformed Church and the New Englanders were Congregationalists. Besides, there were now a few adherents of the Anglican denomination, which was to be the established church, and the proprietor was a Catholic.

Nicolls as first governor: his difficulties

Such a lack of homogeneity in the population made it evident that absolutism would have to be tempered by a prudent concession to local feeling. Nicolls appreciated this and was thus able to perform the difficult feat of making Stuart autocracy acceptable to the citizens, a large part of whom were imbued with the tradition of self-government. He owed his success in large measure to his geniality of disposition and personal magnetism, which enabled him to make his contacts with the people without friction.

Nicolls's policy was to establish English institutions in the province as soon as circumstances would permit. Immediately he gave a number of places English instead of Dutch names; for example, New Netherland was changed to New York, and New Amsterdam and Fort Orange became, respectively, New York

English institutions established

[28] Father Isaac Jogues, a Catholic priest who visited New Amsterdam in 1646, said that at that time there were eighteen different languages spoken in the town (JAMESON, F., *Narratives of New Netherland*, p. 259).

and Albany, in honor of the duke's titles. For about a year he made no change in the government of New Amsterdam, leaving the administration in the hands of the Dutch officials. Then by order of the duke he put an end to the old government and substituted for it one by a mayor, aldermen, and sheriffs. It would have been impossible for Nicolls to carry out the instruction in his commission to establish the Anglican as the state church.[29] There was such a great variety of religious beliefs that toleration of all denominations was the only possible course. It was, therefore, this policy of tolerance that he adopted, though he required every community to support a church.

System of government under Nicolls

For the English colonists Nicolls organized a government like that of the counties in England. Westchester, Staten Island, and Long Island were united in a district called "Yorkshire." For this district the governor compiled a collection of laws known as the "Duke's Laws," which were taken largely from the codes of Massachusetts and New Haven. These laws were submitted to an assembly of deputies chosen by Westchester and the towns of Long Island.[30] The deputies were at first inclined to object to a body of laws which the people's representatives had had no voice in framing. Besides, the constitution did not provide for the kind of local government that they had been accustomed to. But Nicolls's diplomacy won over the opposition and the new code was accepted.

The "Duke's Laws"

The "Duke's Laws" were both a code of laws and a constitution, in that they applied to relations between individuals and also provided for a system of government. According to this constitution, the local government in each town was to be in the hands of a constable and a board of eight overseers, elected by the freeholders but responsible to the governor. There were also to be justices of the peace, appointed by the governor. These were to perform the ordinary judicial duties of the office and were to meet in a body once a year as a Court of Assize, which body could make laws with the consent of the governor. This, however, was not a representative assembly, as the justices did not represent

[29] For Nicolls's commission, see BRODHEAD, J. R., *History of the State of New York*, ii, appendix, p. 653.

[30] *Documents Relating to the Colonial History of the State of New York*, usually cited as *New York Colonial Documents* (old ed.), xiv, pp. 564-565.

certain districts, nor did the people have any voice in choosing them.[31]

This constitution not only failed to give the people a voice in the provincial government, but the system of local government provided for by it was not satisfactory to the New Englanders on Long Island, who wanted the town-meeting plan. There was, therefore, some objection to it on Long Island, but it never developed into a serious opposition. The "Duke's Laws" at first applied only to "Yorkshire," but in a few years they were in force throughout the whole province.

In 1670 Charles II signed with Louis XIV the disgraceful Treaty of Dover. By this secret agreement Charles was to receive financial support from the king of France, who was to be compensated by receiving the aid of England against Holland. A war with Holland followed (1672-74), in the course of which a strong Dutch fleet appeared before New York and demanded its surrender. The town was defenseless and was forced to yield after only a few volleys had been fired (1673). New Netherland now passed back under the authority of the Dutch, but was returned to England by the Peace of Westminster (1674). *Dutch reconquer New York*

James was restored to the proprietorship when New Netherland was returned to the British. He sent over as his deputy another army officer, Edmund Andros. Andros was an honest man of average ability and tried to carry out the commands of the proprietor faithfully; but he was untactful and did not have his temper under good control. His lack of tact, together with the absolutist policy he was forced to carry out, made him unpopular and he was recalled by James. *Andros as governor*

The next governor was Colonel Thomas Dongan, an Irish Catholic. His religion was a drawback to him, as the people were strongly prejudiced against Catholics. As a counterpoise to this objection, he brought an instruction from the duke to establish a legislative assembly. This was a wise step for the proprietor to take, as the people were loudly demanding a voice in the government. James made this concession to public sentiment reluctantly, for he was autocratic in his notions and had no sympathy with democratic ideas. But he had had considerable trouble in collecting *A representative assembly set up and then abolished*

[31] For the text of the Duke's Laws, see *Collections* of the New York Historical Society, 1st series, i, pp. 307-397. For alterations and amendments later made while Nicolls was governor, see pp. 398-428.

his revenues and he thought that the people would be more inclined to pay taxes if they were voted by an assembly of their own choosing. So in his instructions to Dongan, there was the provision that laws in New York should be made, as in Virginia, by a legislature consisting of the governor, council, and representatives of the freeholders, subject to a veto by the proprietor.[32]

In compliance with this instruction an assembly met in October, 1683, and enacted a number of measures, the most important of which were the *Charter of Liberties and Privileges.* These laws embodied the beliefs of the representatives as to popular rights and religious toleration.[33] The charter received the approval of the proprietor; but before it was returned to New York Charles II had died and James had become king (February 6, 1685). James was planning a radical change in the administration of the northern colonies by uniting them under a single jurisdiction and he felt that a popular assembly in New York would be an obstacle to his scheme. Accordingly, the *Charter* was disallowed by the Privy Council and later (1687) the assembly came to an end.[34]

The able administration of Governor Dongan

Dongan was a man of exceptional ability and his administration was very acceptable to the people. His policy was also favorable to the interests of the proprietor and the extension of British influence in America.

The Iroquois brought under British influence

In his correspondence with the French governors of Canada he boldly upheld British rights. His greatest achievement for the empire was the establishment of British authority over the territory of the Iroquois. This was effected by an agreement with the Iroquois chieftains entered into by them at Albany with Governor Dongan and Lord Howard of Effingham, governor of Virginia. The Iroquois, through other Indians controlled by them, had been attacking the frontiers of Virginia and Maryland. They now agreed to desist from such raids in the future and also to acknowledge themselves as subjects of England. As a token of their allegiance to the English government they promised to put up the arms of the Duke of York in their fortified villages.[35] By this

[32] For Dongan's instructions, see *New York Colonial Documents,* iii, pp. 331-334.

[33] BRODHEAD, J. R., *History of the State of New York,* ii, appendix, pp. 659-661.

[34] *New York Colonial Documents,* iii, pp. 354, 357; ANDREWS, *Colonial Period,* iii, ch. 3.

[35] *New York Colonial Documents,* iii, pp. 448, 509.

treaty and the agreement entered into with Penn, referred to above, the boundary of New York was pushed southward to its present limits and westward to the French possessions.

NEW JERSEY

The region now known as New Jersey was a part of New Netherland, and so it passed under British control at the time New Netherland was wrested from the Dutch. It was also included in the grant that was made to the Duke of York by the king that same year (1664). The duke had received such a princely domain that he was willing to give a good slice of it to two of his friends. Soon after receiving his patent, he granted to Lord John Berkeley and Sir George Carteret that portion of his land lying south of Manhattan Island and between the Delaware River and Bay and the Atlantic Ocean. The land thus granted was called New Jersey, being so named because of the heroic defense of Jersey Island that had been maintained by Sir George Carteret against the forces of Cromwell in the Civil War. *New Jersey granted to Sir George Carteret and Lord Berkeley*

When the English took over New Netherland there were only a few settlements within the present limits of New Jersey. The Dutch had failed in their efforts to colonize this region, largely on account of the hostility of the Indians. There were at that time some Dutch settlers on the west shore of the lower Hudson, and a few Swedes, Finns, and Dutch on the Delaware.[36] These were the only white people in the province. The English occupation gave an impetus to settlement; and Puritans from New England and Long Island began to come in at once. Some of them received land grants from Governor Nicolls, of New York, and settled near Elizabethtown and at Middletown and Shrewsbury.[37] The proprietors welcomed these New Englanders and encouraged others to come. In 1665 Philip Carteret, a relative of Sir George, came over as governor, bringing about thirty colonists with him. These settled at Elizabethtown, which was made the capital of the province. *Early settlements*

Immigration to New Jersey was encouraged by the liberal policy of the proprietors, who offered the settlers religious freedom, a voice in the making of the laws, and grants of land on easy terms. As a result of these promises, the province had a considerable increase in population during the first decade. Some

[36] *Ibid.*, iii, p. 71.
[37] *New Jersey Archives*, 1st series, ii, pp. 14-19, 43-46.

of the newcomers were from the mother country, but most of them were from New England.

Political
authority
of the pro-
prietors

The New Jersey proprietors contended that their patent conferred upon them not only the right to dispose of the land granted to them, but also the authority to govern their colony. They proceeded, therefore, to issue (February 20, 1665) a statement of principles known as the "Concession and Agreement," by which the people were to be governed. According to this plan, there was to be a governor appointed by the proprietors, and he was to be assisted by a council of his own appointment and by an assembly composed of representatives chosen by the freemen. No one was to be molested on account of his religious opinions.[38]

The
division
of New
Jersey

In 1674 Lord Berkeley sold his interest in New Jersey to two English Quakers, John Fenwick and Edward Byllynge. These new proprietors became involved in debt and had to turn over their lands to the management of three trustees, one of whom was William Penn. In 1676 the Quaker proprietors entered into an agreement with Carteret whereby New Jersey was divided into two parts. A line was drawn from the lower middle coast to the Delaware River which divided the territory into East Jersey and West Jersey.[39] Carteret received the former and the Quaker proprietors the latter.

The le-
gality of
the New
Jersey
govern-
ment
questioned

The government organized by the proprietors did not rest on a strictly legal basis. For in the original New Jersey patent there was no clause specifically stating that the proprietors were to exercise governmental powers in their province. Probably the Duke of York, in issuing the patent to Carteret and Berkeley, did not intend to divest himself of any of his governmental rights over New Jersey. But he did not at first protest against this usurpation of his rights, and the New Jersey proprietors were allowed to consolidate their authority over their province. It was not long, however, before he decided to assert his political authority over New Jersey, and Andros was sent over as governor with a commission that covered New Jersey as well as New York. Andros insisted on his right to collect duties on goods brought into the Jerseys and also tried to exercise governmental power over both of these provinces. This caused a good deal of friction, especially between Andros and the governor of East Jersey. The

[38] For the "Concession and Agreement," see MacDonald, W., *Select Charters,* no. 31; also Thorpe, F.N., *Charters,* pp. 25, 35ff.
[39] *New Jersey Archives,* 1st series, i, pp. 205-219, 232, 326-327.

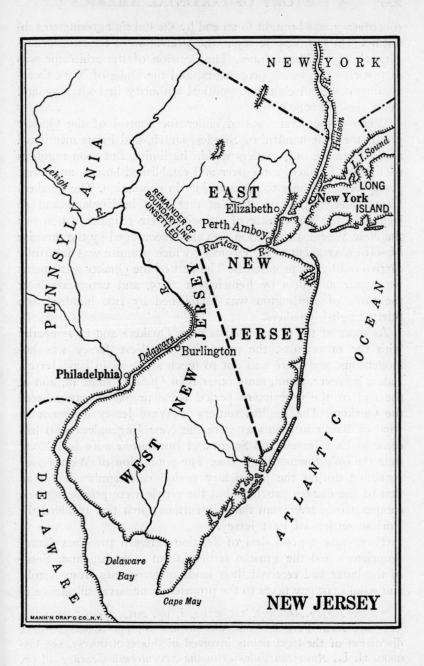

controversy was brought to an end by the duke's agreeing to submit his rights in New Jersey to the arbitration of the ex-attorney-general, Sir William Jones. The decision of the arbitrator was in favor of the Jersey proprietors, and the Duke of York thereupon gave up all claims to political authority in both East and West Jersey (1680).[40]

When West Jersey passed under the control of the Quaker proprietors, the handful of Swedes, Dutch, and Finns mentioned above were the only settlers within its limits. But soon numbers of English Quakers came over and established homes, and West Jersey began at once to grow rapidly in population. The Quakers were undergoing persecution at that time in England and so welcomed the opportunity of enjoying their religion in peace in the New World. Emigration was also encouraged by the promise of self-government to the colonists, which promise was faithfully carried out by the proprietors. The first of the Quaker settlements was made at Salem by Fenwick in 1675, and two years later the town of Burlington was established by two hundred and thirty English Quakers.

As most of the early colonists were Quakers and in sympathy with the proprietors, the population of West Jersey was homogeneous, and there was not so much strife as in East Jersey. Later, however, immigrants other than Quakers came in, and at the end of the proprietary period these probably outnumbered the Quakers. The English settlers in West Jersey were not so fond of living in towns as were the New Englanders who had come to East Jersey, and Salem and Burlington were for a long time the only towns of any size. The population of West Jersey remained during the proprietary period considerably less than that of the eastern province, but the people were prosperous and comparatively free from that contentious spirit that troubled the Puritan settlers of East Jersey.

Friction between the Puritan settlers and the proprietors

There was a good deal of friction between the East Jersey proprietors and the Puritan settlers from New England. Some of the latter had received their lands under grants from Nicolls and would not pay taxes to the proprietors or swear allegiance to

[40] *New Jersey Archives*, 1st series, i, pp. 291, 293-295, 299-318, 323-324; *New York Colonial Documents*, iii, pp. 284-285. For a discussion of the legal points involved in this controversy, see Osgood, H. L., *American Colonies in the Seventeenth Century*, ii, pp. 169-173.

them. They contended that inasmuch as they had bought their lands from the Indians and had received their titles from the Duke of York through Governor Nicolls, they were independent of the proprietors.

Another cause of dispute was the land policy of the proprietors. In New England the practice had been to turn over a large area of land to a town, which in turn would dispose of it to its citizens. The plan of the East Jersey proprietors was to grant land to individuals and to require the grantees to pay them quit rents. The Puritan colonists insisted on the New England method of disposing of land and especially objected to paying the quit rents. In 1670, when the proprietors attempted for the first time to collect the quit rents, a storm of opposition arose which lasted for two years. Two of the towns that had received their land grants from Nicolls asserted their independence of the proprietary government and went so far as to set up an assembly and governor on their own authority. The proprietors sustained their own governor in his resistance to this defiance of his authority, and the movement was crushed, though not without some concessions having been made to the malcontents.

East Jersey was sold in 1682 to William Penn and eleven other Quakers, who soon afterward admitted into the partnership twelve other gentlemen, some of whom were prominent Scotchmen.[41] In March, 1683, the Duke of York issued a patent to these twenty-four proprietors, conferring upon them the right to govern the people. At this time the Scotch Covenanters were being persecuted by their king, and many of them were easily induced by the Scotch partners to emigrate to New Jersey. As these Lowland Scotch and the Scotch-Irish who came later were Presbyterians, their theological beliefs were very similar to those held by the Puritan colonists who had come from New England. These various religious elements were, therefore, able finally to coalesce to make the Presbyterian Church the leading religious denomination of East Jersey. This adjustment, however, did not take place immediately, and for a time there was considerable strife between the newcomers and the old inhabitants growing out of differences in their political ideals.

The troubles of the proprietors did not cease when their authority was acknowledged by the Duke of York. In East Jersey

East Jersey sold to Penn and other proprietors

[41] *New Jersey Archives*, 1st series, i, pp. 366-369, 383-394.

New
Jersey put
under the
authority
of Andros

the difficulty of collecting revenue duties brought them into con-flict with the collector of customs in New York, and complaint was made against East Jersey to the Commissioner of Customs in London. James, who had now become king, was trying to centralize his authority over the northern colonies and took ad-vantage of these complaints to bring the Jerseys under the control of the crown. Proceedings were instituted against the proprietors with the view of annulling their charters. As the king was push-ing these proceedings, the proprietors of both East and West Jersey felt that their fight was hopeless and so surrendered their political authority (1688) but retained their landed rights. Both provinces, together with New York, now passed under the juris-diction of Andros, who was already governor of New England, and so became a part of the Dominion of New England.

New
Jersey
a royal
province

When Andros was deposed in New England and his deputy overthrown in New York, the Jerseys passed back under the con-trol of the proprietors. This change, strange to say, was effected without any disturbance. However, the proprietors were able to enjoy their restored authority for only a few years. For some time there had been considerable complaint against the govern-ment of the Jerseys, as well as that of other proprietary prov-inces. The charge was made that in these jurisdictions pirates and smugglers were given too free a rein. Besides, the Jersey proprietors had lost control of their people as a result of the controversy over quit rents. It seemed desirable, therefore, for the crown to take over the government of these two provinces. As the proprietary government had never rested on a firm legal basis, the crown had a good case. Most of the proprietors were not inclined to fight for their political rights, but tried only to save their title to their land. So after some negotiations they gave up their governmental authority, but were allowed to retain their rights as to quit rents. Both of the Jerseys were now united into one royal province (1702).

SELECTED READINGS

1. The Netherlands at the Beginning of the Sixteenth Century.—Blok, P. J., *A History of the People of the Netherlands*, part iii, chs. *11 and *13.
2. Hudson's Voyage up the Hudson.—Bacon, E. M., *Henry Hud-son*, *chs. 6-8.
3. Sports, Festivals, and Pastimes in New Amsterdam.—Singleton,

Esther, *Dutch New York*, *ch. 13; Goodwin, M. W., *Dutch and English on the Hudson*, *ch. 6.

4. Courtship and Marriage.—Goodwin, *op. cit.*, *ch. 10.
5. Dutch Days and Ways.—Wilson, R. R., *New York*, i, *ch. 4.
6. Schools and Schoolmasters in New Netherland.—Griffis, W. E., *The Story of New Netherland*, *ch. 18; Goodwin, *op. cit.*, *ch. 5.
7. Patroons and Lords of the Manor.—Goodwin, *op. cit.*, *ch. 3.
8. The English Conquest of New Netherland (contemporary account).—Jameson, J. F., ed., *Narratives of New Netherland*, pp. *451-453.
9. The Founding of New Sweden (contemporary accounts).— Myers, A. C., ed., *Narratives of Early Pennsylvania, West New Jersey, and Delaware*, pp. *57-64 and *86-89.
10. The Dutch Conquest of New Sweden (contemporary account). —*Ibid.*, pp. *170-176.
11. New York under Proprietary Rule.—Goodwin, M. W., *op. cit.*, *ch. 8.
12. Administration of Richard Nicolls in New York.—Channing, E., *History of the United States*, ii, pp. *37-44; Andrews, C. M., *Colonial Self-Government*, pp. *79-89.
13. Administration of Thomas Dongan in New York.—Channing, E., *History of the United States*, ii, pp. *143-152; Andrews, C. M., *Colonial Self-Government*, pp. *95-100.
14. The Beginnings of New Jersey.—Fisher, S. G., *The Quaker Colonies*, *ch. 8; Channing, E., *History of the United States*, ii, pp. 44-48, *55-59.
15. Question of the Legality of the Grant to Berkeley and Carteret. —Osgood, H. L., *American Colonies in the Seventeenth Century*, ii, pp. *169-173; Tanner, E. P., *The Province of New Jersey*, *ch. 8, especially pp. *124-132.
16. Planters and Traders of Southern Jersey.—Fisher, E. J., *New Jersey as a Royal Province*, *ch. 9.
17. Scotch Covenanters and Others in East Jersey.—Fisher, E. J., *op. cit.*, *ch. 10.

CHAPTER XI

THE FOUNDING OF THE CAROLINAS

Carolina claimed by both Spain and England

WHEN Charles II became king in 1660 a few bold pioneers were living on the Chowan River, near Albemarle Sound, and in this same year some New Englanders made a temporary settlement on the Cape Fear River. These frontiersmen were the only white people then to be found in all that vast region lying between the present state of Virginia and the Spanish possessions in the south. It was hardly to be expected that a monarch who was so much interested in imperial expansion as was the younger Charles would overlook so fruitful a field for colonization. Even had he been blind to the opportunities offered by this favored region, there were plenty of courtiers around him who would not be slow to point out the possibilities for gain both to themselves and to the empire that would result from the exploitation of this wide area of unappropriated land. Spain claimed this territory, but for more than three-quarters of a century had made no effort to settle it. England had already staked off for herself most of this region, and it had been at the disposal of the king since the charter of the Virginia Company was annulled in 1624.

Carolina granted to eight proprietors

In 1629 Charles I granted to Sir Robert Heath, the attorney-general, all the land between the thirty-first and thirty-sixth degrees of north latitude. To this region was given the name Carolina, in honor of the king.[1] Sir Robert failed to support his title by settlement, and Charles II gladly availed himself of this as an excuse to regain this princely domain. He could now reward with land grants in America some prominent men who had remained faithful to him in his exile or who had helped him back to his throne.

It was in keeping with this policy that he gave Carolina to a group of eight of his favorites (1663) and made them pro-

---

[1] For the text of this patent, see *North Carolina Colonial Records,* i, pp. 1-13, or THORPE, F. N., *Colonial Charters,* pp. 69-76.

The term *Carolina* is derived from the Latin *Carolus,* Charles.

prietors of this vast territory with all the rights and privileges that Lord Baltimore was enjoying in Maryland. These grantees included in their number some of the leading statesmen and politicians of the day. Among them were Edward Hyde, Earl of Clarendon, Lord High Chancellor of England; George Monk, the Duke of Albemarle; Anthony Cooper, Lord Ashley, Chan-

THE CAROLINAS

cellor of the Exchequer; and Sir William Berkeley, Governor of Virginia. The proprietors were given authority to govern the settlers, dispose of the land, and confer titles of nobility, provided they did not employ titles then in use in England. Their power over the settlers was limited by the important provision that laws were to be made with the consent of the freemen or their delegates or deputies. Churches were to be "dedicated and consecrated according to the ecclesiastical laws of our Kingdom of England," but the proprietors were authorized to grant liberty of conscience to all persons who might not be able conscientiously to conform to the practices and beliefs of the Anglican Church.[2]

At first sight it seems strange that such a liberal policy was allowed in Carolina with reference to dissenters by a government that showed such a narrow attitude toward them at home. The explanation lies in the fact that such concessions were deemed necessary to attract settlers to the province. Besides, it was thought that the distance from the new colony to the homeland was so great that religious irregularity in Carolina would not jeopardize the privileged position of the established church in England. They were doubtless right in this view. For the early Carolinians were not inclined to submit to church conventions that reined them up too tightly. Nor was there any danger that nonconformity would develop enough enthusiasm to enable it to spread its contagion to the mother country and thereby menace its orthodoxy.

The proprietors receive a second charter

Two years later (1665) a second charter was granted to the same proprietors, extending the limits of the province on the north to the parallel of 36° 30′ and on the south to the 29th parallel.[3] The northern extension was made to include the settlement on the Chowan River, which was outside of the first Carolina patent.

The first settlements in North Carolina

Before the proprietors received their charter, colonization had begun in the northern portion of their grant, the region now known as North Carolina. The first settlement was the one on the Chowan River, near Albemarle Sound, and was made about 1653 by adventurers from Virginia, who had pushed into the wilderness in search of new home sites.[4] The land on which the colony was planted was level and fertile, and there were a number of large navigable rivers, which abounded in fish and also served as an easy means of communication.

Slow growth of the colony

Despite these favorable circumstances, however, the colony grew slowly, and by 1677 the population was only about three thousand. One of the main reasons for its backwardness was its

---

[2] The full text of this patent is given in THORPE, *op. cit.*; the patent in abbreviated form is given by MACDONALD, W., *Select Charters*, pp. 120-125.

[3] The provisions of the second charter were about the same as those of the first, except those defining the territorial bounds.

[4] CARROLL, B. R., *Historical Collections of South Carolina*, ii, pp. 282-283.

isolation, being separated from the Virginia settlements by wide areas of swamp lands. The rivers, although they promoted communication within the colony, discouraged intercourse with neighboring provinces, for many of them were too wide to be forded, and as they flowed eastward it was impossible to construct roads of any length to the north and south. The roads were, therefore, very poor even as measured by colonial standards. Besides, the harbors were too shallow for large ocean vessels, and so the settlers had little or no trade with the mother country.[5]

It was not long after the Chowan plantation was established before two attempts at colonization were made in southeastern North Carolina. The first of these was made by emigrants from New England (1660), who settled near the mouth of the Cape Fear River. The venture, however, was not a success, and the colony was abandoned in a few years either because of the infertility of the soil or the hostility of the Indians.[6] Another effort to occupy the Cape Fear region was made a few years later (1664), when a group of emigrants from Barbados received a grant from the Carolina proprietors and planted a settlement not far from the scene of the New England failure. The colony started off promisingly and in one year had attained a population of eight hundred.[7] There was, however, a good deal of dissension in the plantation, and in 1667 the enterprise was given up, the settlers going to Albemarle, Virginia, and Massachusetts.[8] *Temporary settlements on the Cape Fear River*

The colony on the Chowan River was slow in expanding southward, and it was not until 1690 that there was any permanent occupation of that portion of North Carolina that lies south of Albemarle Sound. The first settlement permanently established in this region was the one made on the Pamlico River (1690) by French Huguenots from Virginia. Other adventurers soon found their way into this section from Albemarle, Virginia, and Europe, many of the European emigrants being French Huguenots. In 1704 a group of the last-named foreigners planted a settlement on (or near) the Pamlico River, which they called Bath and which enjoyed the distinction of being the first incorporated town *Later settlements in North Carolina*

[5] *North Carolina Colonial Records*, i, p. 54.
[6] Massachusetts Historical Society *Collections*, 3rd series, i, p. 58; LAWSON, JOHN, *The History of Carolina*, pp. 73-74; SALLEY, A. S., *Narratives of Early Carolina (Original Narratives)*, p. 53.
[7] *North Carolina Colonial Records*, i, pp. 153-156.
[8] *Ibid.*, i, pp. 159-161; SALLEY, *op. cit.*, p. 67.

in North Carolina, though it never became anything more than a sleepy village. A few years later other Huguenots from Virginia, probably attracted to the country by the favorable reports of their brethren who were already on the Pamlico, pushed into the North Carolina wilderness and established themselves on the Neuse and Trent rivers. The Huguenots were especially desirable emigrants on account of their character, thrift, and skill, and the proprietors encouraged them to settle in their province.

The German settlement at New Bern

Hardly had the French Protestants become settled on the Neuse, when their colony was reinforced by another group of religious refugees from Europe. These were Swiss and German emigrants, the latter being known as Palatines, as most of them had come originally from the Palatinate.[9] A syndicate headed by a Swiss nobleman, Baron de Graffenried, and another Swiss gentleman, Ludwig Michel, bought a large boundary of land from the Carolina proprietors. As a result of the active efforts of these energetic leaders, about six hundred and fifty German refugees from the Rhine Palatinate and one hundred Swiss emigrants were sent to North Carolina. They were badly treated by the shipmaster on the voyage, and about half of their number died before they reached their destination.

Arriving at their new home on the Neuse River (1710) in the midst of the sickly season, without any provision having been made to receive them, they were again subjected to great suffering, this time from disease and famine. They were so reduced by poverty that they had to sell their tools and clothes to the neighboring inhabitants in order to get enough food to keep them from starvation. Finally, however, they overcame their difficulties, and under the leadership of Graffenried laid the foundations of a flourishing town between the Neuse and the Trent. This they named New Bern, in honor of Graffenried's native city (Bern) in Switzerland. But about the time they had become well established, the Tuscarora War broke out, which was the most horrible Indian conflict ever experienced in North Carolina. The awful struggle lasted two years, during which time the Palatines suffered so greatly in the loss of cattle, the destruction of their homes and crops, and in the loss of life that they never recovered from it. The weakened remnant had to abandon the settlement

[9] For an account of the Palatine exodus and the motives that prompted it, see pp. 349-352.

and Graffenried returned to Europe.[10] The survivors were scattered throughout southeastern North Carolina and ultimately were so completely absorbed by the English population as to lose their racial identity.

In the first attempts at colonization in North Carolina the initiative was taken by the settlers without any assistance from the proprietors. But it was not long before the latter began to take an active interest in the colonization of their province. As a result of their efforts, which included the expenditure of about four thousand pounds in money, three vessels were fitted out and sent from England (1669), carrying a considerable number of emigrants with a liberal supply of guns, ammunition, tools, and provisions. The expedition sailed to Barbados, where it picked up a few recruits. It then proceeded to the Carolina coast under the command of William Sayle, a Bermudian planter, who became the first governor of the new colony. The emigrants touched at Port Royal, a short distance above the mouth of the Savannah River, as that was the place designated for the settlement. But as they were not favorably impressed with this location, they sailed farther northward and entered Charleston Harbor in April, 1670. They chose for their settlement a location on the Ashley River, a short distance above its mouth, which they named Albemarle Point. Here "they entrenched themselves and began to lay out streets and town lots, and to build fortifications and homes."[11] The Indians in the immediate neighborhood gave them a cordial welcome, as they wanted them as allies against their enemies, a tribe living in the vicinity of Port Royal. The colony endured some of the hardships incident to pioneer life, but it did not pass through a period of famine and suffering like that experienced by

The South Carolina colony founded

[10] For an excellent short account of the settlement at New Bern, see CONNOR, R. D. W., *History of North Carolina*, pp. 78-82. For Baron de Graffenried's account, see *Publications of the North Carolina Historical Commission; North Carolina Colonial Records*, i, p. 718.

[11] McCRADY, E., *South Carolina under Proprietary Government*, p. 129. For contemporary accounts of the voyage from Barbados to Port Royal and thence to Albemarle Point, with a brief statement as to conditions in the settlement in the early months of its existence, see SALLEY, *op. cit.*, pp. 114-124, 166. See also *Calendar of State Papers, America and West Indies*, secs. 54, 55, 163; *Shaftesbury Papers*, pp. 117 ff.; *North Carolina Colonial Records*, i, p. 207; and CARROLL, B. R., *Historical Collections of South Carolina*, ii, pp. 296 ff

Virginia and Plymouth. They did not have to depend upon the mother country for their outside food supplies, as did the first settlers in the older colonies, but received them from Virginia and Barbados.

The founding of Charleston

The site of the original settlement was not healthful, and soon some of the colonists went over and settled at the point where the Ashley and Cooper rivers unite to form Charleston Harbor. There were, however, only a few houses at the new site until 1680, when by order of the proprietors it became the seat of government and was given the name of Charlestown.[12] The new town grew rapidly, having a hundred houses in two years, and the old settlement at Albemarle Point began to be abandoned.[13] A contemporary (in 1682) describes Charleston as follows: "The Town is regularly laid out into large and capacious streets, which to Buildings is a great Ornament and Beauty. In it they have reserved convenient places for Building of a Church, Town House, and other Public Structures, an Artillery Ground for the Exercise of their Militia and Wharf's for the Convenience of their Trade and Shipping."[14] The rapid growth of the new town was due in large measure to its fine location on the best harbor on the Atlantic coast south of Virginia. It was protected from the sea by sandbars, but these did not impede access to the harbor by the small vessels of that day. Charleston was, therefore, fitted by nature to be the center of commerce for all the region south of Norfolk, Virginia, and during the eighteenth century it enjoyed the distinction of being the most important city in the South.[15]

Rapid development of the province

Charleston, however, was not the only community that grew rapidly in the decade of the 'eighties. During this period other sections in the colony also had a great increase in population. The proprietors had advertised the advantages of their province and pointed out its superiority in climate and soil to some of the more northerly regions.[16] Events in England at that time were also

[12] The city was known as Charlestown by all colonial writers; but it is thought best to use the modern spelling when referring to it hereafter.

[13] SALLEY, op. cit., p. 167. See also footnote, p. 167.

[14] CARROLL, B. R., Historical Collections, ii, p. 82; quoted by McCRADY, op. cit., p. 183.

[15] For an account of Charleston in 1708 by a contemporary, see SALLEY, op. cit., pp. 362-365.

[16] For contemporary descriptions of Carolina, praising its soil climate, vegetation, etc., see SALLEY, op. cit., pp. 141-156, 168-176

creating conditions that were favorable for an exodus to the New World. The excitement incident to the Catholic scare in 1678,[17] and the fears aroused among radical Protestants by the prospect of a Catholic succession to the throne,[18] made dissenters uneasy and restless in the homeland, and so a goodly number of them came to South Carolina. Five hundred emigrants from England came over in one month, and the population of the province doubled in the two-year period from 1680 to 1682.

The immigrants who came to South Carolina during this decade were not all from England; many of them came from the other continental colonies and from the West Indies, especially Barbados. Prominent among the European emigrants were a band of French Huguenots, who arrived at Charleston in 1680. These Frenchmen had been encouraged to go to Carolina by the English king, who had furnished the two vessels that brought them over.[19] Others came later, and soon these high-class foreigners formed an important part of the population. As they had that exceptional adaptability which is so characteristic of Frenchmen, they easily adjusted themselves to their surroundings and were welcomed by the older inhabitants. The Huguenots settled in a number of the English colonies, but South Carolina got a larger share of them than any other province. The descendants of these religious exiles have played a very important and honorable part in the history of South Carolina and the nation.

French Huguenots in South Carolina

Another good class of emigrants who came over in the early part of this decade were the Scotch, who planted a colony at Port Royal (1683).[20] Their settlement, called Stewart's Town, enjoyed separate government, and this aroused the jealousy of the Charlestonians. Unfortunately, too, Stewart's Town was within

[17] This Catholic scare was a false alarm raised by a lying scoundrel, Titus Oates. He claimed to have knowledge of a plot made by the Catholics to kill the king, burn London, and massacre the Protestants. His unsustained statements were accepted as facts, and a number of innocent Catholics had suffered death before it was discovered that the charges were without foundation. For a good brief account of the so-called "Popish Plot," see CROSS, A. L., *History of England*, pp. 377-380; or LUNT, W. E., *History of England*, pp. 498-499.

[18] At his death Charles II would be succeeded by his brother James, who was a Catholic.

[19] *North Carolina Colonial Records*, i, p. 243.

[20] *Calendar of State Papers, America and West Indies, 1681-85*, secs. 809, 1774.

the limits of the territory claimed by Spain, and a band of Spanish soldiers came up from Florida and attacked the settlement before it had had time to become firmly established (1686). The authorities at Charleston in the beginning showed an inexcusable indifference to the fate of their neighboring colony and failed to send any troops to its aid. The result was an easy victory for the Spaniards, who killed and captured a number of the inhabitants and destroyed the buildings. The few survivors moved to Charleston, and no effort was made by the Scotchmen to rebuild their town.

The Carolinians now forgot their petty jealousies and determined to avenge the wrongs of their fellow-countrymen and forestall further attack by sending an expedition against the Spaniards in Florida. The assembly voted money for an army, and four hundred men were ready to sail for St. Augustine, when the newly-appointed governor arrived and put a curb on this belated enthusiasm by threatening to hang anyone who should participate in the attack.[21] So the angry Carolinians were, as they regarded it, cheated out of their revenge. The governor's reason for holding his people back was that a dependency should not attack a power with which the mother country was at peace.

South Carolina influenced by the British West Indian colonies

South Carolina, more than any other continental colony, was influenced by the social ideals of the West Indian planters. Indeed, the founding of this colony was a sort of westward movement from the British island colonies. The lands in the English sugar islands had begun to wear thin, and the planters there were looking to the Carolina mainland as a virgin field for their industry. Barbados especially was interested in this westward expansion, as the little island was overcrowded with her numerous population, and so took a prominent part in the colonization of South Carolina. Several of the leading men in the early settlements and many of the first colonists came from this island. The connection between South Carolina and the West Indies was strengthened by the fact that in 1670 the Carolina proprietors had the Bahama Islands added to their land grant, and so they were now interested in the development of trade between these islands and their province on the mainland.

It was largely due to this influence that slavery soon became firmly established in South Carolina. At the time Charleston was settled, Barbados had a large slave population—about two

[21] SALLEY, A. S., ed., *Narratives of Early Carolina*, pp. 205-206.

Negroes to one white man—and a very rigid slave code was deemed necessary to keep the blacks under proper subjection. The Barbadian attitude toward slavery was brought over to the Ashley River colony, where conditions of soil and climate favored its perpetuation. For this reason and the additional one that in South Carolina the slaves also became more numerous than the freemen this province imposed greater restraints on its Negroes than did any other continental colony.

When Charles II granted the Carolina charter he was disposing of territory claimed by the Spanish crown. In support of this claim Spanish mission stations, protected by small military forces, were established along the coast all the way from St. Mary's River to Port Royal, South Carolina. In 1587 the northern limit of Spanish occupation retired to a point near the present site of Savannah. The coast of Georgia, which was known as Guale, was held for nearly a century longer, when (in 1680) the Spanish frontier was pushed southward to the St. Mary's River. The Carolinas and Georgia were thus left open for the occupation of a rival power.

Friction between the South Carolinians and the Spaniards in Florida. Basis of the Spanish claim to the South Carolina-Georgia coast

Though Spain had withdrawn her missions, she had not given up her claim to Georgia and South Carolina. In 1676 a treaty was signed between England and Spain by which each power agreed to recognize the right of the other to all territory held by it at that time. As the colony on the Ashley River had been started by the English before this time, Spain gave up all her claim to lands north of this settlement. But she still asserted her rights to southern South Carolina and all of Georgia. It was on the basis of this claim that the Spanish attack on Port Royal had been made in 1686. Thus the boundary between the English colony of South Carolina and the Spanish province of Florida was in dispute, and this disagreement led to considerable strife between the English and Spanish colonists.

The dispute over the boundary between Florida and South Carolina

While the Spaniards made only occasional attempts to assert their claim to South Carolina, the early Carolinians lived in constant dread of them. There was no love lost between Catholic Spaniards and Protestant Englishmen, to begin with, and the former kept feeding the flames of this ill-will by intriguing with the Indian enemies of the latter and by harboring their runaway slaves. The feeling of uneasiness on the part of the South Carolinians was enhanced by the fact that the neighboring English colonies were too far away to render prompt assistance, and so

The Spanish danger retards the development of South Carolina

they would have to depend upon themselves in case of attack. This fear of the Spaniards and their savage allies had the effect of discouraging emigration to South Carolina and thus of retarding the development of the colony.

Attacks of the Spaniards on South Carolina

The Spaniards began at once to challenge the right of the English colonists to Carolina. Hardly had the latter established themselves at Albemarle Point when an expedition from St. Augustine came up to attack them. But when they learned that the English had fortified themselves and were in a position to make a vigorous defense they gave up the attempt and turned back before reaching the settlement. They were, however, more successful in their next attack on the colony, as it was on this occasion that they captured and destroyed the Scotch settlement at Port Royal (1686).

South Carolina takes an active part in Queen Anne's War

South Carolina and Florida were eager for a fight and were only waiting for Europe to give the signal, which was done when England took up the sword against Spain in the War of the Spanish Succession, or Queen Anne's War, as the American part of it was called. The South Carolinians, therefore, took an active part in this war (see p. 377).

Organization of the government in North Carolina

In the same year in which the proprietors received their first charter they arranged for a temporary government for the backwoodsmen living on the Chowan River. Governor William Berkeley, of Virginia, one of the proprietors, was directed to appoint a governor and six councilors for the settlement. His choice for governor fell on William Drummond (1664), who afterward attained notoriety as a leader in Bacon's Rebellion. An assembly was organized, probably the next year, and soon there grew up in the little colony a system of administration modeled after that of the mother colony, Virginia.[22] It consisted of a governor, a council, and an assembly, which at first was probably composed of the freeholders but which two years later became a representative body.

Soon after Drummond took over the administration of the colony the proprietors adopted (1665) a plan of government for the entire province, known as the Concessions and Agreement. It provided for an executive like that already organized in North Carolina and an assembly to be chosen by the freemen, which had

[22] CARROLL, B. R., *Historical Collections*, ii, pp. 283-284; *North Carolina Colonial Records*, i, pp. 48-50, 56; HAWKS, F. L., *History of North Carolina*, ii, pp. 144, 452.

uthority to make laws, levy taxes, and perform certain administrative duties.[23] In their commission to Drummond's successor the proprietors instructed him to put the Concessions in force in the Chowan settlement.

The proprietors had shown good judgment in thus adopting a liberal policy toward their province. But, unfortunately, they considered the Concessions and Agreement as a temporary scheme to be superseded by an elaborate constitution. They had John Locke draw up a complicated plan for the government of the entire province known as the "Fundamental Constitutions." In this governmental scheme there were to be two ranks of nobility below the proprietors, and these new noblemen were to be differentiated from the common people by the titles of landgrave and cacique. These terms were borrowed, respectively, from the Germans and the Indians, as the charter forbade the use of English titles for this wilderness nobility. The whole territory was to be divided up into counties, and these subdivided into seigniories, baronies, and colonies. Two-fifths of the land were to be reserved for the proprietors and the nobility, and the remaining three-fifths were to be granted to the commonalty. But manors from 3,000 to 12,000 acres could be created out of the land left to the people, and these big estates were to be kept intact by the law of primogeniture. On the manors there was to be a class of people, called "leet-men," who were to be under the authority of the lord of the manor and so would have about the same status as that of the mediæval serf.

The machinery of government was complicated and cumbersome. At its head were the eight proprietors, who were to meet as a court and have general oversight and control over the affairs of the province. The oldest proprietor was known as the Palatine, and his seven associates were assigned offices with the high-sounding titles of the highest British officials. There were also to be a number of courts, a Grand Council, and a Parliament, the two last-named to be resident in Carolina. The Parliament was to

(margin) The "Fundamental Constitutions"

[23] For the text of the Concessions, see *North Carolina Colonial Records*, i, pp. 75-92. For a good summary of their provisions, see Osgood, H. L., *American Colonies in the Seventeenth Century*, ii, pp. 204-205.

This constitution was almost an exact duplicate of the one issued in the same year by the New Jersey proprietors for the government of their province (Osgood, *op. cit.*, ii, p. 173).

consist of the proprietors or their deputies, the noblemen, and the representatives of the people, with the three groups sitting together as one body.[24]

The "Fundamental Constitutions" not suited to Carolina

In preparing this plan of government John Locke evidently did not employ that superior wisdom that afterward entitled him to rank among the world's greatest philosophers. It was too undemocratic for any English-speaking community even for that day, and too elaborate and artificial for any society of any age. Besides, it was made in England without regard to measurements taken in America, and no amount of tailoring could make this ready-made constitution, cut on a pattern of feudal aristocracy, fit a young and growing society where the whole tendency was toward democracy. If we did not know that they were sincere in this attempt, we might conclude that the proprietors were trying to perpetrate a joke when they undertook to foist this piece of outworn feudalism on the bold-spirited planters that lived on the Ashley and Chowan rivers.

The Constitutions not carried out

The proprietors had the good sense to suspend the Constitutions in the early years, and changes in them were made from time to time. But despite these revisions the settlers were not satisfied with this cumbersome system of government. The South Carolina legislature suggested still further modifications, and the proprietors thereupon withdrew the Constitutions and made no further effort to force them on the people. By the end of the seventeenth century governmental institutions more in harmony with actual conditions had taken root, and from this time on the "Fundamental Constitutions" played no part in the government of the Carolinas though they were in the background as a menace to the liberties of the people and a cause of friction between them and the proprietors. A few of the principles of this document were, however, put into practice in both North Carolina and South Carolina.

Actual government in the Carolinas

The system of government in both North Carolina and South Carolina was in actual practice quite similar to that in the royal provinces, except that proprietors held about the same relation to

[24] The proprietors changed the "Fundamental Constitutions" several times and so they appear in a number of forms. For the second draft, abbreviated—the one originally presented to the Carolinas—see MacDonald, *op. cit.*, pp. 150-168; also *North Carolina Colonial Records*, i, pp. 187-206. For the first draft of the *Fundamental Constitutions*, see *Shaftesbury Papers*, pp. 93-117

the Carolinas as the king did to the crown colonies. Prior to 1691 the northern and southern sections were administered as two separate jurisdictions. During this period, the provincial government in each division consisted of a governor, a council, and an assembly. The governor was the representative of the proprietors and was appointed by the leading proprietor, or Palatine, as he was called. The council consisted of ten members, one half of whom were appointed by the proprietors as their deputies, and the other half were elected by the provincial assembly.[25]

In both provinces the assembly was composed of the governor, council, and representatives chosen by the freeholders. In the early years in both colonies the representatives of the people sat with the governor and council as one body, but later the assembly was divided into two houses, the governor and council constituting the upper house, the people's representatives the lower. The organization of local government was a slow development in the Carolinas. North Carolina was divided up into precincts (which were really counties) in the last part of the seventeenth century, and a system of county government grew up quite similar to that in Virginia. In South Carolina, however, the county did not play an important part in local administration until near the end of the colonial period.

In the Carolinas, as well as in most of the other continental colonies, there were frequent quarrels between the assembly and the proprietors or the representatives of the proprietors, the governor and their deputies in the council. One cause of dispute was the claim put forth by the proprietors that they alone had the right of initiating legislation and that, therefore, all laws must be proposed by the council. The assembly refused to recognize this

Friction between the assembly and the proprietors and and their representatives

[25] This arrangement for choosing the council was in vogue from 1670 to 1691 only. Before 1670 the number of councilors in North Carolina varied. From 1663 to 1665 it was six, from 1665 to 1670 it could be six or any even number between six and twelve. After 1691 there were no elective members of the council. From 1691 to the end of proprietary rule in South Carolina and until 1724 in North Carolina, the council consisted of seven members appointed by the seven proprietors individually and were regarded as their representatives, or deputies, the governor being the representative of the Palatine. In 1724 the system of deputies was abolished and the council in North Carolina consisted of twelve men appointed by the proprietors jointly (CONNOR, *op. cit.*, pp. 42-43).

privilege, and finally (1693) the proprietors yielded the point and agreed that the power to initiate laws should be exercised by the assembly as well as by the governor and council.

All the territory on the mainland owned by the proprietors was in the early years designated under the term Carolina. They at first distinguished the two divisions of their province by calling the northern portion "our colony northeast of Cape Fear," and the southern "our colony southwest of Cape Fear." By the end of the seventeenth century the term North Carolina, as applied to the northern settlements, had come into use. North Carolina had a separate executive up until 1691, at which time Philip Ludwell became governor of the whole province of Carolina. He resided at Charleston and appointed a deputy for the northern province. Ludwell and his successors, however, paid little or no attention to their deputies in North Carolina. The bonds that held the northern and southern communities together were very slight. This nominal union of the two provinces continued until 1712, when a governor was appointed for North Carolina, and from that time until the end of the proprietary period the northern colony remained a separate province.

There was really no reason why these two distinct centers of colonization should ever have been united. For not only were they separated by a vast expanse of tractless forest, but the economic and social life in the two sections was quite different. In the southern province slavery took deep root quite early, while it developed slowly in the northern settlements. South Carolina carried on trade with the West Indies and Europe and had few dealings with the other English colonies on the mainland. The introduction of rice culture in South Carolina drew it into closer relations with Europe. Northern Carolina, on the other hand, traded with her sister colonies to the northward, and for a long time had hardly any commercial relations directly with the Old World. In South Carolina there was a prosperous town which was the center of life for the whole province; whereas in North Carolina there were no towns for a long time, and even as late as 1709 the only place that was called a town was a hamlet of twelve houses. In the former province, the social ideals were aristocratic; in the latter they were democratic.

The proprietors took little interest in their northern province and left it to a great extent to work out its own destiny. They did not keep in close touch with the governors whom they had chosen and generally let them assert such authority as they North Carolina neglected by the proprietors could. The result was a weak administration, which frequently lapsed into a condition verging on anarchy. The unmanageable character of the people was doubtless both a cause and an effect of this policy of neglect. For such intercourse as was held between the settlers and the proprietors was usually of an unfriendly sort; while on the other hand, the proprietors by shirking their responsibilities encouraged the very spirit of lawlessness that defied their authority and made their relations with the colony so unpleasant.

The Carolinians had other grievances to complain of besides Insurrections in North Carolina the neglect of the proprietors. Among these the most outstanding were the land question and the Navigation Acts. The vacillating policy of the proprietors as to quit rents caused a good deal of dissatisfaction among the settlers, who considered the quit rents too high and feared for the security of their land tenures. Moreover, the Navigation Acts were especially unfair to the North Carolinians. The clause in the Act of 1660 providing that certain "enumerated" articles, tobacco among them, could be sent from the colonies only to England, Ireland, or other British possessions would have worked a severe hardship to the Carolina tobacco growers had it been strictly enforced. They could not ship their tobacco directly to England, because the shallow harbors and shifting sands on the North Carolina coast made navigation dangerous for the large vessels engaged in the transatlantic trade. But the small New England vessels plying the coastwise trade were not discouraged by these obstacles, and so most of the tobacco and other exports from North Carolina went to New England. Much of this tobacco was transshipped from New England to the continental European ports in plain violation of the law of 1660. The tobacco thus smuggled into Europe was escaping taxation, while that which was sent to England and reshipped to continental Europe had to pay a high import duty. This practice, therefore, deprived the government of revenue and gave the bootlegger in the tobacco trade a great advantage over his legitimate competitor in the continental European markets. To discourage such illegal trade Parliament passed the Act of 1673, which imposed a tax on enumerated articles sent from one English colony to another. The enforcement of this law would have made the smuggling trade in tobacco less profitable to the New England merchants, and therefore would have restricted the export of tobacco from North Carolina. The proprietors, however, largely because of ignorance of geographical conditions in North Carolina, wanted to discourage the trade with New England and promote a direct intercourse between the colony and the homeland. They, therefore, favored the enforcement of the unpopular law of 1673.

These and other grievances caused a good deal of dissatisfaction in North Carolina. Owing to the unsettled character of the government, occasioned by the neglect and indifference of the proprietors, this discontent frequently carried the people into rebellion. Riots and revolts followed each other in rapid succession and several governors were deposed and the authority of others was contested. Of these revolts the one that has attracted the most attention of historians was that led by George Durant and John Culpeper (1677-79). This insurrection was caused by an effort made by the proprietors to execute the Act of 1673 and to enforce the collection of quit rents. The insurgents deposed the deputy governor and for about a year had control of the government. Culpeper was then arrested and brought to trial in England on the charge of treason. He was acquitted on the ground that treason could not be committed in North Carolina, "for there was no settled government in that colony."[26]

Bad reputation of the early North Carolinians

The disregard of the Navigation Acts soon brought the North Carolinians into disrepute as smugglers. They were also accused of harboring pirates, and the two Carolina provinces had the worst reputation for piracy of all of the continental colonies. The charge was also made that they were dishonest in their dealings with outsiders, and the Chowan settlement was said to be a refuge for runaway debtors. There was some basis for these accusations. The numerous insurrections showed that the people did not have the proper respect for law and order, and the enactment of a measure in 1669 by the assembly prohibiting for five years the collection of debts owed to persons outside of the colony gives ground for the charge of dishonesty. But apparently the laws of the neighboring provinces as to the payment of debts to outside creditors were just as lax as were those of North Carolina; for the North Carolina Act of 1669 was an exact copy of a Virginia statute and was similar in character to the debtor laws of Maryland and South Carolina.

[26] For references to primary sources for these revolts, see ASHE, S. A., *History of North Carolina*, i, pp. 115-117, 171-178. For an excellent discussion of the causes of these revolts, see CONNOR, *op. cit.*, pp. 52, *et seq.*

These charges, made mainly by contemporary Virginians, were doubtless inspired to some extent by the ill-feeling that existed between Virginia and North Carolina for a considerable period during the colonial era (see p. 242). Then, too, people living in older and settled communities are always inclined to look down upon their neighbors on the frontier and to exaggerate their faults and shortcomings.[27] But after making due allowance for the exaggeration of contemporary accounts, it seems that the first settlers on the Chowan River were exceptionally poor, and were undoubtedly hard to manage. Their faults, however, were those that are incident to pioneer life, for backwoodsmen are usually impatient of restraint, neglectful of conventions, and boldly assertive of their individuality. In North Carolina, owing to the isolation of the settlements, the frontier moved westward very slowly, and so pioneer characteristics clung to the people longer than they did in the other colonies. The neglect of the colony by the proprietors and the consequent weakness of the

[27] The bad reputation of the early North Carolinians was in large measure fastened upon them by Colonel William Byrd, of Virginia, who in his *History of the Dividing Line* (1728) gives an account of the country and the people. He uses an unfriendly pen in describing the shortcomings of his southern neighbors, and it is not unlikely that his statements were biased by a prejudice against them aroused by the boundary dispute. They are represented as being not only very poor, but also as shiftless and indolent. In speaking of their failure to observe the Sabbath, he says that they had so many rest days during the week that they did not need to stop work on Sunday. This account by Colonel Byrd was doubtless more of a caricature than a portrayal. The writer was a man of exceptional wealth and culture, and being accustomed to the refinements of the social life that then characterized the exclusive Virginia aristocracy, he could hardly be expected to view sympathetically and appraise correctly a people who did not know or refused to practice the amenities of polite society. Moreover, his literary efforts are marked by a noticeable attempt at humor, and so some of the exaggerated statements of an uncomplimentary nature that appear in his writings are in all probability only attempts at good-natured joking. He also speaks in a like uncomplimentary strain of his fellow-Virginians who lived along the southern border, attributing their indolence, as well as that of the North Carolinians, to the easy way in which they could procure a living (BASSETT, J. S., ed., *The Writings of Colonel William Byrd*, p. 61; BOYD, W. K., ed., *William Byrd's Histories of the Dividing Line betwixt Virginia and North Carolina*, pp. 51, 304).

government established by them encouraged lawlessness. Then, too, the poverty and isolation of the first settlers made it impossible for them to establish churches and schools for some years. Education and religion were thus slow to begin their work of toning down the crudities that crop out under frontier conditions. This early backwardness was, however, only a temporary condition, for in the period just prior to the Revolution North Carolina was growing rapidly in population and was making long strides in education.[28]

Rivalry between Virginia and North Carolina

Virginia at an early age entered upon her career of being the mother of colonies and states, and North Carolina was her second daughter, her oldest being the province of Maryland. Unfortunately, both of these communities were born under such circumstances as were not favorable to the good feeling that should characterize the relation of parent and child. In both cases the new community in departing from the parental roof took from the mother province territory that the latter felt should rightfully belong to her. Therefore, neither of these two colonies enjoyed the parental blessing during the early years of its separate existence.

Another cause of friction between Virginia and North Carolina was the fact that these two provinces were economic rivals, both being producers of tobacco. To complicate matters, there was for a long time a boundary dispute, which was not settled until 1728. The early Virginians spoke of the Albemarle settlement as "Rogues Harbor," and called the settlers "idle debtors," "theeves," "pyrates," and "runaway servants."[29]

Not only did the Virginians give their southern neighbors a bad name, but they adopted a policy that struck a serious blow at their economic prosperity. Tobacco was the chief article of export from North Carolina, but it could not be shipped directly from the Carolina coast, owing to the shallowness of the harbors and the danger of navigation. A considerable amount of it was, therefore, carried first to Virginia and shipped from her ports to England. To put a stop to this competition the Virginia assembly passed laws (1679, 1705, 1726) prohibiting the bringing in of tobacco from North Carolina to Virginia or its exportation

[28] CONNOR, R. D. W., *History of North Carolina*, pp. 68-73.
[29] *Ibid.*, p. 69.

from Virginia ports. "It was a hard blow to North Carolina and did not tend to improve her relations with her neighbor."[30]

The first Indian war of any consequence in North Carolina broke out in 1711, for before this time only petty disputes had arisen between the whites and the Indians. In 1711 the Tuscaroras, numbering one thousand, two hundred warriors, rose up against the settlers and in one day killed one hundred and twenty of them. A rebellion led by Thomas Cary was probably the occasion of this uprising, though the main reason for it was that the English settlements had extended to the interior and were thus encroaching upon the hunting-grounds of the natives. The Indians had probably been incited by Cary or at any rate they were encouraged by the weakness of the colony caused by the rebellion. The North Carolinians received aid from South Carolina and were able to win a decisive victory over the Tuscaroras. The latter were so badly defeated that they caused the whites no more trouble. A few of the Tuscaroras remained in North Carolina and the rest went north to join the Five Nations.[31]

Religion did not play a prominent part in the early history of North Carolina. The first settlers at Albemarle were not religious refugees, nor were they especially interested in religion. However, the promise of religious tolerance given in the charter and confirmed by the practice of the proprietors was an inducement that attracted settlers to both the northern and southern divisions of Carolina. The policy of the proprietors seems to have been to make the Anglican the established church and at the same time grant toleration to dissenters, but the provisions in the charter as to religion were not carried out in North Carolina during the seventeenth century. Nothing was done to hinder the growth of dissenters or to promote the Anglican Church. In fact, for nearly twenty years the Albemarle settlers were entirely without the means of worship. It was not until 1672 that the first preacher appeared in the colony, and it was thirty years later when the first church building was erected (1702).

The first ministers to visit this frontier settlement were Quaker

Marginal notes: Indian troubles

Religious conditions in North Carolina

---

[30] *Ibid.*, pp. 69-70; *North Carolina Colonial Records*, i, p. 243; HENING, W. W., *Virginia Statutes at Large*, i, p. 445; iii, p. 253; iv, pp. 175-176.

[31] For a full account of this war, see HAWKS, F. L., *History of North Carolina*, ii, pp. 525-553. For sources, see footnotes, *ibid.*, p. 551, and OSGOOD, *op. cit.*, ii, p. 429.

missionaries, George Fox, the founder of Quakerism, being one of them. As the Friends were the first on the ground, they became the leading denomination in the infant colony.[32] In 1694 the governor was a Friend, and for the last five years of the seventeenth century the Quakers controlled the government. No Anglican ministers had come to the colony by the end of the seventeenth century.

During the seventeenth century the dissenters were given a free hand in the northern province. They were unmolested in their religious practices, and there was no competition by the Anglican Church. At the beginning of the eighteenth century the Church of England began to take steps to get a hold in North Carolina. The principal agency behind this movement was the Society for the Propagation of the Gospel in Foreign Parts. The first Anglican minister came over in 1700. But he and some of his immediate successors were unworthy representatives of the denomination and so accomplished little. Even if they had been earnest and active in their efforts they could not have made much headway, as the obstacles to travel were almost insuperable. The planters all lived on the navigable streams, and the only way to go from one river to another was over roads that were virtually impassable in the winter season.[33] A few Anglican churches were, however, organized in the early part of the eighteenth century, and a house of worship was erected at Bath in 1702. This was the first church built in North Carolina, for the Quakers had been holding their meetings in the houses of private families.

Efforts to make the Anglican the established church   The Anglicans mustered enough strength in the assembly to pass a law (1701) establishing the Church of England in the colony. The salary of each minister was to be thirty pounds a year and was to be raised by a poll tax on all the people.[34] The Quakers were strongly opposed to the law, and they were able to influence enough votes in the assembly to secure its repeal in 1703. But in the meantime the act had been disallowed by the proprietors on the ground that the salary mentioned was inadequate.

This unsuccessful effort to establish the Anglican Church, to-

---

[32] *North Carolina Colonial Records,* i, pp. 215-218, 571-572, 687, 711; WEEKS, S. B., *Religious Development in the Province of North Carolina* (Johns Hopkins University *Studies*), pp. 32-33.

[33] SALLEY, ed., *Narratives of Early Carolina,* pp. 214, 217.

[34] *North Carolina Colonial Records,* i, pp. 544-545.

gether with the missionary zeal that this denomination was exhibiting under the leadership of Rev. Dr. John Blair, aroused the dissenters and caused them to consolidate into a party of opposition. Shortly afterward another attempt was made to favor the Anglicans by an act of the assembly. In 1704, or early in 1705, a law was passed making the Anglican the established church and taxing dissenters as well as others for its support. About the same time the act of Parliament requiring all persons to swear allegiance to the queen was reënacted by the North Carolina assembly. As the Quakers did not swear at all, they, of course, declined to take this oath, and were thereupon dismissed from the assembly, council, and courts of justice. They then became a party of opposition. They were strengthened in their opposition by an act of 1711, which again provided for the establishment of the Anglican Church. The discontent came to a head in Cary's Rebellion, the main causes of which were the act requiring the oaths and the effort to make the Anglican the state church. From this time to the end of the colonial period the Anglican was, in theory, the established church of North Carolina. But in a considerable portion of the province there were either no Anglicans or else not enough to justify the maintenance of a church. In such localities the establishment did not function and no church taxes were collected. In those sections in which the Anglican was the strongest denomination the law of the establishment was carried out but not without some opposition. The revenues raised from taxation were not sufficient for the proper maintenance of church worship, and the levying of church rates antagonized the people and made the Anglican Church unpopular. The supporters of the establishment had to find other sources of income to supplement the revenue from taxation. This additional income came from private donations, lotteries, the funds of the Venerable Society, and other sources.

SELECTED READINGS

1. The Settlement at New Bern.—Connor, R. D. W., *History of North Carolina*, i, pp. *78-82.
2. Religion and Learning in North Carolina.—Hawks, Francis L., *History of North Carolina*, ii, ch. 5.
3. Manners and Customs in North Carolina.—Hawks, *op. cit.*, ii, *ch. 7.
4. Agriculture and Industrial Arts in North Carolina.—Hawks, *op. cit.*, ii, *ch. 3.

5. Laying the Foundations of South Carolina.—McCrady, E., *The History of South Carolina Under the Proprietary Government*, ch. 6; Ravenel, Harriott H. (Mrs. St. Julien), *Charleston, the Place and the People*, pp. *1-9.
6. The Founding of Charleston.—Ravenel, *op. cit.*, pp. *9-25.
7. Charleston as a Center for the Trade in Skins and Hides.— Crane, V. W., *The Southern Frontier*, ch. 5.
8. The Capture and Destruction of the Scotch Settlers at Port Royal.—Ravenel, *op. cit.*, pp. *26-31.

CHAPTER XII

PENNSYLVANIA AND DELAWARE

THE Friends, or Quakers, were a sect of radical Protestants that The
arose in England about the middle of the seventeenth century Friends
under the leadership of George Fox. They carried the doctrine or
of private judgment in religion to the extreme limit. They regarded the ordinances of baptism and the Lord's Supper and all
other rites and ceremonies as unnecessary. According to their
doctrine, every Christian is taught by the Holy Spirit within him
what is the truth, and it is unnecessary to have preachers trained
in the schools to act as spiritual guides. They had, therefore, no
paid ministers. The essence of worship, according to their view,
consists in communion with God. Twice a week they met for
public worship and at such times would sit together in quiet
contemplation until some one moved by the promptings of the
Spirit within him felt inclined to share his spiritual experience
with his brethren and sisters. Women had the same privileges in
the church as men. They believed in the Bible as the revelation
of God, but thought that God still reveals himself to his children
and that Christ is being reincarnated today in the lives of
Christians.

In their daily relations they insisted on sincerity of speech,
and refused to use any sort of titles in addressing others. The
pronouns "thou" and "thee" were employed in speaking to all
persons, although these terms were at that time generally used
only in addressing servants or persons of inferior rank. By this
method of speech they wished to show their disregard for class
distinctions. They were opposed to war and declined to take oaths
when summoned to testify in the courts. They also refused to
pay tithes for the support of the established church. Capital
punishment was opposed by them at a time when the English
code recognized two hundred offenses as punishable by death.

The Society of Friends had a very simple form of church
organization. The highest authority in the denomination was the
Yearly Meeting, composed of delegates from all over England.

Next in importance to the Yearly Meeting was the Quarterly Meeting, which had jurisdiction over a number of associated churches. In each congregation there was a Monthly Meeting, at which such business was transacted as was of interest to the local membership. Although the Friends had no complicated ecclesiastical machinery, yet they were able to rein up their members and keep them under strict discipline. At the Monthly Meetings the business affairs and private conduct of individuals were inquired into and criticized in a way that would not be tolerated by the membership of any church of today.[1]

A truly spiritual faith is always unconventional and in every age clashes with the prudential and worldly respectability that encases church and state. The history of the Friends shows no exception to this rule. From the first they were the victims of greater persecution than fell to the lot of ordinary dissenters. Heavy fines were imposed upon them, and many of them were imprisoned in the loathsome jails of the day. In their refusal to pay tithes to the established church and to take oaths in court and in their opposition to war they were, it was thought, striking at the very foundations of authority in both state and church. Besides, at times they carried their unconventional practices so far as to interrupt other congregations in their worship. Sometimes their most emotional preachers would tremble or quake while delivering their message. Hence the name Quaker. It was not, however, from this radical element that the emigrants to America were mainly recruited.

The Quakers persecuted in England and America

The Friends were persecuted not only in England, but also in a number of the colonies.[2] In some places in the New World, however, they were allowed to live in peace and practice their religion without molestation.

On the island of Aquidneck (R. I.), they were numerous and for some time had control of the government. In North Carolina they were the first of the religious denominations on the ground and were able to exert a considerable influence on that frontier colony.

The Quaker leaders coveted a more secure footing for their denomination and were desirous of securing in the New World

[1] For an excellent account of the belief of the Quakers, see an article by JONES, RUFUS M., in the *Religious History of New England*, pp. 179-200.

[2] For an account of these persecutions, see pp. 147-148, 529-530.

a grant of land on which they could establish a colony controlled by Quakers and thus be free from all restraints on their religion. George Fox planned such a settlement in America as early as 1661. But it was hardly to be expected that a government that was persecuting these heretics at home would encourage them to multiply in America. To get such a grant required influence at court, and the humble Quakers had no such influence. These plans, therefore, had no chance of fulfillment until some of their number, either through wealth or the favor of the king, could procure a large area of land. These dreams were partially realized when West Jersey passed under the control of Penn and other Quakers; they were completely fulfilled when the Pennsylvania colony was founded. The most important event in bringing about the realization of these dreams was the conversion of William Penn to Quakerism. The Quakers wish to establish a colony in America

William Penn was the son of Admiral Sir William Penn, who had fought on the side of Parliament in the Puritan Revolution, but had changed over and lent his influence toward restoring Charles II to the throne. He was, therefore, in good standing with the king and, having considerable means, was in a position to give his son a career in the fashionable life of the day. He sent him to Christ College, Oxford, and expected him to acquire the polish and conventional religious notions that would fit him for the high social position he was expected to fill. But young Penn had had in childhood a profound religious experience of the mystic type and out of it had come unconventional views regarding religion. At the time of this experience his emotions had been deeply stirred by the preaching of Thomas Loe, an earnest Quaker minister. Penn was conscientiously opposed to the ritualism of this High Church college and would not obey its regulations in religious affairs. It was probably because of this nonconformity that he was expelled from Oxford. His father was scandalized at what he considered his son's folly and did all he could to cure him of it. He whipped him and drove him away from home. Afterward the admiral became reconciled to his son and tried another method of weaning him away from his unfashionable convictions. He sent him to France in the hope that the gay life of Paris would soon cause him to forget his religious ideals. Part of his sojourn abroad was spent in travel and some of it at a Huguenot college at Saumur.[3] The admiral's policy was for a time suc- The early career of Penn

[3] DOBRÉE, BONAMY, *William Penn*, pp. 6-29.

cessful; for young William relapsed into worldliness, and when he returned to England his religious oddities had been supplanted or covered over by a veneer of conventional polish.

After having wasted several years in an aimless way William Penn was brought again in contact with the Quaker preacher who had twelve years before appealed to his spiritual impulses. By this earnest minister he was influenced to accept the doctrines of the Friends, and thereafter he was identified with that "despised sect which was everywhere spoken against." He became a preacher of this faith and suffered imprisonment at the hands of the authorities. However, contact with the world had rubbed off those angles of fanaticism in his personality which this faith then tended to produce in its adherents, and so William Penn never went to the unreasonable extreme in his religious views as did his more radical religious brethren.

Pennsylvania granted to Penn by Charles II When William Penn was thirty-six years old his father died. Young Penn was in favor with the king and his brother, James, the Duke of York, for he had fallen heir to the warm friendship that had existed between his father and the Stuart family. He had also inherited a claim against the crown that amounted to about $80,000. Charles preferred to discharge this obligation by a grant of land in America rather than by a money payment, as he had more of the former than of the latter commodity. This arrangement suited Penn, who saw in it an opportunity to establish an asylum for his persecuted coreligionists and to try out that experiment in religion and government that he had in mind. He had been interested for some years in American colonization and was at this time one of the proprietors of both East and West Jersey. Circumstances had thus combined to provide in America a refuge for the Quakers more satisfactory than the one they enjoyed in West Jersey.

The charter granted to Penn by the king In March, 1681, Charles II gave to Penn a charter conferring upon him proprietary rights in a large tract of land extending from the Delaware River westward for five degrees of longitude and from "the beginning of the fortieth degree of northern latitude" on the south to the beginning of the forty-third degree on the north. This was a princely domain and was almost as great in area as England and Wales combined. This territory was one of the finest regions for agriculture in America, and in mineral resources was one of the richest areas in the world. The king, of course, did not realize the value of his gift, nor did any one else at the time. To the province created by this grant Charles gave the name Pennsylvania, against the protest of Penn, who feared that the name would be attributed to an un-Quakerlike vanity on his part. In the following year Penn received from the Duke of York a grant of what is now Delaware.

By the royal charter Penn was made both landlord and ruler of his domain. He could dispose of the land to such persons and on such terms as he wished and could make laws for the people and appoint governors and other officials to administer them. But there were certain limitations on the exercise of his powers as a ruler. The laws in the province had to be in harmony with those in England and could be made only by the consent of a majority of the freemen or their representatives. Laws enacted and published in the province had to be sent to England within five years to be passed upon by the Privy Council. All measures were to be void that were vetoed by this body within six months after having been delivered to it. The proprietor was given authority to establish courts of justice and appoint judges and justices. He could also grant pardons in all criminal cases except those of treason and willful murder and could allow reprieves in those cases. All persons in the province were to have the privilege of appealing from the decisions of the provincial courts to the king in council.[4]

The limits of Pennsylvania as laid down in Penn's grant overlapped those of both New York and Maryland. This was due to the fact that the framer of Penn's charter was ignorant of the geography of America and was also not familiar with the details of previous patents. Besides, the wording of the charter was vague. A controversy thus arose at once over both the northern and southern boundaries of the new province. Penn had to agree to the forty-second parallel as the northern limit of his province instead of the forty-third, as was called for in the charter. As he had accepted the forty-second as the "beginning of the forty-third parallel," so he contended that the thirty-ninth should be taken as the beginning of the fortieth parallel. But this claim brought him into conflict with Lord Baltimore, whose grant extended to the fortieth parallel. As Lord Baltimore's patent was

Boundary disputes

[4] For the full text of the charter, see THORPE, F. N., *Colonial Charters*, pp. 3035-3044. The charter in abbreviated form is given in MACDONALD, *op. cit.*, pp. 184-190.

issued before Penn's he undoubtedly had the better technical right to the disputed territory.

The controversy between Maryland and Pennsylvania was carried on for more than three-quarters of a century, when it was finally settled (1760) by an agreement between the proprietors of the two provinces. A few years later a line was run in accordance with this agreement by two English surveyors, Charles Mason and Jeremiah Dixon. By the famous Mason and Dixon's Line the southern boundary of Pennsylvania was fixed at nineteen miles south of the fortieth parallel.[5]

The grant to Penn also conflicted with the charters that had been given to Virginia and Connecticut, and each of these colonies set up a claim to a portion of the Quaker province. Had these claims been allowed, Pennsylvania would have been reduced to very narrow limits. But Thomas Penn, who was managing proprietor after the death of his parents, put up a stubborn fight for the rights of his family, and Virginia and Connecticut were unable to get a decision in their favor. These controversies continued until after the end of the colonial period and were finally settled in favor of Pennsylvania.[6]

The settlement of the province
When Penn received his patent there were already some Swedish, Dutch, and a few English settlers living in Pennsylvania, who were located in the region between Upland and the mouth of the Schuylkill River. Penn encouraged these first settlers to remain in his province and promised that they should enjoy freedom under laws of their own making.[7] He also made vigorous efforts to induce emigrants from Europe to go to Pennsylvania. He published a pamphlet describing his province and pointing out the advantages of colonization. This pamphlet was translated into Dutch, German, and French, and widely scattered over Wales, Ireland, Germany, and Holland. It was favorably received by prospective emigrants in these countries, especially by religious

---

[5] For documents bearing on the Pennsylvania-Maryland boundary dispute, see *Pennsylvania Archives*, 2nd series, vii, pp. 321-425, and xvi.

[6] The dispute with Virginia was settled by the continuation of the Mason and Dixon Line (1784). The controversy with Connecticut went on until 1782, when an agreement was reached.

[7] SHEPHERD, W. R., *History of Proprietary Government in Pennsylvania*, p. 9; MYERS, A. C., ed., *Narratives of Early Pennsylvania, West New Jersey, and Delaware*, pp. 237-238. 252.

sects in Germany like the Mennonites, who held religious views similar to those of the Quakers. His method of advertising his project was quite successful, and many of the early settlers in Pennsylvania came from the non-English countries of Europe, particularly from Wales and Germany.

Penn sent over his first colonists in 1681, and by the end of the year there were about one thousand inhabitants in the province. In October of the next year the proprietor himself arrived on the Delaware, bringing about one hundred new settlers with him. He was very much impressed with the beauty of the scenery as he sailed up the river through the virgin forest. He stopped at the Swedish settlement of Upland, the name of which he changed to Chester. He had a very favorable opinion of the Swedes at Upland and spent the winter there.

Before leaving England, Penn had sent over commissioners to select a site for the capital of the province and there to lay out a city. This was done in the summer of 1682, and when he reached Pennsylvania a town was rapidly growing up on the west shore of the Delaware River, to which he gave the name of Philadelphia. The streets were laid out with stiff regularity and lots were offered for sale. While the houses were being built the settlers lived in log or bark huts or caves. The site was well chosen. It was at the junction of the Schuylkill and Delaware rivers and could be reached by ships on two fronts. The town grew rapidly, and in two years is said to have numbered about six hundred houses. Many of these homes were neatly built of red brick and surrounded by ample lawns and gardens.[8]

The founding of Philadelphia

Shiploads of Quakers kept arriving, and by the summer of 1683 about three thousand settlers had come over. The Quaker emigrants were usually industrious and thrifty and, therefore, prosperous. For those who came to Pennsylvania belonged principally to the propertied class, who were suffering from heavy fines in the homeland. These well-to-do settlers were able to bring plenty of supplies with them. Besides, the climate was healthful, the soil fertile, and fish and game plentiful. These natural advantages could all be exploited by the early settlers without any fear of molestation by the Indians, who were friendly from the begin-

Prosperity of the colony

[8] For interesting contemporary accounts of early Philadelphia, see MYERS. ed., *op. cit.*, pp. 239-240, 242-244, 260-262, 269-272, 329-331. For a contemporary plan of the city, made in 1683, see opposite p. 242.

ning. For these reasons Pennsylvania never passed through a period of famine and sickness as did the older colonies.

One important reason for the success of Penn's experiment in colonization was the friendship of the Indians. The Indians in the neighborhood of Philadelphia had been kindly treated by the Dutch and Swedish settlers and the agents of the Duke of York. Consequently, they were favorably disposed toward the whites when Penn's colonists arrived. This friendship was perpetuated by the fair treatment accorded the natives by Penn and his Quaker brethren. Penn entered into a number of agreements with them by which land purchases were made. One of these land treaties—probably the one made in June, 1683—has figured prominently in later historical writing as "Penn's Treaty with the Indians." These agreements were more important than those usually made between the red men and the whites because they were scrupulously observed by the Quaker settlers. They were also kept by the Indians, and for more than half a century the two races dwelt together in peace and maintained the most cordial relations. Penn traveled among the savages unarmed, and Quaker farmers would leave their children in care of Indians when they went away from home.

Unfortunately, these friendly relations did not continue until the end of the colonial period. Penn's policy of fairness in dealing with the Indians was abandoned by his sons, who in 1737 and again in 1754 obtained from them large tracts of land by fraud. As a result of these sharp practices the Indians on the frontier allied themselves with the French in the French and Indian War.[9]

[9] It would not be correct, however, to say that the unjust treatment accorded the natives by the later proprietors was the only cause of the hostilities that started soon after the middle of the eighteenth century. Nor is it true that the fair dealing of the first proprietor entirely explains the friendship that existed between the red men and the whites during the first seven decades of the colony's history. In both cases, the attitude of the Pennsylvania Indians was influenced by factors that entered into the larger problem of general relations between the English and the natives. It is doubtless true that the conciliatory policy inaugurated by William Penn was an important cause of the long peace of the earlier period, yet this policy might not have been successful if it had not been reinforced by favorable conditions growing out of Indian politics outside the province. For during this time the Pennsylvania Indians were under the subjection of the Iroquois, allies of the English, and were less as-

The Pennsylvanians thus lost the friendship of the natives at a time when their hostility proved to be the most dangerous. For the possession of western Pennsylvania was one of the main objectives of the French, and its frontier was open to attack by the French and their savage allies. Thus did the Pennsylvanians pay a dear price for the short-sighted injustice of their proprietors.

Before leaving England Penn prepared, with the advice of some prominent landholders who were to emigrate to Pennsylvania, a constitution and body of laws for his colony. These laws, with some emendations and omissions, were adopted by an assembly representing the freemen in Pennsylvania (1682) and constituted the Great Law of Pennsylvania.[10] This code in its final form was very mild and humane for the age. It provided that prisons should be workhouses and reformatories rather than mere places of punishment, and prisoners were not required to support themselves or pay fees. It was especially liberal as to religious tolerance. All law-abiding persons who believed in "one Almighty and Eternal God" were to be free to worship God as their consciences might dictate, though officeholding was to be limited to Christians. This broad principle of religious liberty was practiced in Pennsylvania throughout the colonial period, except that in later years, owing to pressure from the British government, Catholics were deprived of the right to hold office. It was this generous religious policy that made Pennsylvania the asylum of many persecuted sects from Europe.

The constitution on which the government of Pennsylvania and Delaware was based were the Frames of Government promulgated by Penn in 1682 and 1683 and the Charter of Privileges of 1701. The First Frame was the one that was prepared by Penn

The Great Law of Pennsylvania

The First and Second Frames of Government

sertive of their rights than they would have been if they had not been overawed and to some extent cowed by their more powerful neighbors. On the other hand, when the French and Indian War broke out, and especially after Braddock's defeat, the savages might have joined the French alliance and have attacked the Pennsylvanians, as belonging to the common enemy, even if the latter had given them no special cause for complaint. The later proprietors by cheating the natives out of their lands gave them a cause of war and so added fuel to a flame that had been ignited by the French and Indian War.

[10] PROUD, ROBERT, *History of Pennsylvania*, i, pp. 206-207. These laws are given in full in HAZARD, SAMUEL, *Annals of Pennsylvania*, pp. 619-634.

and his advisers in England in 1682. It was superseded by the Second Frame, which, though prepared by the proprietor, embodied some important suggestions of the assembly,[11] and went into effect as the organic law of the province.[12]

The constitution as thus amended provided for a government in which the people had a strong voice. The proprietor reserved the right to appoint as his representative the governor or deputy governor, but this official had less power than was usually enjoyed by the chief executive of an American colony. He was scarcely more than president of the council and had no right of veto over the acts of the council or assembly. The governor and council acting together exercised considerable power. They performed the ordinary executive duties and made appointments to office. Besides, they alone had the right to initiate legislation. The councilors were elected by the freemen, as were the members of the assembly.

By the Second Frame the assembly was to consist in the beginning of thirty-six members, six from each county, and the number of representatives should increase as the colony developed. The members of the assembly were to be chosen by the "freemen," by which term was meant taxpayers or property-owners. Six counties were organized, three of which were in Delaware, as the latter had been united with the rest of the province by the assembly at a meeting in 1682. The assembly could pass on all laws and could amend proposals made by the council but could not initiate legislation, although it made a persistent effort to secure this right. Penn was sometimes represented in the colony by a governor or deputy governor chosen by himself. At other times a board of commissioners or the council as a whole had charge of the administration, with the president of the council acting as deputy governor.

Penn regarded his colonial enterprise as a "Holy Experiment." It was an effort to establish a colony in which he could prove that a state could be run successfully in accordance with Quaker principles; that prosperity and peace could be maintained with-

[11] SHEPHERD, W. R., *Proprietary Government in Pennsylvania*, pp. 250-251.

[12] For the full text of the First Frame, see POORE, B. P., *Colonial Charters*, pp. 1517-1523; for the Second Frame, pp. 1527-1531. They are also given in slightly abbreviated form in MACDONALD, *op. cit.*, pp. 193-199 and 200-204.

out oaths and wars; and that religion and morality could flourish in a society where there was no established church and everybody enjoyed freedom of conscience. His experiment was undoubtedly a success.

Pennsylvania attracted more foreigners than did any other colony. This was due partly to the tolerant attitude of the Quaker government toward religious dissent and partly to the efficient advertising methods of Penn. The liberal land policy was another inducement. Large tracts were sold to settlers of means and small allotments to others, both on very reasonable terms. Five thousand acres were sold for one hundred pounds, with a reservation of a quit rent of fifty shillings a year. Small landholders had to pay a rental of only one penny a year per acre for their land. Indentured servants were granted fifty acres each at the end of their terms of service.[13] The fertile soil and a climate favorable to agriculture also did much to make this province attractive to the Europeans from the Continent as well as those from the British Isles.

Non-English colonists in Pennsylvania

In the first two decades the Welsh were the most numerous of the immigrants who spoke a foreign language. They procured a large tract of land west of Philadelphia and established an independent barony there. They tried to hold on to their mother tongue, but they were unable to do this, and after a generation or so the English speech was generally used by them. These early Welsh settlers were mostly Quakers, and many of them were prosperous and enjoyed a high standard of living.

The Welsh

Another class that came over in considerable numbers during the early years were the Germans. In Germany there were many Protestant sects more or less like the Quakers, though differing in some important respects from them. It was from this class that these early German immigrants were mainly drawn. They settled mostly in the country some distance beyond Philadelphia. One of the most important of these denominations was the Mennonites. They affiliated with the Quakers and were so like them in their religious views that they were known as German Quakers. Their leader, David Pastorius, was a man of education and influence. These early Germans, though often extravagant in their religious notions, were usually men of education and as a class were a very choice lot of colonists. About the end of the first

The Germans

[13] MYERS, A. C., ed., *Narratives of Early Pennsylvania, West New Jersey, and Delaware*, pp. 208-209, 374.

decade of the eighteenth century a second wave of German immigration, more important than the first, began to reach the shores of America, and this movement led to a great increase in the German population of Pennsylvania (see pp. 349-353).

The Anglicans hostile to the Quakers

Not all of the early colonists in Pennsylvania were in sympathy with the Quaker belief. Some of them were Anglicans, or Episcopalians, who settled mainly in Philadelphia among the Quakers. They did not get along well with the latter, but on the contrary were in perpetual opposition to them. They opposed Penn during his lifetime and were the main critics of his administration. When Penn's sons, who had been converted to the Anglican faith, succeeded to the proprietorship, the Anglicans became the government party and supported the proprietors, but they kept up their opposition to the Quaker assembly.

The Scotch-Irish

Another important class of colonists whose religious views were not in harmony with those of the Quakers were the Scotch-Irish. In the second decade of the eighteenth century, a great stream of Scotch-Irish Presbyterians began to flow to America, and Pennsylvania received a large share of them. These newcomers did not always maintain the most cordial relations with their Quaker neighbors, for they did not accept the doctrine of inner illumination held by the latter, nor did they indorse the Indian policy of the Friends. They regarded the Indians in about the same light that the old Hebrews looked upon the pagan Canaanites, and felt that they ought not to buy their lands from them, but should exterminate them. Such an attitude meant war. As they were usually on the frontier, they served not only to stir up the Indians, but also to act as a buffer to protect the rest of the settlements from attacks by the savages. They were brave fighters, were fond of liberty, and sometimes rather impatient of the restraints of law.[14]

The Quakers control the government in Pennsylvania

It can be seen that the population of Pennsylvania was not homogeneous. The Quakers, the Church of England party, the Scotch-Irish, the Welsh, and the Germans were separated from one another by religious and racial prejudices, and in the case of the Germans and the Welsh by language. The legislature, however, was until the middle of the eighteenth century controlled by the Quakers, though they were in the minority. At the end of the colonial period it was estimated that about one-third of the

[14] For a fuller account of the Scotch-Irish in Pennsylvania, see pp. 353-357.

population was German, one-third Quaker, and the other third composed of Anglicans and other elements. But the Germans usually voted with the Quakers and thus gave them control of the government. Besides, the method of apportioning seats in the assembly was favorable to the Quakers and gave them a voting strength in this body out of proportion to their numbers.

Penn spent only a few years in his colony. On his first visit he remained in Pennsylvania only two years and then returned to England. He felt that his Quaker brethren needed his protection in the homeland, and his contest with Lord Baltimore over the boundary line demanded his presence at the court. He did not return to his province until 1699, and then remained there only two years. It would have been better for both himself and the settlers if he could have stayed in Pennsylvania and directed the colony in person.

The later career of Penn

While Penn was in England he was on very friendly terms with King James II, and this association did much harm to his reputation. Penn had for a long time entertained a kindly feeling for James, as the latter when he was Duke of York had secured the release of Penn from prison (1669). As king, James pursued a policy of leniency toward the Quakers and other dissenters and even went to the extreme of setting aside laws of Parliament against Catholics and dissenters. We know now that his liberality toward the latter did not arise from any broad spirit of tolerance, but from the desire to shield his fellow Catholics from the penalties prescribed by the laws. Besides, in thus disregarding the laws against dissenters and Catholics he was overriding the authority of Parliament and usurping power not belonging to the crown. The dissenting leaders of that day saw this and refused to support a policy of religious tolerance purchased at the price of political tyranny. So most of them were opposed to the unconstitutional acts of the king, although by them they were granted exemption from unjust laws.

William Penn, however, believed in the sincerity of James and supported his religious policy. After his return to England he became a courtier and adviser of the king and thus shared in the odium that rightly attaches to the latter's arbitrary measures. This intimacy with the unpopular ruler brought Penn into disrepute with the liberal party in both religion and politics and caused him to lose to a considerable extent the esteem and affection of his Quaker brethren. He was judged by the company he kept.

Many honest people actually believed that he was a Jesuit in disguise and was doing all he could to help the king put the Catholic Church in power in England. Unfortunately, there was some basis for a part of this impression; for while he had no Catholic leanings, he approved of some of James's unconstitutional measures and acquiesced in others. His cordial relations with the king were not due altogether to personal friendship, but partly to the belief that the policy of the crown was favorable to religious toleration. He was undoubtedly wrong in his estimate of the motives of James, though doubtless sincere in his attitude toward his policy. His mistake lay in his effort to reconcile his rôle as courtier with his principles as a Christian. For in attempting to approve the acts of a Stuart tyrant and at the same time follow the teachings of Christ he was trying to perform the impossible feat of serving both the God of justice and the Mammon of unrighteousness.

This friendship between Penn and James is not easy to explain, for Quaker religion and Stuart politics made strange bedfellows. Penn used his influence with his sovereign to secure the release of a number of people who had been imprisoned on account of their religious convictions. It is very much to his credit that he showed such active sympathy for the oppressed, but it does not justify or atone for the support that he gave James in overriding the constitution. The most charitable view that we can take is that he was led too far by his desire to serve his persecuted fellow-countrymen and so allowed the softness of his heart to go to his head.

Pennsylvania a royal province

While Penn was having his ups and downs in England, affairs were taking a bad turn in his province. His governor had gotten into a controversy with the assembly, and the Anglicans, who were still in opposition, were now charging Penn with neglect of the province as a result of his long absence. It was also urged that the Quakers were not making any provision for the defense of the colony, which would thus be helpless in case of attack by the French. The Delaware counties were in revolt and had chosen a governor of their own. King William took advantage of this situation to deprive Penn of his governmental powers (1692). Two years later (1694) he regained his old position in the government of the province, and he and his heirs remained proprietors until the Revolutionary War broke out. During the two years (1692-94) when Penn's authority as proprietor was suspended, Pennsylvania was a royal province. The government during this period assumed the form that was usual for the crown colonies.

When Penn was reinstated as proprietor (1694), the form of government temporarily established was about the same as that under the Second Frame except that the assembly now exercised the right of initiative in legislation. The government was put on a permanent basis by another constitution, known as the Charter of Privileges, which was accepted by both the proprietor and the assembly (1701). This Charter remained the organic law of Pennsylvania to the end of the colonial period. Under it the council ceased to be elective and became appointive. It now lost its legislative function and henceforth was only an administrative body. From this time to the Revolution the assembly was a body of one house. The council, however, still exerted influence in lawmaking as it advised the governor concerning proposed legislation.[15]

Proprietary rule restored

DELAWARE

When New Netherland passed under English control the territory of the present States of Delaware and New York was placed under the jurisdiction of the Duke of York. He ruled the Dutch and the Swedes on the Delaware with absolute authority, just as he did the Dutch on the Hudson. The governor of New York or his appointees had entire control over them, but the settlers were unmolested in their religious beliefs and were given the right of trial by jury. After the English conquest some Scotch-Irish and a few English Quakers came to Delaware, but when Penn came to America the Swedes were still in the majority in the Delaware region. The Swedish settlements were all close to the Delaware and Schuylkill rivers and their navigable tributaries. One important reason for this was that the people wanted to be within easy reach of their Lutheran churches, for they used the rivers as their principal means of transportation.

Delaware under the proprietary rule of the Duke of York

Penn received from the Duke of York (1682) a grant of Delaware, or the Territories, as they were called. Penn did not derive from this patent any strictly legal right to govern the Territories,

Delaware as a proprietary province under William Penn

[15] The abbreviated text of the Charter of Privileges is given in MACDONALD, *op. cit.*, pp. 224-229; the full text, in THORPE, *op. cit.*, pp. 3076-3081.

but he proceeded as if there was no question as to his authority.[16] The three counties of Delaware were by an act of the legislature (1682) incorporated into the province of Pennsylvania, and were represented in both the council and assembly, just as were the other counties of Pennsylvania.

By the Charter of Privileges (1701) Delaware was given authority to form a separate assembly if she desired to do so. In two years (1703) the Territories took advantage of this privilege and organized an independent assembly. From that time until the Revolution Delaware had an assembly of her own, but remained under the governor of Pennsylvania.

Selected Readings

1. The Beliefs of the Quakers.—Article by Jones, R. M., in the *Religious History of New England*, pp. *179-200.
2. George Fox.—Jones, R. M., *Life and Message of George Fox* (this short account of twenty-nine pages is brilliantly written and is an excellent appraisal of the spirit and work of the founder of Quakerism).
3. William Penn.—Hodges, George, *William Penn*.
4. Old Roads out of Philadelphia.—Faris, J. T., *The Romance of Old Philadelphia*, *ch. 1.
5. Life in Philadelphia.—Fisher, S. G., *The Quaker Colonies*, *ch. 3.
6. Penn as a Courtier.—Fisher, S. G., *The True William Penn*, *ch. 17.
7. Delaware in the Colonial Period.—Fisher, S. G., *The Quaker Colonies*, *chs. 12-13.

[16] The land originally granted to the Duke of York extended westward only to the Delaware River and, therefore, did not include the present state of Delaware. The duke, however, laid claim to this region on the ground that it was a part of the territory held by the Dutch, all of which was, he contended, granted to him. In 1683 he received another patent from the king giving him the Delaware counties. (For this patent, see Hazard, S., *The Register of Pennsylvania*, ii, pp. 27-28.) But the deeds by which Penn secured a claim to the Lower Counties were executed the year before. These deeds, therefore, conferred no legal authority and no strictly legal title to the land. (For the deed to Penn by the Duke of York, see *ibid.*, i, pp. 429-430.) The king's acquiescence in Penn's assumption of authority over the Lower Counties was probably due to their comparative unimportance.

CHAPTER XIII

THE "GLORIOUS REVOLUTION" IN ENGLAND AND AMERICA

THE republican government established in England by the Puritans in alliance with the Parliamentary party was never able to secure a strong hold on popular opinion. Oliver Cromwell was an able executive, and his policy was characterized by vigor in both domestic and foreign affairs. But during the half-decade of his rule, quiet at home and prestige abroad were purchased at the cost of high taxes and military rule, both of which were very objectionable to the people. Moreover, the people chafed under the restraints which the Lord Protector in his zeal for Puritanism had imposed upon their amusements. For Cromwell in his effort to make his subjects live up to the outward forms of a rigid ethical code had enacted and enforced certain "blue laws" which they regarded as an unwarranted interference with their personal freedom. British virtue was not equal to the strain to which it was subjected, and the average Englishman soon became tired of being good, or at least he was bored with the Puritan brand of goodness. The malcontents were, however, kept under control as long as the strong hand of Cromwell was at the helm, but at his death (1658) the Protectorate collapsed. There followed a short period of uncertainty during which the army was in control. The experiences of this time strengthened the "opinion which had been forming for some time, that the only way to end military despotism was to restore the Stuarts."[1] Charles II was well qualified by both character and experience to lead his subjects back to easy-going habits in moral behavior. The "Merry Monarch" was, therefore, welcomed to the throne of his fathers by a cordiality that was inspired as much by his faults as by his virtues.

A reaction against Puritan rule

The new ruler was frivolous and immoral and his court was a disgrace to any self-respecting nation. But, happily, the Eng-

[1] LUNT, W. E., *History of England*, p. 486.

263

The immorality of Charles's court

lish character was sounder at heart than it appeared, and it soon settled down into moral respectability after having taken a vacation from what was considered Puritan super-goodness. The bad influence of the court did, however, permeate the upper layer of English society and succeeded in lowering the moral tone of the aristocracy. Unfortunately, too, the intellectuals were tainted with the low ethical standards of the age, and some able literary men used their genius in dressing up in artistic garb the fashionable filth of the day. In this way the badness of the Restoration period was given undue publicity, and so the morals of the day appear to us in worse light than they deserve.

James II violates the constitution to favor the Catholics

Charles, being a Stuart, was naturally autocratic in his notions and doubtless would have been despotic in his policy if circumstances had been favorable. But the hardships that he had experienced while in exile had shown him by contrast how soft a seat the throne of a ruler makes, and he was determined to do nothing that would cause him to lose his newly-acquired comforts and "send him on his travels" again. So he managed to get along with Parliament without any serious trouble. At his death (1685) his brother James became king. Charles had secretly been a Catholic, but had not publicly announced his allegiance to this faith until he was on his death-bed. James II, on the other hand, had all along been an avowed Catholic. As the king was the head of the Anglican Church and was bound by oath to enforce the laws against the Catholics, James found his position a very difficult one. His loyalty to his own church caused him to disregard the laws by appointing Catholics to office. Finally he issued a Declaration of Indulgence suspending the measures enacted by Parliament against dissenters and Catholics. By thus setting aside an act of Parliament he was clearly violating the rights of that body.

The Revolution of 1688 in England

The people were inclined to submit to the high-handed policy of James, since he was getting along in years and would probably soon be succeeded by his daughter, Mary, who was a Protestant and was married to William, Stadtholder of the Dutch Netherlands. But about the time the excitement was high over the indulgence controversy, it was announced that a son was born to James. According to English law, this son would succeed to the throne instead of Mary. As he would be educated as a Catholic, it looked as if the Catholic dynasty would become permanent. Under these circumstances, a few noblemen invited William to come to England and head the movement against his father-in-law (1688). William came and was warmly received by all classes of the people. James fled to France and William and Mary became joint rulers of England. This is known as the "Bloodless Revolution," as it was won without any bloodshed in England proper. It is also sometimes spoken of as the "Glorious Revolution."

William had no hereditary right to the throne and owed his position to Parliament. By thus accepting the crown at the hands of Parliament, the king acknowledged this body as sovereign. This precedent ended the divine-right theory of the kingship. The Revolution of 1688, together with the Puritan Revolution that had preceded it, settled for all time the question as to whether Parliament or the king is sovereign and the decision was in favor of the former. Parliament passed the Bill of Rights (1689), which clearly defined the powers of Parliament and set at rest any misunderstanding as to its authority. In the same year, it also passed the Toleration Act, which granted freedom of worship to Protestant dissenters, but withheld religious toleration from the Catholics.

When Charles II ascended the throne (1660) he found that New England had only a nominal connection with the British empire. The Puritan Revolution in England and the events preceding and following it had so engaged the attention of the home authorities that they had left the New England settlements to go their own way, and as a result they had developed into little autonomous republics. Such a situation was undesirable from the point of view of the empire, and it was probably not to the best interests of the colonials. As soon as Charles was seated on his throne numerous complaints against Massachusetts came before the Privy Council. The provincial government had persecuted Quakers in violation of English law and had limited the franchise to church members. The grandsons of Mason and Gorges complained, and justly so, that New Hampshire and Maine had been unlawfully annexed to Massachusetts in disregard of their proprietary rights. There were also boundary disputes between the New England colonies which they were unable to settle. Two of the regicides (the judges who had sentenced the king's father to death) were harbored in New England, and all of the colonies except Rhode Island had refused to proclaim the new ruler.

Conditions in New England at the time of the Restoration

Besides, throughout New England the Navigation Laws were violated.[2]

The government in Massachusetts was now, and had been from the beginning, in the hands of a small minority of the leading men, prominent among whom were the ministers. The practice of restricting the privilege of voting for representatives in the assembly to members of the Congregational Church disfranchised a large proportion of the people. The ruling class in Massachusetts contended that the king had no powers in their colony except those expressly reserved to him in the charter. Such a theory as to the relation of the colony to the mother country was untenable; for when the patent was granted it was never intended that the British government should divest itself of all authority over the territory covered by this charter. Besides, the charter had a provision that all laws made under it should be in harmony with the laws of England. This implied that the authorities in the homeland would have the right to decide whether statutes passed by the assembly in Massachusetts met this requirement. Then, too, some of the measures in force in Massachusetts were undoubtedly in violation of the laws of England. The position taken by the Bay Colony was, therefore, a defiance of imperial control, and if the British government had accepted this contention and had applied the same principle to the rest of the overseas dominions, the result would have been a complete disintegration of the British empire. The Massachusetts authorities had thus raised an issue that the crown could not afford to ignore.

As the British government had no representative in New England, it was not in a position to make a just appraisal of the situation. Massachusetts had agents in England, but they were so hampered by instructions and lack of instructions that the home authorities could not carry on satisfactory negotiations with them. The king decided, therefore, to send over a commission to make investigations and carry out certain necessary measures. In 1664 four royal commissioners were sent to America to reduce the Dutch colony of New Netherland and to investigate conditions in New England. They were also to hear appeals, settle disputes, and see that the Navigation Laws were enforced and religious freedom allowed.[3] The Massachusetts government regarded the

[2] *Calendar State Papers, America and West Indies, 1661-68,* nos. 45, 49, 64, 80.

[3] *New York Colonial Documents,* iii, pp. 51-65.

appointment of this commission as a challenge to its authority and an infringement of its rights. The General Court passed orders for garrisoning the fort on Castle Island and preventing the landing of the soldiers who were coming over with the commissioners.[4]

The commissioners, as we have seen, were successful in reducing New Netherland to British authority, but they got into a controversy with the authorities of Massachusetts and did not succeed in bringing that colony into a proper relation with the empire.[5] In their report to the king three out of the four members recommended the annulment of the Massachusetts charter.[6] The king was also displeased with the attitude of Massachusetts and he expressed himself to that effect in a circular letter to the colonies (1666). He commanded the Bay Colony to send representatives to England to answer the charges that had been brought against it. This the General Court flatly refused to do.

The commissioners recommend annulment of the Massachusetts charter

Massachusetts was now virtually in open rebellion, and it was expected that the crown would proceed at once to bring the recalcitrant colony to terms. But a war with both France and Holland now broke out, and for a decade the British authorities allowed the rebellious colony to go her own way. In the fight between the Massachusetts oligarchy and the crown, the people stood to lose regardless of the outcome. If the king won, the rights covered by the charter would be lost to the colony as a whole. On the other hand, if the oligarchy won it would be strengthened in its position and the old policy of intolerance and limited suffrage would continue.

Action of the crown delayed by war with France and Holland

In 1674, the war with Holland being over, the British government decided to turn its attention to the knotty New England problem. The English authorities did not, however, want to take action without sufficient information, and so they ordered Massachusetts to send over agents to present her case. This demand was to be transmitted by a special messenger, who was to receive the reply of the General Court and also to investigate trade and

Randolph's mission

[4] Osgood, H. L., *American Colonies in the Seventeenth Century*, iii, pp. 174-175.

[5] *Massachusetts Colonial Records*, iv, p. 210; *New York Colonial Documents*, iii, pp. 99-100; Osgood, *op. cit.*, iii, pp. 183-186.

[6] *New Hampshire Provincial Papers*, i, p. 254.

other conditions in New England. Edward Randolph was chosen for this important mission.[7]

Randolph was coolly and even rudely received by the magistrates of the Bay Colony. The governor told him that laws passed by the Parliament of England did not apply to Massachusetts.[8] However, after some delay a meeting of the General Court was held to consider the king's letter. Acting on the advice of the clergy, whose opinion, as usual, had been asked, the assembly decided to yield, and so appointed agents and transmitted a reply to the king.[9]

The charter of Massachusetts annulled

Randolph on his return reported that the Navigation Laws were not being observed and that English citizens had been put to death for their religious views. Besides, the Massachusetts authorities denied the right of appeal to the Privy Council and refused the oath of allegiance to England.[10] Randolph was naturally prejudiced against the leaders in Massachusetts, owing to the way he had been received, and he made exaggerated statements in his charges, but these accusations were substantially true. He recommended that Massachusetts be made a royal province with a guarantee of religious freedom.

The agents were unable to clear the Bay Colony of these charges. They were told by the British authorities that Massachusetts would have to ask pardon for having coined money, promise to enforce the Navigation Laws, accept a supplementary charter, repeal the laws that were repugnant to those of England, and agree to the appointment of a royal revenue official. The agents were also given to understand that the king did not propose to deal with his own subjects as if they were foreigners.

The Massachusetts oligarchy showed no signs of accepting these terms, and the British government was forced to the alternative of acquiescing in the virtual secession of the colony from the empire or of annulling the charter. So after a long time of patient but fruitless negotiation it was finally decided to appoint Randolph as Collector of Customs for New England and to begin

[7] OSGOOD, H. L., *American Colonies in the Seventeenth Century*, iii, pp. 311-312.

[8] HUTCHINSON, THOMAS, *Papers* (Prince Society *Publications*), ii, p. 243; OSGOOD, *op. cit.*, iii, pp. 314-315.

[9] *Massachusetts Colonial Records*, v, pp. 99-101, 106-108, 113-114.

[10] For Randolph's account of Massachusetts, October, 1676, see RANDOLPH, EDWARD, *Letters and Papers*, ii, pp. 225-259.

judicial proceedings looking to the forfeiture of the charter.[11] The proceedings were successful and the charter was annulled October, 1684.[12]

An eminent authority on New England thinks that if the leaders had been willing to give up their trade in violation of the Navigation Laws and to meet the British government halfway in its effort to make an adjustment between the colony and the empire, they might have saved their charter,[13] but after they had taken the stand they did and refused to yield, the king was forced to have the charter withdrawn or else acknowledge the independence of Massachusetts. It seems that the British government was reluctant to take the step which ended the autonomy of the colony, but it could not afford to allow one section of the realm to flaunt its authority and ignore the trade laws of the empire. Besides, in future conflicts with the French it was important that the imperial officials should be in direct communication with and have the active coöperation of the largest and most important province on the French border.

The annulment of the charter did not necessarily mean the loss of the liberties of the people. The immediate effect of the change was to deprive a minority—the members of the Congregational Church—of the privilege of ruling the majority of the people and of forcing them by persecution to conform to their ideas of religion. It was thus a victory for religious tolerance; and as it ended the requirement of church membership for voting, it might also prove to be a victory for political liberalism. The latter result would depend, however, on the character of the king. The new arrangement made possible a scheme of government for the colony under a wise and able king that would give the people greater freedom than they could ever enjoy under the Puritan theocracy. But when an empire has such rulers as the later Stuarts, and especially James II, any change that invests the crown with greater power is usually to be deprecated.

After the Massachusetts charter was canceled the Privy Council was confronted with the problem of devising a plan of government for the province. The scheme, as finally adopted, provided

The Dominion of New England

---

[11] Osgood, H. L., *American Colonies in the Seventeenth Century,* iii, p. 324; *Massachusetts Colonial Records,* v, pp. 421-423.

[12] For the order of court annulling the charter, see Osgood, H. L., *op. cit.,* iii, pp. 333-334.

[13] Adams, J. T., *The Founding of New England,* p. 101.

for a governor and a council appointed by the crown.[14] All executive and judicial powers were to be exercised by these officials, except that appeals in cases involving three hundred pounds were to lie to the king in council. These royal appointees were also to have the power to make laws and levy taxes, as there was no provision for an assembly. It seems that the Lords of Trade and other advisers of the king were opposed to leaving out the assembly, but James insisted on its discontinuance. This was a very unwise decision and was one of the main causes of discontent. The people had had an assembly for fifty years, and while it had been controlled by the clergy and the privileged class, it gave the constitution an element of liberalism, both actual and potential.

The first governor was Joseph Dudley, and he and all but two of his council were New Englanders. His appointment was only temporary, and at the end of seven months he was succeeded by Sir Edmund Andros (December, 1686).[15] Andros had already been serving as governor of New York and had performed the duties there with honesty and ability. Under Dudley, New Hampshire had been joined with Massachusetts, and now New Plymouth was added to the jurisdiction of Andros. It was the purpose of the British government to put all of New England, New York, and the Jerseys under the control of Andros. Connecticut and Rhode Island had charters which stood in the way of this plan of consolidation. Their charters would, therefore, have to be annulled or else these two colonies would have to accept the new authority. Proceedings were started looking to such annulment when Rhode Island submitted and afterward Connecticut acquiesced in the new arrangement.[16] Six months later New York and the Jerseys were put under the control of Andros. The annexation of the latter colonies offered no difficulties, as New York was already a royal province and the governmental authority

[14] In the original plan of government, which was in effect for only seven months, there was no provision for the enactment of new laws.

[15] Andros's commission is given in *Rhode Island Colonial Records*, iii, pp. 212-218.

[16] For proceedings against Connecticut, see *Cal. State Papers, America and West Indies*, nos. 304, 319; *Connecticut Colonial Records*, iii, pp. 350-351. For the proceedings against Rhode Island, see *Colonial Records of Rhode Island*, iii, p. 193; for the compliance of Connecticut, see *Connecticut Colonial Records*, iii, pp. 375-378.

of the Jersey proprietors rested on a basis of doubtful legality. Andros's authority now extended over all the territory from the Delaware River to the French possessions in Canada. This aggregation of provinces was known as the Dominion of New England.

If the plan could have been carried out successfully there would have been decided advantages from the point of view of the empire in having so much territory under single control. It would guarantee a uniform policy with reference to the Indians and would make it easier for the people within that wide area to present a united front against the common enemy. But the difficulties of keeping so many colonies under one government were insuperable. Local patriotism and religious and other differences rendered coöperation well-nigh impossible. Besides, the greatness of the area coupled with the scarcity of the means of communication made it very difficult for the rulers and very inconvenient for the people to have the administration of the whole Dominion carried on from one central point. This experiment in government would probably, therefore, have failed even if conditions in other respects had been favorable. *Objections to the new plan of government*

But conditions in other respects were most unfavorable. No royal governor would have been acceptable to the deposed oligarchy in New England even though he had been in a position to give the people a wise rule. Moreover, under the new arrangement, the chief executive of the province was by instruction from the king committed to an unwise and autocratic policy. Any program, therefore, that he might map out was predestined to arouse enough opposition to cause its failure. Besides, Andros had an impulsive temper and a lack of tact that aggravated the difficulties of the situation.

As was to be expected, Andros soon antagonized the leaders. They complained of a number of grievances, some of which were real and others fanciful. One cause of dissatisfaction was his religious policy. Andros was directed in his instructions to grant religious tolerance to all Protestants, but to encourage the Anglican Church. In carrying out this instruction he showed more zeal for the cause of Anglicanism than knowledge of the Puritan temperament; for he forced the Congregationalists to allow the Anglicans to worship in one of their meeting-houses once every Sunday. The Congregational service was usually very long, and it was not convenient to have two services in one church on the *Unpopularity of Andros's administration: Reasons* same day. But the main objection was that the Puritans felt that it was a sin for them to encourage an erroneous system of worship like that of Anglicanism. If Andros had exercised the proper tact he would have had the Anglicans defer the beginning of their public worship until they had built a church for themselves, which, as it proved, they were able to do in a few years. The strict Puritans were also shocked by the laxity of the governor in keeping the Sabbath and by his observance of Christmas, which they regarded as a Catholic custom.

A grievance that touched all the people was the land question. In New England each town had originally acquired a boundary of land either by the tacit consent of the colonial assembly or by a formal grant from it, and this title had usually been reinforced by purchase from the Indians. Part of the territory so obtained was divided among the citizens of the village, and part of it was held by the local community as common pasture or woodland or for future allotments. Now, the New England colonial charters did not provide for the incorporation of towns, and there was no clause in any of them that authorized this method of disposing of real estate. Therefore, practically all lands were held by a tenure that was not technically legal. By his instructions Andros was to appropriate to the royal domain all unclaimed areas and could re-grant for a small quit rent all tracts that had not already been legally acquired. This meant that all landed property owned by the towns might be taken from them, and individuals might also lose their holdings unless they paid this quit rent. The amount of the quit rent was small (less than one-third of a shilling an acre), but there was strong objection to paying this charge. It is true that in only a few cases were individual titles challenged, but the possibility that any one's title might be questioned gave rise to a general feeling of uncertainty as to tenures.[17] Andros was thus called on to carry out a foolish policy, which upset the people without profiting the crown. Even though the old system of landholding was not technically legal, still it had existed without challenge for two generations and should not have been disturbed. But for the folly and injustice of this policy the king's instructions are more to blame than Andros's interpretation of them, though he might have avoided much of

[17] *Andros Tracts*, ii, pp. 180, 284; *New York Colonial Documents,* iii, pp. 722-726.

the opposition aroused by this unwise measure if he had exercised wisdom and tact in dealing with this difficult problem.[18]

The people had another real grievance when the governor and his council, in accordance with instructions, proceeded to levy taxes. In New England taxes, except for local purposes, had always been imposed by a vote of the colonial assembly, in which sat deputies chosen by the people, and there was strong opposition to a tax levied without the consent of the people's representatives, although taxes were lower under Andros than they had been before. The dissatisfaction was particularly strong in Essex County and especially in the town of Ipswich, both in Massachusetts. In the latter place some of the citizens under the leadership of the Rev. John Wise said that the tax imposed by the governor was a violation of their rights as Englishmen and that they would pay no taxes except those voted by an elected assembly.[19] Twenty-eight of these malcontents were arrested and six of them were imprisoned and heavily fined.

At first the town meetings went on as usual, but as a result of the opposition to the objectionable tax shown in the meetings in Essex County, the council limited these local assemblies to one meeting a year and restricted its business to the election of local officers.[20]

In addition to these real grievances there were certain trumped-up charges that were an important cause of the unpopularity of the governor. Andros had in 1688 been put in charge of Indian affairs for a large part of the English continental colonies. This duty added to the burdens which were already too great for one man, especially one whose staff of assistants was made up largely of greedy placemen, interested only in the emolu-

[18] For a statement of the grievances that the people had against Andros drawn up by the leaders of the revolt and read from the balcony of the town house at the time Andros was deposed, see *Andros Tracts*, i, pp. 11-19. This is a bitter and biased arraignment of the governor's administration. An answer to these charges, made by one of Andros's sympathizers, is given in *ibid.*, pp. 71-131. Charges brought against the governor by five members of his council are given in pp. 137-147. The accusations brought against Andros before the Privy Council, and his answer to the same, are given in pp. 176-182.

[19] *Andros Tracts*, i, pp. 83-86.

[20] *Connecticut Colonial Records*, iii, p. 427.

ments of office. There were minor Indian troubles in several
sections of New England, and Andros led an expedition into
Maine and chastized the savages there. But his Indian policy kept
him away from Boston for a good part of his time, and these
absences gave his enemies the opportunity to charge him with
being in favor of bringing in popery, of betraying the colonies
to France, and of plotting to have the Iroquois attack Boston.
Of course there was no basis for any of these accusations, but
the people, not only in America but also in the homeland, were
at this time nervous about a possible Catholic danger because of
the unconstitutional acts of their Catholic king, and it was easy
to work on their fears and prejudices. The result was that many
believed the unreasonable rumors about Andros spread by his
enemies.

One influential class in Boston, the wealthy merchants, might
have been won over to the support of the new régime if their
interests had not been antagonized. Some of these merchants
were not Puritans and so were not allowed a voice in the colonial
government. They were dissatisfied with the rule of the oligarchy
and were not averse to a change that would lessen its power and
influence. But Andros made a strenuous effort to enforce the
Navigation Laws and this policy struck a severe blow at the
prosperity of the merchants. They, therefore, joined the orthodox
Puritans in their opposition to the royal government.

Andros
deposed
by a revo-
lution in
Boston

Andros's government was so unpopular that it probably would
not have lasted long even if there had been no outward event to
hasten its fall. The immediate occasion of the deposition of the
governor was the downfall of his master, James II, brought on
by the Revolution of 1688. Soon after the news came (March,
1689) that the Prince of Orange had landed in England, a mob
arose in Boston and captured Randolph and others prominent in
the government and lodged them in jail (April 18, 1689). Andros
escaped to the fort, but soon surrendered to avoid bloodshed.[21]
It is not known to what extent, if at all, the old leaders were
responsible for this uprising. Though they denied previous knowledge of it, there is some evidence that they had planned the revolt.
Andros and his associates were kept in prison in Castle William

[21] An account of the revolt, written by a man who was in Boston
at the time, is given in the *Andros Tracts*, i, pp. 3-8. For another
account, written about a month after the outbreak, see *ibid.*, ii, pp.
191-201.

on an island in Boston Harbor until February of the next year, when they were sent to England.

After the downfall of Andros the old régime was for the time being restored in New England. In a few weeks Plymouth, Connecticut, and Rhode Island went back to the same forms of government that they had had before the Dominion of New England had been created. In Massachusetts there was a provisional government for a short time, and then the administration was turned over to the officials who had held office at the time the charter was annulled. The old governments temporarily restored in New England

This was only a temporary arrangement, but Massachusetts was governed in this way for two years. The government of the colony under this plan was weak and unsatisfactory. It was not able to cope with the Indian troubles on the frontier, and the economic condition of the colony was bad. The war with the French (King William's War) was going on, and Massachusetts was unable to coöperate effectively with the other colonies against the French or even to protect its own frontiers against Indian raids. It was evident that a stronger government was needed in the commonwealth.

As the territory over which Andros ruled was more than could be properly administered by one man, Captain Francis Nicholson was appointed as deputy governor for New York. There was no representative assembly, and Nicholson, with the aid of the three local members of the council, was intrusted with the government. Nicholson was not the proper man for this responsible position. He was not without ability, but at times he exhibited a childish lack of self-control that made it impossible for him to command the respect of the people. It was also unfortunate that practically all the important places in the administration were held by Catholics. Besides, Nicholson himself had shown a leaning toward Catholicism, it was thought, for on one occasion he knelt while mass was being celebrated. Unpopularity of Governor Nicholson in New York

The position he was called on to fill was a difficult one. The racial and religious differences among the people, the tradition in favor of self-government on the part of the English settlers, and the prejudice against Catholics made it well-nigh impossible for any representative of a Catholic monarch with absolutist views to be acceptable to all classes. But for an untactful army officer the situation was hopeless. There was, however, no outbreak until news came that James II had been driven from the throne of England and his representative, Andros, had been deposed in New England. Both the props by which Nicholson had hitherto been supported were now removed and there was no outside power to bolster up his weak position. With such an insecure footing he was bound soon to be toppled over by events. There was apparently a real fear on the part of the citizens that Nicholson and the Catholic officials were intriguing with the Catholic French in Canada against the Protestants in New York. While there were no grounds for this belief, still it did not appear improbable at that time. Besides, war might quickly come (as it did), and people are not accustomed to weigh evidence scientifically in the face of a military danger.

Revolution in New York

In an atmosphere so highly charged with excitement and discontent a slight occurrence might easily lead to an outbreak. It was not long, therefore, before a match was struck to start the explosion. The immediate cause of the uprising was a foolish remark made by Nicholson. On one occasion, being goaded to anger by the ignorance or impudence of a subordinate officer, he lost his self-control and imprudently said, "I would rather see the city on fire than commanded by an impudent fellow like him." This heedless statement was misconstrued and exaggerated so as to leave the impression that the governor would like to see the town burned.[22] The people rose in revolt and asked Jacob Leisler to act as their leader. He accepted the offer and took charge of the fort in the name of William and Mary, and Nicholson left for England.[23]

Leisler was of German birth and was a strong Protestant. It is difficult to form a true estimate of his real character, owing to the bitterness of feeling that characterizes the accounts of his contemporaries. According to his enemies, he was an ignorant, coarse demagogue; his friends represent him as a man of education and a real tribune of the people. He was doubtless honest, courageous, and patriotic, but high-tempered, untactful, and bigoted. His leadership was opposed not only by the few Catholic officials, but also by the aristocratic class among the Protestants.

Affairs took a turn in his favor when in December, 1689, there came from the new sovereigns dispatches addressed to "Our Lieutenant-Governor and Commander-in-Chief of our Province of New York, or in his absence to such as for the time being

[22] *New York Colonial Documents*, iii, pp. 593-594, 640.
[23] New York Historical Society *Collections*, 1868, pp. 324-325.

take care to keep the peace and administer the laws." Two members of the council who were opposed to Leisler contended that these dispatches should be turned over to them. But Leisler, more nearly than anyone else, was keeping the peace and administering the laws, and was, therefore, entitled to the dispatches. This, at any rate, seems to have been the view of the messenger, for after some hesitation he turned the papers over to him.[24] Leisler now assumed the title of lieutenant-governor and tried to govern the colony according to the instructions given by the sovereigns in these dispatches.

Leisler's authority was not accepted at Albany, where the Dutch inhabitants, led by the aristocracy, held out against him. But soon a blow struck by the French and their Indian allies showed the colonists the danger of being divided. King William's War was now on, and Frontenac, the able French governor, sent a raiding party of French and Indians against the New York frontier. In February, 1690, this band appeared before Schenectady, a frontier village not far from Albany. They caught the people off their guard and killed sixty of them and captured twenty-seven. A score or more escaped and found their way to Albany to report the terrible tragedy. The people of Albany now saw the necessity of both factions presenting a united front against the common enemy, and so they recognized the authority of Leisler.[25]

The rule of the Lords Baltimore during the three decades (1657-89) that preceded the outbreak of the Revolution of 1689 was not satisfactory to the people of Maryland. The proprietors were absentee landlords, and the terms on which land was granted were not so liberal as they were in Virginia and Pennsylvania. During this period there was a good deal of friction between the proprietors and the representative assembly. The council, which constituted the upper house of the assembly, was dominated by friends and relatives of Lord Baltimore and was usually ready to do his bidding; but the lower house was more assertive of the rights of the people and consequently was often at odds with the upper house and the governor.

This dissatisfaction of the people was increased by certain

The Revolution of 1689 in Maryland: The people are dissatisfied with the rule of the proprietors

---

[24] *Ibid.*, pp. 325-326.

[25] For an account of the part played by Leisler in these events, written by contemporaries who were favorable to him, see *ibid.*, pp. 314-318, 324-327, 398-412.

unwise measures of the proprietor, who, in the management of
his province, acted too much as if it were his private estate. He
felt that he must dominate the government if his interests and
the rights of his Catholic coreligionists were to be properly safeguarded. In his effort to control the administration he had the
suffrage restricted (1670) to freeholders and owners of personal
property to the value of forty pounds. He also tried to increase
his influence over the assembly by limiting the number of representatives to two from each county and by bribing representatives
to support his measures by gifts of office. Laws were also set
aside by the proprietor that had been enacted by the assembly and
been approved by him.[26]

The third Lord Baltimore was in the later years of this period
encouraged in the policy of annulling laws passed by the provincial assembly by the example set by his royal master, James II,
who lost his throne by suspending and disregarding acts of Parliament. The position of the proprietor was also weakened by the
fact that he was a Catholic. The Protestants were in the majority
and they contended that the Catholics had more than their share
of the offices. This was a just complaint, for the proprietor
appointed his relatives and Catholic friends to most of the lucrative offices. Even his policy of religious tolerance was not acceptable to the Protestants, most of whom did not approve of allowing
freedom of worship to the Catholics. The Quakers were one
Protestant sect, however, that did not have this intolerant attitude, and they were willing to accord religious freedom to all
Christians, including Catholics. But they, too, had a grievance
against the government, for their repeated requests to be excused
from taking oaths in court had been denied through the influence
of the proprietor.

The discontent went to the limit of rebellion in 1676, the
insurgents being encouraged by the initial success of Bacon's
Rebellion in Virginia. But the revolt had not made much headway before it was discouraged by the final collapse of Bacon's
uprising in the neighboring province and was easily stamped out
by the authorities. The punishment meted out to the leaders of
the revolt and others who had opposed the policy of the proprietor aroused a spirit of bitterness in certain prominent men,

[26] For a declaration of grievances as recounted by the Protestant
leaders of the revolt (November 28, 1689), see ANDREWS, C. M.,
Narratives of the Insurrections, pp. 305-314.

who were ever afterward looking for an opportunity to even scores with the proprietor and his representatives and stood ready to lead an uprising whenever the time should come. Prominent among those who were nursing a grievance against Lord Baltimore was John Coode, who felt that he had been unfairly dealt with by the proprietor. He had a following among the people that made him a dangerous opponent. Under such conditions Lord Baltimore's authority could hardly hope to stand the strain of revolution, and all that was needed to start a rebellion was the proper encouragement from England.

Such encouragement came early in 1689 when the rumor began to spread that James II had been driven from the throne and William and Mary had been received as rulers of England in his stead. The proprietor was represented in Maryland at that time by the council, at the head of which was an inexperienced man who did not know how to handle the difficult situation. Lord Baltimore had promptly recognized William and Mary as sovereigns of England, but his instructions to his representatives in Maryland to proclaim the new joint rulers were delayed, owing to the death of the messenger by whom they had been sent.[27] This delay was most unfortunate for the proprietor's cause, as the council not only declined to proclaim William and Mary in Maryland, but, it was charged, publicly denied their right to the crown of England.

Revolt in Maryland precipitated by the revolution in England

The opponents of Lord Baltimore took full advantage of the mistake made by his representatives in the province. In April, 1689, there was organized "An Association in arms for the defense of the Protestant Religion, and for Asserting the Right of King William and Queen Mary to the Province of Maryland and all the English Dominions." John Coode was at the head of this organization. As time went on and the colonists learned of the state of affairs in England and saw the unwillingness of the council to proclaim William and Mary, men who had hitherto supported the government joined the Association. The cause of the insurgents was also strengthened by the prospect of war with the French colonies. It was expected that as the king of France was supporting the dethroned English ruler, the Canadian subjects of the former would attack the English colonists in America, and this expectation was soon justified when the first of the inter-

[27] *Maryland Archives, Council Proceedings, 1688-1693*, pp. 67-69, 112-114.

colonial wars broke out. There was also a fear that in this war the Catholics in Maryland would unite with the French Catholics and their Indian allies against their Protestant neighbors. This fear was exploited to the full by the insurgents in the interest of their cause, and wild rumors of Catholic plotting with the French and Indians were circulated. We know now that these rumors were utterly without foundation, but the excitement that animates any people when they are facing the probability of a war is never conducive to a judicial appraisal of evidence, and so these incredible stories were believed by many of the people.

The outbreak

The Association, therefore, had no difficulty in overthrowing the proprietary government. A band of insurgents led by Coode took St. Mary's, the seat of the provincial government (July, 1689). Their example was quickly followed by the Protestants throughout the province, and soon Lord Baltimore's authority was overthrown in every county but one. "The council was able to raise but a few troops, and these, the officers excepted, were not willing to fight."[28] A representative assembly, or convention, was now called, which chose a committee to administer the government until a governor appointed by the new sovereign should arrive to take charge of the administration.

The English Revolution occasions no revolts in the other colonies

In the other American colonies there were no disorders caused by the English Revolution of 1688. When the Dominion of New England collapsed the Jerseys went quietly back under the authority of the proprietors. There was also no outbreak in Pennsylvania, though Penn was for two years (1692-94) deprived of his governmental authority as proprietor in the province. This was done, however, not in response to any action on the part of the Pennsylvania settlers, but because the new British government distrusted Penn on account of his intimate relations with the dethroned monarch. When James II succeeded to the throne there was still smoldering in Virginia some of the discontent that had been aroused by the maladministration of the representatives of Charles II. The accession of a Catholic king only made matters worse, and when news came of Monmouth's Rebellion[29] the governor was disturbed over the sympathy for the rebel shown by

[28] Sparks, F. E., *Causes of the American Revolution of 1689*, p. 102.

[29] Monmouth's Rebellion was an unsuccessful revolt which broke out in the first year of James's reign under the leadership of the Duke of Monmouth, a natural son of Charles II.

the people. Nothing came of this, however, as Monmouth was soon overcome. Some excitement also arose when it was known that William of Orange had landed in England. In North Carolina the people at this time revolted against a disreputable governor and induced the assembly to depose him, and it is not unlikely that the uprising was encouraged by the revolution in England.[30]

Selected Readings

1. Massachusetts in 1676 by a Contemporary.—*Letters and Papers of Edward Randolph* (Prince Society *Publications*, vol. xxiv), ii, pp. *225-229.
2. The Stuart Dominion in New England.—Channing, E., *History of the United States*, ii, *ch. 6.
3. Andros as a Man and Governor.—Andrews, C. M., *Narratives of the Insurrections*, pp. *223-228.
4. The English Revolution in America.—Channing, E., *History of the United States*, ii, *ch. 7.
5. Leisler's Revolt.—Andrews, C. M., *Narratives of the Insurrections*, pp. *317-319; Channing, E., *History of the United States*, ii, pp. *202-209; Goodwin, M. W., *Dutch and English on the Hudson*, *ch. 8.
6. The Revolution of 1689 in Maryland.—Andrews, C. M., *Narratives of the Insurrections*, pp. *301-303; Channing, E., *History of the United States*, ii, pp. *209-213.

[30] Connor, R. D. W., *History of North Carolina*, p. 105.

CHAPTER XIV

THE NORTH BETWEEN TWO REVOLUTIONS

Great movements in the eighteenth century

THE period between the English and American revolutions (1689-1776) is an important one in the history of the English continental colonies. A considerable portion of this era was taken up by the intercolonial wars, which won for Britain the supremacy of the continent. It was in this period, too, that there occurred the great religious revival and the German and Scotch-Irish immigrations, with the consequent extension of the area of settlement westward. During this entire period there was also going on an important development in agriculture, manufacturing, and commerce, which was accompanied by important changes in the social and educational life of the people. These movements are too broad to be properly treated in the accounts devoted to individual provinces and so are discussed with reference to the colonies as a whole. Of the events other than those that are connected with these important movements, those of chief interest for us are the ones that center in the constitutional controversies that were waged between the representatives of the people and the agents of the imperial authorities. These political contests are of special significance because out of them there developed that attitude of mind on the part of the people which furnished the psychological basis of the final struggle for American independence. Of the political disputes of this era none are of greater interest or importance than those of Massachusetts and New York.

The policy of William in reconstructing the colonial governments

When William and Mary came to the throne they were confronted with the problem of reconstructing the government in each of the colonies that had revolted against the Stuart régime. The uprisings in America were all close imitations of their prototype, the Revolution of 1688 in England, and were all carried out in the name of the new rulers. King William, therefore, had to approve them or else admit that his own action in accepting the English crown was unjustifiable. The governments established in all the revolutionary colonies were temporary, and it remained for the king to outline a scheme of administration that would put them on a settled basis. William's wars and other interests took so much of his time that he could not at once devote much thought to the American portion of his empire. By 1691, however, his plans for his overseas dominions were matured, and he was ready to inaugurate a policy for their administration.

The Dominion of New England was given up, and a number of jurisdictions were organized in its stead. New Hampshire was made a separate royal province, and the governments that had been restored in Connecticut and Rhode Island according to their old charters were continued. These charters had never been annulled, as the judicial proceedings against them were still pending when Andros was deposed. In Massachusetts the leaders and probably a majority of the people were in favor of a return to the political system that existed before 1684. Increase Mather, who had been in London for some time as agent for the colony, urged the king to restore the charter of 1629. But there were important reasons why the old government should not be restored without some modifications. If the original charter were revived, the government would be placed in the hands of a minority, the members of the Congregational Church, who would be dominated by the clergy. A majority of the people would be disfranchised, and there would be no guarantee of religious freedom. Besides, the enforcement of the Navigation Laws and the effective prosecution of the war against the French demanded that Massachusetts should be linked up more closely with the empire. *Reconstruction in New England*

A compromise arrangement would thus have to be made for Massachusetts if the desire for local autonomy were to be reconciled with the interests of the empire. Accordingly, a charter was granted to the colony (1691), making it a royal province but giving the people a stronger voice in the government than they had in other crown colonies. To Massachusetts were joined Plymouth, Maine, and, for a short time, Nova Scotia.[1] The governor was to be appointed by the king and was to have power to veto acts of the assembly. Laws passed by the General Court and assented to by the governor could be vetoed within three years by the king in council, as was the practice in other royal *Massachusetts granted a new charter (1691)*

[1] Nova Scotia, or Acadia, had been taken from the French the year before, but was recaptured by them in this same year (1691). So the jurisdiction of Massachusetts over Nova Scotia lasted for only a short time.

provinces. Appeals from the decisions of the provincial courts could lie to the Privy Council in cases involving three hundred pounds or more. The General Court, as under the old charter, was to consist of two houses. The upper house was to be composed of the governor and the council, and the lower, of representatives chosen by the people. The first councilors were appointed by the king, but their successors were to be chosen annually by the assembly as a whole—consisting of the council and the representatives of the people sitting in joint session—and any appointment so made could be vetoed by the governor. The charter did away with the religious test for voting and substituted for it a property qualification. The old system of local government by town meetings was continued with no substantial change.[2]

This plan of administration was, in some respects, better than that provided for by the old charter. It brought the colony into more direct contact with the outside world and thus helped to break up provincialism. Under the new charter the power of the clergy could not be so great as it had been under the old, though they were not immediately deposed from authority. The new governor and councilors were appointed at the suggestion of Increase Mather, a prominent Congregational minister, and were, therefore, of the old clerical party. But the principle of basing suffrage on property holding rather than on membership in the Congregational Church was unfavorable to the perpetuation of the old theocracy.

William Phips the first royal governor   The first governor of Massachusetts under the new, or Province, Charter, as it was called, was Sir William Phips, who had been born and reared in Maine. Phips was well and favorably known in the province. He had played a worthy part in the local Indian troubles and had won a baronetcy by finding in the West Indies a wrecked Spanish treasure ship and conveying its valuable cargo safely to England. As a reward for this feat he was not only honored by his sovereign, but was also allowed enough of the spoils to make him a wealthy man. He had attained prominence as a military leader by heading the expedition that had taken Port Royal from the French (1690), though this prestige had been considerably dimmed by the failure of a later

---

[2] For the text of this charter in abbreviated form, see MacDonald, W., *Select Charters*, pp. 205-212. For the text unabridged, see Thorpe, F. N., *Colonial Charters*, pp. 1870-1886.

attempt to capture Quebec. The British authorities, therefore, had reason to think that in the selection of this distinguished native son they had made a choice that would be eminently satisfactory to both the leaders and the people.

Phips, however, was not a successful governor, despite the auspicious circumstances under which he entered office, and after a short administration of two and a half years (May, 1692-November, 1694), he was called to England by the king to answer important charges that had been preferred against him. This failure was due partly to his instructions, which required him to insist on a permanent supply for the government and on appropriations for the maintenance of the forts on the northern frontier. The assembly would not comply with these requests, and so considerable friction developed between the governor and the people's representatives. But a good deal of Phips's trouble grew out of his own ineptitude as an executive. He had an uncontrollable temper, which at times led him into acts that compromised his dignity and detracted from his prestige. It also embittered his relations with the leaders of the opposition and aroused in them a greater antagonism than would have been caused by a more tactful advocate of an unpopular policy. Moreover, he sometimes allowed personal spite to influence his stand on questions of public interest.

The most important event of Governor Phips's administration was the outbreak of the Salem witchcraft delusion. Intellectual conditions were favorable at the time for this lapse into superstition. The general level of culture in New England was probably lower during the second half of the seventeenth century than it has been at any other time in its entire history. The generation then living had been brought up under the hardest pioneer conditions and had had, therefore, little opportunity to acquire the kind of education that is obtained in the schools. In this respect the men of that period were less fortunate than both their fathers and their sons. The former had come from England, and many of them had enjoyed the educational advantages of an old civilization. The latter lived at a time when the conditions of life in America afforded more time and opportunity for intellectual training and when schools and other agencies of culture were better developed. By the beginning of the eighteenth century there were a number of schools and two colleges in America. There was also more wealth and leisure, and commerce had begun to broaden the

Intellectual conditions in the last half of the seventeenth century

minds of the colonials by bringing the people of one section in contact with those of another and by leading them into the current of European culture.

Moreover, in Massachusetts during the last decade of the seventeenth century the intellectual leaders were so narrow that they were not competent to steer the people safely through the dangers that always arise from ignorance. Puritanism and the discipline acquired in the wilderness school of hard knocks combined to stamp upon these leaders a narrow and conservative view of life. Even the schools that had been established were so closely allied with a narrow theology that they had little, if any, broadening influence. The Mathers, Increase and Cotton (father and son), and other distinguished ministers were out of touch with the scientific movement that had arisen in England under the leadership of Boyle, Newton, and others. The most prominent clergymen were champions of an out-of-date obscurantism and made every effort to identify it with religion. The people naturally accepted the views of their spiritual guides, not knowing that these opinions were a century or more behind their age.

The Mathers   The stoutest champions of the old Puritanism were Increase Mather and his son Cotton. These two ministers were true types of the orthodoxy that had developed in New England under the narrowing influences of the seventeenth century. Both were born and reared in Massachusetts, both were graduates of Harvard, and they shared between them the distinction of being the best-educated men in New England. The younger Mather entertained a respect for his father that was exceptional even in that age of reverence for parents and elders, and the mutual affection that characterized the relations between father and son gave a beautiful human touch to their austere Calvinism. In their loyalty to the faith of the fathers, the infallibility of which they never doubted, they felt impelled to fight modernism wherever it showed its head. Both father and son read extensively and wrote voluminously. Cotton Mather had a library of nearly three thousand volumes,[3] and was the author of about four hundred books and pamphlets.[4] Neither his study and reading, nor that of his father,

[3] WENDELL, BARRETT, Cotton Mather, p. 179.
[4] For excerpts from the writings of Cotton Mather, see STEDMAN, E. C., and HUTCHINSON, E. M., Library of American Literature, ii, pp. 114-166. For specimens of the writings of Increase Mather, see ibid., pp. 75-106.

however, broadened their views to any considerable extent but rather confirmed them in the opinions that they had imbibed in childhood and youth.

Of the two, Increase Mather had the greater ability and the more successful career. He was for sixty-two years minister to the Second Church in Boston, which had a membership of fifteen hundred,[5] and for sixteen years during this same period he was also president of Harvard College. The people of Massachusetts showed their appreciation of his ability by sending him as their agent to England (1688) to secure a renewal of their charter, which had been canceled a few years before. While on this mission he showed considerable diplomatic skill in handling the affairs of the colony; and though he did not succeed in having the old theocracy restored, he was able to get a new charter which gave the Bay Colony a more liberal government than that enjoyed by any other royal province.[6] His sojourn in England brought him in contact with some of the leading men of his day. The impact of these outside influences was strong enough to break a few fissures in the conservatism that incased his view of life, and through these openings there came in a little light from the new age that had already dawned in the homeland.

Increase Mather

No such opportunity came to Cotton Mather, whose mentality was entirely the product of Puritan heredity and New England environment. He, therefore, embodied in his personality most of the virtues and some of the faults of the Calvinism of seventeenth-century New England. Although he led a life of activity and was often engaged in controversy, his religion was of that mystic type that was better suited to a life of contemplation than to the turmoil of the American wilderness. His diary speaks of numerous prayers and fastings, of moments of religious ecstasy alternating with seasons of depression, and of a sense of peace and assurance following a consciousness of sin and an uncertainty as to his acceptance with God. Anyone who has made even a hasty perusal of this diary must be convinced of his deep piety and of his firm conviction that the other world and this are in constant communication. It was this latter belief that was the foundation for some of his finest virtues as well as the basis of his greatest

Cotton Mather

[5] *The British Journal*, October 19, 1723; quoted by MURDOCK, K. B., in his *Life of Increase Mather*, pp. 246-257.

[6] For an account of Increase Mather written by his son, see MATHER, COTTON, *Parentator*.

mistakes. He not only believed that God's people can commune with Him, but he was equally sure that the devil also keeps in touch with witches, who are his emissaries on earth. It is easy for us to understand how such a view would lead him into the witchcraft delusion. On the other hand, the conviction that the children of God can take their problems to their Heavenly Father for solution fortified him in times of stress and trouble and enabled him to weather storms that would have wrecked an ordinary character. For it must not be forgotten that this vain and emotional Puritan divine received more hard blows from life than fall to the lot of the average mortal. He witnessed the disappointment of the most cherished hopes of his beloved father, as well as many of his own; he buried two wives and all but two of his fifteen children; and he had to acknowledge defeat in the great contest waged by his father and himself for the cause of fundamentalism. But through it all he fought a brave fight and to the end he kept the faith.

The Salem witchcraft delusion

The belief in witchcraft was still firmly held as late as the middle of the seventeenth century in both Old and New England. About this time (1645-47) scores of witches were executed in the Puritan counties of eastern England, and the first witchcraft frenzy broke out in New England. The Puritans of Massachusetts and Connecticut, probably inspired by the executions in England, did not lag behind their overseas brethren in their zeal for the punishment of Satan's emissaries. Consequently, in these two colonies fourteen persons were hanged as witches during the period from 1647 to 1662. After the Restoration the belief in witchcraft gradually declined in the homeland, and there have been only two executions for this crime in England since that time.[7] Nor was there any serious excitement in New England over witches during the quarter-century following the panic that ended in 1662. Outside of New England there were probably no executions for witchcraft in any of the colonies,[8] though in some of them trials for this crime were held.

[7] For a good brief statement as to the rise and decline in Europe of the belief in witchcraft, see BURR, G. L., *Narratives of the Witchcraft Cases*, pp. xv-xvii.

[8] In 1654 a woman was executed for sorcery near Barbados on board a ship that was bound for Maryland, and there is some evidence which points toward two other executions for witchcraft on the high seas by persons on their way to Maryland (see HALL, C. C.,

For the recrudescence of this superstition in New England and the dangerous turn it took, the conservative ministers were largely responsible. They were disturbed over the lack of piety and the liberal views exhibited by many of their parishioners, and were afraid that the clergy would be deposed from their power in the government. Moreover, it seemed that the Lord was displeased with New England, as He had recently subjected the land to such harrying experiences as King Philip's War, a smallpox epidemic, and two fires. The ministers felt, therefore, that something must be done to bolster up their influence and arrest the general tendency toward error in opinion and laxity in moral conduct. It was to meet this need that Increase Mather, at the request of a synod of Massachusetts divines, wrote his essay on "Illustrious Providences" (published in 1684). This is a compilation of accounts of "witchcrafts, diabolical possessions, remarkable judgments upon noted sinners, (and) eminent deliverances" in answer to prayer. The effect of this work was to turn the attention of the people toward supernatural occurrences and to revive their superstitious fears of the devil. This book must, therefore, have aided greatly in the creation of the psychological background for the witchcraft craze that broke out a few years later.[9]

The frenzy was started in the summer of 1688 by the strange antics of some children in Boston. Cotton Mather, who was a firm believer in witchcraft, took a great deal of interest in these pranks and gave them undue prominence by writing a book in which were described in minute detail the experiences of these children and of others similarly afflicted.[10]

It was at Salem, however, that the delusion went to the greatest

ed., *Narratives of Early Maryland*, pp. 117, 141). BROWNE, W. H., in his *Maryland, the History of a Palatinate*, p. 83, note, says that a man was executed in Maryland for witchcraft in 1685. But we cannot be sure that this statement is correct, as the Maryland records for that year are lost.

[9] Mather's *Illustrious Providences* is given in part in BURR, G. L., *Narratives of the Witchcraft Cases*, pp. 8-38.

In fairness to Increase Mather, it ought to be said that he did not approve of the unfair methods used by the court in the trial of witch suspects (*ibid.*, pp. 180, 184).

[10] For Cotton Mather's account of the experiences of the Boston children he thought bewitched, see BURR, *Narratives of the Witchcraft Cases*, pp. 99-126. For the account written by the father of the children, see *ibid.*, pp. 126-131.

length and had the most tragic results. Early in 1692 some young girls in Salem began to pretend that they were bewitched and were able to counterfeit the symptoms which victims of the Black Art were supposed to exhibit. Two of these young people belonged to the household of Rev. Samuel Parris, and they probably learned their tricks from a book on witchcraft which was in the minister's library. Mr. Parris was not on good terms with some of his neighbors, and it has been charged that the desire to even scores with some of his enemies was a motive that prompted his activity in stirring up the excitement.[11] The frenzy swept on so rapidly that when Governor Phips arrived in Boston he found that over one hundred persons had been imprisoned and were awaiting trial.

If Phips had been a man of progressive ideas he might have taken the lead in awakening the people from the influence of this superstition and thereby have saved them from the torturing memories of a terrible nightmare, with which their enlightened consciences afterward afflicted them. But he was an ignorant and conventionally-minded man, thoroughly under the influence of the clergy, and so could not be expected to be forward in challenging the infallibility of a public sentiment that was supported by respectability and religion. Instead, therefore, of opening the jails and setting at liberty the victims of this superstition, he constituted a special tribunal which proceeded to try the prisoners. The court rapidly sentenced a number of them to death, most of whom were convicted on evidence that no present-day judge would consider for a moment. "When a score of persons had been executed, when eight more were under sentence, when fifty others had confessed themselves to be witches, when one hundred and fifty were in prison and two hundred accused, things came to a sudden halt."[12] The afflicted girls had in the meantime

[11] The contemporary literature on the Salem witchcraft delusion is voluminous. The contemporary accounts that are most accessible are those in BURR, *Narratives of the Witchcraft Cases*. An excellent modern account of witchcraft in the colonies and of the European background of the delusion is given in WERTENBAKER, T. J., *The First Americans*, ch. 6. An interesting short account, hostile to the clergy, is given in ADAMS, J. T., *The Founding of New England*, pp. 451-456.

[12] WERTENBAKER, T. J., *The First Americans*, p. 161.
Of the persons executed, nineteen were hanged and one was pressed to death with weights.

begun to accuse persons of high standing, and the magistrates began to see that they had gone too far. A reaction set in, and there quickly grew up a feeling that many of the victims were innocent. The governor now put an end to the special court and the executions were stopped (September, 1692).[13]

When the community returned to its normal sanity it realized its terrible mistake, though some of the leaders persisted in their belief in witchcraft. One judge of the special court, Samuel Sewall, was so overcome with the enormity of his error that he made public confession of his mistake in church.[14]

The effect of the delusion was to lower the prestige and influence of the clergy. For the ministers on the whole had given moral and active support to the witch persecutions, though some of them had protested against the unfair methods employed in the trials. After the reaction had come, quite a number of the people felt that their spiritual leaders had acted as blind guides in the unfortunate affair and were inclined to lay at the door of the clergy the responsibility for the great mistake.

The successor of Phips was Richard Coote, Earl of Bellomont, whose authority was at a later date extended over New York and New Hampshire, and he was also put in command of the militia of Connecticut, Rhode Island, and New Jersey.[15] In thus placing one man over such a wide district William was reverting to the policy of the deposed James, for the jurisdiction of Lord Bellomont was the Dominion of New England restored in modified form. This later experiment in colonial union did not, however, arouse opposition as did the creation of the Dominion of New England. Some of the New England leaders were in favor of the arrangement, as they thought that it might enable the English colonists to coöperate more effectively against the common enemy and thereby compete more successfully with the French for the

The administration of the Earl of Bellomont

[13] BURR, G. L., *Narratives of the Witchcraft Cases*, pp. 200-201.

[14] This confession was made in the Old South Meeting-house in Boston (January 14, 1696). Judge Sewall stood while some one read a paper prepared by him in which he expressed his sorrow for his sin and a desire for prayers for forgiveness. For this paper and a brief contemporary account of the incident, see BURR, *Narratives of the Witchcraft Cases*, pp. 386-387.

[15] *Cal. State Papers, America and West Indies, 1693-1696*, nos. 1917, 1964, 2068; *1696-1697*, no. 762; *New York Historical Documents*, iv, pp. 266-273.

trade in fish and furs along the coast from Newfoundland to New York. There was merit in the new plan, and if it had been carried out as a permanent policy it might have enabled the northern colonies to present a more united front against the enemy in the subsequent French and Indian wars. It proved to be, however, a temporary arrangement, as the jurisdiction thus created lasted only until the death of Lord Bellomont (1701).

The chief executive of so large a dominion could not give all the provinces the amount of attention that effective administration demanded. As a good deal of his time was taken up with affairs in New York, he could not supervise the government in Massachusetts very closely and was able to spend only fourteen months in Boston. While absent he kept in touch with affairs to some extent by correspondence with Lieutenant-Governor Stoughton, who was his representative in Massachusetts. Lord Bellomont's brief sojourn in the Bay Colony was characterized by an absence of friction between him and the assembly that is remarkable when we consider how much trouble other governors had there. This is explained by the exceptional integrity and tact displayed by the governor, coupled with the fact that he did not have to make many contacts with the representatives of the people.

For the first twenty-five years under the Province Charter all the governors of Massachusetts except Lord Bellomont were natives of the colony, and, as we have seen, Bellomont's connection with New England was little more than nominal. But the long contest between the assembly and the representative of the crown went on with nearly all of them, and sometimes it was as violent when the governor was of New England origin as when he was of English birth. One of the most unpopular of them all was

Joseph Dudley as governor of Massachusetts

Joseph Dudley, who had been reared in Massachusetts. His administration lasted fourteen years (1702-15) and covered approximately the period of Queen Anne's War. He entered office under a serious handicap, as his record prior to receiving his appointment had been such as to cause the people of Massachusetts to distrust him. He was the first royal governor after the old charter had been annulled, and he had been associated with Andros in his government of the Dominion of New England. He had thus taken a prominent part in the effort made by James II to foist Stuart tyranny upon New England. By aiding and abetting Andros in establishing his autocratic rule he had caused his fellow-citizens to regard him as a traitor to New England. At the downfall of Andros he was, therefore, imprisoned and later driven from Massachusetts. For the past ten years he had been living mainly in England, during which time he had taken an active part in English politics. He had imbibed British ideals during his long sojourn in the motherland and had become more of an Englishman than a New Englander. He had even acquired leanings toward the Anglican Church that compromised his orthodoxy and good standing as a Congregationalist. Moreover, he was thoroughly in accord with the imperialistic notions of the British government and stood ready to sacrifice the interests of his home province to those of the empire, provided he could by so doing advance his own political fortunes.

On receiving the appointment as chief executive of Massachusetts Dudley felt that he had realized the dream of his life, for his highest ambition was to return as governor of the land from which he had formerly been expelled. He soon learned, however, that his new honor had brought with it the opportunity for more trouble than glory. As events proved, his appointment was unfortunate both for the people and for himself. His instructions and his own imperialist inclinations caused him to take a stand against the position of the assembly on practically all the questions that were at issue between it and the executive. However, he was energetic and capable and gave the province an able administration. He had exceptional capacity for politics, and his native gifts in the art of dealing with men had been trained by his experiences in England. His political sagacity could easily have risen to the rank of high statesmanship had it not been fettered by a narrow ambition that was always looking out for his own interests. The able way in which he conducted the war extorted from the people a reluctant admiration for his efficiency, though nothing that he ever did could win their good will.

The political history of Massachusetts from the accession of Dudley until the Revolutionary era is marked by an almost continuous controversy between the governor and the lower house of the assembly. This controversy runs through the events of this period not like a silver thread, but rather like a knotted cord. It goes along from one administration to another with a sameness that is positively tiresome. Indeed, these perennial disputes between the executive and the legislature, if given in detail, would "bore the modern reader as much as they annoyed the provincial

Controversies between the governors and the assembly

Causes of dispute

executive."[16] Among the chief causes of the long contest were the insistence of the lower house of the assembly on the sole right to select its speaker, the attitude of the assembly toward bills of credit, and its refusal to appropriate money for frontier forts and to vote a regular salary to the governor, as it was directed to do by the royal instructions.

Paper money

The controversy over paper money became acute during the administration of Jonathan Belcher (1730-40). The majority of the people of both Massachusetts and New Hampshire were at this time in debt, and many of them had been impoverished by the war. They were, therefore, in favor of extending the time limit for the redemption of the bills of credit that had been issued by the provincial government, as in this way they could be supplied with a cheap medium of exchange. The House of Representatives in Massachusetts supported the people in their demand for more money, but the governor, in obedience to rigid instructions from the Board of Trade, took a firm stand in favor of a contraction of the volume of paper currency. He was supported in this position by the council and the wealthy merchants, who, being creditors and thus interested in a dear money, wanted the currency put on a silver basis. The governor and Board of Trade were right in contending for a sound and stable medium of exchange, but their great mistake lay in their failure to provide a proper substitute for the bills of credit. The effect of the governor's "policy, taken as a whole, was to reduce the medium of exchange of Massachusetts to an amount which was quite inadequate to its needs."[17]

At this juncture (1739) a group of men organized a land bank for the purpose of issuing notes. These notes were to be secured by mortgages on land, and while they were not to be a legal tender in the payment of debts, it was hoped that they would circulate freely and thus relieve the money stringency. As there was no adequate provision for redemption, these notes would, of course, soon depreciate in value. The governor and the sound-money party were violently opposed to the scheme, feeling that it would further complicate and aggravate the bad currency situa-

[16] Quoted from Mayo by BURNS, J. F., in his *Controversies between Royal Governors and Their Assemblies in the Northern American Colonies*, p. 278.

[17] OSGOOD, H. L., *American Colonies in the Eighteenth Century*, iii, p. 347.

tion. The House of Representatives supported the people in their demand for the bank, and now the issue was clearly drawn between the debtor and creditor classes. The controversy was fought out fiercely in the newspapers, and there developed a very strong feeling between the opposing parties. Massachusetts had probably not been in such a state of violent agitation since the days of Andros. The English merchants finally took a hand in the quarrel and used their influence with the British authorities to have the land bank destroyed. The Board of Trade appealed to Parliament, which voted that the operations of the land bank were illegal and void.

The maintenance of the forts on the northern frontier gave rise to a long-continued disagreement between the governor and the House of Representatives,[18] but the most stubborn of all the causes of dispute between the agents of the crown and the people's representatives was the question of appropriating money for the governor's salary and for meeting the other expenses of the provincial government. Under the old charter, the General Court in Massachusetts had always voted an annual appropriation for the governor. This practice had become so well established that the assembly was determined that it should continue under the Province Charter. The governors, however, were required by their instructions to insist upon a regular salary. If the royal instructions on this point were complied with, the income of the governor would be certain and he would be independent of the legislature. The legislature was quick to note the advantage that the control of the provincial purse gave it over the executive, and was resolved not to part with so valuable a weapon. Consequently, it disregarded the orders of the crown and continued to make annual, and sometimes semiannual grants for the governor's

The governor's salary

[18] A fort had been built at Pemaquid, Maine, at the time when this district was under the control of the Catholic Duke of York. The British government was anxious that this fort be kept in the proper state of repair, as it would strengthen England's hold on the territory between the Kennebec River and Acadia. The governors were, therefore, instructed, one after another, to have the assembly vote appropriations for the upkeep of this post. But as it was some distance from any of the settlements and was thus not a protection to the frontier, the Massachusetts lower house insisted that the maintenance of the fort was an obligation resting on the imperial rather than the provincial government. It was, therefore, persistent in its refusal to vote the money asked for by the governor for this purpose.

salary. The amount voted was also frequently smaller than that fixed in the governor's instructions. Moreover, the salary, instead of being voted in advance, was usually given as a "present" at the end of the year. As the amount of the present depended upon the behavior of the governor, the legislature could use it as a species of bribe to make him do its bidding. By such a practice the independence of the executive could easily be destroyed and the king's representative would be reduced to a condition of subservience to the provincial legislature.

As was natural, the governors often refused to accept these presents and protested against the assembly's disregard of the royal orders. Frequently, too, they dissolved the assembly, only to find that the lower house of the new body was of the same temper as the old. The legislature thus had the advantage over the executive in the contest, despite the fact that the latter had behind it the support of the home government. The wars with the French and Indians increased this advantage, as they called for money and gave the assembly more opportunities to wield the power conferred by its control of the purse. By imposing conditions when making grants of money, it was often able to force the governor to accede to its demands. The quarrel over the salary question went on continuously until it was finally settled by a victory for the people's representatives. Governor Belcher received permission from the British authorities to accept an annual appropriation (1731), and for the next four years this permission was renewed. After that time Governor Belcher accepted the annual grant without even waiting for such permission. In this way the British government yielded the point for which the Massachusetts House of Representatives had all along been contending.

Election of the speaker of the lower house

A minor cause of dispute was the method of electing the speaker of the lower house of the assembly. The members of this body contended that they had the sole right to select their own presiding officer and, therefore, that the governor had no authority to approve or disapprove of their choice. Governor Dudley and his successor maintained that their power of veto extended to all acts of the legislative assembly, including the choice of the speaker of the lower house. They urged in support of their position the old English practice of submitting to the king for his approval the name of the person chosen by the House of Commons for the speakership, although this old "practice had become a mere formality, both in England and in most of the royal provinces."[19] This contest came to an end in 1725 by a ruling of the crown in favor of the governor's contention.

The dispute between the legislature and the executive went on in New Hampshire very much as it did in Massachusetts, the questions at issue being about the same in both provinces. The controversy, however, was not so continuous in the smaller province as it was in the larger one, and, in fact, there were periods of harmony between the governor and assembly in New Hampshire, during which the representative of the crown almost enjoyed popularity. For a number of years (from 1702 to 1742) New Hampshire and Massachusetts had the same royal governor, though each province had a separate assembly. In New Hampshire the population was much smaller and the people poorer than was the case in the Bay Colony. The poverty of the province was due in part to the paucity of its natural resources and in part to the ravages made by the wars.

The constitutional struggle in New Hampshire

In Connecticut and Rhode Island the governor, as well as both houses of the assembly, was chosen by the people and so both the executive and the legislature were trying to serve the same master. No serious constitutional controversy, therefore, could arise between the two branches of the government, though there was disagreement between them at times.

No constitutional fight between the legislature and the executive in Rhode Island and Connecticut

At the bottom of these long and tiresome disputes there was an antagonism between two important constitutional principles. The assemblies were contending for the right of the colonists to govern themselves, and the governors were trying to uphold imperial control. It was a struggle between the doctrine of states' rights and that of nationalism. If the contest could always have been kept on the lofty plane of principle it would have been waged with more dignity than actually characterized many of the petty quarrels between the governor and the lower house of the assembly. Unfortunately, however, personal feeling entered into the contest, and both sides indulged in little acts of spite that were unworthy of a constitutional conflict. Not only were the governors sometimes untactful and incompetent and generally more anxious to serve their royal master than their constituents, but the assemblies in their championship of the people's rights sometimes showed a selfish particularism that disregarded the interests of the empire.

Nature of the constitutional controversy

[19] GREENE, E. B., *Foundations of American Nationality*, p. 271.

Attitude
of the
council
toward
the con-
stitutional
struggle

In the struggle between the executive and the people's representatives in Massachusetts the council was often on the side of the former. At first sight this seems strange, as the councilors were chosen by the assembly and were thus indirectly responsible to the people. Their support of the governor might be explained on the ground that he could veto their election and thus to some extent control their tenure of office. A more natural explanation, however, lies in the fact that they belonged to the wealthy and conservative class, whose prosperity was bound up to a considerable extent with imperial interests. It was natural, therefore, that they would oppose a policy that would create unnecessary political agitation and economic unrest at home or would tend to loosen the bond that held the province to the empire.

In the contest between the upholders of local autonomy and the champions of imperial control, the British government acted the part of a grumbling parent, who complains of the disobedience of his children but makes no effective effort to enforce their obedience. The Massachusetts assemblymen soon discovered this flaw in imperial control and proceeded to flaunt the parental authority, meanwhile salving their consciences by protestations of loyalty to the crown.

NEW YORK

Party
strife

It will be remembered that the revolution which overthrew the Stuart régime in New York was led by Jacob Leisler and that his leadership was not accepted by the official and aristocratic class. The revolution thus gave rise to two political parties, the supporters and opponents of Leisler. Personal feeling was the main cause of the division between the two factions, and it was so bitter that for half a generation it formed the basis of political organization. As the Leislerians were recruited mainly from the common people and the anti-Leislerians from the wealthy class, the question of democracy *versus* aristocracy also figured as an issue. The first governors of this period helped to keep the ill-feeling alive by taking sides in the conflict and using the influence of their office to advance the interests of the favored party.

Recon-
struction
in New
York

Both factions sent representatives to England to present their case to the king and queen. It was easily seen that there was great bitterness between the two parties, and it would not do to choose a governor from either side. The king, therefore, wisely decided to select as Nicholson's successor someone who had had no connection with the revolution in New York. But in naming Colonel Henry Sloughter for the place he made an unfortunate choice; for Sloughter was a "profligate, needy, and narrow-minded adventurer." Along with him was sent a body of soldiers, which by some accident arrived at New York ahead of the governor. The commander of the military force demanded that Leisler surrender the fort to him, but did not show any commission from the king. Leisler quite properly refused to comply with this request, for the military leader had no authority to take charge in the absence of the new governor. When Sloughter arrived he at once called upon Leisler to give up the command of the fort. Leisler had not been shown the governor's commission and at first refused to surrender, but later agreed to do so. This hesitation gave Leisler's enemies the opportunity to fix upon him the charge of treason.

Unfortunately, the king, who probably did not realize how bitter the feeling was between the factions, had failed to insert in his commission to Sloughter any provision for the protection of Leisler. Owing to this negligence on the part of William, the man to whom he was most indebted for the success of his cause in New York was left to the mercy of his enemies. They haled him before the council and secured a sentence of death against him and his son-in-law. Sloughter signed the death warrants and both were hanged. The followers of Leisler felt that a gross injustice had been done their leader, and their hatred of the other faction was greatly intensified by these judicial murders. A few years after Leisler was executed his son got Parliament to pass an act (1697) reversing the decision of the court as to the forfeiture of his property. This was in effect declaring that the decision against his father was unjust.

Sloughter brought with him instructions to establish an assembly after the model of that in other royal provinces. This was done, and from this time (April, 1691) until the end of the colonial period the government of New York was about the same as that of other crown colonies. Laws passed by the assembly had to be sent to England within three months and could be vetoed by the king.

New York granted a representative assembly

The great majority of the governors sent to New York after the revolution were unsuited to the important position they were called to fill. Indeed, the British authorities displayed less wisdom in selecting their representatives for New York than for any

Character
of the
New
York gov-
ernors

other province. A very small number of them were men of ability, integrity, and tact, and were as successful as could be expected under the circumstances. Others were honest and moderately capable, but were lacking in the tact and adaptability that were requisite for success in colonial administration. A few of them, however, cannot be listed in either of these groups, but belong in the class of downright grafters and rogues.

The ad-
ministra-
tion of
Fletcher

To this third list historians have consigned the successor of Sloughter, Colonel Benjamin Fletcher, who doubtless merited the classification. Like his predecessor, he allied himself with the anti-Leislerians, probably because he felt that his administration could not succeed without the support of this influential party. His friends shared in the gains accruing from the corrupt practices of his administration and a number of fortunes were created or enlarged during his term. Favoritism and fraud were practiced in granting lands and piracy was winked at for a consideration. When the governor realized that he was soon to be recalled he redoubled his efforts to enrich his political henchmen at the expense of the province, and in the last days of his term made illegally a number of large grants of land to his political supporters.

Lord
Bello-
mont's
adminis-
tration

The next governor was Richard Coote, the Earl of Bellomont, who deserves to rank as one of the able administrators of the province (1698-1701). He was honest and capable and indefatigable in his efforts to carry out what he had undertaken. He set himself a big task as the goal of his administration, which included putting down piracy and smuggling, locating and rooting out corruption, promoting friendly relations with the Indians, encouraging the production of naval stores, making adequate provision for defence, and inducing the assembly to make appropriations for long periods. This extensive program was attacked with energy and enthusiasm, but, of course, all of it could not be carried out. The governor could not devote all of his time to New York affairs, as he had to pay some attention to the other provinces that were under his jurisdiction. Despite this drawback, however, his record of achievement was a creditable one for so short a term. Something was accomplished by his effort to put a stop to piracy and smuggling and to encourage the production of naval stores, while the honesty of his administration raised the governorship to a high level of respectability.

Bellomont identified himself with the Leislerians and thus

aroused the opposition of the anti-Leislerians. As we have seen, the attainder of Leisler and his son-in-law had been reversed by a vote of Parliament, but Governor Fletcher had not done anything to make the act of removal effective. Bellomont ordered the bodies of these two victims of party spite to be taken up from the place near the scaffold and reinterred with honor in the Dutch church (1698). This ceremony stirred up a good deal of feeling and was witnessed by a vast throng of people, though no violence was attempted. By this act the governor enraged the anti-Leislerian faction, and from that time on his administration was strongly partisan, being supported by the Leislerian and opposed by the anti-Leislerian party.

In the list of dishonest and inefficient representatives of the crown the first place belongs easily to Edward Hyde, Lord Cornbury, governor of New York and New Jersey (1702-08). He owed his appointment to his prominent family connections, for he was the grandson of the great Earl of Clarendon and the nephew of Queen Anne. History has properly "exhibited Lord Cornbury as a mean liar, a vulgar profligate, a frivolous spendthrift, an impudent cheat, a fraudulent bankrupt, and a detestable bigot."[20] This "black sheep of a noble house" did "probably more than any other royal governor to bring British administration in America into disrepute."[21] By his graft he made the New York executive disreputable, and by his frivolous conduct he made it ridiculous. Although he was instructed to do all he could to allay factional strife, he helped to keep alive the ill-feeling between the parties by allying himself with the anti-Leislerians. Such a caricature of a governor would have been an easy prey for the assembly but for his influential connections in England. Despite this advantage, however, the assembly took a bold stand against him and tried to put a strong curb on his rascality.

Lord Cornbury as governor

It is quite a relief to turn from this spoiled child of fortune and take a glance at one of the best administrators that ever represented the British government in America. This successful executive was Robert Hunter, governor of New York and New Jersey (1708-16). "Hunter was a Scotchman of good family and training, honest, tactful, and possessed of a considerable

---

[20] BRODHEAD, J. R., in the *Historical Magazine*, November, 1863; quoted by WINSOR, *op. cit.*, v, p. 241.

[21] OSGOOD, H. L., *American Colonies in the Eighteenth Century*, ii, p. 62.

degree of culture."[22] He was a staunch upholder of imperial authority and in consequence was, like the other royal governors, at odds with the assembly during a good part of his administration. Finally, however, a compromise was effected by which the executive and legislative branches were brought into harmonious relations with each other. The prestige of Hunter's administration was discounted to some extent by the failure of the effort made by him to found a colony of German Palatines in New York. (See page 351.)

Cosby's administration

Of the later royal governors, one, William Cosby (1732-36), deserves a brief mention in this narrative. He ranks along with Fletcher and Cornbury as a greedy proconsul, and was appointed governor because of the difficulty he found in maintaining the high standard of living that his social position in England required. He was probably not quite so bad as Fletcher or Cornbury, but by his time the newspaper had developed to the point of being a channel through which the shortcomings of a corrupt or inefficient official could be well advertised. The people were, therefore, better informed as to the ineptitude of his administration than had been the case with his more blameworthy predecessors. One of the most important events of his four-year term was a noted trial, which resulted in making the newspaper a still more effective instrument in opposing the royal government. This was the Zenger case.

The Zenger case

It was not long before the new governor got into a controversy with a strong party of opposition, which included some of the influential merchants and lawyers of New York City and near-by places. These opponents of the governor were organized into a sort of political club and were in a position to wield a wide influence in the province. To strengthen still further their hold on the people, this group founded (1733) an opposition newspaper, the *New York Weekly Journal*, which was edited by John Peter Zenger, a son of one of the German immigrants who had come over in 1709.

In this paper there appeared a number of articles attacking the government, which had been written by leaders of the anti-administration party. As Zenger was the publisher as well as the editor of the *Journal*, he was legally responsible for these articles. The government party decided to put a stop to this manner of attack by having Zenger arrested for libel. The poli-

[22] *Ibid.*, p. 97.

ticians who were backing Zenger felt that this was an attack on their party and so determined to put up a strong fight in behalf of their champion. To defend Zenger they employed Andrew Hamilton of Philadelphia, probably the ablest attorney in America at that time. This venerable lawyer was now approaching the advanced age of eighty, and though his bodily powers were failing, his mental vigor had been no whit impaired by the years, as his success on this occasion proved.[23]

Hamilton admitted that his client had published the statement with which he was charged, but offered to produce evidence to show that it was true and, therefore, not libelous. Chief Justice De Lancey, who presided at the trial, ruled that this evidence could not be admitted and that the jury could only pass on the fact of publication, leaving the court to decide whether or not it was libelous. If this ruling had been accepted—and it was correct according to the usage of that time—there was nothing left for the jury to do but to bring in a verdict of guilty.

Hamilton, however, was not willing to give up the fight because his case was so weak in point of law. He made an eloquent plea for the right of the jury to pass upon the truth or falsehood of the statements, which "proved to be the greatest oratorical triumph won in the colonies prior to the speech of James Otis against writs of assistance."[24] In his appeal to the jurors he represented to them that if they refused to pass upon the nature of the publication and to consider its truthfulness or falsehood in rendering their verdict, they would sacrifice the liberty of writing and speaking freely and would go far toward destroying for themselves and their posterity those safeguards of freedom that are inherent in the sacred right of trial by jury. As the jurors were citizens of the community and were convinced that the statements published were true, this was equivalent to urging them to defy a ruling of the court and declare that the writing was not libelous. Retiring under the flush of Hamilton's oratory, the jury did what any other typical American jury would have done under like circumstances—returned promptly with a verdict of not

[23] For a good short account of the Zenger case, see OSGOOD, H. L., *American Colonies in the Eighteenth Century*, ii, pp. 452-462. For a contemporary account of the trial (first published in 1738), see RUTHERFURD, LIVINGSTON, *John Peter Zenger, his Press, his Trial*.

[24] OSGOOD, H. L., *American Colonies in the Eighteenth Century*, ii, p. 460.

guilty. This decision was warmly indorsed by public sentiment, as was shown by the loud cheers with which Hamilton's speech was punctuated and the ovation given to him at its close.

The verdict in this case was of more than local significance. It was a precedent in favor of the practice which grew up in America of allowing juries and not judges to decide as to whether publications are libelous. It is true that often in subsequent colonial trials for libel the principle laid down in this case was not followed; nevertheless, the victory for justice won on this occasion went far toward liberalizing the procedure against libel, thereby giving a greater freedom to the press. Owing to this new freedom the newspapers of the later colonial period became an important agency for informing the people on political questions. In them were published the proceedings and discussions of assemblies and town meetings, and their columns were used by able publicists and clever literary men as a sort of open forum for the discussion of American rights. The later newspapers, therefore, played a prominent part in arousing and crystallizing that discontent with imperial management that finally developed into a desire for independence.

Constitutional controversies in New York   In New York, as in Massachusetts, the period between the two revolutions (1689-1776) was characterized by an almost continuous struggle between the governor, as the representative of imperial authority, and the assembly, the champion of the people's rights. The final outcome of the contest was a victory for the assembly as complete as the one scored by the General Court in Massachusetts. There were a number of causes of dispute, some of which, however, only led to temporary quarrels of lesser importance. The one outstanding source of persistent friction between the legislature and the executive in New York, as in Massachusetts, was the question as to how the governor's salary should be paid and other financial obligations should be met. Here, as in the Bay Colony, the governor was dependent upon the assembly for his salary, and the legislature used this advantage to wrest one concession after another from the executive, and so finally usurped authority that originally belonged to the latter.[25]

[25] In 1748, Governor Shirley of Massachusetts, after perusing the *Journal* of the New York assembly, expressed the opinion that that body had left no part of the royal prerogative untouched and had

The governors, in obedience to their instructions, insisted that the assembly should provide a permanent salary for their office. This the latter refused to do. At first it was willing to make a grant for a period of five years, but later would only vote annual allowances. The corruption of the early governors caused the legislature to distrust the honesty of the executive and to assert the right to supervise expenditures. It still further strengthened its hold on disbursements by adopting the practice of making appropriations for specific purposes. Not content with this, it also undertook to control appointments by voting salaries to individuals instead of to offices. The governors were compelled by their instructions to resist these claims of the assembly, and so the struggle went on almost continuously. In this contest the people's representatives had the whip hand, for by withholding their salaries they could bring strong pressure to bear on the agents of the crown. The long contest over the salary question was finally ended by the virtual acceptance (1756) on the part of the British authorities of the position of the assembly.

This period was also marked by disagreements between the upper house of the legislature, composed of the councilors, appointees of the crown, and the lower house, made up of representatives of the people. The most important dispute between the upper and lower houses of the assembly grew out of the attempt of the former to amend money bills passed by the latter. In 1711 the council changed several measures that had been adopted by the representative branch of the assembly. The latter body refused to accept these changes, contending that the upper house could not amend money bills. Governor Hunter warmly supported the claim of the upper house in the controversy, and its position would undoubtedly have been sustained by the British authorities. In answer to the contention that the king's instructions gave the council equal authority with the assembly in financial as well as other legislation, the representatives took the advanced ground that the council, since it derived its power "only from the meer Pleasure of the Prince," was not equal in authority on money questions with the assembly, whose "inherent right" "to dispose of the money of the Freemen of this Colony, does not proceed

---

"gone great lengths toward getting the government, military as well as civil, into their hands" (*New York Colonial Documents*, vi, p. 436).

from any Commission, Letters Patent or other grant from the Crown, but from the free Choice and Election of the People, who ought not to be divested of their Property (nor justly can) without their consent."[26] This was a bold assertion of the natural rights of the people that existed independently of any chartered privileges conferred by the crown, a doctrine that was proclaimed half a century later by Revolutionary leaders to justify an opposition that resulted in secession from the empire.

Selected Readings

1. The Salem Witchcraft.—Adams, J. T., *The Founding of New England*, pp. *451-456; Fiske, John, *New France and New England*, *ch. 5.
2. Samuel Sewall.—Parrington, V. L., *The Colonial Mind*, pp. *88-97.
3. The Mather Dynasty.—*Ibid.*, pp. *98-117.
4. New York in the Eighteenth Century.—Goodwin, M. W., *Dutch and English on the Hudson*, *ch. 11.
5. Privateers and Pirates.—Goodwin, *op. cit.*, *ch. 10.
6. The Zenger Trial.—Goodwin, *op. cit.*, *ch. 12; Rutherfurd, L., *John Peter Zenger, etc.*, pp. 173-246 (Zenger's account of the trial).

[26] *Assembly Journal*, i, pp. 307 ff., quoted in Burns, J. F., *Controversies between Royal Governors and Their Assemblies*, p. 307. See also Osgood, H. L., *American Colonies in the Eighteenth Century*, ii, pp. 104-106.

CHAPTER XV

THE MIDDLE COLONIES IN THE EIGHTEENTH CENTURY

NEW JERSEY

THE right of the New Jersey proprietors to govern their territory had from the beginning rested on a basis of doubtful legality. When the effort was made by James II to annex the Jerseys to the Dominion of New England, the proprietors yielded without resistance. These two provinces were, however, under the control of Andros, the governor of the Dominion, for only about two months, and he did not exercise much authority over them during this short period. After the Dominion of New England was overthrown there was no general government in the Jerseys for about three years.

The Jerseys a part of the Dominion of New England

The authority of the proprietors was restored in 1692, but their rule proved inefficient and in a few years collapsed. Their hold on the provinces was weakened by the temporary loss of their power while the Jerseys were a part of the Dominion of New England, and was still further lessened by the fact that the proprietors were so numerous that they were unable to agree upon a firm, united policy. There were twenty-four proprietary overlords for East Jersey, most of whom lived in Great Britain, and they were divided as to policy and often worked at cross purposes. In West Jersey the proprietors were still more numerous and included a large proportion of the people.[1] The Quaker influence was dominant in West Jersey, and their pacifism rendered the security of the colony uncertain in time of war. Moreover, it was necessary to bring these two colonies under royal control if an effective policy against piracy and illicit trading was to be en-

Collapse of proprietary rule

[1] Professor Osgood thought that the proprietors included the whole body of freeholders (see his *American Colonies in the Eighteenth Century*, i, p. 383). Another high authority says that no definite statement can be made "as to the exact number holding proprietary interests down to 1702" (see TANNER, E. P., *The Province of New Jersey*, p. 16).

forced. Therefore, both local and imperial interests demanded that the government of the Jerseys should be turned over to the crown.

The proprietors appreciated this and expressed a willingness to surrender their jurisdiction, provided their landed rights were protected and certain other conditions were met. Accordingly, an agreement was made (1702) whereby the king assumed control of both Jerseys, which were to be united into one royal province under the name of New Jersey. The assembly was to consist of an equal number of representatives from East and West Jersey, and its sessions and those of the supreme court were to be held alternately at Perth Amboy and Burlington.[2] The proprietors were to retain their title to all unoccupied lands and have the right to collect the quit rents on the lands that had already been granted.

The government of New Jersey as a royal province   The last years of the proprietary régime were characterized by factional disputes and there was a good deal of feeling between the opposing parties. As the leading men of the province were identified with one faction or the other, the British government felt that harmony could more easily be restored if an outsider were named as chief executive. Lord Cornbury was already governor of New York, and New Jersey was also put under his jurisdiction. The form of government provided for by the instructions to Cornbury and his successors was quite similar to that established in other royal provinces.[3] The governor was given the usual powers, and was to be assisted by a council appointed by the king on the nomination of the governor. Here, as elsewhere, the councilors were men of wealth and influence and were granted the administrative, judicial, and legislative powers that were usually enjoyed by the provincial council in the crown colonies. The assembly was composed of two houses; the councilors constituted the upper house, and representatives chosen by the people the lower.

Lord Cornbury as governor   From 1702 to 1738 New Jersey, though a separate royal province, had the same chief executive as New York. From the latter date until the end of the colonial period its government was administered by its own royal governor. The character of Lord

[2] The assembly continued to meet alternately at these two towns until the end of the colonial period, except for a few sessions that were held at Trenton and Elizabethtown on account of the illness of the governor.

[3] For Cornbury's instructions see *New Jersey Archives*, 1st series, ii, pp. 506-536.

Cornbury was such as to give the people of New Jersey, right at the start, a bad impression of the representatives of the crown. With such a scapegrace of a governor, it is only natural that the first administration under royal control should have been characterized by considerable strife between the legislature and the executive. The people breathed a sigh of relief when Cornbury was recalled, and the lower house of the assembly expressed its thanks to the queen for "putting an end to the worst administration New Jersey ever knew."[4]

However, friction between the people's representatives and the royal governor did not end with the retirement of Lord Cornbury. During subsequent administrations disputes arose from time to time of a very similar character to those that ran through the later history of New York and Massachusetts. In New Jersey, as in these provinces, the assembly had control of the purse-strings and often refused to grant money except at the price of concessions wrung from the executive. However, the friction here between the governor and the lower house was not so persistent as it was in the northern colonies. This was due largely to the fact that the governors prior to 1738 devoted most of their time and attention to New York and treated their southern province with comparative indifference. Owing to this neglect, the occasions for unpleasant contacts between the legislative and executive branches of the government were reduced to a minimum. By the end of this period of union a number of the important questions at issue between the governor and the assembly had been decided in favor of the latter and so did not figure prominently in the later controversies.

There were a number of causes of dispute between the governor and the lower house of assembly. One of the most important of these was the question of the governor's salary. There was no permanent fund out of which the crown could remunerate its representative for his services, and so he was dependent upon the assembly for his salary. The governors, in obedience to their instructions, insisted on a regular permanent allowance. The lower house refused to comply with this request and made its grants for five years and sometimes for only one year. In New Jersey, as well as in New York, there was also a controversy between the upper and lower houses of assembly over the claim made by the latter of the exclusive right to initiate all measures

Friction between the governor and the assembly

Causes and outcome of these disputes

[4] *New Jersey Archives*, 1st series, iii, p. 363.

appropriating money. Because of its control of the purse the lower house was victorious in the struggle with the council over financial measures and with the governor over the salary question and nearly all the other issues that had arisen between them. "In New Jersey, then, as in all of the American colonies, the whole trend of the political development was in the direction of making the governor the executor of the wishes of the assembly rather than its master."[5]

PENNSYLVANIA

Quakers as legislators: The controversy over judicial oaths   It was sometimes rather difficult to apply the Quaker doctrine to practical politics, and Quaker officials and legislators were often hampered in the discharge of their public duties by inconvenient religious scruples. Conscientious Friends would neither take oaths themselves nor administer them to others. The Pennsylvania assembly was dominated by Quaker influence until the middle of the eighteenth century, and laws were repeatedly voted by this body to relieve Friends from the necessity of taking oaths. For a number of years these laws were vetoed by the home authorities because they were contrary to English practice, according to which oaths were generally required of officials and always of witnesses in criminal cases and jurymen in all cases. This deadlock was finally broken when the king approved two laws of the Pennsylvania assembly (passed in 1718 and 1724) which allowed the substitution of a solemn affirmation for an oath. Strict Quakers were, however, still excluded from the bench, as the law required the judges to administer oaths to such witnesses and other persons as should prefer an oath to an affirmation.

The problem as to military service   But the greatest embarrassment came when the wars with the French subjected Quaker pacifism to a very severe strain. It now became extremely difficult to harmonize their religion with their patriotism. For example, in 1745, at the time of the war with France (King George's War), the home government asked the Pennsylvania assembly to vote money to aid in supplying Louisbourg with arms and ammunition. The Quaker assembly wished to comply with this request, but to do so would be to give up the position of their denomination with reference to war. They tried to reconcile their patriotism with their pacifism by appropriating a sum of money for the purchase of "bread, beef, pork, flour, wheat, or other grain." The governor used a part of this money

[5] TANNER, E. P., *The Province of New Jersey*, p. 456.

for buying gunpowder on the ground that it came under the head of "other grain," and the assembly made no objection to this method of escaping from their dilemma.

When the French and Indian War broke out, the home government felt that it would not be safe for Pennsylvania to remain under the control of the Quakers. In order to exclude them from the Pennsylvania assembly a bill was offered in Parliament requiring all members of the Pennsylvania legislature to take the oath of allegiance. As the Friends would not take any sort of oath this law would automatically exclude them. Before this proposal was finally acted upon by Parliament the London Quakers agreed that if the measure were postponed they would try to persuade their coreligionists in Pennsylvania not to offer for seats in the legislature. This promise was kept, and partly of their own accord and partly as a result of the persuasions of their English brethren, enough Friends refused to be candidates so that a majority of the legislature became non-Quaker.[6]

The philosophy of non-resistance was not practiced by the Quaker assembly in its relations with the proprietors. There was a good deal of friction between the assembly and the proprietors, especially over the effort of the Penns to have their lands and quit rents exempt from taxation. This controversy finally reached such a stage that the assembly voted to send Benjamin Franklin to England to present its claims before the king. Franklin "succeeded in having the proprietary lands taxed equally with the lands of the colonists. But the proprietors attempted to construe this provision so that their best lands were taxed at the rate paid by the people on their worst. This obvious quibble, of course, raised such a storm of opposition"[7] that the legislature again sent Franklin to England (1764), this time with instructions to use his utmost endeavors to have the government of the province transferred from the proprietors to the crown. As Parliament was about to pass the Stamp Act and was thus arousing opposition in the colonies to its policy, Franklin presented the request of the assembly but did not urge it. The assembly had now come to fear that the people's liberties would be in greater danger as a

Friction between the assembly and the proprietors

[6] For a contemporary account of the action of the London Quakers and its effect on their brethren in Pennsylvania, see SHARPLESS, ISAAC, *Quaker Government in Pennsylvania*, i, pp. 250-256.

[7] FISHER, S. G., *The Quaker Colonies*, p. 118.

crown colony than as a proprietary province. They, therefore, instructed Franklin to drop the plan.

Benjamin Franklin   Although the attempt to have the authority of the proprietors annulled was not carried out, it brought Pennsylvania's most gifted citizen into prominence and gave him an opportunity to enter upon his remarkable career as a diplomat. Franklin was the most outstanding man in public life throughout the entire colonial period. The part he played in the War for Independence gave him his chief title to fame, but even before that he had to his credit a record of achievement that was unsurpassed by any of his contemporaries. Coming to Philadelphia from Boston in early young manhood, he began his career in the latter city as a printer, but soon developed into a journalist. He was the editor and owner of *The Pennsylvania Gazette*, which he made the best weekly paper in English America. In its columns he advocated many progressive measures, some of which he was able to persuade his fellow-countrymen to carry out in the Quaker city. Among these was the organization of a fire department, as well as a police and militia system, the creation of a public library, and the founding of the Academy, which became the University of Pennsylvania. His interest in science and the affairs of everyday life led him to experiment with electricity and to invent a stove, which we know as the open "Franklin stove." Franklin had left school at the age of ten, but by careful reading and close study he became a well-educated man. His wide knowledge of the best literature, his genial temperament, and his sense of humor, which was reinforced by a great fund of anecdote, made him one of the most brilliant conversationalists of his time. He was "one of the most widely and thoroughly cultivated men of his age."[8] By the time the French and Indian War broke out, he had won a prominent place in the civic life of the province. He had been postmaster of Philadelphia and was now one of the two postmasters-general who had charge of the postal service for all the English continental colonies. For several years he had been a leading member of the Pennsylvania assembly, and in this body had fought in the face of Quaker pacifism for a policy of military preparedness. When hostilities began he took an active part in the plans for prosecuting the war.

[8] *Cambridge History of Modern Literature*, p. 91.

MARYLAND

The revolution in Maryland (1689) had given the king the opportunity to assume control of another American colony. William welcomed this turn of events, as it was his policy to convert proprietary into royal provinces whenever the change could be effected without violating any vested rights. The war that was just beginning between England and France made this policy especially desirable at this time, as it would enable the English government to mobilize more effectively the resources of the colonies in the fight against the French in Canada. The chief justice in England gave an opinion to the effect that the king had the right to take over the government of Maryland, but that all the revenues accruing from the sale of lands and other sources would have to be turned over to the proprietor.[9] This suggestion was accepted and the colony was placed under the control of the crown (1691). *Maryland becomes a royal province*

The government of Maryland under the new régime was closely modeled after that of the other royal provinces. Lord Baltimore lost all authority as a ruler, but retained his rights as a landlord. He was still to receive one-half of the export duty on tobacco and the tonnage duties levied on foreign ships entering the Maryland ports. All vacant lands were to be retained by him, and the revenue accruing from the collection of quit rents was to go into his treasury. *Government*

The king was indebted to the leaders of the revolution in Maryland for creating the occasion that led to the desired change. Despite this obligation, however, he did not name one of the Maryland insurgents as the first royal governor, but his choice for this position fell upon Lionel Copley, an Englishman who was a loyal supporter of the new sovereigns. William probably felt that in Maryland, as in New York, party strife would continue if the chief executive were chosen from and identified with one of the opposing factions. After a short administration of less than three years, Copley died and was succeeded by Francis Nicholson (1694). *Copley the first royal governor*

Governor Nicholson had had some experience in colonial administration, as he had recently served as lieutenant-governor of Virginia and had been the ill-fated deputy governor of New York *The administration of Francis Nicholson*

[9] The opinion of Chief Justice Holt is quoted by Channing, *op. cit.*, ii, pp. 226-227, note. See also *Maryland Archives*, viii, p. 185.

when that province was a part of the Dominion of New England.
He was very religious and was earnest in his desire to promote
the growth of the Anglican Church. He was also interested in
public education and gave generously toward the establishment of
a free school. On his arrival he convened his first assembly, not
at St. Mary's, the capital, but at the town of Anne Arundel, the
name of which was afterward changed to Annapolis. This assembly was very hostile to the Catholics and voted to move the
capital from St. Mary's, their social and political center, and
establish it permanently at the Protestant town of Annapolis.
The residents of St. Mary's sent a petition to the assembly giving
a number of reasons for keeping the seat of government at their
town, but this request was flatly and even rudely refused.[10]
Nicholson got along with his assembly without serious friction,
and at the end of his term he received a vote of approval from
this body.

Estab-
lishment
of the
Anglican
Church

The most important change inaugurated by the new régime
was the establishment of the Anglican, or Episcopal, as the
state church of Maryland. In 1692 a law was passed dividing the
province into parishes and requiring every taxpayer to contribute
forty pounds of tobacco for the support of the ministers.[11] The
act was disallowed by the home authorities, but was reënacted in
a modified form a decade later (1702).[12] It now had a provision
extending freedom of worship to Protestant dissenters, but they
were still required to pay the tax for the support of the established church. This law, with slight modifications made from
time to time, was the basis of the religious policy of the government from this time until the end of the colonial period.

Unfair
treatment
of the
Catholics

The toleration allowed dissenters was not extended to Catholics, against whom there was a strong popular prejudice. The
Catholics were, however, afterward granted freedom of worship
on condition that all their meetings should be held in private
houses. The hostile public sentiment against Catholics in Maryland was inspired by the fear that they would join their coreligionists in Canada in plotting with the Indians against their

[10] For the text of this petition and the answer of the assembly, see
SCHARF, J. T., *History of Maryland*, i, pp. 345-348.

[11] For a summary of this act, see BACON, THOMAS, *Laws of
Maryland at Large*, Acts of 1692, ch. 2.

[12] For the full text of this law, see BACON, *op. cit.*, Acts of 1702,
ch. 1.

fellow-countrymen. There was no ground for these suspicions, but the fact that the powerful king of France favored the Catholic Stuarts affords some excuse for this fear.

The effort to establish the Anglican Church met at first with strong opposition. The Anglicans were greatly in the minority, and devout Catholics and dissenters were opposed to giving support to a denomination whose doctrines and practices they abhorred. The irreligious and indifferent also objected to the tax as an unnecessary financial burden. By some strange oversight, the quality of the tobacco to be paid was not specified, and so only the poorest grade was received. The remuneration of the ministers was thus so small that it was well-nigh impossible to attract worthy Anglican clergymen to the Maryland field. As a partial offset to these disadvantages, the church received the active support of Governor Nicholson and was aided by the energetic and sacrificial efforts of Rev. Dr. Thomas Bray, who had been appointed commissary of Maryland by the Bishop of London. Dr. Bray devoted his time and most of his fortune toward building up the church. He sent over missionaries, bought books and established libraries in the parishes, and advised the assembly as to its religious policy.

The religious policy of the government unpopular

During the period of royal control there was some friction between the governor and the lower house of the assembly, but not so much as there was in the northern royal provinces. The assembly here as elsewhere had control over appropriations and the burgesses, or people's representatives, tried at times to use this power to force the executive into an acceptance of their measures. But the lower house could not flourish this stick over the head of the governor so menacingly in Maryland as that body could do in the crown colonies of the North. For a considerable portion of the revenue came from indirect taxation, and so there was a permanent fund large enough to provide for the salary of the governor and other officials. The governor's salary, therefore, never figured in Maryland as a cause of dispute between the legislature and the executive, as it did so often in other royal provinces. The council was also able to put up a more effective fight against the claims of the lower house than was done in some of the other provinces. During the royal period the upper house acquiesced in the practice of having all financial measures originate in the lower house, but exercised the privilege of amending money bills, and it was not until 1740 that it was denied this right.

Friction between the legislature and the executive

Restoration of the Palatinate

Benedict Leonard, who at the death of his father became the fifth Lord Baltimore, abjured the faith of his fathers and announced his adhesion to the Anglican Church. His conversion was apparently prompted by policy rather than principle, as he was looking to the restoration of his political authority in Maryland. Nor was he disappointed in this expectation. In 1715 he was restored to his full proprietary rights, which were retained by him and his heirs to the end of the colonial period. When we remember that the practice of the British authorities at this time was to change proprietary into royal provinces whenever it could legally be done, the revival of the Maryland Palatinate is not easy to explain. The return of the Calvert family to the Anglican communion was not of sufficient importance to justify this reversal of policy. As a matter of fact, it was a step backward, from the point of view of imperial interests, and can be accounted for only on the ground of the indifference to colonial affairs that characterized British administration under the early Hanoverians.

The return to proprietary rule in Maryland was not marked by any perceptible change in the government. The last royal governor, John Hart, was continued in office for some years by the restored Calverts. Public opinion was still running against the Catholics, and the governor and the assembly shared the prejudices of the masses. Consequently, two severe anti-Catholic laws were passed (1716, 1718), which disfranchised and excluded from office all Catholics except those who were willing to compromise their principles by subscribing to certain oaths which conscientious Catholics could hardly take.[13] Later, public sentiment became less hostile and the laws against Catholics were not rigidly enforced, though they never regained all their rights until after the end of the colonial period.[14]

The last Lord Baltimore

Frederick, the sixth and last Baron of Baltimore, was a disreputable character whose only interest in Maryland was the income he derived from the province and spent in dissipation in

[13] For excerpts from the laws of 1716 and 1718, see SCHARF, J. T., *History of Maryland*, i, pp. 382-383. For the full text of these laws, see BACON, *op. cit.*, Acts of 1716, ch. 5, and Acts of 1718, ch. 1.

[14] A contemporary writing at the end of the colonial period (1769-77) says that Catholics at that time did not hold office in Maryland and had no political importance (EDDIS, WILLIAM, *Letters from America*, p. 46).

London.[15] But Frederick was represented in Maryland by two excellent governors, Horatio Sharpe (1753-68) and Sir Robert Eden (1768-76).

An important event of the second proprietary period was the founding of the city of Baltimore. In 1729 the assembly appointed commissioners to lay out a town on the northern shore of the Patapsco River.[16] Accordingly, in the following year a tract of sixty acres of land was bought and divided by streets and alleys into sixty lots of equal size. These were offered for sale and soon a small hamlet sprang up. The growth of the village was slow for the first twenty years, and by the middle of the century it numbered only about twenty-five houses and a hundred inhabitants. A few years later, however, it began to develop more rapidly. The Germans had settled in the upland region west of the town, and so it now had a hinterland to draw from. Its good harbor and favorable location on a navigable stream made it the natural outlet for the wheat raised in the back country. Consequently, it soon began to grow in size, and by the end of the colonial period it was the largest town in Maryland.

The founding of Baltimore

VIRGINIA

As has already been seen, Lord Howard of Effingham was the representative in Virginia of James II at the time the latter was driven from the throne of England. He was incompetent, greedy, and corrupt and had shared the political notions of his royal master.[17] The people of Virginia expected, therefore, that William on his accession would depose this dishonest henchman of the repudiated Stuart king. Lord Howard, however, was not deprived of his office, but was allowed to retire to England with the title and half of the pay of governor, and Francis Nicholson was sent to Virginia to act as lieutenant-governor.

Lord Howard retained as governor by William

Nicholson served as Lord Howard's deputy less than two years and then became governor of Maryland. A few years later

Nicholson's administration

[15] The last Lord Baltimore died in 1771. A dispute then arose as to whether his sister or natural son had succeeded to the proprietorship. This dispute was still pending in chancery when Maryland became an independent state (1776).

[16] BACON, THOMAS, *Laws of Maryland*, Acts of 1729, ch. 12.

For a contemporary account of the origin and early development of Baltimore, see EDDIS, WILLIAM, *Letters from America*, pp. 95-98.

[17] BEVERLEY, R., *History of Virginia*, pp. 77-79.

(1698) he was returned to Virginia, this time as governor in his own right. Nicholson was an administrator of experience and ability, with a breadth of vision greater than that of the ordinary royal executive. He carried out a vigorous policy against piracy and instituted other measures that showed a real concern for the welfare of the people. He was deeply interested in the promotion of religion and education and gave liberally of his own means to establish William and Mary College and to found schools.[18]

The capital removed to Williamsburg

After Jamestown had been destroyed by Bacon it was rebuilt by Lord Culpeper, but was again burned, this time accidentally. The location of Jamestown was unhealthful, as its proximity to a large swamp made mosquitoes and malaria prevalent. The people, therefore, were not inclined to rebuild the village, and there has never been any town since then on the site of the "Cradle of the Republic." Nicholson removed the seat of government to Middle Plantation, which was only seven miles distant from Jamestown. The name of the little village that grew up around the college and the capitol was changed to that of Williamsburg, and, according to the original plan, the streets were to be laid out in the shape of a W and M in honor of the king and queen. This scheme was abandoned, however, on account of the inconvenience.[19]

Personality of Nicholson

Nicholson's good qualities were bound up with some eccentricities of character that greatly marred his usefulness and gave his opponents ground at times for questioning his sanity. His violent temper, over which he had no control, often compromised his dignity, and despite his sincere piety frequently led him into outbursts of profanity that would have disgraced a convict muledriver. Being provoked to anger on one occasion by the attorney-general, he seized him by the lapel of his robe and said, "I know no laws of Virginia! I know my commands are going to be obeyed here!" At another time he abused the aristocratic and dignified councilors, calling them "mere brutes who understand not manners" and saying that "he would beat them into better manners and make them feel that he was governor of Vir-

[18] *Ibid.*, pp. 79-81, 83-88.

[19] It might be more correct to say that the original plan was modified rather than abandoned, as the arrangement of the streets even today is such that by a little aid of the imagination one can trace a W at the end of the town at which the capitol was located, and an M at the location of the college (BEVERLEY, R., *op. cit.*, p. 84).

ginia."[20] Apparently, however, the people did not take the out-bursts of their scolding governor seriously, for he got along well with his assembly, which supported him in his quarrel with the council.

Unfortunately for him, however, he incurred the ill-will of the Rev. Dr. James Blair, who used his great influence in England to secure the removal of Nicholson from the governorship (1705). In antagonizing Dr. Blair, Nicholson had come into disagreeable contact with the ablest and most influential man in Virginia. To understand the part he played in the events of his day we have to take a glance at religious conditions at the time he came to the province. The established church was in a state of decline that called loudly for reform. In a number of parishes there were no ministers, and in those in which there was a rector the spiritual needs of the people were sadly neglected.[21] The Bishop of London, who had authority over the American church, decided to institute some much-needed reforms. He appointed Dr. Blair as his representative in Virginia, with the title of commis-sary, and directed him to put the Anglican Church on a better basis. Blair took up the duties of his task with energy, courage, and enthusiasm, and determined to do all in his power to effect the desired reforms. He tried to discipline the clergy and make them lead more exemplary lives. He advocated measures that would increase the salaries of the rectors and make their tenure more secure by lessening their dependence upon the planters who dominated the vestries. A college was also to be established for the education of young men who were candidates for the ministry.

Commissary Blair's efforts at church reform were at first ably seconded by Governor Nicholson, who, despite his loose morals, was a warm friend of the Anglican Church. But Sir Edmund Andros, who became governor at the end of Nicholson's first term, opposed Blair's program of reform, as he feared that it would result in diverting revenue from the state to the church. This aroused Blair's Scotch combativeness and he determined to get rid of this obstacle by having the governor removed. Accord-ingly, by using his influence in England he secured the recall of

Condition of the Anglican Church in Virginia

Commis-sary Blair tries to reform the church

Friction between the com-missary and the governor

[20] Quoted by FISKE, JOHN, *Old Virginia and Her Neighbors,* pp. 115-116; see also *William and Mary College Quarterly,* i, p. 66.

[21] For contemporary accounts of religious conditions in 1720 and 1724, respectively, see BEVERLEY, *op. cit.,* pp. 210-213, and JONES, *The Present State of Virginia,* pp. 65-74.

Andros. When Nicholson returned to Virginia as governor, the commissary hoped for a vigorous prosecution of his plans. He was disappointed in this expectation, as Nicholson during his second term did not give him satisfactory support in the furtherance of his aims. Blair now turned against his former ally and had him removed from the governorship.[22]

The titular governors of Virginia

When Nicholson was recalled (1705), the Earl of Orkney was commissioned governor and for forty years was allowed more than half of the salary of the office, though he never came to Virginia during the entire period and did nothing to earn the generous income that was allowed him. The real work of administering the province was intrusted to deputies, who had the title of lieutenant-governor. The policy of allowing titular governors resident in England to turn over the responsibilities of their office to deputies in Virginia and to receive pay for rendering no service continued until 1768, at which time there was a return to the practice of requiring the chief executive to reside in the province. This unjust method of squandering the public funds was one of several instances of the policy which the British government had of using colonial offices as berths for politicians in the homeland, and was in keeping with the political jobbery that characterized the administration in the homeland during the eighteenth century.

Spotswood an able governor

Of the deputy governors of the eighteenth century, the ablest was Colonel Alexander Spotswood, a Scotchman, whose administration of more than a decade (1710-22) was the best that Virginia enjoyed during the entire colonial period. He not only upheld the authority of the empire, but he also identified himself

[22] By a foolish exhibition of imprudence Nicholson had incurred the personal enmity of a prominent Virginia family and thereby weakened his cause both in the province and in England. Major Lewis Burwell, an influential planter living near Williamsburg, had a number of attractive daughters, with one of whom the governor had become madly infatuated. When she refused to reciprocate his feeling and declined his attentions, he showed his chagrin by acting like an inmate of Bedlam. He threatened that if the young lady should marry anyone else he would cut the throat of the groom, the justice who should issue the license, and the minister who should perform the ceremony. Such silly behavior as this enabled Nicholson's enemies to laugh away every shred of dignity that his violent temper had left him (*William and Mary College Quarterly*, i, pp. 66-68).

with the colony and showed real concern for the welfare of the people. He took an interest in education and did what he could to promote the growth of William and Mary College. His program of education included schooling for the Indians as well as for the whites, and he induced quite a number of the former to attend a mission school that he had established for them.[23]

It was due to his encouragement that the manufacture of iron was started in Virginia. Four furnaces were established by him, which turned out pig-iron and some of the simpler cast-iron products. Another important service performed by him was the putting down of the pirates that infested the coast. Robert Teach, generally known as "Blackbeard," was the leader of a band of sea robbers who were terrorizing the Virginia and Carolina coasts and robbing the people whenever opportunity offered. Two war-vessels were sent against these cut-throats by the governor, and after a bloody battle the pirate chief was killed and all his crew captured and hanged.

Spotswood's policy was cut on a broad pattern and embraced the interests of the empire as a whole as well as the welfare of the province over which he had control. He sent troops to help South Carolina in her fight with the Yamassee Indians and favored measures that would aid in putting all the colonies in a state of defense against the expected attacks of the French. In urging the Virginians to help their southern neighbors, he was actuated partly by the desire to aid a sister colony engaged in a great struggle for self-preservation and partly by the feeling that such a policy of coöperation was necessary for the defense of his own province. "The readiest way to save ourselves," he wrote, was "to run immediately to check the first kindling flames."[24]

His broad states-manship

Spotswood's interest in the westward movement was prompted by the desire to guard against French encroachments upon British territory. He argued that England's claim to the trans-Alleghany region was menaced by the expansion of the French, who already had colonies in Canada and Louisiana. If these centers of colonization were connected by a sufficient number of settlements along the Mississippi River, the French would be intrenched in

[23] A contemporary, writing in 1724, says that he had seen some seventy Indian children at a school at Fort Christiana, which had been established by Spotswood at his own expense (JONES, HUGH, *The Present State of Virginia*, pp. 14-15).

[24] SPOTSWOOD, ALEXANDER, *Official Letters*, ii, pp. 124-125.

the rear of the British provinces and would be able at any time to arouse their Indian allies against them. Indeed, with such an advantage, France might be able to push England off the Atlantic seaboard and take over the latter's possessions. To prevent these dangers the English should plant settlements on the Great Lakes and take possession of the mountain passes.[25]

It was with the hope of inaugurating such a policy that Spotswood led an expedition across the Blue Ridge Mountains into the Valley of Virginia. The expedition (1716) was little more than a picnic excursion, with plenty of wine and other liquors to soothe the tired feelings of the excursionists, but it is significant as showing Spotswood's interest in the westward movement. Fifty gentlemen, accompanied by Negro slaves and Indian guides, followed their leader over the Blue Ridge at Swift Run Gap and descended to the Shenandoah Valley. In going over the rough Indian trails they found that their horses, which in the low country could get along without shoes, had now to be shod. So upon their return the governor gave to each of his companions a golden horseshoe as a souvenir of the occasion. The recipients of these badges have since been known as Knights of the Golden Horseshoe.[26]

Friction between the governor and the assembly

Spotswood's administration was characterized by exceptional honesty, courage, initiative, and energy. To us it seems strange that such an administrator should have encountered as much opposition as he did from both the assembly and the council. In Virginia, the lower house of the assembly, the House of Burgesses, could not control the governor's salary, as that was provided for out of a permanent fund, but it could withhold appropriations for other purposes. The burgesses used this power over the provincial purse from time to time to secure or force concessions from the executive. In these contests the people's representatives were usually led by men who belonged to the wealthy, patrician class.

When Spotswood first arrived in the province he was gladly received because he was authorized by his instructions to extend the right of the writ of *habeas corpus* to the people of Virginia. The assembly expressed its cordiality by a vote of thanks and a liberal appropriation for completing the governor's mansion. But

[25] *Ibid.*, ii, pp. 295-297.

[26] For a brief contemporary account of this expedition, see JONES, HUGH, *The Present State of Virginia* (1724), p. 14.

the harmony between governor and assembly had lasted only about a year when it was marred by the refusal of the latter to vote money for defending the colony against an expected attack by the French. Four years later (1715) the governor and the House of Burgesses were again at loggerheads when the governor insisted on an appropriation to assist South Carolina in her struggle against the Yamassee Indians.

Much of the friction between Spotswood and the House of Burgesses was due to the fact that the former was trying to uphold the interests of the empire while the latter was acting as the advocate for the people of Virginia. Some of it, however, was due to the narrow particularism of the burgesses, which kept them from rising to the broad statesmanship of the governor and bound them down to a niggardly policy that was willing to sacrifice imperial to local interests. Then, too, Colonel Spotswood was autocratic in his notions and showed a high-handed impatience with all opposition to his measures. It must be remembered, too, that he had been in the military service before coming to Virginia, and that in fighting the battles of his country he had developed the temperament of a military commander. He was, therefore, not so tactful in dealing with the local politicians who found seats in the assembly as a mild-mannered civilian would have been. He regarded many of the burgesses as ignorant and incompetent demagogues, and he did not hesitate to express this opinion to them in language that was more candid than courteous.[27]

Spotswood also met with opposition from the council. This was led by Dr. Blair, who was strongly opposed to the stand that the governor had taken on church affairs. Blair had the courage, the combativeness, and the stubborn loyalty to principle of the typical Scotchman, but not the self-effacement and serenity of temper of the ideal Christian minister. As commissary he was the deputy of the Bishop of London and head of the established church in Virginia. The influence conferred by this important office was reinforced by Blair's close association with the political leaders of Virginia, and he was thus a formidable opponent. The contest went against Spotswood and he lost his position as deputy

Friction between the governor and the council

[27] See SPOTSWOOD, ALEXANDER, *Official Letters*, ii, p. 129; FISKE, J., *Old Virginia and Her Neighbors*, ii, pp. 371-372.

governor in 1722, though he continued to live in the colony to the end of his life.

Colonel William Byrd

Next to Blair, the most noted contemporary of Governor Spotswood was Colonel William Byrd, the second of that name. Although he was born and reared in Virginia, he attended school in England and studied law at the Middle Temple. His interest in science brought him into friendly association with Sir Robert Boyle and other noted scientists and won for him membership in the Royal Society of Great Britain. He was well versed in the social amenities and was always welcomed to the fashionable drawing-rooms of London. At Westover, his magnificent estate on the James River, he dwelt in a spacious mansion that housed the finest and largest collection of books in Virginia. His wealth and literary tastes offered every inducement for a life of ease and idleness, but such a life made no appeal to the ambitious and energetic colonel, who took an active interest in the political affairs and the economic development of the province. He established mills at the falls of the James River, and the little colony he planted there later grew into the city of Richmond. He was one of the surveyors that ran the boundary line between Virginia and North Carolina and wrote an interesting account of it, which is an important source of information not only for that event, but also for the life of the people at that time. This work and his other writings are in a clear and pleasing style and more nearly measure up to the standards of real literature than anything else written in Virginia prior to the decade preceding the outbreak of the Revolution.

His participation in political affairs brought him into conflict with Governor Spotswood, and for a while he was his staunch opponent. This disagreement did not cause a permanent breach in their friendship, and in later years they were on amicable terms. One of the most pleasing incidents in the history of the relations of these two eminent men was a visit that Colonel Byrd made to Colonel Spotswood after the latter had retired from the governorship and had settled down on his estate at Germanna, on the Rapidan River. Colonel Byrd's account of the cordial hospitality accorded him on this occasion shows that both of these men were big enough to disregard their former antagonisms.[28]

[28] For Byrd's account of this visit, see BASSETT, J. S., ed., *The Writings of Colonel William Byrd*, pp. 356 *et seq.*

Selected Readings

1. The Colonial Gentlemen.—Chandler, J. A. C., and Thames, T. B., *Colonial Virginia*, *ch. 20.
2. Benjamin Franklin, Personal Traits.—Bruce, W. C., *Benjamin Franklin*, ii, *ch. 1; Parrington, V. L., *The Colonial Mind*, pp. *164-178.
3. Religion in Virginia.—Stanard, Mary N., *Colonial Virginia*, *ch. 14.
4. Courtship and Marriage in Virginia.—*Ibid.*, *ch. 5.
5. Recreations and Pastimes in Virginia.—Beverley, Robert, *The History of Virginia,* *ch. 21 (a contemporary account).
6. Governor Alexander Spotswood.—Bruce, P. A., *The Virginia Plutarch*, i, *ch. 9.
7. Colonel William Byrd.—Bruce, P. A., *The Virginia Plutarch*, i, *ch. 10.
8. The Beginnings of Baltimore.—Eddis, William, *Letters from America*, pp. *95-98 (a contemporary account).

CHAPTER XVI

THE SOUTH UNDER THE EARLY HANOVERIANS

NORTH CAROLINA

Accession of the Hanoverians marks a turning-point in North Carolina history

ON THE death of Queen Anne in August, 1714, George I, Elector of Hanover, became king of England. The change of rulers in the homeland had no immediate influence on events in either North Carolina or South Carolina, but the date of the accession of the new king proved to be a turning-point in the development of the former colony. Two years before this time Edward Hyde had become governor of North Carolina, and his installation marks the final separation of the northern from the southern Carolina province. The war with the Tuscarora Indians was over, and thereafter the natives gave little trouble in the region east of the mountains. This vast area was now open to settlement. Just prior to this time, too, the last of the formal rebellions (Cary's) came to an end, and the people settled down to a measure of order.

North Carolina remains under proprietary rule for a decade after South Carolina becomes a royal province

The authority of the proprietors in North Carolina was slight, and there was a good deal of dissatisfaction with their rule. They had done nothing to help the people in their life-and-death struggle with the Tuscaroras, and they "never meddled with Carolina affairs but when they should not."[1] Under such circumstances one would expect that the North Carolinians would not be behind-hand with their neighbors in the south in snapping the weak bond that held them to their useless overlords. But such was not the case. When the South Carolinians rose in revolt in 1719 and renounced their allegiance to the proprietors, no attempt to follow their example was made in the northern province. In North Carolina the people had recently gone through the experiences of a rebellion and an Indian war, and were doubtless in the midst of a reaction against strife and disorder. Moreover, the council was loyal to the proprietors, the assembly was not in session, and Moseley, the ablest leader of the people, was discredited at the time. The governor, therefore, had no difficulty in getting a state-

[1] HAWKS, F. L., *The History of North Carolina*, ii, p. 553.

ment from the council that they "detest the proceedings of that province [South Carolina] . . . and that they are entirely easy and satisfied under their lordships' government."[2]

North Carolina remained under proprietary rule for another decade, and then the proprietors surrendered to the king all their governmental powers in the northern province and all but one of them sold to the crown their landed interests in both Carolinas. Lord Carteret held on to his eighth interest in the land for fifteen years, when he exchanged his claim for a large individual grant of territory, which was marked off for him in northern North Carolina. In this section, which was about one-third of the entire area of the province, Lord Carteret was the owner of all unoccupied lands and was given the exclusive right to collect quit rents on all tracts that had been granted to individual owners. The privileges enjoyed by this great landlord and his assigns deprived the provincial government of a large portion of its revenue and prevented the administration of a uniform land policy. There was a great deal of just complaint against this arrangement, as the corrupt and inefficient agents of the proprietor defrauded the people by charging excessive fees, collecting illegal quit rents, and issuing fraudulent deeds.[3]

North Carolina becomes a royal province. Lord Carteret granted a large portion of North Carolina

The transfer of the Carolinas from proprietary to royal rule made no change in the local government and led to only a slight modification of the machinery of provincial administration. The king now took the place of the proprietors as the supreme authority and received the power to appoint the governor and councilors. The people in both provinces, however, welcomed the change, and they were right in preferring the new régime to the old, for while there was very little "change in the outward form of government, there was a marked change in its purpose and spirit. The interests of the lords proprietors centered in dividends, those of the crown in the development of the British Empire. Financial returns, therefore, inspired the spirit of the one, imperial interests that of the other." The transfer of control "meant that a single executive, capable of a sustained policy, had succeeded a many-headed executive, of constantly varying personnel and ever-changing policy; that a tried and proven plan of administration had displaced an experiment which had failed. The

The change from proprietary to royal control a step forward

---

[2] *Journals of Council*, February 22, 23, 1719; quoted by HAWKS, *op. cit.*, ii, p. 561.

[3] CONNOR, R. D. W., *History of North Carolina*, p. 223.

change made possible a stability of purpose, promptness of action, and vigor of administration of which the proprietary government was incapable."[4]

The administration of Gabriel Johnston

The first governor by royal appointment was George Burrington, who had formerly held the same position under the proprietors. In a few years he was superseded by Gabriel Johnston, who in the course of a long administration (1734-52) succeeded to some extent in asserting imperial authority over the hitherto unruly province. When Johnston assumed his administrative duties in North Carolina he at first received the coöperation of the lower house of the assembly as well as the council. But it was not long before a controversy arose between him and the people's representatives, and for the greater part of his term he was at loggerheads with them. The two main causes of this dispute were the governor's policy with reference to quit rents and land grants and his effort to secure equal representation in the assembly for all sections of the province.

The controversy over land patents

At his accession he found that a number of blank patents had been granted by former governors to certain persons, conferring on them large areas of land. These grants had been signed by the governor, but had not received the seal of the province. About half a million acres of land had been disposed of in this way before he arrived in Carolina. By these wholesale grants a few privileged planters were allowed to monopolize a large share of the land and shut out the actual settlers. Moreover, the grantee either paid no quit rents on these great areas or else less than was required by the royal instructions. Such a policy, therefore, retarded the development of the colony and cut down the revenue of the province.

The governor very properly tried to have these blank patents annulled, but in doing so he encountered in both the council and the lower house of the assembly all the opposition that the interested parties and their friends could muster. Besides, he was not supported as strongly by the home government as he deserved, and the result was a compromise by which the large landholders retained most of their holdings.

Quit rents

In his effort to prevent a monopoly of the land by the privileged few the governor had aroused the opposition of an influential group of great landholders; in his policy with reference to quit rents, he antagonized the small as well as the large planters. The

[4] *Ibid.*, p. 210.

people generally were behind in the payment of their quit rents, and the result was that there was not enough revenue to pay the salaries of the governor and the other higher officials. In 1746 Johnston wrote that his salary was eight years in arrears and that other officials were no better off. The condition of the finances was partly responsible for the difficulty in collecting quit rents. North Carolina, unlike Virginia, where tobacco was the only farm product used as currency, recognized a number of commodities as money, and the people insisted on paying their quit rents in these commodities at a high price.

The governor, on the other hand, acting on his instructions, contended that quit rents must be paid in sterling money or in paper money at a rate of exchange fixed by the governor and council. The assembly would not accord this right to the governor and council and insisted on the payment of quit rents in commodities or in paper money, the value of which was to be determined by a committee of its own choosing. As the council supported the governor in his position, the upper and lower houses were for a while deadlocked on this question. Finally, however, a compromise was agreed upon and the governor signed a measure passed by the assembly that settled the dispute. Unfortunately, the act was disallowed by the Privy Council in England, and so the controversy remained unsettled.

The royal government in North Carolina was more efficient and stable than the administration had been under the proprietors, and this improvement in law and order quickly led to an increase in immigration to the province. New settlers came in so rapidly that by 1730 North Carolina had outstripped her southern neighbor in population. But the colony was still backward in its social and economic development because of its isolation from the outside world, due to the lack of a harbor deep enough for ocean-going vessels. This need was met by the occupation of the southern part of the province and by the opening up of the harbor at the mouth of the Cape Fear River. The colonization of the Cape Fear region had begun before Johnston's accession, and the village of Brunswick had been established near the mouth of the river. Governor Johnston encouraged the further development of this section, and soon the southern and middle portions of the province began to fill up rapidly with emigrants from Europe and the other colonies. These newcomers included Swiss, Irish, and Scotch immigrants. After the failure and defeat of the

The province increases in population under royal rule

Young Pretender in 1745, a number of the Highland Scotch came over and found homes in the Cape Fear district.[5] Through the influence of the governor, Wilmington was incorporated as a town (1739), and North Carolina now had a window through which she could look out upon the outside world.

A sectional dispute over representation

This policy of expansion gave rise to a sectional issue which involved the governor in another controversy. By a law of 1715 the Albemarle precincts, or counties, were to have five representatives each in the lower house of assembly, and all other counties two each. For a time there was no substantial injustice in this apportionment, as the bulk of the population lived in the Albemarle region. But after the southern part of the colony had been occupied, this plan occasioned a marked inequality in representation. The southern section was thus arrayed against the northern and demanded a fairer distribution of seats in the assembly, contending that the discrimination against their section was unfavorable to its development.

Governor Johnston sympathized with the contention of the southerners and called the assembly to meet at Wilmington (1746), hoping that some of the Albemarle representatives would fail to attend the session at so great a distance from their homes, and a bill could be passed providing for equal representation. To forestall such action the Albemarle delegates decided to prevent a quorum by refusing to attend, and so there were only fifteen representatives from the entire province. As this was a minority of the whole body, the people of the northern section contended that it was not a quorum and, therefore, could not enact any legislation. The governor, however, recognized this rump parliament as a legal assembly and had it pass a measure providing for

[5] When James II was driven from the English throne, a number of his supporters remained loyal to his cause and never recognized the legality of William's accession. These were known as Jacobites (*Jacobus* being the Latin word for James). At the death of James, the Jacobites recognized James's oldest son, usually known as the Old Pretender, as the rightful king of England and took part in an unsuccessful revolt in his interest in 1715. Thirty years later (1745) another uprising was made under the leadership of James's grandson, the Young Pretender, as he was called. The Highland Scots took sides with the Jacobites in this unfortunate rebellion and were defeated at Culloden Moor (1746). See LARSON, L. M., *History of England*, pp. 482, 503-504, or LUNT, W. E., *History of England*, pp. 549-550, 560.

equal representation and another fixing New Bern as the permanent capital of the province.[6]

Both of these measures were wise, though their legality was questioned. Not only was the old system of representation unfair to the growing southern section, but there was also an urgent need of a fixed seat for the government. At that time the provincial government had no public offices and the records were scattered about in private houses. New Bern was centrally located, and it would greatly aid the convenience of the people of the province to have the public offices located and the meetings of the assembly and council held there. The northern part of the province would not recognize the assembly that was organized on the new plan and declined to send representatives to it. The people also refused to pay taxes and the law courts were suspended. Albemarle was thus in a state of anarchy. The southern counties could not pay all the taxes, and so for a time no revenue was collected in the entire province.

The law of 1746 equalizing the representation in North Carolina was disallowed by the Privy Council on the ground that it was enacted under irregular circumstances and should not have been signed by the governor. The Albemarle region was thus restored to its old privilege of having more representatives for each county than was allowed other portions of the province. But the number of counties soon increased so rapidly that the newer sections gained control of the assembly. The law fixing the capital at New Bern was also annulled by the Privy Council, but owing to the accessibility of this town, it was not long before the provincial government settled down there permanently. *New Bern becomes the permanent capital of the province*

The most important event, or series of events, in the history of the Carolinas and Georgia during the quarter-century preceding the outbreak of the American Revolution was the occupation of the upland, or Piedmont, region (see pp. 355-356). *Occupation of the Carolina-Georgia Piedmont*

SOUTH CAROLINA

At the time of George I's accession to the English throne, the South Carolinians were on the verge of a great struggle with the Indians. They had had no serious trouble with the natives until 1715; but in that year the Yamassee Indians, living on the south- *The Yamassee War*

[6] By the governor's instructions fifteen members were to constitute a quorum, but the assembly had always insisted that a majority was necessary.

ern border, having been incited by the Spaniards, made a sudden attack on the whites and killed two hundred of them. The proprietors did nothing to help the colonists in this trying emergency, but their representative, Governor Craven, took vigorous action against the red men. The settlers in the outlying districts were brought together in Charleston, and the Indians were attacked by bands of soldiers. Help came from Virginia and North Carolina and the Indians were thoroughly overcome.[7]

The cost of the war was a heavy burden on the South Carolinians. A year or so after their victory over the Yamassees, they were called on to clean out the nest of pirates that had been made on their coast. They successfully performed this task, and in doing so showed the same energy and valor that characterized their campaigns against the Yamassees. But the attack on the pirates added greatly to the financial burden to which the province had been subjected by the Indian war, and the assembly tried to meet its financial difficulties the easy way by issuing bills of credit.

Friction between the proprietors and the colonists

The proprietors showed considerably more interest in South Carolina than they did in their northern province. They hoped that the southern colony would produce wine, olive oil, and silk and thus be a source of considerable revenue to them. They were disappointed in this expectation, for the land did not prove to be adapted to these products. In fact, the colonists did not produce any great staple for the English market at first, and later when rice was grown the profits from the province never met the expectations of the proprietors.

Dissatisfaction in England and South Carolina with proprietary rule

The colonists, as well as the proprietors, were disappointed over conditions in the province, and the latter were blamed for their mismanagement of its affairs. This little oligarchy of eight men were trying to govern a state according to the principle of private gain, and this could not be done except at the cost of injustice to the governed. It is not surprising, therefore, that there was a great deal of friction between the people and the proprietors, and the former were encouraged in their attitude of opposition by leaders of exceptional ability. This friction between the colonists and the proprietors, together with the trouble with

[7] For a good account of the Yamassee War, see McCrady, E., *South Carolina as a Proprietary Province*, pp. 531-548. For short contemporary statements regarding the Indian war, see Carroll, B. R., *Historical Collections*, ii, pp. 570-572, 574-576.

the pirates and the fear of the Indians and the Spaniards, had the effect of discouraging emigration to the province and of retarding its development.

The first clash between the South Carolinians and their proprietors occurred in 1681. In that year the people revolted against their governor, deposed him, and set up another in his stead. The proprietors asserted their authority by refusing to accept the governor chosen by the rebels, but failed to punish the offenders. The result of the revolt was that the malcontents had succeeded in ridding themselves of an unpopular governor and had lowered the prestige of the proprietors, although victory was nominally with the latter.

The revolt of 1681

A more serious cause of trouble arose out of the religious situation. It will be remembered that the charter to the proprietors provided for the establishment of the Anglican Church in Carolina and also for religious tolerance for dissenters. For some years no action was taken to enforce either provision, but dissenters were tolerated because no regulations against them had been adopted. In 1696 a law was passed by the assembly guaranteeing religious freedom to all Christians except Roman Catholics. It was, however, nearly a decade after this before an act providing for the establishment of the Anglican Church was passed. The question of the establishment came up in 1704, at which time Sir Nathaniel Johnson, a High Churchman, was governor. The governor called a special meeting of the legislature, which in May, 1704, passed a bill taxing dissenters for the support of the Anglican Church and excluding from membership in the assembly all who were not Anglicans. This assembly was, if the charge of the opposition is to be credited, a packed body, being chosen by unqualified voters, including Negroes, Jews, and sailors belonging to vessels that happened to be in Charleston Harbor.[8] By an act passed later in the same year a provision was added that church affairs in each parish were to be under the supervision of a committee of laymen. As these laymen could remove ministers, it struck at the authority of the Bishop of London, who was supposed to have jurisdiction in such cases.

The religious controversy

The dissenters, who were numerous and influential in the province, would not submit to this unjust discrimination and resolved to carry their fight against these measures to England.

[8] SALLEY, A. S., ed., *Narratives of Early Carolina*, pp. 248, 251-252. For the text of this act, see *ibid.*, pp. 253-256.

They sent over an agent to represent them, who first presented their case to Lord Granville, the Palatine, or chief proprietor. But Lord Granville was a narrow-minded High Churchman and his party in England was trying to restrict the rights of the dissenters by having Parliament enact a new measure against them. As he had no sympathy with religious dissent either in England or in America, naturally he gave the Carolina agent no satisfaction. The latter then presented his case to the House of Lords, supporting it by a petition signed by one hundred and seventy South Carolina planters. He was also aided by prominent dissenters and merchants in England. By calling attention to the provision in the law that deprived the Bishop of London of his authority in Carolina he won the support of this influential functionary, as well as that of the Society for the Propagation of the Gospel. Such influences had the desired effect, and the House of Lords voted an address to the queen showing the unwisdom and injustice of these laws and their inconsistency with the principles of the charter.

Proprietary rule weakened by the controversy

The Board of Trade, which supervised colonial affairs, was looking for an opportunity to cancel the charter and make the Carolinas a royal province, and so it advised the queen not only to annul the laws, but also to revoke the charter. The queen was not willing to go so far at this time, but allowed the proprietors to continue their control, with the understanding that the objectionable laws would be annulled. The proprietors consented to this arrangement and the assembly in Charleston repealed the laws (1706). This was in effect a veto by the crown of an important measure of the proprietors. This action of the British authorities had a significant bearing on the relations between the proprietors and the colonists. It was not only a victory for religious tolerance, but it also strengthened the malcontents in their struggle with their overlords. It revealed to them the possibility of going over the heads of the proprietors to the crown.[9]

Final settlement of the controversy

The dissenters had the good sense to use their victory wisely. When the assembly, controlled by the party in sympathy with their position, repealed the objectionable measures, it enacted others that provided for the establishment of the Anglican

[9] For contemporary accounts of this religious controversy and the events that led up to it written by dissenters, see SALLEY, A. S., ed., *op. cit.*, pp. 233-264, 269-276, 339, 344-351. See also FORCE, PETER, *Tracts*, ii, no. 10.

Church. The province was divided into parishes, each of which was to have a church and a minister supported by taxes levied on the people of the parish. The minister, as well as the vestry-men and the churchwardens, was to be chosen by the Anglicans residing in the parish. By this arrangement dissenters were taxed to support the established church.

Fortunately for the maintenance of the harmony thus restored, Lord Granville died about this time, and his place as Palatine was filled by Lord Craven, who appointed his brother, Charles Craven, as governor. The latter was an able and public-spirited man, and he won the high esteem of the Carolinians, while at the same time he looked after the interests of the proprietors. The people also enjoyed prosperity during his wise administration. The culture of rice had by this time been well established, and it furnished the southern colony with a valuable staple for export. As Negroes were better adapted to the cultivation of rice than white people, slavery had also become firmly rooted.

The proprietors never had had a very strong hold on their province, and their grasp had relaxed as a result of the events of recent years. Their inability to control the settlers in North Carolina, and the bad reputation both provinces had for smuggling and for piracy, had brought proprietary rule into disfavor with the home government. The proprietors had also forfeited the confidence of the colonials by their failure to aid them in the Indian war and protect them against Spanish raids.[10]

South Carolina becomes a royal province

When the struggle with the Yamassees was at its height the Commons House (the lower house of the assembly) asked that South Carolina be taken over by the crown, and the Board of Trade urged the proprietors to surrender their governmental rights in the province and advised the Privy Council to assume control of the Carolinas. But terms could not be agreed upon, and the influence of the proprietors was sufficient to prevent immediate action by the crown. At this juncture, too, Queen Anne died, and the new Hanoverian king, George I, soon had his hands full with the Jacobite uprising of 1715, and so did not turn his attention seriously to the Carolina problem. In this way proprietary rule was given another lease of life.

[10] Edward Randolph in his official report to the Board of Trade in 1699 said that during the entire period of King William's War the proprietors never sent the colonists "one barrel of powder or a pound of lead to help them" (SALLEY, *op. cit.*, p. 206).

The lull in the strife indicated above did not last long. It broke out afresh in 1716. Up until that year the members of the Commons House, though apportioned among the districts, were elected by the voters assembling in Charleston.[11] After the colony had begun to spread out, this was obviously an inconvenient practice. Moreover, it permitted the officials and wealthy Charlestonians a louder voice in the government than would have been the case if voting had been carried on in the precincts. To remedy these objections the assembly in 1716 passed a law providing that elections to the assembly for the future should be held in the precincts. This law was accepted by the council, which was composed of appointees of the proprietors. The South Carolinians thereupon put the new law into practice without waiting for the action of the proprietors. The latter vetoed the law and ordered the governor, Robert Johnson, to dissolve the assembly and order the election of a new one according to the old method. The colonists denied the legality of this veto. They contended that inasmuch as the councilors, as representatives, or deputies, of the proprietors, had sanctioned the law, the latter could not reverse this action, for they had granted to their deputies a sort of power of attorney.

While the tension was high, Governor Johnson was embarrassed by the threat of a Spanish invasion. To meet this emergency he called together the militia. Now the popular party had effected a strong organization under the leadership of an able planter from Barbados, and it had no difficulty in winning over the militia to its support. A new assembly had in the meantime been elected. But the members, instead of meeting as a legislative assembly, resolved themselves into a revolutionary convention and assumed control of the province. They asked Governor Johnson to remain at the head of the administration, with the understanding that he act in the name of the king until His Majesty's pleasure could be known.

Johnson declined the offer, and the assembly then sent an agent to England to present its case to the authorities there. The agent

[11] In 1683 the proprietors had instructed the governor of South Carolina to allow elections to be held both at Charleston and at another place for the choice of members of the assembly; but this instruction seems never to have been carried out. See McCRADY, E., *op. cit.*, pp. 198, 200, 559; RIVERS, W. J., *A Sketch of the History of South Carolina*, p. 135.

first made an appeal to the proprietors, but, receiving no encouragement from them, he carried his case up to the Privy Council. The Board of Trade welcomed this revolt as an opportunity to bring Carolina under the direct control of the crown, and so approved of the action of the insurgents. The proposal of the colonists was accepted, and Sir Francis Nicholson was appointed governor by the Privy Council.[12]

In this way the governmental authority of the proprietors ended (1719) in South Carolina, though it continued for another decade in North Carolina. During this decade the proprietors were, however, still landlords in the southern province. In 1729 Parliament passed an act putting an end to their jurisdiction in both provinces, and providing for the purchase of their claims as landlords.

Nicholson was well qualified by experience for his position, as he had already served a number of years as chief executive in various colonies. He was received by demonstrations of joy by the Carolinians, who felt a sense of relief at the termination of proprietary rule. The transfer of authority from the proprietors to the king made no greater change in the governmental machinery in the southern than it did in the northern province. Moreover, the constitutional history of the colony under the new régime was very much the same as it had been under the old. It was still characterized by dissensions between the assembly, which championed the rights of the colonials, and the governor and council, who were the representatives of the crown. The two most persistent causes of dispute were paper money and the effort of the council to assert its right to amend money bills.

Little change in the governmental machinery when South Carolina becomes a royal province

The colony was already committed to a policy of paper money when Nicholson assumed control. The first issue of bills of credit was voted in 1703 to defray the expenses incurred by the unsuccessful attack on St. Augustine.[13] The aid given the North Carolinians in their fight against the Tuscaroras and their own war with the Yamassees had imposed additional financial burdens on the South Carolinians. To meet these new obligations

The controversy over paper money

[12] For contemporary accounts of the events that led up to the ending of proprietary rule, see FORCE, PETER, *Tracts*, ii, no. 10; CARROLL, B. R., *Historical Collections*, ii, pp. 143-192.

[13] For the text of this law, see COOPER, THOMAS, ed., *Statutes of South Carolina*, ii, pp. 662-680.

the assembly on both occasions ordered reissues of paper money. Other issues were voted, and the volume of paper money in circulation was greater than the needs of legitimate trade demanded. Provisions were made for redeeming the bills of credit; but these measures were not carried out, and only a small proportion of them was retired. Consequently, paper money declined rapidly in value.

As the bills of credit were made a legal tender in the payment of debts, creditors were opposed to and debtors were in favor of increasing the volume of paper currency. The former class was made up principally of wealthy merchants of Charleston, while the latter constituted the majority of the people. The Commons House, being composed of the people's representatives, was naturally responsive to the wishes of the majority and so favored new issues of paper money and was generally opposed to the carrying out of the measures in favor of redemption. The council, which was recruited entirely from the wealthy class, was in sympathy with the creditor merchants and, therefore, was opposed to all new issues and in favor of a reduction of the amount in circulation by gradual retirement.

These two positions were irreconcilable, and there arose a controversy between the two houses of the assembly which lasted about a decade. During the last years of the dispute there was a deadlock between the two bodies that put a stop to all legislation. As most of the laws were of a temporary nature, many of them lapsed and the province was heading toward anarchy. The Board of Trade now interfered and instructed the governor to put an end to the deadlock. This was done by an act of the assembly (August, 1731), which continued the paper money then in circulation without authorizing any increase in the amount, and fixed its value in sterling at the ratio of 7-1. From this time until the end of the colonial period the assembly was more conservative in its paper-money policy.[14]

When we consider this controversy in the light of modern fiscal science, we are inclined to condemn the policy of inflation advocated by the assembly. It certainly was unfair to the South Carolina merchants to force them to receive a cheap money in payment of the debts due them, when they could discharge their obligations to their London creditors only by the use of metallic money. On

[14] For laws providing for later issues of paper money, see COOPER, *op. cit.*, iii, pp. 305-307, 702-704.

the other hand, the scarcity of specie in the province necessitated the use of some kind of a circulating medium in addition to gold and silver, and paper was the only one available. The British government did not help the people to solve their financial difficulties. It should either have allowed a mint in the province for the coinage of money or else have provided a proper medium of exchange for the dominions. Moreover, South Carolina was a border province and, consequently, had to spend a large amount of money in proportion to her population in the wars with the Spaniards and Indians. This meant a high tax rate on the people. Then, too, many of the Charleston merchants and their allies, the public officials, were greedy profiteers, who squeezed every penny they could out of the people for their goods and services. It is not surprising, therefore, that so many of the planters were in debt. If a plan of redemption for the bills of credit had been carried out the currency would have risen in value, causing a corresponding decline in prices, and the evils of deflation would have been added to the burdens already borne by the debtor class.

A few years after the controversy over paper money was ended by the Compromise Act of 1731, another dispute arose between the upper and lower houses of the assembly as to the powers of the former over money bills. It started in 1735 when the council amended a measure that had been passed by the Commons House. The latter claimed that the upper house was usurping powers belonging exclusively to the lower house. The Commons House, it was contended, had the same place in the Carolina assembly that the House of Commons had in the British Parliament. At that time the right of the British House of Commons to initiate all money bills was unchallenged, and its contention that the House of Lords could not amend money bills had so often been acquiesced in by the latter that it had virtually become a recognized principle. The lower house in South Carolina maintained that the council had no more authority over money bills than the Lords had in England. *The dispute between the upper and the lower houses of assembly over the power of the former to amend money bills*

Against this contention the council cited a clause in Governor Nicholson's instructions in which the king clearly recognized the upper house as being on an equality with the lower with reference to revenue bills, as well as to all other legislation. To this the lower house replied that the Carolinians enjoyed the great fundamental rights of Englishmen and that these rights could not be disregarded even by the crown. The dispute finally reached a stage at which the assembly was deadlocked, and that at a time when coöperation between the two houses was badly needed; for Oglethorpe was calling for troops against the Spaniards, and there was danger of attack from both the Spaniards and the Indians. At this juncture a compromise was effected (1739) whereby the council was allowed the right to submit amendments to money bills, a power which it held theoretically for the remainder of the colonial period, though it had become merely nominal before the middle of the century.

The culture of indigo introduced into South Carolina: Eliza Lucas Pinckney

In the decade of the 'forties, South Carolina made an important contribution to southern agriculture by successfully introducing the culture of indigo. It is to Mrs. Eliza Lucas Pinckney that we are indebted for this important service. Eliza Lucas, the daughter of Lieutenant-Colonel Lucas, governor of Antigua, was a young woman of exceptional intelligence, who had been trained by an education in England. At the age of nineteen she came to South Carolina, and from that time until her death (1792) she took an active interest in the development of the province. She married Chief Justice Pinckney and became the mother of General Thomas and Charles C. Pinckney.

The ill-health of her mother and the absence from South Carolina of her father imposed upon her the responsibility of managing her father's estate near the Ashley River. It was in this way that she became interested in the experiments that resulted in indigo becoming one of the great staples of southern agriculture. Her first efforts to raise indigo were unsuccessful, because her managers purposely caused the failure of the first attempt to extract the dye from the plants. Their reason for doing this was that they were from Montserrat and they feared that if indigo should be successfully produced in South Carolina the competition there would lessen the profits derived from the industry in their native West Indian island.

When they were dismissed and a Negro manager secured from one of the French West Indies, a good crop was raised and the success of the experiment was assured. By 1747 enough of the dye plant was harvested to have a consignment of indigo for export to England. Its production was encouraged by a bounty offered by both the British and the provincial governments. The cultivation of indigo quickly became profitable, and soon it took its place along with rice as a great staple in Georgia and the Carolinas.[15]

GEORGIA

The long contest between the English and the Spaniards in the south caused the South Carolinians to realize the importance of having a buffer colony on the Spanish border, and the Yamassee War (1715) accentuated this need. It was to found such a colony that James Edward Oglethorpe and a group of other philanthropists received a charter from King George II granting to them authority over the territory between the Altamaha and Savannah Rivers (1732), which was named Georgia in honor of the king. Oglethorpe had been a member of the House of Commons for ten years and had favored an aggressive policy toward Spain. He had the reputation of being an able military leader, as he had served with distinction under Prince Eugene. He was, therefore, just the man to uphold the claims of England against Spain in a buffer colony. But Oglethorpe and his associates had other reasons for founding a new English colony. There were a number of people in England who were confined in the loathsome prisons because they were unable to pay their debts. As chairman of the committee of the House of Commons that investigated the prison system in England, Oglethorpe had become informed as to the condition of his fellow-countrymen of the poorer class and was anxious to relieve them of their sad plight. The desire to give them a new opportunity and to found a refuge for persecuted Protestants from the continent of Europe was an additional motive that prompted him to enter upon his colonial venture.[16] It was also expected that the new colony would serve as a convenient base for the fur trade and give the English settlers in the south an advantage over their Spanish competitors in the race for the skins and furs supplied by the Indians of the interior.

By the charter the government was intrusted to a group of

Reasons for the founding of Georgia

The charter

[15] See Holbrook, Mrs. Harrison Pinckney, ed., *Journal and Letters of Eliza Lucas.*

[16] In a recent work, *New Viewpoints in Georgia History* (see pp. 3-42), A. B. Saye challenges the traditional view and shows that very few of the early settlers of Georgia (not over a dozen) had ever been imprisoned debtors. Many of them, however, had been unemployed and therefore were poor. See also *American Colonial Tracts Monthly*, i, no. 2, pp. 4-5.

proprietors who were to act as trustees for the colony. They were to derive no benefits from the administration of the province and were not allowed to own any land in it. The colony was to be under their control for twenty-one years, and at the end of this period was to revert to the crown. All laws ordained by the trustees must be in harmony with those of England and must be sent to England for the king's approval. The governor and other officials were to be appointed by the common council, which was a committee of the trustees. But the appointment of the governor had to be approved by the king, and he was required to give security for the enforcement of the laws of trade and navigation. All persons except Catholics were to enjoy religious freedom.[17]

Savannah founded

Oglethorpe got together about one hundred and thirty emigrants, including men, women, and children, and started for the New World in the autumn of 1732. They arrived at Charleston in January, 1733, but soon went south and a month later settled at the mouth of the Savannah River. Here they laid out the city of Savannah with its broad avenues and with parks at the points of intersection.[18] Every ship from England brought new arrivals, some of whom were Scotch Highlanders and some Germans. A settlement was made at Augusta (1737), which soon grew into importance as a center of trade with the Cherokee Indians.[19] Military posts were established south of the Altamaha River on land claimed by the Spaniards, who protested strongly against this encroachment upon their territory.[20]

The Salzburgers settle at Ebenezer

One of the most successful of all the German settlements in America was the one made at Ebenezer by the Lutheran Salzburgers. These Protestants had originally lived in the principality of Salzburg, in the Tyrolean Alps, but had been driven into exile by the persecutions of their Catholic ruler (1729-32). Great numbers of them streamed into the German states for refuge. A small band of these refugees were brought to America under the leadership of Baron von Reck. Through the assistance of the London Society for Promoting Christian Knowledge they were provided with free passage and given lands in Georgia for settle-

[17] For the text of the charter, see *American Colonial Tracts Monthly*, i, no. 4, pp. 2-19.

[18] *Ibid.*, no. 2, pp. 8-10; no. 4, p. 22.

[19] *Ibid.*, no. 4, p. 86.

[20] *Ibid.*, i, no. 4, pp. 30-31.

ment. With this assistance they were able to establish a plantation on the Savannah River about twenty-five miles above its mouth (1734). They were so rejoiced over the outcome of their voyage that they set aside the time of their arrival as a day of thanksgiving. In this same spirit of thanksgiving they called the place Ebenezer, meaning, "Hitherto hath the Lord helped us."[21]

The location selected for their colony was unhealthful and otherwise unsuitable for a plantation. The first contingent of immigrants numbered only about seventy or eighty, and the Alpine peasants were not adapted to pioneering in the lowlands of Georgia. The first year was a time of sickness and distress, and many deaths occurred. But soon others of their fellow-countrymen joined them, including a score or more of Moravians. A more healthful site was chosen, and it was not long before a prosperous settlement was established.[22] By 1741 there were about twelve hundred Germans in Georgia.

For the first five years Oglethorpe acted as a benevolent despot in the infant colony, being not only its judge and lawgiver, but also its military leader against the Spaniards. The people had no voice in the government, as there was no representative assembly until near the end of the proprietary period (1751), and it did not have the power to pass laws, but could only suggest them to the proprietors.

Paternal rule of the proprietors

The new colony started out under the most sanguine hopes of its promoters, and funds were supplied by Parliament and private donations. As the emigrants were poor, provision was made for their transportation and sustenance out of these funds. The soil of Georgia was thought to be very fertile and the climate exceptionally mild. The enthusiastic promoters of the colonizing venture pointed out that the new colony was in the same latitude as that of Palestine, and like the latter, was a Land of Promise, having been especially blessed by a divine Providence.[23] The settlers, however, soon found that the glowing accounts of the new country were based more on optimism than correct information, for neither the climate nor the fertility of the soil measured up to their expectations. On the contrary, they learned that the

The colony grows slowly

[21] HART, A. B., *American History Told by Contemporaries*, ii, pp. 114-116.

[22] *American Colonial Tracts*, i, no. 4, p. 81, and no. 3, p. 5.

[23] *Ibid.*, i, no. 1, pp. 7-8.

fertile regions were malarial and the healthful regions sterile.[24] The colony was, therefore, slow in getting on its feet.[25]

But there were other reasons to account for the slow development of the colony in the early years. These immigrants, many of whom had been unable to earn enough in the homeland to pay their debts, now proved unsuccessful in coping with pioneer conditions. They might have done better, however, if they had not been hampered by unwise restrictions imposed upon them by the trustees. The amount of land allotted to each settler was smaller than that usually held by planters in the other southern colonies, and the quit-rent charge was higher. Other conditions, some of them unreasonable, had to be complied with by the planter or his land would be forfeited. Slavery and even free-Negro labor were prohibited because of the fear that the Negroes might be incited to revolt by the Spaniards who lived near by in Florida. The importation of rum was prohibited.[26] The small planter of Georgia, with little capital and no slaves, could not successfully compete with the wealthy slaveholder of South Carolina, who had plenty of labor and capital for large-scale production. The result was that many of the colonists left for South Carolina,[27] and as late as 1760 the white population of the entire province did not exceed five or six thousand.[28]

The settlers charged their misfortunes to the restraints imposed upon them by the trustees, and clamored for their removal. The

[24] PHILLIPS, U. B., *American Negro Slavery*, p. 94.

[25] For a statement made by a grand jury, September, 1737, showing unsatisfactory conditions in the colony, see *American Colonial Tracts*, i, no. 4, pp. 37-38.

[26] A contemporary makes a loud complaint against the regulation that prohibited the importation of rum. He says that "the experience of all the inhabitants of America will prove the necessity of qualifying water with some spirit." Moreover, he says that while the law gave the magistrates power "to lay hardships upon every person who might be otherwise under their resentment," the law was not enforced; for "as it is the nature of mankind in general, and of the common sort in particular, more eagerly to desire and more immoderately to use those things which are most restrained from them, such was the case with respect to rum in Georgia" (*American Colonial Tracts*, i, pp. 21-23).

[27] *Ibid.*, no. 4, pp. 40, 43, 44, 74.

[28] For an excellent contemporary account of Georgia in 1740, see *Georgia Colonial Records*, iv, pp. 663-676.

great preacher, George Whitefield, who had established an orphan asylum in the province and who had entered upon his remarkable career as an evangelist, lent his support to the request for a modification of the prohibitive measures against slavery, and finally the proprietors removed all these restrictions (1749-50).

But these changes did not put an end to the discontent of the colonists, and the trustees were so discouraged that they surrendered their rights to the crown in 1751. From this time until the Revolution Georgia was a royal province, with a government like that of other crown colonies, consisting of a governor, council, and assembly.

Spain still claimed all the territory occupied by the Georgia settlers and looked upon them as trespassers upon her lands, and Oglethorpe's aggressive policy aggravated the ill-feeling of Spain toward England which had been aroused by the planting of the colony. For not only did Oglethorpe establish the military outpost of Frederica on the southern border of the Georgia grant, but he also erected some small forts as far south as the St. John's River. These encroachments upon Spanish claims led to a controversy, which brought on hostilities between the colonists of Georgia and Florida when war was declared between England and Spain (1739).

The first royal governor of Georgia was John Reynolds, an officer in the British navy. He held the position for only a few years, and during this time there was considerable friction between him and the council and also between the executive and the assembly. The council contended that the governor issued proclamations without asking its advice, whereas the governor complained that the councilors were trying to reduce his position to that of president of the council. One reason for these disputes was that the lines separating the duties and powers of the governor, council, and assembly were not sharply drawn. Under the benevolent despotism of the proprietors few if any precedents had been established that would be useful in guiding the authorities under a system of representative government. The two governors who came after Reynolds were wise and tactful and got along with the assembly without friction.

The Altamaha River marked the southern boundary of Georgia as it was defined in the patent to the trustees. The territory between the Altamaha and Florida was under dispute, being claimed by both the English and the Spaniards. The forts estab-

Georgia becomes a royal province

Strife between the Georgians and and the Spaniards

Relations between the royal governors and the council and the assembly

lished by Oglethorpe in this region were afterward withdrawn, and for a while the land was left unoccupied. Then some unruly frontiersmen went into this disputed area and planted rude settlements. There was a danger that these outlaws, as they were called, would bring on trouble between England and Spain and arouse the hostility of the Creek Indians, who claimed a portion of the land. William Pitt, therefore, directed the governors of South Carolina and Georgia (1758) to order the removal of these settlers, and this was done.

Selected Readings

1. Social and Economic Conditions in Colonial North Carolina.—Holladay, A. R., in the *North Carolina Booklet*, vol. iii, no. 10 (quotes from Col. William Byrd's charges against the North Carolinians and answers them); Connor, R. D. W., *History of North Carolina,* *ch. 10.

2. Manners and Customs in Colonial North Carolina.—Connor, R. D. W., *op. cit.,* *ch. 11.

3. The War of the Regulation in North Carolina.—Connor, R. D. W., *op. cit.,* *ch. 17; Bassett, J. S., in the American Historical Association, *Annual Report*, 1894, pp. 141-212.

4. The Moravian Settlement at Wachovia, North Carolina.—Connor, R. D. W., *op. cit.,* pp. *171-176. For a contemporary account see Mereness, N. D., *Travels in the American Colonies*, pp. *325-364 (the diary of the Moravian leaders who came from Bethlehem, Pa., to Wachovia).

5. The Yamassee War.—McCrady, E., *South Carolina under the Royal Government*, pp. 531-548.

6. The Introduction of the Culture of Indigo in South Carolina.—Ravenel, Harriott H., *Eliza Pinckney*, pp. *7-9, 102-106; Eggleston, George C., *Life in the Eighteenth Century*, pp. *45-48; *The South in the Making of the Nation*, v, pp. *178-183.

7. Charleston in 1763.—Milligen, George, *A Short Description of the Colony of South Carolina*, pp. *31-37 (contemporary account).

8. The Founding of Georgia.—Coulter, E. M., *A Short History of Georgia,* *ch. 3.

9. Early History of Georgia.—Channing, *History of the United States*, ii, pp. *363-365.

10. The Government of Georgia.—*The Colonial Records of Georgia*, xiii, preface, pp. *3-5.

11. Contemporary Account of Early Georgia (1740).—*Ibid.*, iv, pp. *663-680.

12. The Utopia Fails.—Coulter, *op. cit.,* *ch. 7.

CHAPTER XVII

THE OLD WEST

IN THE colonization of the cis-Alleghany region there have been two separate stages. In the first, which continued through the greater part of the seventeenth century, the Europeans occupied the eastern fringe of the present United States, all of which was fairly accessible to the Atlantic Ocean or to navigable waterways leading to it. The second stage lasted from the latter part of the seventeenth century to the end of the French and Indian War (1763). During this period a new region was occupied, which extended from the old settlements westward to the Alleghany Mountains. It comprised the back country of New England, the Mohawk Valley, the Great Valley in southeastern Pennsylvania, a portion of central and western Maryland, the Virginia-Carolina Piedmont, and the Valley of Virginia. By the end of this period the colony of Georgia had also been established and a few bold pioneers had pushed over the mountain barrier into the trans-Alleghany country. The area of settlement cleared out during this second stage of colonization is known as the Old West.

The region occupied during this second period of colonization was, except for its relative inaccessibility, better adapted to settlement than was the eastern belt that had already been appropriated. The Appalachian Valley throughout its entire extent had an exceptionally fertile soil with a limestone base, and in the south the Piedmont was superior to the Tidewater belt in the healthfulness of its climate and the productivity of its lands. The rolling character of its surface gave it good drainage and it was comparatively free from the malaria-breeding swamps that curse the lowlands. In its original state the country had an abundance of fine timber, though there were treeless areas on which grew sufficient wild grass or cane to sustain the great herds of cattle of the early pioneers.

The most distinctive portion of the Old West is the great Appalachian Valley and the Carolina Piedmont, which are closely associated geographically. The Great Valley extends across Penn-

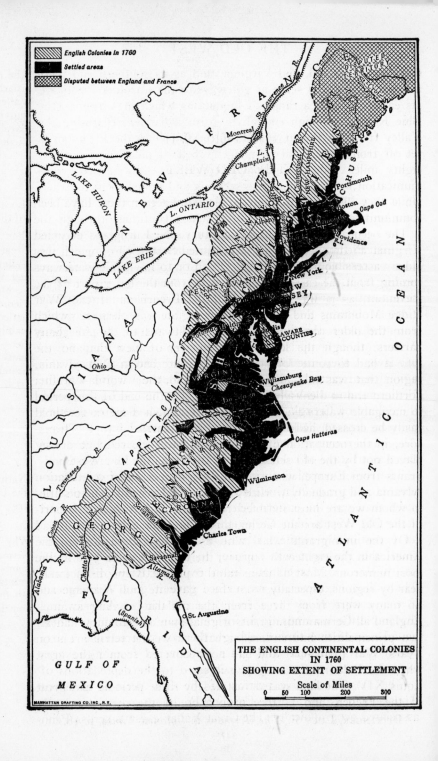

THE ENGLISH CONTINENTAL COLONIES
IN 1760
SHOWING EXTENT OF SETTLEMENT

Scale of Miles
0   50   100   200   300

English Colonies in 1760

Settled areas

Disputed between England and France

sylvania, Maryland, and Virginia, and at its southern end there are water gaps that serve as gateways to the Carolina Piedmont. Its eastern wall is a range of mountains which in Virginia (the Blue Ridge) are high enough to form a barrier separating the Valley from the Piedmont belt. In the Carolinas the Piedmont is set off from the coastal plain by the belt of pine barrens, about eighty miles wide. Geographical conditions thus favored communication between these two sections and linked them together, while they discouraged intercourse between them and the older communities on the east.

The Appalachian Valley and the Carolina Piedmont

The occupation of the back country of New England and the Virginia Piedmont resulted largely from the expansion of the older eastern communities. But the first wave of colonization coming from the east did not reach the Valley and the Carolina Piedmont, as it was broken against the barriers of the Blue Ridge Mountains and the pine barrens. Some settlers, however, from the older communities came to this section despite these barriers, though the larger stream of emigration that flowed into it had to come from another source. The portion of this region that was most accessible to the outside world was the northern end in Pennsylvania. Here it made its nearest approach to navigable waterways and here the mountain ridge could most easily be crossed, as it was low and intersected by gaps. Therefore, in the occupation of this fruitful land the chief part was played not by the old settlers from the east, but by fresh immigrants from Europe, who entered the northern opening in Pennsylvania and gradually worked their way southward. The peoples to whom we are most indebted for the colonization of this part of the Old West are the Germans and the Scotch-Irish.

The Great Valley and the Carolina Piedmont settled mainly by Germans and Scotch-Irish

Of the immigrants who came from continental Europe to America in the eighteenth century, the Germans were by far the most numerous. Most of them came from the Rhine district and near-by regions, especially from the Palatinate and Würtemberg. So many were from the former country that in America and England all German immigrants were known as Palatines.[1] These two principalities had suffered greatly from the terrible Thirty Years' War (1618-48) and had not recovered from its ravages when the Palatinate was again subjected to the depredations of Louis XIV. The land was devastated by these periodic invasions of the French, and a large proportion of the population was

Why the German immigrants left the homeland

*Economic
Religion*

[1] BITTINGER, LUCY F., *The Germans in Colonial Times*, p. 18.

reduced to poverty. To make matters worse, the people were exploited by their selfish and incompetent rulers. Religious conditions were also bad, as there was in the Palatinate a number of Protestant sects who were persecuted by their Catholic rulers.

There was also a good deal of dissatisfaction among the Swiss with conditions in the homeland, and many of them wished to emigrate to America. Switzerland had not suffered from invasion, as had some of the German states, and economic conditions there were not so bad as they were in Germany. But the peasants were oppressed by their feudal lords, and often were hampered in the exercise of their religious beliefs. Protestant sects with unconventional beliefs and practices were subjected to persecution. To those who were dissatisfied in both Germany and Switzerland, America appeared as the land of promise, offering both freedom and economic opportunity. That the New World should figure as a fairyland in their dreams is only natural, since interested promoters of colonization were advertising the advantages and pointing out the opportunities in the colonies with unblushing exaggeration. These efforts were reinforced by the favorable accounts sent home by their fellow-countrymen who had earlier gone to America.

Despite these various hardships, the Germans did not begin to migrate in great numbers until about the end of the first decade of the eighteenth century. One reason for this wholesale emigration was the devastation of Würtemberg by the War of the Spanish Succession (1701-13), but the immediate occasion of it was the suffering caused by the cold winter of 1708-09. During this terrible winter beasts and birds froze in the forests and fruit-trees and vineyards were killed. While all of Europe suffered from the severe cold, it fell especially heavy on the Germans in Würtemberg and the Palatinate because of their impoverished condition.

The great German exodus

In the spring of 1709 about fifteen thousand Germans left home and pressed down the Rhine to Holland, and from there they went to England. They were kindly received by Queen Anne, whose policy was to welcome persecuted Protestants to the British realm. But so large a number of poor people with little or no income was an embarrassment to the authorities. They were settled in camps and for a while provided for by private charity and by appropriations made by Parliament. Such an arrangement could only be temporary and was unsatisfactory while it lasted. The Germans were, therefore, anxious to go to America, where they hoped to find a permanent home.

In 1710 two efforts were made to found German colonies in America. Baron de Graffenried sent over about six hundred and fifty Palatines who planted a settlement at New Bern, North Carolina. The plantation started off promisingly, but before it was two years old it was attacked and nearly destroyed by the Indians (see pp. 228-229). The other attempt of this year to colonize the Palatines in the New World was planned on a big scale. Three thousand of them were sent over to New York with Robert Hunter, the new governor of the province, and were located on the Hudson River, where they were to engage in the production of naval stores. The British government advanced their transportation, supplied them with tools, and promised to furnish them with provisions until they were able to sustain themselves. This experiment in the production of naval stores was not a success, as the German immigrants had been husbandmen and vine-dressers at home and did not take readily to the new occupation. The British authorities failed to keep their promise to furnish them with supplies, and they were exploited by their profiteering landlord. They, therefore, became dissatisfied and a large number of them wished to seek new homes. These moved farther into the wilderness and settled in the Schoharie Valley. Here they had trouble with the authorities over the titles to their lands, and were again unfairly dealt with by grasping landowners. In a few years the majority of them, refusing to submit to this injustice, left Schoharie and planted settlements elsewhere. Some of them located in the Mohawk Valley, where they were later joined by so many of their fellow-countrymen that the Mohawk for thirty miles was a German river.[2] But the greater number of those who left the Schoharie villages moved down the Susquehanna River and settled on one of its tributaries in Bucks County, Pennsylvania (1723).

The Palatines sent to North Carolina and New York

In the meantime a new stream of German immigrants had begun to flow into Pennsylvania from the homeland. "The great migration to that province begins about 1717 and continues with almost unabated vigor until the Revolutionary period."[3] The unjust treatment accorded the Palatines in New York and the

Most of the German immigrants came to Pennsylvania

[2] *Ibid.*, p. 86.

[3] CHANNING, E., *History of the United States*, ii, p. 407.

tragic fate of the Palatine settlement in North Carolina tended to make those two provinces unattractive to prospective German settlers. In pleasing contrast to these unhappy experiences was the history of the Germans who had been living for a generation in Pennsylvania and who were now happy and prosperous. Moreover, by the promise of cheap lands and religious freedom the Quaker colony was able to offer strong inducements to Europeans who were emigrating to America. Pennsylvania, therefore, received more emigrants from Germany than did any other colony, and the Germans constituted about one third of her population at the end of the colonial period. They were located mainly in the zone stretching diagonally across the province from Bucks County to the Maryland line.

Many of these German immigrants were poor when they left home and others were robbed and cheated into poverty by sea captains and others with whom they came in contact before they reached the New World. Therefore, most of those who arrived at Philadelphia after a sea voyage of terrible suffering were unable to pay the transportation charges for themselves and their families. To meet this obligation they sold themselves out to service for a few years. Persons bound out in this way were known as "redemptioners," that is, indentured servants. After their term of service had expired they purchased good lands in the limestone region in the Great Valley, and by industry and thrift soon became prosperous. They held on to their language and German customs and their descendants still are known as Pennsylvania Dutch (*Dutch* being a corruption of *Deutsch—German*). The immigrants who came in the eighteenth century belonged mostly to three Protestant churches, the Lutheran, the German Reformed, and the Moravian (*Unitas Fratrum*), though some of them were Catholics, and quite a number of them belonged to the smaller denominations, such as the Mennonites and the Dunkards.

Industries in the German settlements

The Germans were prominent in the development of colonial industries. Most of the early ironmasters in Pennsylvania were Germans, and they were also active in type-founding and in the manufacture of woolens and paper. Pack-horses carried their manufactured commodities along the frontier all the way from Maryland to Georgia. Their chief industry, however, was farming, in which occupation they had exceptional success, as the men and women were both hard workers. The women not only did the cooking and housekeeping, but they also spun and wove in winter and helped in the fields in the summer. The comfortable homes and the large and well-filled barns that were everywhere typical of the Palatine settlements attest the industry, thrift, and good management of the German farmer.

Pennsylvania was also the province to which most of the Scotch-Irish came on arriving in America. The immigrants of this stock were the descendants of the Scotch Presbyterians who had been living in the northern counties of Ireland (Ulster) since the early part of the seventeenth century. They had originally been settled on lands taken from the Irish under Elizabeth and James I. Later confiscations were made by Cromwell and other settlements were established. As these outsiders were seated on lands of which the native Irish had been unjustly deprived, the latter naturally regarded them with ill-will. The fact that the Scotch-Irish were Protestant and the Celtic Irish Catholic also helped to keep alive the feeling of hatred between them. Therefore, there was constant strife and frequently war between the Scotch-Irish and their neighbors, and they came to look upon war as a normal condition of living. The combative side of their character had thus been overdeveloped, and they brought with them to the New World an attitude of antagonism toward conditions in general that sometimes degenerated into contentiousness. Accordingly, the relations of the Scotch-Irish with their neighbors in America were often far from harmonious. They were brave fighters, but at times they showed impatience at the restraints of the law and were inclined to resort to mob violence. As a class they were energetic and intelligent, with strong moral and religious convictions, and they usually proved a valuable addition to the communities in which they lived. They had suffered persecution as a result of the efforts made by the English kings to establish the Anglican Church in Ireland, and so they came to America with a strong prejudice against Anglicans as well as against Catholics.

There was some Scotch-Irish emigration to America in the seventeenth century, but the great exodus did not begin until about 1718. From that time until the end of the colonial period there was almost a constant stream of emigration from Ulster to America, and at the time of the outbreak of the Revolution

The Scotch-Irish in Ulster

The Scotch-Irish emigration to America

the Scotch-Irish constituted a large and important part of the population of the thirteen continental colonies.

The main reason for their leaving home was economic oppression, though religious restrictions were also a cause of dissatisfaction. By laws passed by the British Parliament in the latter half of the seventeenth century the farm products of Ireland were excluded from the English and Scottish markets. These measures discouraged agriculture in Ireland and caused the people to engage in manufacturing. The wool grown on the island was of an especially high quality, and Irish woolens soon enjoyed a reputation that enabled them to find a ready sale. Capital was coming into Ireland for the woolen business from England, Scotland, and the Continent. The English manufacturers now became alarmed at this competition and secured the passage of an act by Parliament (1699) prohibiting the Irish, as well as the American colonials, from exporting woolen goods to England or to any other country. By this law the principal industry of Ireland was destroyed.

Another grievance was the exactions of the landlords. A good many Scotchmen had gone to Ulster after the Revolution of 1688, largely because land could be leased for a long period at a low rental. By 1717 the terms of these leases began to expire and the landlords would not renew the leases without a great increase in rent—sometimes double and treble the original figure.

The people not only had this heavy burden to carry, but also, in addition to maintaining their own Presbyterian worship, had to pay taxes for the support of the Anglican Church. Besides, in 1704 an act was passed which debarred Presbyterians from holding office and prohibited their ministers from celebrating marriages.

There was also a good deal of distress occasioned by bad harvests. In 1740 and 1741 there were famines, and the suffering caused by them gave a great impetus to emigration. A later exodus, which came just before the American Revolution, was caused partly by the spirit of dissatisfaction that was characteristic of the time. The Scotch-Irish shared in this unrest, especially as the linen industry in Ireland had begun greatly to decline about 1771 as a result of the interruptions in the commercial intercourse with America caused by the friction between England and the colonies. These Scotch-Irish brought with them to America their grievances against the British government, and when the break came most of them supported the cause of independence.[4]

. The Presbyterians of Ulster were Puritans, and their religious beliefs were very similar to those of the Congregationalists of New England. It was natural, therefore, that they should have selected New England as the place to which they would go when they first emigrated to America. During the earliest years of the immigration (1714-20) many of them went to New England. But they did not receive a warm welcome by their Puritan brethren in Massachusetts, who were suspicious of foreigners and were alarmed at the number of the newcomers. Most of the Ulsterites, therefore, who came to the New World after this period found homes in the colonies south of New England.

Ulsterites not cordially welcomed in New England

Quite a number settled in New York and New Jersey, but the great body of them turned toward Pennsylvania, where they found conditions quite to their liking. Land was easily obtained and there were no taxes for the support of an established church. Consequently, great numbers of them came over from year to year and settled in this province. Some of them sat down as squatters on lands in the region that was in dispute between Maryland and Pennsylvania and could never be induced to pay for them. A number also settled in the Susquehanna and Cumberland valleys and at other places in the province.

The Scotch-Irish were of a roving disposition, and soon many of them began to branch out from the Pennsylvania settlements. Rich lands could be had in Maryland and the Valley of Virginia on still better terms than were offered in Pennsylvania. The authorities in the Old Dominion encouraged them to locate on their western frontier, despite their Presbyterianism, as they would protect the older settlements from attack by the Indians. So we soon find them gradually moving southward in the trough of the valleys, occupying western Maryland, the Valley of Virginia, and later the frontier regions of the Carolinas. The Pennsylvania Germans also took an important part in this trek to the southern uplands, and the two peoples occupied approximately the same region, except that the Scotch-Irish were usually located nearer the western frontier than were the Germans. The Germans began to move into the Valley of Virginia about 1726, and

The Scotch-Irish and Germans move southward from Pennsylvania into western Maryland, the Valley of Virginia, and the Carolina Piedmont

[4] For an excellent discussion of the reasons for the Scotch-Irish exodus from Ulster, see FORD, H. J., *The Scotch-Irish in America*, pp. 181-187.

the Scotch-Irish six years later. Gradually going up the Shenandoah Valley, both of these groups later found their way through the water gaps in southwest Virginia into the Carolina Piedmont.[5] They were attracted to this latter region by the cheapness of the lands and the mildness of the winter climate. The desire to settle in this favored land was greatly accelerated by the Indian atrocities on the frontiers of Virginia and Pennsylvania that followed Braddock's defeat.[6] Some of the Germans also settled east of the Blue Ridge in the middle section of Maryland and in the Virginia Piedmont.

Living conditions on the frontier   As the Germans and Scotch-Irish trekked southward they brought with them their seeds, farm implements, and furniture, packed in their big wagons. The women and small children also rode in the wagons, while the men and boys drove their hogs, sheep, and cattle along in true pioneer fashion. Having arrived at a suitable place for settlement, they at once entered upon the task of building the log cabin. "This was the work of a day or two. With a jug of cider or whisky to make merry, the pioneer invited his neighbors to lend a helping hand. The logs were cut near by in the forest, roughly hewn, and fitted into place. The cabin usually consisted of a single room with the natural earth for a floor, a single door swinging rather lopsidedly on two sagging leather hinges; a loophole or two to let in the sunshine and the summer breeze served as windows. Into the rear wall was built the large stone or clay chimney, all out of proportion with the dimensions of the little cabin, so that it looked as though the house had been built for the chimney instead of the chimney for the house. Just under the roof was the loft, which served as a sleeping-room. It was reached by a ladder from the inside

[5] Some of the Scotch-Irish in the Carolinas came there directly from Ulster, but most of them moved southward into this region from Pennsylvania. The Germans who occupied the North Carolina Piedmont also came mainly from the north, while the Palatines in the South Carolina Piedmont came directly from the homeland through the port of Charleston.

[6] One of the most important settlements made by the Germans in the Carolinas was at Wachovia, at the present site of Winston-Salem, North Carolina. For a contemporary account of the founding of this settlement, see the *Journal of the Moravian Brethren*, and SMYTH, J. F. D., *A Tour in the United States of America*, i, pp. 214-217. An excellent account by a recent writer is given in CONNOR, R. D. W., *History of North Carolina*, pp. 171-176.

or by a series of wooden pegs driven into holes, bored an easy step apart, into the logs of the inner wall. The furniture was scarce, but the faithful rifle always hung in the chimney corner within easy reach."[7]

After the occupation of the Old West, the cis-Alleghany region was divided into two distinct areas of settlement. The eastern communities had kept in constant touch with England, and the tendency of a wilderness environment to modify the ideas and habits of an old civilization was held in check to some extent by this intercourse with the homeland. The western zone, on the other hand, was separated from the Atlantic coast by a wide expanse of territory with no navigable streams to form an outlet to the ocean. There was thus very little communication with the Old World, and the frontier was free to do its perfect work of modifying European ideals and customs and adjusting them to wilderness conditions. In its new home the Old World civilization quickly cast aside its European dress and donned the garb of the backwoods. *Contrast between the East and the West*

That portion of the Old West that comprised the Great Valley and the Carolina Piedmont was made up of a homogeneous group of settlements, bound together by a similarity in social conditions and a community of economic interests. The entire region was culturally, as well as geographically, an extension of the Pennsylvania frontier. The Scotch-Irish Presbyterians received their ministers from the College of New Jersey (Princeton), and to it they sent their sons for their higher education. Missionaries from Pennsylvania kept in touch with the German religious bodies and accustomed them to look to their northern leaders for guidance. *Social and economic solidarity of the up-country*

The contrast between East and West was greatest in the Chesapeake and southern colonies. Here the westward movement had created a New South, which was more closely assimilated to the North than to the southern provinces of which it formed a part. The Valley of Virginia and the Carolina Piedmont were shut off from the older eastern communities by distinctive physi- *The New South*

---

[7] SCHAPER, W. A., *Sectionalism in South Carolina*, pp. 277-278. This is an account of frontier conditions in South Carolina, but it will apply equally as well to other sections of the Old West in the earliest stages of its occupation. For an account of life on the frontier in western Pennsylvania written by a contemporary (the Rev. Joseph Doddrige), see FORD, H. J., *op. cit.*, pp. 278-285.

cal features, and the people of the one section were differentiated from those of the other by marked divergencies in economic interests and social ideals. In the East, plantations were large, a few great staples were raised, and slavery and white servitude were the chief types of labor. In the West, landholdings were comparatively small, farming was diversified, and slavery and bond labor unimportant. In the East, the people were mostly of English origin and were inclined to accept the Episcopal, or Anglican, as the state church. In the West, the non-English stocks were predominant, and the people were affiliated with a number of dissenting sects and were all opposed to a union between church and state.

Results of the formation of the Old West   The settlement of the Old West resulted in the creation of a fighting frontier which extended "all along the line from New England to Georgia, which bore the brunt of French and Indian attacks, and gave indispensable service during the Revolution."[8] The new society in the West was so different from the old society in the East that antagonism necessarily arose between them. This antagonism was due to the fact that two areas were united politically which divergent economic and social conditions were tending to separate; that is, government was trying to join together what nature had put asunder. These two sections were not only unnaturally but also unequally yoked together. In every province the local and provincial administration was dominated by a clique of eastern politicians who were unwilling to accord the western communities their rightful share in the government. Usually, the frontier was not properly represented in the provincial assembly and had to bear more than its share of the common burdens. In Pennsylvania and South Carolina the large western counties did not have nearly as many representatives in the assembly as did the eastern counties. In Virginia the counties were all equally represented, but those in the West were much larger than those in the East. Often, too, the upland districts were neglected or exploited by incompetent and grafting local officials who were henchmen of the provincial bosses.

Under such conditions controversies between upland and lowland were inevitable. These controversies took in general the following forms: "contests between the property-holding class of the coast and the debtor class of the interior, where specie was lacking and where paper money and a readjustment of the basis

[8] TURNER, F. J., *The Old West*, p. 218.

of taxation were demanded; contests over defective or unjust local government in the administration of taxes, fees, lands, and the courts; contests over unfair apportionment in the legislature, whereby the coast was able to dominate, even when its population was in the minority; contests to secure the complete separation of church and state; and, later, contests over slavery, internal improvements, and party politics in general. These contests are also intimately connected with the political philosophy of the Revolution and with the development of American democracy. In nearly every colony prior to the Revolution, struggles had been in progress between the party of privilege, chiefly the eastern men of property allied with the English authorities, and the democratic classes, strongest in the West and the cities."[9]

Unfortunately, the struggles between coast and interior were not always kept within constitutional limits. In South Carolina the local administration had by the end of this period become so inefficient and corrupt in the western districts that the people organized themselves into associations (1764) and took the law into their own hands. The "Regulators," as the members of these associations were called, not only administered lynch law, but on one occasion (1769) defied the authorities by meeting the government party in arms. This show of force frightened the ruling clique into making concessions, and so the danger of rebellion passed.[10]

The Regulators

About this same time there was also great dissatisfaction in the hill country of North Carolina because of unjust taxes, the contraction of the currency, and the corrupt practices of the sheriffs. Associations were formed here as in South Carolina (1766 to 1768), and soon the Regulators were up in arms against the provincial government. Governor Tryon sent the militia against the rebels and a pitched battle was fought at Alamance Creek (1771). The Regulators were defeated in the battle and their movement collapsed, though many of the measures they advocated were embodied in the constitution of 1776.[11]

[9] TURNER, F. J., *op. cit.*, pp. 221-222. For an excellent short discussion of the results of the formation of the Old West, see *ibid.*, pp. 218-233.

[10] TURNER, F. J., *The Old West*, pp. 226-227; SCHAPER, W. A., in American Historical Association *Report*, 1900, i, pp. 334-338.

[11] TURNER, *op. cit.*, pp. 227-229; BASSETT, J. S., in American Historical Association *Report*, 1894, pp. 141-212.

Selected Readings

1. The Significance of the American Frontier.—Turner, F. J., *The Frontier in American History*, *ch. 1.
2. Results of the Formation of the Old West.—Turner, *op. cit.*, pp. *106-125.
3. Life on the Frontier.—Ford, H. J., *The Scotch-Irish in America*, pp. *278-285 (a contemporary account). For other contemporary accounts, rather unfavorable, see Callender, G. S., *Selected Readings in the Economic History of the United States*, pp. *601-617.
4. The Scotch-Irish Emigration from Ulster to America.—Hanna, C. A., *The Scotch-Irish*, *ch. 39; also Ford, *op. cit.*, *ch. 5.
5. The Germans in the Colonies.—Adams, J. T., *Provincial Society*, pp. *170-171, 173-186.
6. Conditions in Germany that Led to the Emigration of the Palatines.—Bittinger, Lucy F., *The Germans in Colonial Times*, *ch. 1; Faust, A. B., *The German Element in the United States*, i, pp. *53-63.
7. The Great Exodus of the Palatines.—Bittinger, *op. cit.*, *ch. 8.
8. The Attempt to Colonize the Palatines in New York.—Osgood, H. L., *Eighteenth Century*, i, pp. *512-516.
9. German Methods of Farming in America.—Faust, *op. cit.*, i, pp. *131-138 (a contemporary account).
10. Pennsylvania German Traits.—Knauss, J. O., *Social Conditions among the Pennsylvania Germans in the 18th Century*, *ch. 6.

CHAPTER XVIII

NEW FRANCE AND THE FIRST TWO INTERCOLONIAL WARS

FRENCH OCCUPATION OF CANADA AND THE MISSISSIPPI VALLEY

IT WAS about four decades after its tragic failure at colonization (1565) in Florida (see pp. 48-49) before the French government succeeded in getting a permanent foothold in America. During all this time, however, Frenchmen were going regularly to the Newfoundland waters for fish and to the St. Lawrence region for furs, and to facilitate the fur trade rude huts were erected on the shores of Anticosti Island. By the beginning of the seventeenth century France had made a good start toward recovering the position which she had lost by reason of the religious wars. She was now blessed with the benevolent rule of Henry IV, one of the ablest of her sovereigns, and the great gaps in her economic life made by the civil wars were rapidly filling up. At this time France was in a better position than she had ever been to enter upon an era of colonization. *France renews her effort at colonization in America*

Circumstances had brought to the front a man who was particularly fitted by character, temperament, and experience to lead his country in the attempt to establish its authority in the New World. This man was Samuel de Champlain, properly known as the Father of New France. Like so many of the great men of that day, he had the faith and religious seriousness characteristic of the Middle Ages and the daring, initiative, and enthusiasm that is typical of the modern era. He could easily adapt himself to any situation and was equally at home in the château of a French nobleman or in the wigwam of an Indian brave. While still a young man he had to his credit a fine record as a seaman and soldier and was in high favor with the king. He could doubtless have made his fortune as a courtier, but he had too much energy and ability to be tempted by such an empty and useless career. The call of the wild was strong within him, and the thrills incident to life in the American wilderness had a great charm for him. Besides, the opportunity of converting the Indians and *Champlain* bringing them into the Catholic fold made a strong appeal to his religious sense and invested the American enterprise with the spiritual glamour of a missionary undertaking or a holy crusade. He, therefore, cheerfully devoted the greater part of the latter half of his life to the work of exploring and promoting settlements in New France.

Explorations by Champlain

Champlain's first exploring venture was made in 1603, when he led a trading expedition to Canada and ascended the St. Lawrence River to the falls above Montreal. Later he sailed along the New England coast from below Cape Cod to Acadia. But his most noteworthy explorations were those in which he struck boldly into the interior and visited regions into which no white man had ever penetrated. On one of these expeditions he came into the beautiful lake which now bears his name. Later he ascended the Ottawa River into the heart of Canada (1613) and finally pushed across from the Ottawa River to Georgian Bay and Lake Huron (1615).

If France were ever to get a real hold in the New World it was necessary to follow up these explorations with permanent occupation, and in the work of colonization also Champlain played a leading part. An attempt to plant a French settlement on Sable Island, off the coast of New Brunswick, had been made at the end of the sixteenth century (1598) by the Marquis de la Roche, but this effort was unsuccessful, as the colony was abandoned a few years later. Soon after Champlain's return from his first expedition (1603) the Sieur de Monts received from the king of France a grant of the territory between the fortieth and forty-sixth degrees of north latitude, or from the present site of Philadelphia to the northern part of Nova Scotia. This region was known as La Cadie, or Acadia. The charter gave him a trade monopoly and the right to plant settlements anywhere in Acadia and to govern them as the representative of the king.

Settlement at St. Croix

In 1604 de Monts with the assistance of Champlain made a settlement on the island of St. Croix at the mouth of the river of the same name. The site was an unfavorable one for a colony, and when winter set in the people suffered terribly from cold and disease. The weather was so severe that "cider and wine froze in the casks, and were served out by the pound." To make their misery complete they were attacked by an epidemic of scurvy, which carried off nearly one-half of their number. In this time of awful distress the sick and discouraged survivors were saved from despair by the stout-hearted optimism of Champlain, which held up despite all the untoward circumstances.

In the spring the survivors took fresh courage with the melting of the ice and the coming of the birds, and de Monts decided to choose a better location for his settlement. The colonists thereupon moved across the Bay of Fundy and located at Port Royal, the present site of Annapolis, Nova Scotia (1605). The settlers did not undergo such hardships here as they had at St. Croix,

The settlers move to Port Royal

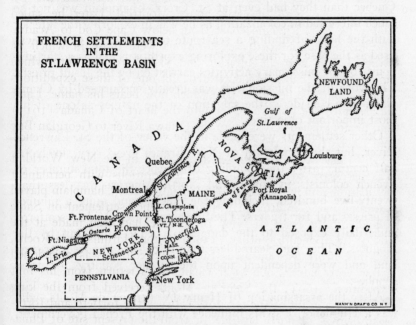

FRENCH SETTLEMENTS
IN THE
ST. LAWRENCE BASIN

but the little colony had a checkered career. This settlement was abandoned in 1607,[1] but was reëstablished a few years later.

[1] The reason for giving up the settlement in 1607 was that the patent of de Monts expired at this time. The place was reoccupied three years later and had taken a new lease on life when Captain Argall came up from Virginia and destroyed the village, claiming that it was on territory owned by England (1613). Despite these discouragements Port Royal was soon afterward rebuilt by the French. Acadia fell into the hands of the British in 1628, but was returned to the French four years later. England again gained possession of Acadia in 1654 and held it this time for more than a decade. France regained control of the province in 1667 and held it until 1690. At that time King William's War was going on and the

Quebec founded

In the meantime Champlain had planted at Quebec the first permanent French settlement in America (1608). The colonists underwent hardships here during the first winter very similar to those endured at St. Croix. We are not informed as to the details regarding the sufferings of the settlers, but we know that they too had to contend with the scurvy, and we judge from the fact that in the spring only eight of the original twenty-eight colonists were alive that the Frenchmen endured greater hardships at Quebec than they had even at St. Croix. Champlain was not so much interested in colonization as he was in exploring the interior with the hope of finding a sea route to the Indies. Quebec was used as the base for these exploring expeditions and as a starting-point for the missionary activities carried on by the Jesuit priests. The work of the missionaries was greatly encouraged by Champlain, who considered the salvation of the natives as one of his most important objectives.

Slow development of New France

Other settlements were made in the valley of the St. Lawrence River, but the population of New France grew very slowly. A half century after the founding of Quebec the total number of French colonists in continental North America was less than twenty-five hundred, including the officials and quite a number of priests and fur traders. The inhabitants were widely scattered and "daily exposed to the danger of being wiped out by the Iroquois." They had cleared less than thirty-five hundred acres of land and were dependent upon the mother country for food supplies.

Part played by Champlain in New France

After the assassination of Henry IV (1610) de Monts, who was a Huguenot, lost his influence with the French government, now in the hands of a regency that was strongly anti-Protestant. His patent had been canceled, and for some years the government of New France was intrusted to a succession of noble favorites. Then in 1627 the entire control of the American colony with a monopoly of the trading privileges was turned over to an association known as the Company of One Hundred Associates. During the early years of this period (until his death in 1635) Champlain had charge of affairs in America, first as the deputy of the noble viceroys and later of the Company. He discharged his responsi-

---

English wrested Port Royal from the French. The latter, however, recovered it a short while later and held it until the English and colonial troops captured it in Queen Anne's War (1710). This time it was permanently retained by England.

bilities with exceptional vigor, and if he had been properly supported the development of New France would probably not have been arrested as it was. But neither the viceroys nor the Company were equal to the great opportunity offered them and failed to back up the heroic efforts made by Champlain to lay the foundations of a French empire in the New World.

Champlain himself added to the difficulties of the situation by allying himself with Indian tribes that were hostile to the Iroquois, or the Five Nations, the most powerful political organization among the natives in North America. As a result of this alliance, Champlain and his savage allies had attacked and defeated a party of the Iroquois on the shores of Lake Champlain (1609). This attack and the alliance that gave rise to it started an enmity between the French and the Iroquois that lasted during the greater part of the colonial period. Shortly after the intrepid French explorer incurred the ill will of this powerful confederacy, Henry Hudson, an English seaman in the service of the Dutch East India Company, made his famous voyage up the Hudson River. He too encountered a band of Iroquois Indians, but instead of fighting them he entertained them with rum and biscuit and succeeded in winning their good will. The Dutch thus started out on good terms with the Five Nations, and this friendship passed on to the English when the latter got possession of New York. The English were able to hold them to this alliance by buying their furs and selling them firearms and "firewater" on better terms than the French could offer. This friendship for the English and hatred of the French was an important factor in colonial history. The Iroquois held the territory on both sides of the Mohawk River, thus controlling the region to the south of the St. Lawrence, and retarded the advance of the French toward the heart of the continent in that direction. Besides, they protected the English of New York from attack and so kept the French from wiping out the northern colonies.

An era of prosperity opened for New France when Louis XIV attained his majority and assumed control in France (1658). Both he and his great minister, Colbert, were interested in colonization and proceeded to take measures that infused new life into the colonial enterprise. The old company was deprived of its rights (1663) and the control of New France was taken over by the crown. The government as now organized was modeled after that of the French province. At the head of the administration

The administration reformed by Louis XIV

was the governor, who was generally a nobleman sent over from the homeland. Next to him in dignity and sometimes above him in real authority was the intendant, who held the chief place in the administration of justice and acted as a check on the governor.[2] A third important official was the bishop. He supervised the work of the parish clergy and had general charge of the religious affairs of the province. These three officials, together with a number of councilors appointed by the crown, constituted the Superior Council. To this body was intrusted the government of the settlers in the St. Lawrence basin, and it became and remained the chief governing body in New France from this time until the end of French control in continental North America.

Talon, the Great Intendant   The first intendant, Jean Talon, was an able man and he did a great deal toward setting the colony on its feet. A band of soldiers (nearly one thousand in number) was sent over to quiet the Iroquois and make America safe for French colonization. These measures started New France on a career of prosperity. In a decade the population tripled and agriculture was greatly increased. The fur trade, too, was flourishing, and the Indian menace was removed for the time being, thanks to the presence of the soldiers. Talon was unwilling, however, to confine his energies to the development of the colony already established. He dreamed of building up a vast empire in the New World and laid plans for exploiting the Great West. It was in pursuance of this aim that three expeditions were sent out to explore the region of the upper lakes. The leader of one of these expeditions stopped at Sault Sainte Marie and in a dramatic way took possession of all the western lands in the name of King Louis XIV (1671). This scene was enacted in the presence of representatives from fourteen Indian tribes, who probably looked on with intense interest in the dramatics of the occasion but with little or no comprehension of their significance.

Frontenac, the "Iron Governor"   At this juncture Louis de Baude, Count Frontenac, was sent to America as governor of the French dominions (1672). He was a man of exceptional ability, industry, and courage, and gave New France an administration characterized by force and vision. But Frontenac had the faults as well as the virtues of greatness. An uncontrollable temper, a feeling of superiority toward men of lesser size, and a too firm belief in the infallibility of his own judgment made his relations with his colleagues

[2] GREENE, E. B., *Foundations of American Nationality*, p. 200.

far from agreeable. Consequently, he had a genius for making enemies and was always hampered by the opposition of those who were associated with him.[3] This disagreement between Frontenac and his opponents was not due altogether to defects in his temperament. Behind all the petty personal bickerings there was a difference of principle between his policy and that advocated by the bishop and the Jesuits, who were his bitter opponents. One cause of strife between him and the Jesuit missionaries was his alleged acquiescence in the sale of brandy to the Indians, which was violently opposed by the priests, as it interfered with their missionary efforts. The friction between Frontenac and his colleagues developed to such an extent that the king finally removed both the governor and his chief opponent, the intendant (1682).

After Frontenac's departure troubles with the Indians arose, and soon New France was fast relapsing into the old conditions. The king thereupon sent him back to serve another term (1689). The war between England and France (known in America as King William's War) was just beginning, and Frontenac proved to be an able military leader as well as an efficient civil administrator. In a few years he had set the colony to rights and had restored it to its former condition of prosperity. He remained in office until his death in 1698. It was the success of this second term of his administration that won for him the distinction of being the greatest governor of New France.

The policy of Frontenac, like that of Talon, was to extend French influence westward and thus rivet the claim of his country to the Great Valley of the Mississippi. This purpose, however, was contrary to the instructions he had received from Colbert, which directed him to consolidate the authority of France in the territory already occupied rather than spread over a wide area the limited resources at his command. But the enthusiastic dreams of the governor could not be restrained by this practical suggestion, and so he disregarded his instructions and encouraged the exploration of the Mississippi Valley and the occupation of the Illinois country. It was due in large measure to his vision that French America grew from a narrow strip on the St. Lawrence into a great empire embracing in its claims half a continent.

In the work of blazing new trails in the Mississippi region the

Frontenac's policy

[3] For an excellent brief appraisal of Count Frontenac, not altogether favorable, see WRONG, G. M., *The Conquest of New France,* pp. 3-5.

Jesuit missionaries and the fur traders took an important part.
In coöperating with the traders the missionaries were forming a
strange partnership. They were primarily interested in saving the
souls of the natives and in lifting them to a higher plane of living.
To accomplish this purpose they underwent all sorts of hardship
and suffering and asked for themselves no material reward in
return. The traders, on the other hand, were usually concerned
only with the profits afforded by their business and in pursuit of
this aim would stoop to the most unscrupulous methods. They
debauched the character of the Indians by selling them brandy
and set an example of licentiousness that tended to debase their
morals. The Jesuits protested strongly against these practices and
did all they could to restrain them. But they could not, as they
considered, afford to break entirely with their sinful fellow-countrymen. For, it was argued, if the Indians could not get French
brandy they would buy English rum, and the traffic with the English might lead to the bringing in of the dangerous Protestant
heresy.

To us the task of occupying the Mississippi Valley looms up as
a vast undertaking, especially when we consider the greatness of
the area and the smallness of the French population in the New
World. At the time of Frontenac's appointment to the governorship, the French possessions in continental North America consisted of the settlements in the St. Lawrence basin and some
mission stations in the lake region, one of which was located on
the western shore of Lake Superior. France had by 1664 also
occupied a part of Haiti and a number of the smaller West Indian
islands. By the middle of the century (1653) the white population
of the French West Indies numbered about fifteen thousand.
There were thus two bases from which Frenchmen might operate
in the work of exploiting the Great West. The southern part of
the Mississippi Valley could easily be approached from the island
colonies and the northern from the Canadian settlements and lake
posts. In the occupation of the Great Valley both plans were
pursued.

Frontenac had no difficulty in finding bold leaders who were
willing to coöperate with him in making discoveries in the West.
Prominent among the voyages into this region was the one made
by the fur trader, Louis Joliet, accompanied by Father Marquette.
Joliet and Marquette left Green Bay (May, 1673) and ascended
the Fox River to the point where it makes its nearest approach to

the Wisconsin. Carrying their canoes over the short portage (only about two miles), they descended the Wisconsin to the Mississippi. Continuing their journey, they floated down the Mississippi to the mouth of the Arkansas. By this time they were thoroughly convinced that the great river does not enter the Gulf of California, as had been thought before, but empties into the Gulf of Mexico. Since they had gained the knowledge for which the expedition had been made, they now turned back and after a difficult journey reached Green Bay (September, 1673).

The greatest of all the French explorers of the Great West was La Salle René Robert Cavelier, Sieur de La Salle. Like Frontenac, he dreamed of extending French influence through the Mississippi Valley and strengthening it by the establishment of forts at strategic points. La Salle was one of those romantic characters that have from time to time enlivened the history of the French people and made it read like highly imaginative fiction. With the courage, energy, and perseverance of a modern business magnate he combined the dreaming enthusiasm of a mediæval crusader. He was thus eminently fitted by both character and temperament for playing the rôle that he had assumed in opening a way for French expansion. In 1674 he received a license from the king to explore the Mississippi to its mouth. He was also encouraged in this venture by Frontenac, though the cost of his equipment was borne by himself and his friends. In his effort to carry out his plan he met with obstacles which would have discouraged any man of average persistence. Nothing daunted, however, by the ill luck that seemed to dog his movements, he continued his efforts and was able finally to start out on the voyage that took him to the mouth of the Mississippi. On arriving at the point where the great river divides into branches just before emptying into the Gulf, he took formal possession of the country in the name of the king of France. In honor of the sovereign who had encouraged him he called the country Louisiana (1682).

The explorations of La Salle, Joliet, and others revealed the Forts and possibilities for colonization afforded by the rich lands of the mission Mississippi Valley. The Catholic missionaries and fur traders, as stations well as the agents of the Quebec government, were interested in the occupation of this vast region by the French; and by the beginning of the eighteenth century a number of fortified posts and mission stations had been established in the territory now comprised within the states of Wisconsin, Minnesota, Michigan, and

Illinois.[4] Some of these posts were held only temporarily, while others became centers of permanent settlements. One of the most important of these permanent settlements was Detroit, which was founded in 1701 by Lamothe Cadillac to guard the water route from Lake Erie to Lake Huron. This village at once became the center of an active trade in furs and "was a most important link . . . in the welding of the chain that was to bind the Mississippi Valley to Canada."[5]

Settlements in the Illinois region

The Illinois region was, however, the scene of the most important experiment in colonization by the French in the upper portion of the Great Valley. In the winter of 1691-92 a fort (Fort St. Louis) was built near Lake Peoria and shortly afterward a Jesuit mission station was established at the same place. It was not long before some French settlers began to locate at this post, and it became the first permanent French settlement in the Illinois region. There were other mission stations and military posts in this region which became nuclei of French villages.[6]

The Illinois villages were located in a region that was noted for the fertility of its soil, and it was hoped that they would be the chief source of supply of grain and cattle for the other settlements. This expectation was in large measure realized, as the farmers in this section raised agricultural products in large quantities. Some of these were sold in Detroit, while a considerable portion of them was sent down the Mississippi to New Orleans and Mobile, to be consumed in these towns or to be transshipped to the West Indies and Europe. It was a question for a time as to whether the middle region should be attached to New France on the north or Louisiana on the south. At first it belonged to the northern province and most of its early inhabitants came from there. But its economic interests were tied more closely to the southern colony, owing to the fact that the Mississippi River bound the two sections together. So in 1717 Illinois, except the

[4] In the establishment of these posts a prominent part was played by La Salle, Father Marquette, and Henri de Tonti.

[5] ALVORD, C. W., *Centennial History of Illinois*, i, p. 114.

[6] Four of these posts were on the Mississippi River, three of them (Cahokia, Fort Chartres, and Kaskaskia) being on the Illinois side and one (Sainte Genevieve) on the Missouri side of the river. One of the settlements (Fort Vincennes) was on the Wabash in the present state of Indiana.

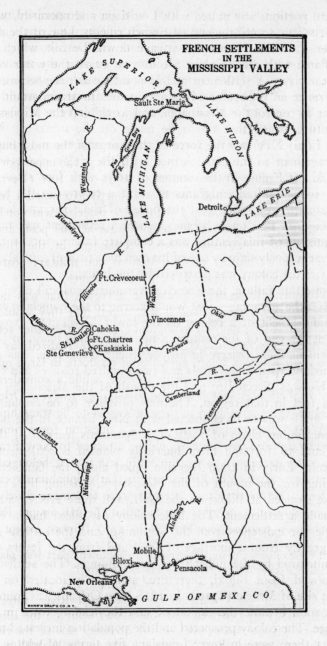

FRENCH SETTLEMENTS
IN THE
MISSISSIPPI VALLEY

LAKE SUPERIOR

LAKE HURON

LAKE MICHIGAN

LAKE ERIE

Sault Ste Marie

Detroit

Green Bay

Fox R.

Wisconsin R.

Mississippi R.

Illinois R.

Ft. Crèvecoeur

Vincennes

Wabash

Ohio R.

Missouri R.

St. Louis

Cahokia

Ft. Chartres

Kaskaskia

Ste Geneviève

Iroquois R.

Cumberland R.

Tennessee R.

Arkansas R.

Mississippi R.

Alabama R.

Mobile

Biloxi

Pensacola

New Orleans

GULF OF MEXICO

MANN'N DRAF'G CO., N.Y.

northern portion, was united with Louisiana and remained under this jurisdiction until the end of French rule in the Great Valley.

La Salle's unsuccessful attempt at colonization

After La Salle's successful voyage down the Mississippi, he was aflame with zeal to plant a colony at or near the mouth of the great river. A settlement at this point would, it was argued, give France an important advantage in the fur trade, would enable her to control the Mississippi, and would serve as a base for any future attack that might be made on the mines of New Spain. Louis XIV saw the force of these arguments and gave his encouragement to the plan. Armed with the king's commission, La Salle left France in the summer of 1684 with four ships and nearly four hundred emigrants to plant a colony on the lower Mississippi. They sailed past the outlet of the river and landed at Matagorda Bay (now Texas), where a settlement was made. The outcome of this venture was a complete failure, for La Salle was treacherously slain by one of his own men (1687), and shortly thereafter the colony was destroyed by the Indians.

The founding of Louisiana

Despite this failure, the French government was still unwilling to forego the advantages that would accrue to the homeland from the establishment of a colony on the lower Mississippi. Accordingly, at the end of the century a new effort was made to plant a settlement there. Pierre le Moyne, Sieur d'Iberville, was sent to Louisiana with four vessels and two hundred soldiers and colonists. He was directed to find the mouth of the Mississippi and erect a fort in that region. The new province to be established in the south was to be connected with New France in the north by a continuous chain of forts. The Spaniards learned of these plans, and to forestall them hurriedly planted a settlement at Pensacola. Early in 1699 Iberville sailed along the Gulf coast, searching for the mouth of the Mississippi. Passing by Pensacola, he stopped at Biloxi on the Gulf, and there erected a fort and made a settlement. The little colony of Biloxi had a hard struggle for existence from the beginning, and the settlers suffered greatly from a shortage of food and from the fevers that were nurtured by the unhealthful surroundings. The settlement was moved from Biloxi, therefore, and finally located on the present site of Mobile (1710). In 1718 New Orleans was founded and it soon became the capital of and the leading town in the province. The colony prospered and the population increased until by 1731 there were in lower Louisiana five thousand whites and two thousand blacks.

The French continued their active efforts to occupy the Great West right up to the time of the outbreak of the French and Indian War. By the middle of the eighteenth century their explorers had reached the Rocky Mountains both in the Northwest and the Southwest. A number of forts had been established in strategic places both east and west of the Mississippi River. There was a chain of military posts connecting the settlements on the lower Mississippi with those in the Illinois country and the lake region, and another extending westward from Lake Superior almost to the Rocky Mountains.

The First Two Intercolonial Wars

The overlapping of French and English claims in America was the occasion of some conflict in the early and middle decades of the seventeenth century. Port Royal passed back and forth several times between the rival claimants (see p. 363, note), and Quebec was captured in 1629 and held for a short time by the English. But these events were only incidents growing out of rivalry or war between England and France and were not caused by ill feeling between their colonies. During the six decades immediately preceding the Revolution of 1688 there was no serious strife between the French and the English colonies. This long peace is explained partly by the absence of any great conflict between the interests of the French and English settlements, owing to the distance that separated them, and partly by the turn that European politics had taken during this period. It had been the policy of England during these six decades to remain at peace with France as far as possible, and Charles II and James II were especially inclined to be friendly with the French king, as they were pensioners of Louis XIV.[7]

No serious strife between the English and French colonials before the Revolution of 1688

The Revolution of 1688, however, marks a turning point in the relations between England and France and also in the attitude of their colonies toward each other. By this time the rivalry between English and French fur traders was becoming tense. Each group was on the watch for opportunities to get ahead of the other. Both were bidding for the friendship of the Iroquois Indians, who acted as middlemen in the trade between the western

The Revolution of 1688 a turning point in intercolonial relations

[7] There was, however, in the reign of Charles II a short war between England and France despite Charles's desire to live on good terms with Louis (Cross, A. L., *A Shorter History of England and Greater Britain*, pp. 367-368).

Indians and the white settlers. The English were able to beat their French competitors in this race, for by an agreement in 1684 the Iroquois declared their allegiance to British rule.

There was also a real conflict of interests between the New Englanders and the French Canadians over the Newfoundland fisheries. Religious prejudice figured as an additional cause of intercolonial strife, for in the Puritan ministers of New England and the Jesuit priests of New France the ill feeling between Protestant and Catholic reached its highest point. Moreover, the English colonists both on the northern and southern frontiers felt insecure as long as their Indian neighbors were encouraged in their hostility toward them by French or Spanish allies. But these various causes of dispute would probably not have led to war had not the heat caused by local friction been reinforced by that produced by international conflict.

In the second half of the seventeenth century England had been taking a more active part in general European politics, and this new interest was increased by the change of dynasty that came with the Revolution of 1688. For the new king, William III, was ruler of the Netherlands and was anxious to preserve the balance of power on the Continent, which was at that time menaced by the imperial ambitions of Louis XIV, king of France. Under the new leadership England entered upon a foreign policy that entangled her in continental quarrels and involved her in a series of wars. The American colonies of both England and her rivals were drawn into these conflicts, and so for each war in the Old World there was a corresponding struggle in the New. This epoch of strife is divided into two periods, separated from each other by a quarter century of peace. In each period there were two wars, with a short interval of peace between them.

King William's War

The long series of European conflicts started soon after the accession of William III with a war between England and France, the American part of which was known as King William's War (1689-97). Louis XIV was trying to extend the boundaries of his country, and in pursuit of this ambition was quite willing to disregard the rights of other nations. This policy of ruthless imperialism had aroused the powerful antagonism of William before he had come to the English throne, for he regarded it as a menace to his beloved Holland. He feared that if Louis were not checked in his aggressions the Spanish Netherlands (now Belgium) and the German states would be swallowed up by him.

In that event there would be no barrier between France and the Dutch Netherlands and the independence of the latter country would be in imminent danger. As stadtholder of the Netherlands he had led the Dutch in a brave fight against French aggression, and from that time until his death he remained the unwavering enemy of Louis XIV.

When William was called to the throne of England Louis made the mistake of refusing to acknowledge him as the rightful sovereign and of supporting the lost cause of James II. This brought England into war against France and into the coalition which had been formed by a number of European states against Louis.

The French and English colonies took up the European quarrel and King William's War was the result. Both England and France were so absorbed by the war in Europe that they could give but little help to their subjects in America. England sent over a few regular troops to New York and convoyed the merchant ships that passed between the colonies and the homeland. The English navy also gave special protection to the British West Indies. The French king could spare no troops, but he returned to Canada as governor and director of military affairs Count Frontenac, the ablest man for the position that the French empire afforded. The fighting was, therefore, done almost entirely by the colonists and their Indian allies. *Method of fighting*

The plan of the French was to protect themselves from English attacks and make raids with their Indian allies on the small settlements on the frontiers of New York and New England. This policy was carried out with ruthless severity, and the people living in the outlying districts were terrorized by the brutal atrocities committed by the French and their savage allies.[8]

In an effort to put a stop to this guerrilla warfare the northern colonists made retaliatory attacks on the Indians and attempted to paralyze the efforts of the enemy by striking at the French strongholds in the St. Lawrence region. An expedition was sent against Port Royal, Acadia (1690), under the leadership of Sir *English attempts to take Port Royal and Quebec*

[8] One of the most noted of these raids was the attack on Schenectady, a town a few miles west of Albany, New York (February, 1690). A band of French and Indians surprised this village early in the morning of a cold February day and killed sixty of the garrison and captured eighty or ninety more. Attacks were also made on Haverhill, Massachusetts, and Dover, New Hampshire, and indescribable cruelties were perpetrated at other places.

William Phips, a prominent New Englander. The town was taken by the English and the province was held by them for a short time, when it was recaptured by the French. The colonists also arranged for two attacks on Canada, one to be made on Quebec by a naval force from Massachusetts and Plymouth, and the other on Montreal by troops from New York and Connecticut marching overland from Albany. Both of these attempts proved disastrous failures.

The war confined to New York and New England

In this war fighting was carried on on a very small scale and was confined to New York and New England, as the frontier settlements of these colonies were the only places that were exposed to attack. The Mohawk Valley was an easy road of approach to the English colonies from Canada, and the British authorities saw the importance of putting up a strong defense against the enemy in the province of New York. In the fall of 1692 the English government issued a requisition on the colonies as far south as Virginia for men and money to aid in the cause. No troops were ever furnished by any of the colonies south of New York in response to this requisition and other similar requests, though Maryland and Virginia did make money contributions. This indifference and lack of coöperation is explained by the fact that the French as yet had not occupied the Mississippi region, and the Delaware and Chesapeake provinces felt that their frontier was beyond the reach of the enemy.

The Peace of Ryswick

The war was ended by the Peace of Ryswick (1697), which left conditions in America as they were before the conflict started.

The Peace of Ryswick proved to be only a short truce, as an international difficulty soon arose over the Spanish succession.

The War of the Spanish Succession: Cause

When the king of Spain died the Spanish possessions passed to Philip of Anjou, a grandson of Louis XIV. As Philip was quite young, it was everywhere felt that his policy would be dominated by his grandfather. This virtually united the two crowns of Spain and France and destroyed the balance of power in Europe. Although William was opposed to this union, neither Holland nor England was willing to go to war on this issue. Europe would thus have acquiesced in the arrangement if Louis had not aroused further opposition by his subsequent measures. French soldiers had been sent to the Belgian Netherlands and were menacing the Dutch Netherlands. Louis also announced that the old regulations prohibiting foreign merchants from trading with the Spanish colonies would be enforced. These restrictions had hitherto been

largely disregarded by the English and Dutch merchants, as the
Spanish navy was not strong enough to keep down smuggling.
But as Louis now had at his command the combined naval force
of the two powers, he would be able to put a stop to the illicit
trade carried on by the English and Dutch seamen with the
Spanish-American dominions. And finally Louis, on the death of
James II, recognized the son of James as the rightful king of
England. Public sentiment was aroused in England and war was
declared against France (1701). William was able to unite sev-
eral European rulers into a Grand Alliance against Spain and
France, and the result was a general European conflict, known
as the War of the Spanish Succession.

King William died before the outbreak of hostilities and was
succeeded by Queen Anne; the war in America, therefore, is
known as Queen Anne's War (1701-13). The Iroquois as allies
of the English had played an important part in King William's
War and had suffered greatly from French attacks. They were
therefore loath to renew the contest with their old enemies, and
in 1701 they signed a treaty of peace with the French and their
Indian allies. As a result of this agreement the Iroquois remained
neutral during the greater part of this war. To encourage them
in this policy of neutrality the French refrained from attacking
their friends, the New Yorkers. By this arrangement New York
was relieved from attack for the first seven years of the war,
and Lord Cornbury, the incompetent and unpatriotic governor of
the province, was unwilling to hazard this immunity by aiding
the neighboring colonies in their struggle with the enemy. The
Middle colonies were so far removed from the danger that they,
too, took little interest in the contest. The brunt of the fighting,
therefore, in the north fell on New England and in the south on
South Carolina.

Two expeditions were sent out from South Carolina against
Florida, in the course of which several small towns and St.
Augustine were captured, though the latter was quickly aban-
doned. An attack on Charleston made by a joint French and
Spanish fleet was bravely repulsed, and the besiegers were driven
off with a loss to them of two hundred and thirty prisoners.

In New England the French made border raids, as in King
William's War. The New Englanders were now, as in the previous war, fired with the desire to wrest Canada and Acadia from
the enemy. In 1709 great preparations were made for an attack

Queen
Anne's
War
Neutrality
of the
Iroquois

War in
the south

Border
raids: At-
tempts to
conquer
Canada

on Montreal by land from New York and on Quebec by sea from New England. New York now abandoned the rôle of slacker and joined heartily in the enterprise with the New Englanders. Enthusiasm was raised to such a pitch that even the authorities of New Jersey and Pennsylvania stretched their Quaker consciences and promised to help with men and money. The colonial troops were to be assisted by a large contingent of regulars sent over from England. When all was in readiness to start there came the discouraging news that the expected British regulars would not be sent, as they were needed in Portugal. The plan of attacking Canada at this time was therefore abandoned.

Two years later (1711) the attempt was renewed on a grand scale, the initiative this time being taken by the British authorities. A strong naval force was sent against Quebec and a large land force was organized to attack Montreal. Both plans ended in complete failure, largely as the result of incompetent leadership.

Port
Royal
captured
by the
English

As an offset to these failures the English had to their credit one important victory, for the efforts to take Acadia were finally crowned with success. After two attempts to capture Port Royal had failed, the last effort was made (1710) by a large force consisting of fifteen hundred New England militiamen and four hundred British marines. The expedition was commanded by Colonel Francis Nicholson, and the soldiers were transported to Port Royal in vessels under convoy of British warships. The French garrison was greatly outnumbered by the assailants and after a few days' resistance was forced to surrender to the English. The name of the town was now changed from Port Royal to Annapolis Royal, in honor of the English queen. This victory was especially gratifying to the New Englanders, for they felt that they could never be at peace with their Indian neighbors as long as Acadia was held by the French. Besides, if Port Royal, the principal town of Acadia, were in possession of the British, the New England fishermen could prosecute their trade to much better advantage.

The
Treaty of
Utrecht

The war was ended by the Treaty of Utrecht (1713). By the terms of the peace England was placed in a favorable position in both Europe and America. From Spain she received Gibraltar and the island of Minorca, and her merchants were granted the exclusive privilege of supplying the Spanish-American colonies with slaves for a period of thirty years. France ceded to the

British empire Acadia, Newfoundland, and the Hudson Bay region, and recognized the British protectorate over the Iroquois. English control of the Hudson Bay region and Newfoundland gave to the English fur traders and New England fishermen, respectively, a decided advantage over their French-Canadian competitors.

The first period of intercolonial strife was a time of economic depression for the English colonies. The fishing industry suffered and the trade with the West Indies declined. The dangers to shipping increased the cost of transporting tobacco to England and thereby lowered the price received by the colonial planter. This brought poverty and distress to the tobacco colonies. The great drain made on their finances caused two of the colonies, Massachusetts and South Carolina,[9] to resort to bills of credit to meet their obligations. In this way was started the dangerous practice of issuing paper money, a practice which was destined to become widely prevalent in the colonies. The wars had also checked western expansion on the part of the English colonies. The border warfare that had been going on for twenty years had virtually closed the frontier for that length of time. During this period there had been only a slight increase in the area occupied by the English settlements, whereas the population had almost doubled. This would indicate a rapid increase in the density of population, which "meant increasing clashing of wills and thoughts, and a keener competition for subsistence or for wealth."[10]

The first two, as well as the last two, intercolonial wars revealed the weak hold that the British imperial administration had on the American dominions and also accentuated the weakness of the bonds that held the latter to the mother country. The failure on the part of the colonial authorities to honor the requisi-

Results of the first two intercolonial wars

[9] Massachusetts was the first of the colonies to resort to paper money, and the occasion of her first issue was the unsuccessful attempt to capture Quebec (1690). To finance the undertaking a heavy indebtedness had been incurred, which, it was hoped, would more than be met by the booty to be secured. The failure of the expedition left the colony saddled with a debt which it felt unable to pay and gave the government the excuse to issue bills of credit.

South Carolina first issued bills of credit to meet the extra expenses incurred in the expedition against St. Augustine in Queen Anne's War.

[10] ADAMS, J. T., *Provincial Society*, p. 168.

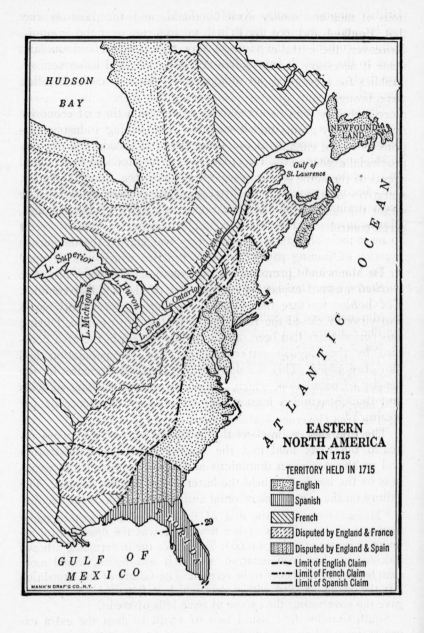

**EASTERN
NORTH AMERICA
IN 1715**

TERRITORY HELD IN 1715

English

Spanish

French

Disputed by England & France

Disputed by England & Spain

– · – · Limit of English Claim

– ·· – Limit of French Claim

——— Limit of Spanish Claim

HUDSON

BAY

NEWFOUND-
LAND

Gulf of
St. Lawrence

NOVA SCOTIA

L. Superior

L. Michigan

L. Huron

L. Ontario

St. Lawrence R.

L. Erie

A T L A N T I C   O C E A N

FLORIDA

29

GULF   OF
MEXICO

MANH'N DRAF'G CO.,N.Y.

tions of men and money made by the home government showed that England did not have her colonies under good control. Moreover, the extra expenses incurred by the wars frequently made it necessary for the provincial governors to call on the assemblies for appropriations of money. In this way the assemblies were brought into greater prominence and were able to assert more authority than they could have done in peace times. For in making money grants they were often able to impose such conditions as would enhance their own power and weaken that of the provincial executive. As the governors in the royal provinces were agents of the home government and the assemblies were the representatives of the people, the increased importance of the latter meant the development of local autonomy at the expense of imperial control.

SELECTED READINGS

1. De Monts and Champlain.—Channing, E., *History of the United States*, i, pp. *100-106; Munro, W. E., *Crusaders of New France*, *ch. 3.
2. Marquette and La Salle.—Munro, *op. cit.*, *ch. 6.
3. The Capture of Louisbourg.—Wood, W., *The Great Fortress*, *ch. 2.
4. The Deerfield Massacre.—Parkman, Francis, *A Half-Century of Conflict*, i, *ch. 4.
5. Friction between Frontenac and the Bishop and the Intendant.— Colby, G. W., *The Founding of New France*, ch. 5.
6. The Iron Governor.—Munro, *op. cit.*, *ch. 5.
7. The Coureurs de Bois.—*Ibid.*, *ch. 9.

CHAPTER XIX

ENGLAND WINS SUPREMACY IN NORTH AMERICA

The period of peace

FOR about a quarter of a century after the Treaty of Utrecht (1713) there was peace in both Europe and America. France and England had been well-nigh exhausted by the previous conflicts and welcomed this respite from war as an opportunity to devote their energies to domestic affairs. This period was characterized by rapid expansion on the part of the English colonies. It was during this time that the great German and Scotch-Irish immigrations began which extended the frontiers of the older settlement toward the west. England also pushed her area of occupation southward by the establishment of the new colony of Georgia (1733). France strengthened her hold on the Great West by establishing trading posts, missions, and settlements in the Mississippi region.

The Anglo-Spanish conflict

During the period of peace there was, however, considerable friction between England and Spain, enough ultimately to bring on war between these two powers. The loss of Gibraltar in the recent contest was a great humiliation to Spain and gave a smart to her pride that helped to keep alive that ill feeling which she had held against the British empire since the days of Hawkins and Drake. Then, too, the British merchants were constantly violating Spanish trade regulations and bringing down upon themselves heavy penalties inflicted by Spanish customs officials. There was also a controversy between the two powers over the southern boundary of South Carolina, and this land dispute was aggravated when the English planted the colony of Georgia (1733) on territory which Spain felt that she had every right to claim as her own. The English merchants complained loudly of the severe reprisals visited upon them by Spanish officials because of their illicit trade in Spanish-American waters and urged the government to take measures for the redress of their grievances. This pressure became so great that the peace-loving premier, Sir Robert Walpole, had to yield, and England and Spain went to war (1739).

The struggle in Europe led to a contest between the Spaniards in Florida and the English settlers in Georgia. General Oglethorpe led two expeditions against St. Augustine (1740, 1743), both of which were unsuccessful. The Spaniards from Florida and Cuba in turn attacked the coast of Georgia, and were defeated in their attempt to capture Frederica, on St. Simon's Island. Fighting in the south between English and Spanish colonials

The Anglo-Spanish war soon merged into a European conflict known as the War of the Austrian Succession. This widening of the war area was occasioned by the aggression of Frederick the Great, king of Prussia, who had seized Silesia, a province belonging to the Austrian Queen, Maria Theresa. She resented this and tried to get allies that would enable her to win it back. France saw an opportunity to get the Austrian Netherlands (formerly the Spanish Netherlands, now Belgium) and so joined in with Prussia. England was bound by honor and self-interest to protect Austria against the loss of the Netherlands; for then, as in 1914, she was opposed to a strong power controlling the little country at her front door. She joined with Austria against Prussia and France, and a general European conflict was again started.

The beginning of war between England and France was the signal for the renewal of strife between New England and New France. In this intercolonial conflict, which was known as King George's War, the method of warfare was about the same as it had been in the previous contests. Again the French and their Indian allies raided the New England frontier, causing great suffering to women and children but without affecting the military situation in any important way. The only military event of importance in the north was the capture of Louisbourg. After the loss of Acadia the French fortified Louisbourg, on Cape Breton Island, and made it one of the strongest military posts in America. The possession of this stronghold gave the French a good lead in the contest with the New Englanders for the control of the Gulf of St. Lawrence and the fishing interests that centered in it. Besides, in time of war it could serve as a starting point for French privateers and for military and naval expeditions against the English colonies. Its strategic value was appreciated by both the French and the New Englanders, and the latter felt that as long as this important place remained in the hands of the French their fishing interests in the Gulf of St. Lawrence would be in danger and their frontier would be exposed to Indian raids. King George's War: The capture of Louisbourg

The Great Awakening had just swept over New England, and the renewed interest in religion aroused by it had led to a revival of anti-Catholic sentiment. This anti-Catholic feeling had also been intensified by the recent Indian raids by tribes among whom the Jesuits were active. Therefore, in the desire to take this important post from the heretic enemy, the religious prejudices of the New Englanders were allied with their economic interests.

William Shirley, governor of Massachusetts, took the lead in arousing interest in the attempt to capture Louisbourg and worked out a plan of attack that was readily accepted by the New England colonies. Accordingly, a force of forty-three hundred men was assembled and ships were provided to transport the troops to the scene of action (1745).[1] William Pepperrell, of Maine, was selected as commander of the expedition. He had had little or no experience as a military leader, but was a man of sound judgment and knew how to secure the coöperation of his colleagues and subordinates. The soldiers were also untrained, and a contemporary in speaking of the enterprise said that "it had a lawyer [Shirley] for contriver, a merchant [Pepperrell] for general, and farmers, fishermen, and mechanics for soldiers." The expedition was joined by three British warships under the command of Commodore Warren, who had come up from the West Indies. Pepperrell and Warren were able to coöperate effectively and the town was besieged and briskly bombarded. The amateurish way in which the attack was made would have been laughable to military experts. But the place was captured (June 17, 1745) thanks partly to good luck and the energy of the assailants and partly to the incompetence exhibited by the French in their conduct of the defense.

Treaty of Aix-la-Chapelle

The French felt humiliated over the loss of this their strongest port on the Atlantic coast, and made two strenuous but unsuccessful efforts to regain it. The war, in both Europe and America, was brought to a close by the Treaty of Aix-la-Chapelle (1748). By the terms of the treaty all conquests were to be returned to their original owners, and Louisbourg was thus restored to France, much to the disappointment of the New Englanders. The British commissioners tried to retain Louisbourg, but France

[1] New York also aided in the equipment of the expedition by furnishing twenty cannon. New Jersey and Pennsylvania sent supplies, but they did not arrive until after the siege was over. OSGOOD, H. L., *The American Colonies in the Eighteenth Century*, iii, pp. 521-522.

would not agree to this. She was in a position to force England to yield on this point, as she had a hold on the Netherlands which she would not relax without compensation.

The Treaty of Aix-la-Chapelle proved to be only a truce, for after six years of peace there broke out another great war, which was destined to decide whether England or France was to enjoy political supremacy in India and North America. This final contest, unlike the preceding intercolonial wars, all of which were of European origin, started in the New World and spread to Europe. It also had a more marked influence on American history than had any of the previous conflicts.

In the final struggle for primacy in continental North America, Spain, the weakest of the contestants, played only a minor part. As a world power she was outclassed by both of her great rivals, and was, therefore, not in a position to assert aggressively her claim to the disputed area. Besides, she was already in unchallenged possession of Florida, southwestern North America, a goodly portion of the West Indies, and most of South America. She had thus already staked off in the New World more land than she could successfully appropriate and develop. The real fight was, therefore, between France and England, though Spain was drawn into the struggle as it neared its close.

As world powers these two contestants were almost equally matched. France had the stronger army, but England in the very beginning had the larger navy, and this superiority on the sea grew as the war advanced. In America, Britain had a decided advantage over her opponent. The population of the French colonies on the continent of North America was only about one-fifteenth that of the English provinces, and this inequality in numbers was accentuated by the fact that the French settlements were widely scattered and, therefore, could not coöperate easily in a concentrated military effort. *Relative strength of France and England*

This failure of the French to keep pace with their English neighbors in America was due partly to the unwise policy with reference to the colonies pursued by the authorities at home. The government was still an absolute monarchy, and social life in France had been characterized by religious intolerance and by many of the restrictions and inequalities of the feudal régime. These political and religious notions had by this time outlived their day in France and were destined to be swept aside by the great Revolution before the close of the century. But they were even less suited to the American wilderness, where nature had ordained that a measure of religious and political freedom was necessary to colonial development. The political leaders of France, however, did not see this and imposed upon their American colonies a system of absolutism in government and intolerance in religion. No dissent from the views held by the Roman Catholic Church was tolerated there, and so the religious dissenters who left the homeland were excluded from the colonies. The English government was for a long time just as narrow, perhaps, in its attitude toward nonconformity in religion in the homeland as was that of the French, but the English colonies welcomed religious and political dissenters not only from England, but from other European countries as well.

But the main reason for the slow development of New France was geographical. To quote the historian Parkman, "France in America had two heads, one amid the snows of Canada, the other amid the canebrakes of Louisiana." In the St. Lawrence basin, where most of the population of the mainland dwelt, the climate was rather cold for successful agriculture, and the contour of the country favored fur trading. The rivers and lakes furnished waterways into the interior of the continent and afforded access to the fur-bearing regions. But the trade growing out of these favorable conditions did not encourage settled pursuits and permanent occupation, for traders and trappers are not essentially home-builders. Besides, the land occupied by the French was comparatively level and there were no insurmountable mountain barriers to check expansion. For these reasons the settlements were more widely scattered than were those of the English. The English colonies, on the other hand, not only had the advantage of their rival in population, but their settlements were also more compact; for they had the Appalachian Mountains at their back and were held in between this barrier and the sea.

As the main occupation of the British colonies was agriculture, they were independent of the outside world for food supplies. The French settlers in Canada, on the other hand, were not self-supporting, and had to buy a good portion of their food from the English colonies. The British government hoped that by withholding these supplies from the French colonials the latter could be starved into submission. But this advantage was in large measure thrown away by the unpatriotic conduct on the part of the Americans. They had for a long time been accustomed to trade with the French possessions in violation of the law, and this habit was so strong that they continued to smuggle goods to the enemy colonies in time of war. As a consequence the struggle was prolonged.

Moreover, these advantages were offset by certain disadvantages. The British colonies had always been accustomed to managing their own affairs without much interference from the mother country. The people had had a large share in their government and were very jealous of their rights. They were inclined to regard any effort on the part of the imperial government to control them as an unwarranted restraint upon their liberties. The provinces were also too jealous of one another to coöperate effectively against the common enemy. There was no political bond holding the thirteen provinces together except that all were members of the British empire. It was, therefore, an impossible task to hitch up these thirteen autonomous republics to the war in such a way that they would exert their full strength in pulling together. The provincial governments were frequently more alive to their rights than to their duties. At times when the military exigencies called for sacrifices in the way of money and troops the colonial legislatures, instead of exerting themselves to meet their obligations, spent valuable time in contending with the governors for their constitutional rights. As a result the requisitions for men and money were never met, and most of the troops had to be supplied from the mother country. Such a political organization is favorable to liberty in time of peace, but is impossible of transformation into an effective military machine in time of war.

The French colonies, on the other hand, had always been ruled autocratically. The colonial government centered at Quebec, and it could mobilize all the resources of New France without being hindered by the assertion of states' rights on the part of quasi-independent provinces. There were, however, certain weaknesses in this military autocracy. Power was divided between the governor, the intendant, and the general in command. France's leading commander in the war, General Montcalm, was really a great man and a patriot and could have accomplished much more if he had had a free hand. But he was hampered by the unwise policy of the governor, who was too small a man for his position, and by the rascality of the intendant, who was a downright grafter. It can thus be seen that the odds were not overwhelmingly against either side, and each of the rivals had grounds for hoping for success whenever the issue should be joined. Both were, therefore, willing to assert their alleged rights to the extent of going to war. In such a situation a cause for quarrel could easily arise.

Points of contact between the rival claimants

On the Gulf of Mexico the French and the Spaniards were near neighbors, as the French settlements in Louisiana had extended eastward to Mobile, and the Spaniards in Florida had pushed westward as far as Pensacola. In the south the unoccupied zone separating the English from the Spanish settlements had also been very much narrowed by the foundation of the colony of Georgia.

In the north there were several points at which French and British interests came in close enough contact to develop friction and possible strife. One of these was at Louisbourg, on the island of Cape Breton. This important stronghold of the French interfered with the New England fisheries and was a menace to the British occupation of Acadia.

The English occupation of Acadia afforded a second cause of possible conflict. The British had been left in possession of this province at the end of Queen Anne's War by the Treaty of Utrecht (1713), but there had never been any agreement between England and France as to what territory was comprised within Acadia. The English contended that it included all that area of land that extended northeastward from Maine to the Gulf of St. Lawrence. The French, on the other hand, maintained that it included only the peninsula of Nova Scotia. To make good their claim they built Fort Beauséjour on the isthmus that connects Nova Scotia with New Brunswick. The people in Acadia remained French at heart and were never loyal to their British masters. In order to strengthen their hold on the province the English brought over new settlers, established the town of Halifax, and fortified Beaubassin, near the French fort.

A third danger point was the region about Lake George and Lake Champlain, for these lakes and the portages leading from them to the Hudson constituted the connecting link between the Richelieu and Hudson rivers. The French were in unchallenged possession of the Richelieu, and the English of the navigable portion of the Hudson. But the land lying around these lakes and between these two rivers was debatable ground. The French were the first to occupy it, for they had built Fort Crown Point on Lake Champlain.

The rival powers were also coming into hostile contact with each other in the region of the Great Lakes. These lakes afforded unusual opportunity for the fur trade which both nations were anxious to control. The French got the start of their competitors here and built three forts, Frontenac, Niagara, and Detroit. But the English had pushed westward up the Mohawk Valley and had established a thriving trading post at Oswego on Lake Ontario. The English at Oswego had lately been more successful than their competitors at Niagara in the race for furs, owing largely to the fact that the Iroquois had been brought under the authority of the British. The French realized this and were anxious to detach the Iroquois from the English alliance and bring them under their own influence. The conflict of interests between the rivals was thus sufficient to give rise to a quarrel on slight provocation. This danger was enhanced by the fact that the width of Lake Ontario was the only barrier between the English post of Oswego and the French fort of Frontenac.[2]

The friction at these points, however, did not generate enough heat to start an international conflagration, though it did contribute a good deal to the background of ill feeling that was behind the war. The quarrel that was the occasion of the war started in a quarter where French and English settlements were not in close proximity to each other. A dispute as to the ownership of the trans-Alleghany region in general and the Ohio Valley in particular was the immediate cause of the conflict known in America as the French and Indian War.

That vast expanse of territory stretching from the Alleghany Mountains on the east to the Mississippi River on the west was claimed by both England and France, but by the middle of the eighteenth century most of it had not been occupied by permanent settlements. The French colony of Louisiana on the lower reaches of the Mississippi numbered only a few thousand white inhabitants, and in the Illinois country there were only a few hundred settlers. Outside of these two centers of population the French had established scattered posts along the Mississippi and the Great Lakes, but the people living in them were nearly all fur

England and France set up rival claims to the trans-Alleghany region

[2] For an excellent brief account of the points of hostile contact between the English and French colonials, see GREENE, E. B., *Foundations of American Nationality*, pp. 367-368.

traders, officials, soldiers, or missionaries, and were thus not permanently located. Of this vast region north of Louisiana, the French had thus occupied little more than the western and northern fringes.

The English had not gone even so far as the French in supporting their claim by occupation. At this time no permanent settlements had been made by the English west of the Alleghanies, though there had been established in the trans-Alleghany country a number of trading posts which were centers of an active fur trade with the Indians both north and south of the Ohio River. As the French trader was also active throughout the trans-Alleghany region, he was now coming into close competition with his British rival. Each group of competitors felt that control of the disputed area by their own government would give them an advantage in forming alliances and making deals with the Indian tribes who procured the furs and skins. The competition between the English and French fur traders was, therefore, changing an academic difference of opinion into an active dispute as to the rightful ownership of the Great West.

The English and French plans of expansion also involved a more deep-seated conflict of interests. The Ohio River and the few short portages connecting it with Lake Erie is by far the shortest route from the lower Great Lakes to the middle Mississippi. The French were naturally anxious to control this river, as it would serve as a connecting link between their Canadian settlements and those in Louisiana and the Illinois country. This would enable the French in the north and in the south to "join hands behind the backs" of the English.[3] On the other hand, if the French were to gain possession of the Ohio Valley or even to retain their hold on the eastern border of the Mississippi River, the English colonies on the Atlantic seaboard could never hope to expand very far westward. Moreover, they would have as back-door neighbors colonials of a rival power, who could at any time easily stir up against them the hostility of the western Indians. Such a condition would not only restrict the limits of the English colonies, but would subject their frontiers to the constant dread of Indian attack.

During the short peace that followed the Treaty of Aix-la-Chapelle, both claimants adopted aggressive measures to strengthen their hold on the disputed territory. About the middle

[3] WOOD, W., *The Fight for Canada*, p. 35.

of the century prominent men in Virginia were given large grants of land in the Ohio region, on which they were to plant a colony. The French in Canada also began to assert their claims more aggressively. In 1749 Céloron de Bienville, acting under orders from the governor of Canada, passed from Lake Erie and Lake Chautauqua down the Allegheny and Ohio rivers to the mouth of the Miami and then by way of the Miami and Maumee rivers back to Lake Erie. He buried leaden plates at various points with inscriptions asserting France's right to the country. It was in this ceremonious way that the French reaffirmed their claim to the upper Ohio region. This expedition did not, of course, strengthen the hold of France on the disputed territory, but it showed that the French were determined to take possession of the land. It also revealed to the French authorities the necessity of more vigorous action if they were not to lose the territory, for everywhere Bienville met English traders.

Aggressive measures of the English and French

Three years later the Marquis Duquesne de Menneville became governor of Canada. He at once decided upon a vigorous policy of upholding French rights in the disputed area. Fort Presqu' Isle was built on the southern shore of Lake Erie, and two other forts were erected on French Creek, all within the present state of Pennsylvania. This was occupying territory claimed by the English, and one of these new forts, Venango (now Franklin, Pa.), was located on the site of a trading post that had been seized from the English. The latter felt that they could not allow these acts of aggression to go unchallenged.

In the summer of 1753 the British Secretary of State who had charge of colonial affairs sent instructions to the colonial governors directing them not to take the offensive, but to repel by force any attempt on the part of the French to infringe upon the undoubted territorial rights of the British. Lieutenant-Governor Robert Dinwiddie, of Virginia, was the first to act on these instructions. In the fall of this same year he sent a message to the commander of the new French forts protesting against the occupation of English lands. For this difficult mission he selected George Washington, a young Virginian just twenty-one years old.

Washington's mission

Washington was especially fitted for this mission. Born and reared in the patrician atmosphere of Tidewater Virginia, he knew the amenities of diplomatic courtesy. Besides, he had been a surveyor of western lands and had gained experience in frontier life which qualified him for dealing with the Indians. But despite the wisdom with which the negotiations were conducted, the effort to settle the dispute by mutual agreement failed. The French commanders politely but firmly asserted France's right to the territory that had been occupied.[4]

Beginning of hostilities

As diplomacy had not succeeded, warlike measures were now demanded. The key to the Ohio region was the forks of the Allegheny and Monongahela Rivers, and this point, therefore, had more strategic importance than any other place in the Western country. The English and the French both realized this and each side was anxious to take possession of this important place. Even before Washington had returned from his mission some Virginians had gone out there and had started to erect a fort. They had not proceeded far with their plans before a strong band of Canadians appeared and drove them away. The Canadians then followed up their success by completing the unfinished post and giving to it the name of Fort Duquesne.

In the meantime, Governor Dinwiddie had sent forward for the protection of the English fort a small force under the command of Colonel Fry and Washington, the advance guard being led by Washington. A few miles west of Great Meadows Run Washington met a small body of French skirmishers and fired on them. In this encounter the French commander and twenty of his soldiers were killed.[5] This was the first bloodshed of the French and Indian War, though hostilities had really begun when the French took the English post at Venango. Washington now fell back to Great Meadows and hastily constructed a rude stockade, to which he gave the name of Fort Necessity. He was soon attacked by a large body of troops from Fort Duquesne and was forced to capitulate. By the terms of the surrender his men were allowed to march out with the honors of war (July 4, 1754).

The Albany Congress

If the war was to be carried on successfully it was necessary to have the coöperation of all the colonies. Indian relations and military activities could not be successfully managed unless some

[4] For the *Journal* of Christopher Gist, Washington's companion, relating the events of this mission, see Massachusetts Historical Society, *Collections*, 3rd series, v, pp. 102-108. See also SPARKS, J., *The Writings of Washington*, ii, pp. 428-447 (Washington's *Journal* and other papers).

[5] For Washington's account of this skirmish, see FITZPATRICK, J. C., *The Diaries of George Washington*, pp. 87-88.

arrangement was made whereby unity of action could be achieved. Leaders in both England and America were, therefore, in favor of some sort of an intercolonial union. An effort in this direction was made by the congress which met at Albany in June, 1754. This body was composed of commissioners from Pennsylvania, Maryland, New York, and all the New England colonies, who had come together in obedience to instructions from the British government to negotiate an agreement with the Iroquois, or Six Nations.[6] They came to an understanding with the representatives of the Iroquois and also discussed the question of colonial federation. A plan of union proposed by Benjamin Franklin was accepted by the congress, but was unanimously rejected by the colonial legislatures. It provided for a federal council composed of delegates from all the colonies. This council was to have power to levy taxes, pass laws, raise armies, and manage Indian affairs.[7]

[6] By 1745 the Iroquois Confederacy had been greatly reduced in numbers and importance. Their numerous wars had taken a great toll of lives, and quite a considerable portion of them had been drawn off to the French mission, which had been formed especially for Iroquois converts. These Christianized Iroquois sometimes helped the French against their pagan relatives. The morale of the warriors had also been weakened by an over-indulgence in whisky and brandy. Moreover, dissensions had arisen in the councils of the Confederacy, as some of the leaders had been opposed to the policy of fighting in remote regions at the risk of their own safety at home.

When the French and Indian War broke out both sides tried to win the support of the Iroquois. According to the law of the Confederacy any tribe could take part in any war without the coöperation of the others, provided such participation did not involve the fighting against another tribe in the league. Now the Mohawks, being under the influence of Sir William Johnson, wanted an alliance with the English, while the other tribes were more inclined to the French. The council of the Confederacy, therefore, favored neutrality and decided to expel from the league any member that took sides with either belligerent. Despite this, however, quite a number of the Mohawks, under the leadership of their war-chief Hendrick, joined the forces of Johnson. (MacLeod, W. C., *The American Indian Frontier*, pp. 289-291.)

[7] For a good account of the Albany Congress, see Osgood, H. L., *The American Colonies in the Eighteenth Century*, iv, pp. 306-328. For contemporary accounts, see Smyth, A. H., ed., *The Life and Writings of Benjamin Franklin*, iii, pp. 197-206; and *New York*

The plan was objected to by the provincial assemblies on the ground that it restricted too much the rights of the colonies. A scheme of union suggested by the Board of Trade also failed to go into operation.[8] However, some measure of unity in military affairs was provided for in that it was suggested at the congress that a commander-in-chief of all the American forces be appointed, and this suggestion was later put into effect.

Strategic positions held by the French

The French had occupied and fortified certain strategic positions which guarded the approaches to Canada, menaced the security of the English settlements, and restricted their expansion. The most important of these posts were Fort Frontenac on Lake Ontario; Fort Duquesne, the key to the upper Ohio region; Fort Niagara, which controlled the portage between Lake Erie and Lake Ontario; Crown Point, which dominated the water route to Canada by way of Lake Champlain and the Richelieu River; Louisbourg, on Cape Breton Island, the strongest port on the Atlantic coast of North America; Fort Beauséjour which threatened England's authority over her French subjects in Acadia; and Quebec, which seemed all but impregnable, perched high on its inaccessible rock. The British could not hope to overcome the French until these places had been wrested from the latter.

British plans for 1755

The British plan for the year 1755 was to send troops from the homeland to coöperate with the colonials and attempt to drive the enemy from four of these strongholds. The British fleet under Admiral Boscawen was to prevent the French from landing any troops in Canada. Although England was stronger on the sea than France, this part of the plan was not a success. For all the French ships but two slipped by Admiral Boscawen and succeeded in landing a large force of regular soldiers in Canada. The French were, therefore, in a position to offer strong resistance to the British scheme.

British failures

In attempting to carry out their plan the British sent an expedition against Fort Niagara. The effort was unsuccessful and the expedition was abandoned. The French were not driven away from Crown Point, although the English won a battle at Lake George.

Colonial Documents, vi, pp. 853-909 (Franklin's Plan of Union is given in pp. 889-891).

[8] For this scheme of union, see *New York Colonial Documents*, vi, pp. 903-906; for several plans offered, including this plan and that of Franklin, see *American Historical Leaflets*, no. 14.

The British attained only one part of their objective, and that at a moral cost that outweighed any military advantage that might accrue from it. Fort Beauséjour was captured and the inhabitants of Acadia, about six thousand in number, were removed from their homes and scattered throughout the English colonies from Maine to Georgia. Such a policy of dealing with noncombatants necessarily entailed great suffering on its victims. Many of them died and others sank into pauperism in the new and unfavorable environment into which they had been thrust. Some, however, were able to work their way to the friendly French settlements in Louisiana, and quite a number returned to their own country at the end of the war. The English have been justly criticized for this act of inhumanity, and Longfellow's "Evangeline" has accentuated the condemnation of modern public opinion. But it ought to be remembered that the Acadians were disloyal to the British cause, and if their country had been invaded by a French army, they would in all probability have turned against their British masters. It was to guard against a contingency of this kind that the British military authorities resorted to transportation.[9]

The greatest of all the humiliations suffered by the British in this unlucky year of 1755 resulted from an attempt to capture Fort Duquesne. General Edward Braddock, who had been appointed commander-in-chief in America, arrived in February of this year with two regiments of British troops and a staff of officers. With a force of about twenty-five hundred men, composed of both regulars and provincials, Braddock proceeded slowly toward Fort Duquesne, cutting a road through the forest as he went. When a selected task force of nearly fourteen hundred men, which had been sent ahead of the main army, reached a point about eight miles from the fort, it was attacked by a smaller body of French and Indians. The assailants, fighting from behind trees and under cover of thickets, soon drove the panic-stricken British soldiers, confused and blinded by the smoke of battle, into headlong flight.[10] General Braddock was mortally wounded,

[9] For a good account of the expulsion of the Acadians, see DOUGHTY, A. G., *The Acadian Exiles*, chs. 8-10.

[10] The responsibility for this defeat has been and still is under dispute by the authorities. According to Dr. Stanley Pargellis, General Braddock was mainly responsible for this disaster. The British general,

and his successor did not make any further advance toward Fort
Duquesne.

After this defeat the Indians were more active than ever in
their support of their French allies. The frontier of Virginia,

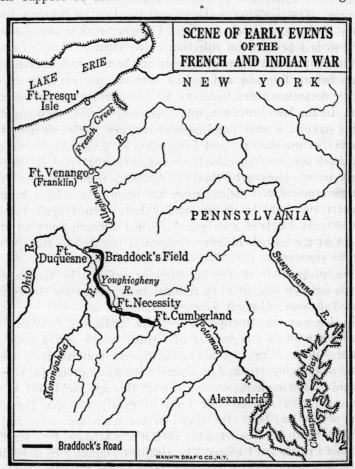

SCENE OF EARLY EVENTS
OF THE
FRENCH AND INDIAN WAR

LAKE ERIE

Ft. Presqu'
Isle

French Creek

R.

NEW YORK

Ft. Venango
(Franklin)

Allegheny

R.

PENNSYLVANIA

Ohio R.

Ft.
Duquesne

× Braddock's Field

Youghiogheny
R.

Ft. Necessity

Ft. Cumberland

Monongahela R.

Potomac R.

Susquehanna R.

Chesapeake Bay

Alexandria

——— Braddock's Road

MANH'N DRAF'G CO., N.Y.

Maryland, and Pennsylvania for four hundred miles was left
almost at the mercy of the savages. The defense of this long

he declares, had at this fateful time relaxed his usual caution and for
the last day had proceeded blindly without finding out whether the way
was clear. On the other hand, Professor L. H. Gipson places most of
the blame on two of Braddock's subordinates. References for these
discussions are given on p. 405, Selected Readings, no. 4.

line was intrusted to Washington, who had only about fifteen hundred men. Washington performed the duties thrust upon him with remarkable wisdom and courage. The young officer and his small force could not, of course, successfully guard so long a frontier. The outlying settlements, therefore, suffered greatly from Indian massacres, and the English frontier was pushed back to and beyond the Alleghany Mountains.

The British and French colonials had been fighting about two years before England and France declared war on each other. In the meantime there had been a diplomatic revolution in Europe. In the last European war England and Austria had been allied against France and Prussia. But the queen of Austria, Maria Theresa, had continued to brood over the loss of Silesia, the Austrian province that Frederick the Great of Prussia had lately seized. Hoping to regain this lost province, she persuaded the government of France to suspend its historic enmity toward Austria and join this power and Russia in an alliance against Prussia. As England was now fighting France in America, and as the king of England, who was also ruler of Hanover, feared for his Hanoverian possessions, there was nothing left for Britain to do but to form an alliance with her former enemy, Prussia. After this new alignment of powers was made England declared war on France (May 18, 1756). *The diplomatic revolution*

In this way the American quarrel developed into a world war. Fighting went on not only on the continent of North America but also in the West Indies, in Europe, and in India. It had thus become a mighty struggle to decide whether England or France should be the leading power in the world. The American phase of the contest is known as the French and Indian War; the European conflict as the Seven Years' War. *The American war widens into a world war*

The French followed up their victories of 1755 by other marked successes in the next two years. They owed these later triumphs to the able leadership of their new general, the Marquis of Montcalm, who was sent over early in 1756 to take command of the Canadian forces. Montcalm was not only a general of great ability, but was also a man of piety, learning, refinement, and high character. He had an abundance of that hopeful optimism and exuberant enthusiasm that is so characteristic of the French temperament. *Montcalm in command of the French forces*

When Montcalm viewed the military situation in America he found that the English, despite their reverses of the previous

Fort Os-
wego cap-
tured by
the
French

year, were still in a position to make a vigorous offensive against the French posts. They held Fort Oswego, on the south shore of Lake Ontario, which could easily serve as a base for an attack on the French Fort Frontenac on the opposite side of the lake. If the latter post were taken by the English, the French line of communication with the west would be cut, and a road would be open to the enemy into the heart of Canada. With the hope of eliminating this dangerous possibility, Montcalm decided to attack Fort Oswego. After some time spent in organizing and disciplining his troops, he succeeded in capturing and destroying it, taking valuable military stores and sixteen hundred prisoners. This victory gave the French undisputed control of the entire lake region and closed to the enemy one of the avenues to Canada. It also made a very favorable impression on the Indians and caused great numbers of them to flock to the French standard.

Fort
William
Henry
captured
and de-
stroyed

A year later Montcalm won another important victory when he captured and destroyed Fort William Henry (August, 1757).[11] As a result of these two victories and the failure of the British in their effort to capture Louisbourg, the French were still in possession of all three of the approaches to Canada.

Pitt in-
trusted
with the
manage-
ment of
the war

The British failures of the first two years were due largely to the weak and inefficient policy of the Ministry in the management of the war. Birth, seniority, and political pull were given too much consideration in making naval and military appointments, with the result that many incompetent officers were holding responsible positions of leadership in the army and navy. Some of the officers sent to America were also untactful and were unable to get along with the colonial authorities. Often, too, they an-

[11] As this fort was located at the lower end of Lake George, it was thus at the starting-point of the route to Canada by way of Lakes George and Champlain and the Richelieu River. Despite its strategic importance the post was now in a weakened condition, owing to the fact that most of the troops had been taken away to join Lord Loudoun, the English commander-in-chief, who had led an unsuccessful expedition against Louisbourg. When Montcalm appeared with a superior force and laid siege to the fort there was nothing for its commander to do but surrender, on the promise that the garrison would be conducted safely to the English Fort Edward, sixteen miles away. Montcalm could not control his Indian allies, despite strong efforts to do so, and a number of the captives were killed by the savages and about two hundred more were carried off as prisoners.

tagonized their American subordinates by their supercilious bearing toward them and thus failed to secure their hearty coöperation.

The French victories and the issues at stake on the Continent and in India awakened in England a realization of the danger of such a policy and of the need for a more efficient management of the war. In this emergency public sentiment turned to William Pitt, the "Great Commoner," as the man best qualified to lead his country to victory and urgently demanded that he be put in command of the war. The clamor was so insistent that the king could not disregard it, and so Pitt was called to the Ministry in the fall of 1756. Next year he was given entire control of the war and was virtually dictator of the British empire.

Pitt proved quite equal to the great responsibilities and opportunities of his high position. Efficiency was his watchword, and it was the main consideration in assigning responsibility in the army and navy. Important places in the conduct of the war were now given to young men of ability rather than to old men of social standing and political influence. Being a man of exceptional self-reliance, courage, energy, initiative, and enthusiasm, he was able to inspire his subordinates with his own faith, and under his wise guidance the fortunes of war everywhere took a decided turn in favor of the English. Up to this time the plan had been to preserve the British possessions in America against French encroachments; his plan was to expel the French from the continent. In carrying out this great aim he was eminently successful in securing the coöperation of the colonial military and civil officials. *His plan and policy*

It was not until the year 1758 that the English began to reap the fruits of Pitt's new policy. In this year Louisbourg was captured and destroyed and Fort Frontenac was taken. This last victory deprived the French of their control over Lake Ontario and cut their communications with their western posts. Near the end of the year Fort Duquesne fell into the hands of the British. These victories were, however, offset by one severe defeat, the failure of an attack on Fort Ticonderoga made by General Abercrombie. *English victories in 1758*

Pitt had a very able ally in Frederick the Great, king of Prussia. His policy was to assist Frederick by subsidies, and in this way he could, as he expressed it, win America in Germany. Frederick's activity engaged the attention of the French to a considerable extent and left Pitt free to center his forces on America, *Pitt gives financial aid to Frederick the Great*

India, and naval supremacy. The only troops sent to aid Frederick were from Hanover.

English victories in 1759

The year 1759 opened with every prospect that the English would soon bring the war to a victorious close, the main objective in the British plan in America being the capture of Quebec. For this important task Pitt chose General James Wolfe to lead the land forces and Admiral Saunders to have charge of the fleet which was to transport the troops. In making these selections Pitt showed his usual ability to judge men, as each was eminently suited for his place, and they were able to coöperate effectively.

General Wolfe

Wolfe was only thirty-two years old, but already he had to his credit a fine record of achievement. He had won distinction in Europe and had been second in command when Louisbourg was captured. With his military ability were combined certain fine traits of character which would have won for him an important place of usefulness in civil life.[12] He was intensely patriotic and always lived up to a rigid standard of loyalty to his country and its cause. His health was poor, but he never allowed his diseased body to handicap his intrepid spirit. It is more than likely, however, that the state of his health was responsible for a strain of seriousness in his temperament that sometimes bordered on melancholy.

Niagara, Ticonderoga, and Crown Point captured by the English

The British plan for 1759 also included the capture of the frontier posts that were still held by the French. These were Forts Niagara, Crown Point, and Ticonderoga. Fort Niagara was defended by a small force and was easily taken by a strong detachment of British troops under the command of General Prideaux and Sir William Johnson. General Jeffery Amherst, the commander-in-chief of the British armies in America, was ordered to take Ticonderoga and Crown Point and proceed down the Richelieu and St. Lawrence rivers and join Wolfe before Quebec. He had no difficulty in capturing the forts, but was detained so long by a French force at Isle aux Noix that he was unable to go to Wolfe's assistance. Wolfe, however, went ahead

[12] Wolfe was interested in literature, and on the night before his great victory, while floating down the St. Lawrence with his men, he entertained his fellow-officers by reciting Gray's "Elegy in a Country Churchyard," probably noting especially the line which reads "The paths of glory lead but to the grave." At the end of his recital he said, "Gentlemen, I would rather have written those lines than take Quebec."

with his plans without waiting for the aid of Amherst, being ably supported by the British fleet under the command of Admiral Saunders. The English navy was by this time very much superior to that of the French, and was able to control the St. Lawrence.

By the end of June Wolfe's army, transported by Admiral Saunders, appeared before Quebec and proceeded to land. The city was situated on a high bluff and could be reached on the river side only by precipitous cliffs or narrow ravines guarded by French troops. It was, therefore, almost impossible to take the place by assault. It was defended by Montcalm, who had an army larger than Wolfe's, though not nearly so well disciplined. The greatest of the French generals was now pitted against the ablest of the English commanders. Montcalm, however, did not have a free hand, as his authority was hampered by that of the governor of the province. But he had only to act on the defensive within his strong fortifications and wait for winter, for then the English would have to raise the siege.

The capture of Quebec

For more than two months Wolfe tried to entice his opponent into a battle, but Montcalm was disposed to play safe and declined the challenge. During this time, however, Wolfe bombarded the town and destroyed a number of buildings and silenced the French batteries. This destruction of private property did not aid at all in the capture of the city, but the silencing of the batteries enabled him to take his ships up the river. As the autumn season was now approaching, Wolfe saw that a bold stroke would have to be made or winter would soon compel him to abandon the attack. On September 13, he landed his forces on the northern shore about two miles above the city and began to ascend the all but inaccessible cliffs by way of an insufficiently guarded ravine. The effort was successful and Montcalm was surprised to learn that his opponent was on the Plains of Abraham, just west of Quebec.

Wolfe was now on the side of the town which was most weakly fortified and was in a position to cut off Montcalm's supplies, which came into Quebec from up the river. It was, therefore, necessary for the French to attempt to drive him away from this position. Montcalm made the mistake of attacking him too hurriedly with the forces under his immediate command, without waiting to be reinforced by other contingents of troops that were only a few miles away. His reason for being so precipitate was that he feared a delay would give Wolfe time to bring up more troops; but in this he was mistaken, as Wolfe already had with him his entire fighting force. The battle had lasted scarcely fifteen minutes when the French had begun to retreat. It was a decisive victory for the British, and Quebec fell into their hands four days later.

The joy of the English over their triumph was tempered by sorrow over the death of their beloved general, who was shot down after the victory had virtually been won. Montcalm, too, was mortally wounded and died next morning. He was thus spared the humiliation of witnessing the surrender of Quebec.

The end of the war

Next year (1760) Montreal was captured by Amherst and all of Canada was surrendered to the British. Pitt was in favor of continuing a vigorous prosecution of the war until England could dictate the terms of peace. Up until this time he had been able to have his own way in the management of affairs, but now his opponents were able to muster enough strength to thwart his policy. The opposition was strengthened by the death of George II (1760) and the accession of George III, for the latter was in favor of peace. Pitt now resigned (1761), as he was unwilling to remain in office unless he could control the policy of the government.

The war continued, however, and in 1762 Spain entered the conflict as an ally of France. Spain had come in too late to save the day for her ally, but in time to bring upon herself some humiliating losses at the hands of the British. Cuba and the Philippines were both wrested from Spain by the English (1762), and in this same year the West Indian island of Martinique was taken from the French. The British had won the war and all the belligerents were ready for peace.

The Treaty of Paris

The final treaty of peace was signed at Paris on February 10, 1763. By the terms of this treaty France surrendered to England all but two of her colonies in India. England retained some of the French West Indian islands that she had captured in the war and restored the others to France. Canada and all the French possessions east of the Mississippi, except the island of Orleans, were ceded to England.[13] Some of the English statesmen of the time were inclined to value the French West Indian colonies more highly than Canada and were in favor of retaining them at the

[13] For the text of that part of the Treaty of Paris which relates to North America, see KINGSFORD, W., *The History of Canada*, iv, pp. 505-507.

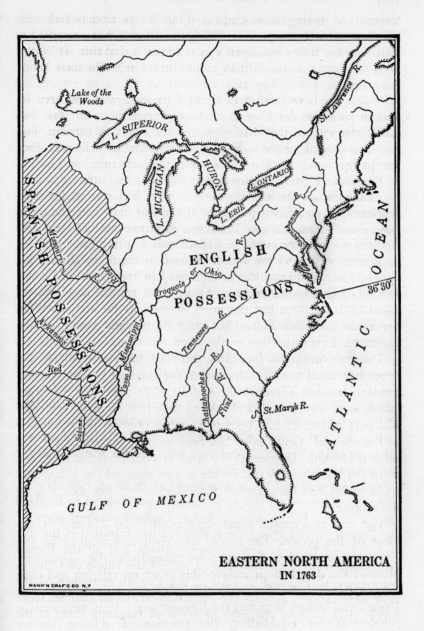

expense of giving back Canada. Franklin pointed out the unwisdom of this policy. The Philippine Islands were restored to
Spain by the treaty because it was not known that they had fallen
into the hands of the British at the time the preliminary treaty
was signed. Cuba was also returned to Spain in return for
Florida, which was ceded to Great Britain. Spain was very reluctant to surrender Florida, and as compensation for this loss
Louisiana west of the Mississippi and the island of Orleans were
ceded to Spain by France. France had thus lost all her possessions
on the mainland, but she was allowed to retain two small islands
in the Gulf of St. Lawrence to be used as fishing stations.

Results
of the
wars

At the end of the last intercolonial war England was the leading colonial and naval power in the world. Her supremacy in
both North America and India was now assured. The colonies
had, by the victory over the French and Pontiac, been relieved
to a great extent of the Indian menace in the Ohio Valley and
the chief barrier to westward expansion had been removed. "With
the fall of Quebec began the history of the United States" (Parkman). During these last two wars, as well as the first two, the
fur trade had declined and the risks of foreign commerce had
increased. This restriction on the intercourse between the colonies
and Europe worked a special hardship on Maryland, which was
dependent upon the French market for the sale of her cheaper
grade of tobacco. The wars also stimulated privateering and speculation, especially in land and commerce. From nearly every colonial port privateers had been sent out to prey on the commerce
of the enemy.[14] Great gains had been won by war contracts and
illicit trade with the enemy. The large amount of funds sent over
from the homeland to sustain the troops changed the balance of
trade which had been against the colonies into one that was in
their favor.

The war also caused some changes in social life and in the
ideas of the people. The spread of deism and atheism by the
English troops, many of whom were imbued with the rationalistic
ideas of the day, had an unfavorable effect on religion and contributed toward the decline in the influence of the clergy. The
French and Indian War and the Revolutionary War were mainly
responsible for establishing the practice of dueling among
Americans. Before the French and Indian War very few duels

[14] ADAMS, J. T., *Provincial Society*, pp. 293-296.

had ever been fought in the English continental colonies. "Contact with British officers in that war had shown young American officers that the duel was the hallmark of military sophistication."[15] American military officers were confirmed in this belief by their contact with French officers during the Revolutionary War, and the practice became so deeply rooted that it persisted in some sections of the country almost to the Civil War.

SELECTED READINGS

1. Washington's Mission to the French Forts.—Fitzpatrick, J. C., *The Diaries of George Washington*, i, pp. *43-67 (account by Washington).
2. The Albany Congress.—Osgood, H. L., *American Colonies in the Eighteenth Century*, iv, pp. *306-328. (For the plan of union adopted by the Congress, see *American History Leaflets*, no. 14.)
3. The Expulsion of the Acadians.—Wrong, G. M., *The Conquest of New France*, *ch. 7, and *The Rise and Fall of New France*, ii, pp. *761-783. (For a fuller account, with quotations from and specific references to the sources, see Doughty, A. G., *The Acadian Exiles*, chs. 8-10.)
4. Braddock's Defeat.—*Pennsylvania Magazine of History*, xx, pp. 409-411; xxiii, pp. 310-328; xxvii, pp. 499-501; *Colonial Records of North Carolina*, v, pp. 429-436 (contemporary accounts). For recent discussions presenting opposite views as to Braddock's responsibility for his defeat, see an article by Stanley Pargellis in the *American Historical Review*, xli, pp. 253-269; and ch. 4 of L. H. Gipson's *The Great War for the Empire: The Years of Defeat* (1946).
5. The Battle of Quebec.—Wood, W., *The Passing of New France*, *chs. 6 and 7.
6. The Management of the War under Pitt.—Wrong, *Rise and Fall of New France*, ii, pp. *800-813.
7. The Requisition System during the War.—Beer, G. L., *British Colonial Policy, 1754-1765*, *ch. 4.
8. Colonial Trade with the Enemy.—Beer, *op. cit.*, *ch. 6.
9. Relation of the Intercolonial Wars to the Fishing Industry in New England.—McFarland, Raymond, *A History of New England Fisheries*, pp. *72-101.

[15] JAMESON, J. F., *The American Revolution Considered as a Social Movement*, p. 122.

Part II:

ECONOMIC AND SOCIAL LIFE

CHAPTER XX

POPULATION AND LABOR

By 1760 settlements had spread until they extended from the
middle coast of Maine to southern Georgia and westward into
the Appalachian valleys. The total population of the thirteen
colonies at this time was a little more than a million and a half.
Of this number about one-fourth were Negro slaves, who were
found in all the colonies, but mainly in the South. In 1640 the
white population was only about 25,000. It had increased to
80,000 by 1660, to a half million by 1721, and to a million by
1743. The population had thus been doubling itself about every
twenty-three years. This growth in numbers was due partly to
immigration but mainly to natural increase.[1]

The majority of the people even at the end of the colonial
period were of English descent, though a large number of them
had sprung from foreign stocks. The Dutch were numerous in
New York, and there were a few Swedes along the Delaware
River. The other non-English elements included Welshmen, a
few Irishmen, Jews, French Huguenots, Germans, Scotchmen,
and Scotch-Irishmen. But the foreigners had generally accepted
British ideals as to law and government, and many of them had
taken up the English language. Bancroft says that in 1775 only
one-fifth of the American people had for their mother tongue
some language other than English. In New England, where the
foreign infusion was the slightest, it is estimated that at the end
of the colonial period ninety-eight per cent of the people were of
pure English descent.

Of the immigrants that came from Europe outside of England
proper, the Germans and the Scotch-Irish played the most important part in colonial history. Another valuable addition to the

*Growth of popula-
tion in the
colonies*

*Foreign
elements
in the
population*

---

[1] For the growth of population in each of the thirteen colonies to
1790, see DEXTER, F. B., "Estimates of Population in the American
Colonies," in American Antiquarian Society *Proceedings*, v, pp. 22-
50; also *A Century of Population Growth, 1790-1900*, pp. 3-11,
especially tables on p. 9.

population of the colonies was made by the incoming of the Huguenots, or French Protestants. They began to leave France in large numbers in the latter part of the seventeenth century because of the violent persecutions to which they were subjected by their king, Louis XIV. In twenty years about a million of them had left France. France could ill afford to lose them, as they constituted the very cream of her population. The Huguenots who left their native land were about seven per cent of the entire population, but in this number were included "a far higher proportion of skilled craftsmen, prosperous merchants, professional men, and scholars." Many of the colonies received a share of these choice emigrants, but South Carolina was more fortunate than any of the others. A good many also settled in Rhode Island, New York, and Virginia. Everywhere they were received with a hearty welcome. Their religion made no difficulty, as they got along well with both the Anglicans of the South and the Puritans of the North.

The Jews   The Jews had begun to come to continental North America by about the middle of the seventeenth century. At this time some Jewish emigrants landed at New Amsterdam, having come from Brazil, where they had not been receiving fair treatment. Peter Stuyvesant, the Dutch governor, was narrow and intolerant and soon let the Jews know that they were not wanted in his province. He had begun to take measures for their banishment when he was directed by the Dutch West India Company to encourage them to settle in New Amsterdam.[2] Others soon came to New Amsterdam from Brazil, Holland, Germany, and Poland. They were granted freedom and protection, not only by the Dutch, but also by their English successors, and they grew in numbers and prosperity. By 1682 they had organized a synagogue and were holding their services in a rented building.[3]

Newport also soon became an important center for the Jews, to which place they were attracted by the freedom allowed them in Rhode Island. Other cities soon numbered Jews in their population, such as Charleston and Philadelphia, but New York was then, as now, the chief center of the Jewish population. In 1733

[2] DALY, C. P., *The Settlement of the Jews in North America*, pp. 8-10.
For the text of the order of the Company (1655) directing the governor not to molest them, see p. 9, note.
[3] *Ibid.*, pp. 64-70.

a party of Jews came to Georgia and were welcomed by Oglethorpe. But while he was away from Georgia persecution was
aroused and they gradually went to Charleston. The Jews lived
mainly in the cities, though some of them settled on the frontier
of Pennsylvania. Many of them had become prosperous by the
time of the Revolution. Most of them were loyal to the patriot
cause.

There was a great demand for labor everywhere during the
colonial period. It required an immense amount of work to clear
the forests, build bridges and roads, and erect barns and dwelling-
houses. The burden on labor was increased by the lack of machinery and labor-saving devices, and the supply was kept down
because workers were constantly deserting the ranks of the employees and joining those of the employers. Land was so cheap
that an efficient hired man could soon save enough money to set
up farming for himself. Even the manufacturing industries required little capital, and any enterprising laborer could in a few
years get together enough money to start as an independent
artisan. Besides, labor was more remunerative in America than
it was in any of the European countries. For over here it was
engaged in exploiting the inexhaustible natural resources of a
virgin continent and there was no limit to its productivity. As a
result of these conditions, the supply of labor tended constantly
to lag behind the demand, and so there was always a scarcity of
free labor.

Scarcity of free labor in the colonies

There were some free laborers in all the colonies, though the
number was comparatively small on the big plantations in the
South after slavery had become well established. In the North
and in the frontier settlements of the South most of the work
was done by the farmer or artisan. On the small farms in all
sections every member of the family was a worker. The wives
and daughters not only performed the household duties, including
spinning and weaving, but at times lent a hand at the outdoor
tasks. Children were put to work at an early age, and there were
no laws or public sentiment against child labor. Sometimes the
farm owner was assisted by hired help, in which case he worked
alongside his employees. Neighbors coöperated with one another
in putting up buildings, in harvesting the crops, and in performing other tasks that required the joint labor of several hands. A
house-raising, log-rolling, or "corn-shucking" was usually a pleasant social occasion as well as an important business event. On

Members of the family the chief laborers on small farms

these occasions liquors were generously dispensed, and there was an abundance of food prepared by the hostess, assisted by other women of the neighborhood. The interval of rest at the noon hour afforded an opportunity for conversation regarding the prospect for crops and an interchange of views on topics of local interest. By bringing the people together in a pleasant and helpful relation the working-bees served to relieve the monotony of country life and keep alive the spirit of coöperation.

Wages high in colonial times

The scarcity of labor, together with its marked productivity, caused wages to be much higher in the New World than they were in the Old. Besides, wage-earners did not suffer from unemployment in America as they did in England. There was thus no labor problem in colonial times. Labor was entirely unorganized and, owing to the property qualification for voting, exerted little, if any, influence on the local and provincial government, which was almost completely dominated by the employer, or capitalist, class. As was to be expected under such conditions, laws were often enacted that were unfavorable to the workingmen, and efforts were sometimes made to keep down wages by legislative enactment. The General Court of Massachusetts several times during the seventeenth century passed laws fixing a maximum wage scale, and other colonial legislatures attempted the same policy. But these efforts at regulation were not in harmony with economic conditions, and so the provincial statutes were unable to override the stronger law of supply and demand. Consequently, these unwise measures were disregarded by both employers and employees.

No ill feeling between labor and capital

There seems to have been no ill feeling to speak of between free labor and capital at any time during the colonial period. Employers and employees were not separated by any sharp dividing line as they are today. Usually the capitalist was also a laborer and the employee hoped soon to become an employer. Besides, there was no social barrier separating the hired laborer from the small farmer or skilled artisan who employed him and worked by his side. Especially was this true in New England, where the daughters of prominent men sometimes served as maids in the families of their neighbors.

WHITE SERVITUDE

White servitude

The scarcity of free labor led the colonials at an early period to resort to bond labor. The unfree workers were of two classes—

servants and slaves. There were in all the colonies white persons who had been bound to service to a master for a term of years. These were known as indented, or indentured, servants. They were divided into two classes, voluntary and involuntary. Voluntary indented servants were those who came to America of their own accord and bound themselves out to serve an employer for a specified time in payment for transportation and maintenance. This contract between the servant and master was an indenture, hence the word "indented," or "indentured," as applied to servants. Strictly speaking, the term indented servant should apply only to those persons who had bound themselves voluntarily to service, but it is generally used for all classes of bond-servants. The contract was usually made in England with the representative of the colonial employer or with a shipmaster, who transferred his agreement to someone in the colonies. Voluntary servants were usually men and women who wanted to come to America and were too poor to pay for their transportation. Most of the servants of this class came from the British Isles, but there were some from the continental countries. The most numerous of the latter class were the Germans, who settled in Pennsylvania. Classes of white servants: Voluntary servants

Apprentices may also properly be classed with the voluntary indented servants. Many apprentices were boys who were bound to a master for a term of years in order to learn a trade. Others were poor children bound out to service because they had no near relatives who were able or willing to provide for their support. In Pennsylvania and the southern colonies, the difference between an apprentice of this class and an indented servant was only one of age. Apprentices

Involuntary servants were insolvent debtors, paupers, or criminals who were sentenced to long terms of service in America in lieu of more serious punishments to be inflicted if they remained in the homeland. Another class consisted of those who had been kidnapped in England and carried to the colonies and sold.[4] Children were the chief victims, being lured into captivity by sweetmeats and other like inducements. This practice of stealing persons and selling them into service was known as "spiriting." During the reign of Charles II the practice became widely prevalent, especially in Bristol and London. At one time the ladies of Involuntary servants: "Spiriting"

[4] STEDMAN, E. C., and HUTCHINSON, E. M., *A Library of American Literature*, ii, pp. 285-286.

the court and the mayor of Bristol were suspected of sharing in the profits from this business.[5]

Criminals as servants

In the lists of criminals were those who had committed political offenses, such as participation in the Monmouth Rebellion or in Tory plots in Ireland or Scotland. During the seventeenth and eighteenth centuries, the penal code of Great Britain defined as crimes offenses that would not be so considered at the present day. The criminals sent over were, therefore, not altogether a bad lot. But still, people who come under the censures of the criminal law are, as a rule, not a desirable class in any age. We are, therefore, not surprised to find that some of the colonies were strongly opposed to the importation of these convicts. Virginia and Pennsylvania tried to protect themselves by law from the inflow of British criminals, and also urged the English government to stop sending persons of that class to America. The acts passed in Virginia prohibiting or restricting the traffic in criminal servants were all vetoed by the home government. The practice was discontinued, however, for a while, but was revived in the early part of the eighteenth century and continued throughout the remainder of the colonial period.

Length of term of service

The length of the term of service varied in the different colonies. The usual term for a voluntary servant was from four to five years in Virginia; in New England it was longer. The convicts had to serve from seven to fourteen years, depending upon the nature of the offense committed by them.

Treatment of servants

The treatment of servants was on the whole as just as could be expected, considering the spirit of the times and the circumstances under which these unfortunate persons were placed. Beverley, the historian of Virginia, writing in the first part of the eighteenth century, says that servants in the Old Dominion were accorded as good treatment as were free laborers in England at the same time.[6] As a rule, servants were more restricted in their privileges in the later colonial period than they were in the earlier, and this change for the worse was due to the influence of slavery. After slavery was firmly established, the relation between the planter and his white servant tended to become more and more like that existing between the master and his black slave.

[5] One authority says that "in 1670 as many as ten thousand persons were spirited from England in one year" (CHANNING, E., *History of United States*, ii, p. 369).

[6] BEVERLEY, R., *History of Virginia*, p. 220.

The laws were made by and for the masters and, of course, their interests rather than those of the servants were primarily considered. But employers were largely dependent upon white servants for labor, especially before slaves had become numerous. A policy of justice would attract desirable voluntary servants and would thereby increase the number of laborers. Cruelty and injustice, on the other hand, would repel desirable workers and thereby decrease or lower the standard of the labor supply. In this way economic policy joined with humanitarian considerations in protecting the servants against inhuman treatment.

The servants had many privileges of citizenship enjoyed by freemen, and in Plymouth during the first sixteen years of its history they had the right to vote. If they were ill cared for or otherwise mistreated by their masters, they had access to the justices of the peace and local courts for redress.[7] Masters had to provide their servants with maintenance, medical attention, and proper religious training. The servant could own property, could sue and be sued, and could give evidence in court if he were not a convict. At the end of his term of service he usually received from his master a certain amount of corn and clothing or an equal value in money as freedom dues. In some of the colonies he was entitled to a claim of fifty acres of land from the public domain.[8] On the other hand, he had to submit to many of the restraints of the unfree. He could not marry without his master's consent. For an offense ordinarily punishable by a fine if committed by a freeman, he received a whipping, publicly administered by the local authorities, or had his term of service extended. His master could also inflict reasonable corporal punishment on him in the exercise of his ordinary powers of discipline.

Other provisions of the penal codes did not usually show much greater severity toward servants than toward freemen, except those that applied to runaways. The punishment for absconding was very severe. The servant who ran away from his master had his term lengthened by double the time he was away and sometimes more. All expenses, like sheriff fees, jail fees, and others of like character occasioned by his desertion were charged up to the fugitive and had to be discharged by an extension of his time. Expenses incurred by the authorities in apprehending a

Severe punishment of runaways

[7] HURD, J. C., *The Law of Freedom and Bondage in the United States*, i, p. 255.

[8] BEVERLEY, R., *History of Virginia*, pp. 220-222.

runaway were also charged to him, unless assumed by his master, and had to be paid by service to the public after all his obligations to his master had been met. In extreme cases service in irons had to be performed to the public for terms ranging from two to seven years. For a long time the law in Virginia for runaway servants was the same as that for runaway slaves (see pp. 423-424).[9]

Freedmen quickly absorbed by other classes

At the end of his term, the freedman had all the rights of a freeman. He was quickly absorbed by the other classes and lost his identity, and so there was no separate class that was recruited from the white servants. Apparently there was no stigma attaching to the status of servitude, even in the South, as is indicated by the frequent intermarriage of servants and free persons. The servants, like the slaves among the ancient Greeks, were frequently men of intelligence and education, and many of the teachers of the "old field" schools were taken from their class. The economic opportunity for the freedman was also good. If energetic and reliable, he could easily secure a position as a hired workman or could rent or buy a small tract of land in the old settlements or take up one on the frontier. While most of the indented servants in the South at the expiration of their terms became overseers, hired laborers, tenants, or small farmers, a few ultimately won their way to patrician rank. In Virginia in 1654 several members of the House of Burgesses were former servants. A contemporary said in 1662 that the burgesses who represent the people "are usually such as were sent over servants thither."[10]

Evils of white servitude

One bad effect of white servitude was that it hardened the feelings of the masters toward their unfree laborers and paved the way for slavery. The system also increased crime and pauperism, for the convicts were as a rule an undesirable lot of immigrants from which the criminal and pauper classes were largely recruited. The women servants of this class were frequently im-

[9] HENING, W. W., *Statutes at Large* (Va.), i, pp. 254-255; ii, pp. 116-117, 266, 277-279; iii, p. 458; BALLAGH, J. C., *White Servitude in the Colony of Virginia*, p. 57. For a valuable summary of the laws relating to bond service in all the colonies, see HURD, *op. cit.*, i, pp. 228-311.

[10] NEILL, E. D., *Virginia Carolorum*, pp. 279, 290.

While the statement quoted above is doubtless an exaggeration, it was not uncommon for ex-servants to be elected to membership in the Virginia House of Burgesses.

moral, and this tended to lower the standard of morality of masters and other freemen.

Among the good results of the system may be mentioned the following:

(1) It acted as an immigration agency to bring settlers to the colonies.

(2) White servitude met the demand for skilled and unskilled labor before slavery was well established and furnished a large proportion of the skilled labor after that time. It had an advantage over free labor in that it gave employers the assurance of a constant supply of workers for long periods of time. This enabled them to make their plans for several years ahead without fearing a labor shortage.

(3) It recruited the yeomanry and thereby increased the numbers and importance of the middle class. By increasing the number of small farmers, especially in the frontier districts, it strengthened the influences favorable to democracy and helped to check the tendency in the South toward the centralization of land into large estates.

(4) It enabled the mother country to relieve itself in a humane way of a class of people who were socially undesirable. By draining off the surplus of labor it helped to solve the problem of unemployment in Europe and thereby bettered the condition of those workers who remained at home.

(5) It saved many criminals from severe and sometimes unjust punishments. It gave worthy poor people the opportunity to enter upon successful careers in the New World, which would have been denied them in Europe.[11]

SLAVERY

In colonial America slavery was more important as a system of labor than white servitude, especially in the Southern colonies. There were two kinds of slaves—Indians and Negroes. The main source of supply for the former class was the numerous wars carried on between the natives and the English settlers. From a very early period it was the practice to sell into slavery the women and children captured in Indian wars. But the Indian did not make a good slave. He was immoral and unruly and inclined to intrigue with his free kinsmen and incite them to revolt. Conse-

[11] BALLAGH, J. C., *White Servitude in the Colony of Virginia*, pp. 89-95.

quently, Indian slavery was not successful and did not become a permanent institution.

The slave trade

Negro slavery, on the other hand, was well adapted to conditions in the New World and so took deep root in the economic life of colonial America. Like most other colonial institutions, this labor system was an importation from Europe. For before America was settled or even discovered, Negro slavery had been introduced in Europe and there had begun that traffic in human beings that is responsible for the transplanting of slavery from the Old to the New World. The African slave trade was started by the Portuguese, under the leadership of Prince Henry, about the middle of the fifteenth century (1442). Early in the sixteenth century (1517), Spanish merchants began to engage in the traffic, and about the middle of the same century Sir John Hawkins, the great English seaman, entered upon his remarkable career as a slave-dealer. It was not long after this before the merchants of all the great commercial nations were engaging in this profitable trade. Great Britain took the lead in this nefarious business and held on to it during the entire colonial period. The English slave trade was greatly encouraged by that provision in the Treaty of Utrecht (1713) which gave to British seamen the exclusive right to furnish the Spanish-American colonies with slaves.

The "triangular trade"

For some years the English slave trade was monopolized by great companies, the most important being the Royal African Company. But in 1697 the right to share in this trade was allowed to all British subjects, and in the eighteenth century a good many American ships, mostly from New England, were engaged in the slave trade. The New England merchants linked up the slave trade with the manufacture and sale of rum in such a way as to make the combined business quite profitable. Rum was shipped from New England to the west coast of Africa and bartered for Negroes. These were taken to the West Indies and exchanged for molasses and other commodities. From the molasses brought back to the home ports was manufactured the rum that was used as cargo on the first part of the three-sided voyage, which was known as the "three-cornered" or "triangular" trade. The trip from Africa to the West Indies was called the "Middle Passage," as it was the second or middle lap of the triangular voyage.

Some of the Negroes were sold in England, Spain, and Portugal, but most of them were taken to the colonies of the various European powers. The Spanish-American colonies were at first the most important market for them, but later there grew up a great demand for slaves in the British West Indies and still later in the British continental colonies. The Negroes were procured by the slave-dealers on the west coast of Africa. They were kidnapped by the slave merchants themselves or else bought from native chiefs who were engaged in the business of capturing or stealing their fellow-beings. Often the methods employed in entrapping the native blacks were horribly brutal and unprincipled, but these brutalities were encouraged by the Christian slave-dealers, who were always ready to buy likely Negroes and never rebuked their African confederates for the means they used in procuring the supply. The captives also suffered greatly on the voyage across the ocean, as they were chained down in close quarters and did not get sufficient fresh air and exercise. The horrors of the "Middle Passage" were proverbial.[12] The slave-traders tried to salve their consciences and justify themselves in the eyes of their contemporaries by saying that the Negroes were benefited by being taken from a heathen and savage land to a new country where they would be brought under the influence of civilization and Christianity.

How the Negroes were procured and transported

Colonial public sentiment seems in general to have been satisfied with this sophistry, as there was no strong opposition to the slave trade on moral grounds. But when the blacks began to multiply rapidly in America, the leaders in some of the colonies saw a social danger in the large proportion of slaves to freemen, and advocated provincial legislation that would restrict the traffic. Laws were passed in Massachusetts, Maryland, Virginia, and South Carolina imposing a duty on slaves brought into these provinces, with a view to discouraging their importation. In South Carolina, where the disproportion between whites and blacks was greatest, the people were especially apprehensive of slave insurrections, and this fear was accentuated by an outbreak in 1739.[13]

Colonial efforts to restrict the slave trade

[12] "Peter Faneuil, one of the most honored and public-spirited citizens of Boston, made his fortune in the slave trade. Faneuil Hall, his gift to the city of Boston, was the scene of many patriotic meetings at the time of the Revolution and has been appropriately called the 'Cradle of Liberty.' These two facts led to the witty observation that the 'Cradle of Liberty rocks on the bones of the Middle Passage'" (FAULKNER, H. U., *American Economic History*, p. 75, note).

[13] CARROLL, B. R., *Historical Collections*, ii, pp. 357-358.

The assembly thereupon began the attempt to check the inflow of slaves by levying an import duty on all that should be brought into the province. Some time before this (1716) the legislature had also made an effort to raise the proportion of whites to blacks by passing a law requiring every planter to own one-tenth as many white servants as slaves.[14]

But the London merchants, regarding the colonial enactments in restraint of the slave trade as a menace to their source of gain, brought pressure to bear on the British authorities and succeeded in having all these restrictions annulled. This was done either by royal veto or by instructions to the royal governors to disallow all such measures. The king's assent was withheld from as many as thirty-three different acts of the Virginia assembly against the slave trade.[15] This disposition of the home government to disregard the reasonable wishes of the Americans in order to advance the selfish interests of the British merchants helped to bring about the final estrangement between them and the mother country and was thus a cause of the Revolution. This narrow and selfish policy also justified, in the opinion of a noted modern historian (Channing), the indictment brought against the British king in the first draft of the Declaration of Independence by Jefferson, in which he said, "He has prostituted his negative for suppressing every legislative attempt to prohibit or restrain this execrable commerce."[16]

Slavery in the West Indies

American slavery had its birth in the West Indies. These islands were the nursery in which it first took root and from which it was transplanted to the continental colonies. In the Spanish West Indies there grew up at an early date a system of forced labor that was a virtual enslavement of the natives. The Indians died rapidly under servitude, and the islands were soon threatened with a serious shortage of labor. To meet this emergency the Spanish planters resorted to Negro slavery. Great numbers of blacks were brought in from Africa and located on the sugar plantations. As the experiment proved to be a success, in due time Negro slavery spread from the Spanish to the English

[14] COOPER, THOMAS, *Statutes at Large of South Carolina*, pp. 646-649.

[15] BALLAGH, J. C., *History of Slavery in Virginia*, p. 11; HENING, W. W., *op. cit.*, iii, pp. 193, 225, 233.

[16] BECKER, CARL, *The Declaration of Independence*, p. 167.

West Indies, and soon the blacks in the latter greatly outnumbered the whites.

The first Negroes brought to the English continental colonies were landed at Jamestown in 1619 from a Dutch privateer. John Rolfe's brief account of this event was as follows: "About the last of August came in a Dutch man of War that sold us twenty negars."[17] Other blacks were brought in from time to time, mainly from the West Indies, but the number increased so slowly that there were only three hundred in the colony in 1649. It was not until about the end of the seventeenth century that they began to come in in considerable numbers. In the meantime slavery had spread to other sections on the continent and was finally established in all the English colonies. When the first Negroes were brought to Jamestown, there was no law in Virginia for establishing slavery and they may have been accorded the status of indented servants.[18] It was not long, however, before laws began to appear in the colonial codes which recognized the blacks as slaves.

Introduction of slavery into the continental colonies

The number of slaves in any locality—except in those colonies in which the Quaker influence was strong—was always determined by economic conditions. In New England the proportion of blacks to whites was comparatively small because most of the farmers in this region were not able to buy many slaves and could not profitably employ a large number of them on their small farms, which demanded intensive cultivation. There was, however, one exception to this rule. In the southern part of Rhode Island, on the west coast of Narragansett Bay, there was an area of fertile land on which were located large plantations with numerous slaves. Proximity to Newport, the great entrepôt for slaves in New England, was partly responsible for the large proportion of slaves in this district. For doubtless the slave merchants of Newport often had left-overs that they were willing to dispose of at bargain prices.

How the slaves were distributed among the various sections

Slavery was encouraged in New Netherland by the Dutch West India Company, which was a slave-trading corporation. The institution did not, however, take deep root while the colony was in the hands of the Dutch, as the settlers were more interested in trading with the Indians than in farming. But later, after the province had passed under English control, there were a con-

[17] TYLER, L. G., ed., *Narratives of Early Virginia*, p. 337.
[18] BALLAGH, J. C., *History of Slavery in Virginia*, pp. 28-34.

siderable number of slaves on the big estates on the Hudson and in the city of New York. In Pennsylvania and New Jersey the proportion of slaves to freemen was smaller than it was in the adjoining colonies, New York and Maryland. This was due to the dislike of slavery by the Germans in Pennsylvania and by the Quakers in both colonies. Besides, in Pennsylvania white laborers, both free and bond, were more numerous than elsewhere, and so the demand for slave labor was not so great.

The South was the section in which slaves were most numerous. Here climatic conditions and the economic system were both most favorable to Negro labor. The cultivation of the great southern staples, tobacco, rice, and indigo, was especially well adapted to slave labor (see p. 448). Virginia and South Carolina were respectively the leading tobacco and rice colonies, and in these provinces the proportion of blacks to whites was greater than in any of the other continental colonies. At the end of the colonial period Negro slaves constituted nearly one-half of the entire population of Virginia and more than two-thirds of the population of South Carolina.[19]

The legal status of the slave   The laws regarding slavery, when viewed in the light of present-day public opinon, seem unduly harsh. Nor was this severity confined to the southern codes, for the slave laws in the North were as severe as in the South, when the proportion of blacks to whites in the two sections is considered. In a few of the colonies instances are given of burning Negroes alive, but apparently this inhuman method of punishment was not often resorted to, and when inflicted it was usually for participation in revolts or for other grave offenses.[20] Besides, it should be remembered that in

[19] For a brief description of slavery in Virginia in 1724 by a contemporary, see JONES, HUGH, *The Present State of Virginia*, pp. 36-38.

[20] The records show that this method of carrying out the death sentence was practiced once each, or oftener, in Massachusetts, Virginia, New York, North Carolina, and South Carolina, and if our records were complete other colonies might have to be put in this same class. In New York in 1712 a slave revolt caused great excitement, and the people were aroused to such a frenzy by fear that they went far beyond the bounds of reason in punishing those who were accused of complicity in the plot. One Negro was convicted after he had been twice acquitted. Of those sentenced to death one was broken on the wheel and twenty hanged or burned. One of these was sentenced "to be burned with a slow fire, that he may continue in

the seventeenth and eighteenth centuries punishment for crime was everywhere more severe than it is in the present age, and that white as well as black criminals were subjected to brutalities that would not be tolerated today.

But all the injustice to the slaves cannot be charged to the opinion of the age as to how crime in general should be punished. There was a good deal of discrimination in the statutes against the unfree blacks, and this inequality before the law was one of the incidents of slavery. One grave objection to bond service is that society cannot be made safe for slavery unless the unfree workers are deprived of some of those individual rights to which all human beings are entitled. If the black servant had been free in his leisure hours to come and go whenever he wished, runaways would have been more numerous and the danger of servile uprisings greater than it was. Moreover, if the master had been bound by law to respect the rights of his slave as completely as those of any other free citizen, he could not have maintained as rigid a discipline over him as the success of the institution demanded. We thus find laws in some of the colonies forbidding slaves to leave the plantations of their masters without written permission unless they were dressed in the livery of their owners. In South Carolina the law required overseers to whip all slaves found on their plantations without these means of identification.[21] If a white man should assist a slave to run away from his master

torment for eight or ten hours and continue burning in said fire until he be dead and consumed to ashes." About thirty years later (1741) the whites were again aroused by a robbery and a number of fires, and a great number of Negroes were punished for an alleged conspiracy. Twenty-nine Negroes were hanged or burned on this occasion (McCRADY, E., article in *Annual Report of the American Historical Association* for 1895, p. 659; CHITWOOD, O. P., *Justice in Colonial Virginia* [Johns Hopkins University *Studies*], p. 101; *Virginia Gazette*, February 18, 1737; BASSETT, J. S., *Slavery and Servitude in the Colony of North Carolina*, p. 61; O'CALLAGHAN, E. B., ed., *New York Colonial Documents*, v, pp. 341, 342, 346, 356-357, 371; *New York Genealogical and Biographical Record*, xxi, pp. 162-163; PHILLIPS, U. B., *American Negro Slavery*, pp. 469-471, especially footnote, p. 471).

[21] McCRADY, E., in *Annual Report of American Historical Association* for 1895, p. 647.

and leave the province, both he and the slave were to be punished by death.

There was also a very severe law against runaways in New York because of the proximity of this province to Canada and the ease with which slaves could escape to a foreign jurisdiction. By a statute passed early in the eighteenth century (1705), it was provided that all slaves found forty miles north of Albany should be put to death. Everywhere runaways were severely dealt with. In Virginia when a runaway slave was caught, he was taken from one constable to another until he was returned to his owner. Each constable who took part in conveying him back to his master whipped him before turning him over to the next constable. If it was not known to whom the fugitive belonged he was confined in the county jail and a notice of his capture was posted on the court-house door. At the end of two months—if he was not claimed by his owner—he was sent to the public jail at Williamsburg and was kept in the custody of the sheriff there until his master was found. In the *Virginia Gazette* were published notices of all such runaways, in which minute descriptions of their personal appearance were given. The practice in North Carolina with reference to runaways was about the same as that in Virginia.[22]

The laws in some of the colonies afforded the slaves inadequate protection against mistreatment by their masters. In the Carolinas and Virginia, if a master killed his slave in carrying out a legal punishment, the act was regarded as an accidental homicide and was, therefore, not punishable. North Carolina seems to have had no law protecting slaves from willful murder by their masters until the end of the colonial period (1774). At that time a law was passed providing for the punishment of masters who should willfully and maliciously kill their slaves. For the first offense the murderer was to be imprisoned for twelve months, and for the second, the death penalty was inflicted. In South Carolina the willful murder of a slave by his master was punished by a fine of fifty pounds and three months' imprisonment.[23] The law in

---

[22] CHITWOOD, *Justice in Colonial Virginia*, p. 97; BASSETT, J. S., *Slavery and Servitude in the Colony of North Carolina*, pp. 34-36; HENING, W. W., *Statutes at Large*, iii, pp. 456-457; iv, pp. 168-171; v, pp. 552-555; vi, pp. 363-366; *Virginia Gazette*, June 3, 1737; July 7 and September 29, 1768; December 7, 1769.

[23] HURD, J. C., *The Law of Freedom and Bondage in the United States*, i, pp. 232, 296, 297.

Virginia also prescribed penalties for the willful killing of slaves by masters.

In a number of the colonies slaves accused of capital offenses were tried by special courts without the aid of a jury. These courts usually consisted of certain justices of the peace designated for this purpose by the governor, with whom were sometimes associated a few prominent citizens who were not magistrates.[24] But no injustice was done the slaves by thus debarring them from the right of trial by jury. The justices and their associates, who were generally among the leading men of the county and were accustomed to hear causes, would be less apt than a jury of twelve average men to be swayed by prejudice and excitement in passing upon the guilt or innocence of Negroes charged with grave crimes.

In the Southern colonies the evidence of Negroes, mulattoes, and Indians could not be admitted by the courts except in those cases to which a Negro, Indian, or mulatto was a party. This exception to the general rule of evidence made it possible for a slave to be unjustly convicted of a crime on unreliable testimony. To guard against this danger the law in Virginia (after 1723) and North Carolina (after 1741) provided that the evidence of this class of witnesses to be accepted must be supported by "pregnant circumstances or the testimony of one or more credible witnesses." The accused was still further protected against false testimony by the threat to the witness that he would be severely punished if he failed to tell the truth. If a non-Christian Negro, Indian, or mulatto should give false testimony, his ears were to be nailed to the pillory one hour each and were then to be cut loose from the nails, after which he was to receive thirty-nine lashes "on his bare back, well laid on."[25]

The Negro, however, seems to have been happier under slavery than one would suppose from his legal status. His lot was hardest on the big rice and sugar plantations in South Carolina and the West Indies, where his contacts with his master were too few to enable the latter to appreciate fully the human side of the relationship. For the large landowners in these colonies seldom lived on their plantations all the year round, and the West Indian

Slave courts

Relation of master and slave

[24] *Ibid.*, i, pp. 237-238, 244, 305; BASSETT, *op. cit.*, pp. 28-29; HAWKS, F. L., *History of North Carolina*, ii, p. 205.

[25] BALLAGH, *History of Slavery in Virginia*, p. 83; BASSETT, *op. cit.*, p. 29.

sugar-growers often spent all of their time in England. The slaves were thus placed under the control of overseers, whose wages were generally determined by the amount of sugar and rice produced at small cost rather than by the kind of treatment accorded to the slaves. Under such a system, an ambitious overseer was tempted to overwork his men and to make inadequate provision for their needs. But in all the colonies there were many slaveholders who owned a comparatively small number of slaves and were thus able to come in daily contact with them. This was especially the case in the Northern colonies and in the tobacco provinces. In the latter there was virtually no absenteeism, but the planters lived on their estates all the year round. There were, however, some tobacco-growers who had so much land and so many slaves that they could not keep in close touch with all of them. But the masters who did not have direct contact with their slaves were not nearly so numerous in the tobacco colonies as they were in the sugar and rice provinces.

Generally when the master and slave were brought in close association, a mutual feeling of kindliness and affection sprang up between them, which restrained the former from undue harshness toward the latter. Even when the master was too coarse-grained to be touched with sympathy for his slaves, he was often constrained to treat them justly by the thought that it was bad business to abuse his laborers. For an excess of ill treatment would render a laborer unfit for efficient service. But in the case of the Negro, the margin between the demands of economic efficiency and the moral obligations imposed upon the master by the natural rights of his dependent fellow-beings was broad enough to permit a good deal of injustice. And so we find that there were always some brutal masters who treated their black servants inhumanly, but they were doubtless few in number.

Good feeling between master and slave was promoted in large measure by the happy disposition and docile temperament of the Negro. Seldom was he surly and discontented and rarely did he harbor a grudge against his master for depriving him of his liberty. On the contrary, as a rule he accepted his inferior status as a matter of course and went about his daily tasks cheerfully, often singing while at work. It was these qualities that gave the Negro the greatest adaptability to slavery of all the races known to history. The fact that he had never known the ease and comforts of civilization in his homeland made it less difficult for him

Patrick Henry. (*The Bettmann Archive.*)

Drafting the Declaration of Independence. Shown here are Franklin, Jefferson, Adams, Livingston, and Sherman. (*Culver Service.*)

Ratification Ceremony of the Constitutional Convention in Philadelphia, 1787. (*From a painting by Herter. The Bettmann Archive.*)

The Signing of the Declaration of Independence, July 4, 1776. (*From a painting by Trumbull. The Bettmann Archive.*)

Shelb-ns Sacrifice, or the Recommended Loyalists, a Faithful Reproduction of a Tragedy Shortly to Be Performed on the Continent of America. (*From an old print published in 1783. Culver Service.*)

The Surrender of General Burgoyne. (*From a painting by Trumbull. The Bettmann Archive.*)

The Introduction of Slavery. (*Culver Service.*)

The First Legislative Assembly in Kentucky, May 23, 1775. This assembly, which included Daniel Boone, met under a huge elm tree in Boonesborough. (*The Bettmann Archive.*)

The Pillory. (*Culver Service.*)

The Stocks. (*Culver Service.*)

In **ADAM'S** Fall
We finned all.

Heaven to find,
The Bible Mind.

Chrift crucify'd
For finners dy'd.

The Deluge drown'd
The Earth around.

ELIJAH hid
By Ravens fed.

The judgment made
FELIX afraid.

As runs the Glass,
Our Life doth pass.

My Book and Heart
Must never part.

JOB feels the Rod,—
Yet bleffes GOD.

Proud Korah's troop
Was fwallowed up

LOT fled to *Zoar*,
Saw fiery Shower
On *Sodom* pour.

MOSES was he
Who *Israel's* Hoft
Led 'thro' the Sea.

NOAH did view
The old world & new

Young **OBADIAS**,
DAVID, **JOSIAS**
All were pious.

PETER deny'd
His Lord and cry'd.

Queen **ESTHER** fues
And faves the *Jews*.

Young pious **RUTH**.
Left all for Truth.

Young **SAM'L** dear
The Lord did fear.

Young **TIMOTHY**
Learnt fin to fly.

VASTHI for Pride,
Was fet afide.

Whales in the Sea,
GOD's Voice obey.

XERXES did die,
And fo muft I.

While youth do chear
Death may be near.

ZACCHEUS he
Did climb the Tree
Our Lord to fee.

An Alphabet Including Both Religious and Secular Jingles.
(From a primer printed in Boston about 1800. *The Bettmann
Archive.*)

The Hartford Wits: Tory Pandemonium. McFingal's Mock Epic by John Trumbull. (*The Bettmann Archive.*)

An Illustration from Benjamin Franklin's *Poor Richard's Almanac.*
(*The Bettmann Archive.*)

Southern Hospitality. (*The Bettmann Archive.*)

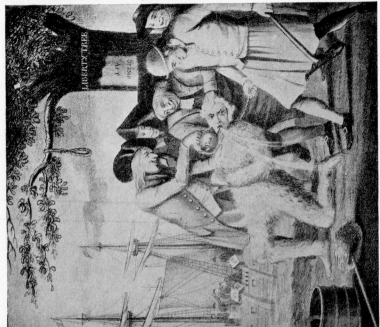

The Bostonians Paying the Excise-Man, or Tarring and Feathering. (Copied on stone by D. C. Johnston from a print published in 1774. Culver Service.)

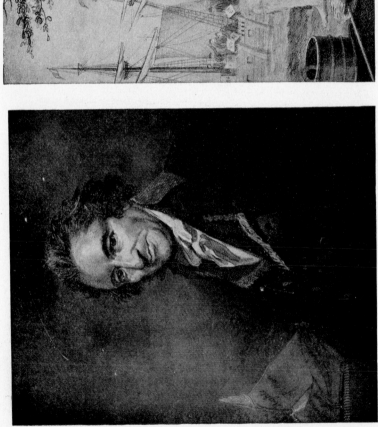

Thomas Paine. (From a painting by Romney. The Bettmann Archive.)

A Picturesque View of the State of the Nation for February, 1778. (*Culver Service.*)

The Windmill in Easthampton, Long Island, One of the Oldest in the
Country. (*The Bettmann Archive.*)

The Horse America, Throwing His Master. (*From an old print published in 1779. Culver Service.*)

The Battle of Lexington. (*From a painting by Alonzo Chappé. Culver Service.*)

St. Augustine, Florida. (*Culver Service.*)

La Salle's Landing in Texas. (*Reduced facsimile from Hennepin. The Bettmann Archive.*)

Colonial Schoolroom. (*From a painting by Curran. The Bettmann Archive.*)

Jack England Fighting the Four Confederates. (*From an old print published in 1781. Culver Service.*)

Pre-Revolutionary Mill, with Water Wheel. (*Culver Service.*)

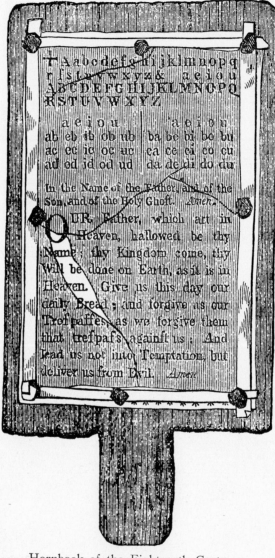

Hornbook of the Eighteenth Century.
(*Brown Brothers.*)

Life in North Carolina. (*Culver Service.*)

A Dame School. (*Brown Brothers.*)

A Quilting Bee. (*Brown Brothers.*)

A New England Kitchen, Around 1780. (*The Bettmann Archive.*)

Whipping Quakers at the Cart's Tail. (*Culver Service.*)

A Puritan Church. (*The Bettmann Archive.*)

The First House Erected in Connecticut.
(*Culver Service.*)

Agricultural Implements at the End of the Eighteenth Century. (*The Bettmann Archive.*)

New Haven in 1637. (*Culver Service.*)

Site of Marietta, Ohio, in 1788. (*Culver Service.*)

The Repeal, or the Funeral Procession, of Miss Americ-Stamp. (*Culver Service.*)

Uprising of the New England Yeomanry Early in the American Revolution. (*Culver Service.*)

Hooker and His Friends Reach
the Connecticut.
(Culver Service.)

The Marriage of Pocahontas.
*(From an engraving by John
C. McRae. Culver Service.)*

Governor Berkeley and the Insurgents—Bacon's Rebellion. (*Culver Service*.)

The Town of Secola—an Indian Village. (*Reproduced from* The History and Present State of Virginia *by Robert Beverley, Edited with an Introduction by Louis B. Wright, by permission of* The University of North Carolina Press. *Copyright, 1947, by The University of North Carolina Press.*)

Boston. (*From an old print, 1768. Culver Service.*)

The Iron Foundry in Salisbury, Connecticut, Built Before the Revolution.
(*Culver Service.*)

An Old Mill. (*Culver Service.*)

Sawmill and Block House on Fort Anne Creek. (*From Ambere's* Travels Through America, *published in 1789. The Bettmann Archive.*)

Johns St. Theatre, New York, During Washington's Administration.
(*From an old wood cut. Culver Service.*)

to submit to the hardships and inferior position of his condition. In this respect the American Negro was better off than the slave of ancient Rome, who was often the intellectual equal and sometimes the superior of his master.

The only effective opposition to slavery in the colonial period was made by the Quakers. Apparently, even this denomination at first raised no objection to the institution, and William Penn himself owned a few Negroes. But it was not long before the Quaker conscience began to be troubled by the bondage of their fellow human beings. The Quaker fight against slavery was started in April, 1688, by Daniel Pastorius and a few other German Friends living at Germantown, Pennsylvania. In the Monthly Meeting held at this time they declared that it was contrary to Christian principles for one class of people to be held in bondage by another and presented arguments to show that it is just as wrong for the whites to deprive the blacks of their liberty as it is for Turks to enslave Christians. This protest was sent up to the Quarterly Meeting of Philadelphia and later to the Yearly Meeting held at Burlington, New Jersey. But the denomination was not yet ready to take a radical stand against slavery, and so the Yearly Meeting declined to accept the recommendations of the Germantown church.

In less than a decade, however (1696), the Yearly Meeting adopted the policy of advising members of the denomination to "be careful not to encourage the bringing in of any more negroes." This policy was too mild to put an end to the practice of buying slaves by the Quakers, and in 1755 the Yearly Meeting adopted the rule that all Friends who should thereafter import slaves would be excluded from the denomination.[26] Three years later it further advised Friends to set their slaves at liberty, " 'making a Christian provision for them,' and appointed a committee to visit Friends who owned slaves and labor with them to set them free."[27]

These efforts did a great deal toward ridding the Quaker denomination of slavery, as most of the Friends gave freedom to their blacks, though many of them disobeyed the orders of the Meetings and retained their slaves or else compromised with their consciences by selling them to non-Quaker masters. By 1776 the Quakers were committed to the principle of abolition, and,

Opposition of the Quakers to slavery

[26] Pennsylvania Historical Society's *Memoirs*, i, p. 377.
[27] SHARPLESS, ISAAC, *Quaker Government*, i, p. 32.

what is most remarkable, they had reached this advanced position without occasioning a breach in their denomination. In every step taken toward this goal the progressives had induced the conservatives to yield by persuasion without arousing any bad feeling on either side. It will also be noted that by their plan of abolition all financial losses entailed by the reform were assumed by themselves.

In colonial days, there was very little active opposition to slavery on moral grounds except among the Quakers, though the Baptists and Methodists did not approve of it. The other denominations seem to have accepted the institution without any qualms of conscience. The Venerable Society bought slaves and used some of them to teach other Negroes. George Whitefield, the great evangelist, also indorsed slavery. He not only owned Negroes himself, but he was instrumental in getting the trustees to relax the measures that prohibited slavery in Georgia. There were, however, a few protests against slavery outside of the Quaker denomination, but they were mostly of an academic character and did not make any lasting impress on public sentiment.[28]

Advantages and disadvantages of slavery

As a system of labor, Negro slavery had advantages and disadvantages as compared with white labor, both bond and free. In the first place, it gave the employer complete control over a constant supply of labor. He could make his plans for a long period ahead with reasonable assurance that they would not be hindered by a shortage of labor. But the supply of workers was

---

[28] The earliest of these protests was an act passed by the joint government of Providence and Warwick in 1652, providing that all slaves within the jurisdiction of these two towns should be freed at the end of ten years' service (*Rhode Island Colonial Records*, i, p. 243). This law was probably never enforced, and after slaves became numerous in Rhode Island the black code there was not any milder than that of the other New England colonies. Another protest came from New England in the beginning of the eighteenth century (1701), when Samuel Sewall published at Boston his tract entitled "The Selling of Joseph." In this pamphlet the author argues that slavery is both morally wrong and socially inexpedient (Massachusetts Historical Society *Proceedings*, 1863-64, pp. 161-165). Some years later (1736) Colonel William Byrd of Virginia pointed out objections to slavery in that it encouraged idleness in the whites and necessitated the enactment of harsh measures to keep Negroes in bounds (HART, A. B., *Source-Book of American History*, pp. 119-121).

inelastic as well as constant and could not be readily adjusted to the demand for the commodities produced. For as the cost of maintaining slaves was the same whether they produced much or little, the master could not expand or contract production to meet the rise or fall in the demand for his crops.

In the second place, slave labor was cheap. The biggest item in its cost was the purchase price of the Negro, but this initial outlay was not great when we consider that the owner could command his services for a lifetime. Besides, a large proportion of the blacks were raised by the masters on their own plantations at a small cost. For on every farm or plantation there were a number of light duties to which Negro children were assigned, and they began to earn their maintenance at a very early age. The standard of living of the Negro was low and the cost of feeding, clothing, and housing him was less than it was for the white laborer. This cheapness, however, was partially offset by the unskilled character of the labor and by the lack of interest and the reluctance with which work is always performed by those who are forced to do it. The master was thus put to the expense of hiring high-priced overseers to direct the work of his slaves and keep them from shirking their tasks. Slavery also tended to discourage free labor both by attaching a social stigma to it and also by lowering its compensation. The white laborer had to compete with the Negro slave, and this competition kept his wages down to a low level. Moreover, in those communities where slaves were numerous, most of the manual labor was performed by them and, therefore, to work with one's hands was considered degrading and not proper for a gentleman.

Thirdly, slavery relieved the members of the wealthy families of the drudgery of household and farm routine and gave them more time to devote to intellectual pursuits and the social amenities. In some cases this leisure was wasted by the men in idle recreation, and in others it was spent in luxury and dissipation. But in the main the upper classes used their spare time in promoting the higher interests of society. It is true that in colonial America the privileged class produced no masterpieces of art, literature, or philosophy to justify a leisure purchased at the price of human freedom, as was the case in ancient Greece; but they did devote a good deal of their time to public affairs and received an experience in practical government that trained them for leadership in political affairs. It is to this training that we are largely indebted for the ability and sanity that characterized the leadership of the American people in their struggle for independence. The women seem to have profited even more than the men by the exemption from drudgery. The responsibility of managing the household with its numerous activities (which often included spinning and weaving) afforded the matron on a big plantation a dignified employment that lifted her above the frivolities which are so often the curse of the idle rich. The interchange of hospitalities and the practice of the amenities occasioned by it gave the patrician ladies a charm of manner that would be an ornament to the social life of any age. But the number of families who enjoyed these advantages was very small, and their superiority in culture helped to widen the social gulf that already separated the families of the small farmers from those of the big planters. In this way slavery helped to accentuate the aristocratic tendencies of the day.

Fourthly, the Negro was better adapted to the climate of the Tidewater section of the lower South than was the white man. It was thought that white men could not work in the rice-fields because of the prevalence of malaria in the low, swampy regions where it was grown. If colored laborers (who were considered partially immune from malaria) could not have been procured for the cultivation of this plant, the development of the South would undoubtedly have been retarded.

Fifthly, slavery was in some ways a blessing to the Negro himself. It taught him the rudiments of civilization and Christianity, especially on the plantations that were small enough to permit close contact between the slave and the members of his master's family. The Negro was very religious by temperament and religious ecstasy made a strong appeal to his emotional nature. When the imagination of a pious Negro contrasted the happiness after death promised believers with the hardships of this life, he experienced a spiritual joy that unemotional people of this age find it difficult to understand. His enthusiasm sometimes overleaped all the restraints imposed by his untutored intellect and went to the extreme of excitement that would seem utterly irrational today—except on the occasion of a football game. But despite these emotional excesses there were a great many slaves who enjoyed the blessing of a sincere and fervent piety.

Sixthly, slavery trained the Negro in habits of industry and taught him a rudimentary knowledge of farming and primitive industry. It helped to curb his savage instincts and discipline him into the self-restraint demanded by civilization. Slavery was thus a schoolmaster to prepare the savage African for the responsibilities of American civilization. But as is often the case with schoolmasters, it carried its policy of discipline too far, even to the point of cramping individuality and destroying initiative. In demanding deference toward the whites by the blacks it expected a servile attitude of the latter toward the former. This attitude of servility tended to weaken that self-respect which is the foundation stone of all real strength of character.

Lastly, to appraise correctly the benefits and evils of slavery, we have to consider the ethical aspect of the question. When we do this we find one objection to the institution that outweighs all its merits—the wrong of depriving any class of human beings of the right to personal liberty. Slavery thus rested on a foundation of unrighteousness and had to be propped up by codes discriminating unfairly against slaves because such unfairness was necessary to preserve the institution. Masters were granted by law a power over their slaves with which there was not coupled a commensurate responsibility. And whenever responsibility is divorced from authority there is always the possibility of tyranny. While many masters never abused this power, there were always some brutal ones that did. The morals of the Negro were quite low to begin with, and slavery did little, if anything, to improve them. It is even charged that slavery tended to debase the morals of the Negroes. It could hardly be expected that the slaves would be bound strictly by the marriage tie when the laws permitted the master to break it at will by separating husband and wife. It is true that this was not very often done, but there was always the possibility that it might be done.

SELECTED READINGS

1. Huguenot Home Life in America.—Fosdick, L. J., *The French Blood in America*, *ch. 6.
2. Jewish Pre-Revolutionary Settlements.—Peters, M. C., *The Jews in America*, *ch. 2.
3. Method of Capturing Slaves in Africa.—Spears, J. R., *The American Slave Trade*, *ch. 5.
4. Domestic Service.—Salmon, L. M., *Domestic Service*, *ch. 3.
5. Education of the Negro.—Woodson, C. G., *The Education of the Negro Prior to 1861*, ch. 2.

6. The Negro Church in Colonial Days.—Article by DuBois, W. E. B., in the Atlanta University *Publications*, no. 8, pp. *1-22.

7. Advantages and Disadvantages of White Servitude.—Ballagh, J. C., *White Servitude in the Colony of Virginia* (Johns Hopkins University *Studies*, 13th series), pp. *89-95.

8. White Servitude in South Carolina.—Schaper, W. A., *Sectionalism in South Carolina*, pp. *299-303.

9. Arguments in Favor of Slavery.—Hart, A. B., *Slavery and Abolition*, *ch. 10.

10. Arguments against Slavery.—*Ibid.*, *166-169.

11. The African Slave Trade.—Ingram, J. K., *A History of Slavery and Serfdom*, *ch. 6.

CHAPTER XXI

AGRICULTURE AND LAND TENURE

FARMING is generally the principal occupation of all new and undeveloped countries, as this industry is favored by the abundance, fertility, and cheapness of the virgin soil. The American colonies were no exception to this rule. (In all of them farming was the main business throughout the entire colonial period.) Not only was agriculture profitable, but it was absolutely essential to the very existence of the people.) Ships were small when the early settlers came, and the cargoes of food supplies landed by them could not have been large after the demands of passengers and crew had been met. It was, therefore, imperative that the colonists depend upon themselves for the means of living.

Importance of agriculture in colonial times

The two main crops of the Indians were corn, or maize, and tobacco. They usually selected for tillage the most fertile spots and, as far as possible, those that were free from trees, though they sometimes cleared out fields in the primeval forest. In this case they would kill the trees by cutting away the bark with a stone ax and then burning around the roots. The dead trees were allowed to stand in the field until they fell, when they were burned up by the women. The smaller trees were either broken down or cut off with stone hatchets.

Indian agriculture: How the land was cleared

The raising of corn required much labor, and this task was, in the main, turned over to the women. After the land was sufficiently cleared, holes were dug in the ground about four feet apart, and in each were planted from four to six grains of corn and two beans. Between the hills there were later planted peas, pumpkins, cymlins, gourds, and May apples. The plants were cultivated with crude hoes, which the women used sitting down. These hoes were made of shells, crooked pieces of wood, or the bones or horns of deer or other animals fastened to wooden handles. With these implements they dug up the weeds, stirred the soil, and later piled up the dirt around the stalks. No manure was used on the ground, but in some sections a dead fish or crab was put in each hill as a fertilizer. The birds were so numerous

433

that a field of corn unprotected from them would have yielded a very small return. To guard against their depredations, a watch tower was built in the field, and in it a young Indian slept in order that he might begin early in the morning to frighten away the birds. This method of raising corn was the one adopted by the first settlers and is still employed with little modification in many sections of the country. Mr. Bruce says that a field of maize planted on the James River long before the English came "was almost the exact counterpart of the same field, planted with the same grain, three hundred years afterward by the modern Virginia farmer."[1]

The cultivation of tobacco

Tobacco was another plant held in high esteem by the Indians. They regarded it as a special gift from the Great Spirit and thought it possessed medicinal qualities. It was the one farm product which the men could cultivate without lowering their sense of dignity.

Methods of farming employed by the colonists

Colonial methods of farming were generally more backward than those practiced in England during the same period. The plowing was not well done and the fences were not carefully looked after, especially in the South. There was no scientific inquiry to lend interest to farming and promote progressive methods. "Hard work was the order of the day into which neither poetry nor science ever entered."[2] The lack of progress was not due entirely to an ignorance of science, but also in part to the conventional attitude of mind of the farmers. Crops were planted and cultivated according to the practices of their fathers. If a bold innovator tried a new and unconventional method he was made uncomfortable by the frowns and ridicule of public opinion.

"Earth-butchery"

The early settler not only learned from the Indians how to raise the native plants, but he also brought with him the European methods of cultivating the crops of the homeland. In the seventeenth century and the first part of the eighteenth, the English were making some noted improvements in farm management. The most important of these was the introduction of turnips, clovers and grasses, and other crops. By the use of these

[1] For an excellent account of Indian agriculture, see BRUCE, P. A., *Economic History of Virginia in the Seventeenth Century*, i, pp. 150-155. For a brief contemporary account, see BOGART, E. L., and THOMPSON, C. M., *Readings in the Economic History of the United States*, p. 29.

[2] BOLLES, A. S., *Industrial History of the United States*, p. 12.

plants the fertility of the soil could be restored and sustained by a scientific rotation of crops. This was a great advance over the old plan of every few years allowing a field to lie idle for a season. The colonials were, of course, acquainted with these discoveries, but they did not profit by them to any great extent. Land was tilled year after year with little or no regard for its future productivity. Nor did the colonial farmer appreciate the value of manure in maintaining the fertility of the soil and increasing the yield of the crops. Live-stock ran at large and little manure was made, and the little that collected was considered a nuisance rather than a valuable asset.[3] As a result of such methods the lands were rapidly worn out. This practice of killing land is known as "earth-butchery."[4] The main reason for this was that land was plentiful and cheap, and it was considered more profitable to clear new grounds than to incur the expense and trouble of preserving or restoring the productivity of old fields. "Earth-butchery" was practiced everywhere, but was especially flagrant in the South, where the staple crops of tobacco, indigo, and rice were grown. Tobacco and indigo require rich soils, and the finer grades of tobacco do especially well on fresh land.

The successful cultivation of tobacco required, therefore, the constant clearing of new lands. Besides, the method of paying overseers was favorable to land-killing. They usually received a part of the crop as compensation for their services, and were more interested in getting large returns than in preserving soil fertility. The farmers in this period thus contracted a habit which they passed on to their descendants.

One reason why the colonists were backward in agriculture was that their farm implements were so crude. There were no plows either at Jamestown or at Plymouth in the first few years of these settlements. By 1617 there was only one plow in Virginia, and in 1637 there were only thirty-seven in the colony of

Farm implements

[3] A story is told by a contemporary of a colonial farmer who was advised by one of his neighbors to move his barn to get away from the manure that had accumulated in it (BIDWELL, P. W., and FALCONER, J. I., *History of Agriculture in the Northern United States*, p. 87).

[4] For a contemporary account of farming methods in colonial times, made by a very competent observer (1775), see *American Husbandry*, i, pp. 75, 78, 80, 114, 143, 147-148, 171-172, 173-174, 176, 247, 265-266, 339-340, 349; ii, pp. 4-32.

Massachusetts Bay,[5] Sometimes one plow did service for a whole neighborhood, going from farm to farm as the threshing-machine does today. The scarcity of plows in the early years was due not only to their cost, but also probably to the fact that the land was not sufficiently cleared of stumps and trees to justify their use. The plow in colonial times was made mainly of wood, though the share was of iron and often the mold-board was covered over with strips of sheet iron. It was very heavy and, owing to its shape, encountered more friction than was necessary. It took a strong team to pull it, and this explains in part why the slow, heavy ox was so often used in plowing. In short, the plow of colonial times was not much better than the one which was drawn by the oxen of Elisha, the Hebrew prophet, more than twenty-four centuries earlier. Other implements in common use were the spade, wooden fork, and harrow, the teeth of which were frequently made of wood but often of iron. Grain was cut by the reap-hook, or sickle, and threshed with the flail or by having oxen tread it out, as was done in the time of Moses.[6]

Live-stock   In the early years some of the colonists were very scantily supplied with live-stock, as the Indians had no domestic animals (except the dog) from which they could draw, and it was difficult to transport them from England.[7] After the settlements were firmly established cattle, horses, and sheep increased rapidly in number, but they were much smaller than they are now. This was true not only of American live-stock, but of English as well, though in England in the eighteenth century horses, cows, sheep, and hogs were all generally larger than they were in America. One reason that horses and cattle were so small in the colonies was that they were poorly fed and housed. In New England and the Middle colonies there were good meadows on which were raised the cultivated grasses and clovers for hay and pasturage and dairying was an important industry. But horses were over-

[5] FLINT, C. L., in *Eighty Years' Progress,* p. 11.

[6] In BIDWELL, P. W., and FALCONER, J. I., *History of Agriculture in the Northern United States,* pp. 34-35, are given lists from contemporary documents of the farm implements owned by typical New Englanders in the early period. For a picture of farm implements in use in 1790, see KETTEL, T. P., ed., *Eighty Years' Progress,* p. 28.

[7] The Pilgrims at Plymouth had no cattle for the first three years and no horses or sheep as late as 1627 (BRADFORD, W., *History of Plymouth Plantation, Original Narratives,* pp. 166, 217).

worked, and both horses and cattle badly treated here as everywhere else. Cattle, hogs, and poultry were left unsheltered at night even when the snow was on the ground, not only in the South, but also as far north as New Jersey.[8]

The Germans in Pennsylvania were an exception to this rule, for they usually had large barns and were able to house their cattle in the winter. In the Southern colonies cattle were turned out in the woods to fine pasturage and were given little or no feed even in the winter-time. Milch cows were usually fed a little, partly to get them in the habit of coming to the milking-place. A contemporary observer says that the farmers in Virginia in the seventeenth century thought that if cattle were fed in the wintertime "it would pave the way for their destruction."[9] As a result of such treatment the butter that was made was usually small in amount and poor in quality. Besides, a good many animals died when the winters were severe. In Virginia during the winter of 1673, which was unusually cold, 50,000 head of cattle are said to have died, probably from exposure to the cold and because of the dearth of vegetation.

Another reason for the scrubbiness of live-stock was the custom (prevalent both in New England and in the South) of allowing horses and cattle to run at large, for there was no possibility of improving the breed as long as there was a general intermingling of the stocks. Horses were employed mainly for riding, as oxen were the principal draft animals. Even during the latter half of the eighteenth century considerably more oxen were used in New England than horses, though the latter were frequently used in light plowing and as leaders of ox teams. Despite the neglect with which they were treated, domestic animals were in the eighteenth century numerous everywhere, and in the South horses, hogs, and cattle ran wild. Hunting wild horses, sometimes with the aid of dogs, was a favorite sport of the young men of Virginia in the seventeenth century. The wild cows were still more numerous, but they had such a keen scent for the hunters that it was difficult to get near a herd of them. So in hunting them the young men used guns, as they did in the case of elk and deer.

The principal plants found in America by the colonists were maize, or Indian corn, tobacco, squashes, gourds, pumpkins, beans,

[8] *American Husbandry*, i, pp. 99, 133-134, 164, 338, 350-351; BIDWELL and FALCONER, *op. cit.*, p. 107; KETTEL, *op. cit.*, p. 20.

[9] KALM, PETER, *Travels into North America*, i, p. 207.

Native
plants:
Potatoes

peas, and sweet potatoes. The white, or Irish, potato seems not
to have been known to the Indians of continental North America,
but was raised in the West Indies. From these islands it was
taken to Ireland, whence it was brought back to America. It was
cultivated in Pennsylvania before the end of the seventeenth
century, but was not grown in New England until the second
decade of the eighteenth century (about 1718), being introduced
by the Scotch-Irish.[10] The white potato proved to be an invaluable food plant because it is easy to keep through the winter and
its yield per acre is great. It was grown profitably in New York
and all the colonies to the south. A planter in Georgia in the
eighteenth century asserted that he had raised as many as three
hundred bushels of potatoes on a quarter of an acre of land.[11]
The native crops played a very important part in the economic
life of the people, as they could be raised from the very beginning
without costly experimentation as to when and where they should
be planted and how cultivated.

Maize

(The most valuable of all the native plants to the colonials, as
well as to the Indians, was Indian corn, or maize. Two years after
the Jamestown settlement began, Captain John Smith, who was
in charge in the colony, had forty acres of land planted in corn
according to directions which two captive Indians were forced
to give.[12] Thirteen years later a friendly Indian performed voluntarily the same service for the Pilgrim settlers.[13] These were among
the most important events in the early history of our country,
for they mark the beginnings in English America of the culture
of a plant on which the very existence of the settlers depended.
Mr. Bruce thinks that the infant colony at Jamestown would have
perished in the cradle had it not been for this important food
product. It was raised everywhere in the colonies except the ex-

[10] BIDWELL, and FALCONER, op. cit., pp. 16, 97, 98; CARRIER,
LYMAN, Beginnings of Agriculture in America, pp. 81-87.
There is some disagreement among the authorities as to the original
habitat of the potato. For a view as to how the potato was taken to
Europe at variance with the statement made above, see BLACKMAN,
V. H., in Encyclopedia Britannica, xviii, pp. 326-327. See also
FAULKNER, op. cit., p. 59.
[11] American Husbandry, ii, pp. 22-23.
[12] TYLER, L. G., ed., Narratives of Early Virginia (Original Narratives), p. 185.
[13] BRADFORD, W., op. cit., pp. 115-116.

treme northern part of New England. It was the most valuable of the grains for several reasons. Its yield is greater per acre than that of any other. It is more easily ground than wheat, and can be prepared for food in several different ways. The grain is fine feed for horses, cattle, poultry, and hogs, and the husks and fodder are also good forage for animals. The time for gathering in the ripened grain is much longer than that of the small cereals. This makes it possible to harvest as large a crop as can be raised. The time for cutting wheat, on the other hand, is very short and before modern reaping machinery was invented was never long enough to admit of the harvesting of large crops. Corn is well adapted to virgin soil and could be planted immediately after the forests were cleared by the first settlers. But in Virginia wheat could not be successfully raised in the earliest times on the rich lands until their fertility had been somewhat reduced by crops of corn or tobacco. In the fresh rich soil the growth went to the straw rather than to the grain.

Tobacco ranked next to corn as an agricultural product in **Tobacco** colonial times. When Columbus landed on the island of Cuba in 1492 he had hardly gotten ashore when a native chief showed his hospitality by giving him and his men cigars to smoke. The natives called these cigars *tobaccos*. This was the first acquaintance that a European had with this fragrant weed. In a little while tobacco was as popular with the Europeans as it was with the Indians. The settlers at Jamestown, however, were so much engrossed with the problem of getting food that it was five years before they began the successful cultivation of tobacco. In 1612, John Rolfe (afterward the husband of Pocahontas) succeeded in raising a crop of tobacco. At that time the Jamestown settlement was about to fail because the farmers had no money crop to export. Grain could never be exported in large amounts because England at that time was a farming country and was raising all the wheat, barley, and oats that she needed. There was even talk of abandoning the colony, when it was discovered that tobacco was a paying crop. It became at once the most important export from Virginia and remained so throughout the entire colonial period.

The colony now rested on a firm economic basis and took on new life at once. There was a danger, however, that so much attention would be given to the cultivation of tobacco that corn and other food products would be neglected. To guard against this danger measures were adopted and enforced by both the home and local governments to encourage the production of corn and restrict that of tobacco. But despite these restrictions tobacco continued throughout the colonial period to be the principal crop in Virginia and Maryland and an important one in northern North Carolina. (The main reason for this was that the land yielded a greater money return per acre when planted in tobacco than when used for corn or other grains.) Then, too, tobacco could be transported to the European markets without taking up much ship space because its bulk in proportion to value is less than that of other farm products. It could also be conveyed to the wharves and loaded on the ships without much difficulty. The cured leaves were tied in bundles and packed into a hogshead at a time when the moisture in the atmosphere made them soft enough to be handled without being crumbled. An iron rod was then put through the hogshead and horses or oxen hitched to it. By this method it was rolled over the rough and uneven dirt roads to the warehouse, where it was stored until ready for export. The storage buildings were known as "rolling-houses."[14] Very often the plantations bordered on navigable streams and the planter could in such cases load his hogsheads in boats at his own wharf. Even though at times the price of tobacco was low, the planters continued to raise it, partly through force of habit and partly because of the hope that prices would be higher. The fact that tobacco was used as money also put a premium on its production. (Tobacco was the most important of all the colonial exports, constituting at different times from one-fourth to one-half of the value of all products sent out of the English continental colonies.

Fruits   The first settlers on the Atlantic seaboard found in abundance walnuts, chestnuts, and other varieties of nuts, plums, cherries, probably blackberries, black raspberries, whortleberries, cranberries, wild grapes, and wild strawberries. The last named were so plentiful in Virginia and Maryland that in these provinces one could hardly walk through the forest in the strawberry season without staining his shoes red with their juice.[15] The apple was brought to Virginia from England at an early date, and in due time there were planted numerous apple orchards in the various

[14] For a picture of rolling tobacco to the warehouse (imaginary), see Bolles, *op. cit.*, p. 8.

[15] Hall, C. C., ed., *Narratives of Early Maryland (Original Narratives)*, p. 45.

colonies. It was the fruit most generally cultivated in colonial times because cider and brandy could be made from it easily,) and these beverages enjoyed a wide popularity. Other fruits were imported from Europe, the peach being one of the most useful of them. In New Jersey and Pennsylvania and all the colonies south of them, peaches were in such abundance that they were used to fatten hogs.

One important service performed by the settlers was to find **Foreign** out by experimentation what foreign plants could be raised here **plants** and in what sections they could be profitably cultivated. The similarity of the summer climate of our Atlantic coast to that of western Europe reduced the hazards of this experimentation to the minimum, and yet many attempts to introduce foreign plants were costly failures. In Virginia, for example, attempts were made in the seventeenth century to raise West Indian fruits, such as lemons, almonds, pomegranates, olives, and ginger, and the culture of rice, cotton, and indigo was tried in New England. It is needless to say that these efforts were disappointing failures. The colonists, however, did succeed in bringing in a great many valuable plants from Europe and other countries and in determining what sections were adapted to each. They performed this service so well that very little was done from the end of the colonial era to the beginning of the twentieth century in adapting foreign vegetation to our soil and climate. This is about their only contribution to the science of agriculture. "There was, however, practically no improvement in the plants, vegetables, and fruits by culture and selection after they were once introduced."[16]

The principal plants brought to America from other lands were wheat, barley, buckwheat, oats, rice, hemp, and indigo.)Wheat was grown in all the colonies, but was cultivated with especial success in New York and the Delaware region. In New England rye and buckwheat ranked next to maize in the list of the principal food crops. Wheat, oats, and barley were also raised here, but not very successfully. All of these grains (except rice) were produced in all the other colonies, and hemp and flax (the latter a native plant) were cultivated generally throughout the colonies. Rice was the great staple of the Carolinas and Georgia. Its culture in this country began in 1694, when the governor of South Carolina successfully raised a small patch in his garden. It was grown in the swamps in the hot malarial regions of the South and was

[16] Bogart, E. L., *Economic History of the United States*, p. 41.

cultivated mainly by Negro slaves. Indigo was grown in the Carolinas and Georgia and was one of their most important exports. Its production was stimulated by the bounty paid by the British government on all of it that was sold in England.

Landholding in New England

In New England the usual practice in disposing of land was for the colonial government to grant a certain area, usually from eight to ten square miles, to a group of people who wished to make a new settlement.[17] Such a tract would constitute a township and would be under the entire control of the grantees, who were to be the citizens of the new town. As a rule the title to this land was confirmed by purchase from the Indians. Near the center of the grant a village would be laid out. In surveying the town they would usually reserve a large square for the church, the cemetery, the minister's house-lot, the market place, and the school. Around this square or adjacent to it there would be a plot of ground divided into house-lots, each of which would front one of the streets intersecting it, and one of these lots would be granted to each proprietor. Then a portion of the arable and mowing lands would be divided up. Large fields of several hundred acres were marked off and cut up into a number of small strips. These were assigned to the settlers by lot, each one getting a number of sections scattered about in different fields and in different places in the same field. Some of the meadow and tillable land would remain under joint ownership for future divisions. From these reserved areas distributions would be made from time to time after the manner of the first allotments.[18]

The reserved portion of the tract, including the forest, pasture, and undistributed arable and mowing lands, also belonged to the community, and all the residents of the town had the privilege of getting lumber and firewood from the forests and of grazing

[17] In Massachusetts this grant was generally made by the colonial assembly, the General Court, but in Rhode Island and frequently in Connecticut the towns bought their lands from the Indians and took possession of them without any authorization from the General Court (BIDWELL and FALCONER, op. cit., pp. 49-50).

[18] For contemporary accounts of the laying out of towns in the seventeenth century, see ibid., pp. 51-52.

Each townsman enjoyed absolute ownership of the house-lot and usually of the sections that had been assigned him; but in some cases the allotments in some of the fields were made only for temporary use, the ownership of the land being retained by the town.

stock on the common pastures. The cows were under a cowherd, who brought them to and from the village twice a day to be milked. This system combined the advantages of both individual and communal ownership. It brought the people together and made them feel more their mutual dependence and obligations and thus kept alive the social instinct. It also made possible the regulation of the forests by preventing the destruction of them by the community. At the same time it kept alive the energy and individual initiative that are encouraged by the private ownership of land.[19]

In distributing the lands no attempt was made, even in the beginning, to give equal shares to all. The house-lots were usually about the same in size, "but in the distribution of other land-holdings the right of some to receive more than others was invariably recognized. There were two criteria of distribution: (1) the investment of the settler in the original enterprise, and (2) his ability to use land."[20] These inequalities were not great, however, and so in the early years no one citizen owned an amount of land greatly in excess of that held by the average townsmen. But it was inconvenient for the farmer to have his small acreage divided up into a number of strips scattered all around the township, and it was not long before holdings began to be consolidated by purchase and exchange. This made it possible for the wealthy to buy up the lots of the poor, and so in time the substantial equality as to land ownership of the early days disappeared, though the tendency toward large landed estates never went so far in New England as it did in the South.

This system of land distribution was in some respects like the one that our Teutonic ancestors had when they lived in the wilds of Germany. The similarity was due not to any conscious imitation, but to the fact that the early New Englanders were environed by conditions of the same character as those under which the German mark was developed. It was a case of primitive methods of living calling for primitive social institutions. Just as the German mark was held together by the common bond of religion and the fear of neighboring enemies, so the New England township owed its existence largely to the dread of the Indians and the importance attached to church attendance by the

---

[19] For an excellent account of the New England town, see WERTENBAKER, T. J., *The First Americans*, pp. 55-61, 75, 83-86.

[20] BIDWELL and FALCONER, *op. cit.*, p. 52.

Puritans. In both cases the people could more easily ward off the attacks of their enemies and more conveniently perform their acts of public worship if they should live together in villages. The New England township was thus more the creature of environment than of heredity.

It can readily be seen that the method of landholding in New England would cause the farms to be small, at least in the beginning. The social reasons for the township system were also reinforced by certain economic conditions that tended to discourage the growth of great landed estates. The economic reasons for small farms in New England were as follows: (1) The land suited to agriculture was limited in amount. Expansion toward the north was bounded by the French possessions and toward the west by the mountains, which are much nearer the sea than they are in the South. Besides, all the land east of the mountains is not adapted to farming, as considerable portions of it are sandy or swampy. (2) The population increased more rapidly in New England than it did in the South, and if the farms had been large, land for all the people could not have been obtained. (3) The farmers had no great staple like tobacco or rice to export to other countries, and the cereals and hay cultivated by them were bulky and not easy to transport. Moreover, the foreign demand for them was not great, as the other colonies raised them, and England, who was trying to produce her own food supplies, was levying a heavy tax on all grain imported into Britain. There was, therefore, not the incentive to large-scale production that there was in the South. (4) The land, owing to the rocky character of its surface, required more careful tillage than it did on a southern plantation. This meant that intensive farming paid better than extensive. (5) The farmers frequently had some other occupation as a side line, such as fishing, lumbering, and manufacturing. (6) Labor was scarce in New England, and slavery never got a firm footing as it did in the South.

In every town there were some newcomers who had not inherited any land from the original proprietors, and who, therefore, had no legal right to use the land owned by the community as a whole. But in the seventeenth century land was so plentiful and cheap that these unprivileged residents were allowed the use of the common pastures and forest along with the proprietors. In the eighteenth century, however, land became more valuable, and there was a growing tendency to withhold these privileges from non-proprietors. Moreover, new distributions were made from time to time which gradually absorbed all the reserve, and so the common lands by degrees dwindled away. The poorer people thus found it harder and harder to earn a livelihood in the old settlements, and many of them moved into the unoccupied region in the West. During the eighteenth century, however, it became increasingly difficult for farmers of small means to get land even on the frontier. For by the end of the first quarter of this century the old practice of granting lands to a group of prospective settlers had given way to that of selling whole townships to land speculators, who sold it again in small tracts to the actual settlers. In such cases the purchasers were not proprietors and, therefore, did not have all the rights of townsmen, though they did have a voice in the town meeting. The original grantees, many of whom sometimes lived in distant towns, were able, by virtue of their favorable economic position, to exert a strong influence on the town meetings. As they often used this power to secure the enactment of tax laws and other measures that were favorable to themselves, the pioneers living in the villages felt that they were being exploited by wealthy capitalists who were getting profits from their lands without bearing their share of the burdens. The hard-working settlers began to harbor feelings of resentment toward the absentee speculators, who were reaping where they had not sown. During the middle and later decades of the eighteenth century there grew up, therefore, on the frontiers of Connecticut and Massachusetts a bitter class hatred between the small farmers living in the villages and the prosperous owners of large estates who controlled the administration of local affairs.[21]

The system of landholding in the Middle colonies was in one respect similar to that of the South, and in another to that of New England. The grants were made by the king or proprietor to individuals and not to townships, but often the people would group themselves into towns after they had received their lands, though the group system of landholding was not so universal in this section as it was in New England. It was also the practice to require landowners to pay to the proprietors a small sum each year, which was known as a quit rent.[22] The farms were on an

Landholdings in the Middle colonies

---

[21] ADAMS, J. T., *Provincial Society*, pp. 246-250.

[22] Some lands were granted in Pennsylvania that were not subject to quit rents. Nor were quit rents collected in West Jersey or in

average larger than in New England, but not so large as the southern plantations. There was one noted exception to the rule as to moderate-sized farms. In New York the Dutch granted large feudal estates to individuals who were called patroons. When the English took over the colony they confirmed these grants and made other large ones. But this effort to establish patroonships was confined to the valley of the Hudson and its tributaries and was not successful there. These great estates could not procure tenants, and large portions of them "remained uninhabited and uncultivated until separated in later times into small holdings."[23]

The custom as to inheritances in the New England colonies and the Middle provinces, except New York, were not so favorable to the growth and perpetuation of large landed estates as was the case in the South. In New York the English practice of having the oldest son inherit all the land of his father was established by law in 1687; but in the other Middle and Northern colonies it was the custom for persons making wills to distribute their land equally among all the heirs, or at most to leave the oldest son only a double portion. At times, too, the laws made provision for an equal division of estates left by persons without wills.

In the Chesapeake and Southern colonies land grants were all made to individuals and were subject to the payment of quit rents. The authorities were lavish in their patents, and so great tracts were easily obtained. The practice of granting lands in Virginia may be taken as typical of the Chesapeake and Southern colonies. It was the custom here to give to anyone a claim to fifty acres of land for every person he transported to Virginia, provided the person brought over remained there for three years. The only other conditions attaching to this grant were that the land must be occupied, nominally at least, for a year and a quit rent of one shilling had to be paid to the sheriff. The disbursement of the

New Netherland while this latter colony was under Dutch rule. In other places there was strong opposition to paying this charge, and the proprietors and royal authorities had a great deal of trouble in collecting it.

[23] BALLAGH, J. C., *White Servitude in the Colony of Virginia*, p. 110.

For an account of the origin of the land system in the Middle colonies and a comparison of it with that of New England, see OSGOOD, H. L., *American Colonies in the Seventeenth Century*, ii, pp. 6-18, 24-25, 34, 47-52.

quit rents was controlled by the governor, but the revenue derived from them seems to have been all spent for the benefit of the colony.

If these conditions had been complied with, the expense of transporting emigrants would have kept down the size of the grants. But by fraudulent means large estates were frequently acquired without incurring the expense of bringing over the requisite number of emigrants. Land was so plentiful and the desire to have the country settled so great that these frauds were winked at by the authorities. The claim to land acquired by transporting an emigrant was called a head right. It was easy to have head rights allowed on false lists. Shipmasters would sometimes get head rights on lists of their crews. A very common method of cheating the land office was to present a list of names copied out of old record books and get claims on the basis of this list. "The perversion was pushed so far that head rights were granted upon the presentation of lists of names copied from old books of record, and it ended in the clerks in the office of the secretary of the colony falling into the grossly illegal habit of selling these rights to all who would pay from one to five shillings for each right, without any pretension being made that the buyer had complied with the law either by bringing in immigrants himself or by purchasing certificates from persons who had done so."[24]

In Maryland, the Carolinas, and Georgia they had about the same system of granting lands that was in vogue in Virginia, differing generally only in some unimportant details. In all of them head rights were obtained by emigrating or transporting emigrants to America. In Maryland there was an exception to the general practice, in that some manorial estates were established there (see pp. 189-190) somewhat like the patroonships of New Netherland.

The head-right system of granting lands continued until the end of the colonial era, but in the eighteenth century the most usual way of acquiring land was by purchase. This method was more favorable to the creation of large estates than was the head-right system. The law of primogeniture, by which all the land of a deceased parent should descend to the oldest son, was, with modifications,[25] in force in the Chesapeake and Southern prov-

[24] BRUCE, *op. cit.*, i, pp. 523-524.

[25] In Virginia, and probably in other colonies as well, parents in their wills often bequeathed land to their younger sons.

inces, and this helped to perpetuate the large estates thus established. Besides, the English feeling brought by the settlers to
America, that large landed possessions were a badge of social
distinction, doubtless helped also to keep these big estates intact.

Economic
reasons
for large
estates in
the South
The main causes, however, for the continuance of the big plantation in the South were economic. They were as follows:

(1) The principal crops were the great staples, tobacco, rice,
and indigo. There was a strong demand in foreign countries for
these, and so they could be raised in unlimited quantities. These
staples demand a fertile soil, and the finer grades of tobacco
require fresh lands. Its culture thus necessitated the constant
clearing of new grounds. The successful planter would therefore have to own enough land for present and future tillage.
Then, too, the slaves to be kept busy all the year had to have the
opportunity of cutting timber in the winter time. This meant
that a plantation must be large enough to include a good deal of
land that would never be used except for lumbering and pasturage.
Such lands were usually back from the rivers, constituting in
part the upland portions of the plantations. Most plantations were
located on the rivers on account of the fertility of the bottom
land and because of the better transportation facilities. Lands
back from the streams were not only infertile as a rule, but were
well-nigh inaccessible on account of poor roads. They were,
therefore, of small value unless attached to river plantations.

(2) Another cause of large plantations was slavery. The Negro
was not an efficient worker unless he was supervised by a white
overseer. But an overseer commanded such high wages that a
planter could not afford to employ him unless he had a considerable number of slaves to put under his immediate supervision.
Therefore, to be profitable, slave labor should be used on a large
scale. The great staples were especially adapted to slave labor.
Rice was grown in hot malarial swamps where white workers
did not thrive. Indigo was profitably raised in connection with
rice, as the latter did not keep the slave busy all the year. Negroes
were well suited to tobacco culture, for in a tobacco field they
could be grouped so that one white man could look after quite a
number of them. These crops, therefore, made Negro labor profitable and gave an economic basis for slavery in the seventeenth and
eighteenth centuries, as did cotton culture in the nineteenth. So
while cotton is responsible for the perpetuation of slavery, tobacco and rice are responsible for its introduction.

While there were a number of immense estates in the South, there were also a great many small farms. In Virginia and Maryland in the seventeenth century the majority of the planters were sturdy yeomen, who owned small farms and cultivated them without the aid of slave labor. But in the beginning of the eighteenth century the increase in the number of slaves was putting the small landowner at a great economic disadvantage by forcing him to compete with Negro labor. The yeomanry now began to decline in importance in the old, established communities, and many of them were compelled to find homes in the back country or in the more northerly colonies, where conditions were not so unfavorable.[26] In the eighteenth century, therefore, small farms were most numerous in the upland region—the Piedmont section and the Great Valley. There were, however, throughout the entire colonial era quite a number of small landowners interspersed among the big planters in the Tidewater belt. They frequently bought the land that the great planter had used and given up for fresh lands farther west. As they usually had few, if any, slaves, they raised mostly corn and other food products, which they could easily sell to the neighboring tobacco and rice planters. In addition to these small landowners, there also grew up in Virginia and Maryland in the eighteenth century a class of tenant farmers. These were persons who were not able to buy even small tracts of land and were forced to rent portions of the land that had been absorbed by the large planters or speculators.[27]

The colonial farmer was, as a rule, largely independent of the outside world. On his farm were generally produced most of the food and clothing needed by his family and dependents, as well as building material for houses and barns. This was true of the Northern and Middle colonies more than of the Southern, because in the latter more attention was devoted to money exports. But even in the South there were on every large plantation blacksmith and carpenter shops for making and repairing farm implements. Flax and wool grown at home furnished the raw materials, which were usually spun and woven and then made into clothing by the wives and daughters of the small farmer or by the slaves of the large planter. Hides were tanned and made into shoes at home. The farmer also had allied occupations to which *over*

Versatility of the colonial farmer

---

[26] WERTENBAKER, T. J., *The First Americans*, pp. 30-34, 41-44; ADAMS, J. T., *Provincial Society*, pp. 29-30.

[27] *Ibid.*, p. 199.

he devoted his spare time. In the winter he got out staves and shingles or other kinds of lumber. Hunting and fishing were not only recreational sports, but were also sources of gain, especially in the early years of the settlements. In New England the farmer frequently found time to go on fishing trips as far away as the Grand Banks of Newfoundland. This playing the part of a Jack of all trades developed versatility in the farmer, and his mind was freed from the narrowing influence of over-specialization. In this one respect his business was better as an educational agency than the ordinary occupation of today.

¶ Everywhere the energetic farmer lived in comfort, having few of the luxuries but an abundance of the necessaries of life. Land was so cheap and plentiful that anyone with average industry could soon own a farm. There was little or no poverty and great wealth was rare. Taxes were low and little or nothing had to be contributed for the support of the needy. As a rule farmers had large families, but as children were put to work at an early age, they were not an economic burden but an addition to the producing force.

¶ see paper

Selected Readings

1. Indian Agriculture.—Bruce, P. A., *Economic History of Virginia in the Seventeenth Century,* i, pp. 150-155; Gabriel, R. H., *Toilers of Land and Sea,* pp. *29-31; Jameson, J. F., ed., *Narratives of New Netherland,* pp. *107-108.

2. How the Middle-class Farmer Lived.—Gabriel, *op. cit.,* *ch. 4 (excellent pictures).

3. Methods of Farming Employed by the Colonists: Earth-Butchery. —Flint, C. L., in *Eighty Years' Progress,* pp. 21-24; Bolles, A. S., *Industrial History of the United States,* pp. *5-14.

4. Importance of Indian Corn.—Smith, J. R., *Industrial and Commercial Geography,* pp. *82-83.

5. Tobacco Culture.—Bruce, *op. cit.,* i, pp. *438-442; Smith, *op. cit.,* *312-315; *American Husbandry,* i, pp. *223-224, 229-231, 237-238 (contemporary account).

6. Rice Culture.—Gabriel, *op. cit.,* pp. *55-58; Phillips, U. B., *American Negro Slavery,* pp. *88-90; *American Husbandry,* i, pp. *391-394.

7. Farming in Georgia (at the end of the colonial period).—*American Husbandry,* ii, pp. *4-32.

8. Farm Implements.—Kettel, T. P., ed., *Eighty Years' Progress,* pp. *26-32; Bolles, *op. cit.,* pp. *32-33 (for picture of farm implements in 1790, see Kettel, *op. cit.,* p. 28).

9. Indigo Culture.—Gray, L. C., and Thompson, Esther K., *History of Agriculture in the Southern United States to 1860*, i, pp. *290-297.
10. Live-stock Husbandry.—Gray and Thompson, *op. cit.*, i, *ch. 9; *American Husbandry*, i, pp. *80, 133-134, 266-267, 338, 350-351 (contemporary account).
11. Land Tenure in the Northern Colonies.—Bidwell, P. W., and Falconer, J. I., *History of Agriculture in the Northern United States*, *ch. 5; Weeden, W. B., *Economic and Social History of New England*, i, pp. *60-67.
12. The Quit-Rent System in the American Colonies.—Article by B. W. Bond in the *American Historical Review*, xviii, pp. *496-516.

CHAPTER XXII

COLONIAL INDUSTRY

Primary and secondary manufactures

MANUFACTURES are divided into two classes, primary and secondary. The former are those in which raw materials are only slightly changed, such as flour, bread, lumber, naval stores, and pig-iron. The latter are those that have been considerably changed from the natural state, such as cloth, clothing, hats, paper, furniture, steel, and iron implements. Primary manufactures can be carried on profitably in a new and undeveloped country where raw materials are abundant. But for the successful development of secondary manufactures, there must be transportation facilities, a currency system, foreign or domestic markets, and an adequate supply of labor and capital. Good transportation is needed both to convey the finished products to market and to get the raw materials together. An effective monetary or credit system is necessary because labor cannot be employed and the sale of finished products negotiated on a basis of barter.

The colonies had poor transportation facilities and a very imperfect system of currency. There was also a great scarcity of capital and labor, both skilled and unskilled. Especially was there a limited supply of skilled craftsmen who were needed in building up manufacturing industries. This was due in part to the fact that the English emigrants to America came from the farming and laboring classes rather than from the artisan. Moreover, the economic opportunity held out by farming and independent land ownership was greater than that offered by industry. For these reasons secondary manufactures never attained importance in the colonies. The British government also discouraged colonial manufactures of this class. But even if there had been no restrictions the manufacture of finished products would never have made much headway.

Conditions in the colonies were favorable to primary manufactures, as they usually are in new and undeveloped countries. Raw materials were abundant and the mother country encouraged those colonial industries in which raw products were slightly changed in the process of manufacture. Pioneer conditions also call into being those primitive secondary industries that supply the people with the ordinary necessaries of plain living. Thus in the American colonies certain simple, small-scale manufactures were stimulated by the very conditions that rendered manufacturing on a large scale impossible. For example, the scarcity of money and capital in the early years, which was so unfavorable to large-scale industry, necessitated the production at home of most of the clothing, furniture, tools, and household utensils used by the settlers, who were too poor to buy these things from England with the extra costs entailed by the high freight charges.

Conditions in the colonies favorable to primary and primitive secondary manufactures

In all the colonies the spinning and weaving of flax and coarse wool into cloth, the tanning of leather, and the making of shoes, farm implements, rude furniture, and other similar articles, were carried on in the home or in connection with the other farming operations. These activities are known as homespun or household industries. They are naturally allied to farming, for by them the men are afforded employment in bad weather, and women and children given an opportunity to help in the task of meeting the needs of the family. Such industries are stimulated rather than discouraged by poor transportation facilities and the lack of markets. For in backward and isolated communities raw materials cannot be easily sold and so must be worked up into finished products at home. Besides, manufactures are difficult to procure from without and must be made by the community that uses them.

Household industries

One of the most important of the household industries was cloth-making. Spinning and weaving were carried on in the home in all the colonies almost from the beginning. In many homes there was a loom and in nearly all a spinning-wheel. The women of the household usually did the spinning, but often the men assisted at the weaving. In the South the spinning and weaving were done by the slaves on the big plantations, and by the members of the family on the small farms.

Cloth-making

While cloth-making was an important business in all sections, it, as well as manufacturing in general, reached its highest development in the Northern and Middle provinces. In the North agriculture did not make such a drain on the supply of labor and capital as it did in the South. The North had no great staple to sell in England and, therefore, could not procure its manufactures in the homeland, as the South was able to do. This imposed upon the New England and Middle colonies the necessity of producing at home many things that the plantation provinces imported from Europe. Then, too, in the North, town life had made more headway than it had in the South, and so labor and capital could coöperate there more effectively than they could in those sections where population was widely diffused. Moreover, the Middle and Northern colonies were better supplied with skilled craftsmen than were those provinces in which the greater part of the laborers were ignorant slaves.

While most of the English settlers had come from the farming rather than the manufacturing classes, many of the non-English emigrants had been trained in the craft of spinning and weaving in their European homes. This was particularly true of the Scotch-Irish, the French Huguenots, and the German Palatines, and where they settled in considerable numbers the textile industries especially flourished. In the eighteenth century Pennsylvania held a leading place in the production of textiles, and she owed this position largely to the Germans who had settled in the province. The only sections in the South where spinning and weaving attained any importance were the frontier regions occupied by the Germans and Scotch-Irish. These foreigners were inclined to the household industries by the traditions they brought with them from Europe, and their economic isolation forced them to make at home most of the clothing and many of the farm implements they needed. The distance of the upland districts from market towns and the poor means of transportation made it very hard for the people to sell their own products or buy those produced in the seaboard communities.

Materials used in clothmaking
The materials used in making homespun cloth were flax and hemp, wool and cotton. Flax was more widely used than either cotton or wool, as linen in large measure took the place now filled by cotton. Hemp was also used in making coarse cloth. Flax and wool were frequently mixed to make a kind of cloth that was known as linsey-woolsey. The importance of flax and hemp was appreciated by the colonial assemblies, and laws were often passed by them with the aim of encouraging or compelling the people to raise them.

It has been estimated that the household industries supplied the continental possessions as a whole with about three-fourths of the textiles consumed by them. It was only the coarser grades of cloth, however, that were manufactured in the colonies. These cheap homespun fabrics were used in making the clothing for the poorer classes in the North and the slaves in the South, while the well-to-do in both sections used the finer woolens imported from England.

The products of the home loom and spinning-wheel were used mostly by the families producing them. Especially was this the case in the seventeenth century. But by the beginning of the eighteenth century many homes were turning out enough cloth not only for their own needs, but also a considerable amount for the domestic market and even for the intercolonial trade. In many cases in the Middle and Northern sections the industry had outgrown the home and established itself in small factories. A woolen and fulling mill was started at Rowley, in Massachusetts, in 1643, and the first fulling mill in Virginia was erected in 1692. By the middle of the eighteenth century there were a good many fulling mills in Pennsylvania. Philadelphia and Lancaster were the principal centers of the industry in this province. In Lancaster, which was the leading inland town in America, about one-third of the population was engaged in the cloth industry. "By the end of the colonial period in New England some faint beginnings of the factory system could be seen in the grouping of several weaving machines under the same roof."[1]

Another important household industry was the making of leather and the working of it up into shoes, clothing, and harness. Tanning was carried on in every community from the earliest times, as bark suitable for tanning was everywhere easily obtained, and there was always a great demand for leather. It was used not only for shoes and harness, but also for making the breeches and waistcoats of the men and the petticoats and jerkins worn by the women of the lower and middle classes. Tanning was often an auxiliary business of farming, but like weaving it gradually grew into such importance that in many cases it separated from agriculture and became an independent industry. In the manufacture of leather, Pennsylvania, New Jersey, and the New England colonies took the lead. Leather was an important article in the intercolonial trade.[2]

Leather-working was a widespread industry in all the colonies.

Tanning and leather-working

[1] FAULKNER, H. U., *American Economic History*, p. 89.

[2] CLARK, V. S., *History of Manufactures in the United States*, i, p. 115; BISHOP, J. L., *A History of American Manufactures*, i, pp. 446, 461.

In every community of any importance saddles, harness, and coarse shoes were manufactured to supply local needs. Shops for making and repairing boots and shoes could be found everywhere, on the plantations in the South as well as on the farms in the North. In the Southern, as well as in the Middle and Northern provinces, the small farmer often made or repaired the shoes for his own family, usually doing this sort of work on rainy days, winter evenings, or at other odd times. On the big plantations slaves specially trained to work in leather devoted all their time to this craft.

Shoemaking often became an independent occupation, and one man would do the work for the community. Generally the shop of the local shoemaker was small and he worked alone without the aid of hired assistants. His shoes were made for customers in the neighborhood on advanced orders. This was especially true up until the middle of the eighteenth century. By that time shoe manufacturers had in some places begun to engage the services of a few journeymen and apprentices. While shoes were exported from Massachusetts as early as the middle of the seventeenth century, the practice of producing for distant markets was unusual. Transportation facilities were so poor that the manufacturing of shoes, except for the local trade, had not made much progress by the end of the colonial period. The chief seat of the shoe industry was Lynn, Massachusetts. By the middle of the seventeenth century the manufacture of shoes had become the principal business of the town, which became noted for its ladies' shoes, owing to some improvements in their manufacture introduced by a Welshman. A contemporary in 1764 wrote that "shoes for women were made at Lynn exceeding in strength and beauty any that were usually imported from London."[3]

Importance of the forests in industry

The forests constituted one of the most valuable of all the natural resources that were available for the colonists. To them the early settlers were indebted not only for firewood and materials for building their houses and making their furniture and farm implements, but also for game, food, and furs for clothing and export. Besides, the forests furnished pasturage for cattle and hogs. Cattle ran wild in the woods surrounding the frontier settlements, and everywhere hogs in great numbers fed on the mast dropped by the numerous oak and chestnut trees. The forests were also a source of the raw materials for some of the leading

[3] BISHOP, J. L., op. cit., pp. 451-452.

colonial industries. Lumbering, shipbuilding, and the manufacture of naval stores and pot- and pearl-ashes were all forest industries.

Timber was so plentiful that the colonists did not realize the importance of conserving it. It was not always convenient to get logs to sawmills, and often lumber was destroyed in a most wasteful manner, especially in the settlements that were not accessible to navigable streams or water-power. Logs were piled up and burned in order to clear the land. Pot- and pearl-ashes, used in England for bleaching woolens, were the only products derived from this wholesale method of destroying forests. The manufacture of pot- and pearl-ashes

The leading manufacturing industry in the colonial period was lumbering, and it was an important business in all the colonies almost from the beginning. In every community there was a great demand for lumber for building houses and making rough furniture and farming implements. This demand was usually met by working up the timber that was within easy reach of every settlement. Lumbering thus started as a household industry, and was closely allied to farming. The farmer hewed out the timbers for his house and sometimes in the early years the planks for the floors. Besides, he made furniture, household utensils, shingles, and pipe and barrel staves by hand, often devoting odd hours, winter evenings, and rainy days to this kind of work. But the early settlers soon realized the importance of sawmills, and these were in time set up in sufficient number to supply the home demands in all the colonies. The first sawmill in Virginia was erected in 1652, and the first in New England was set up near Portsmouth, New Hampshire, probably as early as 1635. These mills were often run by wind, but more often by water-power. Frequently a corn- or flour-mill was operated in connection with the sawmill. The sawing of lumber for local needs was more important than the manufacture of it for export. Lumbering

The colonists were not slow, however, to discover that timber was one of their most valuable exports, and commercial lumbering became an important enterprise in some settlements in the earliest years. In some localities the production of lumber for export was begun before agriculture had started. Commercial lumbering was carried on more extensively in New England, and especially in New Hampshire and Maine, than in any other section. This was due partly to the fact that agriculture here was not so strong a competitor for labor and capital as it was in those more favored sections where warmer climate and more fertile soil made farming more profitable. Moreover, in New England the conditions for both the production and the marketing of lumber were exceptionally good. There was an abundance of fine timber near the falls of the rivers, where the sawmills were erected. As the fall line in New England is close to the coast, the logs could be carried to the mills without much difficulty and the sawn lumber could easily be sent down the rivers to the ocean ports. Lumber was also exported from the Middle and Southern colonies. Timber in considerable quantities was cut in the forests bordering the Hudson, Delaware, Schuylkill, and Susquehanna rivers and transported down these streams to Albany, New York, Philadelphia, and Baltimore, either to be used in these cities or to be sent to foreign markets. Among the Southern colonies Georgia and North Carolina took the lead in the exportation of lumber.

Lumber was exported mainly in the form of hoops, staves, and headings for barrels; masts and spars for ships; shingles, clapboards, and framing for houses; and sawn lumber in other forms. Timber was becoming scarce in England and the shipbuilders there were anxious to supply their needs as largely as possible from the American forests. The tall white pines in the colonies furnished excellent material for ship masts. To prevent the destruction of this valuable timber the British government sent agents to America to select trees in the public forests to be reserved for the use of the British navy. Trees so selected were marked with a broad arrow and a heavy fine was imposed for cutting them. Unfortunately, the colonists did not support the mother country in this laudable effort at conservation, but on the contrary frequently cut down and destroyed these fine trees in utter disregard of the imperial prohibition. They even complained of this policy as an unwarranted restriction upon their rights.

Laws were passed by the British Parliament for the purpose of encouraging the colonists to send their lumber to the mother country. In the first quarter of the eighteenth century (1722) the duty on American lumber imported into England was removed, and a premium was put on masts and spars. Later (1764) lumber was put on the "enumerated" list—that is, it was named as one of the colonial products that could be exported only to England or her possessions, or if sent to other European countries must first pass through a British port. These inducements caused an increase in the amount of lumber sent to Great Britain, but despite this encouragement most of the lumber exports from the continental colonies went to the West Indies or to Spain and Portugal rather than to England. One reason for this was that the demand in England was mainly for unsawn lumber, while the West Indies took the finished products.[4] Staves, hoops, and heads for barrels were sold, and often the barrels were put together on board the ship while it was *en route*. Ready-framed houses were sometimes sent to the West India Islands.

Pitch, tar, rosin, and turpentine were made in America from the white pine in the North and the yellow pine in the South. The manufacture of these products was usually carried on in those localities where the timber was not accessible to water-power or navigable streams. There was a great demand in England for these commodities, as large quantities of them were needed for the building and repairing of the ships of the British navy and merchant marine. _{Naval stores}

In the seventeenth century England bought her naval stores mainly from Norway and Sweden and northern Russia. The amount of goods exported to these countries from England was not sufficient to pay for the naval supplies imported from them. This unfavorable balance of trade caused a stream of gold and silver to flow from England to the Baltic regions. According to the Mercantilist doctrine such a trade was unprofitable and was condemned by the economists of the day. If these commodities could be bought in the dominions they could be paid for by English manufactures. Then, too, if the New Englanders could be induced to manufacture naval stores in large quantities they would have a staple export with which to buy English goods and would not be tempted to make them at home. Moreover, as long as Britain was dependent upon outside countries for naval supplies the strength of the navy would be to some extent at the mercy of foreign powers. So both the economists and the statesmen felt that it would be best for England to purchase her naval supplies in her American possessions. To encourage the colonies to produce them in larger quantities, Parliament (1705) offered a bounty of four pounds per ton on tar and pitch sent over from America, three pounds per ton on rosin and turpentine, and six pounds per ton on hemp. Some of the colonial legislatures also offered bounties to stimulate the production of these commodities. In order that all colonial naval stores might be sent to England they were put on the enumerated list at the time of the War of

[4] CLARK, V. S., *op. cit.*, pp. 94, 98.

the Spanish Succession (1706).[5] This policy acted as a stimulus to the production of naval stores in the overseas dominions and was especially successful in the Carolinas, where the pines were most numerous. North Carolina produced more pitch and tar than did any of the other colonies.[6]

Ship-
building

Shipbuilding was one of the oldest of the colonial industries. The first decked vessel ever built within the present limits of the United States was constructed by the Dutchman, Adrian Block, at Manhattan in 1614. In this same year John Smith built some fishing-vessels on the coast of Maine. The Plymouth colony was only four years old when it started on its career of shipbuilding, and the Massachusetts settlers built their first ship in 1631. In the other New England colonies and in the Middle provinces shipbuilding was begun soon after the first settlements were made.[7]

This industry was carried on most extensively in New England, though it also flourished in the Middle colonies, especially Pennsylvania. Some small vessels were built in Virginia before 1621, but shipbuilding did not make much progress in this province or the Carolinas in the seventeenth century, although there was in both sections an abundance of good timber suitable for shipbuilding. The culture of tobacco and rice was profitable, and so much capital and labor were attracted to this business that there was little left for other occupations. But in the latter half of the eighteenth century it was discovered that live-oak was better suited to the construction of ships than any other kind of timber, and Virginia and the Carolinas then became important centers of the industry.

New England's lead in shipbuilding was due to the great demand in that section for vessels for commerce and fishing. There was also an abundance of timber suitable for shipbuilding near the coast and the navigable portion of the Connecticut River. Not all of the ships built by the New Englanders were used by their own merchants and fishermen, but many of them were sold in Old England, as ships could be constructed in America more cheaply than in the British Isles. It is estimated that vessels could be built in the colonies at a cost per ton of from one-fifth to one-half less

[5] *Ibid.*, p. 24.
[6] FAULKNER, H. U., *op. cit.*, p. 83.
[7] BISHOP, J. L., *op. cit.*, pp. 37, 58, 59. See also WINTHROP, J., *Journal (Original Narratives)*, p. 65.

than in the mother country. We are not surprised, therefore, to find that at the end of the colonial period one-third of England's merchant marine had been built in America.

Colonial shipbuilding was encouraged by the Navigation Acts of 1651 and 1660. By these laws ships flying the British flag were given a monopoly of a large part of the carrying trade of the empire, and colonial vessels shared in this monopoly.

Mining never became an important industry during the colonial period. The great mineral resources that have in recent decades given the United States her primacy in world industry were unknown or unexploited, and even the few metals that were mined were obtained mainly from sources that are now unused. No attempt was made to tap the rich stores of gas and oil, and the great coal, iron, and copper deposits were hardly touched. The metals that were mined were lead, copper, and iron. Lead was mined in southeastern Missouri after 1720.[8] Most of the lead procured here was molded by the frontier hunters into bullets, and only a small amount was available for export. Lead mines were also worked in Virginia and Pennsylvania at the time of the Revolution. Copper was mined for short periods in several of the colonies, but the quantity produced was small. At Symesburg, Connecticut, a mine was operated with varying success from about 1707 to 1773. In Hudson County, New Jersey, a copper mine was also successfully run by the Schuyler family for a number of years beginning in 1719. One reason for the failure of copper-mining to develop into an important business was the fact that there was no industry resting on copper in colonial times.

In some respects conditions in the colonies were unfavorable and in others favorable to the manufacture of iron. The production of iron required considerable capital and could not be carried on as a side line of agriculture. The industry was also handicapped by poor transportation facilities. The ore had to be carted over poor roads to the furnaces and bloomeries, and the heavy pigs or other iron products conveyed in the same way to market. On the other hand, there was always a great demand at home for iron for making household utensils and farm implements, and the scarcity of money in the colonies ruled out the possibility of buying those articles to any great extent from England. There were also iron-ore deposits in workable quantities in all the colonies,

Mining

The iron industry

[8] FAULKNER, H. U., *op. cit.,* p. 93.

and everywhere there was plenty of wood for making the charcoal needed in smelting.

In the production of iron two kinds of ore were used in the colonial period—bog ore and rock ore. The former was found in the peat bogs in eastern Massachusetts and in the Tidewater region of the Middle and Southern colonies. The latter was mined and used by the furnaces in the "uplands from the Connecticut River, in a circle north of New York City, through northern New Jersey and eastern Pennsylvania southward."[9] Bog ore was of an inferior quality and usually the deposits were limited in amount; but it was easily obtained and was good for making castings and hollow ware.

The first effort to manufacture iron was made by the Virginia Company at Falling Creek, near Jamestown, as early as 1620. A large sum of money was invested in these works, and one hundred and fifty skilled workmen were sent over to operate the plant. A mine was opened and the furnace was started up. But hardly had they begun when the venture was brought to an untimely end by the Indian massacre (1622), in which the iron works were destroyed and the operatives all killed. No other attempt at smelting ore was made in Virginia for about one hundred years, when Governor Spotswood established his furnaces on the Rappahannock River. The first successful effort to manufacture iron in New England was made in 1643 by a company which erected a furnace and a forge at Lynn, after having received special privileges from the General Court of Massachusetts. Bog ore was obtained near the plant and this was worked up into pig-iron, pots, kettles, and other hollow ware. Ironworks were erected in other colonies from time to time, and by the beginning of the Revolution "a line of furnaces and forges extended from New Hampshire to South Carolina." These were most numerous in Pennsylvania. This was due partly to the superior skill of the German craftsmen and partly to the superiority of the upland ores which had begun to be worked extensively by the middle of the eighteenth century.

Rolling-mills and puddling-furnaces for refining were unknown, but there were a few triphammers, plating forges, and slitting-mills in the colonies. By these bar-iron was flattened out into sheets and cut up into small narrow strips or other shapes and sizes that were convenient for making nails and rough imple-

[9] CLARK, V. S., op. cit., p. 76.

ments. On every farm of any consequence there was a blacksmith shop furnished with a small forge and anvil. In these shops the farmers hammered out nails and other implements from the nail rods and iron strips cut out by the slitting-mills. The list of iron products made in the colonies included farming implements, stoves, pots and other household utensils, common wire, and iron and steel work for carriages. Cannon were made by first casting a solid cylinder and then boring it out.

Another important industry was milling. At first grain was ground by hand, but soon wind- and water-mills were erected in all the colonies, often, as has been seen, in connection with saw-mills. In every community there was a mill to grind the grain for local consumption. The miller was usually paid for his services by receiving a certain part of the grain ground. The rate of toll was fixed by law and ranged from one-sixteenth in New England, where the mills were comparatively numerous, to one-sixth in Maryland, in which province they were scarce. By the end of the seventeenth century commercial milling had become important and flour had come to rank as one of the leading colonial exports. The colonies that were tributary to Philadelphia and New York took the lead in the export of flour because more wheat was grown in this region than elsewhere. Grain and flour were sent from one continental colony to another and also to the West Indies and to Europe.[10]

Milling

There were many other industries carried on in the colonies, such as brick- and tile-making, the manufacture of glass, liquors, furniture, candles, and hats, book-binding, paper-making, and printing. A glass factory was erected at Jamestown (1609) when the settlement was only two years old. This the first manufacturing plant ever constructed in English America lasted only thirteen years, as it was destroyed by the Indians in the uprising of 1622. Glass works were established in some of the other colonies, but the high price of labor discouraged this industry and it made little progress before the Revolution.[11] The bricks first used in the early settlements were brought over from England. But the cost of transportation was almost prohibitive, and soon brick kilns were set up in every settled community to supply the local needs. By the time of the Revolution the continental colonies as a whole

Other industries

[10] *Ibid.*, pp. 63-64; BISHOP, J. L., *op. cit.*, pp. 40, 133, 137-138, 143, 145, 148-149.

[11] BISHOP, J. L., *op. cit.*, pp. 232-237.

were not only making enough bricks to meet their own wants, but were also exporting a small surplus to the West Indies. Another widespread industry was the manufacture of furniture. In every locality there was a cabinet-maker who made furniture to order. Some of these artisans were quite skilled and much of their handiwork is still in use. There was, however, no large-scale production of furniture by factories.

The formation of a "trust" in the candle business

In the latter half of the eighteenth century the manufacture of spermaceti candles became an important business. Newport, Rhode Island, took the lead in this industry, and by 1760 seventeen candle-factories were in operation in this town. The candle-makers formed a combination which included all the manufacturers of spermaceti candles in New England and Philadelphia. As a result of this organization they were able to control the price of both the candles and the raw materials used in their manufacture.[12]

The manufacture of rum and other beverages

The distillation of liquors was a universal business in colonial times. The manufacture of beer, cider, ale, brandy, and whisky was frequently carried on as a household industry. There was a great home demand for these beverages, for our ancestors indulged quite freely their appetites for alcoholic stimulants. Corn and fruit were everywhere plentiful, and whisky and brandy could be made from them with little outlay of capital. But not all of the liquor manufactured in the colonies was consumed at home, as much of it was sold in foreign markets. Beer, cider, and ale were exported to the West Indies, but rum was the most important of the liquors manufactured for commercial purposes. The distillation of rum was a profitable industry in New England, especially in Rhode Island.

Colonial legislation affecting manufactures

Laws were passed in the various colonies at different times having as their aim the encouragement of local manufactures. Bounties and premiums were offered, protective import duties were placed on competitive foreign products, and other favors were granted home manufacturers for the purpose of stimulating colonial industry.[13] The purpose of these laws was to promote the development of such essential manufactures as would give the colonies some degree of economic independence and thereby lessen

---

[12] ADAMS, J. T., *Provincial Society,* p. 297; Massachusetts Historical Society *Collections,* series 7, ix, pp. 88-92, 97-102.

[13] For a lengthy discussion of colonial laws affecting manufactures, with specific references to documents, see CLARK, V. S., *op. cit.,* ch. 3.

the hardships that would come to them if they were at any time cut off from the foreign source of supply. In adopting these measures the Americans were imitating the policy of the mother country and trying to practice the philosophy of Mercantilism.

Colonial laws were also enacted to regulate industries in such a way as to protect the consumer against goods of an inferior quality. These regulations were more numerous in the New England colonies than elsewhere, because the Puritan ideal was not unfavorable to restrictions on individuality. However, the efforts made by the provincial legislatures to promote and regulate manufactures had little effect on their development. This was due partly to the fact that the laws were of a temporary nature and were often in effect for short periods only. But the main reason was that the economic life of the colonies was determined by natural forces which were stronger than the artificial restraints. Economic law usually predominates over legislative enactment unless the latter is backed up by the compulsion of a powerful state. The laws of the colonial legislatures did not have behind them a sanction strong enough to override the economic forces and so they did not have much effect on industry.

The policy of the British government with reference to American manufactures was strictly in keeping with the doctrine of Mercantilism. The general principle underlying this policy was the desire to have the colonies supply the English manufacturers with raw materials and buy from them manufactured articles. Laws were passed by Parliament to encourage such primary manufactures as pig- and bar-iron, lumber, naval stores, etc., and to discourage the production of finished articles like those turned out by English mills, such as cloth, hats, and hardware. Manufactures of the former type were encouraged because they were really raw materials slightly changed and were used as raw materials by the more developed industries of the homeland. There were two reasons why manufactures of the latter type were discouraged: (1) If the Americans should engage extensively in the manufacture of such articles they would produce less of the raw materials desired by English manufacturers and would consume what they produced. (2) The demand in America for British manufactures would be supplied by home industries, and the British manufacturers would lose the colonial market. Indeed, colonial manufactures might develop to the extent of competing with British products in European markets.

Policy of the British government toward colonial manufactures

The
Woolens
Act
of 1699

It was not, however, until about the end of the seventeenth century that American manufactures began to attract the unfavorable notice of the British government. By that time the New England colonies had developed the manufacture of coarse woolen cloth to the extent of supplying in part the needs of their own people and were selling cloth to other colonies. The English manufacturers on learning this urged Parliament to destroy this industry in its infancy. In compliance with this request Parliament passed a law (1699) prohibiting the Americans from sending their raw wool or woolen cloth from one colony to another or to foreign countries.[14] This law was generally obeyed, and the woolen industry, even in the North, never advanced beyond the embryonic stage in colonial times. Coarse woolens were woven at home and worn by the masses, but the wealthy classes bought their woolens from England. The law, however, worked no serious hardship to the people, as conditions in the New World were not favorable to manufacturing except on a small scale, and the trade with the West Indies afforded the Northern colonies an economic opportunity that more than compensated for the loss entailed by the restraints imposed by the Woolens Act.

The Hat
Act of
1732

The manufacture of felt hats had become quite an industry in New York and New England by the beginning of the eighteenth century. The American hat-maker could procure beaver more cheaply than could his English competitor, and so had a considerable advantage over him. As a result beaver hats were sent from Boston and New York to Europe and the West Indies in such quantities as to alarm the hatters of London and cause them to petition Parliament (1731) to give them some relief from American competition. They complained that American hats were almost entirely supplying the foreign markets and quite a number of them were being sold in England. It was in response to their request that Parliament passed a law the following year (1732) forbidding the exportation of hats from one colony to another and to foreign countries, and limiting each colonial hat-maker to two apprentices.[15]

The Iron
Act of
1750

By the beginning of the third decade of the eighteenth century, pig- and bar-iron were being exported in small quantities from Virginia and Maryland to England. The Northern colonies smelted a small amount of crude iron, but used more than they

[14] RUFFHEAD, OWEN, *Statutes at Large*, iv, p. 12.
[15] *Ibid.*, vi, pp. 89-91.

produced in shipbuilding and in making finished iron commodities. True to the policy of Mercantilism, Parliament decided to encourage the colonies to produce raw iron, which England wanted, and to discourage the further manufacture of it into the finished product. English forests were being denuded and charcoal was becoming expensive. It cost more, therefore, to make pig-iron in the British Isles than it did in America, and so the British iron manufacturers wanted to procure their raw materials overseas. They also desired a monopoly of the colonial market for the sale of their steel and rolled-iron products. To meet their demands Parliament enacted the law of 1750, which provided that "no mill or other engine for slitting or rolling iron, or any plating forge to work with a tilt hammer, or any furnace for making steel, shall be erected, or after such erection, continued in any of his Majesty's Colonies in America." The production of bar-iron and pig-iron was encouraged by the provision that after 1757 they should be admitted into England free of duty.[16] This law worked a slight hardship on New England, but not a serious one, because agriculture and fishing were more profitable occupations than the iron industry. Besides, the restrictions did not apply to the making of farm implements and nails in the forges. On the other hand, the law was favorable to Virginia and Maryland, for it stimulated the production and export of pig- and bar-iron.

FISHING

The fishing industry started in America a century before the first permanent English settlement was made in Virginia. John Cabot's voyage (1497) revealed to the world the value of the Newfoundland fisheries, and in a few years (by 1504) French seamen were exploiting the great fishing possibilities of the Grand Banks. Soon Portuguese, Spanish, and later English seamen were also going regularly to Newfoundland for fish. At the beginning of the seventeenth century the English began to fish off the coast of New England. Cape Cod was so named by an English explorer, Bartholomew Gosnold (1602), because of the abundance of this fish in its vicinity. In order to promote the fisheries in this region a number of settlements were established in New England between 1620 and 1630. By 1636 Massachusetts had come to realize the importance of her fisheries, and three

Early American fisheries

[16] *Ibid.*, vii, pp. 261-264.

years later the industry was encouraged by exempting from duty for seven years all ships engaged in this business.

Fishing ranked next to agriculture as a colonial industry, and was followed in all the colonies to supply local needs. Oysters, too, were harvested in the Middle colonies, especially Virginia and Maryland. But fishing for export was carried on exclusively in New England.

There were several reasons to account for the primacy of New England in this industry. In the first place, agriculture was not so profitable here as it was in the Middle and Southern colonies, and the people had to engage in other occupations to gain a livelihood. But a more important reason was that the waters of New England and the neighboring regions to the north constituted the finest fishing-grounds in America. The submerging of the North Atlantic coast in prehistoric times had left a fringe of shallow water from Long Island to Newfoundland. The water here was kept cool by currents coming down from the Arctic regions. These were ideal conditions for fish, and cod, mackerel, halibut, and other varieties were very numerous. The fishing industry was also greatly aided in New England by the numerous inlets and harbors which afforded shelter to the fishermen in times of storm and furnished places for drying the fish. The advantages enjoyed by the New Englanders in shipbuilding also promoted the fishing business, and it in turn encouraged shipbuilding.

In the early years the New Englanders carried on their fishing ventures off their own coast, but later (after 1670) they went up into the Gulf of St. Lawrence and off the shores of Nova Scotia and Newfoundland. The Grand Banks of Newfoundland were the finest of the fishing-grounds. There were many varieties of fish taken, but the most important were mackerel and cod, the latter especially being valuable as an export. Of the fish caught on these expeditions the better class was sold to the Catholic countries of Spain and Portugal. The poorer kinds were shipped to the West Indies and sold to the sugar planters for their slaves. The "middlings" were usually disposed of in the home market, or else sent to the Canaries and the Madeira Islands.

There were also whales in the New England waters, and whaling had become an important industry by the end of the seventeenth century. Whales were valuable chiefly for the oil made from their blubber, which was used in making candles and lubricants; for the ambergris procured from them, which was an important ingredient in the manufacture of perfume; and for whalebone, used in making stays for the wearing apparel of the women of that day. At first whaling consisted in catching the few whales that drifted ashore. But by the end of the seventeenth century, vessels engaged in this industry had begun to venture out into the deep seas in pursuit of their prey. When in the latter part of the colonial period the whales had left the New England waters for the northern seas, the fishermen pursued them into the Arctic regions. Whalers ventured as far north as Baffin Bay and Davis Strait. Citizens of Provincetown and Nantucket were especially prominent in this far-off whale-fishing.[17]

The fishing industry had a very important place in the economic life of New England. It stimulated shipbuilding and commerce and afforded a training-school for sailors. Commerce and navigation brought the people in contact with the outside world and gave them a broader outlook on life. It promoted the cooperage industry and the manufacture of salt. New England was indebted to this business for a valuable staple of export in the form of codfish and mackerel. Fishing was also the basis of the important trade with the West Indies, as fish was one of the most valuable products exported to these islands from the New England colonies.

Importance of the fishing industry in New England

Selected Readings

1. Colonial Manufactures.—Wells, L. R., *Industrial History of the United States,* *ch. 6; Webster, W. C., *General History of Commerce,* pp. *328-333; Keir, M., *Manufacturing Industries in America,* pp. *30-41.
2. Lumbering.—Moore, J. R. H., *An Industrial History of the American People,* *ch. 3 (readable, though elementary).
3. Fisheries.—Johnson, E. R., and others, eds., *History of Domestic and Foreign Commerce of the United States,* i, *ch. 9 (this article was written by T. W. Van Metre). There is also an excellent short account in his *Economic History of the United States,* pp. *94-96.
4. Cloth-making in the Home.—Earle, Alice M., *Home Life in Colonial Days,* chs. 8-10.
5. The Age of Homespun.—Keir, M., *The Epic of Industry,* *ch. 1.
6. The Coming of the Artisan.—Keir, M., *The Epic of Industry,* *ch. 2.
7. Scarcity of Labor.—Clark, V. S., *History of Manufactures in the United States,* i, pp. *152-155.

[17] For the relation of the fishing industry to the wars between the French and the English colonies, see pp. 378-379.

CHAPTER XXIII

TRANSPORTATION AND TRADE

Modes of Travel

Water transportation

THE continental colonies were favored by geographical conditions for commerce both among themselves and with foreign countries. There were a number of fine harbors on the coast of the Northern and Middle colonies, and everywhere navigable rivers or bays led back into the interior. During the seventeenth century nearly all the population lived within easy reach of waterways, and even in the eighteenth century, except for the back country, no large proportion of the people were located so far inland as to have no access to navigable streams. Water was thus the chief means of trade and transportation in colonial times. The rivers were more valuable for navigation than they are now; for a great deal of the land was still covered with forests, and the streams, being fed gradually, had a comparatively even flow and never became so shallow in times of drought as they do today. Besides, the boats of that period were small and did not require deep water. Nearly every family living on a stream had some kind of a boat, which was used on the rivers as we use the automobile on the roads of today. These boats were sometimes large enough to be propelled by sails, but frequently they were small bark or log canoes.

Roads

The great convenience of the rivers enabled the people to get along without any good roads. This was fortunate, as it would have been impossible in the colonial period to construct highways that could have accommodated the whole volume of traffic even of that day. The scarcity of labor and capital and the sparseness of the population precluded all means of land communication in the country except the dirt road. There were, therefore, no hard-surfaced turnpikes in any of the colonies during the entire colonial period.[1]

[1] There was, however, a hard-graveled road leading out from Portsmouth, Maine, as early as 1760 (ANDREWS, C. M., *Colonial Folkways*, p. 215).

The first roads in America were Indian trails. These were usually well located and lay along the shortest and best routes across the country. This is shown by the fact that, in the main, these trails have been followed in building many of the highways of today. The Indian trails were usually from twelve to eighteen inches wide and were sometimes worn to a depth of a foot. After the English settlers came, these paths were widened by travel and later were made into roads by order of the provincial or local authorities. These roads were very poor. They were uncomfortably dusty in the summer and fall and on account of the deep mud almost impassable in the spring and winter. There were few bridges, and often large streams had to be forded, sometimes when they were swollen by floods. There were numerous mudholes and washouts in which vehicles could be stuck or overturned. Traveling was, therefore, not only uncomfortable and dangerous, but for a long time was well-nigh impossible if attempted in vehicles. During the seventeenth century interior travel and transportation was mostly on foot or by horseback.[2] Women sometimes rode behind their husbands or near relatives on pillions, and sometimes separately on side-saddles. A fine breed of horses was developed in Virginia and also in Rhode Island, and the prices of horses were high everywhere in colonial times.

Indian trails were widened into roads

In the Middle and Northern colonies much of the inland travel was done in the winter-time because there was more leisure then and also because the roads and streams in these regions were frozen and easily traversed by sleighs. Sleighs had been introduced quite early and by 1700 they were in general use. Snowshoes were also used in going short distances.

In the cities wealthy people began at an early date to use sedan-chairs, according to the European custom. These were carried by servants or sometimes by horses. Later on in the seventeenth century, wheeled vehicles came into use in the cities, and by the end of the century there were a dozen or so of horse-drawn conveyances in each of the larger towns of Philadelphia, Boston, and

Vehicles in the city

[2] For a typical account by a contemporary of the trials incident to travel in the early part of the eighteenth century, see WINSHIP, H. A., ed., *Journal of Madam Knight*. A portion of this journal, describing the journey of Sarah Kemble Knight from Boston to New Haven (1704), is given in HART, A. B., *American History Told by Contemporaries,* ii, pp. 224-229.

New York. Some of these carriages were like the heavy English coaches of the day and were pulled by two horses. But there were two other types of carriage that were more popular because they were better adapted to conditions in America. These were the chair and the chaise, each drawn by one horse. The former was a light two-wheeled vehicle with a seat for two. Sometimes there was an additional small seat in front at the end of the shafts for the driver. The chaise was just a chair with a top. When vehicles drawn by horses were introduced in Boston (1687) there was a strong sentiment against them as a sign of worldly luxury and extravagance. They grew in popularity, however, despite this feeling, though their use was for quite a time confined to the towns.

The stage-coach   By 1730 road development had gone forward to such an extent that carriages were quite common throughout the colonies. In Virginia the wealthy planter frequently rode in a carriage drawn by six horses and attended by a black coachman, a postilion, and a footman. The stage-coach also made its appearance about the same time. The first stage line for the conveyance of the public was opened in 1732 between Burlington and Amboy, New Jersey. From Amboy to New York and from Burlington to Philadelphia the connections were made by boat. By 1756 there was a through stage between Philadelphia and New York, and the trip was made in three days. This journey must have subjected the passengers to considerable strain, as they suffered from cold in winter and heat in summer. The coach was going about eighteen hours a day, and the passengers usually did not arrive at the taverns until ten at night, although they were called up at around three in the morning. By the beginning of the Revolution there were a number of stage lines in operation.

Road construction at the end of the colonial period   By the end of the colonial period a good many long roads had been constructed. The principal cities were all linked together by roads and there was a continuous system of highways extending from Boston to Savannah.[3] The western frontier was also connected with the east by two military roads built in the French and Indian War by Generals Braddock and Forbes. Both of these led to the present site of Pittsburgh, the former going across

---

[3] For a contemporary account of roads in America in 1732, see *Vade Mecum for America.*

western Maryland and southern Pennsylvania and the latter across
the middle portion of Pennsylvania.[4]

TAVERNS

Taverns were common in all the colonies, and were especially
important in New England. The town governments here were
suspicious of outsiders, and in Boston there were at one time strict
regulations forbidding townsmen from entertaining strangers
without permission from the authorities.[5] As private hospitality
toward outsiders was thus hampered, there was a great need for
places of public entertainment. The inn was everywhere a social
center. Not only could the traveler find food and shelter for himself and his horse at the tavern, but he could also get liquid re-
freshments here with which to arouse his drooping spirits. It is
true that in New England, as elsewhere, the innkeeper was restricted in the dispensing of both food and drink by governmental
regulations, but there was still room inside these limits for considerable sociability at the taverns.

The tavern was generally near the church and was regarded as
a convenient aid to it. In the nooning period the people on cold
winter days could assemble before its roaring fire to exchange
conversation, get the news, and refresh themselves with food and
drink. At such times the meeting-houses were terribly cold, as
they usually had no stoves or any other means of heating except
the small foot-warmers used by the women. The tavern was the
club of that day, and its attractions appealed to some people more
strongly than did those of the church. In its large public room
Yankee curiosity could be regaled with stories told by travelers,
who would usually have news from the outside world. The regulations for segregating the classes did not apply here, but men of
low degree might jostle their neighbors of the highest rank.
Democracy thus found a home in the drinking rooms at a time
when it was excluded from the church. We are not surprised,
therefore, to learn that in every community there were men who
preferred to loiter around the comfortable fire of the inn to sitting
in an unheated meeting-house with nothing but the minister's
fervor to keep them warm. To prevent this neglect of worship
a law was passed in early Massachusetts requiring all the tavern-

Taverns
in New
England

[4] For map showing the location of these roads, see VOLWILER,
A. T., *George Croghan,* frontispiece.
[5] EARLE, ALICE M., *Stage Coach and Tavern Days,* pp. 1-2.

keepers within a mile of any church to turn out all persons during service who were able to go to church.

In New York

In New York the taverns were used sometimes as meeting-places for the social clubs, and in them were held concerts, balls, and public receptions.

In Virginia

As a rule, every county-seat in Virginia had a tavern, which served as the political and social center of the community. Some-times sessions of the county court and other public meetings were held in it before the court-house had been erected. The amuse-ments of the taverns were not always harmless, for gambling as well as drinking was encouraged by them. They were usually equipped with pool-tables and bowling-alleys, and betting on these games was a very common pastime. The drinking public was protected against profiteering landlords by governmental regula-tion of the price of drinks. The most famous of all the inns in Virginia was the Raleigh Tavern, in Williamsburg. It had a banqueting-hall, known as the "Apollo Room," in which were held fashionable balls and important public meetings. It was in this room that the Phi Beta Kappa Society was organized. Just prior to the outbreak of the Revolution, meetings were held in the Apollo Room by the leaders of the patriot cause, and so important were these meetings that Raleigh Tavern contested with Faneuil Hall for the honor of being the "Cradle of Liberty."

THE COLONIAL POST OFFICE

Periods in the history of the colonial post office.

The history of the American post office prior to the outbreak of the Revolution is divided into three periods. The first extends from the beginning to the year 1691; the second from 1691 to 1707; the third from 1707 to 1775. The few post offices that were established in the first period were controlled by the colonial governments. During the second period the post-office system was under the management of a proprietor who was given a complete monopoly of the postal business. Throughout the third period the American post was under royal control and was a part of the postal system of the British empire.

First period: No organized postal system in the early years

In the earliest years there was no organized arrangement in any of the colonies for transmitting and distributing letters and packages. Letters were sent by friends, merchants, and other pri-vate messengers, and Indians were frequently employed in this service. Ship captains were intrusted with the mail between the possessions and the mother country. Letters sent to England and

Holland from America were turned over to the post offices in the home ports and distributed by the postal authorities there.

There was, however, no arrangement to provide for the distribution of letters coming to the colonies from the homeland. It was to remedy this lack that the first steps were taken to establish a postal system in the dominions. In 1639 the General Court of Massachusetts passed a law designating the tavern of Richard Fairbank in Boston as the place to which all letters going abroad could be brought and from which those from abroad should be distributed to the persons to whom they were addressed. Fairbank was to receive one penny for each letter delivered by him. He was not, however, given a monopoly of the collection of letters, as the order expressly stipulated that "no man shall be compelled to bring his letters thither except as he please."[6] Some years later (1652) a similar provision was adopted by the Dutch West India Company for New Netherland.[7]

Apparently, nothing further was done for some time to facilitate the transmission and distribution of private letters. For several decades there was not much need of an organized agency to handle the small amount of mail that passed between the settlers, practically all of whom lived on the sea coast or on the banks of navigable streams and were more concerned about the means of communication with the mother country than with other sections of America.

The first step toward the establishment of an internal postal system was taken to meet the necessity of forwarding government letters and dispatches. By 1658 there had grown up a practice in Virginia of requiring planters to send all official papers from one plantation to another until they reached the person to whom they were addressed.[8] In Massachusetts and Connecticut laws were passed (1673, 1674, respectively) providing for the carrying of official documents by riders, who were to be paid out of the public funds. This service was performed in Pennsylvania by the constables, sheriffs, and justices of the peace.

Massachusetts was the first of the colonies to provide a plan for carrying and distributing private mail within the province. In

Side notes:
Beginnings of a postal system in Massachusetts

First organized plan for transmitting mail within the colonies limited to public letters and dispatches

[6] *Collections* of the Massachusetts Historical Society, 3rd series, vii, p. 48; WOOLLEY, MARY E., *Early History of the Colonial Post-Office*, pp. 270-271.

[7] *New York Colonial Documents*, xiv, pp. 186, 446.

[8] HENING, W. W., *Statutes at Large*, i, p. 436.

1677 the General Court passed a law setting the price at which private letters were to be carried and also appointed a postmaster. A like system was established in Pennsylvania in 1683.

The first attempt to establish an intercolonial postal route

In the meantime an effort had been made to link some of the colonies together by an intercolonial postal system. For some years there was no urgent demand for this, as the different colonies had little intercourse with each other. But in 1672 the threat of war between England and Holland made it desirable for New York and New England to keep in touch with each other if they were to coöperate effectively in warding off the common danger. To this end Governor Lovelace of New York at the instance of the king established a mail route between New York and Boston over which a carrier was to go once a month.[9] There was no road at that time between these two towns, and Governor Winthrop was asked to "discourse with some of the most able woodmen, to make out the best and most facile way for a post, which in process of tyme would be the King's best highway."[10] The carrier had made only a few trips when the project was brought to an untimely end by Indian troubles and the recapture of New York by the Dutch. When New York was returned to the English in 1674 the mail route was not reopened, as the need for coöperation against a common enemy no longer existed.

Second period: The post office put under proprietary management

Within the next decade and a half two other efforts were made to establish an intercolonial postal system, but these attempts were only partially and temporarily successful. In 1691, however, the American post office entered upon a new career, for it was at this time that King William made Thomas Neale postmaster-general for all the British possessions in America, with "authority to establish within the chief parts of their Majestie's colonies and plantations in America, an office or offices for the receiving and despatching of letters and pacquets, and to receive, send and deliver the same."[11] His patent gave him a monopoly of the right to carry letters, with certain exceptions, for a period of twenty-one years.

Neale chose as his deputy in America Andrew Hamilton of

[9] Massachusetts Historical Society's *Collections*, 5th series, ix, pp. 83-84.

[10] Quoted by WOOLLEY, MARY E., *op. cit.*, p. 272. See also RICH, W. E., *History of the United States Post-Office*, p. 7.

[11] For Neale's commission, see WOOLLEY, MARY E., *Early History of the Colonial Post-Office*, appendix.

New Jersey, a very able man, who was for some years governor of that province. He enlisted the coöperation of the colonial legislatures and had them pass laws fixing rates and confirming the privileges that had been granted to Neale by the crown.[12] Encouraged by this support, Hamilton was soon able to establish a line of posts from Portsmouth, New Hampshire, to Philadelphia, with a weekly mail service each way between these two points.

It was expected that the American post office would be a source of revenue to Neale, who was allowed all the profits accruing from the business. But there were no profits. On the contrary, there was always a deficit, which Neale had to make good out of his own private funds. He was, therefore, willing to give up his patent, and in 1707 the American postal system was taken over by the crown and was henceforth run by the British postal authorities.

In 1710 an act was passed by Parliament (effective 1711) centralizing the control of the postal system for all the British dominions. By this law the postmaster of London was made postmaster-general for the whole empire. Deputy postmasters-general were to be appointed for Edinburgh, Dublin, New York, and the West Indies. The deputy postmaster-general residing in New York was given authority to appoint deputies, and he and his employees were to have charge of all postal business in the continental colonies. The rates of postage were fixed in the act and they were higher than they had been before. These rates were in the nature of a tax, for it was expected that they would not only cover operating expenses, but would yield a surplus revenue which could be used for helping to defray the expenses of the War of the Spanish Succession. *Third period: The colonial post office linked up with the imperial postal system*

While the colonial post was under the proprietary control of Neale and his assigns, Virginia and Maryland were not included in the system established by him. But the plan of reorganization provided for by the Act of 1710 contemplated the extension of the colonial post to include the Southern provinces. Accordingly, by 1717 postmasters had been appointed for Virginia and routes opened in all of the more populous counties. But it was not long before the people of Virginia awoke to the realization that the rates charged by the postal authorities for letters brought from

[12] For references for these laws see an article by SMITH, WILLIAM, in the *American Historical Review*, xxi, p. 262, note 13.

overseas were considerably higher than those they had been accustomed to pay. They then objected to the increased rates and raised the protest that they were being unlawfully taxed without the consent of their assembly. The assembly thereupon virtually nullified the Act of 1710 by imposing conditions for its enforcement that could not be met. The post-office system was, therefore, not extended to Virginia until ex-Governor Spotswood became postmaster-general in 1732.

The colonial post efficiently managed by Franklin as deputy postmaster-general

A very important step forward was taken in 1753 when Benjamin Franklin and William Hunter were appointed joint postmasters-general for the colonies. Franklin had already been serving as postmaster of Philadelphia for sixteen years and was exceptionally well fitted by experience and ability for this responsible position. He at once set about making reforms in the service. After an extended tour of investigation, in the course of which he visited all the offices in the Northern and Chesapeake colonies, he began to open up new and shorter routes, to speed up the service, and to make other important improvements. The time required for letters to go from Philadelphia to Boston was reduced by one-half. This was done by requiring the riders on this route to travel by night as well as by day. In a few years (by 1757) the revenues were in excess of the expenditures for the first time in the history of the American post office.[13]

Provisions for conveying mail overseas

Up to the Seven Years' War there were no regular mail-ships plying between England and the continental colonies and no regular schedule for the mail service. The postal authorities delivered the mail-bags to any ship that happened to be going to America, and the captain had to turn over the bags to the postmaster in the port at which he first landed. Such a system had its drawbacks in time of peace and was utterly inadequate in time of war.

After Braddock's defeat (1755) the Board of Trade realized the need of better communication between the dominions and the mother country, and in this same year instructed the postmasters-general to arrange for regular monthly trips to New York and to restore the West Indian service, which had been discontinued in 1749. The packet boats engaged in carrying the mail were armed and were not allowed to take on any other freight. The service was continued after the war, despite the fact that it was very expensive.[14]

[13] SMITH, WILLIAM, *ibid.*, xxi, p. 270.
[14] *Ibid.*, pp. 270-271.

Franklin held the office of postmaster-general for over twenty years. The greater part of this time was spent in England, first as the agent of Pennsylvania and later as the agent of Massachusetts. This long absence exposed him to criticism in London, and the part he played in the events that preceded and led to the Revolution aroused antagonism toward him in influential circles. This opposition reached its climax when he made public the Hutchinson letters, and he was removed from office (1774).[15]

Franklin dismissed from the postmaster-generalship

The dismissal of Franklin marks the end of the colonial period for the American post office. Soon thereafter it was declared independent of the imperial system and was definitely allied with the patriot cause.

The colonial post had by the outbreak of the Revolution been extended until it embraced all the thirteen provinces. It was, therefore, a useful agency in binding the colonies together. Stamps were not in use and postage was paid on receiving letters. The rates were based on distance and the size of the letters. Letters were classed as single, double, and treble, depending on whether they consisted of one, two, or three sheets. The rate for the double and treble sizes were, respectively, twice and three times as high as those of the single, and the charges for letters weighing an ounce or more were still higher. No envelopes were used and letters were so folded that an unwritten part of the sheet was always on the outside. On this free space the address was written. Postmasters were expected to insist on cash payment for all pieces of mail delivered, but they failed to observe this regula-

Condition of the American postal system at the end of the colonial period

[15] There had come into Franklin's possession some private letters that had been written by Governor Hutchinson and Lieutenant-Governor Oliver of Massachusetts. These letters showed that these officials were using their influence to inflame the minds of the British authorities against the colony. As Franklin was the agent of Massachusetts, he felt that he should send these papers to the speaker of the Massachusetts assembly. Upon the receipt of these letters, the assembly sent an address to the king, asking the removal of Hutchinson and Oliver from office. When this petition came before the Privy Council (January, 1774) the Solicitor-General made a savage attack on Franklin, charging that he had committed a most dishonorable act in divulging the contents of private letters. Franklin felt deep humiliation over the insult, but always maintained that he had done no wrong in forwarding the letters to Boston. A few days later he was removed from his place as postmaster-general (TREVELYAN, G. O., *The American Revolution*, part i, pp. 169-174).

tion and frequently their customers were greatly in arrears on their dues for letters.[16]

Newspapers admitted to the mails

For a long time newspapers were not admitted to the mails, though they were carried by the riders, who received extra pay for this service. The postmasters usually printed newspapers, and often would not allow their riders to carry any newspapers except their own. When Franklin was publishing a newspaper in Philadelphia, he complained that he was hampered by this monopoly while the owner of a rival sheet was city postmaster. On becoming postmaster-general Franklin did away with this monopoly (1758) by instructing deputy postmasters to admit newspapers to the mails at fixed rates.

FUR TRADING

Fur trading

In the seventeenth century the only commerce of any importance between the coast settlements and the interior was the fur trade. Some furs were procured by hunting and trapping on the part of the colonists, but the greater part of the supply was purchased from the Indians. There were a number of fur-bearing animals, such as the otter, marten, fox, and beaver, the last-named being by far the most important. Fur trading was an important activity in all the colonies during the seventeenth century; but by the beginning of the eighteenth century beaver was becom-

[16] We have an account of the American post office as it appeared to a competent observer at the end of the colonial period. This was written by Hugh Finlay, who was sent out in 1773 by the British postal authorities as surveyor of the American post office. He traveled through the continental colonies from Portland, Maine, to Savannah, Georgia, and wrote an account of his impressions in his journal. He found everywhere that the postal laws were being violated, especially by the carriers. They lost time because they carried packages and performed other business for people living on their routes. At one place he heard many inquiries as to whether he had seen the carrier driving some oxen, which evidently he had engaged to do. The riders also carried letters without putting them in the mail-bag, taking for themselves the pay for conveying them and thus depriving the office of postage. Many persons of standing would make a private bargain with the carrier for taking their dispatches rather than send them by mail, which was more expensive.

See *Journal Kept by Hugh Finlay*, pp. 1-99. In the Introduction, pp. v-xxv, there are important documents, including postal laws passed by various colonial legislatures.

ing relatively scarce, and the business in the Northern and Middle sections (except in Pennsylvania) had begun to decline.

New York was the most successful of all the English colonies in procuring beaver from the Indians. Fur trading was the main object that prompted the settlement of the province by the Dutch West India Company, and it was the principal industry of the colony during the period of the Dutch occupation. In New Sweden and Pennsylvania fur trading was also a profitable business. It was promoted in the latter colony by the friendship that existed between the Indians and the Quakers. In New England, owing to the fact that the rivers except the Connecticut were navigable for only a short distance, the fur trade did not attain the importance that it did in some of the other sections.

An extensive trade in skins was carried on in the lower South both in the seventeenth and in the eighteenth century, especially in the latter period. In the early years, before rice became an important product, hides procured from the Indians were the chief exports from South Carolina. Beaver skins in this region were not of as good quality as they were in the Northern colonies, and so the trade in beaver was comparatively unimportant. Deer were, however, very plentiful, and the hides of these animals constituted the bulk of the fur trade. From 1720 on, trade in skins was a growing source of profit to the Charleston merchants and English traders who were engaged in the business. Fort Moore, on the Savannah River, opposite the present site of Augusta, was the center of the trade. From this point a road ran to Charleston, and another into the Indian country. Later another post was established near the present site of Columbia, and still later other trade centers were located on the frontier. After the business was well organized pack-mules were used in conveying the skins to the seacoast. Sometimes trains of eighty mules could be seen going eastward loaded with furs, or westward bearing the trinkets and goods with which furs were to be purchased. In 1748 approximately 160,000 deer skins were exported from South Carolina. The fur trade was not only a source of profit to the settlers, but was also valued as a means for keeping the Indians friendly to the English and preventing their becoming allies of the French and Spaniards.[17]

[17] CRANE, V. W., *The Southern Frontier*, pp. 110-112, 115, 127-128; LOGAN, J. H., *History of Upper South Carolina*, i, p. 382; McCRADY, EDWARD, *South Carolina under Royal Government*, p. 270.

Fur trading was a very profitable business. There was always a great demand for furs in Europe, and the prices were high. The margin of profit for the American trader was wide, as he could usually procure peltries from the Indians at a price far below their real worth. Often in the early period the natives were tricked into exchanging furs of great value for cheap or worthless trinkets. In later years the Indians came to understand better the value both of their own product and of the goods that the English had to barter for it, and so it became more difficult to cheat them. But even then, by getting them drunk and by taking advantage of their necessities, unscrupulous traders were often able to get beaver at such rates as would permit of an enormous profit.

Importance of the fur trade

Furs and skins held an important place in the economic life of the colonies. In the first place, they furnished the settlers with a salable article of export. They were of high value in proportion to bulk and could be easily transported. The demand in England for them was so great that there was never any difficulty in disposing of them for gold or silver or in exchange for goods bought in the mother country. England was so anxious to get all the beaver produced in the colonies that Parliament in 1764 put furs and skins on the enumerated list (see p. 506). Besides, the traffic in furs aided in the exploration and settlement of the West. As the cleared areas encroached more and more on the original forest, the fur-bearing animals gradually moved into the western wilds, where the forests had been untouched. Traders and trappers thus had to penetrate farther and farther into the unexplored West in search of their valued product. In this way a knowledge of the wilderness was gained, and it proved useful to the settlers who followed the traders and hunters. The trading posts, which were at first only temporary depots for the collection of skins, became permanent settlements. Thirdly, fur trading helped to precipitate the conflict between the French and the English (see p. 390).

Foreign Commerce

Countries that the colonies traded with

The foreign commerce of the colonies soon grew into considerable importance, and by the time of the Revolution its value was about one-seventh of that of all the trade of the British empire.[18]

[18] Bogart, E. L., *Economic History of the United States* (1923 ed.), p. 73. For statistics showing the value of this trade, see tables

This trade was carried on with the British Isles, Holland, and other European countries, the Azores, Canary, and Madeira Islands, the West coast of Africa, and the British and foreign West Indies. These avenues of commerce were all opened up before the end of the seventeenth century, and during the eighteenth century there was a great expansion of trade along these lines. The exports and imports of the various sections were (with a few exceptions) about the same in the eighteenth century as in the seventeenth, except that they were greater in amount in the later period.

The most important branch of colonial foreign commerce was the trade with England. At the beginning of the eighteenth century the exports from all the continental possessions to the mother country were slightly less in value than the imports from it, but by the end of the colonial period the value of the imports from the homeland was considerably above that of the exports.[19] This is accounted for by the fact that all of the colonies north of Maryland bought a good deal more from the British Isles than they sold to them. The English people were trying to raise their own food supplies, and in order to encourage agriculture in Britain the government imposed a high tax on foodstuffs imported into the island. This duty was so high that it excluded the farm products of the Northern dominions. On the other hand, these colonies, as well as those in the South, bought woolen and linen goods and other manufactures in large quantities from England. The result was that in 1700 the value of the exports from New England to the mother country was only one-half of that of the imports, and the excess of the imports over exports was still greater for Pennsylvania and New York. But the exports from Virginia and Maryland to England were greater in value than the imports from the homeland. This favorable balance was caused by the large shipments of tobacco from these two provinces. Tobacco was the principal farm product of this section, and the bulk of the crop was sent to England, only a small amount being smuggled into Holland and other European countries. In

Trade with England

given in JOHNSON, E. R., and others, *History of Domestic and Foreign Commerce of the United States*, i, pp. 92, 118, 119.

[19] For tables showing the value of colonial imports from and exports to England by decades during the first eight decades of the eighteenth century, see FAULKNER, H. U., *American Economic History*, p. 111. See also JOHNSON, E. R., *op. cit.*, i, pp. 89, 90.

the eighteenth century the rice, indigo, and naval stores shipped from the Carolinas and Georgia helped to swell the excess of Southern exports over imports from Great Britain.

The West Indian trade

The trade between the continental colonies and the West Indian islands constituted an important part of colonial commerce. It was carried on between all the mainland possessions and the sugar islands. Maryland, Virginia, and the other Southern provinces received slaves, rum, molasses, sugar, ginger, and other tropical products from these islands and sent to them furs, corn, cattle, pork, pitch, tar, and clapboards. These exchanges were sometimes made directly by the southern planters with their West Indian agents, but often they were effected through merchants from the northern towns, whose ships touched at southern ports going to and coming from the sugar islands.

Especially important was the commerce carried on between the West Indies and the New England and Middle colonies. A regular trade had grown up between New England and the West Indies by the middle of the seventeenth century, and it continually grew in importance as both sections increased in wealth and population. This interchange of products was at first confined to the English West Indies, but later it was extended to the Dutch, French, and Spanish islands. During the eighteenth century the commerce with the sugar islands was a leading factor in the economic life of all the Northern and Middle colonies (those north of Maryland). The chief exports from these sections were fish, Indian corn, wheat, flour, lumber, and live animals. Wheat and foodstuffs were exported from the Delaware and Hudson region in greater quantities than from New England or any other section. So much was this the case that the Middle provinces were known as the "bread colonies." For these commodities there were received in exchange rum, molasses, sugar, ginger, and other tropical products, as well as bills of exchange from the English and money from the foreign islands.[20]

[20] JOHNSON, E. R., *op. cit.*, i, pp. 94-95.

A bill of exchange is "an unconditional order in writing, signed by the person giving it (the drawer), requiring the person to whom it is addressed (the drawee) to pay on demand or at some fixed time a given sum of money to, or to the order of, a named person (the payee), or to bearer." It is unlike a check in that it is usually drawn on a private person and not a bank, and is not usually payable on sight or on demand, but at a definite date. A bill of exchange is not

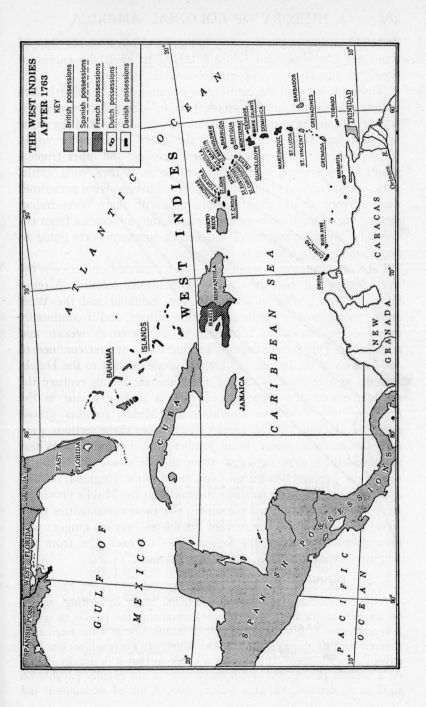

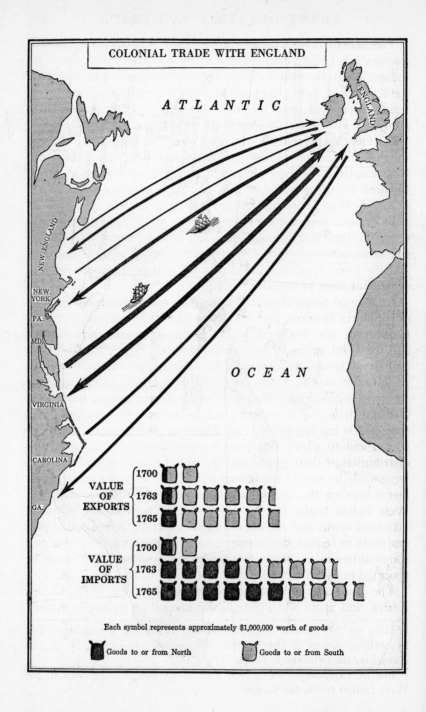

COLONIAL TRADE WITH ENGLAND

ATLANTIC

ENGLAND

NEW ENGLAND

NEW YORK

PA.

MD.

VIRGINIA

CAROLINA

GA.

OCEAN

VALUE
OF
EXPORTS

1700
1763
1765

VALUE
OF
IMPORTS

1700
1763
1765

Each symbol represents approximately $1,000,000 worth of goods

Goods to or from North   Goods to or from South

The economic prosperity of the New England and Middle colonies was largely dependent upon the commerce with the West Indies. As their most valuable exports, fish and food supplies, were excluded from England by high import duties, they were mainly dependent upon the sugar islands for a market for these products. To this trade they were indebted for the money and bills of exchange with which they paid for English goods and for the molasses on which rested the flourishing rum industry of New England. As the rum bought in the West Indies or manufactured from the molasses procured there was used extensively in buying skins from the Indians and Negroes from the African slave-dealers, both the fur trade and the slave trade were closely related to the West Indian commerce. Besides, to it more than to any other economic factor the fishing industry in New England and the grain-growing business of the Middle colonies were indebted for their prosperity.

In colonial times there was always a considerable interchange of products between the various continental colonies, but this home trade was not so valuable as the commerce with Europe and the West Indies. The South sold to the North tobacco, rice, and naval stores, and received in return rum, flour, fish, beef, pork, and European goods. A considerable portion of this business consisted in collecting American products for export to Europe and in distributing European goods to the various colonies. There were a few leading ports from which colonial products were exported and to which European commodities were brought. The distribution of these goods and the collection of colonial products were made by small vessels engaged in the coastwise trade. Commerce between the mainland colonies was also stimulated by the West Indian trade, for the vessels plying between the northern mainland towns and the sugar islands generally stopped at southern ports to receive rice, tobacco, naval stores, and other southern commodities in exchange for the wares brought from home or procured in the West Indies. *The coastwise trade*

The coastal trade and the commerce with the West Indies, Africa, and Spain and Portugal was carried on mainly in Ameri-

binding on the drawee until the latter indicates his acceptance of it by writing across it the proper endorsement (CRUMP, N. E., in *Encyclopedia Britannica*, iii, pp. 575-576).

For an explanation as to how bills of exchange were used in the West Indian trade, see p. 490.

American and British ships used in foreign and domestic trade

can vessels, most of which were owned by merchants of the northern towns. British vessels, on the other hand, had most of the carrying-trade between the dominions and the mother country, though a few planters sent their staples to England in their own vessels. Some of the southern exports were also carried to the homeland by northern ships through northern ports, and some European products were imported into the southern provinces in this indirect way. In colonial times shipowners were also merchants, who bought and sold the commodities they transported. The dangers from pirates and privateers and those incident to the numerous wars that were going on prevented the organization of commerce on a big scale. The merchant would stock up his vessel and go from one port to another exchanging his wares without attempting to keep within a prearranged and advertised schedule.[21]

Regulation of commerce by colonial legislation

The colonies as a rule believed in freedom of trade and considered that commerce should not be taxed unless it was absolutely necessary. Yet practically all of them at one time or another collected import duties on some commodities, and all of them but two (Delaware and Rhode Island) levied export duties at times. These restrictions were imposed mainly to raise revenue, but they were also sometimes voted to encourage shipping, to retaliate against the tax measures of other provinces, or to encourage direct trade with the country or countries producing certain desired articles. Bounties were given on certain exports by nearly all the colonies. The articles thus favored were flax and hemp and those products on which the British government paid a bounty when they were sent to England.

Expansion of commerce in the eighteenth century

Commerce in the first three-quarters of the eighteenth century encountered obstacles that today would be considered almost insurmountable. Wars were going on between France and England and their American colonies for a good part of this period. These wars not only made commerce dangerous on the high seas, but also encouraged piracy and privateering. The warring nations were so busy fighting one another that they could not properly police the high seas, "and piracy was able to disguise itself as legitimate privateering. . . . Smuggling was undoubtedly stimu-

[21] In the eighteenth century the shipowner could protect himself against these losses by taking out insurance, for marine insurance was sold in the colonies as early as 1721. See DAVIS, J. S., *Essays in the Earlier History of American Corporations,* pp. 231-233.

lated by both piracy and privateering, and these practices in turn were encouraged by the ease of evading the customs officials, for as long as it was possible to dispose of captured goods readily and at a fair price there were always those willing to risk the gallows to obtain them."[22] But war did not interfere with commerce then as seriously as it does today. There were no cablegrams or wireless messages to locate ships, and the small vessels of that day could thread their quiet way through war dangers more easily than can the great liners of our age, whose whereabouts are generally known. Besides, the American merchants did not scruple at trading with the enemy as well as with neutrals in time of war. Even with hindrances of war, piracy, and privateering, American commerce, instead of declining, enjoyed a steady increase in volume and in value. Nor did this expansion in trade stop in 1763, at which time the British government entered upon a more rigid enforcement of its commercial restrictions. Despite the attempt to enforce the Molasses Act of 1733 and the enactment of the Sugar Act of 1764,[23] the colonial merchants continued to prosper. For along with these discouragements of trade there went certain compensations. Most of the duties on whalebone imported into Great Britain by the Americans were taken off in 1764, and a year later a bounty was put on colonial lumber. Moreover, in 1766 the objectionable Sugar Act was modified by substituting for the duty of threepence a gallon on foreign molasses a duty of one penny a gallon on all molasses imported into the continental colonies.[24]

COLONIAL FINANCE

Commerce in colonial times was hampered by a scarcity of metallic money. The inconvenience resulting from the scarcity of gold and silver coins was increased by the absence of banking facilities. There were no banks in the modern sense of the term, and so the bank check, which is so important a medium of exchange today, was not employed at all in the business transactions of the colonial era. *Scarcity of money*

This scarcity of money was due mainly to the following causes: (1) In the dominions, as in all new and undeveloped countries, the exploitation of natural resources required considerable outlays *Reasons*

[22] FAULKNER, *op. cit.*, pp. 104-105.
[23] See pp. 625-626.
[24] CHANNING, E., *History of the United States*, iii, p. 78.

of capital. Houses, barns, and sawmills had to be erected and farms had to be equipped with tools and supplied with stock. A considerable portion of the money by which these demands were met was borrowed from England, where capital was abundant and the opportunities for its use not so remunerative. Therefore, the colonies were in debt to the homeland, as they should have been. To meet these debts a constant stream of money had to flow from America to the mother country. (2) The value of the goods imported by the Northern colonies from England was greater than the value of the products sent thither by them, and the balance had to be paid in gold or silver. This caused a constant drain on their supply of money. (3) Efforts were made in the various colonies to remedy the money stringency by issuing bills of credit. These rapidly depreciated in value, and this cheap paper money drove the good metallic money out of circulation.

"Pine-tree shillings"   For these reasons the overseas dominions not only failed to procure money from the homeland, but had to send thither a considerable portion of the coin received from other countries. There was thus practically no English money in circulation in the continental American colonies. Weeden says that when an English shilling was dug up on Long Island in 1647, it was regarded as an object of curiosity by the people, many of whom had never seen a similar coin before.

From 1652 to 1684 a mint was operated at Boston at which silver shillings and smaller coins were struck off, and this was the only attempt to coin money made by the colonies. The shillings turned out by this mint had the picture of a pine tree stamped on them and were known as "pine-tree shillings." Their value was only three-fourths that of the English shillings, and it was hoped that this depreciation would cause them to remain in America. But they too were drained off by the demands of British commerce. The coining of money is one of the incidents of sovereignty, and by striking off her own coins Massachusetts was acting like an independent state. The king resented this assumption of authority on the part of the Puritan commonwealth, and when the charter was annulled (1684) the privilege of coining money was withheld from the province.

Foreign coins   Foreign commerce brought in Portuguese, French, and Spanish coins, and these constituted practically all the metallic money that circulated in the colonies. The most important of the silver coins was the Spanish "piece of eight" (eight reals), or the Spanish milled dollar, which took its place after 1728. The piece of eight, with its successor, the Spanish dollar, was the monetary unit throughout the colonial period and thus became the ancestor of our dollar. When Congress (1786) accepted it as the monetary standard of the United States it was only recognizing by law a practice that was almost as old as the country itself. For small change the colonies had the Spanish fractional money, the four-real piece (the half-dollar), the two-real piece (the quarter-dollar), the one-real piece, and two small coins valued, respectively, at one-half and one-fourth reals. The principal gold coins were the Portuguese johannes, or joe, and the moidore, and the Spanish and French pistole. The first of these was valued at sixteen Spanish dollars, the second at about six, and the last named at a little less than four.[25]

The terms "pounds," "shillings," and "pence" were used in valuing the foreign coins and the farm products that took the place of money. As these English coins were not in circulation in the colonies, the shilling was, as Weeden terms it, "a medium of expression" rather than a medium of exchange. This practice of using the currency of one country and the monetary terminology of another caused confusion, for the various provinces did not employ the same standard in adapting the foreign currency to the English system of nomenclature. For example, the real value of the piece of eight was four and a half shillings, but the rating it received in the different colonies varied from four shillings eight pence in South Carolina and Georgia to eight shillings in New York and North Carolina. *(English monetary terms in use)*

In the early period wampum was used as a substitute for money in New England and the Middle colonies. Wampum was valued highly by the Indians and was readily received by them in exchange for furs. As furs could be disposed of in European markets as easily as gold itself and as wampum was thus practically redeemable in furs among the Indians, it served as a fairly good substitute for money until the development of the country pushed back the sources of the supply of furs. Its value was regulated from time to time by acts of the colonial legislature.[26] *(Substitutes for money: Wampum)*

[25] For table showing the value of foreign coins in 1765, see CHANNING, *op. cit.*, ii, p. 498, note. See also *Authentic Account of the Stamp Act Congress*, p. 31.

[26] Wampum was the name applied to shell beads strung on a strand of hemp or a tendon of an animal. The beads were cylindrical

"Coun-
try pay"

Various agricultural and manufactured products were used in the place of money. Their value was fixed in terms of English shillings and at times some of them were received for taxes and some were even made a legal tender in the payment of debts. Produce used in exchange in this way was known as "country pay." This method of conducting exchanges was really only a sort of regulated barter. Such a medium of exchange is not only very inconvenient, but, owing to its rapid fluctuations in value, is also very unreliable. Wheat in Pennsylvania; tobacco in Virginia, Maryland, and North Carolina; rice in South Carolina and Georgia; beaver, grain, and other products in New England— were all used as substitutes for money. In Virginia by 1734 it had become the practice for planters to deposit their tobacco in the public warehouses and receive certificates entitling them to the amount of the tobacco mentioned in the receipt. These certificates were known as "crop notes" and could be passed from one person to another like silver certificates of today.[27] In Pennsylvania they had a like practice with reference to wheat.

Bills of
exchange

Bills of exchange received in the trade with the British West Indian plantations also performed the services of money. A northern merchant would sell a cargo of fish or other produce to a sugar-planter and receive for it a bill of exchange, which was an order on a London merchant. The New Englander receiving such a bill could use it in purchasing goods in England or else sell it to a fellow-American merchant, who could so use it. These drafts were not very useful in the ordinary exchanges between individuals, but they were a great aid in the trade with England.

---

in shape and were about a quarter of an inch in length and one-eighth of an inch in diameter. To bore the hole through the shell cylinders and polish them required skilled and patient labor. They were worn as ornaments on the wrists and necks of warriors and women and children. Sometimes the beads were embroidered on strips of deerskin and thus made into belts and scarfs. Wampum was also used in certain ceremonies, and the kings wore wampum in abundance as a sign of their dignity. It thus took the place among the Indian royalty of the crown jewels among European rulers. For these reasons it had a value among the Indians and they were willing to exchange furs for it (WEEDEN, W. W., *Economic and Social History of New England,* i, pp. 32-46).

[27] HENING, W. W., *Virginia Statutes at Large,* iv, pp. 386-388; v, pp. 132-134; vi, pp. 163-164.

But all the devices mentioned above did not adequately supply Paper
money the need for a medium of exchange and the colonies resorted to paper money. The first paper money was issued by Massachusetts in 1690 to meet an extraordinary expense incurred in an unsuccessful effort to capture Quebec (see p. 379, note).[28] The example of Massachusetts was followed by other colonies, and so in time all of them tried the experiment of paper money. If they had restricted the amounts issued and had provided a fund by taxation for redeeming the bills of credit, they could have kept them at par. But instead of doing this they reissued the notes that were received in payment of taxes and kept increasing the amount of paper money, with the result that everywhere it depreciated in value. In Pennsylvania a more cautious policy was carried out than in other colonies, and the evils resulting from depreciation there were not very great. A provision was made for paying the interest on the notes and a promise of redemption was held out. So paper money was kept up to par in this province until the outbreak of the French and Indian War.

The evils of depreciation were realized by the business interests, but the majority of the people, who were generally in debt, usually wanted cheap money. In New England this latter class had such a hold on the representative assemblies that the rich merchants were unable to put a stop to the issuance of fiat money.[29] They, therefore, appealed to Parliament and procured the enactment of a law (1751) prohibiting the issuance of bills of credit in New England except in time of war or other emergencies.[30] In 1764 Parliament passed another law forbidding all the colonies to issue paper money to be used as legal tender.[31] These measures were very unpopular with the masses of the people

[28] For the text of one of these Massachusetts notes and a brief contemporary account by Cotton Mather of the action of the assembly in providing for their issue, see DEWEY, D. R., *Financial History of the United States*, p. 22. For a fuller account, see HUTCHINSON, THOMAS, *History of Massachusetts*, 3rd ed., i, p. 357.

[29] For arguments in favor of paper money advanced by a royal governor of Massachusetts, see HART, A B., *American History Told by Contemporaries*, ii, pp. 251-253. See also O'CALLAGHAN, E. B., ed., *New York Colonial Documents*, v, pp. 736-738.

[30] RUFFHEAD, OWEN, *Statutes at Large* (24 Geo. II, cap. 53), vii, p. 403.

[31] See p. 626.

and figured as an important cause of that dissatisfaction with the home government that led to the Revolution.

Selected Readings

1. The West Indian Trade.—Johnson, E. R., and others, eds., *History of Domestic and Foreign Commerce of the United States*, i, pp. *93-100 (an excellent account), and Beer, G. L., *Commercial Policy of England*, *ch. 6.
2. Colonial Commerce (a short discussion).—Schlesinger, A. M., *The Colonial Merchants and the American Revolution*, pp. *15-32.
3. The Fur Trade.—Moore, J. R. H., *An Industrial History of the United States*, pp. *61-89.
4. Money in Colonial Times.—Van Metre, T. W., *Economic History of the United States*, pp. *106-111.
5. Scarcity of Money in the Colonial Era.—Clark, Victor S., *History of Manufactures in the United States, 1607-1860*, pp. *123-129.
6. Wampum as Money.—Weeden, W. B., *Economic and Social History of New England*, pp. *32-46.
7. The Indian System of Transportation.—Ringwalt, J. D., *Development of Transportation Systems in the United States*, pp. *5-8.
8. Old-time Taverns.—Earle, Alice M., *Stage Coach and Tavern Days*, *ch. 2.
9. The Colonial Post Office.—*American Historical Review*, xxi, pp. *258-275.
10. Pirates along the Carolina Coast.—Davis, J. E., *Jamestown and Her Neighbors*, *ch. 5.
11. Commodity Money in the Colonies.—Nettels, C. P., *The Money Supply of the American Colonies before 1720*, *ch. 8.
12. Commerce, Currency, and Credit.—*Ibid.*, pp. *278-283 (an excellent summary).
13. The West India Trade before the American Revolution.—Article by H. C. Bell in the *American Historical Review*, xxii, pp. 272-287.

CHAPTER XXIV

IMPERIAL SUPERVISION OF THE COLONIES

General Character of Colonial Administration

THROUGHOUT the entire colonial period, except during the Interregnum (1649-60), the chief authority over the American possessions was claimed and exercised by the king. All patents granting lands and all charters conferring governmental powers were issued in the name of the crown. In the early years the king had entire control of the plantations in the New World. While Parliament did not acknowledge the exclusive authority of the king over the dominions, it did not legislate for the colonies or make any successful effort to take part in colonial affairs until the Long Parliament started on its career of opposition to the crown. When the Civil War came and the king was deposed, Parliament took over the management of the colonies. In the early years of the Commonwealth, the supervision of the overseas possessions was intrusted by Parliament to the Council of State,[1] and later, when the Protectorate was established, was given over to the Lord Protector. With the Restoration the crown regained administrative control of the dominions, which it held until the end of the colonial era.

The colonies are under the authority of the crown

But during the Commonwealth period, Parliament had acquired a power in colonial affairs which the later Stuarts could not ignore. The laws regulating American commerce during the Restoration period were the work of Parliament and constituted a successful assertion of the right of that body to legislate for the colonies. After the Revolution of 1688 Parliament gradually became more powerful in the homeland and increasingly active in American affairs.

Part played by Parliament in colonial administration

One of the great problems connected with imperial administration was that of determining how much authority the mother

[1] The Council of State was a body created by Parliament to perform the executive functions of the British government during the period intervening between the downfall of the king and the establishment of the Protectorate.

Imperial
adminis-
tration
under the
early
Stuarts
and dur-
ing the
Interreg-
num
country should assert over the dominions. The question was, Should the overseas possessions be united with the empire by strong political ties, or should the connection between them and the homeland be maintained less by political bonds than by economic interest and sentimental attachment? In the policy actually carried out neither of these ideas was consistently followed. After a period of vacillation, during which colonial administration veered first toward the one theory and then the other, a compromise scheme was adopted which embodied some of the features, both good and bad, of both plans. Under the early Stuarts there was a tendency to bring the colonies under the direct and real control of the king. Virginia was made a royal province (1624), and the British imperial officials planned to assert the authority of the crown over New England. This tendency was arrested by the Puritan Revolution and the downfall of the king which resulted from it. During the Interregnum Parliament and Cromwell allowed the American continental colonies virtual freedom in the management of their own affairs.

Under the
later
Stuarts
With the Restoration there came a return to the policy of imperial control. The desire of the home authorities to enforce the commercial regulations in order to favor the merchant class necessitated a closer supervision of the dominions by the British government. It was difficult, however, to make this supervision effective in the chartered colonies, as the leading officials in them were not directly responsible to the king, but were chosen by and were responsible to the proprietors or the people. The new policy, therefore, demanded that no more chartered colonies be created and that those which had already been established should be converted into royal provinces as soon as the opportunity for making the change should arise. If Charles II had been consistent in his colonial measures this plan would have been pursued from the beginning. But in the early years of his reign a number of charters were granted. Two of these were issued to colonies (Connecticut and Rhode Island) and others to individuals, making them proprietors of provinces. (The proprietary provinces thus established were New Jersey, New York, Pennsylvania, and the Carolinas.) The spoils system was responsible for this inconsistency —that is, the desire of Charles to reward his political friends by grants of land. It was, therefore, not until the last decade of Stuart rule that an attempt was made to carry out fully the original plan. Representative assemblies were now abolished, char-

ters suspended, and colonies consolidated and brought under the direct control of the crown. The creation of the Dominion of New England was an attempt to carry out this new imperial policy.

The Revolution of 1688 put an end to the Stuart experiment and brought in still another plan of colonial administration. Under the new arrangement the policy of the later Stuarts was partially abandoned and partially followed. The assemblies that had been destroyed were all restored, but there was a return to the Stuart practice of strengthening the provincial executives and of linking up the colonies more closely with the rest of the empire. If this plan were to be successful, it would be necessary for the crown to keep in close touch with the authorities in America. This could be done more easily in the royal provinces than in the chartered colonies, and so from the Revolution of 1688 to the end of the colonial era there was a constant tendency to annul charters whenever they could be legally canceled and to change chartered colonies into royal provinces.[2] The self-governing and proprietary colonies were also brought within the general supervision of the British government, and an attempt was made to enforce within them the acts of Parliament regulating trade and manufacturing. The plan of binding the dominions more closely to the homeland was favored by the powerful commercial and landed interests that dominated the British government in the eighteenth century because they hoped to profit greatly by the monopoly of the colonial trade which they would enjoy under the new policy. The new arrangement was also advocated by the Anglican Church, and especially by the Society for the Propagation of the Gospel in Foreign Parts, because they felt that the Anglican cause in America would be promoted by a closer union between England and her colonies.

The plan inaugurated by William and followed by his successors was a compromise between the practice of Cromwell and that of the later Stuarts. If the Cromwellian practice of allowing the colonies to manage their own affairs had become a permanent policy, the overseas possessions would have been held to the homeland only by sentimental, economic, and nominal political ties. If the later Stuart idea had prevailed, they would have been so closely incorporated in the empire as to lose their local autonomy. In the former case the American possessions would have enjoyed the

The plan inaugurated by William III

A compromise plan

[2] The only reversal of this general tendency was the restoration of proprietary rule in Maryland in 1715 (see p. 316).

privileges of self-government, but might not have enjoyed to the full extent the prosperity that would result from a close identification with the empire. In the latter case the dominions would have forfeited their right of self-government, but would have enjoyed the oversight of the empire and with it a larger measure of prosperity than would have come to them as separate political entities.

Merits
and defects of
the system
The compromise policy carried out by William and the Georges was preferable to either of these extreme plans, both from the point of view of the dominions and the empire as a whole. By it the American possessions were to be kept securely within the empire and at the same time enjoy a large measure of local autonomy. In this way neither liberty nor security would be sacrificed. Politically speaking, each province was to rotate on its own axis, but all of them were to revolve around England as the center of the imperial system. Unfortunately, however, the orbit in which each was to move was marked out by British economic interests. The great difficulty in carrying out this political scheme was that of keeping the provinces in the path that had been mapped out for them. A sentimental attachment on the part of the colonials for the mother country was not a sufficient attraction; it had to be and was bolstered up by force and self-interest. These three influences combined kept the American colonies in the British system for more than eight decades after the Revolution, though they did not always follow closely the orbit that had been marked out for them.

This arrangement might have lasted much longer if the British authorities had used a little more wisdom in planning the system and a little more force and vigor in carrying it out. The initial mistake was made when American interests were largely disregarded and British interests mainly considered in determining the relations that the colonies should sustain to the mother country. This error, however, was a very natural one, as Britain, as well as other European countries, was obsessed at that time with the Mercantilist idea that colonies exist primarily for the benefit of the homeland. Despite the injustice of this theory, the overseas dominions could have been held to obedience if the measures adopted to keep them in line had been vigorously enforced. But this was not done. During a good portion of the time that intervened between the Revolution of 1688 and the Peace of Paris (1763), the home government exhibited an amazing indifference to colonial affairs and winked at a policy of laxity in overseas administration. Even when the British authorities made an earnest attempt to enforce the regulations their efforts were often rendered abortive by the corruption, ignorance, or incompetence of imperial officials in England or their agents in America.

THE MACHINERY OF IMPERIAL ADMINISTRATION

When the annulment of the charter of the Virginia Company (1624) imposed upon the British government the responsibility of administering colonial affairs, it entered upon the task without creating any new governmental machinery. The members of the Privy Council were the official advisers of the king, and to this body was intrusted the authority over the dominions. Thereafter the Privy Council appointed and gave instructions to royal governors and other crown officials and exercised a general supervision over the New World possessions. This power was retained by the Privy Council, technically at least, as long as continental America remained a part of the British empire, except for the short period of the Interregnum.

The authority of the crown over the colonies delegated to the Privy Council

As the Privy Council was a large body and had a great many other duties to perform, it could hardly be expected to look after the details of colonial administration. It had, therefore, to be guided by the recommendations of advisory commissions. In the early years special committees were appointed, and to them was delegated the duty of conducting investigations and of making recommendations in certain specific cases, to be acted on finally by the Privy Council.[3] In 1634 a permanent board was constituted, which was known as the Lords Commissioners for Foreign Plantations, and to it was given the supervision and management of all the British colonies. It included in its membership men who held the highest positions in church and state and was presided over by William Laud, Archbishop of Canterbury. This commission made recommendations as to the appointment and removal of governors, judges, and other officials and as to the solution of other problems that arose in connection with the dominions. It was, however, only a standing committee of the Privy Council, and all its decisions had finally to be confirmed by that body.

The Lords Commissioners for Foreign Plantations

[3] BEER, G. L., *The Origins of the British Colonial System*, pp. 307, 308, 311.

Imperial
adminis-
tration
during the
Interreg-
num

During the Interregnum the machinery of colonial administration was rather elaborate, with special standing committees to advise the Council of State and the Lord Protector, though the home government exercised little or no authority over the continental American colonies.[4] When Charles II came to the throne he returned to the former practice of transacting colonial business through the Privy Council, which was guided by the recommendations of special and permanent committees.[5] As these advisory councils proved unsatisfactory, they were dispensed with and their functions were absorbed (1675) by a permanent board, known as the Committee for Trade and Foreign Plantations, or the Lords of Trade. This board had a permanent secretariat, kept a record of its proceedings, and held meetings once a week. As the active members were the leading officials in the British government, its recommendations were usually approved by the Privy Council. It corresponded with governors, sent them their instructions, made inquiries regarding conditions in the colonies, saw to the enforcement of the navigation laws, and maintained a general oversight over the dominions.

The
Lords
of Trade

The
Board of
Trade

For more than twenty years the colonies were under the control of the Lords of Trade. At the end of that period (1696) a new body was created by order of the king, which is generally known as the Board of Trade. It consisted of eight active members, who were paid a regular salary and did the work, and a number of prominent men who held high positions in the government. When the Board was first organized two of its influential members were Councilors, and so the Board was in a sense a committee of the Privy Council. Large powers were delegated to this newly-created body, one of the most important of which was the authority to supervise the administration of the plantations. It was to examine all laws passed by colonial legislatures and make recommendations as to which should be confirmed and which disallowed, as well as hear all complaints from the overseas possessions and make reports thereon. The Board also sometimes made recommendations as to the appointment of officials in America, though often its advice was not asked when royal governors were appointed and removed. The chief aim in creating

[4] *Ibid.*, pp. 312-317, 340, 347-352, 418, 421.
[5] BEER, G. L., *The Old Colonial System*, i, pp. 230-258.

the Board was "to make the colonies commercially profitable to the mother country."[6]

The powers of the Board of Trade varied from time to time, but it continued to look after colonial affairs until near the end of our colonial era. In 1768 its president was raised to the rank of Secretary of State for the Colonies.[7] From that time until 1779 the Board performed the clerical duties of the new department and acted as a sort of cabinet to its head. In 1779 the Secretary of State for the Colonies was relieved of the presidency of the Board of Trade and a new official took his place. The Board had thus been separated from the Colonial Department and three years later was abolished.

The king and the Privy Council could pass upon the laws voted by the assemblies in all the American colonies. The legislative enactments of a royal province could be rejected at any time, but those coming up from the chartered colonies, both self-governing and proprietary, could be disallowed only within a definite time stated in the charter.[8] The failure to veto the law in the given time was equivalent to an acceptance. In the charters of Maryland, Rhode Island, and Connecticut there was no provision requiring the laws to be submitted to the king, but these colonies usually sent up to the Privy Council measures voted by their assemblies when they were insistently requested to do so. Unless the act itself contained a provision to the contrary, it was effective until disallowed by the king.

The royal veto

Theoretically, the laws were reviewed by the king in council, and the Privy Council formally passed on every one submitted to it. But the real decision was usually rendered (after 1696)

[6] DICKERSON, O. M., *American Colonial Government,* pp. 21-26; BASYE, A. H., *The Board of Trade,* p. 54.

For the text of the commission creating the Board of Trade, see O'CALLAGHAN, E. B., ed., *New York Colonial Documents,* iv, pp. 145-148. For the same, given in abbreviated form, see HART, A. B., *American History Told by Contemporaries,* ii, pp. 129-131.

[7] For the later history of the Board of Trade, see BASYE, A. H., *Lord Commissioners of Trade and Plantations,* pp. 122-127, 146, 150-160, 165-175, 178, 182, 204-205, 212-213; also a book review by ANDREWS, C. M., in the *American Historical Review,* xxxiv, pp. 849-853.

[8] DICKERSON, O. M., *op. cit.,* pp. 225-228, 234-236, 264-265, 273-274.

by the Board of Trade, which with the advice of official counsel considered each case carefully, and made a recommendation regarding it to the Privy Council. The colonies found it to their interest to have an agent to represent them before both the legal adviser and the Board.[9] Generally the assent to or veto of a measure was in accordance with the recommendation of the Board, though sometimes the Privy Council reversed the decision of the Board.

One of the main reasons for disapproving laws was that they infringed upon the prerogative of the crown. Colonial laws were not to be inconsistent with the common law of England or the statutes of Parliament, and the Privy Council, acting on the advice of the Board of Trade or (before 1696) of other advisory bodies, had to decide whether colonial statutes conformed to these requirements. Moreover, the charters gave certain rights to the legislatures of the charter colonies, and the Board and the Privy Council had to decide whether they had exceeded these powers. The Privy Council was thus passing on the constitutionality of the laws voted by the colonial legislatures just as the Supreme Court does on the acts of Congress today. In this way our legislatures were accustomed to a limitation of their authority that paved the way for their acceptance of the modern doctrine that all legislation is subject to review by the courts. This practice also enabled the imperial government to exercise some restraint on the acts of the colonial assemblies and tended toward a certain degree of uniformity in American jurisprudence.

Appeals from the colonial courts

The Privy Council was the highest court of appeal for the colonies, and to it appeals could be taken from the provincial courts of all the colonies. As a rule, only civil causes involving

[9] The colonial agents were the unofficial representatives of the colonies in London. They were usually chosen by a vote of both houses of the assembly, with the approval of the governor. Not only did they advocate the interests of their respective colonies before the Board of Trade, but they also kept an eye on Parliament to prevent any action by that body that would be unfavorable to their constituents. Many of the measures favorable to the dominions that were adopted by the British authorities were secured through their influence. Although the direct compensation of the colonial agent was small and his responsibilities were great, the office was one of dignity and influence and prominent men were willing to accept it. (For recent works discussing in a scholarly way the part played by the colonial agent see Bibliographical Notes, p. 822.)

large amounts and exceptional criminal cases could be carried up by appeal, but sometimes cases of lesser importance were heard by the Council.[10] The appellant had to give bond of sufficient amount to guarantee the prosecution of the case and to cover all damages that might accrue to the appellee in the event the decision should be in the latter's favor. Therefore, the expense of prosecuting appeals in England was so great that the practice would have been limited to important cases even if there had been no imperial regulation imposing such a restriction on it.

In the determination of judicial causes, as well as in the transaction of other business, the Privy Council had the advice of the Board of Trade and usually, though not always, accepted its recommendations. The king often sat in the Privy Council (Charles II attended seventy-one of the eighty-one meetings held in 1672). Cases in which wrong decisions had been rendered by a provincial court were heard directly by the Committee of the Privy Council without being referred to the Board of Trade.[11] But in all cases involving constitutional points, such as the interpretation of charters or the action of an imperial official, an examination and report were made by the Board. The Board also had sometimes to decide whether an appeal should be allowed from a colonial court.

Complaints made to the Privy Council were usually referred to the Board for a report. These complaints were gone into very carefully and were not sustained unless backed up by sufficient evidence. This sometimes meant delay. It was also difficult to get adequate evidence in case the complaints were lodged against a governor; for owing to the influence he wielded and the patronage he controlled, witnesses were generally reluctant to testify against him. Then, too, the cost to the complainant of transporting his witnesses to England, along with other expenses, put him at a

[10] HAZELTINE, H. D., *Appeals from the Colonial Courts to the King in Council,* pp. 308, 315.

[11] Early in the eighteenth century it had become the usual practice for the Privy Council to refer judicial appeals and complaints from the colonies, as well as other business, to a committee of the whole Council. While in theory all the members of the Privy Council belonged to this committee, only a few of the most active members attended regularly. This committee had several names, varying according to the character of the business transacted, but the personnel, so far as the regular attendants were concerned, seems to have been about the same, regardless of the name under which it went.

disadvantage. For these reasons it was not always easy to convict an official who was really guilty of injustice or malfeasance in office. On the other hand, the practice of carrying important cases before the king in council by appeal afforded individuals in the colonies a measure of protection against injustice arising from political prejudice or other local causes.

The imperial administration of the colonies inefficient

The complicated machinery outlined above did not prove to be an efficient system of administration. There was an overlapping of powers and a division of responsibility not only as between the different departments of the imperial administration, but also between Parliament and the crown. After 1688 Parliament played a larger part in the management of the colonies, and its policy was usually short-sighted and unwise. This overlapping of authority and consequent division of responsibility, coupled with the ignorance of conditions in America on the part of responsible British officials and their dilatoriness in transacting business, the distance from America, and the low ideals of political morality in the eighteenth century, all combined to render weak and inefficient the management of the colonies by the English government.

IMPERIAL REGULATION OF COLONIAL COMMERCE

The doctrine of Mercantilism

During the seventeenth and eighteenth centuries international relations were based on the principle of national selfishness and were characterized by a spirit of intense rivalry. As each power was striving to outstrip its neighbor in the race for wealth and power, the European states were always rivals in trade and industry and potential, if not active, enemies in war. It was thought that the gain of one country always meant the loss of another, and good patriotism, therefore, demanded not only the strengthening of one's own country, but the weakening of its possible rivals. No practical statesman advocated the doctrine that cooperation between nations is as mutually helpful and profitable as between individuals. In short, European international usage had been little affected in actual practice by either religion, morality, or a sane political theory.

In such a condition of world organization, or rather lack of organization, each state had to look to itself for protection against the actual and possible attacks, both economic and military, of its neighbors. As there was no international police, every nation, however peace-loving it might be, had to be prepared to defend its rights whenever they were assailed. Under such conditions weakness in a government would be the unpardonable sin and strength the one virtue toward the attainment of which all efforts should tend. It was such a philosophy that was behind the political and economic policy of the governments of Europe in the seventeenth and eighteenth centuries. During this period each country tried to become wealthy and powerful at the expense of other countries, especially their rivals. The best measure of wealth, it was thought, was gold and silver, and every nation was interested in the accumulation of the precious metals. To be powerful, a people must be economically self-sufficient and be able to create a strong army and navy. And so a policy looking toward military preparedness was always pursued.

This policy, which is known as Mercantilism, or the Mercantile System, was accepted by the political economists of the day and was acted upon by all the nations of Europe. It is not in harmony with either the ethical or the economic canons of today, but traces of it still linger in our modern political philosophy. In that age of international chaos and anarchy it was considered the only safe and sane philosophy.

The aims of the Mercantile System as pursued by the British government were as follows: (1) to increase the amount of gold and silver in the country; (2) to encourage the growth of population, particularly the increase in the number of sturdy and strong men who would make good soldiers and sailors; (3) to encourage agriculture and manufacturing because these industries would not only make the country economically self-sufficient in time of war, but would afford employment to the people and thereby favor the growth of population; besides, agriculture is an occupation that tends to develop strong bodies, and it is thus a training-school for soldiers; (4) to build up a strong navy and a large merchant marine as an aid to the navy; (5) to support the fishing industry, because it would develop the merchant marine and serve as a training-school to men who might be needed to serve in the navy in time of war; (6) to encourage commerce as a stimulus to shipbuilding and as a source of revenue to the government through the customs duties.[12]

For the realization of this program the British government did

The Mercantile System in England

[12] For a brief statement by a contemporary writer (1747) of the aims of British Mercantilism, see JOHNSON, E. R., and others, *History of Domestic and Foreign Commerce of the United States*, i, pp. 36-37.

The Mer-
cantile
System as
applied to
the Eng-
lish colo-
nies

not scruple at infringing on the rights of foreign nations and was willing, if necessary, to subordinate the real interests of the dominions to the supposed interests of the mother country. So the policy of Mercantilism was carried out with reference to the American colonies as well as to foreign countries. The laws of the seventeenth and eighteenth centuries imposing restrictions on American trade and industry all had the aim of making the overseas possessions contribute toward the increase of the wealth and power of the mother country. The colonies were to sell to England what she wanted and buy from her what she had to sell. She wanted raw materials for manufacturing and lumber and naval stores for shipbuilding. The dominions were expected to produce these articles and were encouraged or compelled to sell them exclusively in England. Such agricultural products as Britain herself raised in abundance were not wanted from America, and their importation was prohibited by high import duties. On the other hand, products that could not be raised successfully at home, like tobacco and sugar, had to be sent to the English ports. The laws also required that commodities of European origin bought by Americans, and many of those sold to Europe by them, should pass through English ports.

The plantations were also expected to furnish a market for the manufactures of the homeland. In order to give the English manufacturers a monopoly of the colonial market and protect them from the possible competition of American wares in European markets, manufacturing in the dominions was discouraged. If this policy could be carried out English commerce and manufacturing would be stimulated and the balance of trade as between England and America would be in favor of the former. For the colonies would buy from England more than they would sell, and the difference would have to be settled by the payment of money. In this way the overseas possessions would aid in the accumulation of precious metals in the mother country.

To carry out this policy Parliament passed a number of navigation and trade laws in the seventeenth and eighteenth centuries. Most of these acts contained provisions that were unfair to the colonies, and if they had been strictly enforced would have brought serious hardship upon them. In the effort to excuse this unwise and unjust policy it was contended that the dominions owed something to the parent state as compensation for the expense incurred in affording them protection. The British navy was the main reliance for the protection of the whole empire, and the cost of maintaining it constituted a heavy burden on the English taxpayer. As the overseas possessions enjoyed the security afforded by it, they should bear some of the sacrifices entailed by the imperial policy. Besides, as England was the heart of the empire it should be kept prosperous and strong; for if the heart could not perform its functions properly, the outlying members of the empire could not be adequately nourished. Then, too, these laws had some provisions that conferred benefits on the plantations that went far toward compensating them for any grievances that might lurk in them.

The policy of the first two Stuarts with reference to the colonies tended toward economic centralization as well as political. Both of these tendencies were arrested by the Civil War. High wages and high taxes as a result of the war increased the cost of production and hence the price of English goods. While the struggle was going on between Parliament and the king, the adherents of both contestants seized one another's merchant-ships in both English and American waters. Commerce with England was thus insecure. For these reasons trade between the colonies and foreign countries increased, and by the end of the war the Dutch had appropriated the bulk of the English colonial trade. The Dutch had a vast accumulation of capital, good banking and commercial facilities, and could carry freight at low rates. They were, therefore, monopolizing the carrying-trade of the world.[13]

Importance of the Dutch carrying-trade

As soon as Parliament had its hands free by the victory over the king, it entered upon the attempt to turn the British carrying-trade from Dutch- to English-owned shipping. In 1650 an act was passed as a war measure forbidding foreign vessels to trade with the colonies, and next year the famous Navigation Law was passed. This was the first of a series of acts by which Parliament tried to apply the Mercantile System to the dominions. By this law all products sent from the colonies to England or from one colony to another had to be carried in vessels owned either by Englishmen or by colonials. All commodities brought into England or the colonies from European countries must be carried either in English ships or in the ships of the country from which

The Navigation Act of 1651

[13] Beer, G. L., *The Origins of the British Colonial System,* pp. 352-358, 372-373.

the commodities came.[14] In this way the Dutch were to be entirely excluded from the British carrying-trade, and a monopoly of it was given to British and colonial ships. This law would have been a terrible blow to Dutch prosperity had it been enforced, but during the Interregnum little heed was paid to it in the colonies. The possession of New Amsterdam by the Dutch made evasion of the law less difficult.

The Act of 1651 had been passed in response to the demands of the influential merchant class, which in the main had been aligned with Parliament against the king. When Charles II was restored to the throne this class supported the new régime and used its influence to get legislation in its favor. The merchants were able to enlist the support of some leading politicians, who saw that the aims of the merchants were in line with the Mercantilist notions of the day, and a series of navigation laws were passed by Parliament. These laws were the basis of the policy that determined commercial relations between Great Britain and her colonies from this time until the end of the colonial period.[15]

The first of these laws was that of 1660, which reënacted in substance some of the clauses of the Act of 1651 and added some other provisions of importance. By this law exports from and imports into the colonies must be carried by English, Irish, or American ships. As the Act of 1660, like its predecessor of 1651, gave British subjects a monopoly of the carrying-trade between America and the British Isles, and as the colonies shared in this monopoly, shipbuilding was stimulated in America, and so these laws were favorable to the northern seafaring colonies.

"Enumerated" articles

One of the provisions of the law of 1660 not found in the former act was that of listing certain exports from the colonies, known as "enumerated" articles, which could be sent only to the British Isles and the English possessions. The commodities so listed in the Act of 1660 were sugar, tobacco, ginger, cotton-wool, fustic, and other dye-woods.[16] Some of these commodities,

[14] *Ibid.*, p. 374. For the text of this act in abbreviated form, see MacDONALD, W., *Select Charters,* pp. 107-110.

[15] GREENE, E. B., *Foundations of American Nationality,* pp. 180-185.

[16] For the text of this act, see PICKERING, DANBY, *Statutes at Large,* vii, pp. 452-460. For the abbreviated text, see MacDONALD, W., *Select Charters,* pp. 110-115.

like cotton-wool and dye-woods, were enumerated in order that the English manufacturer might have a monopoly of these colonial raw materials. Others, like sugar and tobacco, were put on for the sake of the revenue, as an import duty was paid by them on entering the British ports.

Of the commodities put on the original list, tobacco was the only one grown in the continental colonies. This restriction was opposed by the Maryland and Virginia planters and was partially responsible for the decline in the price of tobacco. Another grievance complained of by the planters was the tax on tobacco imported into England. It was gradually increased from 1d. a pound in 1657 to 7⅓d. in 1747. This tax was at times as much as 250 per cent *ad valorem*. From the beginning, one-half of the import duty and later all of it was remitted when tobacco was reëxported from England to the Continent, but in all such cases of reëxportation there was the additional expense caused by the break in the voyage. This expense considerably increased the cost of marketing tobacco on the Continent and cut down or completely absorbed the profits of the producer.[17] However, tobacco enjoyed certain privileges that helped to offset these restrictions. The English people were forbidden to raise it (not only by the law of 1660, but by previous laws going back to James I), and the duty on Spanish and Portuguese tobacco was much higher than on that brought from the colonies. The colonies thus had a monopoly of the British market, with the privilege of selling it anywhere else without duty, provided they landed it in England and reëxported it. Despite these compensations, however, the price of tobacco declined in the seventeenth century until by 1704 it was only one-eighteenth of what it was in 1619. This was due partly to overproduction and partly to the tax. Moreover, the provision confining the colonial carrying-trade to English and American ships also worked a hardship on the tobacco-growers, for it deprived them of the right of having their product transported in Dutch vessels, whose rates were lower than those charged by British and colonial merchants.

The number of enumerated articles was increased from time to time. In 1706 rice was put on the list. The cultivation of this cereal was begun in South Carolina in 1688, and, the soil and climate proving favorable to its growth, it was not long before

Tobacco

Rice

[17] BEER, G. L., *The Commercial Policy of England Toward the American Colonies,* pp. 45-49.

it became the staple product of this province and later of Georgia also. The rice grown in the South was of good quality and was able to compete successfully with Brazilian and Egyptian rice in the markets of Spain and Portugal. It soon drove out all competitors from the markets of the latter country and held its own with its rivals in the former. Rice was unwisely enumerated because it was thought that the direct sale of it to Portugal would injure the trade of the British merchants, Parliament being persuaded to this view by a man who had a private interest at stake. Enumeration increased the freight charge to such an extent that American rice lost the Portuguese market except at those times when the Italian and Egyptian crops were failures. To remedy the situation laws were passed in the reign of George II allowing rice to be sent directly to countries south of Cape Finisterre, and immediately the American product regained its position in the European market.[18]

The Staple Act of 1663

The law of 1660 had given "English, Irish, and colonial shipping a monopoly of the carrying-trade within the Empire" and had made "England the staple for tobacco and the West Indian products." It had not, however, prohibited the direct importation of European goods into the plantations. This omission enabled continental Europe to share in the advantages derived from trade with the colonies and prevented England from enjoying a monopoly of the colonial market for her manufactures. To remedy this defect in the previous statute, the law of 1663, known as the "Staple Act," was passed. It provided that goods imported into the dominions from European countries should pass through English ports. That is, they would have to be landed in England and, after paying the customs duties, be reloaded for shipment to the colonies.[19] Exceptions were made as to a few products, such as salt, so badly needed in New England for the fishing industry, and wines from the Azores and Madeira Islands.

There were several reasons for enacting such a measure, as is shown by the preamble of the law. It was hoped that it would make England the staple for commodities sold to the dominions by Europe and would give greater employment to English ship-

[18] Other articles were put on the enumerated list as follows: naval stores, tar, pitch, turpentine, hemp, masts, and yards, in 1706; copper ore, beaver and other furs, in 1722; molasses in 1733; whale fins, hides, iron, lumber, raw silk, and pearl-ashes in 1764.

[19] PICKERING, DANBY, *Statutes at Large,* viii, pp. 160-167.

ping. The inconveniences incident to this indirect method of communication would to some extent discourage trade between Europe and America and to a like extent encourage commerce between the colonies and the mother country. Moreover, this policy would also lead to an increase of revenue from the customs receipts. Colonial commerce would be limited to certain channels and could be more easily protected by the British navy than if allowed to scatter itself without restraint over the entire ocean. In short, the law would bring the overseas possessions into closer economic dependence upon the homeland, and this would tend to strengthen the political bond between England and America.

This law, though unfair in principle, did not in actual practice work any serious injustice to the colonies. It was not observed so well as the preceding act, though most of the goods imported from Europe passed through English ports. There were three conditions that rendered the measure less burdensome than it would have been otherwise. They were these: (1) Americans generally found British manufactures cheaper than foreign wares. (2) Most of the manufactures sent from continental Europe to the British dominions would naturally have passed through the ports of England even if there had been no legal restrictions on this trade. American merchants as a rule preferred to buy European goods as far as possible in English markets, owing to their difficulty with foreign languages and because of the conveniences afforded by the banking facilities in London. (3) Besides, the tariff duties remitted on goods reshipped to the colonies were so great as to make some European commodities cheaper to Americans than to the English.

The navigation laws were not strictly obeyed by the colonists. Goods were brought directly from European to colonial ports contrary to the Staple Act of 1663, and enumerated articles were sent directly to Europe in violation of the law of 1660. The latter act imposed upon colonial governors the duty of requiring owners of ships bound for European ports to give bond guaranteeing that all enumerated goods would be landed in England. But no such conditions were imposed upon ships leaving one colonial port for another, as there was no restriction at first on the intercolonial trade in enumerated products. Often colonial vessels would take sugar or tobacco from the West Indies or Virginia to a northern port and there reload for a European voyage. The

The Acts of 1672 and 1696

governors in the New England colonies did not require a bond covering enumerated articles bound for Europe, as the law required, probably because it was presumed that no tobacco or sugar would be shipped from these ports. These ships would thus be free to go directly to continental European ports, and would thereby avoid paying the customs duty in England and the cost of loading and unloading. But this gain to the American trader meant a loss of business to the English middleman and a reduction of the revenue that accrued to the British Exchequer.

In order to put a stop to this practice and to enforce more effectively all the trade laws, supplementary acts were passed in 1672 and 1696. The Act of 1672 (effective 1673) put an export duty on enumerated articles sent from one colony to another, which was usually about the same as the import duty levied on these articles in England.[20] It was thought that this would make the indirect, illegal trade with Europe in enumerated goods less profitable, and would promote the direct trade with England. This measure, however, did not put an end to the illicit trade, though it did raise the price of sugar brought into the continental colonies. The law of 1696 was passed to clear up a doubt as to the interpretation of the Act of 1672 and to create admiralty courts, the Board of Trade, and other machinery to assist in the enforcement of the laws.[21]

There was no general restriction in these laws on the sale of colonial products not on the enumerated list. These commodities could be sold wherever a market could be found for them. But the corn laws prohibited by high duties the importation into England of foodstuffs from foreign countries. While these laws were not aimed at the dominions, they applied to them and had the effect of excluding from the English markets the food exports from the New England and Middle colonies, such as fish, wheat, corn, flour, and meat.

Rivalry between the sugar-growers in the British and French West Indies

It has already been seen that the trade between the continental colonies and the West Indies was at first confined to the English islands, but had later been extended to the Dutch, Spanish, and French possessions. Early in the eighteenth century (about 1717) the sugar-planters in the French colonies entered upon a period of prosperity owing to the adoption of a liberal policy toward them by the home government. About this same time the English

[20] MacDonald, W., *op. cit.*, pp. 169-170.
[21] *Ibid.*, pp. 213-217.

sugar-growers began to lag behind their French rivals in success and prosperity. This was due partly to their extravagant method of living, partly to the exhaustion of the soil, and partly to the fact that sugar was on the enumerated list. The French islands now had the European markets for their sugar, while the English plantations sold only to the mother country and the English continental colonies. The French planter could, therefore, sell his sugar and molasses at a lower price than could his British competitor. Besides, the English islands did not produce a large amount of molasses, and could not supply all the needs of the continental possessions. The mainland colonies, therefore, were buying rum and molasses extensively from the foreign West Indies.

To escape from this competition the English sugar-growers appealed to Parliament for help. Many of the men who owned sugar plantations in the West Indies were English capitalists who had considerable influence with Parliament. They were, therefore, able to procure the enactment of a law the object of which was to protect them against the competition of their foreign rivals. This measure was adopted in 1733 and is known as the Molasses Act. It imposed a duty which was virtually prohibitory on sugar, molasses, rum, and spirits imported into the continental colonies from the foreign sugar islands.[22]

The Molasses Act of 1733

The act was not enforced with reference to the Northern colonies, but it seems to have been observed fairly well in the Southern provinces. The reason for this was that the West Indian trade was not so important in the latter section as it was in the former, for the economic prosperity of the people in the South was not dependent upon it. Consequently, the temptation to disregard the law was not so great in the Southern as it was in the Northern colonies. If the latter had been forced to comply with its requirements they would have been brought down almost to the verge of economic ruin. They would not have found a market for all their fish and lumber, and would have been unable to obtain all the molasses needed for the manufacture of rum. The source of their money supply would thus have dried up and they would have been unable to buy English manufactures as they had

[22] *Ibid.*, pp. 249-251. For a readable and scholarly discussion of the Molasses Act of 1733, see BEER, G. L., *The Commercial Policy of England Toward the American Colonies*, ch. 6.

hitherto done.[23] As the enforcement of the law would have worked a hardship on the English manufacturers, the British government was willing to acquiesce in its virtual nullification. Then, too, in a few years (1739 and 1742) sugar was taken off the enumerated list and other favors were granted to the sugar-growers. They could now ship their sugar directly to Europe and conditions were greatly improved for them. Therefore, they apparently did not insist on the enforcement of the law, and so it became practically a dead letter so far as New England and the Middle colonies were concerned.

But the law was a serious blunder. Its non-enforcement permitted wholesale smuggling, which was condoned by public sentiment in the Northern provinces. It, therefore, changed many law-abiding men into smugglers. The habitual disregard of an unjust statute on the part of a people leads to a lack of reverence for all law. We are not surprised, therefore, to learn that the habit of smuggling, acquired as a result of this unjust measure and others of similar character, was continued in times when patriotism demanded its cessation. When the colonies and the mother country were engaged in a great contest with France (the French and Indian War, 1754-63), the continental commercial colonies gave aid to the enemy by keeping up their illegal trade with the French dominions and thereby furnishing them with the supplies that enabled them to protract the struggle.

Enforcement of the commercial regulations: The governor

The governors in all the colonies, self-governing and proprietary as well as royal, were made responsible for the enforcement of the navigation and trade acts. They were required by law to pledge themselves under oath to enforce these regulations. A failure to carry out these measures was punishable by a fine of one thousand pounds and removal from office. But in the chartered colonies the governor was not directly responsible to the home government, and in the early years there was no imperial official in these provinces to supervise his conduct. On the other hand, he was anxious to please the people or the proprietor, to whom he owed his appointment, and generally the people and often the proprietor did not want a rigid enforcement of the imperial restrictions on commerce. Consequently, during the first

[23] For an excellent brief statement as to the arguments against the law that were urged by the colonials, see JOHNSON, E. R., and others, *History of Domestic and Foreign Commerce of the United States*, i, p. 95.

half of the Restoration period, the governors in the autonomous and proprietary colonies did not usually take the oath, nor did they carry out the trade regulations strictly. Even in the royal provinces the governor was generally unable or unwilling to enforce these acts effectively. The failure of the governor to obey this part of his instructions was due partly to the pressure of other duties, which kept him from devoting much attention to this business, and partly to his reluctance to enforce a policy that would antagonize his local constituency.[24]

The negligence on the part of colonial executives was preventing a full collection of the customs duties and causing the treasury to suffer. This weak link in the chain of imperial administration was early discovered, and in the latter part of the Restoration period an attempt was made to strengthen it. Collectors of the customs were appointed for all the dominions (1673-78), usually one for each colony, with authority to appoint deputies. In 1683 a Surveyor-General of the Customs in the American Colonies was appointed to superintend the work of the various colonial customs officials.[25] *Revenue officials in America*

These tax-gatherers were charged not only with the collection of the revenues, but also with the enforcement of the trade laws. Their duties thus overlapped those of the governors, and there was considerable friction between the revenue officers and the colonial executives even in the royal provinces. But the friction between the customs officials and the provincial government in the proprietary and charter colonies was more deep-seated. Here it was not merely personal, but was also political. The presence of the revenue collectors was resented by the proprietors and the people as an interference with their rights. These officials were entirely separate from the provincial government and were the only imperial representatives in these colonies.

During the period from 1660 to 1696 the plan of the British government for regulating trade with the dominions was not carried out effectively, mainly because the machinery of enforcement was not perfected. But at the end of this period a more vigorous policy was inaugurated. By the Trade Act of 1696 the Board of Trade was created, whose principal duties were to be the supervision of imperial commerce. This law also gave the admiralty courts a more important place in the colonial judi- *Admiralty courts*

[24] BEER, G. L., *The Old Colonial System*, i, pp. 264-267, 272.
[25] *Ibid.,* i. pp. 277-280.

ciary.[26] Under it admiralty courts were soon established in most of the colonies and were given jurisdiction in cases involving violations of the trade laws. This was done because it was easier to secure a prosecution for trade offenses in an admiralty court, which had no jury, than in an ordinary court, where public opinion could have weight in favor of smugglers. Because they did not make use of juries, the admiralty courts were unpopular, although the decisions of their judges were usually fairer than would have been the verdicts of prejudiced juries. Appeals from colonial admiralty courts lay to the king in council and to the High Court of Admiralty in England.[27]

The policy of "salutary neglect"   The policy of attempting a vigorous enforcement of the navigation laws was pursued throughout the reigns of William III and Anne but was terminated by the accession of Walpole to power. Walpole believed that the commerce of the colonies ought not to be hampered but should be encouraged. Freedom in trade would make America more prosperous and more able to buy British goods. The management of colonial affairs was turned over to the Duke of Newcastle, whose policy was that of "salutary neglect" of the colonies. This loose method of administra-

[26] The jurisdiction of the English admiralty had been extended to the colonies at an early date, but it was not used to any extent until the Commonwealth period. During this time and after, it was employed in passing on seizures of enemy ships and of foreign ships for violating the trade laws. At the Restoration, James, Duke of York, was made High Admiral of England, and in 1662 his authority was extended to America. Deputies were appointed by him and courts of admiralty were established in the crown colonies. Even before this time admiralty courts had been established in some of the colonies by the provincial governments. These courts were, however, irregular and illegal.

During the Restoration era no effort was made to extend the jurisdiction of the English admiralty to the charter and proprietary colonies. In these colonies admiralty courts were occasionally set up by the provincial governments. In the royal provinces the governors were commissioned as vice-admirals by the Duke of York and authorized to establish admiralty courts in their respective jurisdictions. For some time there was little need of admiralty courts in the continental royal provinces and they were confined practically to the West Indies until near the end of the period (BEER, G. L., Commercial Policy, pp. 129-130).

[27] WASHBURNE, G. A., Imperial Control of Justice in the American Colonies, pp. 170-172.

tion lasted until 1763, when a more rigid observance of the laws was again attempted.

The Old Colonial System

The plan of administering the overseas possessions employed by the British government from 1660 to 1763 is generally known as the Old Colonial System. The arrangement was not an ideal one for determining the relations that should exist between the mother country and the dominions, but under it no grievous injustice was perpetrated against the latter by the parent state. Throughout the entire period the colonies of England enjoyed a larger measure of self-government and more political freedom than those of any other European power. The navigation and trade laws before 1763 did not give ground for serious complaint against the homeland, as under them trade flourished and the colonies prospered. A modern scholar considers the century ending in 1763 as the golden age of the American merchant.[28]

Some provisions of these laws were not harmful, and others were beneficial to colonial interests. Those that would have been objectionable if enforced were largely disregarded, and so the injustice of the policy was reduced to a minimum. However, the system was based on a wrong economic theory and was motivated by a narrow selfish nationalism that was willing to subordinate American to British interests. A potential grievance, therefore, lay concealed in the colonial policy, and there was always present the possibility that it might be aroused to activity by some act of misgovernment. Passive discontent could easily be organized into active opposition, because the popular branch of the provincial assembly was an agency through which the people could make their wishes known.

SELECTED READINGS

1. The Colonial Agent, General Activities.—Lilly, E. P., *The Colonial Agents of New York and New Jersey,* *ch. 6 (excellent summary, p. 224).
2. The Aims of Mercantilism.—Andrews, C. M., *Colonial Self-Government*, pp. *6-9.
3. History of Enumerated Commodities.—Beer, G. L., *Commercial Policy of England Toward the American Colonies*, *ch. 3.
4. The Administration of the Trade Laws.—*Ibid.*, *ch. 7.
5. The Molasses Act of 1733.—*Ibid.*, *ch. 6.
6. Effects of the Acts of Trade.—*Ibid.*, pp. *35-37 (an excellent summary).

[28] SCHLESINGER, A. M., *The Colonial Merchants and the American Revolution*, pp. 15-22.

CHAPTER XXV

ORGANIZATION OF THE COLONIAL CHURCH

Denominations THE principal denominations among the English-speaking settlers were the Congregationalists, the Presbyterians, the Baptists, the Anglicans, or Episcopalians, and the Quakers.) The Dutch of New Netherland belonged mainly to the Dutch Reformed communion, *i.e.,* the state church of Holland and the established church of New Netherland. The Swedes of New Sweden held to the Swedish Lutheran Church. Among the Germans there were a number of denominations. Of these the Lutheran, German Reformed, and Moravian (*Unitas Fratrum*) were the strongest, but there were also a number of other sects such as the Tunkers, or Dunkards, and the Mennonites.

The Anglicans: Chaplain Hunt (To the Anglican Church belongs the credit of making the first effort to establish Christianity in English America.)With the first contingent of immigrants to Virginia there came as chaplain the Rev. Robert Hunt, a most worthy representative of this denomination. He seems to have possessed to an unusual degree the rare virtues of patience and fortitude, for we are told that despite the sufferings he experienced from illness and the hardships which he endured during the terrible first years at Jamestown, no one ever heard him complain or repine.[1] His calmness of temper and poise of character were a mollifying influence among the quarrels and bickerings that characterized the relations of the early leaders at Jamestown.

The establishment of the first church in the colonies The following extract from John Smith's writings relates how the Anglican Church, as well as Christianity in general, had its beginning in Virginia:

"I well remember wee did hang an awning (which is an old saile) to three or foure trees to shaden us from the Sunne, our walles were rales of wood, our seats unhewed trees, till we cut plankes; our Pulpit a bar of wood, nailed to two neighboring trees. This was our Church till wee built a homely thing like a

[1] TYLER, L. G., ed., *Narratives of Early Virginia*, pp. 122, 125, 135-136.

barne, set upon Cratchets, covered with rafts, sedge, and earth; so was also the walls. Yet wee had daily Common Prayer morning and evening, every Sunday two Sermons, and every three moneths the Holy Communion, till our Minister died."[2]

Chaplain Hunt lived only a few years, but in this short time he made a record for sacrificial service not excelled by any of the English pioneer ministers. There were other clergymen, all Anglicans, who in the early trying years of the Jamestown settlement showed the same spirit of self-sacrifice and devotion to religion. Among these should be mentioned the Rev. Alexander Whitaker, who came to Virginia in 1611. Although he was a graduate of St. John's College, Cambridge, and had every hope of preferment at home, he sacrificed these brilliant prospects in order that he might help establish Christianity among the settlers and natives of the New World. (The most noted of his Indian converts was Pocahontas, the daughter of the great chief, Powhatan.)

Other ministers in the early years

The later history of the Anglican Church in Virginia and throughout the colonies generally was not in keeping with this auspicious beginning. By the end of the seventeenth century (1697), the Anglican denomination was well established in Maryland and Virginia, but outside of these two provinces it had only a few scattered churches. These were located in Charleston, Philadelphia, New York, and Boston. There were not a half-dozen Anglican ministers outside of Maryland and Virginia, and less than fifty in all the colonies.

Later developments of the church

An effort had been made by the British authorities to establish the Anglican Church in New England when Andros was sent over as governor of that region. It was unfortunate for the denomination that this attempt was made, as Andros was the representative of Stuart tyranny, and the Church of England by virtue of this association came in for a share of the odium that attached to his administration. The unpopularity of Anglicanism was increased by the attempt made by Andros to requisition a Puritan meeting-house for the Anglican services against the wishes of those who had charge of the building. Consequently, when Andros was overthrown Anglicanism collapsed in New England.

The Anglican Church in New England

At the beginning of the eighteenth century the prospects for the Church of England were not at all bright in America. Its influence on the people generally was slight compared with that

Anglicanism not popular in America

[2] ARBER, E., and BIDLEY, A. G., *Works of Captain John Smith,* ii. pp. 957-958.

enjoyed by the dissenting denominations. Such a condition was not in keeping with the aims of the British government, which was at this time attempting to tighten the bonds that held the colonies to the mother country. The failure on the part of the Americans to recognize the established order in religion might easily lead to a denial of the authority of the empire in government, and ecclesiastical independence might thus pave the way for political independence. Unfortunately for imperial interests, the Anglican Church was not in a position to put up a very effective fight against dissent in America. Its moral tone had suffered by the low ethical standards brought in by the Restoration, and the leaders of the denomination had attained a feeling of security as a result of its final victory over Puritanism and Catholicism. Anglicanism was thus well on the way toward that spiritual decline of which it was generally accused during the greater part of the eighteenth century. An organization that had been coddled by prosperity could hardly be expected to be inspired by the burning zeal exhibited by sects that had been disciplined by persecution.

The work of the Venerable Society

As an offset to this disadvantage, the Church of England enjoyed the encouragement and support of the government officials in the royal provinces and received encouragement and financial aid from the establishment in England. From the beginning of the eighteenth century to the end of the colonial period Anglicanism made a serious and continuous effort to win a place for itself in the overseas dominions. To this movement the royal governors, backed by the home authorities, lent a helping hand, but the most efficient agency employed in transplanting the Anglican Church to American soil was the Society for the Propagation of the Gospel in Foreign Parts, frequently spoken of as the Venerable Society. It was organized in 1701, with the Archbishop of Canterbury as its first president, and numbered among its patrons King William III and many distinguished churchmen, both lay and clerical. The purpose of the society was to do missionary work among the Indians and Negroes and establish churches for the white people in those colonies where religious destitution was especially great, and particularly where the Anglican cause was weak. It entered upon its work with zeal and energy and played a very worthy part in promoting religion and education in the colonies. A great number of missionaries were sent to America by the Society, virtually all of whom were men of energy, zeal, and devotion to the cause of Christianity. They underwent great hardships in traveling through wild sections to preach and teach Indians and Negroes, as well as the white settlers. New churches were founded, prayer-books, Bibles, and tracts were distributed, and numbers of the Negroes and Indians were converted. The Venerable Society did not, however, confine its activities to those localities where there was a dearth of religious instruction. On the other hand, a considerable attempt was made in some places to convert dissenters and bring them into the orthodox fold. In New England this purpose held a large place in their program and aroused the active hostility of the Congregationalists to the Society.[3]

The efforts of the Society were crowned with the greatest success in South Carolina. Its work here was ably seconded by the colonists, and as a result the church soon took deep root in the province. In this colony, too, the competition of the dissenters was strong enough to prod the churchmen into a wholesome activity and to keep them from feeling at ease in Zion. In North Carolina for a long time the results were rather discouraging. The difficulties of travel, owing to poor roads and the absence of bridges, together with the ignorance and indifference of the people, proved to be obstacles that the zeal and self-sacrifice of the missionaries were unable to overcome. So, for a long time the Anglican cause made little headway in this colony. By the end of the colonial period, however, there were a number of Anglican churches in this province and a few flourishing ones in the cities of Brunswick and Wilmington. By this time, too, there were Anglican (or Episcopal, which term was sometimes used synonymously with Anglican[4]) churches in all the colonies, though the number in New Hampshire and Georgia was very small, being smallest of all in Georgia.

[3] For a good short account of this society, see TIFFANY, C. C., *History of the Protestant Episcopal Church in the United States of America,* pp. 278-280. See also OSGOOD, H. L., *American Colonies in the Eighteenth Century,* ii, pp. 30-37.

[4] After the colonies separated from the mother country the American branch of the Church of England was organized into the Protestant Episcopal Church of today. But long before this separation was effected the term *Episcopalian* was used to designate a member of the Church of England. Just when *Episcopalian* began to be used synonymously with Anglican we cannot say, but such usage certainly goes back as far as 1738. See *New English Dictionary.*

Colonies in which the Anglican was the established church

It was the aim of the British government to establish the Church of England in all the royal colonies, and the governors were instructed to carry out this policy. The Anglican was the established church in Virginia throughout the entire colonial era, except for a few years during the Commonwealth period, when the province was under Puritan control. It was also established in Maryland at the end of the seventeenth century (1692)[5] and in the Carolinas a few years later. The establishment in Maryland and South Carolina was effective, but in North Carolina it was only nominal so far as a good portion of the province was concerned. In many sections there were either no Anglicans or else not enough to justify the organization of a church. In such cases the vestrymen usually failed to obey that part of the law that directed them to provide for the Anglican worship. There was considerable opposition to the establishment in North Carolina, as the dissenters were so largely in the majority. This dissatisfaction finally led to an insurrection known as the Cary Rebellion (see page 245). The attempts to make the Episcopal the state church in New York and New Jersey were not successful, as the dissenters greatly outnumbered the Anglicans in these two provinces.[6] In Georgia a law was passed by the assembly

[5] For a summary of the Act of 1692 establishing the Church of England in Maryland, see BACON, THOMAS, *Laws of Maryland at Large* (1692), ch. 2.

[6] In New York the law on which the establishment rested (passed 1693) provided for vestries, chosen by the freeholders, who were to select ministers and provide for their support by taxation. Nothing was said in the law as to the denominational affiliation of these ministers except that they must be "good and sufficient Protestants." The assembly, therefore, contended that dissenting clergymen were eligible for appointment, though the governors maintained, and correctly so, that the phrase "good and sufficient Protestants" had a technical meaning and applied only to Anglicans. See TIFFANY, *op. cit.,* pp. 165-166; also OSGOOD, H. L., *The American Colonies in the Eighteenth Century,* ii, pp. 15-16. For the text of this law see *Ecclesiastical Records of the State of New York,* ii, pp. 1076-1079.

When East and West Jersey were united and made a royal province (1702) the governor was instructed by the queen to make the Anglican the established church of the province. But the Presbyterians and Quakers were very strong and put up a vigorous fight against the establishment. As a result, the assembly never passed an act establishing the Anglican Church, and so there was in reality no

(1758) establishing the Anglican Church, but there were only two churches of this denomination in the colony as late as 1769.

(In those provinces in which the Church of England was established, the salary of the minister and other expenses incurred in connection with public worship were paid out of funds raised by taxing all the people, dissenters as well as Episcopalians) In Virginia the vestries fixed the salaries of ministers and virtually controlled their appointment.[7] Anglican ministers were chosen by the proprietor in Maryland and by the people in South Carolina.

There was never a resident bishop in America, and the colonial churches were under the supervision of the Archbishop of Canterbury until about 1673 and of the Bishop of London after that date. The Bishop of London could, however, exert very little direct influence over his American charge, owing to its extent and its distance from England. From the latter part of the seventeenth century to the end of the colonial period he was represented in America by deputies known as commissaries. The commissary could perform all the duties of a bishop except that of consecrating priests and confirming members, and he was expected to supervise and discipline the clergy under his charge. But his powers were not equal to his duties and responsibilities, and seldom was he able to accomplish much in the way of toning up the ministry to a larger measure of efficiency or a higher standard of moral conduct. It was also a great handicap to the church that all candidates for the priesthood had to be ordained in England. This practice discouraged the building up of a native ministry, for the expense and trouble of crossing the Atlantic for ordination deterred many young men from taking up the calling. This meant that too many of the preachers were Englishmen, who could not fit into the work so perfectly as native workers would have been able to do.

The commissary

The remedy for such a situation was to send over one or more bishops or suffragan bishops to the overseas dominions. The

A resident bishop needed in America

establishment at all, though in the instructions to all the governors there was kept up the fiction that the Church of England was established.

[7] In the early years the governor in Virginia had the authority to present ministers and contended for this power later on. He was not, however, able to make good this claim in the face of the opposition of the vestries (COBB, S. H., *The Rise of Religious Liberty in America*, pp. 87-88).

friends of the Anglican cause both in the colonies and the homeland realized this and earnestly recommended that such a step
be taken. The plan was favored by the clergy, the missionaries of
the Venerable Society in America, and by prominent church
leaders in England, including Queen Anne and the Archbishop
of Canterbury. With such support the advocates of the plan had
every reason to hope that it would succeed, and at one time it
looked as if their expectations would certainly be realized. But
in the meantime there had grown up an opposition to the plan
that was able to muster considerable strength. This opposition
came mostly from lay Anglicans and dissenters in the colonies.
The former did not want an American bishop, because they
thought that he would reprove them for their moral laxity and
interfere with their control over the clergy. The dissenters were
strongly opposed to any change that would strengthen the Anglican denomination in America and were able to bring considerable pressure to bear on the home government through their
friends among the English dissenters. The authorities in England
were hesitant and cautious in the face of this opposition, and
nothing had been done when the sudden death of Queen Anne
gave a severe setback to the cause. Under the Hanoverian rulers
the question was agitated at times, but never reached the stage of
a practical issue. This failure to take a step that would have
strengthened the established church in the New World was due
partly to the indifference toward colonial affairs that characterized
imperial administration under the early Hanoverian rulers and
partly to the opposition that influential Whigs in England waged
against a policy that was displeasing to their fellow-dissenters
overseas.

The
Anglican
Church
weak in
the colo-
nies

At no time during the colonial period did the Anglican Church
have a strength in America commensurate with the efforts made
in its behalf. There are several reasons to account for this fact.
Prominent among these causes is the one that has already been
discussed, namely, the failure of the home authorities to provide
the colonial church with an effective organization by placing a
resident bishop at its head. It must be borne in mind, however,
that the eighteenth century was not an age of faith and that
throughout western Europe religion was at a low ebb during the
greater part of this period. The Church of England shared in this
general decline and did not have enough live coals on its own

altars to light up brightly those erected by it in the overseas dominions.

The Anglican denomination was also handicapped by its alliance with the royal government. This union frequently compromised the church leaders and tempted religion into an alliance with politics. Too often preachers were actuated by prudence rather than by an adventurous faith and were more interested in carrying out the program of the local and provincial administration than in extending the kingdom of God. It is true that the church owed to this union an assured income and an enhanced prestige that came from the association with the ruling class. But sometimes the revenue derived from taxation was not adequate for the support of the church, and the taxation by which it was raised aroused an antagonism on the part of the people which weakened its hold upon them. Then, too, the patronage of the governing cliques and the privileged class had a tendency to impart to it a worldly character that lowered its spiritual tone. When such disreputable officials as Governors Fletcher and Cornbury held a high place in the counsels of the Anglican Church, an outsider might easily conclude that the union of church and state was an unholy alliance.[8]

The church not benefited by its union with the state

In colonial times there were two communions in addition to the Anglican that enjoyed the support of the state. These were the Congregational and the Dutch Reformed, which were the established churches in New England (except in Rhode Island) and New Netherland, respectively. The connection of the latter with the state ended, however, when Dutch rule in New Netherland gave way to English control, while the establishment in New England lasted until after the dawn of the nineteenth century. From the beginning, church and state were closely associated in all the New England colonies except Rhode Island. In every town in New Plymouth, New Haven, Massachusetts, and Connecticut there was at least one Congregational church and more than one in the larger towns. Each of these churches was presided over by a minister who had been chosen by the voters in town meeting.[9] In the early years these churches were all financed by

The Congregational the established church in New England

[8] For conditions in the established church in Maryland and Virginia, see pp. 315, 319.

[9] This statement would also apply to the majority of the towns of New Hampshire. In the eighteenth century ministers were often chosen by the church members meeting as an ecclesiastical organization.

voluntary contributions; but by about the middle of the seventeenth century (1657) all of these colonies had adopted a plan for supporting public worship by taxation. These taxes were for a long time imposed upon all the people regardless of their religious beliefs. But in the first third of the eighteenth century laws were passed in Connecticut and Massachusetts exempting the Anglicans and dissenting Protestant sects from taxation to support the Congregational ministers. In New Hampshire the Congregational Church was also supported by taxation, and in this province, as well as in Massachusetts and Connecticut, church and state continued their union until after the Revolution.

But these exemptions applied only to the Quaker, Anglican, and Baptist denominations, nor did they give as much relief to these communions as would be inferred from the letter of the statutes. Persons desiring exemption had to procure certificates showing their membership in one of these denominations and were thus put to a good deal of trouble. Besides, the law was so enforced as to make it hard for the dissenters to prove their case and often they were taxed to support the establishment despite the apparent liberality of the law. Just on the eve of the Revolution (1770), Baptists in Massachusetts were still complaining that some of their membership who had conscientious objections to paying taxes to support the state church had been fined and imprisoned, and they threatened to appeal to the king if their grievances were not redressed. In 1774 a delegation of prominent Baptists appeared before the Continental Congress to complain of the unfair treatment that their denomination was receiving at the hands of the Massachusetts authorities.[10]

In Rhode Island, Pennsylvania, and Delaware no attempt was ever made to unite church and state.

The Congregationalists and the Presbyterians

Throughout the entire colonial period the Congregationalists were overwhelmingly in the majority in all of the New England colonies except Rhode Island, but they had no strength to speak of outside of this section. The Puritan denomination most closely allied to them was the Presbyterian. These two religious bodies had very similar doctrinal beliefs, as both adhered firmly to the teachings of Calvin, but differed as to their mode of government. According to the Congregational plan each church had the right

[10] *The Religious History of New England* (*King's Chapel Lectures*), pp. 158-161.

of self-government and the authority of the denomination as a whole resulted from a loose association of the churches. The Presbyterian churches, on the other hand, were federated into a system of government similar to that of the United States under our present Constitution. Thus the general government of the Presbyterians was that of the federal state; that of the Congregationalists of the loose confederation, somewhat like that of the United States under the Articles of Confederation.

As these two Calvinistic denominations were so close together, it seems strange to us that they did not join forces as one great Puritan organization. An effort to bring about such a union was made in New England. It was not a complete success in Massachusetts, though it did result in modifying there the Congregational system of church government in the direction of Presbyterianism.[11] In Connecticut it was almost entirely successful; for by the adoption of the Saybrook Platform (1708), the Connecticut Congregationalists put themselves under a system of government quite similar to that of the Presbyterians and remained under it until after the end of the colonial period.

Congregationalism in New England modified in the direction of Presbyterianism

There were a few Presbyterians on Long Island by the middle of the seventeenth century, and a few Scotch immigrants of this faith had come to several of the colonies in the period between the Restoration and the Revolution of 1688. But the denomination had gotten no real hold in the New World until the coming of Francis Makemie (1683), who deserves the credit of establishing the church in America. He made evangelistic tours through the colonies from South Carolina to New York. As a result of his labors the denomination grew rapidly in numbers and importance, and in 1708 the first presbytery was organized. A few years later (about 1714) the Scotch-Irish emigration to America began, and it gave a great impetus to the growth of Presbyterianism.

Growth of the Presbyterian denomination

The Baptists were a radical branch of the Separatists. Their first church in England was organized about 1611 or 1612, and

[11] The plan of church government finally adopted in Massachusetts was a compromise between the Presbyterian and Congregational systems. By it the local churches surrendered some of their independence to the association of churches and allowed their ministers and elders to exercise more authority than accorded strictly with the Congregational ideal (GREENE, E. B., *Foundations of American Nationality*, p. 107).

the first in America in 1639 in Rhode Island. In that year Roger Williams and Ezekiel Holliman immersed each other and these two leaders, with eleven others who were baptized at the same time, formed themselves into a church society. This was probably the first Baptist church organized in America. Soon afterward (or before, some scholars believe) another church of the same faith was organized at Newport under the leadership of John Clarke, who was a prominent physician as well as a clergyman.

From these beginnings the Baptists spread, despite their unpopularity and the antagonism they aroused, until at the time of the Great Awakening they had churches in all the colonies from Massachusetts to South Carolina. They were especially strong in Rhode Island and the Quaker colonies of Pennsylvania, Delaware, and New Jersey, as they had never suffered persecution there. It was in Philadelphia that the churches first grouped themselves together and acted as an association. This association dates from 1707 and was an important agency in building up the denomination in the Middle and Southern colonies.

The Baptists held that church membership should be confined to Christians only, and that baptism should be administered only to those who had already been converted. This ruled out children, and so they were strongly opposed to infant baptism. In fact, they regarded the baptism of infants as no baptism at all, and all candidates for admission into the church who had been baptized in infancy had to have this rite performed a second time. Hence they were called by their enemies Re-baptists, or Anabaptists. They also contended that inner convictions cannot be influenced by outward coercion; therefore, any effort on the part of the civil or ecclesiastical authorities to regulate the beliefs of people are not only wrong but futile. This position led them to advocate absolute religious liberty and the complete separation of church and state. At first there were differences of opinion among the English Baptists as to the mode of baptism; but from the first the American Baptists, and by the middle of the seventeenth century the English Baptists also, had come to agree upon immersion as the only proper mode of baptism. The Baptists had in colonial times, as now, the congregational form of church government. Many of them held to the Calvinistic idea of predestination and election, while others believed in the Arminian doctrine that salvation is offered to all who are willing to repent and accept it.

The Quakers were not so numerous as the denominations already discussed, but they played an important part in the history The Quakers of the colonies. As has already been shown, they were during the entire colonial period the dominant group in Pennsylvania, and were influential in the government of New Jersey as long as it was under proprietary control. They played an important part in the administration of Rhode Island and North Carolina, and were also numerous in Maryland and New England. (For beliefs of Quakers, see pp. 247-248).

The number of Catholics in the English colonies was always The Catholics small. In Maryland they had a stronger hold than elsewhere, but even in this province they were in the seventeenth century outnumbered by the Protestants, and during the eighteenth century they constituted only a small minority of the population. But as many of them belonged to the wealthy and cultured class, they exerted during the first proprietary period an influence greater than their numbers would indicate. Outside of Maryland they were most numerous in Pennsylvania. According to a report made by Bishop Challoner in 1756, there were from four to seven thousand Catholics in Maryland and Pennsylvania (the estimates varying between these figures), with twelve Jesuit missionaries in Maryland and four in Pennsylvania. These priests administered also to the few Catholics in New Jersey and on the Potomac River in Virginia. In the reign of James II there were a few adherents of this faith in New York, and there may have been a few straggling Catholics in this province and in New England at other times.[12]

One of the cardinal beliefs held by the leaders of the Prot- Religious tolerance estant Reformation was that the individual can approach God directly without the intermediary agency of a priest. If this doctrine had been carried to its logical conclusion it would have led to freedom of conscience. But in actual practice the early Protestant theologians were as a rule not ahead of their time in religious tolerance, and so a narrow policy toward religious dissent was pursued after the Reformation as before in both Protestant and Catholic countries. This disparity between the theory and the practice of the first Protestant leaders has caused an English historian (Gooch) to observe that "religious tolerance is the child of the Reformation but not of the Reformers."

The spirit of intolerance still had a strong grip on the European mind during the seventeenth century, and in this period the

[12] For an account of the Methodists, see pp. 701-702.

Americans shared in the spirit of the age. Prior to the Revolution of 1688, dissent from the established church was usually punished by persecution in those provinces where church and state were united. But conditions in America were not favorable to the enforcement of religious uniformity. In all the colonies except the Puritan commonwealths of New England there were a number of denominations, and these could not have lived together in peace if they had not agreed upon a policy of give and take in religious affairs. Moreover, often settlers could not be induced to brave the hardships of pioneer life without the promise, or at least the hope, of freedom of conscience. So even in the seventeenth century considerable progress toward religious toleration was made in some of the colonies.

In Rhode Island, Delaware, and Pennsylvania   The colonies having the finest record for religious tolerance were Rhode Island, Delaware, and Pennsylvania, as no attempt was ever made to establish a state church in any of these provinces. In Pennsylvania and Delaware all believers in God were permitted to worship Him in any way that their consciences might prescribe, but only believers in Christ could vote and hold office. From the beginning of the eighteenth century (1702) to the end of the colonial period Catholics and Jews were also excluded from holding office in Pennsylvania. This narrow policy was adopted as a result of pressure from the British government and was strongly opposed by Penn. Rhode Island, while dominated by the liberal ideas of Roger Williams, went to the full limit in religious toleration. Persons of every faith, even Jews and Turks, were allowed complete freedom of conscience. But during the last century of the colonial period this broad principle seems to have been considerably narrowed by the government, for there appeared (after 1719) in the list of legislative enactments a statute which excluded Catholics from the right to vote and hold office. There is, however, some doubt as to whether this law had ever been passed by the assembly, and even if it had, there were no Catholics in Rhode Island to suffer from its provisions.[13]

[13] This law was found in a revised list of the statutes of Rhode Island which was made apparently in 1744. The compilers of this collection of statutes claimed that this anti-Catholic law had been enacted sometime after 1688. Bancroft thinks that the law was interpolated by revisers and was never a real statute. At any rate it was only of academic interest, as there were no Catholics in Rhode Island

In Maryland, while the Catholic proprietors were in control, freedom of worship was allowed to all Christians. Religious toleration was also allowed in New Jersey, and in the Carolinas during the seventeenth century. The charter to the Carolina proprietors provided for the establishment of the Anglican Church and the toleration of Protestant dissenters. This would imply that the Catholics were not to enjoy freedom of worship; but there were very few if any Catholics in the Carolinas in this century, and so there was no interference with the right to worship in these provinces until the early part of the eighteenth century (1707 in North Carolina and 1706 in South Carolina).

The Revolution of 1688 secured to Protestant dissenters a considerable measure of religious freedom both in the homeland and also in the overseas dominions. The Toleration Act passed by Parliament in 1689 provided that all Protestants should be allowed to worship God as their consciences might prescribe. It is a disputed point as to whether this act applied to the colonies, but at any rate its principle was soon put in force in all the American possessions. Soon after the Revolution laws were passed in all the colonies providing for freedom of worship for all Protestants, but these laws were sometimes administered in such a way as to admit of considerable persecution of unpopular sects. Neither the Toleration Act, however, nor the colonial statutes based on it offered any relief to Catholics, who remained under the ban of the law until the end of the colonial era.

The most unpopular of all the Protestant denominations and those that were subjected to the severest persecutions were the Quakers and the Baptists. The Quakers interpreted literally the injunction "Swear not at all," and would not take the oath of allegiance required by the English government. By a law passed by Parliament in the reign of Queen Elizabeth such a refusal was to be punished by banishment and by death in case of return. In Virginia there were in the seventeenth century laws prescribing banishment for Quakers and the death penalty if they returned. Despite the severity of these laws, no Quakers or other heretics ever suffered death in the Old Dominion, though many Quakers were severely punished by fines, whippings, imprison-

The other colonies

Persecution of the Quakers

---

until the French soldiers came over to aid in the American cause, and then it was expunged by act of the legislature (BANCROFT, GEORGE, *History of the United States,* ii, p. 65; COBB, S. H., *The Rise of Religious Liberty in America,* pp. 437-438).

ment, and banishment. Even in Maryland under the tolerant rule of Lord Baltimore, the Quakers came in conflict with the authorities because of their refusal to take the oath as jurors, give evidence in court, bear arms, or even pledge their fidelity to the government. At one time, near the middle of the seventeenth century, there was a regulation providing for their expulsion from the colony. If they returned they were to be "whipped from constable to constable out of the province." The Dutch of New Netherland were liberal in their attitude toward religious dissent, and refugees from persecution came to New Amsterdam from many foreign countries. But even in New Netherland Baptists and Quakers were persecuted by Governor Stuyvesant, being fined and whipped and otherwise unjustly treated.[14] Persecution went to greater lengths in Massachusetts than in any other colony. Not only were such prominent heretics as Roger Williams and Anne Hutchinson banished, but four Quakers were executed, one of them being a woman.[15] In New Hampshire three Quaker women were severely whipped (1659). Connecticut had laws against Quakers, but there was not much persecution under these laws. Even in New Plymouth, which was more inclined toward tolerance than her sister Puritan colonies, one Quaker was whipped and a few fined and banished from the colony.[16]

Persecution of the Baptists

One reason that the Baptists came in for so large a share of persecution was that they had to suffer for the bad reputation of the Anabaptists of Germany, with whom they were identified in the opinion of the colonial church authorities. Some of these German Anabaptists had engaged in revolutionary outbreaks against the social order and were looked upon in the same light as anarchists are with us today. Moreover, the denial by the Baptists of the efficacy of infant baptism struck at the foundations of those churches which engaged in this practice. The acceptance of this doctrine would be to unchurch all who belonged to these denominations.

In Massachusetts

The policy of Massachusetts was very severe against the Baptists (see page 147). In 1679 the Massachusetts government was directed by King Charles II to allow liberty of conscience to

[14] JAMESON, J. F., ed., *Narratives of New Netherland,* pp. 400-401.
[15] See pp. 147-148.
[16] FELT, J. B., *Ecclesiastical History of New England,* ii, pp. 168, 313; COBB, S. H., *The Rise of Religious Liberty in America,* pp. 142, 259-261, 293.

all Protestants. The authorities were at first inclined to disregard this order, and in 1681 a Baptist church was temporarily closed. But soon thereafter they ceased to interfere with their worship, and by 1714 a Baptist minister was invited by some of his colleagues of the Congregational Church to assist them in the celebration of Thanksgiving.

The Baptists were persecuted in Virginia right up to the Revolution. As late as January, 1774, James Madison wrote that there were in an adjacent county "not less than five or six well-meaning men in close jail for publishing their religious sentiments, which, in the main, are very orthodox."[17] There were, however, no imprisonments in 1775, as the ruling class wanted the aid of the Baptists in the struggle with the mother country. The Baptists joined heartily in the fight for independence and practically all of them supported the patriot cause. In Virginia

The English Toleration Act of 1689 granted freedom of worship to dissenters on condition that their places of worship were licensed. Now many of the Baptist clergymen were itinerant preachers and, therefore, could not easily comply with the licensing clause of the law. Besides, the General Court in Virginia seems to have been loath to grant these licenses to ministers of this denomination, as they would allow them only one place of worship in each county. Many of the preachers, therefore, went ahead with their services without a license.

This might have been overlooked if the adherents of this sect had not been unpopular with the ruling class. But Baptist preachers had little regard for the fox-hunting rectors of the Anglican Church and were unsparing in their criticism of them. As these rectors were hand in glove with the ruling aristocracy, the ire of the governing class was easily aroused against their critics. It seems, too, that the Baptists were unpopular with the crowd, and sometimes their preachers would be insulted while conducting public worship, and their baptismal services would be profaned and ridiculed by ruffians riding in while the ceremony was being performed. Moreover, the enthusiasm of their emotional leaders sometimes overleaped the bounds of conventional decorum and thus subjected them to the charge of holding disorderly meetings.

By their technical violation of the law they laid themselves liable to persecution, and the planter aristocracy was inclined to

[17] RIVES, W. C., *Life and Times of James Madison*, i, p. 44.

press its advantage over them. So some of the ministers were arrested and thrown into prison. The persecuted clergymen, however, had the true spirit of martyrs, and some of them preached from their jail windows to crowds of enthusiastic listeners and sometimes converted their persecutors.

Intoler-
ance
toward
Catho-
lics

A more intolerant spirit than that exhibited toward Protestant heretics found expression in the laws against Roman Catholics, and these laws remained on the statute books until the end of the colonial period, though they seem not to have been strictly enforced during the later decades. Catholics were excluded from New England and New York and were restricted as to their rights in Virginia and Maryland. The proximity of the French in Canada to New York and New England, and their activity in converting the Indians to the Catholic faith, caused the people in these colonies to fear the Catholics, although there were very few, if any, of them in their midst. In Maryland after 1689 the laws against them were more severe than in any other colony, because they were more numerous there than elsewhere.[18] The newspapers and pamphlets would frequently stir up feeling against them by calling attention to their increase in numbers and wealth and by pointing out the menace of this to the Protestant population. There seems to have been a constant fear that the Catholics in Maryland would help the French whenever war should break out between England and France, though there is no evidence of any disloyalty on the part of the Catholics toward the English cause. So uncomfortable were the Maryland Catholics that at one time some of the wealthy leaders were considering a plan for leaving the province for Louisiana.

The main reason for this intolerant attitude was the belief held by Protestants that an increase in the number of Catholics would jeopardize their political liberty. The head of the Roman Catholic Church had at one time claimed and exercised authority over the rulers of Europe, and Protestants feared that he would again assert his power over the governments of the world if his following should ever become large enough to warrant it. The Englishman of that day, whether he lived in the homeland or in the dominions, was a strong nationalist and was impatient of any claim on the part of a foreign prelate to temporal power.

[18] *Archives of Maryland,* viii, p. 448; BACON, THOMAS, *Laws of Maryland,* ch. 1. Also see pp. 314, 316.

Selected Readings

1. Calvinism as Believed by the Puritans of New England.—Wendell, Barrett, *Life of Cotton Mather*, pp. *5-6 (an excellent brief statement).
2. An Appraisal of Puritanism.—Adams, J. T., *The Founding of New England*, *ch. 4 (unsympathetic). For sympathetic accounts, see Bancroft, George, *History of the United States* (1876 ed.), i, pp. *370-377; and Morison, S. E., *Builders of the Bay Colony*, pp. *54-58.
3. Condition of the Established Church in Maryland (1770).—Eddis, William, *Letters from America, 1769-1777*, pp. 45-51 (a favorable account by a contemporary).
4. Condition of the Established Church in Virginia (1724).—Jones, Hugh, *Present State of Virginia*, part iii, pp. *65-74 (an unfavorable account by a contemporary). For a favorable modern view, see Goodwin, E. L., *The Colonial Church in Virginia*, pp. *90-97.
5. The Baptists.—*The Religious History of New England (King's Chapel Lectures)*, pp *137-176.
6. Beliefs and Church Organization of the Quakers.—*Ibid.*, pp. *179-201; Sweet, W. W., *Religion in Colonial America*, pp. *163-166.
7. Colonial Catholicism after 1700.—Sweet, *op. cit.*, pp. 181-184.
8. The Unchurched Liberals.—*Ibid.*, pp. *334-339.
9. Francis Makemie.—*Ibid.*, pp. *254-259.
10. The Jews.—Thompson, C. L., *The Religious Foundations of America*, *ch. 11.
11. A Church Service in Early New England.—Crawford, M. C., *Social Life in Old New England*, pp. *147-148 (a contemporary account).
12. The Venerable Society.—Osgood, H. L., *American Colonies in the Eighteenth Century*, ii, pp. *30-37.
13. The Scotch-Irish Presbyterians.—Sweet, *The Story of Religions in America*, ch. 8.

CHAPTER XXVI

THE DECLINE AND REVIVAL OF RELIGION

The people generally religious

OUR ancestors of the colonial era, as a rule, took a serious interest in religion, especially during the seventeenth century. This was the case not only in those colonies whose first settlers had come to America to find a refuge from religious persecution in the homeland, but it was likewise true in those that had been planted for economic or social reasons. In practically every home there was a copy of the Bible, and there was generally a reverential attitude toward religion. The Bible was accepted as the word of God and no question was raised as to its infallibility. The Puritans at first used Calvin's Bible, but later the King James translation was universally accepted. Other religious works that were very popular, especially among the Puritan denominations, were Bunyan's *Pilgrim's Progress* and Baxter's *Call to the Unconverted*.

The meeting-house

The first houses used for public worship were generally built of wood, and the later ones of wood, brick, or stone. In Virginia the larger and better churches were sometimes constructed in the form of a cross, thus imitating in a small way the plan of the European cathedral. In the earlier years the meeting-house in New England was usually a plain square or rectangular building with doors at one end and on both sides. The pews inside were so high that when closed only the tops of the heads of the occupants could be seen. The church buildings were usually not heated or lighted, except in a few instances near the end of the colonial period. The men probably suffered more in these cold buildings than the women, as the latter sometimes brought with them to church little charcoal stoves that served as foot-warmers. The church, or meeting-house, was everywhere an important political and social, as well as religious, center. In New England the town-meeting was often held in the church building. The people attended divine service not only for religious reasons, but also to meet their neighbors and exchange political and theological opinions and engage in friendly local gossip. In an age when few amusements were possible and those that could be had were restricted by a Puritanical public sentiment, the social attractions connected with church-going were a strong incentive to many who could not be reached by the higher appeal.

In Virginia and Maryland the sermon was usually short—a sort of moral essay, which did not greatly perturb the consciences of the hearers. In New England, on the other hand, church attendance was a serious business, if not a strenuous experience. The congregation was summoned to services by the beat of a drum in the early years and in later times by the ringing of the church bell. The people on assembling took the seats that had been assigned them by a committee chosen by the town-meeting. In front sat the deacons and elders. The other pews had been distributed to the rest of the membership according to their rank, which was supposed to be determined according to "property, virtue, and intelligence." It was not, however, always easy for a committee to draw the lines properly, and a good deal of opposition to their decisions was manifested from time to time. The sermon was not only long, but it frequently pointed out the terrors of the law and the eternal punishment threatening the transgressor. Nor was the gloom relieved by gladsome music. Organs were frowned upon until late in the eighteenth century, and in the early years only Psalms were sung, though Watts' hymns were later used.

A church service in New England

The New England congregation was reined up to right living by the supervision of the deacons, elders, and tithingmen, as well as by the admonitions of the pastor. The tithingman was expected to look after the spiritual welfare of about ten families, assist in catechising them, and supervise their conduct during the week. It was likewise his duty to see that his protégés listened to the sermon with proper interest. For the discharge of this duty he was supplied with a long white wand with a knob at one end and a fox tail at the other. When he discovered anyone drowsing under the long, tiresome sermon, he would arouse him by tickling him with the fox tail, or, if that failed, by giving him a rap with the hard end.[1]

Puritan discipline

Sunday was generally observed as a day of rest in all the colonies. In the seventeenth century a rigid observance of the Sabbath was required by law in New England, Virginia, New

Sabbath observance and Blue Laws

[1] WEEDEN, W. B., *Economic and Social History of New England*, i, pp. 279-280.

Netherland, and in Maryland while under Puritan control.[2] But
the strictest regulations regarding the Sabbath were made and
carried out in the Puritan colonies of New England. The strait-
laced rules as to the observance of the Sabbath were a part of
a general plan carried out by the government for the regulation
of the conduct of the individual. Attempts were made to fix
prices and wages, to restrain extravagance in dress, to regulate
drinking and restrict the use of tobacco. On Sundays, "no one
. . . could make mince pies, dance, play cards, or play any instrument of music, except the drum, trumpet, and Jew's harp."

These regulations and others of like character, known as Blue
Laws, grew out of the belief that many, if not most, of man's
natural instincts are evil and must be suppressed for the good of
his soul. This doctrine is responsible for the asceticism of the
mediæval monk and the unreasonable self-denial of the later

The Puri-
tan ideal

Puritan. The Puritan ideal based on this philosophy was both
right and wrong. It was right in that it taught purity, self-control,
frugality, faith in the absolute sovereignty of God, and a belief
in the equality of His elect children. Some of the noblest characters in history have held to this ideal as the guiding principle
of their lives. In New England there were nurtured on this

---

[2] In 1624 the Council in Virginia punished Thomas Sully, who had
gone hunting on Sunday, by requiring him to pay a fine toward the
support of the church and to "acknowledge his fault in the presence
of the congregation." In 1679 a man was indicted by the grand jury
of Henrico County for playing cards, and another for playing
checkers, on Sunday. See STANARD, MARY N., *Colonial Virginia*,
p. 328.

The code of New Netherland contained a law passed in 1696 which
punished by fine ordinary labor and hunting and fishing on the Sabbath as well as "any lower or unlawful exercise and amusement,
drunkenness, frequenting taverns or tippling houses, dancing, playing
ball, cards, tricktrack, tennis, cricket, or ninepins, going on pleasure
parties in a boat, car, or wagon before, between or during divine
service on penalty of a double fine" (O'CALLAGHAN, E. B., *Laws of
New Netherland*, p. 211; quoted in CHANNING, *op. cit.*, i, p. 536).

President Washington was stopped in Connecticut by the tithingman (1789) for riding a few miles on Sunday, and was not allowed
to proceed on his journey until he explained that it was necessary for
him to do so in order to attend divine service (the Columbia *Sentinel*
for December, 1789; quoted by BROOKS, HENRY M., *The New
England Sunday*, pp. 1-2).

philosophy dutiful and respectful children, chaste women, and serious-minded men dominated by deep-seated convictions. "One might dwell there from year to year and not see a drunkard, or hear an oath, or meet a beggar."[3] The Puritan conception of ethics and religion has undoubtedly done a great deal to stiffen the moral fiber of the American people.

Puritanism, however, cramped individuality by subjecting it too greatly to external control. It acted on the false assumption that inner character can be developed by outward restraint, that one can be frightened into goodness by the fear of punishment. By branding as sinful certain enjoyable practices that were harmless, it deprived the people, and especially the youth, of much innocent pleasure and narrowed too closely the opportunities for recreation and diversion. Even religion, which under normal conditions is a great source of joy to those who comply with its conditions, was often presented in such a way as to add to the gloom of life. Frequently the minister in his sermon had too much to say about the terrors of the law and the punishment of the unsaved, and not enough about the love and mercy of God and His willingness to forgive the penitent sinner. Such a mode of preaching sometimes led sensitive young people into a habit of morbid introspection which clouded their lives with useless depression. In every age there are a few choice spirits who derive their greatest happiness from religious ecstasy and who do not object to the restraints imposed by Puritanism or even mediæval asceticism. But, unfortunately, these saints are always few in number. Many people of average virtue never rise to so high a standard of spirituality, and much of their enjoyment is of a worldly nature. To impose upon such the burdens of asceticism when they are not endowed with the spiritual compensations is to defy both human and divine law. This is the flaw in the Puritan philosophy.

It ought to be said, however, that the first generation of New England Puritans were never conscious of these defects in their theology. Conditions in early New England were such as to impress the settlers with the seriousness of life, to rule out extravagance and luxury in living, and to allow little or no time for idle recreation. A religion, therefore, that insisted upon rigid

[3] For an excellent discussion of the strong points of Puritanism, see BANCROFT, GEORGE, *History of the United States,* i, pp. 316-322. See also MORISON, S. E., *The Builders of the Bay Colony,* pp. 54-58.

self-control and thrift and narrowly restricted amusements was only giving a theological sanction to what nature herself had already decreed. The practice of the Puritan virtues was thus not only good religion, but also sound economics. The frontier, however, was gradually moving toward the interior, leaving an ever-widening strip of territory on the coast in which pioneer conditions no longer prevailed. In this older portion of the Puritan colonies there had emerged before the end of the seventeenth century a prosperous class of merchants and others who had money enough to buy the good things of the world and leisure enough to enjoy them. There were quite a number in this favored class who regarded the old ideas as to luxury and amusements and the Spartan discipline of the early days as an unnecessary restraint on legitimate enjoyment. To many of the rich and worldly the old gateway to church membership had now become a needle's eye through which they found it impossible to pass.

The "Half-Way Covenant"   By the beginning of the second half of the seventeenth century some of the Puritan leaders had begun to feel that the requirements for admission to the church would have to be lowered, as a good many of the people could not meet the high entrance conditions that were prescribed by the orthodoxy of the time. It had been the custom from the earliest times in the New England churches for applicants for membership to give evidence of their regeneration before being admitted. The practice was for the candidate to relate publicly his religious experience. But when the second generation of Puritans reached maturity it developed that there were quite a number of people who were of good moral character but who were not conscious of having experienced a spiritual rebirth. If these were denied all the benefits of church membership their children could not be brought forward for baptism. To avoid this dilemma a compromise arrangement was made whereby all persons of blameless life who would accept the main doctrines of Christianity and promise obedience to the church discipline would be allowed to present their children for baptism, even though they themselves had not been converted. Their status was that of a sort of associate membership, as they were not allowed to partake of the communion.[4] This compromise was

[4] The Rev. Solomon Stoddard, grandfather of Jonathan Edwards and the latter's predecessor as pastor of the Northampton Church, allowed the associate members under the Half-Way Covenant to partake of the communion.

known as the Half-Way Covenant. It was endorsed by a small assembly of Congregational ministers from Connecticut and Massachusetts, meeting in Boston in 1657, and by a larger synod of Massachusetts divines five years later. The Half-Way Covenant was widely adopted in New England, though there was at first considerable opposition to it by the more conservative leaders. Later (1699) the Brattle Street Church, Boston, departed still farther from the orthodox practice by receiving candidates into full membership without requiring them to relate publicly their religious experiences.

By the beginning of the eighteenth century there had also grown up a tendency toward liberalism in theology. The liberals were objecting to those tenets of Calvinism which represented man as being unable to do anything toward his own salvation. They contended that salvation was open not to a select few only —the elect—but to all who were willing to repent, that everyone is capable of accepting or rejecting the offer of salvation, and that man thus can in a sense aid God in his own salvation. This doctrine is known as Arminianism.

Rise of liberalism

These changes in faith and practice did not, however, spring from a deeper interest in religion, but rather arose from the desire to adjust the church to new social and economic conditions. For the first three decades of the eighteenth century were a period of decline in religion in America as well as in England. The ministers in New England were still educated and continued to afflict their audiences with long sermons, but these often had the ring of sounding brass or a tinkling cymbal. As a brilliant writer on New England history has said, the spiritual needs of the people were demanding bread, while the ministers of the established churches in New England and elsewhere were giving them polished stones.[5] In other sections, too, the standard in religion was being lowered. In the early decades of the eighteenth century religion in many places had become conventionalized and wealth had brought in materialism and spiritual coldness. Not only had worldliness crept into the Anglican Church in Virginia and Maryland, but in the Middle colonies also religion had settled down into a comfortable and complacent respectability and prosperity, and in many places had lost much of the zeal that had characterized the founders of the dissenting denominations. The skepticism that was undermining orthodoxy in Europe and creating

[5] ADAMS, J. T., *Provincial Society*, p. 284.

there the age of reason was finding expression in a deistical literature, which by 1730 was appearing in America and bringing in its wake deism and atheism. Everywhere in the colonies, therefore, the spiritual leaders felt the need of a revival that would create or renew within the hearts of the people a deeper interest in the cause of Christianity.

The Great Awakening: Beginnings

At this juncture came the Great Awakening, which was a series of revivals that began in the seventeen-thirties and swept over the colonies. Indeed it was international in scope, for the spiritual awakening in America was preceded by the Pietistic movement in Germany and the Methodist revival in England. "Underlying all these religious movements was the fundamental idea that personal piety and reformation of conduct were more important than correctness of belief."[6] The American revival began in a church at Northampton, Massachusetts (1734), the

Jonathan Edwards

pastor of which was Jonathan Edwards, one of the most intellectual men that America has ever produced. To the earnestness that comes from deep convictions he added other qualities that are valuable aids to effective public speaking, such as a vivid imagination, a logical method of presentation, and an unusual command of language. He had a strain of mysticism in his piety which fired it with zeal and earnestness. Although he was a graduate of Yale College and had made an exceptional record as a student, his education had not awakened within him any tendency toward liberalism. Indeed, his reading and studies had accentuated his belief in an out-of-date Puritan philosophy, and his brilliant mind never got out of the groove that had been hollowed out by a narrow seventeenth-century Calvinism. But the extreme conservatism of his theology never impaired his usefulness as a leader in the Great Revival, as this movement was conservative in aim, however radical it became at times in its methods. On the contrary, the lack of breadth in his intellectual views gave greater depth and force to his piety. A minister with such views and with a genius for presenting them could easily arouse the people to a realization of the terrors of the old Puritan theology. In his preaching he described with awful vividness the everlasting torments of the unsaved, and paralyzed his hearers with the fear thus inspired.[7]

[6] JERNEGAN, M. W., *The American Colonies,* p. 408.

[7] For extracts from Edwards's famous sermon, *Sinners in the Hands of an Angry God,* see TYLER, M. C., *A History of American Literature, 1607-1765,* ii, pp. 189-191.

There was a lull for a few years, when the revival started up again under the preaching of George Whitefield, an eloquent minister from England. He traveled through the colonies preaching to immense audiences and arousing the greatest emotional excitement. Whitefield was not so intellectual as Edwards and was less restrained in his methods, but he made a strong appeal to the masses. His great enthusiasm, his oratory, and his reputation for sincere piety made a wonderful impression on them. In his preaching he would supplement his oratory with unconventional gestures and attitudes. His audiences were too large for the churches, and often he preached in groves and in the fields. Sometimes the house would be so full that he would have to be admitted at a window and be passed over the heads of the people to the pulpit. *White-field*

Both Edwards and Whitefield believed that the religious life is entered through the gateway of a psychological experience known as conversion. The first step toward conversion was the realization of one's utter sinfulness and unworthiness in the sight of God. Along with this conviction there frequently went a fear of eternal punishment that kept the penitent awake at nights. Then came a consciousness of pardon that filled the heart with peace, joy, and love. This spiritual experience was so ecstatic that often those who had it felt impelled to shout their thanks to God. *Revival methods*

Whitefield, as well as Edwards, accepted the orthodox views of the day as to eternal rewards and punishment. They drew gruesome pictures of the tortures to which the unsaved were subjected in the other world, and mightily convinced their hearers of the folly and danger of risking a destiny of everlasting suffering. Under the spell of their preaching people were so wrought up that they would cry aloud for mercy. A contemporary relates that he had seen their hearers roll around in the snow in bitterly cold weather while under the influence of this excitement.

Their meetings were remarkably successful. Hundreds professed conversion and the membership of many of the churches was greatly increased. But there was considerable opposition to the methods of the revival. Whitefield believed that no one was a Christian unless he had had an emotional experience similar to his own. As a great many of the church members, including a number of preachers, had never had such an experience, he regarded them as still in their sins and did not hesitate to say so. He also attacked the colleges, which had begun to be the nurseries *Opposi-tion to the revival* of liberal opinions. He was uncompromising in his opposition to the luxury indulged in by the wealthy classes and the amusements practiced by them. Consequently, he aroused against his movement a number of opponents, many of whom held positions of influence.

Some of this opposition arose from an honest objection to the emotional extravagances indulged in by the converts and the methods employed by the evangelists; some of it came as a protest against Whitefield's attack on the ministers and the colleges; but a good deal of it was due to the fact that the higher standard of spirituality upheld by the revivalists was a stern rebuke to the worldliness of the period. Wealth and culture wanted an easy religion, one that would not restrict the amusements and extravagances in dress indulged in by the patrician families. The higher classes had draped around themselves a conventional type of religion that imparted to its professors a smug respectability, but seldom fired the heart with religious ecstasy. The Great Revival gave a rude shock to this conventionalized religion. There was, therefore, considerable opposition to Whitefield among the wealthy and educated classes, while the common people heard him gladly and considered him a powerful messenger of God. The opponents of the movement included not only the worldly-minded, who always chafe at the restraints of religion, but also many of the conservative church leaders, both Puritan and Anglican, as well as most of the college professors.

Results of the Great Awakening   As both Whitefield and Edwards were Calvinistic in theology and strongly opposed to Arminianism, the Great Awakening was decidedly a fundamentalist movement. It was marked not only by a revival of spirituality in religion, but also by a renaissance of Calvinism in theology. It, therefore, accentuated the difference between the liberals and the conservatives. It also caused a schism in the two great Puritan communions, the Congregationalists and the Presbyterians. In both of these denominations there were quite a number of people who believed with Whitefield and Edwards, while there were others who did not approve of the methods of the revival nor accept the view that one must have a certain type of emotional experience to be born into the Kingdom of God. Congregationalists of the latter type were called Old Lights; those of the former, New Lights. The opponents of the revival methods in the Presbyterian Church were known as the Old Side; those who favored it, the New Side. Some of the New

Light Congregationalists formed independent Congregational churches and many of them went over into the Baptist fold. Among the Presbyterians this difference grew until it widened into a division of the denomination. The opposing factions organized separate synods and the breach lasted for seventeen years (1741-58). Finally a compromise was agreed upon (1758), and from this time on the Presbyterians had the most effective intercolonial organization of all the denominations.

The great revival was also an important event in the history of the Baptists, as it deepened their spiritual life and led to a rapid growth in their numbers. The Baptists had suffered along with the other religious bodies from the general decline in religion that characterized the early decades of the eighteenth century. But inasmuch as they had all along insisted on a regenerated membership they had not cooled off in religious fervor to the same extent as had the more conventionalized denominations. The Baptists at first seemed hesitant about linking up with the movement, but soon entered enthusiastically into it. They, therefore, reaped a rich harvest of converts. The revival also turned them away from Arminianism and Unitarianism, toward which many of them had been drifting, and brought them back to the orthodox Calvinistic doctrines.

The Quakers seem not to have been influenced greatly by the general awakening. The demonstrative emotionalism of Whitefield's converts jarred upon their quiet piety, and so they did not lend their support to the movement. The Anglicans were also not in sympathy with the methods of the revivalists and opposed the movement more than any other Protestant group. The Anglican churches were usually closed to Whitefield, and some of the strongest articles against him were written by Anglican clergymen. When a prominent Anglican minister met Whitefield in Boston he frankly showed his disapproval of his methods by saying, "Mr. Whitefield, I am sorry to see you here," to which the latter replied, "Yes, and so is the devil."

This opposition was due in large measure to the fact that although Whitefield had been ordained as a minister of the Church of England, he disregarded the orders and canons of the church. Besides, his unconventional methods and the emotional extravagancies indulged in by his converts outraged their sense of decorum. The Anglican Church was, however, strengthened by the revival. This was due to the fact that into this communion were gathered many of those of other denominations who were opposed to the methods or views of the great revivalist and his helpers.

It is difficult to appraise the results of this great religious movement. Even today there are those who doubt whether the good accomplished by the revival outweighed the evil that resulted from it. Some modern writers contend that it led to little or no permanent improvement in the religious and moral condition of the people.[8] Its opponents charge that the excitement incident to the movement made such a drain on the emotions that a reaction of indifference to religion was the ultimate result. We cannot estimate with even an approximation to accuracy what proportion of the converts remained faithful to the professions made under the excitement of the meetings. Edwards seems to have thought that quite a number of them were mistaken in thinking that they had been converted. For in 1751 he wrote as follows: "I cannot say that the greater part of the supposed converts give reason by their conversation to suppose that they are true converts. The proportion may, perhaps, be more truly represented by the proportion of blossoms on a tree, which abide and come to mature fruit, to the whole number of blossoms in the spring."[9] But after proper allowances are made for the backslidings of those in whose hearts the word did not take deep root, a good deal in the way of spiritual progress can rightfully be claimed for the movement. Much of the seed fell on good ground and bore an abundant harvest. A great number of people exchanged a religion of cold complacent formalism for one of joyous hope and active zeal. Even when the high tide of emotional excitement had subsided it is probable that the church as a whole was still on a higher spiritual plane than it had been before the movement started.[10]

The revival also gave a new impetus to higher education which resulted in the establishment of four new colleges. These were the College of New Jersey at Princeton (Presbyterian), Brown

[8] JERNEGAN, M. W., *The American Colonies*, p. 411; OSGOOD, H. L., *The American Colonies in the Eighteenth Century*, iii, p. 451.

[9] OSGOOD, H. L., *op. cit.*, iii, pp. 447-448; DWIGHT, S. E., *Life of President Edwards*, pp. 298 ff.

[10] For a favorable view of the results of the revivals, see GEWEHR, W. M., *The Great Awakening in Virginia, 1740-1790*. See also ADAMS, J. T., *Provincial Society*, p. 284.

(Baptist), Dartmouth (Congregationalist), and Rutgers (Dutch Reformed).

As the Great Awakening was a revolt against the established order in religion, it broke the hold of the conservative element on the church and gave the common man a greater influence in religious affairs. It favored the old congregational principle of allowing each local church to be governed by a majority of its members rather than by supervisory councils dominated by the clergy. This theory tended toward decentralization in church government and the weakening of church establishments. According to the teachings of the revivalists all who had experienced the new birth were equal before God. This theory put the uneducated and humble convert on the same spiritual level with the educated and trained leader. The "Popular Denominations," such as the Baptist, the Presbyterian, and later the Methodist, which were strengthened by the movement, became liberal in their political views. The revival, therefore, fostered the tendency toward democracy which the westward movement was promoting.

The converts were bound together by a fraternal feeling that overleaped denominational lines and provincial boundaries. This led to a breaking down of local prejudices. There was a tendency for the denominations with which the New Lights were affiliated to cease to be provincial and become American in their aims and plans. "It was the first great and spontaneous movement in the history of the American people."[11] The revival was also favorable to the growth of religious tolerance, as Whitefield was a believer in toleration. "I am," he said, "of a catholic spirit, and if I see a man who loves the Lord Jesus in sincerity, I am not very solicitous [as] to what outward communion he belongs."[12]

The spiritual upheaval occasioned by the revival released a feeling of pity for the unfortunate and a sense of responsibility for their betterment. This feeling found expression in humanitarianism, "and the humanitarian movement in the colonies may be traced mainly from this time forward." Whitefield's interests were largely humanitarian. He established a flourishing orphan asylum in Georgia and spent a good deal of effort and time in raising funds for its support. This sympathy for the unfortunate

[11] Osgood, H. L., *The American Colonies in the Eighteenth Century,* p. 409.

[12] Quoted by Jernegan, M. W., in *The American Colonies,* pp. 411-412.

led to a more kindly treatment of servants and slaves and aroused within the New Lights a greater desire for the conversion of the Indians to Christianity.[13]

Efforts to convert the Indians: The University of Henricus

Efforts were made from time to time all through the colonial period to bring the natives within the Christian fold. We have already seen that Rev. Alexander Whitaker, one of the early ministers at Jamestown, succeeded in converting a number of Indians to the Christian faith. The Virginia Company was interested in this good work and directed Governor Yeardley (1618) to establish a college at Henricus. This college was to be for both white and Indian students, and it was hoped that young Indians trained here would go back as missionaries to their own people. A good deal of interest was shown in this school, and benevolent people in England were generous in gifts to it. An able man, Mr. George Thorpe, was chosen as head of the college and prospects were bright for its success, when they were suddenly blighted by the Indian massacre of 1622. This outbreak not only put an end to all plans for the University of Henricus, but it caused the settlers to change their attitude toward the natives and put a stop for the time being to Indian missions. The early optimism as to the possibility of civilizing them was now gone.

John Eliot

The Puritans of Massachusetts also had missionaries among the Indians in the seventeenth century. The first and most noted of these was John Eliot. Beginning about the middle of the century (1646) he was for more than forty years engaged in preaching to the natives. He also translated the Bible and other religious books into the Massachusetts dialect of the Algonquian language. Probably no other man in colonial times better deserved the title of "Apostle to the Indians." There were other missionaries sent out among the natives, and by 1674 it is estimated that there were four hundred Christian Indians in New England. King Philip's War checked for a time this interest in the spiritual welfare of the natives.

Other efforts to educate and evangelize the Indians

In the eighteenth century all the denominations showed an interest in the education and evangelization of the Indians. Many of the missionaries sent to America by the Venerable Society

[13] For excellent short accounts of the results of the Great Awakening, see ADAMS, J. T., *Provincial Society,* pp. 283-286, and JERNEGAN, M. W., *The American Colonies,* pp. 410-412. For a lengthy discussion of the results of the revivals in Virginia, see GEWEHR, W. M., *The Great Awakening in Virginia, 1740-1790.*

were zealous in their efforts to teach the natives and bring them to a knowledge of the truth. The Presbyterians, despite the friction that often characterized their relations with their savage neighbors, also had missionaries among them. The most noted of these was David Brainerd, who labored (1743-47) with great zeal and heroic devotion among the Indians in Pennsylvania and New Jersey. The Protestant missionaries founded schools for the natives in various sections and made an earnest effort to educate them. In the middle of the eighteenth century there were several of these schools in New England, one of which developed into Dartmouth College. Governor Spotswood established an Indian school on the frontier of Virginia, and William and Mary College was open to Indians. Harvard and the College of New Jersey also received Indians, though only one Indian graduate is recorded in colonial times from the former institution. The Roman Catholics in Maryland also took an active interest in the conversion of the natives. The Jesuit priests began to preach to them immediately after landing at St. Mary's and were able to report to their superior officer quite a number of conversions in a few years. In 1681 the Catholics had a mission school for the Indians.[14]

These efforts, however, were not crowned with the success that one would expect from the circumstance that the natives were for more than a century and a half in touch with Christian settlers, many of whom had come to the New World from religious motives. One reason for this poor showing was that when the whites came to America the temptation to exploit the Indians was for the majority greater than the desire to serve them. And while a few choice spirits were teaching them by precept and example the Christian doctrine of sacrificial service, their compatriots were by their practices proclaiming the opposite doctrine of exploitation. They would sell them the dangerous "firewater" and cheat them out of their furs and lands by buying them for trinkets. It is not unlikely, therefore, that the simple natives, noticing this glaring inconsistency, questioned the efficacy of the white man's religion and the sincerity of those who proclaimed it. But the main cause of the failure was the ill feeling engendered by the wars between the two races.

At the time the first English colonies were planted, it seems to have been the generally accepted opinion that one Christian

14 HALL, C. C., ed., *Narratives of Early Maryland*, p. 143.

should not hold another Christian in bondage. If this doctrine were carried to its logical conclusion it would mean that slaves on accepting Christianity would have to be freed. The fear of such a result caused many masters to discourage their slaves from uniting with the church. To relieve these fears and thus encourage the Christianization of the Negroes, laws were passed in some of the colonies especially providing that the conversion of slaves to Christianity did not alter their status. In New England the fact that church membership carried the right to vote caused the Puritans there to discourage the evangelization of the Negroes. For these reasons there was very little effort made in the seventeenth century to convert the blacks.

Despite these drawbacks, however, some Negroes were Christianized and admitted into the membership of the churches. As early as 1624 a Negro was baptized at Jamestown, and from that time on they continued to join the Virginia churches.

The problem of church membership also presented another difficulty. The Negroes might be admitted into the white churches as inferior members or could be allowed to form churches of their own to be run under the supervision of the whites. Both practices were at first followed. But later it was feared that if the slaves were allowed independent meetings these gatherings would be used to foment discontent and might lead to slave riots. So in 1715 North Carolina passed a law forbidding the Negroes to have meeting-houses of their own, and other Southern colonies followed this precedent.

In the eighteenth century there was considerable missionary activity among the Negroes in the various colonies. The Society for the Propagation of the Gospel in Foreign Parts took the lead in this worthy endeavor, but the dissenting sects were also active. Schools were founded in which Indians and Negroes could be taught to read. One of these was established in Charleston (1743) to train Negroes to engage in missionary work. Often, too, slaves were instructed in the Bible by the members of their master's household. However, the efforts put forth by the various denominations to educate and evangelize the slaves were never commensurate with the opportunity, and so the spiritual interests of the blacks were comparatively neglected.

The ritual of the Episcopal Church was too complicated for the Negro to understand it fully, and the services of the Quakers were too simple to satisfy his dramatic instincts. More to his liking were the Baptist, and later the Methodist, denominations, for they not only made a strong appeal to his emotions, but were also able to win his favor by their disapproval of slavery.

SELECTED READINGS

1. The Half-Way Covenant.—Sweet, W. W., *Religion in Colonial America*, pp. *105-109.
2. The Great Awakening.—Adams, J. T., *Provincial Society*, pp. *279-286 (a fine short account) ; Walker, W., *Creeds and Platforms of Congregationalism,* *ch. 3 ; and *Religious History of New England (King's Chapel Lectures)*, pp. *42-51. See also Jonathan Edwards's account of his conversion in his *Religious Experiences*.
3. George Whitefield.—*Religious History of New England*, pp. *45-47.
4. Jonathan Edwards.—*Religious History of New England*, pp. *42-45 ; Tyler, M. C., *A History of American Literature, 1607-1765*, ii, pp. *177-192 ; Wendell, B., and Greenough, C. N., *A History of Literature in America*, part ii, *ch. 5 ; Parrington, V. L., *The Colonial Mind*, pp. *148-163.
5. The Log College Evangelists.—Sweet, W. W., *Revivalism in America*, *ch. 3.
6. Revivalism and the Common Man.—*Ibid.*, pp. *91-118.
7. The Negro Church in Colonial Times.—Woodson, C. G., *The History of the Negro Church*, pp. *1-22.

CHAPTER XXVII

INTELLECTUAL LIFE

Schools in England at the beginning of the seventeenth century

AT THE beginning of the seventeenth century Oxford and Cambridge were richly endowed and flourishing institutions, and offered good opportunities for the training of scholars, church leaders, and statesmen. The Renaissance was at its height in England about this time, and the upper classes were keenly alive to the intellectual progress of the day. Educational practice, however, as well as social relations, was based on aristocratic notions, and there was a feeling that schooling was not for the masses, but only for the privileged few. Consequently, the state made no effort to provide free education for all. There were, however, a good many schools, both primary and secondary, but the state assumed no responsibility for them except to require that the teachers be licensed by the king or bishop. The purpose of this restriction was to guard against instruction that might impart heretical or otherwise improper notions. Poor children were apprenticed to masters, who were compelled to teach them a trade, the materials, flax, etc., used in learning this trade being provided for out of funds raised by taxation. This was the only contribution made by the state toward the education of the youth in England.

The secondary, or Latin Grammar, schools were supported by private endowments, and the elementary schools were sustained either by church funds or by private benefactions. To enter a Latin school it was necessary to be able to read and to repeat in English the Lord's Prayer, Apostles' Creed, the Ten Commandments, and the Angelic Salutation. Latin constituted the main part of the curriculum, though instruction was also given in religion and in the art of disputation. The American colonies borrowed their school system from England, and in effecting the transfer they did not modify it sufficiently to make a perfect adaptation to New World conditions.

The school system in New England was far in advance of that of any other section. This was due not to any difference in the

550

character of the people, but to the fact that circumstances there were most favorable for the establishment of schools. The people lived in towns and villages and, except in Rhode Island, the great majority of them belonged to the same religious denomination. It was, therefore, easier for them to coöperate in founding and maintaining schools than it was in rural communities, and in those in which the people were divided up into numerous religious sects.

In education as in other activities Massachusetts took the lead and set the pace for the other New England colonies. A school had been established in Boston when the town was only five years old. A few years later (1642) a law was passed by the General Court providing that all parents should have their children taught how to read as well as how to ply a trade. Parents who failed to meet this requirement were to be fined and the children of such parents as could not comply with it were to be apprenticed to masters who would teach them.[1] This measure was based on the English poor-law of 1601, which required that all indigent children be taught a trade. The Massachusetts law thus went further than its English prototype in that it made primary education compulsory on all parents, whereas the latter only required the teaching of a trade to poor children.

Five years later an act was passed by the General Court of Massachusetts which provided for a general system of public education for the entire colony. By the famous law of 1647 every township of fifty families was required to support a school in which all the children who wished to attend could be taught reading and writing. Every town having a hundred families or more was compelled to establish a grammar school which was to offer such courses as would prepare the youth for college.[2] This plan for public education was later adopted by all the New England colonies except Rhode Island.

This law, however, represented an ideal rather than an actual practice, and was in fact about two centuries ahead of its time. The towns were either unable or unwilling to carry out its provisions, and especially was this the case in outlying settlements

[1] For the text of this law, see DEXTER, E. G., *History of Education in the United States*, pp. 584-585.

[2] For the text of this law, see *Massachusetts Colonial Records*, ii, p. 203; also given in BOONE, R. G., *Education in the United States*, pp. 44-45.

like those of Maine. In the earlier years the penalties for disregarding the law were so light that the towns found it cheaper to pay the fines than to maintain the schools. Later (1671) the fines in Massachusetts were increased, but the constables were not willing to enforce the act rigidly.[3] Consequently, Boston was the only town in the Bay Colony that complied with the requirement at all times.

The common school and the dame schools

Although the ideal behind the law of 1647 was never attained, schools were established in a number of towns throughout New England. In the great majority of these the only subjects taught were reading, writing, arithmetic, and religion. Instruction, still more elementary, was often given by women teachers to groups of girls and small boys. In these dame schools, as they were called, the pupils were taught the alphabet, the Catechism, and sometimes the rudiments of reading and writing. The teacher was usually poorly educated and often could barely read. Sometimes a mother would teach her own family and sometimes a maiden lady would be employed to instruct the children of the neighborhood.

Grammar schools

In a few of the towns, there was, in addition to the common school, a higher one, whose function was to prepare boys for college. This was the grammar school—that is, the English Latin school transplanted to America. Latin held the chief place in its curriculum, though writing, mathematics, and other branches were also taught. The grammar school did not offer the type of instruction that was most needed in a pioneer community, where Latin did not figure to any important extent in the affairs of ordinary life. During the seventeenth century, however, the social ideals of Old and New England were so similar that this objection was not raised and the grammar school was regarded as a success. But by the time the eighteenth century was well under way, the divergence in social conditions between the mother country and the colonies was so great that the people in New England began to realize the unwisdom of their copying slavishly an educational policy that was designed for an old and established society. So the grammar school now began to fall into disfavor as a training-school for life. Besides, it had never been a success as a preparatory school, for the number of boys who went to college was always small for any one town. The requirement that each town of one hundred families maintain a school for this select few proved to be a heavy burden in many cases, and so this provision

[3] See DEXTER, E. G., *op. cit.*, Appendix B, pp. 586-587.

of the law of 1647 was often disregarded, and finally it became a dead letter. The grammar schools, therefore, declined in importance, and by the end of the Revolution there was "scarcely a Latin grammar school worthy of the name existing anywhere in New England."[4] Their place had been taken by the academy, which admitted both boys and girls and offered a more practical course of study.

In New England the opportunities for education offered the girls were very meager. During the seventeenth century and a good part of the eighteenth, girls in most of the towns did not go beyond the dame schools. They were taught reading, writing, sewing, embroidery, and good conduct. In some of the towns they were admitted to the boys' schools either during the short summer term or at odd times, like the noon hour or after school. This practice became more prevalent toward the end of the colonial period, but even then it was not widespread, as is evidenced by the fact that a careful study of two hundred towns shows that in less than a dozen of them were girls admitted to grammar-school instruction prior to the opening of the nineteenth century.

Education of women

In New England some of the schools were private, some public, and some partly public and partly private. The private schools were, of course, supported entirely by tuition fees. The public schools were sustained by voluntary contributions on the part of public-spirited men and by funds voted by the towns or the General Court. They were open to all classes of children, and generally no tuition fees were charged. These were the free schools and were found in all the New England colonies except Rhode Island. In this colony the practice was to collect tuition fees, even in the schools that were partially supported by public funds, from all except poor children. In the other New England provinces there were also some schools in which children whose parents were able to do so were required to pay fees, though the children of the poor were admitted free.

How the schools were supported

It is needless to say that the schools of colonial New England were not up to the standard of the primary and secondary schools of today, but they were as good as could be expected under the circumstances. Next to the meeting-house the schoolhouse was the most important public building in the town. It was generally near the church and was regarded as a sort of annex to it. Religion had a large place in the Puritan school. The pupils read

[4] SMALL, W. H., *Early New England Schools*, p. 29.

the Catechism and selections from the Bible, the Psalms, and a gruesome collection of rhymes called the "Day of Doom." The sentences in grammar to be parsed were taken from the Psalms, and the reading material of the primers consisted largely of religious rhymes. School discipline was unnecessarily severe. Not only were boys flogged and punished in other cruel ways, but initiative and innocent self-expression on the part of the pupils were rigorously suppressed. In an age when grown-ups were forced to accept ready-made opinions it could hardly be expected that schoolboys would be allowed to act or think except along the lines marked out for them by their elders. The schools in New England, therefore, were not an agency for giving the mind of the youth a larger freedom, but rather an instrument used by the leaders for fastening upon it the fetters of a narrow conventional orthodoxy.

Textbooks   During the seventeenth century nearly all the textbooks in use in the colonies were brought over from England. The chief texts used in the primary and secondary schools were the hornbook,[5] the A B C manual, the primer, and the "Book of Manners." In the latter part of the century English texts began to be printed in New England. The most famous of these reprints was the "English Protestant Tutor," which was printed in Boston about 1690 under the title of the "New England Primer." Its contents included all that the hornbook, A B C manual, and other primers contained, together with additional material. It was popular in all the colonies and was "the most widely used book in America." It held its own until after the end of the Revolution, when it was supplanted by readers and by Webster's "Blue Back Spelling Book." The primer and the hornbook were the main and about the only textbooks for most children. Both were based on the Bible, and the former has been called "the little Bible of New

[5] The hornbook was "a sheet of paper pasted on a flat piece of wood and covered with transparent horn so as to save the printing underneath." It had a handle at one end which gave it the appearance of a paddle, and it was sometimes used as such by the master or dame in punishing the children. On the printed sheet was the alphabet, the Lord's Prayer, verses from the Scriptures, and scraps of religious doggerel, with little pictures sometimes placed on the margins (MERIWETHER, COLYER, *Colonial Curriculum*, pp. 29-30). For a picture of a hornbook, see WERTENBAKER, T. J., *The First Americans*, facing p. 246.

England."[6] The Bible was used as the reading text for those few pupils who went beyond the hornbook and the primer. Spelling as well as reading was taught from the primer, as there was no spelling-book in New England in the seventeenth century. In the eighteenth century they began to use a separate spelling-book, which was also based on the Bible.[7]

The Dutch were very much interested in education, but they were rather slow in organizing an educational system in New Netherland. Their first school was not established until 1638, and by the middle of the century (1656) there seem to have been only three schools in the entire province. It was not long, however, before the number began to increase, and by the end of Dutch rule (1664) there was a public school in practically every town of any consequence in New Netherland. These schools were supported in part by public funds and in part by tuition fees, paid by those patrons who were able to contribute, while the poor pupils were admitted without charge. Instruction in these schools was mostly of an elementary character, as the tendency among the Dutch was to offer primary education to the many rather than advanced training to the few. New Amsterdam, however, could boast of one Latin school, which enjoyed such a fine reputation that it attracted students from Delaware and Virginia.[8]

Education in New York

In New Netherland, as in New England, the school was closely associated with the established church. Not only was a good deal of time devoted to religious instruction, but the teacher was partially supported by the church and was a sort of assistant to the preacher. In addition to his school duties he read the Ten Commandments and other selections from the Bible, acted as chorister, set the Psalm, catechised the children, rang the church bell, provided a basin of water for baptism, furnished bread and wine for the communion, and performed other like duties.[9] Besides, the Bible was read, Psalms were sung, and prayers were

[6] MERIWETHER, COLYER, *Colonial Curriculum*, p. 19.

[7] DEXTER, E. G., *op. cit.*, pp. 211-213.

[8] KILPATRICK, W. H., *The Dutch Schools of New Netherland and Colonial New York*, pp. 39 ff. Some authorities give 1633 as the date of the first Dutch school.

[9] For the text of a contract with a Dutch schoolmaster (1682), which enumerates his duties, see DEXTER, E. G., *op. cit.*, Appendix A, pp. 581-582. For the duties of a New England teacher (1661), see BOONE, R. G., *Education in the United States*, p. 12, note.

recited at each daily session of school. Despite these religious associations, the teachers were frequently bad examples of conduct for the pupils to follow, as drunkenness seems to have been rather a common fault among them.

The British occupation was unfavorable to educational development in New York, for the public-school system inaugurated by the Dutch was not continued under the new régime. However, private schools, both primary and secondary, were established from time to time, and some of the Dutch schools were kept up by private support. Quite a number of the elementary schools were founded and sustained by the Society for the Propagation of the Gospel in Foreign Parts. The schools established by this missionary organization of the Anglican Church were used primarily as agencies for promulgating the doctrines and extending the influence of that denomination. In them instruction was given to poor children without charge, not only in the Catechism and the Anglican ritual, but also in reading, writing, and arithmetic. Owing to the zeal and generosity of this missionary society, many indigent children were grounded in the rudiments of learning, but this valuable service was performed at the cost of attaching the stigma of pauperism to free education.

Education in New Jersey

New Jersey, while under Dutch rule, had a public school at Bergen as early as 1661 or 1662, and public schools were established in some of the towns while the province was under the control of the English proprietors. In 1693 and 1695 laws were passed by the East Jersey assembly authorizing the towns to establish schools and support them by taxation. When the two Jerseys were united to form one royal province (1702), the attempt to create a system of public education was abandoned, and thereafter New Jersey had to rely on private schools for the education of its youth. As the eighteenth century advanced, a number of schools were founded by private initiative. While most of these were of an elementary character, in some of them the more advanced branches were taught. The Presbyterians took the lead in education in New Jersey, and it was under their auspices that the College of New Jersey was established at Princeton.

Education in Pennsylvania

The schools in Pennsylvania, both primary and secondary, were about as good as they were in other colonies, though the Quakers as a class probably did not attach as much importance to higher education as did the Puritans of New England. The reason for this was that the Quakers did not think that a knowledge of the classics was a necessary qualification for the ministry. They believed that spiritual understanding comes to the believer by inner illumination, and that religious truth cannot be learned at college. They, therefore, did not require a college training for their ministers. George Fox, the founder of the Quaker denomination, "used to say that 'God stood in no need of human learning,' and that 'Oxford and Cambridge could not make a minister.' Quakers, in studying the Bible, depended upon their Inner Light rather than that critical interpretation of texts to which the orthodox Puritans attached so much importance. A knowledge of Hebrew, therefore, was not highly valued; and as for Greek and Latin literature, it was the unsanctified work of pagans."[10]

Fox did, however, believe that schools are important agencies in imparting moral and religious instruction to children and in giving them the training needed in making a living. The Quakers in Pennsylvania adopted this idea and their church organization tried to carry it out. There was also a law requiring all parents to have their children taught reading and writing. These efforts must have been fairly successful, for by the end of the eighteenth century it is estimated that sixty or seventy schools had been established according to the Quaker standard, as well as a considerable number not measuring up to this requirement.[11] The most famous school in the province was the Penn Charter School, founded in 1689 and chartered eight years later.

In Maryland, as well as in the provinces south of the Potomac River, the English tradition in favor of private schools was strong, and so the public-school system never took deep root

Schools in
Maryland

[10] FISKE, JOHN, *The Dutch and Quaker Colonies,* ii, p. 320.

[11] The Quaker standard demanded that education should be useful and practical, with the major emphasis placed on religious and moral instruction. The teacher had to be competent, of good moral influence, and a member of the Quaker denomination, and the school had to be under the supervision of the Monthly Meeting of the Society (WOODY, THOMAS, *Early Quaker Education in Pennsylvania,* pp. 172-176, 268-271).

The earlier schools were not free except to poor children, and all pupils whose parents could afford to do so had to pay tuition. A very few instances are recorded, however, in which tuition rates were lowered because of appropriations out of the public funds. Later on, as sentiment in favor of public education grew, many Quaker schools were taken over as public schools.

during the colonial period. In 1696 an attempt to inaugurate a system of public education was made, when a law was passed creating a corporation and authorizing it to receive gifts of land for the endowment of schools.[12] This corporation, or board, was to establish a grammar school at Annapolis and at other places as soon as sufficient funds were available.[13] The plan was not an entire success, as only one school, King William's at Annapolis, was established under it. The assembly next voted that certain fines and the import duties on certain products and the export duties on certain others should be set aside as a fund to be used in establishing schools. By 1723 this fund was considered large enough to justify the assembly in taking another important step in the creation of a school system. In this year a school board was appointed for each county and the accumulated school fund was divided equally among these boards. With these funds and others accruing from private gifts the boards were to establish a school in every county. The masters in the schools were to be members of the Church of England and able to teach mathematics, grammar, and good writing, "if such can conveniently be got."[14] Under this law some public schools were founded, and in addition to these a few successful private schools were organized from time to time.

These various agencies, however, did not adequately meet the educational needs of the province, and Maryland was one of the most backward of all the English colonies as to the opportunities offered for education. It was difficult to get teachers for the poor salaries paid, and those that were secured were often incompetent and unfitted by character for their responsible position. It seems that quite a number of the teachers were indentured servants. A contemporary writer, even as late as 1773, said that "at least two-thirds of the little education we receive are derived from instructors who are either indentured servants or transported felons." "Not a ship arrives," he continues, "either with redemptioners or convicts in which schoolmasters are not regularly advertised as weavers, tailors, or any other trade; with little other difference that I can hear of, excepting perhaps that the former do not

[12] Two years before this a school law had been passed by the assembly, but its provisions are not given in Bacon's collection. See BACON, THOMAS, *Laws of Maryland,* 1694, ch. 31.

[13] For provisions of this act, see *ibid.,* 1696, ch. 17.

[14] For the text of this law, see *ibid.,* 1723, ch. 19.

usually fetch as good a price as the latter."[15] While this statement is doubtless an exaggeration, still there is enough other evidence to show that the schools in this province were exceptionally scarce and poor. One reason for this was that in the eighteenth century the teachers were required by law to be Anglicans, while most of the people were dissenters. In 1750 the lower house of the legislature of Maryland pronounced the schools a failure. The governor in an official statement made in 1763 said that there was not a good grammar school in the province.[16]

It was difficult to maintain a satisfactory school system in the South, owing to the fact that the settlers were so widely scattered. There were, therefore, few schools in the Southern provinces in the early years of their history. But after the colonies were firmly established, schools sprang up, and soon the people in this section were, as a rule, able to solve their educational problems as well as did their fellow colonials of the North, due account being taken of the greater obstacles that they had to overcome.

Educational conditions in the South

The agencies for primary and secondary education in the provinces south of the Potomac were private tutors, public and private schools, and the classical schools or academies. It was quite common in England in the seventeenth century for families in the upper classes to employ tutors to teach their own children. This practice was widely adopted by the southern planters, many of whom had tutors for their children, girls as well as boys. A room in an outbuilding was usually set aside for the school. Other children in the neighborhood, as well as those of friends and relatives from a distance, also frequently attended, the latter boarding or visiting at the plantation. The tutor might be an indentured servant of slight education, an Anglican minister, or a graduate of an English university. In the eighteenth century women were sometimes employed as tutors in Virginia, and this practice was the nearest approach that the South made to the system of dame schools that was characteristic of New England. Boys were prepared by tutors for the classical schools, for William and Mary College, or for the universities abroad.

Agencies for education in the South

There were also numerous small private schools scattered throughout the Southern provinces. A common location for these

[15] Quoted by STEINER, B. C., in *History of Education in Maryland*, p. 38.
[16] MERENESS, N. D., *Maryland as a Proprietary Province*, p. 141.

schools was a worn-out field in the plantation, and so they were called "old field schools." They were usually taught by the local Anglican minister, who was frequently a college-bred man from England, or a scholar who had come from England with credentials from the Bishop of London. In the districts occupied by the Scotch-Irish, the teacher was often a Presbyterian clergyman, and the schoolhouse and the church were frequently built together. In South Carolina the qualifications required of teachers were especially high. By a law passed as early as 1712 teachers had to be able to teach Greek and Latin.[17] The subjects taught in these schools were usually reading, writing, and arithmetic, though Greek, Latin, and more advanced mathematics were sometimes included.

As a rule the schools in the South charged tuition fees, though there were quite a few in South Carolina and Virginia that were free to poor children. Most of these were founded and maintained by endowment funds, usually left as legacies by public-spirited property-owners.[18] There were, however, some free schools that were sustained by public funds. South Carolina took the lead in the support of public education among the Southern provinces. An appropriation was made by the legislature for a

[17] MERIWETHER, COLYER, *History of Higher Education in South Carolina* (American Educational History, ii), pp. 22-23.

[18] In 1671, Governor Berkeley in a report to the home government made the following statement: "But I thank God there are no free schools nor printing, and I hope we shall not have these hundred years, for learning has brought disobedience and heresy and sects into the world and printing has divulged [them] and libels against the best government. God keep us from both." Many scholars assume that this statement is a correct account of educational conditions in Virginia at this time and a true indication of the attitude of the people toward free schools. As a matter of fact, it is neither. There were at the time of this report at least two and probably more flourishing free schools in the province. It is also a well-known fact that Governor Berkeley, who was a hidebound reactionary and at this time in his dotage, was not in harmony with public opinion in Virginia. This is shown by the fact that a few years later (1676) he was repudiated by the people, who rose in rebellion against him and under the leadership of Nathaniel Bacon drove him across Chesapeake Bay. See *William and Mary College Quarterly Historical Magazine*, v, pp. 112-113; MADDOX, W. A., *The Free School Idea in Virginia before the Civil War*, p. 1; and BRUCE, P. A., *Institutional History of Virginia in the Seventeenth Century*, pp. 350-356.

public school in Charleston in 1712. In this same year a law was passed providing that ten pounds be given annually from the public funds for the support of a schoolmaster in each parish.[19] We do not know to what extent this law was enforced, but a high authority on the colonial history of South Carolina, in speaking of educational conditions at the end of the colonial period, says, "In each parish there were pupils who were taught free at the public expense." In North Carolina prior to the Revolution there was no effective legislation for public schools. The governors were apparently not interested in public education, except Gabriel Johnston, who in 1736 urged the legislature to provide for schools, but nothing was done by the assembly to carry out this suggestion. However, under the apprenticeship system inherited from England masters were required to teach their wards the rudiments of learning.

About the same time that the academy was superseding the Latin school in New England it was also playing an important part in southern education. This new type of school had a place between the small private school and the college. There was no sharp line separating it from the "old field school" below or the college above, for in its curriculum it overlapped both. The "old field school" frequently offered courses in Latin and Greek, and in some of the academies the elementary branches were taught, as well as Greek, Latin, science, mathematics, and other subjects listed in the college curriculum. The academy had an especially important place in the educational system of North Carolina in the latter part of the colonial period. During the decade and a half just preceding the outbreak of the Revolution, Presbyterian ministers established several academies in this province. These academies served both as preparatory schools for Princeton and other colleges and as "people's colleges," giving young men their final academic training. Many men prominent in the ministry and other professions in North Carolina received their education in these schools.[20] Of one of these academies (founded about 1766 by Rev. Dr. David Caldwell) it was said that for many years

The academy

[19] COOPER, THOMAS, *Statutes of South Carolina*, ii, pp. 389-396.
[20] *Colonial Records of North Carolina*, iv, pp. 977, 979, 980, 993, 994; SMITH, C. L., *History of Education in North Carolina*, pp. 13, 23-26, 32-35; CONNOR, R. D. W., *History of North Carolina*, pp. 202-204.

"his [Dr. Caldwell's] log cabin served North Carolina as an academy, a college, and a theological seminary."[21]

Higher education in the South

For their higher education young men went to William and Mary College, to schools in England, or to colleges in the Northern and Middle colonies. Every large planter in the South had an ambition to educate his sons at either Oxford or Cambridge, and quite a number of young men of wealthy families from all the Southern provinces went to England to complete their education. South Carolina sent more of her sons to England in proportion to population than any other American province. This was due partly to the fact that there was no institution of higher learning in the colony and partly to the close intercourse kept up between Charleston and the mother country.[22] From Virginia, too, many young men went to England to study despite the fact that they had a college in the province all during the eighteenth century. It was also the custom in North Carolina for men of means to send their children off to school. In the northeastern section they went to England; in the Cape Fear region (where there was a settlement of New Englanders), Harvard was the most popular college; while among the Presbyterians in the upland regions, not only of North Carolina but also of South Carolina and Virginia, Princeton was the favorite.

Part played by the church in education in the South

The church was active in its support of education in the Southern as well as in the Northern and Middle colonies. The most important agency of the Anglican Church in promoting education was the Society for Propagating the Gospel in Foreign Parts. This missionary society established a number of schools in all the Southern provinces. Among the Scotch-Irish settlers in the upland regions the chief impulse to education was given by Presbyterian missionaries and preachers. The ministers were usually graduates of Princeton and believed firmly not only in the value of elementary instruction, but also in the importance of a knowledge of the higher branches, especially Greek and Latin, the languages of the New Testament and western Christianity. Through their influence many small schools were established in connection with the churches, and the teachers in these schools were frequently clergymen. As has already been seen, the ministers were also instrumental in establishing academies, and to them Princeton College was entirely indebted for the hold it main-

[21] SMITH, C. L., *History of Education in North Carolina*, p. 27.
[22] McCRADY, E., *Colonial Education in South Carolina*, pp. 232-235.

tained on the settlers of the upland regions. The Baptists were also active in supporting education after the middle of the eighteenth century. Among the royal governors who encouraged education, Francis Nicholson probably deserves the first place. He was not only one of the main promoters of William and Mary College, but as governor of South Carolina (1721-24) he also encouraged the establishment of schools by making generous donations and thereby setting an example that other public-spirited men were inclined to follow.

The Colonial College

Quite a number of the leaders of early New England were graduates of the University of Cambridge, while a few had attended Oxford.[23] The fact that more came from the former than from the latter university is easily understood when we recall that Puritanism had gotten quite a hold on Cambridge, while Oxford, being at the time largely under the influence of Laud, the arch-opponent of ecclesiastical irregularity, was not sympathetic with any kind of religious dissent. As many of these college-bred men were clergymen and the clergy dominated public opinion in New England, it is only natural that Massachusetts should have taken steps to establish a college for the training of ministers before anything to speak of had been done toward organizing a system of primary education. This disposition to put the capstone on the educational structure before the foundations were well laid was characteristic not only of the Congregationalists of New England, but of other denominations in other sections as well. The colonial college, therefore, outran the primary and secondary school in development. The scheme of education in colonial days was inspired by the notion that it was more important to provide higher education for the leaders than elementary instruction for the masses. This aristocratic idea of education was responsible for the birth of Harvard College and the later establishment of other similar institutions in an age when the common people had very inadequate opportunities for schooling.

[23] "In 1638 there were in the four or five settlements of Massachusetts and Connecticut forty or fifty graduates of Cambridge and not a few Oxonians; roughly, one in every two-hundred and fifty of the inhabitants was university bred; a proportion three times as large as at the present day" (DEXTER, E. G., *op. cit.*, p. 223).

Colleges   At the end of the colonial period there were nine institutions of higher learning in English America. They were, in the order of seniority, Harvard, William and Mary, Yale, the College of New Jersey (now Princeton), the "Academy" (now the University of Pennsylvania), King's (now Columbia), Brown, Queen's (now Rutgers), and Dartmouth.

Harvard   Harvard College was founded in 1636, when the legislature of Massachusetts made a liberal appropriation for the establishment of a college at Newtown,[24] the name of which was soon changed to that of Cambridge in honor of the University of Cambridge in England. Two years later John Harvard, a young Charlestown minister, died and left half his property and all his library to the infant institution. This was a liberal bequest and in appreciation of it the college was at once given the name of this generous patron. In a sense the beginning of the college dates from this legacy, as the appropriation made by the General Court had not as yet been received and it is very doubtful as to whether it was ever paid. Later appropriations, however, were paid and the support of the Massachusetts government was generous, considering the financial condition of the colony. John Harvard's example was quickly followed by others, and soon the college was the recipient of a number of private benefactions. These included small gifts by the poor, as well as large donations by the wealthy.[25] As the main purpose of Harvard was to train young men for the ministry, it was supported by all the Puritan colonies of New England. At one time every family in each of the colonies contributed at least a peck of corn or its equivalent in value for its support.

The new institution was housed "in a fair and comely edifice, having in it a spacious hall and a large library with some books in it." The age limit for entrance was low and some of the students were only about eleven years old. Students were given seats at commons and arranged in classes according to their social position, just as their parents were seated in church according to the same plan. Each tutor heard recitations in all subjects, and not until 1776 were instructors assigned separate branches.

William and Mary   The College of William and Mary was founded in 1693, mainly

[24] *Massachusetts Bay Colony Records*, i, p. 183.
[25] For lists of private donations made in the seventeenth century, see QUINCY, JOSIAH, *History of Harvard University*, i, Appendix, pp. 506-513.

through the efforts of Governor Nicholson and James Blair, the Commissary for Virginia. Governor Nicholson, who was always the friend of education, not only exerted his official influence in support of the college, but he also contributed generously toward the endowment out of his own private means. A productive fund was started in 1690 by subscriptions made by London merchants at the solicitation of Dr. Blair, and it was enlarged by liberal contributions made by Virginians. Blair then went to England as the agent of the Virginia assembly to get financial aid and a charter for the college. He succeeded in interesting King William and Queen Mary and a charter was granted by them (1693), and the quit rents that had accumulated in the colony were added to the endowment. The institution was also given twenty thousand acres of land, the right to farm the office of surveyor-general, and a penny tax on every pound of tobacco exported from Virginia and Maryland. To these sources of income was added by the colonial assembly an appropriation of more than one hundred pounds a year, to be paid out of an export duty on skins and furs.[26]

The college was very properly named William and Mary in honor of its royal benefactors. A building was erected at Middle Plantation (afterwards Williamsburg) and the college was organized with Dr. Blair as president, which position he held for fifty years. In a few years the capital was moved to Williamsburg and the town became the chief social center of the province. One of the motives for establishing the college was the hope that it would be an aid to religion and a strong ally of the Anglican Church in the province. This purpose was emphasized by Blair[27] and it made a strong appeal to the early supporters of the move-

[26] For a contemporary account of the founding of William and Mary College, see HARTWELL, BLAIR, and CHILTON, *The Present State of Virginia and the College* (1727), pp. 67-71. For the text of the charter of the college, see *ibid.*, pp. 72-95. See also HENING, W. W., *Statutes at Large*, iii, p. 123, and ADAMS, H. B., *The College of William and Mary*, p. 15.

[27] A story is told which would indicate that this appeal was not always effective with worldly-minded officials. Seymour, the Attorney-General, was one of those who did not favor the project. Blair tried to win him over by reminding him that the colonists had souls to save. His blunt reply was: "Souls: Damn their souls: Make tobacco" (SPARKS, J., *Life and Writings of Franklin*, x, pp. 110-111).

ment in England. In the beginning all the professors were members of the Church of England and most of them were ministers who served neighboring churches. A number of young men who were studying for the Anglican ministry were aided by being given free board and tuition. The preparatory school was opened before the college proper, and in the early years the institution was only a grammar school. In 1723 a building to be used as an Indian school was erected on the campus out of funds left by the English scientist, Sir Robert Boyle. It was hoped that the Indians educated here would return as missionaries to their own people. This expectation, however, was not realized, as the Indian students, after leaving college, usually reverted to paganism and barbarism. The college building was destroyed by fire in 1705, and for some years thereafter the institution had to struggle to keep on its feet. Rev. Hugh Jones, one of the professors, spoke of it in 1724 as "a college without a chapel, without a scholarship, and without a statute, having a library without books comparatively speaking, and a president without a fixed salary till of late."[28] The college became more prosperous later, and during the greater part of the eighteenth century it was an important agency for higher education in the Old Dominion. Many of the Virginians who took a leading part in the Revolution were trained at William and Mary.

Yale   Yale College was founded in 1701, when a charter for a college was granted by the legislature of Connecticut and an appropriation made for its support.[29] The initial step, however, had been taken the year before, when ten ministers met at Branford and gave forty books from their libraries to establish a college. The population of New England had by this time increased sufficiently, it was thought, to justify the establishment of another Puritan institution for higher learning. The people of Connecticut, and especially the ministers, wanted a college nearer than Harvard. Besides, Harvard had come under the control of those who were liberal in theology and the conservatives favored the establishment of a more orthodox institution. The new college opened its doors with an enrollment of eight students. It had a checkered career for the first seventeen years, and a recent president of Yale, in speaking of this early period, said that "for many years

[28] JONES, HUGH, *Present State of Virginia*, p. 83.
[29] The text of this act is given in DEXTER, E. G., *op. cit.*, pp. 20-23.

it was difficult to say what it was and where it belonged."[30] Jealousy between the towns prevented an agreement as to a permanent location, and for a time instruction was given at several places at once. Finally, in 1716 the college settled down at New Haven as its permanent abode, though the location here was still contested by Wethersfield and a rival commencement was held there in 1718.[31] The competing towns, however, soon accepted the New Haven site, and donations of money and books began to come from various sources.

The most important early contribution to the endowment was made by Elihu Yale, a New Englander by birth, who had acquired wealth in India and had held the important position of Governor of the East India Company at Madras. The name of this liberal benefactor was assumed by the college at the commencement in 1718. The main purpose of the institution was to train young men for the ministry. The governing body was composed entirely of ministers, who by a later regulation must be free from all taint of "Arminian and Prelatical Corruptions." The orthodoxy of the institution being thus safeguarded, it grew in prosperity and became "the academic headquarters of thoroughgoing Calvinism both for New England and the Middle colonies."

The increased interest aroused in religion by the Great Awakening stimulated a greater activity in higher education on the part of the Baptists and the Presbyterians. As a result of this educational revival a college was established by each of these denominations, the College of New Jersey by the New Side Presbyterians (1747) and the College in Rhode Island[32] by the Baptists (1764). The College of New Jersey was founded primarily for the training of ministers, and in the beginning all of

Princeton and Brown

[30] HADLEY, President ARTHUR T., quoted by ADAMS, J. T., *Provincial Society,* p. 135.

[31] STEINER, B. C., *History of Education in Connecticut,* pp. 77-79; DEXTER, F. B., *Documentary History of Yale University,* pp. 159-163.

[32] The Baptist college in Rhode Island was at first known as Rhode Island College. In 1804 it assumed the name of Brown University in honor of Nicholas Brown, the first of its generous benefactors (DEXTER, E. G., *op. cit.,* pp. 260, 262; BRONSON, W. C., *The History of Brown University,* pp. 155-157).

For a contemporary account of the founding of the college, see BRONSON, *op. cit.,* pp. 15-19.

the trustees were clergymen. This new seat of learning proved to be an important factor in promoting the cause of the New Side Presbyterians, and it soon became the leading institution of higher learning not only for the young men of New Jersey, but also for those of the upland regions of the South. Brown was exceptionally liberal in its attitude toward other denominations. The charter provided that the president and a majority of the trustees should be Baptists, but other denominations were to be represented on the board.[33]

King's (Columbia)

Before the middle of the eighteenth century the Anglicans had come to realize that they must increase their activity in the field of higher education if they were to hold their own with the dissenters. So it was decided to establish in the town of New York a college for the Anglicans. Lotteries were held, beginning in 1746, to raise funds for the prospective college, and in five years seventeen hundred dollars had been procured in this way. A board of trustees was now organized, and a few years later (1754) a charter was obtained from George II.[34] Other funds were raised by private subscription, and in this same year King's College, as it was called, opened its doors to the eight students who came to be under the tutelage of the president and only instructor, Dr. Samuel Johnson. King's College was closed from 1776 to the end of the Revolutionary War, and when it reopened (1784) it took the name of Columbia College.

In 1749 Franklin drew up a plan for a school of higher learn-

[33] The exceptional liberality of this college even in the beginning is attested by the following clause in the charter: "Into this liberal and catholic institution shall never be admitted any religious tests. But, on the contrary, all the members hereof shall forever enjoy full, free, absolute, and uninterrupted liberty of conscience; and that the places of professors, tutors, and all other officers, the president alone excepted, shall be free and open for all denominations of Protestants; and that youths of all religious denominations shall and may be admitted to the equal advantages, emoluments, and honors of the college or university . . . and that the public teaching shall in general respect the sciences; and that the sectarian differences of opinion shall not make any part of the public and classical instruction" (BRONSON, op. cit., p. 506).

For the full text of the charter of 1764, see ibid., pp. 500-507. For early laws of the college, see ibid., pp. 508-518.

[34] For a brief history of King's College to 1784, see HATHAWAY, F. A., History of Higher Education in New York, pp. 133-139.

ing in Philadelphia, which was to be free from sectarian influ- The Uni-
ence and in which instruction of a practical character was to be versity of
given. According to the plan, English was to be put on a par Pennsyl-
with Latin, the modern languages were to be taught, and history, vania
economics, and politics were to be emphasized. Funds for the new
school were soon available, having been raised by lotteries, private subscriptions, and appropriations by the town council, and
the "Academy," as the institution was called, was ready to open
by 1751, though it was not chartered until three years later.
Franklin's ideal was not completely realized, as the trend of the
times was against it, and Latin received more attention than
English in the Academy. He had, however, succeeded in establishing a school that was free from denominational control. In
1791 the Academy became the University of Pennsylvania.

The last two colonial institutions of higher learning were Rutgers
Queen's (Rutgers) College, established by the Dutch Reformed and Dart-
Church (1766) for the training of ministers, and Dartmouth mouth
College (chartered in 1769), which grew out of a successful
Indian school that had been established by Rev. Dr. Eleazar
Wheelock. The school was originally located at Warren, Con-
necticut, and was moved to its present site, Hanover, New Hamp-
shire, in 1770.

The college curriculum in the seventeenth century included The
Greek, Latin, Hebrew, and elementary Chaldee and Syriac; arith- college
metic and geometry; history, politics, logic, and ethics; the Bible; curricu-
rhetoric, composition, and oratory; astronomy, physics (very lum
elementary), and botany (nature of plants). These same subjects
are found in the eighteenth-century courses of study, except that
Chaldee and Syriac have dropped out and elementary French has
been added. There was some improvement in the method of teaching Latin during the latter century, as an attempt was made to
give the student an appreciation of the literary merits of the
Latin classics.[35]

Strict discipline was enforced in the colonial college. Students College
were held to systematic habits and a conventional standard of discipline
behavior by the regulations of the governing bodies. They were
required to rise early, to attend all lectures and recitations, indulge in no questionable conduct, and show proper deference to
their superiors. At Harvard discipline was maintained for a long

[35] For the college curricula of the seventeenth and eighteenth
centuries, see MERIWETHER, COLYER, *Colonial Curriculum*, p. 11.

time by flogging, but after 1734 violations of college rules were punished by fines.[36] In addition to the requirements imposed by the authorities, there were campus regulations prescribed by the students that still further restricted their freedom. Upper classmen domineered over under classmen in a way that would be quite understandable to a modern freshman. For example, there was a campus rule at Yale in 1764 according to which freshmen were to perform "all reasonable errands for any superior."

The extreme youthfulness of many of the students accounts in part for these restrictions. They also grew naturally out of the belief that human nature is deeply tainted with depravity and that inner impulses must be curbed by outward restraints if virtue is to have a chance. Such a régime, it was hoped, would rub off all angularities in personality and achieve complete regularity in outward behavior. But it also discouraged legitimate self-expression and afforded small opportunity for individuality to assert itself. Fortunately, however, the exuberance of youth was frequently too much for the artificial restraints and often showed a sensible impatience with the straitjacket in which it had been placed. For we find that students in colonial days performed very much the same sort of pranks as did their ancestors in earlier times and their descendants in modern days. Among the improper practices indulged in by the young men in Princeton in 1770, a contemporary mentions the following: "strewing the entries in the Night with greasy Feathers; freezing the bell; Ringing it at late Hours of the Night; . . . Picking from the neighborhood now and then a plump fat Hen or Turkey; . . . Darting Sunbeams upon the Town-People."[37]

Extra-curricular activities There was little or no place for organized athletics in the colonial college. Just before the Revolution (1770) a student in

[36] BUSH, G. G., *History of Higher Education in Massachusetts,* pp. 29-30. For the law permitting the Harvard authorities to punish students by fine or whipping, see *Massachusetts Bay Colony Records,* iv, pp. 278-279. For the text of the rules governing student conduct at Harvard adopted just prior to the middle of the seventeenth century, see QUINCY, JOSIAH, *History of Harvard University,* i, Appendix, pp. 515-517.

[37] Quoted by SLOSSON, E. E., in *The American Spirit in Education,* p. 63. For other freshmen regulations see STEINER, B. C., *History of Education in Connecticut,* p. 111. For freshmen rules in force at Harvard during the seventeenth century, see BUSH, G. G., *The History of Higher Education in Massachusetts,* pp. 25-26.

Princeton relates that the faculty prohibited shinny on the ground that it was dangerous and because there were "many amusements both more honorable and more useful in which they are indulged."[38] There were no Greek-letter fraternities, but literary societies took their place in a way.

The first newspaper in America was started at the beginning of the eighteenth century by William Campbell, the postmaster of Boston. His position gave him an opportunity to keep informed as to the news of the day. In order that others might share this advantage with him, he wrote news letters and sent them to his friends in different sections of New England. Writing by hand was slow and tedious, and so in 1704 he began to print his letter. *The Boston News Letter* thus became the first newspaper printed in America. It was fifteen years before another publication was established, but before the middle of the century a number of weekly papers were in circulation in the various colonies. The newspapers of the half century preceding the Revolution frequently discussed political questions, and in this way exerted a great influence in preparing the minds of the people for the revolt against the mother country.

Books were not numerous in the colonial period, but as a rule there were some in every family except the poorest. In the homes of the wealthy there were sometimes libraries of considerable size. The library of Westover, on the James River, the home of the noted Byrd family, had in 1788 nearly four thousand volumes.[39] The most important attempt to put good books within the reach of the people was made by the Anglican Church. Dr. Thomas Bray, who became Commissary of Maryland in 1696, succeeded in placing a library in nearly every one of the thirty parishes in that province. The Venerable Society was also active in establishing parochial libraries in Virginia and the Carolinas. One of these in the village of Bathtown, North Carolina, had at one time a larger collection of books than could be found in all New England outside of Boston. In 1700, South Carolina, on the

News-papers

Libraries

---

[38] *The Diary of Philip Fithian,* quoted by SLOSSON, *op. cit.,* p. 60.
[39] For a list of books in the library at Westover, the largest collection in the South, see BASSETT, J. S., ed., *The Writings of Colonel William Byrd,* Appendix A. For other documents showing size of colonial private libraries, see *William and Mary College Quarterly,* ii, pp. 169-175, 247-251; and *Massachusetts Bay Colony Records,* i, p. 183.

receipt of two hundred and twenty-five volumes, established a provincial library and passed the earliest library law in the colonies, making the use of the library open to the people.[40] A public library was also established in Philadelphia (1731) through the efforts of Benjamin Franklin. These worthy examples were followed by other towns in other provinces and, as Franklin tells us, "reading became fashionable; and our people having no public amusements to divert their attention from study, became better acquainted with books, and in a few years, were observed by strangers to be better instructed and more intelligent than people of the same rank generally in other countries." There was practically no light literature in that day and reading of books had a higher educational value than at the present time. One book that was especially popular was that masterpiece of English literature, the King James version of the Bible.

Public meetings as educational agencies

Another important agency for broadening the minds of the people was the public meeting, which brought men of all classes together. Our colonial ancestors, in the performance of their civic duties, had to attend town meetings, legislative assemblies, public elections, musters, county courts, or vestry meetings. There was thus frequent occasion for bringing the poor and unlettered in contact with the rich and learned. In this way there was afforded a fine opportunity "for the mind of man to polish that of his fellow."

In the seventeenth century the ministry was the only profession that was composed largely of educated men. Lawyers were few in number and generally were without legal education. "Mercenary attorneys" were everywhere the objects of suspicion, and the incompetent bar of that day doubtless merited much of the opprobrium that attached to it. In all the colonies some of the highest positions on the bench were held at the beginning of the eighteenth century by men who had had no special training in the law. By the middle of this century, however, a very noticeable improvement had been made in this profession, and in the pre-Revolutionary decade there were quite a number of prominent lawyers, many of whom were leaders in the political activity of the day. No law school was established in America prior to the Revolutionary War.

Professional schools

It has been said that the seventeenth century was the period of twilight when alchemy was passing into chemistry. The science

[40] ADAMS, J. T., *Provincial Society*, p. 118.

of medicine had made little progress during the past seven centuries. The belief generally held that diseases were the result of diabolic influences was responsible for the use of magic formulas in the practice of medicine. Bleeding was often resorted to, and patients were subjected to other forms of treatment that aggravated the ills from which they suffered. The science of medicine was still more backward in America than it was in Europe, and colonial physicians were generally poorly educated. As a rule they were not trained in colleges or in hospitals, but learned their art as apprentices to those who were already engaged in practice. A young man would take a short course of reading in medical books, would ride with an old physician, gather herbs and do other errands for him, and in this way be initiated into the mysteries of healing. At the end of his term of apprenticeship, with this inadequate training, he was turned loose on the public. His fees were small and frequently he had to engage in some other occupation as a side line. The trade of the barber seems to have been the one most closely allied to his profession. At one time we find the surgeons in New Netherland trying to get a monopoly of the business of shaving. As he made most of his own medicine, the old-fashioned doctor also had to have considerable skill in cooking, and in the seventeenth and eighteenth centuries many of the cook-books were written by physicians. The colonial doctor borrowed some of his remedies from the Indian medicine-men, and some of the herbs used by the latter were widely popular not only in the colonies, but also in Europe. One important advance in medicine was the introduction of cinchona bark. By 1671 it was in use in Virginia and was greatly reducing the mortality from malaria.[41]

Conditions in the medical profession were improved in the eighteenth century. There were, even in the seventeenth century, a few physicians in the colonies who had received a regular medical education in England. This number increased as the eighteenth century advanced, and two medical schools had been established in America by the end of the colonial period. These were the Medical College of Philadelphia, founded in 1765 and affiliated with the University of Pennsylvania since 1791, and the medical department of King's College, established in 1767.

[41] For a very readable and scholarly account of the colonial physician of the seventeenth century, see WERTENBAKER, T. J., *The First Americans*, ch. 7.

AMERICAN LITERATURE IN COLONIAL TIMES

Paucity of real literature in colonial times

The English American colonies produced very little literature worthy of the name prior to the pre-Revolutionary decade. There were a number of writers like John Smith, William Bradford, John Winthrop, the Mathers, William Byrd, and others, whose works are valuable as sources of historical information, but are not characterized by the originality of thought or the charm of expression that entitle them to rank as literature.

It is difficult to explain this dearth in letters in a people whose contemporaries in the homeland experienced in the time of Queen Anne the literary outburst known as the Augustan Age and whose recent ancestors in the reign of Elizabeth had created the Golden Age of English literature. The utter lack of great writers in the seventeenth century is easily accounted for on the ground that it was a period during which frontier conditions of living left little or no leisure for any activities other than those associated with earning a livelihood. But the eighteenth century had not advanced far before there had grown up in every section a favored class who had sufficient wealth and leisure to devote a considerable part of its time to intellectual pursuits. At first sight it seems strange that the culture of this class did not flower out in literature; but this privileged group was very small, even in the eighteenth century, and its members were usually closely identified with the civic or religious life of their respective communities. Their extra-vocational interests, therefore, found expression in political rather than literary activity. Moreover, the frontier, on retiring from the eastern settlements to push into the western wilderness, had left as a cultural sediment a utilitarian view of life that was not favorable to the nurture of the contemplative idealism on which literature is based.

Jonathan Edwards

There was not, however, a complete blank in American letters in the colonial era, for two names stand out with sufficient prominence to merit a place in the list of the world's great writers. These are Jonathan Edwards and Benjamin Franklin. Edwards was the author of a number of works, but the one on which his fame chiefly rests is the treatise *On the Freedom of the Will*. This is an exposition of Calvinism as interpreted by a typical American orthodox Puritan, and it is the ablest argument in favor of conservative New England Puritanism known to our literature. Indeed, it is probably the most masterly discussion of

Protestant theology that has been published since the appearance of Calvin's *Institutes*. In closely-knit logic and clarity and forcefulness of expression this work is a masterpiece and has won for its author the distinction of being America's greatest metaphysician. But it has never made a strong appeal to the reading public except that small part of it that belongs intellectually and spiritually to the elect. For when it was written interest in theology was on the wane and since that time it has steadily declined, until today the average reader is not attracted to a theological treatise of any sort.

Franklin owes his fame as a literary man mainly to his *Autobiography* and *Poor Richard's Almanac*. The *Autobiography* was written in the latter part of his career and does not belong to the colonial period; the *Almanac* was published, under the name of Richard Sanders, annually for twenty-six years, beginning in 1732. This series of little pamphlets contained a great number of wise sayings, expressed in clear, forceful, and often epigrammatic style, which deserve to rank with Bacon's *Essays* and the Proverbs of Solomon. Like the crisp writings of the great English essayist, they went straight to "men's homes and businesses," and the *Almanac* was more widely read in colonial times than any other book, with the possible exception of the King James translation of the Bible. "The philosophy of *Poor Richard's Almanac* was rather a collection of popular wisdom than an original contribution,"[42] but it was so cleverly phrased and fitted in so well with American ideals that it made a strong appeal to the common man. It inculcated industry and thrift and lauded other virtues that have a high utilitarian value in a new community.

Edwards and Franklin were in strong contrast to each other, both as to personality and as to the nature of the influence wielded by each. They were contemporaries in that they lived about the same time, but they were a century or more apart in their views of life. Edwards in his private life measured up to a high standard of morality based on a religious creed that magnified the importance of the next world and placed a comparatively low estimate on the material values of this life. Franklin, on the other hand, was rather lax in the practice of a not very rigid moral code, resting on a liberal philosophy that had little concern for the other world, and insisted on making the best possible use of the good things of this one. He was "less concerned with the

Benjamin Franklin

Poor Richard's Almanac

Contrast between Edwards and Franklin

[42] *Cambridge History of American Literature,* p. 104.

golden pavements of the City of God than that the cobblestones of Chestnut Street in Philadelphia should be well and evenly laid."[43] Edwards's conservatism caused him to look backward and glorify the thought of the past; Franklin's progressivism impelled him to look forward, to accept the views of the advanced thinkers of his day, and to repudiate some of the fundamental beliefs of his father's generation. The wide appeal that Franklin's apothegms made to the masses was due to the fact that they, in language easily understandable to everyone, gave practical advice as to how to obtain the good things of this life; while the abstruse and finely-spun reasoning of Edwards was understood and enjoyed only by the intellectual aristocracy, and its discussions were concerned not with the acquisition of wealth in this world, but only with the laying up of treasures in heaven.

Selected Readings

1. The New England Primer.—Dexter, E. G., *History of Education in the United States,* pp. *211-213.
2. The Elementary Course.—Meriwether, Colyer, *Colonial Curriculum,* *ch. 1.
3. The Hornbook.—*Ibid.,* pp. *29-32; Dexter, E. G., *op. cit.,* p. *209.
4. The Grammar Schools of England.—Brown, E. E., *The Making of Our Middle Schools,* *ch. 1.
5. The Grammar School in New England.—Grizzell, E. D., *Origin and Development of the High School in New England,* pp. *1-27.
6. Rise of Elementary Schools in Virginia.—Heatwole, C. J., *History of Education in Virginia,* *ch. 3.
7. Attempts to Establish Free Schools in Virginia.—*Ibid.,* *ch. 4.
8. Harvard College.—Thwing, C. F., *A History of Higher Education in America,* *ch. 1.
9. Yale.—*Ibid.,* ch. 3; Boone, R. G., *Education in the United States,* pp. *37-42.
10. William and Mary.—Heatwole, *op. cit.,* *ch. 6; Tyler, L. G., *Williamsburg,* ch. 3.
11. Princeton.—Dexter, E. G., *op. cit.,* pp. *245-250.
12. University of Pennsylvania.—*Ibid.,* pp. *250-252.
13. King's College (Columbia).—Goodwin, Maud, and others, *Historic New York,* pp. *323-331; Dexter, E. G., *op. cit.,* pp. *253-257.
14. Brown.—Bronson, W. C., *The History of Brown University,* chs. 1-2.

[43] Parrington, V. L., *The Colonial Mind,* p. 178.

15. Rutgers.—Dexter, E. G., *op. cit.*, pp. *263-265.
16. Dartmouth.—*Ibid.*, pp. *265-267.
17. Higher Education in South Carolina.—Meriwether, Colyer, *History of Higher Education in South Carolina* (United States Bureau of Education, ii), pp. *13-27.
18. Newspapers.—Dexter, E. G., *op. cit.*, pp. 503-507; *Cambridge History of American Literature*, i, *ch. 7; Faris, J. T., *When America Was Young*, *ch. 3.
19. Literature in the Seventeenth Century.—Williams, S. T., *The American Spirit in Letters*, *ch. 1.
20. Literature in the Eighteenth Century.—*Ibid.*, *ch. 2.
21. Jonathan Edwards.—Trent, W. P., *A History of American Literature, 1607-1865*, pp. *113-122; Tyler, M. C., *A History of American Literature, 1607-1765*, ii, pp. 177-192; *Cambridge History of American Literature*, i, *ch. 4; Parrington, V. L., *The Colonial Mind*, pp. *152-163.
22. Benjamin Franklin.—Trent, *op. cit.*, pp. *122-128; *Cambridge History of American Literature*, i, *ch. 6; Bruce, W. C., *Benjamin Franklin*, ii, *ch. 5; Becker, Carl L., *Benjamin Franklin* (an outline of his career and an excellent appraisal of his personality, 1946); and Van Doren, Carl, *Benjamin Franklin*, pp. *260-262 (an excellent appraisal).
23. Extracts from *Poor Richard's Almanac, ibid.*, pp. *266-267.

CHAPTER XXVIII

MANNERS AND CUSTOMS

LIFE IN THE COLONIAL TOWN

Colonial cities and towns

As AGRICULTURE was by far the most important occupation in colonial days, the great majority of the people lived in the country, either on separate farms or plantations, as was the rule in the South, or in villages or small towns, as was the custom in New England and to a considerable extent in the Middle colonies. However, as commerce grew in importance, certain trade centers developed into towns of considerable size. By the end of the colonial era five of these—Philadelphia, Boston, Newport (Rhode Island), New York, and Charleston—compared quite favorably in wealth and population with the European cities of their day. There had also grown up by this time a number of other thriving towns, such as Salem in Massachusetts, New Haven in Connecticut, Baltimore in Maryland, Norfolk in Virginia, and Wilmington in North Carolina.[1] In addition to these, Annapolis and Williamsburg, though small of size and of no great commercial importance, enjoyed a political and social prestige that was the envy of some of their larger rivals. These two little provincial capitals were centers around which rotated the charming social life of the Maryland and Virginia aristocracy.[2]

Philadelphia

During the last few decades of the colonial era Philadelphia was the largest and most important of the American cities. Its location on the navigable portion of the Delaware River, in the center of a fine wheat-growing region, with good roads to connect it with the prosperous farms of the hinterland, made it the best center for the export of grain in the English dominions. Its population numbered about thirty thousand at the outbreak of the Revolution. Most of the houses were built of brick and many

---

[1] *A Century of Population Growth, 1790-1900*, pp. 11-14.

[2] For good contemporary accounts of Williamsburg, see BURNABY, A., *Travels through North America*, pp. 33-35, and JONES, HUGH, *The Present State of Virginia*, part ii, ch. 2. For a contemporary account of Annapolis, see BURNABY, *op. cit.*, pp. 80-82.

of them were three stories high. The dwelling-houses were very much alike, and visitors complained of the smallness of the rooms as well as the monotony of the architecture. The streets, which crossed one another at right angles, were well paved, were provided with sidewalks, and were lighted at night by lamps.[3]

For a long time Boston was the largest of the colonial cities, Boston and even after Philadelphia deprived it of this rank it held second place in commercial activity and general importance, being only a few thousand behind its successful rival in population. "It stood upon a rocky peninsula, and from the sea appeared to lie in crescent form, with the country issuing gently behind it to sunny fields and green woods."[4] For the convenience of the numerous vessels that entered and went out of its harbor there was a wharf two thousand feet in length, which was regarded as one of the greatest wonders in America. On the north side of this wharf were built warehouses for the storage of freight, and adjacent to it were the shops in which the retail merchants and artisans plied their trades. The humbler tradesmen and craftsmen lived in the rooms above their shops, but the homes of the wealthy class were located some distance from the business district on lots large enough to afford ample space for flower and vegetable gardens. The houses of the well-to-do were large but were not noted either for comfort or architectural beauty. The open fires used in heating them never raised the temperature of the rooms in severe winter weather to the point of comfort. By the time of the Revolution, Puritanism had lost much of its religious severity but had not yet taken on an appreciation of beauty. Consequently, the dwelling-houses of Boston at the end of the colonial period, as well as the Congregational churches, were characterized by a plainness that verged on ugliness. The more important streets were paved, but many of them were narrow and crooked and all were laid out with little or no regard for any general plan.[5]

[3] For a contemporary account of Philadelphia as it was about the middle of the eighteenth century, see BURNABY, *op. cit.*, pp. 88-92. For earlier accounts of Philadelphia written by contemporaries, see MYERS, A. C., ed., *Narratives of Early Pennsylvania, West New Jersey, and Delaware*, pp. 239-240, 260-262.

[4] HOCKETT, H. C., *Political and Social History of the United States,* p. 62.

[5] For a contemporary account of Boston, see BURNABY, *op. cit.*, pp.

New York   Much that has been said about Boston would also apply to New York. The latter town was not quite so large as the former, having at the end of the colonial period a population of about twenty-two thousand. The houses were built mostly of brick and many of them were large structures, three or four stories high. There were at the time of the Revolution still quite a number of dwellings of the old Dutch type with their gable ends facing the street. As in Boston, the streets were narrow and crooked, though they were generally paved except in high places, where pavement was not so much needed, and were usually kept clean.[6]

Charleston   Charleston was the only city in South Carolina during the entire colonial period, and was, therefore, able to monopolize the social, commercial, and political life of the province more completely than did any other colonial capital. The surrounding country had a fertile soil and the sea breezes gave it, in the early years, an exemption from malaria that was not shared by the other communities in Carolina. At the beginning of the dull and sickly season the big planter usually took his family away from his country residence, to which the numerous mosquitoes from the near-by swamps brought malaria, and went to the city, not only to find better health conditions, but also to enjoy the social gayeties afforded by the provincial metropolis. Owing to the part played by Charleston in the life of the people, South Carolina was more nearly a city-state than any other American colony.[7]

Life in the colonial town   As the colonial city owed its importance to commerce rather than to manufacturing,[8] it was free from many of the nuisances that are commonplaces of this industrial age. There were no screaming whistles to upset sensitive nerves and no coal smoke to

132-134. For an interesting account by a modern writer, see HOCKETT, op. cit., pp. 62-69.

[6] For a contemporary account of New York, see BURNABY, op. cit., pp. 111-113. For a fine description of the town by a modern writer, see SINGLETON, ESTHER, Social New York Under the Georges, pp. 3-48.

[7] For an excellent contemporary account of Charleston as it appeared in 1763, see MILLIGEN, GEORGE, A Short Description of the Colony of South Carolina, pp. 31-37.

[8] In some instances, however, manufacturing played a part in the development of the towns. Newport, Rhode Island, for instance, at one time had thirty rum distilleries and seventeen candle and spermoil factories. See EGGLESTON, E., in Century Magazine, vi; also ADAMS, J. T., Provincial Society, p. 297.

shut off the light of the sun. The machinery used in industry never disturbed the quiet of the night, and even in the daytime about the only noises that the people had to endure were those occasioned by the hammering of ship-carpenters, the lazy rumbling of grist-mills, and the rasping whir of sawmills. On the other hand, the townsmen of that age had to forego certain comforts which we now consider necessities. In none of the cities was there running water in the houses, and there was probably not a bathroom in any American home before the Revolution. Water was obtained from surface wells and was always liable to pollution by disease germs. As illuminating gas had not come into use and coal oil was also still unknown, candles were generally used for lighting, although in the homes of the wealthy there were lamps in which sperm or lard oil was used on rare occasions.

By 1742 Boston, New York, and Philadelphia had made some provision for cleaning their streets, with New York taking the lead in this improvement. By that time, too, the construction of sewers had started in all five of the cities, and Boston was probably the best-drained city in the English-speaking world. These arrangements were not adequate, however, and ashes and garbage were thrown into unsanitary heaps in the alleys and on vacant lots. In all the cities and towns prior to 1742, and in some of them after that time, hogs were allowed to roam through the streets and act as scavengers by eating up the scraps of meat and vegetables that had been thrown out by the housewives.[9] In Charleston the buzzards were the scavengers. They hovered around the marketplaces and were quite tame because they were protected by law. These unsanitary conditions persisted long after colonial times and were matters of comment by travelers in the middle of the nineteenth century.[10]

CLASS DISTINCTIONS

The first settlers in the English colonies brought with them from the Old World aristocratic notions regarding social distinctions. Social lines were therefore clearly drawn in colonial times, despite the tendency of pioneer conditions to obliterate them. Freemen (excluding paupers and criminals) were roughly divided

Classes of people

[9] See BRIDENBAUGH, CARL, *Cities in the Wilderness* (1938), pp. 18, 158-161, 165-167, 318-319, 321-323.

[10] See RAEDER, O. M., *America in the Forties*, p. 78.

into three classes, the aristocracy, the middle class, and the lowest class. The aristocracy consisted of the provincial officials, ministers of the established churches, the wealthy merchant princes of New England and the middle colonies, the owners of large landed estates in New York and Rhode Island, and the big planters of the South. This group furnished most of the political leaders and monopolized all of the important offices. The members of this privileged class were known as gentlemen and were honored with the titles of "Mister" and "Esquire." The middle class, which constituted the bulk of the white population, consisted of the artisans, tradesmen, and small landholders (the yeomanry). In New England the men and women who belonged to this middle class were designated by the titles of "Goodman" and "Goodwife," the latter usually abbreviated into "Goody."[11] On the bottom rung of the social ladder was the class of unskilled laborers who as a rule were addressed without titles. This group was small, for the economic opportunities were so good that any healthy man of average character and industry could soon raise himself and his family to the rank of the yeomanry.

Class distinctions accentuated by law and customs   In New England in the early years social distinctions were accentuated by laws which were intended to put a stamp on each person, showing to which class he belonged. Not only were there regulations against extravagance, as would be expected in Puritan communities, but there were also laws restraining the yeomanry from dressing in a manner not in keeping with their position in society. Even the church and the college, which ought to be the chief agencies of democracy, lent their aid in maintaining these unnatural distinctions. People were seated in church according to their social standing, and students in college were listed in the catalogue and seated at commons in the order of their social rank.[12]

In the South the wealthy patrician families held themselves

---

[11] In ordinary conversation the term "Mister" was employed in Virginia in speaking of both yeomen and gentlemen, but in legal records (certainly in the seventeenth century) it seems to have been used only of the latter. "Esquire" applied only to councilors (BRUCE, P. A., *Social Life of Virginia in the Seventeenth Century*, pp. 115, 117, 121; WEEDEN, W. B., *Economic and Social History of New England*, i, pp. 418-419).

[12] WEEDEN, *op. cit.*, i, pp. 74-75, 279-280, 417-418; ii, 528-529, 699.

proudly aloof socially from their plebeian neighbors, who tilled their small farms with their own labor. But here, as well as in other sections, the classes tended to merge into one another, as the lines separating the great planter from the small landowner, or the latter from the hired laborer or renter, could not always be sharply drawn. Besides, there was abundant opportunity for an energetic plebeian of ability to acquire the property that would qualify him for admission into the higher social rank. There was apparently little, if any, bitter feeling in the early years between the classes, and the plebeians seem to have accepted their lower status without complaint. Indeed, a qualified friendship frequently existed between the aristocrat and the common man. All classes were thrown together on terms of equality at the taverns and on public occasions. The rule of hospitality allowed the humble stranger to sit at the fireside and even eat at the table of the wealthy planter. A certain degree of good-fellowship and friendly intercourse could thus be practiced between the upper and lower classes without overstepping the social barriers that separated them. But if the relations between the wealthy and the poorer classes were as a rule friendly in the early decades of the colonial period, this had ceased to be the case by the middle of the eighteenth century. For by this time there had grown up in a number of colonies a feeling of class hatred between the upper and lower economic groups. This was due to the fact that the privileged minority who dominated the provincial government in every colony were appropriating more than their share of the lands and were ruling in the interest of their class to the detriment of the rights of the common people.

It seems strange to us that our fathers, who in the struggle of subduing a wilderness stood face to face with stern reality, should have tolerated such artificial distinctions. One would think that these inequalities would all have been ironed out by pioneer conditions, as was the case later in the settlement of the West. But we must remember that the first settlers were Europeans who brought their Old World prejudices with them to America. For generations they had taken feudal inequalities as a matter of course; to question their rightness would be to find fault with the laws of nature. Such a view as to the social order cannot be modernized in one generation, even if environmental conditions are most favorable to a change.

THE COLONIAL HOUSE

Houses of the first settlers

The houses of the first settlers were probably modeled after those of the peasants in England. A high authority on colonial architecture thinks that "many of the early houses were of wattle, with or without a daubing of clay," and that the first timber buildings were of planks stood vertically as palisades. In New England in the early days the roof was frequently, if not generally, made of thatch. In the last decades of the seventeenth century we find the log cabin in the English settlements, probably having been brought to America by the Swedes who settled in New Sweden. As the colonies developed, the log cabin moved to the frontier, being largely superseded in the old settlements by more pretentious structures. It remained, however, in the older communities as the dwelling of the poorer people, and was the usual type of house for the poor white and Negro in the South.[13]

European architecture adapted to conditions in America

Colonial architecture was European in origin. The Dutch, the Swedes, the Germans, and the English all brought with them to the new country the architectural ideas of their respective homelands. But the house plans of the Old World could not be copied closely in the New. Pioneer conditions necessitated certain modifications, and as a result the colonial house showed marked differences from its prototype in the Old World. This was especially the case in the seventeenth century. The modifications of the European designs were usually determined by climatic conditions and the abundance or scarcity of certain building materials. In making these changes beauty was usually sacrificed to comfort and convenience. A great many houses in all the colonies were one-story structures, sided with unpainted boards that had been sawed or rough-hewed.

Most of the colonial houses were built of wood. Stone was

[13] The authorities do not agree as to the types of houses built by the early settlers. The views given above are those of S. Fiske Kimball. See his *Domestic Architecture in the American Colonies,* pp. 3-7; and *American Architecture* (1928), pp. 19-20. See also KIMBALL, S. F., and EDGELL, C. H., *A History of Architecture,* p. 533; and WEEDEN, W. B., *Economic and Social History of New England,* i, pp. 212-213, 283-284. For brief contemporary accounts of early Virginia houses, see WERTENBAKER, T. J., *The First Americans,* pp. 284, 286.

used sometimes and brick frequently by the wealthy classes, especially in the eighteenth century. Stone houses were more common in the North than in the South because of the scarcity of building-stones in the latter section.[14] One drawback to using both stone and brick was the difficulty in procuring lime for making mortar. Limestone was known in New England by the end of the seventeenth century, but was not used in the Tidewater region of the South for making lime at any time during the colonial period, lime in this section being obtained by burning oyster shells. The bricks used in building houses were mostly manufactured at home, and brickmaking was carried on in all the colonies. A few bricks, however, were imported from England and Holland all during the colonial period, but not enough to affect appreciably the brickmaking industry in America.[15] Houses were covered with thatch, shingles, slate, tiles, or lead. Most of the lead roofs were taken off at the time of the Revolution to be molded into bullets.

Nails, glass, and paint were scarce in the seventeenth century. In the town of Kennebec, Maine, there was not a pane of glass in any house as late as 1745, oiled paper being used as a substitute for glass. So valuable were nails that in Virginia in the first half of the seventeenth century owners of small houses, on moving, sometimes burned their dwellings for the nails.[16] For a long time the houses had only casement windows of small, diamond-shaped panes. Single- and double-sashed windows came into use in the eighteenth century.

In this century, too, the houses were larger and more comfortable in all the colonies. During this period the type of house most common in Virginia was a story-and-a-half dwelling, built of brick or sawed lumber, sometimes having a wing and generally a small front porch and a shed-room kitchen. There was usually a big stone chimney at each end of the building. In New England the houses of the better class, as a rule, had two stories and frequently gambreled roofs and dormer windows. Sometimes the

Materials used in building houses

Scarcity of nails and glass

Types of houses in the different sections

[14] There was, however, not a scarcity of stone all over the South. In the Valley of Virginia limestone was used for building purposes, and in Winchester about the middle of the eighteenth century there were a number of stone houses.

[15] For an article by G. A. Townsend, showing to what a limited extent imported bricks were used in the colonies, see Columbia Historical Society *Records*, vii, pp. 195-210.

[16] HENING, W. W., *Virginia Statutes at Large*, i, p. 291.

roof was very steep, and when it extended over a lean-to kitchen at the back, it came within a few feet of the ground. This type of roof was very common also among the Dutch of New Netherland.

The houses in New Netherland were usually a story and a half high, with the gable end fronting the street. On the first floor were low-ceiled rooms, the most important being the kitchen and parlor. The half-story had bedrooms, and a large attic above them. The parlor was frequently furnished with a bed and used also as a guest-room. The walls and furniture were kept scrupulously clean and the floor was adorned with figures made in the sand that covered it. The garret and cellar were also important parts of the home. The garret was used as a place for drying clothes in the winter. In it there was also a kind of smokehouse, in which were hung hams, bacon, and other kinds of meat after they had been cured. The cellar was used as a storeroom for potatoes, turnips, apples, parsnips, beets, firkins of butter, barrels of salt pork, tubs of hams, and many other food supplies.

Georgian houses in the eighteenth century

In the eighteenth century (after about 1720) the wealthy in all sections began to copy the Georgian style of architecture. Houses of this type were very much alike in all the colonies, differing only in details in the various sections, as all of them followed in general principles the European pattern. They were usually large and imposing in appearance, having wide halls and numerous high-pitched rooms wainscoted to the ceiling and ornamented with beautiful balustrades and mantels carved in relief. These fine residences were generally the homes of the merchant princes of New England and the central colonies, the owners of the large manors in New York, or the great planters in the South. The most common type of plantation mansion in the South was a large square house, two stories high, with or without an attic. It was built of wood or brick, usually with numerous broad fireplaces and with four rooms and a spacious hall on each floor. There were also outbuildings, such as the schoolroom, the office, the laundry, and the kitchen. At a short distance from the main building were the stables, the poultry-house, and the carriage-house, and still farther away, hidden by the trees, were the Negro cabins.[17]

The tall-columned portico (like the one at Mount Vernon),

[17] For a picture of a house of this type, see STANARD, MARY N., *Colonial Virginia,* p. 74.

which is usually associated with the colonial type of architecture, was not introduced in Virginia until near the end of the colonial era and did not come into general use until after the Revolution. Wall paper was little known in the colonial period, and when used was hung or tacked on the walls. In Virginia the farmhouse of the better class usually had a front yard adorned with shade trees, shrubs, and flowers arranged around a semicircular driveway. The approach to the mansion was frequently an avenue bordered on each side by a row of stately trees. There were also flower gardens and mazes and walks of boxwood.[18]

The porch was not known in the early years, but it became a feature of some of the later colonial houses. In fact, this important addition to the house seems to have been a contribution to architecture that was made by our ancestors of the colonial period. It is true that certain features of the piazza were known to both England and continental European architecture before America was settled, but the porch as we now have it was not used by them. Our porch, it is believed, was evolved from the wide eaves of the Dutch house in New Netherland. At first there was a platform built under the shelter of the long-projecting front eaves, and then later a separate roof was made for the platform. The two-storied porch originated in South Carolina. *The porch*

In the seventeenth century the utensils and furnishings of the average colonial home were meager. In the early days they had no chinaware, no forks, and few knives. There were pewter dishes, wooden platters, some tin vessels, and a little earthenware. The lack of forks was especially inconvenient. Madam Knight, who traveled in Connecticut in the early part of the eighteenth century, complained of the farmers there for eating with their Negro slaves to save time. "Into the dish," she said, "goes the black hoof as freely as the white hand." Convenient utensils, such as forks and chinaware, became more common as the eighteenth century advanced, and silverware was used in the homes of the wealthy. *House furnishings*

Our ancestors enjoyed some comforts that are denied the present generation. Their large open fireplace with its cheery flames playing behind brass andirons would be an expensive luxury today. But big wood fires were the rule everywhere in those days, and our forefathers could enjoy them without being troubled with a conscience accusing them of waste and extravagance.

[18] For picture of boxwood maze, see *ibid.*, p. 68.

For not only was wood cheap and easy to get, but in many places trees were an obstacle to farming and the destruction of them was considered a real aid to progress. The colonists also had comfortable arrangements for sleeping. Many of them had soft feather beds and high four-poster bedsteads. The small children usually slept in a low trundle-bed, which was kept under the big bed in the daytime and rolled out at night. In Virginia there were often two or three large beds in one room. Among the Dutch in New York the bed was frequently placed in an alcove or closet, which was closed in the daytime and the bed was thus hidden from view. A warming-pan was sometimes used to warm the beds in cold rooms.

FOOD AND CLOTHING

Food

After the first few years of struggle were over, there was generally plenty of food in all sections. The people enjoyed very few luxuries, but practically everyone was bountifully supplied with the necessaries. Meat was plentiful because there were not only domestic animals in abundance to slaughter, but wild game and fish could easily be procured. Corn was widely used for making bread, especially among the poorer classes in the South. Corn bread, hominy, and salt pork were the main articles of food among the poor whites and the Negroes. They had, of course, everywhere garden vegetables and fruits in great plenty in the summertime. Strange to say, however, butter was scarce and regarded as a luxury. As late as 1690 there was only one churn in the entire district of Maine. Tea and coffee were coming slowly into use in the first quarter of the eighteenth century, while chocolate had by this time become quite common.

Our ancestors of the colonial era came of a race of hard drinkers and they brought their thirst for alcoholic beverages with them to the New World. Cider and beer were very popular drinks in all sections. In Virginia they made a kind of beer from persimmons, which grew in great abundance. But the stronger liquors, like rum, brandy, whisky, and imported wines, were also popular, especially the last-named. "In Virginia, a julep before breakfast was believed to give protection against malaria, and a toddy or a glass of wine, punch, or beer at almost any time of the day or night to be good for the body as well as cheering to the spirit and indispensable to the practice of hospitality."[19] But drinking

[19] *Ibid.*, pp. 126-127.

was not confined to Virginia and the South; even the staid Puritan of New England and the quiet Quaker of Pennsylvania sipped his rum and Madeira wine.

The colonials attached more importance to dress even than we **Dress** do today, as the first settlers brought with them from the homeland the idea that dress is a badge of social rank. Our forefathers placed a high value on social prestige and often tried to purchase it at the cost of dressing beyond their means. But the upper and ruling classes did not want the "common people" to wear the badges of the aristocracy. So in the early years laws were passed to prohibit the wearing of extravagant apparel by all classes except the privileged families who had wealth or official position. Such regulations appear in Virginia in the first half-century of its history, but apparently the most rigid laws regarding dress were passed and enforced in Puritan New England. In 1651 the General Court of Massachusetts expressed its "utter detestation that men and women of mean condition, education and calling, should take upon them the garbe of gentlemen by wearing of gold or silver lace, or buttons or pognots at their knees, or walke in great boots, or women of the same ranke to wear silke or tiffany hoods or scarfs."[20] At one time thirty-eight women in Connecticut were brought before the court for dressing more extravagantly than the size of their estates would warrant. It was always difficult to enforce these restrictions, and in the eighteenth century the attempt was abandoned. By this time wealth had accumulated sufficiently to admit of expensive dressing in many families, and the colonists were indulging in extravagance in dress, especially in the cities and among the large planters in the South.

The colonials in the eighteenth century tried to follow the London styles in dress, though they did not always keep up-to-date in the effort. There were no fashion magazines and it was not easy for the Americans to follow European fashions. The task would have been well-nigh hopeless but for the fact that the styles did not change so often then as now. Dolls dressed in London were sold in the colonies to keep the dressmakers informed as to the latest European modes.

Leather breeches were in common use among servants, laborers, and hunters. Another garment that was quite popular,

---

[20] Quoted by EARLE, ALICE M., in her *Home Life in Colonial Days,* p. 283.

especially among hunters and frontiersmen, was an attractive and picturesque hunting-jacket made of deerskin. Wealthy men frequently wore silk stockings and breeches made of brocade, velvet, plush, or silk, with shoe-buckles and knee-buckles of silver or gold, set with paste jewels. The black frock coats worn by the rich were generally ornamented with decorative trimmings, which were sometimes made of gold lace. The material used in making these coats was usually broadcloth imported from England. For a long time wigs were frowned upon by the Puritans, but in the eighteenth century they were popular in New England, as they were everywhere else in the English colonies. Even slaves and children were allowed to wear them. The women were not behindhand with the men in their indulgence in finery. Costly dresses and furs were as much coveted by the colonial dames as they are today by their female descendants. The wearing of hoop-skirts came into fashion early in the second quarter of the eighteenth century. It seems that umbrellas did not find their way to New England until the second quarter of the eighteenth century. When the first one was seen in Windsor, Connecticut, about 1740, the lady who had it was mocked by her neighbors, who carried in derision sieves on broom handles.

AMUSEMENTS

Amuse-
ments
in New
England

In New England during the greater part of the seventeenth century the social life, according to Weeden, "was bare and spiritless beyond the possibility of description." This is doubtless an exaggerated statement and yet the Puritan attitude of mind in the seventeenth century was such as to rule out many of the amusements that are natural for young people. But youth can under all circumstances find ways of enjoying itself, and the Puritan boys and girls were not entirely without the pleasures to which they were entitled. There were corn-huskings, apple-parings, quilting parties, weddings, and other like social occasions, when the young people could get together. The older people, too, had their house-raisings and other working parties, congregated at the village store, and assembled at town meetings and in taverns. The church also afforded all, young and old, the opportunity of social intercourse. Not only were services held regularly on Sundays, but a lecture on some religious topic was given once a week, usually on Thursday. These lectures were very popular despite their length, which was sometimes as much as five hours. On these occasions wedding banns were published and other announcements made and criminals publicly punished. The Thursday lectures are said to have held the place in the social life of New England now filled by the opera. The fact that the people got so much enjoyment from them is strong evidence of the scarcity of other kinds of amusement.

Opportunities for recreation were also afforded by college commencements, musters, and elections. Elections were such noteworthy events that not only the day on which they were held, but the entire week had an air of holiday. Training-days, of which there were usually six a year for each township, were also times of pleasant social intercourse. All men of military age were required to attend the musters, and with them there usually came the older men and the women and children. During the day the men practiced the use of arms and engaged in shooting contests for prizes. Excitement was afforded by the firing of guns, and the occasion was made festive by a dinner bountifully prepared.

The Puritans were opposed to the observance of Christmas, which they regarded as a Catholic custom, and during the colonial period, Christmas was, therefore, not a New England holiday except in Rhode Island. For the orthodox Puritan, Thanksgiving day, or rather week, took the place of Christmas. While the practice of setting aside a day for thanksgiving did not originate with the Puritans, the New Englanders took up the custom at an early date and gave it a large place in their recreational life.[21] Before the end of the seventeenth century the Thanksgiving season had become a regular annual holiday in Connecticut and Massachusetts. It lasted about a week and was the most important series of holidays that the Puritans had. It was not specially a religious celebration, but a time of festivity like the English yuletide. It is

Thanksgiving holidays

[21] The practice of setting aside a day for thanksgiving had its origin in Europe before the Reformation and was continued by certain Protestant bodies, especially by the Anglicans. The first American Thanksgiving was celebrated at Plymouth in the fall of 1621, after the first harvest had been gathered in. The account of this event, written by Edward Winslow (afterward governor of the colony), is familiar to every modern schoolboy and girl. It was a festival of several days' length, during which time the Pilgrims and their Indian guests feasted in the open air on the meat, wild fowl, and deer that had been barbecued for the occasion. See YOUNG, A., *Chronicles of the Pilgrim Fathers*, p. 231; also USHER, R. G., *The Pilgrims and their History*, p. 93.

thought that Thursday was chosen as Thanksgiving day because of its popularity as lecture day.

By the early part of the eighteenth century, Puritan rigor had begun to relax and more amusements were allowed. Dancing was now engaged in, and as the century advanced, tea parties were given by the ladies, and even plays were at times allowed in Boston.

Amusements in New York

The people of New York City, both Dutch and English, seem to have been exceptionally cheerful and fond of amusement. They had social clubs, private theatricals, picnics for young people, and dancing, sleighing, and fishing parties. The religious notions of the Dutch were not hostile to games, and there were numerous holidays in which to indulge in sport and recreation. The most popular holidays were New Year's and May Day. On these days visits among friends were exchanged and family reunions held. When the English got control of the province such sports as fox-hunting, cock-fighting, and card-playing became popular.

In the South

The people of the Southern provinces were also fond of amusements, and except among the dissenters, they were not restrained in their pleasures by any Puritanical religious notions. Like the New Englanders, they frequently combined social pleasure with their work by performing coöperatively certain tasks that required the labor of a number of men. Such coöperation was especially common among the small farmers in the back country. In the South, as well as in the North, house-raising, log-rolling, and other similar kinds of work gave opportunity for neighborhood gatherings at which business and social intercourse were pleasantly combined. On these occasions the work to be done did not take the whole day, and there was usually left plenty of time to enjoy the mint juleps and the abundance of food prepared by the solicitous housewives and their servants. A like opportunity for feasting and merrymaking was afforded the Negroes by the corn-shuckings. After the corn had been pulled and hauled to the barn, all the Negroes of the neighborhood were brought together to take part in the shucking. A typical scene was that of a high pile of corn surrounded by a group of happy Negroes, interspersing their work with rude jokes, laughter, loud talk, or singing. The Negroes also had plenty to eat at these working parties.

The most popular amusement in the South for the white people was dancing. Everybody danced, young and old, patrician and plebeian.[22] Learning to dance was considered an important part of education and dancing-masters were numerous. Among the popular dances were jigs, square dances, and the Virginia reel, the party being usually ended with the last named. The Virginians brought with them from the homeland a fondness for outdoor sports. They liked fishing, fox-hunting, but best of all horse-racing, which was considered the one sport most proper for a gentleman. Cock-fighting was also very popular with all classes, not only in the South, but in other sections as well. Gambling was a very common vice in the colonial period. The men would bet on games, on horse-races, and other sporting contests. The lottery was another very common form of gambling, which was employed extensively in all sections, even in Puritan New England. It was used to raise money for bridges, roads, and other public improvements, for building churches, and for securing endowment funds for colleges. Ministers were particularly fond of this form of gambling, though it was indulged in by all classes.

Visiting among friends was another means of social enjoyment, especially in the South. In this section all classes, the poor whites as well as the rich planters, were noted for their hospitality. Strangers were cordially received and well treated, and friends and relatives were entertained in royal fashion. Many of the great families were related or connected by marriage, and there was an easy camaraderie between the patricians that made social intercourse natural and charmingly delightful. Friends had to make long journeys to visit one another and they generally went in large numbers, as several servants as well as members of the family usually composed the party. An ordinary visit, therefore, was something like a modern house party. The exchange of hospitality in those days did not subject the lady of the home to the strain which such social functions would impose upon the modern

[22] A contemporary, writing in 1773, describes a ball given by "Squire" Richard Lee in Virginia, which lasted from Monday morning until Thursday night. When his seventy guests were finally so tired out that they could dance no longer, their host insisted that they protract their visit to a still greater length. Quoted by STANARD, MARY N., *op. cit.*, p. 146.

The German Lutherans and the Scotch-Irish Presbyterians in the Valley of Virginia also allowed dancing among their young people. Sometimes dancing among them went on night after night for weeks. See KERCHEVAL, SAMUEL, *History of the Valley of Virginia*, p. 57.

housewife. Food was cheap and plentiful and the numerous slaves stood ready to do the work. The exercise of hospitality relieved the loneliness which would otherwise have settled down on the plantations, widely scattered as they were. Anyone coming in from the outside and breaking the tedium of isolation was a welcomed guest, whether he was a patrician friend, a plebeian stranger, or even a peddler.

Social clubs One important form of amusement common to all the colonies in the eighteenth century was the social club. Before the end of the second decade of this century there had sprung up in all sections numerous organizations whose membership consisted generally, though not always, of men. These groups held frequent meetings in taverns or private residences "for social intercourse, the interchange of ideas, and the generous absorption of liquor." While the chief value of these clubs lay in the opportunities offered by them for social contacts, they also served as an agency for disseminating news and informing public opinion. By 1715 the order of Free Masons had been established in America, and by the middle of the century there were lodges in the principal towns of all the colonies except North Carolina.[23]

THE COLONIAL THEATER

We know practically nothing of the colonial theater in the seventeenth century. A leading authority on Virginia history thinks it not improbable that plays were acted at Jamestown during the administration of William Berkeley, as this stanch old Cavalier was fond of the drama and was a writer of plays.[24] But this is all conjecture, as we have no evidence of any dramatic performances by professional actors in any of the colonies in the seventeenth century.

Just when the English theater first found its way to the do-

[23] ADAMS, J. T., *Provincial Society,* pp. 260-263.

[24] The earliest mention of play-acting in America is found in the county court records of Acomac County, Virginia, in 1665. In that year a complaint was made to the court against several persons for acting a play called "Ye Bare and ye Cubb." The court had the performance repeated in its presence and, finding it unobjectionable, released the defendant and made the complainant pay the costs. In 1690 the students of Harvard College gave a dramatic presentation. But in each of these cases the play was the performance of amateurs and so had no bearing on the history of the professional stage (TYLER, L. G., *Williamsburg,* p. 224).

minions we are unable to say, but it certainly had come by the beginning of the eighteenth century. We know that Anthony Ashton was playing in New York about 1702, and there are other scattered references to actors during the first half of this century. In 1716 a play-house was built in Williamsburg, which was the first one erected in America. We have, however, very little information regarding the colonial theater before the middle of the eighteenth century. But this lack of knowledge does not prove that theatricals had no place in the life of the American townsmen. There were no newspapers in the seventeenth century, and those of the eighteenth century contained very few notices of plays. This failure to give the drama a proper place in their columns might be explained on the ground that public sentiment was usually against the theater, and the newspapers did not want to antagonize their constituency by giving undue publicity to an unpopular amusement. It may be, too, that the stage managers of that day were not so alive to the opportunities for publicity afforded by the press as are their descendants of today.

While occasional plays were doubtless given in the larger and more important towns during the first half of the eighteenth century, it was not until about the middle of this century that the colonial stage was put on a well-organized basis. The English drama had sloughed off much of the filth with which it had been besmirched in the Restoration period, and men of ability and standing were now engaged in writing and acting plays. Peg Woffington and David Garrick were in their prime, and the theater enjoyed eminent respectability and great popularity in England. By this time there had arisen a wealthy and leisure class in all the colonies, who followed the fashions and indulged in the amusements of the homeland. The time was therefore opportune for transplanting the English theater to America and giving it a permanent footing there.

The agents by which the transfer was effected were two joint-stock companies. The first of these, the Murray-Kean Company, came to Philadelphia in 1749, and for several seasons gave performances in that city, in New York, at Annapolis, and at Williamsburg and other places in Virginia.[25] But the company which did most to give the stage a permanent place in colonial life was

[25] The Murray-Kean Company, under different names and with changes in the personnel of the actors, continued to play in America for twenty years.

the one organized in London by William Hallam and his brother Lewis. This group of players consisted of twelve adult actors and three children. Arriving in Virginia in June, 1752, they received a cordial welcome at Williamsburg, and after a successful season at this provincial capital and other Virginia towns, they left for a tour of the northern cities. In the North they encountered the opposition of prominent churchmen, but except for this were everywhere accorded a cordial reception. After the death of David Hallam, his widow, who had been one of the leading actresses in the original cast, married David Douglass. The latter reorganized the company (1758) and entered upon a tour of all the important towns from Williamsburg to Providence, Rhode Island. Despite the opposition of religious leaders in certain quarters, his company continued its performances until the Revolution put an end to its activities.

Theaters were rude structures in New York in the early days. They were usually log rooms, accommodating about three hundred people. They were not heated except by a stove in the anteroom, and the audience in cold weather would usually crowd around it in the intervals between acts. Foot-warmers were used as in church, and candles were employed for light and for footlights. Sometimes in the midst of a love scene or exciting tragedy the stage hand would interrupt the scene by snuffing the smoking candle wicks of the footlights. In Williamsburg it was the custom to have servants go to the theater about four in the afternoon to hold the seats of their masters for the performance, which usually began about six.[26]

The colonial theater was altogether an importation from the homeland. With a few insignificant exceptions, all the plays presented in America were both written and acted by Englishmen. The English drama of the latter half of the eighteenth century, though cleaner than it was under the later Stuarts, had not entirely freed itself from the taint of licentiousness acquired in the

[26] The following announcement appeared in the *Virginia Gazette*, under date of August 21, 1752: "The Company [the Hallams] lately from London . . . will open on the first Friday in September with a play called 'The Merchant of Venice,' written by Shakespeare. Ladies engaging seats in the boxes are advised to send their servants early on the day of the performance to hold them and prevent trouble and disappointment" (quoted by HORNBLOW, ARTHUR, *A History of the Theatre in America*, i, pp. 80-81).

Restoration period; for in both England and America the immoral comedies of Congreve, Farquhar, and Wycherly were presented, as well as the tragedies of Shakespeare and Addison. So the theater made both a high intellectual and a low sensual appeal to its patrons. To enjoy drama, therefore, was to partake of the fruit borne by the tree of the knowledge of good and evil. For this reason moral and religious leaders in America, especially among the Quakers and Puritans, regarded such an indulgence as a great sin and resorted to the thunders of the moral law and the rigors of the penal code to save the people from its baleful influence. In 1750 the Massachusetts General Court passed a law prohibiting theaters in Massachusetts; Pennsylvania did the same in 1759, Rhode Island in 1761, and New Hampshire in 1762. These acts were, however, probably passed only as a concession to the Puritan sentiment among the middle and lower classes. By this time the wealthy classes in the cities were not allowing their Puritanism to hamper seriously their amusements, and these laws were probably not enforced. While in New England, Douglass seems at times to have steered clear of the prejudice against the drama by camouflaging his plays under the title of "moral dialogues."[27]

The people in the provinces south of the Potomac River apparently did not share the prejudices entertained by their northern neighbors against dramatic performances, and there were no laws in Virginia and Maryland against them. Indeed, the South "was a Paradise without a forbidden fruit" for all devotees of the stage and other like amusements. The easy-going Anglicanism of the wealthy planters who dominated this section saw no objection to theater-going, and Quakerism and Puritanism were not strong enough to secure legislative enactments against them. In vain,

[27] As an example of this clever subterfuge, we might cite the following play-bill gotten out by him in Newport, Rhode Island, 1761, before the presentation of *Othello*:

"Moral Dialogues
In Five Parts

Depicting the Evil Effects of Jealousy and other Bad Passions, and Proving that Happiness can only Spring from the Pursuit of Virtue. Mr. Douglass will represent a noble and magnanimous Moor named Othello, who loves a young lady named Desdemona, and after he had married her, harbors [as in too many cases] the dreadful passion of jealousy" (quoted by HORNBLOW, ARTHUR, *op. cit.*, pp. 110-111).

too, were their efforts to keep the people away by moral and religious prohibition.

COURTSHIP AND MARRIAGE

Early and frequent marriages

One of the earliest romances recorded in the history of English-speaking America was that of John Rolfe, who fell in love with the Indian princess, Pocahontas, and married her in the spring of 1614. Others, however, followed in rapid succession and the colonists were soon noted for early and frequent marriages. Young men and women generally married at a very early age, and widows and widowers usually remarried after a short period of mourning. Colonel Byrd speaks of his daughter, the beautiful Evelyn, as an "antique virgin," though she was at the time only about twenty years old. A New England contemporary writer alludes to a young woman of twenty-five as an "ancient maid."[28] The governor of New Hampshire married a widow after she had had only six days in which to mourn the loss of her first husband. In Virginia an instance is recorded in which a widow used a part of the meats prepared for the funeral of her first husband at the wedding feast given on the occasion of her second marriage.

One reason for such haste in marrying was that economic conditions and social customs made it very undesirable for either men or women to remain single for any considerable length of time. In the pioneer state of society there was practically no economic opportunity for an unmarried woman, and public opinion aided in making it uncomfortable for maiden ladies. The situation was almost as bad for men who wished to remain single. It was difficult and almost impossible for a bachelor to employ a housekeeper. In New England, even if one could be found, the law

[28] It seems that after the colonies were well established it was exceptional for a woman to go through life unmarried. A contemporary, speaking in 1727, says that in Virginia "an old maid or an old bachelor are as scarce among us and reckoned as ominous as a blazing star" (Colonel William Byrd, quoted by STANARD, MARY N., in *Colonial Virginia*, p. 171).

A traveler in New England in the latter part of the seventeenth century said: "It is true, an old (or superannuated) Maid in Boston is thought such a curse, as nothing can exceed it (and looked on as a *dismal spectacle*)" (DUTTON, JOHN, *Life and Error*, pp. 102, 103; quoted by WEEDEN, W. B., in his *Economic and Social History of New England*, i, p. 299, note).

or public sentiment would not allow him to hire one. Unmarried men there were looked upon with suspicion by the authorities. They were not allowed to live alone or even to choose their places of residence, but were compelled to stay at such places as the court might designate. They were constantly under the spying scrutiny of such officials as the tithingman, constable, and the watchman. In some towns a special tax or an exceptional burden was imposed upon them.[29]

In colonial days courtship was more under parental supervision than it is today. The usual custom among the upper classes was for the young man to get the consent of her father before he declared himself to the lady of his choice. This consent was usually obtained as a result of negotiations carried on by the parents of the young lovers. The agreements arrived at by the older people were very prosaic and business-like. This was especially true in New England, where the ascetic and religious notions of the Puritans robbed courtship of much of its romance. The marriage portion of the prospective bride played a prominent part in the preëngagement negotiations, and the amount of it was sometimes openly discussed. In South Carolina the newspapers would sometimes state in figures the amount of the fortune of the bride-elect. "The pattern of love-making [among the Puritans] was as rigid as that of their cuffs and collars" (Weeden).

Court-
ship

It is more than likely, however, that the young people found means of evading these unnatural restrictions and frequently followed the leadings of a sane sentiment. For men and girls of marriageable age were thrown together at church, dances, house parties, or other like social functions. There were also opportunities for long rides and drives together and walks in shady lanes and flower gardens. As the young people in that day were endowed with the same human traits as they now display, we may safely assume that a good deal of informal love-making went on without the previous consent of parents. However, the exercise of such freedom on the part of young men and women was a defiance of the conventions and in New England at one time a violation of the law. If a man should win the affections of a

---

[29] In Eastham, Massachusetts, there was a law in 1695, which ordained that "every unmarried man in the township shall kill six blackbirds or three crows while he remains single," and he would not be allowed to marry until he had complied with this order (EARLE, A. M., *Customs in Old New England,* p. 37).

young lady without the consent of her parents, he was liable to punishment by fine, imprisonment, or flogging, and there are numerous instances of the enforcement of this law.

Courtship was also regulated sometimes in the name of religion. Some denominations, like the Catholics, Episcopalians, Quakers, Mennonites, and Dunkards, objected very seriously to their members marrying outside the fold, and to prevent this they discouraged courtship between their young people and those belonging to other denominations. Public opinion was the restraint generally used to keep sentiment within the orthodox limits, but among the Quakers a more direct form of compulsion was employed. In their regular Monthly Meetings, they frequently asked each young man whether he was associating with any young woman outside the church with a view to matrimony. If he pleaded guilty, a strong effort was made to induce him to give up the dangerous association before his feelings were too deeply committed. If he paid no heed to the advice of his brethren and married a non-Quaker he was excluded from the fold.

Among the Puritans (except in New Hampshire) the banns were usually published three times before marriage. Marriage was regarded by them as a civil contract and in the early years was always performed by the civil magistrate. In the eighteenth century we find ministers performing the ceremony, but they were probably acting as officials of the civil government, as ministers do today.

Marriage customs

A wedding was an occasion of festivity everywhere in the colonial period. Then as now jokes and unconventional practices were indulged in at the expense of the newly-married couple. In New England they had the custom of stealing the bride. Some young men—usually those who had not been invited to the wedding—would steal the bride and take her off to a near-by tavern. The groom would then have to give a supper to the abductors to redeem her. A custom sometimes followed in Connecticut was for the groom, just before the marriage ceremony was to begin, to feign reluctance and run away, to be seized by the attendant young men and forced back to the place of duty.[30] In this way the young Puritans mixed a little make-believe asceticism even with their amusements.

The Scotch-Irish in New Hampshire and in the South observed the old Scotch custom of running for the bottle. Ker-

[30] *Ibid.*, p. 77.

cheval in his *History of the Valley of Virginia* (p. 59) gives the following account of this old custom as practiced in the Valley of Virginia:

"It was usual for the wedding parties to ride to the residence of the clergyman to have the ceremony performed. In their absence the father or the next friend prepared at the bride's residence a bottle of the best spirits that could be obtained, around the neck of which a white ribbon was tied. Returning from the clergyman's, when within one or two miles of the home of the bride, some three or four young men prepared to run for the bottle. Taking an even start, their horses were put at full speed, dashing over mud, rocks, stumps, and disregarding all impediments. The race, in fact, was run with as much eagerness and desire to win as is manifested on the turf by our sporting characters. The father or next friend of the bride, expecting the racers, stood with the bottle in his hand, ready to deliver it to the successful competitor. On receiving it, he forthwith returned to meet the bride and groom; when met, the bottle was first presented to the bride, who must taste it at least, next to the groom, and then handed round to the company, every one of whom was required to swig it."[31]

Large families were the rule in all of the colonies. Frequently there were ten or twelve children in a family, and from twenty to twenty-five were not unknown. A man in Massachusetts died about the end of the colonial period leaving one hundred and

Large families

---

[31] The Moravians, of Bethlehem, Pa., had a curious method of bringing young people together with a view to courtship and marriage. They regarded marriage as a sacred institution and the church acted as a sort of match-making agency. A writer in 1819 gave the following description of the way in which their matrimonial agency was run:

"The young man who has an inclination to marry makes application to the priest, who presents a young woman designated by the superintendent as the next in rotation for marriage. Having left the parties together for an hour, the priest returns, and if they mutually consent to live together, they are married the next day; if otherwise, each is put at the bottom of the list, containing perhaps sixty or seventy names, and on the part of the girl there is no chance of marriage unless the same young man should again feel disposed for matrimony" (quoted by CALHOUN, A. W., in his *Social History of the American Family*, p. 206, from MACKENZIE, E., *Historical, Topographical, and Descriptive View of the United States of America and of Upper and Lower Canada* (1819), p. 379).

fifty-seven living children, grandchildren, and great-grandchildren. Infant mortality was very high. One mother is mentioned who lost twenty children in early childhood.

Selected Readings

1. Life in the Colonial City:
    A. Social Life in the Towns.—Bridenbaugh, Carl, *Cities in the Wilderness*, *ch. 8.
    B. The Awakening of Civic Consciousness.—*Ibid.*, pp. *298-300 (a fine summary).
    C. The Urban Setting.—*Ibid.*, *ch. 9.
    D. Persistent Problems of an Urban Society.—*Ibid.*, *ch. 11.
    E. Social Maturity.—*Ibid.*, *ch. 12.
    F. One Hundred Years of Urban Growth.—*Ibid.*, pp. *467-481 (an excellent summary).
2. Colonial Cities, Brief Accounts:
    A. Boston.—Burnaby, A., *Travels through North America*, ed. by R. R. Wilson, pp. *33-35 (this and the other references to Burnaby are contemporary accounts).
    B. New York.—*Ibid.*, pp. *111-113.
    C. Philadelphia.—*Ibid.*, pp. *88-92.
    D. Annapolis.—*Ibid.*, pp. *80-82; Wertenbaker, T. J., *The Golden Age of Colonial Culture*, pp. *85-105.
    E. Williamsburg.—Burnaby, *op. cit.*, pp. *33-35; Wertenbaker, *op. cit.*, pp. *105-126.
    F. Charleston.—Wertenbaker, *op. cit.*, pp. *127-150.
3. Character and Customs of the Virginians.—*Ibid.*, pp. *53-58.
4. Perukes and Periwigs.—Earle, A. M., *Two Centuries of Costume in America*, i, *ch. 11.
5. History of Colonial Dress.—Earle, A. M., *Costume of Colonial Times*, pp. *1-42.
6. Child Life.—Earle, A. M., *Customs in Old New England*, *ch. 1.
7. Courtship and Marriage in New Amsterdam.—Singleton, Esther, *Dutch New York*, *ch. 10.
8. Amusements in New Amsterdam.—*Ibid.*, *ch. 13.
9. Doctors and Patients.—Eggleston, G. C., *Life in the Eighteenth Century*, pp. *232-234; Wertenbaker, T. J., *The First Americans*, *ch. 7.
10. Moral Conditions in New England.—Calhoun, A. W., *Social History of the American Family*, i, *ch. 7.
11. The Colonial Theater.—Crawford, Mary C., *Social Life in Old New England*, pp. *19-71; Hughes, Glenn, *The Story of the Theatre*, ch. 17.
12. Houses in the Seventeenth Century.—Kimball, S. F., *Domestic Architecture*, pp. *3-52.

Part III:

SEPARATION FROM THE EMPIRE

CHAPTER XXIX

THE OCCUPATION OF THE TRANS-ALLEGHANY REGION

THE acquisition of vast areas of unoccupied lands as a result of the successful termination of the Seven Years' War had imposed an additional responsibility on the imperial government of Great Britain. The new territory had to be organized politically, and a policy had to be outlined that would keep the western Indians quiet. The Board of Trade addressed itself at once to its new task and had the king issue a proclamation in October, 1763, which offered a solution for both problems. From the southern territory acquired from Spain were created the provinces of East and West Florida, and the Canadian possessions were organized into the Province of Quebec. In each of these three jurisdictions all the powers of government were at first vested in a governor appointed by the crown, though the inhabitants were to have the civil rights enjoyed by the people of the English settlements. At a later date assemblies were to be granted to these new provinces and their government was to take on the form of the older crown colonies. No provision was made at this time for setting up a civil government in the Illinois country, and the few French settlements in that region were left under the control of military officials.[1]

Political organization of the territory gained by the war

The proclamation also provided for a radical change in the management of Indian affairs. Under the old plan, whereby each colony supervised its own relations with the natives, a great deal of injustice was perpetrated against the Indians. They had been left to the tender mercies of unscrupulous traders and speculators, who had cheated them of their furs and robbed them of their lands.[2] Indian relations were now to be handled exclusively by imperial agents, and all future purchases of land from the natives were to be made by these officials. In order to prevent the settlers

A new Indian policy inaugurated

[1] For the text of this proclamation, see MacDonald, W., *Select Charters*, pp. 267-272.

[2] *New York Colonial Documents*, vii, pp. 953-978.

from infringing upon the landed rights of the Indians and thereby producing friction between the two races, the vast region west of the Alleghany Mountains was set off as an Indian reservation. The watershed separating the sources of the rivers flowing westward into the Mississippi from those flowing eastward into the Atlantic was for the time being made the western boundary of colonial expansion. No lands could be bought from the natives and no settlements could be made west of this line without permission of the imperial agents, and settlements already made in the reservation must be abandoned.[3] This barrier to western expansion was not to be permanent, however, as it was expected that land purchases would be made from time to time by the imperial authorities and new areas west of the line would thus be open to colonization.

In assuming the authority to dispose of the western territory the home government was disregarding the claims of those colonies which contended that their charters gave them a right to the unoccupied land of the transmontane region. The land companies, which were interested in the exploitation of the West, were especially opposed to the new arrangement, as it ran counter to their plans for colonization. Moreover, the impatient backwoodsmen chafed at this restriction on their freedom to move westward, and paid little heed to the artificial boundary that had been set up by the British government. The imperial authorities had thus adopted a policy which aroused the antagonism of the prospective settler and the capitalist land dealer, and had supplied both with a grievance against the home government. Apparently, however, the Board of Trade was actuated only by the best motives in erecting this barrier to western settlement. The main purpose of this prohibition seems to have been "to protect the fur trade from the injury which it would sustain from an inrush of settlers," and "to assure the natives that their rights would be respected and encroachments prevented until, by negotiations from time to time with the proper officers, they might agree to relinquish portions of their territory."[4]

[3] MacDonald, W., *Select Charters*, pp. 270-271.

[4] Hockett, H., *Political and Social History of the United States*, p. 114.

According to some authorities, another motive that prompted the British government to put a limit to western settlements was the hope that the colonials might be confined "to such a distance from

The Proclamation Line

Unfortunately, however, these good intentions were not carried out in time to ward off the Indian danger. For before the new policy was formulated news came of a great uprising among the western Indians. The leader of the movement was Pontiac, an able Ottawa chieftain, who had formed a powerful confederacy

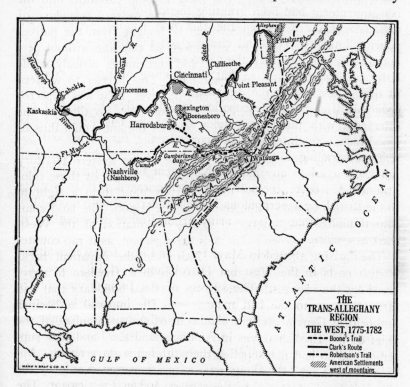

THE
TRANS-ALLEGHANY
REGION
THE WEST, 1775-1782
----- Boone's Trail
——— Clark's Route
-·-·- Robertson's Trail
////// American Settlements
west of mountains.

of the western tribes. So great was the unrest among the natives that one tribe of the Iroquois broke its historic friendship for the British and joined the so-called conspiracy. The savages had

---

the seacoast as that those settlements should lie within the reach of the trade and commerce of this kingdom [Great Britain], . . . and also of the exercise of that authority and jurisdiction which was conceived to be necessary for the preservation of the colonies in due subordination to, and dependence upon, the mother country" (SPARKS, J., ed., *Life and Writings of Franklin*, iv, pp. 305-306). For an opinion contrary to this view, see an article by ALVORD, C. W., on "The Genesis of the Proclamation of 1763," in the *Michigan Pioneer and Historical Collections*, xxxvi, pp. 20-51, especially pp. 41-43.

a number of reasons for uniting in a great struggle with the white intruders. The smoldering discontent caused by the bad treatment that they had suffered at the hands of the English traders was fanned into active hostility at the end of the French and Indian War by the withholding of the presents that the British government had been granting them. But the main cause of dissatisfaction arose from the fact that English settlers were pouring into the West and clearing out the forests which harbored the game on which the natives depended for a living. The latter now came to realize that the planting of English colonies in their midst meant the destruction of the very basis of their economic life. French occupation, on the other hand, had not interfered with the Indian mode of living. The French backwoodsmen were interested primarily in the fur trade, and the scattered trading and military posts established by them had not encroached to any appreciable extent upon Indian hunting-grounds. Moreover, the natives were encouraged in their hostility to the British by unscrupulous French traders, who deceived them into thinking that a large army from France was coming to their assistance.

The uprising started in May, 1763, and in a few weeks all the British posts in the West but Detroit and Fort Pitt were captured by the savages.[5] The success of the Indians was due in large measure to the bad management of the British military authorities. General Jeffery Amherst, who was commander-in-chief of the English forces in America, held the Indians in contempt and so had not supplied the scattered posts with as many men as were needed. A vigorous effort, however, was made by the whites to put an end to the contest, and in 1764 two expeditions were sent into the heart of the enemy's country. One of these succeeded in reaching Detroit, while the other, under the command of Colonel Bouquet,[6] who had won a noted victory over the Indians at Bushy Run, marched from Fort Pitt into the interior of Ohio. Pontiac was now defeated and the backbone of the uprising was thus broken.

A few years after Pontiac's defeat, the imperial agents for

[5] ALVORD, C. W., *The Mississippi Valley in British Politics,* i, p. 187.

[6] For Bouquet's account of this battle, see *Michigan Pioneer and Historical Society Collections,* xix, pp. 219-222.

Indian affairs negotiated two treaties (1768), one with the Iro- The
quois at Fort Stanwix and one with the Cherokees at Hard English
Labor. By the Treaty of Fort Stanwix the Iroquois surrendered acquire
to the English whatever rights they had to a small strip of land lands in
in central New York, a large area covering southwestern Penn- the West
sylvania and the trans-Alleghany portion of West Virginia, and by treaties
the region between the Ohio and Tennessee rivers.[7] The English with the
were also confirmed in their possession of a part of this grant Indians
by the agreement with the Cherokees.[8]

While the right of the Iroquois to a good deal of this land was Vandalia
questionable, the British authorities acted as if their title to it
all was valid, and so a princely domain in the West was open to
colonization. Land speculators had been the prime movers in the
transactions that led to the treaty with the Iroquois, and they
determined to take advantage of this great opportunity. A group
of Americans and Englishmen formed a syndicate and asked
for a large grant of land. Prominent among the Americans who
were interested in the scheme were Benjamin Franklin and Sir
William Johnson, the imperial agent for Indian affairs who had
negotiated the Treaty of Fort Stanwix. Some of the most influential politicians in England were also stockholders in the company, and considerable pressure was brought to bear upon the
British authorities to gain their assent to the cession. Lord Hills-
boro, president of the Board of Trade, was opposed to the plan,
as he considered it a violation of the rights of the older colonies
and contrary to the policy already established for the Indians.[9]
He was removed from the presidency of the Board of Trade,
however, and his successor agreed to the project. Accordingly,
the Board of Trade recommended that most of the territory
within the present limits of West Virginia and eastern Kentucky be granted to this company. A colony was to be planted on
this extensive grant, which was to be called Vandalia.[10] The Privy

[7] For an account of the negotiations with the Indians at Fort Stanwix and the treaty signed by them there, see *New York Colonial
Documents,* viii, pp. 111-137. For a copy of a map made by Sir
William Johnson showing by a red line the boundary of the grant,
see p. 136.

[8] BODLEY, TEMPLE, *History of Kentucky,* p. 40; ALVORD, C. W.,
The Mississippi Valley in British Politics, ii, p. 63.

[9] SPARKS, J., ed., *Life and Writings of Franklin,* iv, pp. 302-303.

[10] For map showing the extent of the Vandalia grant, see VOL-
WILER, A. T., *George Croghan and the Westward Movement,* p. 255.

Council accepted this recommendation, and by the spring of 1775 the patent was ready for the king's signature, but the outbreak of the Revolution put an end to the plan.[11]

The first trans-Appalachian settlements   Although the initial steps in the winning of the West were taken by capitalists interested in land speculation, the chief part was played not by them, but by hardy backwoodsmen, who pushed into the wilderness in search of cheap and fertile lands. By the outbreak of the French and Indian War a number of settlers had moved beyond the first tier of the Alleghany Mountains and located in the eastern portions of the present state of West Virginia. A few bold pioneers had also built cabins west of the Alleghany ranges in the valley of the Monongahela River in what is now northwestern West Virginia and southwestern Pennsylvania. But the trans-Alleghany settlements were, with few if any exceptions, abandoned temporarily, first in the French and Indian War and again in Pontiac's war, and were not reëstablished permanently until after peace had been made with Pontiac. The treaties that ended the war with the French and the conflict with Pontiac gave to the West a quiet and security which led to the gradual extension of the frontier across the Alleghany ridges toward the Ohio River. From about 1766 to 1774 permanent settlements were made on the upper Ohio and on the Monongahela River and other tributaries of the Ohio. By 1770 the youthful town of Pittsburgh could boast of some twenty log houses, and there was the nucleus of a village on the present site of Wheeling.[12]

The peace that came at the end of the wars with the French and the Indians was also the signal for extending the frontier across the Appalachian ranges in the southwest, and before the outbreak of the Revolution cabins had begun to appear in Kentucky and Tennessee. The occupation of this area was encouraged by the treaty with the Iroquois (1768), mentioned above. For the backwoodsmen contended that this treaty removed the barrier that had been erected by the Proclamation Line of 1763.

(In 1769 a settlement was made on the Watauga River by emigrants from southwest Virginia.)Two years later this little

[11] O'CALLAGHAN, E. B., *Documentary History of New York*, ii, pp. 998, 1001.

[12] CALLAHAN, J. M., *History of West Virginia*, pp. 50-56, 69-74; JAMES, A. P., in the *Mississippi Valley Historical Review*, xviii, pp. 55-71.

colony was reinforced by seventeen families from western North
Carolina, which had been led across the mountains by James
Robertson. This trek westward had been made in true pioneer
fashion. The men went in front, driving their cattle and hogs,
while the women and small children, as well as their few household belongings, were borne on pack-horses. Robertson, who was
a typical frontiersman of the better sort, soon became a leader in
the colony. Although his education was very meager, he had the
poise, quiet courage, and firmness of character that are marks of
real greatness, and his fellow-pioneers were quick to recognize
his ability as a leader of men.

A year later (1772) the infant colony received another valuable addition in the person of John Sevier, who with Robertson
was destined to play an important rôle in its later history. He
was the son of a French Huguenot who had emigrated to the
Shenandoah Valley in Virginia. He had a fair education, as
well as exceptional polish and refinement, and was well versed
in the ways of the world. To his French heritage he was indebted
for a gay, pleasure-loving temperament, a free and easy manner,
and that adaptability that is so characteristic of the French people. His unflinching courage and his skill and prowess as an
Indian fighter commanded the respect of his fellow-frontiersmen,
and his tact, unfailing courtesy, and charm of manner won their
warmest affection. He was thus richly endowed with those qualities that are most highly prized on the frontier, and it was only
natural that he should wield a great influence over the backwoodsmen at Watauga (in the present state of Tennessee).

The Watauga colony was within the limits of North Carolina,
but was so far removed from the older settlements that it was
beyond the reach of the governmental authority of that province.
This made it necessary for the inhabitants to devise a scheme of
government for themselves, just as the Pilgrims and other New
England communities had done in the seventeenth century. Under
the leadership of Robertson and Sevier the people from the settlements in the Watauga region met in a mass-meeting and organized themselves into a body politic (1772). A written
constitution was adopted, which provided for a representative
assembly to make laws and a board of five commissioners to perform the judicial and executive functions of the miniature state.[13]

The Watauga settlements: Robertson

Sevier

Organization of the government

[13] RAMSEY, J. G. M., *Annals of Tennessee*, pp. 106-107, 134-136;
PHELAN, JAMES, *History of Tennessee*, pp. 33-34.

This little republic enjoyed complete independence until 1778, at which time North Carolina asserted her authority over Watauga by making it a part of the recently organized county of Washington.

Lord Dunmore's War

For a decade after the signing of the treaty that ended Pontiac's War, the northwestern Indians were nominally at peace with the whites, though during all this time they exhibited a spirit of haughty insolence toward the frontiersmen which might at any time lead to a renewal of strife. The dissatisfaction and uneasiness of the Indians were increased when the backwoodsmen began to build their cabins on Indian hunting-lands south and east of the Ohio. In 1774 the smoldering ill will between the two races that had been kept alive by occasional murders on both sides finally burst into flames. The outbreak occurred on the northwestern frontier of Virginia and was led by the Shawnees, though other tribes in the Ohio region were soon drawn into the conflict. Pennsylvania maintained an attitude of neutrality, and so the burden of the war had to be borne entirely by Virginia. The fact that at this time Virginia claimed all of the southwestern portion of the present State of Pennsylvania doubtless accounts in large measure for the apathy exhibited by the Quaker colony during this Indian conflict.[14]

Lord Dunmore, the last royal governor of the Old Dominion, fully realized the gravity of the situation, and determined to take vigorous measures to reduce the Indians to submission. Two military expeditions, of fifteen hundred men each, were organized and sent to attack the enemy. One of these, under the command of the governor himself, was to proceed to Fort Pitt (Pittsburgh) and then descend the Ohio. The other division was to be led by General Andrew Lewis, who by a more southerly route was to march across the wilderness to join Dunmore at the mouth of the Kanawha River. On arriving at Fort Pitt, Dunmore, acting on the advice of a subordinate, unwisely decided to change his plans. In furtherance of his new purpose he floated his army down the Ohio to the mouth of the Hockhocking River and then moved west until he came to Pickaway Plains, near the Indian town of Chillicothe. Here he built a fortified camp and sent out

[14] For an account of the events that preceded and led up to this Indian war, as related by Lord Dunmore in his official report, see THWAITES, R. G., and KELLOGG, L. P., *Documentary History of Dunmore's War*, pp. 373-382.

raiding parties to destroy the Indian villages in that region. A messenger was also dispatched to General Lewis to announce the change of plan and to direct him to join the governor at Pickaway Plains.[15]

In the meantime General Lewis had assembled his army of frontiersmen at the Great Levels on the Greenbrier River, where the town of Lewisburg, West Virginia, is now located. To this rendezvous had come more men than he had expected, all of them from the frontier settlements west and southwest of the Blue Ridge, including a company from the Watauga country. These raw recruits were typical woodsmen. Dressed in picturesque hunting-shirts and wearing moccasins, they looked more like Indian braves than English soldiers. It was an undisciplined crowd, and their lack of military training, together with their spirit of personal independence, made effective teamwork difficult and rendered impossible the kind of tactics that are demanded by conventional generalship. But their courage, skilled marksmanship, and knowledge of Indian warfare eminently fitted them for individual fighting, and that was the kind that was most needed in encounters with the savages.[16]

The battle of Point Pleasant

Lewis led his army down the Kanawha to its mouth to join forces with Lord Dunmore. Arriving here on October 6, 1774, he selected for the site of his camp the promontory lying between the Kanawha and Ohio rivers, where the town of Point Pleasant is now located. The troops had been here only a few days when the messenger from Governor Dunmore arrived with orders for the army to break camp and join him at Pickaway Plains. Lewis was preparing to obey this order when he learned that near his position there lay nearly a thousand Indians armed and ready for battle. Cornstalk, the able leader of the Shawnees, decided to attack Lewis before the two armies could come together. To carry out this purpose he had marched rapidly to the Ohio River, and during the night of October 9 had his men ferried across the river and placed in position near Lewis's camp. When their presence was discovered early next morning by the Virginians the battle was immediately joined. After a long and bloody contest, in which the backwoodsmen sustained heavy losses, the Indians

[15] *Ibid.*, pp. 181-192.

[16] For a brief account of the war given by Dunmore in his official report. see *ibid.*, pp. 383-386.

withdrew and the battle of Point Pleasant was won for the Virginians.[17]

(The spirit of the savages was now broken and Cornstalk was forced by his council of war chiefs to accept terms of peace. Accordingly, a treaty was signed with Lord Dunmore whereby the Indians surrendered all their prisoners and gave up all their claims to the land south and east of the Ohio River.[18] This battle, which had been fought at a heavy cost to the whites, convinced the Indians that they could not stay the tide of western migration, and, therefore, they became quiet and remained so for a time.

The founding of Kentucky

Kentucky, with its fertile blue-grass lands and salt-licks to attract the elk and the buffalo, was an inviting region to both the hunter and the settler. This fine section of country was not the permanent abode of any Indians, though it was the hunting-ground and battlefield for rival tribes whose titles to the land were shadowy and conflicting. As we have seen, the Iroquois had by the treaty of 1768 surrendered to the English whatever rights they had to the region, and in Dunmore's War the whites had wrested from the Shawnees their claim to the country. The Cherokees also laid claim to the same territory, and their consent would have to be obtained before Kentucky (an Indian name meaning "dark and bloody ground") would be safe for English colonization, for they were so located as to be able to make it dangerous for emigrants going to the new country.

The Transylvania Company

Reports as to the nature of this western paradise were brought to the frontier settlements of the older colonies by hunters,[19] and in 1774 a settlement was begun at Harrodsburg by James Harrod, from Pennsylvania. But the first organized attempt to plant a colony in Kentucky was made by Judge Richard Henderson of North Carolina. Henderson belonged to the planter class and was more closely identified with the patricians in the Tidewater Belt than with the untutored backwoodsmen of the frontier. However, he had an adventurous spirit and dreamed of creating in the wilderness a great province in which he and his associates would

[17] For accounts of the battle, given by men who participated in it, see *ibid.*, pp. 253-297, especially pp. 257-259.

[18] *Ibid.*, pp. 385-386.

[19] In the list of the early explorers of Kentucky a prominent place belongs to Thomas Walker, who found his way into the "dark and bloody ground" as early as 1750.

be able to play the rôle of lords proprietors. In pursuit of this ambition he and some other land speculators formed a partnership (1774) which was known as the Transylvania Company. In the spring of the following year (1775) they bought from the Cherokees all the land between the Kentucky and Cumberland rivers. Next they sent forward a band of thirty men, under the leadership of Daniel Boone, to clear out a trail from the Holston River to the Kentucky River. The trail thus marked out later grew into an important highway, which was known as the Wilderness Road.

In selecting Boone to lead the vanguard of his colonizing expedition, Henderson made a very wise choice. This famous hunter was eminently qualified by both character and experience for this important task. In him was embodied the spirit of the frontier, with practically all of its virtues and few of its faults. His personality was characterized by a combination of mild-mannered kindliness, exceptional courage, self-reliance, and resolute boldness. His skill in extricating himself from a difficult situation was a wonder to the Indians, whose craftiness was no match for his resourcefulness. These qualities, together with his love of adventure, his reverence for the grandeur and beauty of the silent forest, and his iron constitution that enabled him to defy the hardships of outdoor life in all sorts of weather, marked him out as a man "ordained of God to settle the wilderness."[20] He had already penetrated the trackless forest to the blue-grass region on one of his long hunting excursions into Kentucky in 1769-71. Two years later he had attempted to lead a group of emigrants to this new land; but they were attacked on the way by the savages and were forced to abandon the undertaking.[21]

Boone and his men went ahead rapidly with the work of clearing out a road to the Kentucky River and in two weeks they were near their journey's end. At this time they were attacked by the Indians and two of Boone's party were killed. Nothing daunted by this experience, Boone pushed ahead and on April 1, 1775, laid the foundations of the settlement of Boonesborough, on the Kentucky River. Other pioneers had in the meantime come into this region and were erecting their log cabins and were

Daniel Boone

First settlements in Kentucky

---

[20] These are Boone's own words.

[21] For Boone's account of these experiences, as edited by John Filson (1784), see HART, A. B., *American History Told by Contemporaries*, ii, pp. 383-385.

planting corn. Hardly had the newcomers settled down in their homes when they were attacked by the Indians and some of them killed. This threw the community into a panic and Boone sent word to Henderson, who was coming on with more emigrants, to hurry to their assistance. Henderson was prompt to respond to this request, and he and his party soon joined Boone at the fort which the latter had erected at Boonesborough. Other settlers came about the time of Henderson's arrival and soon there were several settlements in the Kentucky community.

Organization of the government of Transylvania

Henderson soon took steps to organize a government for Transylvania, as the new province was called. A convention consisting of representatives from four settlements met under a large elm tree and drew up a sort of written constitution and created the necessary machinery of government for the infant commonwealth.[22] But Transylvania did not long remain under this form of government. Henderson's title to the land based on the treaty with the Cherokees was questioned, and the treaty itself was a violation of the Indian regulations as laid down by the British authorities in the Proclamation of 1763. Moreover, the new colony was within the limits of Virginia, and this province did not recognize the claims of the self-appointed proprietors.[23] The little colony was also threatened with destruction by the Indians, who had been stirred to a menacing restlessness by the outbreak of the Revolutionary War, for Henry Hamilton, the British governor at Detroit, was inciting the savages to attack the Kentucky settlements.

In this unsettled state of affairs it was felt that the wilderness republic should be placed on a firmer political basis if it was to afford its citizens the measure of protection that the unsettled times demanded. Accordingly, two attempts were made to stabilize the government by linking it up with an outside jurisdiction. The proprietors sent a delegate to the Continental Congress and asked that body to recognize Transylvania as one of the united colonies,[24] while the people of Harrodsburg sent a petition to the

[22] For Henderson's account of the convention that drew up this constitution, see BODLEY, T., *History of Kentucky,* pp. 105-106. For the proceedings of this assembly (which met May 23, 1775), see *Filson Club Publications,* no. 16, Appendix, pp. 196-212.

[22] FORCE, PETER, *American Archives,* 4th series, ii, p. 174; *Filson Club Publications,* no. 16, p. 253.

[24] For the text of this petition, see *Filson Club Publications,* no. 16, pp. 214-216, or BODLEY, T., *History of Kentucky,* pp. 582-583.

legislature of Virginia asking that the authority of the Old Dominion be extended over the Kentucky settlements.[25] Congress refused the request of the proprietors,[26] but Virginia responded favorably to the petition of the Harrodsburg settlers. The result was that the greater part of what is now Kentucky was organized into a county of Virginia, and Transylvania ceased to exist as an independent commonwealth (December, 1776).[27]

Selected Readings

1. The Treaty of Fort Stanwix.—Alvord, C. W., *The Mississippi Valley in British Politics,* ii, pp. *68-77.
2. Mode of Living among the Backwoodsmen.—Roosevelt, T., *The Winning of the West,* pp. *126-156; Skinner, C. L., *Pioneers of the Old South-West,* *ch. 2.
3. The House, Furniture, and Diet of the Backwoodsmen.—Doddridge, J., *Notes on the Settlement and Indian Wars of the Western Parts of Virginia and Pennsylvania,* *ch. 10 (a contemporary account).
4. Caravans and Modes of Travel.—*Ibid.,* *ch. 13.
5. Marriage Customs.—*Ibid.,* *ch. 15.
6. The Building of the Cabin.—*Ibid.,* *ch. 16.
7. Games and Diversions.—*Ibid.,* *ch. 20.
8. Law, Morality, and Religion.—*Ibid.,* *ch. 22.
9. Dunmore's War.—Skinner, C. L., *op. cit.,* pp. *114-128.
10. The Founding of Kentucky.—*Ibid.,* *ch. 7; Thwaites, R. G., *Daniel Boone,* *ch. 9.
11. The Watauga Settlement.—Skinner, C. L., *op. cit.,* pp. *164-184.
12. The Founding of Nashville.—*Ibid.,* pp. *184-194.

[25] *Filson Club Publications,* no. 16, pp. 241-247; ALDEN, G. H., *New Governments West of the Alleghanies before 1780,* pp. 59-62.

[26] Dr. Archibald Henderson says that John Adams was opposed to the recognition of Transylvania as one of the colonies for the reason that if the Continental Congress should take under its protection "a body of people who have acted in defiance of the King's proclamation" it would "be looked on as a confirmation of that independent spirit with which we are daily reproached." See pamphlet by HENDERSON, A., entitled *The Transylvania Company and the Founding of Henderson, Ky.,* p. 11.

[27] HENING, W. W., *Statutes at Large,* ix, pp. 257-258. For excerpts from the Journal of the House of Delegates bearing on the question, see BODLEY, T., *op. cit.,* pp. 132-137.

CHAPTER XXX

A DECADE OF DISCONTENT

AT THE end of the colonial era there were marked differences of opinion between Englishmen and Americans regarding the nature of the empire, and there necessarily grew up conflicting theories as to the respective powers of Parliament and the colonial assemblies.[1] As a rule, British publicists contended that Parliament

[1]"In Britain," wrote Governor Bernard in 1765, "the American Governments are considered as Corporations empowered to make by-laws, existing only during the Pleasure of Parliament. . . . In America they claim to be perfect States, not otherwise dependent upon Great Britain than by having the same King" (quoted by VAN TYNE, C. H., in his *Causes of the War of Independence,* pp. 217-218).

For a comprehensive, scholarly discussion of the constitutional basis of American opposition to British colonial policy, see McILWAIN, C. H., *The American Revolution: A Constitutional Interpretation.* Professor McIlwain says that the colonials at different times held to three different constitutional theories in defense of their rights. Prior to 1765 their main argument was based on the privileges granted to them by their charters. From 1765 to 1774 political leaders in America accepted the Whig doctrine that Parliament had authority over the dominions as well as the homeland and that the colonial assemblies were subordinate to Parliament. But in the exercise of this power Parliament was bound by natural right, as natural right was embedded in the English constitution. According to this theory, every man (in America as elsewhere) was entitled to all the rights of Englishmen, regardless of any charters, "by the law of God and nature, by the common law, and by act of Parliament." The weakness of this position was that it accorded unlimited authority to Parliament and left the people no remedy against Parliamentary oppression except "sighs and tears." Even Otis admitted that the only remedy the Americans had against the Stamp Act was that of sending a petition to Parliament. Such a theory was not in harmony with the policy of opposition to the British government which the colonials were pursuing during the years immediately preceding the outbreak. Accordingly, the leaders had by 1774 given

had supreme authority throughout the empire, its powers being
limited only by its own interpretation of the British constitution.
The Americans, on the other hand, contended that their assemblies
had the same power over taxation in the colonies that Parliament had in the homeland, and that Parliament was restricted in
the exercise of its authority not only by the legal precedents of
the British constitution, but also by the higher principle of natural rights. According to this view, any act of Parliament which
was not in harmony with the English constitution or the law of
nature was null and void.[2]   •

This disagreement in opinion might have been confined to the
realm of speculative thinking had the British authorities always
pursued a wise course in dealing with the Americans. But British
imperial administration during the greater part of the third
quarter of the eighteenth century was characterized by ineptitude
rather than by wisdom, and it would have been a miracle if these
opposing theories had not given rise to friction in actual practice. So even before the Seven Years' War had ended, two ominous clashes had occurred between American and British opinion
as to the right of the imperial government to interfere in colonial
affairs.

The first serious challenge to the authority of Parliament was   Writs of
made by James Otis in his argument against Writs of Assistance.   Assistance
The people of New England, as well as those of the other Northern and Middle Colonies, regarded the Molasses Act of 1733[3]
as an unjust law and so paid little or no heed to its provisions.
Smuggling was practiced everywhere in the commercial colonies
and was generally condoned by public opinion. This flouting of
an unwise measure was winked at by the British authorities in
times of peace, but could not be overlooked while the French and
Indian War was being waged. For the illegal trade that went on

---

up this view and were contending that Parliament had no right to
interfere in the internal affairs of the colonies. This was the last
position taken by those patriots who were defending their opposition
to English policy on constitutional grounds. When finally the secession of the colonies from the empire came it was based not on any
constitutional theory but on the natural right of revolution.

[2] For brief quotations showing contemporary English and American opinion on these points, see VAN TYNE, *op. cit.*, pp. 218-219. See
also *American Historical Review*, viii, p. 325.

[3] See p. 511.

between the Northern merchants and the French and Spanish colonists kept the latter supplied with food and other commodities that the British military authorities were trying to withhold from them. Pitt was advised that this source of aid to the enemy would be dried up if the Molasses Act were strictly executed, and so he determined upon a more rigid enforcement of this law.

The ordinary search warrant proved to be an inadequate remedy against smuggling, for it could only be issued on information and could apply only to places specifically designated in the warrant. The Writ of Assistance was a more effective instrument in the hands of a customs official, as it enabled him to search any house or ship for dutiable goods. Accordingly, Writs of Assistance were employed by imperial officials in their search for smuggled goods. This practice was very objectionable to the New Englanders because, as they considered, it violated "the immunity of an English home, where the wind might blow through every cranny, but the King's writ could not enter."[4] The people, however, submitted to the general writs, though with a bad grace, until some months after the death of George II (1760), at which time the old writs lost their validity and new ones had to be granted. When an application for Writs of Assistance was made before the Superior Court of Massachusetts, the Boston merchants made a strong effort to prevent them from being issued. The merchants were represented by James Otis, who delivered a fiery speech (1761) and, according to John Adams, aroused among the people a feeling of resentment that later ripened into the spirit of revolt. In his attack on the Writs Otis argued that "no act of Parliament can establish such an act," for "an act against the Constitution is void" and must be so declared by the courts.[5] Although Otis had implanted in the minds of his hearers the seeds of a radical political philosophy, he did not prevent the granting of the Writs, for in Massachusetts, as in other colonies, they were issued until the outbreak of the Revolution.

The
Parson's
Cause

The blame for the second of these clashes cannot all be laid at the door of the British government, but rather is it to be

---

[4] These are the words of Pitt; quoted by VAN TYNE, in his *Causes of the War of Independence*, p. 175.

[5] *Ibid.*, pp. 175-179, 225. For a contemporary account of Otis's speech, see ADAMS, C. F., ed., *The Life and Works of John Adams*, x, pp. 233, 244-248, 272, 276. For the arguments presented in this case, as reported by John Adams, see *ibid.*. ii, Appendix, pp. 523-525.

explained in part by the fact that an eloquent young lawyer allowed his zeal for the interests of his clients to lead him beyond the limits marked out by a strict sense of fairness and justice. This young advocate was Patrick Henry, and the occasion for this display of oratory was a suit brought in the county court of Hanover County, Virginia. To understand the circumstances that gave rise to this case, which is known in history as the Parson's Cause, we shall have to review briefly the events that led to this famous lawsuit.

As we have already seen, tobacco was the money of account in Virginia, and as its value was subject to marked fluctuations it was a very unsteady medium of exchange. In 1755 there was a great drought in Virginia, and again in 1758 there was a bad season throughout the greater portion of the colony. This meant that for these years the crop of tobacco was short and its price unusually high. If taxes, fees, and salaries were paid in tobacco at the old rating, salaried officials would gain, whereas the planters would have additional burdens imposed upon them at a time when they were already suffering from a shortage of their principal crop. To remedy this situation the assembly enacted measures in 1755 and 1758 (each to be effective for not more than a year) permitting the payment of taxes, fees, and debts contracted while the acts were in effect, in money at the rate of twopence for every pound of tobacco that was due.[6] The clergy of the established church complained that this law was unjust to them, as it deprived them of the advantage that had come as a result of the rise in the price of tobacco, to which advantage they were entitled as a compensation for the losses that they had sustained in previous years from the fall in value of this medium of exchange. They, therefore, brought their grievance to the notice of the Privy Council and that body vetoed the law.

In the meantime the Virginia vestries had assumed that the law was valid and had been making payments in accordance with its provisions. After the king in council had set aside the act, the ministers contended that it had been void from the beginning and that they should receive compensation according to the old rate. Accordingly, some of them brought suit against their vestries for arrears in salary. The most noted of these cases was the one that came before the county court of Hanover County in 1763.

[6] For the text of these laws, see HENING, W. W., *Statutes at Large* (Va.), vi, pp. 568-569; vii, pp. 240-241, 277-278.

The court ruled that the recent act of the Virginia assembly was void and the plaintiff was entitled to back pay. The jury was instructed to fix the amount of compensation to which he was entitled under the old law. Patrick Henry, the attorney for the vestrymen, made a stirring address to the jury. He contended that the Privy Council had acted tyrannically in vetoing the law of 1758 and the people of Virginia were justified in disregarding this veto. By stirring up the prejudice of the jurymen against the established church, he aroused them to a high pitch of excitement. The jury, swept off its feet by this flood of oratory, gave the plaintiff only one penny damage.[7]

This verdict was not only a plain violation of the ruling of the court, but was also a virtual annulment of an act of the king in council. This case is significant in that it showed that the American people would go to the extreme length of attacking the prerogative of the crown in upholding their rights. Moreover, the part played by Patrick Henry in the case gave him a prestige as an orator and agitator which made him eminently available for leadership in the radical opposition to the later policy of the home government.

The two events just narrated did not in themselves lead to a serious breach in the friendly relations that existed between the colonies and the mother country, but they were straws showing which way the wind of opposition was blowing. If the imperial government had been thoroughly awake to their significance, subsequent mistakes might have been averted and the later friction avoided. But this was not to be.

British politics after the Seven Years' War

To understand how the British government made such a blundering effort at solving the colonial problems that arose during the decade following the Peace of Paris, we must take a look at the game of British politics as it was played at that time. When George III came to the throne (1760) he found that the Whigs were so deeply intrenched in power that their opponents, the Tories, had had little or no part in the government for nearly half a century. But, as is generally the case when a party becomes too strong, the Whigs had split up into a number of factions. These divisions were based on the personal ambitions of the politicians rather than on honest differences of opinion as to imperial policy. Under such conditions a ministry could be formed

[7] For an excellent account of the Parson's Cause, see ECKENRODE, H. J., *The Revolution in Virginia*, pp. 9-13.

only by calling in representatives of several factions, and the government was usually in the hands of what was virtually a coalition Cabinet. The ministries were not so stable as they usually are under the bi-party system, and the king often had the opportunity to make new combinations.

In this way George III was able to wield an influence in the government greater than that usually exerted by an English sovereign. His position was still further strengthened by the fact that he could always count on the support of certain members of Parliament whom he had bound to himself by bribery and gifts of office. This situation was very much to the liking of George, who had an ambition to be a real ruler and not a figurehead, as had been his two immediate predecessors. This accession of power to the crown might have been a blessing to the empire had the king made a judicious use of it. But George III was not the type of man to whom it is safe to intrust much power and responsibility, for although he was conscientious and good-intentioned he was too opinionated, ignorant, and narrow-minded for the requirements of statesmanship.

Nor did he have the benefit of wise counsel to guide him through the difficulties that beset the first part of his reign. William Pitt was the one man who might have given wise advice, but, although he was a member of Parliament during the greater part of the decade preceding the outbreak of the Revolution, he was a member of the Cabinet for only a short time during this trying period. The inability of the Great Commoner to come to the aid of his country in this her hour of need is explained in part by certain traits in his character. His overpowering self-confidence caused him to put a low estimate on the views and abilities of other men and to reduce his colleagues to the rank of subordinates. Men of spirit resented being treated as inferiors or nonentities and did not wish to serve under him. Moreover, his strenuous energy was too much for easy-going placemen, and his lofty idealism was too reckless for complacent standpatters. "No careful statesman wished to be tied to the tail of a comet."[8] Besides, the ambitious king did not wish to play the rôle of a *roi fainéant* (a do-nothing king) to this proud mayor of the palace. Moreover, when, despite these drawbacks, the opportunity for leadership came to Pitt he could not take advantage of it on account of ill health.

[8] VAN TYNE, C. H., *Causes of the War of Independence*, p. 122.

As these circumstances were precluding the leadership of England's only political genius, the government had to go along under the guidance of mediocre politicians. In 1763 George Grenville became premier. He was honest and courageous and took the trouble to inform himself as to conditions in the dominions. But his conscientious efforts to enforce the trade regulations complicated rather than solved the difficult problem. Hitherto the saving grace of the imperial administration had been its indifference to American affairs; but ineptitude was now coupled with a sense of duty and had thus become dangerous. The stage was now properly set for a tragedy of errors.

The new colonial policy

The French and Indian War had left England mistress of the seas and the possessor of a world-wide empire. It had also doubled her national debt and greatly increased the tax burdens of her people. There was a rapid growth in industry in the mother country and the British manufacturer was now more anxious than ever to enjoy the exclusive right to buy raw materials and sell finished products in the colonies. It was thought that the new conditions called for a new policy of imperial administration, which would link together the various parts of the empire more closely. The commercial and industrial regulations were to be enforced more effectively and the colonies were to be called on to share the burdens of imperial taxation. This meant for America an abandonment of the policy of "salutary neglect." In short, the mother country was attempting to assume an authority which she had not previously maintained.

Such an experiment would have been hazardous even if times had not changed. But recent events had caused the colonies to desire a looser rather than a closer identification with the empire. The war with the French and the contest with the western Indians had freed the Americans from the French menace and had to a great extent relieved them of the danger of Indian attack. They therefore no longer felt the need of British protection so strongly as they had done before the treaties of peace had been signed.[9] During the war they had also incurred new financial obligations and they felt little inclined to add to these burdens by accepting imperial taxation.

[9] BOGART, E. L., and THOMPSON, C. M., *Readings in the Economic History of the United States,* pp. 143-144. See also KALM, PETER, *Travels into North America,* in PINKERTON, JOHN, *Voyages and Travels,* xiii, p. 461.

In pursuance of the new policy the British government at first The Sugar Act of 1764 began to enforce more rigidly the Molasses Act of 1733 and soon enacted another measure known as the Sugar Act of 1764 to take its place. The new law, like the old one, was passed for the purpose of discouraging trade with the French and Spanish West Indies, though it was also intended as a means of raising revenue. Both measures imposed a duty on sugar, molasses, and other commodities carried from the foreign West Indian plantations to the English continental colonies. The new act provided for a higher duty on refined sugar than did the old one, but lowered the duty on molasses from sixpence to threepence a gallon. The buying of rum and spirits from foreign plantations was prohibited. A tax was put on indigo imported into the colonies in order to protect the infant industry that was growing up in Georgia and South Carolina. The net revenue accruing from the enforcement of the law was all to be used "toward defraying the necessary expenses of defending, protecting, and securing, the said colonies and plantations."[10]

On the face of it the law of 1764 appeared more liberal than that of 1733, for, as has already been seen, the prosperity of the Northern colonies was more dependent upon the purchase of molasses than of sugar from the foreign West Indies.[11] Therefore, the lowering of the tax on molasses meant more to the continental colonies than did the raising of the duty on sugar. But despite this apparent improvement in the new law, the American merchants were more opposed to it than to the old one. The reason for this was that there were now provisions for the enforcement of the trade regulations, whereas the Act of 1733 had become a dead letter. Cases arising from indictments for smuggling were to be determined by British admiralty courts without trial by jury, and British imperial naval officers were to collect the customs duties. Another provision of the law of 1764 that was considered burdensome was the one requiring that the duties collected under the act be paid into the "receipt of His Majesty's

[10] For the text of the Sugar Act of 1764, see PICKERING, DANBY, *Statutes at Large,* xxvi, pp. 33-52 (4 Geo. III, c. 15). The law in abbreviated form is also given in MACDONALD, W., *Select Charters,* pp. 273-281. See also CHANNING, E., *op. cit.,* iii, pp. 40-44.

[11] The reason for this was that the rum industry in New England was dependent upon the purchase of molasses from the French West Indies. See p. 511.

Exchequer." The radicals in America interpreted this clause to mean that duties would have to be paid in metallic money, and these payments, they contended, would drain off from the colonies all their gold and silver. This was, in all probability, a groundless fear, as the net proceeds of the duties collected were to be spent in the colonies.

The colonies forbidden to issue paper money

The same year in which the opposition of the wealthy merchant class was aroused by the Sugar Act, Parliament supplied the common people with a grievance by the act which prohibited the colonies from issuing any more paper money to be used as legal tender. This measure was very unpopular with the masses, and a critic of America said (1776) that the colonials wanted to discharge "their British debts with an American sponge."[12] This was doubtless an unfair accusation, though the desire for an inflated currency was widespread. This attitude toward cheap money is explained in part by the fact that there was very little gold and silver in the colonies, and for America, therefore, the choice was largely between barter and paper money as a medium of exchange.[13]

Taxation

While the commercial restrictions were the worst grievance the colonists had against the British government, taxation was the main cause of discontent and opposition. The colonials had not been accustomed to paying direct taxes except in small amounts and for local purposes. This was due to the fact that the government did little for the individual in the simple conditions of life at that time, and so there was no good reason for making heavy demands on the taxpayer. Besides, the scarcity of specie in the colonies rendered the payment of imperial taxes a heavy burden. The question of taxation also had a political aspect. The political leaders pointed out that, as the dominions were not represented in Parliament, they could not be taxed by that body. And so the cry of "no taxation without representation" was raised.

The Stamp Act

During the intercolonial wars the British military authorities made requisitions of men and supplies on the colonies, but these requisitions were rarely, if ever, fully met. Evidently, it was

---

[12] BOGART, E. L., and THOMPSON, C. M., *Readings in the Economic History of the United States*, p. 165.

[13] For contemporary arguments in favor of paper money, see *ibid.*, p. 147; CALLENDER, G. S., *Selections from the Economic History of the United States*, pp. 67-68; and HART, A. B., *American History Told by Contemporaries*, ii, pp. 251-253.

necessary to devise some other means of maintaining and supporting a military force in the overseas possessions. The English government, therefore, decided to leave in America ten thousand British soldiers to protect the people against the Indians, to keep the French in Canada quiet, and in general to protect the interests of the empire. A secondary consideration was that the presence of regular troops in the dominions would strengthen the hand of the royal governors and aid in the enforcement of the laws against smuggling. The colonials had not asked for these soldiers and apparently did not want them, especially if they were to be taxed for their support.

The tax burdens borne by the Englishman at that time were very heavy. "Landowners were paying in taxes no less than twenty per cent of their incomes from land." The interest on the enormous public debt, the expense of keeping up the navy, as well as the ordinary costs of running the government, were all borne by the taxpayers of the homeland. The colonials were not asked to share in these burdens, although they were protected by the navy, and the public debt had been increased by the French and Indian War, waged partly at least in their behalf. But the British Ministry decided that the Americans should bear a portion of the cost of maintaining an army for their own protection. Grenville, therefore, announced a year in advance that a stamp duty would be imposed on the colonies, the revenue accruing from it to be used toward the partial support of the army stationed in the overseas dominions. He also stated that if the Americans would devise some other means of raising revenue he would accord the plan due consideration.[14] The colonials expressed strong opposition to the proposed stamp tax, but offered no substitute except the old system of requisitions. Indeed, it would have been difficult to devise a plan that would have been both effective and at the same time satisfactory to the overseas possessions.[15]

The Stamp Act was passed in 1765 by a large majority in the House of Commons and without opposition in the House of Lords. It provided that all newspapers, legal documents, and many business instruments should be stamped. The revenue derived from the sale of stamps was to be expended exclusively for

[14] HART, A. B., *American History Told by Contemporaries*, ii, pp. 381-382.

[15] BEER, G. L., *British Colonial Policy*, pp. 284-285; *New York Colonial Documents*, vii, p. 646.

the purpose of "defending, protecting, and securing" the colonies.[16] Americans of good standing accepted the agency for the sale of the stamps, and at first the people seemed to acquiesce in the law. Even such patriots as Otis and Franklin advised their fellow-countrymen to accept the situation, and for a while the opposition was confined mostly to the lawyers.

Patrick
Henry
arouses
opposi-
tion to
the
Stamp
Act

From this attitude of acquiescence the colonies were aroused by the act of the Virginia House of Burgesses under the leadership of Patrick Henry. Since his success in the Parson's Cause the frontiersmen had looked up to this eloquent lawyer as their spokesman and leader. When the question arose in the assembly as to what action should be taken with reference to the Stamp Act, Henry, who had recently been chosen a member, at once took a decided stand in opposition to the measure and offered some very radical resolutions against it. These resolutions were considered too extreme by the patrician conservatives in the assembly —even by some who afterward became leaders in the patriot cause[17]—and a violent debate ensued. Thomas Jefferson, who was a law student in Williamsburg at the time and had slipped away from his studies to listen to the speeches in the House, pronounced the debate over one of these resolutions "most bloody."[18] In a moment of tense excitement Henry gave utterance to a sentiment bolder than any ever yet expressed. "Cæsar," he said, "had his Brutus; Charles the First, his Cromwell, and George the Third——" Being interrupted at this point by numerous cries of "Treason!" he rose to a towering attitude, and finished the sentence by saying, "may profit by their example.[19] If this be

[16] For the full text of this law, see PICKERING, DANBY, *Statutes at Large,* xxvi, pp. 179-204 (5 Geo. III, c. 12). The text is also given in *American History Leaflets,* No. 21, and, somewhat condensed, in MACDONALD, W., *Select Charters,* pp. 282-305.

[17] Among these were George Wythe, Edmund Pendleton, Richard Bland, and Peyton Randolph, the first president of the Continental Congress.

[18] *Historical Magazine,* 2nd series, ii, p. 91.

[19] There is some dispute as to the exact words used by Henry in this famous sentence of his speech. The phraseology given above is that reported by Judge John Tyler (the father of President John Tyler), who was standing by Jefferson and heard the speech (see TYLER, L. G., *Letters and Times of the Tylers,* i, pp. 55-56). Tyler's statement is corroborated by Jefferson (for Jefferson's account of the speech in his own words, see WIRT, WILLIAM, *Life of Patrick Henry,*

treason make the most of it." Henry's eloquence, supported by the sound reasoning of an able colleague, prevailed over the opposition to the extent of securing the passage of all the resolutions but two. One of the resolutions adopted declared "that the general assembly of this colony have the only and sole exclusive right and power to lay taxes and impositions upon the inhabitants of this colony, and that every attempt to vest such power in any person or persons whatsoever, other than the general assembly aforesaid, has a manifest tendency to destroy British as well as American freedom."[20]

These resolutions were published in newspapers and scattered throughout the colonies. They had a great influence in stirring up opposition to the Stamp Act.[21] This opposition found expression in town meetings, discussions in newspapers and pamphlets, and in various other ways. In several of the Northern states there were agreements among merchants to buy no more goods from England until the Stamp Act was repealed. It was hoped that this curtailment of imports from the mother country would result in a serious loss of business to the British merchants and manufacturers and induce them to clamor for its repeal. At the suggestion of Massachusetts an intercolonial congress was held in New York (October, 1765), in which nine colonies were represented. This body formulated a bill of rights and a statement of grievances. It took the position that America cannot be represented in Parliament and therefore cannot be taxed except by the pro-

The Stamp Act Congress

---

pp. 78-79 and note, pp. 83-84). In recent years a document has been found in the French archives which contains an account of Henry's speech given by a Frenchman who was in Williamsburg and heard the oration. This account seems to have been written at the time or soon thereafter as a report to the French government, while the one given above was written in later years from memory by the men who heard it. For this reason some scholars are inclined to accept the Frenchman's report rather than the traditional statement. For the account given by the French agent, see *American Historical Review*, xxvi, p. 745. For a discussion of the speech, see *ibid.*, pp. 726-729. Both contemporary accounts are given in PEASE, T. C., and ROBERTS, A. S., *Selected Readings in American History*, pp. 85-86.

[20] For this resolution and the other six that were adopted, see TYLER, M. C., *Patrick Henry*, pp. 62-63; and WEST, W. M., *Source Book*, pp. 374-375.

[21] Thomas Jefferson said: "Mr. Henry certainly gave the first impulse to the ball of the Revolution" (WIRT, WILLIAM, *op. cit.*, p. 59).

vincial legislatures. Petitions and memorials were drawn up and sent to the king and Parliament.[22]

The Sons of Liberty   In the meantime, revolutionary organizations known as Sons of Liberty had been formed throughout the colonies. At first they acted in secret, but later came out in the open. Their object was to force the stamp agents to resign and to see that the non-importation agreements were enforced. All the stamp agents were compelled or induced to resign and the stamp law was disregarded. A good deal of rioting characterized this period, especially in New England. The burning and pillaging of Chief Justice Hutchinson's house in Boston was the worst example of several disgraceful exhibitions of mob violence in Massachusetts.[23] These and other illegal acts went unpunished because public sentiment favored them.

Repeal of the Stamp Act   As it soon became evident that the Stamp Act could not be enforced, Parliament repealed it. In taking this action Parliament was influenced not only by the opposition in America, but also by the pressure brought to bear on it by the merchants of many English towns, who sent in petitions urging the repeal.[24] The British merchants wanted the Stamp Act rescinded not only because they suffered a loss of trade from the continuance of non-intercourse, but also because they were afraid that the debts owing them by American merchants would not be paid if the strained relations between the homeland and the dominions were not ended. While Parliament was considering the repeal of the act, Benjamin Franklin, who was in London at the time, was called before a committee of the House of Commons (February 13, 1766) to give his views as to the effect of the law on America. He was at his best on this occasion. His ready wit, his sound common sense, and his unusual tact enabled him to make a strong case for his fellow-countrymen without antagonizing those who were in favor of continuing the act.[25]

[22] For the text of the Resolutions of the Stamp Act Congress, see PEASE and ROBERTS, *op. cit.*, pp. 86-88; MACDONALD, W., *Select Charters*, pp. 314-315; and ALMON, J., *Prior Documents*, pp. 27-34.

[23] HART, A. B., *American History Told by Contemporaries,* ii, pp. 397-400. For other contemporary accounts of mob violence against stamp agents, see WEST, W. M., *op. cit.*, pp. 377-380.

[24] For petitions to Parliament of British merchants against the Stamp Act, see CALLENDER, G. S., *Selections from the Economic History of the United States,* pp. 145-148.

[25] For a contemporary report of Franklin's testimony before the

When Parliament rescinded the Stamp Act it coupled with the *The Declaratory Act* act of repeal a resolution declaring its right to make laws binding on the colonies.[26] Even William Pitt, the great friend of the Americans, felt that the authority of Parliament over the dominions should be asserted. The Americans, however, paid little attention to the objectionable Declaratory Act and accepted the annulment of the stamp law with signs of joy and loyalty. At the same time the Sugar Act was modified by Parliament. The duty of threepence a gallon on molasses brought into the continental colonies from the foreign West Indian plantations was changed to a tax of one penny a gallon on all molasses imported into the continental colonies, whether from the British or foreign West Indies. Other changes were also made which rendered the law less objectionable to the colonials.

Soon after the repeal of the Stamp Act, William Pitt, now *The Townshend Acts* the Earl of Chatham, was made the head of a new ministry. This was a coalition cabinet, being composed of Whigs, Tories, and King's Friends. This heterogeneous and uncongenial group could not coöperate effectively, and so was not under the control of Pitt. Besides, it was not long before ill health forced him to retire from the active duties of his important office, and the responsibility for handling the dangerous American situation devolved upon Charles Townshend, Chancellor of the Exchequer. Townshend was not without ability, but he had certain defects of character that rendered him unsuitable for the trying position he was called on to fill. Under his leadership Parliament passed some laws which caused the opposition in America to flare up again.

In their opposition to the Stamp Act the American leaders had made a distinction between an "internal" tax—that is, one collected inside the colonies—and an "external" tax—one collected at the ports. Townshend, therefore, thought that they would submit to an external tax, and so he secured the passage of a law by Parliament (the Townshend Duty Act) imposing a duty on glass, lead, paper, and tea imported into the colonies. One serious objection to the measure was the provision that a part of the

Committee of the House, see PEASE, T. C., and ROBERTS, A. S., *Selected Readings,* pp. 88-96, and SPARKS, J., *Life and Writings of Franklin,* iv, pp. 162-198.

[26] For the text of the Declaratory Act, see PICKERING, DANBY, *Statutes at Large,* xxvii, pp. 19-20 (6 Geo. III, c. 12).

revenue raised under it was to be used to defray the expenses incurred in the administration of justice and in the support of the civil government in those colonies in which it should be found necessary. The revenue accruing from the act could, therefore, be used in paying the salaries of the colonial judges and of the governors. Prior to this time these officials had in the Northern colonies to look to the assemblies for their salaries, and as one branch of the assemblies was chosen by the people, these royal appointees were thus indirectly responsible to the voters. But if their salaries were provided for by a regular fund they would be entirely free from the control of the people's representatives. This law also reaffirmed the legality of the Writs of Assistance and made provision for the granting of them by the colonial courts.

Another one of the unpopular Townshend Acts was a measure which provided for the establishment of a board of customs officials in America. It was hoped that this arrangement would encourage commerce between the mother country and the dominions and facilitate the collection of the rates and duties imposed on commodities exported from or imported into the overseas possessions. Still more objectionable was an act of Parliament (June, 1767) which suspended the assembly of New York because it had refused to make adequate provision for the quartering of the soldiers that were to be stationed there. This act was considered a high-handed measure by the Americans, and one that struck at a fundamental principle of their liberties. For if Parliament could suspend one provincial assembly it might suspend or abolish any or all of the provincial legislatures. The acquiescence in such a practice would involve the giving up of the American contention that the colonial assemblies were independent legislative bodies, acting as little Parliaments in their respective provinces.[27]

"Letters from a Farmer in Pennsylvania"   There were in America at this time some able lawyers who had been educated in England and were well versed in the principles of the English constitution. When the Townshend Acts were made known in America some of the leading lawyers op-

[27] For the text of the Townshend Acts in abbreviated form, see MacDonald, W., *Select Charters,* pp. 321-330. For the full text of these acts see Pickering, Danby, *Statutes at Large,* xxvii, pp. 447-449 (7 Geo. III, c. 41), pp. 505-512 (7 Geo. III, c. 46), pp. 600-605 (7 Geo. III, c. 56).

posed them and brought up strong constitutional arguments against them. Prominent among these able publicists were Charles C. Pinckney and Edward Rutledge of South Carolina, Daniel Dulany of Maryland, and John Dickinson of Pennsylvania. The arguments that exerted the greatest influence were those put forth by Dickinson in a series of pamphlets known as "Letters from a Farmer in Pennsylvania." In these articles, which were written in language simple enough to be comprehended by the uneducated masses, he contended that the new measures were contrary to English law and traditions and should be resisted by the colonials.

If Parliament, as he maintained, could levy a duty on colonial imports, England might, out of selfish considerations, overtax any and all American articles, and in that event "the tragedy of American liberty" would be finished. He boldly declared that "we are only as much dependent on Great Britain as one perfectly free people can be on another."[28] His articles were widely read and his doctrines were accepted by a large proportion of the people throughout the entire country.

The Townshend Duty Act worked an especial hardship on the merchant class, and the opposition to it was strongest in the commercial colonies in the North. Organized resistance was started by the Massachusetts assembly, acting under the leadership of Samuel Adams, for, although he was not a merchant and his own pecuniary interests were not directly affected by the measures, he and his radical followers were more ardent in their opposition to them than were the merchants. A petition to the king was drawn up and letters were sent to the other colonies, asking them to join in expressing disapproval of the law. These letters met with a sympathetic response in many of the colonies. Agreements were entered into by the merchants of Philadelphia, New York, and Boston, and by some of the planters of the Chesapeake and Southern provinces, not to import British goods until the obnoxious measures were repealed.[29] As a result of these non-importation agreements the trade with the mother country was curtailed to a considerable extent; the importation of English

Non-importation agreements

[28] For excerpts from these letters, see TYLER, M. C., *The Literary History of the American Revolution*, i, pp. 235-236.

[29] For the text of the non-importation agreements entered into by the inhabitants of Boston and New York, see CALLENDER, G. S., *op. cit.*, pp. 149-151.

goods into New England and the Middle provinces declined more than sixty per cent.

The "Boston Massacre"

The opposition in Massachusetts took such a violent turn that the British authorities ordered troops to be sent to Boston from Halifax. Two regiments were stationed in the town, against the most urgent protest of the citizens. As the people resented the presence of the soldiers, there was naturally a good deal of friction between them and the townsmen. This culminated in a street fight between a mob and a small band of soldiers in which five civilians were killed and six wounded (1770). In this encounter between soldiers and citizens, the latter were quite as much to blame as the former for the affray. Seven soldiers under the command of Captain Preston were surrounded by a crowd of fifty or sixty men and boys, who insulted the soldiers and, according to some of the evidence, threw snowballs at them and struck one of them with a club. Captain Preston was charged with ordering his men to fire, but this accusation was not proved in the trial. Excitement in Massachusetts was stirred to fever heat by this unfortunate tragedy, which has been improperly termed the "Boston Massacre" by patriotic historians. A distorted account of the occurrence which had been spread abroad did much toward stirring up the people and filling their minds with bitterness toward the mother country.[30]

Partial repeal of the Townshend Duty Act

The amount of revenue collected the first year under the Townshend measure was very little in excess of the cost of collection. Besides, "extraordinary military expenses amounting to $170,000 had in the same period been incurred." The revenue act was evidently a failure and was repealed (April, 1770), except that the tax on tea was retained. This was done to save the principle that Parliament had the right to tax the colonies.

As soon as the Townshend Duty Act was repealed non-importation was given up, except as to tea, and the pledge not to use tea imported from England was regarded rather lightly. The merchants were ready to forego further opposition to the policy of the British government, for the colonials now had no real grievance against the mother country. The conservatives were anxious for peace and quiet and were determined to put a check to the dangerous radicalism that had been aroused. They were afraid that the wind of peaceful opposition started by them

[30] For a contemporary account of this street riot, see HART, A. B., *American History Told by Contemporaries*, ii, pp. 429-431.

would grow into the whirlwind of mob violence. And well might they be uneasy, for the bad feeling caused by the Townshend Acts did not subside when these measures were repealed. It was kept alive by the agitation of radical leaders, who favored a vigorous assertion of colonial rights. In Massachusetts the most outstanding of these agitators was Samuel Adams. But Adams was now handicapped in his fight in that he was without an issue, and he and his party lost popularity and influence during the two years immediately following the repeal of most of the Townshend duties. This change in the situation did not, however, cause any abatement of his opposition to the alleged tyranny of the British government. On the contrary, he continued the attack with the most stubborn persistence, writing forty articles during this period for the radical press, which were characterized by intense bitterness. In this way he hoped to keep alive the spirit of discontent so that it would be ready to flame up again when the next blunder of the British should supply a grievance.

Like Patrick Henry, Samuel Adams was especially fitted for the rôle of revolutionary leader. His experiments in business as a young man had all been failures, and he seemed utterly incapable wherever the handling of finances was involved. But he had exceptional qualifications for political leadership. In the early years of his career as a politician he was identified with the popular party in Boston which was fighting the aristocratic clique that ruled Massachusetts. He was narrow and prejudiced, but very sincere and earnest in his views. He had the courage of his convictions and prejudices and was inclined to fight for both with absolute fearlessness. As a writer he had a clear and straightforward style and was able to present the doctrines borrowed from Locke and other advanced thinkers with unusual vividness and simplicity. The great hold he had upon the people was due not entirely to his sympathy with them and the zeal with which he upheld his views, but in large measure to his great skill in practical politics. He had behind him in Massachusetts a political organization that might well be the envy of the most expert machine politician of today. His zeal for the cause championed by the radical patriots never flagged. He was strongly prejudiced against the British government and felt that its policy was a menace to American liberty. Apparently by 1765 or 1766 he was in favor of autonomy, or legislative independence, for the colo-

Samuel Adams

nies, and he was one of the first among the patriot leaders to advocate separation from England.[31]

Committees of correspondence

In November, 1772, the town meeting of Boston, on the motion of Samuel Adams, appointed a committee to correspond with committees to be appointed by the other towns of the province. These committees were to state the rights of the people and proclaim them to the outside world.[32] The other towns in Massachusetts began at once to appoint the committees, and soon the province was bound together by an organization outside of the law. Other sections followed the example of Massachusetts, and by the middle of the next year six colonies were linked together by committees of correspondence. The foundation was now laid for joint action. After the Boston Tea Party committees of correspondence were formed by the assemblies of the other colonies, and in some of them local committees were also established.

Selected Readings

1. Causes of the Revolution.—Andrews, C. M., *Colonial Background of the American Revolution,* *ch. 3.
2. The New Colonial Policy.—Channing, E., *History of United States,* iii, pp. *29-48.
3. The Sugar Act of 1764.—Beer, G. L., *British Colonial Policy, 1754-1765,* pp. *276-280.
4. The Parson's Cause.—Eckenrode, H. J., *The Revolution in Virginia,* pp. *9-13; Lingley, C. R., *The Transition in Virginia from Colony to Commonwealth,* pp. 27-34.
5. Writs of Assistance.—Van Tyne, C. H., *The Causes of the War of Independence,* pp. *175-179; Fisher, S. G., *The Struggle for American Independence,* i, ch. 4.
6. Taxation as a Cause of Revolt.—Callender, G. S., *Selections from the Economic History of the United States,* pp. *123, 137-140.
7. The Stamp Act.—MacDonald, W., *Select Charters,* pp. 281-305 (the text of the act in abridged form); Howard, G. E., *Preliminaries of the Revolution,* pp. *136-145; Lecky, W. E. H., *The American Revolution,* pp. *67-84.
8. Franklin's Testimony on the Stamp Act.—Bogart, E. L., and Thompson, C. M., *Readings in the Economic History of the United States,* pp. 155-159 (a contemporary account).

[31] For a brief biography of Samuel Adams, see an article by Becker, C. L., in the *Dictionary of American Biography.* For a full and authoritative work on Adams, see Harlow, R. V., *Samuel Adams.*

[32] West, W. M., *A Source Book in American History,* pp. 389-390.

9. The Stamp Act Congress.—MacDonald, *op. cit.*, pp. *313-315; Frothingham, R., *Rise of the Republic of the United States*, pp. 167-190.

10. The Townshend Acts.—MacDonald, *op. cit.*, pp. 320-330; Howard, G. E., *Preliminaries of the Revolution*, pp. *183-192; Fisher, S. G., *The Struggle for American Independence*, i, *chs. 9 and 10.

11. The Virginia Resolutions and Patrick Henry's Speech on Them.— Tyler, M. C., *Patrick Henry*, pp. *57-68.

12. Committees of Correspondence.—Collins, E. D., in the *Annual Report* of the American Historical Association for 1901, i, pp. 245-271.

13. Franklin's Humiliation by the Privy Council.—Trevelyan, G. O., *The American Revolution*, part i, vol. i, pp. *167-174.

14. William Pitt, Earl of Chatham.—Trevelyan, G. O., *George the Third and Charles Fox*, i, pp. *12-35.

CHAPTER XXXI

THE FINAL BREAK

The burning of the *Gaspee*

THE period of calm that followed the partial repeal of the Townshend Acts was soon rudely disturbed by an act of mob violence in Rhode Island. This colony was almost an independent commonwealth and in it imperial authority counted for very little. Smuggling, being easy because of the broken coast line, was widely prevalent, and it was well-nigh impossible to enforce the revenue laws. The British authorities were, however, bent on carrying out the trade regulations in this colony, as well as elsewhere, and Lieutenant Dudingston was sent to Rhode Island in command of an armed schooner, the *Gaspee*. Dudingston was arbitrary and untactful in his methods, and soon public sentiment was strongly aroused against him. One night while the *Gaspee* was grounded on a sandspit, having run aground the afternoon before, a mob boarded her, wounded the commander, overpowered the crew, and burned the vessel (June, 1772).[1] The British authorities were aroused by this highhanded act and were determined to find out and punish its perpetrators. A special court was constituted to inquire into the case and turn over to the British Admiralty all persons found guilty of having participated in the attack. No evidence could be found against anyone, but the measures taken by the imperial authorities were considered a violation of American rights and aroused resentment not only in Rhode Island, but also in other colonies.[2]

The Tea Act

The next occasion of dispute between the colonies and the mother country was the Tea Act (effective May, 1773), which was passed to relieve the financial embarrassment of the East India Company. Prior to the enactment of this measure the East

---

[1] For the primary sources dealing with the destruction of the *Gaspee*, see STAPLES, W. R., *Documentary History of the Destruction of the Gaspee*, or the *Records of the Colony of Rhode Island and Providence Plantations*, vii, pp. 60-192.

[2] See *Rhode Island Colonial Records*, vii, pp. 60-192; ARNOLD, S. G., *History of the State of Rhode Island*, ii, pp. 309-320.

India Company enjoyed the exclusive right to sell tea in the British Isles, but had to pay a heavy revenue tax for the privilege.[3] There was also a requirement that all tea sent to America should pass through English ports, but this provision was disregarded by New England merchants, many of whom bought their supply in Holland and smuggled it into America without paying the high tax. This practice, together with the non-importation agreements in America, cut deeply into the business of the Company. The homeland could not buy all of the Company's output, and there was stored in its warehouses in England a great quantity of tea for which there was no sale. This could be easily disposed of if the Americans could be induced to buy all of their tea in England. It was to bring about this result that the Tea Act was passed. The Company, owing to bad management, the competition of the Dutch, and the expenses incurred in wars with the natives in India, was now in bad financial straits, and the government was anxious to save it from bankruptcy.

The law provided that all duties paid on tea in England should be rebated when it was reshipped to America. The East India Company was also allowed to take from its warehouses the tea stored there and ship it to the colonies without first offering it for public sale as had heretofore been the practice. This provision gave the East India Company a monopoly of the tea trade to America, for with such an advantage it could undersell both the legitimate American merchant and the smuggler, who had to pay a middleman's profit either in England or in Holland. The law, however, did not remit the tax of threepence per pound tha the Townshend Act had placed on all tea brought into the colonies.[4] But this tax was much less than that paid by the English consumers, and so tea in America could be bought at one-half the price paid in England. It was hoped that this low price would cause the colonials to overlook the monopoly feature of the act and buy tea in such quantities as to relieve the East India Company of its financial straits.

By this act Samuel Adams and his radical followers were provided with an issue in their campaign against "British op-

[3] For the text of the law regulating the tea trade of the Company with England, see PICKERING, DANBY, *Statutes at Large* (7 Geo. III, c. 56), xxvii, pp. 600-605.
[4] For the text of this act, see *ibid.* (13 Geo. III, c. 44), xxx, pp. 74-77.

pression." They could now point to a specific grievance and, therefore, could get a hearing when they inveighed against taxation without representation and urged the people to refrain from drinking any tea on which the tax had been paid. They were joined in their opposition by the wealthy class, whose business interests were seriously menaced by the Tea Act, for the monopoly given to the East India Company by the new law struck a severe blow at the prosperity of those merchants who had grown rich by legitimate trade or by smuggling.[5]

The Company appointed agents for the principal American ports, and shiploads of tea were sent over to be received and sold by them. There was, however, so much opposition to the law that the agents in New York, Philadelphia, and Charleston resigned. When the tea-ships arrived at the two first-named cities there was no one to take charge of their cargoes, and so they returned to England without unloading.[6] The arrival of the tea-ships at Charleston led to the calling of mass meetings of the citizens which voted that the tea should not be landed. The consignees were induced to resign and the tea was stored away in the government warehouses by order of the revenue officials because no one appeared to pay the duty. When later (November, 1774) a consignment of seven chests arrived, "an oblation was made to Neptune" of it, as it was emptied into the Cooper River. The tea that had been placed in the government storehouses remained there until after independence was declared, when it was sold at auction and the money appropriated to the patriot cause.[7] When a tea-ship, the *Peggy Stewart*, arrived at Annapolis a mass meeting was

[5] The authorities are not in entire agreement as to whether the merchants or the radicals took the initiative in arousing opposition to the Tea Act. Professor A. M. Schlesinger, in his work, *Colonial Merchants and the American Revolution*, brings forward strong evidence to show that the merchants started the agitation (see pp. 262-264), while R. V. Harlow, in his *Samuel Adams*, contends that in Massachusetts Samuel Adams and his radical associates took the lead in stirring up ill-feeling over the act (see pp. 216-218). See also VAN TYNE, C. H., *Causes of the War of Independence*, pp. 377-378.

[6] *Pennsylvania Magazine of History*, xv, pp. 386-393; WEST, W. M., *A Source Book in American History*, pp. 394-395.

[7] For an account of the tea incident at Charleston, with excerpts from contemporary newspapers, see article by WALLACE, D. D., in the Vanderbilt Southern Historical Society *Publications*, no. 4.

held and it was resolved that the tea should not be landed. Excitement grew more and more intense until finally the ship and its cargo were burned by a mob.

It was in Massachusetts, however, that the opposition assumed the most menacing attitude. The Company made the mistake of choosing as agents in Boston two sons and a nephew of Thomas Hutchinson, the unpopular governor of Massachusetts. When the tea-ships reached Boston the agents would not resign and the governor would not grant the vessels a permit to return to England. The people were determined that the tea should not be received by the consignees or sold at auction for the revenue dues. A large mass meeting was held in Old South Church in Boston (November 29, 1773), at which it was voted that the tea on board the ships then in the harbor should never be landed.[8] In this meeting and in another held on December 19 Samuel Adams took the leading part. At the end of the second meeting a mob of fifty or sixty men, dressed as Indians, went and threw all the tea overboard, while a great crowd of spectators looked on in silence.[9] This destruction of private property was condoned by the Massachusetts government and warmly approved by public sentiment. Nothing was done by the town or provincial authorities to prevent or punish the crime.

The effect that this riot had on sentiment in America and England and on British policy gives it a significance out of all proportion to its character as an unfortunate act of an undisciplined mob. In the other colonies there was considerable public sentiment that indorsed the illegal method of opposition practiced by Boston, though quite a number of moderate men, like Franklin, condemned the act as an unwarranted exhibition of the mob spirit.[10] In England public opinion was strong against the

[8] For the minutes of the tea meeting, see Massachusetts Historical Society *Proceedings,* 1st series, xx, pp. 10-17.

[9] For a brief account of the tea party by an eye-witness, see HART, A. B., *American History Told by Contemporaries,* ii, pp. 431-433.

[10] SMYTH, A. H., ed., *Franklin's Writings,* vi, p. 179.
John Adams regarded the destruction of the tea as a "magnificent movement" and one that was absolutely necessary. The Bostonians, he thought, had no alternative but to destroy the tea or let it be landed (ADAMS, C. F., *The Life and Works of John Adams,* ii, pp. 323-324, Diary).

destroyers, and even friends of America, like William Pitt, condemned "the late illegal and violent proceedings at Boston."[11]

The year 1774 marks the date at which the dispute between the mother country and the dominions ceased to be a family quarrel and became an irrepressible conflict. It was in this year that Parliament undertook to punish Massachusetts for the Boston Tea Party by passing four coercive measures, which were known by the colonials as the "Intolerable Acts." These laws were all very unwise and only aggravated the trouble that they were intended to allay. In entering upon this policy Parliament was acting like a schoolmaster trying to restore order in a school which had gotten beyond his control. The effort to discipline the chief offender into good behavior not only failed, but it resulted in throwing the whole school into commotion. The enactment of these statutes started a train of events that led directly to the separation of the American colonies from the homeland.[12]

The "Intolerable Acts"   The first of these measures (the Boston Port Act) provided that the harbor of Boston should be closed to commerce, except in the bare necessaries, until the tea that had been destroyed was paid for. The second (the Massachusetts Government Act) made a change in the charter of Massachusetts which lessened the power of the people in the government of the province. By the third (the Administration of Justice Act) officials of the crown in Massachusetts who should be accused of capital offenses in connection with the discharge of their duties were to be sent to England or some other colony for trial, provided the governor should think that they would not receive a fair trial in the local courts. The fourth and last of the objectionable coercive measures (the Quartering Act) applied not to Massachusetts alone, but to all the British dominions in North America. This law authorized the governor of any province to requisition for the use of the British soldiers any barns, outhouses, or vacant buildings that might be needed for the proper quartering of the troops, "making a reasonable allowance for the same."[13]

[11] Quoted by CHANNING, op. cit., iii, p. 133, note. See also VAN TYNE, C. H., Causes of the War of Independence, p. 392.

[12] For the discussions in Parliament on three of these measures, see FORCE, PETER, American Archives, 4th series, i, pp. 35-131.

[13] The text of these laws in abbreviated form is given in MACDONALD, W., Select Charters, pp. 337-356. The full text can be found in PICKERING, DANBY, Statutes at Large, xxx, pp. 336-341, 367-371,

The Quebec Act is also sometimes classed as one of the "In- tolerable Acts" and was "regarded at the time as one of the most serious grievances of the colonies." By this measure provision was made for the organization of civil government in the Illinois region and for a better administration of the other territory acquired from France by the Treaty of 1763. The boundaries of Quebec were extended southward to include the territory between the Ohio and Mississippi rivers and the Great Lakes. French law was to be used in the decision of civil suits, which meant that such cases were to be tried without a jury. Religious freedom was guaranteed to the Catholics, and their clergy were allowed to collect tithes from the people. The administration of the province was centralized under the control of the king, as the people had not been accustomed to and were not yet ready for self-government.[14] In passing the law Parliament had acted from the best of motives and with no thought of persecuting or punishing the complaining colonies. It was an honest and wise effort to give the French people religious freedom and a good form of government. Since 1763 the eighty thousand French Canadians had been governed according to the provisions of the hastily-drawn Proclamation of 1763. They were put under English law and court procedure, and the promise of religous freedom made in 1763 had not been fully kept. As Catholics they were subject to certain disabilities under English procedure and could not always get justice in the courts. Moreover, nothing had been done toward establishing a civil government in the Illinois region. It was, therefore, necessary to change the administration in Canada and the Northwest if the people there were to be fairly dealt with.

Unfortunately, however, the new law, coming as it did about the time of the coercive acts (1774), was considered a punitive measure and strong opposition was voiced against it. Objection was made to the clause providing for the collection of tithes, on the ground that it conferred a special favor on the Roman Catholic Church. The leaders appealed to the anti-Catholic prejudices of the masses and held up before them the bogey of papal domi-

---

381-390, 410. A good brief account of the Parliamentary debates on these acts is given in VAN TYNE, C. H., *Causes of the War of Independence*, pp. 393-401.

[14] For the text of this law, see PICKERING, DANBY, *Statutes at Large*, xxx, pp. 549-554. A brief summary of the provisions of the act is given in CHANNING, E., *History of the United States,* iii, p. 153.

nation. It was also contended that the law would establish an autocratic government and would deprive Englishmen of the right of trial by jury. The extension of the boundaries of Quebec southward so as to include the Northwest was especially resented, as it shut off further expansion westward on the part of the older colonies. Massachusetts, Connecticut, and Virginia, which claimed the western territory, felt that they were being deprived of lands that had been granted to them by their charters.

The coercive measures rigidly enforced

For the enforcement of the punitive measures, General Gage was sent to Massachusetts as governor with four regiments of soldiers. Gage was a mild-mannered man with an American wife, and it was hoped that he would not be very strict in the performance of his disagreeable duty. This expectation, however, was dispelled when he began to carry out his instructions to the very letter. The coercive measures as enforced by Gage aroused the antagonism of all the other colonies, for they felt that Massachusetts was being punished too severely for her offense. To organize this sympathy and make it effective for united resistance the first Continental Congress was convened in Philadelphia in September, 1774. The call for this meeting was issued by the Virginia Burgesses acting in an unofficial capacity at Raleigh Tavern after the assembly had been dissolved by Governor Dunmore. The governor had dissolved the House of Burgesses because of its adoption of a resolution setting aside June 1 (the date on which the Boston harbor was to be closed) as a day of fasting and prayer.[15]

Radicals and conservatives

During the long, intermittent quarrel between the colonies and the mother country there had grown up in America two distinct parties—the radicals, who advocated an aggressive policy of opposition to the English government, and the conservatives, who were inclined to hold back and favor conciliation. In the Northern and Middle colonies the former party was recruited mainly from the lower and middle classes, while the latter group was made up largely of persons of wealth and education. This cleavage in parties was not due entirely to a difference of attitude toward imperial policy, but was occasioned in part by the desire of the unprivileged class to gain for itself a voice in the provincial government. Members of the privileged group, which had hitherto exercised an unchallenged leadership in colonial administration, were menaced with the loss of their power at home. They also

[15] WEST, W. M., *A Source Book in American History*, pp. 396-401.

feared that if the resistance to the recent measures of Parliament were not checked it would degenerate into mob violence. In that event government would become unsettled and the security of their property would be jeopardized. Some of them, therefore, called for a halt in the policy of opposition to British authority and were branded as unpatriotic Tories by their more ardent fellow-countrymen. Others of them went along with the tide, though rather reluctantly, and supported the patriot cause.

In the tobacco colonies the large planters were also identified with the radical movement. Many of them were heavily in debt and so were dissatisfied with British rule. Moreover, they had always been very impatient of any restraint on their individual freedom, and they regarded the recent laws of Parliament as an unwarranted interference with their personal rights. In the Carolinas those who were opposing British control—Whigs, as they were called—were in the majority in the Tidewater Belt, while the Tories had considerable strength in the back country.[16] The infant colony of Georgia was still in leading strings to the mother country and did not feel like straining the ties that bound it to the homeland. Moreover, the hostile Creek Indians at their back made the Georgians cautious in their effort to stand alone. Prior to 1774, men in America could argue about their grievances "without calling for pistols and coffee for two."[17] Now the lines were sharply drawn between radicals and conservatives, and the feeling between the two parties had become too strong for compromise.

All the colonies except Georgia sent representatives to the first Continental Congress. It included in its small membership of fifty-six some of the leading men in America.[18] This assembly had no legal authority and was only an advisory body. There were two main parties, one favoring conciliation and the other resistance. The latter, ably led by the Virginia and Massachusetts representatives, were in the ascendancy.[19] Early in the session

The first Continental Congress

[16] VAN TYNE, C. H., *The Loyalists in the American Revolution*, pp. 96-98.

[17] VAN TYNE, C. H., *Causes of the War of Independence*, p. 449.

[18] When the first meeting was held in Carpenter's Hall, only forty-five members were present, representing all the colonies but North Carolina and Georgia (FORD, W. C., ed., *Journals of the Continental Congress*, i, pp. 113-114). See also HART, A. B., *American History Told by Contemporaries*, ii, pp. 434-439.

[19] The Virginia delegation included in its membership Patrick

they secured the indorsement by Congress of the "Resolves" that had been adopted by Suffolk County, Massachusetts. These resolutions declared that Massachusetts should not obey the recent acts of Parliament and threatened the British government with forcible resistance.

The conservatives, led by Joseph Galloway of Pennsylvania, favored a policy of reconciliation that would safeguard the rights of the colonies and keep them in the British empire. Galloway proposed a plan of union which provided for a president-general over the colonies to be appointed by the king, and a grand council, the members of which were to be chosen by the colonial assemblies. This council was to have "legislative authority to regulate all affairs in which Great Britain, the colonies as a whole, or any two colonies might be interested." Acts of the grand council were not to be effective until approved by the president-general. Galloway's plan was tabled and afterwards deleted from the minutes.[20]

The delegates affirmed their loyalty to the king and sent a petition to him asking a redress of grievances. Addresses were sent out to the people of England, Quebec, and the thirteen colonies, setting forth the rights of the Americans and the grievances they had suffered at the hands of the British government.[21] A "Declaration of Rights and Grievances" was voted, in which the body set forth the ideals and political theory of the colonials. In these resolutions it was stated that the rights of the Americans "to life, liberty, and property were secured by the principles of the British Constitution, the unchanging laws of nature, and their colonial charters." They could be taxed only by their own representative assemblies, though their external commerce might be regulated by Parliament, provided that in such regulation there was no "idea of taxation, external or internal."[22] It was also agreed that a second congress should meet in May of the next

---

Henry, Washington, and Peyton Randolph, the last named being chosen president of the Congress. The leading representatives from Massachusetts were John and Samuel Adams (*Journals of the Continental Congress,* i. p. 14).

[20] BOYD, J. P., *Anglo-American Union,* pp. 32-38, 112-114 (text of the Galloway Plan).

[21] *Journals of the Continental Congress,* i, pp. 81-101, 115-121.

[22] VAN TYNE, C. H., *Causes of the War of Independence,* p. 440; WEST, W. M., *A Source Book in American History,* pp. 421-426.

year, provided the British government had not redressed their grievances in the meantime.[23]

The most important act of the Congress was the signing of a non-intercourse agreement, known as the Continental Association. By this agreement the members entered into a solemn pledge in behalf of themselves and their constituents not to import goods from England after December 1, 1774, nor to export any of their own commodities except rice to the British Isles after September 10, 1775. Committees were to be appointed in every community to look after the enforcement of the agreement.[24] Although the Association did not rest on any legal sanction, it was strongly indorsed by public sentiment and was carried out more widely and successfully than had been any of the other attempts to boycott England. Effective machinery for enforcing the Association was organized in all the colonies except Georgia, and the people were more obedient to its provisions than they were to the laws of the provincial legislatures.[25]

The Association

In the meantime conditions in Massachusetts were drifting rapidly toward revolution. The coercive policy of the British government left only two alternatives, submission or rebellious resistance to the authority of the government. The people in Massachusetts, urged on by Samuel Adams and other radical leaders, determined on the latter policy. A revolutionary government was established, an army was raised, and the authority of General Gage, the legal governor, was defied. Gage learned that the insurgents were collecting military stores at Concord, a village about eighteen miles from Boston, and sent a small body of troops to seize these supplies. In the early morning of April 19, 1775, the British soldiers had reached Lexington on their march. Here a body of armed men was encountered who refused to lay down their arms when ordered to do so. Firing ensued and

Lexington and Concord

[23] For an excellent discussion of the sources of information for the first Continental Congress, see WINSOR, J., *Narrative and Critical History*, vi, pp. 98-104.

[24] For the text of the Association, see *Journals of the Continental Congress*, pp. 75-80; also WEST, W. M., *A Source Book in American History*, pp. 427-432; also PEASE, T. C., and ROBERTS, A. S., *Selected Readings in American History*, pp. 116-122.

[25] HART, A. B., *American History Told by Contemporaries*, ii, pp. 439-441.

eight militiamen were killed and ten wounded.[26] The British went on to Concord and destroyed the supplies there; but meanwhile the country around had been aroused and a number of militiamen had assembled to strike at the British. Hiding behind trees, rocks, and fences, they fired at the redcoats on their return march, and "there was a crimson trail from Concord to Boston."[27] At once armed men hurried to Boston from all quarters in New England and besieged Gage in the town. The war had now begun, and the news of bloodshed flew like wild-fire, arousing the people in all the provinces. Patriotic resolutions were voted and preparations for war were made throughout the country. The most outspoken of these resolutions were those adopted by the people of Mecklenburg County, North Carolina.[28]

The second Continental Congress

In the midst of this excitement the second Continental Congress met at Philadelphia on May 10, 1775. This body had charge of federal affairs until March 1, 1781, at which time the Articles of Confederation went into effect. In it sat representatives from all the colonies, though in some cases they were chosen by only a very small minority of the people. The governors had been instructed by the British authorities not to permit the choice of delegates to another congress,[29] and so the representatives attending the first session were selected by revolutionary conventions. Owing to this method of election the delegates of radical sympathies were in the majority, which might not have been the case if they had been chosen by the regular colonial assemblies. The predominance of the radical element in the new Congress is also explained in part by the fact that the conservative, aristocratic leaders did not, as a rule, take an active part in the election of delegates. They failed to do so partly because they were intimidated by the radicals and partly because they were unwilling to stoop to the undignified practices that characterized political campaigns in that day. One faction of the representatives, ably led by John Adams, favored a declaration of independence. But

[26] We do not know by which side the first shot was fired. For an excellent collection of documents on the events at Lexington and Concord, see McLaughlin, A. C., *et al.*, *Source Problems in United States History*, pp. 13-54.

[27] Van Tyne, C. H., *Causes of the War of Independence*, p. 455.

[28] For the text of these bold resolutions, see *North Carolina Records*, ix, pp. 1282-1284.

[29] *Ibid.*, ix, p. 1108.

the more conservative element, led by John Dickinson of Pennsylvania, was opposed to a complete break with the mother country. Through the influence of the conservatives, an address reiterating loyalty to the king was again voted by the body. The radical party, however, were able to carry through some measures that virtually meant a declaration of war on England. The army that had gathered around Boston was taken over by Congress, and provision was made for enlarging it by the addition of ten companies to be raised in Pennsylvania, Maryland, and Virginia. George Washington was appointed commander-in-chief of the army. This was done at the suggestion of John Adams, who wanted to win the support of the South to the cause of Massachusetts.[30]

Congress was particularly fortunate in its choice of a commander-in-chief, for Washington was easily the best man in America for the place. Not that he excelled all of his compatriots in intellectual ability, for in mental attainments he was outranked by Franklin and other prominent statesmen. Nor was he the most noted and experienced military leader that favored the patriot cause, as both Charles Lee and Thomas Conway (who were later officers in the American army) had achieved a fame on the battlefields of Europe which outshone the prestige won by him in the trans-Alleghany wilderness. But no other American at that time possessed in so large a degree those qualities of mind and character that were needed in the chief commander of the loosely-organized forces known as the Continental Army. To inspire the respect of the undisciplined rabble placed under his command and direct its energies into effective service required more than technical skill—it called for moral qualities of the highest order; and it was in loftiness of character that Washington towered above most men of his and every other age. His fine qualities, however, did not appear on the surface, and a casual appraisal would have led to an underestimate of his ability. "His mind was not quick or remarkably original. His conversation had no brilliancy or wit," and "he was entirely without the gift of eloquence." Exceptionally modest and taciturn, he would have appeared to the superficial observer only as a distinguished-looking country gentleman whose behavior was characterized by dignity and courtesy.

Washington

[30] See Adams's Diary in ADAMS, C. F., *The Life and Works of John Adams*, ii, pp. 415-418.

But the keen analyst of personality would have also noted his sterling honesty, his sound judgment, and his unusual self-control. Always a gentleman and ever actuated by a high sense of honor, "he carried into public life the severe standards of private morals." He had the physical courage that could face danger without panic, and the moral fortitude that could meet misfortune without discouragement and defeat without despair. During those trying times when the prospects of the American cause were most gloomy he maintained a calm optimism and an unruffled serenity that held out hope to those of little faith; and when victory had come and the plaudits of the world were laid at his feet, he received his honors with a quiet modesty that ruled out all self-complacent exultation. Although he presented to strangers an exterior of stiff dignity and cold formality, he revealed to those who were privileged to know his inner life a warm emotional temperament that attracted the intimate friendship of romantic enthusiasts like Lafayette and other young dreamers.[31]

Despite the protestations of loyalty on the part of Congress, war was now definitely launched. It is not easy to understand why England and America had to resort to a long, fratricidal war to settle their differences.[32] A partial explanation lies in the fact that the grievances against the mother country came at a time when the dominions were suffering from economic depression, which was a part of the aftermath of the Seven Years' War. The commercial classes in the New England and Middle colonies were especially affected by the hard times experienced by nearly all the colonies during the decade preceding the outbreak. The economic situation was aggravated by the commercial restraints imposed by the British government and the non-intercourse agreements entered into by the colonials themselves.

The crisis was also awkwardly handled by the British government. The policy of the mother country toward the colonies was that of a vacillating parent toward an obstreperous child. It was irritating enough to arouse opposition, but not firm and severe

[31] For an excellent appraisal of Washington's character, very favorable, by an Englishman, see LECKY, W. E. H., *The American Revolution*, pp. 208-214.

[32] For a declaration by Congress (July 6, 1775) giving the reasons that compelled that body to declare war, see FLÜGEL, F., and FAULKNER, H. U., *Readings in the Economic and Social History of the United States*, pp. 4-9.

enough to compel obedience. The situation called for the active exercise of all the political wisdom that the empire could command. But conditions in England were such that the best statesmanship of the time was employed not in solving the problem, but in further complicating it. The wise and statesmanlike policy advocated by Pitt, Burke, and the other friends of America was not adopted. On the other hand, their advocacy of this policy had the effect of encouraging the opposition on the part of the Americans, who entertained an exaggerated notion as to the strength of English sentiment in their favor.

In joining battle with the strongest of the European powers, the American colonies showed a hardihood of spirit that few prudent countries would dare emulate. Britain had a man-power which was five times as great as that of the thirteen colonies, and could point to one hundred fighting ships to their one. There was a still greater inequality as to the financial resources of the contestants. England was the richest country in the world and had good credit and a well-oiled tax machine that enabled the government to raise adequate sums of money. In the dominions, on the other hand, there was very little surplus capital, and the credit of the government was too poor to attract what little there was into the public coffers. Moreover, the lack of federal machinery for imposing and collecting taxes, coupled with the strong feeling on the part of the people against taxation, made the raising of a sufficient revenue an impossible undertaking.

There was also a woeful lack in America of that military preparedness without which the waging of war becomes a hazardous enterprise. As the basis for an army there were about three hundred thousand militiamen scattered throughout the thirteen provinces, but they were little better than raw recruits, as they had received only from two to four days' training a year. The fortifications had been neglected and allowed to fall into disrepair, and there was an "utter dearth of every weapon suited to the iron hand of Mars."[33] It was very difficult to overcome these handicaps after the war had started, for England's control of the sea in the beginning enabled her to shut off to a great extent the war supplies that otherwise would have been brought to the colonies from Europe. This disadvantage was not entirely overcome even after Spain and France had entered the lists against Great Britain and had challenged her naval supremacy.

[33] VAN TYNE, C. H., *England and America*, p. 128.

The men who constituted the American forces were in large measure undisciplined as well as untrained. General Montgomery in the early part of the war complained that the soldiers were licentious and mutinous and that the "privates [were] all generals."[34] The men were enlisted for short periods, and often they could not be induced to remain with the army after their terms had expired. It was difficult to secure sufficient enlistments to keep the regular army up to the requisite strength, although bounties were offered to volunteers, and late in the war drafting was tried in several of the states. One cause of the difficulty in securing recruits was the fact that the army could not offer the inducements held out by the occupations of civil life. There was a great demand for labor, and much better wages were paid in industry than in the service. Besides, enterprising civilians had excellent opportunities for profiteering, for "many caterpillars were allowed to hang on the branches of commerce."[35] In competition with the strong bids that industry and trade were making for men, the army could only offer promises of small wages, the payment of which was often six months in arrears. So much was this the case that the soldiers were said to be "fed with promises" and clothed "with filthy rags." The hospital service was "badly organized, ill-supplied, [and] dishonestly administered."[36] Much unnecessary suffering resulted from this poor management, as in the camps there were thousands of the sick that were not properly cared for.

There were, to be sure, quite a number of patriots who were fighting not for pay or any other kind of material reward, but for their home altars and a righteous cause. The men of this type constituted a reliable nucleus on which the commanding officer could always depend and without which the army could not have held together. They were not "summer soldiers and sunshine patriots," but remained true to the cause under the most adverse circumstances. Their steadfastness was not shaken by the gloom that attended Washington's retreat across New Jersey or by the terrible sufferings endured at Valley Forge. Unfortunately, however, this Gideon's band was too small to overthrow the hosts of Midian without the aid of less worthy associates.

The regular army was supplemented at times by the state

[34] Quoted by VAN TYNE, *op. cit.*, p. 133.
[35] *Ibid.*, p. 131.
[36] *Ibid.*, p. 141.

militia. This part of the fighting force was especially unsatisfactory. The militiamen were not only untrained, but often acted in a cowardly and unpatriotic manner. They would leave at the end of their terms of enlistment despite the urgency of the need. "Even in the hour of supreme danger they would not wait a few days to save the cause." They were adept in making excuses to get away and great numbers of them deserted. Such an unreliable soldiery was of little or no value for long-continued military operations, though it was often useful in short campaigns. The militiamen were usually good marksmen and fought well in defending their farms and villages in border warfare.

When we consider that the undisciplined and unmanageable groups of men which constituted the American army were pitted against a military machine which some decades earlier had won under Marlborough the victories of Blenheim and Malplaquet and was destined a few decades later to encompass under Wellington the downfall of Napoleon, it seems a miracle that they could have held their own in a struggle that lasted seven long years. But a closer view reveals the fact that the inequalities were not so great as they appear from a casual observation.

In prosecuting the war Great Britain was at a disadvantage that could not be easily overcome by numbers, wealth, and efficient organization. The greatest drawback to English success in the contest was that of distance. To hold a large military force at arm's length is a difficult feat even for a rich nation to perform. With the seagoing vessels of that day it was a stupendous undertaking to transport a large army across seas and sustain it three thousand miles from its base. The costs and hazards of the transatlantic voyages were greatly enhanced by official corruption. Even after the ships approached the American shore, they were still beset with difficulties and dangers, as there were no lighthouses to guide them along the ill-charted coast. After the troops had overcome all of these difficulties and had safely landed, they were confronted with new obstacles growing out of the nature of the country. There was no strategic center which would prove a key to the whole military situation, but, on the contrary, a wide expanse of country, all of which would have to be overrun before victory could be assured. The British forces, therefore, had to be divided up between a number of posts, and no operations on a big scale could be carried on. Climate, as well as physical geography, was on the side of the patriots. "The winter rigors of the North, the torrid summers in the South, malaria over great areas of the seaboard, fought in the main on the side of the rebellion."[37]

It was difficult to secure enlistments in the British service, for the treatment accorded the private soldier was such as to make life almost unendurable for men of spirit. A wide social gulf separated officers from privates, and the latter were treated with haughty injustice and overbearing cruelty. They were kicked and caned by petty officials and cowed into discipline by methods that no reasonable man of today would think of applying to dumb animals. On shipboard they were crowded into uncomfortable quarters and were served with unpalatable and unhealthful food, which frequently brought on the scurvy. "His [the private soldier's] daily bread was often full of vermin, his bacon sometimes four or five years old. War profiteers furnished meat that had lain in salt for years."[38] To these objections to enlisting in the service must be added the disinclination that the average Englishman had to fighting his kinsmen in America. It is no wonder, therefore, that volunteering was so slow that the British military authorities had to hire many of their troops from the German princes. It is true that Howe had, when he landed at New York in 1776, a force larger than the one with which Wellington afterward defeated Napoleon at Waterloo, yet Britain was never able to keep in the field as many troops as the task required. When Clinton's army was at its greatest strength it numbered only thirty-four thousand men, and they were scattered over the mainland and island colonies.

The Americans also seem to have had some advantage over their opponents as to the ability and efficiency of their military leaders. Washington, true to his aristocratic instincts, tried to recruit all of his officers from the class of gentlemen, feeling that only men of dignity could command the respect of the soldiers. This aim was not realized, however, for many of the subordinate officers fell far below the standard that their great commander had set for them. As the lower officials were chosen by their own men, they often resorted to cheap demagoguery to secure their election. They would permit their soldiers to indulge in practices that were destructive of discipline and would sometimes even encourage them in pillage. In speaking of the officers

[37] *Ibid.*, pp. 122-123.
[38] *Ibid.*, p. 124.

in 1776, Washington said that "except in a few instances [they were] not worth the bread they eat." But Washington was more fortunate in his subordinates of higher rank. Some of the generals who served under him were military leaders of real ability, while several of the others performed their duties with average efficiency. In the former class belong Montgomery, Greene, and Arnold, the last named being especially noted for daring initiative, dashing courage, and heroic endurance.

The English army, on the other hand, could not boast of an able leadership. Howe was well trained in the science and art of war, but for some reason, not fully understood, in conducting his campaigns in America he displayed a lack of energy and promptitude which often kept him from reaping the fruits of successful operations. The policy of his successor, Clinton, was characterized by the same inactivity. It was this dilatoriness that was mainly responsible for Cornwallis's downfall at Yorktown. For six weeks Clinton was advised by his subordinates in a council of war to send aid to Cornwallis, and if this wise suggestion had been promptly acted on, the result for the American cause might have been quite different. As a rule, the British commanders were better trained both in theory and by practice than were their colonial rivals, but the experience acquired in Europe was not often of much practical value in America, owing to the great difference in the way in which war was conducted on the two continents.

At the beginning of the year 1775 the majority of American leaders were opposed to independence, although the Continental Congress was soon to issue a declaration of war on England. The radicals in Congress who favored separation were in the first half of the year largely in the minority. But it was not long before King George and Parliament entered upon a policy that aroused still further resentment in America and greatly strengthened the party in the dominions that favored separation. The king in a proclamation (issued August 23), and in an address made before Parliament two months later, took the position that the colonials were rebels and should be treated as such.[39] This suggestion of the king was followed by an act of Parliament prohibiting all trade and intercourse with the continental colonies

Independence declared

[39] See FORCE, PETER, *American Archives*, 4th Series, iii, pp. 240-241, or American Antiquarian Society's *Transactions*, xii, pp. 228-229.

as long as they were in a state of rebellion.[40] Under these condi
tions it was both inconsistent and unwise for the American dominions to continue to declare their loyalty to the British empire. If
they should assert their independence they would be in a position
to get recognition of their rights as belligerents by foreign powers and might be able to make military alliances or commercial
treaties with them. Early in 1776 sentiment in favor of independence was widespread throughout the colonies. This sentiment had been greatly increased by a pamphlet written by Thomas
Paine, an Englishman who had been living in Philadelphia for
about a year. In this pamphlet, which he styled *Common Sense*,
he made a powerful appeal for independence. It was written in a
clear but brilliant style and had an immense circulation.[41] The
radical party was now in control in Congress and that body was
ready to break the bonds that held the colonies to the British
empire.

North Carolina instructed her delegates in Congress (April
12) to support independence,[42] and like instructions were issued by
other colonies. But before the Congress had voted in favor of
independence, Virginia, one of the most influential of the provinces, had announced her separation from the mother country.[43]
Her example exerted a powerful influence on those colonies that
were hesitating to break the political bonds that held them to the
homeland. Virginia also instructed her delegates in Congress
(May 15) to move the adoption by that body of a declaration of
independence for all the colonies. In obedience to this instruction,
Richard Henry Lee moved (June 7, 1776) that the united colonies be declared "free and independent states."[44] A committee,
consisting of Jefferson, John Adams, Franklin, Roger Sherman,
and Robert R. Livingston, was appointed to draft a declaration
of independence. The famous document in its original form was

[40] PICKERING, DANBY, *Statutes at Large*, xxxi, pp. 135-154.

[41] For an excellent paraphrase of *Common Sense*, which adheres
closely to the original text, see TYLER, M. C., *The Literary History
of the American Revolution*, i, pp. 462-468.

[42] For the text of this resolution, see CHANNING, *op. cit.*, iii, pp.
191-192, note. See also *Records of North Carolina*, x, p. 512.

[43] Virginia adopted her Bill of Rights on June 12 and her Constitution June 29. For the text of the Virginia Bill of Rights and Constitution, see THORPE, F. N., *Constitutions, Charters*, etc., pp. 3812-
3819.

[44] *Journals of Congress*, v, p. 425.

entirely the work of Jefferson, except for a few verbal changes made by John Adams and Franklin.[45] The draft thus prepared was presented to Congress, and its acceptance was warmly urged by John Adams. On July 4, 1776, the Declaration was adopted by that body by a vote of twelve colonies after some rather important changes had been made in the first draft.

In making its revisions Congress struck out of the original document certain "passages which conveyed censures on the English people" and a clause that brought a severe indictment against George III for forcing African slaves on the colonies.[46] The former elision was made because it was feared that if the allusions to the English people were retained it would alienate some of the friends of America in the homeland. The latter clause "was struck out," as Jefferson wrote, "in complaisance to South Carolina and Georgia, who had never attempted to restrain the importation of slaves, and who, on the contrary, still wished to continue it. Our Northern brethren also, I believe, felt a little tender under those censures; for tho' their people have very few slaves themselves, yet they had been pretty considerable carriers of them to others."[47]

Two weeks after the Declaration was adopted, Congress voted (July 19) that it should be engrossed on parchment and signed by the members of the body. This order was carried out, and on August 2 all of the members who were present signed the Declaration, and those who were absent later attached their signatures to the famous document.[48] The Act of July 4 was greeted by the ringing of bells, the booming of cannon, or other like signs of rejoicing in all the colonies. It was a great victory for the radical leaders. Hereafter all who remained loyal to the king were classed as enemies of their country.

The Declaration states the natural rights of man, enumerates the grievances suffered by the colonies which justify their sepa-

[45] For Jefferson's statement regarding the authorship of the Declaration, see BECKER, CARL, *The Declaration of Independence*, p. 136.

[46] The original text with the emendations made by Congress is shown in *ibid.*, pp. 174-184.

[47] FORD, W. C., ed., *Writings of Thomas Jefferson*, i, p. 28; quoted by BECKER, CARL, *op. cit.*, pp. 171-172.

[48] BECKER, *op. cit.*, pp. 184-185. The engrossed and signed copy of the Declaration of Independence is now on exhibition in the Library of Congress.

ration from the mother country, and declares that "these United Colonies are, and of right ought to be, free and independent states." The doctrines enunciated in it were drawn largely from Locke's writings, especially his "Second Essay of Government," and many of them, therefore, were not new, even to the Americans of that day. But in arranging them and giving them clear and forceful expression Jefferson displayed marked originality. He was quite happy as a phrase-maker, and he succeeded in casting familiar ideas into a form that makes the Declaration of Independence a literary masterpiece.

SELECTED READINGS

1. Burning of the *Gaspee.*—Channing, E., *History of the United States*, iii, pp. *124-127.
2. The Boston Tea Party.—Howard, G. E., *Preliminaries of the Revolution*, ch. 15; Van Tyne, C. H., *Causes of the War of Independence*, pp. *376-390; *Old South Leaflets*, iii, *no. 68; Fisher, S. G., *Struggle for American Independence*, i, *ch. 14.
3. The Coercive Acts.—Van Tyne, C. H., *Causes of the War of Independence*, pp. *390-401; Howard, *op. cit.*, pp. *272-279; Lecky, W. E. H., *The American Revolution*, pp. *165-170.
4. The Quebec Act.—Van Tyne, C. H., *Causes of the War of Independence*, pp. *401-407; Alvord, C. W., *The Mississippi Valley in British Politics*, ii, pp. 216-247, especially pp. 234-247.
5. The First Continental Congress.—Van Tyne, C. H., *Causes of the War of Independence*, pp. *432-443; Howard, *op. cit.*, *ch. 16; MacDonald, W., *Select Charters*, pp. *166-171, 176-183; Fisher, *op. cit.*, i, *chs. 19 and 20.
6. The Continental Association.—Van Tyne, C. H., *Causes of the War of Independence*, pp. *441-449; Fisher, *op. cit.*, i, pp. *234-237.
7. First Session of the Second Continental Congress (1775).—Channing, *op. cit.*, iii, pp. *161-163, and Fisher, *op. cit.*, i, *ch. 27.
8. *Common Sense* by Thomas Paine.—Trevelyan, G. O., *The American Revolution*, part ii, vol. i, pp. *147-155; Tyler, M. C., *Literary History of the American Revolution*, i, pp. *462-481; Van Tyne, C. H., *Causes of the War of Independence*, pp. *323-333.
9. The Philosophy of the Declaration of Independence.—Friedenwald, H., *The Declaration of Independence*, *ch. 9.
10. Drafting the Declaration.—Becker, C. L., *The Declaration of Independence*, *ch. 4; Van Tyne, C. H., *Causes of the War of Independence*, *ch. 17.
11. Historical Antecedents of the Declaration.—Becker, C. L., *The Declaration of Independence*, chs. 2 and 3.

CHAPTER XXXII

THE WAR FOR INDEPENDENCE

ON RECEIVING his appointment as commander-in-chief of the American forces, Washington proceeded to Boston to take charge of the army there. It consisted of about sixteen hundred volunteers from the New England states and later of about three thousand additional troops from Pennsylvania, Maryland, and Virginia. It was an undisciplined and unorganized body of men, and the officers were dissatisfied and jealous of one another. General Gage with about six thousand soldiers was shut up in Boston, and the first task was to drive him out. The only way to do this was for the besieging army to seize one of the heights near Boston that would command Gage's position. On the north of Boston there were the elevations of Bunker Hill and Breed's Hill; on the south, those of Dorchester Heights. Battle of Bunker Hill

Before Washington's arrival the patriot army under the leadership of Colonel William Prescott had fortified Breed's Hill with a view to forcing Gage out of Boston. Gage appreciated his danger and drove the patriots away from their position after a battle that cost him heavily in the loss of men, his success being due to the fact that the latter had run short of ammunition. This first important engagement of the war is known as the battle of Bunker Hill, though it was fought (June 17) on the near-by eminence of Breed's Hill.[1]

When Washington took charge of the army (July 3, 1775) it was in a state of confusion. Supplies were lacking, the enthusiasm of the men was cooling, and many of the soldiers were dropping out of the ranks at the end of their terms of enlistment. General Howe had succeeded Gage in command of the British troops in Boston. If he had attacked Washington's army while it was in this disorganized condition he might have driven the Americans away and thus have relieved the siege. This, however, Boston evacuated by the British

---

[1] For a plan of the battle of Bunker Hill reproduced from a contemporary map made by a British officer, see CHANNING, E., *History of the United States*, iii, p. 166.

he failed to do. New life and hope were breathed into the army under Washington's management. In the meantime Ethan Allen and Benedict Arnold had captured Forts Ticonderoga and Crown Point, on Lake Champlain. Cannon and other military supplies were secured at these places and sent to Boston over the snow on sleds. In the spring of 1776 Washington fortified Dorchester

BUNKER HILL

BREEDS HILL

Charlestown

BOSTON

Dorchester Heights

**BOSTON
AND ENVIRONS**

MANH'N DRAF'G CO., N.Y.

Heights and his artillery commanded the position of Howe's army and fleet. The British commander therefore withdrew from Boston and went to Halifax, Nova Scotia.

Unsuccessful attempts to conquer the Carolinas

There were a good many Loyalists, or Tories, as they were called, in the Carolinas. It was thought that if these Loyalists were properly supported by a British fleet these two colonies could be restored to imperial control. Accordingly, ships were sent to Wilmington, N. C., and Charleston, S. C. But before the belated

fleet arrived at the coast of North Carolina the Tories were
defeated by the Whigs at Moore's Creek Bridge, near Wilmington (February 27, 1776), and the patriot cause was greatly
strengthened by this victory. Six weeks later Sir Henry Clinton
arrived at Wilmington with the British ships, but realizing that
the delay had ruined all chances for success in North Carolina,
he moved on to attack Charleston (June, 1776), which was
bravely defended by six hundred militiamen under Colonel Moultrie. The American soldiers, who were sheltered in a fort made
of green palmetto logs, fired into the British ships so briskly
that the latter were forced to retire. The Carolinas were thus
saved to the patriot cause and the Whigs were very much
encouraged.

The Americans thought that if an expedition were sent into
Canada the French there would join them against the English
government. Accordingly, Montgomery attacked Montreal and
captured it. Montgomery and Arnold then made an unsuccessful
attack on Quebec, in which Montgomery was killed (1775).
Arnold, after having spent the winter before Quebec, was in the
spring pushed slowly southward by Sir Guy Carleton. By the
resistance offered by Arnold, Carleton was delayed in his progress
and was thus prevented from coöperating with Howe in New
York.

The
expedition
against
Canada

After a few months' sojourn in Halifax, Howe sailed southward and prepared to attack New York. This city occupied a
strategic position of great importance, as its possession by the
British would divide the American confederacy into two isolated
sections. Washington realized this and had already transferred
his army to New York. He strengthened the defenses and determined to hold the place if possible. A part of his army commanded by General Putnam was badly defeated on Long Island.
If Howe had followed up his advantage promptly he might have
captured about nine thousand of Washington's men, who were
hemmed in on the island. But the delay on his part and the
friendly aid of a heavy fog gave Washington time to get his army
out of the trap and escape.

New York
City cap-
tured
by the
British

The defeat of the patriot forces on Long Island was followed
by other British victories around New York. In one of these
(Fort Washington) the Americans were forced to surrender
over twenty-eight hundred of their best troops. As a result of
these successes the British got control of New York, which they

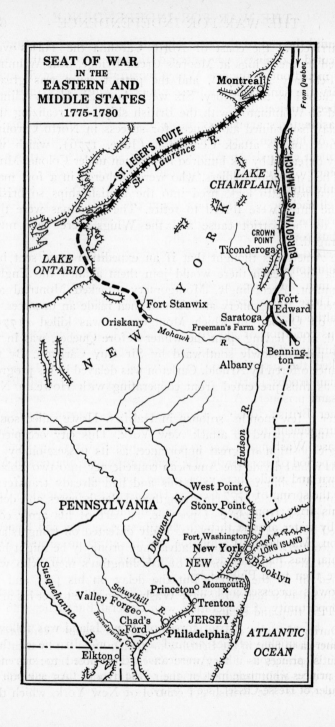

SEAT OF WAR
IN THE
EASTERN AND
MIDDLE STATES
1775-1780

Montreal

From Quebec

St. Lawrence R.

ST. LEGER'S ROUTE

LAKE
CHAMPLAIN

BURGOYNE'S MARCH

CROWN
POINT

Ticonderoga

LAKE
ONTARIO

Fort Stanwix

Fort
Edward

Oriskany

Mohawk R.

Saratoga

Freeman's Farm ×

N E W

Bennington

Albany

Hudson R.

PENNSYLVANIA

Delaware R.

West Point

Stony Point

Susquehanna R.

Schuylkill R.

Valley Forge

Fort Washington

New York

LONG ISLAND

Brooklyn

NEW

Princeton

Monmouth ×

Trenton

Chad's
Ford

JERSEY

Brandywine Cr.

Philadelphia

ATLANTIC
OCEAN

Elkton

held until the end of the war. The city now became a refuge for persecuted Loyalists, who flocked thither from all the states. They meted out to the few Whigs remaining in the town and its vicinity the same kind of persecution to which they themselves had been subjected.

Washington's army was disorganized and undisciplined, and many of his men were deserting or leaving when their term of enlistment expired. An American officer spoke of the army as "a receptacle of ragamuffins." Retreat to a place of safety was now the only alternative left the patriot army. Accordingly, Washington fell back across New Jersey and crossed the Delaware River at Trenton (December, 1776). Howe's forces were in hot pursuit but could not get across the Delaware because Washington had seized all the boats for some distance up and down the river. Washington's army had now dwindled down to about three thousand men, and many people felt that the American cause was lost. There was a great panic at Philadelphia, and Congress fled to Baltimore. *Washington's retreat across New Jersey*

This condition of gloom was relieved by two bold strokes of Washington. On Christmas night he recrossed the Delaware and attacked the surprised British force at Trenton (composed of Hessian troops[2]). He defeated the enemy and carried off one thousand prisoners. A little later (January 3, 1777) he defeated another British force at Princeton. These victories gave great encouragement to the patriot cause, and enlistments began to increase. Washington was given dictatorial powers by Congress for a period of six months. He went into winter quarters at Morristown and while there reorganized his army. *Battles of Trenton and Princeton*

In the spring of 1777 General Howe unwisely decided to transfer his army from New York to Philadelphia. His troops were sent by water around through the Chesapeake Bay and landed at Elkton, Maryland. Washington, in the effort to protect Philadelphia, was met and defeated by Howe at Brandywine Creek. Howe then took Philadelphia. *Philadelphia taken by the British*

Howe's successes in Pennsylvania were gained at the cost of the opportunity of coöperating with General Burgoyne, who was

[2] During the war nearly thirty thousand Germans were brought to America to fight in the British army, being hired out by their petty absolutist princes as if they were slaves. The most notorious of the little princes who made merchandise of the lives of their subjects was the ruler of Hesse-Cassel (see p. 654).

coming down toward the Hudson River from Montreal. The chief aim of Burgoyne's expedition was to reënforce Howe and thereby strengthen his army for an attack on Washington. Colonel St. Leger was to go down the Mohawk Valley to Albany and there unite his forces with those of Howe. If these plans were successfully carried out New York State would be under the control of the British and New England would be completely separated from the rest of the country.

The plan failed for several reasons. St. Leger was defeated and driven back to Canada; and Howe, for some unaccountable reason,[3] led his army southward instead of going north to unite with Burgoyne. Moreover, Burgoyne's line of march passed through a wide stretch of country, in which swamps and forests made marching difficult. It also skirted the frontier of New England, where the people were enthusiastic in their support of the patriot cause. Supplies were hard to get, and he had to lessen his fighting force by keeping up a long line of communication with his base in Canada. Burgoyne was still further weakened by the defeat at Bennington, Vermont, of two detachments of German and Indian troops, which had been sent eastward to take the food supplies stored at that place. On this ill-fated expedition he lost over nine hundred men in killed, captured, wounded, and missing.

Opposed to Burgoyne there was an American army composed of Continental troops and militia commanded at first by General Schuyler and later by General Gates. The opposing forces met at Freeman's Farm, near Saratoga, in two battles (September 19 and October 7, 1777). The first engagement was indecisive, but the second was a decisive victory for the patriots. On these occasions Arnold won the chief laurels.[4] Burgoyne, who had been

---

[3] The reason often given by historians for Howe's failure to coöperate with Burgoyne is that he never received instructions to go north, owing to the fact that the order of the War Minister was overlooked and never sent. Professor Van Tyne, however, says that there is no proof of this, and shows that Howe was informed of Burgoyne's plans and could have rendered him invaluable assistance had he chosen to do so. See VAN TYNE, C. H., *The War of Independence*, pp. 411-417.

[4] There is a difference of opinion among historians as to whether Arnold deserved the credit usually accorded him for the part he played in these battles. See FISHER, S. G., *The Struggle for American Independence*, ii, pp. 93, 96-97. For an account favorable to Arnold and

greatly outnumbered for some time, was now surrounded and forced to surrender (October 17, 1777).[5] His entire army, about fifty-eight hundred men, laid down their arms at Saratoga. This was by far the greatest victory won by the patriots up to this time, and it had a very important bearing on the ultimate success of their cause. It not only greatly encouraged them, but was also the decisive factor in inducing the French to come to their aid.

Just before our Revolution started, some noted French writers —Voltaire, Rousseau, Montesquieu, and others—argued ably and brilliantly in favor of simplicity in living, liberalism in government, and freedom in religion. The ideas of these writers, or philosophers, became very popular in France. It was natural, therefore, for the French people to sympathize with the Americans in their struggle for independence, for they regarded it as a movement in the direction of that political and religious freedom of which their recent prophets had spoken. The fight that the colonies were making for independence made a strong appeal to the Gallic imagination and aroused a good deal of genuine enthusiasm among the devotees of the new philosophy. A great many Frenchmen offered their services in the cause of American independence. Many of these were irresponsible enthusiasts and adventurers whose applications were declined.[6] Of those who were sincerely devoted to the cause, the most noted was Lafayette. He was a man of wealth and high social position and had recently married. Sacrificing all of these opportunities for enjoyment and preferment at home, he came to America in 1777 and offered to serve in Washington's army in any capacity. This enthusiastic young nobleman had seriously taken to heart the teachings of the French philosophers, and he saw in the fight that Washington and his ragged soldiers were waging an effort to realize the ideals of freedom proclaimed by Rousseau and the other French radicals. Washington gave him a cordial welcome to his army, and he was elevated to the high rank of major-general.

The French Alliance

---

unfavorable to Gates, see BOLTON, H. E., and MARSHALL, T. M., *Colonization of North America*, pp. 497-498.

[5] For an account of the surrender and the events that preceded it, written by the wife of a British officer, see HART, A. B., *American History Told by Contemporaries*, ii, pp. 565-568.

[6] SPARKS, JARED, ed., *Diplomatic Correspondence of the American Revolution*, i, p. 71; WHARTON, FRANCIS, ed., *Revolutionary Diplomatic Correspondence of the United States*, ii, pp. 98, 286.

Other foreigners who should be mentioned in this connection were Thomas Conway and Johann Kalb, French officers[7] who were given important positions in the American service; Thaddeus Kosciusko and Count Pulaski, Polish officers who held and merited high rank as military leaders under Washington; and Baron von Steuben, a Prussian general who had served with distinction under Frederick the Great.[8] Steuben performed an especially valuable service in drilling and organizing our raw and undisciplined troops into the semblance of an army.[9]

The French government was at this time on the verge of that financial crisis that in a few years precipitated the French Revolution, and could not, therefore, afford another war. The king, Louis XVI, who had recently come to the throne (1774), was a young man of the best intentions, but was lacking in the judgment and will power needed to guide his country through the difficulties that it was facing. Although he was in theory an absolute ruler, his policy both in domestic and in foreign affairs was determined by the ministers who enjoyed his confidence. During the greater part of the period of our Revolution his chief adviser in foreign affairs was Count de Vergennes, Secretary of State for Foreign Affairs.

Vergennes was smarting under the humiliation that his country had been forced to endure by the English success in the Seven Years' War, and was longing for a chance to even scores with France's old enemy. He saw in the American Revolution an opportunity to strike a successful blow at British prestige and restore the balance of power in Europe. For if Great Britain should suffer the loss of her overseas dominions or were forced to carry on with them a long and costly war, her position as a world power would be weakened and that of France relatively strengthened.[10] In short, his purpose was to call on the New World to

[7] Conway was a native of Ireland and Kalb of Germany, but Conway had been reared and educated in France and both had been for some time in the French military service.

[8] SPARKS, JARED, op. cit., i, pp. 73, 76, 97-100.

[9] For a very readable popular account of the part played in the American army by Steuben, see an article in *Harper's Magazine* for September, 1928, pp. 456-466. For Steuben's impression of America and references to his career, see HART, A. B., *American History Told by Contemporaries*, ii, pp. 583-585.

[10] For an excellent discussion of the motives that prompted France to give aid to the revolting American colonies, see an article by COR-

aid in redressing the balance of the Old. He, therefore, urged the king (March, 1776) to give the insurgents secret aid in munitions and money. In arriving at this decision Vergennes was influenced largely by the arguments of Caron de Beaumarchais, a brilliant play-writer, who had won his way to a place of influence in court and political circles by his musical talent, his literary ability, and his grace of manner. He was liberal in his ideas and was fanatical in his desire that the disgrace to his country recorded in the Treaty of 1763 might be wiped out. For these reasons he espoused the cause of the insurgents with intense zeal and enthusiasm. He argued that both the French and Spanish West Indian possessions were in danger; for if England were successful in putting down the revolt she would at the end of the war be tempted to appropriate the island colonies of Spain and France in the New World. On the other hand, if the Americans should win their independence without the aid of France and Spain, they would feel at liberty to take over the Spanish and French possessions. These arguments made a strong appeal to Vergennes and the young king, who decided that secret aid should be extended to the colonies and that all business with them should be transacted through the agency of Beaumarchais.[11] No better agent could have been found to act as an intermediary between the French government and the representatives of the new republic. He established a mercantile firm in Paris, known as Hortelez & Co., and through it disbursed to the Americans quantities of arms and clothing.

The Continental Congress had in the meantime taken steps to capitalize French sympathy and enlist the support of other foreign powers in the cause of the Revolution. After independence was declared some of the leaders in Congress were in favor of sending ministers to European countries to seek out friendships and alliances that would aid in upholding American independence. This idea was combated by others, who felt that no representatives to foreign capitals should be sent until there were assurances that they would be officially received. Of this latter opinion was Franklin, who said: "A virgin state should preserve the virgin character, and not go abroad suitoring for alliances; but wait with

---

WIN, E. S., in the *American Historical Review*, xxi, pp. 33-61. The main points of the article are summarized in pp. 59-61.

[11] LATANÉ, J. H., *A History of American Diplomacy*, p. 7; FOSTER, J. W., *A Century of American Diplomacy*, pp. 11-12.

decent dignity for the application of others."[12] This wise advice was not heeded, and commissioners were sent to several European countries. Most of these envoys were never received by the governments to which they were accredited and were forced to congregate in Paris, where they embarrassed Franklin by giving him unasked advice and in other ways interfering with his work.[13] France was the only one of the European powers which in the early years of the Revolution manifested a cordial sympathy with the American cause.

In the spring of 1776 Silas Deane was sent by the Continental Congress as its agent to Paris. In the fall of the same year Arthur Lee and Benjamin Franklin were appointed to serve with Deane as commissioners to France.[14] They were not officially received but were able to present the claims of their country indirectly. Franklin after his arrival took the leading part in the negotiations, and Deane was afterward recalled (by an act of Congress passed December 8, 1777).[15] Franklin took Paris completely by storm. His fine common sense, his wise and pithy sayings, his reputation as a scientist and writer, and the Quaker-like simplicity of his taste in dress, at once gave him the highest rank as a philosopher of the Rousseau type. "His reputation was more universal than that of Leibnitz or Newton, or Frederick [the Great] or Voltaire, and his character more beloved and esteemed than any or all of them. . . . His name was familiar to government and people, to foreign countries, nobility, clergy, and philosophers, as well as plebeians, to such a degree that there was scarcely a peasant or a citizen, a *valet de chambre*, coachman, or footman, a lady's chambermaid or a scullion in a kitchen, who was not familiar with it and who did not consider him a friend to humankind."[16] It goes without saying, therefore, that Franklin was as successful as anyone could be in urging the claims of America before the French court and in pointing out to it the advantages of an alliance with the new republic.

Vergennes was cautious, however, and would not commit his

[12] Quoted in *ibid.*, p. 9.

[13] See LATANÉ, *op. cit.*, pp. 14-15.

[14] Jefferson was at first appointed, but owing to illness in his family he could not serve and Lee was appointed in his place (*Journal of the Continental Congress*, vi, p. 897).

[15] *Ibid.*, ix, pp. 1008-1009; v, p. 827; vi, pp. 884, 897.

[16] The above quotation is from a letter written by John Adams; quoted by LATANÉ, *op. cit.*, p. 11.

government to a formal recognition of the independence of the colonies. He was not willing to risk a break with England without some assurance that the insurgents would win the war, and for a time he would do no more than give secret aid to the revolutionary government in the form of loans and gifts of money. Finally there came the news of Burgoyne's surrender, and then he decided definitely in favor of the alliance.[17]

Two treaties were signed on February 6, 1778. One was an agreement as to trade, and the other a political and military alliance. By these treaties France recognized the independence of the United States and pledged her support in maintaining this independence. In case war should break out between Great Britain and France, both France and the United States were to make it a common cause, and neither of the two parties was "to conclude either truce or peace with Great Britain without the formal consent of the other first obtained." France renounced forever all rights to her former possessions in the Bermudas and on the mainland of North America, but reserved the right to conquer from England any of her islands in or near the Gulf of Mexico. Each of the signatories guaranteed to the other all the American possessions that it then held or might acquire by the treaty of peace.[18]

France went to war at once with England as the ally of Amer-

Spain and Holland drawn into the war

[17] For a brief statement made by Vergennes himself as to the motives that prompted him to form the alliance, see *American Historical Review*, xxi, pp. 532-533. For a corroboration of this statement by other French statesmen, see *ibid.*, footnotes, pp. 533-534.

Professor Van Tyne, in an article in the *American Historical Review* (xxi, pp. 528-541), contended that Vergennes was led to take the final step in forming the alliance by the fear that England would make terms with her revolting colonies and probably enlist their aid in an attack on the French American possessions. As both the king and his Minister of Foreign Affairs were convinced that war with England was inevitable, whether France entered the American alliance or not, they felt "that it was the better policy to join with America and thus win her support rather than wait for England to make peace with America, and then make war in company with her upon the House of Bourbon, whose insular possessions would lie so completely at their mercy" (p. 541). See also Van Tyne, C. H., *The War of Independence*, pp. 498-501.

[18] For the text of these two treaties, see Malloy, W. M., *Treaties, Conventions, etc., between the United States and Other Powers*, i, pp. 468-482.

ica. Spain also declared war on England the next year, though on her own account and not in alliance with the United States. Not only did England now have to cope with these two new enemies, but she also had to take into account the hostile sentiment that prevailed against her in the neutral European countries. This ill feeling was shown by an alliance entered into in the spring of 1780 by Denmark, Sweden, Holland, Portugal, and Russia, which was known as the Armed Neutrality. The alliance was based on a declaration of Catherine II of Russia, defining the rights of neutrals in time of war. The rights claimed for neutrals in the agreement were such as Great Britain was unwilling to recognize, and the declaration itself was a gesture of strong disapproval of British methods in conducting the war. Serious friction soon developed between England and Holland because of the latter's accession to the Armed Neutrality and other causes of dispute, and by the last of the year 1780 these two powers were at war. The American conflict had thus led to a European struggle, and England's enemies had increased until they challenged her control of the sea. This increase in naval strength against Great Britain was an important factor in determining the outcome of the war in favor of American independence.

Washington at Valley Forge   Washington's army spent the winter of 1777-78 at Valley Forge. During this time the soldiers endured terrible sufferings because of a lack of food and clothing.[19] These sacrifices were entirely unnecessary, as there was plenty of food in the states. The failure on the part of the authorities to look after the needs of the soldiers was due partly to the weakness and inefficiency of Congress. Paper money was also a cause. The army of Howe stationed in Philadelphia fared sumptuously because British gold could procure supplies in abundance, while the Pennsylvania farmers refused to sell food to Washington's soldiers for cheap paper money. But the main cause of the suffering was poor transportation facilities. In this trying time Washington's greatness shone in unusual splendor. He had to face the suffering and just complaints of the soldiers, the indifference and selfishness of the civilian population, the lack of support of a helpless and incompetent Congress, and intrigues to deprive him of his command

[19] FORD, W. C., ed., *Writings of Washington*, vi, p. 267. See also HART, A. B., *American History Told by Contemporaries*, ii, pp. 568-573.

carried on by subordinate officers. And yet he did not despair. In the midst of it all he stood erect and serene as the one commanding figure in an environment of littleness and jealousy.

After spending the winter in Philadelphia the British army was ordered back to New York, Clinton having in the meantime superseded Howe. Washington followed Clinton and attacked him at Monmouth. He probably would have won a victory here but for the unwise or treasonable conduct of Charles Lee. This was the last battle of importance fought in the North. The British still held New York and Newport, Rhode Island. The Americans and their French allies united in an attack on the latter place, but were defeated (1778). **The British evacuate Philadelphia**

George Rogers Clark, acting on a commission granted him by Patrick Henry, governor of Virginia, led a small band of soldiers into the Illinois region. The French living there were indifferent as to whether the political control of the country was in the hands of the British or Americans, and when they learned that the latter were in alliance with the French king they gave their allegiance to the American government. Clark was thus able to conquer the whole Illinois region (1778-79). Hamilton, the British governor of the Northwest, known as the "hair-buyer" because of the large number of scalps he paid the Indians to procure, was defeated and captured. Clark's successful campaigns in the West were among the most important events of the war. The states claimed this region on the basis of charters granted to them by the crown when they were colonies, and these claims were now supported by the fact of possession. The region north of the Ohio River was organized into the County of Illinois by the Virginia legislature.[20] **Conquest of the Northwest**

[20] Clark's force consisted of one hundred and seventy-five men, mostly Virginians. The little band floated down the Ohio River to Fort Massac and then marched overland to attack the French villages. Kaskaskia, Vincennes, and other places fell into their hands. Hamilton moved down from Detroit and made an effort to regain the lost posts, but succeeded only in recapturing Vincennes. In February, 1779, Clark marched over the flooded prairies and attacked Vincennes. Hamilton was taken completely by surprise and was compelled to surrender his entire force. For an authoritative account of the capture of Kaskaskia and Vincennes, see JAMES, J. A., *The Life of George Rogers Clark*, chs. 6 and 7. For an excellent map showing Clark's route, see *ibid.*, opposite p. 216, also *Harper's Atlas of American History*, p. 19.

Part
played by
the navy

England enjoyed the unchallenged mastery of the seas before France and Spain entered the conflict. The American navy, therefore, was not able to play a large part in the war. There were, however, some small warships provided by both Congress and the state governments. There were also numerous privateers— that is, vessels owned by private persons but commissioned by the government. A good many prizes were captured by the privateers, and the owners, who were mainly New Englanders, grew wealthy from the British ships and cargoes seized. The friendship of France for America made it possible for the latter's privateers and warships to use French ports as sheltered bases of operation, both before and after the alliance was formed.

The most noted American naval commander was John Paul Jones. He was put in command of a squadron of five vessels, four of which were furnished by the French king. While cruising along the east coast of Scotland he encountered (September, 1779) two English warships convoying forty merchantmen. A battle ensued in which Jones defeated his antagonist and captured both of his vessels.

War in
the South

The South became the scene of the war in the last part of 1778. There were a good many Tories in Georgia and the Carolinas, and the British expected to be more successful in the South than they had been in the North. Savannah was captured (December, 1778) and the whole state of Georgia was overrun. The Americans under the leadership of General Lincoln, aided by the French fleet, made an attempt (October, 1779) to retake Savannah, but were unsuccessful. The British then attacked Charleston. General Lincoln, who defended the city, was defeated and his army of five thousand men compelled to surrender (May, 1780).

South Carolina and Georgia were now in the hands of the British. For some time the only opposition offered by the Americans was that of small isolated bands of soldiers commanded by such partisan leaders as Marion, Pickens, and Sumter. These bold leaders gave the enemy considerable annoyance by irregular and unexpected attacks on small detached bodies of the enemy.

Congress made an effort to assist the patriots in the South. General Gates was sent to their aid with a small army composed of an equal number of militiamen and regulars. He was badly defeated at Camden (August 16, 1780) and lost, in killed and captured, two-thirds of his army. Shortly after this defeat the Americans won a victory at King's Mountain, which checked the advance of the British and greatly encouraged the patriots. It was the turning-point in the war in the South.

General Greene succeeded Gates (December, 1780) in command of the patriot forces in the South. He was an able general and made a wise use of the small force under his command. He was often defeated in battle, but he knew how to conduct a masterly retreat and keep up the morale of his soldiers. In a way

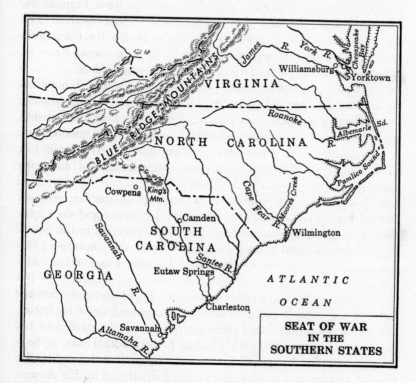

SEAT OF WAR
IN THE
SOUTHERN STATES

he was able to reap from defeat the fruits of victory. He was ably assisted by Colonel Morgan, who won a signal victory over the British at Cowpens.

It can readily be seen that the Americans had reason to be discouraged over the outcome of military events in the South. But there were other causes of discouragement for the patriots besides the defeats their armies had sustained. Congress was gradually becoming more helpless, and the people were growing tired of the war. The paper-money situation had become hopeless, and Congress had in March, 1780, virtually put the country into

Arnold's treason

bankruptcy. Washington's soldiers were without adequate food and clothing and some were deserting and going over to the enemy. "Never were American affairs blacker than during the year which preceded the surrender of Cornwallis. Even Washington had almost ceased to hope."

In the midst of this gloom the country was called on to experience another great discouragement. This was the treason of Benedict Arnold. After the British left Philadelphia, Arnold was stationed there because the wound that he had received near Saratoga made him inactive. While there he lived extravagantly and engaged extensively in speculation, and in consequence became involved in financial difficulties. His second wife was a beautiful and attractive young woman who belonged to a prominent Tory family, and many of his associates were of Loyalist sympathies. He, therefore, became unpopular with the patriots, and charges, both serious and trivial, were brought against him by his enemies. A committee of investigation exonerated him from the serious charges, but a court martial declared him guilty of some petty offenses and directed Washington to reprimand him for them. Washington in executing this order virtually turned his reprimand into a eulogy of his past services. In the meantime Congress had refused to allow some claims based on expenditures alleged to have been made by him in connection with the expedition against Quebec, and he was faced with financial ruin.

Washington still had entire confidence in Arnold and intrusted him, at the latter's request, with the command at West Point, one of the most important strategic positions held by the Americans. Arnold arranged with Clinton to betray this post to him. In payment for his treachery he was to receive a considerable sum of money and a colonelcy in the British army. His purpose would have been carried out had not Major André, who was conducting the negotiations between him and the enemy, been seized with the papers that revealed the plot (September, 1780). As it was, Arnold made good his escape and joined the British Army.[21] Had he remained true to the patriot cause a little more than a year longer, his place as a hero of the Revolution would in all probability have ranked second to that of Washington only.

[21] For source materials on Arnold's treason see VAN DOREN, CARL, *Secret History of the American Revolution*, and the *Pennsylvania Magazine of History and Biography*, xxii, pp. 410-414.

In the spring of 1781 Cornwallis, who had been in command of the British forces in the Carolinas, moved northward into Virginia. He was here joined by Arnold, who had been harrying the state for five months. Cornwallis's army was now large enough to give him control of the Old Dominion. Lafayette with a force about half the size of that of his antagonist was unable to offer an effective resistance to his movements. After chasing Lafayette unsuccessfully for some time, Cornwallis finally settled down at Yorktown.

About this time Washington received word from Count De Grasse, commander of the French fleet in the West Indies, offering to coöperate with him. Washington saw an excellent opportunity to entrap Cornwallis, and so requested De Grasse to bring his fleet up to the Chesapeake Bay, where he could prevent the escape by water of Cornwallis's army and fight back a relieving squadron. In the meantime the French troops under the command of Rochambeau, stationed at Newport, joined Washington in front of New York. Clinton, the British commander in New York, was made to believe that the Americans were preparing to attack him. While Clinton was in this attitude of watchful waiting, Washington moved southward rapidly with his army. He was joined by Lafayette, and the combined armies sat down in front of Yorktown. Washington's forces now numbered sixteen thousand, a large portion of which were French regulars. Cornwallis with less than half that number was surrounded and besieged in the village of Yorktown.

Evidently Cornwallis's army was doomed unless aid were despatched to him from Clinton. Admiral Graves was sent with nineteen ships to his assistance, but was defeated at the mouth of Chesapeake Bay by Count De Grasse and driven back. Clinton's second effort to relieve Corwallis was made too late to help him.

The American and French soldiers captured two redoubts near the British lines, and the prospect of escape for Cornwallis was now hopeless. He surrendered on October 19, 1781, his entire army of about eight thousand men. This victory virtually ended the war, although the treaty of peace was not signed until a year later.

Offers of peace had been made to the revolting colonies by the British authorities on two occasions before the victory at Yorktown. When Lord Howe arrived at New York with his fleet (1776), he brought the olive branch as well as the sword, for he had been commissioned by the British government to make an effort at conciliation. This mission was very acceptable to him, for he had a very kindly feeling toward America and was anxious for the war to end. Probably no other naval officer in England at that time was better fitted to make peace overtures than was Lord Howe. His brother had been killed while fighting in America, and Lord Howe himself had spoken in Parliament in favor of the American cause. After the victory on Long Island he had an informal meeting with three commissioners of the Continental Congress.[22] The Declaration of Independence had been adopted at this time and the American commissioners insisted on the recognition of the independence of the states as a necessary condition of peace. Lord Howe had no authority to treat on this basis, and nothing was accomplished by the conference.[23]

After the defeat of Burgoyne the British prime minister was again anxious to end the war. Commissioners were sent to America to offer pardon and liberal terms. They offered the Americans practically everything that they had asked except independence.[24] Again the United States would accept nothing short of independence, and so the second peace mission failed.

The victory at Yorktown had decided that the United States was to be independent, and peace negotiations were begun in the spring of 1782. John Adams had been appointed by Congress in 1779 as sole commissioner to negotiate a treaty of peace with England.[25] The selection of Adams was not altogether a wise choice, for he was not fitted by temperament for the delicate task of peace-making. His honesty, patriotism, and courage were beyond question, but he was lacking in the tact which is so needful for oiling the wheels of diplomacy. Adams, however, was not conscious of this limitation and so entered upon his new responsibilities with hopeful enthusiasm. He went to Paris and there awaited an opportunity to open negotiations with the British

[22] These commissioners were John Adams, Franklin, and Edward Rutledge.

[23] For a good short account of this conference, see TREVELYAN, G. O., *The American Revolution*, part ii, vol. i, pp. 253-266. For a contemporary account, written by Lord Howe's secretary, see *Atlantic Monthly*, lxxvii, pp. 759-762.

[24] These proposals are given in part in PEASE, T. C., and ROBERTS, A. S., *Selected Readings in American History*, pp. 149-151.

[25] *Journals of the Continental Congress*, xv, p. 1113.

authorities. During his sojourn in the French capital he busied himself with problems that were arising between his country and France, and assumed a rather haughty attitude toward our ally. In his correspondence with Vergennes so much friction developed that the French foreign minister finally declined to have any further relations with him.

Shortly afterwards Adams went to Holland and again tried his hand at diplomacy, this time with marked success. At first Holland was not inclined to receive an envoy from the new republic, although she was already at war with England. It was not long, however, before her reluctance was overcome by the news of Cornwallis's surrender, and the independence of the American states was formally recognized (April, 1782). Adams was also able to secure from the bankers of Holland a loan of $2,000,000 and to negotiate a treaty of commerce with the government.

In the meantime Congress had changed its plans for negotiating the peace. Adams was no longer to be sole plenipotentiary, but four other men were to be associated with him as joint commissioners to treat with England (June 15, 1781). These envoys were, besides Adams, Franklin, John Jay, Thomas Jefferson, and Henry Laurens. Jefferson did not go to Paris, and Laurens was captured by the British and was released just in time to attach his signature to the treaty. So the negotiations were conducted by Franklin, Adams, and Jay.

Congress, in issuing its instructions to the commissioners, showed the timidity that was characteristic of that weak body. The hope was expressed that the Mississippi River would be secured as the western boundary, but no positive instruction was given to the envoys to insist on it. As a result of the influence exerted on Congress by the French minister, the commissioners were directed "to make the most candid and confidential communications, upon all subjects, to the Ministers of our generous ally, the King of France; to undertake nothing in the negotiations for peace or truce without their knowledge and concurrence; and ultimately to govern yourselves [themselves] by their advice and opinion."[26] Fortunately, our commissioners were possessed of a much bolder spirit than that which informed these overcautious instructions.

[26] LATANÉ, *op. cit.*, p. 40; for these instructions, see *Journals of the Continental Congress*, xx, pp. 651-654.

While Adams was still in the Netherlands and Jay at Madrid, where he had been trying unsuccessfully to represent American interests since the autumn of 1779, Franklin was beginning to enter upon the negotiations for peace with the British authorities. In the spring of 1782 letters passed between Franklin and Lord Shelburne, Minister of the Colonies, with the result that the latter agreed to send a special representative to Paris to confer with Franklin (April, 1782). For this delicate mission Shelburne selected Richard Oswald, a Scotchman, who was on very friendly terms with Franklin and was kindly disposed toward America. The negotiations were well under way when Jay arrived at Paris (June, 1782), and four months later Adams came from Holland to join his colleague in the work of formulating peace terms.

Jay soon began to suspect that Vergennes was giving the negotiations such a turn as to sacrifice American interests, and he had what he considered good grounds for these suspicions. Our commissioners were determined to secure, if possible, for their country all of that vast territory between the Alleghany Mountains and the Mississippi River, although their instructions did not order them to insist on this. Spain also laid claim to a portion of this region. The alliance between Spain and France had imposed obligations on the latter country which could not easily be met if America should get all she wanted in the peace treaty. Vergennes, the French foreign minister, was, therefore, embarrassed by the conflicting claims of the allies of his government. As a solution of the difficulty, Rayneval, his private secretary, proposed a division of the western country that would have been very unsatisfactory to America. According to this plan the region between the Mississippi River and the Alleghany Mountains should be divided into two parts, with the Ohio River as the boundary between them. The northern portion should go to England, and the southern should be left in possession of the Indians, who were to be under the protection of Spain and the United States.[27]

It was evident from this proposal that Vergennes was willing to support Spain's claims to the Mississippi Valley at a sacrifice of American interests in that region. In taking this stand Vergennes was actuated partly by the desire to satisfy France's ally,

[27] For map showing how the West was to be divided according to Rayneval's proposal, see *Harper's Atlas of American History*, p. 20.

Spain, and probably also in part by the fear that the United States would become too powerful if given all the western territory. Lord Shelburne, on the other hand, was willing for the United States to have the Northwest, as England preferred the American Confederation to Spain as a neighbor of Canada. The new republic was thus in the anomalous situation of having its claims supported by the enemy and opposed by its ally.

Jay's suspicion that Vergennes was trying to barter away the territorial rights of the United States for concessions in favor of Spain and his own country was so strong that he determined to break his instructions and open up secret negotiations with the representative of Great Britain. Adams concurred fully in Jay's views and policy and tried to win Franklin over to them. Franklin did not share Jay's distrust of Vergennes, but after a slight hesitation acquiesced reluctantly in his plan for separate negotiations. The British government welcomed this opportunity of widening the breach between France and her ally, and a treaty between England and America was signed November 30, 1782. It was not, however, to be effective until France and Great Britain had come to an understanding. The final treaty between Great Britain and the United States, which was signed on September 3, 1783, after England and France had agreed upon terms, was the same as the preliminary treaty, except that a secret clause in the latter was omitted from the former.[28]

By these treaties the United States were recognized as independent states. The northern boundary was the same as it is at present; the western boundary was the Mississippi River; the southern, the northern boundary of the Floridas, which were given to Spain. Spain also retained the Isle of Orleans and the territory west of the Mississippi River. The Americans were given the right to fish on the banks of Newfoundland and in the Gulf of St. Lawrence. The navigation of the Mississippi was

[28] The secret clause in the preliminary treaty provided that, in case Great Britain should get West Florida in the final treaty, the northern boundary of West Florida should be a line extending from the mouth of the Yazoo River due east to the Apalachicola River. But if some power other than England should receive the Floridas, then the southern boundary of the United States should be a line running along the thirty-first parallel and what is now the northern boundary of Florida (MALLOY, W. M., comp., *Treaties, Conventions, etc., between the United States and Other Powers,* i, p. 584).

to be free to both England and the United States, despite the fact that Spain controlled not only the western bank, but also the mouth of the river.

There were two points on which the British and American commissioners had considerable difficulty in reaching an agreement. One of these was the question of debts due British subjects by American citizens; the other was the problem of the Loyalists whose property had been confiscated. The English commissioners insisted on a provision in the treaty guaranteeing the payment of all debts to British citizens contracted by Americans before 1775. This guarantee was not given, but it was agreed that "creditors on either side shall meet with no legal impediment to the recovery of the full value in sterling money of all *bona fide* debts heretofore contracted." As has already been seen, the property of the Loyalists, or Tories, had been confiscated by the states during the war. The English commissioners stoutly contended for a provision in the treaty that would secure to the American Loyalists a restoration of their property and other rights, as they were in honor bound to do. Our commissioners maintained that Congress had no authority to enact measures that would be effective in compensating Tories for their losses by confiscation, but that such measures could be adopted only by the individual states. The controversy was finally settled by the American commissioners agreeing to a clause which pledged the American Congress earnestly to recommend to the state legislatures the enactment of such provisions as would lead to the restoration of the just rights of Tories whose property had been confiscated.[29]

[29] Congress made the recommendation to the states that was promised in the treaty, but little heed was paid to it by the state governments. Confiscations still went on, and in nearly every state Tories were disfranchised. It was not until after the War of 1812 that the laws against Tories had all been repealed. A good many Tories who had not been conspicuous in their loyalty to the British cause remained in the United States after the war. This was especially the case in the larger cities, where they could more easily lose their identity. But most of those who took part in the war were forced into exile during or immediately after the war. The greater portion of those who left at the close of hostilities went to Canada. The British government reimbursed those Loyalists who had been deprived of property or office during the war. The needy were furnished with supplies, and to the humbler classes liberal grants of land were made. They were also fur-

The treaty was a great diplomatic victory for the Americans, who got practically all they asked. In signing the preliminary treaty without the knowledge of Vergennes the commissioners had plainly violated their instructions and had acted in opposition to the spirit of the treaty of alliance with France. After learning that a separate treaty had been signed by the American envoys, Vergennes wrote to Franklin, reproving him and his colleagues for what they had done. Franklin in a rather lame defense pointed out to him that as the treaty would not go into effect until agreed to by France, they had "been guilty only of neglecting a point of *bienséance*."[30] The treaty received the unanimous approval of Congress, but there was a strong feeling among the majority of the members that the commissioners should not have disregarded their instructions and signed the provisional treaty without the knowledge of the French foreign office. The insertion of the secret article was also generally condemned.[31]

SELECTED READINGS

1. Relative Strength of the British and American Armies.—Van Tyne, C. H., *England and America,* *lecture v. See also Van Tyne, *The War of Independence,* *chs. 5-6.
2. The Character of Washington (an English estimate).—Lecky, W. E. H., *The American Revolution,* pp. *208-214.
3. Loyalists and Patriots.—Van Tyne, C. H., *The War of Independence,* *ch. 2.
4. Franklin in Paris.—Trevelyan, G. O., *The American Revolution,* part iii, pp. *450-466.
5. The French Alliance.—Wrong, G. M., *Washington and His Comrades,* pp. *182-193; Van Tyne, C. H., *The American Revolution,* *ch. 12; *England and America,* pp. *155-177; Latané, J. H., *A History of American Diplomacy,* *ch. 1.
6. Lafayette.—Trevelyan, *The American Revolution,* part iii, pp. *218-223.

---

nished with tools and building materials (VAN TYNE, C. H., *The Loyalists in the American Revolution,* pp. 298-303).

For the text of the provisional treaty, see MALLOY, *op. cit.,* pp. 580-584; for the definitive treaty, *ibid.,* pp. 586-590.

[30] For Vergennes's letter and Franklin's reply, see FOSTER, J. W., *A Century of American Diplomacy,* pp. 67-68; WHARTON, F., *The Revolutionary Diplomatic Correspondence of the United States,* vi, pp. 140, 143-144.

[31] FOSTER, J. W., *op. cit.,* pp. 68-69.

7. Washington at Valley Forge.—Channing, E., *History of the United States,* iii, pp *394-396; Trevelyan, *The American Revolution,* part iii, pp. *289-301 (with this reference there should be read Fitzpatrick, J. C., *The Spirit of the American Revolution,* ch. 6).

8. Motives that Prompted the French Government to Aid the Americans.—Articles by E. S. Corwin and C. H. Van Tyne in the *American Historical Review,* pp. *33-63, *529-541, respectively.

9. The Capture of Kaskaskia.—Temple, B., *George Rogers Clark,* *ch. 7 (mostly in Clark's own words).

10. Supplying the Army.—Hatch, L. C., *The Administration of the American Revolutionary Army,* *ch. 6.

11. Hospitals and Prison Ships.—Bolton, C. K., *The Private Soldier Under Washington,* *ch. 8.

12. Arnold's Treason.—Fisher, S. G., *The Struggle for American Independence,* ii, *ch. 84; Fiske, John, *The American Revolution,* i, *ch. 14.

13. The Battle of Yorktown.—Articles by R. G. Adams and William B. Willcox in the *American Historical Review,* xxxvii, pp. 25-49, and lii, pp. 1-35, respectively (new and conflicting views as to the responsibility for Cornwallis's failure).

14. The Peace Negotiations.—McLaughlin, A. C., *The Confederation and the Constitution,* *chs. 1-2; Foster, J. W., *A Century of American Diplomacy,* *ch. 2; for the text of the treaties, see Malloy, W. M., comp., *Treaties, Conventions, etc., between the United States and Other Powers,* i, pp. 580-584 (provisional treaty); i, pp. 586-590 (definitive treaty).

CHAPTER XXXIII

POLITICAL AND SOCIAL ASPECTS OF THE REVOLUTION

THE events recorded in the foregoing chapters show clearly that by the end of the third quarter of the eighteenth century England and America had come to the parting of the ways. The common origin from which they had sprung no longer constituted a bond strong enough to keep them together. The economic and social life of both peoples was rooted in the institutions of early seventeenth-century England; but a century and a half of separation with differences in environmental conditions had produced marked divergencies in the culture of each group. In England, civilization had developed under Old World conditions and had reached a point at which it was exhibiting not only the attractive characteristics of maturity, but also some of the weaknesses of senility. In the New World, on the other hand, the culture of Elizabethan England had renewed its youth in the wilderness and had taken on not only the fresh spontaneity and cheerful optimism, but also something of the crudity and awkwardness, of undisciplined adolescence.

America and England at the parting of the ways

In the first place, there was a decided difference in the primary occupations of the two peoples. In England manufacturing and commerce were developing rapidly, while in America manufacturing had attained no great importance, and agriculture was the leading occupation in all sections of the country. In the colonies, therefore, all the people but a small percentage lived in the rural districts or in small villages, whereas in the homeland the recent economic changes had effected a transfer of a considerable portion of the population from the country to the towns and cities.

Secondly, on the intellectual side of their civilization the two groups had also developed away from each other. America had borrowed her school system from England, and the educational opportunities of the masses were probably as good in the dominions as they were in the homeland. But the upper classes in the mother country could boast of a broader and more liberal culture than that possessed by the colonial aristocracy. The English universities were better than the American colleges, and the extra-curricular agencies for the promotion of culture were finer and more numerous in the old society than in the new. At a time when American architecture was "bare and square" and the best public buildings we could point to were Independence Hall in Philadelphia, Trinity Church in New York, and Faneuil Hall in Boston, England had Westminster Abbey, a number of imposing cathedrals and castles, and hundreds of beautiful private residences. The colonials were also far behind their transatlantic brethren in the creation and appreciation of other forms of art, such as painting, music, and literature.

Even in law and government the two peoples had grown apart. While the English constitution and the common law had crossed the Atlantic and every colonial government was modeled after that of the mother country, yet frontier modes of living in the New World had brought about a modification of English political and legal institutions. The common law was never adopted in its entirety in the dominions, and such portions of it as were in use there were often modified to suit local conditions. Local government in the Northern and Middle colonies showed considerable divergencies from the pattern furnished by the homeland. In both England and America suffrage was restricted to property-owners, but in America it was much easier for a man to acquire land and thereby qualify as a voter than it was in the mother country. There was thus a tendency toward democracy in the colonies.

The cultural divergencies that grew up between the overseas possessions and the homeland were not due entirely to differences in environmental conditions. These diversities owed their origin in part, at least, to dissimilarities in the character of the people who had gone to America and of those who had remained at home. In the very beginning the political and religious beliefs of a large proportion of the emigrants who came to the New World were different from those held by their brethren in England, and many of them had made the change because they were out of harmony with the social order of the homeland. Moreover, at the outbreak of the Revolution a large proportion of the population of the thirteen colonies was of non-English origin. These foreigners brought with them to their new home the political and social ideals of France, Scotland, Germany, and the Netherlands.

The contrasts between the social order in England and that of the American dominions show that the latter had grown into a separate economic and political entity, which was separated from the mother country by a gulf that could not be permanently bridged.[1] America had thus achieved her cultural independence before she had asserted her political freedom. By the beginning of the last quarter of the eighteenth century the thirteen original colonies had attained their majority and wished to set up house for themselves.

The Revolution was a struggle between two parties, both of which were represented in England and America. It was a fight between conservatives and liberals, or radicals, as their opponents regarded the latter. In the early stages of their opposition to the policy of Parliament the American radicals were supported by some influential leaders of the Whig party in England. The English conservatives, members of the Tory party, were usually opposed to liberal concessions to the colonies. It is said that some of the most important battles of the Revolution were fought in Parliament. Prominent in the list of British friends of America were William Pitt, the Earl of Chatham, and Edmund Burke, the great orator.

Whigs and Tories

On the other hand, there were many Americans who were opposed to the Revolution. They are known as Loyalists, though their enemies called them Tories. The Americans who espoused the cause of the Revolution were known as patriots and Whigs. The Loyalists were numerous in all the colonies and in some they may have been in the majority. John Adams, who would be inclined to underestimate rather than overestimate the number of the Loyalists, thought that a third of the people in the colonies and more than a third of the influential class were opposed to the Revolution.[2] Some of the Tories were opposed to the Stamp Act and other measures passed by Parliament in the decade preceding the Revolution, but were unwilling to go beyond the limits of legal resistance. Others, being prosperous and comfortable, and having, as was charged, "too great an attachment for property," feared the hazards of war and governmental experiments. Still

[1] VAN TYNE, C. H., *Causes of the War of Independence,* pp. 327-345.

[2] Statements regarding the number of Loyalists, or Tories, have of necessity to be guarded, as all contemporary estimates are little more than guesswork.

others believed that America's highest interests were bound up with the British empire and that for the colonies to secede from it would be to jeopardize the liberty and prosperity so long enjoyed by them. As a class they seem to have been actuated by as high and patriotic motives as were the revolutionists.

But honest convictions were not a protection against cruel persecution at the hands of the patriots. The Loyalists were subjected to harsh and unjust treatment with a view to their conversion or for the purpose of wreaking vengeance upon them. Their property was confiscated by the state governments; some were moved from one locality to another to lessen their influence; others were forced into exile; and a few were hanged for treason. Tar and feathers were sometimes used as a means of punishment. Those that were banished from the country went to England, the West Indies, Canada, or some American city under British control. A great many of them enlisted in the British army and fought against their fellow-countrymen.[3]

The Tories, however, showed a like feeling of bitterness toward the Whigs when they had the opportunity to even scores with the latter. The ruthless depredations committed by the Tories were largely responsible for the bitter hatred that characterized the later period of the war. At Wyoming Valley, Pennsylvania, and Cherry Valley, in central New York, massacres and depredations were perpetrated by the Tories and their Indian allies.

The organization of the new state governments
The secession from the empire necessitated the establishment of new governments for the colonies, now transformed into commonwealths. Even before the Declaration of Independence was adopted the states had begun to form new constitutions, and by the spring of 1777 a temporary or permanent government had been organized in each of them. In every case but two a new constitution had been adopted. These two exceptions were Rhode Island and Connecticut, whose old charters were so liberal that they were continued as state constitutions.

In laying the political foundations of the new commonwealths the statesmen of that day exercised a sound conservatism that is

[3] For an example of the feeling that existed toward the Tories, see MOORE, FRANK, *Diary of the American Revolution*, ii, pp. 166-169. See also PEASE, T. C., and ROBERTS, A. S., *Selected Readings in American History*, pp. 122-124; also VAN TYNE, C. H., *The Loyalists in the American Revolution*, ch. I.

rare in revolutionary leaders. Instead of tearing down the old institutions and erecting entirely new political structures, they used in every instance the framework of the colonial constitution and contented themselves with making what they regarded as much-needed repairs. The political leaders were guided in these revisions partly by experience and partly by the new French philosophy, especially that advocated by Montesquieu.

One of the principles ably upheld by Montesquieu was that the three branches of government, the executive, legislative, and judicial, should be kept as distinct from one another as possible. The Revolutionary fathers adhered to this principle in theory, but failed to carry it out in actual practice, for in the state constitutions the executive was subordinated to the legislature. The creators of the new political order were obsessed with a great fear of their administrative officers, especially the governors, and so hedged their authority around with such restrictions that the executive was weak and inefficient. In eight states the governor was chosen by the legislature and was thus made subservient to it. "Ten states limited his term of office to a year; in eleven states he had no veto. A number of states contrived a council of state to advise the governor. The legislature, as a rule, chose this council and the civil officers upon whom the governor must depend for administrative service."[4] The fear that dictated these restrictions on the executive had grown out of the unpleasant experiences that the people had had with their royal governors. Having been treated in an arbitrary way by imperial officials, they were determined not to be domineered over by their own appointees. Unfortunately, however, in trying to render their governors impotent for evil, these constitution-makers tied their hands so completely that they could not efficiently perform any very useful function in the administration.

Most of the state constitutions were prefaced by or had incorporated in them elaborate bills of rights, in which were enumerated certain natural rights to which every individual was entitled. The doctrines enunciated in these bills of rights were very much the same as those proclaimed in the Declaration of Independence. They included guaranties of the personal liberty of the individual, freedom of speech and of religious worship, trial by jury, and security against unreasonable search, excessive

[4] VAN TYNE, C. H., *The American Revolution,* p. 144.

bail and fines, and unusual punishments.[5] The bills of rights were based on liberal principles, and if these principles had been actually carried out radical changes would have been effected in the political institutions of the states. But the doctrines proclaimed in the declarations of rights were not always accepted at face value by the practical politicians who framed the first state governments. The idealism preached by the advocates of natural rights could not, however, go entirely unheeded, and so a few steps toward democracy were taken at this time. There was a slight broadening of the suffrage, though voting was restricted in all of the thirteen original states to property-owners, renters of houses, or taxpayers. Only in the revolutionary state of Vermont was there universal manhood suffrage.

The second Continental Congress

The second Continental Congress was the organ of the federal government from its first meeting in 1775 until the Articles of Confederation went into effect in 1781. It was a revolutionary creation and had behind it no legal sanction, as there was no constitution to define its powers or limitations. Its authority rested on the acquiescence and support of the people, and it could exercise only such powers as the states were willing to delegate to it. The general government was weak and the state governments were strong because the people willed such a distribution of power. The states as the successors of the colonies were rooted in historic tradition, whereas the confederation was a new and artificial arrangement. Besides, the colonies had seceded from the empire into which they had been born and reared because their rights, as they believed, had been assailed. They were, therefore, determined not to jeopardize these rights by making the states subordinate to a new empire of their own creation. Moreover, sectional jealousies prevented an effective coöperation among the representatives. Usually, too, the personnel of the Continental Congress was not of a high order, as the most capable men of the country generally preferred to devote their abilities to foreign affairs or to the concerns of their respective states rather than spend their time in the discussions, often fruitless, of this federal debating society.[6]

[5] The first and most important of the bills of rights is the one that prefaces the Virginia Constitution. See THORPE, F. N., ed., *Colonial Charters*, pp. 3812-3814.

[6] SPARKS, JARED, *The Writings of Washington*, v, pp. 508-509; see also HART, A. B., *American History Told by Contemporaries*, ii, pp. 543-545 (Hamilton's opinion).

The exigencies of war demanded a more effective coöperation on the part of the states than was possible as long as the general government was exercised by a weak Congress unsupported by constitutional sanction. Early in the struggle, therefore, the need was felt of adopting a constitution for the general government. Lee's resolution for independence, offered on June 7, 1776, carried with it a motion "that a plan of confederation be prepared and transmitted to the respective Colonies for their consideration and approbation."[7] In this same month a committee of thirteen, one from each colony, was appointed to draft a constitution for the general government. Prominent members of this committee were John Dickinson, now of Delaware, Samuel Adams of Massachusetts, Edward Rutledge of South Carolina, Roger Sherman of Connecticut, and Robert R. Livingston of New York. A month later (July 12) the committee reported to Congress a draft of the Articles of Confederation, which had been written mostly by Dickinson.

Owing to the stress of other business, interruptions caused by the war, and differences of opinion, Congress did not take action immediately on the report of the committee. The new frame of government, after having been fully discussed and considerably revised, was finally accepted by Congress on November 15, 1777.[8] But the constitution was not to go into effect until it had been ratified by the legislatures of all the states. Most of the states had ratified it before the end of 1778, but Delaware and Maryland held out longer, the former accepting it early in 1779, and the latter on March 1, 1781.[9] Maryland's delay in ratifying the Articles was due to her fear of the states which had claims to western territory. If these states were to retain their western lands they would soon become so large and important that the smaller states with no such possessions would be dwarfed into comparative insignificance. A political union composed of commonwealths differing so greatly in area and population would be a partnership of giants and pygmies, and the latter might fare badly from the association.[10] By 1781 Maryland's fears on this score were re-

[7] *Journals of Congress,* v, p. 425.

[8] *Journals of Congress,* v, pp. 433, 546. For the discussion in Congress on the Articles, as reported by John Adams, see ADAMS, C. F., *The Life and Works of John Adams,* ii, pp. 492-502.

[9] HART, A. B., *op. cit.,* ii, p. 604.

[10] For an able argument in favor of Maryland's position, see *Journals of the Continental Congress,* xiv, pp. 619-622.

lieved, because New York had turned over to the federal government her shadowy claims to her western lands, and it was expected that the other six states which had rights in the West would surrender them to the Confederation.

The new constitution did not materially strengthen the general government. The states were recognized as sovereign and the federal government had only such authority as was delegated to it. In framing the Articles, the members of Congress were ever mindful of the fact that most of the friction between the colonies and the mother country had grown out of the attempt made by the latter to tax the possessions and regulate their commerce. The power wielded by the royal governors was another source of trouble between the American people and the British government. To avoid similar dangers in the future it was decided that in the new constitution there should be no provision for a strong federal executive, and the power to raise taxes and regulate commerce should be left with the states. No adequate arrangement was thus devised for enforcing the measures adopted by Congress, though this defect was afterward partially remedied by legislation. During the greater part of the war Congress had performed its administrative functions largely through committees. But this arrangement was not satisfactory, and in the early part of 1781 provision was made for the creation of four new offices. These were Superintendent of Finance, Secretary of War, Secretary of Marine, and Secretary of Foreign Affairs. This plan was continued after the adoption of the Articles of Confederation, and in this way the foundations were laid for the executive departments the heads of which now constitute the Cabinet. By allowing the states the right to lay import duties and regulate commerce, as well as levy direct taxes, the Confederation forfeited every direct source of revenue and yielded a power that should always belong to the general government. Congress was given power to vote taxes and apportion them among the states, but was not clothed with any authority to enforce collection.

Each state was to have one vote in Congress, and all important measures required the assent of nine states. Amendments could not be made without the consent of the legislature of all the states. A committee, called the Committee of the States, composed of

This protest is given in abbreviated form in HART, A. B., *American History Told by Contemporaries,* ii, pp. 591-593.

one delegate from each state, was to act in the interim of Congress and exercise such functions as that body by a vote of nine states should delegate to it. Delegates from the states were to be appointed and paid in such manner as the legislatures should direct, and could be recalled by the states. The powers of Congress included the "right and power of determining on peace and war"; "of sending and receiving ambassadors; entering into treaties and alliances"; of establishing rules for deciding upon the legality of captures on land and water and the manner of disposing of prizes taken by the land and naval forces; "appointing courts for the trial of piracies and felonies committed on the high seas"; and of establishing admiralty courts for the trial of appeals in all cases of captures. There was also a rather elaborate arrangement for the arbitration of disputes between the states. These last-mentioned clauses constituted the only provision made in the Articles for the establishment of a federal judiciary.[11]

The cost of the war, as measured in specie, was $65,863,825, according to the best estimates. This amount came mainly from four sources: namely, bills of credit, or Continental currency; requisitions on the states; domestic loans; and foreign loans. An effort was made to raise money by lotteries, but with little success, owing to the fact that the prizes were in the form of paper money and, therefore, were not attractive enough to tempt the people into the hazards of this form of gambling. *How the war was financed*

In June, 1775, Congress authorized the issue of bills of credit to the amount of two million dollars.[12] These were certificates entitling the holder to a given number of Spanish dollars, though the time and place of redemption were not stated. At first the denominations of the notes ranged from one dollar to eight; later certificates were issued in denominations as high as sixty-five dollars and as low as one-sixth of a dollar. As the Continental Congress had no power to compel the payment of taxes, it could not guarantee the redemption of this paper currency. The obligation to redeem the notes was turned over to the states, and the *Bills of credit, or Continental money*

[11] BOLTON, H. E., and MARSHALL, T. M., *The Colonization of North America*, p. 553.

The text of the Articles of Confederation can be found in the *Old South Leaflets*, no. 2; in PEASE, T. C., and ROBERTS, A. S., *Selected Readings*, pp. 141-148; and in WEST, W. M., *A Source Book in American History*, pp. 475-484 (slightly abbreviated).

[12] *Journals of Congress*, ii, p. 103.

proportion assigned to each state was determined by its population, including Negroes. It was recommended that the notes be redeemed gradually from 1779 to 1782. Very little was done by the states to meet the obligation imposed upon them by Congress, and only a very small amount was redeemed.

If the Continental currency had been restricted in amount its value might have been kept up almost to the level of metallic money, despite the failure of the redemption policy. For a while it was at a parity with specie. But later other issues were made until the total amount put in circulation went beyond the mark of $241,552,000. In addition to this, the states also issued paper money to the amount of over two hundred million dollars. Virginia and the Southern states were the greatest sinners in this respect. New England and the Middle states, probably because they were profiting by their earlier experiences, did not issue so much. The Continental currency was easy to imitate, and a great many counterfeit notes were thrown into circulation by unscrupulous Americans and by the British military authorities.

Under such conditions depreciation was inevitable.[13] The Continental notes declined so rapidly that by the beginning of 1781, fifty cents in paper were worth less than one cent in specie. Finally, in 1780, Congress frankly admitted the depreciation of the paper money and repudiated its obligations by making a provision for calling in the Continental notes, receiving them in place of silver at one-fortieth of their nominal value. This was nothing but bankruptcy.[14] Under the operation of this law, notes to the amount of $119,400,000 were called in and destroyed. New notes were issued in their stead to the amount of $4,400,000. They were to be redeemed in silver in six years and were to bear interest at the rate of five per cent. This new regulation failed to arrest the decline of the old paper money, and the new notes also began to depreciate rapidly. By the end of May, 1781, both kinds of notes had become worthless and had ceased to circulate as money.

In 1791, when the finances of the United States were put on a solid basis, the new tenor bills were exchanged in small amounts for good government securities and were thus redeemed. The old issue notes were also received for these same securities at the rate of 100 to 1. But only about six million dollars of them were

[13] HART, A. B., *American History Told by Contemporaries*, ii, pp. 601-603.

[14] *Journals of Congress*, xvi, pp. 262-267.

sent in for government stock, though the amount outstanding was estimated at seventy-eight million dollars. "The remainder had probably been lost or destroyed." A contemporary writer, in speaking of the Continental money, said that it "gently fell asleep in the hands of its last possessors." A modern economist thinks that a more correct way to describe the end of this paper money would be to say that "it passed out of the world like a victim of delirium tremens."[15]

As the states all declared the Continental money a legal tender, creditors were compelled to receive it in payment of debt. This gave dishonest debtors the opportunity of robbing their creditors by paying them off with cheap or worthless money. Many of them took advantage of the opportunity. A contemporary wrote: "For two or three years we constantly saw and were informed of creditors running away from their debtors, and the debtors pursuing them in triumph, and paying them without mercy."[16]

Prices rose rapidly despite futile efforts to regulate them. This encouraged speculation and extravagance, and enabled sharpers and rascals to become rich at the expense of honest and less clever people. It put the government in the attitude of setting an example of dishonesty to the people. According to Pelatiah Webster, a contemporary, this paper money "polluted the equity of our laws; turned them into engines of oppression and wrong; corrupted the justice of our public administration; destroyed the

[15] BULLOCK, C. J., *The Finances of the United States, 1775-1789*, p. 73. See also RAMSAY, D., *History of South Carolina*, ii, pp. 180-181.

[16] WITHERSPOON, J., *Works*, ix, p. 36.

For an excellent short account of the Continental currency, see an article by HARLOW, R. V., in the *American Historical Review*, xxxv, pp. 46-68. The author is not so severe in his condemnation of the paper-money policy of the Revolutionary government as are most of the writers on this subject. He admits that it was confiscation, but says that it was necessary as a means of financing the war and was no worse than other war activities, such as propaganda and other forms of misrepresentation. He quotes Franklin as saying that as the notes passed rapidly from hand to hand, no one usually lost much by their depreciation except creditors and persons with fixed incomes. Moreover, the losses resulting from depreciation acted as a gradual tax upon the people (pp. 62-63). In this way the people were able to bear at the time more than half the cost of the war (p. 68).

fortunes of thousands who had most confidence in it; and went far to destroying the morality of the people."[17]

But however bad the plan, it was a necessary evil. Congress could not have financed the war even so imperfectly as it did but for the expedient of paper money. The amount of money derived from all the other sources amounted to only about one-third, or a little more, of the total cost of the war.

Requisitions on the states   Beginning in November, 1777, Congress tried to raise money from time to time by making requisitions on the states. Only a part of the amount asked for on each occasion was voted by the state legislatures. The total amount collected in this way, as measured in specie, was less than six million dollars. It was difficult for the states to raise money by taxation. The people had not been accustomed to paying taxes except in small amounts, and these mainly for local purposes, and the machinery of taxation was not adequate for the collection of large sums of money. Besides, the people had rebelled against England largely on account of taxes. They could not, therefore, be expected to assent to taxes by a new central government. In 1780 Congress made requisition on the states for specific supplies of corn, beef, pork, rum, hay, etc. There was a good deal of waste in connection with the delivery of these supplies, and the plan was not a success.

Domestic loans   After the war had been going on about a year, Congress made an effort (October, 1776) to float a domestic loan of five million dollars.[18] The rate of interest was fixed at first at four and later at six per cent. But there was very little free capital at home to lend, and during the first year less than four million dollars of the amount was subscribed. About this time a loan was contracted in France which enabled Congress to pay in specie the interest on the bonds held by our own people. These bonds now became more attractive to American investors, and subscriptions to the loan were obtained more easily. The total amount raised in this way was $63,289,000 in paper, or $7,684,000 as measured in specie. To this amount should be added $1,272,284 which was supplied in the form of short-time loans by the Bank of North America in 1782 and 1783. Officers in the army were also au-

---

For an account by a contemporary, see FLÜGEL, F., and FAULKNER, H. U., *Readings in the Economic and Social History of the United States*, pp. 13-21.

[17] WEBSTER, PELATIAH, *Political Essays*, pp. 175-176, note.

[18] *Journals of Congress*, v, pp. 845-846.

thorized to impress food supplies, horses and wagons, and other transportation facilities. A certificate of value was given to the owner for these supplies. This was a kind of forced loan.

France and Spain secretly aided the United States by subsidies before the former had made an open alliance with us. A small amount was received from Spain in this way, and nearly two million dollars from France. These money grants were virtually gifts and were made with the hope of injuring their old enemy, England. In addition to these subsidies the United States borrowed from the French government over six million dollars and from Spain a small amount. Most of this money was spent in France for supplies and clothing for the soldiers. By 1782 the credit of the United States had become good enough for it to borrow money from private banks in the Netherlands. In that year and the next loans amounting to more than a million and a quarter dollars were contracted in that country. *Foreign loans*

At the end of the colonial period the American post office was still a part of the British imperial postal system, and this connection was an important strand in the cord that held the dominions to the mother country. There had arisen, however, even before the beginning of the quarrel with the homeland, considerable dissatisfaction with the Royal Mail Service in America, owing to the arrogance displayed by postal officials and the high rates charged for handling mail. This feeling of dissatisfaction grew quickly into a spirit of rebellion as a result of the policy carried out by the imperial post office after the controversy arose over the Stamp Act. "The Royal Post Office interfered in every possible way that could block the efforts of the colonies to obtain unanimity of action. It delayed and suppressed news and mishandled mail. Letters were opened, read, and destroyed, and the information thus obtained was transmitted to the royal authorities."[19] *The Revolutionary post office*

The only way to put an end to this intolerable situation was to organize an American postal system to supersede the Royal Mail Service. This the second Continental Congress proceeded to do. In May, 1775, a committee was appointed by that body to devise a plan for uniting the colonies under a new postal system.[20] The committee proposed the creation of a post office department that would have charge of the business of conveying and

[19] FITZPATRICK, J. C., *The Spirit of the Revolution*, p. 237.
[20] *Journals of the Continental Congress*, ii, p. 71.

distributing letters throughout the colonies. This report was adopted by Congress on July 26, 1775,[21] and in this way there came into being the second of the executive departments, the first being that of Indian affairs. The separation of the colonial from the imperial post office was thus effected nearly a year before political independence was declared. Under the new arrangement offices were established in all the colonies, with postmasters to collect and distribute the mail and post-riders to carry it on all routes from Maine to Georgia. The general management of the system was intrusted to a Postmaster-General, with headquarters at Philadelphia, and with him were associated a Secretary and a Comptroller, or Auditor. Benjamin Franklin, who had been the most successful administrator of the Royal Mail Service, was chosen as the first Postmaster-General.

In establishing the American post office Congress did not appropriate the machinery of the Royal Mail Service, but took over and developed a postal system that had been organized by William Goddard, an enterprising newspaper publisher. Goddard was the owner of a weekly paper, the *Maryland Journal and Baltimore Advertiser*, in whose columns the rights of the colonies were upheld with courage and ardent enthusiasm. The editor's criticism of British policy was so severe that finally the paper was refused the use of the mails. Goddard was not, however, the man to yield to imperial highhandedness, and he determined to publish and distribute his newspaper in spite of the opposition of the British authorities. Accordingly, he formed a plan for delivering copies of his weekly by sending out his own riders, who covered routes extending from Maine to Georgia. His riders were more reliable than those of the Royal Mail Service, and it was not long before the people living along their routes began to intrust them with the carrying of their letters and small packages. This competition soon cut heavily into the receipts of the royal post office, and "there were frequent personal encounters and much bad blood displayed by the competing riders when they chanced to meet upon the road. These were, in effect, the preliminary skirmishes of the war that was soon to break forth."[22]

In organizing the Revolutionary postal system Franklin showed the energy and efficiency which usually characterized his efforts, and by the end of 1776, at which time he left for France,

[21] *Ibid.*, ii, pp. 208-209.
[22] Fitzpatrick, J. C., *The Spirit of the Revolution*, p. 238.

the American post office was well established. Postal rates, as well as the compensation allowed postmasters and the higher officials, were fixed by Congress, and this body promised to make good any deficits that might arise, a pledge which it generally found difficult to redeem.

After establishing a postal system of its own, Congress had to decide whether it would allow its rival, the Royal Mail Service, to remain in the field. There was considerable debate on a proposal to suppress the British post office, but no action was taken.[23] Nor was it necessary for Congress to act, for events soon caused the Royal Mail Service to end its career in the colonies. When hostilities began, feeling against everything British became so intense that the imperial post office had very little business. Finley, the royal Postmaster-General, reported that the rebels were robbing and rifling the mails and were keeping the public from using them by declaring that it was unconstitutional to send letters and packages through the royal postal system.[24] Finally, on Christmas Day, 1775, it was announced that owing to interruptions in the service in various parts of the country the royal post office would be closed.[25]

The doctrines taught by the patriot leaders also resulted in some important social changes. The severe criminal code of the old days was mitigated, and a broader justice in social relations was generally advocated. Thinkers like Jefferson noted the inconsistency of their views with the continuance of Negro slavery and regretted that the blessing of liberty might not be enjoyed by blacks as well as whites. This feeling found expression in state laws prohibiting or restricting the importation of slaves. Like action was also taken by the general government. The Association, or non-importation agreement, adopted by the first Continental Congress contained a clause forbidding the further importation of slaves, and this clause seems to have been well enforced. As a result of these restrictions the African slave trade was almost entirely stopped during the period of the Revolution. There was also a strong sentiment in favor of emancipating the blacks, and measures providing for the gradual or immediate abolition of slavery were adopted in all the states in which the number of

Social results of the Revolution: Effect on slavery

[23] *Journals of the Continental Congress*, iii, pp. 488-489.

[24] See an article by SMITH, WILLIAM, in the *American Historical Review*, xxi, p. 275.

[25] FORCE, PETER, *American Archives*, 4th series, iv, p. 453.

slaves was small. Even in the South there was considerable opposition to human bondage, and many slaves were freed south of Mason and Dixon's Line.[26] When a movement was finally inaugurated that led to the extinction of slavery in the entire country, the doctrines of the Revolutionary period were invoked to justify and support it.

Changes in the land policy

The Revolution also led to some significant changes in the land policy of the states. It put an end to the payment of quit rents, thereby relieving landowners of a tax of about one hundred thousand dollars a year, which amount was being paid to the king and the proprietors at the end of the colonial period. It was not long after the treaty of peace before most of the states had abolished entails, and a few years later in all of the states the law of primogeniture had been repealed.[27] By these reforms the bequeathing of land to a succession of heirs was forbidden, and all the sons of a deceased parent were put on an equality in the distribution of real property. These changes, therefore, tended to promote a wider distribution of real estate and to discourage the concentration of landholdings in the hands of a few wealthy families. The confiscation of the property of Tories also accentuated this tendency, for some princely estates were taken from the Loyalists and divided up into moderate-sized farms. The states also took over and sold the unoccupied lands belonging to the crown, and most of this land ultimately came into the possession of small farmers.

Religion as a cause of revolt

Religion played an important part in the American Revolution. At first thought it would seem that religion would serve as a cultural tie to reinforce the political bond that held the dominions to the British Isles. For every denomination in America was the counterpart of an ecclesiastical organization of the same faith and order in the homeland. In the case of the dissenters, however, the only connection between the English denominations and

[26] The number of slaves freed in eight years in Virginia was twice as large as the number emancipated by the Massachusetts constitution, and was equal to the whole number of slaves in both Connecticut and Rhode Island at the outbreak of the Revolution (JAMESON, J. F., *The American Revolution Considered as a Social Movement*, pp. 37-38).

[27] An entail was an estate that was limited to a particular class of heirs, and the holder of it could not sell or give it away. Under the law of primogeniture all the landed property of a father who died without a will went to the oldest son.

their American adherents was a fraternal feeling arising from a community of beliefs and a uniformity of practices. The Anglicans in the colonies, it is true, were bound to the mother church by ecclesiastical organization, as well as sentimental ties, but the adherents of this faith were greatly in the minority in the overseas possessions. The church, as a whole, therefore, was not an agency that promoted loyalty to the empire on the part of the colonials.

The great majority of the English-speaking colonists belonged to sects that would not affiliate with the national church. In thus asserting their ecclesiastical independence the American dissenters were entering a path that might lead to political separation from the empire. Inasmuch as the imperial government, both in England and in the dominions, was allied with the Anglican Church, any dissatisfaction with the latter would naturally give grounds for complaint against the former. It was for this reason that there was a religious as well as a political side to the revolutions in England in the seventeenth century and also to our revolt against the mother country. In the case of the Puritan Revolution, the dissenters were allied with Parliament against the king; in the American Revolution they were identified with the radical patriots who were in opposition to the British government. It is true that religion did not play as important a part in the latter struggle as it did in the former, but on its religious side our Revolution was a faint echo of its prototype of the seventeenth century. The Congregational ministers in New England and the Presbyterian and other dissenting clergymen in the Middle and Southern colonies were the spiritual descendants of the men who prayed for the success of Cromwell's army and of those bold Scotch Covenanters who signed in their blood an agreement to oppose the establishment of Anglicanism in their own country.

We are not surprised, therefore, to learn that the New England ministers took a prominent part in proclaiming the rights of the colonists and in opposing any encroachment upon these rights by the imperial authorities. These clergymen did not have the political power in the eighteenth century that they had wielded in the seventeenth, but they still exerted a mighty influence in molding public opinion. Most of them had been indoctrinated with the liberal political views of Milton, Locke, and Algernon Sidney. From Locke they had imbibed the "doctrine that it was the people's right to choose their own rulers and to fix the bounds of their authority."[28] This advanced philosophy was not always confined to the realm of academic speculation, but was sometimes preached from the pulpit as a part of the political gospel. In this way some of the liberal ideas of Locke and other advanced thinkers found their way into the minds of the plain people.

The primacy of the dissenters in the Northern and Middle colonies was never seriously threatened by the Anglicans, but there was always a lurking fear that Anglicanism would with government support secure a dangerous footing in this region. This fear arose partly from the attempt made by Andros to favor the Anglicans in New England, partly from the abortive endeavors to establish the Church of England in New York, and largely from the efforts that were made from time to time to secure the appointment of a bishop for America. The dissenters feared that the establishment of a bishopric in the colonies would give the Anglican Church in the dominions a more effective organization and thereby make it a more formidable rival of the other denominations.

When we remember that the imperial government was the chief prop of the Church of England in America, we can readily see how easy it was for the New England clergy to link up their fight against the latter with opposition to the former, and how likely they were to carry a large proportion of their parishioners with them. The Presbyterians, because of the unjust treatment to which they had been subjected in Ireland by the Anglican party, came to the New World with a strong feeling against Anglicanism, which they transmitted to their posterity. Their disagreement with the English Church could easily be converted into an attitude of hostility to the English government, and so the Presbyterian ministers were almost unanimous in their support of the Revolution. Nor did the Baptists lag behind their fellow Puritans in opposing Anglicanism. Their persecutions in Virginia by the establishment just on the brink of the Revolution gave a new zeal to their opposition to the Anglican Church and the political order that upheld it, and their ministers, almost to a man, were aligned with the patriot cause.

As an offset to the influence of the dissenting clergy, many of the Anglican rectors urged loyalty to the British government, and some of them went to the extreme of proclaiming the antiquated doctrine of the divine right of kings. They could do little,

[28] Van Tyne, C. H., *Causes of the War of Independence*, p. 356.

however, to counteract the liberal notions set afloat by their rivals, as they were not in a position to make an effective appeal to any large portion of the people. In the Northern and Middle colonies the adherents of the Anglican cause were comparatively few in number; and even in the South, outside of South Carolina, the ministers of the established church did not exert a potent influence in molding public opinion, as many of them did not have the strength of character or independence of spirit that are necessary for leadership. Seldom did a proud-spirited Virginia planter pay much heed to the opinions of an impoverished rector, whose salary he named and whose opinions he often controlled.

The Revolution dealt a serious blow to the Church of England. It was disestablished in those provinces in which it had enjoyed recognition as the state church. Moreover, the sentiments of loyalty to the British cause held by many of the Anglican clergy rendered them objects of suspicion to the patriots. When the Declaration of Independence was voted, the Anglican ministers were embarrassed by the fact that it was now disloyal to the new republic to use that part of the liturgy which requires that prayers be said for the king. Under such unfavorable circumstances the church necessarily declined very rapidly in numbers and influence. The support of the Venerable Society was withdrawn, church buildings were closed, and many ministers were forced to give up their work. At the end of the war there were only six Anglican preachers left in all New England, and in Georgia the church had completely disappeared. There was at one time only one Anglican clergyman in the entire province of Pennsylvania, and even in Virginia and Maryland the Anglican cause had greatly declined.

Effect of the Revolution on the Anglican Church

The Methodists had not yet separated from the Anglican Church, and they came in for a full share of the opprobrium that was meted out to the Anglicans. The first Methodist to come to America was Philip Embury, who landed in New York in 1760. Six years later he began to preach in his own house and gathered around himself a few converts, who formed the first Methodist society in America. About the same time a society was formed in Baltimore under the preaching of Robert Strawbridge. Missionaries were sent over by Wesley, and as a result of their preaching and that of local assistants the society grew rapidly. In 1771 the number had increased to nearly five thousand.

Effect on the Methodists

When the break with the mother country came, the Methodists

were all regarded as Tories and so were looked upon with suspicion and disfavor. The reason for this was that most of the preachers were Englishmen and the society acknowledged the leadership of Wesley. Wesley was now strongly disliked in America because he had come out in a pamphlet against the patriot cause, although he had previously expressed sympathy with it. The English missionaries all went back to England except Francis Asbury,[29] and he was in hiding for a while. Some of the Methodists were imprisoned for their alleged disloyalty, while others were fined or whipped because their consciences would not let them fight. Despite these untoward circumstances, however, the society continued to grow in numbers, and after the Revolution it developed into a separate denomination.

Effect on the other denominations — The war had also an unfavorable effect on the spiritual condition and material prosperity of the dissenters, as well as of the Anglicans. Many churches were destroyed or desecrated by the armies, and there was a tendency toward spiritual decline among the Presbyterians, Congregationalists, and Baptists. The historian of the Virginia Baptists in speaking of them said, "With some few exceptions, the declension was general throughout the state. The love of many waxed cold. Some of the watchmen fell, others stumbled, and many slumbered at their posts."[30] It looked as if it were "impossible for men to serve Mars and Christ at the same time." As an offset to this loss in spiritual fervor there was a decided gain in religious toleration, for the liberal principles embodied in the bills of rights of the states (see p. 687) were plainly in conflict with the spirit of religious intolerance. It is true that in some of the states there were still religious tests for officeholding, but "in most cases these restrictions disappeared before many years, and substantially the battle for religious freedom was won."[31]

"It [the Revolution] was in truth an economic, social, and intellectual transformation of prime significance—the first of those modern world-shaking reconstructions in which mankind has

[29] Francis Asbury became the first bishop of the American Methodists after they were organized into a separate denomination.

[30] SEMPLE, R. B., *History of the Rise and Progress of the Baptists in Virginia* (1810); quoted by JAMESON, J. F., *The American Revolution Considered as a Social Movement*, p. 148.

[31] *Ibid.*, p. 142.

sought to cut and fashion the tough and stubborn web of fact to fit the pattern of its dreams."[32]

The one important economic resource of the colonies in the contest with the mother country was their foreign commerce. They used it as a weapon in the fight with England, just as the South expected to use cotton in its struggle for independence. In the eighteenth century, owing to the Mercantilist notions then prevailing, colonial trade was considered a most valuable asset for the mother country. England, it was thought, owed in large measure her wealth and position as a great sea power to the trade with her American colonies. If this trade were cut off economic decline would result.

Relation of commerce to the Revolution

Acting on this belief, the colonies first tried the policy of non-intercourse with England. It was hoped that this suspension of commerce between America and England would mean great loss to the trading and manufacturing interests in the latter country. Pressure would then be brought on Parliament and the objectionable measures would be repealed. This policy might have succeeded if the commercial and manufacturing classes had at that time been represented in Parliament in proportion to their numbers and wealth.

When the colonies saw that they could not force the British government to yield to their demands by withholding their trade, they decided to offer it to some foreign power for military aid. But they could not hope to negotiate a commercial treaty with a European power as long as they were a part of the British empire. It was, therefore, thought necessary to declare the independence of the colonies if their best economic weapon was to be used most effectively.

The war at first caused a decided interruption of foreign commerce. Relations between England and America were at one time forbidden by both Parliament and Congress. Later, however, Congress opened American ports to British ships. It was also the policy of the British to prevent the colonies from trading with European countries. At first American foreign commerce was almost driven off the seas, and considerable hardship to the people was the result. There was especially a scarcity of woolen clothing, which caused much suffering among the soldiers. But in a few years American privateers and neutral ships that had learned

[32] BEARD, C. A., and MARY R., *The Rise of American Civilization*, 1, p. 296.

how to escape the watching British cruisers opened up to some extent the lanes of foreign commerce. Foreign trade, however, had to be carried on by circuitous routes and was still subject to great risks, and so the cost of transportation and insurance was high. Despite these handicaps, however, foreign supplies began to come in in considerable amounts by 1777 and continued until the end of the war. By 1783 the people of New England were enjoying more comforts than they had even before the outbreak of the war. Conditions, however, were different in the South, where the British armies had overrun the country, destroyed property, and taken away slaves.[33]

Effect of the Revolution on industry

"Within a short time after the outbreak of the war a serious economic depression swept over the country. New England lost heavily from the destruction of the fisheries; the indigo-planters were sorely affected by the withdrawal of bounties; and the tobacco and rice growers suffered for want of an adequate market. It was not long, however, until the country adjusted itself to the new conditions which the war had produced."[34] Indeed, the ultimate effect of the Revolution on agriculture was favorable, for it enabled the Americans to come in touch with the improvements in farming that had been made in France and England during the middle portion of the eighteenth century. Better methods in tillage were employed, more up-to-date implements were used, and efforts were made to improve the breeds of livestock. Moreover, the people during the contest with the mother country had become accustomed to forming organizations for political purposes, and this practice led soon after the war to the creation of numerous much-needed agricultural societies. By means of these organizations the new ideas borrowed from Europe and others found out by experiment and comparison were broadcast over the country.

In some respects the war had a tendency to discourage manufacturing. Before the Revolution the manufacture of pig-iron was carried on extensively in all the colonies. American pig-iron was admitted to England duty free, while that coming from other countries had to pay a tax. A ready market was, therefore, found in the mother country for all the pigs and bars cast in America.

---

[33] For the relation of industry and commerce to the Revolution, see CALLENDER, G. S., *Selected Readings in the Economic History of the United States*, pp. 122-137, 143-165.

[34] FLÜGEL, F., and FAULKNER, H. U., *Readings in the Economic and Social History of the United States*, p. 3.

This market was entirely closed by the war. There was also a greater scarcity of labor than ever, owing to enlistment in the army, the expulsion of the Tories, and the cutting off of the source of supply of indentured servants and slaves. Shipbuilding, which had been a very important industry before the outbreak of hostilities, was for the time being virtually destroyed.

But manufacturing on the whole was encouraged rather than discouraged by the war. The restrictions on commerce hampered foreign competition to a considerable extent, and this gave the American manufacturer a good home market. One of the industries greatly stimulated by the interruption of foreign commerce was the manufacture of salt. The colonials had always consumed a vast amount of salt, nearly all of which was procured from southern Europe, and the Canary, Madeira, and West Indian Islands. These sources of supply were now cut off to a great extent, and the scarcity of salt and its high price gave a strong impetus to its manufacture. Besides, the demand for supplies was greater than ever on account of the needs of the war. Munitions of war, woolen clothing, canvas for tents, and shoes and socks (which were rapidly worn out) were all needed. The constant decline in the value of money and the corresponding rise in prices made it easy to sell commodities and thus created an artificial demand for goods of all kinds. These conditions stimulated home production and new industries sprang up in every section of the country. There was also perfect freedom in industry, as the colonial restrictions imposed by the British government were now inoperative.[35]

It is interesting to speculate on what might have been the course of all later world history if English statesmen had been more conscious of the necessity of a new policy and colonial leaders had been more patient before forcing the issue of secession. It is quite likely that a partnership, profitable to both sides, might have been maintained indefinitely between England and America, if the British empire had in 1763 been organized on its present basis. If the colonies had been granted the status now enjoyed by Canada, separation from the empire might have

[35] For the effect of the Revolution on manufactures, see CLARK, V., *History of Manufactures in the United States*, i, pp. 215-227, and JAMESON, J. F., *The American Revolution Considered as a Social Movement*, pp. 81-97.

meant going backward instead of forward, for it would have been giving up the benefits of imperialism without acquiring any compensating advantages. Such a solution, however, was impossible at that stage of the world's acceptance of the truth regarding economic and political problems. To heap adverse criticism on either the mother country or the colonies for not agreeing upon a plan of adjustment like that recently made with reference to Ireland, would be to complain that the twentieth century had not dawned in the last quarter of the eighteenth.

Selected Readings

1. American Women (a British estimate).—Trevelyan, G. O. *The American Revolution*, part i, vol. i, pp. *97-99.
2. The Social and Intellectual Gulf between England and America. —Van Tyne, C. H., *The Causes of the War of Independence,* *ch. 12; Greene, E. B., *Foundations of American Nationality,* pp. *347-355.
3. The Religious Aspects of the Revolution.—Trevelyan, *The American Revolution*, part ii, vol. ii, pp. *297-328; Van Tyne, C. H., *England and America,* *lecture iii; *Causes of the War of Independence,* *ch. 13.
4. The Post Office of the Revolutionary Period.—Fitzpatrick, J. C., *The Spirit of the Revolution,* *ch. 17.
5. Part Played by Lawyers in the Revolution.—Van Tyne, C. H., *England and America,* *lecture iv.
6. Organization of the New State Governments.—Van Tyne, C. H., *The American Revolution,* *ch. 9.
7. The Articles of Confederation.—Bolton, H. E., and Marshall, T. M., *The Colonization of North America,* pp. *539-544.
8. War Finances.—Flügel, F., and Faulkner, H. U., *Readings in the Economic and Social History of the United States,* pp. *13-21; Bullock, C. J., *Monetary History of the United States,* pp. *60-73; Dewey, D. R., *Financial History of the United States,* *ch. 2; Oberholtzer, E. P., *Robert Morris, Patriot and Financier,* *ch. 3.
9. Relation of Industry and Commerce to the Revolution.—Channing, E., *History of the United States,* iii, ch. 13; Callender, G. S., *Selections from the Economic History of the United States,* pp. *122-137, 143-165; Van Metre, T. W., *Economic History of the United States,* pp. *146-152; Jameson, J. F., *The American Revolution Considered as a Social Movement,* *ch. 3; Flügel, F., and Faulkner, H. U., *op. cit.,* pp. *9-13.
10. Effect of the Revolution on Manufactures.—Clark, Victor, *History of Manufactures in the United States,* i, pp. 215-227.

11. Effect of the Revolution on Thought and Feeling.—Jameson, J. F., *The American Revolution, etc.,* *ch. 4.
12. Moral Effects of the War.—Adams, J. T., *New England in the Republic,* *ch. 3.
13. The Influence of the New England Clergy on the American Revolution.—Van Tyne, C. H., article in the *American Historical Review,* xix, pp. *44-64.

PART IV

THE CONFEDERATION

CHAPTER XXXIV

THE FIRST REPUBLIC

Government under the Confederation

The United States, since independence, has gone through three stages of political development. These periods might properly be designated as the First, Second, and Third Republics. In the first period (1776-1789) the general government was weak, with sovereignty, or supreme power, residing in the states. During the second period (1789-1861) it was a disputed point as to whether the federal union was a confederation, as it was before 1789, or a national state, as it has been since the early eighteen-sixties. The War of Secession marked the death of the Second and the birth of the Third Republic, which has continued until the present time. With the inauguration of the new government under the present Constitution the First Republic ended its short-lived career.

As has already been shown,[1] the Articles of Confederation were the constitution of the First Republic during the last eight years of its existence. When this constitution was subjected to the strain of actual practice its defects soon became apparent. These defects in the main grew out of the weakness of the general government, which did not rest directly on the people but on the states. Among the shortcomings that were generally recognized were the dependence of the inadequate executive on the legislature, the absence of a well-organized federal judiciary, and the inability of Congress to levy taxes and regulate interstate and foreign commerce. *Weaknesses of the Articles of Confederation*

The general government was especially hampered by its lack of authority to raise an adequate revenue. Since Congress could not levy taxes, the income of the Confederation was derived solely from the sale of public lands and from requisitions on the states. The states, however, failed to meet the payments that were asked of them, and the amount of revenue which came into the federal *Financial difficulties*

[1] See pp. 689-691.

treasury was pitiably small.[2] There was not enough to pay the running expenses of the government and interest on its indebtedness, and therefore the public debt was constantly increasing.[3]

Discontent in the army   Besides, the soldiers were in an angry mood because of arrearages in the payments due them. In the army stationed at Newburg on the Hudson discontent had almost reached the point of mutiny (1783) and but for the influence of Washington might have led to an outbreak.[4] Not all the soldiers, however, were so amenable to good advice. There was a mutiny among the Pennsylvania troops quartered at Lancaster and about eighty of them marched to Philadelphia.[5] Instead of dealing firmly with the situation, the Philadelphia authorities showed their timidity by negotiating with the malcontents. Partly as a protest against this weak policy, Congress left Philadelphia for Princeton (June, 1783), where it held its sessions for some time.[6]

Inadequate regulation of commerce   It was unfortunate too that the control of commerce between the states and with foreign countries was vested in the government of the states rather than in that of the Confederation. Such an allocation of authority prevented the country from presenting a united front in its commercial dealings with outside powers and fostered jealousy and competition among the states in both their domestic and their foreign commercial relations.

Failure of efforts to amend the Articles of Confederation   These defects might all have been remedied by amendments to the constitution but for the unwise provision of the Articles of

[2] *Journals of the Continental Congress*, xxvi, p. 194; xxx, pp. 73-74.

[3] WRIGHT, CHESTER W., *Economic History of the United States*, p. 237.

[4] In an address to the officers of the army Washington spoke so feelingly and made such a strong appeal to their patriotism that they abandoned all idea of resorting to force, if they had ever harbored such an intention. For the documents covering the Newburg affair and Washington's skillful handling of it, see *Journals of the Continental Congress*, xxiv, pp. 291-311; and SPARKS, JARED, ed., *The Writings of George Washington*, viii, pp. 551-566. The more important of these documents can also be found in the appendix of HATCH, L. C., *The Administration of the American Revolutionary Army*, pp. 197-209.

[5] FITZPATRICK, J. C., ed., *The Writings of George Washington*, xxvii, pp. 32-36.

[6] *Journals of the Continental Congress*, xxiv, pp. 410-411; xxv, pp. 971, 973-974.

Confederation which made such revision practically impossible. All amendments proposed by Congress failed of ratification, in one case by the adverse vote of only one state legislature.[7]

As a result of these and other weaknesses, the Articles of Confederation lasted less than a decade, although the framers of the instrument declared the Union under it to be perpetual. If the constitution had included a plan for future changes the result might have been very different, but this attempt to fit a changing society into a fixed mold was doomed to failure. To the growing young republic the constitution soon became a strait jacket instead of a comfortable suit of clothes.

Diplomatic Problems

After independence the new nation was confronted with the important problem of making the proper adjustments with foreign powers. In the peace treaty itself lay the germs of controversy.

Relations with England: Controversy over the terms of the peace treaty

[7] In February, 1781, Congress asked the states for authority to levy a 5 per cent tax on imports, the money to be used for the payment of interest and principal on the federal debt. Most of the states promptly complied with this request, but Rhode Island refused her assent. Virginia had accepted the proposal, but after Rhode Island's refusal she withdrew her consent for fear of jeopardizing the sovereignty of the state. *Journals of the Continental Congress,* xix, pp. 112-113; xxiii, p. 643; Hening, W. W., *Statutes at Large* (Va.), x, pp. 409-410, 451; xi, p. 171; *Annual Report* for 1894 of the American Historical Association, pp. 351-359.

Two years later (April, 1783) Congress again proposed a change in the Articles by which Congress would be granted for a period of twenty-five years the authority to levy a small duty on imports, the money to be used solely for the payment of interest and principal on the public debt. Finally, after a delay of more than three years, all the states but New York ratified the amendment (before the end of 1786). The New York legislature took no action regarding it and so the amendment was lost. *Journals of the Continental Congress,* xxiv, pp. 257-262; xxx, 70-76.

In April, 1784, Congress adopted a resolution asking the states to grant it authority for fifteen years to pass acts regulating foreign commerce. This request was renewed in October, 1786. Although the northern and middle states were in favor of such an amendment, there was enough opposition in the South to defeat it. McLaughlin, A. C., *The Confederation and the Constitution,* pp. 84-85; *Journals of the Continental Congress,* xxvi, pp. 318-322; Hunt, G. A., ed., *Writings of James Madison,* ii, p. 180.

It had been stipulated that Congress would earnestly recommend to the state legislatures the enactment of provisions restoring the just rights of Tories, or Loyalists, whose property had been confiscated, and removing all legal impediments to the full recovery of all debts justly owing to British creditors in America. Although Congress made the promised recommendation, the states did not obey the injunction as to the rights of either Tories or British creditors. In clear violation of the spirit of the pledge given by the American commissioners, state legislatures passed laws hampering the collection of pre-war debts.[8] In a circular sent to the states, Congress urged them to repeal such statutes, and by 1789 most of the states had complied with this request.

When the new Constitution went into effect (1789) it annulled all laws in violation of the treaty and opened the courts to British creditors. Nothing but legal delays then stood in the way of the collection of debts due Englishmen, but these delays were so great that it was considered necessary to insert in Jay's Treaty (1794) a clause providing for a mixed commission to pass upon all uncollected debts.[9] This commission failed to agree, and it was not until 1802 that a final settlement was effected. At that time the United States government paid to British creditors a lump sum of 600,000 pounds, in complete satisfaction of all debts, principal and interest.[10]

British posts in the West

Although Britain had promised in the treaty to withdraw her garrisons from American soil "with all convenient speed," she nevertheless maintained for twelve years seven military posts in the Northwest, south of the Canadian border. The excuse offered for this plain violation of the terms of the treaty was that the Americans had violated them also, notably as to English debts and the treatment of Loyalists. Probably the real reason was the desire of the British to use these posts as centers for the promotion of the Canadian fur trade and for controlling the western Indians in their interests.[11]

[8] For the action of the states regarding Tories, see p. 680 n.; also JOHNSTON, HENRY P., ed., *The Correspondence and Public Papers of John Jay*, iii, p. 214.

[9] For this provision in Jay's Treaty, see MALLOY, W. M., *Treaties, Conventions . . . between the United States of America and Other Powers*, i, pp. 594-595.

[10] *Ibid.*, p. 611.

[11] For a good discussion of the relation of the debt question to the retention of the British posts, see MCLAUGHLIN, A. C., "The West-

To John Adams, first minister of the United States to England, was assigned the task of grappling with these difficulties. He went to London in 1785 hoping to negotiate a commercial treaty with the British government, to persuade it to withdraw its troops from the western posts, and to secure an indemnity for slaves seized in America after the peace treaty had been signed. He was cordially received by the king but could make no progress with the foreign office. He was told that the military posts would not be removed until the debts had been paid. Refusal of the American demands was not softened by diplomatic suavity, but Adams was a match for the British ministers in blunt candor. He was unable, however, to make the slightest dent in the British self-complacency.

Adams's unsuccessful mission

Adams returned home, therefore, in 1788 without having realized any of his three aims, and with the feeling that his failure had been due largely to the weakness of our federal government. The British authorities knew that a commercial treaty with America could not be enforced since Congress had no power to regulate foreign commerce. They knew also that the American government was not able to offer any inducements for a liberal treatment of its citizens or to retaliate if their rights were infringed. Hence they refused to sign a treaty of commerce with the United States.[12]

The peace treaty between England and the United States provided that the boundary between Spanish West Florida and the United States should be the thirty-first parallel and that the Mississippi River should be free for the use of both the British and the Americans. This treaty soon gave rise to disputes between Spain and the United States; for Spain contended that Britain had exceeded her authority in making such promises and that therefore they were not binding upon herself. During the war Spain had seized West Florida and still held this territory, including the area as far north as the mouth of the Yazoo River. She also claimed virtually all the land west of Georgia and south of the Cumberland River. The Spanish government therefore maintained that England had no right to dispose of West Florida

Relations with Spain: Causes of dispute

---

ern Posts and the British Debts," *Annual Report* of the American Historical Association for 1894, pp. 413-444.

[12] SPARKS, JARED, ed., *Diplomatic Correspondence, 1783-1789* (3 vol. ed.), ii, pp. 478-482, 484, 581.

or any part of it. This overlapping of claims was a source of considerable trouble to the American settlers in the Southwest because the Spanish authorities encouraged the powerful Indian tribes there to shut American traders and settlers out of the region. Consequently, the entire southwestern frontier was in constant danger of Indian attack.

Both sides of the Mississippi for two hundred miles above its mouth were in the unchallenged possession of Spain, and the land on both sides was claimed by her to a considerably greater distance to the north. She was therefore in a position to control navigation on the "Father of Waters." While the United States contended for the *right* of her Westerners to navigate the river, Spain allowed them to use it only as a *privilege* to be granted under such terms and regulations as her own policy might from time to time dictate.[13]

Negotiations between Jay and the Spanish representative

In the hope of settling these disputes between the United States and Spain, negotiations were begun in the summer of 1785, when Don Diego de Gardoqui, the Spanish chargé d'affaires, arrived in Washington. John Jay, the American Secretary for Foreign Affairs, had been instructed to induce the Spanish minister (1) to agree to a commercial treaty between the two countries, (2) to accept the thirty-first parallel as the northern boundary of West Florida, and (3) to grant to our citizens the right of free navigation of the Mississippi River. Jay's chief handicap in the negotiations was his inability to offer anything of commensurate value in exchange for these demands. Nor could he frighten Gardoqui by the threat of war, for the Spanish representative knew that the new country was in no position to engage in another military contest.[14]

[13] In 1784 the Spanish authorities at New Orleans announced that thereafter the Mississippi River would be closed to American trade. Four years later the river was opened to the use of the Westerners, but only on condition that they pay duties on goods sold at New Orleans or transshipped from there to other ports. There was a reduction in these duties in favor of individuals who by letters from James Wilkinson could show that they were disposed to promote Spanish interests in the West. BEMIS, S. F., *A Diplomatic History of the United States*, pp. 74, 81.

[14] *Secret Journals of Congress*, Aug. 25, 1785; Feb. 28, 1786; Aug. 3, 1786.

With the idea that even partial success in dealing with these Jay's pro-
posals problems would be preferable to a complete failure, Jay asked Congress to authorize him to make a more acceptable offer. He felt that if a favorable commercial treaty could be agreed upon, the United States might well afford to postpone her claims regarding the other two points in dispute. As a compromise measure the United States could for twenty-five or thirty years suspend her right to navigate the Mississippi River; for by the end of that period the population of the West would be great enough to frighten Spain into accepting the American demands as to the use of the great river.[15] A proposal in Congress that Jay be instructed to make the concessions he had suggested led to a heated debate. In the North, where·commerce was important, it was felt that a treaty with Spain would greatly benefit not only that section but the country as a whole. The northern representatives were therefore willing to waive for the time being the right to navigate the Mississippi. The southern states, on the contrary, opposed the proposal. They still had western lands and their representatives in Congress realized more fully than did Jay and the Northerners generally how impossible it would be to keep the Westerners from using the Mississippi as an outlet for their commerce. The discussions in Congress showed that the proposal could not win the support of two-thirds of the states. Since no treaty could be ratified without such a vote, Jay gave up the plan.[16]

HARD TIMES

During the war the American people were in the main fairly Prosperity
during the
war prosperous, except in the regions that were overrun by enemy troops. Manufactured goods and farm products found a home market created by the needs of the various armies. For many shipowners the gains from privateering afforded at least partial compensation for the loss of ocean commerce. French and British soldiers brought in gold and silver currency and money was therefore plentiful. The coming of peace was expected to bring still better times. Out of this expectation came a brief season of

[15] For Jay's proposal to Congress, see *Journals of the Continental Congress,* xxxi, pp. 473-481.

[16] It was this experience that caused the southern delegates to the Philadelphia Convention (1787) to insist that the new Constitution should include a requirement of a two-thirds vote by the Senate for the ratification of treaties.

extravagance and artificial prosperity, followed, as usual, by a period of financial depression. Times remained hard until about 1787.

The dislocation of the country's economic machinery and a severe financial strain were the inevitable results of the long war. Peace and independence required a new adjustment of commerce, agriculture, and industry. The breaking of the connection with a great commercial empire necessarily involved economic loss and some obstruction of the channels of business.

Some ports in the French and Spanish West Indies were open to American products and ships, but tax restrictions greatly handicapped trade with these islands. The commercial regulations of Great Britain, however, struck the greatest blow to the prosperity of the new republic. The American whaling industry was virtually ruined by the exclusion of fish oil and whale products from England, which, up to that time, had been the only market for these articles. British regulations regarding trade with the British West Indies had an even worse influence on American commerce. Before the Revolution the continental colonies sold in large amounts fish, lumber, grain, and other products in the English and foreign sugar islands. In exchange for these products they received not only sugar and molasses but English and foreign coins and commodities not produced at home. Molasses was processed into rum, which in turn was exchanged with the Indians for furs and with African slave-dealers for Negroes. Therefore, upon the American trade with the West Indian islands depended to a large extent the prosperity of the grain grower, the fur-trader, the fisherman, the lumberman, and the slave-trader, all of whom suffered when the trade was obstructed.[17]

After the Revolution the British navigation laws operated against the states much as they did against other foreign nations. A royal proclamation of July 2, 1783, forbade imports into and exports from the British West Indies except when transported in British ships. The carrying of lumber, live-stock, grain, vegetables, and certain other articles from American ports to the islands was forbidden, as was also the exporting of rum, sugar, molasses, and some other products from the islands to the states. These restrictions therefore had the effect of giving the British ship-

[17] For the importance of the West Indian trade to the continental colonies in the pre-Revolutionary era, see pp. 484 f.

owners a monopoly of the carrying-trade between the United States and the British West Indies and of placing an embargo upon all products that might compete with Canadian exports to these islands. The damage to American commerce due to the British policy would have been much greater but for the easy access afforded American ships to the Dutch and Danish West Indies. These places were used by smugglers as back doors to the English islands.

American agriculture was also discouraged during this period, not only by this narrowing of the West Indian outlet, but in other ways. The home market, which had been expanded by war demands, was now contracted to pre-war dimensions. The war had, of course, cut off the British bounty on indigo and annulled the favors which American-grown tobacco had enjoyed in the English market, resulting in a lowering of prices on both articles. The infant manufacturing industries were crippled by the competition of floods of cheap foreign goods.

Condition of agriculture and industry

The year 1786 marked the depth of the post-Revolutionary depression. In the next year hard times began to give way to prosperity as the people gradually learned how to fit into a new political and economic situation. Old commercial channels had been reopened, and the new ones to the west coast of North America, China, and the East Indies were gradually attracting many of our merchant ships. American farm crops came into greater demand because of crop shortages in France and her West Indian colonies. Not only was American agriculture thus restored but industry also revived and prospered.

Prosperity returns; reasons

Many people who lived under the government of the Confederation and some historians since have unjustly blamed that government for the hard times. As a matter of fact, it did not bring on the depression, nor could the best of governments have prevented it. Some economic critics have maintained that a stronger general government could have forced more favorable trade concessions from foreign powers, could have regulated interstate commerce, and through a uniform tariff policy could have protected our infant industries against the products dumped upon the country by English manufacturers. Although there is some ground for this contention, the economic shortcomings of the Confederation government have been greatly exaggerated. Because the new government under the present Constitution was fortunate enough to start off in a period of prosperity, it has re-

Alleged responsibility of the government for the hard times

ceived too much credit for the good times, and the old government too much blame for the bad times.

PAPER MONEY

Deflation

By the end of the war, as has already been seen, the Continental currency had gradually declined in value until it had ceased to circulate as money. The country was therefore on a specie basis except in the states that were still using their own bills of credit as money. During the short post-war boom the extravagant buying of foreign goods by the American people led to a severe drain on the country's supply of gold and silver. Hence money became scarce and prices fell. Debtors who had bought goods, land, or tools on credit at peak prices had now to pay for them when their own goods were a drug on the market. In other words, inflation had given way to deflation, which meant that creditors were benefited while debtors were exploited.

The demand for paper money; reasons

During this period of hard times farmers, laborers, tradesmen, and debtors generally were unable to pay their debts and the taxes which in many cases had been unfairly imposed upon them. Foreclosures of mortgages, bankruptcies, and imprisonments for debt were the logical results of such an economic situation. As could only be expected, the distressed portion of the population sent up loud cries for relief. "Stay laws," or moratoria on debts, reforms of the courts making the dispensing of justice less costly, and particularly the issuance of paper money, were among the chief demands of the malcontents. Mingled with the reasonable demands of those who had real grievances were the complaints of the idle and shiftless who advocated such revolutionary changes as the abolition of all debts and the redistribution of private property. These radical ideas were to some extent an outgrowth of the philosophy that was behind the revolt against British authority.[18]

Paper money in Rhode Island

Yielding to this pressure, seven states decided to issue paper money, in effect scaling down debts by depreciation. Of the various experiments in paper money made by the states, that of Rhode Island commanded the greatest attention. The legislature of this state made its paper money legal tender, which meant that

[18] DRAKE, FRANCIS S., *Life and Correspondence of Henry Knox* (1873), pp. 91-93; HART, A. B., *American History Told by Contemporaries*, iii, p. 192; LIBBY, O. G., *The Geographical Distribution of the Vote of the Thirteen States on the Federal Constitution*, p. 58.

creditors were forced to accept it in payment of debts (1786). A later act in the same year defined as a penal offense the refusal to accept paper money in ordinary business transactions.[19] A noted legal case, Trevett vs. Weeden, resulted from this last provision. John Weeden, a butcher of Newport, refused to accept the paper money offered by John Trevett in payment for meat. Trevett then brought suit against Weeden as a violator of the law. The supreme court of the state acquitted Weeden on the ground that this law was contrary to the state constitution and therefore void. This was one of the first cases (and the most noted of the early ones) in which a court decided that an act of a state legislature could be set aside on the ground of unconstitutionality.[20]

In six of the states the legislatures, under the dominance of property owners and prosperous business men, disregarded the demands of the radicals for paper money and continued the policy of deflation. The leaders saw that the issuance of irredeemable paper money meant inflation, by which debtors would be able to rob their creditors. The advocates of hard money apparently overlooked the fact that the continuance of deflation would allow creditors to exploit their debtors. The proper remedy, a monetary system so regulated as to insure justice to both groups, was not worked out in any of the states.

In Massachusetts, the evils of deflation seem to have gone to the greatest length. There, the farmers, owing to the narrowing of the West Indian trade and the general stagnation caused by the depression, could find no sale for their products. They were staggering under unbearable debt burdens, and creditors were demanding their pound of flesh. Justice was slow and costly, with lawyers charging exorbitant fees for their counsel. The state government, in the hands of the prosperous classes, had placed too great a proportion of the tax burden upon the shoulders of the farmers and laborers. Some of the money so raised went to pay off the state's indebtedness and thus found its way into the pockets of speculators who had bought up the state's paper at a low figure. The poor debtor class was becoming desperate. With those who had real

Shays's Rebellion

[19] BATES, FRANK G., *Rhode Island in the Formation of the Union*, pp. 123-131.

[20] *Ibid.*, pp. 131-138 (quotations from the arguments for the defense); MCLAUGHLIN, *op. cit.*, pp. 151 ff.

grievances were associated many of the shiftless and dishonest who were agitating, as usual, on general principles.[21]

A feverish discontent among the common people expressed itself in town meetings, county conventions, and petitions to the legislature. The malcontents asked that the public debt be reduced, that the privileges of the propertied class be lessened, that the judiciary and the tax system be reformed, and that debtors be afforded relief in the form of paper money. When the legislature refused to grant these demands mob violence broke out and courts were prevented from holding their sessions by groups of infuriated farmers, laborers, and mechanics. The insurrection, led by Daniel Shays, a veteran of the Revolutionary War, was suppressed in the winter of 1787 by state troops sent out by Governor Bowdoin and commanded by General Benjamin Lincoln.[22]

Result of Shays's Rebellion

The result of Shays's Rebellion and of lesser similar disorders in other states was to fill the conservatives with a dread of radicalism. A strong central government, one which could assist the states in maintaining law and order, now seemed to these conservatives more necessary than ever. Particularly did they desire to uphold the sanctity of property, to guarantee the observance of contracts, and to prevent the further issuance of irredeemable paper money.

THE WESTERN PROBLEM

State claims to western territory

As has already been shown,[23] the ownership of the unoccupied West was one of the important early problems with which the Confederation had to deal. The western territory was originally claimed by the states of Massachusetts, Connecticut, New York, Virginia, North Carolina, South Carolina, and Georgia. New York's rights were based on her suzerainty over the Iroquois Indians, who at times had exercised a measure of authority over some of the Indian tribes as far west as the Mississippi. The titles of the other states rested on grants made to them by royal charters during the colonial era. These grants overlapped, however, so that some claims conflicted with others,[24] and there was the further

---

[21] HART, A. B., *Contemporaries*, iii, p. 191; MINOT, GEORGE R., *The History of the Insurrections in Massachusetts* (1810), pp. 5-36, 82-86.

[22] For a contemporary account of Shays's Rebellion, see MINOT, *op. cit.*, the entire volume.

[23] See p. 689.

[24] For this overlapping, see the accompanying map.

STATE CLAIMS TO WESTERN LANDS

question as to whether the British government had not really repudiated them all in 1774 when it extended the limits of the province of Quebec as far south as the Ohio. During the Revolution France and Spain maintained that it had. Actually, Virginia had strengthened her claim by sponsoring the expedition of George Rogers Clark, who had conquered the Northwest. But Maryland contended that Clark's success had been due to the opposition of all the colonies to the British armies in the east and that the West should therefore belong to all the colonies jointly.

In 1780 New York yielded to the Confederation her claims to the western territory. The other states followed her example, and by 1802 the ownership of the entire West had passed to the Confederation. The acquisition of these lands created two new problems for Congress. First, it had to formulate a policy for the disposal of the land, and second, it had to adopt a plan of government for the settlers. The responsibility of solving these problems was placed upon two committees, with Thomas Jefferson as chairman of each. A scheme of government growing out of the report of one of these committees was adopted by Congress as the Ordinance of 1784. By this plan the western territory was divided into eighteen districts, each of which was to be admitted into the Union as a state when it reached the population of the least populous of the old states. Prior to statehood the people were to enjoy the right of partial self-government under the supervision of Congress. The Ordinance was to go into effect when all the lands had been ceded to the general government. But before this happened, this plan was superseded by the Ordinance of 1787 and so was never carried out.[25]

The Ordinance of 1784

A plan for disposing of the land to settlers, drawn up by the other committee, was adopted by Congress in the Land Ordinance of 1785. This ordinance provided that from time to time considerable areas of land were to be surveyed and divided into townships, rectangular tracts six miles square. Each township was to be divided into thirty-six sections of 640 acres each. Section 16 in every township was to be reserved for the use of schools. After each area had been surveyed, the land was to be auctioned off to the highest bidder. The minimum single purchase was to be one section and the minimum price one dollar an acre. At least $640 in cash was therefore required for each purchase.[26] As few individual

The Land Ordinance of 1785

---

[25] *Journal of the Continental Congress,* xxvi, pp. 275-279.
[26] *Ibid.,* xxviii, pp. 375-381.

settlers could raise such a large sum, most of the land was sold to speculators who could cut up the land into smaller tracts and sell them on credit.

Land sale to the Company of Ohio Associates

Since the government was in great need of funds and anxious to dispose of as much land as possible, it was willing to sell large tracts at a reduced price. Of the various purchasers who took advantage of this situation, the best known was the Company of Ohio Associates, a group of New England Revolutionary veterans who held certificates of indebtedness issued by Congress.[27] Congress sold to the Reverend Manasseh Cutler and Major Winthrop Sargent, as agents for the Ohio Company, about one and a half million acres for one million dollars, to be paid in veterans' certificates worth about twelve cents on the dollar.[28]

A settlement at Marietta

The Ohio Company at once began the work of actual settlement. In the spring of 1788 the superintendent of the colony, General Rufus Putnam, led a band of settlers to the mouth of the Youghiogheny River. There they built a boat, the *Mayflower*, and in it and other smaller vessels floated downstream on the Ohio to the mouth of the Muskingum. Here they established the town of Marietta, the first authorized settlement in what is now the state of Ohio. In accordance with the terms prescribed by Congress in the sale and in keeping with the terms of the Ordinance of 1785, one section in every township was reserved for the support of schools.

The Ordinance of 1787

Before the land sale to the Ohio Company had been consummated, Congress passed a second act for the government of the West, the Ordinance of 1787. This new measure applied not to the entire West, as did the Ordinance of 1784, but only to the Northwest Territory—a vast area lying between the Ohio River and the boundary of Pennsylvania on the east, the Mississippi on the west, the Ohio on the south, and the Canadian border on the north. The

The bill of rights

Ordinance consisted of governmental provisions and a bill of rights. The latter was similar to the bills of rights in the constitutions of the old states. The inhabitants were guaranteed freedom of worship, the benefits of the writ of habeas corpus and trial by jury, and exemption from unusual and excessive punishments. Private contracts were not to be interfered with, judicial proceed-

---

[27] CUTLER, W. P., and JULIA P., eds., *Life, Journals, and Correspondence of Rev. Manasseh Cutler*, i, pp. 181-186.

[28] *Ibid.*, i, pp. 230, 237, 239, 305, 471-473; *Journals of the Continental Congress*, xxxiii, pp. 399-401, 427-430.

ings were to be in accordance with the common law, and no one was to be deprived of life, liberty, or property "but by the judgment of his peers or the law of the land." There was to be no slavery or involuntary servitude in the entire territory.

The whole region was to be governed temporarily as one Territory but later was to be divided into not less than three nor more than five districts. The Territory was to pass through three governmental stages. In the first, the laws were to be made and administered by a governor and three judges appointed by Congress. The governor was to be assisted in his duties by a secretary, also chosen by Congress. During this initial period the people were to have no share in the government. As soon, however, as the Territory attained a population of 5000 adult males this autocratic government would be replaced by a legislature with a lower house chosen by the people and an upper house selected by Congress from nominations made by the lower house. At this stage the Territory could send a delegate to Congress to take part in the deliberations of that body but without power to vote. Whenever any one of the three or five districts into which the Territory was to be divided had a free population of 60,000, it was to be admitted into the Union as a state on an equal basis with the older states.[29]

Governmental provisions

The Ordinance of 1787 inaugurated a policy in the government of our territories which has been followed in principle ever since. This was the decision to treat the new territory not as a colonial dependency but as an integral part of the country. It meant that the settlers in the West were to have from the beginning all the rights of citizenship enjoyed by the inhabitants of the older states and that ultimately the new states to be carved out of the Territory would be put on the basis of political equality with the original thirteen. This wise decision settled at once—and in the right way—the problem as to whether we should or should not have a colonial system.

The Land Ordinance of 1785 and the Northwest Ordinance of 1787 were the most noted pieces of legislation enacted by the Congress of the Confederation. When the latter measure was passed in New York, a convention was in session in Philadelphia framing the present Constitution of the United States. Congress, though not old in years, had developed symptoms of premature senility. That many of the members had lost interest in it and did

[29] *Ibid.*, xxxii, pp. 334-343. For the text of the Ordinance, see *Old South Leaflets*, no. 13.

not regularly attend its sessions is shown by the fact that when the Northwest Ordinance was voted only eighteen members were present and only eight states were represented. The enactment of these two ordinances was a remarkable achievement for so decrepit a body. Indeed, it is surprising that the senile Congress could prop itself up on its deathbed and pass these two important measures.

SELECTED READINGS

1. Urban Life in the Postwar Period:
   A. Boston.—McMaster, J. B., *A History of the People of the United States,* i, pp. *11-17.
   B. New York.—*Ibid.,* pp. *52-57.
   C. Philadelphia.—*Ibid.,* pp. *64-67.
2. The Virginia Gentleman.—*Ibid.,* pp. *71-75.
3. The Articles of Confederation.—McLaughlin, A. C., *A Constitutional History of the United States,* *ch. 12. For the text of the Articles, see Commager, H. S., *Documents of American History,* i, pp. 111-116; Pease, Theodore C., and Roberts, A. S., *Selected Readings in American History,* pp. 141-148; or *Old South Leaflets,* no. 2.
4. Weaknesses in the Government of the Confederation.— Johnson, Allen, *Readings in American Constitutional History,* pp. *84-92 (extracts from *The Federalist*); Farrand, Max, *The Framing of the Constitution of the United States,* *ch. 3.
5. Commercial Problems.—McLaughlin, A. C., *The Confederation and the Constitution,* pp. 71-80.
6. Financial Difficulties of the Confederation.—Curtis, G. T., *History of the Origin, Formation, and Adoption of the Constitution of the United States,* i, pp. *172-189; Fiske, John, *The Critical Period of American History,* pp. *165-169; McLaughlin, A. C., *The Confederation and the Constitution,* *ch. 9.
7. Shays's Rebellion.—McMaster, *op. cit.,* pp. *306-330; Fiske, *op. cit.,* pp. *177-186; McLaughlin, *The Confederation and the Constitution,* *ch. 10. (For a brief document on the rebellion, see Commager, *op. cit.,* i, pp. 126-128.)
8. Relations with Spain.—Fiske, *op. cit.,* pp. *207-211; Bailey, Thomas A., *A Diplomatic History of the American People,* pp. *44-50; Bemis, S. F., *A Diplomatic History of the United States,* pp. *73-81.
9. Relations with England.—Bailey, *op. cit.,* pp. *38-42; Bemis, *op. cit.,* pp. *69-73.
10. The Ohio Company and the Settlement at Marietta.—McMaster, *op. cit.,* i, 504-515; Channing, E., *A History of the United States,* iii, pp. 540-544, 548-550.

11. The Ordinance of 1787.—McLaughlin, *The Confederation and the Constitution*, pp. 119-122. (For the text of the Ordinance, see Commager, *op. cit.*, i, pp. 128-132; Pease and Roberts, *op. cit.*, pp. 171-176; or *Old South Leaflets*, no. 13.)

CHAPTER XXXV

THE CREATION OF A NEW GOVERNMENT

THE FRAMING OF THE CONSTITUTION

Agitation in favor of strengthening the general government

As HAS already been seen, during the first half-decade after the war there was growing dissatisfaction with the government of the Confederation owing to the commercial and financial confusion and the general instability of conditions throughout the country. This discontent was greatest among the upper classes, who dominated economic, social, and political life in the states. There soon arose therefore, among the leaders of these classes, an agitation in favor of granting more authority to the general government. Propaganda directed toward this aim was carried on by means of private correspondence and the circulation of printed pamphlets. Among those who took a prominent part in this movement were Alexander Hamilton, James Madison, Pelatiah Webster, and Washington. These statesmen and others who supported them in this agitation felt that not only would a new constitution promote the economic prosperity of all classes, but only by strengthening the federal government could the states be held together in the Union.

How to convert this sentiment into action was now the important problem. To do this it would be necessary to overcome the political inertia of the country, which constituted a serious obstacle to change. There was also a deep-seated fear in the minds of a large portion of the population, especially in the rural sections, that change would result in depriving the states of their rights and in conferring upon the general government power which would be a menace to popular liberty. A centralized government with enlarged powers in the hands of the aristocracy might easily deprive the masses of all the gains won by the war. To exorcise these fears and overcome this inertia would not be an easy task. Fortunately for the cause, the leading advocates of a strong general government skillfully handled the events that preceded and led to the calling of the Constitutional Convention.

One favorable circumstance in this series of events was the disagreement between Maryland and Virginia over the navigation of
the Potomac River and the Chesapeake Bay. Each of these states
was in a position to hamper the commerce of the other, and only
by mutual agreement could their trade and navigation be relieved
of undue restraints. An attempt at such an agreement made in
1777 had been unsuccessful. A later effort led to a meeting of
commissioners in 1785, first at Alexandria and then at Mount
Vernon. The commissioners came to an understanding which was
accepted by the legislatures of both states.

The
Mount
Vernon
Confer-
ence

The Maryland legislature also suggested that Pennsylvania and
Delaware be invited to enter into a commercial agreement with
them. The Virginia assembly not only was favorable to this
proposal but was willing to broaden it into a like invitation to all
the states. Taking advantage of this favorable sentiment, James
Madison wrote a resolution inviting all the states to send commissioners to Annapolis to consider in joint meeting the problem
of uniform commercial regulations among them. This resolution
was offered by John Tyler (father of the tenth President) and
was unanimously adopted by the Virginia assembly (January,
1786).[1] In response to this invitation, at the appointed time
(September 11, 1786) commissioners from five states appeared at
Annapolis. In view of the meager representation, the convention
declined to take any action except to make a recommendation to
the states.[2] The members present unanimously agreed to a report
written by Hamilton which suggested that all the states should
appoint delegates to a convention to be held at Philadelphia on the
second Monday of May, 1787, "to devise such further provisions
as shall appear to them necessary to render the constitution of the
Federal Government adequate to the exigencies of the Union." The
commissioners had no authority to make recommendations to the
states except to the five represented by them at Annapolis, but
"from motives of respect" they sent a copy of their suggestions

The An-
napolis
Conven-
tion

[1] FARRAND, MAX, *The Records of the Federal Convention of 1787,*
iii, p. 544.

[2] The five states represented by commissioners were New York,
Pennsylvania, New Jersey, Delaware, and Virginia. Four other states
(New Hampshire, Massachusetts, Rhode Island, and North Carolina)
had chosen delegates, but they were not present. The delegates from
Massachusetts and Rhode Island were on the way to Annapolis when
they learned that the convention had adjourned.

to Congress and to the executives of all of the thirteen states.[3]

Response
of the
states to
the call of
the An-
napolis
Con-
vention

Virginia and New Jersey were the first states to accept the invitation issued by the Annapolis Convention. The legislature of Virginia chose seven deputies, any three of whom were to meet with deputies from other states for the purpose of making such changes in the Articles of Confederation as would render that constitution "adequate to the exigencies of the Union." Other states followed this example and appointed deputies with like instructions. The movement soon made such headway that Congress decided to take action. Accordingly, it passed a resolution (February 21, 1787) calling a convention to meet at the time and place suggested by the Annapolis Convention "for the sole and express purpose of revising the Articles of Confederation." All amendments that might be offered by this convention were to be reported to Congress and the various state legislatures for acceptance or rejection.[4]

By the time the Philadelphia Convention met (or shortly thereafter), all the states except New Hampshire and Rhode Island had chosen delegates to it. New Hampshire did not appoint her delegates until late in June, and so they did not arrive at Philadelphia until July 23, after most of the controversial questions had been settled. Rhode Island refused to send any representatives; hence this state had no share in the work of constitution-making.

The Con-
stitutional
Conven-
tion:
Member-
ship

In all, seventy-four delegates to the Convention were selected. Nineteen of them did not serve, and so the total number in attendance was fifty-five. Some of these were absent for a good portion of the time, and the average attendance was only about thirty. The number that signed the finished document was thirty-nine.[5] In choosing delegates Virginia set a high standard by naming her most distinguished sons. The other states emulated her example; consequently the list of appointees included most of the outstanding political leaders of the country. Membership in the prospective convention was regarded as such a distinction that the state legislatures in making their selections were able to skim the cream of

[3] For the proceedings of the Annapolis Convention, see TANSILL, C. C., comp., *Documents Illustrative of the Union of the American States,* pp. 39-43. See also JOHNSON, ALLEN, *Readings in American Constitutional History, 1776-1786,* pp. 96-98.

[4] *Journals of the Continental Congress,* xxxii, pp. 71-74.

[5] FARRAND, MAX, ed., *The Records of the Federal Convention* (hereafter referred to as Farrand, *Records*), iii, pp. 557-559.

American statesmanship. Thomas Jefferson, then in Paris, was deeply impressed with the roster of names and, with an exaggeration which he probably afterwards regretted, spoke of the convention as "an assembly of demigods." About one-half of them were college graduates, and most of them had had practical experience in governmental affairs. The list included thirty-nine former members of Congress, eight signers of the Declaration of Independence, twenty-one veterans of the Revolutionary War, seven who had been governors of states, and eight who had aided in the framing of state constitutions.[6]

The delegates in the main belonged to the wealthy and educated classes and were aristocratic in their political opinions. They held the view, then generally accepted by the ruling class, that one of the most important functions of government is to protect property rights. Furthermore, a considerable portion of them owned federal and state bonds.[7] If a strong general government were established, the value of this paper would be greatly enhanced. Then, too, a stabilized government, state and federal, would be favorable to the growth of commerce and industry and would therefore promote the prosperity of the wealthy classes and of the people generally. To what extent the framers were influenced by these selfish considerations it is impossible to say. It is more than likely, however, that they were actuated by higher and more patriotic motives. They were doubtless firm in the conviction that what was good for their group would be good for the country as a whole.

The belief of the deputies in the sanctity of property, together with their aristocratic notions, was a guaranty that the work of the Convention would be of a conservative character. Their idealism had been tempered by experience in actual government, and so

[6] WARREN, CHARLES, *The Making of the Constitution,* pp. 55-56.

[7] C. A. BEARD, in *An Economic Interpretation of the Constitution of the United States,* gives a long list of members of the Convention who presented federal bonds for redemption in 1791. Just how many of these bonds were purchased after 1787 and how many belonged to clients whom these former Convention deputies represented, we are unable to say. But after all due allowances are made, it is quite probable that a considerable number of the deputies owned state or federal paper while they were sitting in the Convention. This fact has given occasion for some "debunking" writers to charge them with having been prompted by selfish motives. For a discussion of the economic interests of the members of the Convention, see ch. v, especially pp. 150-151.

they were able to differentiate between the desirable and the attainable. Moreover, their conservatism had been accentuated by Shays's Rebellion and other recent disorders. They were therefore in general agreement as to the desirability of establishing a political system that would not only safeguard liberty but also protect property, with emphasis on the latter.

Washington

The most illustrious member of the Convention was George Washington, placed by Virginia at the head of her distinguished delegation. He preferred not to serve, but was induced to overcome his reluctance and accept the appointment. At the height of his fame at the time, he was easily the most noted man in America. He was looked up to with awe and reverence by the people, and if his great prestige could be linked up with the Convention it would give assurance that its work would be for the good of the country.[8] As he was president of the body, he did not participate in the debates, except for one short speech,[9] but he took a deep interest in the proceedings and voted as a member of the Virginia delegation. Furthermore, it was charged (maybe falsely) that his attitude on important measures was shown from the chair by smiles of approval or frowns of disapproval. Since he favored a strong general government, his silent influence was a support to the nationalist party.[10]

James Madison

Although less conspicuous than some of his colleagues, James Madison proved to be the most effective member of the Convention. Now at the age of thirty-six, he brought to his task a college-disciplined mind (he was a graduate of Princeton) which had been trained by experience in the art of government as a member of Congress and of the Virginia assembly. For some years this scholar in politics had been advocating an increase in the power of the general government and had qualified as a conservative by successfully opposing the issuance of paper money in Virginia. Although not a brilliant orator, he was a clear thinker and a logical debater. In preparation for his work in the Convention, he had studied the experiments in federation made by the ancient Greeks, and was thus armed with historical information as well as with

[8] For contemporary correspondence regarding the desirability of Washington's acceptance of the appointment, see WARREN, CHARLES, op. cit., pp. 61-67.

[9] FARRAND, Records, ii, p. 644.

[10] McLAUGHLIN, A. C., A Constitutional History of the United States, p. 149.

the knowledge that comes from experience. His efforts, both within and outside the Convention, in behalf of a stronger general government won for him the deserved honor of being known as the "Father of the Constitution."

Next to Madison in the work of the Convention came James Wilson of Pennsylvania. He was born and educated in Scotland, but had lived in this country long enough to become one of its ablest lawyers. He had served a number of years in Congress and had signed the Declaration of Independence. He was now forty-five years old and thus in the prime of life. More brilliant than Wilson was his young colleague in the Pennsylvania delegation, Gouverneur Morris. Clever, aristocratic in his notions, and gifted with a fine style but hampered somewhat by a reputation for laxity in morals, Morris played a more conspicuous than useful part in the proceedings.

Wilson and Morris

All of the above-mentioned leaders were advocates of a strong general government.[11] The opponents of nationalism could also point to able leaders. Members of this group who deserve particular mention were William Paterson of New Jersey, a good debater, who had been a member of the Continental Congress, a signer of the Declaration of Independence, and for eleven years attorney-general of his state; and Roger Sherman of Connecticut, an able politician of sound judgment, who had been in succession a shoemaker, almanac-maker, lawyer, and judge.[12]

Paterson and Sherman

The opponents of a strong centralized government did not act merely as obstructionists but performed a valuable service in the framing of the Constitution. By their opposition they kept the

[11] In this list also belongs Rufus King of Massachusetts. Possessing unusual personal charm, marked ability, and a fine voice, he impressed the Convention as a pleasing orator and successful debater. Others who advocated a strong government, though not so ardently or consistently as did those previously mentioned, were Edmund Randolph, the handsome and polished governor of Virginia, who was a successful lawyer and a good debater; George Mason, a Virginian of the old school, author of the constitution of his state and one of the ablest debaters in the country; and Charles Pinckney of South Carolina, who, only twenty-nine years of age, was one of the youngest members of the Convention.

[12] Among the others who opposed a strong general government should be mentioned the following: Robert Yates and John Lansing, Jr., of New York, the former an able judge of the state supreme court, the latter "a young lawyer of moderate ability"; William

trend toward nationalism from going to such lengths as to sacrifice unduly the rights of individuals and the powers of the states. Their insistence upon the rights of the states led to certain compromises but for which the Constitution might not have been ratified by the states.

Franklin and Hamilton

Two other names that have a high place in American history should be listed—Benjamin Franklin and Alexander Hamilton. The former could look back to an illustrious career, and the latter forward to a brilliant record in the service of his country. But neither of them exerted any considerable influence in the Convention. Franklin's eighty-one years had taken toll of his vigor, and his temperament, always conciliatory, had now been softened with age. He therefore did not take an aggressive stand on the questions at issue. His chief service consisted in pouring oil on the troubled waters when controversy reached the danger point. Owing to a manner which seemed conceited and overbearing, Hamilton did not enjoy personal popularity and he did not exert the influence that might be expected from his exceptional ability. Besides, his extreme nationalism handicapped his usefulness, for the majority of the members were unwilling to consider the creation of a government as highly centralized as he suggested. His two colleagues from New York were especially opposed to his views and he was usually outvoted in his delegation. Furthermore, he was absent from the sessions for a good part of the time.

Noted absentees

Conspicuous for their absence were John Adams and Samuel Adams of Massachusetts, and Thomas Jefferson and Patrick Henry of Virginia. John Adams and Jefferson were on foreign missions, the former at London and the latter at Paris. Samuel Adams was not chosen as a delegate. Patrick Henry's name was put on Virginia's list next to that of Washington, but he declined the appointment; he was not in sympathy with the trend toward nationalism. His reason for not going to Philadelphia, as given by him later, was that "he smelt a rat."[13]

Samuel Johnson, recently elected president of Columbia College, who was considered the most learned man at the Convention; and Oliver Ellsworth, a judge of the supreme court of his state, who was greatly "respected for his integrity, and venerated for his abilities." The last two were representatives from Connecticut.

[13] For good short sketches of the members of the Convention, see FARRAND, MAX, *The Framing of the Constitution of the United States,* pp. 15-41; WARREN, CHARLES, *op. cit.,* pp. 55 ff.

By May 14, the time set for the opening of the Convention, only a few of the deputies had reached Philadelphia, and it was not until eleven days later that delegations from a majority of the states arrived. The Convention was then organized (May 25), with Washington the unanimous choice for president. Rules of procedure were adopted, one of which pledged the members to the strictest secrecy.[14] The debates were thus free from the influence of outside clamor and from the motive of speaking for effect on listening constituencies. Each state had one vote, which was determined by the voice of a majority of its representatives. Owing to the smallness of the Convention, important questions could be thoroughly debated, and opinions were molded by discussion more than is customary with representative assemblies. *Organization of the Convention*

The rule of secrecy prevented newspaper reporters from attending the sessions and therefore the press of the day is not a source of information as to the proceedings. The secretary was not efficient and the record kept by him is very meager and unsatisfactory. Fortunately we have a much fuller and better account in the *Notes* of James Madison. He took down in abbreviated form what was said and done and wrote up his notes in full between sessions. His manuscript was thus completed a few days after the last meeting of the Convention.[15] This account is by all odds the fullest and best we have of the work of the Convention. The statements are clear and fair and not warped by feeling. Motions and the votes on them are recorded, and also the arguments for and against them. *Sources of information regarding the work of the Convention*

Next in importance to the notes of Madison are those which were taken by Robert Yates. These stop, however, on July 10, for he did not attend the sessions after that time. There has also lately come to light the journal of his colleague in the New York

[14] FARRAND, MAX, *The Records of the Federal Convention of 1787,* i, pp. 1-17.

[15] The careful way in which these notes were taken is explained by Madison himself as follows:

"I chose a seat in front of the presiding member, with the other members on my right and left hand. In this favorable position for hearing all that passed I noted in terms legible and in abbreviations and marks intelligible to myself what was read from the Chair or spoken by the members; and losing not a moment unnecessarily between the adjournment and reassembling of the Convention I was enabled to write out my daily notes during the session or within a few finishing days after its close." Quoted by Max Farrand in *op. cit.,* i, p. xvi.

delegation, John Lansing, Jr.[16] In addition to these, we have brief accounts by other delegates[17] and items of information gleaned from the letters and speeches of members.

The Virginia Plan

While waiting for latecomers to arrive, the Virginia delegation had daily meetings and agreed upon a set of resolutions which were to be offered as the basis for the new constitution. These resolutions were presented to the Convention by Randolph, who made a brilliant speech showing the need of a strong government.[18] The scheme of government embodied in them was known as the Virginia, or Randolph, Plan. It was in all probability mainly the work of Madison. This plan provided for a strong federal government. There was to be a legislature of two houses—each to be based on proportional representation—a national executive, and a national judiciary.[19]

The Virginia Plan was discussed for two weeks by the delegates sitting as a committee of the whole house. As a result of these discussions some important changes were made in the original resolutions. The Virginia Plan as thus amended was accepted by the Committee of the Whole and reported to the Convention in the form of nineteen resolutions (June 13).[20]

The New Jersey Plan

During the discussions on the Virginia Plan the delegates gradually divided into two parties, those from the large states supporting it and those from the small states opposing it. So dissatisfied were the delegates of the latter group with this plan

[16] Lansing's notes were edited and published (1939) by Joseph R. Strayer under the title of *The Delegate from New York*. They give a brief account of the proceedings of the Convention until July 9, the day before Yates and Lansing withdrew.

[17] Of the delegates who have left brief accounts, other than those already named, the following should be mentioned: King, Paterson, James McHenry, Hamilton, Charles Pinckney, Mason, and William Pierce. The notes of the last-named are valuable because of the character sketches of delegates in them. In 1819 the seal of secrecy was broken, when by order of Congress the official account of the secretary was published. Madison's *Notes* were published in 1840. These and the other sources mentioned above (except Lansing's notes) can be found in Farrand's *Records*.

[18] Farrand, *Records,* i, pp. 16, 18-19; iii, pp. 409, 525.

[19] For the text of the Virginia Plan see *ibid.,* i, pp. 20-22; iii, pp. 593-594.

[20] *Ibid.,* i, pp. 33, 235. For the text of these nineteen resolutions, see pp. 228-232.

and the resolutions based on it that they asked the Convention to postpone action on the report of the Committee of the Whole until they could present alternative proposals. This request was granted and the next day (June 15) William Paterson of New Jersey offered as a substitute another scheme of government. These proposals were embodied in a series of resolutions offered by him and are known as the Paterson, or New Jersey, Plan. According to this plan the Articles of Confederation would be amended and Congress given greater powers, but the federal government would not be clothed with sovereignty. A federal judiciary and executive would be created and Congress would have power to regulate interstate and foreign commerce and levy import duties and stamp taxes. The old system of raising money by requisitions on the states would be continued but would be made effective by giving Congress power to direct the collection of an assessment whenever a state failed to comply with the requisition within a specified time. The acts of Congress and federal treaties would be the supreme law of the land and the state courts would be bound by them. Force could be used to compel the states to obey the treaties and laws of the United States.[21]

For three days (June 16, 18, 19) it was warmly debated in the Committee of the Whole whether the New Jersey Plan should supersede the amended Virginia Plan. This was a crucial period in the deliberations. The acceptance of the New Jersey Plan would have meant a union in which sovereignty would still reside in the states. The larger states wanted a stronger federal government than would thus be provided for. As the strong-government party had a majority over the states' rights group, the latter were again outvoted and the New Jersey Plan was rejected by the committee (June 19).[22] The original proposal of the committee—the nineteen resolutions based on the Virginia Plan—was now taken up by the Convention.

Rejection of the New Jersey Plan

The victory of the large states was not final, however, for their scheme of government had received the endorsement only of the Committee of the Whole and had yet to be passed upon by the Convention. The small-state party was now solidified and was determined to put up a vigorous fight against nationalism on the

[21] *Ibid.*, i, pp. 240-242. For the text of these resolutions, see i, pp. 242-245, and iii, pp. 611 ff.

[22] *Ibid.*, ii, p. 312.

floor of the Convention. The issue that caused the greatest controversy was representation.

The Great Com- promise: Repre- sentation in the lower house

It was decided, without serious opposition, that the federal legislature should consist of two houses (June 21).[23] Next came the
question of apportioning representation in the lower house. The
large-state group insisted that membership in this house should
be based on proportional representation. The small-state party
demanded equal representation. Each side was so unyielding that
a hopeless deadlock seemed to have been reached. It was at this
critical juncture that Franklin offered his motion that "prayers
imploring the assistance of Heaven . . . be held in this Assembly
every morning. . . . The longer I live," said he, "the more con-
vincing proofs I see of this truth—*that God governs in the affairs
of men.* And if a sparrow cannot fall to the ground without his
notice, is it probable that an empire can rise without his aid?"[24]
The proposal was not accepted. One objection urged against it was
that to begin this practice so late in the session might cause the
people on the outside to feel that the Convention was on the verge
of a dangerous crisis. Indeed, a situation so serious as to cause
politicians to resort to prayer might quite properly alarm the general public. Probably the real reason, however, for not engaging
the services of a chaplain was that the Convention had no funds
with which to pay one.

The danger passed and it was decided "that the rule of suffrage
in the first branch ought not to be according to that established by
the Articles of Confederation, but according to some equitable
ratio of representation."[25] This was, in awkward phraseology, the
virtual acceptance of the principle of proportional representation
in the lower house of the assembly.

Repre- sentation in the upper house

The large-state party having won the victory as to representation in the lower house, the small states put up a vigorous fight for
equal representation in the upper house. Their delegates contended
that proportional representation in both houses would put the

[23] *Ibid.,* i, p. 353.

[24] *Ibid.,* i, pp. 450-452, 458.

According to one authority, which Farrand does not consider very
trustworthy, Hamilton in a flippant way, which brought a look of
surprise and censure to Washington's face, said that inasmuch as the
Convention was a body of such wisdom, talent, and experience "he
did not see the necessity of calling in *foreign* aid." *Ibid.,* iii, p. 472.

[25] *Ibid.,* i, pp. 460, 468.

small states entirely at the mercy of the large ones. The latter would combine into a predominant party and thus completely control Congress. In reply Madison argued ably to show that party lines in the future would be drawn not with reference to the size of states but in accordance with geographical and economic conditions. Political alignments would be based on sectionalism, and the large and small states of one section would combine against those of another. Furthermore, he pointed out the injustice of allowing the people of a little state the same voice in the government as those of a large one. To do this would be to give each citizen of a small state a voting power several times as great as that enjoyed by a citizen of a large state.[26]

The vote on this heated question resulted in a tie, five to five, with Georgia divided.[27] To break the deadlock a committee of one from each state was chosen and instructed to report a plan of compromise. The personnel of this compromise committee was favorable to the small states, since it did not include any of the stoutest opponents of equal representation.[28] The plan suggested by the committee was that in the upper house of the federal assembly (the Senate) each state should be allowed two representatives, and in the lower house one representative for every 40,000 inhabitants. There was also a provision that all bills for raising and appropriating money and for fixing salaries must originate in the lower house, and such bills could not be amended by the upper house. This clause was added to ease the forebodings of the large-state delegates, who were afraid that the small states, acting through the upper house, would impose unnecessary tax burdens upon the country. Before it was finally incorporated in the Constitution this provision was changed to read as follows: "All bills for raising revenue shall originate in the House of Representatives; but the Senate may propose or concur with amendments as on other bills."[29]

The proposals of the committee were warmly debated for a week, being strongly opposed by the large-state delegates. There was some modification of these proposals, but the important provision of equal representation in the upper house and proportional representation in the lower remained without substantial change. Finally (July 16) the amended report was accepted by the narrow

The final decision

[26] *Ibid.,* i, pp. 463-465, 485-487.
[27] *Ibid.,* i, p. 509.
[28] *Ibid.,* pp. 510, 516.   [29] *Ibid.,* pp. 524 ff.

vote of five to four, with Massachusetts divided. The vote of
New York was not counted, as two of her delegates had left the
convention.[30] This agreement on representation in Congress is
known as the Great Compromise.

The compromise on slave enumeration

In the debates over the apportionment of representatives in the
lower house a dispute arose as to whether and how slaves should be
counted in determining the number of representatives each state
should be allowed. Some of the delegates from the deep South contended that all the slaves should be counted. Certain northern
members, on the other hand, were opposed to counting any of
them. The fact that the slaves were property strengthened the
argument in favor of including them, since there was a feeling that
property should be one of the bases of representation. By coupling
taxation with representation a plan was found that was acceptable
to the Convention. It was agreed that in apportioning representation and direct taxation three-fifths of the slaves would be
counted.[31] In adopting the three-fifths ratio the Convention was
following a precedent set by the Confederation Congress, for the
revenue amendment proposed by Congress in 1783 provided that
this same ratio was to be used in apportioning direct taxes.[32]

The place of the West in the Union

While the discussions on the report of the Compromise Committee were in progress the question was raised as to what place
the West should have in the Union. Morris contended that this
section should not be given equality with the East in the government of the republic. Madison and George Mason strongly opposed
any discrimination against the West. They wanted the new states
to be admitted to the Union on the same terms as the original
states. If Morris were consistent, declared Madison, he would
determine human character by the points of the compass.[33] Although Morris did not entirely succeed in his endeavor he was able
to prevent the inclusion in the Constitution of a guarantee of
equality to the western states. Instead of such a guarantee, this
rather vague clause was finally adopted: "New States may be

[30] *Ibid.,* ii, pp. 13 ff.

[31] FARRAND, *Records,* i, pp. 580, 581, 589, 591-593.

[32] *Journals of the Continental Congress,* xxiv, p. 260.

[33] FARRAND, *Records,* i, pp. 533-534, 584.

While Morris was contending for a limitation of the rights of the
Westerners, Congress was formulating the Ordinance of 1787 (passed
July 13) by which the West would eventually be given equality with
the East.

admitted by the Congress into this Union." Whether Congress could limit the power of new states by prescribing conditions for their admission was left as an open question to be decided in later years.

By July 26 the Convention had agreed upon a number of general principles which were embodied in twenty-odd resolutions. A Committee of Detail, consisting of five members, had already been appointed, and to it was assigned the task of breaking down these general principles into specific clauses and thus giving in detail a plan for a constitution.[34] The Convention then adjourned for ten days to give the Committee time to do its work. By working continuously, including Sunday, the Committee was ready with its report by the end of the allotted time. The report was in the form of a plan of government similar to that finally adopted, although the arrangement and some of its provisions were different from those in the present Constitution.[35]

The Committee of Detail

Instead of adopting in its entirety the plan suggested by the Committee, the Convention on reassembling on August 6 entered upon a discussion of its provisions which lasted five weeks. The proposals were taken up item by item and were thoroughly thrashed out. Disagreements continued and compromises were necessary. None of the later controversies, however, were as sharp as had been the one over representation. Sectionalism played a part in some of these later disputes, as it had in the debates over western representation and slave enumeration. In the disputes between the North and the South slavery figured to some extent but not so importantly as was at one time supposed.

Minor controversies and compromises

A serious line of cleavage between North and South developed in the discussions over the question of giving Congress the power to regulate commerce. The southern delegates feared that if Congress, by a mere majority, could pass navigation laws it might require all American exports and imports to be carried in American bottoms. Such a monopoly would mean high freight rates for agricultural products sent abroad from the South and thus favor the northern shipowner at the expense of the southern farmer and planter. Burdensome duties might also be imposed on southern exports, such as tobacco and rice.

Navigation acts and the importation of slaves

The South therefore contended that navigation laws should require the assent of two-thirds of both houses of Congress. The

[34] *Ibid.*, ii, pp. 95, 96, 97, 106, 117-118, 128-133.
[35] *Ibid.*, ii, pp. 176-189.

northern delegates opposed this, maintaining that one of the principal reasons for calling the Convention was to give Congress the right to regulate commerce. The situation was further complicated by the demand in Georgia and the Carolinas for more slaves. The deputations from these states insisted that the federal government should not have the power to prohibit the importation of slaves.

Evidently these different points of view could be reconciled only by a policy of give-and-take. To relieve the South of the fear that its staples would be overburdened with taxation in their passage to foreign markets, it was moved that Congress be prohibited from levying export duties. Wilson strongly protested against this limitation of the power of Congress to regulate commerce. Sectional lines, however, were not sharply drawn on this point, and the provision was accepted without great difficulty.[36]

It was not so easy to settle the question raised by the deep South regarding the slave trade. Representatives from this section declared that their states would not ratify the Constitution if their demands were not met. The delegations from the middle region, including Virginia, opposed further importation, but some of the New England deputies were willing to allow the continuance of the traffic rather than jeopardize the acceptance of the Constitution. A compromise was agreed to whereby Congress could not prohibit the slave trade prior to January 1, 1808, but could levy an import duty of $10 each on all slaves imported. These concessions having been made to the South, it was agreed that navigation acts, like other laws, could be passed by a majority vote of both houses of Congress with the consent of the President.[37]

Other provisions relating to Congress
After the Great Compromise was accepted, the other provisions regarding the legislature were adopted without controversy. The first and second branches of Congress were to be known respectively as the House of Representatives and the Senate. The new Congress was to have the powers exercised by the old Congress, namely, those of borrowing money, coining money and regulating the value thereof; establishing post offices and post roads; punishing piracies and felonies committed on the high seas; declaring war and granting letters of marque and reprisal; raising and supporting armies; and providing and maintaining a navy.

To this group of powers were added certain others not exercised by the Congress of the Confederation. Prominent in this latter list

[36] *Ibid.,* ii, pp. 360-364.
[37] *Ibid.,* ii, pp. 364 f., 369-375, 400, 409, 414-417.

were the right to "lay and collect taxes, duties, imposts, and excises, to pay the debts and provide for the common defense and general welfare of the United States"; to regulate interstate and foreign commerce; to exercise exclusive legislation over the territories and the federal district in which the seat of government should be located; and "to make all laws which shall be necessary and proper for carrying into execution of the foregoing powers, and all other powers vested by this Constitution in the government of the United States, or in any department or officer thereof." All laws were to receive the assent of both houses, and the two houses were to be equal in other respects, with a few important exceptions.

One of the knottiest of all the problems which confronted the Convention was providing for a proper federal executive. At one time a plural executive was advocated by some of the delegates, but the final decision was in favor of a single executive with the title of President, who should be independent of the legislature and be given large powers. He was made commander-in-chief of the army and navy; was given power, "by and with the advice and consent of two-thirds of the Senate," to make treaties; and with the advice and consent of a majority of the Senate, to appoint judges of the federal courts, ambassadors, ministers, and consuls, and other important public officers. Considerable authority in legislation was also conferred upon him. It was his duty to keep Congress informed as to the state of the Union and recommend measures for its consideration. He could exercise a tentative veto on any bill passed by Congress, and this tentative veto would be final unless the vetoed bill were reconsidered and passed by a two-thirds majority of both houses of Congress.

The federal executive: Powers

To devise a method of selecting an officer with such powers and responsibilities proved to be a most difficult task. Many plans were offered and rejected, and the Convention reversed itself several times on proposals that had been presented. If the President were chosen by Congress he would be dependent upon that body, and the principle of the separation of powers would not be upheld. Since the deputies were aristocratic in their notions, there was a strong feeling among them that the people were not qualified to make so important a choice. Even George Mason, though more liberal than many of his colleagues, thought that to call upon the people to elect the President would be like asking a blind man for a judgment as to colors.

Method of choosing the President

Finally it was decided that the President should be chosen by electors, these electors to be selected in such manner as the state legislatures might prescribe. The electors were to meet in their respective states and vote for two persons for President. The candidate who received the highest number of votes would be declared President, provided the number received by him were a majority of all the votes cast. The candidate receiving the next highest number of votes would be accepted as Vice-President. In the event that no candidate should receive a majority in the electoral college, the House of Representatives would make a selection from a list of the five candidates who had received the highest vote. The election in the House would be by states, each state having one vote.[38]

A minor compromise between the large and small states

In the provision for electing the President there cropped out again the idea of compromise between the large and small states. It was thought that a majority of the electors would seldom agree on a candidate and that more often than not the House of Representatives would be called upon to act. In such cases, the large states, because of their predominance in the electoral college, would make the preliminary slate; the small states would have a strong voice in the final election, owing to their overrepresentation in the House when it was acting in its electoral capacity.[39]

The Convention was proud of the scheme devised by it for the election of the President and Vice-President. In fact, it was one of the few original features of the Constitution. But the provision did not work out as the Fathers had expected. The electors, instead of acting independently in the selection of the President and Vice-President, soon became rubber stamps obediently registering the will of their respective parties. So, after having been tried out for a decade and a half, the plan was changed by the Twelfth Amendment, which provided for the election of the President and the Vice-President by separate ballots.

The federal judiciary

One of the clearly apparent weaknesses of the Articles of Confederation was the lack of a real federal judiciary, and the Convention was therefore in general agreement that this defect should be remedied. Nor was there any difference of opinion as to the jurisdiction of the Supreme Court of the United States. A dispute

[38] Accounts of the discussions regarding the executive are scattered over a good portion of Farrand's *Records*. The best guide for finding them is the index.

[39] Farrand, *Records*, iii, pp. 458-459.

arose, however, over the proposal to establish inferior federal courts. Some of the deputies opposed the creation of such tribunals and advocated the use of state courts as such, with appeals from them to the United States Supreme Court. The Convention side-stepped the question by declaring: "The judicial power of the United States shall be vested in one Supreme Court, and in such inferior courts as the Congress may from time to time ordain and establish." Since this clause gave Congress an option rather than an obligation, the final responsibility as to inferior courts was imposed upon that body.

The Constitution was not a new creation. It did not spring full-armed from the brain of the Jovian Fathers, as Mr. Gladstone once indicated. Nearly all its provisions were borrowed from one source or another. The work of the framers was therefore mainly one of selection, adaptation, and organization. Most of the stones had been shaped by experience before they found a place in the new structure. The principles embodied in the Constitution came from a variety of sources. Among them the following should be mentioned: *Sources of ideas embodied in the Constitution*

(1) The Articles of Confederation and the experience of the general government under them. A considerable portion of the old constitution was transferred to the new, some of it with little or no change in wording. Some of the most important of the new provisions were added because experience under the Articles revealed the desirability of such changes.

(2) The state constitutions and the lessons learned from actual government under them. The similarity in the framework of the government of the Union and that of the states was due not to coincidence but to conscious borrowing. The states had been running their own affairs for more than a decade and were revealing the strong and weak points in their political institutions. The framers of the federal Constitution were able, therefore, to distinguish between the good and the bad in the state constitutions and from these observations to gain useful ideas to be embedded in the new organic law.

(3) Colonial practice. The state governments were generally modeled after the colonial governments, and hence the principles taken from the former were indirectly borrowed from the latter. Furthermore, certain colonial practices had grown into traditions which were perpetuated in the federal and state governments. To this source, for example, we are indebted for the idea that bills

for raising revenue should originate in the lower house of the assembly and that enactments of legislative bodies should be subject to judicial review.

(4) The English Constitution. Since the colonial governments were more or less imitations of the British government, many of the political ideas contributed by the former came indirectly from the latter. Besides, some of the features of the American Constitution were borrowed directly from the British Constitution. For example, the division of governmental functions between the Union and the states was similar to the distribution of power between the British colonies and the homeland.

(5) Political theories current at the time. There were embodied in the Constitution some ideas which the Fathers had gleaned from the writings of English and French philosophers. Especially marked was the influence of Montesquieu, whose doctrine of the separation of powers and of checks and balances was generally accepted in America.

The Fathers did not regard their handiwork as a perfect instrument of government. The infallibility attributed to them by later generations would doubtless have made a strong appeal to their sense of humor. The Constitution was a bundle of compromises, and probably not one of its framers approved of it in its entirety.[40] It was, however, the best scheme available by which a real union and an effective general government could be established, and its advocates accepted it for that reason. They also believed that the imperfections could be worked out in the future by the amending process.

Provision for amendments

Amendments could be proposed in two ways: first, by Congress by a two-thirds vote of both houses, and second, by a national convention called by Congress. The call for a national convention must be issued by Congress whenever the legislatures of two-thirds of the states shall by petition ask it to do so. The framers probably

[40] Charles Biddle of Philadelphia, who was acquainted with most of the members of the Convention, was told by some of the best-informed deputies that "they did not believe a single member was *perfectly* satisfied with the Constitution, but they believed it was the best they could ever agree upon, and that it was infinitely better to have such a one than break up without fixing on some form of government, which I believe at one time it was expected they would have done." Quoted from Biddle's *Autobiography* (1802) by FARRAND, MAX, *Fathers of the Constitution*, p. 141.

thought that national conventions would be used at times not only to propose amendments but also to give the Constitution a general overhauling. This expectation has never been realized, for no second national convention has ever been held.

After an amendment has been proposed, by either the first or second method, it has to be ratified by the legislatures of three-fourths of the states or by conventions of three-fourths of the states. Congress has to decide as to which method of ratification shall be employed. So far, only one amendment, the twenty-second, has been ratified by state conventions; all the others have been ratified by state legislatures.

In creating the new government the framers of the Constitution were performing a noble experiment. This new government as well as that of the states rested directly on the people. The problem was to make the federal government strong enough to take care of general interests and at the same time leave to the states such authority as was needed for dealing with local interests. This attempt to create a political machine made up of wheels within a wheel was no easy task. The difficulty was to keep the wheels running smoothly without any jamming of cogs. Certain powers were allocated to the federal government and others to the states. But the line that separated the one group of powers from the other was not sharply drawn, and for seven decades there was more or less controversy as to the location of this dim line. *General character of the new government*

Owing to the vagueness of the Constitution in this particular and in other respects, there have arisen from time to time important differences of opinion as to its meaning. For the settlement of these differences numerous appeals have been made to the federal judiciary. In these decisions the courts have at times stretched and even changed the Constitution to make it fit new conditions. As these opinions are accepted as fundamental law, the Supreme Court has been able virtually to amend the Constitution by judicial interpretation. *Amendment by judicial interpretation*

The Constitution did not clearly state whether sovereignty, or supreme authority, resided in the states, as it did under the Articles of Confederation, or in the Union, as it does today. It took a terrible fratricidal war to settle this disputed question. And yet the Fathers are not to be severely censured for thus by-passing this important issue. If it had been definitely understood in 1787 that the new Constitution was creating a national government such as we have today, in all probability it would not have been accepted *Location of sovereignty* by the state conventions. On the other hand, if the Constitution had contained a straightforward declaration in favor of state sovereignty, the federal government might never have gained the power necessary to meet the problems with which it has had to cope.[41]

Short-comings of the Constitution

Some of the shortcomings of the original Constitution were doubtless due to inadvertence. A case in point was its failure to confer upon the Union any definite authority to acquire new territory or any power to regulate manufacturing. These may have been oversights—*casa omissa*, as Jefferson afterwards termed them. At that time commerce was more important than industry. The confusion that arose from state control of commerce demonstrated the necessity of giving the general government the power to regulate foreign and interstate commerce. But the problems that grew out of the small-scale industry of that day could be properly handled by state and local authorities. No one could then foresee that industry would become nation-wide in scope and would, as much as commerce, demand national regulation.

Not all of the omissions in the Constitution, however, can be laid to inadvertence. In two instances at least, the Convention consciously refused to grant the federal government a power which has since been considered one of its proper functions. At one time Franklin made a motion to give Congress authority to construct canals. At another time Madison suggested that the general government be allowed to issue charters of incorporation for the purpose of encouraging internal improvements. Neither of these proposals was accepted.

Limitations on the federal government

The Constitution did not at first contain a formal bill of rights, but it did list a few individual rights which were to be protected against governmental interference. The privilege of the writ of habeas corpus was not to be suspended "unless when in cases of

---

[41] This view is ably contested by Professor McLaughlin, who is firmly of the belief that it was "the intention of the framers to establish a national government and to abandon a Confederation of sovereign states." Furthermore, it was, he says, clearly pointed out in the discussions in the state conventions and in the controversial literature of the period that the acceptance of the Constitution would mean the end of state sovereignty. That such arguments were frequently used in the state conventions and in newspaper discussions cannot be denied. It does not follow, however, that these views were generally accepted at the time. McLaughlin, A. C., *The Constitutional History of the United States*, pp. 214-216.

rebellion or invasion the public safety may require it." No bill of attainder or ex post facto law could be passed by either the federal or a state legislature.

The states were also forbidden to "coin money; emit bills of credit; make anything but gold and silver a tender in payment of debts; . . . or [pass any] law impairing the obligation of contracts." These restrictions were placed on the states for the protection of the propertied interests. They insured creditors against the scaling-down of the indebtedness due them or its payment in cheap money. With these provisions should be classed the following clause: "All debts contracted and engagements entered into, before the adoption of this Constitution, shall be as valid against the United States under this Constitution as under the confederation." This guaranteed that holders of United States bonds would be paid in full. It is this clause especially on which rests the charge that the Fathers (those of them who owned government paper) were looking out for their own selfish interests. And yet if the new government had not assumed the indebtedness of the old, the credit of the country would have been greatly impaired. *Limitations on the powers of the states*

In recent years some historians, especially those who are classed as "revisionists," have had much to say about the undemocratic features of the original Constitution. That the Fathers were members of an aristocratic class which had little confidence in either the wisdom or the virtue of the masses cannot be doubted. It ought to be pointed out, however, that by leaving the regulation of the suffrage to the states they did nothing to limit the exercise of this privilege. Furthermore, the Constitution put the people in direct or indirect control of all branches of the federal government. *Did the Constitution advance or retard democracy?*

By September 8 the Convention had come to a final agreement as to the provisions of the Constitution, but there was still the need of giving these general principles suitable arrangement and of putting them in the proper literary form. For this final task a committee of five was selected; Dr. Samuel Johnson, president of Columbia College, was chairman. Within a few days it finished its work. The writing of the Constitution in its final form was the work of Gouverneur Morris, with the probable assistance of James Wilson.[42] *The Committee of Style*

[42] The members of the Committee, besides Dr. Johnson and Morris, were Hamilton, Madison, and King. Although James Wilson was not a member, there is reliable evidence that he gave substantial aid to Morris in preparing the final draft of the Constitution. FARRAND,

Adoption
of the
Constitu-
tion

On September 17, the Constitution came up for adoption. A few of the members were unwilling to sign it; hence the document could not be sent out with the unanimous approval of the delegates. To give the action of the Convention the semblance of unanimity, the resolution of adoption was worded as follows: "Done in Convention by the unanimous consent of the States present. . . ." This resolution, which had been written by Morris and offered by Franklin, was adopted by a vote of all the state delegations. The engrossed copy of the Constitution was then signed by all but three of the delegates present.[43]

The Ratification of the Constitution

Provision
for rati-
fication

The Constitution contained this provision for its ratification: Conventions were to be held in the states; and as soon as nine of these conventions had ratified the new instrument of government, it would go into effect in the states which had accepted it. To be left out were the states which were unwilling to come under the "New Roof," as the Constitution was called. The launching of the new government under such an arrangement would therefore be an act of revolution. Under the old constitution changes in the fundamental law could be made only with the consent of the *legislatures* of *all* the states. The important innovations suggested by the proposed Constitution were to be effective when accepted by *conventions* of *some* of the states. Furthermore, the Articles of Confederation declared that the old union was to be perpetual, whereas it was now to be destroyed by the secession of the ratifying states.

The Con-
stitution
submitted
to state
conven-
tions

The Constitution was sent to Congress with the request that it be submitted to the state conventions for their acceptance or rejection. The Confederation government was thus invited "to light its own funeral pyre." At first Congress showed no enthusiasm over the new plan. But despite objections raised by some of the members, the eleven states present voted unanimously to forward the new instrument to the state legislatures to be submitted by them to the state conventions.[44] In so doing, the old government was virtually announcing its own abdication.

Records, ii, pp. 547, 553, 582; iii, p. 553. See also documents given by Warren, Charles, *The Making of the Constitution,* pp. 687-688.

[43] Farrand, *Records,* ii, pp. 641-643, 647.

[44] *Journals of the Continental Congress,* xxxiii, p. 549.

The Constitution, now before the people, was the issue which gave rise to two political parties. Those who favored ratification called themselves Federalists. This term was a misnomer, for most of the advocates of ratification were working for a stronger general government than was possible under a federation of states. The word "National" would more nearly have defined their position. But since the latter term was in disfavor with the people, the friends of the new system appropriated the more acceptable name, Federalists. There was left then for the opponents of ratification nothing but the designation "Anti-Federalists." They were thus under the disadvantage of having to wear a label that had only a negative connotation. *Federalists and Anti-Federalists*

In some of the states there were heated contests between the supporters and the opponents of ratification. These disputes were carried on not only in the state conventions, but also in state legislatures, on the stump, and in the press. Numerous articles on both sides, many of them over Latin or fanciful pseudonyms, appeared in the newspapers. These discussions were not always kept on the high plane of principle, but frequently degenerated into personal abuse and appeals to prejudice. Indeed, this campaign of agitation was in some instances carried on in a manner more becoming ward heelers than revered patriots.

The basis of the opposition to the Constitution was the contention that it gave the federal government too much power and left too little to the states. It would, so the Anti-Federalists maintained, change a confederation into a nation and thus reduce the states to a position of undue subordination. It would give the President and Congress greater power over the states than that formerly exercised by king and Parliament over the colonies. The Federalists, on the other hand, denied that a consolidated national government would be created and that the states would be deprived of any rights needful for the control of their legitimate interests. The new union, so the Federalists contended, would be a cross between a league of states and a consolidated nation. *Objections to the Constitution*

Itemizing their general objections, the Anti-Federalists pointed out a number of specific features in the new Constitution with which they found fault. Throughout the country there was pretty general agreement among them that the absence of a bill of rights was a serious shortcoming. Owing to this omission there was no guarantee that religious freedom, freedom of the press, and other natural rights of the individual would be respected by the general government. No provision had been made for trial by jury in civil cases in the federal courts. Debtors and the poorer classes generally objected to the provisions which prevented the states from impairing the obligation of contracts and issuing paper money. Class feeling was also a cause of opposition to the new plan of government. The land speculators, merchants, manufacturers, lawyers, and wealthy persons as a whole in the coast towns as a rule were for ratification. In some localities these prosperous classes were cordially hated by their poorer neighbors in the towns and by the small farmers of the interior. The advocacy of any measure by the wealthy group—usually called with a spice of malice the "well-born"—tended to arouse the suspicion, if not the opposition, of the poorer people.

Early ratifications

The Constitution was promptly ratified by the smaller states with little or no opposition. One large state, Pennsylvania, also accepted it at an early date (December 12, 1787), although the Anti-Federalists put up a vigorous fight in opposition. Before the middle of January, 1788, ratification had been voted by the states of Delaware, Pennsylvania, New Jersey, Georgia, and Connecticut, in the order named. The vote in Delaware, New Jersey, and Georgia was unanimous. In Pennsylvania it was two to one, and in Connecticut more than three to one. Then came ratification by Massachusetts, Maryland, South Carolina, and New Hampshire. By the action of New Hampshire (June 21) the new union was assured, as she was the ninth state to accept the Constitution. New Hampshire thus became the keystone of the arch of the Union.[45]

The contest over ratification in Massachusetts

The opposition offered by the Anti-Federalists was particularly strong in Massachusetts, New York, and Virginia. In Massachusetts the intense feeling behind the late disorders had not subsided and the small farmers of the interior and the poorer classes generally felt bitter toward the merchants, lawyers, and others among the "well-born" in the East. This hang-over from Shays's Rebellion was an important factor in the deliberations of the convention; since the latter classes were for ratification, the former were inclined to be against it.

Moreover, the two most popular of the Revolutionary leaders,

[45] For the order in which the states accepted the Constitution and the date of each ratification, see ELLIOT, JONATHAN, *The Debates in the Several State Conventions on the Adoption of the Federal Constitution*, i, pp. 319 ff.

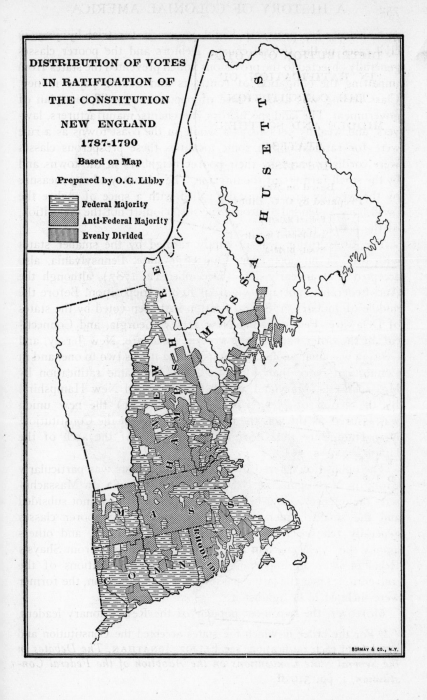

DISTRIBUTION OF VOTES
IN RATIFICATION OF
THE CONSTITUTION

NEW ENGLAND
1787-1790

Based on Map
Prepared by O. G. Libby

▤ Federal Majority
▨ Anti-Federal Majority
▥ Evenly Divided

BORMAY & CO., N.Y.

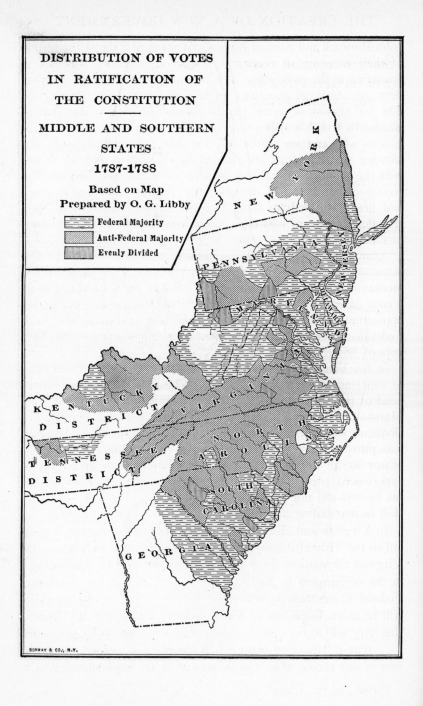

DISTRIBUTION OF VOTES
IN RATIFICATION OF
THE CONSTITUTION
—
MIDDLE AND SOUTHERN
STATES
1787-1788

Based on Map
Prepared by O. G. Libby

Federal Majority
Anti-Federal Majority
Evenly Divided

NEW YORK

PENNSYLVANIA

NEW JERSEY

MARYLAND

KENTUCKY DISTRICT

VIRGINIA

TENNESSEE DISTRICT

NORTH CAROLINA

SOUTH CAROLINA

GEORGIA

BORMAY & CO., N.Y.

John Hancock and Samuel Adams, did not at first throw the weight of their influence in favor of ratification. Hancock was late in appearing at the convention, although he had been elected its president. An attack of gout was given as the excuse for his absence. The real reason, however (in the opinion of some), was that he wanted to trim his sails properly and to do this it was better for him to wait and see which way the wind of public opinion was blowing. Later he took his place in the convention and fell in line with the advocates of ratification after the convention had voted to recommend certain amendments to the federal Constitution which had been proposed by him. The Federalists, it has been said, appealed to his vanity by dangling before him the Vice-Presidency of the new republic.

Adams too was anxious to be on the popular side. He was at first dissatisfied with the Constitution; but when the shipwrights and mechanics of Boston adopted resolutions in favor of ratification, a copy of which they sent to him by Paul Revere, he gave up his opposition and climbed up on the band wagon. Finally the Anti-Federalists were defeated, and the Constitution was accepted by a vote of 187 to 168.[46]

In the Virginia convention the Anti-Federalists had a number of able leaders, such as George Mason and Patrick Henry. At the head of the Federalist delegation were James Madison and John Marshall. The contest was a battle royal between giants. The eloquence of Henry, who was the most polished orator in America, was pitted against the clear reasoning of Madison, who was no orator but an able debater. In this convention, made up largely of experienced politicians, Henry's ability to stir the emotions of his hearers did not make so effective an appeal as did Madison's skill in marshaling arguments. *In Virginia*

In Virginia and elsewhere Washington's influence was a great aid to the Federalist cause, although he was not a member of the Virginia convention. In a private letter which had been printed in the newspapers he had said: ". . . and clear I am if another Federal Convention is attempted the sentiment of the members will be more discordant or less Conciliatory than the last, in fine, that they will agree upon no genl. plan. . . . I am fully persuaded . . . that it [the Constitution] or disunion is before us; if the first is our choice when the defects of it are experienced a Con- *Washington's influence*

46 *Ibid.*, ii, pp. 1-204.

stitutional door is open for amendments and may be adopted in a peaceable manner without tumult or disorder."[47]

The Anti-Federalists in the Virginia convention stoutly maintained that the Constitution would change the confederation of states into a consolidated government. Mason objected to allowing a continuance of the slave trade for twenty years and bitterly assailed the unrestricted right of Congress to regulate commerce. The Anti-Federalists contended that the danger of losing the right to navigate the Mississippi would be increased under the new regime. This argument appealed strongly to the members from the Kentucky region, who voted against ratification. But after a long and earnest discussion, the Constitution was accepted by a vote of 89 to 79.[48]

In New York

The New York convention was at first under the control of the Anti-Federalists. George Clinton, who was strongly opposed to ratification, was its president. Hamilton, though not entirely satisfied with the Constitution because it did not go far enough toward nationalism, was one of the outstanding leaders of the Federalists. The Anti-Federalists could have defeated ratification by prompt action; but as they were hesitant about pushing their advantage, a heated discussion characterized by abusive speeches was carried on for two weeks. They lost their opportunity by this delay; for before a final decision was reached, news was received of the favorable action of New Hampshire and Virginia. The Union was now a certainty, and New York would have to come in or be subjected to the great difficulty of maintaining a separate political existence in the center of the new republic. Accordingly, ratification was accepted, but only by a narrow majority. The convention also voted unanimously to send a circular letter to the other states recommending a second constitutional convention.[49]

The convention of North Carolina adjourned without accepting the Constitution, deciding to await further developments. Massachusetts, Virginia, and other states had proposed lists of amendments and it was thought that changes would soon be made in the Constitution. In response to the circular letter sent out by New

[47] FITZPATRICK, J. C., ed., *The Writings of George Washington*, xxix, p. 340.

[48] For a report of the debates in the Virginia convention, see Elliot, *op. cit.*, iii (the entire volume is devoted to this convention).

[49] For a report of the New York convention, see ELLIOT, *op. cit.*, ii, pp. 205-414.

York, a second federal convention might be held for a general revision of the federal instrument. In view of such possibilities, North Carolina felt that it would be best for her to postpone action. For some time Rhode Island declined even to call a convention. The new Union, therefore, went into effect with a membership of eleven instead of thirteen states.[50]

The most important of the newspaper articles that figured in the propaganda for and against ratification were a series of learned essays in support of the Constitution which are known as *The Federalist*. They were published in certain New York papers in the period from October, 1787, to August, 1788. All of them bore the signature "Publius." The authors who used this pen name were Hamilton, Madison, and John Jay. Free from the abuse and personal allusions so noticeable in many of the newspaper articles of the day, these essays were characterized by sound argument, logical arrangement, and a clarity of expression that rendered an abstruse subject understandable to the ordinary citizen. *The Federalist* is an interpretation of the Constitution by able contemporaries, and is the best commentary that we have on that document. An eminent present-day historian has rated it "one of the greatest works ever written in the realm of political science."[51]

The Federalist

In the preamble of the Constitution is the statement, "We the people of the United States . . . do ordain and establish this Constitution." The people did not, however, participate as individuals in either framing or ratifying the Constitution. In both steps they acted through their respective states. All votes on the various questions that arose in the Philadelphia Convention were by states and all ratifications were by states. It was thus by the states, rather than by the people, that the Constitution was ordained and established. Besides, the majority of the people did not share even indirectly in the building of the "New Roof." Owing to the limitations then imposed on the suffrage, a good portion of the adult male population was not allowed to vote, and a majority of those who were qualified refused to exercise the privilege. It is estimated, therefore, that "no more than one-fourth of the adult white males

Was the Constitution established by the people?

[50] North Carolina ratified the Constitution January 11, 1790; Rhode Island, June 16, 1790.

[51] McLaughlin, A. C., *The Confederation and the Constitution*, p. 308. *The Federalist* has been published a number of times. The editions edited by P. L. Ford (1898) and E. H. Scott (1898) are good.

in the country voted one way or the other in the elections at which delegates to the state ratifying conventions were chosen."[52]

On September 13, 1788, the Confederation Congress adopted a resolution providing for the installation of the new government. Dates were set for the choosing of electors, for their meeting to vote on presidential candidates, and for the organization of the new Congress.[53]

SELECTED READINGS

1. The Annapolis Convention.—McLaughlin, A. C., *The Confederation and the Constitution*, pp. 179-183; Commager, H. S., *Documents of American History*, i, pp. 132-134; Channing, E., *A History of the United States,* iii, pp. *496-473; Johnson, Allen, *Readings in American Constitutional History, 1776-1876*, pp. *93-98.

2. The Organization of the Philadelphia Convention.—Bancroft, George, *History of the Formation of the Constitution of the United States* (1885), ii, pp. *2-17; Warren, Charles, *The Making of the Constitution*, pp. *99-127; Farrand, Max, *The Framing of the Constitution of the United States*, *ch. 4.

3. Personnel of the Convention.—Farrand, Max, *op. cit.*, *ch. 2; McLaughlin, A. C., *Readings in the History of the American Nation*, pp. *87-92 (an estimate of his colleagues by William Pierce, a member of the Convention).

4. Economic Motives of the Fathers.—Beard, C. A., *An Economic Interpretation of the Constitution of the United States*, ch. 5.

5. James Madison.—Curtis, George T., *History of the Origin, Formation, and Adoption of the Constitution of the United States,* i, *ch. 9.

6. James Wilson.—*Ibid.*, pp. *462-465. (For lengthy excerpts from a great speech Wilson made on the Constitution, see pp. 465-479.)

7. Compromises of the Constitution.—Farrand, Max, in the *American Historical Review,* ix, pp. 479-489.

8. The Great Compromise.—McLaughlin, *The Confederation and the Constitution*, *ch. 14; Farrand, *The Framing of the Constitution*, *ch. 7.

9. Objections to the Constitution.—Commager, *op. cit.*, i, pp. 149-150; McLaughlin, *op. cit.*, pp. 279-280, 287-290, 298-304, 306-309.

[52] McLAUGHLIN, A. C., *A Constitutional History of the United States*, pp. 220-221; BEARD, C. A. and MARY R., *The Rise of American Civilization*, i, p. 332.

[53] *Journals of the Continental Congress*, xxxiv, pp. 521-523.

10. The Ratification of the Constitution.—McLaughlin, *op. cit.*, *chs. 17-18; McLaughlin, *A Constitutional History of the United States,* *ch. 15.

11. *The Federalist,* excerpts from.—Johnson, *op. cit.*, nos. 18-21, 31, 39; Pease and Roberts, *Selected Readings in American History,* pp. 176-179.

BIBLIOGRAPHICAL NOTES

GENERAL WORKS ON AMERICAN HISTORY

MOST of the fuller works concerned with the general history of the United States devote considerable space to the period prior to 1789. Some of them carry along the narrative of events and others give a continuous discussion of certain aspects of historical development. The more important titles in both groups are listed herewith as part of the Bibliography of the early period of American history.

General histories of the United States: Single works

One of the outstanding general histories of the United States is Edward Channing's *A History of the United States*, 6 vols. (1905-1925), covering the period 1492-1865. The first three volumes are devoted to the period prior to 1789. Although these volumes are concerned primarily with narrative history, considerable attention is given to social and economic life. The numerous references to sources and the interesting appraisals of bibliographical material given at. the end of the chapters make the work a useful guide for the special student. Another well-known general history is E. M. Avery's *A History of the United States and Its People*, 7 vols. (1904-1910; later editions have more than seven volumes). The narrative is illustrated and adorned with a large number of good pictures, maps, and plans, which add greatly to its value. Woodrow Wilson's *A History of the American People*, Documentary Edition (1917, 1918), is useful both for the general reader and for the special student. Each of the ten volumes contains important documents and numerous illustrations. The style of the text is clear and interesting. All of the first four volumes and part of the fifth are given over to the period prior to 1789. The student of colonial history may also wish to consult vols. i and ii of W. E. Chancellor and F. W. Hewes' *The United States, A History of Three Centuries* (1904-1905; numerous small maps).

Coöperative works

A readable series of books is *The Chronicles of America*, 50 vols. (1918-1921), edited by Allen Johnson. The first twelve volumes are devoted to the colonial and Revolutionary periods, and the two volumes on Education and Literature begin back in the colonial era. These little treatises vary as to the amount of scholarship behind them, but most of them are interesting. There are no references to sources, but the bibliographical notes in some of the volumes are helpful. Of less interest to the general reader but of more value to the special student is an older series, *The American Nation; A His-*

tory from Original Sources, 28 vols. (1904-1918), edited by A. B. Hart. The first ten volumes cover the period to 1789. The numerous references to the sources in the footnotes of these volumes make them a useful guide for special study. But probably the best starting-point for the serious student of colonial history is *The Narrative and Critical History of America*, 8 vols. (1884-1889), edited by Justin Winsor. The greater part of these volumes is devoted to the colonial and Revolutionary eras. This scholarly work, though old and in some respects out-of-date, gives the best appraisal we have of the primary and secondary authorities that were available at the time of its publication. Besides, the numerous reproduction of old maps and contemporary pictures constitute valuable source materials. The series, *The South in the Building of the Nation*, 12 vols. (1909; an extra index volume, 1913), is the product of a group of six editors-in-chief and numerous contributors. It deals with social and economic as well as political conditions; considerable space is devoted to the period prior to 1789.

The Pageant of America, 15 vols. (1925-1929), edited by Ralph H. Gabriel and others, is a useful work for both the general reader and the special student. The first volume of this series is given over entirely to the colonial period, and most of the others devote considerable space to the discussion of colonial topics. As this work is planned to give a pictorial history of the United States, each of the volumes has a great number of important pictures. Many of these are imaginary, though a number are reproductions of old portraits and prints. Another easily accessible collection of pictures is *The Album of American History*, edited by J. T. Adams and others (1944-   ; in progress; 3 volumes to 1893; mostly a reproduction of historical pictures).

Picture books

Important documents bearing on the general history of the United States are easily accessible in the following works: Commager, H. S., *Documents of American History*, 2 vols. in one (1934, 1943); Commager, H. S., and Nevins, Allan, *The Heritage of America* (1939; extracts from contemporary accounts; good illustrations); Pease, T. C., and Roberts, A. S., *Selected Readings in American History* (1928); and MacDonald, William, *Documentary Source Book of American History, 1606-1926* (1926). Other collections are: Hart, A. B., ed., *American History Told by Contemporaries*, 5 vols. (1897-1929); Thorpe, Willard, Curti, Merle, and Baker, Carlos, eds., *American Issues*, 2 vols. (1941; an anthology of intellectual history; semi-historical documents in vol. i); Preston, H. W., ed., *Documents Illustrative of American History, 1606-1863* (1886; more than half on the period prior to 1789); and Stedman, E. C., and Hutchinson, E. M., *A Library of American Literature from the Earliest Settlement to the Present Time*, 11 vols. (1889-1890, 1894; the first three to

Source books

1788). All the colonial charters are given in F. N. Thorpe's *The Federal and State Constitutions, Colonial Charters, and Other Organic Laws of the States and Territories and Colonies,* 7 vols. (1909), and most of them are also given in Benjamin P. Poore's *Federal and State Constitutions, Colonial Charters, and Other Organic Laws of the United States,* 2 vols. (1877, 1878). Some of the charters and other documents are given in abbreviated form in William MacDonald's *Documentary Source Book of American History, 1606-1926* (1926).

Economic histories of the United States

In recent years there have been published a number of single-volume economic histories which serve as useful supplements to the general treatises on American history. In this list should be included the following works: Bogart, E. L., and Kemmerer, D. L., *Economic History of the American People* (1942; a revision of Bogart's *Economic History of the American People*); Carman, H. J., *Social and Economic History of the United States,* 2 vols. (1930-1934); Faulkner, H. U., *American Economic History* (5th ed., 1943); Hawk, E. Q., *Economic History of the South* (1934); Homphrey, E. F., *An Economic History of the United States* (1937); Jennings, W. W., *A History of Economic Progress of the United States* (1926); Kirkland, E. C., *A History of American Economic Life* (1934); Lippincott, Isaac, *Economic Development of the United States* (1921); McGrane, R. C., *The Economic Development of the American Nation* (1942); Sakolski, A. M., and Myron, L. H., *American Economic Development* (1936); Shannon, Fred A., *Economic History of the People of the United States* (1934); Thompson, C. M., and Jones, F. M., *Economic Development of the United States* (1939); VanMetre, T. W., *Economic History of the United States* (1921); and Wright, Chester W., *Economic History of the United States* (1941). A dip into the primary sources of economic history is afforded by Bogart, E. L., and Thompson, C. M., *Readings in the Economic History of the United States* (1916).

Social life

There is no complete work which deals satisfactorily with the whole field of American social life. The nearest approach to an adequate treatment of this subject is *A History of American Life,* edited by A. M. Schlesinger and D. R. Fox, 12 vols. (1929-1944; first four volumes to 1790). The best discussion of life in the cities is to be found in Bridenbaugh, Carl, *Cities in the Wilderness* (1938). The student interested in urban life will find this scholarly work indispensable. For the everyday life of the people, see Langdon, W. C., *Everyday Things in American Life, 1607-1776,* 2 vols. (1937-1941; many valuable pictures); Dulles, E. R., *America Learns to Play: A History of Popular Recreation, 1607-1940* (1940); Coad, O. S., and Mims, Edwin, Jr., *The American Stage* [*The Pageant of America,* xiv] (1929; pictures); and Hornblow, Arthur, *A History of the Theatre in America,* 2 vols. (1919; numerous quotations from the sources;

pictures); Calhoun, A. W., *Social History of the American Family*, 3 vols. (1917-1919); and McClellan, Elizabeth, *History of American Costume, 1607-1870* (1904, 1937; excellent pictures; an invaluable work).

A very readable brief history of education in the United States is E. E. Slosson's *The American Spirit in Education* [*The Chronicles of America,* xxxiii] (1921). Fuller accounts are: Grant, E. G., *A History of Education in the United States* (1904), and Noble, Stuart G., *A History of American Education* (1938). Other useful general works are: Dexter, E. G., *A History of Education in the United States* (1904); Knight, Edgar W., *Education in the United States* (1929, 1941); and Thwing, C. F., *A History of Higher Education in America* (1906). Education and religion

The whole field of religion in the United States is covered by Sweet, W. W., *The Story of Religions in America* (1930); *The American Church History*, 13 vols. (1893-1897; a co-operative work; the 13th volume, *A History of American Christianity*, by L. W. Bacon, gives a summary of the entire subject); and Weigle, Luther A., *American Idealism* [*The Pageant of America,* x] (1928). In the last-named volume the brief narrative is supplemented with valuable pictures.

Useful map books are: Fox, D. R., ed., *Harper's Atlas of American History* (1920); Paullin, C. O., *Atlas of Historical Geography of the United States* (1932); Adams, J. T., *Atlas of American History* (1943); and Lord, C. L. and B. H., *Historical Atlas of the United States* (1944). The following works show the influence of geography on American history: Brigham, A. P., *Geographic Influences in American History* (1903); McCarty, H. H., *The Geographic Basis of American Economic Life* (1940); and Semple, E. C., *American History and Its Geographic Conditions* (rev. ed., 1933). Good descriptive geographies are: Bowman, Isaiah, *Forest Physiography* (1911); and Fenneman, N. M., *Physiography of Eastern United States* (1938), *Physiography of Western United States* (1931), and "Physiographic Divisions of the United States" [Association of American Geographer's *Annals,* xviii]. Historical geography

Useful and easily accessible books of reference are: Johnson, Allen, and Malone, Dumas, eds., *The Dictionary of American Biography*, 20 vols. (1928-1937); Adams, J. T., ed., *The Dictionary of American History*, 6 vols. (1940); and Seligman, E. R. A., and others, eds. *Encyclopedia of the Social Sciences*, 15 vols. (1930-1935). Reference works

Most of the works already listed contain extensive bibliographies which will prove helpful to serious students. Of the works devoted entirely or mainly to bibliography, the following should be mentioned: Channing, E., Hart, A. B., and Turner, E. J., *Guide to the Study and Reading of American History* (1912; hereafter referred to as Channing, Hart, and Turner's *Guide*); Larned, J. N., *Literature of Amer-* Bibliographies *ican History* (1902); and Griffin, Grace C., and others, *Writings on American History*, a series of volumes, one each year, which have been published since 1918 as a part of the *Annual Report* of the American Historical Association. In these volumes are listed the books and articles on United States and Canadian history published each year. A noted collection of bibliographical material can be found in *A Dictionary of Books Relating to America from Its Discovery to the Present Time*, 29 vols. The first edition of this monumental work was compiled by Joseph Sabin and published in 1868. It has been brought up to the latest date of publication (1936) by Wilber Eames and R. W. G. Vail. See also Bradford, T. L., *Bibliographer's Manual of American History*, 4 vols. (1907-1909; a brief account of all the state, county, and town histories). An excellent guide to source materials and other literature of American history (probably the best) is Beers, Henry P., *Bibliographies in American History* (1942). This is a bibliography of bibliographies, and is so organized that with it one can easily locate the literature on any subject in the field of United States history.

EARLY AMERICAN HISTORY (TO 1789)

Comprehensive works

The student of early American history should have access to historical literature that gives a fuller treatment of this period than can be found in the titles already listed. There are a number of comprehensive works which are devoted mainly or entirely to early America. Of these the first place should be accorded to Andrews, C. M., *The Colonial Period of American History*, 4 vols. (1934-1938). It is probably the best general history of the American colonies, but there is less emphasis on social and institutional history than in some of the older writings. It is valuable for the special student, but in many places it is too detailed to hold the interest of the general reader. Another useful general work, this one by an English author, is Doyle, J. A., *English Colonies in America*, 5 vols. (1880-1907). For colonial institutions the best authority is Osgood, H. L., *The American Colonies in the Seventeenth Century*, 3 vols. (1904), and the *American Colonies in the Eighteenth Century*, 4 vols. (1924-1925). George Bancroft's *History of the United States* (6 vols., 1891-1892) is devoted entirely to the period to 1789. The chief value of this classic lies in its high literary quality. An interesting volume which appeals to the general reader is Frank J. Klingberg's *The Morning of America* (1941; emphasis on personalities and good stories).

Briefer works

Useful one-volume books are: Bolton, H. E., and Marshall, T. M., *The Colonization of North America* (1920; considerable space given to Spanish and French colonies); Greene, E. B., *Foundations of American Nationality* (rev. ed., 1935); Jernegan, M. W., *The American Colonies* (1929); Nettles, C. P., *The Roots of American Civilization*

(1938; emphasizes British background); Savelle, Max, *The Foundations of American Civilization* (1942); and Sanders, J. B., *Early American History, 1492-1789* (1938; has a full bibliography, including a valuable list of historical articles).

The best account of Britain's possessions during our colonial era is given by L. H. Gipson in his definitive work, *The British Empire Before the American Revolution,* 6 vols. (in progress, 1936-   ). A valuable feature of the work is the attention paid to the insular colonies. Some space is also devoted to the British West Indian plantations by Savelle in *The Foundations of American Civilization* and by Andrews in *The Colonial Period of American History.* See also Pitman, F. W., *The Development of the British West Indies, 1700-1763* (1917). The British West Indies

In addition to the bibliographies already listed, two which are devoted mostly to the colonial period should be mentioned: Waldman, Milton, *Americana: The Literature of American History* (1925; an interesting discussion of the old writings, mostly on the colonial period); Greene, E. B., and Morris, R. B., *A Guide to the Principal Sources for Early American History (1600-1800) in the City of New York* (1929; an invaluable work; hereafter referred to as Greene and Morris's *Guide*); and Beers, H. P., *Bibliographies in American History,* pp. 32-57. Bibliographies

In addition to the general sources discussed on pages 759-760, certain others concerned exclusively with the early period should be listed. The most valuable collection of contemporary narratives on the colonial period that is easily accessible to all readers is the *Original Narratives of Early American History,* 18 vols. (1906-1917), edited by J. Franklin Jameson and an able corps of associates. Some interesting and important source materials are also scattered throughout the *Old South Leaflets* and the *American History Leaflets.* A most useful collection of treaties relating to early American history is *European Treaties Bearing on the History of the United States and Its Dependencies,* 4 vols. (1917-1937), edited by Frances G. Davenport and C. O. Paullin. The original texts and English translations of the treaties are given. The text of each is preceded by explanatory comment and references to both primary and secondary authorities. These four volumes cover the period to 1815. Peter Kalm's *Travels into North America,* 2 vols. (1772), is an account by an observant contemporary of the manners and customs of the people at the end of the colonial period, and of the natural history and the civil, ecclesiastical, and commercial state of the country. George Chalmers's *Political Annals of the Present United Colonies from their Settlement to the Peace of 1763* (1780) might be considered a contemporary work, as the author spent the greater part of the first half of his life in the colonies (from his birth in 1742 to the outbreak of the Revolution). Besides, he was clerk of the Board of Trade after 1786 and had access to valuable docu- Source materials ments. The acts of the British Parliament regarding the American colonies can be found most easily by using Leo F. Stock's *Proceedings and Debates of the British Parliaments Respecting North America,* 5 vols. (1924-1930; a 6th vol. is in preparation). Useful one-volume source books, giving well-known documents or excerpts from them, are: West, W. M., ed., *A Source Book in American History to 1787* (1913); and MacDonald, William, *Select Charters and Other Documents Illustrative of American History, 1606-1775* (1899).

Other collections of value to the special student are: Sainsbury, W. N., and others, eds., *Calendar of State Papers, Colonial Series, America and West Indies* (1860-   ; in progress; thirty-odd volumes by 1939); Grant, W. L., and Munro, James, eds., *Acts of the Privy Council of England, Colonial Series,* 6 vols. (1908-   ); Force, Peter, comp., *Tracts and Other Papers,* 4 vols. (1836-1846), and *American Archives,* 4th and 5th series, 9 vols. (4th series, 1837-1846; 5th series, 1848-1853); and Hazard, Ebenezer, ed., *Historical Collections,* 2 vols. (1792-1794). For a fuller list of primary sources, well selected, see A. B. Hart's *American History Told by Contemporaries,* i, pp. 9-15; ii, pp. 11-21.

Contem-
porary
maps For reproductions of old maps, see the following collections: Hulbert, A. B., collector, *The Crown Collection of Photographs of American Maps* (1904-1908; these folios are unwieldy and rare, for only twenty-five copies were originally printed; 1st series, 5 vols.; 2nd series, 5 vols., in portfolio; 3rd series, 250 sheets; nearly all of the maps in the three series date from the eighteenth century, the greater part of them from the latter half of that century); Stevenson, E. L., *Maps Illustrating Early Discovery and Exploration in America, 1502-1530* (1906; twelve maps in 124 sheets; there are only eighteen sets in all, which are located in a few of the leading libraries throughout the country). An exhaustive list of maps, old and new, is given by P. L. Phillips in his *List of Geographical Atlases in the Library of Congress,* 2 vols. (1909).

CHAPTER I.—THE BACKGROUND OF COLONIAL AMERICAN HISTORY

European
back-
ground FOR a good discussion of the European background of American history, giving political, economic, and social conditions, see Sellery, G. C., and Krey, A. C., *Medieval Foundations of Western Civilization* (1929), chs. 17-25. A good account of political conditions in Europe at the beginning of the sixteenth century is given in C. J. H. Hayes's *Political and Social History of Modern Europe* (1916, 1924), i, ch. 1. For an interesting short discussion of social conditions in Europe at the same period, see Higby, C. P., *History of Europe, 1492-1815* (1927), pp. 1-27. E. P. Cheyney, in his *Industrial and Social History of England* (1920 ed.), ch. 6, and his *Social Changes in England in the Sixteenth Century* (1895), describes the changes in the social and industrial life of England that grew out of and were incident to the transition from the mediæval to the modern age. *The History of England, 1588-1603*, 2 vols. (1914-1926), by the same author, is an excellent history of the reign of Elizabeth. See also Lunt, W. E., *History of England* (1928, 1938), chs. 16-21; Hall, W. P., and Albion, R. G., *History of England and the British Empire* (1937); Mullet, Charles F., *The British Empire* (1938); Davies, Godfrey, *The Early Stuarts* (1937); and vol. i of *The Cambridge History of the British Empire*, 8 vols. (1929-1936).

The events in the development of Europe that help to explain our early history are presented in readable form in E. P. Cheyney's *European Background of American History* (1904). For more detailed discussions of the European and English backgrounds, see Seeley, John R., *Expansion of England* (1911), and *Growth of British Policy* (1922), i; and Abbott, W. C., *The Expansion of Europe* (1924 ed.), i, especially ch. 16 (social conditions in England at the end of the sixteenth century). Other works that are useful for a study of economic and social conditions in England at the beginning of the period of colonization are: Traill, H. D., ed., *Social England*, 6 vols. (1894-1898), iv-v; Ashley, W. J., *The Economic Organization of England, an Outline History* (1914, 1935), ii, chs. 3-5; Bradley, Harriette, *The Enclosures in England* (1918); and Hart, A. B., *American History Told by Contemporaries*, i, pp. 145-152 (a contemporary account).

The economic, social, and cultural life of the Indians is discussed at length in Clark Wissler's valuable works, *The American Indian* (1922), and *Indians of the United States: Four Centuries of their History and Culture* (1940; of interest to both the special student and the general reader). Other accounts of the aborigines that may prove useful are: Radin, P., *The Story of the American Indian* (1927, 1934); Hodge, F. W., ed., *Handbook of American Indians North of Mexico* (1907-1910; in two parts; an encyclopedia with numerous illustrations); Farrand, Livingston, *Basis of American History* [*The American Nation*, ii; 1904], chs. 5-17; and Embree, E. R., *Indians of the Americas* (1939). `Indians`

Chapter II.—The Discovery of America

The following works give good general accounts of the period of discovery, and they are all easily accessible to college students: Bourne, E. G., *Spain in America* [*American Nation Series*] (readable and scholarly, with specific references to the sources); Richman, I. B., *The Spanish Conquerors* [*Chronicles of America Series*] (in- `General` `accounts` teresting; no references to sources, but has a useful bibliography); Fiske, John, *The Discovery of America*, 2 vols. (is brilliantly written and is probably the most interesting work covering the entire period. On a few points, however, it is not in complete harmony with the conclusions of the most recent scholarship). Excellent brief accounts are: Channing, E., *History of the United States*, i, chs. 1-5; and Wissler, C., Skinner, C. L., and Wood, W., *Adventures in the Wilderness* [*The Pageant of America*], chs. 1-5. For collections of documents and a list of older secondary authorities, with an appraisal of both, see Larned, J. N., *Literature of American History*, pp. 50-66. Other references useful for an intensive study of this period can be found in Justin Winsor's *Narrative and Critical History of America*, ii, chs. 1-3, and iii, ch. 1. For an appraisal of the primary and secondary authorities in this valuable work, see p. 729.

The Norse discoveries
There is a good short account of the Norse discoveries in E. Channing's *History of the United States*, i, pp. 1-16, with bibliographical notes on pp. 27-28. For a discussion of the sources of information regarding these discoveries, see Reeves, Arthur M., *The Finding of Wineland the Good* (1895). English translations of the texts of the sagas and other documents are given at length. There are also a number of pages of facsimiles of the sagas, with the printed texts opposite. Other works of value are: Gathorne-Hardy, Geoffrey, *The Norse Discoveries of America* (1921; gives an English translation of the sagas and an elaborate discussion of the evidence in favor of the Norse discoveries); Holand, H. R., *Westward from Umland* (1940; contains a lengthy discussion as to the genuineness of the Kensington Stone); Fraser, A. D., *Norse Discoveries* (1943); and Haugen, Einar, *Voyages to Vinland* (1942; a new translation of the old manuscripts with arguments in favor of the historicity of the Norse traditions). For other primary sources see footnotes for this chapter. An excellent evaluation of the sagas as source materials is given by J. E. Olson and E. G. Bourne, eds., *The Northmen, Columbus, and Cabot* (1906), pp. 3-13; for English translations of the sagas and other documents on the Norse discoveries, see pp. 14-74. See also Lawrence, A. W., and Young, J., eds., *Narratives of the Discovery of America* (1931).

Work of Prince Henry
For the work of Prince Henry of Portugal, see Major, R. H., *The Life of Prince Henry of Portugal, Surnamed the Navigator* (1868). For a brief account, see an article in the *American Historical Review*, January, 1912, xvii, pp. 252-267 (especially pp. 263-267), by C. R. Beazley, who has also published a fuller work, *Prince Henry the Navigator* (1895).

Trade-routes to the East
A good readable account of the trade-routes to the East is given in E. P. Cheyney's *European Background of American History*. However, it presents the old view of the relation of these routes to the events that led to the early discoveries and should be checked up by

referring to two articles by A. H. Lybyer which are based on later research. For these articles, see the *English Historical Review*, xxx, pp. 577-588, and the *Annual Report* of the American Historical Association, 1914, i, pp. 127-133.

The general accounts of the period of discovery mentioned above (pp. 765 f.) all devote considerable space to the career of Columbus. The references listed under Selected Readings (p. 37) also cover the principal events of his life. A valuable supplement to these is S. E. Morison's *Admiral of the Ocean Sea: A Life of Christopher Columbus*, 2 vols. (1942; scholarly and readable). From the works thus listed and those given on pp. 762 f. can be obtained all the information that the general reader or the average college student will want. In addition to these the special student may wish to consult the following: Harrisse, H., *The Discovery of North America* (1892), and *Christophe Colomb*, 2 vols. (1884-1885); Winsor, Justin, *Christopher Columbus* (1891, 1892); Vignaud, H., *Toscanelli and Columbus* (1903), and other works by the same author mentioned below; Thacher, J. B., *Christopher Columbus*, 3 vols. (1903-1904); Markham, C. R., *Life of Christopher Columbus* (1902); Humboldt, A., *Examen Critique*, 5 vols. (1836-1889); and Young, F., *Christopher Columbus and the New World of His Discovery*, 1912 ed. (documents in the appendix, pp. 425-450).

Columbus: Secondary authorities

A friendly attitude toward Columbus and the traditional view regarding his career were generally maintained by Columbists until the middle eighteen-eighties (1884-1885), when Henry Harrisse published his *Christophe Colomb*. After years of study Harrisse brought to light new documents and subjected old ones to rigid criticism. He questioned the authenticity of the *History of Ferdinand Columbus* as we now have it, and stripped the Great Admiral's picture of the aureole of sanctity with which the hero-worship of former generations had adorned it. The views of Harrisse were accepted by Justin Winsor and can be found in his *Christopher Columbus*. Since Harrisse started the ball of hostile criticism rolling, there has been an immense amount of controversy among scholars over the various phases of the career of Columbus.

Another critic of the traditional view regarding Columbus's motives is the French scholar, Henry Vignaud. He has written several books about the great navigator, the most important being his *Histoire Critique de la Grande Enterprise de Christophe Colomb*, 2 vols. (1911). The contention of this work has been summarized in a pamphlet in English entitled *The Columbian Tradition on the Discovery of America and the Part Played Therein by the Astronomer Toscanelli* (1919). This pamphlet is all that the average reader needs to get the author's point of view. It is a labored and, in places, over-refined argument to show that Columbus's motive in making his first voyage was not to find a sea-route to the East, but to discover a new island, or islands, the general location of which he had received information about from an unknown sailor or other sources. Vignaud thinks also that the map and letter attributed to Toscanelli are forgeries. Most of the fine points raised by Vignaud are of interest only to scholars and meticulous students and are of little concern to the general reader. For a popularization of Vignaud's theory, see M. André's *Christopher Columbus* (English translation, 1928). For an excellent summary of the conclusions of recent scholarship on the Columbist dispute, see a scholarly article by Charles E. Nowell in the *American Historical Review*, July, 1939, xliv, pp. 802-822.

Sources on Columbus

The most important collection of sources is *Raccolta di Documenti e Studi*, 14 vols. (1892-1896). These contain the writings of Columbus and numerous other valuable documents. Other important sources are: Major, R. H., *Select Letters of Columbus* (1890) ; Las Casas, Bartholomew, *Historia de las Indias,* 5 vols. (1875). Las Casas was a friend of Columbus, and in the preparation of his history he had the use of Columbus's *Journal* and other documents that are no longer extant. He lived in the West Indies and probably accompanied Columbus on his fourth voyage. Another contemporary of Columbus was Peter Martyr, who was at one time Isabella's chaplain. He wrote 812 letters that have come down to us. Some of them describe the early events of American history and were written at the time the news of these events first came to court. The letters and a work called *De Orbe Novo,* which is a treatise on the discoveries in the New World, were published in 1530. The *De Orbe Novo* has been translated into English by F. A. McNutt, 2 vols. (1912). Another well-known work is the *History of the Life and Actions of Columbus*, which bears as its author's name Ferdinand Columbus, the son of the Great Admiral. It was first published in 1571 in Italian ; the original Spanish version (if there ever was one) has been lost. Harrisse denied the claim that this work was written by Ferdinand Columbus. For his views see Winsor, *Christopher Columbus*, pp. 44-46. This history can be found in John Pinkerton's *Voyages* (1812), xii, pp. 1-155 ; and in Robert Kerr's *Voyages and Travels* (1811), iii, pp. 7-242.

The following sources are the most accessible: *Old South Leaflets*, nos. 29, 33, 71, and 102 ; Hart, A. B., *American History Told by Contemporaries*, i, pp. 35-40 ; Olson, J. E., and Bourne, E. G., eds., *The Northmen, Columbus, and Cabot* (1906; see footnotes for page references). There are some valuable source materials in Thacher's voluminous work. It gives the full text (so far as we have it) of Columbus's *Journal* of his first voyage ; letters to Columbus, with a number of facsimiles of his handwriting ; and other important documents. A fine collection of sources is the one edited by Cecil Jane entitled *Select Documents Illustrating the Four Voyages of Columbus, 2 vols. (1930-1933).

The definitive work on the Cabots is James A. Williamson's *The Voyages of the Cabots and the English Discovery of North America Under Henry VII and Henry VIII* (1929; fair to Sebastian Cabot; some documents and reproduction of old maps). Other secondary authorities are: Winship, G. P., *Cabot Bibliography* (1896), pp. xi-xvi (an excellent short account of the career of John Cabot); Olson and Bourne, *op. cit.,* pp. 423-450; and *Old South Leaflets,* nos. 37 and 115. Bibliographies: Harrisse, Henry, *John Cabot, the Discoverer of America, and Sebastian, His Son* (1896), pp. 387-469; and Winship, *Cabot Bibliography.* An interesting short discussion of the career of Vespucius is to be found in an article by E. G. Bourne in the *American Historical Review,* x, pp. 41-51. This is a hostile view; with it should be read either Fiske, *The Discovery of America,* ii, pp. 25-76, or H. Vignaud's *Americ Vespuce* (1912; so far as I know, there is no English translation of the French edition). Vignaud's work discusses at great length the voyages of Americus Vespucius. He concludes that Vespucius made an expedition in 1497-1498, in which he sailed along the coast of North America from Honduras to Florida. He contends that Vespucius was the first one to discover that America was a new world and not part of Asia. The views of the work are summarized on pp. 299-301. A brief account of the voyages of Vespucius, with a critique of the evidence, is given in an article entitled "Americ Vespuce," published in the *Journal de la Société des Américanistes de Paris,* nouvelle serie, tome viii, pp. 23-54. A recent discussion of the Vespucian question can be found in F. J. Pohl's *Amerigo Vespucci: Pilot Major* (1944). For source materials, see *Old South Leaflets,* nos. 34 and 90; and Northup, George T., *Vespucci Reprints, Texts and Studies,* iv.

CHAPTER III.—EARLY EXPLORATIONS AND INTERNATIONAL RIVALRIES IN AMERICA

SPANISH EXPLORATIONS

THERE are many readable and useful works on early Spanish exploration in America. Of these the following should be listed: Bourne, E. G., *Spain in America* (1904), pp. 133-174; Richman, I. B., *The Spanish Conquerors* (1919), pp. 64-215; Bolton, H. E., *The Spanish Borderlands* (1921); Fiske, J., *The Discovery of America* (1795), ii, chs. 8-12; Lowery, Woodbury, *The Spanish Settlements Within the Present Limits of the United States, 1513-61* (1911); Winsor, J., *Narrative and Critical History of America,* ii, chs. 3-7; Priestley, H. I., *The Coming of the White Man, 1492-1848* (1929), chs. 1-6; and Wissler, C., Skinner, C. L., and Wood, W., *Adventures in the Wilderness* [*The Pageant of America*] (1925), chs.

6 and 18. The special student will also wish to consult Theodore Maynard's *De Soto and the Conquistadores* (1930; "a delightfully written narrative"); and both the special student and the general reader will find interest in two later works: A. G. Day's *Coronado's Quest: The Discovery of the Southwestern States* (1940), and George P. Hammond's *Narratives of the Coronado Expedition, 1540-1542* (1940; best collection of documents).

Sources   The best collection of sources that is easily accessible is to be found in the two volumes of the *Original Narratives of Early American History: Spanish Explorers in the Southern United States, 1528-1543* (1907), edited by F. W. Hodge and T. H. Lewis; and *Spanish Explorations in the Southwest, 1542-1706* (1925), edited by H. E. Bolton. Other accessible sources are certain volumes of the *Trail Makers* Series. These little books are English translations of accounts of explorations written either by the explorers themselves or by their companions. The volumes in this series bearing on this period are: *The Journey of Alvar Nuñez Cabeza de Vaca and His Companions from Florida to the Pacific, 1528-1536*, written by Cabeza and translated by Fanny Bandelier (1905); Long, Hanil, ed., *Nuñez Cabeza de Vaca* (1944; Cabeza de Vaca's story of his journey from Florida to the Pacific, 1528-1536); *Narratives of the Career of Hernando de Soto in the Conquest of Florida, 1539-1542* (1904, 1929; these narratives were written by three men who had been with de Soto on his Florida expedition; they have been translated by E. G. Bourne); *The Journey of Coronado, 1540-42*, written by himself and some of his followers and edited by G. P. Winship (1904). For lists of other authorities and sources, see Bolton, H. E., *Spanish Explorations*, pp. 297-300, and the Critical Essays at the end of each chapter in Winsor's *Narrative and Critical History*, ii. For reproductions of contemporary maps, see *Narrative and Critical History*, ii, and Stevenson, E. L., *Maps Illustrating Early Discovery and Exploration* (rare).

FRENCH EXPLORATIONS

General accounts   The greatest authority on the part played by the French in the New World is Francis Parkman. His works include a number of volumes, all of which are interesting and scholarly. The two volumes on *The Pioneers of France in the New World* (1865, 1895) deal with the early French explorations. Parkman's historical writings have been condensed into one volume by Edgar Pelham, under the title of *The Struggle for a Continent* (1916). This is a very useful work for those who do not have time to read the voluminous writings of Parkman himself. Readable accounts of the early French explorers are John Fiske's *New France and New England* (1902), ch. 1; W. B. Munro's *Crusaders of New France* [*The Chronicles of America*] (1918); and G. M. Wrong's *The Rise and Fall of New France*, 2 vols. (1928).

Other useful works are: Thwaites, R. G., *France in America* [*The American Nation Series*] (1905); Leacock, S., *The Mariner of St. Malo, A Chronicle of Jacques Cartier* [*Chronicles of Canada Series*] (1914); Winsor, J., *Cartier to Frontenac*, chs. 2 and 3 (1904; this volume contains a number of reproductions of contemporary maps that are valuable); and Wissler, C., Skinner, C. L., and Wood, W., *Adventures in the Wilderness*, ch. 7, and ch. 17, sec. I.

Henry S. Burrage, ed., *Early English and French Voyages* [*Original Narratives*] (1906), pp. 4-103, gives an account of Cartier's three voyages. These same accounts (the first of which was written by Cartier himself, the second by one of his men, and the third by Hakluyt) are given in J. P. Baxter's *A Memoir of Jacques Cartier* (1906), pp. 75-231; H. P. Biggar's *The Voyages of Jacques Cartier* (1924); and H. B. Stephens's *Jacques Cartier and His Four Voyages to Canada* (1891). The last work gives an account of a fourth voyage which Cartier is said to have made but about which there is some doubt. Baxter reproduces a portrait which is supposed to be that of Cartier, but there is some doubt as to its authenticity. This portrait is also reproduced in Winsor, *Narrative and Critical History*, ii, p. 45. In Richard Hakluyt's *Early English Voyages to America* (1889 ed.) there are also some important contemporary accounts of French explorations. These include the expedition of Verrazano, the voyages of Cartier (ii, pp. 77-168) and Roberval (pp. 163-168), and the careers of Laudonnière (pp. 402-508), Ribaut (pp. 508-523), and Captain Gourgues in Florida (pp. 524-533). For lists of other authorities and a critical discussion of primary and secondary sources, see Thwaites, R. G., *op. cit.*, pp. 296-303, and Munro, W. B., *op. cit.*, pp. 229-231.

Sources

ENGLISH EXPLORATIONS

For general accounts of early English explorations see: Wood, William, *Elizabethan Sea-Dogs*. [*Chronicles of America Series*] (1918); Tyler, L. G., *England in America, 1580-1662* [*American Nation Series*] (1904), chs. 1 and 2; Corbett, Julian S., *Drake and the Tudor Navy*, 2 vols. (1898, 1899); Wagner, H. R., *Sir Francis Drake's Voyage Around the World* (1926); Walling, R. A. J., *A Sea-Dog of Devon* (1907; a good biography of John Hawkins); Williamson, J. A., *Sir John Hawkins; the Time and the Man* (1927); Waldman, Milton, *Sir Walter Raleigh* (1928); Anthony, Irvin, *Raleigh and His World* (1934); Chidsey, Donald B., *Sir Walter Raleigh* (1931); and Wissler, C., Skinner, C. L., and Wood, W., *Adventures in the Wilderness*, ch. 8.

General accounts

The most accessible collection of sources on this topic are: Burrage, H. S., ed., *Early English and French Voyages, 1543-1608* [*Original Narratives*] (1906), pp. 106-419; and Hart, A. B., ed., *American History Told by Contemporaries*, i, ch. 4. A few contemporary accounts

Sources

are given in the *Old South Leaflets*, nos. 116-119. One of the most valuable collections of documents for the special student of this period is Hakluyt's *Principal Navigations, Voiages, Traffiques, and Discoveries*. They are contemporary accounts not only of English but also of Spanish and French voyages. They were first collected and published by Richard Hakluyt in 1589. The Hakluyt Society has reprinted and edited these documents and published others. Its publications cover a great number of volumes and are an invaluable mine of information for the period of discovery and exploration. Of this vast collection we may note especially the two following: *The World Encompassed by Sir Francis Drake* and the *Hawkins Voyages*. The former was written by the chaplain and others who were with Drake on his famous voyage; the latter contains original accounts of the achievements of three generations of Hawkinses. For this last work see C. R. Markham, ed., *The Hakluyt Society Publications*, 1878 ed., lvii. E. J. Payne, in his *Voyages of Elizabethan Seamen to America*, gives extracts from Hakluyt on the voyages of Hawkins, Frobisher, Drake, Gilbert, Amadas and Barlow, and Cavendish, and on Raleigh's voyage to Guiana. There are three editions of this work, 1880, 1900, 1907. Another convenient place in which to find some contemporary accounts is C. R. Beazley's *Voyages and Travels*, 2 vols. (1903). Vol. i, pp. 29-130, contains documents on the voyages of Hawkins; vol. ii, pp. 221-294, on those of Drake. C. W. Sams in *The Conquest of Virginia* (1924) gives the texts of contemporary accounts of Raleigh's attempts at exploration and colonization. For a further discussion of the sources, see Winsor's *Narrative and Critical History of America*, iii, pp. 78-84 (Hawkins and Drake), 121-126 (Raleigh). Important contemporary maps are reproduced on pp. 124-126. For a reproduction of pictures made by John White and Jacques Le Moyne and engraved by Theodore De Bry in 1590, see Stefan Lorant's *The New World: The First Pictures of America* (1946).

CHAPTER IV.—VIRGINIA FROM PLANTATION TO ROYAL PROVINCE

Secondary authorities: General accounts

SOME of the general histories listed above are very good for this period. Of these, special mention should be made of the writings of Doyle, Channing, Tyler, Osgood, and C. M. Andrews. To this list may be added Matthew P. Andrews's *Virginia, the Old Dominion* (1937), chs. 1-19. See also an article, "Some English Conditions Surrounding the Settlement of Virginia," by E. P. Cheyney in the *American Historical Review*, xii, pp. 507-528. Among the works dealing entirely or mainly with colonial Virginia, the following are useful: Fiske, John, *The Old Dominion and Her Neighbors*, 2 vols. (1897; brilliantly written; the most readable of all the accounts); Bruce, P. A.,

History of Colonial Virginia (1923; the first volume of a three-volume co-operative history of the Old Dominion) ; Brown, Alexander, *The First Republic in America* (1898; gives a detailed account of the history of Virginia to 1627) ; Tyler, L. G., *The Cradle of the Republic* (1900, 1906; contains a great deal of information regarding the early history of Virginia; a number of illustrations, good map and chart, pp. 22, 101) ; and Stanard, Mary N., *The Story of Virginia's First Century* (1928).

There are also a number of scholarly monographs on certain phases of Virginia history. These are all well documented and the numerous specific references in the footnotes enable the student easily to find his way to the sources. Of these monographs the following may prove useful: Craven, Wesley W., *Dissolution of the Virginia Company: The Failure of a Colonial Experiment* (1932; a definitive account of the last six years of the Virginia Company) ; Wertenbaker, T. J., *Virginia Under the Stuarts* (1914), *Patrician and Plebeian in Virginia* (1916), and *The Planters of Colonial Virginia* (1922) ; Flippin, P. S., *The Royal Government in Virginia* (1919), and *The Financial Administration of the Colony of Virginia* (1915) ; Bruce, P. A., *Economic History of Virginia in the Seventeenth Century*, 2 vols. (1896), *Social Life of Virginia in the Seventeenth Century* (1907), and *Institutional History of Virginia in the Seventeenth Century*, 2 vols. (1910) ; Chitwood, O. P., *Justice in Colonial Virginia* (1905) ; Chandler, J. A. C., *History of Suffrage in Virginia* (1899), and *Representation in Virginia* (1896) ; and Ingle, E., *Virginia Local Institutions* (1885). The last four monographs are published in the Johns Hopkins University *Studies in Historical and Political Science*. See also an article by T. A. Wright in the *American Historical Review* for April, 1920, entitled "Spanish Policy Toward Virginia, 1606-1612."

Other works that should be listed are: Bruce, P. A., *The Virginia Plutarch*, 2 vols. (1929; biographies of noted Virginians, with reproductions of contemporary portraits; first volume on the colonial and Revolutionary periods) ; Davis, J. E., *Jamestown and Her Neighbors* (1928) ; Fletcher, John G., *John Smith also Pocahontas* (1928) ; and Chatterton, E. K., *Captain John Smith* (1927; favorable to Smith; thinks his narrative substantially correct, even accepts the Pocahontas story). For other works on colonial Virginia history, see Swem, E. G., *A Bibliography of Virginia* [Virginia State Library *Bulletin*], i, and ii, pp. 1-35; and Boyd, W. K., and Brooks, R. P., *A Selected Bibliography and Syllabus of the History of the South, 1584-1876* (pp. 7-81 on the colonial and Revolutionary periods).

The most accessible collections of sources for the period covered by this chapter are: *The Narratives of Early Virginia* [*Original Narratives of Early American History*] (1907), edited by L. G. Tyler; *The Genesis of the United States*, 2 vols., edited by Alexander Brown

Monographs

Sources

(1891; a voluminous collection of documents on the early history of Virginia); *The Records of the Virginia Company of London*, 4 vols., edited by Susan M. Kingsbury (1906-1935; a valuable collection of documents including the proceedings of the Virginia Company and other papers, mainly on the period 1619-1624); *The Travel and Works of Captain John Smith*, 2 vols. (originally printed in 1629; edited and published by Edward Arber in 1910; contains the *True Relation*, the *General History of Virginia and the Summer Isles, Smith's Travels*, and other documents); *Calendar of Virginia State Papers and Other Manuscripts* in the Capitol at Richmond, 11 vols., edited by W. P. Palmer (vol. i covers the period 1651-1781); *Journals of the House of Burgesses of Virginia*, 13 vols. (1906-1915; contain such portions of the journal of the House of Burgesses from 1619 to 1776 as have been found. They also contain petitions, letters, and statements sent by the House or by the assembly to the authorities in England and communications made to the assembly); *Minutes of the Council and General Court of Colonial Virginia* (1924; one volume covering incompletely the periods 1622-1632 and 1670-1676); and *Legislative Journals of the Council of Colonial Virginia*, 3 vols. (1918-1919). All these important documents (except one volume of the *Journals of the House of Burgesses*, by J. P. Kennedy) have been collected and edited by H. A. McIlwaine. Another series of valuable papers of like character is the *Executive Journals of the Council of Colonial Virginia* (1925-in progress). The first four volumes were collected by McIlwaine, and the series is being continued by W. L. Hall. The fifth volume (1945) carries the record up to 1754.

Other collections that may be mentioned are: Wynne, T. S., and Gilman, W. S., eds., *Colonial Records of Virginia, 1619-80*; and Clemens, W. M., ed., *Virginia Wills Before 1799* (1924). Some well-selected source materials bearing on this chapter are given in West, W. M., *A Source Book in American History* (1913), pp. 4-92; Stedman, E. C., and Hutchinson, E. M., *A Library of American Literature*, 10 vols. (1888-1890), i, pp. 3-43; Hart, A. B., *American History Told by Contemporaries*, i, ch. 10; and the *Old South Leaflets*, no. 167. Another valuable source, though not so accessible as those mentioned above, is W. W. Hening's *Statutes at Large, 1619-1792*, 13 vols. (1823). William Stith's *History of Virginia* to 1624 (first published in 1747; follows the documents closely) is also generally regarded as a source. Other source materials are scattered throughout the *Virginia Magazine of History and Biography*, the *Virginia Historical Register and Literary Advertiser, The William and Mary College Quarterly*, the *Collections* of the Virginia Historical Society, and such collections of documents as Force's *Tracts* and *Purchas's Pilgrims*. An indispensable guide in locating data given in Hening and the Virginia historical magazines is E. G. Swem's *Virginia Historical Index*, 2 vols. (1934-

1936). For an appraisal of the source materials for Virginia history, see Winsor, J., *Narrative and Critical History of America*, iii, pp. 153-168. For other sources see Greene and Morris's *Guide*, pp. 52-56.

CHAPTER V.—THE OLD DOMINION AND MARYLAND

VIRGINIA

MOST of the primary and secondary authorities mentioned in the preceding chapter apply also to the portion of Virginia history covered by this chapter. To this list should be added: T. J. Wertenbaker's *Torch Bearer of the Revolution: The Story of Bacon's Rebellion and Its Leader* (1940; an interesting and scholarly account); *Virginia Colonial Decisions—Reports of Randolph and Barradall of the Decisions of the General Court of Virginia*, 2 vols. (1728-1741); and *Narratives of the Insurrections* (1915), edited by C. M. Andrews. This latter work gives three contemporary accounts of Bacon's Rebellion, one of which is a report made in 1677 by the commissioners sent over by the king. In reading the last-named account it must be remembered that the commissioners were hostile to Berkeley and his party and were inclined to lay a good deal of the blame on them. The colonial laws are also valuable source materials. The best collection of Virginia laws for the colonial era is Hening's *Statutes at Large,* 13 vols. For other collections, see Channing, Hart, and Turner's *Guide*, p. 149; Greene and Morris's *Guide*, pp. 53-54; and Boyd, W. K., and Brooks, R. P., *A Selected Bibliography and Syllabus of the History of the South*, pp. 7-81.

[margin: Secondary and primary authorities]

MARYLAND

The general histories referred to in the Bibliographical Notes for Chapter IV cover the early period of Maryland with sufficient fullness for the average reader. Of these accounts, the most interesting is John Fiske's three chapters in his *Old Virginia and Her Neighbors*. For good brief accounts see W. T. Brantley's article in J. Winsor's *America*, iii, ch. 13, and C. Wissler, C. L. Skinner, and W. Wood's *Adventures in the Wilderness*, ch. 13. A fuller and better account is M. P. Andrews's *The Founding of Maryland* (1933). See also his *History of Maryland: Province and State* (1929), a good portion of which is devoted to the period prior to 1789. Other histories of Maryland are: Browne, W. H., *Maryland, The History of a Palatinate* [*American Commonwealths*] (1884; the whole volume is on the colonial and Revolutionary periods); Scharf, J. T., *History of Maryland*, 3 vols. (1879; numerous lengthy quotations from the sources); and Mereness, N. D., *Maryland as a Proprietary Province*

[margin: Secondary authorities]

(1901; discusses political, economic, and social institutions; scholarly; specific references to primary sources). C. M. Andrews has two good chapters on proprietary Maryland in vol. ii of his *Colonial Period of American History.*

Monographs

There are a number of monographs in the Johns Hopkins University *Studies in Historical and Political Science* (hereafter listed as the Johns Hopkins *Studies*) that deal with certain phases of Maryland history. Most of these are valuable for the special student, as they give numerous specific references to the sources. These monographs are as follows: Wilhelm, L. W., *Maryland Local Institutions,* 3rd series; Petrie, George, *Church and State in Maryland,* 10th series; Latané, J. H., *The Early Relations Between Maryland and Virginia,* 13th series; and Steiner, B. C., *Beginnings of Maryland,* 21st series, *Descriptions of Maryland,* 22nd series, *Maryland During the English Civil Wars,* 24th and 25th series, and *Maryland Under the Commonwealth,* 29th series. Other works on special topics: Wroth, L. C. A., *A History of Printing in Colonial Maryland, 1686-1776* (1922); and Claiborne, J. H., *William Claiborne of Virginia* (1917; discusses at length the controversy between William Claiborne and Lord Baltimore).

Sources

The best single volume of sources on this period of Maryland history is C. C. Hall's *Narratives of Early Maryland* (1910). Each contemporary document is preceded by an explanatory account by the editor, which is very helpful. There is one chapter on Maryland in Hart's *Contemporaries,* and a few pages in West's *Source Book in American History.* A contemporary account of early Virginia and Maryland, though not very accessible, is John Hammond's *Leah and Rachel* (printed in 1656; reprinted in 1844). Portions of this work are reprinted in C. C. Hall's *Narratives of Early Maryland* and A. B. Hart's *American History Told by Contemporaries.* The Maryland Historical Society has published a large number of volumes under the title, *Fund Publication,* which contain some documents on the colonial period. Among these are the *Calvert Papers.* These papers are printed in vols. xxviii and xxxiv-xxxv, and a calendar of them is given in vol. xxviii, pp. 61-126. Other collections: Baldwin, J., comp., *Maryland Calendar of Wills, 1635-1738,* 7 vols.; Browne, W. H., and others, eds., *The Archives of Maryland* (in progress since 1883; 58 volumes by 1941; a voluminous collection of documents, all on the colonial period; published by the state). The last-named collection contains the proceedings and acts of the assembly, proceedings of the Council of Maryland, an account of the judicial and testamentary business of the Provincial Court, and other important documents. Some source material is also scattered throughout the numerous volumes of the *Maryland Historical Magazine.* For law and government, see *Votes and Proceedings of the Lower House of Assembly of the Province of Maryland* (April-May, 1757) ; and Thomas Bacon, *Laws of Maryland at Large, 1637-1763.* Other collections of laws are listed in Channing, Hart, and Turner's *Guide,* p. 137; and in Greene and Morris's *Guide,* p. 17. For an appraisal of the sources by W. T. Brantley, see Winsor's *Narrative and Critical History,* iii, pp. 553-562.

CHAPTER VI.—THE MIGRATION OF PURITANISM FROM
OLD TO NEW ENGLAND

NEW ENGLAND

MOST of the general histories covering the entire colonial era (see above, pp. 762ff.) are useful for a study of this period. Of these we may mention especially Bancroft, Andrews, Channing, Doyle, Eggleston, and Osgood. In addition to these there are a number of excellent works on New England. Prominent in this list are *The History of New England* by J. G. Palfrey, 5 vols. (1858-1890). This history, though old, is still valuable not only for the general reader but also for the serious student. The narrative is interesting, and there are many references to and quotations from the documents. The author, of course, belongs to the orthodox school of historians and is a strong advocate of Puritanism. Later works of great value are J. T. Adams's *The Founding of New England* (1921) and *Revolutionary New England* (1923). These two discussions are brilliant and interesting, but, although well documented, are not entirely free from bias; they are severe in their excoriations of the Puritan clergy. Along with them should be read S. E. Morison's *Builders of the Bay Colony* (1930), especially pp. 339-346.

A fine short account is given in C. M. Andrews's *The Fathers of New England* [*The Chronicles of America Series*] (1921; no specific references to sources, but bibliographical notes at the end). A good short account, profusely illustrated, is C. Wissler, C. L. Skinner, and W. Wood's *Adventures in the Wilderness* [*The Pageant of America*], ch. 10. An excellent work on social and economic history is W. B. Weeden's *Economic and Social History of New England, 1620-1789,* 2 vols. (1891; specific references to sources; interesting). The following general works should be mentioned: Fiske, John, *The Beginnings of New England* (1899; very readable) ; Wright, Thomas G., *Literary Culture in Early New England* (1920) ; Lawrence, Robert M., *New England Colonial Life* (1927) ; Merriam, T. M., *The Pilgrims, Puritans, and Roger Williams* (1892) ; Lauer, P. E., *Church and State in New England* [Johns Hopkins *Studies,* 10th series] ; MacLear, Anne B., *Early New England Towns* (1908) ;

General accounts

Akagi, R. H., *The Town Proprietors of the New England Colonies* (1924) ; and Sly, J. F., *Town Government in Massachusetts, 1620-1930* (1933). For other titles, see "Bibliography of Historical Publications of Massachusetts," in the Colonial Society of Massachusetts *Publications*, iii, pp. 114-117.

Sources   The *Original Narratives of Early American History* devote to New England four entire volumes and portions of three others. A. B. Hart's *American History Told by Contemporaries* devotes eight chapters of vol. i to seventeenth-century New England. Useful and accessible source materials can also be found in W. M. West's *A Source Book in American History, The American History Leaflets,* and *The Old South Leaflets.* A contemporary account especially valuable for its description of the soil, climate, and animal and vegetable life of New England is Thomas Morton's *New English Canaan,* edited by C. F. Adams (printed in 1637; reprinted 1838, 1883). Cotton Mather's *Magnalia,* or the *Ecclesiastical History of New England,* 2 vols., first published in 1702, is also a contemporary work. It covers the period from 1628 to 1698 and gives a good deal of biographical and other information, but is thoroughly uncritical. A contemporary account of much greater value is the *General History of New England,* from the discovery to 1680, by the Rev. William Hubbard.

Charters and land patents are given in full in Poore and Thorpe and in part in MacDonald, West, and other source books. The *Records of the Council for New England* are given in the American Antiquarian Society *Proceedings* (1867), pp. 59-131.

Bibliographies   For further bibliographical material, see the footnotes and Selected Readings for this chapter; Greene and Morris's *Guide,* pp. 18-25 ; and the critical essays and editorial notes on sources by competent scholars in Winsor's *Narrative and Critical History,* iii, pp. 185-218, 244-256, 283-294, 340-384. For reproductions of old maps, see *ibid.,* pp. 303, 306, 333, 382, 383.

NEW PLYMOUTH

Secondary authorities   For the background of the history of New Plymouth, H. M. and M. Dexter's *The England and Holland of the Pilgrims* (1905) is indispensable. This is a scholarly work with numerous specific references to the sources. A short and very readable account of the Pilgrims by one of these authors is M. Dexter's *The Story of the Pilgrims* (1894; presents the traditional sympathetic view). A later work on the English background of the Pilgrims is C. E. Banks's *The English Ancestry and Homes of the Pilgrim Fathers* (1929; gives short biographical sketches of some of the passengers on the *Mayflower* and other early Pilgrim ships). Other works are: Usher, R. G., *The Pilgrims and Their History* (1918; sympathetic, but more inclined to the modern view than Dexter; readable and scholarly, though no references to sources; some space devoted to the life of the people); Powell, Walter A., *The Pilgrims and Their Religious, Intellectual, and Civic Life* (1923; unfriendly; rather interesting; gives the general history and also an account of the life of the people); Crawford, Mary C., *In the Days of the Pilgrim Fathers* (1920; deals with the life of the people); Sawyer, J. D., *History of the Pilgrims and Puritans,* 3 vols. (1922; good print and attractive illustrations; colorful; no footnotes to sources); Willison, G. F., *Saints and Strangers* (1945; a detailed history of New Plymouth to 1691); and Hart, A. B., ed., *Commonwealth History of Massachusetts,* i, ch. 4, by T. E. Busfield.

The most valuable and accessible contemporary account dealing   Sources with the early history of the Pilgrims is Governor William Bradford's *History of the Plymouth Plantation, 1606-1646.* There are a number of editions of this work, but the one especially recommended is that edited by William T. Davis [*Original Narratives of Early American History*] (1908). Next to Bradford's *History* in value and accessibility is Alexander Young's *Chronicles of the Pilgrim Fathers of Plymouth, 1602-1625* (1841, 1844). This collection of contemporary accounts includes a part of Bradford's *History,* the journal written by Bradford and Winslow covering the period from November 9, 1620, to December 11, 1621 (known as *Mourt's Relation*), and other primary sources. Another contemporary account that should be listed is Nathaniel Morton's *New England's Memorial* (1903; borrows freely from Bradford's *History;* the most accessible edition is the one by A. Lord). Good collections of contemporary narratives are: Arber, Edward, ed., *The Story of the Pilgrim Fathers, 1606-1623,* as told by themselves, their friends, and their enemies (1897); Masefield, J., ed., *Chronicles of the Pilgrim Fathers;* Hart, A. B., ed., *American History Told by Contemporaries,* i, chs. 14-15; and West, W. M., ed., *Source Book in American History,* pp. 109-128. The most valuable collection of sources for the serious student is the *New Plymouth Colony Records,* 12 vols. These contain the proceedings of the General Court and Court of Assistants, judicial acts, laws, deeds, and miscellaneous documents. Some interesting source material is contained in *Days of the Spinning Wheel* and *Some Strange and Curious Punishments,* edited by H. M. Brooks [*The Olden Time Series,* 1886].

CHAPTER VII.—THE ESTABLISHMENT OF PURITANISM
IN NEW ENGLAND

THE general accounts of New England and many of the special works   Second- listed under New Plymouth devote considerable space to the history   ary au- of the Massachusetts Bay Colony. In addition to these, the following   thorities titles should be listed: Adams, Brooks, *The Emancipation of Massachusetts* (1887, 1919; severely critical of the Puritan oligarchy); Winsor, J., *Memorial History of Boston,* i (1880-1887; a valuable work; a good deal of space devoted to the life of the people); Murdock, K. B., *Increase Mather* (1925; scholarly, fair, but inclining to a favorable view of the Puritans); Osgood, H. L., "The Political Ideas of the Puritans," in *Political Science Quarterly,* vi, pp. 1-28; and Bolton, C. K., *The Real Founders of New England, 1602-1628* (1899). Later works of value are the *Commonwealth History of Massachusetts,* edited by A. B. Hart, 5 vols. (1927-1930; vols. i-iii on the colonial and Revolutionary eras); and *Builders of the Bay Colony,* by S. E. Morison (1930; a brilliant account of the leading personages in the early history of the Bay Colony). Two biographies of Anne Hutchinson should be listed: Augur, Helen, *An American Jezebel: The Life of Anne Hutchinson* (1930); and Rugg, Winnifred K., *Unafraid: A Life of Anne Hutchinson* (1930). A valuable history of early Massachusetts is *The History of the Colony and Province of Massachusetts Bay* by Thomas Hutchinson. The first two volumes of this work were published by the author (2nd ed., 1765-1768) and they have been reprinted, with the addition of the third in manuscript, under the editorship of Lawrence S. Mayo (1936). Hutchinson's *History* is in a sense a primary source not only because the author was contemporary with and took part in some of the events described, but also because he refers to and quotes from documents that have since been lost.

Sources   The most valuable and accessible contemporary account of early Massachusetts is Winthrop's *Journal,* 2 vols., edited by J. K. Hosmer [*Original Narratives of Early American History*] (1908). Another work in this same series is Johnson's *Wonder-Working Providence, 1628-1651* (1910), edited by J. F. Jameson. A number of important documents are given in R. C. Winthrop's *Life and Letters of John Winthrop,* 2 vols. (1864). The second volume covers Winthrop's career in New England. The *Winthrop Papers,* 4 vols. (published by the Massachusetts Historical Society, 1929-1944), is a voluminous collection of documents, mostly letters to and from members of the Winthrop family. Most of this correspondence deals with events of the seventeenth century, though it covers the period to 1728. Vol. lxii of the *Proceedings* of the Massachusetts Historical Society contains some documents on early Massachusetts History. Alexander Young's *Chronicles of the First Planters of the Colony of Massachusetts Bay* (1846) gives in one volume some important source material covering the period from 1623 to 1636. Other valuable collections of documents are: *The Hutchinson Papers,* 2 vols., compiled by Thomas Hutchinson and reprinted by the Prince Society (1865; covers the period from 1629 to 1789); the *Mather Papers,* published in the Massachusetts Historical Society *Collections,* 4th series, viii (letters to and from Increase Mather and other prominent persons, covering the period from 1651 to 1734). The *Massachusetts Bay Colony Records, 1628-1686,* 6 vols., are indispensable for the student who wishes to make an intensive study of early Massachusetts history. They contain the proceedings of the General Court, and the first volume also gives proceedings of the Court of Assistants. For a list of the colonial laws of Massachusetts, see Channing, Hart, and Turner's *Guide,* p. 138; for a list of town records, *ibid.,* p. 139. See also Greene and Morris's *Guide to the Principal Sources for Early American History,* pp. 19-20, 22-25.

CHAPTER VIII.—EXPANSION OF PURITANISM IN NEW ENGLAND

CONNECTICUT

THE general histories of New England given in Chapter VI are all concerned with Connecticut and New Haven. Of these, probably the most valuable is Andrews's *Colonial Period of American History,* ii, chs. 3-5. To this list should be added a few works devoted entirely to Connecticut. Of these a prominent place should be given to Benjamin Trumbull's *Complete History of Connecticut to 1764,* 2 vols. (1818). Other useful authorities are: Clark, G. L., *A History of Connecticut* (1914); Johnston, Alexander, *Connecticut* [*American Commonwealths*] (1887, 1903); Morgan, Forest, and others, eds., *Connecticut as a Colony and as a State,* 4 vols. (1904; first volume on the colonial period; interesting; no references to sources; gives some space to life of the people); Osborn, Norris G., ed., *The History of Connecticut,* 5 vols. (1925; the first volume, written by ex-Governor Simeon E. Baldwin, covers the colonial period; quotes at length from the documents and devotes a good deal of space to the life of the people); Andrews, C. M., *Connecticut's Place in Colonial History* (1924), and *River Towns of Connecticut* [Johns Hopkins *Studies,* 7th series] (specific references to the sources); Coleman, C. V., *The Old Patent of Connecticut* (1936); and Mead, Nelson P., *Connecticut as a Corporate Colony* (1906). The Tercentenary Commission of the State of Connecticut has published sixty brief essays on Connecticut history (1933-1936). Some of these may be of interest to students of early Connecticut history. — Secondary authorities

The war with the Pequot Indians is discussed in the following works: Bradstreet, Howard, *The Story of the Pequot War Retold* (1933); and Orr, Charles, ed., *History of the Pequot War* (1897; a reprint of a contemporary account). — The Pequot War

NEW HAVEN

For the colony of New Haven see: Calder, Isabel M., *The New Haven Colony* (1934) ; Atwater, E. E., *History of the Colony of New Haven* (1881 ; old but valuable because of the numerous lengthy quotations from the documents) ; Levermore, C. H., *The Republic of New Haven* [Johns Hopkins *Studies,* extra vol. i] ; and Andrews, C. M., *The Rise and Fall of the New Haven Colony* [The Tercentenary Commission Series] (1936).

Sources for Connecticut and New Haven   The most valuable collections of documents relative to the early history of Connecticut and New Haven are, respectively, the *Connecticut Colony Public Records, 1653-1776,* 15 vols., and the *New Haven Colonial Records, 1636-1649, 1653-1665,* 2 vols. These contain proceedings of the General Court and the Court of Assistants, laws, and other documents. A few passages are also scattered throughout Bradford's *History,* Winthrop's *Journal,* and Johnson's *Wonder-Working Providence* that deal with early Connecticut and New Haven history. W. Hubbard's *General History of New England* devotes some space to Connecticut and New Haven. Useful source material on New Haven can be found in Isabel M. Calder's *Letters of John Davenport, Puritan Divine* (1937). For the laws of Connecticut, Maine, New Hampshire, and Rhode Island, see Channing, Hart, and Turner's *Guide,* pp. 133, 137, 141, 145; and Greene and Morris's *Guide,* pp. 10-11, 27, 46-47. See also J. H. Trumbull, *The True Blue-Laws of Connecticut and New Haven and False Blue-Laws Forged by Peters* (1876). Brief contemporary accounts of early events in Connecticut and New Haven are given in A. B. Hart's *American History Told by Contemporaries,* i, pp. 410-422. For other sources on Connecticut, see Greene and Morris's *Guide,* pp. 10-13.

RHODE ISLAND

Secondary works   For good brief discussions of the early history of Rhode Island, see the general histories listed on pp. 762 f., especially Andrews's *Colonial Period,* chs. 1-2. One of the most valuable histories of colonial Rhode Island is I. B. Richman's *Rhode Island: Its Making and Its Meaning,* 2 vols. (1902; a full, scholarly account, with specific references to primary sources). See also *Rhode Island, A Study in Separatism* (1905), by the same author. Other useful works are: Bicknell, F. W., *History of Rhode Island,* 3 vols. (1920; a good deal of space is given to the colonial period; quotes at length from the sources; has chapters on the life of the people) ; Weeden, W. B., *Early Rhode Island* (1910; specific references to sources) ; Field, Edward, *The State of Rhode Island and Providence Plantations* (1902), i; and Merriman, T. M., *The Pilgrims, Puritans, and Roger Williams* (1892). For a list of other works on colonial Rhode Island, see Field, *op. cit.*, iii, pp. 653-681. There are a number of works on Roger Williams that discuss the early history of Rhode Island. Prominent among these are: Straus, O. S., *Roger Williams* (1936); Ernst, James E., *Roger Williams, New England Firebrand* (1932; a full-length biography); Easton, Emily, *Roger Williams, Prophet and Pioneer* (1930; quotes at length from Williams's letters); Brockunier, Samuel H., *The Irrepressible Democrat: Roger Williams* (1940). For other authorities, see Brigham, C. S., *Bibliography of Rhode Island History* (1902), and Chapin, H. M., *Bibliography of Rhode Island Bibliography* (1914).

The sources on the career of Roger Williams are full and many Sources of them are easily accessible. Winthrop's *Journal* gives some valuable information regarding the banishment of Roger Williams and other events in the early history of Rhode Island. The biographers of Williams also quote freely from the documents. Williams's writings have been published by the Narragansett Club in vols. i to vi of its *Publications*. Of these, his letters, in vol. vi, are valuable for the early history of Rhode Island. The most accessible and useful collection of source materials is the *Documentary History of Rhode Island*, edited by H. M. Chapin. There are two volumes of this work. The first, published in 1916, gives the history of all four of the plantations from 1636 to 1647; the second, published in 1919, covers the island plantations to 1647. These volumes contain numerous brief excerpts from the documents arranged topically. Samuel Gorton, in his *Simplicities Defence Against Seven-headed Policy* (1646), gives an account in vigorous English of his controversy with the Massachusetts authorities. Less accessible but very valuable sources are: *Rhode Island Colonial Records, 1636-1776*, 7 vols.; *Early Records of the Town of Providence* (to about 1722), 21 vols.; and *Early Records of the Town of Portsmouth*, 1 vol. Excerpts from a few documents are also given in W. M. West, *Source Book in American History*, pp. 267-272. For short contemporary accounts, see Hart, A. B., *American History Told by Contemporaries*, i, pp. 397-409. For other primary sources on Rhode Island, see Greene and Morris's *Guide*, pp. 46-48.

NEW HAMPSHIRE AND MAINE

For a good short account of the early history of Maine and New Second- Hampshire, see *Encyclopædia Britannica*. One of the most scholarly ary au- of the works on New Hampshire is W. H. Fry's *New Hampshire as* thorities *a Royal Province* (1908). Only one chapter, however, is devoted to the period prior to 1679, the volume being primarily an institutional history of the province after 1679; specific references to sources. Other accounts of colonial New Hampshire can be found in F. B.

Sanborn's *New Hampshire* [*American Commonwealths*] (1904), and John N. McClintock's voluminous *History of New Hampshire* (1889).

The colonial period in Maine is discussed at length in W. D. Williamson's *History of the State of Maine,* 2 vols. (1832, 1839). All of the first volume and more than half of the second are devoted to the colonial era. An exhaustive treatment of the early history of Maine is found in J. P. Baxter's *Sir Ferdinando Gorges and His Province of Maine,* 3 vols. H S. Burrage's *The Beginning of Colonial Maine* (1914) is useful (references to sources). For other works on Maine, see J. Williamson, *Bibliography of the State of Maine,* 2 vols. (1892).

Sources   The most valuable collection of documents for the study of the colonial history of New Hampshire is the *Provincial Papers,* 7 vols., covering the period to 1764. They contain records of the council, journals of the assembly, messages of the governors, and other documents. Abundant source materials on colonial Maine are given in the *Collections* of the Maine Historical Society. The first series (10 vols., including one volume of index) contains some documents on the colonial period, and the second series (*Documentary History*) is especially rich in source materials for colonial Maine. All of vols. i-xiii and xxiii and portions of vols. xiv and xxiv are devoted to the colonial period. A later series published by this society is *Province and Court Records of Maine,* 2 vols. (1928-1931), edited by C. T. Libby. For other sources on Maine and New Hampshire, see Greene and Morris's *Guide,* pp. 15-16, 26-28.

THE NEW ENGLAND CONFEDERATION AND KING PHILIP'S WAR

For lengthy discussions of these topics, see Frothingham, Richard, *Rise of the Republic of the United States,* pp. 33-100 (1872, 1910); Hart, A. B., ed., *Commonwealth History of Massachusetts,* i, ch. 9; Adams, J. T., *The Founding of New England,* ch. 9; and Sylvester, H. M., *Indian Wars of New England,* 3 vols. (1910). For briefer discussions by secondary authorities and for sources, see the Selected Readings and the reference notes for this chapter.

CHAPTER IX.—GOVERNMENT AND LAW

Secondary authorities: General accounts   AN EXCELLENT brief account of local government in England at the time colonization began in America is given in E. P. Cheyney's *A History of England from the Defeat of the Armada to the Death of Elizabeth* (1913), ii, chs. 37-41. For governmental institutions in America, the best authority is Osgood. A good deal of valuable information on both local and provincial government is scattered throughout both his *Seventeenth Century* and his *Eighteenth Century*. The detailed tables of contents make it easy for the reader to find the information he desires on any particular topic. The special student may also wish to consult the following works: Tyler, Alice F., *Freedom's Ferment: Phases of American Social History to 1860* (1944); and Morris, Richard B., *Government and Labor in Early America* (1946), and *Studies in the History of American Law* (1930; special reference to the 17th and 18th centuries).

There are also a number of monographs and other works that deal with certain phases of colonial government. Of these the following are useful: Bishop, C. F., *History of Elections in the American Colonies* (1893; useful for advanced students; specific references to sources); McKinley, A. E., "English and Dutch Towns of New Netherland," an excellent article in the *American Historical Review*, vi, pp. 1-18; *The Suffrage Franchise in the Thirteen English Colonies in America* (1905), by the same author (voluminous; specific references to sources); Porter K. H., *A History of Suffrage in the United States* (1918); Greene, E. B., *The Provincial Governor in the English Colonies of North America* (1898; well documented; scholarly; the appendix contains a valuable list of instructions and commissions of royal governors, with specific references as to where the originals can be found); Labaree, Leonard W., ed., *Royal Instructions to British Colonial Governors, 1670-1776*, 2 vols. (1935); Clarke, Mary P., *Parliamentary Privilege in the American Colonies* (1943; a scholarly work of value); Burns, John F., *Controversies Between Royal Governors and Their Assemblies in the Northern American Colonies* (1923; numerous specific references to primary sources); Lloyd, William H., *The Early Courts of Pennsylvania* (1910); Shepherd, William R., *History of Proprietary Government in Pennsylvania* [Columbia University *Studies*] (1896; specific references to sources; too voluminous except for the special student); Raper, Charles L., *North Carolina, a Royal Province, 1729-1775* (1901), and *Social Life in Colonial North Carolina* (1903); Wallace, David D., *Constitutional History of South Carolina from 1725 to 1775* (1899); Sly, J. F., *Town Government in Massachusetts, 1620-1930* (1933); Griffith, Ernest S., *History of American City Government: Colonial Period* (1938); Borgeaud, Charles, *Rise of Modern Democracy* (1894); Proper, E. E., *Colonial Emigration Laws* (1900); Bruce, P. A., *Institutional History of Virginia in the Seventeenth Century*, i, part i, chs. 6-9, part iii, chs. 1-16; MacLear, Anne B., *Early New England Towns*; and Myers, G., *Ye Olden Blue Laws* (1921).

In the Johns Hopkins *Studies* there are a number of valuable monographs dealing with government in the colonies. Most of these are of a scholarly character, with numerous specific references to the

Special works

Monographs

documents. One of the most useful for our purposes is G. E. Howard's *Local Government in the Colonies: An Introduction to the Local Constitutional History of the United States*; special vols., no. 4. Of those published in the regular series, the following should be mentioned: Adams, H. B., *The German Origin of the New England Town*, Ingle, Edward, *Parish Institutions of Maryland*, Johnson, J. H., *Old Maryland Manors* (1st series) ; Engle, E., *Virginia Local Institutions*, and Wilhelm, L. W., *Maryland Local Institutions* (3rd series) ; Elting, I., *Dutch Village Communities on the Hudson River*, Foster, W. E., *Town Government in Rhode Island*, and Holcomb, W. P., *Pennsylvania Boroughs* (4th series) ; Lauer, P. E., *Church and State in New England*, and Petrie, G., *Church and State in Maryland* (10th series) ; Weeks, S. B., *Church and State in North Carolina* (11th series) ; Bassett, J. S., *Constitutional Beginnings of North Carolina*, and Haynes, G. H., *Representation and Suffrage in Massachusetts* (12th series) ; Moran, T. F., *The Rise of the Bicameral System in America*, and Whitney, E. L., *Government of the Colony of South Carolina* (13th series) ; Chandler, J. A. C., *Representation in Virginia*, and Riley, F. L., *Colonial Origins of New England Senates* (14th series) ; Kaye, P. L., *The Colonial Executive prior to the Restoration* (18th series) ; Chandler, J. A. C., *History of Suffrage in Virginia* (19th series) ; Sioussat, St. G. L., *The English Statutes in Maryland* (21st series) ; and Chitwood, O. P., *Justice in Colonial Virginia* (23rd series).

To this list of monographs should be added the following articles: Carpenter, A. H., "Habeas Corpus in the Colonies" (*American Historical Review*, viii, pp. 18-27) ; Kellogg, L. P., "The American Colonial Charter" (*Annual Report* of the American Historical Association, 1903, i, pp. 187-341) ; Tanner, E. P., "Colonial Agencies in England in the 18th Century" (*Political Science Quarterly*, xvi, pp. 24-49) ; and Franklin, W. N., "Some Aspects of Representation in the American Colonies" (*North Carolina Historical Review*, January, 1929). See also Labaree, L. W., *Royal Government in America: A Study of the British Colonial System Before 1783* (1930), and *Royal Instructions to British Colonial Governors, 1670-1776*, 2 vols. (1935; a valuable collection of documents) ; Karraker, C. H., *The Seventeenth Century Sheriff* (1930; in England and in the Chesapeake colonies) ; and Miller, Elmer I., *The Legislature of the Province of Virginia* (1907; specific references to the sources).

Laws   An excellent treatise on the English common law in the colonies is P. S. Reinsch's *English Common Law in the Early American Colonies* [University of Wisconsin *Bulletin*, no. 31] (1899). For a list and appraisal of other works on law and legal institutions, see Adams, J. T., *Provincial Society*, pp. 336-337.

The proceedings of the assemblies and the minutes of the councils of the various colonies afford a rich mine of information for the study of colonial government. For lists of these documents, see the Bibliographical Notes on the various colonies listed above. There are also a number of collections of colonial laws. For these, see Channing, Hart, and Turner's *Guide,* pp. 131-149. Among the easily accessible sources, the following deserve mention: Brooks, Henry M., *Some Strange and Curious Punishments [Olden Times Series]* (excerpts from newspapers and laws, mostly on New England; interesting); Dillon, John B., *Oddities of Colonial Legislation in America* (1879), pp. 21-269; Stokes, Anthony, *A View of the Constitution of the British Colonies in North America and the West Indies at the Outbreak of the Revolution* (1783; the author lived in the colonies before the Revolution and fought on the British side in the war; numerous lengthy excerpts from the laws and other documents); Earle, Alice M., *Curious Punishments of Bygone Days* (1896); Hart, A. B., *American History Told by Contemporaries,* i, chs. 7-11; West, W. M., *A Source Book in American History,* pp. 178-245, 267-278, 290-364; and Wright, Benjamin F., *A Source Book of American Political Theory* (1929). For printed collections of the laws of the various colonies, see Greene and Morris's *Guide,* pp. 10-55. Manuscript sources for laws, courts, and lawyers are listed in *ibid.,* pp. 207-223.

Miscellaneous documents

CHAPTER X.—NEW NETHERLAND AND NEW SWEDEN

NEW NETHERLAND AND NEW YORK

READABLE accounts of the period covered by this chapter are Maud W. Goodwin's *Dutch and English on the Hudson [The Chronicles of America]* (1919); and John Fiske's *Dutch and Quaker Colonies in America,* 2 vols. (1899), chs. 1-11. Good brief discussions can be found in H. I. Priestley's *The Coming of the White Man* (1929), chs. 11-12; E. Channing's *History,* i, chs. 16-17, and ii, ch. 2; J. Winsor's *Narrative and Critical History,* iv, ch. 8; C. Wissler, C. L. Skinner, and W. Wood's *Adventures in the Wilderness,* ch. 11 (pictorial); and an article by A. E. McKinley, "The English and Dutch Towns of New Netherland," in the *American Historical Review,* vi, pp. 1-18. An excellent discussion embodying the latest results of scholarly research is given by C. M. Andrews in his *Colonial Period of American History,* iii, ch. 3. For governmental institutions H. L. Osgood's *Seventeenth Century,* ii, chs. 5-7, is the best authority. Of the special works that deal exclusively with New York history, the following deserve mention: Roberts, Ellis, *New York [American Commonwealths],* 2 vols. (1887, 1904; the first volume is on the colonial period); Griffis, W. E., *The*

Secondary authorities

Story of New Netherland (1909; readable; gives general history, with a few chapters on social life); O'Callaghan, E. B., *History of New Netherland*, 2 vols. (1846-1848, 1855; detailed; some lengthy quotations from the sources; a valuable work); Brodhead, J. R., *History of the State of New York*, 2 vols. to 1690 (1853-1871; specific references to sources; valuable); Janvier, T. D., *Dutch Founding of New York*; Flick, Alexander C., ed., *History of the State of New York*, 10 vols. (1933-1937; a coöperative work; first four volumes concerned with the period prior to 1789; illustrations); Fox, D. R., *Yankees and Yorkers* (1940); and Thompson, B. F., *History of Long Island*, 4 vols. (published first in 1839; later edited by R. H. Dodd and published in 1918; some documents on the colonial period are scattered throughout the four volumes). An old work of value is William Smith's *History of the Province of New York*, 2 vols. The author was a prominent lawyer who lived in New York City in the decades immediately preceding the Revolution. A useful work on New York history is James Sullivan's *History of New York State, 1523-1927*, 5 vols. (first two volumes and about one-half of the third are on the colonial and Revolutionary periods).

Histories of New York City   There are also a number of histories of the city of New York which give a good deal of useful information. These are: Innes, J. H., *New Amsterdam and Its People* (1902; devotes considerable space to the life of the people); Van Rensselaer, Mrs. Schuyler, *History of the City of New York in the Seventeenth Century*, 2 vols. (1909; covers period to 1691; no specific reference to sources, but has lengthy bibliographies); Lamb, Martha J., *History of the City of New York*, 3 vols. (1877-1896; first volume on the colonial period); Roosevelt, Theodore, *New York [Historic Towns Series]* (1891, 1895); Wilson, James, *Memorial History of the City of New York*, 4 vols. (1892-1893; first two volumes on colonial and Revolutionary periods; some space given to social life); Leonard, John W., *History of the City of New York, 1600-1909* (1910); and Wilson, R. R., *New York: Old and New*, 2 vols. (1902; chs. 1-9 of vol. i on colonial period; some space given to social life).

There are also two biographies that deserve a place in this list: Tuckerman, Bayard, *Peter Stuyvesant* (1893, 1904), and Bacon, E. M., *Henry Hudson; His Times and His Voyages* (1907; lengthy quotations from the sources; chs. 6-8 especially valuable because they describe the voyage on which he discovered the Hudson). For other references, see Flagg, C. A., and Jennings, J. T., *Bibliography of New York Colonial History* (1901); Channing, Hart, and Turner's *Guide*, pp. 76-79. Other bibliographies are listed in Greene and Morris's *Guide*, pp. 30-31.

Sources   The source materials for early New York that are most accessible are: Hart, A. B., *American History Told by Contemporaries*, i, chs.

22 and 23; *Narratives of New Netherland* (1909), edited by J. F. Jameson; and *The Journal of Jasper Danckaerts* (1913), edited by B. B. James and J. F. Jameson. The last two belong to the series, *Original Narratives of Early American History.* The most valuable collection of documents is *Documents Relative to the Colonial History of the State of New York,* usually cited as *New York Colonial Documents.* The materials for the first ten volumes of this series, covering the period 1603-1774, were procured by J. R. Brodhead in England, France, and Holland, and edited by E. B. O'Callaghan. Vol. xi is an index of the preceding volumes; vol. xii deals with the Dutch and Swedish settlements on the Delaware River (1624-1682), and vol. xiv with those on Long Island (1630-1683). The last-named volumes are made up of papers copied from the original records in the royal archives of Sweden and the office of the Secretary of State at Albany. They were compiled and translated by B. Fernow.

Other important collections of documents are: O'Callaghan, E. B., *Documentary History of New York,* 4 vols. (the first three volumes and a part of the fourth devoted almost entirely to the colonial period) ; *Ecclesiastical Records of the State of New York,* 7 vols. (the first five volumes and part of the sixth on the colonial period) ; the *Van Rensselaer Bowier Manuscript,* translated and edited by A. J. F. van Laer (this voluminous collection contains the letters of Killiaen van Rensselaer, 1630-1643, and other documents relating to the colony of Rensselaerswyck, the only successful patroonship in the province. These papers not only portray the life of the people on this patroonship, but also give a good deal of information regarding the colony of New Netherland as a whole) ; *Laws and Ordinances of New Netherland* (1638-1674), compiled and translated by E. B. O'Callaghan; *Minutes of the Executive Council of the Province of New York* during the administration of Governor Francis Lovelace (1668-1673), 2 vols., compiled and edited by V. H. Palsits (in addition to the minutes of the council, certain collateral documents referred to in the minutes are given) ; *A Calendar of Council Minutes,* covering the entire period from 1668 to 1776, prepared by B. Fernow, and published as a bulletin (no. 58) of the New York State Library; *Calendar of Historical Manuscripts in the office of the Secretary of State,* 2 vols., by E. B. O'Callaghan (the first volume covers the Dutch period, 1630-1664; the second, the English period, 1664-1776) ; the New-York Historical Society *Collections* (some documents on the colonial period) ; and *The Records of New Amsterdam,* 7 vols., edited by Berthold Fernow (contain the minutes of the Court of Burgomasters and Schepens from 1653 to 1674; the first volume also contains ordinances of the Director General and Council of New Netherland). These have also been published in *Laws and Ordinances of New Netherland; Affairs and Men of New Amsterdam in the Time of Governor Peter Stuyve-*

sant, compiled and translated by J. Paulding; and *Documents Relating to the Early History of Long Island,* edited by B. Fernow (a variety of valuable papers chronologically arranged, covering the period to October, 1683).

For a lengthy discussion of the sources, see Winsor's *Narrative and Critical History,* iv. pp. 409-442. See also Larned, J. N., *Literature of American History.* For lists of public documents and other sources, see Greene and Morris's *Guide,* pp. 31-39.

DELAWARE

Secondary authorities

The early history of Delaware is given in brief but readable form by Fiske, Goodwin, and Channing, in the works mentioned above. S. G. Fisher, in *The Quaker Colonies* [*Chronicles of America*] (1921), devotes two chapters (12 and 13) to colonial Delaware. An older work that is useful though inaccurate is J. T. Scharf's *History of Delaware,* 2 vols. (1888). Another old work that should be mentioned is J. C. Clay's *Annals of the Swedes on the Delaware* (1835; mostly about churches; gives extracts from the primary sources). A good short account of early Delaware is given by H. M. Jenkins, *Pennsylvania, Colonial and Federal* (1903), i, chs. 3 and 4. But the definitive work on early Delaware, the one that supersedes all others for the special student, is Amandus Johnson's *The Swedish Settlements on the Delaware, 1638-1664,* 2 vols. (1911; voluminous; numerous references in the footnotes to sources; many illustrations; a good deal of space given to social and economic life; some documents in the appendix; lengthy bibliography; in short, the last word on the subject). Other titles that may be listed are: Ward, Christopher, *New Sweden on the Delaware* (1938), and Garber, John P., *The Valley of the Delaware and Its Place in American History* (1934).

Sources

In the *Narratives of New Netherland* there are short discussions of certain events in the history of the Dutch and Swedish occupation of the Delaware region, but more satisfactory contemporary accounts of early Delaware are given in the *Narratives of Early Pennsylvania, West New Jersey, and Delaware* (1912), edited by A. C. Myers. Good collections of documents are: *Documents Relating to the History of the Dutch and Swedish Settlements on the Delaware River* [*New York Colonial Documents,* xii], compiled and translated by B. Fernow; and *Papers Relating to the Colonies on the Delaware* [*Pennsylvania Archives,* 2nd series, v]. A valuable contemporary description is the *Geographia Americæ,* written in 1691 by Peter Lindeström. In it are discussed the mode of living of the Indians, the animal life, the climate, and the agriculture of New Sweden. It also gives the location of the settlements and has two maps of New Sweden, a large one (opposite p. 156) and a small one (opposite p. 152).

Another account of New Sweden that is valuable, though not contemporary, is Israel Acrelius's *Description of the Former and Present Condition of the Swedish Churches in What Was Called New Sweden.* This was written a little after the middle of the eighteenth century (1758). The author was a prominent minister in the region formerly known as New Sweden and had a good opportunity to gather the data on which his account is based. He discusses the ecclesiastical affairs of the Swedish congregations and gives the civil and political history of the country. Acrelius's work was translated and published (1874) by the Rev. W. M. Reynolds in *Memoirs* of the Historical Society of Pennsylvania, vol. ii. A portion of his treatise is given in *Narratives of Early Pennsylvania*, pp. 57-81. Another description of New Sweden, similar in character to but not so valuable as Acrelius's work, is *A Short History of New Sweden* by T. G. Holm (1702), translated by P. S. Du Ponceau (uncritical; gives excerpts from some valuable sources. Ponceau's translation is in *Memoirs* of the Historical Society of Pennsylvania, vol. iii). For other primary sources on Delaware, see Greene and Morris's *Guide*, pp. 13-14.

NEW JERSEY

Short readable accounts: Channing, *op. cit.* (ii, pp. 44-48, 55-59), and Fisher, S. G., *The Quaker Colonies* (chs. 8-11). For political institutions, see Osgood, H. L., *Seventeenth Century,* ii. ch. 8. Special works: *The Swedes and Finns in New Jersey* [Federal Writers' Project] (1938; illustrations); Lee, F. B., and others, eds., *New Jersey as a Colony and as a State,* 4 vols. (1902; the first volume on the colonial period; considerable space given to the economic and social life of the people; attractively printed); Whitehead, W. A., *East Jersey Under the Proprietary Governments* (1846, 1875; "narrative of events connected with the settlement and progress of the province, until the surrender of the government to the crown in 1702"; the latter part of the work, pp. 241-333, contains documents that were first printed in 1685); Tanner, Edwin P., *The Province of New Jersey, 1664-1738* [Columbia University *Studies in History, Economics and Public Law*] (1908; specific references to sources; voluminous; a good deal of space to government); Fisher, E. J., *New Jersey as a Royal Province, 1738-1776* [Columbia University *Studies*] (1911; mostly on government, but one chapter on religious and social conditions; some little attention to general history; specific references to sources); and Smith, Samuel, *The History of the Colony of Nova Cæsaria, or New Jersey,* to the year 1721, published in 1765 (the narrative part of the work is inaccurate, but the volume is valuable because there are a number of documents in the appendix, and lengthy excerpts from the sources are scattered throughout the narrative). Two useful monographs published in the Johns Hopkins *Studies* are: Scott, Austin,

Secondary
authorities

Influence of the Proprietors in the Founding of New Jersey (1885), and Cooley, H. S., *Study of Slavery in New Jersey* (1896).

Sources The sources for the history of New Jersey that are easily accessible are not so numerous as they are for most of the other colonies. The charters are given in full by Poore and Thorpe and in abbreviated form by W. MacDonald, and there are some source materials in Hart's *American History Told by Contemporaries*, i, ch. 25, and in the *Narratives of Early Pennsylvania*, pp. 182-185, 191-195, 338-352. The most valuable collection of documents is the *New Jersey Archives*, 1st series (1631-1800), 27 vols.; 2nd series (1776-1779), 3 vols. There are also a few documents on the colonial history of New Jersey in the *Collections* of the New Jersey Historical Society. Vol. v of the *Collections* is given over entirely to an *Analytical Index to the Colonial Documents of New Jersey* in the State Paper Offices of England. Each item states what the corresponding document is and where it is, but the abstracts are usually too brief to be of any value except as indicating where the documents referred to can be found. Other collections of documents that should be mentioned are: Leaming, A., and Spicer, J., *Grants and Concessions and Original Constitutions of New Jersey; Journal and Votes of the House of Representatives of New Jersey;* and *Votes and Proceedings of the General Assembly, 1750-1751* (1770). For other documents, see Greene and Morris's *Guide*, pp. 28-30.

CHAPTER XI.—THE FOUNDING OF THE CAROLINAS

NORTH CAROLINA

General accounts THE general histories on the colonial period discuss the Carolinas with sufficient fullness for the average reader. Of these, Channing, Osgood, Andrews, Winsor, and Doyle deserve special mention. A brief account of the early Carolinas is given in Wissler, C., Skinner, C. L., and Woods, W., *Adventures in the Wilderness,* ch. 14. For an appraisal of both primary and secondary authorities (published before 1899), see Larned, J. N., *Literature of American History*, pp. 100-106.

Secondary accounts One of the best general histories of North Carolina is a coöperative work, entitled the *History of North Carolina,* 3 vols. R. D. W. Connor is the author of the first volume (1923), which covers the colonial and Revolutionary periods. One chapter is devoted to society, religion, and education. Another modern work is S. A. Ashe's *History of North Carolina,* i (1908), ii (1925). The first volume gives some useful information on the period covered by this chapter. Another good general history is Archibald Henderson's *North Carolina: The Old North State and the New,* 2 vols. (1941). Several older histories are useful. Prominent among these are: Hawks, Francis L., *History of*

North Carolina, 2 vols. (1857, 1858; the second volume covers the proprietary period; besides giving the general history of the colony, it discusses agriculture, manners and customs, government, etc. Every chapter but one is preceded by a collection of documents; a very valuable work) ; Williamson, Hugh, *The History of North Carolina*, 2 vols. (1812; both volumes on the colonial period; some documents at the end of each volume) ; and Moore, J. W., *History of North Carolina*, 2 vols. (1880; about one-third of the first volume is devoted to the colonial period).

For the religious history of the province, the best discussion is Stephen B. Weeks's *The Religious Development in the Province of North Carolina* [Johns Hopkins *Studies*, 10th series] (numerous references to primary sources) ; and his *Church and State in North Carolina* (11th series). For political development, see Raper, C. L., *North Carolina, a Study in English Colonial Government* (1904) ; and Bassett, J. S., *Constitutional Beginnings of North Carolina* [Johns Hopkins *Studies*, 12th series]. Brief discussions: Andrews, C. M., *Colonial Self-Government*, chs. 8-10; and Hamilton, P. J., *The Colonization of the South* (1904), ch. 7. The *North Carolina Booklet*, a monthly publication, contains a number of articles by competent scholars bearing on the political, economic, and social life of the people. There are also a few good articles on certain phases of the political institutions of colonial North Carolina in the *James Sprunt Historical Publications*. These are given in the first number each of vols. xi, xii, and xiii.

For other works on North Carolina, see Channing, Hart, and Turner's *Guide*, p. 79; Weeks, Stephen B., *Bibliography of the Historical Literature of North Carolina* [Harvard University Library, *Bibliographical Contributions*, no. 48] (1895) ; Larned, J. N., *Literature of American History*, p. 12; Boyd, W. K., and Brooks, R. P., *A Selected Bibliography and Syllabus of the History of the South, 1584-1876* (1918) ; and Boyd, W. K., and Hamilton, J. G., *A Syllabus of North Carolina History, 1584-1876* (1913), pp. 1-63 (the last two are invaluable aids for the intensive study of southern history). **Bibliographies**

The finest collection of sources is the *Colonial Records of North Carolina, 1662-1776*, 10 vols. They contain extracts from the journal of the council, acting in both its administrative and its legislative capacity; letters to and from public officials and other prominent men; and numerous miscellaneous documents. The series is continued as the *State Records, 1776-1790*, 16 vols. Other collections of documents are: Grimes, J. B., comp., *Abstract of North Carolina Wills, 1663-1760; Public Acts of the General Assembly of North Carolina, 1715-1803; North Carolina Historical and Genealogical Register*, iii (nearly all of this volume is devoted to sources on the colonial period; contains abstracts of wills, records of Albemarle County, and other contem- **Sources**

porary papers); and *Index to Documents Relating to North Carolina*
during the colonial period now on file in the offices of the Board of
Trade and State Paper Offices in London.

Contem-
porary ac-
counts

Contemporary accounts: Gent, T. A., *Carolina, or a Description of
the Present State of That Country* (printed 1682; a glowing account
of the natural advantages of the country); *A Brief Description of the
Province of Carolina* (first printed in 1666); and Graffenried, Christoph von, *Account of the Founding of New Bern* [*Publications* of the
North Carolina Historical Commission] (1920; German and French
editions given, with a translation of each into English; edited by Vin-
cent H. Todd, and others). Two histories written in the early part of
the eighteenth century should also be ranked as contemporary
accounts: Lawson, John, *The History of Carolina*, published in 1714
(it gives "an exact description and natural history of that country
with the present state thereof," as well as an account of the manners
and customs of the Indians); and Brickell, John, *The Natural History
of North Carolina*, published in 1737 ("an account of the trade, manners, and customs of the Christian and Indian inhabitants." This work
is based on Lawson's *History*, but is fuller than the latter. The editor,
J. B. Grimes, says that Brickell's *History* "is the best description we
have of the natural, social, and economic conditions in the colony of
North Carolina." The frontispiece is a contemporary map of North
Carolina). Some source material on colonial North Carolina is given in
A. S. Salley's *Narratives of Early Carolina* [*Original Narratives
Series*] (1911). For a list of other primary sources, see Greene and
Morris's *Guide*, pp. 39-40. There is a fine discussion of primary
sources, with reproductions of old maps, in Winsor's *Narrative and
Critical History*, v, pp. 335-356.

SOUTH CAROLINA

The early history of the two Carolinas is so closely related that
many of the authorities, both primary and secondary, that are concerned with either one of these colonies are useful for a study of the
other. Hence many of the titles listed above under North Carolina
should be included in the bibliography of South Carolina.

Secondary
authori-
ties:
Histories

One of the best of the general histories of South Carolina is David
D. Wallace's *The History of South Carolina,* 4 vols. (1934-1935; the
fourth volume entirely biographical). Among the other works that
relate primarily or exclusively to South Carolina, the most valuable
for this period are McCrady, Edward, *The History of South Carolina
Under the Proprietary Government, 1670-1719* (1897; numerous
specific references to the sources); Snowden, Yates, and Cutler, H. G.,
eds., *History of South Carolina,* 2 vols. (1920; readable; most of
the first volume on the colonial and Revolutionary periods); and
Childs, St. Julien R., *Malaria and Colonization in the Carolina Low*

Country, 1526-1696 (1940). Of the older histories, the following should be mentioned: Rivers, William J., *A Sketch of the History of South Carolina* (1856; covers period to 1719; references to sources in footnotes; a long appendix of 157 pages is made up entirely of documents) ; Ramsay, David, *History of South Carolina,* 2 vols. bound in one, written in 1808, published in 1858 (covers period to 1808; first volume devoted to general history; second to economic, constitutional, and social history) ; and Hewatt, A., *An Historical Account of the Rise and Progress of the Colonies of South Carolina and Georgia,* 2 vols. (1779; mostly on South Carolina; mainly general history; no footnotes and few quotations from sources).

Of the monographs that discuss certain phases of South Carolina history, the following deserve special mention: Schaper, W. A., *Sectionalism and Representation in South Carolina* (1901; part ii deals with the colonial period; it gives a short account of the general history and discusses economic life and political institutions; scholarly and readable) ; Ravenel, Mrs. St. Julien, *Charleston, the Place and People* (1931; first eleven chapters on the colonial period; some quotations from sources; pictures of churches; something about the life of the people) ; Whitney, E. L., *The Government of the Colony of South Carolina* [Johns Hopkins *Studies,* 13th series] ; Crane, V. W., *The Southern Frontier, 1670-1732* (1928) ; and Hirsch, A. H., *The Huguenots of Colonial South Carolina* (1928). For other works, see Whitney, E. L., "Bibliography of the Colonial History of South Carolina," in the *Annual Report* of the American Historical Association for 1894, pp. 563-586.

Monographs

The best single volume of documents on the Carolinas (mostly on South Carolina) that is easily accessible is A. S. Salley's *Narratives of Early Carolina.* To appraise these contemporary accounts correctly it is necessary to read the editor's prefatory explanations and the footnotes, for some of the statements made by these old writers were biased by partisan feeling, and others were based on inaccurate information. These errors are pointed out and corrected in the prefaces and footnotes. Another valuable group of source materials is the *Collections* of the Historical Society of South Carolina, especially vols. i, ii, and v. Vols. i and ii consist, in the main, of lists and abstracts of papers in the State Paper Offices, London. Although the abstracts are generally brief, in many cases they are full enough to be of value. Pp. 75-107 of vol. ii are devoted to documents bearing on the French Protestants of the Abbeville district. Vol. v is given over almost entirely to the *Shaftesbury Papers.* These consist of the council journals, instructions to governors, letters to and from governors and other officials, and other documents; a very valuable collection.

Sources

Two other collections of sources of importance, both edited by A. S. Salley, are *Commissions and Instructions from the Lords Pro-*

prietors of Carolina to Public Officials of South Carolina, 1685-1715, and *Journal of the Grand Council of South Carolina* (there are two small volumes on the period prior to 1776, one covering the years from August 25, 1671, to June 24, 1680, and the other extending over the months from April 11, 1692, to September 26, 1692). There should also be added to this list: *Journal of the Commons House of Assembly of South Carolina for the Sessions 1692, 1693, 1696, 1697, 1698,* 2 vols.; *Statutes at Large of South Carolina, 1682-1875,* 15 vols.; and B. R. Carroll's *Historical Collections of South Carolina,* 2 vols. (the first volume is a history of South Carolina; the second is made up of contemporary accounts and documents).

For a contemporary account of the events that immediately preceded and caused the downfall of proprietary rule in South Carolina, see F. Yonge's *Proceedings of the People in South Carolina in 1719* (1837). Other valuable contemporary accounts are contained in two pamphlets, each of which gives an interesting description of the climate, soil, natural resources, and the life of the people of South Carolina. The first is entitled *The Present State of Carolina with Advice to the Settlers,* by R. F., and printed in London in 1680. The second is *A Letter from South Carolina,* written by a Swiss gentleman and printed in 1710. A few documents bearing on the colonial period are also scattered throughout the numerous volumes of the *South Carolina Historical and Genealogical Magazine* and the *Transactions* of the Huguenot Society of South Carolina. Other sources are listed in Greene and Morris's *Guide,* pp. 48-50. For a discussion of the source materials for this colony, see W. R. Smith's "Literature for the Study of the Colonial History of South Carolina," in *South Atlantic Quarterly,* i, no. 2.

Chapter XII.—Pennsylvania

Secondary authorities: General accounts

The period covered by this chapter is discussed in a brief and scholarly way in E. Channing's *History of the United States,* ii, chs. 4 and 11; and by C. M. Andrews in *Colonial Self-Government,* chs. 11-12, and in *The Colonial Period of American History,* iii, ch. 7. Very readable accounts are: Fisher, S. G., *The Quaker Colonies* [*Chronicles of America*], chs. 1-7, 12-13 (1921; the last two chapters are on Delaware); Fiske, John, *The Dutch and Quaker Colonies,* chs. 12, 16, and 17; and Wissler, C., Skinner, C. L., and Wood, W., *Adventures in the Wilderness,* ch. 14 (pictorial). The following histories of Pennsylvania deserve mention: Dunaway, Wayland F., *A History of Pennsylvania* (1935; a good deal of space to economic and social development); Bolles, A. S., *Pennsylvania, Province and State, 1609-1790* (1899; mostly narrative; no references to sources); Proud, Robert, *The*

History of Pennsylvania, 2 vols. (1797; valuable because of the lengthy excerpts from the sources) ; Donehoo, George P., ed., *Pennsylvania, a History*, 4 vols. (1926; first volume on colonial period; specific references in the text to the primary sources; the most valuable work on the general history of colonial Pennsylvania) ; Hazard, Samuel, *Annals of Pennsylvania, 1690-1682* (1850; quotes freely from documents; virtually a source book) ; and Jenkins, H. M., *Pennsylvania, Colonial and Federal* (1903; first volume on colonial period). Information of interest to the special student can be found in S. G. Fisher's *The Making of Pennsylvania* (1896), and *Pennsylvania; Colony and Commonwealth* (1897).

The best volume on the history of the Quakers during the colonial period is R. M. Jones's *The Quakers in the American Colonies* (1911). A later work by the same author, *The Faith and Practices of the Quakers* (1927), is useful for a study of the religious beliefs and practices of the Friends. There are a number of lives of William Penn. Those that deserve mention are: Janney, S. M., *The Life of William Penn* (1852; sympathetic; lengthy quotations from Penn's correspondence and autobiography) ; Buck, W. J., *William Penn in America* (1888; valuable for the numerous quotations from letters to and from Penn, and other documents) ; Fisher, S. G., *The True William Penn* (1900; readable) ; Hodges, George, *William Penn* (1901; a very readable short account, sympathetic; deserves first place in a list of biographies of Penn for the general reader) ; Comfort, W. W., and others, eds., *Remember William Penn, 1644-1944* (1944; in general, Penn speaks for himself) ; Dobree, Bonamy, *William Penn, Quaker and Pioneer* (1932; for the general reader) ; and Pound, Arthur, *Penns of Pennsylvania* (1932; illustrations).
The Quakers and William Penn

There are several works on Philadelphia that give information of value for the special student of Pennsylvania colonial history. Of these the following should be listed: Watson, J. F., *Annals of Philadelphia*, 2 vols. (1830, 1908; full on the life of the people; some quotations from the sources; a useful mine of information) ; Faris, J. T., *The Romance of Old Philadelphia* (1918; numerous quotations from the sources bearing on the manners and customs of the people) ; Repplier, Agnes, *Philadelphia, the Place and the People* (1898; first ten chapters on the colonial period; colorful and readable; gives a good deal of space to the life of the people) ; Lippincott, H. M., *Early Philadelphia; Its People, Life and Progress* (1917; some quotations from sources; a good account of the life of the people).
Philadelphia

Monographs dealing with certain phases of Pennsylvania history are: Diffenderffer, F. R., *The German Immigration into Pennsylvania, 1700-1775* (1900) ; Sharpless, Isaac, *A History of Quaker Government in Pennsylvania*, 2 vols. (1902; first volume on colonial period; gives a number of lengthy quotations from the sources), and
Mono graphs

Political Leaders of Provincial Pennsylvania (1919); Shepherd, W. R., *History of Proprietary Government in Pennsylvania* [Columbia University *Studies*] (1896; scholarly, with numerous specific references to sources, but too detailed to be of interest to any readers except special students); Root, W. T., *The Relations of Pennsylvania with the British Government, 1696-1765* (1912; scholarly; specific references to sources; detailed). In the Johns Hopkins University *Studies in Historical and Political Science* there are several useful monographs that should be included in this list: Holcomb, W. P., *Pennsylvania Boroughs* (4th series); Allinson, E. P., and Penrose, B., *City Government of Philadelphia* (5th series); and Applegarth, A. C., *The Quakers in Pennsylvania* (10th series). With these studies should be listed E. R. Turner's *The Negro in Pennsylvania* (1910). For other works on Pennsylvania, see Channing, Hart, and Turner's *Guide*, pp. 82-83, and Winsor's *Narrative and Critical History of America*, iii, pp. 495-516. For the general history of Delaware, see Bibliographical Notes for Chapter X.

Sources   The best single volume of contemporary accounts relating to this period is A. C. Myers, ed., *Narratives of Early Pennsylvania, West New Jersey, and Delaware, 1630-1707* [*Original Narratives of Early American History*] (1912). A. B. Hart's *American History Told by Contemporaries,* i, ch. 24, also gives some source material on Pennsylvania and Delaware. The largest and most complete collection of sources on the history of Pennsylvania is the *Pennsylvania Archives.* These run through several series, each with a considerable number of volumes. Of these the following are concerned with the colonial period: 1st series, vols. i-iv (miscellaneous documents); 2nd series, vol. v (a collection of papers relating to the settlements on the Delaware, 1614-1682); vol. vii (contains papers relating to provincial affairs in Pennsylvania and Maryland, 1734-1760, pp. 305-400, and the Dutch and Swedish settlements on the Delaware, 1630-1682, pp. 459-820); vol. xvi (the whole volume given over to documents on the boundary dispute, and a statement of the case in favor of the Penns; at the beginning of the volume there is an excellent map of the disputed territory made in 1740); 3rd series, vols. viii-x (contain land patents, commissions to sheriffs, justices of the peace, etc.); 4th series, vols. i-iii (a collection of papers of the governors from 1681 to 1785, including the Charter, Frames of Government, and the Great Law).

Other collections of source materials are: the Pennsylvania Historical Society *Memoirs* (some of the volumes contain documents on the colonial period; vol. v has the journal of Braddock's expedition; vol. xi, the *History of New Sweden* by Israel Acrelius; vols. ix and x, the Penn-Logan Correspondence); *Statutes at Large of Pennsylvania from 1682 to 1801,* 12 vols.; the *Pennsylvania Magazine of History* (some documents of interest to the student of colonial history are scattered throughout its volumes); *Pennsylvania Colonial Records, 1683-1790*, 16 vols. (give the records of the Provincial Council from 1683 to 1776); *Votes and Proceedings of the House of Representatives of the Province of Pennsylvania, 1682-1776*, 6 vols.; Hazard, S., *Register of Pennsylvania*, 16 vols. (there are a few documents on the colonial era scattered throughout this voluminous work, but they are hard to find unless a citation is given to them); *Laws of the State of Delaware, 1700-1797*, 2 vols.; and *Records of the Court of New Castle on Delaware, 1676-1681*. For a list of other primary sources on Pennsylvania, see Greene and Morris's *Guide*, pp. 42-46.

For the writings of William Penn, see the Penn-Logan Correspondence referred to above and the *Select Works of William Penn* (of the several editions that have been published, the 4th [1825] is especially recommended). Maria Webb's *The Penns and Penningtons of the Seventeenth Century* gives a number of letters to and from Penn, and other contemporary documents (1867). The journal of George Fox is useful for a study of the Quakers. There are a number of editions of this work; the briefest is Norman Penny's *The Journal of George Fox* (1925; a small volume giving extracts from the original manuscript). Penn's writings

CHAPTER XIII.—THE "GLORIOUS REVOLUTION" IN ENGLAND AND AMERICA

NEW ENGLAND

FOR a brief account of the Revolution of 1688 in England, see W. E. Lunt's *History of England*, pp. 500-509. Good short accounts of Stuart rule in New England and the revolt against it are given in Osgood, H. L., *American Colonies in the Seventeenth Century*, iii, chs. 6, 10, 13, 14; Channing, E., *History of the United States*, ii, pp. 155-202; Andrews, C. M., *Colonial Self-Government*, chs. 3, 4, 16, and pp. 273-279; Winsor, J., *Memorial History of Boston*, i, ch. 10, and ii, ch. 1; and Adams, J. T., *The Founding of New England*, chs. 13-16. The best single volume on the Revolution in New England and the events that preceded and led to it is Viola Barnes's *The Dominion of New England* (1923). This work is both scholarly and readable, with numerous references to the sources in the footnotes and an excellent appraisal of source materials in the bibliography at the end of the volume. The first three chapters of Everett Kimball's *The Public Life of Joseph Dudley* (1911) discuss the Revolution in New England. This is also a scholarly account, with numerous specific references to the primary sources and a lengthy bibliography. Secondary authorities

The best available collection of sources bearing on Andros's administration and the Revolution can be found in C. M. Andrews's *Narra-* Sources *tives of the Insurrections* (1915), pp. 170-219, 229-267. For more detailed discussions, see *The Dudley Records* in the Massachusetts Historical Society *Proceedings*, 2nd series, xiii, pp. 226-286 (covering the period from May to December, 1686), and the *Publications* of the Prince Society. In the latter series the following deserve special mention: The *Andros Tracts*, 3 vols., and the *Edward Randolph Papers*, 7 vols., edited by A. T. S. Goodrich and R. N. Toppan. The first volume and a good part of the second of the *Randolph Papers* are devoted to a memoir of Randolph; the rest of the work consists of documents covering the period from 1676 to 1703. It is a very valuable collection of source materials for the Dominion period and the events that immediately preceded it. *The Hinckley Papers, 1676-1699* [Massachusetts Historical Society *Collections,* 4th series, v, pp. 1-308] is valuable for a study of the workings of the Dominion in New Plymouth.

NEW YORK AND MARYLAND

Secondary authorities   Channing, *op. cit.* (ii, pp. 202-213), Osgood, *American Colonies in the Seventeenth Century* (iii, chs. 15-16), and Andrews, C. M., *Colonial Self-Government* (pp. 279-287) serve as good starting-points for the study of the Revolution in New York and Maryland. A lengthy account of the Andros régime in New York and the Leisler revolt is given in Mrs. Schuyler Van Rensselaer's *History of the City of New York in the Seventeenth Century,* chs. 24-29 (1909; lengthy bibliographies listing primary sources). For the Revolution in Maryland, see Sparks, F. E., *Causes of the Maryland Revolution of 1689* [Johns Hopkins *Studies,* 14th series], and Steiner, B. C., "The Protestant Revolution in Maryland," in the *Annual Report* of the American Historical Association for 1898, pp. 281-353.

Sources   Several contemporary accounts of Leisler's revolt are given by Andrews in his *Narratives of the Insurrections* (for accounts hostile to Leisler, see pp. 320-354, 360-372; a friendly view is given in pp. 375-401). For other contemporary material bearing on the Revolution in New York, see *Documents Relating to the Administration of Jacob Leisler,* i, pp. 241-246 [New York Historical Society *Collections,* Publication Fund, 1868]. The *Narratives of the Insurrections,* pp. 305-314, gives a contemporary statement of the Protestant side of the controversy. The editor cautions against accepting these statements as facts, but says that they are valuable as showing the thoughts and feelings of the time.

CHAPTER XIV.—THE NORTH BETWEEN TWO REVOLUTIONS

MANY of the references in the Bibliographical Notes for the chapters dealing with the early history of New England and New York are useful for this period. It is not necessary to repeat them here. The authorities mentioned below, both primary and secondary—most of which are concerned with only the later period—are intended as a supplement to the lists of references given above.

NEW ENGLAND

Useful secondary authorities: Osgood, H. L., *American Colonies in the Eighteenth Century*, i, part i, chs. 8-9; ii, part i, ch. 20; iii, part ii, chs. 12-16, and part iii, ch. 4; Hart, A. B., ed., *Commonwealth History of Massachusetts*, ii, chs. 1-14; Kimball, Everett, *Public Life of Joseph Dudley*; Matthews, L. K., *The Expansion of New England* (1909); Burns, J. F., *Controversies Between Royal Governors and Their Assemblies in the Northern American Colonies*, chs. 1-4 (1923; numerous specific references to and quotations from the sources; valuable for the special student; too detailed for the general reader); and Adams, Brooks, *Emanicpation of Massachusetts* (1887, 1919). The most readable single volume on New England for this period is J. T. Adams's brilliant work, *Revolutionary New England* (1923). It is scholarly but is affected with an anti-Puritan bias that in places mars its perspective. Along with it should be read K. B. Murdock's *Increase Mather* (1925), which upholds the orthodox pro-Puritan view. W. H. Chamberlin's *Samuel Sewall and the World He Lived In*; Barrett Wendell's *Cotton Mather, the Puritan Priest* (1891, 1926; numerous quotations from his diary); and *Cotton Mather, Keeper of the Puritan Conscience* (1928), by Ralph and Louise Boas, are useful for the special student. *(margin: Secondary authorities)*

A work of value on witchcraft in England and America is George L. Kittredge's *Witchcraft in Old and New England* (1929). Of the other numerous writings on this topic, these should be mentioned: Hart, A. B., ed., *Commonwealth History of Massachusetts*, ii, ch. 2; and Taylor, J. M., *The Witchcraft Delusion in Colonial Connecticut, 1647-1697* (1908; numerous quotations from the documents; a good source book). For a discussion of the literature on witchcraft in New England, see notes in J. Winsor's *Memorial History of Boston*, ii, ch. 6, and an article by the same author in American Antiquarian Society *Proceedings*, n.s., x, pp. 351-373. *(margin: The witchcraft delusion)*

The Massachusetts Historical Society *Collections* constitute a regular library of documents, many of which are valuable for this period. Running through several volumes of this collection are the *Winthrop Papers*, some of which bear on this chapter and some on the earlier history of New England. Of the other numerous documents in this vast collection, the following should be listed: *The Hinckley Papers*, 4th series, v, pp. 1-308 (the letters and papers of Thomas Hinckley, governor of the colony of New Plymouth; they cover the *(margin: Sources: Massachusetts and New Plymouth)* period from 1676 to 1699) ; the *Diary of Samuel Sewall* from December, 1673, to October, 1729 (5th series), v-vii; the *Letter Book of Samuel Sewall* (6th series), i and ii; the *Diary of Cotton Mather, 1681-1727* (7th series), vii and viii; the *Belcher Papers, 1731-1743* (6th series), vi and vii (letters of Jonathan Belcher, governor of Massachusetts).

Other useful sources are: Murdock, K. B., *Selections from Cotton Mather* (1926) ; Weeks, L. H., and Bacon, E. M., *Historical Digest of the Provincial Press* (issues of the *Boston News Letter*) ; *Journals of the House of Representatives of Massachusetts* (a number of volumes on the periods 1715-1727 and 1745-1775) ; Mather, Cotton, *Magnalia Christi Americana,* or the *Ecclesiastical History of New England* (covers the period from 1620 to 1698. "A work that is still a storehouse of ill-compiled and ill-digested matter, not without real historical importance"; first published in 1702) ; Brooks, Henry M., *Some Strange and Curious Punishments* [*Olden Times Series*] (1886; excerpts from newspapers and laws; interesting) ; *Publications* of the Colonial Society of Massachusetts, ii, iv, ix (vol. ii contains commissions and instructions to governors and other colonial officials from 1681 to 1774) ; and Hart, A. B., *American History Told by Contemporaries,* ii, ch. 3.

The witchcraft cases

The best collection of easily accessible source materials on the witchcraft delusion is G. L. Burr's *Narratives of the Witchcraft Cases, 1648-1706* [*Original Narratives*] (1914). Other collections are: Upham, W. P., *Salem Witchcraft;* Stedman, E. C., and Hutchinson, E. M., *Library of American Literature,* ii, pp. 114 *et seq.;* Nevins, W. S., ed., *Witchcraft in Salem Village in 1692* (1892, 1916; numerous extracts from the documents; virtually a source book; in appendix, pp. 207-260, is given Governor Phips's account of the trials and of his stopping the special court of oyer and terminer) ; and Drake, S. G., ed., *Annals of Witchcraft in New England and Elsewhere in the United States* [*Woodward Historical Series,* no. viii] (1869; a collection of cases; very complete).

Connecticut and Rhode Island

In the Connecticut Historical Society *Collections* there are also a number of documents bearing on this period. Of these the following should especially be noted: *Talcott Papers* (letters and documents covering the period of Joseph Talcott's governorship of the colony of Connecticut, 1724-1741 ; vols. iv and v of the series) ; the *Law Papers* (correspondence and documents relating to Jonathan Law's administration as governor of Connecticut, 1741-1750; vols. xi, xii, and xv) ; the *Wolcott Papers* (correspondence and documents relating to Roger Wolcott's governorship of Connecticut, 1750-1754; vol. xvi) ; the *Fitch Papers* (letters and papers dealing with Thomas Fitch's administration as governor of Connecticut, 1754-1766; vols. xvii and xviii) ; the *Pitkin Papers* (documents on the administration of William Pitkin, 1766-1769; vol. xix); and *The Correspondence of the Colonial Governors of Rhode Island, 1723-1775,* 3 vols., edited by G. S. Kimball. The colonial records of Connecticut and Rhode Island mentioned in Chapter VIII extend over a part or all of this period.

NEW YORK

Good secondary authorities: Channing, *op. cit.,* ii, pp. 294-310; Greene, E. B., *Provincial America,* chs. 5, 12, and *The Provincial Governor,* chs. 8-10; Burns, J. F., *Controversies Between Royal Governors and Their Assemblies,* ch. 5; Osgood, H. L., *American Colonies in the Eighteenth Century,* i, part i, chs. 7-8; ii, part i, chs. 18-19, and part ii, chs. 4-5; and iv, part i, ch. 10. The accounts in Osgood's work are valuable for the special student, but too detailed for the general reader. See also Irving Mark's *Agrarian Conflicts in Colonial New York, 1711-1775* (1940). — *Secondary authorities*

Many of the voluminous collections of sources given for Chapter X extend over this period. To this list should be added: *Letters and Papers of Cadwallader Colden, 1711-1775* [New York Historical Society *Collections* for 1917-1923], 7 vols.; Colden, Cadwallader, *History of the Five Indian Nations,* 2 vols. (1902); and Rutherfurd, L., *John Peter Zenger* (1904; lengthy account of the Zenger Case and events related to it, interspersed with excerpts from the documents; ch. 5 and pp. 173-246 give original reports of the trial). — *Sources*

CHAPTER XV.—THE MIDDLE COLONIES IN THE EIGHTEENTH CENTURY

MANY of the works listed in the Bibliographical Notes for Chapters IV, V, and XII will be found useful for the study of the events narrated in this chapter. Other secondary authorities are: Greene, E. B., *Provincial America,* chs. 2-6, and *The Provincial Governor,* chs. 8-10; Osgood, H. L., *American Colonies in the Eighteenth Century,* i, pp. 328-398; ii, pp. 85-94, 118-125, 159-289, 431-442, 530-534; iii, pp. 3-113, 222-237; Barker, Charles A., *The Background of the Revolution in Maryland* (1940); and Dodson, Leonidas, *Alexander Spotswood, Governor of Colonial Virginia, 1710-1722* (1932). — *Secondary authorities*

Among the sources dealing with this period not given in preceding lists, the following should be mentioned: Eddis, William, *Letters from America, 1769-1777* (1792); *Votes and Proceedings of the Lower House of Assembly of the Province of Maryland, 1754-1758,* 7 vols.; Bacon, Thomas, *Laws of Maryland at large, 1637-1763*; Allinson, Samuel, comp., *Acts of the General Assembly of the Province of New Jersey, 1702-1776*; Paterson, William, *Laws of the State of New Jersey, 1703-1798*; *The Papers of Lewis Morris,* governor of — *Sources* the province of New Jersey from 1738 to 1746 (these constitute the 4th volume of the *Collections* of the New Jersey Historical Society; valuable); Hartwell, Henry, Blair, James, and Chilton, Edward, *The Present State of Virginia and the College* (originally published in 1727; a recent reprint, edited by Henry D. Farish, appeared in 1940); Jones, Hugh, *The Present State of Virginia* (1724); Beverly, R., *The History and Present State of Virginia* (first published in 1705; recent edition edited by Louis B. Wright was published in 1947); Keith, Sir William, *The History of the British Plantations in America*, 1738 (part i gives the history of Virginia); *The Official Letters of Alexander Spotswood*, lieutenant-governor of Virginia, 1710-1722, 2 vols.; *The Official Records of Robert Dinwiddie*, lieutenant-governor of the colony of Virginia, 1751-1758, 2 vols. (the last two were published by the Virginia Historical Society); and Thomas Jefferson's *Notes on the State of Virginia* (1787; a valuable description of Virginia at the end of the colonial period by an observant contemporary). For other documents, see Channing, Hart, and Turner's *Guide*, p. 137.

CHAPTER XVI.—THE SOUTH UNDER THE EARLY HANOVERIANS

THE CAROLINAS

Secondary authorities

PRACTICALLY all the bibliographical references in Chapter XI apply to this chapter as well. In addition, a few works should be mentioned that deal only with the later period. Of these the following are useful: McCrady, Edward, *The History of South Carolina Under the Royal Government, 1719-1776* (1899; specific references to sources as in his previous volume); Smith, W. R., *South Carolina as a Royal Province* (1903; deals mostly with institutional history; numerous specific references to sources including unpublished manuscripts; a valuable volume); Meriwether, Robert L., *The Expansion of South Carolina, 1729-1765* (1940; maps; scholarly); and Foote, W. R., *Sketches of North Carolina* (1846; has some chapters on the Scotch-Irish). Briefer accounts of Georgia and the Carolinas of this period are given in Greene, *The Provincial Governor*, chs. 8-10; Osgood, *Eighteenth Century*, ii, pp. 347-411; iii, pp. 34-75; iv, pp. 201-221, 238-278; Weeks, S. B., *The Press of North Carolina in the 18th Century* (1891); Hewatt, A., *An Historical Account of the Rise and Progress of the Colonies of South Carolina and Georgia*, 2 vols. (1779); Voight, G. P., *The German and German-Swiss Element in South Carolina, 1732-1752* [*Bulletin* of the University of South Carolina]; and Schaper, W. A., *Sectionalism and Representation in South Carolina* (1901), part ii.

A good brief collection of documents is W. K. Boyd's *Some Eight-* Sources
eenth Century Tracts Concerning North Carolina (1927). The laws
of North Carolina from 1715 to 1788 are given in vols. xxiii and
xxiv of the *State Records of North Carolina*. Two good contemporary
descriptions of South Carolina in the later colonial period are James
Glen's *A Description of South Carolina* (1761, 1836); and George
Milligen's *A Short Description of the Province of South Carolina,*
written in 1763 and printed in 1770 (gives a description of the physical features and climate of the country, an excellent description of
Charleston, and an account of the inhabitants, with emphasis on the
diseases of the people; chs. 3 and 4 are particularly good). For other
contemporary accounts, see B. R. Carroll's *Historical Collections of
South Carolina* (1836), ii. Other documents that should be listed
are: Weston, P. C. J., ed., *Documents Connected with the History
of South Carolina* (1856); Trott, Nicholas, ed., *Laws of the Province
of South Carolina before 1734*, 2 vols.; Cooper, Thomas, and McCord,
D. J., eds., *Statutes at Large of South Carolina*, 10 vols.

GEORGIA

The following histories cover all or a portion of the colonial period Secondary
in Georgia: Greene, E. B., *Provincial America*, ch. 15; Wissler, C., authorities
Skinner, C. L., and Wood, W., *Adventures in the Wilderness*, ch. 15
(pictorial); Howell, Clark, *History of Georgia* (1926; about half of
the volume is on the colonial period); McCain, James R., *Georgia
as a Proprietary Province* (1917; emphasis on government and social
life, though some general history is given; specific references to
sources); Flippin, P. S., *The Royal Government in Georgia* (1923);
Mitchell, F. L., *Georgia, Land and People* (1900); Coulter, E. M.,
A Short History of Georgia (1933); Johnson, Amanda, *Georgia as
Colony and State* (1938); and Saye, Albert B., *New Viewpoints in
Georgia History* (1943; takes issue with the older authorities as to
part played by debtors in the settlement of Georgia). There are also
four biographies of Oglethorpe that should be mentioned: Ettinger,
Amos A., *James Edward Oglethorpe, Imperial Idealist* (1936);
Cooper, Harriet C., *James Oglethorpe, the Founder of Georgia*
(1904); Bruce, Henry, *Life of General Oglethorpe* [*Makers of
America Series*] (1890; numerous excerpts from the sources); and
Wright, Robert, *A Memoir of General James Oglethorpe* (1867; ex-
tracts from the sources). For other authorities, see R. P. Brooks's "A
Preliminary Bibliography of Georgia History" in University of
Georgia *Bulletin*, x, no. 10A.

Of the Georgia Historical Society *Collections*, practically all of vols. Sources
i, ii, and vi are made up of documents on the colonial period. But the
most valuable collection of documents is *The Colonial Records of
Georgia*, a voluminous work edited by Governor Allen D. Candler.

These volumes are all printed in large clear type, with an index for each. Some of the volumes are prefaced by short explanatory statements which are of great value to the student. The statements prefacing vols. xiii and xvi constitute an excellent short account of the provincial government. But for the absence of a table of contents and general index, this work would be a model of historical publication, but this omission seriously impairs its availability for all students except those who have time to specialize on this period. The following are some of the documents reprinted in this remarkable collection: *A Journal of the Proceedings in Georgia, 1737-1740*, by William Stephens (Stephens was sent out by the trustees, with the title of "Secretary to the Trustees in Georgia," to study the situation in the province and report to them. The journal was the result of his three years' work in this capacity; it is to be found in vol. iv and supplementary volume); *Journal of the Earl of Egmont, First President of the Board of Trustees*, from June 14, 1738, to May 25, 1744, v; *Proceedings of the President and Assistants*, vi; *Proceedings and Minutes of the Governor and Council, 1754-1782*, vii-xii; *Journal of the Commons House of Assembly from 1755 to 1782*, xiii-xv (these three volumes contain all the records of the proceedings of the Commons House that are extant. They are full and complete to April, 1772; after this period they are meager and fragmentary); *Journal of the Upper House of Assembly, 1755-1774*, xvi-xvii (these two volumes of the *Records* contain all the journals of the upper house that are extant; they are complete up to the Revolutionary disturbances. In the preface to vol. xvi, pp. 3-4, there is an excellent account of the upper house). The statutes for the years 1768 to 1805 are given in vols. xviii and xix; and the correspondence of the trustees, General Oglethorpe, and others appears in vols. xxi-xxv.

Another valuable collection of contemporary accounts bearing on the early history of Georgia is the *American Colonial Tracts Monthly*, i. Short excerpts from contemporary accounts are given in A. B. Hart's *American History Told by Contemporaries*, ii, ch. 6. For the Spanish settlements on the Carolina-Georgia coast and the long controversy between the English and Spanish colonists, see Antonio de Arredondo's *Spain's Title to Georgia* (1925), edited by H. E. Bolton. This valuable work includes a general statement of the facts by Professor Bolton (pp. 1-110); Arredondo's statement of facts and the arguments built upon them (1742) in Spanish (pp. 225-235); and an English translation of Arredondo's discussion. For other documents on colonial Georgia, see Greene and Morris's *Guide*, p. 14.

Chapter XVII.—The Old West

THE pioneer in the study of the western movement is Professor F. J. Turner. His article, "The Significance of the Frontier," first published in the *Annual Report* of the American Historical Association for 1893, pp. 199-227, is one of the finest specimens of historical writing produced in the past six decades. This treatise and others subsequently published by him have opened the eyes of students of history to the importance of the westward movement. Some of his essays, including this article, have been collected and published in one volume under the title of *The Frontier in American History* (1921). The first three chapters of this work afford an excellent approach to the study of that phase of western expansion known as the Old West, and I have leaned heavily on them in writing the chapter on this subject. Other works concerned with the westward movement are: Hansen, Marcus L., *The Atlantic Migration, 1607-1860* (1940); and Wittke, Carl, *We Who Built America* (1939).

Secondary authorities: General works

For a good short account of the German and Scotch-Irish emigrations, see H. L. Osgood's *American Colonies in the Eighteenth Century,* ii, ch. 6. Of the fuller works the following should be listed: Ford, H. J., *The Scotch-Irish in America* (1915; detailed and rather diffuse; no footnotes, but lengthy quotations from the sources); Bolton, C. K., *Scotch-Irish Pioneers in Ulster and America* (1910; quotes at length from the sources); Hanna, Charles A., *The Scotch-Irish*, 2 vols. (1902; is of little value for the colonial period except that ch. 39 gives an excellent account of the emigration from Ulster to America); Faust, A. B., *The German Element in the United States*, 2 vols. (1909; probably the best work on the German settlements in America; scholarly; references to primary sources); Bittinger, Lucy F., *The Germans in Colonial Times* (1901; popular account; readable); Kuhns, Oscar, *The German and Swiss Settlements of Colonial Pennsylvania* (1901); Rosenberger, Jesse L., *The Pennsylvania Germans* (1923; popular; good deal of space to life of the people); Rush, B., *Manners of the German Inhabitants* [Pennsylvania-German Society *Proceedings*, xix] (1910; written in 1789; a contemporary account; brief but valuable); Knauss, J. O., *Social Conditions Among the Pennsylvania Germans in the 18th Century* [*Proceedings* of the Pennsylvania-German Society, xxix] (1922; numerous specific references to sources; bibliography, pp. 212-217); Schuricht, Hermann, *History of the German Element in Virginia* (1898-1900); Wayland, J. W., *The German Element of the Shenandoah Valley of Virginia* (1907); and Bernheim, G. D., *History of German Settlements and of the Lutheran Church in North and South Carolina* (1872; first half on colonial and Revolutionary periods).

Special works

For brief discussions see the following articles: Hoskins, J. P., "German Influence on Religious Life and Thought in America During the Colonial Period," *Princeton Theological Review*, v, pp. 49-79; Faust, A. B., "Swiss Emigration to the American Colonies in the 18th Century," *American Historical Review*, xxii, pp. 21-24; and Voight, G. P., "German and Swiss Element in South Carolina," *Bulletin of the University of South Carolina*, no. 113. For other references on the German settlers, see bibliographical notes in Faust, *op. cit.*, ii, pp. 479-562; and Turner, F. J., and Merk, F., *List of References on the History of the West* (1922).

Sources   There are no accessible collections of primary sources that bear on this topic as a whole. Some material of value will be found scattered throughout the voluminous *Proceedings* of the Scotch-Irish Society Congresses, 10 vols. (1889-1901), and the *Proceedings* of the Pennsylvania-German Society. *Christoph von Graffenried's Account of the Founding of New Bern* [*Publications* of the North Carolina Historical Commission, 1920], translated and edited by V. H. Todd, is a good contemporary account of the founding of the first German settlement in North Carolina. Documents bearing on the Moravian settlement in North Carolina are given at length in *Records of the Moravians in North Carolina* [*Publications* of the North Carolina Historical Commission] (edited by Adelaide L. Fries; in progress; 4 vols. to 1922). See also A. B. Faust, ed., "Documents Relating to Swiss Emigration to America," *American Historical Review*, xxii, pp. 98-132. Other sources can be found by using the footnotes in the best secondary authorities listed above.

CHAPTER XVIII.—NEW FRANCE AND THE FIRST TWO
INTERCOLONIAL WARS

NEW FRANCE

Secondary authorities   THE *Chronicles of Canada*, 32 vols. (1914-1921), edited by G. M. Wrong and H. H. Langton, have five interesting volumes on this subject. They are: Colby, C. W., *The Founder of New France* (a chronicle of Champlain); Marquis, T. G., *The Jesuit Missions* (a chronicle of the Cross in the Wilderness); Chapais, Thomas, *The Great Intendant* (a chronicle of Jean Talon in Canada); Munro, W. B., *The Seigneurs of Old Canada*, (a chronicle of New World feudalism); and Colby, C. W., *The Fighting Governor* (a chronicle of Frontenac). Other accounts that should be listed are: Wissler, C., Skinner, C. L., and Wood, W., *Adventures in the Wilderness*, ch. 17, secs. 2-3; Thwaites, R. G., *France in America* [*American Nation Series*] (1905), chs. 1-5; Kingsford, William, *History of Canada*

(1887-1898), i, chs. 1-12; Tracy, F. B., *The Tercentenary History of Canada* (1908, 1913), i, chs. 3-16, 20; Lucas, C. P., *A Historical Geography of the British Dominions*, v—Canada, part i (also covers the intercolonial wars); Burt, Alfred L., *A Short History of Canada for Americans* (1942); Shortt, Adams, and Doughty, A. G., eds., *Canada and Its Provinces*, 22 vols.; i, pp. 1-198, and ii (1914, 1917; all of vol. ii is on economic and social history; reproduction of contemporary portraits); Priestley, H. I., *The Coming of the White Man*, chs. 8-10; Winsor, J., *Cartier to Frontenac* (1894; has numerous reproductions of contemporary maps that are valuable); Fiske, J., *New France and New England*, chs. 1-4; Wittke, Carl, *History of Canada* (1933), ch. 2; Parkman, Francis, *Frontenac and New France Under Louis XIV* (1894), and *Pioneers of New France* (1865, 1895); Douglas, James, *New England and New France* (1913); and Wrong, G. M., *The Rise and Fall of New France*, i (1928; readable; no footnotes, but bibliographies are given at end of volume). Short general accounts can be found in Channing's *History of the United States*, ii, ch. 5; and in W. M. Sloane's *The French War and the Revolution* (1893).

For the French explorations and settlements in the West and Southwest, see Ogg, Frederic A., *The Opening of the Mississippi* (1904); Steck, F. B., *The Joliet-Marquette Expedition, 1673* (1927, 1928; numerous excerpts from the documents); Gayarre, Charles, *History of Louisiana*, 4 vols. (1852, 1903; first two volumes on the colonial and Revolutionary periods); Wallace, Joseph, *The History of Illinois and Louisiana Under the French Rule*, with some account of the English occupation of Illinois (1893); Hamilton, P. J., *Colonial Mobile* (1897, 1910; first thirty-five chapters on the colonial and Revolutionary periods); and Vandiveer, C. A., *The Fur-Trade and Early Western Exploration* (1929), chs. 4-8. For other references, see Turner, F. J., and Merk, Frederick, *List of References on the History of the West*; and the bibliographical notes in G. M. Wrong's *Rise and Fall of New France*.

In the *Trail Makers* Series there are English translations of two *Sources* important contemporary works. These are *The Voyages and Explorations of Samuel de Champlain* (1600-1616), as narrated by himself and translated by Anne Nettleton Bourne, 2 vols. (1906, 1922); and *The Journeys of La Salle*, written by his associates and friends and edited by I. J. Cox, 2 vols. (1905, 1922). A valuable collection of sources bearing on the career of Champlain in America is W. L. Grant's *Voyages of Samuel Champlain, 1604-1618* [*Original Narratives Series*] (1917). Another collection of contemporary accounts in the same series is L. P. Kellogg's *Early Narratives of the Northwest, 1634-1699* (1917). Other important sources are: Lescarbot, Marc, *Nova Francia, A Description of Acadia*, trans. by P. Erondelle (writ-

ten in 1608; gives an account of the settlements at St. Croix Island
and Port Royal in part i, chs. 1-18; part ii is devoted to manners and
customs of the Indians); Shea, J. D. G., *Discovery and Exploration
of the Mississippi Valley* (1852, 1903; documents and contemporary
accounts, pp. 197-267); and French, B. F., *Historical Collections of
Louisiana*, 1st series, 5 vols., 2nd series, 2 vols. (1869-1875; historical
memoirs and narratives). For lists of other primary sources with an
appraisal of their value, see Winsor, J., *Narrative and Critical History*, iv, pp. 130-134, 149-162, 196-262, 290-316, 356-394; v, pp.
63-86.

THE FIRST TWO INTERCOLONIAL WARS

Secondary   Brief accounts of the first two intercolonial wars: Greene, E. B.,
authorities *Provincial America*, chs. 8 and 9; Wrong, G. M., *The Conquest of
New France [Chronicles of America]* (1918), chs. 1-3; and Tracy,
F. B., *Tercentenary History of Canada*, i, chs. 17 and 18. A more
detailed discussion of these wars can be found in two scholarly and
interesting works by Francis Parkman, *Frontenac and New France*
(1877, 1903), and *A Half-Century of Conflict*, 2 vols. (1894; discusses Queen Anne's War and King George's War). In the *Chronicles
of Canada* Series there are two interesting popular treatises on the
first two intercolonial wars: Colby, C. W., *The Fighting Governor*
(1915; a chronicle of Frontenac); and Doughty, A. G., *The Acadian
Exiles* (1916; a history of Acadia). A later account of Acadia is J.
B. Brebner's *New England Outposts* (1927). An excellent general
work for the special student is H. L. Osgood's *American Colonies in
the Eighteenth Century*. The greater part of the first three volumes
is taken up with the discussion of these wars, conditions in the colonies during the wars, and the English and French background of the
long conflict. The numerous footnotes enable the student easily to
check from the sources all statements of fact.

Other works that should be included are: Crane, V. W., *The
Southern Frontier, 1670-1732* (1921; a scholarly work emphasizing
the relation of Indian trade to intercolonial conflict in the South),
and "The Southern Frontier in Queen Anne's War," an article by
the same author in the *American Historical Review*, xxiv, pp. 379-
395; Wood, G. A., *William Shirley, Governor of Massachusetts,
1741-1756*, 2 vols. (1920; numerous specific references to sources);
Parsons, Usher, *Life of Sir William Pepperrell, Bart.* (1856; chs. 3-6
are devoted to the siege and capture of Louisbourg; number of documents given); Griffis, W. E., *Sir William Johnson and the Six Nations* (1891); Andrews, C. M., "Anglo-French Commercial Rivalry,
1700-1750," *American Historical Review*, xx, pp. 539-556, 761-780;
Drake, S. A., *The Border Wars of New England* (1897; King Wil-

liam's War and Queen Anne's War) ; and Sylvester, H. M., *Indian Wars of New England*, 3 vols. (1910).

C. H. Lincoln's *Narratives of the Indian Wars* [*Original Narratives Series*] (1913), pp. 179-300, gives Cotton Mather's account of King William's War. S. Penhallow's *The History of the Wars of New England with the Eastern Indians, 1703-1713* (1726, 1859) is a good contemporary account by a competent observer of Queen Anne's War. Collections of sources: Hart, A. B., *American History Told by Contemporaries*, ii, ch. 19; Colden, Cadwallader, *History of the Five Indian Nations*, 2 vols. (1747, 1922), edited by P. G. Winship; Lincoln, C. H., ed., *The Correspondence of William Shirley*, 2 vols. (good portion of the first volume on the first three intercolonial wars). For reproductions of contemporary maps and plans of forts, see Hulbert, A. B., collector and editor, *The Crown Collection of Photographs of American Maps*, three series (rare). For other sources, both primary and secondary, on the first three wars, see the Bibliographical Notes for the next chapter; and Winsor, J., *Narrative and Critical History*, v, pp. 418-482.

Sources

Chapter XIX.—England Wins Supremacy in North America

An excellent brief account of King George's War and the French and Indian War is given in E. Channing's *History of the United States*, ii, pp. 546-599. H. L. Osgood, in his *American Colonies in the Eighteenth Century,* iii, part iii, ch. 3, and iv, part iii, chs. 12-17, gives a lengthy discussion of these two wars, with emphasis on their administrative phases, that is valuable for the special student. The special student will also want to consult vols. iv, v, and vi of L. H. Gipson's *The British Empire before the American Revolution*, in which will be found an authoritative discussion of the last two intercolonial wars from the British as well as the American point of view. A work of great value on the French and Indian War is Francis Parkman's *Montcalm and Wolfe*, 2 vols. (1884, 1896; scholarly and interesting). Other full accounts that should be listed are: Bradley, A. G., *The Fight with France for North America* (1900) ; Wood, W., *The Fight for Canada* (1906; a valuable work; a very full bibliography of sources, pp. 346-360) ; and Sloane, W. M., *The French War and the Revolution,* chs. 4-9. G. L. Beer's *British Colonial Policy, 1754-1763* (1907, 1933), chs. 1-9, is an excellent discussion of British policy toward America during the French and Indian War. See also E. I. McCormac's *Colonial Opposition to Imperial Authority During the French and Indian War* (1911).

A very interesting popular narrative of both wars is G. M. Wrong's

Secondary authorities

The Conquest of New France [*Chronicles of America*], chs. 4-11 (a good brief bibliography at the end of the volume). In the *Chronicles of Canada* there are four interesting volumes that discuss certain phases of King George's War and the French and Indian War. These are: Wood, W., *The Great Fortress* (1915; a chronicle of Louisbourg); Doughty, A. G., *The Acadian Exiles* (a chronicle of the Land of Evangeline); Wood, W., *The Winning of Canada* (1914; a chronicle of Wolfe); and *The Passing of New France* (1914; a chronicle of Montcalm). For an excellent pictorial history of these two wars, see Wissler, C., Skinner, C. L., and Wood, W., *Adventures in the Wilderness*, ch. 17, sec. 4. Short accounts: Adams, J. T., *Provincial Society*, ch. 11 (an account of economic and social conditions at the time of the French and Indian War); Bradley, A. G., *Britain Across the Seas, America* (1911), ch. 3; and Wrong, G. M., *Rise and Fall of New France*, ii, chs. 25 and 27. For the part played by Washington in the French and Indian War, see Hughes, Rupert, *Life of Washington,* i (1926); and Ambler, C. H., *George Washington and the West* (1936).

Special topics   Other secondary authorities that may prove useful, especially to the serious student, are: Bailey, K. P., *The Ohio Company of Virginia and the Westward Movement, 1748-1792* (1939); Winsor, J., *The Mississippi Basin* (1895, 1898); Hulbert, A. B., *Braddock's Road* (1904; emphasis on Braddock's campaign; quotes at length from contemporary accounts; reproduces on p. 69 a contemporary map of Braddock's Road made about 1759); MacLeod, W. C., *The American Indian Frontier* (1928), ch. 26; Volwiler, A. T., *George Croghan and the Westward Movement* (1924); Mayo, L. S., *Jeffery Amherst* (1916; chs. 3-9 on the French and Indian War); Tracy, F. B., *Tercentenary History of Canada,* i, chs. 19, 21-29; Doughty, A. G., and Parmelee, G. W., *The Siege of Quebec*, 6 vols. (1901; a voluminous work; a good deal of source material and an endless bibliography); Black, J. W., *Maryland's Attitude in the Struggle for Canada* [Johns Hopkins *Studies*] (1892); Baker-Crothers, Hayes, *Virginia and the French and Indian War* (1928; numerous specific references to sources; good bibliography); Koontz, L. K., *The Virginia Frontier, 1754-1763* (1925; quotations from and specific references to sources; a good account of the part played by Washington and Governor Dinwiddie in the French and Indian War); Hurst, G. B., *The Old Colonial System,* chs. 1-3 (1905; numerous specific references to sources); Hotblack, Kate, *Chatham's Colonial Policy* (1917; some of the chapters are concerned with imperial policy during the intercolonial wars; numerous specific references to sources); Corbett, J. S., *England in the Seven Years' War*, 2 vols. (1907); Stone, W. L., *Life and Times of Sir William Johnson and the Six Nations* (1865); Clarke, T. W., *The Bloody Mohawk* (1940); Wood,

G. A., *The Public Life of William Shirley*, governor of Massachusetts, 1741-1746, 2 vols. (1920). For other references for King George's War, see Bibliographical Notes for Chapter XVIII.

There are a number of collections of papers bearing on the French Sources and Indian War and the other intercolonial wars. Among these should be mentioned: *The Journal of Sir William Pepperrell*, kept during the expedition against Louisbourg, March 24-August 22, 1745 [American Antiquarian Society *Proceedings*, new series, xx], pp. 139-176; *The Papers of Sir William Johnson*, 6 vols., edited by James Sullivan (vols. i, ii, iii, and a small portion of vol. iv deal with King George's War and the French and Indian War; a calendar of these papers has been published by the New York State Education Department); *Correspondence of William Shirley* (1731-1760), 2 vols., edited by C. H. Lincoln; *Washington's Journal*, edited by J. M. Toner (covers Washington's expedition across the Alleghanies in 1754, including the attack on Jumonville and the surrender at Fort Necessity); Darlington, W. M., ed., *Journals of Christopher Gist and Thomas Walker* (1893); Fitzpatrick, John C., ed., *The Diaries of George Washington*, 4 vols. (1925); *The Writings of George Washington from the Original Manuscript Sources, 1745-1799*, 37 vols. (1931-1940; the best collection of Washington letters); *Official Records of Robert Dinwiddie, 1751-1758* [Virginia Historical Society *Collections*, new series, iii and iv]; Sargent, Winthrop, ed., *The History of an Expedition Against Fort Duquesne in 1755* (1855, 1856); Pargellis, Stanley M., ed., *Military Affairs in North America, 1748-1765: Selected Documents from the Cumberland Papers in Windsor Castle* (1936); Pouchot, M., *Memoir upon the Late War in North America Between the French and the English, 1755-60* (published in French in 1781, translated into English by F. B. Hough, and published in 2 vols., 1866; a valuable contemporary account by a French officer, based on his own observations and those of other eye-witnesses; a valuable source from the French point of view); *The Journal of Captain Knox*, 3 vols., edited by A. G. Doughty (Captain Knox was a soldier in both King George's War and the French and Indian War; his *Journal*, covering the period 1757-1760, was first published in 1769); and Mante, *The History of the Late War in North America* (1772).

Useful source materials on the management of the war can be found in the following collections: Fortescue, Hon. Sir John, ed., *The Correspondence of King George the Third*, 1760-1780, i-ii; and the *Correspondence of William Pitt*, 2 vols., edited by Gertrude S. Kimball (1906; correspondence with colonial governors and military and naval commissioners in America).

There are some documents and contemporary accounts in A. B. Hart's *American History Told by Contemporaries*, ii, ch. 20; *Virginia*

Historical Register, v; Pennsylvania Historical Society *Memoirs,* v (Journal of Braddock's expedition); and Reuben G. Thwaites, ed., *Early Western Travels,* i (1904-1907; Journals of Conrad Weiser and George Croghan). For reproduction of contemporary maps and plans of forts, see A. B. Hulbert's *The Crown Collection of Photographs* listed in the Bibliographical Notes for the preceding chapter. For lists of other primary sources, see Channing, Hart, and Turner's *Guide,* pp. 289-290, and Winsor's *Narrative and Critical History,* v, pp. 452-482, 569-622.

PART II.—ECONOMIC AND SOCIAL LIFE

General works

THE economic development of the colonies is given in outline by the economic histories listed on p. 760. A good deal of information on social life to 1789 can be found in the general works listed on pp. 760 f.

CHAPTER XX.—POPULATION AND LABOR

Secondary authorities: Population

FOR the growth of population in the colonies, see Dexter, F. B., "Estimates of Population in the American Colonies," in American Antiquarian Society *Proceedings,* v, pp. 22-50; Greene, E. B., and Harrington, Virginia B., *American Population Before the Census of 1790* (1932); Sutherland, Stella H., *Population Distribution in Colonial America* (1936); and *A Century of Population Growth, 1790-1900* (1909; published as a part of the report of the Twelfth Census). See also Proper, E. E., *Colonial Emigration Laws* [Columbia University *Studies,* xii].

Jewish and non-English settlers

References for the Scotch-Irish and German elements in the population are given in the Bibliographical Notes for Chapter XVII. For the part played in colonial history by the other peoples, see the following works: Peters, M. C., *Jews in America* (1905), chs. 2-3; Cohen, George, *The Jews in the Making of America* (1924), chs. 1-4; Daly, C. P., *The Settlement of the Jews in North America* (1893); Rosengarten, J. F., *French Colonists and Exiles in the United States* (1907); Hirsch, A. H., *The Huguenots of Colonial South Carolina* (1928); Fosdick, L. J., *The French Blood in America* (1906), pp. 25-376, 407-415; Baird, C. W., *History of Huguenot Emigration to America,* 2 vols. (1885).

Labor

Short accounts of the colonial labor system can be found in the economic histories listed on p. 760. For fuller discussions of certain aspects of the labor situation in the colonies, see: *Government and Labor in Early America* (1946), by Richard B. Morris; and *Laboring and Dependent Classes in Colonial America, 1607-1783* (1931), a group of studies by Marcus W. Jernegan.

An authoritative account of colonial slavery is given by U. B. Phillips in *American Negro Slavery*, chs. 1-6 (1918; scholarly; specific references to sources in footnotes). There is an article by the same author in the *Political Science Quarterly*, xx, "The Economic Cost of Slave-holding." Other useful works on slavery are: Williams, George W., *A History of the Negro Race in America from 1619 to 1880* (1882, 1883; part ii, pp. 115-323, on colonial period); Ingram, John K., *History of Slavery and Serfdom* (1895), ch. 6; Woodson, C. G., *The Negro in Our History*, 1941 ed. (gives in a popular form a good deal of information about the Negro in colonial times as well as in a later period); Spears, J. R., *American Slave Trade* (1900, 1907; readable); and Du Bois, W. E. B., *Suppression of the Slave Trade* (1896; scholarly and readable; specific references to sources). An excellent work on white servitude is Lucy M. Salmon's *Domestic Service* (1897, 1901; scholarly; numerous references to sources; excerpts from contemporary accounts). See also Butler, J. D., "British Convicts Shipped to American Colonies," *American Historical Review*, ii, pp. 12-33; and Smith, A. E., "Transportation of Convicts to the American Colonies in the Seventeenth Century," *American Historical Review*, January, 1934, xxxix.

There are a number of good monographs that deal with white servitude and certain phases of Negro slavery. Those published in the Johns Hopkins *Studies* hold high rank. These articles are valuable for the special student, as they give numerous references to the sources in the footnotes. Those bearing on the colonial period are as follows: Steiner, B. C., *History of Slavery in Connecticut* (11th series); Ballagh, J. C., *White Servitude in the Colony of Virginia* (13th series); Bassett, J. S., *Slavery and Servitude in the Colony of North Carolina* (14th series); Cooley, Henry S., *A Study of Slavery in New Jersey* (14th series); McCormac, E. T., *White Servitude in Maryland* (22nd series); Ballagh, J. C., *A History of Slavery in Virginia* (extra volume); Brackett, Jeffrey S., *The Negro in Maryland* (extra volume); and Weeks, S. B., *Southern Quakers and Slavery* (extra volume). A good short account is given in an article in the *Annual Report* of the American Historical Association for 1895, entitled "Slavery in the Province of South Carolina," 1670-1770, by Edward McCrady. Other monographs that should be listed are: Greene, Lorenzo J., *The Negro in New England* (1942); Henry, H. M., *The Police Control of the Slave in South Carolina* (1914; portions of this work are useful for the colonial period); Johnston, W. D., *Slavery in Rhode Island, 1755-1776* (1894); Turner, E. R., *The Negro in Pennsylvania* (1911); West, G. M., *The Status of the Negro in Virginia During the Colonial Period* (1889); Bruce, P. A., *Economic History of Virginia in the Seventeenth Century*, chs. 9-11; Wilson, H., *Rise and Fall of the Slave Power in America* (1872-

Marginal notes: Slavery and white servitude; Monographs

1877), ch. i; and Lauber, A. W., *Indian Slavery in Colonial Times Within the Present United States* (1913), chs. 4-12. For an extensive bibliography of the American Negro prepared by W. E. B. Du Bois, see Atlanta University *Publications* (some of the works listed are on the colonial period).

Sources   A good starting-point for an intensive study of slavery is the *Journal of Negro History*. This publication contains articles on the Negro, extracts from the sources, and reviews of books that have come out since it began publication (1916). Most of this material deals with the later history of the Negro, but some of it will be of interest to the student of colonial slavery. For discussions bearing wholly or in part on the colonial period, see i, pp. 349-360; ii, pp. 1-20; iii, pp. 134-232, 335-354; v, pp. 1-4; viii, pp. 41-47. For documents, see i, pp. 164-216, 399-435; viii, p. 333. A number of short excerpts from contemporary discussions of labor and population are given in E. L. Bogart and C. M. Thompson's *Readings in the Economic History of the United States*, pp. 82-96, 106-114. For source materials on the slave trade, see Donnan, Elizabeth, ed., *Documents Illustrative of the History of the Slave Trade to America*, 4 vols. (1930-1935). A valuable collection of laws regarding slavery is John C. Hurd's *The Law of Freedom and Bondage,* 2 vols. (1858; vol. i, pp. 228-311, contains abstracts of the laws relating to slavery in all the colonies, arranged chronologically by colonies). Some extracts of laws bearing on colonial slavery and servitude are also given in John B. Dillon's *Oddities of Colonial Legislation in America*, pp. 190-243. For court decisions regarding slaves, see Helen F. Catterall's *Judicial Cases Concerning American Slavery and the Negro,* 5 vols. (1926-1937). Other source materials on colonial slavery are given in the *Documentary History of American Industrial Society*, edited by R. T. Ely, J. R. Commons, and others. Those that deal with the colonial period can be found in i, pp. 339-374 (white servitude); ii, pp. 29-30, 33-34, 43-44 (slavery); ii, pp. 51-53, 56-58, 81-83, 86, 88-89, 93, 118-119 (slave trade). Contemporary accounts of two voyages of Dutch slavers (1659, 1663) and other papers relating to the Dutch slave trade will be found in *New York Colonial Tracts*, iii, edited by E. B. O'Callaghan.

CHAPTER XXI.—AGRICULTURE AND LAND TENURE

Secondary authorities: General   THE best treatment of colonial agriculture is to be found in two works published by the Carnegie Institution: The *History of Agriculture in the Northern United States, 1620-1860*, by P. W. Bidwell and John I. Falconer (1925; pp. 1-144 deal with the colonial period); and the *History of Agriculture in the Southern United States to 1860*,

2 vols., by L. C. Gray and Esther K. Thompson (1933; all of the first volume on the colonial period). These are scholarly works with specific references to and quotations from the sources. Brief accounts are given in Sanford, A. H., *The Story of Agriculture,* chs. 1-8; Carrier, Lyman, *The Beginnings of Agriculture in the United States* (1923; valuable); and Gabriel, R. H., *Toilers of Land and Sea* [*Pageant of America*] (1924), chs. 2-4 (very readable; gives an interesting account of farm life; numerous pictures, some contemporary, some imaginary). For other short discussions, see chapters by C. L. Flint on "Agriculture in the United States, 1607-1860," in *Eighty Years' Progress,* edited by T. P. Kettel; Carver, T. N., "Historical Sketch of American Agriculture," in L. H. Bailey's *Cyclopedia of American Agriculture* (1907-1909), iv, pp. 39-50; *The South in the Building of the Nation,* v, pp. 43-53, 158-163, 178-183; Wertenbaker, T. J., *The First Americans,* chs. 2-3; Adams, J. T., *Provincial Society,* ch. 2; and the chapters on colonial agriculture in the economic histories listed on p. 760.

Of the special studies the following deserve mention: Bruce, P. A., *Economic History of Virginia in the Seventeenth Century,* i, chs. 4-8 (an interesting and scholarly discussion of agriculture in Virginia); Weeden, W. B., *Economic and Social History of New England,* 2 vols. (1891); Connor, L. G., *A Brief History of the Sheep Industry* (1918); Salley, A. S., Jr., *The Introduction of Rice Culture into South Carolina* (1919); Myer, Jacobstein, *The Tobacco Industry in the United States* [Columbia University *Studies,* 1907, xxvi, no. 3]; Craven, A. O., *Soil Exhaustion as a Factor in the Agricultural History of Virginia and Maryland, 1606-1860* [University of Illinois *Studies,* 1926, xiii, no. 1]; Ballagh, J. C., "The Land System in the South," *Annual Report* of the American Historical Association for 1897, pp. 101-129; Osgood, H. L., *The American Colonies in the Seventeenth Century,* i, ch. 11, and ii, ch. 2; Akagi, R. H., *The Town Proprietors of the New England Colonies;* MacLear, Anne B., *Early New England Towns* (1908); Egleston, Melville, *The Land System of the New England Colonies* [Johns Hopkins *Studies,* 4th series, 1883]; Ford, Amelia C., *Colonial Precedents of Our National Land System as It Existed in 1800* [University of Wisconsin *Bulletin, Historical Series,* 1910, ii]; and Bond, B. W., *The Quit Rent System in the American Colonies* (1919). If other references are desired, they can be found by consulting Schmidt, L. B., *Topical Studies and References on the Economic History of American Agriculture* (1919, 1940), chs. 3-7, and parts of 9-10; and Edwards, E. E., *A Bibliography of the History of Agriculture in the United States* (1930).

We have an excellent contemporary account of American agriculture at the end of the colonial period by a competent English observer who traveled through the English continental colonies and wrote

Special studies

Sources

down his impressions as to agricultural conditions. His observations were published in a work entitled *American Husbandry*, 2 vols. (1775; reprinted in 1939 under the editorship of H. J. Carman). The author of this interesting work is unknown, but its value is beyond question. Excerpts from *American Husbandry* and other sources are given in *Readings in the Economic History of the United States* by E. L. Bogart and C. M. Thompson, pp. 28-41; and H. J. Carman's *Social and Economic History of the United States*, i, ch. 2. A few documents on colonial agriculture are also scattered through the first volume of the *Documentary History of American Industrial Society*, edited by J. R. Commons, U. B. Phillips, and others. For these sources, see pp. 109-115, 186-191, 245-251, 293-298, 300-307, 309, 319-322, 324-329, 339-374. An easily accessible collection of documents is Schmidt, L. B., and Ross, E. D., eds., *Readings in the Economic History of American Agriculture* (1925). For lists of manuscript sources on land systems, see Greene and Morris's *Guide*, pp. 224-239; on agriculture, pp. 273-274.

CHAPTER XXII.—COLONIAL INDUSTRY

Secondary authorities: General works

THE best work on colonial manufactures for the special student is V. S. Clark's *History of Manufactures in the United States*, 3 vols. (1939; scholarly; specific references to sources; lengthy bibliography; chs. 1-9 on the colonial era; ch. 10 on the Revolutionary period). There are also some older works that have not been entirely superseded by later publications. These are: Bolles, A. S., *Industrial History of the United States* (1887); Bishop, J. L., *A History of American Manufactures from 1609 to 1860*, 3 vols. (1866; gives an immense amount of valuable information so arranged as to be easily found by the student of any special topic); and Kettel, T. P., ed., *Eighty Years' Progress in the United States*. Good short accounts are: Keir, Malcolm, *The Epic of Industry* [*Pageant of America*], chs. 1 and 2 (1926; a great number of valuable pictures showing how the homespun and other industries were carried on); Wells, L. R., *Industrial History of the United States*, chs. 1-6 (1922, 1926; readable); Forman, S. E., *The Rise of American Commerce and Industry* (1927; first hundred pages on colonial and Revolutionary periods); and the chapters on colonial industry in the American economic histories listed on p. 760.

Special works

Other works of value for the special student are: Durfee, William F., "Early Steps in Iron Manufacturing" [*Popular Science Monthly*, xxxviii, pp. 145-172]; Tryon, R. M., *Household Manufactures in the United States, 1640-1860* (1917; scholarly; numerous specific references to sources in footnotes; also a number of quotations from contemporary accounts and other documents; the best authority on the subject; first three chapters on the colonial period); Bagnall, W. R.,

The Textile Industries of the United States (1893), i; Ballagh, J. C.,
ed., [*Southern*] *Economic History* [*The South in the Building of the
Nation*, v], pp. 299-312 (article on colonial manufactures by V. S.
Clark); Lord, E. L., *Industrial Experiments in the British Colonies
of North America* [Johns Hopkins *Studies,* 17th series]; Bining,
A. C., *British Regulation of the Colonial Iron Industry* (1933); and
Wright, Carroll, D., *The Industrial Evolution of the United States*
(1897, 1902), chs. 1-8. P. A. Bruce, in his *Economic History of
Virginia in the 17th Century,* and W. B. Weeden, in his *Economic
and Social History of New England,* give a good deal of valuable
information regarding industries in Virginia and New England,
respectively.

The authorities on whaling and fishing, in general, are: McFarland,
Raymond, *A History of the New England Fisheries* (1911; scholarly,
with some references to sources in footnotes; too long and detailed
except for the special student); Spears, J. R., *The Story of the New
England Whalers; A History of American Whale Fishing* [University
of Pennsylvania *Studies,* no. 23]; Chatterton, E. K., *Whalers and
Whaling* (1931); and Hohman, E. P., *The American Whalemen*
(1928), ch. 2. Of the other monographs on special phases of industry,
the following should be mentioned: Pearse, J. B., *A Concise History
of the Iron Manufacture of the American Colonies up to the Revolution* (1876); Abbott, Edith, *Women in Industry* (1910); Abbott,
W. J., *American Ships and Sailors;* Dexter, *Elizabeth, Colonial
Women of Affairs* (1924); and Hazard, B. E., *The Organization of
the Boot and Shoe Industry in Massachusetts Before 1875* (1921; the
first chapter and part of the second on the colonial period).

There are no large collections of sources on colonial industry. The Sources
scattered source materials can be found by the special student by
following the directions in the reference notes indicated in the fuller
works mentioned above. Short contemporary accounts are given in
Bogart, E. L., and Thompson, C. M., *Readings in the Economic History of the United States* (1916), pp. 42-81; Callender, G. S., *Selections from the Economic History of the United States* (1909), pp. 29-
44; Commons, J. R., Phillips, U. B., and others, eds., *Documentary
History of American Industrial Society,* ii, pp. 169-176, 314-328,
350-352. For manuscript sources for industry, see Greene and
Morris's *Guide,* pp. 269-273; and H. J. Carman's *Social and
Economic History of the United States,* i, ch. 3.

CHAPTER XXIII.—TRANSPORTATION AND TRADE

WE HAVE no full account of the roads in colonial days. Seymour Travel
Dunbar, in his *History of Travel in America,* 4 vols. (1915), devotes

some space in the first part of the first volume to colonial roads, but the treatment is inadequate. W. B. Weeden, in his *Economic and Social History of New England, 1620-1789,* 2 vols., gives considerable attention to transportation and commerce, as does also P. A. Bruce, in his *Economic History of Virginia in the Seventeenth Century,* 2 vols. *The Vade Mecum for America,* or a *Companion for Traders and Travelers,* published in 1732, describes the principal roads at that time from the mouth of the Kennebec River to the James River in Virginia. A list of these roads, with names of the towns through which they passed and the name of a tavern in each town, is given on pp. 195-203. There are several interesting accounts of the colonial tavern which incidentally give us information regarding methods of travel. Of these the following are readable: Field, Edward, *The Colonial Tavern* (1897; no specific references to documents, but numerous quotations from the documents; deals only with New England); Earle, Alice M., *Stage Coach and Tavern Days* (1900; frequent quotations from the sources); Crawford, Mary C., *Little Pilgrimages Among New England Inns* (1907); Lathrop, Elsie, *Early American Inns and Taverns* (1926, 1935); and Bayles, W. H., *Old Taverns of New York* (1915).

The colonial post office   An excellent brief account of the colonial post office, both scholarly and interesting, is an article by William Smith, entitled "The Colonial Post-Office," in the *American Historical Review,* xxi, pp. 258-275; a fuller account by the same author is found in the *History of the Post-Office in British North America* (1920), chs. 1-2. For a later discussion, see Harlow, A. F., *Old Post Bags* (1928), chs. 14-16. Two scholarly works are: Rich, W. E., *The History of the United States Post Office to the Year 1829* (1924; pp. 3-60 deal with the period prior to 1783); and Woolley, Mary E., *Early History of the Colonial Post-Office* [Rhode Island Historical Society *Publications*] (1893-1894), pp. 270-291. For a list of other authorities, see Rich, *op. cit.,* pp. 173-179. A valuable source is the *Journal* kept by Hugh Finlay. (For an account of this *Journal* see text, p. 480, note 16.) Other source materials can be found in the *Official Letters* of Alexander Spotswood [*Collections* of the Virginia Historical Society, n.s., i and ii]; and the *Writings* of Benjamin Franklin, 10 vols., edited by A. H. Smyth. There are also numerous references to other sources in the footnotes in the works by Rich, Smith, and Woolley.

Commerce   The best work on colonial commerce is the *History of Domestic and Foreign Commerce of the United States,* 2 vols. (1915), edited by Emory R. Johnson and others and published by the Carnegie Institution of Washington. There are a number of specific references in the footnotes, though these are not all to primary sources. The period to 1783 is covered in chs. 1-8 and 10-11 of the first volume. Short discussions can be found in Day, C., *History of Commerce* (1907);

Andrews, C. M., *Colonial Self-Government* [*American Nation Series*], ch. 19; Greene, E. B., *Provincial America* [same series], ch. 17; Keir, M., *The March of Commerce* [*Pageant of America*] (1927), ch. 2 (pictures); and the economic histories listed on p. 760. An elaborate and scholarly treatise on colonial commerce, with emphasis on its relation to the American Revolution, is A. M. Schlesinger's *The Colonial Merchants and the American Revolution* (1918). There are two good articles by C. M. Andrews in the *American Historical Review*, 1914-1915, xx; these are "Colonial Commerce," pp. 43-63, and "Anglo-French Commercial Rivalry, 1700-1750," pp. 539-556, 761-780. The first is largely interpretative and there are no references to sources; the second is well documented in both installments. For the West Indian trade see Pares, Richard, *War and Trade in the West Indies, 1739-1763* (1936); Pitman, F. W., *The Development of the British West Indies, 1700-1763* (1917), chs. 9, 11-14; and Bell, H. C., "The West Indian Trade Before the American Revolution," *American Historical Review*, xxii, pp. 272-287.

The merchant marine of the colonies is discussed in W. L. Marvin's *The American Merchant Marine* and G. F. Dow's *The Sailing Ships of New England* (1922). For the fur trade, see the following: Vandiver, C. A., *The Fur-Trade and Early Western Exploration* (1929), chs. 1-10; Crane, V. W., *The Southern Frontier, 1670-1732*; and Stevens, W. E., *The Northwest Fur Trade, 1763-1800* [University of Illinois *Studies in the Social Sciences*, xiv] (1928), chs. 1-3. — Merchant marine and the fur trade

For source readings on colonial commerce, see *Readings in the Economic History of the United States* by E. L. Bogart and C. M. Thompson, pp. 69-81, 96-106; Callender, G. S., *Selections from the Economic History of the United States, 1765-1860*, pp. 51-68; Hart, A. B., *American History Told by Contemporaries*, ii, ch. 13; and Jameson, J. F., ed., *Privateers and Piracy in the Colonial Period*. — Source readings

The financial experience of our country prior to 1789 is outlined in the first three chapters of D. R. Dewey's *Financial History of the United States* (1936 ed.). A fuller and much better discussion of colonial finance (up to 1720) is given in the authoritative work of C. P. Nettels, *The Money Supply of the American Colonies Before 1720* (1934). Works that may be useful for the special student are: Bezanson, Anne, and others, *Prices in Colonial Pennsylvania* (1935); Davis, A. McF., *Currency and Banking in the Province of Massachusetts Bay* [American Economic Association *Publications*, 1900-1901, ii, part ii]; Bruce, P. A., *Economic History of Virginia in the Seventeenth Century*, ii, ch. 19 (an excellent account of the medium of exchange in Virginia); Bullock, C. J., *Essays on the Monetary History of the United States* (1900; good for North Carolina and New Hampshire); and Phillips, Henry, Jr., *Historical Sketches of the Paper Money of the Colonies* (1865-1866). A. McF. Davis's *Colonial* — Colonial currency

Currency Reprints, 1682-1751, 4 vols. (1910-1911), is a valuable collection of documents. Some source material on this topic can be found in E. L. Bogart and C. M. Thompson's *Readings in the Economic History of the United States*, pp. 96-105. For manuscript sources on commerce, see Greene and Morris's *Guide*, pp. 247-269.

CHAPTER XXIV.—IMPERIAL SUPERVISION OF THE COLONIES

Secondary authorities VERY readable and scholarly discussions of the policy of the home government in dealing with the colonies will be found in G. L. Beer's works. These are: *The Origins of the British Colonial System, 1578-1660* (1908, 1933); *The Old Colonial System, 1660-1754*, 2 vols. (1912); *British Colonial Policy, 1754-1765* (1907); and *Commercial Policy of England Toward the American Colonies* (1893). See also Osgood, H. L., *American Colonies in the Seventeenth Century*, iii, chs. 1, 3, 5-7, and *Eighteenth Century*, i, chs. 1, 4-6. Other useful works are: Andrews, C. M., *Colonial Self-Government*, chs. 1 and 2; and *British Commissions, and Councils of Trade and Plantations, 1622-1657* [Johns Hopkins *Studies*, 26th series]; Egerton, H. E., *A Short History of British Colonial Policy*, chs. 1-9, and *Colonial Administration of Crown Colonies in the Seventeenth Century* [Royal Historical Society *Transactions*, 4th series, i, pp. 190 *et seq.*]: Dickerson, O. M., *American Colonial Government, 1696-1765* (1912; a study of the British Board of Trade in its relation to the American colonies; scholarly; well documented with specific references to sources); Biebe, Ralph P., *The Lords of Trade and Plantations, 1675-1696* (1919; numerous specific references to sources); and Basye, A. H., *The Board of Trade, 1748-1782* [Yale University *Historical Publications*] (1925; scholarly; the best single work on the Board of Trade).

Imperial administration of the colonies For the part played by the colonial agent in the administration of colonial affairs, see three scholarly and authoritative works: Burns, J. J., *The Colonial Agents of New England* (1935); E. P. Lilly's *The Colonial Agents of New York and New Jersey* (1936); and Ella Lonn's *The Colonial Agents of the Southern Colonies* (1945). Other references that should be listed are: Kaye, P. L., *English Colonial Administration Under Lord Clarendon, 1660-1667* [Johns Hopkins *Studies*, 23rd series]; Greene, E. B., *The Provincial Governor* and *Provincial America*, chs. 2-4; Root, W. T., *Relations of Pennsylvania with the British Government* (1912), chs. 1-6, and "Lords of Trade and Plantations," *American Historical Review*, xxiii, pp. 20-41; Hurst, G. B., *The Old Colonial System* (1905); Adams, J. T., *Revolutionary New England*, chs. 2 and 4; Becker, C., *Beginnings of the American People*, pp. 134-160 and ch. 5; McClellan, W. S., *Smuggling in the American Colonies at the Outbreak of the American Revolution*

(1912); Guttredge, G. H., *The Colonial Policy of William III in America and the West Indies* (1922; detailed; specific references to sources; summary, pp. 179-181); Russell, Elmer B., *The Review of American Colonial Legislation by the King in Council* [Columbia University *Studies*] (1915; numerous specific references to sources); Washburne, G. A., *Imperial Control of the Administration of Justice in the Thirteen American Colonies, 1684-1776* (1923; references to primary sources); Hazeltine, H. D., *Appeals from the Colonial Courts to the King in Council, with special reference to Rhode Island* (1896); Crump, Helen J., *Colonial Admiralty Jurisdiction in the Seventeenth Century* (1931); Schmoller, Gustav, *The Mercantile System and Its Historical Significance* (1896, 1931); and Pitman, F. W., *The Development of the British West Indies, 1700-1763* (1917), chs. 9, 11-14. On the Privy Council, see E. R. Turner's *The Privy Council, 1603-1784*, 2 vols. (1927-1928).

There are a number of magazine articles that discuss certain phases of this general subject. Some of these are: Ashley, W. J., "The Commercial Legislation of England and the American Colonies, 1660-1760," *Quarterly Journal of Economics*, xiv, pp. 1-29; Andrews, Charles M., "Colonial Commerce," *American Historical Review*, xx, pp. 43-63; Bell, H. C., "The West Indian Trade Before the American Revolution," *American Historical Review*, xxii, pp. 272-287; McGovney, D. O., "The Navigation Acts as Applied to European Trade," *American Historical Review*, ix, pp. 725-734; Kellogg, L. P., "The American Colonial Charter," *Annual Report* of the American Historical Association, 1903, i, pp. 187-341; and Tanner, E. P., "Colonial Agencies in England during the Eighteenth Century," *Political Science Quarterly*, xvi, pp. 24-49. For other works of this character, see Jernegan, M. W., *The American Colonies*, pp. 242-244.

Magazine articles

Most of the sources on the subject of this chapter are not easily accessible, but the serious-minded student can find his way to them by following the directions in the footnotes of the above-mentioned authorities. A discussion of the topic by a well-informed contemporary is Thomas Pownall's *The Administration of the British Colonies* (1777). See also Jeremiah Dummer's *A Defence of the New England Charters* (first published in 1721). Useful brief collections of documents are: Hart, A. B., *American History Told by Contemporaries*, ii, ch. 7; and Bogart, E. L., and Thompson, C. M., *Readings in the Economic History of the United States*, ch. 4. Larger collections are: Brigham, C. S., "British Royal Proclamations Relating to America, 1603-1783" [*Transactions and Collections* of the American Antiquarian Society, xii]; Grant, W. E., ed., *Acts of the Privy Council, Colonial; Journal of the Commission for Trade and Plantations* (the Board of Trade), 5 vols. (1933-1936); and Stock, L. F., ed., *Proceedings and Debates of the British Parliament Respecting North*

Sources

America, 5 vols. (1924-1941; 6th vol. in preparation). The Navigation Acts are given, in part, in W. MacDonald's *Select Charters*, nos. 22, 23, 25, 28, 34, 43, 50, 56. For specific references to the full text of these acts, see footnotes for this chapter. For lists of collections of English statutes and other British documents, see Hart, Channing, and Turner's *Guide*, p. 130. For guides to source materials in foreign archives, see *ibid.*, p. 181.

Chapter XXV.—Organization of the Colonial Church

Secondary authorities: Denominational histories

THE best single volume on the colonial church is William W. Sweet's *Religion in Colonial America* (1942). There is also a brief discussion of colonial religion by the same author in *The Story of Religions in America* (1931). A detailed history of the various denominations is given in *The American Church History* Series, 13 vols. (1893-1897; a coöperative work). The first nine volumes and the last one are of value to the student of the colonial period. An extended bibliography is given in each volume, but there is no appraisal of the various works listed. In the last volume, *A History of American Christianity* by L. W. Bacon, chs. 1-12 present a general discussion of the colonial church. Each of the following denominational histories devotes considerable space to the period prior to 1789: Manross, William W., *A History of the American Episcopal Church* (1935; largely on the colonial period); McConnell, S. D., *History of the American Episcopal Church* (1916; readable and scholarly); Corwin, E. T., *History of the Dutch Reformed Church* (1895); Dexter, H. M., *The Congregationalism of the Last Three Hundred Years* (1880); Walker, Williston, *History of the Congregational Churches in the United States* (1894); Briggs, C. A., *American Presbyterianism; Its Origin and Early History* (an excellent work; number of documents in the appendix); Newman, A. H., *A History of the Baptist Churches in the United States* (1894); Maynard, Theodore, *The Story of American Catholicism* (1941, 1943; the best single volume on the history of American Catholicism; first nine chapters on the period to 1783); and Sweet, W. W., *Methodism in American History* (1933).

Of the denominational histories that are concerned with the colonial and Revolutionary periods alone, the following should be mentioned: Anderson, J. S. M., *The History of the Church of England in the Colonies and Foreign Dependencies of the British Empire*, 3 vols. (1845; specific citations to authorities and sources, and some documents in the appendices; an interesting book of value); Goodwin, E. L., *The Colonial Church in Virginia* (1927; a friendly view; scholarly; numerous references to the sources and some quotations from the documents) ; Jones, R. M., *The Quakers in the American Colonies* (1911) ; Qualben, Lars P., *The Lutheran Church in Colonial America* (1940) ; and Shea, J. G., *The Catholic Church in Colonial Days* (1886).

For full discussions of certain aspects of colonial religion, see the following works: Cross, A. L., *The Anglican Episcopate and the American Colonies* [*Harvard Studies*, ix] (1902; specific references to sources; documents in the appendix) ; Hallowell, R. P., *Quaker Invasion of Massachusetts* (1883, 1884) ; Gates, Everett, *Religious Liberty in Massachusetts* (1905) ; Greene, M. L., *The Development of Religious Liberty in Connecticut* (1905) ; Zwierlein, E. J., *Religion in New Netherland*; Bittner, L. F., *German Religious Life in Colonial Times*; Walker, G. L., *Some Aspects of the Religious Life of New England*; Meade, (Bishop) William, *Old Churches, Ministers, and Families of Virginia* (1857) ; Byington, E. H., *The Puritan in England and New England* (1896) ; Platner, J. W., and others, *Religious Life of New England*; Morgan, Edmund S., *The Puritan Family: Essays on Religion and Domestic Relations in Seventeenth Century New England* (1944) ; Miller, Perry, *Orthodoxy in Massachusetts, 1630-1650* (1933; explains why Congregationalism was established) ; Earle, Alice M., *The Sabbath in Puritan New England* (1891) ; Murdock, K. B., *Increase Mather* (1925; friendly to Puritanism; scholarly) ; Boas, R. P., and L. S., *Cotton Mather, Keeper of the Puritan Conscience* (1928) ; Wendell, B., *Cotton Mather, the Puritan Priest* (1891, 1926) ; Child, F. S., *The Colonial Parson of New England* (1896) ; Felt, J. B., *Ecclesiastical History of New England*, 2 vols. (1855-1862) ; Hawks, F. L., *Contributions to the Ecclesiastical History of the United States*, 2 vols. (1836-1839).

A scholarly and readable account of religious conditions in colonial New England is given in the *Religious History of New England* [*King's Chapel Lectures*] (a collection of articles contributed by several authors). Useful works on the relation of church and state are: S. H. Cobb's *The Rise of Religious Liberty in America* (1902; specific references to sources and authorities) ; and James, J. F., *Documentary History of the Struggle for Religious Liberty in Virginia* (1900; numerous quotations from documents; valuable; mainly on the Baptists). For relation of the churches to the Revolution, E. F. Humphrey's *Nationalism and Religion in America* is useful (1774-1789; citations to and extracts from the sources). Numerous pictures illustrative of the religious history of the colonial and Revolutionary periods are given in L. A. Weigle's *American Idealism* [*Pageant of America*] (1928), chs. 2-5.

A number of monographs bearing on the colonial church have been published in the Johns Hopkins University *Studies in Historical and Political Science*. These scholarly studies give specific citations to

Special topics

Monographs

sources and quote at length from the documents. They are: Lauer, P. E., *Church and State in New England* (10th series); Weeks, S. B., *Religious Development in the Province of North Carolina* (10th series); Petrie, George, *Church and State in Maryland* (10th series); Weeks, S. B., *Church and State in North Carolina* (11th series); and McIlwaine, H. R., *The Struggle of Protestant Dissenters for Religious Freedom in Virginia* (12th series). For other authorities, see Wertenbaker, T. J., *The First Americans*, pp. 325-328.

Sources   The source materials for the history of the colonial church are scattered throughout a number of books and collections. Of these the following are of value: Cornelison, I. A., *The Relation of Religion to Civil Government in the United States of America* (mostly excerpts from the laws and charters; pp. 1-88 deal with the colonial period); Hawks, F. L., and Perry, W. S., *Documentary History of the Protestant Episcopal Church in the United States of America*, 2 vols. (1863-1864; covers the period to 1789); Perry, W. S., ed., *Historical Collections Relating to the American Colonial Episcopal Church*, 5 vols.; Dillon, John B., *Oddities of Colonial Legislation in America*, pp. 21-103; and *Ecclesiastical Records of the State of New York*, 7 vols., including one volume of index, published by the state (this is a voluminous collection devoted mostly to the colonial and Revolutionary periods). Accounts by contemporary writers: Mather, Cotton, *Magnalia Christi Americana*, or *The Ecclesiastical History of New England*, 2 vols.; first published in 1702 (it is both a civil and an ecclesiastical history of New England, with numerous biographies of governors, ministers, and other prominent men; should be read with caution, as it is thoroughly uncritical); Bishop, George, *New England Judged by the Spirit of the Lord* (1703; an indictment of the Puritan oligarchy by a Quaker); Gummere, Amelia M., *The Journal and Essays of John Woolman* (1720-1722); Johnson, E., *Wonder-Working Providence of Sion's Savior, or a History of New England* [*Original Narratives*] (a defense of Puritanism); and Backus, Isaac, *A History of New England*, 3 vols., with particular reference to the Baptists and their persecutions (1777-1796; a two-volume edition was published in 1871).

A fine collection of documents illustrative of the life of the early New England Puritans is *The Puritans*, compiled by Perry Miller and Thomas H. Johnson (1938; excerpts from the writings of Puritan leaders). A good deal of information regarding the beliefs and practices of the New England Puritans can also be gleaned from the diaries of Samuel Sewall and Cotton Mather. The diary of the former, who was a typical Puritan layman, is given in the Massachusetts Historical Society *Collections*, 5th series, v-vii; the diary of the latter, who was a typical Congregationalist minister of the later seventeenth century, is also published in the *Collections*, 7th series, vii-viii. Numerous extracts from Mather's diary are also given in Barrett Wendell's *Cotton Mather*.

For other primary sources, see Allison, W. H., *Inventory of Unpublished Materials for American Religious History in Protestant Church Archives and Other Repositories* (1910) ; Mode, P. G., ed., *Source Book and Bibliographical Guide for American Church History* (1920; excerpts from the documents and numerous citations to the sources) ; and Schneider, H. W., *The Puritan Mind* (1930). An excellent appraisal of both primary and secondary authorities is given in J. N. Larned's *Literature of American History,* pp. 337-357. Greene and Morris's *Guide* lists printed sources (pp. 4-5) and manuscript materials (pp. 279-313).

CHAPTER XXVI.—THE DECLINE AND REVIVAL OF RELIGION

MANY of the works, both primary and secondary, listed in the Bibliographical Notes for the preceding chapter apply to this chapter also. In addition to these, the following references should be given: Winslow, Ola E., *Jonathan Edwards, 1703-1758: A Biography* (1940; "by far the most complete and scholarly account of Edwards's career") ; Allen, A. V. G., *Jonathan Edwards* (1889) ; Sweet, W. W., *Revivalism in America: Its Origin, Growth and Decline* (1944) ; Osgood, H. L., *The American Colonies in the Eighteenth Century,* iii, pp. 407-451 ; Tracy, Joseph, *The Great Awakening* (1842) ; Maxson, C. H., *The Great Awakening in the Middle Colonies* (1920; the bibliography contains a long list of titles with no attempt at appraisal) ; and Gewehr, W. M., *The Great Awakening in Virginia, 1740-1790* (1929; good account, really a religious history of Virginia for this period). For other references see footnotes and Selected Readings for this chapter. *(margin: The Great Awakening)*

The best contemporary account of the Great Revival is *The Christian History,* edited by Thomas Prince, 1744-1745 (a weekly publication detailing the events of the revival). Jonathan Edwards in his *Conversions in New England* gives an account of a number of conversions during the Great Awakening. This work is also a defense against the criticisms of the revival. See also A. Wright's *Life and Character of Jonathan Edwards* (1764; gives Edwards's diary and extracts from his writings, including seventeen select sermons). To get the point of view of those who were opposed to the movement, the works of Charles Chauncey should be consulted. These are: *Enthusiasm Described and Cautioned Against* (1742) ; *A Letter from a Gentleman in Boston to Mr. Geo. Wishart* (1742) ; and *Some Seasonable Thoughts on the State of Religion in New England* (1743). *(margin: Sources)*

The
Negro
Church

Religious conditions among the Negroes in colonial days are well discussed in Carter G. Woodson's *The History of the Negro Church* (1921; pp. 1-22 on the colonial period; a good readable account without references to the sources).

CHAPTER XXVII.—INTELLECTUAL LIFE

Secondary
authori-
ties:
General
accounts

ALL OF the general histories of education in the United States listed on p. 761 devote some space to intellectual conditions in the colonies. Any one of these accounts is a good starting-point for the study of colonial education.

Special
studies

There are a number of special studies on various phases of intellectual life in the colonies. Of these the following should be listed: Earle, Alice M., *Child Life in Colonial Days* (1899), chs. 3-6; Wright, T. G., *Literary Culture in Early New England, 1620-1730* (1920; numerous quotations from and citations to the sources); Martin, G. H., *The Evolution of the Massachusetts Public School System* (1894), chs. 1-2; Carroll, Charles, *Public Education in Rhode Island* (1918; first chapter on colonial period; scholarly but too statistical for the general reader; good summaries and general statements, pp. 13-16, 33-36); Jackson, George L., *School Support in Colonial Massachusetts* [Columbia University *Contributions to Education,* Teachers College series, no. 25] (scholarly, but too detailed except for the special student; good summaries and generalizations, pp. 32-33); Woody, Thomas, *Early Quaker Education in Pennsylvania* [same series, no. 10] (scholarly, but too voluminous and detailed for general reading; good summaries, pp. 172-176, 268-271), and *Quaker Education in the Colony and State of New Jersey* (1923; a source book); Kemp, W. W,. *The Support of Schools in Colonial New York by the Society for the Progagation of the Gospel in Foreign Parts,* no. 16 (1913; a useful study); Small, Walter H., *Early New England Schools* (1914; detailed; numerous quotations from the sources; almost a source book); Brown, E. F., *The Making of Our Middle Schools* (1903, 1907), chs. 1-9; Clews, Elsie W., *Educational Legislation and Administration of the Colonial Governments* (1899; quotes at length from the documents; covers all the colonies except Georgia; valuable for advanced students doing intensive work); Meriwether, Colyer, *Colonial Curriculum* (1907); Knight, E. W., *Public Education in the South* (1921; first three chapters on colonial period, good summaries at the beginning of chapters, also pp. 40-44); Heatwole, C. J., *History of Education in Virginia* (1916; interesting); Wells, G. F., *Parish Education in Colonial Virginia* (1923); Kilpatrick, William H., *The Dutch Schools of New Netherland and Colonial New York* (1912); Bruce, P. A., *Institutional History of Virginia in the Seventeenth Century,* i, part ii;

Grizzell, Emil D., *Origin and Development of the High School in New England Before 1865* (1923; some quotations from the sources; pp. 1-27 an excellent account of the Latin Grammar school); and Raper, C. L., *The Church and Private Schools of North Carolina* (1904).

See also articles in the *School Review* by M. W. Jernegan, xxvi, pp. 731-749; xxvii, pp. 27-43, 360-376, 405-425; xxviii, pp. 127-142 (these articles are scholarly, and of interest to those who are making an intensive study of the subject).

The United States Bureau of Education, under the editorship of H. B. Adams, publshed a series of monographs under the general title *Contributions to American Educational History*. Of the monographs in this series, which cover most of the colonies, the following should be mentioned: Adams, H. B., *The College of William and Mary*, no. 1; Steiner, B. C., *The History of Education in Connecticut*, no. 14 (first part of the work deals with Yale College and the primary and secondary schools of colonial Connecticut); Bush, G. G., *The History of Higher Education in Massachusetts*, no. 13; Tolman, W. H., *History of Higher Education in Rhode Island*, no. 18; Steiner, B. C., *History of Education in Maryland*, no. 19; Smith, C. L., *The History of Education in North Carolina*, ii, no. 4 (pp. 13-27 on colonial period; fine account). The appendix of this volume, pp. 211-235, contains a discussion by Edward McCrady which corrects some mistaken notions regarding educational conditions in South Carolina during the colonial and Revolutionary periods. *(margin: Monographs)*

Good readable accounts of the colonial colleges are given in C. F. Thwing's *A History of Higher Education in America*. An excellent account of Harvard in the early period is given by S. E. Morison in his definitive works: *The Founding of Harvard College* (1935) and *Harvard College in the Seventeenth Century* (1936). The best history of Princeton is T. J. Wertenbaker's *Princeton, 1746-1896* (1946). There are no definitive histories of William and Mary and of Yale. Good brief but old accounts can be found in the works of Adams and Steiner mentioned in the preceding paragraph. See also Edwin Oviatt's *The Beginnings of Yale, 1701-1726* (1916). For short accounts of the other colleges see Selected Readings, pp. 576-577. *(margin: The colonial college)*

For insight into the intellectual attitude of the colonials the following works may prove helpful: Miller, Perry, *The New England Mind: The Seventeenth Century* (1939); and Hall, T. C., *Religious Background of American Culture* (1930; an extensive bibliography). *(margin: Intellectual attitude of the colonials)*

Excellent short accounts of colonial literature are given in Bliss Perry's *The American Spirit in Literature* [*Chronicles of America*] (1918; written in an interesting and even brilliant style); and W. P. Trent's *A History of American Literature, 1607-1805* (1903; pp. 1-186 on the colonial and Revolutionary periods). A work of great value *(margin: Literature)* to both the general reader and the special student is S. T. Williams's *The American Spirit in Letters* [*Pageant of America*] (1925; chs. 1-3 on the colonial and Revolutionary periods; readable; the numerous reproductions of contemporary portraits and other old pictures make it a source book). For fuller discussions, see Trent, W. P., and others, eds., *The Cambridge History of American Literature*, 8 vols. (1917-1921; vol. i on colonial and Revolutionary periods); Tyler, M. C., *A History of American Literature, 1607-1765*, 2 vols. (1878-1879); Parrington, V. C., *The Colonial Mind, 1620-1800* (1927), vol. i of *Currents in American Thought* (brilliantly written; a literary masterpiece; fine characterization of men); and Wendell, B., *A Literary History of America* (1901, 1928), i and ii. See also the following biographies of colonial writers: Winslow, Ola E., *Jonathan Edwards, 1703-1758;* and Van Doren, Carl, *Benjamin Franklin* (1938).

Newspapers   For the colonial newspaper see: McMurtrie, Douglas C., *A History of Printing in the United States* (1936); Kobre, Sidney, *The Development of the Colonial Newspaper* (1944); Mott, Frank L., *American Journalism* (1941; first five chapters to 1783); Cook, Elizabeth C., *Literary Influences in Colonial Newspapers, 1704-1750* [Columbia University *Studies in English and Comparative Literature*] (1912); Weeks, S. B., *The Press of North Carolina in the Eighteenth Century* (1891); Richardson, L. N., *A History of Early American Magazines, 1741-1789* (1931); and Schuyler, L. R., *The Liberty of the Press in the American Colonies Before the Revolutionary War* (1905), with special reference to New York. C. A. Duniway's *The Development of the Freedom of the Press in Massachusetts* [*Harvard Historical Studies*, 1916, xii] is the best history of the freedom of the press that we have. For a discussion of the Zenger Case, see L. A. Rutherfurd's *John Peter Zenger, His Press, His Trial, and a Bibliography of Zenger Imprints* (1904). For lists of colonial newspapers now extant, see Channing, Hart, and Turner's *Guide*, pp. 126-127; *Check List of American Newspapers in the Library of Congress*, compiled by A. B. Slosson; and Greene and Morris's *Guide*, pp. 56-84.

Libraries   The only general account of public libraries in colonial days is H. E. Scudder's *Public Libraries a Hundred Years Ago* [*Public Libraries in the United States*, 1876, part i]. For a list of other works on colonial libraries, see Adams, J. T., *Provincial Society*, p. 34, and Jernegan, M. W., *The American Colonies*, p. 386.

Bibliography   For an appraisal of works published prior to 1899, see J. N. Larned's *Literature of American History*, pp. 331-337.

Sources: Colleges   As has already been indicated, considerable source material can be found in some of the secondary authorities listed above, and references in the footnotes indicate numerous other sources. Aside from these, there are no important collections of source materials that are easily accessible. A. B. Hart's *American History Told by Contemporaries*, ii, ch. 13, gives a few excerpts from colonial writings on intellectual life. *The William and Mary College Historical Quarterly* (1st series), ii-iii, v-vii, gives some valuable primary information regarding educational conditions in Virginia. The *Journal* of the Meetings of the President and Masters of William and Mary College is given in vols. i-v, xiii-xv. Franklin B. Dexter's *Documentary History of Yale University, 1701-1745,* gives the principal documents relating to the history of Yale to 1745. The Colonial Society of Massachusetts has published two volumes of *Harvard College Records* [*Corporation Records,* 1636-1750] that are of value to the special student. Josiah Quincy's *History of Harvard University,* 2 vols. (1840, 1860), gives a good deal of documentary material in the appendices.

First-hand information regarding the earliest newspapers can be had from *An Historical Digest of the Provincial Press* by L. H. Weeks and E. H. Bacon (1911). This work is a very ambitious one in purpose for it was planned to give an "exact reproduction of the text of the American newspapers, other than their reprints of foreign intelligence in the English journals," from the appearance of the first American newspaper to 1783. The first series is to cover the Massachusetts press. Unfortunately, however, as yet only one volume of the first series has appeared and it covers only the period from 1689 to 1707. Extracts from the newspapers of colonial South Carolina are given in W. L. King's *The Newspaper Press of Charleston, South Carolina* (1872), chs. 1-3. Vols, xi, xii, xix of the *Archives of the State of New Jersey* (1st series) are given over entirely to extracts from newspapers. A useful guide to the colonial newspapers is C. S. Brigham's *Bibliography of American Newspapers, 1690-1820,* 6 vols. (1913-1929). Newspapers

For manuscript materials on the intellectual life of the colonists, see Greene and Morris's *Guide,* pp. 313-328.

CHAPTER XXVIII.—MANNERS AND CUSTOMS

AN EXCELLENT short account of colonial life is given in C. M. Andrews's *Colonial Folkways* [*Chronicles of America*] (1919). This little volume is scholarly and readable, but is without specific references to sources. This lack is partially compensated for by an extended bibliography of both primary and secondary authorities. An older work, written in attractive and readable style, is Edward Eggleston's *Transit of Civilization* (1901). Fuller than either of these are *The First Americans, 1607-1690,* by T. J. Wertenbaker, *Provincial Society, 1690-1763,* by J. T. Adams, and *The Revolutionary Generation, 1763-1790,* by E. B. Greene (1943). These three volumes [*A History of American Life,* ii-iv] are scholarly, give specific references to sources, and contain bibliographies. An interesting collection of books on Secondary authorities colonial life are the works of Mrs. Alice Morse Earle. They give numerous extracts from the sources and include the following titles: *Two Centuries of Costume in America*, 2 vols. (1903; numerous reproductions of contemporary portraits showing the styles of dress); *Costume of Colonial Times* (1894); *Colonial Days in Old New York* (1896); *Customs and Fashions in Old New England* (1893); *Child Life in Colonial Days* (1899); *Colonial Dames and Good Wives* (1895); *Home Life in Colonial Days* (1898); and *Stage Coach and Tavern Days* (1900).

Other works concerned with colonial life in general are: Langdon, W. C., *Everyday Things in American Life*, 2 vols. (1937; first volume, 1776-1876; a valuable work; good pictures); Calhoun, A. W., *Social History of the American Family*, 3 vols. (1917-1919; the first volume covers the period to 1776; readable and scholarly; specific references to sources and a lengthy bibliography); Fisher, S. G., *Men, Women, and Manners in Colonial Times*, 2 vols. (1898); Dexter, Elizabeth A., *Colonial Women of Affairs* (1931; specific references to and numerous extracts from the sources); Holliday, Carl, *Woman's Life in Colonial Days* (1921; readable; numerous quotations from the sources); McClellan, Elizabeth, *History of American Costume, 1607-1870* (1904, 1937), and *Historic Dress in America, 1607-1800* (1904; numerous pictures showing styles of dress); Wharton, Anne H., *Colonial Days and Dames* (1895), and *Through Colonial Doorways* (1893); Benson, Mary S., *Women in Eighteenth Century America* (1935); and Deutsch, Albert, *The Mentally Ill in America: A History of their Care and Treatment from Colonial Times* (1937).

Life in the colonial town and city

The best account of social life in the cities is Carl Bridenbaugh's *Cities in the Wilderness: The First Century of Urban Life in America, 1625-1742* (1938). This scholarly work discusses at length economic and social problems and the life of the people in the five colonial cities (Boston, Newport, New York, Philadelphia, and Charleston). Other works dealing with city life are: Wertenbaker, T. J., *The Golden Age of Colonial Culture* (1942; account of cultural conditions in six cities at the middle of the eighteenth century); Eberlein, Harold D., and Hubbard, Cortlandt V., *Portrait of a Colonial City: Philadelphia, 1670-1838* (1939; many valuable pictures); and Bowes, Frederick P., *The Culture of Early Charleston* (1942).

The colonial house

The literature on the colonial house and its furnishings is most voluminous. Of the numerous works on this topic, the following deserve mention: Shurtleff, Harold R., *The Log Cabin Myth: A Study of the Early Dwellings of the English Colonists in North America* (1939); Eberlein, H. D., *The Architecture of Colonial America* (1924), and *The Manors and Historic Homes of the Hudson Valley* (1924); Kimball, Sidney F., *American Architecture* (1928), chs. 1-6, and *Domestic Architecture of the American Colonies and of the Early*

Republic (1922, 1927; "perhaps the best work on architecture in the colonies") ; Hamlin, T. F., *The American Spirit in Architecture* [*Pageant of America*] (1926), chs. 3-8 (contains a large number of pictures of colonial structures; a valuable work) ; Jackson, J., *American Colonial Architecture* (1924) ; Chandler, J. E., *The Colonial House* (1924) ; Sanburn, Kate, *Old Time Wall Papers* (1905), chs. 3-4; and Glenn, T. A., *Some Colonial Mansions*, 2 vols. (1898, 1900; gives numerous portraits of people and pictures of houses with interior views). For the architecture of different sections, see : Sale, Edith T., *Manors of Virginia in Colonial Times* (1909) ; Coffin, L. A., Jr., and Holden, A. C., *Brick Architecture of the Colonial Period in Maryland and Virginia* (1919; numerous pictures and plans) ; Cousins, Frank, and Riley, P. M., *Colonial Architecture of Philadelphia* (1920) ; Westcott, T., *The Historic Mansions and Buildings of Philadelphia* (1877) ; Mills, W. J., *Historic Houses of New Jersey* (1902); and Wertenbaker, T. J., *The Founding of American Civilization: The Middle Colonies* (1938).

There are a number of descriptions of colonial furniture. Of these the following titles should be listed : Shea, John G., and Wenger, Paul N., *Colonial Furniture* (1935; numerous illustrations) ; Lockwood, L. V., *Colonial Furniture in America*, 2 vols. (1901, 1926; "best work on furniture") ; Singleton, Esther, *The Furniture of Our Forefathers*, 2 vols. (1901, 1913; valuable as a source book) ; Lyon, I. W., *Colonial Furniture of New England*; and Nutting, Wallace, *Furniture of the Pilgrim Century, 1620-1720* (1921, 1924; about fifteen hundred illustrations). Colonial furniture

The most useful single volume on the colonial theater is Arthur Hornblow's *A History of the Theatre in America*, 2 vols. (1919). The first six chapters of the first volume are devoted to the colonial period. This work gives numerous quotations from the sources, some of them lengthy, and has a number of good illustrations. Other works that may be of interest to the special student are: Seilhamer, George O., *History of the American Theatre*, 3 vols. (1888-1891; covers the period 1749-1797; quotes extensively from the sources; virtually a source book) ; Quinn, A. H., *A History of the American Drama from the Beginning to the Civil War* (2nd ed., 1943; first three chapters on the period prior to 1790) ; Irelan, J. N., *Records of the New York Stage from 1750 to 1860*, 2 vols. (1866-1867; first chapters of the first volume on the colonial period; numerous excerpts from the sources) ; Daly, C. P., *First Theatre in America* [Dunlap Society *Publications*, new series, i] (1896; quotes from documents) ; Crawford, Mary Caroline, *The Romance of the American Theatre*, pp. 19-71 (1925; quotations from sources; colorful and very readable) ; Tyler, L. G., *Williamsburg*, ch. 8 (1907; a good account of the theater in Virginia). The theater

There are a number of special works that discuss the social life of the various regions. High in this list stands T. J. Wertenbaker's two volumes on *The Founding of American Civilization*. The subtitles of these volumes are: *The Middle Colonies* (1938) and *The Old South* (1942; deals mainly with the Chesapeake colonies). Both volumes are fully illustrated. Of the numerous other works in this class the following should be listed: Spruill, Julia C., *Woman's Life and Work in the Southern Colonies* (1938; illustrations); and Wright, Louis B., *The First Gentlemen of Virginia: Intellectual Qualities of the Early Ruling Class* (1940; extends to middle of the eighteenth century). Interesting and useful discussions of life in the Old Dominion are also given in Mary N. Stanard's *Colonial Virginia, Its People and Customs* (1917); and in the scholarly works of P. A. Bruce, all of which give specific references to the sources. These latter are: *The Economic History of Virginia in the Seventeenth Century*, 2 vols.; *Institutional History of Virginia in the Seventeenth Century*, 2 vols.; and *Social Life in Virginia in the Seventeenth Century*. For North Carolina, see an article by C. L. Raper, "Social Life in Colonial North Carolina," *North Carolina Booklet*, iii.

Certain aspects of New England social life are discussed in an interesting and useful way by the following treatises: Crawford, Mary C., *Social Life in Old New England* (1914; gives quotations from the sources and a number of important pictures); Dow, G. F., *Domestic Life in New England in the Seventeenth Century* (1925); Felt, J. B., *The Customs of New England* (1853); Lathrop, Elsie, *Early American Inns and Taverns* (1926); Field, E., *The Colonial Tavern* (of value for the general reader; deals only with the taverns of New England); and Weeden, W. B., *Economic and Social History of New England*, 2 vols. (a very valuable work; specific references to sources). For life in colonial New York, see Goodwin, Maud W., Royce, Alice R., and Putnam, Ruth, eds., *Historic New York*; and Singleton, Esther, *Social New York Under the Georges* (1902; numerous pictures; quotations from the sources). For the manners and customs of the German-Americans, see: Knauss, J. O., *Social Conditions Among the Pennsylvania Germans* (1922); and Rush, B., *Manners of the German Inhabitants* (written in 1789).

For a discussion of morality in New England, see an article by C. F. Adams in Massachusetts Historical Society *Proceedings*, 2nd series, vi, pp. 477-516. An account of the curious practice of bundling and its relation to immorality is given in H. R. Stiles's *Bundling, Its Origin, Progress, and Decline in America* (1869, 1928).

The sources for this subject are not easily accessible. Some excerpts from contemporary writings are given in A. B. Hart's *Colonial Children* (a source reader), and *American History Told by Contemporaries*, ii, ch. 12; and in J. T. Faris's *When America Was Young*

(1925). Other accounts by contemporaries that are fairly accessible are: Smith, J. F. D., *A Tour in the United States of America*; Kalm, Peter, *Travels into North America*, 2 vols. (1772); Burnaby, A., *Travels Through North America* (1759-1760), edited by R. R. Wilson (gives an account of the physical conditions of the country, the cities, the government, educational conditions, and the character of the people; interesting); and Crèvecœur, St. John de, *Sketches of Eighteenth Century America* (1925). For an insight into the home life of a wealthy Virginia family, see P. V. Fithian's *Journal and Letters, 1773-1774*. The manuscript has now been reprinted in complete form (1943) under the editorship of Hunter D. Farish. Another valuable journal by Fithian, 1775-1776, has been edited and published by Robert G. Albion (1934). This journal was written on the Virginia-Pennsylvania frontier and in the army around New York. It describes the life of the people on the frontier and their reaction to the war. The diaries of prominent colonials are also an important source of information for the life of the people. The best guide to these is Harriette M. Forbes's *New England Diaries* (1923). Scattered documents can also be found in the works of Mrs. Earle and Miss Crawford, and numerous specific references to others are given in the footnotes of Bruce's, Weeden's, and Calhoun's works. In addition, the bibliography in Andrews's *Colonial Folkways* gives a considerable list of source materials.

Pictures of historic houses and their furnishings and reproductions Pictures of old portraits are an important source of information on houses, furniture, and styles of dress. A number of such pictures are given in the works of Miss McClellan and Mrs. Earle. Some of the treatises on the colonial house listed above contain pictures of this kind. Other works on the colonial house which may prove useful on account of their pictures are listed in T. J. Wertenbaker's *The First Americans*, pp. 336-338, and J. T. Adams's *Provincial Society*, pp. 345-346. The best easily accessible collections of pictures are *The Pageant of America* and Adams's *The Album of American History*, i and ii (consult the tables of contents in both works).

PART III.—SEPARATION FROM THE EMPIRE, 1763-1783

GENERAL ACCOUNTS

A BRIEF history of the two decades of this period is given in the general works listed on pp. 758-759. For fuller accounts of the American Revolution, see the general histories of the Revolution on pp. 842 ff.

CHAPTER XXIX.—OCCUPATION OF THE TRANS-ALLEGHANY REGION

General accounts

SOME of the works listed in the Bibliographical Notes on the Old West also apply to this chapter. Of these, special attention should be called to F. J. Turner's *The Frontier in American History*, chs. 7-12. An excellent discussion of the occupation of the trans-Alleghany region is given in Constance L. Skinner's *Pioneers of the Old Southwest* [*Chronicles of America Series*] (1919; a readable small volume with valuable bibliographical notes). A much fuller account, also interesting, is Theodore Roosevelt's *The Winning of the West*, 4 vols. (1889-1896, 1920). Other general accounts are: Henderson, A., *The Conquest of the Old Southwest* (1920); Winsor J., *The Mississippi Basin* (1895, 1898), ch. 12, and *The Westward Movement* (1897), chs. 1-6 (contains a number of contemporary maps); and Alden, G. H., *New Governments West of the Alleghanies Before 1780* [University of Wisconsin *Historical Series*] (1897). Brief accounts: Gabriel, R. H., *The Lure of the Frontier* [*Pageant of America*], chs. 1-2 (1929; numerous pictures); Paxson, F. L., *History of the American Frontier* (1924), ch. 1; Alvord, C. W., "Virginia and the West," *Mississippi Valley Historical Review*, iii, pp. 19-38; and Turner, F. J., "Western State-Making in the Revolutionary Era," *American Historical Review*, i, pp. 70-87. For the geographical background, see Ellen C. Semple's *American History and Its Geographic Conditions* (rev. ed., 1933), chs. 4-5.

Special works

In recent years students of history have devoted a good deal of attention to westward extension, and a number of valuable special works have been published, portions of which are devoted to certain phases of the trans-Alleghany movement. Of these the following deserve mention: Alvord, C. W., *The Mississippi Valley in British Politics*, 2 vols. (1917; a scholarly work of great value to the special student), and "The Genesis of the Proclamation of 1763" [*Michigan Pioneer and Historical Collections*, xxxvi, pp. 20-51]; Carter, C. E., *Great Britain and the Illinois Country, 1763-1764* (1910); Volwiler, A. T., *George Croghan and the Westward Movement, 1741-1782* (1926; scholarly; numerous specific references to primary sources); and Parkman, Francis, *The Conspiracy of Pontiac*, 2 vols. (brilliant and interesting).

The founding of Kentucky

An interesting account of the founding of Kentucky is A. B. Hulbert's *Boone's Wilderness Road* (1903; some excerpts from contemporary accounts). Other works dealing with the early history of Kentucky are: Henderson, Archibald, *The Transylvania Company and the Founding of Henderson, Ky.* (1929; contains a few contemporary pictures), and "Richard Henderson and the Occupation of Kentucky," *Mississippi Valley Historical Review*, ii, pp. 465-483; and

Lester, W. S., *The Transylvania Colony* (1935). The following biographies of Daniel Boone should also be mentioned: Bruce, H. A., *Daniel Boone and the Wilderness Road* (1929); Bakeless, John, *Daniel Boone, Master of the Wilderness* (1939).

For the settlement of Tennessee and western Virginia see: Abernethy, Thomas P., *From Frontier to Plantation in Tennessee: A Study in Frontier Democracy* (1932), chs. 1-6; Driver, Carl S., *John Sevier, Pioneer of the Old West* (1932), ch. 1; Turner, F. M., *The Life of General John Sevier* (1910); and De Hass, Wills, *History of the Early Settlement and Indian Wars of Western Virginia* (1851). Early Tennessee and western Virginia

State histories covering the early history of Kentucky, Tennessee, and western Virginia are: Bodley, Temple, and Wilson, S. W., *History of Kentucky*, 2 vols. (the first volume, by Bodley, is on the colonial period; scholarly and readable; numerous quotations from and citations to the primary sources); Moore, J. T., and Foster, A. P., *Tennessee, The Volunteer State, 1769-1923* (1923); Callahan, J. M., *History of West Virginia* (1923), chs. 3-8; and Ambler, C. H., *West Virginia, The Mountain State* (1940), chs. 5-10.

The sources for the history of the trans-Alleghany frontier are abundant. Excerpts from a few contemporary accounts are given in A. B. Hart's *American History Told by Contemporaries*, ii, ch. 22. Collections of sources valuable for the special student are: Thwaites, R. G., *Early Western Travels, 1748-1846*, 32 vols. (1904-1907; vol. i contains the journal of George Croghan, pp. 72-173); Filson, John, *The Discovery, Settlement, and Present State of Kentucke* (1784-1793; the autobiography of Daniel Boone, put in literary form by John Filson) [Filson Club *Publications*, xvi]; Johnston, J. S., ed., *Journals of Dr. Thomas Walker, 1750, and of Christopher Gist, 1751* [Filson Club *Publications*, no. 13] (for a map showing routes of these explorers see p. 32); Darlington, W. M., ed., *Christopher Gist's Journals* (gives an account of Gist's surveys for the Ohio Company); Hanna, C. A., *The Wilderness Trail*, 2 vols. (1911); Doddridge, J., *Notes on the Settlement and Indian Wars of the Western Parts of Virginia and Pennsylvania from 1763 to 1783* (1824, 1912; portions of this valuable contemporary account are devoted to a description of the daily life of the people in the back country); Alvord, C. W., and Carter, C. E., eds., *The Critical Period, 1763-1765* (1915), and *The New Regime, 1765-1767* (1916; a collection of documents relating to the Illinois region during the first few years of British rule); Withers, Alexander S., *Chronicles of Border Warfare, or A History of the Settlement by the Whites of Northwestern Virginia*, and of the Indian wars and massacres in that section of the state, edited by R. G. Thwaites (1895; based largely on oral statements of his older contemporaries; the treatment of the larger events is there- Sources fore unreliable, but the accounts of local happenings are trustworthy) ; Mante, Thomas, *History of the War* (1772), ch. 12 (a contemporary account of Pontiac's War) ; Smith, William, *Historical Account of Bouquet's Expedition Against the Ohio Indians in 1764* (published in 1765) ; Smyth, J. F. D., *Tour in the United States of America*, 2 vols. (London, 1784; observations on the life of the frontiersmen made by an Englishman) ; Thwaites, R. G., and Kellogg, L. P., eds., *Documentary History of Dunmore's War, 1774* (1905) ; Ramsey, J. G. M., *The Annals of Tennessee* (1853, 1926) ; Haywood, John, *The Civil and Political History of the State of Tennessee* (1823, 1891) ; Williams, S. C., *Early Travels in the Tennessee Country, 1540-1800* (1928) ; and the *Colonial Records of North Carolina.* For other sources see the bibliographical lists and footnotes in the secondary authorities mentioned above.

CHAPTER XXX.—A DECADE OF DISCONTENT

General accounts
THE period covered by this chapter is discussed in a brilliant way by C. L. Becker in *The Eve of the Revolution* (1921; no footnotes, but a full and discriminating bibliography). Other scholarly and readable works are: Van Tyne, C. H., *The American Revolution* (1905), ch. i, and *The Causes of the War of Independence* (1922; references to primary sources; interesting; upholds new view as to England's responsibility) ; Howard, G. E., *Preliminaries of the Revolution* (1905; references to primary sources, with critical essay on sources) ; Channing, E., *History of the United States*, iii, chs. 1-5 (references to sources; leans toward the traditional view) ; Adams, J. T., *Revolutionary New England*; Egerton, H. E., *The Causes and Character of the American Revolution* (1923) ; and Miller, J. C., *Origins of the American Revolution* (1943). Short accounts can be found in the one-volume colonial histories listed on pp. 762 f. For brief discussions of the economic causes of the Revolution, see the economic histories of the United States listed on p. 760. Other general accounts are given in the histories of the Revolution listed in the Bibliographical Notes for Chapter XXXII. See also J. N. Larned's *Literature of American History*, pp. 111-152, for an appraisal of a long list of primary and secondary authorities on the Revolution.

Works on special topics
An able and scholarly defense of the British imperial policy during the two decades preceding the Revolution is given in G. L. Beer's *British Colonial Policy, 1754-1765*, chs. 9-14. British imperial administration is also discussed in a scholarly way in C. W. Alvord's *The Mississippi Valley in British Politics*, 2 vols., and H. E. Egerton's *A Short History of British Colonial Policy* (1897, 1932). For a good clear account of British politics under George III, see W. E. Lunt's

History of England, ch. 30. A. M. Schlesinger's *Colonial Merchants and the American Revolution* (1918) presents a great deal of well-documented new material on the causes of the Revolution. The thesis maintained in this work contradicts the traditional view on some important points. The same author in his *New Viewpoints in American History* (1922), ch. 7, makes some very interesting and useful observations on the Revolution as a whole. To this chapter is appended an appraisal of bibliographical material that is valuable. Schlesinger has a brief article, "The American Revolution Reconsidered," in *Political Science Quarterly*, xxxiv, pp. 61-78. M. C. Tyler's *Literary History of the American Revolution*, 2 vols., gives interesting and useful information on the controversies preceding the outbreak (reprinted in 1941). C. M. Andrews's *The Colonial Background of the American Revolution* is a good discussion of the indirect causes of the Revolution. For the English background of the Revolution, see Namier, L. B., *England in the Age of the American Revolution* (1930). See also Coupland, R., *The American Revolution and the British Empire* (1930). Other special works that should be listed are: Labaree, L. W., *Royal Government in America*; Morris, R. B., ed., *The Era of the American Revolution* [*Studies Inscribed to Evarts Boutell Greene*] (1939); Adams, Randolph G., *Political Ideas of the Revolution* (1922); and Hacker, L. M., "The First American Revolution," *Columbia University Quarterly*, xxvii, pp. 259-295.

The biographies of the Revolutionary leaders throw light on the causes of discontent among the colonials. Of these biographies the following deserve special mention: Henry, W. W., *Patrick Henry: Life, Correspondence and Speeches*, 3 vols. (1891); Tyler, M. C., *Patrick Henry* (1887-1917); Van Doren, Carl, *Benjamin Franklin* (1938); Ford, P. L., *The Many-Sided Franklin* (1899); Bruce, W. C., *Benjamin Franklin, Self-Revealed*, 2 vols. (1918; quotes at length from Franklin's writings; readable); Chinard, Gilbert, *Honest John Adams* (1933); Miller, J. C., *Sam Adams, Pioneer in Propaganda* (1936); and Harlow, R. V., *Samuel Adams, Promoter of the Revolution* (1923). For the biographies and writings of other Revolutionary leaders, see Bibliographical Notes for Chapter XXXII; Channing, Hart, and Turner's *Guide*, pp. 398-399; and Larned, J. N., *op. cit.*, pp. 111-152. *(margin: Biographies)*

Easily accessible documents can be found in the following works: MacDonald, W., *Select Charters and Other Documents*; Bogart, E. L., and Thompson, C. M., *Readings in the Economic History of the United States*, pp. 143-175; Hart, A. B. *American History Told by Contemporaries*, ii, chs. 21, 23, and 24; Callender, G. S., *Selections from the Economic History of the United States*, pp. 125-137, 140-143, 145-151; Hart, A. B., and Channing, E., *American History Leaflets*, nos. 14 and 21; McLaughlin, A. C., and others, *Source* *(margin: Sources)*

Problems in United States History (1918), problem ii; Preston, H. W., *Documents Illustrative of American History, 1606-1863* (1886), pp. 170-191; West, W. M., *Source Book in American History*, chs. 21-22; Niles, H., *Principles and Acts of the Revolution in America* (1822); Pease, T. C., and Roberts, A. S., *Selected Readings in American History*, pp. 75-96; Commager, H. L., *Documents of American History*, i, pp. 45-89; Almon, J., *Collection of Papers Relative to the Dispute Between Great Britain and America, 1777* (usually cited as *Prior Documents*); Force, Peter, *American Archives* (4th series); Moore, F., *Diary of the American Revolution from the Newspapers and the Original Documents* (1860, 1875); Eddis, William, *Letters from America, Historical and Descriptive, 1769-1777* ("best account we have on the rise of Revolutionary principles in Maryland"); Morison, S. E., *Sources and Documents Illustrating the American Revolution and the Formation of the Federal Constitution, 1764-1788* (1923); Mumby, Frank A., *George III and the American Revolution* (made up largely of excerpts from letters; a source collection; goes to 1775); and Pownall, Thomas, *The Administration of the Colonies* (published in 1775; suggests policy to be pursued by British government; author had been governor of Massachusetts and two other colonies; excellent summary of the work in the table of contents).

Controversial pamphlets

Of the numerous controversial pamphlets circulated by the Revolutionary leaders, the following should be mentioned: Otis, J., *Rights of the British Colonies Asserted and Proved*, 1774; Dulany, D., *Considerations on the Propriety of Imposing Taxes on the British Colonies*, 1765; Dickinson, John, *Letters from a Farmer in Pennsylvania to the Inhabitants of the British Colonies*, 1768; Knox, W., *The Controversy Between Great Britain and Her Colonies Reviewed*, 1769 (a pro-British reply to Dickinson's pamphlet); Jenyns, S., *The Objections to the Taxation of Our American Colonies . . . Briefly Considered*, 1765. An excellent summary of these pamphlets and numerous others is given in M. C. Tyler's *The Literary History of the American Revolution, 1763-1783*, 2 vols. (1927).

Other contemporary writings

Other important source materials for this period can be found in the letters and papers of the political leaders and the writings of contemporary historians. Of these, the following are of special value: Adams, C. F., *The Works of John Adams*, 10 vols., 1856 (the Diary and Autobiography of John Adams, in vols. ii and iii, are especially useful for the Revolutionary period); Hutchinson, P. O., *Diary and Letters of Thomas Hutchinson*, 2 vols.; Smyth, A. H., *The Writings of Benjamin Franklin*, 10 vols.; Bigelow, John, *Complete Works of Benjamin Franklin*, 10 vols.; Cushing, H. A., *The Writings of Samuel Adams*, 4 vols.; Ford, P. L., *The Writings of John Dickinson*, 3 vols.; Burnett, E. C., *Letters of the Members of the Continental Congress*, 8 vols. (1921-1936); Gordon, W., *The History of the Rise,*

Progress, and Establishment of the Independence of the Unitel States of America (1788, 1801; portions of it consist of excerpts from the *Annual Register*); Ramsay, D., *History of the Revolution of South Carolina*, 2 vols., 1785; Warren, Mercy, *History of the American Revolution*, 3 vols., 1805 (the author was a sister of James Otis and the wife of James Warren); Hutchinson, T., *History of Massachusetts Bay* (based on documents some of which are no longer extant). For lists of other sources, see Bibliographical Notes for Chapter XXXII; Channing, Hart, and Turner's *Guide*, pp. 296-301; and Winsor's *Narrative and Critical History*, vi, pp. 62-112.

CHAPTER XXXI.—THE FINAL BREAK

MOST of the primary and secondary sources listed for Chapters XXX and XXXII are useful for a study of the topics discussed in this chapter. To these should be added the following titles: Brown, Weldon A., *Empire or Independence: A Study in the Failure of Reconciliation, 1774-1783* (1941; discusses the abortive efforts to prevent a final break); Brown, S. G., *We Hold These Truths*, pp. 18-55 (1941; a few important and well-known documents); Boyd, Julian K., *Anglo-American Union: Joseph Galloway's Plans to Preserve the British Empire, 1774-1788* (1941; gives text of plans of union). For a brief general account of the final break, see: Van Tyne, C. H., *The American Revolution*, chs. 2 and 4; Channing, E., *History of the United States*, iii, chs. 5-7; Adams, J. T., *Revolutionary New England*, chs. 16-18; and Chalmers, George, *Introduction to the History of the Revolt of the American Colonies* (1845). `General accounts`

A good discussion of the Declaration of Independence is C. L. Becker's *The Declaration of Independence*. The lengthy excerpts from the documents it contains virtually make it a source book. But the definitive work on the evolution of the Declaration is J. K. Boyd's *The Declaration of Independence: The Evolution of the Text as Shown in Facsimiles of Various Drafts by Its Author, Thomas Jefferson* (1945). Other lengthy discussions are: Friedenwald, H., *The Declaration of Independence*, and Hazelton, J. H., *The Declaration of Independence: Its History*. John Locke's two *Treatises on Government* (given in his *Works*, 1824 ed., iv, pp. 212-485) should be consulted by the special student, since much of the philosophy of the Declaration was borrowed from them. The second *Treatise* is briefly summarized by H. Friedenwald, pp. 187-193. `The Declaration of Independence`

For sources, see the Bibliographical Notes for Chapters XXX and XXXII. Only a few other collections need be mentioned: West, W. M., *A Source Book in American History*, chs. 22-23; Hart, A. B., *American History Told by Contemporaries*, ii, chs. 25, 30, and pp. `Sources`

454-461; Force, Peter, *American Archives*, 4th series, 6 vols. (a large collection of valuable documents covering the period 1774-1776); Drake, Francis S., *Tea Leaves* (a collection of letters relating to the shipment of tea to the American colonies in 1773); Willard, Margaret W., *Letters on the American Revolution, 1774-1776*; the *Annual Register* for 1776; Fast, Howard, ed., *The Selected Works of Tom Paine* (1945); [Huett, Richard], *Basic Writings of Thomas Paine* (1942); Clark, Henry H., *Thomas Paine:Representative Selections, with Introduction, Bibliography, and Notes* (1944); Toner, Philip S., ed. and comp., *The Complete Works of Thomas Paine*, 2 vols. (1945); and Carter, Clarence E., comp., *The Correspondence of General Thomas Gage with the Secretary of State, 1763-1775*, 2 vols. (1931-1933). For other sources, see the bibliographical notes in Winsor's *Narrative and Critical History*, vi, pp. 172-230, 252-274.

Chapter XXXII.—The War for Independence

"Revi-
sionist"
histories
of the
Revolu-
tion

UNTIL the beginning of the last decade of the nineteenth century American historians in discussing the Revolution, generally took the position that in the quarrel between the colonies and the mother country the former were entirely in the right and the latter altogether wrong. But in recent decades much time has been devoted by scholars to re-examining the sources of Revolutionary history and, in consequence, a more impartial and sounder view of the conflict is now held by most competent historians. The classic champion of the old view is Bancroft, who in his *History of the United States*, 6 vols. (1891-1892), gives us, correctly in the main, the facts, but·with them an interpretation strongly biased by patriotism. Of like character is John Fiske's brilliant and interesting narrative, *The American Revolution*, 2 vols. (1891).

Prominent in the list of the scholars who take the more scientific view is the late C. H. Van Tyne, who was for more than a quarter of a century engaged in the study of this period. In his *Loyalists in the American Revolution* (1902), he showed in a scholarly way that the Tories, so called, were not so bad as they had been painted. Later (1905) he published as one of the *American Nation Series, The American Revolution*, a volume that is valuable for both the general reader and the special student. A later work, *The Causes of the War of Independence* (1922), is a readable and scholarly discussion of the early phases of the contest. His latest works are: *England and America* (1927; a series of lectures discussing in an interesting way certain phases of the Revolution that have been neglected by most historians), and *War of Independence* (1929; discusses the Revolution-

ary War to the French alliance, 1778). The work that is most unsparing in its destruction of our patriotic notions regarding the
Fathers is S. G. Fisher's *The Struggle for American Independence*,
2 vols. (1908). In it facts, well documented by references to the
sources, cut their way through cherished prejudices with merciless
candor. For briefer discussions, see Whitton, E. W., *The American
War of Independence* (1931) ; and Wrong, G. M., *Washington and
His Comrades* [*Chronicles of America Series*] (1921; interesting;
especially adapted to the general reader).

There are two fine discussions of the Revolution by English writ- Other
ers, both of which are eminently fair. These are: Trevelyan, G. O., general
The American Revolution, 4 vols. (1905; a very interesting account, accounts
favorable to America; "on the whole the work of the Revolution best
worth reading") ; and Lecky, W. E. H., *The American Revolution*
(1898; taken from his *History of England in the Eighteenth Century*,
8 vols., and edited by J. A. Woodburn; one of the best single volumes
on the Revolution). Other works that deserve mention are: Greene,
F. V., *The Revolutionary War and the Military Policy of the United
States* (1911; many excellent maps) ; French, Allen, *The First Year
of the American Revolution* (1934) ; Abbott, W. C., *New York in
the American Revolution* (1929) ; Eckenrode, H. J., *The Revolution
in Virginia* (1916) ; and two articles on the battle of Yorktown in
the *American Historical Review*, one by R. G. Adams (October,
1931) and the other by William B. Willcox (October, 1946). For
an explanation of the management, or rather mismanagement, of the
war by the Howes, see T. S. Anderson's *The Command of the Howe
Brothers During the American Revolution* (1936; scholarly; for the
special student, not the general reader; good maps).

Interesting pictures can be found in William Wood and R. H. Pictures
Gabriel's *The Winning of Freedom* [*Pageant of America*] (1927) ;
Benson Lossing's *Pictorial Field Book of the Revolution*, 2 vols.
(1850, 1860; gives useful information for places) ; and J. T. Adams's
Album of American History, i.

For the management of the army and the problems growing out Adminis-
of military affairs see: Bowman, Allen, *The Morale of the American* tration of
Revolutionary Army (1943) ; Bolton, C. K., *The Private Soldier* the Amer-
Under Washington (1902) ; Hatch, L. C., *The Administration of* ican army
the American Revolutionary Army (1904) ; Spaulding, O. L., *The
United States Army in War and Peace* (1937), chs. 2-5; and Johnson, V. L., *The Administration of the American Commissariat During the Revolutionary War* (1941).

If a detailed study of naval operations is desired, the following Naval
works should be consulted: Mahan, A. T., *Major Operations of the* affairs
Navies in the War of American Independence (1913) ; Paulin, C. O.,

The Navy of the American Revolution (1906); Allen, G. W., *A Naval History of the American Revolution*, 2 vols. (1913).

Biographies

A good deal of information on various aspects of the Revolution is to be found in the biographies of the statesmen and military leaders. The biographies of Washington, Lafayette, Jefferson, Hamilton, Madison, and John Jay should be added to the list given in Bibliographical Notes for Chapter XXX. For an appraisal of the older works on the lives of these and other prominent men, see Larned, *op. cit.,* pp. 111-152. The general reader and the average student will, however, be more interested in the later popular biographies, some of which are written in an interesting and brilliant style. Of these the following should be mentioned: Wilson, Woodrow, *George Washington* (1896, 1924); Hughes, Rupert, *George Washington*, 3 vols. (1926-1930; one of the most popular of all of Washington's biographies; vols. ii and iii are concerned with the Revolution); Fitzpatrick, John C., *George Washington Himself: A Common Sense Biography Written from His Manuscripts* (1933); Sears, L. M., *George Washington* (1932); Sawyer, J. D., *Washington* (1927; a large collection of pictures); Stephenson, Nathaniel, and Dunn, W. H., *George Washington*, 2 vols. (1940); Young, Norwood, *George Washington, Soul of the Revolution* (1932); Knollenberg, Bernard, *Washington and the Revolution, A Reappraisal* (1940; more favorable to Gates and Congress than are the orthodox histories; for the special student); Whitlock, Brand, *Lafayette*, 2 vols. (1929; vol. i gives numerous excerpts from the sources); and Tower, Charlemagne, *The Marquis de La Fayette in the American Revolution*, 2 vols. (1895). For the conquest of the Northwest, see J. A. James's *The Life of George Rogers Clark* (1928); and Temple Bodley's *George Rogers Clark: His Life and Public Services* (1926).

New light on Arnold's treason has been shed by the recent work of Carl Van Doren, *Secret History of the American Revolution* (1941; has a valuable collection of documents). Of the biographies of statesmen who played a prominent part in the Revolution, the following should be listed: Muzzey, D. S., *Thomas Jefferson* (1918); Van Doren, Carl, *Benjamin Franklin* (1938; readable); Faÿ, Bernard, *Franklin, the Apostle of Modern Times* (1929); Monaghan, Frank, *John Jay, Defender of Liberty Against Kings and Peoples* (1935); and Jay, William, *John Jay* (1833; a biography by his son, with selections from his correspondence and miscellaneous papers). See also the biographies listed on p. 839.

The diplomacy of the war

The diplomatic history of the Revolution is discussed briefly in a number of one-volume histories of American diplomacy. Of these the following deserve mention: Bemis, S. F., *A Diplomatic History of the United States* (1942), chs. 2-4; Bailey, Thomas A., *A Diplo-*

matic History of the American People (1940), chs. 2-3 (ch. 4 on the period of the Confederation) ; Jones, Robert L., *History of the Foreign Policy of the United States* (1933), chs. 1-4; Sears, L. M., *History of American Foreign Relations* (1935 ed.), ch. 1; Latané, J. H., *History of American Diplomacy* (1934 ed.), pp. 1-46; Foster, J. W., *A Century of American Diplomacy* (1901), chs. 1-3. For fuller discussions relating to the French alliance, see: Bemis, S. F., *The Diplomacy of the American Revolution* (1935); Corwin, E. S., *French Policy and the American Alliance of 1778* (1916); Perkins, J. B., *France in the American Revolution* (1911); Van Doren, Carl, *Benjamin Franklin*; Faÿ, Bernard, *Franklin, the Apostle of Modern Times*; and an article by C. H. Van Tyne in the *American Historical Review* for April, 1916, "Influences Which Determined the French Government to Make the Treaty with America." The negotiations that led to the peace treaty are discussed at length in John Jay's *Peace Negotiations of 1782 and 1783.* Good short accounts of these negotiations are given in A. C. McLaughlin's *The Confederation and the Constitution* (1905), chs. 1-2; C. E. Hill's *Leading American Treaties* (1931), chs. 1-2; and J. W. Foster's *A Century of American Diplomacy*, ch. 2.

For other secondary authorities, see Winsor, J., *The Reader's Handbook of the American Revolution, 1761-1783*; and the bibliographies given by the authorities listed above.

The sources on this chapter, especially on the military events, are so voluminous that it is difficult to make a selection. Brief collections are: Hart, A. B., *American History Told by Contemporaries*, ii, chs. 26-35; McLaughlin, A. C., and others, *Source Problems in United States History*, problem ii; and Preston, H. W., *Documents Illustrative of American History*, 5th ed.; Stedman, E. C., and Hutchinson, E. M., *A Library of American Literature*, iii; Pease, T. C., and Roberts, A. S., *Selected Readings in American History*, pp. 110-162; Commager, H. S., *Documents of American History*, i, pp. 45-119; and Brown, Stuart G., *We Hold These Truths* (1941), pp. 18-65. Sources: Briefer collections

Of the larger collections, the special student may wish to refer to the following: *The Annual Register, 1765-1776* ("an English annual giving summaries of political events supposed to have been prepared by Edmund Burke"); Force, Peter, *American Archives*, 5th series; Morison, S. E., *Sources and Documents Illustrating the American Revolution and the Formation of the Federal Constitution, 1764-1788* (1923); Moore, F., *Diary of the American Revolution from the Newspapers and the Original Documents*; Niles, H., *Principles and Acts of the Revolution in America* (a collection of contemporary speeches, letters, and other documents); Almon, J., *Collection of Papers Relative to the Dispute Between Great Britain and America,* Larger collections

1777 (usually cited as *Prior Documents*), and *The Remembrancer*, by the same author (published monthly from 1775 to 1781).

Documents pertaining to diplomatic negotiations
The part played by France in the American Revolution is discussed at great length by Henri Doniol in *Histoire de la Participation de la France à l'Etablissement des Etats-Unis d'Amérique,* 5 vols. and supplement ("a monumental work, being at once a diplomatic history and a collection of documents covering the events which led to the alliance between France and the United States in 1778, the coöperation of the two powers from that time till the close of the war, and the peace negotiations that followed"). Other valuable collections of sources bearing on the diplomacy of the Revolution are: Sparks, Jared, ed., *Diplomatic Correspondence of the American Revolution,* 4 vols. (1853) ; Wharton, Francis, ed., *The Revolutionary Diplomatic Correspondence of the United States,* 6 vols. (1889) ; and Deane, Silas, *The Deane Papers, 1774-1790,* 5 vols. (1887-1890; valuable as a source of information regarding French aid). The texts of the treaties with France and the peace treaties with England are given in *Treaties, Conventions, International Acts, Protocols and Agreements Between the United States of America and Other Powers,* compiled by William M. Malloy (1910-1937) ; and in *Treaties and Other International Acts of the United States of America,* by David H. Miller (1942; in progress; 7 vols. to 1858).

Other contemporary correspondence
A great number of letters written at the time by men who took a prominent part in the Revolution have also been preserved. Of these, the following collections should be listed: Fitzpatrick, John C., *The Writings of George Washington from the Original Manuscript Sources, 1745-1799,* 37 vols. (1931-1940; a valuable collection) ; Chase, E. P., ed. and trans., *Our Revolutionary Forefathers, The Letters of Francois, Marquis de Barbe-Marbois,* during his residence in the United States as secretary of the French legation, 1779-1785 ; Deane, Silas, *Correspondence of Silas Deane,* 2 vols. (Sidelights on the early history of the Revolution in Connecticut) ; Ballagh, J. C., ed., *The Writings of Richarl Henry Lee* (1911-1913) ; Donne, W. B., ed., *The Correspondence of King George the Third with Lord North from 1768 to 1783,* 2 vols. (1867) ; Fortescue, Sir John, ed., *The Correspondence of King George the Third from 1760 to December, 1783,* 6 vols. (1927-1928; valuable collection of documents, especially vols. iii-vi; vol v contains some important new material on the peace negotiations) ; and Taylor, W. S., and Pringle, J. H., eds., *Chatham Correspondence.* For a brief estimate of the writings of the Revolutionary leaders, see Larned, J. N., *Literature of American History,* pp. 111-112 (John Adams), pp. 124-125 (Franklin), pp. 130-131 (Jefferson), pp. 132-133 (Lafayette), p. 134 (the Lees), pp. 148-151 (Washington).

The following collections of memoirs will prove useful for the Memoirs special student: Albemarle, Earl of (George Thomas, Earl of Albe- and other marle), *Memoirs of the Marquis of Rockingham and His Contem-* contem- *poraries,* with original letters and documents, 2 vols. (1852; made porary up mostly of documents; first five chapters of vol. i on French and accounts Indian War; rest of the work on the Revolutionary War); Lafayette, Marquis de, *Memoirs, Correspondence, and Manuscripts*; Moultrie, W., *Memoirs of the American Revolution so Far as It Related to North and South Carolina,* 2 vols. (1821); Jones, T., *History of New York During the Revolutionary War,* 2 vols. (written between 1783 and 1788 by a prominent Loyalist of New York); Lee, Lt.-Col. Henry, *Memoirs of the War in the Southern Department of the United States,* ed. by Robert E. Lee (1870); Durand, John, ed., *New Materials for the History of the American Revolution* (1889; translated from documents in the French archives); Stedman, Charles, *The History of the Origin, Progress, and Termination of the Ameri-can War, 1763-1783,* 2 vols. (1794; the author was an officer in the British army during the Revolutionary War; "best contemporary ac-count of the war from the British side"); Ramsay, David, *The His-tory of the American Revolution,* 2 vols. (1815), and *The History of the Revolution of South Carolina from a British Colony to an In-dependent State,* 2 vols. (1785; the author was for a while a surgeon in the Continental Army; later he took an active part in the political life of South Carolina and the Confederation).

The primary and secondary authorities for this period are discussed Bibliog- at great length in Winsor's *Narrative and Critical History,* vi, pp. raphies 315-366, 403-468, 507-562, 589-604, 647-684. Channing, Hart, and Turner's *Guide,* pp. 301-315, gives lists of source materials and sec-ondary authorities that are almost endless. Some of these and other works are appraised in J. N. Larned's *Literature of American His-tory,* iii, p. 152. For a list of manuscript sources on this chapter, see Greene and Morris's *Guide,* pp. 143-189. A full list of works on the Revolution and the Confederation can be found in H. P. Beers's *Bibli-ographies in American History,* pp. 54-57 (secondary works), and 52-54 (source materials).

Chapter XXXIII.—Political and Social Aspects of the Revolution

BRIEF discussions of the economic aspects of the Revolution are given Brief in the American economic histories listed on p. 760. There are also a discus- number of references to good secondary authorities on social life in sions the Selected Readings on pp. 706-707. Numerous citations to sources are given in the footnotes for the present chapter. Some of the other works listed in the Bibliographical Notes for the other chapters on the Revolution contain useful information on social history. Of these, special note should be taken of C. H. Van Tyne's *Loyalists in the American Revolution*. See also *England and America* by the same author.

Government   Of the few additional titles that should be listed, the following are concerned with governmental problems: Nevins, Allan, *The American States During and After the Revolution* (1943; treats authoritatively the subject indicated by this title); Jensen, Merrill, *The Articles of Confederation: An Interpretation of the Social-Constitutional History of the American Revolution, 1774-1781* (1940); and Burnett, E. C., *The Continental Congress* (1941; the definitive work on the Continental Congress). The special student may also wish to refer to C. L. Lord's *The Continental Congresses and the Congress of the Constitution, 1777-1789* [*The Atlas of Congressional Roll Calls,* i], (1943). Votes by states are shown by maps. This is the first volume of an ambitious plan to cover the entire voting record of Congress up to date. One drawback to it is that the print is very small. The most valuable collections of source materials on the Continental Congress are: *Letters of Members of the Continental Congress*, 8 vols. (1921-1936), compiled by E. C. Burnett; *Journals of the Continental Congress, 1774-1789*, 34 vols. (1904-1937), compiled by W. C. Ford and others; and *Secret Journals of the Acts and Proceedings of Congress*, 4 vols. (1821).

Economic and social problems.   For a discussion of business and financial problems of the Revolutionary period, see: East, Robert A., *Business Enterprise in the American Revolutionary Era* (1938); Bullock, C. J., *Finances of the United States from 1778 to 1788* (1895); Breck, S., *Historical Sketch of the Continental Paper Money* (1843, 1863); Oberholtzer, E. P., *Life of Robert Morris* (1903); Phillips, Henry, Jr., *Historical Sketches of the Paper Currency of the American Colonies Prior to the Adoption of the Federal Constitution* (1865-1866; "the most detailed study of the Continental Currency in print; generous extracts from contemporaneous documents"). The two best general accounts of the social life of the period are: Greene, E. B., *The Revolutionary Generation, 1763-1790* [*A History of American Life,* iv] (1943; for the special student rather than the general reader); and Jameson, J. F., *The American Revolution Considered as a Social Movement* (2nd printing, 1940; contains much valuable information clothed in a readable style). For a discussion of certain aspects of social life, see: Koch, G. A., *Republican Religion: The American Revolution and the Cult of Reason* (1933); Thornton, J. W., *The Pulpit of the American Revolution* (1860; eight sermons preached from 1750 to 1783); and Baldwin, Alice M., *The New England Clergy and the American Revolution* (1928). Brief source readings are given in Callender, G. S.,

Selections from the Economic History of the United States, 1765-1860 (1909), ch. 4.

PART IV.—THE FIRST REPUBLIC

GENERAL WORKS

THE period from 1783 to 1789 is discussed at considerable length in each of the general histories listed on pp. 758 f. To this list should be added the following: McMaster, John B., *A History of the People of the United States from the Revolution to the Civil War*, 8 vols. (1883-1913; readable and scholarly; social life emphasized; nearly all of vol. i on this period); Schouler, James, *History of the United States of America Under the Constitution*, 7 vols. (1895-1913; stately and ornate style; first three chapters of vol. i on this period); Curtis, George T., *Constitutional History of the United States*, 2 vols. (1889; vol. i on the period of the Confederation); Klingberg, F. J., *The Morning of America* (1941); and Greene, E. B., *The Revolutionary Generation, 1763-1790* [*A History of American Life*, iv, 1943].

CHAPTER XXXIV.—THE CONFEDERATION PERIOD

GOOD brief accounts of the Confederation period are given in Max Farrand's *The Fathers of the Constitution* [*Chronicles of America*, xiii; 1921]; and A. C. McLaughlin's *The Confederation and the Constitution* [*American Nation Series*, x, 1905]. For interesting details, see John Fiske's *The Critical Period of American History* (1888). The last two works, especially *The Critical Period*, lean too far toward the old tendency to exaggerate the shortcomings of the Confederation government. For foreign relations and conditions in the states, see, respectively, *Our Rising Empire, 1763-1803* (1940), by A. B. Darling; and the *American States During and After the Revolution* (1924), by Allan Nevins. For other works on foreign affairs, see the diplomatic histories listed on pp. 844 f. Additional references on government will be found on p. 850. *(General accounts)*

Good insight into the life of the people, especially of the wealthy classes, is given in the diary of Robert Hunter, Jr., a young Scotsman who traveled throughout the States soon after the close of the Revolutionary War. His interesting observations have been edited and published by Louis B. Wright and Marion Tingling, under the title *Quebec to Carolina in 1785-1786* (1943). A contemporary account of Shays's Rebellion is given in George R. Minot's *History of the Insurrection in Massachusetts* (1810). For the work of the Congress of the *(Sources)*

Confederation, see E. C. Burnett's *Letters of Members of the Continental Congress*, 8 vols.; *Journals of the Continental Congress*, 34 vols.; and the *Secret Journals of the Acts and Proceedings of Congress*, 4 vols. For the text of the Articles of Confederation, see *Old South Leaflets*, no. 2; Commager, H. S., *Documents of American History*, i, pp. 111-116; and Pease, T. C., and Roberts, A. S., *Selected Readings in American History*, pp. 141-148.

Western problems   Of the numerous works concerned with the western problems of this period the following may be useful for the special student: Abernethy, T. P., *Western Lands and the American Revolution* (1937); Treat, Payson J., *The National Land System, 1785-1820* (1910); Winsor, Justin, *The Westward Movement* (1897); Ogg, F. A., *The Old Northwest* [*Chronicles of America*, xix; 1919]; Hinsdale, B. A., *The Old Northwest; the Beginnings of Our Colonial System* (1899); Bond, B. W., *The Civilization of the Old Northwest* (1934); Whittaker, A. P., *The Spanish American Frontier, 1783-1795* (1927); and Barrett, Jay A., *Evolution of the Ordinance of 1787* (1927). For the text of the Ordinance of 1787, see *Old South Leaflets*, no. 13; Commager, *op. cit.*, i, pp. 128-132; Pease and Roberts, *op. cit.*, pp. 171-176.

CHAPTER XXXV.—THE CREATION OF A NEW GOVERNMENT

Secondary authorities   GOOD brief accounts of the formation and ratification of the Constitution can be found in the works of Farrand and McLaughlin listed in the preceding chapter. A later discussion of the subject by McLaughlin appears in *A Constitutional History of the United States* (1936), chs. 14-15. This is one of the best of the brief accounts of the work of the Fathers in framing and securing the ratification of the Constitution. Another brief account of this is given in H. C. Hockett's *The Constitutional History of the United States* (1939; in progress; two vols. to 1876). Fuller accounts are: Bancroft, George, *History of the Formation of the Constitution of the United States*, 2 vols. (1885); Curtis, George T., *History of the Origin, Formation, and Adoption of the Constitution of the United States*, 2 vols. (1863-1865); Farrand, Max, *The Framing of the Constitution of the United States* (1913; an excellent account); Warren, Charles, *The Making of the Constitution* (1929; an excellent summary of the proceedings of the Convention of 1787, with numerous excerpts from the documents); Prescott, A. T., *Drafting the Federal Constitution* (1941; documents; rearrangement of *Madison's Notes*); and Schuyler, Robert L., *The Constitution of the United States; an Historical Survey of Its Formation* (1923, 1928). For the motives behind the creation of the Constitution, see Beard, C. A., *An Economic Interpretation of the Constitution of the United States* (1913; see footnote on p. 731). The vote of the various sections in favor of the ratification of the Constitution is shown in *The*

Geographical Distribution of the Vote of the Thirteen States on the Federal Constitution, 1787-88 by O. G. Libby (1894; detailed; large map). See also: Smith, Abbott E., *James Madison, Builder* (1937); and Burns, E. M., *James Madison, Philosopher of the Constitution* (1938).

The best and most easily accessible collection of documents on the Constitutional Convention is *Records of the Federal Convention of 1787*, 3 vols., edited by Max Farrand (see footnote, p. 736). Other useful collections are: Morison, S. E., *Sources and Documents Illustrating the American Revolution and the Formation of the Federal Constitution, 1764-1788*; and Tansill, Charles C., *Documents Illustrative of the Formation of the Union of the American States* (1927). The debates on the Constitution that were carried on in the state conventions, as well as a number of other valuable documents, are given in Jonathan Elliot's *Debates in the Several State Conventions on the Adoption of the Constitution*, 5 vols. (1836-1876). For editions of *The Federalist* see p. 755, footnote 51. Useful brief excerpts from the documents bearing on the formation and ratification of the Constitution are given in the source books by Commager and Pease and Roberts and in Allen Johnson's *Readings in American Constitutional History, 1776-1876* (1912). The text of the Constitution can be found in each of these three source books, in *Old South Leaflets*, no. 1, and in almost any school and college history of the United States.

INDEX

Abercrombie, General James, 399
"Academy," the (University of Pennsylvania), 568 f.
Acadia, 362, 388, 395
Acadians, removal of, 395
Acts of Supremacy and Uniformity, 10
Adam of Bremen, 23
Adams, John, 734; in first Continental Congress, 648 f.; nominates Washington for commander-in-chief, 649; supports independence, 656 f.; aids in peace negotiations, 676 ff.; secures loan in Holland, 677; unsuccessful mission to England, 715
Adams, Samuel, 734; as politician, 635 f.; as writer, 635; committees of correspondence, 636; "Boston Tea Party," 641; incites resistance, 647; attitude toward ratification of Constitution, 753
Administration of Justice Act, 642
Admiralty courts, 513 f., 514 n.
Adolphus, Gustavus, 204
"Adventurers," 78 f.
Agriculture, importance of, in colonial times, 433; Indian, 433 f.; methods of farming, 434 f.; farm implements, 435 f.; live-stock, 436 f.; native plants, 438 ff.; fruits, 440 f.; foreign plants, 441; land tenure, 442 ff.; versatility of colonial farmer, 449 f.; condition of, under the Confederation, 719; bibliography, 816 ff.
Alamance Creek, battle of, 359
Albany, 196, 197, 198
Albany Congress, 392 ff.
Alexander VI, Pope, 32
Alexandria, conference at, 729
Alleghany Mountains, 17, 389, 390, 606, 610
Alleghany region claimed by England and France, 389 ff.
Allen, Ethan, 660
Amadas, Philip, 53
America, naming of, 36 f.; discovery of, see Columbus
Americus Vespucius, 36 f.

Amherst, General Jeffery, 400, 402, 608
Amusements, in New England, 590 ff.; in New York, 592; in the South, 592 ff.
André, Major John, 674
Andrews, C. M., 126 n., 158 n.
Andros, Sir Edmund, governor of New York, 215, 218; governor of Dominion of New England, 270 ff.; deposed, 274 f.; governor of Virginia, 319
Anglican Church, in England, 10 f.; in North Carolina, 244 f.; hostile to Quakers in Pennsylvania, 258; in Maryland, 314 f.; in Virginia, 319, 516 f.; in South Carolina, 333 ff.; in New England, 517; work of the Venerable Society, 518 f.; in New Jersey, 520; in New York and Georgia, 520; the state church in Virginia, Maryland, North and South Carolina, Georgia, 520; the commissary, 521; bishop needed in America, 521 f.; effect of Great Revival, 543 f.; attitude toward American Revolution, 700 ff.; effect of American Revolution on, 702
Anglo-Spanish conflict, 382 f.
Animal life, 18 f.
Annapolis, 104, 189 n., 314, 558, 578
Annapolis Convention, 729 f., 729 n.
Anti-Federalists oppose ratification of Constitution, 751 ff.
Antinomianism in Massachusetts, 145 f,. 145 n.
Apollo Room, 474
Appalachian Highland, 15 f.
Appalachian Valley, 347, 349
Appeals from colonial courts, 501 ff.
Apprentices, 413
Aquidneck, island of, 160
Architecture, colonial, 584; European, 584; bibliography, 778, 779
Arlington, Lord, 91
Armada, defeat of, 57 f.; results, 58
Armed Neutrality, 670
Arminianism, 539

Years' War, 622 ff.; new colonial
policy, 624 f.; taxation of colonies,
625 ff.; colonial opposition to taxation, 626, 628 ff., 632 ff.; "Boston
Tea Party," 640 f.; "Intolerable
Acts," 642 ff.; first Continental Congress, 645 ff.; military events, 647 f.,
659 ff., 671 ff.; second Continental
Congress, 648 f.; Washington chosen
commander-in-chief, 649; relative
strength of contestants, 651 ff.; independence declared, 655 ff.; French
Alliance, 665 ff.; Spain and Holland
drawn into war, 669 f.; Valley
Forge, 670; conquest of Northwest,
671, 671 n.; part played by navy,
672; Arnold's treason, 674; peace
negotiations, 675 ff.; bibliography,
838 ff.
Revolution, American, political and
social aspects, 683 ff.; differences between England and America at end
of colonial period, 683 ff.; Whigs
and Tories, 685 f.; organization of
new state governments, 686 ff.; federal government during, 688 ff.;
Articles of Confederation, 689 ff.;
how financed, 691 ff.; postal system,
695 ff.; social results, 697 ff.; religious aspects, 698 ff.; effect on commerce, 703 f.; effect on industry,
704 f.; bibliography, 847 ff.
Revolution of 1688 in England, causes,
264 f.; James II deposed, 264 f.;
accession of William and Mary, 265;
effect on New England, 274 f.;
effect on New York, 275 f.; effect
on Maryland, 279 f.; effect on other
English colonies, 280 f., 373, 374;
bibliography, 799 f.
Revolution of 1689, in New England,
274 f.; in New York, 275 ff.; in
Maryland, 277 ff.
Reynolds, John, governor of Georgia,
345
Rhode Island, beginning of, 143, 147,
159 f.; organization of government
in Providence, 160; settlements at
Portsmouth, Newport, and Warwick,
160 f.; federation of four colonies,
162 f.; first charter, 163; second
charter, 163; government of confederation, 163 f.; religious freedom,
164; refuses assent to amendment to
Articles of Confederation, 713 n.;
paper money in, 720 f.; refuses to

ratify federal Constitution, 755; rati-
fies federal Constitution, 755 n.; bib-
liography 782 f.
Ribaut, Jean, 48, 49
Rice, 507 f.
Roads, colonial, 470 ff.
Roanoke Island, "Lost Colony" on,
54 f.
Robertson, James, 611
Robinson, John, 111, 112
Rochambeau, Count de, 675
"Rogues Harbor," 242
Rolfe, John, 78, 81, 421
Roses, Wars of, 9
Roundheads, 87
Rousseau, J. J., 665
Royal African Company, 418
Royal Mail Service, 477 ff., 695, 696,
697
Rum industry, 464, 485, 511, 580 n.,
718
Runaways, treatment of, 415 f., 424
Rutgers College, 545, 569
Rutledge, Edward, 633, 689

Sabbath observance, 535 f.
Sagadahoc colony, 65 n.
St. Augustine founded, 45, 49
St. Croix, French settlement, 362
St. Leger, Colonel, 664
St. Mary's, Maryland, settlement at,
99 f.; capital removed from, 314
Salem, Massachusetts, 125 f., 130, 288,
578
Salem witchcraft delusion, 288 ff.
"Salutary neglect," policy of, 514
Salzburgers, 342 f.
Samoset, Indian at Plymouth, 117
Sandys, Sir Edwin, 82, 83, 85, 85 n.
San Salvador, 30
Saratoga, surrender at, 663 ff.
Sargent, Major Winthrop, 724
Saunders, Admiral, 400, 401
Savannah, founded, 342; captured by
British, 672
Say and Sele, Lord, 153
Saybrook settlement, 153, 158 n.
Saye, A. B., 341 n.
Sayle, William, 229
Schools, in England at beginning of
seventeenth century, 550; school
laws in early New England, 551 f.;
dame, 552; grammar, 552 f.; how
supported, 553 f.